Lecture Notes in Computer Science 11892

More information about this series at http://www.springer.com/series/7410

Dennis Hofheinz · Alon Rosen (Eds.)

Theory of Cryptography

17th International Conference, TCC 2019
Nuremberg, Germany, December 1–5, 2019
Proceedings, Part II

 Springer

Editors
Dennis Hofheinz
Karlsruhe Institute of Technology
Karlsruhe, Germany

Alon Rosen
IDC Herzliya
Herzliya, Israel

ISSN 0302-9743 ISSN 1611-3349 (electronic)
Lecture Notes in Computer Science
ISBN 978-3-030-36032-0 ISBN 978-3-030-36033-7 (eBook)
https://doi.org/10.1007/978-3-030-36033-7

LNCS Sublibrary: SL4 – Security and Cryptology

This Springer imprint is published by the registered company Springer Nature Switzerland AG
The registered company address is: Gewerbestrasse 11, 6330 Cham, Switzerland

Preface

The 17th Theory of Cryptography Conference (TCC 2019) was held during December 1–5, 2019, at the DB Museum in Nuremberg, Germany. It was sponsored by the International Association for Cryptologic Research (IACR). The general chair of the conference was Dominique Schröder.

The conference received 147 submissions, of which the Program Committee (PC) selected 43 for presentation. Each submission was reviewed by at least three PC members, often more. The 35 PC members (including PC chairs), all top researchers in our field, were helped by 171 external reviewers, who were consulted when appropriate. These proceedings consist of the revised version of the 43 accepted papers. The revisions were not reviewed, and the authors bear full responsibility for the content of their papers.

As in previous years, we used Shai Halevi's excellent Web-review software, and are extremely grateful to him for writing it, and for providing fast and reliable technical support whenever we had any questions. We made extensive use of the interaction feature supported by the review software, where PC members could anonymously interact with authors. This was used to ask specific technical questions, such as suspected bugs. We felt this approach helped us prevent potential misunderstandings and improved the quality of the review process.

This year's TCC was extended from three to four days of talks, and the lengths of the presentations were accordingly extended from 20 to 25 minutes.

This was the sixth year that TCC presented the Test of Time Award to an outstanding paper that was published at TCC at least eight years ago, making a significant contribution to the theory of cryptography, preferably with influence also in other areas of cryptography, theory, and beyond. This year the Test of Time Award Committee selected the following paper, published at TCC 2008: "Incrementally Verifiable Computation or Proofs of Knowledge Imply Time/Space Efficiency" by Paul Valiant. This paper was selected for demonstrating the power of recursive composition of proofs of knowledge and enabling the development of efficiently verifiable proofs of correctness for complex computations. The authors were invited to deliver a talk at TCC 2019. The conference also featured two other invited talks, by Rachel Lin and by Omer Reingold.

A Best Young Researcher Paper Award was given to Henry Corrigan-Gibbs and Dmitry Kogan for their paper "The Function-Inversion Problem: Barriers and Opportunities."

We are greatly indebted to many people who were involved in making TCC 2019 a success. First of all, a big thanks to the most important contributors: all the authors who submitted papers to the conference. Next, we would like to thank the PC members for their hard work, dedication, and diligence in reviewing the papers, verifying the correctness, and in-depth discussion. We are also thankful to the external reviewers for their volunteered hard work and investment in reviewing papers and answering questions, often under time pressure. For running the conference itself, we are very grateful to the general chair, Dominique Schröder. We appreciate the sponsorship from the IACR, Deloitte, Siemens, Syss, and HGS. We also wish to thank Friedrich-Alexander-Universität Erlangen-Nürnberg and Nuremberg Campus of Technology for their support. Finally, we are thankful to the TCC Steering Committee as well as the entire thriving and vibrant TCC community.

October 2019   Dennis Hofheinz
                                                                     Alon Rosen

TCC 2019

The 17th Theory of Cryptography Conference

Nuremberg, Germany,
December 1–5, 2019

General Chair

Dominique Schröder   University of Erlangen-Nuremberg, Germany

Program Co-chairs

Dennis Hofheinz   Karlsruhe Institute of Technology
Alon Rosen   IDC Herzliya

Program Committee

Adi Akavia   Haifa University, Israel
Joël Alwen   Wickr, USA
Benny Applebaum   Tel Aviv University, Israel
Gilad Asharov   JP Morgan AI Research, USA
Nir Bitansky   Tel Aviv University, Israel
Chris Brzuska   Aalto University, Finland
Kai-Min Chung   Institute of Information Science, Academia Sinica,
                                        Taiwan
Ran Cohen   BU and Northeastern University, USA
Geoffroy Couteau   Karlsruhe Institute of Technology, Germany
Dana Dachman-Soled   University of Maryland, USA
Nico Döttling   CISPA, Saarbrücken, Germany
Marc Fischlin   Technische Universität Darmstadt, Germany
Siyao Guo   NYU Shanghai, China
Julia Hesse   Technische Universität Darmstadt, Germany
Pavel Hubáček   Charles University Prague, Czech Republic
Abhishek Jain   Johns Hopkins University, USA
Bhavana Kanukurthi   Indian Institute of Science, India
Eike Kiltz   Ruhr-Universität Bochum, Germany
Susumu Kiyoshima   NTT Secure Platform Laboratories, Japan
Venkata Koppula   Weizmann Institute of Science, Israel
Mohammad Mahmoody   University of Virginia, USA
Nikolaos Makriyannis   Technion, Israel
Pratyay Mukherjee   Visa Research, San Francisco, USA
Jörn Müller-Quade   Karlsruhe Institute of Technology, Germany

Ryo Nishimaki	NTT Secure Platform Laboratories, Japan
Omer Paneth	MIT, USA
Antigoni Polychroniadou	JP Morgan AI Research, USA
Mariana Raykova	Google, Inc., New York, USA
Ron Rothblum	IDC Herzliya, Israel
Noah Stephens-Davidowitz	MIT, USA
Prashant Vasudevan	UC Berkeley, USA
Muthuramakrishnan Venkitasubramaniam	University of Rochester, USA
Yu Yu	Shanghai Jiaotong University, China

External Reviewers

Nathan Manohar
Daniel Masny
Noam Mazor
Jeremias Mechler
Nikolas Melissaris
Takaaki Mizuki
Ameer Mohammed
Tamer Mour
Marta Mularczyk
Matthias Nagel
Ariel Nof
Bhavana Obbattu
Maciej Obremski
Eran Omri
Michele Orru
Jiaxin Pan
Sikhar Patranabis
Udi Peled
Naty Peter
Oxana Poburinnaya
Sihang Pu
Erick Purwanto
Willy Quach
Samuel Ranellucci
Divya Ravi

Joao Ribeiro
Silas Richelson
Miruna Rosca
Paul Rösler
Pratik Sarkar
Santanu Sarkar
Peter Scholl
Rebecca Schwerdt
Sven Schäge
Adam Sealfon
Mahdi Sedaghat
Sruthi Sekar
Ido Shahaf
Devika Sharma
Sina Shiehian
Kazumasa Shinagawa
Omri Shmueli
Jad Silbak
Yifan Song
Nick Spooner
Akshayaram Srinivasan
Igors Stepanovs
Pierre-Yves Strub
Shi-Feng Sun
Siwei Sun

Xiaoming Sun
Björn Tackmann
Katsuyuki Takashima
Justin Thaler
Junichi Tomida
Rotem Tsabary
Dominique Unruh
Bogdan Ursu
Alexandre Wallet
Yuyu Wang
Mor Weiss
Daniel Wichs
David Wu
Keita Xagawa
Sophia Yakoubov
Shota Yamada
Takashi Yamakawa
Avishay Yanai
Kevin Yeo
Eylon Yogev
Fan Zhang
Jiapeng Zhang
Vassilis Zikas
Giorgos Zirdelis
Akin Ünal

Contents – Part II

Contents – Part I

Succinct Arguments in the Quantum Random Oracle Model

Alessandro Chiesa[1(✉)], Peter Manohar[2], and Nicholas Spooner[1]

[1] University of California, Berkeley, USA
{alexch,nick.spooner}@berkeley.edu
[2] Carnegie Mellon University, Pittsburgh, USA
pmanohar@cs.cmu.edu

Abstract. Succinct non-interactive arguments (SNARGs) are highly efficient certificates of membership in non-deterministic languages. Constructions of SNARGs in the random oracle model are widely believed to be post-quantum secure, provided the oracle is instantiated with a suitable post-quantum hash function. No formal evidence, however, supports this belief.

In this work we provide the first such evidence by proving that the SNARG construction of Micali is unconditionally secure in the *quantum* random oracle model. We also prove that, analogously to the classical case, the SNARG inherits the zero knowledge and proof of knowledge properties of the PCP underlying the Micali construction. We thus obtain the first zero knowledge SNARG of knowledge (zkSNARK) that is secure in the quantum random oracle model.

Our main tool is a new lifting lemma that shows how, for a rich class of oracle games, we can *generically* deduce security against quantum attackers by bounding a natural classical property of these games. This means that in order to prove our theorem we only need to establish *classical* properties about the Micali construction. This approach not only lets us prove post-quantum security but also enables us to prove explicit bounds that are tight up to small factors.

We additionally use our techniques to prove that SNARGs based on interactive oracle proofs (IOPs) with round-by-round soundness are unconditionally secure in the quantum random oracle model. This result establishes the post-quantum security of many SNARGs of practical interest.

Keywords: Succinct arguments · Quantum random oracle model · Probabilistically checkable proofs

1 Introduction

The design and analysis of cryptographic primitives that are plausibly secure against quantum attackers is an increasingly important goal. The expected advent of quantum computers demands the cryptography community to be prepared well in advance, so much so that the National Institute of Standards and

© International Association for Cryptologic Research 2019
D. Hofheinz and A. Rosen (Eds.): TCC 2019, LNCS 11892, pp. 1–29, 2019.
https://doi.org/10.1007/978-3-030-36033-7_1

Technology (NIST) is *already* in the process of selecting, from among many proposals, a new set of cryptography standards that are "post-quantum" [50]. The proposals involve schemes for key agreement, public-key encryption, and digital signatures, and are intended to eventually replace existing standards based on the hardness of factoring or discrete logarithms.

In this paper we study the post-quantum security of a cryptographic primitive that has recently received much attention across theoretical and applied communities: *succinct arguments* [33]. These are argument systems [19] for non-deterministic languages where the communication complexity between the prover and verifier is sublinear in the size of the non-deterministic witness.[1] This notion originates in seminal works of Kilian [43] and Micali [49], which construct succinct arguments for languages in $\mathsf{NTIME}(T(n))$ where communication complexity is $\mathsf{poly}(\lambda, \log T(n))$ and the time complexity of the verifier is $\mathsf{poly}(\lambda, n, \log T(n))$; here λ is the security parameter.

Researchers have studied many aspects of succinct arguments in the last two decades, leading to numerous constructions with different tradeoffs [62], efficient realizations in code [18,24,39,46,55–57], real-world deployments [29,51], and standardization efforts [67]. A particularly useful feature is that many succinct arguments can be made zero knowledge with minimal overhead. At present, however, *most approaches to obtain efficient succinct arguments are "pre-quantum"*, since they rely on the discrete logarithm problem (and more).

A notable exception is a class of succinct arguments obtained by combining two ingredients: (a) probabilistic proof systems, which are unconditionally secure, and (b) cryptographic hash functions, for which we have post-quantum candidates. This class includes the succinct interactive argument of Kilian [43], which use probabilistically checkable proofs (PCPs) [4,5,7,30] and collision-resistant hash functions. It also includes the succinct non-interactive argument (SNARG) of Micali [49], which uses PCPs and random oracles. More generally, by using random oracles one can construct a SNARG from a multi-round generalization of PCPs known as interactive oracle proofs (IOPs) [13,54]. *All of these succinct arguments are widely believed to be post-quantum*, provided the hash function is suitably instantiated [11].[2]

There is, however, no formal evidence that supports the above widely-held belief. Since succinct arguments are a fundamental cryptographic primitive with both theoretical and real-world applications, it is important to prove guarantees on their post-quantum security.

1.1 SNARGs with Random Oracles

In this paper we focus our attention on the SNARG construction of Micali [49], which is unconditionally secure in the random oracle model [10,53]. SNARGs

---

[1] Achieving communication complexity that is sublinear in the witness size is known to *require* relaxing soundness from statistical to computational, provided one assumes standard complexity conjectures [34,35].

[2] There is also a class of lattice-based succinct arguments that is plausibly post-quantum; see Sect. 1.3.

in the random oracle model are not only plausibly post-quantum secure but also enjoy other desirable features. Namely, the random oracle can be heuristically instantiated via hash functions that avoid expensive public-key cryptographic operations. Moreover, the SNARG uses a transparent (public-coin) setup, because the only public parameter needed to produce/verify proofs is the choice of hash function.

We are thus interested in asking: can we establish formal evidence that the SNARG construction of Micali is post-quantum secure? One way to establish formal evidence is to prove security in a quantum analogue of the random oracle model, as we now explain. A quantum attacker can, among other things, evaluate a hash function in superposition when given the hash function's code. This enables the attacker, for instance, to find pre-images [38] or collisions [20] faster than a classical attacker. In light of this, Boneh et al. [15] have argued that, in the quantum setting, the correct way to model a random oracle is to allow the attacker to query the random oracle in superposition. The resulting model is known as the *quantum random oracle model* (QROM), and a line of work has established post-quantum security within this model for a variety of cryptographic primitives; see, e.g., [15,28,58,64,65].

Our goal is to study the SNARG construction of Micali in the quantum random oracle model. We also study the SNARG construction of BCS [13], which yields SNARGs of practical interest.

1.2   Our Results

The main result of this paper is establishing that the SNARG construction of Micali [49] is unconditionally secure in the quantum random oracle model. This is the first formal evidence that supports the widely-held belief that this construction is post-quantum secure when the oracle is instantiated via a suitable post-quantum hash function.

Theorem 1 (informal). *The non-interactive argument of Micali, when based on a PCP with soundness error ϵ, has soundness error $O(t^2\epsilon + t^3/2^\lambda)$ against quantum attackers that make t queries to a random oracle with output size λ. This soundness error is tight up to small factors.*

A key step in our proof, of independent interest, is a *Lifting Lemma* that shows how, for a rich class of "oracle games", we can *generically* deduce security against quantum attackers by bounding a natural classical property of these games, instability, that we introduce. This means that to prove Theorem 1 we only need to bound the instability of the Micali construction. This approach not only yields the theorem but also enables us to prove explicit bounds that are tight up to small factors.

If we base the Micali construction on suitable PCPs, we obtain new statements about the existence of post-quantum non-interactive arguments. First, if the PCP achieves (honest-verifier) zero knowledge and proof of knowledge then through the Micali construction we obtain a zero knowledge non-interactive argument of knowledge that is *unconditionally* secure in the quantum random oracle model. This strengthens a result of Unruh [59], which assumes the existence of a post-quantum Σ-protocol for NP. Moreover, if the PCP has polylogarithmic query complexity and verifier running time then we obtain the first construction of a zero knowledge succinct non-interactive argument of knowledge (zkSNARK) that is secure in the quantum random oracle model.

Theorem 2 (informal). *There exists a zero knowledge non-interactive argument of knowledge for NP in the quantum random oracle model. Moreover, the non-interactive argument is succinct, in the sense that arguments have size λ^c and can be verified in time $(\lambda \cdot n)^c$, where λ is the random oracle's security parameter, n is instance size, and $c > 0$ is a universal constant.*

The above theorem is stated for NP only for simplicity. Analogously to the classical case, a more general statement holds for all non-deterministic time languages by relying on suitable PCPs for non-deterministic time. For example, the PCP in [7] achieves proof of knowledge, can be made (honest-verifier) zero knowledge [27,44], and supports non-deterministic time.

The BCS Construction. We conclude with a result that demonstrates how the tools in this paper can be used to study the post-quantum security of protocols that are of practical interest. Since known PCP constructions are expensive, efficient constructions of succinct arguments in the random oracle model are typically based on the BCS construction [13], which instead uses interactive oracle proofs (IOPs) [13,54], a multi-round extension of PCPs. This extension additionally captures IPs [6,37] and IPCPs [41] as special cases.

We prove that the BCS construction is unconditionally secure in the quantum random oracle model, if applied to public-coin IOPs that have round-by-round soundness [21]. The resulting argument inherits proof of knowledge and zero knowledge properties of the underlying IOP.

Theorem 3 (informal). *The non-interactive argument of BCS, when based on a public-coin IOP with round-by-round soundness error ϵ, has soundness error $O(t^2\epsilon + t^3/2^\lambda)$ against quantum attackers that make t queries to a random oracle with output size λ. Moreover, it is an argument of knowledge if the IOP has round-by-round proof of knowledge, and it is a (statistical) zero knowledge argument if the IOP is honest-verifier zero knowledge.*

Round-by-round proof of knowledge is a natural notion that we introduce, analogous to round-by-round soundness, and is satisfied by many natural protocols. In particular, Theorem 3 enables us to deduce the post-quantum security of succinct arguments based on well-known IPs such as the sumcheck protocol [48] and the GKR protocol [36], as well as zkSNARKs based on recent IOPs such as [3,11,12]. These protocols (among others) are of interest to practitioners, and our result can be used to guide parameter choices in practice.

1.3   Related Work

Argument Systems That Use Random Oracles. Several works study the post-quantum security of zero knowledge non-interactive arguments of knowledge that use random oracles, most notably those obtained by applying the Fiat–Shamir transformation [31] to a post-quantum Σ-protocol. Such arguments are used to achieve post-quantum digital signatures [9,22,42], and underlie constructions submitted to the NIST call for post-quantum cryptography [50].

A security reduction for the Fiat–Shamir transformation in the quantum random oracle model has been recently achieved [26,47]. Obtaining a security reduction had been elusive, as the classical approach of rewinding the adversary to reduce to special soundness of the Σ-protocol does not work for quantum adversaries.[3] Before, researchers were only able to prove security if the underlying Σ-protocol satisfies special properties [23,45,60], or resorted to proving security for alternative, less efficient, constructions such as the Unruh transformation [59].

The question that we study in this paper is complementary to these prior works. On the one hand, prior works study the security of the Fiat–Shamir transformation *given* that the underlying Σ-protocol is secure against efficient quantum attackers. On the other hand, we study protocols such as the Micali construction and BCS construction that can be viewed as applying the Fiat–Shamir transformation to specific public-coin protocols that are known to be unconditionally secure in the (classical) random oracle model. In particular, we establish *unconditional* security in the quantum random oracle model via an approach that considers the protocol as a whole (similarly to the classical analysis of these protocols).

The foregoing differences are reflected in a technical analysis that departs from prior works. Most of the effort in this paper is establishing *classical* security properties of the Micali and BCS constructions, which we then use to generically deduce their quantum security. This approach, besides being intuitive, yields tight bounds that can be used to guide parameter choices in practice.

Succinct Arguments Based on Lattices. Several lattice problems are presumed to remain hard even against quantum adversaries, and researchers have relied on such problems to propose numerous cryptographic constructions that are plausibly post-quantum. A handful of works have used lattices to achieve various notions of succinct arguments that are plausibly post-quantum. Baum et al. [8] rely on the short integer solution (SIS) problem to obtain an argument system for arithmetic circuits where the communication complexity grows with the square-root of circuit size; the argument system is constant-round, public-coin, and honest-verifier zero knowledge. Boneh et al. [16,17] and Gennaro et al. [32] rely on lattice knowledge assumptions to construct designated-verifier SNARGs for boolean circuits, in the preprocessing model [14]. Whether one can use lattices to obtain public-coin argument systems with polylogarithmic communication complexity (as in the construction of Micali) remains an intriguing open problem.

---

[3] Rewinding quantum adversaries is a delicate matter [63] and, more importantly, special soundness does *not* imply post-quantum soundness (relative to some oracle) [2]. These difficulties have been circumvented by using new techniques that enable reducing directly to the (post-quantum) soundness of the underlying Σ-protocol.

2 Techniques

We discuss the main ideas behind our results. In Sect. 2.1 we recall the construction of Micali, and then in Sect. 2.2 we explain the challenges that arise when trying to prove its security in the quantum random oracle model. In Sect. 2.3 we outline our approach to obtain a proof of security for the Micali construction (Theorem 1); we elaborate on our approach in Sects. 2.4 to 2.7. Finally, in Sect. 2.8 we discuss how to further establish zero knowledge and proof of knowledge; we thus obtain the first zkSNARK secure in the quantum random oracle model (Theorem 2).

We conclude in Sect. 2.9 by explaining how our techniques extend to establish post-quantum security for the BCS construction applied to many protocols of practical interest (Theorem 3).

Many of the proofs/sections have been omitted from this version of the paper due space limitations. We refer the reader to the full version of the paper for all relevant details.

2.1 The Construction of Micali

The construction of Micali is a transformation that maps any *probabilistically checkable proof* (PCP) into a corresponding non-interactive argument in the random oracle model. (See Sect. 3.4 for the definition of a PCP, and Sect. 3.3 for that of a non-interactive argument.) The resulting non-interactive argument is *succinct*, i.e. a SNARG, provided the PCP has suitable parameters.

Let $(\mathbf{P}, \mathbf{V})$ be a PCP for a relation $\mathcal{R}$ with soundness error ϵ, proof length ℓ over alphabet Σ, and query complexity q. The honest prover $\mathbf{P}$ takes as input an instance-witness pair (x, w) and outputs a proof string $\Pi\colon [\ell] \to \Sigma$. The honest verifier $\mathbf{V}$ takes as input the instance x, makes q probabilistic queries to a (possibly malicious) proof string $\tilde{\Pi}\colon [\ell] \to \Sigma$, and then accepts or rejects.

The PCP $(\mathbf{P}, \mathbf{V})$ for $\mathcal{R}$ is used to construct a SNARG $(\mathcal{P}, \mathcal{V})$ for $\mathcal{R}$, as follows.

The SNARG prover $\mathcal{P}$ takes as input an instance x and witness w. First, $\mathcal{P}$ uses the random oracle h to commit to the proof string $\Pi := \mathbf{P}(\mathsf{x}, \mathsf{w})$ via a Merkle tree, obtaining a corresponding root rt. Second, $\mathcal{P}$ applies the random oracle h to the root rt in order to derive randomness r for the PCP verifier $\mathbf{V}$. Third, $\mathcal{P}$ simulates the PCP verifier $\mathbf{V}$ with the proof string Π, input x, and randomness r, in order to deduce the queried locations of Π. Finally, $\mathcal{P}$ assembles a SNARG proof π that contains the root rt, answers to the queries, and an authentication path for each answer.

Observe that the SNARG proof π is succinct because it is small (it has size $|\pi| = O(q \cdot (\log |\Sigma| + \lambda \log \ell)) = O_\lambda(q)$ for $\ell, |\Sigma| = 2^{O(\lambda)}$) and it is cheap to validate via the algorithm described next.

The SNARG verifier $\mathcal{V}$ takes as input an instance x and a (possibly malicious) SNARG proof $\tilde{\pi}$. First, $\mathcal{V}$ uses the random oracle h to check that each answer in $\tilde{\pi}$ is certified by an authentication path relative to the claimed root $\tilde{\mathsf{rt}}$. Next, $\mathcal{V}$ applies the random oracle h to the root $\tilde{\mathsf{rt}}$ in order to derive randomness $\tilde{\mathsf{r}}$.

Finally, $\mathcal{V}$ runs the PCP verifier $\mathbf{V}$ on the instance x and randomness $\tilde{\mathsf{r}}$, answering $\mathbf{V}$'s queries using the claimed answers in $\tilde{\pi}$.

The intuition behind the construction is that the soundness guarantee of a PCP holds only if the proof string $\tilde{\Pi}$ to be validated is *fixed* before the randomness $\tilde{\mathsf{r}}$ for the PCP verifier is known, and for this reason the SNARG prover must derive $\tilde{\mathsf{r}}$ by hashing a commitment $\tilde{\mathsf{rt}}$ to $\tilde{\Pi}$.

This construction is unconditionally secure in the random oracle model [13,49,61]:

Theorem 1. *The SNARG $(\mathcal{P}, \mathcal{V})$ has soundness error $O(t\epsilon + t^2/2^\lambda)$ against (classical) attackers that make at most t queries to the random oracle. This soundness error is tight up to small factors.*

A SNARG obtained via the Micali construction also inherits zero knowledge and proof of knowledge properties of the underlying PCP. We discuss these additional properties and how we establish them in the quantum setting later on in Sect. 2.8. We focus on soundness first.

2.2   Challenges in the Quantum Setting

Our goal is to show that the SNARG construction of Micali is unconditionally secure in the *quantum* random oracle model. Suppose that $\tilde{\mathcal{P}}$ is a t-query quantum prover that convinces the SNARG verifier $\mathcal{V}$ with probability δ (over the random oracle). We wish to construct a malicious PCP prover $\tilde{\mathbf{P}}$ that, using $\tilde{\mathcal{P}}$ as a subroutine, outputs a proof string $\tilde{\Pi} \colon [\ell] \to \Sigma$ that convinces the PCP verifier $\mathbf{V}$ with related probability $\epsilon(\delta, t)$ (here the probability is over the randomness of $\tilde{\mathbf{P}}$ and $\mathbf{V}$).

A natural approach to reduce the SNARG prover $\tilde{\mathcal{P}}$ to the PCP prover $\tilde{\mathbf{P}}$ would be to try to adapt to the quantum setting the reduction that is used for the classical setting. Below we recall the classical reduction, and then explain why adapting it to the quantum case is challenging.

The Reduction for Classical Attackers. The reduction from a *classical* SNARG prover $\tilde{\mathcal{P}}$ to a PCP prover $\tilde{\mathbf{P}}$ relies on a *straightline extractor*, as we now explain.

While the SNARG prover $\tilde{\mathcal{P}}$ outputs a short proof π that contains a Merkle root and a few decommitted values, the PCP prover $\tilde{\mathbf{P}}$ must output a "long" proof string $\tilde{\Pi}$. How can $\tilde{\mathbf{P}}$ obtain all this information from seeing only π? The answer is that, when running $\tilde{\mathcal{P}}$ as a subroutine, $\tilde{\mathbf{P}}$ observes the queries that $\tilde{\mathcal{P}}$ makes to the oracle, and these queries reveal the proof string $\tilde{\Pi}$.

This is only a caricature of how $\tilde{\mathbf{P}}$ actually works, though. The reason is that $\tilde{\mathcal{P}}$ need not produce a query sequence from which $\tilde{\mathbf{P}}$ can just read off a proof string $\tilde{\Pi}$ consistent with the Merkle root in π. For example, $\tilde{\mathcal{P}}$ could try to commit to many possible proof strings "in its head", derive the corresponding randomness from each commitment, and then select which commitment to include in π. Even worse, $\tilde{\mathcal{P}}$ could try to commit to a *partial* proof string $\tilde{\Pi}$ via an incomplete Merkle tree and, because the PCP verifier inspects only a small fraction of a proof string, hope that queries will land to leaves of the Merkle tree that do exist.

The proof of Theorem 1 shows that, despite these complications, there is a way for $\tilde{\mathbf{P}}$ to observe all queries and answers of a single execution of the SNARG prover $\tilde{\mathcal{P}}$, and then run an algorithm on these to extract a suitable proof string $\tilde{\Pi}$.

How to Deal with Quantum Attackers? If we now return to the case where the SNARG prover $\tilde{\mathcal{P}}$ is a quantum attacker, we are immediately confronted with a severe problem. Since $\tilde{\mathcal{P}}$ can query the random oracle in superposition, how can $\tilde{\mathbf{P}}$ "observe" queries and answers to the oracle? If $\tilde{\mathbf{P}}$ were to just measure $\tilde{\mathcal{P}}$'s query register, $\tilde{\mathcal{P}}$ may detect this and stop working. This basic problem has made obtaining security reductions against quantum attackers that access random oracles exceedingly difficult when compared to the case of classical attackers. Papers that study the security of cryptographic primitives in the quantum random oracle model have had to develop clever techniques to somehow circumvent this problem in various settings of interest.

Most relevant to this paper is a work of Zhandry [66] that introduces *compressed oracles*, a set of notions and techniques that enables a quantum algorithm to simulate access to a random oracle for a quantum attacker. This is achieved by replacing a random oracle $h\colon \{0,1\}^m \to \{0,1\}^n$ with the action of a specially-crafted unitary $\mathcal{O}$ that implicitly keeps track of queries. This is a quantum analogue of when, in the classical setting, a simulator merely observes the queries made by the attacker and maintains a database of the query-answer pairs. Formally, the classical simulator keeps track of a database D, which is a partial function $D\colon \{0,1\}^m \rightharpoonup \{0,1\}^n$. The database represents the part of the random oracle that has been "revealed" to the attacker by answering its queries. In the quantum setting, the state space of the quantum attacker is augmented with registers to store the database, which (loosely) keep track of the database D in superposition, as it evolves from query to query. Thus, while the original oracle h operates on the state $|\psi_{\mathcal{A}}\rangle$ of the adversary, the unitary $\mathcal{O}$ operates on a bipartite state $|\psi_{\mathcal{A}}, \psi_D\rangle$. This extended state represents a purification of the mixed state of the adversary induced by choosing the oracle h at random.

One may conjecture that compressed oracles, by virtue of "exposing" a quantum attacker's queries, make proving the quantum security of the Micali construction, or indeed of any construction using random oracles, straightforward. This is, unfortunately, not the case.

For example, compressed oracles allow us to argue that, given an adversary that outputs a convincing SNARG proof π with high probability, if we measure the database D after the adversary terminates, then with high probability one can find a convincing SNARG proof π in the database D. This does not allow us to reduce to soundness of the underlying PCP, however, because to do that we need to argue that one can extract a PCP proof Π from D (that is much longer than the SNARG proof π) that convinces the PCP verifier with high probability.

Nevertheless, compressed oracles are a useful starting point for this work, and indeed a basic lemma about compressed oracles plays the role of a hybrid in our security proof.

2.3   Outline of Our Approach

The ideas that we use in this paper to analyze the Micali construction are almost entirely generic, and can be used to analyze any *oracle game*. Informally, given a "base game" $G \subseteq A^k \times B^k \times C$, an adversary with oracle access to a random oracle h wins the oracle game for G if it outputs a tuple $(\mathbf{a}, \mathbf{b}, c) \in G$ where $h(a_i) = b_i$ for each $i \in [k]$. Oracle games are a natural notion that captures many games of interest, such as finding pre-images or finding collisions. Producing a valid proof in the Micali construction can also be cast as an oracle game, and we shall view the soundness property as stating that the value (maximum winning probability) of this game is small.

Our proof of quantum security consists of two main parts. First, we *generically* reduce the value of any oracle game to the *instability* of the game, a purely classical property of the game that we introduce. Second, we analyze the instability of the oracle game induced by the Micali construction. The instability of this oracle game is not too difficult to analyze because it is a classical quantity, and the "hard work" is crisply, and conveniently, encapsulated within our generic reduction. We view bounding values of oracle games via instability as the main technical contribution of this paper.

We now elaborate on our approach: in Sect. 2.4 we recast prior work in the language of oracle games; in Sect. 2.5 we explain what is instability and how we use it to bound game values; in Sect. 2.6 we introduce conditional instability and use it to prove tighter bounds on oracle game values; and in Sect. 2.7 we outline the analysis of instability for the Micali construction.

2.4   From Oracle Games to Database Games

We begin with a sequence of three games whose values are closely related. These games play the role of hybrids in our analysis, and are all defined relative to the given base game $G \subseteq A^k \times B^k \times C$.

- **Oracle game.** This is the game defined earlier that is played in the real world, using a random oracle h. The adversary wins if it outputs a tuple $(\mathbf{a}, \mathbf{b}, c) \in G$ with $h(a_i) = b_i$ for each $i \in [k]$.
- **Simulated oracle game.** The simulator of Zhandry [66] is used to run the adversary and its final state is measured, leading to a tuple $(\mathbf{a}, \mathbf{b}, c)$ *and* a database D. The adversary wins if $(\mathbf{a}, \mathbf{b}, c) \in G$ and $D(a_i) = b_i$ for each $i \in [k]$. (The oracle $h \colon \{0,1\}^m \to \{0,1\}^n$ is now replaced by the database $D \colon \{0,1\}^m \rightharpoonup \{0,1\}^n$ stored by the simulator.)
- **Database game.** Again the simulator of Zhandry is used to run the adversary, leading to a tuple $(\mathbf{a}, \mathbf{b}, c)$ and a database D. However, now we ignore $(\mathbf{a}, \mathbf{b}, c)$ and only consider D. The adversary wins if there *exists* $(\mathbf{a}', \mathbf{b}', c') \in G$ such that $D(a_i) = b_i$ for each $i \in [k]$.

We let $\omega_O^*(G, t)$, $\omega_S^*(G, t)$, and $\omega_D^*(G, t)$ denote the values of the oracle game, simulated oracle game, and database game against quantum adversaries that make at most t oracle queries.

A result of Zhandry [66, Lemma 5], when stated via the notions above, shows that $\sqrt{\omega_O^*(G, t)} \leq \sqrt{\omega_S^*(G, t)} + \sqrt{k/2^n}$. Moreover, $\omega_S^*(G, t) \leq \omega_D^*(G, t)$ holds trivially, because winning the simulated oracle game implies winning the database game, by taking $(\mathbf{a}', \mathbf{b}', c') := (\mathbf{a}, \mathbf{b}, c)$. In sum:

Lemma 1. *For any base game* G,

$$\sqrt{\omega_O^*(G, t)} \leq \sqrt{\omega_D^*(G, t)} + \sqrt{k/2^n}.$$

The above lemma is a conceptualization of prior work, and is the starting point for the technical contributions of this paper. In particular, the lemma tells us that in order to bound the maximum winning probability of a quantum adversary in an oracle game (played in the real world) it suffices to bound the maximum winning probability of the adversary in the corresponding database game.

See the full version of the paper for more details.

2.5   A Basic Lifting Lemma for Database Games

We describe how we use a *classical* quantity $\mathbf{I}(\mathcal{P}_G, t)$ to bound $\omega_D^*(G, t)$, the maximum winning probability of any t-query quantum algorithm in the database game of G. When combined with the hybrids in Sect. 2.4, this reduces the quantum security of oracle games to studying $\mathbf{I}(\mathcal{P}_G, t)$.

Given a base game G, we let $\mathcal{P}_G$ be the set of databases that win the database game of G. In the classical setting, a natural way to bound the maximum winning probability of the database game is to compute, for each possible database $D \notin \mathcal{P}_G$ (a database that is currently losing the game), the maximum probability that adding a query-answer pair to D puts D in $\mathcal{P}_G$. Assuming that the empty database is not in $\mathcal{P}_G$ (for otherwise one can win trivially), this quantity characterizes the probability that the adversary gets lucky and ends up with a winning database D.

We define the *instability* of $\mathcal{P}_G$ with query bound t, denoted $\mathbf{I}(\mathcal{P}_G, t)$, to be the maximum probability that, for any database D containing less than t queries, making one additional (classical) query changes whether or not D is in $\mathcal{P}_G$. *The foregoing argument explains that the classical value of the database game* G *is bounded by* $t \cdot \mathbf{I}(\mathcal{P}_G, t)$. Intuitively this is because each query can increase the probability that the database D is in $\mathcal{P}_G$ by at most $\mathbf{I}(\mathcal{P}_G, t)$.

We prove that an analogous result holds for quantum adversaries as well. We call this lemma a lifting lemma, because it enables us to use the *classical* quantity of instability to prove a bound on the maximum winning probability of *quantum* adversaries. The version below is a "basic" version, because we shall ultimately need a stronger statement, as we discuss in Sect. 2.6. The result below extends an idea of Zhandry sketched in [66, Section 4.3].

Lemma 2 (Basic lifting lemma). *For any base game G,*

$$\omega_{\mathsf{D}}^*(G,t) \le O\big(t^2 \cdot \mathbf{I}(\mathcal{P}_G,t)\big).$$

In particular, combining the above with Lemma 1, we get

$$\omega_{\mathsf{O}}^*(G,t) \le O\big(t^2 \cdot \mathbf{I}(\mathcal{P}_G,t) + k/2^n\big).$$

Even the above basic lifting lemma is a powerful tool. For example, suppose that G is the collision game, where the adversary wins if it outputs an oracle collision. Then $\mathbf{I}(\mathcal{P}_G,t) < t/2^n$, because if D is a database with no collisions and less than t entries, then making one more query produces a collision with probability less than $t/2^n$, and if D has collisions then it is not possible to make an additional query and remove collisions. Then (since $k = 2$ in the collision game) the lifting lemma immediately tells us that $\omega_{\mathsf{O}}^*(G,t) \le O(t^3/2^n)$, which shows that the probability that a t-query quantum oracle algorithm finds a collision is bounded by $O(t^3/2^n)$. This further simplifies the analysis of this fact in [66] and matches the bound of [1] (which is tight [20]).

We now sketch the proof of the basic lifting lemma. The proof sketch differs slightly from the actual proof, as in the actual proof we do a slightly more complicated analysis that gives us smaller constants. The main ideas, however, remain the same.

We let P_G be the operator that projects onto databases that win the database game G: for any basis state $|D\rangle$ in the database register, $P_G |D\rangle = |D\rangle$ if $D \in \mathcal{P}_G$, and $P_G |D\rangle = 0$ if $D \notin \mathcal{P}_G$; P_G acts as the identity on other registers. If $|\phi\rangle$ is the final joint state of the quantum adversary and database, then $\|P_G |\phi\rangle\|^2$ is the probability that $D \in \mathcal{P}_G$ after measurement. We will assume that $\emptyset \notin \mathcal{P}_G$, i.e., that the empty database does not win the database game of G (or else the adversary can win by doing nothing).

We can represent any simulated quantum adversary making at most t queries as a sequence of unitary operators $U = A_t \mathcal{O} A_{t-1} \mathcal{O} \ldots A_1 \mathcal{O}$ applied to an initial state $|\phi_0, \emptyset\rangle := |\phi_0\rangle \otimes |\emptyset\rangle$, where $\mathcal{O}$ is the compressed oracle and $|\emptyset\rangle$ is the state of the empty database. Each A_i acts non-trivially only on the registers of the adversary being simulated and P_G acts non-trivially only on the database registers, so P_G and A_i commute. So, if P_G and $\mathcal{O}$ were to also commute, then we could simply conclude that $P_G U |\phi_0, \emptyset\rangle = U P_G |\phi_0, \emptyset\rangle = 0$, i.e., that the adversary never wins. (Here we used the fact that $\emptyset \notin \mathcal{P}_G$.)

However, it is *not* the case that P_G and $\mathcal{O}$ commute. This should be expected because in general an adversary can win with some positive probability. However, if we could show that they *almost* commute, then we could apply the previous argument to show that $P_G U |\phi_0, \emptyset\rangle \approx U P_G |\phi_0, \emptyset\rangle = 0$; i.e., the adversary wins with small probability. The notion of "almost" commuting we use is that the operator norm $\|[P_G, \mathcal{O}]\|$ of the commutator $[P_G, \mathcal{O}] := P_G \mathcal{O} - \mathcal{O} P_G$ is small.

Unfortunately, for interesting games the operator norm $\|[P_G, \mathcal{O}]\|$ may not be small. For example, if G is the collision game and D is a database with a pre-image of every $y \in \{0,1\}^n$ but no collisions, then $\|[P_G, \mathcal{O}] |x, u, D\rangle\| = 1$. Generally, this norm may be large if D has many entries.

Query-bounded adversaries, however, cannot produce nonzero amplitudes on databases with more entries than the query bound. Hence, intuitively we should not consider states that correspond to large databases when bounding the operator norm of the aforementioned commutator. We follow this intuition by introducing the notion of a *projected oracle*, which acts as the compressed oracle except that it discards databases that do not belong to a certain subset.

Definition 1. *Let P be the operator that projects onto databases that belong to a given subset $\mathcal{P}$ of databases. A* **projected oracle** *is an operator of the form $P\mathcal{O}P$.*

We thus consider the projected oracle $P_t\mathcal{O}P_t$, where P_t is operator that projects onto databases containing at most t queries. For adversaries that make at most t queries, replacing $\mathcal{O}$ with $P_t\mathcal{O}P_t$ has no effect because the adversary cannot create a database that contains more than t entries. Moreover, $\|[P_G, P_t\mathcal{O}P_t]\,|D\rangle\| = 0$ if D contains more than t entries, so the operator norm of $[P_G, P_t\mathcal{O}P_t]$ accounts for the action of $\mathcal{O}$ *only* on databases containing at most t entries.

In sum, projected oracles allow us to cleanly compute the operator norm only over databases that are reachable by an adversary making a bounded number of queries. By carefully analyzing the action of $\mathcal{O}$, we show that

$$\|[P_G, P_t\mathcal{O}P_t]\|^2 \leq O\big(\mathbf{I}(\mathcal{P}_G, t)\big).$$

We additionally prove that $\|P_G U\,|\phi_0, \emptyset\rangle - U P_G\,|\phi_0, \emptyset\rangle\| \leq t\|[P_G, P_t\mathcal{O}P_t]\|$. Combining these two inequalities yields the lifting lemma.

See Sect. 4.1 for more details.

2.6   Stronger Lifting via Conditional Instability

The lifting lemma implies that to prove soundness of the Micali construction, it suffices to bound the instability of the Micali database game. Unfortunately, the instability of the Micali database game is actually large, even given the query bound. For example, suppose that D is a database containing Merkle trees for many different proof strings, but each of these Merkle trees has (miraculously) the same root due to collisions. Then, the probability that querying the root yields a good randomness for the underlying PCP verifier is large, because the answer to the query only needs to be a good random string for any one of the many proofs that D contains.

This counterexample, however, should not be of concern because it relies on the database having many collisions, and we have already argued that creating even a single collision in the database is difficult. To deal with this issue, we introduce the notion of *conditional instability*: $\mathbf{I}(\mathcal{P}\,|\,\mathcal{Q}, t)$. This is a refined notion of instability that allows us to condition on events, e.g., that the database has no collisions. Our main technical contribution is the following stronger variant of Lemma 2.

Definition 2. *A database property $\mathcal{P}$ is a set of databases. The complement of $\mathcal{P}$ is $\bar{\mathcal{P}}$.*

Lemma 3 (Lifting lemma). *For any base game G and database property $\mathcal{Q}$,*

$$\omega_{\mathsf{D}}^*(G, t) \leq O\Big(t^2 \cdot \big(\mathbf{I}(\mathcal{P}_G \mid \bar{\mathcal{Q}}, t) + \mathbf{I}(\mathcal{Q}, t)\big)\Big).$$

In particular, combining the above with Lemma 1, we get

$$\omega_{\mathsf{O}}^*(G, t) \leq O\Big(t^2 \cdot \big(\mathbf{I}(\mathcal{P}_G \mid \bar{\mathcal{Q}}, t) + \mathbf{I}(\mathcal{Q}, t)\big) + k/2^n\Big).$$

The above statement is an "instability analogue" of the standard fact that for any two events E_1 and E_2, $\Pr[E_1] \leq \Pr[E_1 \cup E_2] \leq \Pr[E_1 \mid \bar{E_2}] + \Pr[E_2]$.

The proof of Lemma 3 has three steps. First, we relax the database game $\mathcal{P}_G$ so that the adversary wins if the database is in $\mathcal{P}_G \cup \mathcal{Q}$. Clearly, winning the relaxed game is only easier than the original database game. Lemma 2 then implies that $\omega_{\mathsf{D}}^*(G, t) \leq O\Big(t^2 \cdot \mathbf{I}(\mathcal{P}_G \cup \mathcal{Q}, t)\Big)$. Finally, we show that for any two database properties $\mathcal{P}$ and $\mathcal{Q}$ it holds that $\mathbf{I}(\mathcal{P} \cup \mathcal{Q}, t) \leq \mathbf{I}(\mathcal{P} \mid \bar{\mathcal{Q}}, t) + \mathbf{I}(\mathcal{Q}, t)$, which completes the proof.

We remark that Lemma 3 cannot be proved by simply arguing that $\mathbf{I}(\mathcal{P}, t) \leq \mathbf{I}(\mathcal{P} \cup \mathcal{Q}, t)$ and then applying Lemma 2. This is because $\mathbf{I}(\mathcal{P}, t)$ and $\mathbf{I}(\mathcal{P} \cup \mathcal{Q}, t)$ are in general *incomparable* (see Proposition 5 for examples).

See Sect. 4.2 for more details.

2.7 Instability of the Micali Oracle Game

Armed with our lifting lemma, establishing the quantum security of the Micali construction is now relatively straightforward. Let $\mathcal{P}_{\mathsf{Mic}}$ be the database property for the Micali game, and let $\bar{\mathcal{P}}_{\mathsf{col}}$ be the no-collision property (the set of databases that do not contain collisions). We show that, for a random oracle of the form $h \colon \{0,1\}^{2\lambda} \to \{0,1\}^{\lambda}$,

$$\mathbf{I}(\mathcal{P}_{\mathsf{col}}, t) < t/2^{\lambda} \quad \text{and} \quad \mathbf{I}(\mathcal{P}_{\mathsf{Mic}} \mid \bar{\mathcal{P}}_{\mathsf{col}}, t) < \varepsilon + O(t/2^{\lambda}).$$

Proving each of these inequalities is merely a classical argument.

– $\mathbf{I}(\mathcal{P}_{\mathsf{col}}, t)$: If D is a database containing less than t entries and has a collision, then adding an entry to D cannot remove the collision, so the probability that adding a new entry to D makes D have no collisions is 0. Let D be a database containing less than t entries and no collisions. For any new query x, adding the query-answer pair (x, y) to D for a random y will contain a collision with probability less than $t/2^{\lambda}$. Thus, $\mathbf{I}(\mathcal{P}_{\mathsf{col}}, t) < t/2^{\lambda}$.
– $\mathbf{I}(\mathcal{P}_{\mathsf{Mic}} \mid \bar{\mathcal{P}}_{\mathsf{col}}, t)$: It is impossible to go from a database D in $\mathcal{P}_{\mathsf{Mic}}$ to a database D not in $\mathcal{P}_{\mathsf{Mic}}$ by adding entries. Let D be a database not in $\mathcal{P}_{\mathsf{Mic}}$ containing less than t entries that contains no collisions. There are two ways to make D in $\mathcal{P}_{\mathsf{Mic}}$: either the new query is for the randomness of the PCP verifier in the

Micali construction, in which case this finds a good choice of randomness with probability at most ε, or the new query extends one of the Merkle trees that the adversary is constructing. To extend the Merkle tree the adversary must find a pre-image, which happens with probability less than $O(t/2^\lambda)$. Hence, $\mathbf{I}(\mathcal{P}_{\mathsf{Mic}} \mid \bar{\mathcal{P}}_{\mathsf{col}}, t) < \varepsilon + O(t/2^\lambda)$, completing the proof.

Combining these bounds on instability with the lifting lemma completes the proof of soundness, and completes a proof sketch for Theorem 1. See the full version of the paper for more details.

2.8   zkSNARKs in the QROM

We have so far discussed how to establish soundness of the Micali construction in the quantum setting. We now discuss how to further establish zero knowledge and proof of knowledge, obtaining the first zkSNARKs secure in the quantum random oracle model (and thereby proving Theorem 2).

Zero Knowledge. In the classical setting, the Micali construction achieves statistical zero knowledge provided the underlying PCP is (honest-verifier) statistical zero knowledge (and leaves in the Merkle tree are suitably salted to ensure statistical hiding of unrevealed leaves) [13,40]. In the quantum setting, an analogous statement is immediate simply because the zero knowledge property holds against computationally unbounded verifiers *that make an unbounded number of queries to the random oracle*, and any quantum verifier can be simulated by an unbounded verifier.

Proof of Knowledge. In the classical setting, the Micali construction achieves proof of knowledge provided the underlying PCP is a proof of knowledge [61]. The quantum analogue of this statement, however, does *not* immediately follow from our soundness analysis. Recall that our strategy was to bound the instability of the Micali property for $x \notin \mathcal{L}$, conditioned on no collisions. But when $x \in \mathcal{L}$ this approach will not work, because the instability of the Micali property even conditioned on the absence of collisions is 1 (as witnessed by the existence of the honest prover).

Nevertheless, the tools that we develop in this work are flexible enough that we can apply them to also establish proof of knowledge. We consider the following natural extractor strategy: run the prover until completion, and measure the database. Then, for each entry in the database, try to extract a PCP proof rooted at that entry, and then run the PCP extractor on this proof.

Let $\mathcal{P}$ be the set of databases D where there exists a root rt such that D wins the Micali game with a SNARG proof rooted at rt, but the PCP extractor does not extract a valid witness from the PCP proof rooted at rt. If the prover wins the Micali game but the extractor fails, then D must be in $\mathcal{P}$. We then argue that $\mathbf{I}(\mathcal{P} \mid \bar{\mathcal{P}}_{\mathsf{col}}, t)$ is at most $\mathsf{k} + O(t/2^\lambda)$, where k is the knowledge error of the underlying PCP. Intuitively, this is because if the PCP extractor fails to extract a witness from the PCP proof Π rooted at rt, then Π convinces the verifier with probability at most k, and hence the probability of finding good randomness for

Π is at most k. Combining this with Lemma 3 implies that the probability that the prover wins the Micali game but the extractor fails is at most $O(t^2\mathsf{k}+t^3/2^\lambda)$. Hence, if μ is the probability that the prover wins the Micali game, then the probability that the extractor succeeds is at least $\Omega(\mu - t^2\mathsf{k} - t^3/2^\lambda)$.

See the full version of the paper for more details.

2.9   The BCS Construction: Succinct Arguments Beyond Micali

We apply our techniques to prove post-quantum security of the BCS construction [13], when the underlying public-coin IOP satisfies a notion of soundness achieved by many protocols of practical interest. The notion is *round-by-round soundness*, and was introduced for IPs in [21] for the purposes of facilitating proofs of security of the Fiat–Shamir transformation for correlation-intractable hash functions. The notion can be extended in a straightforward way to any IOP, and this is the notion that we consider in this work. We further show that if the underlying IOP is honest-verifier zero knowledge and/or has round-by-round proof of knowledge, then the BCS argument inherits these properties. Round-by-round proof of knowledge is a type of knowledge property that is analogous to round-by-round soundness (and is also achieved by many protocols of practical interest). Below we sketch our analysis; see the full version of the paper for details.

Soundness. An IOP has round-by-round soundness if, for any partial transcript tr of the protocol, one can tell if tr is "doomed", i.e., that it is highly unlikely to be accepted by the verifier when completed to a full transcript; a doomed full transcript is never accepted by the verifier.

By the lifting lemma, in order to prove the post-quantum security of the BCS construction it suffices to bound the conditional instability of the database property $\mathcal{P}$, where $D \in \mathcal{P}$ if D contains a partial transcript where the last verifier message has flipped the transcript from "doomed" to "not doomed". We argue that $\mathbf{I}(\mathcal{P} \mid \bar{\mathcal{P}}_{\mathsf{col}}, t) < \epsilon + O(t/2^\lambda)$, where ϵ is the round-by-round soundness error of the IOP. The proof is similar to the proof for the Micali construction. If $D \notin \mathcal{P}$, there are two ways to add an entry and make $D \in \mathcal{P}$: either the new query is for the randomness of the next verifier message in the IOP for some doomed transcript tr, in which case we find a message that makes tr not doomed with probability ϵ; or the new query extends one of the Merkle trees that the adversary is constructing, which happens with probability less than $O(t/2^\lambda)$ as this implies finding a pre-image. Hence, $\mathbf{I}(\mathcal{P} \mid \bar{\mathcal{P}}_{\mathsf{col}}, t) < \epsilon + O(t/2^\lambda)$, which completes the proof.

Zero Knowledge. As in the case of Micali, zero knowledge is straightforward, as the BCS construction classically achieves *statistical* zero knowledge when the IOP is honest-verifier zero knowledge.

Proof of Knowledge. Analogously to our analysis of the Micali construction, we define a property $\mathcal{Q}$, where $D \in \mathcal{Q}$ if D contains a partial transcript that is in $\mathcal{P}$ but the BCS extractor fails to extract a valid witness. We then argue that

$\mathbf{I}(\mathcal{Q} \mid \bar{\mathcal{P}}_{\mathsf{col}}) < \mathsf{k} + O(t/2^\lambda)$, where k is the round-by-round knowledge error of the IOP; the proof of this fact is similar to the proof of soundness. We conclude that if the prover causes the verifier to accept with probability at least μ, then the probability that the extractor succeeds is at least $\Omega(\mu - t^2 \mathsf{k} - t^3/2^\lambda)$.

3   Preliminaries

We denote by $\mathcal{R}$ a binary relation of instance-witness pairs (x, w), and by $\mathcal{L}(\mathcal{R})$ its corresponding language, which is the set $\{\mathsf{x} \mid \exists \mathsf{w} \text{ s.t. } (\mathsf{x}, \mathsf{w}) \in \mathcal{R}\}$. We denote by $f \colon X \to Y$ a function from a set X to a set Y; similarly, we denote by $f \colon X \rightharpoonup Y$ a *partial* function from a set X to a set Y, i.e., a function $f \colon X \to Y \cup \{\bot\}$, where $\bot \notin Y$ is a special symbol indicating that $f(x)$ is undefined.

3.1   Quantum Notation

We briefly recall standard quantum notation. We let $|\phi\rangle$ denote an arbitrary quantum state, and let $|x\rangle$ denote an element of the standard (computational) basis. The norm of a state $|\phi\rangle$ is $\||\phi\rangle\| := \sqrt{\langle\phi|\phi\rangle}$. In general, the states that we consider will have norm 1. The operator norm of an operator A is $\|A\|$, defined to be $\max_{|\phi\rangle : \||\phi\rangle\|=1} \|A|\phi\rangle\|$. Note that if A is unitary then $\|A\| = 1$. The commutator of two operators A and B is $[A, B] := AB - BA$. The following proposition relates operator norms and commutators.

Proposition 1. *Let A, B, C be operators with $\|B\|, \|C\| \le 1$. Then*

$$\|[A, BC]\| \le \|[A, B]\| + \|[A, C]\|.$$

Proof. By definition, $[A, BC] = ABC - BCA = ABC - BAC + BAC - BCA = [A, B]C + B[A, C]$. Therefore, $\|[A, BC]\| \le \|[A, B]C\| + \|B[A, C]\| \le \|[A, B]\| + \|[A, C]\|$, as $\|B\|, \|C\| \le 1$.

A projector P is an idempotent linear operator (i.e., $P^2 = P$). Throughout, we will only consider orthogonal projectors of the form $P_S := \sum_{x \in S} |x\rangle\langle x|$, where S is a set of binary strings. Measuring a state $|\phi\rangle$ in the standard basis results in an output that is in S with probability equal to $\|P_S |\phi\rangle\|^2$. Since all P_S are diagonal in the same basis, they commute with each other. Note that for any non-zero orthogonal projector P it holds that $\|P\| = 1$. In particular, since $\|AB\| \le \|A\|\|B\|$, we see that if A is the product of projectors and unitaries then $\|A\| \le 1$.

3.2   Oracle Algorithms

Let $f \colon \{0,1\}^m \to \{0,1\}^n$ be a function. The standard way to model oracle access to f in the quantum setting is via a unitary operator O_f that acts as $|x, y\rangle \mapsto |x, y \oplus f(x)\rangle$ for all $x \in \{0,1\}^m$ and $y \in \{0,1\}^n$. We label the input and output registers X and Y, respectively.

A *t-query quantum oracle algorithm* $\mathcal{A}$ is specified via $m, n \in \mathbb{N}$, t unitary operators $A_1, \ldots, A_t$ and an initial state $|\phi_0\rangle$ on four registers $\mathsf{X}, \mathsf{Y}, \mathsf{S}, \mathsf{T}$. The register X is on m qubits and is for queries to the oracle; the register Y is on n qubits and is for answers from the oracle; the register S is for the output of $\mathcal{A}$; and the register T is for scratch space of $\mathcal{A}$. The initial state $|\phi_0\rangle$ and unitary operators A_i need not be efficiently computable.

We write $|\mathcal{A}^f\rangle$ to denote $A_t O_f A_{t-1} O_f \cdots A_1 O_f |\phi_0\rangle$, the final state of the adversary before measurement. (We implicitly extend O_f to act as the identity on S, T.) We write $\mathcal{A}^f$ to denote the random variable which is the outcome of measuring the register S of $|\mathcal{A}^f\rangle$ in the computational basis. This is the output of $\mathcal{A}$ when accessing the oracle f.

A *random oracle* is a function $h \colon \{0,1\}^m \to \{0,1\}^n$ sampled from $\mathcal{U}(m, n)$, the uniform distribution over functions from $\{0,1\}^m$ to $\{0,1\}^n$. We write $h \leftarrow \mathcal{U}(m, n)$ to say that h is sampled from $\mathcal{U}(m, n)$. In the quantum random oracle model [15], we study $\mathcal{A}^h$ for $h \leftarrow \mathcal{U}(m, n)$.

3.3 Non-interactive Arguments in the Quantum Random Oracle Model

Let $(\mathcal{P}, \mathcal{V})$ be two polynomial-time (classical) algorithms, known as the prover and verifier. We say that $(\mathcal{P}, \mathcal{V})$ is a *non-interactive argument in the quantum random oracle model* (QROM) with soundness error ϵ for a relation $\mathcal{R}$ if it satisfies the following properties.

- **Completeness.** For every $(\mathbb{x}, \mathbb{w}) \in \mathcal{R}$ and function $h \in \mathcal{U}(2\lambda, \lambda)$, $\mathcal{P}^h(\mathbb{x}, \mathbb{w})$ outputs a (classical) proof string π for which $\mathcal{V}^h(\mathbb{x}, \pi) = 1$.
- **Soundness.** For every $\mathbb{x} \notin \mathcal{L}(\mathcal{R})$ and t-query quantum oracle algorithm $\tilde{\mathcal{P}}$, the probability over a function $h \leftarrow \mathcal{U}(2\lambda, \lambda)$ and (classical) proof string $\tilde{\pi} \leftarrow \tilde{\mathcal{P}}^h$ that $\mathcal{V}^h(\mathbb{x}, \tilde{\pi}) = 1$ is at most $\epsilon(t, \lambda)$.

We say that $(\mathcal{P}, \mathcal{V})$ has *argument size* s if a proof π output by $\mathcal{P}^h(\mathbb{x}, \mathbb{w})$ consists of $s(|\mathbb{x}|)$ bits.

We also consider non-interactive arguments that additionally achieve *proof of knowledge* and *zero knowledge*. The first property will hold against query-bounded adversaries (that are otherwise all-powerful), while the second property will hold against unbounded adversaries (and in particular need not refer to quantum algorithms). We define both of these properties below.

Knowledge. The non-interactive argument $(\mathcal{P}, \mathcal{V})$ is an *argument of knowledge* with extraction probability κ if there exists a polynomial-time quantum extractor $\mathcal{E}$ such that, for every instance $\mathbb{x}$ and t-query quantum oracle algorithm $\tilde{\mathcal{P}}$, if, over a random oracle $h \leftarrow \mathcal{U}(2\lambda, \lambda)$, for $\pi := \tilde{\mathcal{P}}^h$ it holds that $\mathcal{V}^h(\mathbb{x}, \pi) = 1$ with probability μ, the probability that $\mathcal{E}^{\tilde{\mathcal{P}}}(\mathbb{x}, 1^t, 1^\lambda)$ outputs a valid witness for $\mathbb{x}$ is at least $\kappa(t, \mu, \lambda)$. Here the notation $\mathcal{E}^{\tilde{\mathcal{P}}}$ denotes that $\mathcal{E}$ has black-box access to $\tilde{\mathcal{P}}$ as defined by Unruh [60]. Informally, this means that if $\tilde{\mathcal{P}} = (A_1, \ldots, A_t)$

with initial state $|\phi_0\rangle$, then $\mathcal{E}$ is given an auxiliary register containing $|\phi_0\rangle$ and may apply, in addition to any efficient quantum operation, any A_i to any of its registers.

Zero Knowledge. The non-interactive argument $(\mathcal{P}, \mathcal{V})$ has (statistical) zero knowledge if there exists a probabilistic polynomial-time simulator $\mathcal{S}$ such that for every instance-witness pair $(\mathsf{x}, \mathsf{w}) \in \mathcal{R}$ the distributions below are statistically close (as a function of λ):

$$\left\{ (h, \pi) \;\middle|\; \begin{matrix} h \leftarrow \mathcal{U}(2\lambda, \lambda) \\ \pi \leftarrow \mathcal{P}^h(\mathsf{x}, \mathsf{w}) \end{matrix} \right\} \quad \text{and} \quad \left\{ (h[\mu], \pi) \;\middle|\; \begin{matrix} h \leftarrow \mathcal{U}(2\lambda, \lambda) \\ (\mu, \pi) \leftarrow \mathcal{S}^h(\mathsf{x}) \end{matrix} \right\}.$$

Above, $h[\mu]$ is the function that, on input x, equals $\mu(x)$ if μ is defined on x, or $h(x)$ otherwise. This definition uses explicitly-programmable random oracles [10]. (Non-interactive zero knowledge with non-programmable random oracles is impossible for non-trivial languages [13,52].)

Succinctness for Non-deterministic Time. A zkSNARK for $\mathsf{NTIME}(T(n))$ in the QROM is a non-interactive argument for $\mathsf{NTIME}(T(n))$ in the QROM such that: (a) it has (statistical) zero knowledge; (b) it has extraction probability $\mathsf{poly}(\mu, 1/t) - \mathsf{poly}(\mu, t)/2^\lambda$; (c) arguments have size $\mathsf{poly}(\lambda, \log T(n))$, the prover runs in time $\mathsf{poly}(\lambda, n, T(n))$, and the verifier runs in time $\mathsf{poly}(\lambda, n, \log T(n))$.

3.4 Probabilistically Checkable Proofs

A *probabilistically checkable proof* (PCP) for a relation $\mathcal{R}$ with soundness error ϵ, proof length ℓ, and alphabet Σ is a pair of polynomial-time algorithms $(\mathbf{P}, \mathbf{V})$ for which the following holds.

- **Completeness.** For every instance-witness pair $(\mathsf{x}, \mathsf{w}) \in \mathcal{R}$, $\mathbf{P}(\mathsf{x}, \mathsf{w})$ outputs a proof string $\Pi \colon [\ell] \to \Sigma$ such that $\Pr[\mathbf{V}^\Pi(\mathsf{x}) = 1] = 1$.
- **Soundness.** For every instance $\mathsf{x} \notin \mathcal{L}(\mathcal{R})$ and proof string $\Pi \colon [\ell] \to \Sigma$, $\Pr[\mathbf{V}^\Pi(\mathsf{x}) = 1] \le \epsilon$.

The quantities ϵ, ℓ, Σ can be functions of the instance size $|\mathsf{x}|$. Probabilities are taken over the randomness of $\mathbf{V}$. The *randomness complexity* is the number of random bits used by $\mathbf{V}$, and the *query complexity* q is the number of locations of Π read by $\mathbf{V}$. (Both can be functions of $|\mathsf{x}|$.)

We also consider PCPs that achieve *proof of knowledge* and (honest-verifier) *zero knowledge*. We define both of these properties below.

Proof of Knowledge. The PCP $(\mathbf{P}, \mathbf{V})$ has knowledge error k if there exists a polynomial-time extractor $\mathbf{E}$ such that for every instance x and proof string $\Pi \colon [\ell] \to \Sigma$ if $\Pr[\mathbf{V}(\mathsf{x}, \Pi) = 1] > \mathsf{k}$ then $\mathbf{E}(\mathsf{x}, \Pi)$ outputs a valid witness for x.

Zero Knowledge. The PCP $(\mathbf{P}, \mathbf{V})$ is (perfect) honest-verifier zero knowledge if there exists a probabilistic polynomial-time simulator $\mathbf{S}$ such that for every instance-witness pair $(\mathsf{x}, \mathsf{w}) \in \mathcal{R}$ the view of $\mathbf{V}(\mathsf{x})$ when given access to a proof string sampled as $\Pi \leftarrow \mathbf{P}(\mathsf{x}, \mathsf{w})$ equals the view of $\mathbf{V}(\mathsf{x})$ when given access to $\mathbf{S}(\mathsf{x})$. In the latter case, $\mathbf{S}(\mathsf{x})$ adaptively answers queries received from $\mathbf{V}(\mathsf{x})$.

3.5   Databases

A *database* mapping X to Y is a partial function $D\colon X \rightharpoonup Y$. The support of a database D is $\mathrm{supp}(D) := \{x \in X\colon D(x) \neq \bot\}$ and its image $\mathrm{im}(D)$ is $\{D(x)\colon x \in \mathrm{supp}(D)\}$. The size of a database is the size of its support: $|D| := |\mathrm{supp}(D)|$. Given two databases D and D', we write $D \subseteq D'$ if $\mathrm{supp}(D) \subseteq \mathrm{supp}(D')$ and $D(x) = D'(x)$ for every $x \in \mathrm{supp}(D)$.

We define two operations on databases, corresponding to deletions and insertions. Given a database D, input values $x, x' \in X$, and output value $y \in Y$, we define the two databases

$$(D - x)(x') := \begin{cases} \bot & \text{if } x = x' \\ D(x') & \text{if } x \neq x' \end{cases} \quad \text{and} \quad (D + [x \mapsto y])(x') := \begin{cases} y & \text{if } x = x' \\ D(x') & \text{if } x \neq x' \end{cases}.$$

For $D\colon \{0,1\}^m \rightharpoonup \{0,1\}^n$ and $t \in \mathbb{N}$ with $|D| \leq t \leq 2^m$, we define the pure quantum state

$$|D_t\rangle := \big|x_1, y_1, \ldots, x_{|D|}, y_{|D|}\big\rangle \otimes |\bot, 0^n\rangle^{\otimes(|D|-t)}$$

where $x_1, \ldots, x_{|D|}$ is the lexicographic ordering of $\mathrm{supp}(D)$ and $y_i := D(x_i)$ for each $i \in [|D|]$. We will write $|D\rangle$ for $|D_t\rangle$ when the bound t is clear from context.

3.6   Compressed Phase Oracle

The standard method to encode a function $h\colon \{0,1\}^m \to \{0,1\}^n$ as a quantum operation is the unitary matrix O_h defined in Sect. 3.2, which acts as $|x,y\rangle \mapsto |x, y \oplus h(x)\rangle$. Another method is to encode h in the *phase* of a quantum state, via the unitary matrix O_h' that acts as $|x,u\rangle \mapsto (-1)^{u \cdot h(x)} |x,u\rangle$. These two encodings are equivalent under an efficient change of basis: $O_h = (I^m \otimes H^n)O_h'(I^m \otimes H^n)$ where I^m is the identity on the first m qubits and H^n is the Hadamard transformation on the other n qubits. Thus, choosing between the *standard oracle* O_h or the *phase oracle* O_h' is a matter of convenience. For example, the Deutsch–Josza algorithm [25] is easier to describe with a standard oracle, while Grover's algorithm [38] is easier with a phase oracle.

In this paper it is more convenient to *always work with phase oracles*. All quantum query algorithms will thus have an oracle phase register U instead of the oracle answer register Y. Moreover, since h is sampled at random from the set of all functions from m bits to n bits, we follow Zhandry [66] and extend the adversary's initial state with a random superposition of all functions h, which represents a purification of the adversary's mixed state relative to the random oracle.

In fact, instead of considering a superposition of functions h, we will consider a superposition of databases D, according to the *compressed oracle* formalism of [66]. Specifically, throughout this paper we will only deal with the *compressed phase oracle* with m input bits and n output bits, which we denote by $\mathcal{O}$. We fix the database query bound of the compressed oracle to be t in advance. For the purposes of this paper, we will only use the fact that $\mathcal{O}$ is a certain unitary matrix, indistinguishable from a real random oracle, whose action is given by the following lemma. We refer the reader to [66] for more details.

Lemma 4 ([66]). *The compressed phase oracle $\mathcal{O}$ (with query bound t) acts on a quantum state $|x, u, z, D\rangle$, where $x \in \{0,1\}^m$, $u \in \{0,1\}^n$, $z \in \{0,1\}^*$, and $D: \{0,1\}^m \rightharpoonup \{0,1\}^n$ is a database with $|D| \leq t$, as follows.*

- *If $|D| = t$ or $u = 0^n$, then $\mathcal{O}|x, u, z, D\rangle = (-1)^{u \cdot D(x)} |x, u, z, D\rangle$, where $u \cdot \perp := 0$.*
- *If $D(x) = \perp$, $|D| < t$, and $u \neq 0^n$, then $\mathcal{O}|x, u, z, D\rangle = |x, u, z\rangle \otimes |\phi\rangle$ where*

$$|\phi\rangle := \frac{1}{\sqrt{2^n}} \sum_{y \in \{0,1\}^n} (-1)^{u \cdot y} |D + [x \mapsto y]\rangle .$$

- *If $D(x) \neq \perp$, $|D| < t$, and $u \neq 0^n$, then $\mathcal{O}|x, u, z, D\rangle = |x, u, z\rangle \otimes |\phi\rangle$ where*

$$|\phi\rangle := (-1)^{u \cdot D(x)} |D\rangle + \frac{(-1)^{u \cdot D(x)}}{\sqrt{2^n}} |D - x\rangle$$

$$+ \frac{1}{2^n} \sum_{y \in \{0,1\}^n} \left(1 - (-1)^{u \cdot y} - (-1)^{u \cdot D(x)}\right) |D - x + [x \mapsto y]\rangle .$$

Given a quantum algorithm $\mathcal{A}$ described by unitaries $A_1, \ldots, A_t$ and initial state $|\phi_0\rangle$, we write $|\mathsf{Sim}^*(\mathcal{A})\rangle$ to represent the final state of $\mathcal{A}$ before measurement when simulated using $\mathcal{O}$ as the oracle. Formally, $|\mathsf{Sim}^*(\mathcal{A})\rangle = A_t \mathcal{O} \cdots A_1 \mathcal{O} |\phi_0, \emptyset\rangle$, where $\emptyset$ denotes that the D register holds the empty database with t slots, and we implicitly extend each A_i to act as the identity on D.

The following lemma of [66] shows simulating $\mathcal{A}$ by using $\mathcal{O}$ as the oracle is perfectly indistinguishable from running $\mathcal{A}$ with access to a random oracle.

Lemma 5 ([66, Lemma 4]). *For any quantum oracle algorithm $\mathcal{A}$ making at most t queries,*

$$\mathrm{Tr}_\mathsf{D}(|\mathsf{Sim}^*(\mathcal{A})\rangle\langle\mathsf{Sim}^*(\mathcal{A})|) = \frac{1}{(2^n)^{2^m}} \sum_{h: \{0,1\}^m \to \{0,1\}^n} |\mathcal{A}^h\rangle\langle\mathcal{A}^h| .$$

I.e., $|\mathsf{Sim}^*(\mathcal{A})\rangle$ purifies the mixed state of $\mathcal{A}$ when interacting with a random oracle $h \leftarrow \mathcal{U}(m, n)$.

The notation Tr_D denotes the partial trace over the D (database) register, defined as the unique linear operator such that $\mathrm{Tr}_\mathsf{D}(|a\rangle\langle a|_\mathsf{Z} \otimes |b\rangle\langle b|_\mathsf{D}) := \langle b|b\rangle \, |a\rangle\langle a|_\mathsf{Z}$ for all vectors $|a\rangle, |b\rangle$. Here Z denotes all the registers of the adversary.

4   A Lifting Lemma for Database Games

In this section we show how to bound the value of a (classical or quantum) database game via the *instability* of the game, a purely classical quantity that we introduce in this paper. As we will see shortly, it is straightforward to argue that for any base game G (Sect. 2.4), the value $\omega_D(G, t)$ is at most t times the instability of G. The goal of this section is to prove that the (quantum) value $\omega_D^*(G, t)$ is at most t^2 times the instability of G. In particular, we enable *lifting* a bound on the (classical) instability of G to a bound on the (quantum) value $\omega_D^*(G, t)$. Combining the lifting lemma with the fact that oracle games can be generically reduced to database games (Lemma 1), we are able to establish the post-quantum security of the Micali construction solely by analyzing classical properties of it.

4.1   Database Properties and the Basic Lifting Lemma

A database property is a more general notion of a database game.

Definition 3. *A **database property** $\mathcal{P}$ is a set of databases $D \colon X \rightharpoonup Y$. The negation of $\mathcal{P}$, denoted $\bar{\mathcal{P}}$, is the set $(X \rightharpoonup Y) \setminus \mathcal{P}$.*

Given a base game, we define a corresponding database property as follows.

Definition 4. *The database property of a base game $G \subseteq A^k \times B^k \times C$ is*

$$\mathcal{P}_G := \{D : \exists\, (\mathbf{a}, \mathbf{b}, c) \in G \text{ with } D(a_i) = b_i\ \forall\, i \in [k]\}.$$

For a base game G, the database property $\mathcal{P}_G$ is closely related to the database game of G. This is because winning the database game is equivalent to the database outputted by $\mathsf{Sim}^*(\mathcal{A})$ being in $\mathcal{P}_G$. In particular, the following proposition holds.

Proposition 2. *For every base game $G \subseteq A^k \times B^k \times C$ and quantum algorithm $\mathcal{A}$,*

$$\Pr[\mathcal{A} \text{ wins } G_D^*] = \Pr\left[D \in \mathcal{P}_G \,\middle|\, ((\mathbf{a}, \mathbf{b}, c), D) \leftarrow \mathsf{Sim}^*(\mathcal{A})\right].$$

We define the *flip probability* of a pair of database properties.

Definition 5. *The **flip probability** $\mathrm{flip}(\mathcal{P} \to \mathcal{Q}, t)$ from property $\mathcal{P}$ to property $\mathcal{Q}$ is the quantity*

$$\mathrm{flip}(\mathcal{P} \to \mathcal{Q}, t) := \max_{\substack{D \colon \{0,1\}^m \to \{0,1\}^n \\ |D| < t,\, D \in \mathcal{P}}} \max_{x \notin \mathrm{supp}(D)} \Pr_y\left[D + [x \mapsto y] \in \mathcal{Q}\right],$$

and $\mathrm{flip}(\emptyset \to \mathcal{Q}, t) := 0$.

Intuitively, this is the maximum probability over all databases $D \in \mathcal{P}$ with less than t entries that making an additional query puts $D \in \mathcal{Q}$. The following properties can be obtained easily from the above definition.

Proposition 3 (Properties of the flip probability). *Let $\mathcal{P}, \mathcal{P}', \mathcal{Q}, \mathcal{Q}'$ be database properties.*

(i) If $\mathcal{P} \subseteq \mathcal{P}'$ and $\mathcal{Q} \subseteq \mathcal{Q}'$ then $\mathrm{flip}(\mathcal{P} \to \mathcal{Q}) \leq \mathrm{flip}(\mathcal{P}' \to \mathcal{Q}')$.
(ii) $\mathrm{flip}(\mathcal{P} \cup \mathcal{P}' \to \mathcal{Q}) = \max\left(\mathrm{flip}(\mathcal{P} \to \mathcal{Q}), \mathrm{flip}(\mathcal{P}' \to \mathcal{Q})\right)$.
(iii) $\mathrm{flip}(\mathcal{P} \to \mathcal{Q} \cup \mathcal{Q}') \leq \mathrm{flip}(\mathcal{P} \to \mathcal{Q}) + \mathrm{flip}(\mathcal{P} \to \mathcal{Q}')$.

The instability of a database property is the following classical quantity.

Definition 6. *The* **instability** $\mathbf{I}(\mathcal{P}, t)$ *of a database property* $\mathcal{P}$ *with query bound* t *is the maximum probability that, for any database D containing less than t queries, making one additional (classical) query changes whether or not D has the property $\mathcal{P}$. Formally, we let*

$$\mathbf{I}(\mathcal{P}, t) := \max\{\mathrm{flip}(\bar{\mathcal{P}} \to \mathcal{P}, t), \mathrm{flip}(\mathcal{P} \to \bar{\mathcal{P}}, t)\}.$$

Note that instability is symmetric: $\mathbf{I}(\mathcal{P}, t) = \mathbf{I}(\bar{\mathcal{P}}, t)$. There is a direct argument that shows that $\omega_{\mathsf{D}}(G, t)$ is bounded by $t\mathbf{I}(\mathcal{P}_G, t)$.[4] Similarly, our basic lifting lemma shows that $\omega_{\mathsf{D}}^*(G, t)$ is bounded by the instability of the database property $\mathcal{P}_G$. Thus, it lifts a *classical* notion to prove a bound on the *quantum* value of a database game.

Lemma 6 (Basic lifting lemma). *For any base game G,*

$$\omega_{\mathsf{D}}^*(G, t) \leq t^2 \cdot 6\mathbf{I}(\mathcal{P}_G, t).$$

Before we proceed to the proof of Lemma 6, we first introduce some quantum notation. Recall that we let $|\mathsf{Sim}^*(\mathcal{A})\rangle$ denote the final quantum state of the simulated adversary. Using the definition of measurement, we can express the probability that the final measured database D is in a database property $\mathcal{P}$ in terms of the state $|\mathsf{Sim}^*(\mathcal{A})\rangle$.

Proposition 4. *For every database property $\mathcal{P}$ and quantum adversary $\mathcal{A}$,*

$$\Pr\left[D \in \mathcal{P} \,\middle|\, ((\mathbf{a}, \mathbf{b}, c), D) \leftarrow \mathsf{Sim}^*(\mathcal{A})\right] = \||P|\mathsf{Sim}^*(\mathcal{A})\rangle\|^2,$$

where $P := I \otimes \sum_{D \in \mathcal{P}} |D\rangle\langle D|$ is the projector that maps all basis states of the form $|x, u, z\rangle \otimes |D\rangle$ to 0 if $D \notin \mathcal{P}$, and is otherwise the identity.

We learn that in order to bound $\omega_{\mathsf{D}}^*(G, t)$ it suffices to bound $\|P_G |\mathsf{Sim}^*(\mathcal{A})\rangle\|$ for every $\mathcal{A} \in \mathcal{C}_t^*$.

Next, define $P_t := I \otimes \sum_{D : |D| \leq t} |D\rangle\langle D|$ to be the projector that maps all basis states of the form $|x, u, z\rangle \otimes |D\rangle$ to 0 if $|D| > t$, and is otherwise the identity.

The proof of Lemma 6 follows from two lemmas. The first lemma shows that $\|P|\mathsf{Sim}^*(\mathcal{A})\rangle\|$ is bounded by $t\|P(P_t\mathcal{O}P_t)\bar{P}\|$. Intuitively, this is because if P and $P_t\mathcal{O}P_t$ almost commute (i.e., P and $\mathcal{O}$ almost commute when acting on databases with at most t entries) then each oracle query cannot change the probability that the database is in $\mathcal{P}$ by too much. The second lemma shows that $\|P(P_t\mathcal{O}P_t)\bar{P}\|^2$ is bounded by $\mathbf{I}(\mathcal{P}, t)$. Combining the two lemmas with Proposition 4 completes the proof of Lemma 6.

---

[4] Let $\mathcal{A}$ be a classical adversary, and let $\mathcal{A}_i$ be the adversary obtained by stopping $\mathcal{A}$ immediately before its i-th query. Then $|\Pr[\mathcal{A}_{i+1} \text{ wins } G_{\mathsf{D}}] - \Pr[\mathcal{A}_i \text{ wins } G_{\mathsf{D}}]| \leq \mathbf{I}(\mathcal{P}, t)$ holds for each $i \in [t]$ by definition of instability, and $\Pr[\mathcal{A}_1 \text{ wins } G_{\mathsf{D}}] = 0$ since $\emptyset \notin \mathcal{P}_G$. Therefore, $\Pr[\mathcal{A} \text{ wins } G_{\mathsf{D}}] \leq t\mathbf{I}(\mathcal{P}, t)$.

Lemma 7. *Let $\mathcal{P}$ be a database property with $\emptyset \notin \mathcal{P}$. For every $\mathcal{A} \in \mathcal{C}_t^*$,*

$$\||P|\mathsf{Sim}^*(\mathcal{A})\rangle\| \leq t \cdot \|P(P_t \mathcal{O} P_t)\bar{P}\|.$$

Lemma 8. *For any database property $\mathcal{P}$,*

$$\|P(P_t \mathcal{O} P_t)\bar{P}\|^2 \leq 6\mathbf{I}(\mathcal{P}, t).$$

Lemmas 7 and 8 strengthen the proof sketch outlined in Sect. 2.5. This is because for any operator A and projector P, $[P, A] = PA - AP = (PAP + PA\bar{P}) - (PAP + \bar{P}AP) = PA\bar{P} - \bar{P}AP$, and so $\|[P, A]\|^2 = \|PA\bar{P}\|^2 + \|\bar{P}AP\|^2$. Hence, Lemma 7 implies that $\||P|\mathsf{Sim}^*(\mathcal{A})\rangle\| \leq t \cdot \|[P, P_t \mathcal{O} P_t]\|$ and Lemma 8 implies that $\|[P, P_t \mathcal{O} P_t]\|^2 \leq 12\mathbf{I}(\mathcal{P}, t)$.

We now prove Lemma 7; the proof of Lemma 8 can be found in the full version of the paper.

Proof (Proof of Lemma 7). Recall that the quantum algorithm $\mathcal{A}$ is described by some unitaries $(A_1, \ldots, A_t)$ and initial state $|\phi_0\rangle$. We can thus describe the quantum algorithm $\mathsf{Sim}^*(\mathcal{A})$ via the cumulative unitary $U := A_t \mathcal{O} A_{t-1} \cdots \mathcal{O} A_1 \mathcal{O}$ acting on the initial state $|\phi_0, \emptyset\rangle$ where $\emptyset$ denotes the empty database. (We abuse notation and implicitly extend A_i to act as the identity on the database register.) The final state is $|\mathsf{Sim}^*(\mathcal{A})\rangle := U|\phi_0, \emptyset\rangle$.

Let $U' := A_t(P_t \mathcal{O} P_t)A_{t-1} \cdots (P_t \mathcal{O} P_t)A_1(P_t \mathcal{O} P_t)$. We have that $U'|\phi_0, \emptyset\rangle = U|\phi_0, \emptyset\rangle$, as applying each P_t has no effect, since the database can only have at most t queries when P_t is applied.

For any operators $C_1, \ldots, C_t$ and projector P, we have that

$$C_t \cdots C_1 = \bar{P}C_t \bar{P}C_{t-1}\bar{P} \cdots C_1 \bar{P} + \sum_{i=0}^{t}(C_t \cdots C_{i+1}) \cdot P \cdot (C_i \bar{P} \cdots C_1 \bar{P}). \qquad (1)$$

To see this, we observe that

$$C_t \cdots C_1 = (C_t \cdots C_2)(C_1 \bar{P}) + (C_t \cdots C_1) \cdot P,$$

which implies Eq. (1) by induction.

Let $C_i = A_i(P_t \mathcal{O} P_t)$. Then we have that

$$\||P|\mathsf{Sim}^*(\mathcal{A})\rangle\| = \|PU'|\phi_0, \emptyset\rangle\|$$

$$= \left\|\left(P\bar{P}C_t \bar{P}C_{t-1}\bar{P} \cdots C_1 \bar{P} + \sum_{i=0}^{t}P(C_t \cdots C_{i+1}) \cdot P \cdot (C_i \bar{P} \cdots C_1 \bar{P})\right)|\phi_0, \emptyset\rangle\right\|$$

$$\leq \sum_{i=0}^{t}\|P(C_t \cdots C_{i+1}) \cdot P \cdot (C_i \bar{P} \cdots C_1 \bar{P})|\phi_0, \emptyset\rangle\|$$

$$\leq \|P(C_t \cdots C_1) \cdot P|\phi_0, \emptyset\rangle\| + \sum_{i=1}^{t}\|P(C_t \cdots C_{i+1})\| \cdot \|P \cdot (C_i \bar{P} \cdots C_1 \bar{P})|\phi_0, \emptyset\rangle\|$$

$$\leq 0 + \sum_{i=1}^{t}\|PC_i \bar{P}\| \cdot \|(C_i \bar{P} \cdots C_1 \bar{P})|\phi_0, \emptyset\rangle\|$$

$$\leq \sum_{i=1}^{t}\|PA_i(P_t \mathcal{O} P_t)\bar{P}\|,$$

where we use the fact that the operator norm of a product of unitaries/projectors is at most 1, and that $\emptyset \notin \mathcal{P}$. Since P and A_i commute for every i, we get that $\|PA_i(P_t \mathcal{O} P_t)\bar{P}\| = \|A_i P(P_t \mathcal{O} P_t)\bar{P}\| \leq \|A_i\|\|P(P_t \mathcal{O} P_t)\bar{P}\| = \|P(P_t \mathcal{O} P_t)\bar{P}\|$. Hence, $\||P|\mathsf{Sim}^*(\mathcal{A})\rangle\| \leq t\|P(P_t \mathcal{O} P_t)\bar{P}\|$.

4.2 Conditional Instability and the Lifting Lemma

Lemma 6 is not quite sufficient to analyze the database game that corresponds to the Micali construction. In fact, the instability of this game is high because we take a maximum over all bounded databases, including those which contain collisions. If we were to only take the maximum over databases that do not contain collisions, then the instability would be low. Moreover, the instability of the "no collision" property is itself low.

In this section, we strengthen the results of the previous section by introducing the notion of *conditional* instability, which allows us to analyze the value $\omega_D^*(G, t)$ by splitting its database property $\mathcal{P}_G$ into subproperties and analyzing the subproperties separately, analogous to conditioning in probability. In particular, we can then analyze the Micali game by analyzing the no collision property and the instability of the Micali database property conditioned on the no collision property.

For the entirety of this section we will let $\mathcal{P}$ and $\mathcal{Q}$ be database properties, and we will analyze quantities about $\mathcal{P}$ conditioned on $\mathcal{Q}$. These results strengthen the results of Sect. 4.1, as the previous results can be recovered by setting $\mathcal{Q}$ to be the database property containing all databases.

Definition 7. *Let $\mathcal{P}$ and $\mathcal{Q}$ be two database properties, and let t be a query bound. We define*

$$\mathrm{flip}(\mathcal{P} \mid \mathcal{Q}, t) := \mathrm{flip}(\bar{\mathcal{P}} \cap \mathcal{Q} \to \mathcal{P} \cap \mathcal{Q}, t).$$

The **conditional instability** $\mathbf{I}(\mathcal{P} \mid \mathcal{Q}, t)$ *is defined as*

$$\mathbf{I}(\mathcal{P} \mid \mathcal{Q}, t) := \max\{\mathrm{flip}(\mathcal{P} \mid \mathcal{Q}, t), \ \mathrm{flip}(\bar{\mathcal{P}} \mid \mathcal{Q}, t)\}.$$

Before we state the lifting lemma, we observe the following properties of instability.

Proposition 5. *Let $\mathcal{P}$ and $\mathcal{Q}$ be two database properties. Then*

1. $\mathbf{I}(\mathcal{P}, t)$ *and* $\mathbf{I}(\mathcal{P} \cup \mathcal{Q}, t)$ *are incomparable.*
2. $\mathrm{flip}(\mathcal{P} \mid \mathcal{Q}, t) \leq \mathrm{flip}(\bar{\mathcal{P}} \to \mathcal{P}, t)$, *and therefore* $\mathbf{I}(\mathcal{P} \mid \mathcal{Q}, t) \leq \mathbf{I}(\mathcal{P}, t)$.
3. $\mathbf{I}(\mathcal{P} \cup \mathcal{Q}, t) \leq \mathbf{I}(\mathcal{P} \mid \bar{\mathcal{Q}}, t) + \mathbf{I}(\mathcal{Q}, t)$.

Proof. To show Item 1, we give database properties $\mathcal{P}, \mathcal{Q}$ such that $\mathbf{I}(\mathcal{P}, t) > \mathbf{I}(\mathcal{P} \cup \mathcal{Q}, t)$ and properties $\mathcal{P}', \mathcal{Q}'$ such that $\mathbf{I}(\mathcal{P}', t) < \mathbf{I}(\mathcal{P}' \cup \mathcal{Q}', t)$. Let $\mathcal{P}$ be the property that $D \neq \emptyset$. Then clearly $\mathbf{I}(\mathcal{P}, t) \geq \mathrm{flip}(\bar{\mathcal{P}} \to \mathcal{P}, t) = 1$. Let $\mathcal{Q}$ be the property that $D = \emptyset$. Now $\mathcal{P} \cup \mathcal{Q}$ is the set of all databases, so $\mathbf{I}(\mathcal{P} \cup \mathcal{Q}, t) = 0$.

On the other hand, let $\mathcal{P}' = \emptyset$ be the empty property, and let $\mathcal{Q}'$ be the property that $D = \emptyset$. Then, $\mathbf{I}(\mathcal{P}', t) = 0$, and $\mathbf{I}(\mathcal{P}' \cup \mathcal{Q}', t) = \mathbf{I}(\mathcal{Q}', t) = 1$.

Item 2 holds since

$$\text{flip}(\mathcal{P} \mid \mathcal{Q}, t) = \text{flip}(\bar{\mathcal{P}} \cap \mathcal{Q} \to \mathcal{P} \cap \mathcal{Q}, t) \leq \text{flip}(\bar{\mathcal{P}} \to \mathcal{P}, t).$$

Finally, for Item 3 we observe that

$$\begin{aligned}
\text{flip}(\overline{\mathcal{P} \cup \mathcal{Q}} \to \mathcal{P} \cup \mathcal{Q}, t) &= \text{flip}(\bar{\mathcal{P}} \cap \bar{\mathcal{Q}} \to \mathcal{P} \cup \mathcal{Q}, t) \\
&\leq \text{flip}(\bar{\mathcal{P}} \cap \bar{\mathcal{Q}} \to \mathcal{P} \cap \bar{\mathcal{Q}}, t) + \text{flip}(\bar{\mathcal{P}} \cap \bar{\mathcal{Q}} \to \mathcal{Q}, t) \\
&\leq \text{flip}(\mathcal{P} \mid \bar{\mathcal{Q}}, t) + \text{flip}(\bar{\mathcal{Q}} \to \mathcal{Q}, t).
\end{aligned}$$

On the other hand,

$$\begin{aligned}
\text{flip}(\mathcal{P} \cup \mathcal{Q} \to \overline{\mathcal{P} \cup \mathcal{Q}}, t) &= \text{flip}(\mathcal{P} \cup \mathcal{Q} \to \bar{\mathcal{P}} \cap \bar{\mathcal{Q}}, t) \\
&= \max(\text{flip}(\mathcal{P} \cap \bar{\mathcal{Q}} \to \bar{\mathcal{P}} \cap \bar{\mathcal{Q}}, t), \text{flip}(\mathcal{Q} \to \bar{\mathcal{P}} \cap \bar{\mathcal{Q}}, t)) \\
&\leq \max(\text{flip}(\bar{\mathcal{P}} \mid \bar{\mathcal{Q}}, t), \text{flip}(\mathcal{Q} \to \bar{\mathcal{Q}}, t)).
\end{aligned}$$

Therefore, we get that $\mathbf{I}(\mathcal{P} \cup \mathcal{Q}) \leq \mathbf{I}(\mathcal{P} \mid \bar{\mathcal{Q}}, t) + \mathbf{I}(\mathcal{Q}, t)$.

We now state the lifting lemma.

Lemma 9 (Lifting lemma). *Let G be a base game. Then for any database property $\mathcal{Q}$,*

$$\omega_{\mathsf{D}}^*(G, t) \leq t^2 \cdot 6 \left(\mathbf{I}(\mathcal{P}_G \mid \bar{\mathcal{Q}}, t) + \mathbf{I}(\mathcal{Q}, t) \right).$$

Proof. Let $\mathcal{P}$ and $\mathcal{Q}$ be two database properties. We show that for every $\mathcal{A} \in \mathcal{C}_t^*$ it holds that

$$\| P \mid \mathsf{Sim}^*(\mathcal{A}) \rangle \|^2 \leq t^2 \cdot 6 \left(\mathbf{I}(\mathcal{P} \mid \bar{\mathcal{Q}}, t) + \mathbf{I}(\mathcal{Q}, t) \right).$$

Let $\mathcal{R} = \mathcal{P} \cup \mathcal{Q}$. Then by Lemmas 7 and 8 we have that

$$\| P \mid \mathsf{Sim}^*(\mathcal{A}) \rangle \|^2 \leq \| R \mid \mathsf{Sim}^*(\mathcal{A}) \rangle \|^2 \leq t^2 \cdot \| [R, P_t \mathcal{O} P_t] \|^2 \leq t^2 \cdot 6 \mathbf{I}(\mathcal{R}, t),$$

where the first inequality holds since $\mathcal{P} \subseteq \mathcal{R}$. Finally, we use the fact that $\mathbf{I}(\mathcal{R}, t) = \mathbf{I}(\mathcal{P} \cup \mathcal{Q}, t) \leq \mathbf{I}(\mathcal{P} \mid \bar{\mathcal{Q}}, t) + \mathbf{I}(\mathcal{Q}, t)$, which completes the proof. $\quad\square$

Acknowledgments. We thank Chinmay Nirkhe for taking part in early stages of this research, and for providing valuable feedback. This research was supported in part by: a Google Faculty Award; the UC Berkeley Center for Long-Term Cybersecurity; the NSF Graduate Research Fellowship Program; the ARCS Foundation; and donations from the Ethereum Foundation and the Interchain Foundation.

This material is based upon work supported by the National Science Foundation Graduate Research Fellowship Program under Grant No. DGE1745016. Any opinions, findings, and conclusions or recommendations expressed in this material are those of the author(s) and do not necessarily reflect the views of the National Science Foundation.

6

References

1. Aaronson, S., Shi, Y.: Quantum lower bounds for the collision and the element distinctness problems. J. ACM **51**(4), 595–605 (2004)
2. Ambainis, A., Rosmanis, A., Unruh, D.: Quantum attacks on classical proof systems: the hardness of quantum rewinding. In: Proceedings of the 55th Annual IEEE Symposium on Foundations of Computer Science, FOCS 2014, pp. 474–483 (2014)
3. Ames, S., Hazay, C., Ishai, Y., Venkitasubramaniam, M.: Ligero: lightweight sublinear arguments without a trusted setup. In: Proceedings of the 24th ACM Conference on Computer and Communications Security, CCS 2017, pp. 2087–2104 (2017)
4. Arora, S., Lund, C., Motwani, R., Sudan, M., Szegedy, M.: Proof verification and the hardness of approximation problems. J. ACM **45**(3), 501–555 (1998). Preliminary version in FOCS '92
5. Arora, S., Safra, S.: Probabilistic checking of proofs: a new characterization of NP. J. ACM **45**(1), 70–122 (1998). Preliminary version in FOCS '92
6. Babai, L.: Trading group theory for randomness. In: Proceedings of the 17th Annual ACM Symposium on Theory of Computing, STOC 1985, pp. 421–429 (1985)
7. Babai, L., Fortnow, L., Levin, L.A., Szegedy, M.: Checking computations in polylogarithmic time. In: Proceedings of the 23rd Annual ACM Symposium on Theory of Computing, STOC 1991, pp. 21–32 (1991)
8. Baum, C., Bootle, J., Cerulli, A., del Pino, R., Groth, J., Lyubashevsky, V.: Sublinear lattice-based zero-knowledge arguments for arithmetic circuits. In: Shacham, H., Boldyreva, A. (eds.) CRYPTO 2018. LNCS, vol. 10992, pp. 669–699. Springer, Cham (2018). https://doi.org/10.1007/978-3-319-96881-0_23
9. Baum, C., Nof, A.: Concretely-efficient zero-knowledge arguments for arithmetic circuits and their application to lattice-based cryptography. Cryptology ePrint Archive, Report 2019/532 (2019)
10. Bellare, M., Rogaway, P.: Random oracles are practical: a paradigm for designing efficient protocols. In: Proceedings of the 1st ACM Conference on Computer and Communications Security, CCS 1993, pp. 62–73 (1993)
11. Ben-Sasson, E., Bentov, I., Horesh, Y., Riabzev, M.: Scalable zero knowledge with no trusted setup. In: Boldyreva, A., Micciancio, D. (eds.) CRYPTO 2019. LNCS, vol. 11694, pp. 701–732. Springer, Cham (2019). https://doi.org/10.1007/978-3-030-26954-8_23
12. Ben-Sasson, E., Chiesa, A., Riabzev, M., Spooner, N., Virza, M., Ward, N.P.: Aurora: transparent succinct arguments for R1CS. In: Ishai, Y., Rijmen, V. (eds.) EUROCRYPT 2019. LNCS, vol. 11476, pp. 103–128. Springer, Cham (2019). https://doi.org/10.1007/978-3-030-17653-2_4. Full version https://eprint.iacr.org/2018/828
13. Ben-Sasson, E., Chiesa, A., Spooner, N.: Interactive oracle proofs. In: Hirt, M., Smith, A. (eds.) TCC 2016. LNCS, vol. 9986, pp. 31–60. Springer, Heidelberg (2016). https://doi.org/10.1007/978-3-662-53644-5_2
14. Bitansky, N., Chiesa, A., Ishai, Y., Paneth, O., Ostrovsky, R.: Succinct noninteractive arguments via linear interactive proofs. In: Sahai, A. (ed.) TCC 2013. LNCS, vol. 7785, pp. 315–333. Springer, Heidelberg (2013). https://doi.org/10.1007/978-3-642-36594-2_18

15. Boneh, D., Dagdelen, Ö., Fischlin, M., Lehmann, A., Schaffner, C., Zhandry, M.: Random oracles in a quantum world. In: Lee, D.H., Wang, X. (eds.) ASIACRYPT 2011. LNCS, vol. 7073, pp. 41–69. Springer, Heidelberg (2011). https://doi.org/10.1007/978-3-642-25385-0_3

16. Boneh, D., Ishai, Y., Sahai, A., Wu, D.J.: Lattice-based SNARGs and their application to more efficient obfuscation. In: Coron, J.-S., Nielsen, J.B. (eds.) EUROCRYPT 2017. LNCS, vol. 10212, pp. 247–277. Springer, Cham (2017). https://doi.org/10.1007/978-3-319-56617-7_9

17. Boneh, D., Ishai, Y., Sahai, A., Wu, D.J.: Quasi-optimal SNARGs via linear multiprover interactive proofs. In: Nielsen, J.B., Rijmen, V. (eds.) EUROCRYPT 2018. LNCS, vol. 10822, pp. 222–255. Springer, Cham (2018). https://doi.org/10.1007/978-3-319-78372-7_8

18. Bowe, S.: bellman: a zk-snark library (2015). https://github.com/zkcrypto/bellman

19. Brassard, G., Chaum, D., Crépeau, C.: Minimum disclosure proofs of knowledge. J. Comput. Syst. Sci. 37(2), 156–189 (1988)

20. Brassard, G., Høyer, P., Tapp, A.: Quantum cryptanalysis of hash and claw-free functions. In: Lucchesi, C.L., Moura, A.V. (eds.) LATIN 1998. LNCS, vol. 1380, pp. 163–169. Springer, Heidelberg (1998). https://doi.org/10.1007/BFb0054319

21. Canetti, R., Chen, Y., Holmgren, J., Lombardi, A., Rothblum, G.N., Rothblum, R.D.: Fiat-Shamir from simpler assumptions. Cryptology ePrint Archive, Report 2018/1004 (2018)

22. Chase, M., et al.: Post-quantum zero-knowledge and signatures from symmetric-key primitives. In: Proceedings of the 24th ACM Conference on Computer and Communications Security, CCS 2017, pp. 1825–1842 (2017)

23. Dagdelen, Ö., Fischlin, M., Gagliardoni, T.: The Fiat–Shamir transformation in a quantum world. In: Sako, K., Sarkar, P. (eds.) ASIACRYPT 2013. LNCS, vol. 8270, pp. 62–81. Springer, Heidelberg (2013). https://doi.org/10.1007/978-3-642-42045-0_4

24. dalek cryptography: A pure-Rust implementation of Bulletproofs using Ristretto (2018). https://github.com/dalek-cryptography/bulletproofs

25. Deutsch, D., Jozsa, R.: Rapid solution of problems by quantum computation. Proc. R. Soc. Lond. A 439(1907), 553–558 (1992)

26. Don, J., Fehr, S., Majenz, C., Schaffner, C.: Security of the Fiat-Shamir transformation in the quantum random-oracle model. In: Boldyreva, A., Micciancio, D. (eds.) CRYPTO 2019. LNCS, vol. 11693, pp. 356–383. Springer, Cham (2019). https://doi.org/10.1007/978-3-030-26951-7_13

27. Dwork, C., Feige, U., Kilian, J., Naor, M., Safra, M.: Low communication 2-prover zero-knowledge proofs for NP. In: Brickell, E.F. (ed.) CRYPTO 1992. LNCS, vol. 740, pp. 215–227. Springer, Heidelberg (1993). https://doi.org/10.1007/3-540-48071-4_15

28. Eaton, E.: Leighton-Micali hash-based signatures in the quantum random-oracle model. In: Adams, C., Camenisch, J. (eds.) SAC 2017. LNCS, vol. 10719, pp. 263–280. Springer, Cham (2018). https://doi.org/10.1007/978-3-319-72565-9_13

29. Electric Coin Company: Zcash Cryptocurrency (2014). https://z.cash/

30. Feige, U., Goldwasser, S., Lovász, L., Safra, S., Szegedy, M.: Interactive proofs and the hardness of approximating cliques. J. ACM 43(2), 268–292 (1996). Preliminary version in FOCS '91

31. Fiat, A., Shamir, A.: How to prove yourself: practical solutions to identification and signature problems. In: Odlyzko, A.M. (ed.) CRYPTO 1986. LNCS, vol. 263, pp. 186–194. Springer, Heidelberg (1987). https://doi.org/10.1007/3-540-47721-7_12

32. Gennaro, R., Minelli, M., Nitulescu, A., Orrù, M.: Lattice-based zk-SNARKs from square span programs. In: Proceedings of the 25th ACM Conference on Computer and Communications Security, CCS 2018, pp. 556–573 (2018)

33. Gentry, C., Wichs, D.: Separating succinct non-interactive arguments from all falsifiable assumptions. In: Proceedings of the 43rd Annual ACM Symposium on Theory of Computing, STOC 2011, pp. 99–108 (2011)

34. Goldreich, O., Håstad, J.: On the complexity of interactive proofs with bounded communication. Inf. Process. Lett. **67**(4), 205–214 (1998)

35. Goldreich, O., Vadhan, S., Wigderson, A.: On interactive proofs with a laconic prover. Comput. Complex. **11**(1/2), 1–53 (2002)

36. Goldwasser, S., Kalai, Y.T., Rothblum, G.N.: Delegating computation: interactive proofs for muggles. J. ACM **62**(4), 27:1–27:64 (2015)

37. Goldwasser, S., Micali, S., Rackoff, C.: The knowledge complexity of interactive proof systems. SIAM J. Comput. **18**(1), 186–208 (1989). Preliminary version appeared in STOC '85

38. Grover, L.K.: A fast quantum mechanical algorithm for database search. In: Proceedings of the 28th Annual ACM Symposium on Theory of Computing, STOC 1996, pp. 212–219 (1996)

39. iden3: websnark: A fast zkSNARK proof generator written in native web assembly (2019). https://github.com/iden3/websnark

40. Ishai, Y., Mahmoody, M., Sahai, A., Xiao, D.: On zero-knowledge PCPs: limitations, simplifications, and applications (2015). http://www.cs.virginia.edu/~mohammad/files/papers/ZKPCPs-Full.pdf

41. Kalai, Y.T., Raz, R.: Interactive PCP. In: Aceto, L., Damgård, I., Goldberg, L.A., Halldórsson, M.M., Ingólfsdóttir, A., Walukiewicz, I. (eds.) ICALP 2008. LNCS, vol. 5126, pp. 536–547. Springer, Heidelberg (2008). https://doi.org/10.1007/978-3-540-70583-3_44

42. Katz, J., Kolesnikov, V., Wang, X.: Improved non-interactive zero knowledge with applications to post-quantum signatures. In: Proceedings of the 25th ACM Conference on Computer and Communications Security, CCS 2018, pp. 525–537 (2018)

43. Kilian, J.: A note on efficient zero-knowledge proofs and arguments. In: Proceedings of the 24th Annual ACM Symposium on Theory of Computing, STOC 1992, pp. 723–732 (1992)

44. Kilian, J., Petrank, E., Tardos, G.: Probabilistically checkable proofs with zero knowledge. In: Proceedings of the 29th Annual ACM Symposium on Theory of Computing, STOC 1997, pp. 496–505 (1997)

45. Kiltz, E., Lyubashevsky, V., Schaffner, C.: A concrete treatment of Fiat-Shamir signatures in the quantum random-oracle model. In: Nielsen, J.B., Rijmen, V. (eds.) EUROCRYPT 2018. LNCS, vol. 10822, pp. 552–586. Springer, Cham (2018). https://doi.org/10.1007/978-3-319-78372-7_18

46. libstark: libstark: a C++ library for zkSTARK systems (2018). https://github.com/elibensasson/libSTARK

47. Liu, Q., Zhandry, M.: Revisiting post-quantum Fiat-Shamir. In: Boldyreva, A., Micciancio, D. (eds.) CRYPTO 2019. LNCS, vol. 11693, pp. 326–355. Springer, Cham (2019). https://doi.org/10.1007/978-3-030-26951-7_12

48. Lund, C., Fortnow, L., Karloff, H.J., Nisan, N.: Algebraic methods for interactive proof systems. J. ACM **39**(4), 859–868 (1992)

49. Micali, S.: Computationally sound proofs. SIAM J. Comput. **30**(4), 1253–1298 (2000). Preliminary version appeared in FOCS '94

50. NIST: Post-quantum cryptography (2016). https://csrc.nist.gov/Projects/Post-Quantum-Cryptography

51. O(1) Labs: Coda Cryptocurrency (2017). https://codaprotocol.com/
52. Pass, R.: On deniability in the common reference string and random oracle model. In: Boneh, D. (ed.) CRYPTO 2003. LNCS, vol. 2729, pp. 316–337. Springer, Heidelberg (2003). https://doi.org/10.1007/978-3-540-45146-4_19
53. Pointcheval, D., Stern, J.: Security proofs for signature schemes. In: Maurer, U. (ed.) EUROCRYPT 1996. LNCS, vol. 1070, pp. 387–398. Springer, Heidelberg (1996). https://doi.org/10.1007/3-540-68339-9_33
54. Reingold, O., Rothblum, R., Rothblum, G.: Constant-round interactive proofs for delegating computation. In: Proceedings of the 48th ACM Symposium on the Theory of Computing, STOC 2016, pp. 49–62 (2016)
55. SCIPR Lab: libsnark: a C++ library for zkSNARK proofs (2014). https://github.com/scipr-lab/libsnark
56. SCIPR Lab: Dizk: Java library for distributed zero knowledge proof systems (2018). https://github.com/scipr-lab/dizk
57. SCIPR Lab: libiop: C++ library for IOP-based zkSNARKs (2019). https://github.com/scipr-lab/libiop
58. Targhi, E.E., Unruh, D.: Post-quantum security of the Fujisaki-Okamoto and OAEP transforms. In: Hirt, M., Smith, A. (eds.) TCC 2016. LNCS, vol. 9986, pp. 192–216. Springer, Heidelberg (2016). https://doi.org/10.1007/978-3-662-53644-5_8
59. Unruh, D.: Non-interactive zero-knowledge proofs in the quantum random oracle model. In: Oswald, E., Fischlin, M. (eds.) EUROCRYPT 2015. LNCS, vol. 9057, pp. 755–784. Springer, Heidelberg (2015). https://doi.org/10.1007/978-3-662-46803-6_25
60. Unruh, D.: Post-quantum security of Fiat-Shamir. In: Takagi, T., Peyrin, T. (eds.) ASIACRYPT 2017. LNCS, vol. 10624, pp. 65–95. Springer, Cham (2017). https://doi.org/10.1007/978-3-319-70694-8_3
61. Valiant, P.: Incrementally verifiable computation or proofs of knowledge imply time/space efficiency. In: Canetti, R. (ed.) TCC 2008. LNCS, vol. 4948, pp. 1–18. Springer, Heidelberg (2008). https://doi.org/10.1007/978-3-540-78524-8_1
62. Walfish, M., Blumberg, A.J.: Verifying computations without reexecuting them. Commun. ACM **58**(2), 74–84 (2015)
63. Watrous, J.: Zero-knowledge against quantum attacks. SIAM J. Comput. **39**(1), 25–58 (2009). Preliminary version appeared in STOC '06
64. Zhandry, M.: Secure identity-based encryption in the quantum random oracle model. In: Safavi-Naini, R., Canetti, R. (eds.) CRYPTO 2012. LNCS, vol. 7417, pp. 758–775. Springer, Heidelberg (2012). https://doi.org/10.1007/978-3-642-32009-5_44
65. Zhandry, M.: A note on the quantum collision and set equality problems. Quantum Inf. Comput. **15**(7&8), 557–567 (2015)
66. Zhandry, M.: How to record quantum queries, and applications to quantum indifferentiability. In: Boldyreva, A., Micciancio, D. (eds.) CRYPTO 2019. LNCS, vol. 11693, pp. 239–268. Springer, Cham (2019). https://doi.org/10.1007/978-3-030-26951-7_9
67. ZKP Standards: Zero knowledge proof standardization (2017). https://zkproof.org/

Delegating Quantum Computation in the Quantum Random Oracle Model

Jiayu Zhang$^{(\boxtimes)}$

Boston University, Boston, USA
jyz16@bu.edu

Abstract. A delegation scheme allows a computationally weak client to use a server's resources to help it evaluate a complex circuit without leaking any information about the input (other than its length) to the server. In this paper, we consider delegation schemes for quantum circuits, where we try to minimize the quantum operations needed by the client. We construct a new scheme for delegating a large circuit family, which we call "C+P circuits". "C+P" circuits are the circuits composed of Toffoli gates and diagonal gates. Our scheme is non-interactive, requires small amount of quantum computation from the client (proportional to input length but independent of the circuit size), and can be proved secure in the quantum random oracle model, without relying on additional assumptions, such as the existence of fully homomorphic encryption. In practice the random oracle can be replaced by an appropriate hash function or block cipher, for example, SHA-3, AES.

This protocol allows a client to delegate the most expensive part of some quantum algorithms, for example, Shor's algorithm. The previous protocols that are powerful enough to delegate Shor's algorithm require either many client side quantum operations or the existence of FHE. The protocol requires asymptotically fewer quantum gates on the client side compared to running Shor's algorithm locally.

To hide the inputs, our scheme uses an encoding that maps one input qubit to multiple qubits. We then provide a novel generalization of classical garbled circuits ("reversible garbled circuits") to allow the computation of Toffoli circuits on this encoding. We also give a technique that can support the computation of phase gates on this encoding.

To prove the security of this protocol, we study key dependent message (KDM) security in the quantum random oracle model. KDM security was not previously studied in quantum settings.

Keywords: Quantum computation delegation · Quantum cryptography · Garbled circuit · Quantum random oracle · KDM security

J. Zhang—Supported in part by NSF awards IIS-1447700 and AF-1763786.
The full version of this paper can be found at http://arxiv.org/abs/1810.05234.

1   Introduction

In computation delegation, there is a client holding secret data φ and the description of circuit C that it wants to apply, but it doesn't have the ability to compute $C(\varphi)$ itself. A delegation protocol allows the client to compute $C(\varphi)$ with the help from a more computationally powerful server. The delegation is *private* if the server cannot learn anything about the input φ during the protocol. After some communications, the client can decrypt the response from the server and get the computation result (see Fig. 1.) This problem is important in the quantum setting: it's likely that quantum computers, when they are built, will be expensive, and made available as a remote service. If a client wants to do some quantum computation on secret data, a quantum computation delegation protocol is needed.

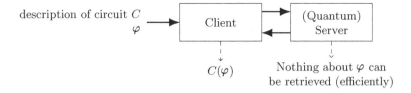

Fig. 1. Delegation of (quantum) computation

Delegation of computation is a central problem in modern cryptography, and has been studied for a long time in classical settings. Related works include multiparty computation, fully homomorphic encryption (FHE), etc. In the study of delegation, there are two key aspects: privacy and authenticity. This paper will focus on privacy.

We want the delegation protocol to be useful, efficient and secure. Previous work falls into two classes: some protocols have information-theoretical security, but they either can only support a small circuit class or require huge client side quantum resources (including quantum memories, quantum gates and quantum communications); other protocols rely on classical fully homomorphic encryption (FHE). This raises the following question:

Is it possible to delegate quantum computation for a large circuit family, with small amount of quantum resources on the client side, without assuming classical FHE?

In the classical world, Yao's garbled circuit answers this question. Garbled circuit is also a fundamental tool in many other cryptographic tasks, like multiparty computation and functional encryption.

Note. When designing quantum cryptographic protocols, one factor that we care about is the "quantum resources" on the client side. The "quantum resources" can be defined as the sum of the cost of the following: (1) the size of quantum memory that the client needs; (2) the number of quantum gates that the client needs to apply; (3) the quantum communication that the client needs to make. Note that if the input (or computation, communication) is partly quantum and partly classical, we only consider the quantum part. Since the classical part is usually much easier to implement than the quantum part, as long as the classical part is polynomial, it's reasonable to ignore it and only consider the complexity of quantum resources. And we argue that it's better to consider the "client side quantum resources" instead of considering only the quantum memory size or quantum gates: on the one hand, we do not know which type of quantum computers will survive in the future, so it's better to focus on the cost estimate that is invariant to them; on the other hand, there may be some way to compose the protocol with other protocols to reduce the memory size, or simplify the gate set.

1.1   Our Contributions

In this paper we develop a non-interactive (1 round) quantum computation delegation scheme for "C+P circuits", the circuits composed of Toffoli gates and diagonal gates. We prove the following:

Theorem 1. *It's possible to delegate C+P circuits non-interactively and securely in the quantum random oracle model, and the client requires $O(\eta N_q + N_q^2)$ quantum CNOT gates as well as polynomial classical computation, where N_q is the number of qubits in the input and η is the security parameter.*

We will give a more formal statement in Sect. 6. The client's quantum circuit size can in fact be bounded by $O(\kappa N_q)$ where κ is the key length of the cryptographic primitives we use. Our current proof of security requires setting $\kappa = \eta + 4N_q$ where η is the actual security parameter. However, we conjecture the same protocol can be proven secure for $\kappa = O(\eta)$, leading to the following conjecture:

Conjecture 1. It's possible to delegate C+P circuits non-interactively and securely in the quantum random oracle model, using the same protocol as Theorem 1, and the client side quantum resources are $O(\eta N_q)$ CNOT gates, where N_q is the number of qubits in the input and η is the security parameter.

We argue that our protocol is important for three reasons: (1) The client only needs small quantum resources. Here we say "small" to mean the quantum resources only depend on the key length and the input size, and are independent of the circuit size. (2) Its security can be proven in the quantum random oracle model, without assuming some trapdoor one-way function. Many protocols before, for example, [11,14] are based on classical FHE and therefore rely on some kinds of lattice cryptographic assumptions, for example, LWE assumption. Our protocol is based on the quantum random oracle (therefore based on hash functions in practice), and this provides an alternative, incomparable assumption on which we can base the security of quantum delegation. (3) Our protocol introduces some new ideas and different techniques, which may be useful in the study of other problems.

Our protocol can be applied to Shor's algorithm. The hardest part of Shor's algorithm is the Toffoli part applied on quantum states, so the client can use this protocol securely with the help of a remote quantum server.

Corollary 1. *It's possible to delegate Shor's algorithm on input of length n within one round of communication in the quantum random oracle model, where the client requires $O(\eta n + n^2)$ CNOT gates plus $\tilde{O}(n)$ quantum gates. Assuming Conjecture 1, the number of CNOT gates is $O(\eta n)$.*

If the client runs the factoring algorithm by itself, the quantum operations it needed will be $\omega(n^2)$, and the exact complexity depends on the multiplication methods.

The security proof for our protocol heavily uses the concept of KDM security, which was not previously studied in the quantum setting. We therefore also initiate a systematic study of KDM security in the quantum random oracle model. We point out that although there already exists classical KDM secure encryption scheme in the random oracle model [5], the security in the quantum random oracle model still needs an explicit proof. We complete its proof in this paper. Furthermore, we generalize KDM security to quantum KDM security, and construct a protocol for it in the quantum random oracle model.

1.2   Related Work

To delegate quantum computation, people raised the concepts of blind quantum computation [7] and quantum homomorphic encryption (QHE) [8]. These two concepts are a little different but closely related: in quantum homomorphic encryption, no interaction is allowed and the circuits to be evaluated are known by the server. While in blind quantum computation, interactions are usually allowed and the circuits are usually only known by the client.

The concept of blind quantum computation was first raised in [3]. And [7] gave a universal blind quantum computation protocol, based on measurement-based quantum computation (MBQC) [17]. What's more, secure assisted quantum computation based on quantum one-time pad (QOTP) technique was raised in [9], with which we can easily apply Clifford gates securely but T gates are hard to implement and require interactions.

Quantum homomorphic encryption is the homomorphic encryption for quantum circuits. Based on QOTP and classical FHE, [8] studied the quantum homomorphic encryption for circuits with low T gate complexity. Later [11] constructed a quantum homomorphic encryption scheme for polynomial size circuits. But it still requires some quantum computing ability on the client side to prepare the evaluation gadgets, and the size of gadgets is proportional to the number of T gates. Recently Mahadev constructed a protocol [14], which achieves fully quantum homomorphic encryption, and what makes this protocol amazing is that the client can be purely classical, which hugely reduces the burden on the client side.

Another viewpoint of these protocols is the computational assumptions needed. With interactions, we can do blind quantum computation for universal quantum circuits information theoretically (IT-) securely. But for non-interactive protocols, [24] gave a limit for IT-secure QHE, which implies IT-secure quantum FHE is impossible. But it's still possible to design protocols for some non-universal circuit families. [13] gave a protocol for IQP circuits, and [23] gave a protocol for circuit with logarithmic number of T gates.

On the other hand, [8,11,14] rely on classical FHE. The current constructions of classical FHE are all based on various kinds of lattice-based cryptosystems, and the most standard assumption is the Learning-With-Error (LWE) assumption.

Table 1 compares different protocols for quantum computation delegation.

Table 1. L is the number of gates in the circuits, N_q is the number of qubits in the input, η is the security parameter.

Protocol	Circuit class	Client's quantum resources	Assumption
QOTP [9]	Clifford	$O(N_q)$ Pauli operations	–
[7]	All	$O(L)$ Rounds: Circuit Depth	–
[14]	All	$O(N_q)$ Pauli operations	FHE
[13]	IQP	$O(N_q)$	–
[23]	Clifford+small number of T gates	Exponential in the number of T gates	–
This paper	C+P	$O(\eta N_q)$(Conjectured) $O(\eta N_q + N_q^2)$(Proved) CNOT operations	Quantum ROM

1.3   Techniques

A Different Encoding for Hiding Quantum States with Classical Keys. In many previous protocols, the client hides a quantum state using "quantum one time pad": $\rho \to X^a Z^b(\rho)$, where a, b are two classical strings. After taking average on a, b, the encrypted state becomes a completely mixed state. In our protocol, we use the following mapping to hide quantum states, which maps one qubit in the plaintext to κ qubits in the ciphertext:

$$\mathsf{Et}_{k_0, k_1} : |0\rangle \to |k_0\rangle, |1\rangle \to |k_1\rangle$$

where k_0, k_1 are chosen uniformly at random in $\{0, 1\}^\kappa$ and distinct.

We can prove for all possible input states, if we apply this operator on each qubit, after taking average on all the possible keys, the final results will be exponentially close to the completely mixed state.

Reversible Garbled Circuits. The main ingredient in our construction is "reversible garbled circuit". In the usual construction of Yao's garbled table, the server can feed the input keys into the garbled table, and get the output keys; then in the decoding phase, it uses an output mapping to map the keys to the result. This well-studied classical construction does not work for quantum states. Even if the original circuit is reversible, the evaluation of Yao's garbled circuit is not! To use it on quantum states, besides the original garbled table, we add another table from the output keys to the input keys. This makes the whole scheme reversible, which means we can use it on quantum states and the computation result won't be entangled with auxiliary qubits. For security, we remove the output mappings. In the context of delegation, these are kept by the client (Fig. 2).

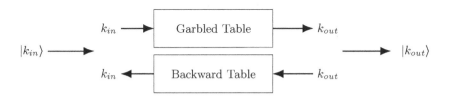

Fig. 2. Reversible garbled table

Note. The proof of security of this scheme is subtle. The extra information included to allow the reversible computation introduces encryption cycles among the keys. We address the problem by studying key-dependent message security in the quantum setting. We show that a KDM-secure encryption scheme exists in the quantum random oracle model, and use this result to prove the security of our reversible garbled circuit construction.

Phase Gates. The reversible garbled circuit allows evaluating Toffoli circuits. To handle phase gates, instead of applying $|k_{in}\rangle \rightarrow |k_{out}\rangle$, we can make the garbled table implement the following transformation (where m is chosen randomly):

$$|k_0\rangle \rightarrow |k_0\rangle |m\rangle, |k_1\rangle \rightarrow |k_1\rangle |m + 1\rangle \tag{1}$$

Then the server can apply a "qudit Z gate" $\sum_i w_n^i |i\rangle \langle i|$ (define $w_n := e^{i\pi/n}$) on the second register, where $i \in \mathbb{Z}_n$ goes through all the integers in $\mathbb{Z}_n$. (This operation can be done efficiently.) This will give us:

$$|k_0\rangle \rightarrow w_n^m |k_0\rangle |m\rangle, |k_1\rangle \rightarrow w_n^{m+1} |k_1\rangle |m + 1\rangle$$

Then it applies (1) again to erase the second register. After removing the global phase the result is the same as the output of applying a phase gate $R_Z(\frac{\pi}{n}) = |0\rangle \langle 0| + w_n |1\rangle \langle 1|$.

1.4   Organisation

This paper is organized as follows. Section 2 contains some background for this paper. In Sect. 3 we discuss the encoding scheme. In Sect. 4 we give our construction of the quantum computation delegation protocol for C+P circuits. In Sect. 5 we prove the security of classical KDM secure scheme in the quantum random oracle model, as the preparation for the security proof of the main protocol. Then in Sect. 6 we discuss the security of our protocol. Section 7.1 turns this delegation scheme to a fully blind protocol, and Sect. 7.2 shows how to use our protocol on Shor's algorithm. Section 8 generalizes KDM security to quantum settings, constructs a quantum KDM secure protocol and proves its security. Then we discuss the open questions and complete this paper.

2   Definitions and Preliminaries

2.1   Basics of Quantum Computation

In this section we give a simple introduction for quantum computing, and clarify some notations in this paper. For more detailed explanations, we refer to [15].

In quantum computing, a pure state is described by a unit vector in a Hilbert space. A qubit, or a quantum bit, in a pure state, can be described by a vector $|\varphi\rangle \in \mathbb{C}^2$. The symbols $|\cdot\rangle$ and $\langle\cdot|$ are called Dirac symbols. A qudit is described by a vector $|\varphi\rangle \in \mathbb{C}^d$.

But a quantum system isn't necessarily in a pure state. When the quantum system is open, we need to consider mixed states. To describe both pure and mixed states, the state of a qubit is described by a density matrix in $\mathbb{C}^{2\times 2}$. A density matrix is a trace-one positive semidefinite complex matrix. The density matrix that corresponds to pure state $|\varphi\rangle$ is $|\varphi\rangle\langle\varphi|$, and we abbreviate it as φ.

For an n-qubit state, its density matrix is in $\mathbb{C}^{2^n \times 2^n}$. The space of density operators in system $\mathcal{S}$ is denoted as $\mathbb{D}(\mathcal{S})$. Note that we use $\mathbb{E}$ for the notation of the expectation value.

A quantum operation on pure states can be described by a unitary transform $|\varphi\rangle \rightarrow U|\varphi\rangle$. And an operation on mixed states can be described by a superoperator $\rho \rightarrow \mathcal{E}(\rho) = \mathrm{tr}_R(U(\rho \otimes |0\rangle\langle 0|)U^\dagger))$. We use calligraphic characters like $\mathcal{D}, \mathcal{E}$ to denote superoperators, and use the normal characters like U, D to denote unitary transforms. We also use Sans-serif font like X, Z, Et to denote quantum operations: When they are used as Et $|\varphi\rangle$ they mean unitary operations (applied on Dirac symbols without parentheses), and when used as Et(ρ) they mean superoperators.

The quantum gates include X, Y, Z, CNOT, H, T, Toffoli and so on. What's more, denote $R_Z(\theta) = |0\rangle\langle 0| + e^{i\theta}|1\rangle\langle 1|$, where i is the imaginary unit. Denote $\omega_n = e^{i\pi/n}$, we can write $R_Z(k\pi/n) = |0\rangle\langle 0| + \omega_n^k|1\rangle\langle 1|$. Since the i will be used as the symbol for indexes and "inputs", we avoid using $e^{i\pi/n}$ in this paper, and use ω_n instead.

The trace distance of two quantum states is defined as $\Delta(\rho, \sigma) = \frac{1}{2}|\rho - \sigma|_{\mathrm{tr}}$, where $|\cdot|_{\mathrm{tr}}$ is the trace norm.

2.2   Encryption with Quantum Adversaries

A quantum symmetric key encryption scheme contains three mappings: $\mathsf{KeyGen}(1^\kappa) \to sk$, $\mathsf{Enc}_{sk} : \mathbb{D}(\mathcal{M}) \to \mathbb{D}(\mathcal{C})$, $\mathsf{Dec}_{sk} : \mathbb{D}(\mathcal{C}) \to \mathbb{D}(\mathcal{M})$ [16].

In this paper, we need to use the symmetric key encryption scheme with key tags, which contains four mappings: KeyGen, Enc, Dec, Ver. The scheme has a key verification procedure $\mathsf{Ver} : \mathcal{K} \times \mathbb{D}(\mathcal{C}) \to \{\bot, 1\}$.

A quantum symmetric key encryption scheme with key tags is correct if:

1. $\forall \rho \in \mathbb{D}(\mathcal{R} \otimes \mathcal{S})$, $\mathbb{E}_{sk \leftarrow \mathsf{KeyGen}(1^\kappa)} |(\mathsf{I} \otimes \mathsf{Dec}_{sk})((\mathsf{I} \otimes \mathsf{Enc}_{sk})(\rho)) - \rho|_{\mathrm{tr}} = \mathsf{negl}(\kappa)$
2. $\forall \rho \in \mathbb{D}(\mathcal{R} \otimes \mathcal{S})$, $\mathrm{Pr}_{sk \leftarrow \mathsf{KeyGen}(1^\kappa)}(\mathsf{Ver}(sk, (\mathsf{I} \otimes \mathsf{Enc}_{sk})(\rho)) = \bot) = \mathsf{negl}(\kappa)$,
   and $\mathrm{Pr}_{sk \leftarrow \mathsf{KeyGen}(1^\kappa), r \leftarrow \mathsf{KeyGen}(1^\kappa)}(\mathsf{Ver}(r, (\mathsf{I} \otimes \mathsf{Enc}_{sk})(\rho)) = 1) = \mathsf{negl}(\kappa)$

Here the encryption and decryption are all on system S, and R is the reference system.

Sometimes we also need to encrypt the messages with multiple keys, and require that (informally) an adversary can only get the message if it knows all the keys. In symmetric multi-key encryption scheme with key tags, $\mathsf{KeyGen}(1^\kappa)$ is the same as the symmetric single-key scheme, $\mathsf{Enc}_{k_1, k_2, \cdots k_i}$ encrypts a message under keys $K = (k_1, k_2, \cdots k_i)$, $\mathsf{Dec}_{k_1, k_2, \cdots k_i}$ decrypts a ciphertext given all the keys $k_1, k_2, \cdots k_i$, and $\mathsf{Ver}(k, i, c) \to \{\bot, 1\}$ verifies whether k is the i-th key used in the encryption of c.

The next problem is to define "secure" formally. The concept of indistinguishability under chosen plaintext attack (IND-CPA) was introduced in [4,12]. Let's first review the security definitions in the classical case.

Definition 1. *For a symmetric key encryption scheme, consider the following game, called "IND-CPA game", between a challenger and an adversary $\mathscr{A}$:*

1. *The challenger runs $\mathsf{KeyGen}(1^\kappa) \to sk$ and samples $b \leftarrow_r \{0, 1\}$.*
2. *The adversary gets the following classical oracle, whose input space is $\mathcal{M}$:*
   (a) The adversary chooses $m \in \mathcal{M}$, and sends it into the oracle.
   (b) If $b = 1$, the oracle outputs $\mathsf{Enc}(m)$. If $b = 0$, it outputs $\mathsf{Enc}(0^{|m|})$.
3. *The adversary tries to guess b with some distinguisher $\mathcal{D}$. Denote the guessing result as b'.*

The distinguishing advantage is defined by $\mathsf{Adv}^{IND-CPA}(\mathscr{A}, \kappa) = |\mathrm{Pr}(b' = 1 | b = 1) - \mathrm{Pr}(b' = 1 | b = 0)|$.

And we call it an one-shot IND-CPA game if the adversary can only query the oracle once. Similarly we can define the distinguishing advantage $\mathsf{Adv}^{IND-CPA-oneshot}(\mathscr{A}, \kappa) = |\mathrm{Pr}(b' = 1 | b = 1) - \mathrm{Pr}(b' = 1 | b = 0)|$.

Definition 2. *We say a protocol is IND-CPA secure against quantum adversaries if for any BQP adversary $\mathscr{A}$ which can run quantum circuits as the distinguisher but can only make classical encryption queries, there exists a negligible function negl such that $\mathsf{Adv}^{IND-CPA}(\mathscr{A}, \kappa) = \mathsf{negl}(\kappa)$. And we call it one-shot IND-CPA secure against quantum adversaries if $\mathsf{Adv}^{IND-CPA-oneshot}(\mathscr{A}, \kappa) = \mathsf{negl}(\kappa)$.*

Note that the "IND-CPA security against quantum adversaries" characterizes the security of a protocol against an adversary who has the quantum computing ability in the distinguishing phase but can only run the protocol classically.

For quantum cryptographic schemes, we use the formulation in [8].

Definition 3. *For a symmetric key encryption scheme, consider the following game, called "qIND-CPA game", between a challenger and an adversary $\mathscr{A}$:*

1. *The challenger runs* KeyGen$(1^\kappa) \to sk$ *and samples* $b \leftarrow_r \{0,1\}$.
2. *The adversary gets the following oracle, whose input space is* $\mathcal{D}(\mathcal{M})$:
   (a) *The adversary chooses* $\rho \in \mathbb{D}(\mathcal{M} \otimes \mathcal{R})$. *The adversary sends system* $\mathcal{M}$ *to the oracle, and keeps* $\mathcal{R}$ *as the reference system.*
   (b) *If* $b = 1$, *the oracle applies* Enc *on* $\mathcal{M}$ *and sends it to the adversary. The adversary will hold the state* $(\mathsf{Enc} \otimes \mathsf{I})(\rho)$. *If* $b = 0$, *the oracle encrypts* $0^{|m|}$ *and the adversary gets* $(\mathsf{Enc} \otimes \mathsf{I})(0^{|m|} \otimes \rho_R)$, *where* ρ_R *is the density operator of subsystem* $\mathcal{R}$.
3. *The adversary tries to guess* b *with some distinguisher* $\mathcal{D}$. *Denote the guessing output as* b'.

The distinguishing advantage is defined by $\mathsf{Adv}^{qIND-CPA}(\mathscr{A}, \kappa) = |\Pr(b' = 1|b = 1) - \Pr(b' = 1|b = 0)|$.

And we call it an one-shot qIND-CPA game if the adversary can only query the oracle once. Similarly we can define the distinguishing advantage $\mathsf{Adv}^{qIND-CPA-oneshot}(\mathscr{A}, \kappa) = |\Pr(b' = 1|b = 1) - \Pr(b' = 1|b = 0)|$.

Definition 4. *A protocol is qIND-CPA secure if for any BQP adversary $\mathscr{A}$, there exists a negligible function* negl *such that* $\mathsf{Adv}^{qIND-CPA}(\mathscr{A}, \kappa) = \mathsf{negl}(\kappa)$.

What's more, we call it one-shot qIND-CPA secure if for any BQP adversary $\mathscr{A}$, there exists a negligible function negl *such that* $\mathsf{Adv}^{qIND-CPA-oneshot}(\mathscr{A}, \kappa) = \mathsf{negl}(\kappa)$.

In the definition of qIND-CPA security, the adversary can query the encryption oracle with quantum states, and it can also run a quantum distinguisher.

Key Dependent Message Security. In the definitions above the plaintexts do not depend on the secret keys. There is another type of security called "key-dependent message (KDM) security", where the adversary can get encryptions of the secret keys themselves. We will need to study this type of security in the proof of our main theorem, but we defer the definitions and further discussions to Sect. 5.

2.3   Delegation of Quantum Computation, and Related Problems

There are three similar concepts: delegation of quantum computation, quantum homomorphic encryption [8] and blind quantum computation [3,7].

The differences of these three concepts are whether the interaction is allowed, and which party knows the circuit. The delegation of quantum computation and blind quantum computation protocols are interactive. For quantum homomorphic encryption, the interaction is not allowed. If we focus on non-interactive protocols, their difference is which party knows the circuit: in blind quantum computation, the circuit is only known by the client but not the server; in homomorphic encryption, the circuit is known by the server but not necessarily known by the client. In our paper, we use "delegation of quantum computation" to mean that the circuit is known by both parties but the input is kept secret.

A non-interactive quantum computation delegation protocol BQC on circuit family $\mathcal{F} = \{F_n\}$ contains 4 mappings:

BQC.KeyGen$(1^\kappa, 1^N, 1^L) \rightarrow (sk)$: The key generation algorithm takes the key length κ, input length N and circuit length L and returns the secret key.

BQC.Enc$_{sk}^C : \mathbb{D}(\mathcal{M}) \rightarrow \mathbb{D}(\mathcal{C})$. Given the encryption key and the public circuit in $\mathcal{F} = \cup\{F_n\}$, this algorithm maps inputs to ciphertexts.

BQC.Eval$^C : \mathbb{D}(\mathcal{C}) \rightarrow \mathbb{D}(\mathcal{C}')$. This algorithm maps ciphertexts to some other ciphertexts, following the instructions which may be contained in $\mathcal{C}$.

BQC.Dec$_{sk} : \mathbb{D}(\mathcal{C}') \rightarrow \mathbb{D}(\mathcal{M}')$. This algorithm decrypts the ciphertexts and stores the outputs in $\mathcal{M}$.

Here we put N, L into the KeyGen algorithm, which are needed in our protocol. We put C on the superscript to mean the circuit is known by both parties.

Definition 5. *The security (IND-CPA, qIND-CPA, etc) of the non-interactive delegation of computation protocol is defined to be the security of its encryption scheme* (KeyGen, Enc)*.*

2.4 Quantum Random Oracle Model

A classical random oracle is an oracle of a random function $\mathcal{H} : \{0,1\}^\kappa \rightarrow \{0,1\}^\kappa$ which all parties can query with classical inputs. It returns independent random value for different inputs, and returns fixed value for the same input. In practice, a random oracle is usually replaced by a hash function.

A quantum random oracle allows the users to query it with quantum states: the users can apply the map $\mathcal{H} : |a\rangle\,|b\rangle \rightarrow |a\rangle\,|\mathcal{H}(a) \oplus b\rangle$ on its state. The quantum random oracle was raised in [6]. It becomes the security proof model for many post-quantum cryptographic scheme [?]. On the other hand, the application of the quantum random oracle in quantum cryptographic problems is not very common, and as far as we know, our work is the first application of it in the delegation-stype problems.

The security definitions in the quantum random oracle model are the same as Definitions 2 and 4. Here we assume the adversary can only make polynomial number of random oracle queries, but the queries can be quantum states. Then by the "Random Oracle Methodology" we can conjecture the protocol is also secure in the standard model, when the random oracle is replaced by a hash function in practice. As with proofs in the classical random oracle model, interpreting these security claims is subtle, since there exist protocols that are secure in the random oracle model but insecure in any concrete initialization of hash function [?].

This paper focuses on the quantum cryptographic protocols in the quantum random oracle model. As far as we know, the assumption of a quantum random oracle is incomparable to any trapdoor assumption. We do not know any construction of public key encryption based on solely quantum random oracle. What's more, in our proof, the random oracle doesn't need to be "programmable" [?].

2.5 Garbled Table

We make a simple introduction of Yao's garbled table [22] here. The garbled table construction will be the foundation of our protocol.

Garbled table is a powerful technique for the randomized encoding of functions. When constructing the garbled circuit of some circuit C, the client picks two keys for each wire, and denotes them as k_b^w, where $b \in \{0, 1\}$, and w is the index of the wire.

The garbled table is based on a symmetric key encryption scheme with key tags. For gate g, suppose its input wires are w_1, w_2, and the output wire is v. The client constructs the following table:

$$\text{Enc}_{k_0^{w_1}, k_0^{w_2}}(k_{g(0,0)}^v) \tag{2}$$

$$\text{Enc}_{k_0^{w_1}, k_1^{w_2}}(k_{g(0,1)}^v) \tag{3}$$

$$\text{Enc}_{k_1^{w_1}, k_0^{w_2}}(k_{g(1,0)}^v) \tag{4}$$

$$\text{Enc}_{k_1^{w_1}, k_1^{w_2}}(k_{g(1,1)}^v) \tag{5}$$

And it picks a random permutation in S_4 to shuffle them.

If the server is given the garbled table for some gate, and given a pair of input keys, it can evaluate the output keys: it can try each row in the garbled table and see whether the given keys pass the verification. If they pass, use them to decrypt this row and get the output keys.

By providing the input keys and the garbled table for each gate in the circuit, the server can evaluate the output keys for the whole circuit. And in the randomized encoding problem the client also provides the mapping from the output keys to the corresponding values on some wires: $k_b^w \to b$, for some set of ws. The server can know the output values on these revealed wires, but the values on other wires are hidden. This construction has wide applications in classical world, for example, it allows an NC^0 client to delegate the evaluation of a circuit to the server.

3   The Encoding for Hiding Quantum States with Classical Keys

Let's first discuss the encoding operator, Et, to "hide" the quantum states. For each qubit in the input, the client picks two random different keys $k_0, k_1 \in \{0, 1\}^\kappa$ and encodes the input qubit with the following operator:

$$\text{Et}_{k_0, k_1} : |0\rangle \to |k_0\rangle, |1\rangle \to |k_1\rangle$$

The dimensions of two sides are not the same, but we can add some auxiliary qubits on the left side. As long as k_0, k_1 are distinct, this operator is unitary.

For pure quantum state $|\varphi\rangle = \sum \alpha_{i_1 i_2 \cdots i_N} |i_1 i_2 \cdots i_N\rangle$, given key set $K = \{k_i^n\}$, where $n \in [N]$, $i \in \{0,1\}$, if we apply this operator on each qubit, using keys $\{k_0^n, k_1^n\}$ for the n-th qubit, we get:

$$\mathsf{Et}_K |\varphi\rangle = \sum \alpha_{i_1 i_2 \cdots i_n} |k_{i_1}^{(1)} k_{i_2}^{(2)} \cdots k_{i_n}^{(N)}\rangle$$

The following lemma shows that if the keys are long enough, chosen randomly and kept secret, this encoding is statistically secure, in other words, the mixed state after we take average on all the possible keys, is close to the completely mixed state with exponentially small distance:

Lemma 1. *Suppose* $\rho \in \mathbb{D}(\mathcal{S} \otimes \mathcal{R})$, $\mathcal{S} = (\mathbb{C}^2)^{\otimes N}$. *Suppose we apply the* Et *operation on system* $\mathcal{S}$ *with key length* κ, *after taking average on all the valid keys, we get*

$$\sigma = \frac{1}{(2^\kappa (2^\kappa - 1))^N} \sum_{\forall n \in [N], k_0^n, k_1^n \in \{0,1\}^\kappa, k_0^n \neq k_1^n} (\mathsf{Et}_{\{k_i^n\}}^{\mathcal{S}} \otimes I)(\rho)$$

then we have $\Delta(\sigma, (\frac{1}{2^{\kappa N}} I) \otimes \mathrm{tr}_{\mathcal{S}}(\rho)) \leq (\frac{1}{2})^{\kappa - 4} N$

Thus such an encoding keeps the input secure against unbounded adversaries. We put the detailed proof in the full version of this paper.

Since Et is a unitary mapping, given K and $\mathsf{Et}_K(\rho)$, we can apply the inverse of Et and get ρ: $\mathsf{Et}_K^{-1}(\mathsf{Et}_K(\rho)) = \rho$. Note that when applying Et we enlarge the space by appending auxiliary qubits, and when applying Et^{-1} we remove these auxiliary qubits.

Fact 1. Et *can be implemented with only* CNOT *operations.*

Proof. First implement mapping $|0\rangle \rightarrow |0^\kappa\rangle$, $|1\rangle \rightarrow |k_0 \oplus k_1\rangle$. This can be done by CNOT the input into the places where $k_0 \oplus k_1$ has bit value 1. Then apply X gates on the places where k_0 has bit value 1. This will xor k_0 into these registers and complete the mapping $|0\rangle \rightarrow |k_0\rangle$, $|1\rangle \rightarrow |k_1\rangle$.

The quantum computation delegation protocol that we will discuss in the next section will use this encoding.

4   A Quantum Computation Delegation Protocol for C+P Circuits

In this section, we use Et encoding and a new technique called "reversible garbled circuit" to design a quantum computation delegation protocol.

4.1   C+P Circuits and the Relation to Toffoli Depth

[19] defined "almost classical" circuits. Here we rename it to "C+P" circuits, abbreviating "classical plus phase".

Definition 6 ([19]). *C+P is the family of quantum circuits which are composed of Toffoli gates and diagonal gates.*

We can prove it's possible to decompose this type of circuits into simpler gates. We put the proof in the full version of this paper.

Proposition 1. *Any C+P circuit can be decomposed to Toffoli gates and single qubit phase gates. Furthermore, it can be approximated by Toffoli gates and single qubit phase gates of the form $R_Z(\frac{\pi}{n}) = |0\rangle\langle 0| + \omega_n |1\rangle\langle 1|, n \in \mathbb{N}_+$, where ω_n is the nth root of unity. To approximate a circuit of length L of Toffoli gates and single qubit phase gates to precision ϵ, we only need Toffoli gates and phase gates in the form of $R_Z(\frac{\pi}{2^d}), d \in [D]$, where $D = \Theta(\log \frac{L}{\epsilon})$.*

We consider D as a fixed value in this paper. Since ϵ depends exponentially on D, a small D in practice should be enough and it will at most add a logarithmic term in the complexity.

{C+P, H} is a complete basis for quantum circuits. Our work implies a delegation scheme whose round complexity equals the H-depth of a given circuit. Previous works on quantum computation delegation generally focused on {Clifford, T} basis. (The exception is [13], which works for IQP circuits.) With the exception of Mahadev's FHE-based scheme [14], their complexity of client side quantum gates increases with the circuit's T-depth.

As far as we know, there is no general way to transform a Toffoli circuit into the {Clifford, T} basis such that its T depth is smaller than the Toffoli depth of the original circuit, without blowing up the circuit width exponentially. We formalize this statement as a conjecture:

Conjecture 2. For any polynomial time algorithm that transforms Toffoli circuits into the {Clifford, T} basis, there exists a sequence of inputs with increasing Toffoli depths for which the algorithm's outputs have T depth $\Omega(d)$, where d denotes the Toffoli depths of the original circuits.

Working with the {C+P, H} basis allows us to design efficient protocols for delegating Shor's algorithm (which has low H-depth). Previously, this was only possible using FHE-based schemes.

4.2   Protocol Construction

We now describe our protocol that supports our main results. This protocol gets a public description of a C+P circuit as well as a secret quantum state.

The idea comes from Yao's Garbled Circuit construction. We have discussed the construction in Sect. 2.5. The garbled circuit construction is commonly used for randomized encodings of classical circuits, but it's not applicable to quantum circuits. In this paper we will show how to do the reversible garbling for C+P circuits. Let's first discuss the ideas briefly.

One big difference of classical operations and quantum operations is in quantum world, the operations have to be reversible. Firstly, we will consider the garbling of Toffoli gates. In classical world, the garbled tables can contain nonreversible gates, for example, AND gate, OR gate. But in quantum world, we have to start with the Toffoli gate, which is reversible, and contains 3 input wires and 3 output wires.

However, even if the underlying circuit is reversible, if we try to use the classical garbled table construction on a quantum circuit, the garbled circuits is still not reversible, and it's not possible to use it to implement the quantum operations. Note that we need two levels of reversibility here: the circuit to be garbled needs to be reversible, and the garbled circuit itself has to be reversible too, even if it calls the random oracle as a black box.

Thus we propose a new garbling technique, which is a reversible garbling of reversible circuits: when constructing the garbled tables, instead of just creating one table for each gate, the client can construct two tables, in one table it encrypts the output keys with the input keys, and in the other table it encrypts the input keys with the output keys! This construction will make the garbled circuit reversible: we will show, the garbled circuit evaluation mapping can be applied on quantum states unitarily.

But another problem arises: If we simply replace the garbled circuit in the randomized encoding problem with "reversible garbled circuit", it's not secure any more. But it turns out, if we remove the output mapping, it becomes secure again, under some reasonable assumptions. And that gives us a delegation protocol.

The full protocol is specified in Protocol 1. Below we give more details.

Reversible Garbling of Toffoli Gates. First recall that in the classical garbled circuit, the evaluation operation on each garbled gate takes the input keys, decrypts the table and computes the corresponding output keys:

$$k_{in} \rightarrow k_{out}$$

This mapping is classical, and there is a standard way to transform a classical circuit to a quantum circuit, by introducing auxiliary output registers, and keeping the input:

$$U : |k_{in}\rangle |c\rangle \xrightarrow{\text{garbled gate}} |k_{in}\rangle |k_{out} \oplus c\rangle \qquad (6)$$

We use the second register as the output register, and c is its original value. This mapping computes the output keys from the garbled table and xors them to the second register.

This mapping is unitary, and we can also put superpositions on the left-hand side of (6). However, when it is used directly on quantum states, the inputs and outputs will be entangled together. Explicitly, for a specific Toffoli gate, we use

$k_u^{w1}, k_v^{w2}, k_w^{w3}$ to denote the keys of the input wires $w1, w2, w3$ which correspond to the input (u, v, w); for the output part the keys are $k_u^{v1}, k_v^{v2}, k_w^{v3}$. If we apply (6) directly, we get:

$$U : |k_u^{w1}\rangle |k_v^{w2}\rangle |k_w^{w3}\rangle |c_1\rangle |c_2\rangle |c_3\rangle$$
$$\to |k_u^{w1}\rangle |k_v^{w2}\rangle |k_w^{w3}\rangle |k_u^{v1} \oplus c_1\rangle |k_v^{v2} \oplus c_2\rangle |k_{w\oplus uv}^{v3} \oplus c_3\rangle$$

But what we need is the following mapping:

$$U : |k_u^{w1}\rangle |k_v^{w2}\rangle |k_w^{w3}\rangle \to |k_u^{v1}\rangle |k_v^{v2}\rangle |k_{w\oplus uv}^{v3}\rangle \tag{7}$$

Which means, we need to disentangle and erase the input registers from the output registers. Note that, again, both sides should be understood as superpositions of different keys. And recall that for each Toffoli gate there are eight possible combinations of input keys, and this mapping should work for all the eight combinations.

To erase the input from the output, we can use two mappings: $|k_{in}\rangle |0\rangle \to |k_{in}\rangle |k_{out}\rangle$ and $|k_{in}\rangle |k_{out}\rangle \to |0\rangle |k_{out}\rangle$. Both operations have the same form as Eq. (6). (For the second step, we could view the k_{out} as the input, k_{in} as c, and get $|k_{out}\rangle |k_{in} \oplus k_{in}\rangle$) So we can use two garbled tables for this "reversible garbled table"!

Assume CL is some multiple key encryption scheme with key tags. The client puts the encryption outputs $\text{CL.Enc}_{k_{in}}(k_{out})$ into a table (there are eight rows in this table), and shuffles them randomly; this is the forward table. And it puts the encryption outputs $\text{CL.Enc}_{k_{out}}(k_{in})$ into a table and shuffles to get the backward table. This construction will allow the server to implement (7), even on superpositions of input keys.

We note that we do not need to consider the detailed operations for decrypting each garbled table, and the existence of such operations comes from quantize the classical mapping as (6).

For the encoding of the inputs, recall that in the usual garble table construction, the client encrypts each bit in the inputs with the mapping:

$$0 \to k_0, 1 \to k_1 \tag{8}$$

To make it quantum, instead of replacing the classical bits with the corresponding keys, the client uses Et operator to hide the inputs. And we notice that (8) is a special case of Et where the input is classical.

Phase Gates. Now the protocol works for Toffoli gates. But what if there are phase gates?

From Proposition 1, we only need to consider the single qubit phase gates in the form of $R_Z(\frac{\pi}{n}), n \in \mathbb{Z}_+$. Suppose we want to implement such a gate on some wire, where the keys are k_0, k_1, corresponding to values 0 and 1, as discussed in the last subsection.

To implement $R_Z(\frac{\pi}{n})$, the client first picks a random integer $m \in \mathbb{Z}_n$. What it is going to do is to create a table of two rows, put $\text{CL.Enc}_{k_0}(m)$ and $\text{CL.Enc}_{k_1}(m+1)$

into the table and shuffle it. When the server needs to evaluate $R_Z(\frac{\pi}{n})$, it will first decrypt the garbled table and write the output on an auxiliary register $|0\rangle$. So it can implement the following transformation:

$$|k_0\rangle \to |k_0\rangle |m\rangle , |k_1\rangle \to |k_1\rangle |m+1\rangle \qquad (9)$$

This step is similar to implementing Eq. (6).

Then it applies a "qudit Z gate" $\sum_i \omega_n^i |i\rangle \langle i|$ on the second register, where $i \in \mathbb{Z}_n$ goes through all the integers in $\mathbb{Z}_n$. (This operation can be done efficiently.) This will give us:

$$|k_0\rangle \to \omega_n^m |k_0\rangle |m\rangle , |k_1\rangle \to \omega_n^{m+1} |k_1\rangle |m+1\rangle$$

Then it applies (9) again to erase the second register. After removing the global phase the result is the same as the output of applying a phase gate $R_Z(\frac{\pi}{n}) = |0\rangle \langle 0| + \omega_n |1\rangle \langle 1|$.

What's more, since m is chosen randomly the garbled gate won't reveal the keys. (This fact is contained in the security proof.)

4.3   Protocol Design

In this section we formalize this garbled circuit based quantum computation delegation protocol. Let's call it GBC.

We index the wires in the circuit as follows: If two wires are separated by a single qubit phase gate, we consider them as the same wire; otherwise (separated by a Toffoli gate, or disjoint), they are different wires. Suppose we have already transformed the circuit using Fact 1 so that there is no controlled phase gate. For a circuit with N input bits and L gates, the number of wires is at most $N + 3L$.

Protocol 1. *The protocol* GBC, *with* CL *being the underlying classical encryption scheme, for a circuit C which is composed of Toffoli gates and phase gates in the form of $R_Z(\frac{\pi}{n})$, is defined as:*

Key Generation GBC.KeyGen$(1^\kappa, 1^N, 1^L)$: *Sample keys* $K = (k_b^l)$, $k_b^l \leftarrow$ CL.KeyGen(1^κ), $b \in \{0,1\}, l \in [N + 3L]$.
Encryption GBC.Enc$_K^C(\rho)$: *Output* $(\text{Et}_{K_{in}}(\rho), \text{TAB}_{\text{CL}}^C(K))$. *(Note that with the reference system, the first part is $(\mathsf{I} \otimes \text{Et}_{K_{in}})(\rho_{RS})$.)*
Evaluation GBC.Eval$^C(c)$, *where $c = (\rho_q, tabs)$: Output* EvalTAB$_{\text{CL}}^C(\rho_q, tabs)$
Decryption GBC.Dec$_K(\sigma)$: *Suppose the output keys in K are K_{out}. Apply the map* Et$_{K_{out}}^{-1}(\cdot)$ *on σ and return the result.*

TAB$_{\text{CL}}^C(K)$ and EvalTAB$_{\text{CL}}^C(\rho_q, tabs)$ appeared in this protocol are defined as follows:

Protocol 2. TAB$_{\text{CL}}^C(K)$, *where K is the set of keys:*
Suppose circuit C is composed of gates $(g_i)_{i=1}^L$. This algorithm returns $(tab_{g_i})_{i=1}^L$, where tab_g is defined as follows:

1. *If g is a Toffoli gate: Suppose g has controlled input wires $w1, w2$ and target wire $w3$, and the corresponding output wires are $v1, v2, v3$. Suppose the corresponding keys in K are $\{k_b^w\}, w \in \{w1, w2, w3, v1, v2, v3\}, b \in \{0, 1\}$:*
   Create table1 as follows: For each triple $u, v, w \in \{0, 1\}^3$, add the following as a row:

$$\mathsf{CL.Enc}_{k_u^{w1}, k_v^{w2}, k_w^{w3}}(k_u^{v1} \| k_v^{v2} \| k_{w \oplus uv}^{v3})$$

   and pick a random permutation in S_8 to shuffle this table.
   Create table2 as follows: For each triple $u, v, w \in \{0, 1\}^3$, add the following as a row:

$$\mathsf{CL.Enc}_{k_u^{v1}, k_v^{v2}, k_{w \oplus uv}^{v3}}(k_u^{w1} \| k_v^{w2} \| k_w^{w3})$$

   and pick another random permutation in S_8 to shuffle this table.
   Return $(table1, table2)$
2. *If g is a phase gate, Suppose g is a phase gate $R_Z(\frac{\pi}{n})$ on wire w:*
   Sample $m_0 \leftarrow_r \mathbb{Z}_n$, $m_1 = m_0 + 1$. Create table1 as follows: For each $u \in \{0, 1\}$, add the following as a row:

$$\mathsf{CL.Enc}_{k_u^w}(m_u)$$

   and pick a random permutation in S_2 to shuffle this table.
   Return table1.

Protocol 3. $\mathsf{EvalTAB}_{\mathsf{CL}}^C(\rho, tab)$: *Suppose circuit C is composed of gates $(g_i)_{i=1}^L$. For each gate g in C, whose corresponding garbled gate is tab_g in tab:*

If g is a Toffoli gate, with input wires $w1, w2, w3$, output wires $v1, v2, v3$: Suppose $tab_g = (tab1, tab2)$, where $tab1$ is the table from input keys to output keys, and $tab2$ is from output keys to input keys. Suppose $\rho \in \mathbb{D}(S_g \otimes S')$, where S_g is the system that is currently storing the keys on the input wires of g, and S' is the remaining systems:

1. *Introduce three auxiliary registers and denote the system as S_g'. Use $tab1$ to apply the following mapping on S_g, as discussed in the Sect. 4.2:*

$$|k_u^{w1}\rangle |k_v^{w2}\rangle |k_w^{w3}\rangle |0\rangle |0\rangle |0\rangle \rightarrow |k_u^{w1}\rangle |k_v^{w2}\rangle |k_w^{w3}\rangle |k_u^{v1}\rangle |k_v^{v2}\rangle |k_{w \oplus uv}^{v3}\rangle$$

2. *Use $tab2$ to apply the following mapping on $S_g \otimes S_g'$, as discussed in the Sect. 4.2:*

$$|k_u^{w1}\rangle |k_v^{w2}\rangle |k_w^{w3}\rangle |k_u^{v1}\rangle |k_v^{v2}\rangle |k_{w \oplus uv}^{v3}\rangle \rightarrow |0\rangle |0\rangle |0\rangle |k_u^{v1}\rangle |k_v^{v2}\rangle |k_{w \oplus uv}^{v3}\rangle$$

3. *Remove system S_g, rename S_g' as S_g. Denote the final state as the new ρ.*

If g is a phase gate on wire w in the form of $R_Z(\frac{\pi}{n})$, : Suppose $\rho \in D(S_g \otimes S')$, where S_g is the system that stores the keys on the input wire of g, and S' is the remaining systems:

1. *Use tab_g to implement the mapping $|k^w\rangle |0\rangle \rightarrow |k^w\rangle |m\rangle$, where m is the decrypted output.*

2. Apply $\sum_i \omega_n^i |i\rangle \langle i|$ on the system of m.
3. Use tab_g to implement the mapping $|k^w\rangle |m\rangle \rightarrow |k^w\rangle |0\rangle$.

The following two theorems summarize its correctness and efficiency:

Theorem 2. *Protocol* GBC *is a correct non-interactive quantum computation delegation protocol for C+P circuits.*

Theorem 3. *In* GBC *protocol, the quantum resources required on the client side are* $O(\kappa N_q)$ CNOT *gates, where* κ *stands for the key length used in the protocol,* N_q *is the size of quantum states in the input, which are independent of the size of the circuit.*

Here we use N_q instead of N because we want to consider the case where some part of the input is classical and some part of it is quantum. To make the protocol secure we may need to choose κ depending on N_q. This is discussed with more details in Sect. 6.

This means the quantum resources of this protocol are independent of the circuit to be evaluated! In practice the size of the circuit may be a large polynomial of the input size, and our protocol will not be affected by this.

4.4 Structure of the Security Proofs

The structure of the security proofs is as follows. First we study the key dependent message security in the quantum world, and design a protocol which we call the KDMP protocol. Note that this part is not about the garbling scheme.

Then for the garbling scheme, we first state Proposition 2, which is the IND-CPA security of our garbling scheme. And we state a lemma about the security of the garbling scheme, which is the Lemma 2. The proofs use a reduction to the security of the KDMP protocol. And the proofs are in the full version.

Then we prove the security of our garbling scheme (Theorem 6) from Proposition 2 and Lemma 2. This part is given in the main content.

5   KDM Security of Classical Encryption Against Quantum Attack

As we can see, in GBC protocol there are encryption cycles. So to make the protocol secure, for the underlying encryption scheme CL, the usual security definition is not enough and we need at least KDM security. In this section, we will first discuss the key dependent message security (KDM security) in quantum world, and give an encryption scheme KDMP that is KDM-secure against quantum adversaries. These results will be the foundation for the security proof of the GBC protocol.

In classical world, KDM security was discussed in several papers, for example, [2,5]. [5] gave a classical KDM secure encryption scheme in the random oracle model, and [2] constructed KDM secure protocols in the standard model, based on some hard problems, for example, Learning-With-Error.

5.1 KDM Security in the Classical World

As a part of the preliminaries, we repeat the definition of the security game of the classical KDM security [2,5].

Definition 7. *The KDM-CPA game is defined similar to the IND-CPA game, except that (1) in the first step the challenger runs* $\mathsf{KeyGen}(1^\kappa)$ *for N times to generate* $\mathcal{K} = \{sk_i\}_{i\in[N]}$, N *is less than a polynomial of the security parameter. (2) the client is allowed to query the encryption oracle with a function $f \in \mathcal{F}$, a message m, and an index i of the keys, and the encryption oracle returns* $\mathsf{Enc}_{sk_i}(f(K,m))$ *or* $\mathsf{Enc}_{sk_i}(0^{|f(K,m)|})$, *depending on b. Note that the outputs of functions in $\mathcal{F}$ should be fixed-length, otherwise $|f(K,m)|$ is not well-defined.*

5.2 KDM Security in the Quantum World

The attack for the KDM security can be adaptive, which means, the adversary can make encryption queries after it receives some ciphertexts. But in our work we only need to consider the non-adaptive setting. What's more, we only need to consider the symmetric key case. To summarize, the game between the adversary and the challenger can be defined as:

Definition 8 (naSymKDM Game). *The symmetric key non-adaptive KDM game naSymKDM for function family $\mathcal{F}$ against a quantum adversary $\mathscr{A}$ in the quantum random oracle model with parameters (κ, L, T, q) is defined as follows.*

1. *The challenger chooses bit $b \leftarrow_r \{0,1\}$ and samples $K = \{sk_i\}_{i=1}^L$, $sk_i \leftarrow \mathsf{KeyGen}(1^\kappa)$.*
2. *The adversary and the challenger do the following T times, non-adaptively, which means, the challenger will only send out the answers in step (b) after it has received all the queries:*
   (a) *The adversary picks index i, function $f \in \mathcal{F}$ and message $msg \in \{0,1\}^*$, and sends them to the challenger. The size of msg should be compatible with f.*
   (b) *If $b = 1$, the challenger gives $c = \mathsf{Enc}_{sk_i}(f(K,msg))$ to the adversary. If $b = 0$, the challenger gives $c = \mathsf{Enc}_{sk_i}(0^{|f(K,msg)|})$.*
3. *The adversary tries to guess b using distinguisher $\mathcal{D}$ and outputs b'. Here $\mathcal{D}$ is a quantum operation and can query the oracle with quantum states. Suppose $\mathcal{D}$ will query the random oracle for at most q times.*

f can also query the random oracle, and it only makes queries on classical states. What's more, the output of functions in $\mathcal{F}$ should have a fixed length, otherwise $|f(K,m)|$ will not be well-defined.

The guessing advantage is defined as $\mathsf{Adv}_{\mathcal{F}}^{naSymKDM}(\mathscr{A}_{(L,T,q)}, \kappa) = |\Pr(b' = 1|b = 1) - \Pr(b' = 1|b = 0)|$.

Definition 9. *A symmetric key encryption scheme is nonadaptive KDM secure for circuit family $\mathcal{F}$ against quantum adversaries in the quantum random oracle model if for any BQP adversary,*

$$\mathsf{Adv}_{\mathcal{F}}^{naSymKDM}\left(\mathscr{A}_{(L(\kappa),T(\kappa),q(\kappa))},\kappa\right) = \mathsf{negl}(\kappa)$$

Where $L(\kappa), T(\kappa), q(\kappa)$ are polynomial functions that may depend on the adversary.

5.3 A KDM Secure Protocol in the Quantum Random Oracle Model

In the quantum random oracle model, we can give a construction of the classical KDM secure encryption scheme KDMP. Here "classical" means the encryption and decryption are purely classical. But the distinguisher may query the quantum random oracle in superposition.

Protocol 4. *We can construct a symmetric KDM secure encryption scheme* KDMP *that has key tags in the quantum random oracle model, where we denote the random oracle as $\mathcal{H}$:*

KDMP.KeyGen(1^{κ}): *Output* $sk \leftarrow_r \{0,1\}^{\kappa}$
KDMP.Enc$_{sk}(m)$: $R_1, R_2 \leftarrow_r \{0,1\}^{\kappa}$, *output ciphertext* $c = (R_1, \mathcal{H}(sk\|R_1) \oplus m)$
    and key tag $(R_2, \mathcal{H}(sk\|R_2))$
KDMP.Dec$_{sk}(c)$: *Output* $\mathcal{H}(sk\|c_1) \oplus c_2$, *where* c_1 *and* c_2 *are from* $c = (c_1, c_2)$.
KDMP.Ver(k, tag): *Suppose* $tag = (tag1, tag2)$, *output 1 if* $\mathcal{H}(k\|tag1) = tag2$,
    and $\perp$ *otherwise.*

Since the execution of this protocol is classical, the correctness can be proved classically and is obvious. We refer to [5] here and write it out explicitly for convenience.

Theorem 4 (Correctness). KDMP *is a correct symmetric key encryption scheme with key tags in the quantum random oracle model.*

The security under classical random oracle model has been proven. But here we study the quantum random oracle, so although the protocol is almost the same, we still need a new proof.

Theorem 5 (Security). *Define $\mathcal{F}[q']$ as the set of classical functions that query the random oracle at most q' times. For any adversary which can query the random oracle quantumly at most q times, we have*

$$\mathsf{Adv}_{\mathsf{KDMP},\mathcal{F}[q']}^{naSymKDM}\left(\mathscr{A}_{(L,T,q)},\kappa\right) \leq \mathsf{poly}(q,q',L,T)2^{-0.5\kappa}$$

where poly *is a fixed polynomial.*

We put the proof in the full version of this paper.

6   Security of GBC Protocol

In this section we discuss the security of protocol GBC. First we need to construct a classical encryption scheme CL as its underlying scheme. The construction is very similar to the KDMP scheme, except that this is multi-key and the KDMP scheme is single-key. We will use it as the underlying scheme of GBC.

6.1   Construction of the Underlying Classical Encryption Scheme

Protocol 5. *The underlying multi-key encryption scheme* CL *is defined as:*

CL.KeyGen(1^κ): *Output* $sk \leftarrow_r \{0,1\}^\kappa$
CL.Enc$_{k_1,k_2,k_3}(m)$: $R_1, R_2, R_3, R_4, R_5, R_6 \leftarrow_r \{0,1\}^\kappa$, *output*

$$(R_1, R_2, R_3, \mathcal{H}(k_1||R_1) \oplus \mathcal{H}(k_2||R_2) \oplus \mathcal{H}(k_3||R_3) \oplus m), \qquad (10)$$

$$((R_4, \mathcal{H}(k_1||R_4)), (R_5, \mathcal{H}(k_2||R_5)), (R_6, \mathcal{H}(k_3||R_6))) \qquad (11)$$

where $\mathcal{H}$ *is the quantum random oracle.*
CL.Dec$_{k_1,k_2,k_3}(c)$: *Suppose* $c = (R_1, R_2, R_3, c_4)$. *Output* $(\mathcal{H}(k_1||R_1) \oplus \mathcal{H}(k_2||R_2) \oplus \mathcal{H}(k_3||R_3) \oplus c_4)$.
CL.Ver(k, i, c): *Suppose the ith key tag in c is* $tag_i = (R_i, r)$. *Output* 1 *if* $r = \mathcal{H}(k||R_i)$, *and* $\perp$ *otherwise.*

We choose not to define and discuss the security of this scheme, but use it as a "wrapper" of the KDMP scheme. In the security proof we will "unwrap" its structure and base the proof on the security of KDMP scheme.

6.2   Security of GBC Against Classical or Quantum Attack

In this subsection we give the security statements of GBC. First, we can show, when used on classical inputs, GBC$_{CL}$ is secure:

Proposition 2. GBC$_{CL}$, *where* CL *is defined as Protocol 5, is one-shot IND-CPA secure against quantum adversary (that is, secure when used to encrypt one classical input) in the quantum random oracle model. Explicitly, if the distinguisher that the adversary uses makes at most q queries to the quantum random oracle, the input size is N and the size of circuit C is L,*

$$\mathsf{Adv}^{IND-CPA-oneshot}_{\mathsf{GBC}^C_{\mathsf{CL}}}(\mathscr{A}, \kappa) \leq \mathsf{poly}(q, N, L)2^{-0.5\kappa}$$

Where poly *is a fixed polynomial that does not depend on* $\mathscr{A}$ *or the parameters.*

The detailed proof is in the full version of this paper.

But we meet some difficulty when we try to prove the qIND-CPA security (that is, the security for quantum inputs). We leave it as a conjecture:

Conjecture 3. GBC$_{CL}$ *is one-shot qIND-CPA secure in the quantum random oracle model.*

But if we use a longer key, we can prove its security.

Theorem 6. *For any BQP adversary $\mathscr{A}$, there exists a negligible function* negl *such that:*

$$\mathsf{Adv}_{\mathsf{GBC}_{\mathsf{CL}}}^{qIND-CPA-oneshot}(\mathscr{A}, \kappa) = \mathsf{negl}(\kappa - 4N_q)$$

where N_q is the size of quantum states in the input.

In other words, denote GBC' as the protocol of taking $\kappa = \eta + 4N_q$ as the key length in the GBC protocol, we can prove GBC' is one-shot qIND-CPA secure with respect to security parameter η. So we prove:

Theorem 7. *There exists a delegation protocol for C+P gate set that is one-shot qIND-CPA secure in the quantum random oracle model, and the client requires $O(\eta N_q + N_q^2)$ quantum* CNOT *gates as well as polynomial classical computation, where N_q is the number of qubits in the input and η is the security parameter.*

Although we don't have a proof for Conjecture 3, we conjecture it is true, since this protocol seems to be a very natural generalization from classical to quantum. We leave it as an open problem. The main obstacle here is its security cannot be reduced to the semantic security of classical garbled circuits easily: the adversary gets many superpositions of keys. We have to prove it using different techniques, which leads to Theorem 6.

From Theorem 6 we know when we take $\kappa \geq 4N_q$ and consider $\kappa - 4N_q$ as the security parameter the security has been proved. So when the circuit size $L = \omega(N_q^2)$ the quantum resources for the client to run this protocol are smaller than running the circuit itself anyway.

What's more, although our proof requires the quantum random oracle model, we conjecture that this protocol is still secure when we replace the random oracle with practical hash functions or symmetric key encryption schemes:

Conjecture 4. When we replace the quantum random oracle in $\mathsf{GBC}_{\mathsf{CL}}$ with practical hash functions or symmetric key encryption schemes, such as versions of SHA-3 or AES with appropriate input and output sizes, the security statements still hold.

6.3   Security Proof

IND-CPA Security of Protocol 1. The proof of Proposition 2 is postponed into the full version of this paper. The proof is based on Theorem 5, which is about KDM security of Protocol 4. The structure of our scheme, when used classically, can be seen as a special case of the KDM function. But the definition of IND-CPA security for protocol GBC is still different from the KDM game security: in GBC we are trying to say the inputs of Et are hidden, but KDM security is about the encrypted messages in the garbled table. So it doesn't follow from the security of KDMP protocol trivially.

Discussions of the qIND-CPA Security. To prove Theorem 6, we use a different security proof technique, which enables us to base the qIND-CPA advantage on the IND-CPA advantage and a classical "hard-to-compute" lemma. This technique enables us to argue about the security of a quantum protocol using only security results in the classical settings.

We need to prove the keys that are not "revealed" are "hard to compute". Then we expand the expression of the qIND-CPA advantage, write it as the sum of exponential number of terms and we can observe that their forms are the same as the probability of "computing the unrevealed keys". We can prove these terms are all exponentially small, thus we get a bound for the whole expression.

Lemma 2. *For any C+P circuit C, $|C| = L$, any adversary that uses distinguisher $\mathcal{D}$ which can query the quantum random oracle q times (either with classical or quantum inputs), given the reversible garbled table and input keys corresponding to one input, it's hard to compute the input keys corresponding to other input. Formally, for any $i \neq j, |\varphi_i\rangle$, we have*

$$\mathbb{E}_K \, \mathbb{E}_R \, \mathrm{tr}((\mathsf{Et}_K \, |j\rangle)^\dagger \mathcal{D}(\mathsf{Et}_K(|i\rangle \langle i|) \otimes \varphi_i \otimes \mathsf{TAB}_{\mathsf{CL}}^C(K, R))(\mathsf{Et}_K \, |j\rangle)))$$
$$\leq \mathsf{poly}(q, N, L) 2^{-0.5\kappa} \quad (12)$$

where poly *is a fixed polynomial that does not depend on $\mathscr{A}$ or the parameters, N is the size of inputs, and R denotes the randomness used in the computation of $\mathsf{TAB}_{\mathsf{CL}}^C(K)$, including the random oracle outputs, the random paddings and the random shuffling. And $\mathsf{TAB}_{\mathsf{CL}}^C(K, R)$ is the output of $\mathsf{TAB}_{\mathsf{CL}}^C(K)$ using randomness R, and since R is given as a parameter there will be no randomness inside.*

Note that since we have already fixed all the randomness, $\mathsf{TAB}_{\mathsf{CL}}^C(K, R)$ is pure. We also note that this can be seen as a classical lemma since $|i\rangle$, $|j\rangle$ are all in computational basis. We postpone the proof into the full version.

Let's prove Theorem 6 from Proposition 2 and Lemma 2. We will expand the the expression of the input state and qIND-CPA advantage, and each term in the cross terms can be bounded by (12).

Proof (of Theorem 6). First, suppose the state that the adversary uses is $|\varphi\rangle = \sum_i c_i |i\rangle |\varphi_i\rangle$, where i is in the input system, $i \in I$ where I is the set of non-zero term ($c_i \neq 0$), $|I| \leq 2^{N_q}$ and $|\varphi_i\rangle$ is in the reference system. Additionally assume c_is are all real numbers and $| \, |i\rangle |\varphi_i\rangle \, | = 1$. We can only consider pure states since we can always write a mixed state as a probability ensemble of pure states.

Then we can assume the distinguisher $\mathcal{D}$ is a unitary operation D on the output and auxiliary qubits, followed by a measurement on a specific output qubit. So we can write $\mathcal{D}(\rho) = \mathrm{tr}_R(D(\rho \otimes |0\rangle \langle 0|)D^\dagger)$, where $|0\rangle \langle 0|$ stands for big enough auxiliary qubits. Let's use $\mathcal{E}_{proj}(\rho)$ to denote the operation of projecting ρ onto the computational basis. Denote the projection operator onto the $|0\rangle \langle 0|$

space as P_0, we have

$$\mathsf{Adv}_{\mathsf{GBC}}^{qIND-CPA-oneshot}(\mathscr{A},\kappa) \tag{13}$$

$$=|\Pr(\mathcal{D}(\mathbb{E}_K\,\mathsf{GBC.Enc}_K(\varphi))=1))-\Pr(\mathcal{D}(\mathbb{E}_K\,\mathsf{GBC.Enc}_K(0^N))=1)| \tag{14}$$

$$\leq|\Pr(\mathcal{D}(\mathbb{E}_K\,\mathbb{E}_R(\rho))=1))-\Pr(\mathcal{D}(\mathbb{E}_K\,\mathbb{E}_R(\mathcal{E}_{proj}(\rho)))=1)|+$$
$$|\Pr(\mathcal{D}(\mathbb{E}_K\,\mathsf{GBC.Enc}_K(\mathcal{E}_{proj}(\varphi)))=1))-\Pr(\mathcal{D}(\mathbb{E}_K\,\mathsf{GBC.Enc}_K(0^N))=1)| \tag{15}$$

Here we write $\rho := (\mathsf{Et}_K \otimes \mathsf{I})(\varphi) \otimes \mathsf{TAB}(K,R)$.

Let's first compute the first term.

$$|\Pr(\mathcal{D}(\mathbb{E}_K\,\mathbb{E}_R(\rho))=1))-\Pr(\mathcal{D}(\mathbb{E}_K\,\mathbb{E}_R(\mathcal{E}_{proj}(\rho)))=1))| \tag{16}$$

$$=|\operatorname{tr}(P_0(\mathbb{E}_K\,\mathbb{E}_R\,D(\rho\otimes|0\rangle\,\langle0|)D^\dagger))-\operatorname{tr}(P_0(\mathbb{E}_K\,\mathbb{E}_R\,D(\mathcal{E}_{proj}(\rho)\otimes|0\rangle\,\langle0|)D^\dagger))| \tag{17}$$

The first term inside can be expanded as

$$\mathbb{E}_K\,\mathbb{E}_R\,D(\rho\otimes|0\rangle\,\langle0|)D^\dagger \tag{18}$$

$$=\mathbb{E}_K\,\mathbb{E}_R\,D((\mathsf{Et}_K\otimes\mathsf{I})(\varphi)\otimes\mathsf{TAB}(K,R)\otimes|0\rangle\,\langle0|)D^\dagger \tag{19}$$

$$=\mathbb{E}_K\,\mathbb{E}_R\,D((\mathsf{Et}_K\otimes\mathsf{I})((\sum_i c_i\,|i\rangle\,|\varphi_i\rangle)(\sum_i c_i^\dagger\,\langle i|\,\langle\varphi_i|))$$
$$(\mathsf{Et}_K\otimes\mathsf{I})^\dagger\otimes\mathsf{TAB}(K,R)\otimes|0\rangle\,\langle0|)D^\dagger \tag{20}$$

Denote $|x_i\rangle = \mathsf{Et}_K\,|i\rangle\otimes|\varphi_i\rangle$, we can simplify the expression:

$$(20)=\mathbb{E}_K\,\mathbb{E}_R\,D(\sum_i c_i\,|x_i\rangle\sum_i c_i^\dagger\,\langle x_i|\otimes\mathsf{TAB}(K,R)\otimes|0\rangle\,\langle0|)D^\dagger \tag{21}$$

$$=\mathbb{E}_K\,\mathbb{E}_R\,D(\sum_i|c_i|^2\,|x_i\rangle\,\langle x_i|\otimes\mathsf{TAB}(K,R)\otimes|0\rangle\,\langle0|)D^\dagger$$
$$+\mathbb{E}_K\,\mathbb{E}_R\,D(\sum_{i\neq j} c_ic_j^\dagger\,|x_i\rangle\,\langle x_j|\otimes\mathsf{TAB}(K,R)\otimes|0\rangle\,\langle0|)D^\dagger \tag{22}$$

$$=\mathbb{E}_K\,\mathbb{E}_R\,D(\mathcal{E}_{proj}(\rho)\otimes|0\rangle\,\langle0|)D^\dagger$$
$$+\mathbb{E}_K\,\mathbb{E}_R\,D(\sum_{i\neq j} c_ic_j^\dagger\,|x_i\rangle\,\langle x_j|\otimes\mathsf{TAB}(K,R)\otimes|0\rangle\,\langle0|)D^\dagger \tag{23}$$

Substitute it into (17), we get

$$(17)$$

$$=|\mathbb{E}_K\,\mathbb{E}_R\operatorname{tr}(P_0 D(\sum_{i\neq j} c_ic_j^\dagger\,|x_i\rangle\,\langle x_j|\otimes\mathsf{TAB}(K,R)\otimes|0\rangle\,\langle0|)D^\dagger)| \tag{24}$$

$$=|\sum_{i\neq j} c_ic_j^\dagger\,\mathbb{E}_K\,\mathbb{E}_R(\langle x_j|\,\langle\mathsf{TAB}(K,R)|\,\langle0|\,D^\dagger P_0 D(|x_i\rangle\,|\mathsf{TAB}(K,R)\rangle\,|0\rangle)| \tag{25}$$

$$\leq \sqrt{\sum_{i\neq j} c_i^2 c_j^{\dagger 2}} \sqrt{\sum_{i\neq j} |\mathbb{E}_K \mathbb{E}_R \langle 0| \langle \mathsf{TAB}(K,R)| \langle x_j| D^\dagger P_0 D |x_i\rangle \otimes |\mathsf{TAB}(K,R)\rangle |0\rangle|^2} \quad (26)$$

$$\leq \sqrt{\sum_{i\neq j} \mathbb{E}_K \mathbb{E}_R |(\langle 0| \otimes \langle \mathsf{TAB}(K,R)| \langle x_j|) D^\dagger P_0 D(|x_i\rangle \otimes |\mathsf{TAB}(K,R)\rangle |0\rangle)|^2} \quad (27)$$

The magic of this technique actually happens between (24) and (25): first we move $\sum_{i\neq j} c_i c_j^\dagger$ out by linearity, then after rotating terms inside the trace, an expression which talks about applying D on some state becomes an expression for the probability of applying $\{D^\dagger P_0 D, D^\dagger P_1 D\}$ on $|x_i\rangle$ and getting $|x_j\rangle$.

By Lemma 2, consider the operation $\mathcal{E}$ defined as follows: expand the space and apply D, make a measurement with operators $\{P_0, P_1\}$, and apply $D^\dagger$. Let $\mathcal{E}_0 = D^\dagger P_0 D(\cdot \otimes |0\rangle \langle 0|) D^\dagger P_0 D$, and $\mathcal{E}_1 = D^\dagger P_1 D(\cdot \otimes |0\rangle \langle 0|) D^\dagger P_1 D$. We have:

$$\mathbb{E}_K \mathbb{E}_R (\mathrm{tr}((\mathsf{Et}_K |j\rangle)^\dagger \mathcal{E}_0 (\mathsf{Et}_K(i) \otimes \varphi_i \otimes \mathsf{TAB}(K,R)) \mathsf{Et}_K |j\rangle)) \quad (28)$$

$$+ \mathrm{tr}((\mathsf{Et}_K |j\rangle)^\dagger \mathcal{E}_1 (\mathsf{Et}_K(|i\rangle \langle i|) \otimes \varphi_i \otimes \mathsf{TAB}(K,R)) \mathsf{Et}_K |j\rangle)) \quad (29)$$

$$\leq \mathsf{poly}(q, N, L) 2^{-0.5\kappa} \quad (30)$$

With this, we can bound the inner part of (27) further:

$$\mathbb{E}_K \mathbb{E}_R |(\langle 0| \otimes \langle \mathsf{TAB}(K,R)| \langle x_j|) D^\dagger P_0 D(|x_i\rangle \otimes |\mathsf{TAB}(K,R)\rangle |0\rangle)|^2 \quad (31)$$

$$= \mathbb{E}_K \mathbb{E}_R |(\langle 0| \otimes \langle \mathsf{TAB}(K,R)| ((\mathsf{Et}_K |j\rangle) \otimes |\varphi_j\rangle)^\dagger$$

$$D^\dagger P_0 D(\mathsf{Et}_K |i\rangle \otimes |\varphi_i\rangle) \otimes |\mathsf{TAB}(K,R)\rangle |0\rangle)|^2 \quad (32)$$

$$\leq \mathbb{E}_K \mathbb{E}_R \mathrm{tr}((\mathsf{Et}_K |j\rangle)^\dagger \mathcal{E}_0 (\mathsf{Et}_K(|i\rangle \langle i|) \otimes \varphi_i \otimes \mathsf{TAB}(K,R) \otimes |0\rangle \langle 0|) \mathsf{Et}_K |j\rangle) \quad (33)$$

$$\leq \mathsf{poly}(q, N, L) 2^{-0.5\kappa} \quad (34)$$

Substitute it back into (27), we will know

$$|\Pr(\mathcal{D}(\mathbb{E}_K \mathbb{E}_R(\rho)) = 1) - \Pr(\mathcal{D}(\mathbb{E}_K \mathbb{E}_R(\mathcal{E}_{proj}(\rho))) = 1)| \quad (35)$$

$$\leq 2^{N_q} \mathsf{poly}(q, N, L) 2^{-0.25\kappa} \quad (36)$$

The second term in (15) can be bounded by Proposition 2. $\mathcal{E}_{proj}(\rho)$ is a classical state so we have

$$|\Pr(\mathcal{D}(\mathbb{E}_K \mathsf{GBC.Enc}_K(\mathcal{E}_{proj}(\varphi))) = 1) - \Pr(\mathcal{D}(\mathbb{E}_K \mathsf{GBC.Enc}_K(0^N)) = 1)|$$

$$\leq \mathsf{poly}(q, N, L) 2^{-\kappa}$$

Combining these two inequalities we have

$$\mathsf{Adv}_{\mathsf{GBC}}^{qIND-CPA-oneshot}(\mathscr{A}, \kappa) \leq \mathsf{poly}(q, N, L) 2^{-0.25(\kappa - 4N_q)}$$

6.4   Standard Model

In the last section we prove the security in the quantum random oracle model. In practice, the random oracle can usually be replaced with hash functions, and we claim that our protocol is not an exception (Conjecture 4). In our protocol, it's more natural to use a symmetric key encryption scheme directly: the usage of the random oracle in our protocol is on the symmetric multi-key encryption scheme with key tags, and the key verification can be replaced with the "point-and-permute" technique from the classical garbled circuit.

When using symmetric key encryption instead of the random oracle, since in our protocol we use affine functions in KDM game, we need at least that the symmetric key encryption is secure against quantum adversaries under KDM game for affine functions. Although this is a strong assumption, it's still reasonable in practice.

7 Applications

7.1 Blind Quantum Computation for C+P Circuits

Protocol 1 is a quantum computation delegation protocol. But since the circuit can be put into inputs, we can turn it into a blind quantum computation protocol, where the server doesn't know either input state or the circuit to be applied. If we only want to hide the type of gates in the circuit, our original protocol actually already achieves it. But if we also want to hide the circuit topology, we need to do more. The adversaries should only know the fact that the circuit is a C+P circuit, the input size and an upper bound on the circuit size. In this subsection we are going to construct a universal machine $\mathcal{U}$ such that for all the C+P circuit C, $C(\rho) = \mathcal{U}(C, \rho)$. What's more, we want $\mathcal{U}$ to be in C+P so that we can use our protocol on $\mathcal{U}$.

Suppose the size of input is N and the phase gates are all in the form of $R_Z(\pi/2^d), d \in [D]$. Then there are $N^3 + ND$ possible choices for each gate. Thus a $\log(N^3 + ND)$ bits description is enough for each gate. For the server-side evaluation, a bad implementation may lead to $N^3 + ND$ extra cost, and we can do a simple preprocessing on the circuit to reduce it: We can first introduce three auxiliary wires, and convert C to a form that only contains three types of gates: (1) $R_Z(\pi/2^d)$ (2) a SWAP operation between a normal wire and an auxiliary wire (3) a Toffoli gate on the auxiliary wires. After this transformation, the number of choices of the gates is only $3N + 1 + ND$. Thus we can describe each gate by a string of length $\log(3N + 1 + ND)$. And given the description of g, the operation of $\mathcal{U}$ is a series of multi-controlled gate operations, where the control wires correspond to the gate description and the target wires are the wires in the original circuit. And this multi-controlled multi-target operation is also in C+P and it can be transformed to the standard form of Toffoli and phase gates.

Since $\mathcal{U}$ itself is a C+P circuit, we can delegate it by applying Protocol 1. Then the original circuit will be indistinguishable from the identity circuit, which means we know nothing beyond some information on its size.

7.2 Delegation of Shor's Algorithm

Shor's algorithm contains two parts: first we apply lots of Toffoli gates on $|+\rangle^{\otimes n} \otimes |M\rangle$, where M is, for example, the number to be factored, and $n = \log M$; then measure, apply quantum Fourier transform and measure again. From [10,18] we know the quantum Fourier transform is actually easy to implement: a quantum Fourier transform on n qubits has time complexity $\tilde{O}(n)$. The main burden of Shor's algorithm is the Toffoli part. ([18] contains resource estimates on the elliptic curve version.) With this protocol we can let the server do the Toffoli part of Shor's algorithm without revealing the actual value of the input.

Explicitly, suppose the client wants to run Shor's algorithm on M while also wants to keep M secret, the client can use the following protocol:

Protocol 6 *Protocol for delegation of Shor's algorithm:*

Suppose ShorToff is the Toffoli gate part of Shor's algorithm, and its length is L.

1. *The client samples $K \leftarrow$ GBC.KeyGen$(1^\kappa, 1^{2n}, 1^L)$. Then the client prepares $(\rho, tab) \leftarrow$ GBC.Enc$_K^{ShorToff}(|+\rangle^{\otimes n} \otimes |M\rangle)$ and sends it to the server.*
2. *The server evaluates GBC_{CL}.Eval$^{ShorToff}(\rho, tab)$ and sends it back to the client.*
3. *The client decrypts with GBC.Dec$_K$. Then it does quantum Fourier transform itself and measures to get the final result.*

So the quantum resources on the client side are only $O(\kappa n)$ CNOT gates plus $\tilde{O}(n)$ gates for quantum Fourier transform, and it can delegate Shor's algorithm to the server side securely.

Theorem 8. *Protocol 6 can be used to delegate Shor's algorithm securely and non-interactively, in the quantum random oracle model (without assuming trapdoor one-way functions), and for n bit inputs, the amount of quantum resources on the client side are quasi-linear quantum gates plus $O(\kappa n)$ CNOT gates (assuming Conjecture 3, $\kappa = \eta$, or under the current security proof, $\kappa = \eta + 4n$).*

For comparison, if the client runs Shor's algorithm locally, the client needs to perform $\omega(n^2 \log n)$ Toffoli gates, and the exact form depends on the multiplication method it uses. Schoolbook multiplication leads to $O(n^3)$ complexity; if it uses fast multiplication method, the complexity is still $\omega(n^2 \log n)$ and it has a big hidden constant.

8 Quantum KDM Security

As a natural generalization of our discussion of KDM-security, we formalize the quantum KDM security and construct a protocol in this section. Previously when we discuss the KDM security the function f and message m are classical; here we further generalize them to include quantum states and operations.

Definition 10. *A symmetric key non-adaptive quantum KDM game naSymQKDM for function family $\mathcal{F}$ in the quantum random oracle model is defined as follows:*

1. *The challenger chooses bit $b \leftarrow_r \{0,1\}$ and samples $K = \{sk_i\}_{i=1}^{N}$, $sk_i \leftarrow$
   KeyGen(1^κ).*
2. *The adversary and the challenger repeat the following for L times, non-adaptively, in other words, the challenger should only sends out the answers in step (b) after it receives all the queries:*
   (a) *The adversary picks index i, function $f \in \mathcal{F}$ and message $\rho \in \mathbb{D}(\mathcal{R} \otimes \mathcal{M})$, and sends system $\mathcal{M}$ to the challenger.*
   (b) *If $b = 1$, the challenger returns $c = \mathsf{Enc}_{sk_i}(f(K, \rho_m))$ to the adversary. If $b = 0$, the challenger returns $c = \mathsf{Enc}_{sk_i}(0^{|f(K,\rho_m)|})$.*
3. *The adversary tries to guess b with some distinguisher $\mathcal{D}$, and outputs b'.*

Note that $\mathcal{F}$ can be quantum operations and can query the random oracle with quantum states. The output of functions in $\mathcal{F}$ should be fixed-lengthed, otherwise $|f(K, m)|$ will not be well-defined.

The guessing advantage is defined as $\mathsf{Adv}^{naSymQKDM}(\mathscr{A}, \kappa) = |\Pr(b' = 1|b = 1) - \Pr(b' = 1|b = 0)|$.

Definition 11. *A symmetric key quantum encryption scheme is nonadaptively qKDM-CPA secure for function $\mathcal{F}$ if for any BQP adversary $\mathscr{A}$,*

$$\mathsf{Adv}_{\mathcal{F}}^{naSymQKDM}(\mathscr{A}, \kappa) = \mathsf{negl}(\kappa)$$

8.1   Protocol Design

Protocol 7. *A Quantum KDM Secure Protocol in the Quantum Random Oracle Model:*

Key Generation QKDM.KeyGen(1^κ): $sk \leftarrow \{0,1\}^\kappa$.
Encryption QKDM.Enc$_{sk}(\rho)$: *Sample $a, b \in_r \{0,1\}^N$, where N is the length of inputs.*
   Output $(\mathsf{X}^a \mathsf{Z}^b(\rho), \mathsf{KDMP.Enc}_{sk}(a, b))$.
Decryption QKDM.Dec$_{sk}((\rho, c))$: *First compute $a, b \leftarrow \mathsf{KDMP.Dec}_{sk}(c)$, then output $\mathsf{X}^a \mathsf{Z}^b(\rho)$*

Theorem 9. *Protocol 7 is nonadaptively qKDM-CPA secure for functions in $\mathcal{F}[\mathsf{poly}]$ in the quantum random oracle model, where $\mathcal{F}[\mathsf{poly}]$ is the function family that makes at most $\mathsf{poly}(\kappa)$ queries to the quantum random oracle.*

We put its proof in the full version of this paper.

9   Open Problems

One obvious open problem in our paper is to prove Conjecture 3, the qIND-CPA security without additional requirement on κ. We believe this is true, but we can only prove the security when $\kappa - 4N_q = \eta$. And another further research direction is to base these protocols directly on the assumptions in the standard model, for example, the existence of hash functions or symmetric key encryption schemes that are exponentially KDM secure for affine functions against a quantum adversary. We can also study how to optimize this protocol, and how efficient it is compared to other protocols based on the quantum one-time pad. One obvious route is to make use of the optimization techniques for classical garbled circuits.

Another open question is whether this protocol is useful in other problems than Shor's algorithm. Lots of previous works studied quantum circuits on $\{\mathsf{Clifford}, \mathsf{T}\}$ gate set, and our work shows $\{\mathsf{C+P}, \mathsf{H}\}$ is also important and worth studying. There are not many works on converting quantum circuits into layers of C+P gates and H gates, and it's possible that some famous quantum algorithms which require a lot of T gates, after converted into $\{\mathsf{C+P}, \mathsf{H}\}$ gate set, can have small H depth. This problem is still quite open, and further research is needed here.

What's more, KDM security in quantum settings is an interesting problem. This paper gives some initial study on it, but there are still a lot of open questions. Is it possible to construct quantum KDM secure protocol in the standard model? Could quantum cryptography help us design classical KDM secure scheme? Again, further research is needed here.

This paper also gives some new ideas on constructing secure quantum encryption schemes without using trapdoor functions. Although there is some result [24] on the limit of information-theoretically secure quantum homomorphic encryption, in our work we use the quantum random oracle and make the circuits available to the client, the limit doesn't hold any more. So here comes lots of interesting problems on the possibility and impossibility of quantum computation delegation: What is the limit for non-interactive information-theoretically secure delegation of quantum computation, where the circuit is public/private, with/without quantum ROM? If we allow small amount of quantum/classical communication, does it lead to something different?

Acknowledgements. The author would like to thank Prof. Adam Smith, NSF funding and anonymous reviewers.

References

1. Aaronson, S., Cojocaru, A., Gheorghiu, A., Kashefi, E.: On the implausibility of classical client blind quantum computing. CoRR abs/1704.08482 (2017)
2. Applebaum, B., Cash, D., Peikert, C., Sahai, A.: Fast cryptographic primitives and circular-secure encryption based on hard learning problems. In: Halevi, S. (ed.) CRYPTO 2009. LNCS, vol. 5677, pp. 595–618. Springer, Heidelberg (2009). https://doi.org/10.1007/978-3-642-03356-8_35
3. Arrighi, P., Salvail, L.: Blind quantum computation. Int. J. Quantum Inf. **04** (2003)
4. Bellare, M., Desai, A., Jokipii, E., Rogaway, P.: A concrete security treatment of symmetric encryption, January 1997
5. Black, J., Rogaway, P., Shrimpton, T.: Encryption-scheme security in the presence of key-dependent messages. In: Nyberg, K., Heys, H. (eds.) SAC 2002. LNCS, vol. 2595, pp. 62–75. Springer, Heidelberg (2003). https://doi.org/10.1007/3-540-36492-7_6

6. Boneh, D., Dagdelen, Ö., Fischlin, M., Lehmann, A., Schaffner, C., Zhandry, M.: Random oracles in a quantum world. In: Lee, D.H., Wang, X. (eds.) ASIACRYPT 2011. LNCS, vol. 7073, pp. 41–69. Springer, Heidelberg (2011). https://doi.org/10.1007/978-3-642-25385-0_3

7. Broadbent, A., Fitzsimons, J., Kashefi, E.: Universal blind quantum computation. In: Proceedings of the 2009 50th Annual IEEE Symposium on Foundations of Computer Science, FOCS 2009, pp. 517–526. IEEE Computer Society, Washington, DC, USA (2009)

8. Broadbent, A., Jeffery, S.: Quantum homomorphic encryption for circuits of low T-gate complexity. In: Gennaro, R., Robshaw, M. (eds.) CRYPTO 2015. LNCS, vol. 9216, pp. 609–629. Springer, Heidelberg (2015). https://doi.org/10.1007/978-3-662-48000-7_30

9. Childs, A.M.: Secure assisted quantum computation. Quantum Inf. Comput. **5**(6), 456–466 (2005)

10. Cleve, R., Watrous, J.: Fast parallel circuits for the quantum Fourier transform, June 2000

11. Dulek, Y., Schaffner, C., Speelman, F.: Quantum homomorphic encryption for polynomial-sized circuits. In: Robshaw, M., Katz, J. (eds.) CRYPTO 2016. LNCS, vol. 9816, pp. 3–32. Springer, Heidelberg (2016). https://doi.org/10.1007/978-3-662-53015-3_1

12. Goldwasser, S., Micali, S.: Probabilistic encryption & how to play mental poker keeping secret all partial information. In: Proceedings of the Fourteenth Annual ACM Symposium on Theory of Computing, STOC 1982, pp. 365–377. ACM, New York, NY, USA (1982)

13. Lai, C.Y., Chung, K.M.: On statistically-secure quantum homomorphic encryption. Quantum Inf. Comput. **18**, 785–794 (2018)

14. Mahadev, U.: Classical homomorphic encryption for quantum circuits. CoRR (2017)

15. Nielsen, M.A., Chuang, I.L.: Quantum Computation and Quantum Information: 10th Anniversary Edition, 10th edn. Cambridge University Press, New York (2011)

16. Okamoto, T., Tanaka, K., Uchiyama, S.: Quantum public-key cryptosystems. In: Bellare, M. (ed.) CRYPTO 2000. LNCS, vol. 1880, pp. 147–165. Springer, Heidelberg (2000). https://doi.org/10.1007/3-540-44598-6_9

17. Raussendorf, R.: Measurement-based quantum computation with cluster states. Int. J. Quantum Inf. **07**(06), 1053–1203 (2009)

18. Roetteler, M., Naehrig, M., Svore, K.M., Lauter, K.: Quantum resource estimates for computing elliptic curve discrete logarithms. In: Takagi, T., Peyrin, T. (eds.) ASIACRYPT 2017. LNCS, vol. 10625, pp. 241–270. Springer, Cham (2017). https://doi.org/10.1007/978-3-319-70697-9_9

19. Selinger, P.: Quantum circuits of t-depth one. Phys. Rev. A **87**, 042302 (2013)

20. Shi, Y.: Quantum and classical tradeoffs. Theoret. Comput. Sci. **344**(2–3), 335–345 (2005)

21. Unruh, D.: Revocable quantum timed-release encryption. In: Nguyen, P.Q., Oswald, E. (eds.) EUROCRYPT 2014. LNCS, vol. 8441, pp. 129–146. Springer, Heidelberg (2014). https://doi.org/10.1007/978-3-642-55220-5_8

22. Yao, A.C.: How to generate and exchange secrets. In: 27th Annual Symposium on Foundations of Computer Science (sfcs 1986), pp. 162–167, October 1986. https://doi.org/10.1109/SFCS.1986.25

23. Ouyang, Y., Tan, S.-H., Fitzsimons, J.: Quantum homomorphic encryption from quantum codes. Phys. Rev. A **98**, 042334 (2015)

24. Yu, L., Perez-Delgado, C.A., Fitzsimons, J.: Limitations on information theoretically secure quantum homomorphic encryption. Phys. Rev. A **90**, 050303 (2014)
25. Zalka, C.: Grover's quantum searching algorithm is optimal. Phys. Rev. A **60**, 2746–2751 (1999)

Tighter Proofs of CCA Security
in the Quantum Random Oracle Model

Nina Bindel[1(✉)], Mike Hamburg[2(✉)], Kathrin Hövelmanns[3(✉)],
Andreas Hülsing[4(✉)], and Edoardo Persichetti[5(✉)]

[1] University of Waterloo, Waterloo, Canada
nlbindel@uwaterloo.ca
[2] Rambus, San Francisco, USA
mhamburg@rambus.com
[3] Ruhr-Universität Bochum, Bochum, Germany
kathrin.hoevelmanns@ruhr-uni-bochum.de
[4] Eindhoven University of Technology, Eindhoven, The Netherlands
andreas@huelsing.net
[5] Florida Atlantic University, Boca Raton, USA
epersichetti@fau.edu

Abstract. We revisit the construction of IND-CCA secure key encapsulation mechanisms (KEM) from public-key encryption schemes (PKE). We give new, tighter security reductions for several constructions. Our main result is an improved reduction for the security of the $U^{\not\perp}$-transform of Hofheinz, Hövelmanns, and Kiltz (TCC'17) which turns OW-CPA secure deterministic PKEs into IND-CCA secure KEMs. This result is enabled by a new one-way to hiding (O2H) lemma which gives a tighter bound than previous O2H lemmas in certain settings and might be of independent interest. We extend this result also to the case of PKEs with non-zero decryption failure probability and non-deterministic PKEs. However, we assume that the derandomized PKE is injective with overwhelming probability.

In addition, we analyze the impact of different variations of the $U^{\not\perp}$-transform discussed in the literature on the security of the final scheme. We consider the difference between explicit ($U^{\perp}$) and implicit ($U^{\not\perp}$) rejection, proving that security of the former implies security of the latter. We show that the opposite direction holds if the scheme with explicit rejection also uses key confirmation. Finally, we prove that (at least from a theoretic point of view) security is independent of whether the session keys are derived from message and ciphertext ($U^{\not\perp}$) or just from the message ($U_m^{\not\perp}$).

1 Introduction

If a general-purpose quantum computer can be built, it will break most widely-deployed public-key cryptography. The cryptographic community is busily designing new cryptographic systems to prepare for this risk. These systems typically consist of an algebraic structure with cryptographic hardness properties, plus a symmetric cryptography layer which transforms the algebraic structure

© International Association for Cryptologic Research 2019
D. Hofheinz and A. Rosen (Eds.): TCC 2019, LNCS 11892, pp. 61–90, 2019.
https://doi.org/10.1007/978-3-030-36033-7_3

into a higher level primitive like a public-key encryption (PKE) scheme, a key encapsulation mechanism (KEM), or a signature scheme. The algebraic structures underlying these so-called "post-quantum" systems have new properties, and the quantum threat model requires changes in the way security is analyzed. Therefore the transformations turning the algebraic structures into cryptosystems have to be freshly examined.

In this work we focus on the construction of secure KEMs. In this setting the algebraic structures usually provide a PKE from which a KEM is derived via a generic transform. A new property of the algebraic structures used in many post-quantum PKEs and KEMs gives them malleable ciphertexts, so they are at risk from chosen-ciphertext attacks (CCA) [HNP+03]. The standard defenses against CCA are variants of the Fujisaki-Okamoto (FO) transform [FO99]. Known security proofs for the FO transform use the random oracle model (ROM) [BR93]. This is for two reasons. First, the FO transform has a circular structure–it chooses coins for encryption according to the message being encrypted. This leads to obstacles which we do not know how to overcome when proving security in the standard model. In the ROM, we circumvent this by re-programming. Second, in the ROM a reduction learns all the adversary's queries to the random oracle. This allows us to formalize the intuition that an adversary must have known a challenge plaintext to extract said plaintext.

Since we are concerned with security against quantum attackers, we need to extend these proofs to the quantum-accessible random oracle model (QROM) [BDF+11]. This comes with two challenges for our setting. On the one hand, in the QROM the adversary can query all inputs in superposition. Hence, it is no longer trivial to break the circular dependency by re-programming, which results in security bounds that do not tightly match known attacks. On the other hand, a reduction cannot learn the adversarial queries by simple observation anymore. The reason is that observation of a quantum state requires a measurement which disturbs the state. Hence, more advanced techniques are required.

1.1   Our Contribution

QROM analysis of KEMs has advanced rapidly over the past several years. The initial solutions were loose by a factor of up to q^6 [TU16, HHK17], where q is the number of times the adversary queries the random oracle. This has improved to q^2 [SXY18, JZC+18] and finally to q [HKSU18, JZM19a, JZM19c]. Some works provide tight proofs under stronger assumptions [SXY18, XY19]. Our work provides a proof of IND-CCA security for KEMs constructed from deterministic PKEs (Theorem 2), which is tight except for a quadratic security loss which might be impossible to avoid [JZM19b]. For KEMs constructed from randomized PKEs our bound is still loose by a factor of up to q (Theorem 1). In this particular case, our bound does not essentially differ from the bound already given in [HKSU18]. In [HKSU18], the proof given is called "semi-modular": it is first shown that derandomization and puncturing achieve the stronger notion that [SXY18] requires to achieve tight security, and the tight proof of [SXY18] is then applied to the derandomized and punctured scheme. The strategy of [HKSU18] was deliberately chosen to deal with correctness errors:

The tight proof of [SXY18] could not trivially be generalized for non-perfect schemes in a way such that the result still would have been meaningful for most lattice-based encryption schemes. Our work deals with correctness errors in a modular way by introducing an additional intermediate notion (called FFC).

At the heart of our bound is a new one-way to hiding (O2H) lemma which gives a tighter bound than previous O2H lemmas (Lemma 5). This comes at the cost of limited applicability. O2H lemmas allow to bound the difference in the success probability of an adversary when replacing its oracle function by a similar function. Previous lemmas lost a factor of roughly the number of the adversary's queries to this oracle or its square-root. Our lemma does not incur any such loss. On the downside, our lemma only applies if the reduction has access to both oracle functions and if the functions only differ in one position. See Table 1 for a comparison.

Some post-quantum schemes feature an inherent probability of decryption failure, say $\delta > 0$. Such failures can be used in attacks, but they also complicate security proofs. As a result, previous bounds typically contain a term $q\sqrt{\delta}$ which is not known to be tight. However, most of the obstacles that arise in our CCA security proof can be avoided by assuming that encryption with a particular public key is injective (after derandomization). This is generally the case, even for imperfectly-correct systems; see Appendix D for a rough analysis of LWE schemes. In that case, the adversary's advantage is limited to the probability that it actually finds and submits a valid message that fails to decrypt. This means that our bounds apply to deterministic but failure-prone systems like certain earlier BIKE [ABB+19] variants[1], but our result is limited by the assumption of injectivity.

Until today several variants of the FO-transform were proposed. We consider the four basic transforms $U^{\perp}, U_m^{\perp}, U^{\not\perp}, U_m^{\not\perp}$ [HHK17] and, in addition, we study $U_m^{\perp}$ in the presence of key confirmation. The two most notable differences reside in the use of implicit rejection $(U^{\not\perp}, U_m^{\not\perp})$ versus explicit rejection $(U^{\perp}, U_m^{\perp})$, and whether the derivation of the session key should depend on the ciphertext $(U_m^{\perp}, U_m^{\not\perp})$ or not $(U^{\perp}, U^{\not\perp})$. Another important decision is the use of key confirmation which we also partially analyze. We come to the following results. Security with implicit rejection implies security with explicit rejection (Theorem 3). The opposite holds if the scheme with explicit rejection also employs key confirmation (Theorem 4). Moreover, security is independent of the decision if the session key derivation depends on the ciphertext (Theorem 5).

Notation. We will use the following notation throughout the paper.

- For two sets X, Y, we write Y^X to denote the set of functions from X to Y.
- Let $H : X \to Y$ be a (classical or quantum-accessible) random oracle. Then we denote the programming of H at $x \in X$ to some $y \in Y$ as $H[x \to y]$.
- Let $\mathcal{A}$ be an algorithm. If $\mathcal{A}$ has access to a classical (resp., quantum-accessible) oracle H, we write $\mathcal{A}^H$ and call $\mathcal{A}$ an oracle (resp., quantum oracle) algorithm.

---

[1] After this paper was submitted, the BIKE team has changed their encryption schemes to be randomized.

2   One-way to Hiding

ROM reductions typically simulate the random oracle in order to learn the adversary's queries. In the classical ROM, the adversary cannot learn any information about $H(x)$ without the simulator learning both x and $H(x)$. In the QROM things are not so simple, because measuring or otherwise recording the queries might collapse the adversary's quantum state and change its behavior. However, under certain conditions the simulator can learn the queries using "One-way to Hiding" (O2H) techniques going back to [Unr15]. We will use the O2H techniques from [AHU19], and introduce a novel variant that allows for tighter results.

Consider two quantum-accessible oracles $G, H : X \to Y$. The oracles do not need to be random. Suppose that G and H differ only on some small set $S \subset X$, meaning that $\forall x \notin S, G(x) = H(x)$. Let $\mathcal{A}$ be an oracle algorithm that takes an input z and makes at most q queries to G or H. Possibly $\mathcal{A}$ makes them in parallel. Therefore, suppose that the query depth, i.e., the maximum number of sequential invocations of the oracle [AHU19], is at most $d \leq q$. If $\mathcal{A}^G(z)$ behaves differently from $\mathcal{A}^H(z)$, then the O2H techniques give a way for the simulator to find some $x \in S$ with probability dependent on d and q.

We will use the following three O2H lemmas.

- Lemma 1 (original O2H) is the most general: the simulator needs to provide only G or H but it has the least probability of success.
- Lemma 3 (semiclassical O2H) has a greater probability of success, but requires more from the simulator: for each query x, the simulator must be able to recognize whether $x \in S$, and if not it must return $G(x) = H(x)$.
- Lemma 5 (our new "double-sided" O2H) gives the best probability of success, but it requires the simulator to evaluate both G and H in superposition. It also can only extract $x \in S$ if S has a single element. If S has many elements, but the simulator knows a function f such that $\{f(x) : x \in S\}$ has a single element, then it can instead extract that element $f(x)$.

We summarize the three variants of O2H as shown in Table 1. In all cases, there are two oracles H and G that differ in some set S, and the simulator outputs $x \in S$ with some probability ϵ. The lemma then shows an upper bound on the difference between $\mathcal{A}^H$ and $\mathcal{A}^G$ as a function of ϵ.

Table 1. Comparison of O2H variants

Variant	Lemma	Ref	Oracles differ	Sim. must know	Bound
Original	Lem. 1	[AHU19]	Arbitrary	H or G	$2d\sqrt{\epsilon}$
Semi-classical	Lem. 3	[AHU19]	Arbitrary	S and ($H\backslash S$ or $G\backslash S$)	$2\sqrt{d\epsilon}$
Double-sided	Lem. 5	this work	One place	H and G	$2\sqrt{\epsilon}$

Arbitrary joint distribution. The O2H lemmas allow (G, H, S, z) to be random with arbitrary joint distribution. This is stronger than (G, H, S, z) being arbitrary fixed objects, because the probabilities in the lemma include the choice of

(G, H, S, z) in addition to $\mathcal{A}$'s coins and measurements. Also, the lemmas are still true if the adversary consults other oracles which are also drawn from a joint distribution with (G, H, S, z).

2.1   Original O2H

We begin with the original O2H which first appeared in [Unr15]. We use the phrasing from [AHU19] as it is more general and more consistent with our other lemmata.

Lemma 1 (One-way to hiding; [AHU19] Theorem 3). *Let $G, H : X \to Y$ be random functions, let z be a random value, and let $S \subset X$ be a random set such that $\forall x \notin S, G(x) = H(x)$. (G, H, S, z) may have arbitrary joint distribution. Furthermore, let $\mathcal{A}^H$ be a quantum oracle algorithm which queries H with depth at most d. Let Ev be an arbitrary classical event. Define an oracle algorithm $\mathcal{B}^H(z)$ as follows: Pick $i \xleftarrow{\$} \{1, \ldots, d\}$. Run $\mathcal{A}^H(z)$ until just before its ith round of queries to H. Measure all query input registers in the computational basis, and output the set T of measurement outcomes. Let*

$$P_{\mathrm{left}} := \Pr[\mathsf{Ev} : \mathcal{A}^H(z)], \quad P_{\mathrm{right}} := \Pr[\mathsf{Ev} : \mathcal{A}^G(z)],$$
$$P_{\mathrm{guess}} := \Pr[S \cap T \neq \varnothing : T \leftarrow \mathcal{B}^H(z)].$$

Then

$$|P_{\mathrm{left}} - P_{\mathrm{right}}| \leq 2d\sqrt{P_{\mathrm{guess}}} \quad and \quad \left| \sqrt{P_{\mathrm{left}}} - \sqrt{P_{\mathrm{right}}} \right| \leq 2d\sqrt{P_{\mathrm{guess}}}.$$

The same result holds with $\mathcal{B}^G(z)$ instead of $\mathcal{B}^H(z)$ in the definition of P_{guess}.

From this lemma we conclude the following result for pseudo-random functions (PRFs, see Definition 10). It intuitively states that a random oracle makes a good PRF, even if the distinguisher is given full access to the random oracle in addition to the PRF oracle.

Corollary 1 (PRF based on random oracle). *Let $H : (K \times X) \to Y$ be a quantum-accessible random oracle. This function may be used as a quantum-accessible PRF $F_k(x) := H(k, x)$ with a key $k \xleftarrow{\$} K$. Suppose a PRF-adversary $\mathcal{A}$ makes q queries to H at depth d, and any number of queries to F_k at any depth. Then*

$$\mathrm{Adv}_{F_k}^{\mathsf{PRF}}(\mathcal{A}) \leq 2\sqrt{dq/|K|}.$$

Proof. The adversary's goal is to distinguish (F_k, H) from (F, H), where F is an unrelated uniformly random function. This is the same as distinguishing $(F, H[(k, x) \to F(x)])$ from (F, H), and the set of differences between these two H-oracles is $S := \{k\} \times X$. By Lemma 1, the distinguishing advantage is at most $2d\sqrt{P_{\mathrm{guess}}}$, where $P_{\mathrm{guess}} = \Pr[\exists(k', x) \in Q : k' = k]$, for a random round Q of parallel queries made by $\mathcal{A}^{F,H}$.

Since $\mathcal{A}^{F,H}$ has no information about k, and in expectation Q contains q/d parallel queries, we have $P_{\text{guess}} \leq q/(d \cdot |K|)$, so

$$\text{Adv}^{\text{PRF}}_{F_k}(\mathcal{A}) \leq 2d\sqrt{q/(d \cdot |K|)} = 2\sqrt{dq/|K|}$$

as claimed.   □

Note that Corollary 1 is the same as [SXY18] Lemma 2.2 and [XY19] Lemma 4, except that it takes query depth into account.

2.2   Semi-classical O2H

We now move on to semi-classical O2H. Here $\mathcal{B}$ is defined in terms of *punctured oracles* [AHU19], which measure whether the input is in a set S as defined next.

Definition 1 (Punctured oracle). *Let $H : X \to Y$ be any function, and $S \subset X$ be a set. The oracle $H\backslash S$ ("H punctured by S") takes as input a value x. It first computes whether $x \in S$ into an auxiliary qubit p, and measures p. Then it runs $H(x)$ and returns the result. Let* Find *be the event that any of the measurements of p returns 1.*

The event is called Find because if the simulator chooses to, it can immediately terminate the simulation and measure the value $x \in S$ which caused the event. The oracle is called "punctured" because if Find does not occur, $H\backslash S$ returns a result independent of H's outputs on S, as shown by the following lemma.

Lemma 2 (Puncturing is effective; [AHU19] Lemma 1). *Let $G, H : X \to Y$ be random functions, let z be a random value, and let $S \subset X$ be a random set such that $\forall x \notin S, G(x) = H(x)$. (G, H, S, z) may have arbitrary joint distribution. Let $\mathcal{A}^H$ be a quantum oracle algorithm. Let* Ev *be an arbitrary classical event. Then*

$$\Pr[\text{Ev} \wedge \neg\text{Find} : \mathcal{A}^{H\backslash S}(z)] = \Pr[\text{Ev} \wedge \neg\text{Find} : \mathcal{A}^{G\backslash S}(z)].$$

Also, puncturing only disturbs the adversary's state when it is likely to Find.

Lemma 3 (Semi-classical O2H; [AHU19] Theorem 1). *Let $G, H : X \to Y$ be random functions, let z be a random value, and let $S \subset X$ be a random set such that $\forall x \notin S, G(x) = H(x)$. (G, H, S, z) may have arbitrary joint distribution.*
  Let $\mathcal{A}^H$ be a quantum oracle algorithm which queries H with depth at most d. Let Ev *be an arbitrary classical event and let*

$$P_{\text{left}} := \Pr[\text{Ev} : \mathcal{A}^H(z)], \; P_{\text{right}} := \Pr[\text{Ev} : \mathcal{A}^G(z)],$$

$$P_{\text{find}} := \Pr[\text{Find} : \mathcal{A}^{G\backslash S}(z)] \overset{\text{Lem. 2}}{=} \Pr[\text{Find} : \mathcal{A}^{H\backslash S}(z)].$$

Then

$$|P_{\text{left}} - P_{\text{right}}| \leq 2\sqrt{dP_{\text{find}}} \quad \text{and} \quad \left|\sqrt{P_{\text{left}}} - \sqrt{P_{\text{right}}}\right| \leq 2\sqrt{dP_{\text{find}}}.$$

The theorem also holds with bound $\sqrt{(d+1)P_{\text{find}}}$ for the following alternative definitions of P_{right}:

$$P_{\text{right}} := \Pr[\text{Ev} : \mathcal{A}^{H \backslash S}(z)]$$

$$P_{\text{right}} := \Pr[\text{Ev} \wedge \neg\text{Find} : \mathcal{A}^{H \backslash S}(z)] \stackrel{\text{Lem. 2}}{=} \Pr[\text{Ev} \wedge \neg\text{Find} : \mathcal{A}^{G \backslash S}(z)]$$

$$P_{\text{right}} := \Pr[\text{Ev} \vee \text{Find} : \mathcal{A}^{H \backslash S}(z)] \stackrel{\text{Lem. 2}}{=} \Pr[\text{Ev} \vee \text{Find} : \mathcal{A}^{G \backslash S}(z)]$$

We might expect that if the adversary has no information about S, then P_{find} would be at most $q|S|/|X|$. But this is not quite true: the disturbance caused by puncturing gives the adversary information about S. This increases $\mathcal{A}$'s chances, but only by a factor of 4, as explained next.

Lemma 4 (Search in semi-classical oracle; [AHU19] Theorem 2). *Let $H : X \to Y$ be a random function, let z be a random value, and let $S \subset X$ be a random set. (H, S, z) may have arbitrary joint distribution. Let $\mathcal{A}^H$ be a quantum oracle algorithm which queries H at most q times with depth at most d.*

Let $\mathcal{B}^H(z)$ and P_{guess} be defined as in Lemma 1. Then

$$\Pr[\text{Find} : \mathcal{A}^{H \backslash S}(z)] \leq 4dP_{\text{guess}}.$$

In particular, if for each $x \in X$, $\Pr[x \in S] \leq \epsilon$ (conditioned on z, on other oracles $\mathcal{A}$ has access to, and on other outputs of H) then

$$\Pr[\text{Find} : \mathcal{A}^{H \backslash S}(z)] \leq 4q\epsilon.$$

2.3 Double-sided O2H

We augment these lemmas with a new O2H lemma which achieves a tighter bound focusing on a special case. This focus comes at the price of limited applicability. Our lemma applies when the simulator can simulate both G and H. It also requires that S is a single element; alternatively if some function f is known such that $f(S)$ is a single element, it can extract $f(S)$.

Lemma 5 (Double-sided O2H). *Let $G, H : X \to Y$ be random functions, let z be a random value, and let $S \subset X$ be a random set such that $\forall x \notin S, G(x) = H(x)$. (G, H, S, z) may have arbitrary joint distribution. Let $\mathcal{A}^H$ be a quantum oracle algorithm. Let $f : X \to W \subseteq \{0,1\}^n$ be any function, and let $f(S)$ denote the image of S under f. Let Ev be an arbitrary classical event.*

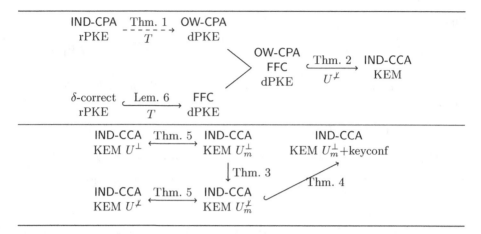

Fig. 1. Relations of our security notions using transforms T and $U^{\not\perp}$ (above) and relations between the security of different types of U-constructions (below). The solid lines show implications which are tight with respect to powers of q and/or d, and the dashed line shows a non-tight implication. The hooked arrows indicate theorems with ϵ-injectivity constraints.

We will define another quantum oracle algorithm $\mathcal{B}^{G,H}(z)$. This $\mathcal{B}$ runs in about the same amount of time as $\mathcal{A}$, but when $\mathcal{A}$ queries H, $\mathcal{B}$ queries both G and H, and also runs f twice. Let

$$P_{\text{left}} := \Pr[\text{Ev} : \mathcal{A}^H(z)], \quad P_{\text{right}} := \Pr[\text{Ev} : \mathcal{A}^G(z)], \quad P_{\text{extract}} := \Pr[\mathcal{B}^{G,H}(z) \in f(S)].$$

If $f(S) = \{w^*\}$ is a single element, then $\mathcal{B}$ will only return $\perp$ or w^*, and furthermore

$$|P_{\text{left}} - P_{\text{right}}| \leq 2\sqrt{P_{\text{extract}}} \quad and \quad \left|\sqrt{P_{\text{left}}} - \sqrt{P_{\text{right}}}\right| \leq 2\sqrt{P_{\text{extract}}}.$$

Proof. See Appendix B.

Note that if $S = \{x^*\}$ is already a single element, then we may take f as the identity. In this case $\mathcal{B}$ will return either $\perp$ or x^*.

3   KEM and PKE Security Proofs

We are now ready to get to the core of our work. All the relevant security notions are given in Appendix A. The implications are summarized in Fig. 1.

3.1   Derandomization: IND-CPA P $\overset{\text{QROM}}{\Rightarrow}$ OW-CPA $T(\mathsf{P}, G)$

The T transform [HHK17] converts a rPKE $\mathsf{P} = (\text{Keygen}, \text{Encr}, \text{Decr})$ to a dPKE $T(\mathsf{P}, G) = (\text{Keygen}, \text{Encr}_1, \text{Decr})$ by using a hash function $G : \mathcal{M} \to \mathcal{R}$, modeled as random oracle, to choose encryption coins, where

$$\text{Encr}_1(\text{pk}, m) := \text{Encr}(\text{pk}, m; \ G(m)).$$

The following theorem shows that if a PKE P is IND-CPA secure[2], then $T(\mathsf{P}, G)$ is one-way secure in the quantum-accessible random oracle model.

Theorem 1. *Let P be an rPKE with messages in $\mathcal{M}$ and random coins in $\mathcal{R}$. Let $G : \mathcal{M} \to \mathcal{R}$ be a quantum-accessible random oracle. Let $\mathcal{A}$ be an OW-CPA adversary against $\mathsf{P}' := T(\mathsf{P}, G)$. Suppose that $\mathcal{A}$ queries G at most q times with depth at most d.*

Then we can construct an IND-CPA adversary $\mathcal{B}$ against P, running in about the same time and resources as $\mathcal{A}$, such that

$$\mathrm{Adv}_{\mathsf{P}'}^{\mathsf{OW\text{-}CPA}}(\mathcal{A}) \leq (d+2) \cdot \left(\mathrm{Adv}_{\mathsf{P}}^{\mathsf{IND\text{-}CPA}}(\mathcal{B}) + \frac{8(q+1)}{|\mathcal{M}|} \right).$$

Proof. See Appendix C.

Second preimages. In the traditional definition of one-way functions, the adversary wins by finding any m' where $\mathrm{Encr}(\mathrm{pk}, m') = c^*$, whereas in our definition (cf. Definition 7) of OW-CPA the adversary must find m^* itself. This only matters if there is a second preimage, and thus a decryption failure. If P is δ-correct and ϵ-injective, it is easily shown that a definition allowing second preimages adds at most $\min(\delta, \epsilon)$ to the adversary's OW-CPA-advantage.

Hashing the public key. Many KEMs use a variant of T which sets the coins to $G(\mathrm{pk}, m)$. This is a countermeasure against multi-key attacks. In this paper we only model single-key security, so we omit pk from the hashes for brevity. The same also applies to the other transforms later in this paper, such as $U^{\perp}$.

3.2 Deterministic P: OW-CPA P $\overset{\mathsf{QROM}}{\Rightarrow}$ IND-CCA $U^{\perp}(\mathsf{P}, \mathsf{F}, H)$

Our OW-CPA to IND-CCA conversion is in the style of [JZM19d]. However, that bound is based on the failure probability δ of a randomized encryption algorithm, whereas ours is based on the difficulty of finding a failure without access to the private key. This means our theorem applies to deterministic but imperfectly-correct algorithms, such as one of the three BIKE variants, BIKE-2 [ABB+19]. So instead we use injectivity and a game where the adversary tries to find ciphertexts which are valid but do not decrypt correctly.

Definition 2 (Valid ciphertext). *Let $\mathsf{P} = (\mathrm{Keygen}, \mathrm{Encr}, \mathrm{Decr})$ be a dPKE. Call a ciphertext c "valid" for a public key pk of P if there exists m such that $c = \mathrm{Encr}(\mathrm{pk}, m)$.*

We introduce a new failure-finding experiment[3], to capture the probability that the adversary can find valid ciphertexts that cause a decryption failure.

---

[2] The theorem actually only requires a weaker notion, IND-KPA-security, in which the challenge messages are chosen at random instead of adversarially.

[3] It is a stretch to even call this an "experiment", because it may not be possible to efficiently determine whether the adversary succeeded. In future work we hope to force the adversary to find failing *message*, but this version is simpler to integrate into our proof.

Definition 3 (Finding Failing Ciphertext). *The find-failing-ciphertexts experiment* (FFC) *is shown in Fig. 2. The* FFC-*advantage of an adversary* $\mathcal{A}$ *is defined by*

$$\mathrm{Adv}_\mathsf{P}^\mathsf{FFC}(\mathcal{A}) := \Pr[\mathrm{Expt}_\mathsf{P}^\mathsf{FFC}(\mathcal{A}) \to 1].$$

$\mathrm{Expt}_\mathsf{P}^\mathsf{FFC}(\mathcal{A})$:

1   $H \xleftarrow{\$} \mathcal{H}$
2   $(\mathrm{pk}, \mathrm{sk}) \leftarrow \mathrm{Keygen}()$
3   $L \leftarrow \mathcal{A}^H(\mathrm{pk})$
4   return $[\exists \mathrm{m} \in \mathcal{M}, c \in L : \mathrm{Encr}(\mathrm{pk}, \mathrm{m}) = c \ \wedge \ \mathrm{Decr}(\mathrm{sk}, c) \neq \mathrm{m}]$

Fig. 2. FFC experiment on a dPKE P. The instantiation of H generalizes to any number of random oracles, including zero.

The $U^{\not\perp}$ transform [HHK17] converts a dPKE P $= (\mathrm{Keygen_P}, \mathrm{Encr}, \mathrm{Decr})$ into a KEM K $= (\mathrm{Keygen}, \mathrm{Encaps}, \mathrm{Decaps})$ using a PRF F $: \mathcal{K}_\mathsf{F} \times \mathcal{C} \to \mathcal{K}$ and a hash function $H : \mathcal{M} \times \mathcal{C} \to \mathcal{K}$, modeled as a random oracle. The PRF is used for implicit rejection, returning $\mathsf{F}(\mathrm{prfk}, c)$ in case of an invalid ciphertext using a secret prfk. The $U^{\not\perp}$ transform is defined in Fig. 3. We also describe variants $U_m^{\not\perp}, U^\perp, U_m^\perp$ of this transform from [HHK17], which make the following changes:

– On Encaps line 3 resp. Decaps line 7, the transformations $U_m^{\not\perp}$ and $U_m^\perp$ compute $H(m)$ resp. $H(m')$ instead of $H(m,c)$ resp. $H(m',c)$.
– On Decaps lines 4 and 6, the transformations $U^\perp$ and $U_m^\perp$ return $\perp$ instead of $\mathsf{F}(\mathrm{prfk}, c)$. These variants also don't need prfk as part of the private key.

The transforms $U^\perp$ and $U_m^\perp$ are said to use *explicit rejection* because they return an explicit failure symbol $\perp$. $U^{\not\perp}$ and $U_m^{\not\perp}$ are said to use *implicit rejection*.

Keygen():	Encaps(pk):	Decaps(sk, c):
1 $(\mathrm{pk}, \mathrm{sk_P}) \leftarrow \mathrm{Keygen_P}()$	1 $m \xleftarrow{\$} \mathcal{M}$	1 parse sk $= (\mathrm{sk_P}, \mathrm{prfk})$
2 $\mathrm{prfk} \xleftarrow{\$} \mathcal{K}_\mathsf{F}$	2 $c \leftarrow \mathrm{Encr}(\mathrm{pk}, m)$	2 $m' \leftarrow \mathrm{Decr}(\mathrm{sk_P}, c)$
3 $\mathrm{sk} \leftarrow (\mathrm{sk_P}, \mathrm{prfk})$	3 $K \leftarrow H(m, c)$	3 if $m' = \perp$:
4 return $(\mathrm{pk}, \mathrm{sk})$	4 return (K, c)	4 return $\mathsf{F}(\mathrm{prfk}, c)$
		5 else if $\mathrm{Encr}(\mathrm{pk}, m') \neq c$:
		6 return $\mathsf{F}(\mathrm{prfk}, c)$
		7 else: return $H(m', c)$

Fig. 3. Transform $U^{\not\perp}(\mathsf{P}, \mathsf{F}) := (\mathrm{Keygen}, \mathrm{Encaps}, \mathrm{Decaps})$.

The next theorem states that breaking the IND-CCA security of $U^{\not\perp}(\mathsf{P}, \mathsf{F}, H)$ requires either breaking the OW-CPA security of P, causing a decapsulation failure, or breaking the PRF used for implicit rejection. In particular, we need P to be an ϵ-injective dPKE as in Definition 6.

Theorem 2. *Let* $H : \mathcal{M} \times \mathcal{C} \to \mathcal{K}$ *be a quantum-accessible random oracle and* $F : \mathcal{K}_F \times \mathcal{C} \to \mathcal{K}$ *be a PRF. Let* P *be an* ϵ-*injective dPKE which is independent of* H. *Let* $\mathcal{A}$ *be an* IND-CCA *adversary against the KEM* $U^{\not\perp}(P, F)$, *and suppose that* $\mathcal{A}$ *makes at most* q_{dec} *decryption queries. Then we can construct three adversaries running in about the same time and resources as* $\mathcal{A}$:

- *an* OW-CPA-*adversary* $\mathcal{B}_1$ *against* P
- *a* FFC-*adversary* $\mathcal{B}_2$ *against* P, *returning a list of at most* q_{dec} *ciphertexts*
- *a* PRF-*adversary* $\mathcal{B}_3$ *against* F

such that

$$\text{Adv}_{U^{\not\perp}(P)}^{\text{IND-CCA}}(\mathcal{A}) \leq 2\sqrt{\text{Adv}_P^{\text{OW-CPA}}(\mathcal{B}_1)} + \text{Adv}_P^{\text{FFC}}(\mathcal{B}_2) + 2 \cdot \text{Adv}_F^{\text{PRF}}(\mathcal{B}_3) + \epsilon.$$

In the common case that $F(\text{prfk}, c)$ *is implemented as* $H(\text{prfk}, c)$ *it holds that if* $\mathcal{A}$ *makes* q *queries at depth* d, *then*

$$\text{Adv}_F^{\text{PRF}}(\mathcal{B}_3) \overset{\text{cor. 1}}{\leq} 2\sqrt{dq/|M|}.$$

Proof. Our proof is by a series of games. In some later games, we will define an outcome "draw" which is distinct from a win or loss. A draw counts as halfway between a win and a loss, as described by the adversary's score w_i:

$$w_i := \Pr[\mathcal{A} \text{ wins: Game } i] + \frac{1}{2}\Pr[\text{Draw: Game } i]$$

$$= \frac{1}{2}\left(1 + \Pr[\mathcal{A} \text{ wins: Game } i] - \Pr[\mathcal{A} \text{ loses: Game } i]\right)$$

Game 0 (IND-CCA). *This is the original* IND-CCA *game against the KEM* $U^{\not\perp}(P, F, H)$, *cf. Definition 12.*

Game 1 (PRF is random). *Game 1 is the same as Game 0, except the simulator replaces* $F(\text{prfk}, \cdot)$ *with a random function* $R \overset{\$}{\leftarrow} \mathcal{K}^{\mathcal{C}}$.

We construct a PRF-adversary $\mathcal{B}_3$ (cf. Definition 10) which replaces its calls to $F(\text{prfk}, \cdot)$ by calls to its oracle, runs $\mathcal{A}$, and outputs 1 if $\mathcal{A}$ wins and 0 otherwise. Now, by construction $\Pr_{k \overset{\$}{\leftarrow} \mathcal{K}}\left[\mathcal{B}^{F(k, \cdot)} = 1\right] = \Pr[\mathcal{A} \text{ wins: Game } 0]$ and $\Pr_{R \overset{\$}{\leftarrow} \mathcal{K}^{\mathcal{C}}}\left[\mathcal{A}^{R(\cdot)} = 1\right] = \Pr[\mathcal{A} \text{ wins: Game } 1]$. Hence,

$$|w_1 - w_0| = \text{Adv}_F^{\text{PRF}}(\mathcal{A}).$$

Game 2 (Draw on fail or non-injective pk**).** *Let* Fail *be the event that one or more of* $\mathcal{A}$'s *decapsulation queries* $D(c)$ *fails to decrypt, meaning that* $c = \text{Encr}(\text{pk}, \text{m})$ *for some* m, *but* $\text{Decr}(\text{sk}, c) \neq \text{m}$. *Let* NonInj *be the event that* $\text{Encr}(\text{pk}, \cdot)$ *is not injective, and let* Draw $:=$ Fail $\vee$ NonInj. *In Game 2 and onward, if* Draw *occurs then the game continues, but at the end it is a draw instead of the adversary winning or losing.*

Let $d_i := \Pr[\mathsf{Draw} : \text{Game } i]$. Then $|w_2 - w_1| \le \frac{1}{2}d_2$. It is important to note that the event Draw is a well-defined classical event and does not depend on H, even though the simulator might not be able to determine efficiently whether it occurred.

Game 3 (Reprogram $H(m,c)$ to $R(c)$). *Game 3 is the same as Game 2, but the simulator reprograms $H(m,c)$ where $c = \text{Encr}(\text{pk}, m)$ to return $R(c)$.*

This produces the same win and draw probabilities as Game 2 as explained next. For each m, the value $H(m, \text{Encr}(\text{pk}, m))$ is changed to a uniformly, independently random value, except when the game is already a draw:

– It is uniformly random because R is uniformly random.
– It is independent of $H(m', c)$ for $m' \ne m$ because $\text{Encr}(\text{pk}, \cdot)$ is injective or else the game is a draw.
– H calls $R(c)$ only for valid ciphertexts $c = \text{Encr}(\text{pk}, m')$. On the other hand, the decapsulation oracle only calls $R(c')$ for rejected ciphertexts c', i.e. ones where $c' \ne \text{Encr}(\text{pk}, \text{Decr}(\text{sk}, c'))$. If a valid ciphertext has been rejected and passed to R in this way, then Draw has occurred and the return value of R does not affect w_i or d_i.

Therefore $w_3 = w_2$ and $d_3 = d_2$.

Game 4 (Decapsulation oracle returns $R(c)$). *Game 4 is the same as Game 3, but the simulated decapsulation oracle simply returns $R(c)$ for all ciphertexts other than the challenge (for which it still returns $\perp$).*

In fact, the decapsulation oracle was already doing this in Game 3: The original decapsulation returns either $H(m, c)$ with $c = \text{Encr}(\text{pk}, m)$ or $\mathsf{F}(\text{prfk}, c)$, but both of those have been reprogrammed to return $R(c)$. Therefore $w_4 = w_3$ and $d_4 = d_3$. As of this game, the simulator does not use the private key anymore.

Bound draw. We now want to upper bound the draw probability. Let $\mathcal{B}_2$ be the algorithm which, given a public key pk, simulates Game 4 for $\mathcal{A}$ and outputs a list L of all of $\mathcal{A}$'s decapsulation queries. Then $\mathcal{B}_2$ is a FFC-adversary against P which runs in about the same time as $\mathcal{A}$ and succeeds whenever a draw occurred during the game. Consequently,

$$d_2 = d_3 = d_4 \le \text{Adv}_{\mathsf{P}}^{\mathsf{FFC}}(\mathcal{B}_2) + \epsilon.$$

Game 5 (Change shared secret). *In Game 5, the shared secret is changed to a uniformly random value r. If $b = 1$, then for all m such that $\text{Encr}(\text{pk}, m) = c^*$, the oracle $H(m)$ is reprogrammed to return r. If $b = 0$, then H is not reprogrammed.*

If $\text{Encr}(\text{pk}, \cdot)$ is injective, then this is the same distribution as Game 4, and otherwise the game is a draw. Therefore $w_5 = w_4$.

It remains to bound $\mathcal{A}$'s advantage in Game 5. The simulation still runs in about the same time as $\mathcal{A}$. Suppose at first that $\text{Encr}(\text{pk}, \cdot)$ is injective, so that the oracle H is reprogrammed only at m^*. Then the $b = 0$ and $b = 1$ cases are now distinguished by a single return value from the H oracle. Hence, we can consider two oracles H and $H' := H[m^* \to r]$ as required by Lemma 5. Then Lemma 5, states that there is an algorithm $\mathcal{B}_1$, running in about the same time as $\mathcal{A}$, such that for all H:

$$
\begin{aligned}
|\Pr[\text{Win} : b = 0] - \Pr[\text{Lose} : b = 1]| &= \left| \begin{array}{l} \Pr[\mathcal{A} \to 0 \wedge \neg\text{Draw} : b = 0] \\ - \Pr[\mathcal{A} \to 0 \wedge \neg\text{Draw} : b = 1] \end{array} \right| \\
&= \left| \begin{array}{l} \Pr[\mathcal{A}^H \to 0 \wedge \neg\text{Draw}] \\ - \Pr[\mathcal{A}^{H'} \to 0 \wedge \neg\text{Draw}] \end{array} \right| \\
&\leq 2\sqrt{\Pr[\mathcal{B}_1(\text{pk}, c) \to m^*]}.
\end{aligned}
$$

The same inequality holds if $\text{Encr}(\text{pk}, \cdot)$ is not injective, for then the game is always a draw and the left-hand side is zero. (The algorithm $\mathcal{B}_1$ still runs with the same efficiency in that case; it just might not return m^*.) The inequality also holds in expectation over H by Jensen's inequality:

$$
\begin{aligned}
\mathrm{E}\left[2\sqrt{\Pr[\mathcal{B}_1(\text{pk}, c) \to m^*]} : H \xleftarrow{\$} \mathcal{K}^{(\mathcal{M} \times \mathcal{C})} \right] \\
\leq 2\sqrt{\mathrm{E}\left[\Pr[\mathcal{B}_1(\text{pk}, c) \to m^*] : H \xleftarrow{\$} \mathcal{K}^{(\mathcal{M} \times \mathcal{C})} \right]} \\
= 2\sqrt{\text{Adv}_\mathsf{P}^{\text{OW-CPA}}(\mathcal{B}_1)}
\end{aligned}
$$

so that

$$
|\Pr[\text{Win} : b = 0] - \Pr[\text{Lose} : b = 1]| \leq 2\sqrt{\text{Adv}_\mathsf{P}^{\text{OW-CPA}}(\mathcal{B}_1)}.
$$

Likewise, for the same adversary $\mathcal{B}_1$,

$$
|\Pr[\text{Win} : b = 1] - \Pr[\text{Lose} : b = 0]| \leq 2\sqrt{\text{Adv}_\mathsf{P}^{\text{OW-CPA}}(\mathcal{B}_1)}.
$$

Since b is either 0 or 1 each with probability $\frac{1}{2}$, we have by the triangle inequality:

$$
|\Pr[\text{Win}] - \Pr[\text{Lose}]| \leq 2\sqrt{\text{Adv}_\mathsf{P}^{\text{OW-CPA}}(\mathcal{B}_1)}
$$

so that $\left| w_5 - \frac{1}{2} \right| \leq \sqrt{\text{Adv}_\mathsf{P}^{\text{OW-CPA}}(\mathcal{B}_1)}$.

Summing up the differences in the previous games, we have

$$
\left| w_0 - \frac{1}{2} \right| \leq \sqrt{\text{Adv}_\mathsf{P}^{\text{OW-CPA}}(\mathcal{B}_1)} + \frac{1}{2}\text{Adv}_\mathsf{P}^{\text{FFC}}(\mathcal{B}_2) + \frac{\epsilon}{2} + \text{Adv}_\mathsf{F}^{\text{PRF}}(\mathcal{B}_3)
$$

and finally

$$
\text{Adv}_{U^{\neq}(\mathsf{P})}^{\text{IND-CCA}}(\mathcal{A}) \leq 2\sqrt{\text{Adv}_\mathsf{P}^{\text{OW-CPA}}(\mathcal{B}_1)} + 2 \cdot \text{Adv}_\mathsf{F}^{\text{PRF}}(\mathcal{B}_3) + \text{Adv}_\mathsf{P}^{\text{FFC}}(\mathcal{B}_2) + \epsilon.
$$

This completes the proof of Theorem 2.   □

Tightness. This bound is essentially tight, since breaking the one-wayness of P and finding decryption failures are both known to result in attacks. Breaking the PRF harms security if and only if implicit rejection is more secure than explicit rejection. For a correct P the bound boils down to the first two terms of the sum. The square-root loss arises from OW being a weaker security notion than IND [MW18], i.e., harder to break, and recent results [JZM19b] suggest that the square-root loss might be unavoidable in the quantum setting.

3.3 Decryption Failures

When the dPKE is constructed by derandomizing an rPKE, we can also bound the FFC advantage.

Lemma 6. *Let* $P = (\mathrm{Keygen}, \mathrm{Encr}, \mathrm{Decr})$ *be a δ-correct rPKE with messages in $\mathcal{M}$ and randomness in $\mathcal{R}$. Let $G : \mathcal{M} \to \mathcal{R}$ be a random oracle, so that $T(P, G) := (\mathrm{Keygen}, \mathrm{Encr}_1, \mathrm{Decr})$ is a derandomized version of P. Suppose that $T(P, G)$ is ϵ-injective. Let $\mathcal{A}$ be a FFC adversary against $T(P, G)$ which makes at most q queries at depth d to G and returns a list of at most q_{dec} ciphertexts. Then*

$$\mathrm{Adv}_{T(P,G)}^{\mathsf{FFC}}(\mathcal{A}) \leq ((4d+1)\delta + \sqrt{3\epsilon}) \cdot (q + q_{\mathrm{dec}}) + \epsilon.$$

Proof. See Appendix E. $\square$

Note that if ϵ is negligible, and if the adversary can recognize which ciphertexts will fail, then this is a Grover bound.

4   Explicit Rejection and Key Confirmation

We now turn to systems with explicit rejection or key confirmation. The next theorem shows that the transform $U^\perp$ (with explicit rejection) never yields KEMs that are more secure than KEMs constructed via $U^{\not\perp}$ (with implicit rejection).

Theorem 3 (Explicit $\to$ implicit). *Let P be a dPKE. Let $\mathcal{A}$ be an IND-CCA adversary against $U^{\not\perp}(P, F, H)$. Then there is an IND-CCA adversary $\mathcal{B}$ against $U^\perp(P, H)$, running in about the same time and resources as $\mathcal{B}$, such that*

$$\mathrm{Adv}_{U^{\not\perp}(P,F,H)}^{\mathsf{IND\text{-}CCA}}(\mathcal{A}) = \mathrm{Adv}_{U^\perp(P,H)}^{\mathsf{IND\text{-}CCA}}(\mathcal{B}).$$

Proof. The only difference between $U^\perp(P, H)$ and $U^{\not\perp}(P, F, H)$ is that where the former would reject a ciphertext c by returning $\perp$, the latter instead returns $F(\mathrm{prfk}, c)$. So the adversary $\mathcal{B}$ can simply choose a random PRF key prfk, run $\mathcal{A}$, and output $\mathcal{A}$'s result. $\mathcal{B}$ forwards all of $\mathcal{A}$'s queries to its oracles and returns the responses with the only difference that in case the decapsulation oracle returns $\perp$, $\mathcal{B}$ returns $F(\mathrm{prfk}, c)$. The algorithm $\mathcal{B}$ perfectly simulates the IND-CCA game for $U^{\not\perp}(P, F, H)$ and hence $\mathcal{A}$ succeeds with the same success probability as in the original game. $\square$

On the other hand, explicit rejection is secure if key confirmation is used. Key confirmation refers to adding a hash of the message to the cipher text. Let τ be the number of bits desired for the key-confirmation tag. For a PKE $P = (\text{Keygen}, \text{Encr}, \text{Decr})$ define the transform $C(P, H_t, \tau) := (\text{Keygen}, \text{Encr}_1, \text{Decr}_1)$ using a random oracle $H_t : \mathcal{M} \to \{0,1\}^\tau$ as in Fig. 4.

$\text{Encr}_1(\text{pk}, m)$:	$\text{Decr}_1(\text{sk}, (c,t))$:
1 $c \leftarrow \text{Encr}(\text{pk}, m)$	1 $m' \leftarrow \text{Decr}(\text{sk}_P, c)$
2 $t \leftarrow H_t(m)$	2 if $H_t(m') \neq t$:
3 return (c,t)	3 return $\bot$
	4 return m'

Fig. 4. Transform $C(P, H_t, \tau) := (\text{Keygen}, \text{Encr}_1, \text{Decr}_1)$.

Theorem 4 (Implicit $\to$ explicit with key confirmation). *Let P be an ϵ-injective dPKE. Consider the KEM $K_1 := U_m^\perp(C(P, H_t, \tau), H_s)$ obtained from P applying the C-transform with random oracle $H_t : \mathcal{M} \to \{0,1\}^\tau$ and the $U_m^\perp$-transform with independent random oracle $H_s : \mathcal{M} \to \{0,1\}^s$. Let $K_2 := U_m^{\not\perp}(P, F, H)$ be the KEM obtained from P applying the $U_m^{\not\perp}$-transform with random oracle $H : \mathcal{M} \to \{0,1\}^{s+\tau}$.*

If $\mathcal{A}$ is an IND-CCA-adversary against K_1 which makes q_{dec} decapsulation queries, then it is also an IND-CCA-adversary against K_2 and there is a PRF-adversary $\mathcal{B}$ against F which uses about the same time and resources as $\mathcal{A}$, such that:

$$\text{Adv}_{K_1}^{\text{IND-CCA}}(\mathcal{A}) \leq 2 \cdot \text{Adv}_{K_2}^{\text{IND-CCA}}(\mathcal{A}) + \frac{q_{\text{dec}}}{2^{\tau-1}} + 2 \cdot \text{Adv}_F^{\text{PRF}}(\mathcal{B}) + 2\epsilon.$$

Proof. Deferred to Appendix F.

Finally, we can show that hashing m is equivalent to hashing (m, c) in the next theorem.

Theorem 5 ($U_m \leftrightarrow U$). *Let P be a dPKE. Let $K_1 = U^\perp(P, H_1)$ and $K_2 = U_m^\perp(P, H_2)$. Then K_1 is IND-CCA secure if and only if K_2 is IND-CCA secure. In other words, if there is an adversary $\mathcal{A}$ against one, then there is an adversary $\mathcal{B}$ against the other, running in about the same time and with the same advantage. The same is true for $U^{\not\perp}$ and $U_m^{\not\perp}$.*

Proof. This is a simple indifferentiability argument. In both the encapsulation and decapsulation functions, the IND-CCA experiment against K_1 only calls $H_1(m, c)$ when $c = \text{Encr}(\text{pk}, m)$. So to simulate the K_1-experiment playing in an IND-CCA experiment against K_2 (with oracle $H_2 : \mathcal{M} \to \mathcal{K}$), sample fresh random oracle $H \xleftarrow{\$} \mathcal{K}^{(\mathcal{M}, \mathcal{C})}$ and set

$$H_1(m, c) := \begin{cases} H_2(m), & \text{if } c = \text{Encr}(\text{pk}, m), \\ H(m, c), & \text{otherwise.} \end{cases}$$

This exactly simulates the IND-CCA experiment against K_1. In the other direction, to simulate the IND-CCA experiment against K_2 it suffices to redirect $H_2(m)$ to $H_1(m, \mathrm{Encr}(\mathrm{pk}, m))$.

The same technique works for $U^{\not\perp}$ and $U_m^{\not\perp}$. It also works for security notions other than IND-CCA, such as OW-CCA, OW-qPVCA, etc. (see for example [JZC+18]). □

Acknowledgements. Part of this work was done while the authors were participating in the 2019 Oxford Post-Quantum Cryptography Workshop. Special thanks to Daniel J. Bernstein, Edward Eaton and Mark Zhandry for helpful discussions; and to the anonymous TCC reviewers for their helpful comments and corrections.

This work was supported by the European Union PROMETHEUS project (Horizon 2020 Research and Innovation Program, grant 780701) and the Deutsche Forschungsgemeinschaft (DFG, German Research Foundation) under Germany's Excellence Strategy (EXC 2092 CASA, 390781972).

References

[ABB+19] Aragon, N., et al.: BIKE: bit flipping key encapsulation (2019). https://bikesuite.org

[AHU19] Ambainis, A., Hamburg, M., Unruh, D.: Quantum security proofs using semi-classical oracles. In: Boldyreva, A., Micciancio, D. (eds.) CRYPTO 2019, Part II. LNCS, vol. 11693, pp. 269–295. Springer, Cham (2019). https://doi.org/10.1007/978-3-030-26951-7_10

[BDF+11] Boneh, D., Dagdelen, Ö., Fischlin, M., Lehmann, A., Schaffner, C., Zhandry, M.: Random oracles in a quantum world. In: Lee, D.H., Wang, X. (eds.) ASIACRYPT 2011. LNCS, vol. 7073, pp. 41–69. Springer, Heidelberg (2011). https://doi.org/10.1007/978-3-642-25385-0_3

[BR93] Bellare, M., Rogaway, P.: Random oracles are practical: a paradigm for designing efficient protocols. In: Denning, D.E., Pyle, R., Ganesan, R., Sandhu, R.S., Ashby, V. (eds.) ACM CCS 93, pp. 62–73. ACM Press, New York (1993). https://doi.org/10.1145/168588.168596

[FO99] Fujisaki, E., Okamoto, T.: Secure integration of asymmetric and symmetric encryption schemes. In: Wiener, M. (ed.) CRYPTO 1999. LNCS, vol. 1666, pp. 537–554. Springer, Heidelberg (1999). https://doi.org/10.1007/3-540-48405-1_34

[HHK17] Hofheinz, D., Hövelmanns, K., Kiltz, E.: A modular analysis of the Fujisaki-Okamoto transformation. In: Kalai, Y., Reyzin, L. (eds.) TCC 2017, Part I. LNCS, vol. 10677, pp. 341–371. Springer, Cham (2017). https://doi.org/10.1007/978-3-319-70500-2_12

[HKSU18] Hövelmanns, K., Kiltz, E., Schäge, S., Unruh, D.: Generic authenticated key exchange in the quantum random oracle model. Cryptology ePrint Archive, Report 2018/928 (2018). https://eprint.iacr.org/2018/928

[HNP+03] Howgrave-Graham, N., et al.: The impact of decryption failures on the security of NTRU encryption. In: Boneh, D. (ed.) CRYPTO 2003. LNCS, vol. 2729, pp. 226–246. Springer, Heidelberg (2003). https://doi.org/10.1007/978-3-540-45146-4_14

[JZC+18] Jiang, H., Zhang, Z., Chen, L., Wang, H., Ma, Z.: IND-CCA-secure key encapsulation mechanism in the quantum random oracle model, revisited. In: Shacham, H., Boldyreva, A. (eds.) CRYPTO 2018, Part III. LNCS, vol. 10993, pp. 96–125. Springer, Cham (2018). https://doi.org/10.1007/978-3-319-96878-0_4

[JZM19a] Jiang, H., Zhang, Z., Ma, Z.: Key encapsulation mechanism with explicit rejection in the quantum random oracle model. In: Lin, D., Sako, K. (eds.) PKC 2019, Part II. LNCS, vol. 11443, pp. 618–645. Springer, Cham (2019). https://doi.org/10.1007/978-3-030-17259-6_21

[JZM19b] Jiang, H., Zhang, Z., Ma, Z.: On the non-tightness of measurement-based reductions for key encapsulation mechanism in the quantum random oracle model. Cryptology ePrint Archive, Report 2019/494 (2019). https://eprint.iacr.org/2019/494

[JZM19c] Jiang, H., Zhang, Z., Ma, Z.: Tighter security proofs for generic key encapsulation mechanism in the quantum random oracle model. In: Ding, J., Steinwandt, R. (eds.) PQCrypto 2019. LNCS, vol. 11505, pp. 227–248. Springer, Cham (2019). https://doi.org/10.1007/978-3-030-25510-7_13

[JZM19d] Jiang, H., Zhang, Z., Ma, Z.: Tighter security proofs for generic key encapsulation mechanism in the quantum random oracle model. Cryptology ePrint Archive, Report 2019/134 (2019). https://eprint.iacr.org/2019/134

[MW18] Micciancio, D., Walter, M.: On the bit security of cryptographic primitives. In: Nielsen, J.B., Rijmen, V. (eds.) EUROCRYPT 2018, Part I. LNCS, vol. 10820, pp. 3–28. Springer, Cham (2018). https://doi.org/10.1007/978-3-319-78381-9_1

[NC00] Nielsen, M.A., Chuang, I.L.: Quantum Computation and Quantum Information. Cambridge University Press, Cambridge (2000)

[SXY18] Saito, T., Xagawa, K., Yamakawa, T.: Tightly-secure key-encapsulation mechanism in the quantum random oracle model. In: Nielsen, J.B., Rijmen, V. (eds.) EUROCRYPT 2018, Part III. LNCS, vol. 10822, pp. 520–551. Springer, Cham (2018). https://doi.org/10.1007/978-3-319-78372-7_17

[TU16] Targhi, E.E., Unruh, D.: Post-quantum security of the Fujisaki-Okamoto and OAEP transforms. In: Hirt, M., Smith, A. (eds.) TCC 2016, Part II. LNCS, vol. 9986, pp. 192–216. Springer, Heidelberg (2016). https://doi.org/10.1007/978-3-662-53644-5_8

[Unr15] Unruh, D.: Revocable quantum timed-release encryption. J. ACM **62**(6), 49:1–49:76 (2015). https://doi.org/10.1145/2817206. http://doi.acm.org/10.1145/2817206

[XY19] Xagawa, K., Yamakawa, T.: (Tightly) QCCA-secure key-encapsulation mechanism in the quantum random oracle model. In: Ding, J., Steinwandt, R. (eds.) PQCrypto 2019. LNCS, vol. 11505, pp. 249–268. Springer, Cham (2019). https://doi.org/10.1007/978-3-030-25510-7_14

[Zha19] Zhandry, M.: How to record quantum queries, and applications to quantum indifferentiability. In: Boldyreva, A., Micciancio, D. (eds.) CRYPTO 2019, Part II. LNCS, vol. 11693, pp. 239–268. Springer, Cham (2019). https://doi.org/10.1007/978-3-030-26951-7_9

A   Security Notions and Definitions

In this section we recall the definition of KEMs and PKEs. Additionally, we recall the respective security notions that are needed in this paper. We begin with a definition of random oracles following [BDF+11] and summarized in Fig. 5.

Classical random oracle $\mathcal{O}_H(x)$:

1. $q_H \leftarrow q_H + 1$
2. return $H(x)$

Quantum random oracle $\mathcal{O}_H(\sum_{x,t,z} \psi_{x,t,z} |x,t,z\rangle)$:

1. $q_H \leftarrow q_H + 1$
2. return $\sum_{x,t,z} \psi_{x,t,z} |x, t \oplus H(x), z\rangle$

Fig. 5. Definition of the classical and quantum random oracle

Definition 4 (Public-Key Encryption Schemes). *A randomized public-key encryption scheme (rPKE) is defined over a finite message space* $\mathcal{M}$, *a ciphertext space* $\mathcal{C}$, *a secret key space* $\mathcal{SK}$ *and a public key space* $\mathcal{PK}$. *It consists of a triple of algorithms* P = (Keygen, Encr, Decr) *defined as follows.*

- Keygen() → (pk, sk) *is a randomized algorithm that returns a secret key* sk ∈ $\mathcal{SK}$ *and a public key* pk ∈ $\mathcal{PK}$.
- Encr(pk, m) → c *is a randomized algorithm that takes as input a public key* pk *and a message* m ∈ $\mathcal{M}$, *and outputs a ciphertext* c ∈ $\mathcal{C}$.
- Decr(sk, c) → {m′, ⊥} *is a deterministic algorithm that takes as input a secret key* sk ∈ $\mathcal{SK}$ *and a ciphertext* c ∈ $\mathcal{C}$ *and returns either a message* m′ ∈ $\mathcal{M}$ *or a failure symbol* ⊥ ∉ $\mathcal{M}$.

A deterministic public-key encryption scheme (dPKE) is defined the same way, except that Encr *is a deterministic algorithm.*

Definition 5 (Correctness and failure probability of PKEs). *A PKE* P = (Keygen, Encr, Decr) *is δ-correct if*

$$E\left[\max_{m \in \mathcal{M}} \Pr[\text{Decr}(\text{sk}, \text{Encr}(\text{pk}, m)) \neq m] : (\text{pk}, \text{sk}) \leftarrow \text{Keygen}()\right] \leq \delta.$$

We call δ the decryption failure probability of P. *We say* P *is correct if δ = 0.*

Note that this definition works for a deterministic or randomized PKE, but for a deterministic PKE the term $\max_{m \in \mathcal{M}} \Pr[\text{Decr}(\text{sk}, \text{Encr}(\text{pk}, m))$ is either 0 or 1 for each keypair.

Definition 6 (Injectivity of PKEs). *A dPKE* P = (Keygen, Encr, Decr) *is ε-injective if*

$$\Pr\left[\text{Encr}(\text{pk}, m) \text{ is not injective} : (\text{pk}, \text{sk}) \leftarrow \text{Keygen}(), H \xleftarrow{\$} \mathcal{H}\right] \leq \epsilon.$$

We say P *is injective if ε = 0. We say that an rPKE is injective if for all public keys* pk, *all m ≠ m' and all coins r, r', we have* Encr(pk, m, r) ≠ Encr(pk, m', r').

Definition 7 (OW-CPA Advantage). *Let* P = (Keygen, Encr, Decr) *be a dPKE or rPKE. The one-way under chosen-plaintext attacks* (OW-CPA) *experiment is shown in Fig. 6. The* OW-CPA*-advantage of an adversary* $\mathcal{A}$ *is defined as*

$$\text{Adv}_{\text{P}}^{\text{OW-CPA}}(\mathcal{A}) := \Pr[\text{Expt}_{\text{P}}^{\text{OW-CPA}}(\mathcal{A}) \to 1].$$

Note that some papers, e.g., [JZM19c], define OW-CPA-advantage this way, and some, e.g., [HHK17], instead use the looser condition that Encr(pk, m') = c*, particularly if Encr is deterministic. We use the definition in Fig. 6 because it is more convenient for our proofs of Theorems 1 and 2.

Definition 8 (IND-CPA Advantage). *Let* P = (Keygen, Encr, Decr) *be an rPKE. The indistinguishability under chosen-plaintext attacks* (IND-CPA) *experiment is shown in Fig. 6. The* IND-CPA*-advantage of an adversary* $\mathcal{A} = (\mathcal{A}_1, \mathcal{A}_2)$ *is defined as*

$$\text{Adv}_{\text{P}}^{\text{IND-CPA}}(\mathcal{A}) := 2\left|\Pr[\text{Expt}_{\text{P}}^{\text{IND-CPA}}(\mathcal{A}) \to 1] - \frac{1}{2}\right|.$$

Note that IND-CPA is unachievable for dPKEs, because $\mathcal{A}$ can just test which message encrypts to c*.

A weakening of IND-CPA is IND-KPA where the challenge messages are chosen by the experiment.

Definition 9 (IND-KPA Advantage). *Let* P = (Keygen, Encr, Decr) *be an rPKE. The indistinguishability under known-plaintext attack* (IND-KPA) *experiment is shown in Fig. 6. The* IND-KPA*-advantage of an adversary* $\mathcal{A}$ *is defined as*

$$\text{Adv}_{\text{P}}^{\text{IND-KPA}}(\mathcal{A}) := 2\left|\Pr[\text{Expt}_{\text{P}}^{\text{IND-KPA}}(\mathcal{A}) \to 1] - \frac{1}{2}\right|.$$

$\underline{\text{Expt}_P^{\text{OW-CPA}}(\mathcal{A}):}$

1   $H \xleftarrow{\$} \mathcal{H}$
2   $(\text{pk}, \text{sk}) \leftarrow \text{Keygen}()$
3   $m^* \xleftarrow{\$} \mathcal{M}$
4   $c^* \leftarrow \text{Encr}(\text{pk}, m^*)$
5   $m' \leftarrow \mathcal{A}^H(\text{pk}, c^*)$
6   return $[m^* = m']$

$\underline{\text{Expt}_P^{\text{IND-KPA}}(\mathcal{A}):}$

1   $H \xleftarrow{\$} \mathcal{H}$
2   $(\text{pk}, \text{sk}) \leftarrow \text{Keygen}()$
3   $m_0, m_1 \leftarrow \mathcal{M}$
4   $b \xleftarrow{\$} \{0, 1\}$
5   $c^* \leftarrow \text{Encr}(\text{pk}, m_b^*)$
6   $b' \leftarrow \mathcal{A}^H(\text{pk}, m_0, m_1, c^*)$
7   return $[b = b']$

$\underline{\text{Expt}_P^{\text{IND-CPA}}(\mathcal{A}):}$

1   $H \xleftarrow{\$} \mathcal{H}$
2   $(\text{pk}, \text{sk}) \leftarrow \text{Keygen}()$
3   $(st, m_0, m_1) \leftarrow \mathcal{A}_1^H(\text{pk})$
4   $b \xleftarrow{\$} \{0, 1\}$
5   $c^* \leftarrow \text{Encr}(\text{pk}, m_b^*)$
6   $b' \leftarrow \mathcal{A}_2^H(\text{pk}, m_0, m_1, c^*, st)$
7   return $[b = b']$

Fig. 6. OW-CPA, IND-CPA, and IND-KPA of a PKE P. The instantiation of H generalizes to any number of random oracles, including zero.

Clearly IND-CPA $\Rightarrow$ IND-KPA as any IND-KPA adversary can be used to break IND-CPA using it as $\mathcal{A}_2$ and simulating $\mathcal{A}_1$ by just sampling random messages.

Definition 10 (PRF Advantage). *Let* $\mathsf{F} : \mathcal{K}_\mathsf{F} \times X \to Y$ *be a pseudorandom function (PRF). We define the* PRF-*advantage of an adversary* $\mathcal{A}$ *as*

$$\text{Adv}_F^{\text{PRF}}(\mathcal{A}) = \left| \Pr_{k \xleftarrow{\$} \mathcal{K}} \left[\mathcal{A}^{\mathsf{F}(k,\cdot)} = 1 \right] - \Pr_{R \xleftarrow{\$} Y^X} \left[\mathcal{A}^{R(\cdot)} = 1 \right] \right|.$$

Definition 11 (Key Encapsulation Mechanism). *A KEM* K *defined over the message space* $\mathcal{M}$, *the public key space* $\mathcal{PK}$, *the secret key space* $\mathcal{SK}$, *and the key space* $\mathcal{K}$, *is a triple of algorithms* $\mathsf{K} = (\text{Keygen}, \text{Encaps}, \text{Decaps})$ *defined as follows.*

- Keygen() $\to$ (pk, sk) *is a randomized algorithm that returns a public key* pk $\in \mathcal{PK}$ *and a secret key* sk $\in \mathcal{SK}$.
- Encaps(pk) $\to$ (c, κ) *is a randomized algorithm that takes as input a public key* pk *and outputs a ciphertext* c *as well as a key* $\kappa \in K$.
- Decaps(sk, c) $\to$ κ *or* $\perp$ *is a deterministic algorithm that takes as input a secret key* sk $\in \mathcal{SK}$ *and a ciphertext* c *and returns a key* $\kappa \in K$ *or a failure symbol* $\perp \notin K$.

As before, we use $\mathcal{H}$ to denote the space of functions from which the random hash function is randomly sampled if a proof for K is being given in the ROM.

Definition 12 (IND-CCA **Advantage**). *Let* K *be a KEM. The security experiment* $\text{Expt}_K^{\text{IND-CCA}}(\mathcal{A})$ *is defined in Fig. 7 for an adversary* $\mathcal{A}$ *against* K, *given access to a (quantum-accessible) random oracle* H *and a classical decapsulation oracle* D.

We define the advantage of a classical (resp., quantum) adversary $\mathcal{A}$ *against a KEM* K *in the classical (resp., quantum-accessible) random oracle model as*

$$\text{Adv}_K^{\text{IND-CCA}}(\mathcal{A}) = \left| \Pr\left[\text{Expt}_K^{\text{IND-CCA}}(\mathcal{A}) = 1 \right] - \frac{1}{2} \right|.$$

$\underline{\text{Expt}_K^{\text{IND-CCA}}(\mathcal{A}):}$ | $\underline{\text{Classical decapsulation oracle } D(c):}$

1   $H \xleftarrow{\$} \mathcal{H}$ 1   if $c = c^*$: return $\bot$
2   $(\text{pk}, \text{sk}) \leftarrow \text{Keygen}()$ 2   return $\text{Decaps}(\text{sk}, c)$
3   $(c^*, k_0^*) \leftarrow \text{Encaps}(\text{pk})$
4   $k_1^* \xleftarrow{\$} K$
5   $b \xleftarrow{\$} \{0, 1\}$
6   $b' \leftarrow \mathcal{A}^{H,D}(\text{pk}, c^*, k_b^*)$
7   return $[b = b']$

Fig. 7. IND-CCA security experiment in the (Q)ROM against an adversary $\mathcal{A}$

B   Proof of Lemma 5

Lemma 5 (Double-sided O2H). *Let* $G, H : X \to Y$ *be random functions, let* z *be a random value, and let* $S \subset X$ *be a random set such that* $\forall x \notin S, G(x) = H(x)$. (G, H, S, z) *may have arbitrary joint distribution. Let* $\mathcal{A}^H$ *be a quantum oracle algorithm. Let* $f : X \to W \subseteq \{0, 1\}^n$ *be any function, and let* $f(S)$ *denote the image of* S *under* f. *Let* Ev *be an arbitrary classical event.*

We will define another quantum oracle algorithm $\mathcal{B}^{G,H}(z)$. *This* $\mathcal{B}$ *runs in about the same amount of time as* $\mathcal{A}$, *but when* $\mathcal{A}$ *queries* H, $\mathcal{B}$ *queries both* G *and* H, *and also runs* f *twice. Let*

$$P_{\text{left}} := \Pr[\text{Ev} : \mathcal{A}^H(z)], \ P_{\text{right}} := \Pr[\text{Ev} : \mathcal{A}^G(z)], \ P_{\text{extract}} := \Pr[\mathcal{B}^{G,H}(z) \in f(S)].$$

If $f(S) = \{w^*\}$ *is a single element, then* $\mathcal{B}$ *will only return* $\bot$ *or* w^*, *and furthermore*

$$|P_{\text{left}} - P_{\text{right}}| \leq 2\sqrt{P_{\text{extract}}} \quad \text{and} \quad \left| \sqrt{P_{\text{left}}} - \sqrt{P_{\text{right}}} \right| \leq 2\sqrt{P_{\text{extract}}}.$$

Proof. The outline of our proof is to use the compressed oracle framework from [Zha19] to instantiate a new random oracle $B : W \to \{0, 1\}$. On query x, the simulator returns $H(x)$ if $B(f(x)) = 0$, or $G(x)$ if $B(f(x)) = 1$. The only value of $B(z)$ that affects the result is $b := B(w^*)$, so at the end of the computation the compressed oracle table for B must be either the empty table or $\{w^* \to b\}$. Our proof quantizes and simplifies this outline.

To begin, suppose that G and H are fixed and $\mathcal{A}$ is unitary. Consider an algorithm $\mathcal{B}_0^{H,G}$ which runs $\mathcal{A}^H$ and $\mathcal{A}^G$ in superposition, with an additional bit b signifying which oracle is being used. Then if $\mathcal{A}^G$ behaves differently from $\mathcal{A}^H$, the state of $\mathcal{A}$ will become entangled with b. We will use $|b\rangle = |+\rangle :=$ $(|0\rangle + |1\rangle)/\sqrt{2}$ to signify that $\mathcal{A}$ is using H, and $|b\rangle = |-\rangle := (|0\rangle - |1\rangle)/\sqrt{2}$ to signify that $\mathcal{A}$ is using G. That is:

$$\mathcal{B}_0^{H,G} := \frac{\mathcal{A}^H \otimes |+\rangle + \mathcal{A}^G \otimes |-\rangle}{\sqrt{2}}.$$

This $\mathcal{B}_0$ can be implemented as $\mathcal{A}$ with only the oracle queries changed. To do this, let b start in the state $(|+\rangle + |-\rangle)/\sqrt{2} = |0\rangle$. When $\mathcal{A}$ queries the oracle, $\mathcal{B}_0$ implements the following map on $|x, y, b\rangle$:

$$U(|x, y, +\rangle) := |x, y \oplus H(x), +\rangle,$$
$$U(|x, y, -\rangle) := |x, y \oplus G(x), -\rangle.$$

This is the same as a conditional evaluation map which queries H if $b = 0$ and G if $b = 1$, with a Hadamard transform before and after.

Let ψ_H resp. ψ_G be the final states of $\mathcal{A}^H$ resp. $\mathcal{A}^G$. The final state of $\mathcal{B}_0^{H,G}$ is

$$\frac{\psi_H \otimes |+\rangle + \psi_G \otimes |-\rangle}{\sqrt{2}} = \frac{1}{2} \cdot \left(\begin{array}{c} (|\psi_H\rangle + |\psi_G\rangle) \otimes |0\rangle \\ +(|\psi_H\rangle - |\psi_G\rangle) \otimes |1\rangle \end{array} \right).$$

Suppose we measure b in the computational basis. This commutes with the final measurement of $\mathcal{A}$'s state. Then, we will measure 1 with probability $\epsilon := \||\psi_H\rangle - |\psi_G\rangle\|^2/4$, and hence,

$$\||\psi_H\rangle - |\psi_G\rangle\| = 2\sqrt{\epsilon}.$$

This $2\sqrt{\epsilon}$ is the claimed probability bound, but we still need a way to extract w^*. The full algorithm $\mathcal{B}^{H,G}$ is the same as $\mathcal{B}_0$, but with a different final measurement and another auxiliary register $w \in \{0,1\}^n$ (i.e. a register that can represent elements of w). The w register is initialized to 0.

We will ensure that except during queries, (b, w) will always be in the state $(0,0)$ or $(1, w^*)$. More formally, let T_w operate on the b and w registers by $T_w(|b, w\rangle) := |b, w \oplus (b \cdot w^*)\rangle$. Therefore T_w swaps $(1, 0)$ with $(1, w^*)$. We will ensure that if at some step in the computation the state of $\mathcal{B}_0^{H,G}$ is ψ, then during the same step the state of $\mathcal{B}^{H,G}$ is $T_w(\psi \otimes |0\rangle)$.

Since $\mathcal{B}_0^{H,G}$ replaces the oracle queries with U, $\mathcal{B}^{H,G}$ should replace them with $U_w := T_w \circ U \circ T_w^\dagger$. (This gives the desired result because T_w commutes with all the steps of $\mathcal{A}$ except for the oracle queries.) To do this, let

$$T_f(|x, y, b, w\rangle) := |x, y, b, w \oplus (b \cdot f(x))\rangle.$$

Then $\mathcal{B}^{H,G}$ replaces $\mathcal{A}$'s oracle queries with

$$U_f := T_f \circ U \circ T_f^\dagger.$$

In fact, $U_f = U_w$. On the subspace where $x \in S$, we have $f(x) = w^*$ by assumption. Therefore $T_f = T_w$ and $U_f = U_w$. On the orthogonal subspace where $x \notin S$, we have $G(x) = H(x)$, so the operation U does not depend on b or w. Therefore on that subspace, U commutes with T_f and T_w, so that $U_f = U = U_w$. In sum, $U_f = U_w$ is an efficient implementation of the oracle by $\mathcal{B}^{H,G}$.

When $\mathcal{A}$ completes, $\mathcal{B}^{H,G}$ measures (b, w) in the computational basis. With probability ϵ it measures $(1, w^*)$, in which case it outputs w^*. Otherwise it measures $(0,0)$, in which case it outputs $\perp$.

The event Ev is classical and well-defined. Therefore whether it occurred is a binary measurement on the final state of $\mathcal{A}$ as a density operator. By [AHU19] Lemmas 3 and 4,

$$\left| \Pr[\mathsf{Ev} : \mathcal{A}^H] - \Pr[\mathsf{Ev} : \mathcal{A}^G] \right| \leq \||\psi_0\rangle - |\psi_1\rangle\| \leq 2\sqrt{\Pr[\mathcal{B}^{H,G} \to w^*]}$$

and likewise

$$\left| \sqrt{\Pr[\mathsf{Ev} : \mathcal{A}^H]} - \sqrt{\Pr[\mathsf{Ev} : \mathcal{A}^G]} \right| \leq \||\psi_0\rangle - |\psi_1\rangle\| \leq 2\sqrt{\Pr[\mathcal{B}^{H,G} \to w^*]}.$$

This completes the proof for unitary adversaries $\mathcal{A}$ with a fixed H and G.

For non-unitary adversaries and for random distributions of H, G, we instead end in a mixture of states Ψ_0 resp. Ψ_1, for which Euclidean distance is not appropriate but the Bures distance [NC00] is. By monotonicity and joint concavity of fidelity (exactly as in [AHU19] Lemma 6 and 9), the same bound holds for the Bures distance:

$$\left| \Pr[\mathsf{Ev} : \mathcal{A}^H] - \Pr[\mathsf{Ev} : \mathcal{A}^G] \right| \leq B(\Psi_0, \Psi_1) \leq 2\sqrt{\Pr[\mathcal{B}^{H,G} \to w^*]}$$

and likewise

$$\left| \sqrt{\Pr[\mathsf{Ev} : \mathcal{A}^H]} - \sqrt{\Pr[\mathsf{Ev} : \mathcal{A}^G]} \right| \leq B(\Psi_0, \Psi_1) \leq 2\sqrt{\Pr[\mathcal{B}^{H,G} \to w^*]}.$$

This completes the proof in the general case. $\qquad\qquad\qquad\qquad\qquad\qquad\square$

C   Proof of Theorem 1

Theorem 1. *Let* P *be an rPKE with messages in* $\mathcal{M}$ *and random coins in* $\mathcal{R}$. *Let* $G : \mathcal{M} \to \mathcal{R}$ *be a quantum-accessible random oracle. Let* $\mathcal{A}$ *be an* OW-CPA *adversary against* $P' := T(P, G)$. *Suppose that* $\mathcal{A}$ *queries* G *at most* q *times with depth at most* d.

Then we can construct an IND-CPA *adversary* $\mathcal{B}$ *against* P, *running in about the same time and resources as* $\mathcal{A}$, *such that*

$$\mathrm{Adv}_{P'}^{\mathsf{OW\text{-}CPA}}(\mathcal{A}) \leq (d + 2) \cdot \left(\mathrm{Adv}_{P}^{\mathsf{IND\text{-}CPA}}(\mathcal{B}) + \frac{8(q+1)}{|\mathcal{M}|} \right).$$

Proof. Let $\mathcal{A}_1$ be the same as $\mathcal{A}$, except that at the end after choosing an output m, it computes and discards $G(m)$. Therefore it makes at most $q + 1$ queries at depth at most $d + 1$. This is a formality so that returning the correct m will count as a Find (cf. Definition 1) later in the proof. Clearly the two algorithms $\mathcal{A}$ and $\mathcal{A}_1$ have the same OW-CPA-advantage against P′.

We actually show a slightly stronger result, constructing an IND-KPA adversary $\mathcal{B}$. The IND-KPA adversary $\mathcal{B}$ (cf. Definition 9) is given the tuple

$$(\text{pk}, m_0, m_1, c) \quad \text{where} \quad c = \text{Encr}(\text{pk}, m_b; r).$$

It wants to determine whether $b = 0$ or $b = 1$. The algorithm $\mathcal{B}$ creates a fresh random oracle G and runs

$$\mathcal{A}_1^{G \setminus \{m_0, m_1\}}(\text{pk}, c).$$

Suppose Find occurs, i.e., a query $x \in \{m_0, m_1\}$ was asked by $\mathcal{A}$ to its oracle G. Then $\mathcal{B}$ measures whether the query x was m_0 or m_1, and returns the corresponding b. If Find does not occur, or if Find occurs but both m_0 and m_1 were queried, then $\mathcal{B}$ guesses b at random.

Let G' be the oracle such that $G'(m_b) = r$ gives the encryption coins used to encrypt m_b, but $G'(m) = G(m)$ for all other messages m. G' is unknown to $\mathcal{B}$, but we can still analyze $\mathcal{A}$'s behavior when run with G' instead of G.

By construction, $\mathcal{A}_1^{G' \setminus \{m_0, m_1\}}$ cannot return m_b without causing Find. Hence,

$$\sqrt{\text{Adv}_{\text{P}'}^{\text{OW-CPA}}(\mathcal{A})} = \sqrt{\Pr[\mathcal{A}^{G'} \to m_b]}$$

$$= \left| \sqrt{\Pr\left[\mathcal{A}_1^{G'} \to m_b\right]} - \underbrace{\sqrt{\Pr\left[\mathcal{A}_1^{G' \setminus \{m_0, m_1\}} \to m_b \wedge \neg\text{Find}\right]}}_{= 0} \right|$$

$$\overset{\text{Lem. 3}}{\leq} \sqrt{(d+2) \cdot \Pr\left[\text{Find} : \mathcal{A}_1^{G' \setminus \{m_0, m_1\}}\right]}.$$

Squaring both sides,

$$\text{Adv}_{\text{P}'}^{\text{OW-CPA}}(\mathcal{A}) \leq (d+2) \cdot \Pr\left[\text{Find} : \mathcal{A}_1^{G' \setminus \{m_0, m_1\}}\right]$$

$$\overset{\text{Lem. 2}}{=} (d+2) \cdot \Pr\left[\text{Find} : \mathcal{A}_1^{G \setminus \{m_0, m_1\}}\right]$$

$$= (d+2) \cdot \Pr[\text{Find} : \mathcal{B}].$$

Now decompose Find as $\text{Find}_b \vee \text{Find}_{\neg b}$, where the former event means that Find occurs and m_b is measured, and latter means that Find occurs and $m_{\neg b}$ is measured. They can both occur if $\mathcal{A}$ makes multiple queries simultaneously, but $\text{Adv}_{\text{P}}^{\text{IND-KPA}}(\mathcal{B}) = |\Pr[\text{Find}_b] - \Pr[\text{Find}_{\neg b}]|$ regardless.

Moreover, since $\mathcal{B}$ measures m whenever Find occurs, we can view $G \setminus \{m_0, m_1\}$ as $G'' \setminus \{m_{\neg b}\} := (G \setminus \{m_b\}) \setminus \{m_{\neg b}\}$. Since $\mathcal{A}$ has no information about $m_{\neg b}$ except from puncturing, it holds for any m that

$$\Pr\left[m \in \{m_{\neg b}\} : \mathcal{A}^{G''}\right] = 1/|\mathcal{M}| =: \epsilon.$$

By (the second statement in) Lemma 4, we have

$$\Pr[\mathsf{Find}_{\neg b} : \mathcal{B}] \leq 4(q+1)\epsilon = \frac{4(q+1)}{|\mathcal{M}|}.$$

Hence,

$$\begin{aligned}
\mathrm{Adv}_{\mathsf{P}'}^{\mathsf{IND\text{-}KPA}}(\mathcal{B}) &= |\Pr\left[\mathsf{Find}_b : \mathcal{B}\right] - \Pr\left[\mathsf{Find}_{\neg b:\mathcal{B}}\right]| \\
&\geq \Pr\left[\mathsf{Find} : \mathcal{B}\right] - 2\,\Pr\left[\mathsf{Find}_{\neg b} : \mathcal{B}\right] \\
&\geq \Pr\left[\mathsf{Find} : \mathcal{B}\right] - 8(q+1)/|\mathcal{M}|.
\end{aligned}$$

Taking into account that $\mathrm{Adv}_{\mathsf{P}}^{\mathsf{IND\text{-}KPA}}(\mathcal{B}) \leq \mathrm{Adv}_{\mathsf{P}}^{\mathsf{IND\text{-}CPA}}(\mathcal{B})$ and combining these results gives

$$\mathrm{Adv}_{\mathsf{P}'}^{\mathsf{OW\text{-}CPA}}(\mathcal{A}) \leq (d+2) \cdot \left(\mathrm{Adv}_{\mathsf{P}}^{\mathsf{IND\text{-}CPA}}(\mathcal{B}) + \frac{8(q+1)}{|\mathcal{M}|}\right)$$

as claimed. □

IND vs. OW. Our $\mathcal{B}$ is a distinguishing adversary, not a one-way adversary. The reason is that $\mathcal{A}$ can check whether a given m is the challenge message, but if P is semantically secure then $\mathcal{B}$ cannot check this. Instead $\mathcal{B}$ would have to pick a random query to measure, which still works using Lemma 1, but with an additional factor of q tightness loss. That is, the one-way problem is potentially harder for a randomized encryption scheme than for a deterministic one. The authors discussed using a new "one-way with confirmation oracle" security game to more tightly capture the OW vs. IND tradeoff, but decided that it is simpler to just reduce to IND-CPA.

We also note that ordinarily distinguishing adversaries are much harder to amplify than one-way adversaries, but $\mathcal{B}$ is constructed to either output with relative certainty if Find, or to fail and guess at random. This means that its advantage will still be high in the Micciancio-Walter notion of cryptographic advantage [MW18]. It is likely that the $8(q+1)/|\mathcal{M}|$ could be reduced to a $4(q+1)/|\mathcal{M}|$ without this requirement.

D   Why Encryption Is Usually Injective for LWE

Here we outline why we expect $\mathrm{Encr}^G(\mathrm{pk}, \cdot)$ to be an injective function for the overwhelming majority of public keys pk in a derandomized PKE based on Learning with Errors (LWE). Consider a typical LWE PKE, where the public key has the form $(A, S = sA + e)$ where s and e are small of dimension n, and ciphertexts have the form $(As' + e', \lceil Xs' + e' + \mathrm{encode}(m) \rfloor)$. Encryption will fail to be injective for some G if there are $(s'_0, e'_0) = G(m_0)$ and $(s'_1, e'_1) = G(m_1)$ such that

$$As'_0 + e'_0 = As'_1 + e'_1 \quad \text{and} \quad \lceil Xs'_0 + e'_0 + \mathrm{encode}(m_0) \rfloor = \lceil Xs'_1 + e'_1 + \mathrm{encode}(m_1) \rfloor.$$

For correctness, the rounded component is always larger than the message space, and is generally larger than $|M|^2$. The unrounded component has size at least q^n which is larger still. The function $(s_0', e_0') \rightarrow As_0' + e_0'$ is almost a universal hash unless s_0' has large nullity, which is highly unlikely for any secure PKE. So the probability of collision with fewer than $|M|^2$ message pairs is not much bigger than q^{-n}, which is negligible.

E   Proof of Lemma 6

To prove Lemma 6, we first show a result about Bernoulli variables.

Lemma 7. *Let $\{e_i : 1 \le i \le n\}$ be a collection of n independent Bernoulli variables. Let $\delta := \max \Pr[e_i]$, and for each integer j let $p_j := \Pr[\sum_{i=1}^{n} e_i = j]$.
Then $p_1 \le \sqrt{3p_0p_2 + \delta^2} \le \sqrt{3p_2} + \delta$.*

Proof. Let $\epsilon_i := \Pr[e_i = 1]$, and without loss of generality let

$$\delta = \epsilon_1 \ge \epsilon_2 \ge \ldots \ge \epsilon_n$$

be given in descending order. Then

$$p_0 = \prod_{i=1}^{n}(1 - \epsilon_i), \quad p_1 = p_0 \cdot \left(\sum_{i=1}^{n} \frac{\epsilon_i}{1 - \epsilon_i}\right), \quad p_2 = p_0 \cdot \left(\sum_{i>j} \frac{\epsilon_i\epsilon_j}{(1 - \epsilon_i)(1 - \epsilon_j)}\right)$$

so that

$$
\begin{aligned}
p_1^2 - 3p_0p_2 &= p_0^2 \cdot \left(\sum_{i,j=1}^{n} \frac{\epsilon_i\epsilon_j}{(1 - \epsilon_i)(1 - \epsilon_j)} - 3\sum_{i>j} \frac{\epsilon_i\epsilon_j}{(1 - \epsilon_i)(1 - \epsilon_j)}\right) \\
&= p_0^2 \cdot \left(\sum_{i=1}^{n} \frac{\epsilon_i^2}{(1 - \epsilon_i)^2} - \sum_{i>j} \frac{\epsilon_i\epsilon_j}{(1 - \epsilon_i)(1 - \epsilon_j)}\right) \\
&\ge p_0^2 \cdot \left(\sum_{i=1}^{n} \frac{\epsilon_i^2}{(1 - \epsilon_i)^2} - \sum_{i=j+1} \frac{\epsilon_i\epsilon_j}{(1 - \epsilon_i)(1 - \epsilon_j)}\right) \\
&\ge p_0^2 \cdot \left(\sum_{i=1}^{n} \frac{\epsilon_i^2}{(1 - \epsilon_i)^2} - \sum_{i=2}^{n} \frac{\epsilon_i^2}{(1 - \epsilon_i)^2}\right) \\
&= p_0^2 \cdot \frac{\epsilon_1^2}{(1 - \epsilon_1)^2} \le \delta^2.
\end{aligned}
$$

Hence, $p_1^2 - 3p_0p_2 \le \delta^2$ and $p_1 \le \sqrt{3p_0p_2 + \delta^2}$ as claimed.   □

We are now ready to prove Lemma 6.

Lemma 6. *Let* $\mathsf{P} = (\mathrm{Keygen}, \mathrm{Encr}, \mathrm{Decr})$ *be a* δ-*correct rPKE with messages in* $\mathcal{M}$ *and randomness in* $\mathcal{R}$. *Let* $G : \mathcal{M} \to \mathcal{R}$ *be a random oracle, so that* $T(\mathsf{P}, G) := (\mathrm{Keygen}, \mathrm{Encr}_1, \mathrm{Decr})$ *is a derandomized version of* P. *Suppose that* $T(\mathsf{P}, G)$ *is* ϵ-*injective. Let* $\mathcal{A}$ *be a* FFC *adversary against* $T(\mathsf{P}, G)$ *which makes at most* q *queries at depth* d *to* G *and returns a list of at most* q_{dec} *ciphertexts. Then*

$$\mathrm{Adv}_{T(\mathsf{P},G)}^{\mathsf{FFC}}(\mathcal{A}) \le ((4d+1)\delta + \sqrt{3\epsilon}) \cdot (q + q_{\mathrm{dec}}) + \epsilon.$$

Proof. Essentially, the idea is at follows: the adversary gets an advantage of about $4dq\delta$ from querying G in search of failing ciphertexts, and at most $q_{\mathrm{dec}}(\delta + 3\sqrt{\epsilon})$ from guessing blindly. The latter term comes from considering ways that some blind guess could be a failing ciphertext: if it is the encryption of one message, then δ is large, and if it is possibly the encryption of more than one message (e.g., as a general "encryption failed" output), then ϵ is large. We will formalize this in what follows.

Generate a keypair $(\mathrm{pk}, \mathrm{sk}) \leftarrow \mathrm{Keygen}()$ and oracle $G \overset{\$}{\leftarrow} \mathcal{R}^{\mathcal{M}}$. Let

$$Y_{\mathrm{m}} := \{r : \mathrm{Decr}(\mathrm{sk}, \mathrm{Encr}(\mathrm{pk}, \mathrm{m}, r)) = \mathrm{m}\}$$

be the set of coins such that decryption of m will succeed. Let $G'(\mathrm{m}) := G(\mathrm{m})$ if $G(\mathrm{m}) \in Y_{\mathrm{m}}$, $G'(\mathrm{m}) \overset{\$}{\leftarrow} \mathcal{R}$ if $Y_{\mathrm{m}} = \emptyset$, and $G'(\mathrm{m}) \overset{\$}{\leftarrow} Y_{\mathrm{m}}$ otherwise. Thus G' is uniformly random in the space $\mathcal{G}$ of oracles where decryption succeeds if possible. Moreover, G' is independent of the behavior of messages and ciphertexts for $T(\mathsf{P}, G)$ which do not decrypt correctly.

Now, fix $(\mathrm{sk}, \mathrm{pk})$ and G' and let

$$\delta' := \max_{\mathrm{m} \in \mathcal{M}} \Pr[\mathrm{Decr}(\mathrm{sk}, \mathrm{Encr}(\mathrm{pk}, \mathrm{m})) \ne \mathrm{m}]$$

be the failure probability for this keypair. Let $\mathsf{DblFail}$ be the event that some ciphertext c is the encryption of two messages m_1 and m_2 such that $\mathrm{Decr}(\mathrm{sk}, c) \notin \{\mathrm{m}_1, \mathrm{m}_2\}$. We define $\epsilon' := \Pr[\mathsf{DblFail}]$. Both δ' and ϵ' are independent of G'. In addition, let Fail be the event that $\mathcal{A}$ wins the FFC game (see Definition 3), and $\mathsf{Ev} := \mathsf{Fail} \wedge \neg \mathsf{DblFail}$. By Lemma 1, it holds that

$$\left| \sqrt{\Pr[\mathsf{Ev} : \mathcal{A}^G(\mathrm{pk})]} - \sqrt{\Pr[\mathsf{Ev} : \mathcal{A}^{G'}(\mathrm{pk})]} \right| \le 2d\sqrt{P_{\mathrm{guess}}}.$$

Since, conditioned on G', $G(\mathrm{m}) \ne G'(\mathrm{m})$ at each m with probability at most δ' and there are q/d guesses (in expectation), it holds furthermore that

$$2d\sqrt{P_{\mathrm{guess}}} \le \sqrt{4d^2 P_{\mathrm{guess}}} \le \sqrt{4dq\delta'}.$$

Next we define for a ciphertext c,

$$p_1(c) := \Pr[\exists \text{ unique } \mathrm{m} \in \mathcal{M} : c = \mathrm{Encr}(\mathrm{pk}, \mathrm{m}, G(\mathrm{m})) \wedge \mathrm{Decr}(\mathrm{sk}, c) \ne \mathrm{m}].$$

(It is important to note that if m exists but is not unique, then $\mathsf{DblFail}$ occurs.) Furthermore, let $p_1 := \max_c (p_1(c))$. Since $p_1(c)$ and p_1 are independent of G', we have

$$\Pr[\mathsf{Ev} : \mathcal{A}^{G'}(\mathrm{pk})] \le q_{\mathrm{dec}} \cdot p_1.$$

By Lemma 7, $p_1 \leq \delta' + \sqrt{3\epsilon'}$. Plugging this in and applying the Cauchy-Schwarz corollary $\sqrt{ab} + \sqrt{cd} \leq \sqrt{(a+c)(b+d)}$ gives

$$\sqrt{\Pr[\mathsf{Ev} : \mathcal{A}^G(\mathrm{pk})]} \leq \sqrt{4dq\delta'} + \sqrt{q_{\mathrm{dec}} \cdot (\delta' + \sqrt{3\epsilon'})}$$

$$\leq \sqrt{((4d+1)\delta' + \sqrt{3\epsilon'}) \cdot (q + q_{\mathrm{dec}})}.$$

Finally, by definition of correctness and injectivity (see Definitions 5 and 6, respectively), it holds that $\delta = \mathrm{E}\left[\delta' : \mathrm{pk}, G\right]$ and $\epsilon \leq \mathrm{E}\left[\epsilon' : \mathrm{pk}, G\right]$. By Jensen's inequality, it holds furthermore that $\sqrt{\epsilon} \leq \mathrm{E}\left[\sqrt{\epsilon'} : \mathrm{pk}, G\right]$. Hence,

$$\mathrm{Adv}_{T(\mathsf{P},G)}^{\mathsf{FFC}}(\mathcal{A}) \leq \mathrm{E}\left[\Pr[\mathsf{Ev} : \mathcal{A}^G(\mathrm{pk})] : (\mathrm{pk}, \mathrm{sk}) \leftarrow \mathrm{Keygen}(); G' \xleftarrow{\$} \mathcal{G}\right] + \epsilon$$

$$\leq ((4d+1)\delta + \sqrt{3\epsilon}) \cdot (q + q_{\mathrm{dec}}) + \epsilon$$

as claimed.   □

F   Proof of Theorem 4

Theorem 4 (Implicit → explicit with key confirmation). *Let* P *be an* ϵ-*injective dPKE. Consider the KEM* $\mathsf{K}_1 := U_m^{\perp}(C(\mathsf{P}, H_t, \tau), H_s)$ *obtained from* P *applying the C-transform with random oracle* $H_t : \mathcal{M} \rightarrow \{0,1\}^{\tau}$ *and the* $U_m^{\perp}$-*transform with independent random oracle* $H_s : \mathcal{M} \rightarrow \{0,1\}^{\varsigma}$. *Let* $\mathsf{K}_2 := U_m^{\not\perp}(\mathsf{P}, \mathsf{F}, H)$ *be the KEM obtained from* P *applying the* $U_m^{\not\perp}$-*transform with random oracle* $H : \mathcal{M} \rightarrow \{0,1\}^{\varsigma + \tau}$.

If $\mathcal{A}$ *is an* IND-CCA-*adversary against* K_1 *which makes* q_{dec} *decapsulation queries, then it is also an* IND-CCA-*adversary against* K_2 *and there is a* PRF-*adversary* $\mathcal{B}$ *against* F *which uses about the same time and resources as* $\mathcal{A}$, *such that:*

$$\mathrm{Adv}_{\mathsf{K}_1}^{\mathsf{IND\text{-}CCA}}(\mathcal{A}) \leq 2 \cdot \mathrm{Adv}_{\mathsf{K}_2}^{\mathsf{IND\text{-}CCA}}(\mathcal{A}) + \frac{q_{\mathrm{dec}}}{2^{\tau-1}} + 2 \cdot \mathrm{Adv}_{\mathsf{F}}^{\mathsf{PRF}}(\mathcal{B}) + 2\epsilon.$$

Proof. The proof is by a series of games. Let w_i be the probability that $\mathcal{A}$ wins Game i. At some point we will have two IND-CCA games running against K_1 and K_2 with different values of the challenge bit b. Call these values b_1 and b_2, respectively.

Game 0 (IND-CCA). *This is the* IND-CCA *game against* K_1, *which is the KEM with explicit rejection and key confirmation.*

Game 1 (Modify decapsulation with random function). *In Game 1, the simulator instantiates a fresh random function* R, *and modifies the decapsulation oracle* D *to the oracle* D' *shown in Fig. 8.*

$D((c,t))$:	$D'((c,t))$:
1 if $(c,t) = (c^*,t^*)$: return $\bot$	1 if $c = c^*$: return $\bot$
2 $m' \leftarrow \mathrm{Decr}(\mathrm{sk},c)$	2 $m' \leftarrow \mathrm{Decr}(\mathrm{sk},c)$
3 if $m' = \bot$:	3 if $m' = \bot$: $(k,t') \leftarrow R(c)$
4 return $\bot$	4 else if $\mathrm{Encr}(\mathrm{pk},m') \neq c$: $(k,t') \leftarrow R(c)$
5 else if $(\mathrm{Encr}(\mathrm{pk},m'), H_t(m')) \neq (c,t)$:	5 else: $(k,t') \leftarrow (H_s(m'), H_t(m'))$
6 return $\bot$	6 if $t' \neq t$: return $\bot$
7 else: return $H_s(m')$	7 else: return k

Fig. 8. Decapsulation oracles for Game 0 and Game 1.

We analyze the difference between D and D' as follows.

- If $c = c^*$, then D' returns $\bot$. If $\mathrm{Encr}(\mathrm{pk},\cdot)$ is injective, then so does D.
- Otherwise, if $\mathrm{Encr}(\mathrm{pk},m') = c$, then both D and D' return $H_s(m')$ if $H_t(m') = t$, and $\bot$ otherwise.
- Otherwise, D returns $\bot$, and so does D' unless t matches t'. Since R is random and is only used for this purpose, this happens with probability at most $q_{\mathrm{dec}}/2^\tau$.

The difference in $\mathcal{A}$'s view is bound by the probability that D' acts different than D. So overall $|w_1 - w_0| \leq q_{\mathrm{dec}}/2^\tau + \epsilon$.

Game 2 (Use PRF instead of R). *In Game 2, the simulator replaces $R(c)$ by $\mathsf{F}(\mathrm{prfk},\cdot)$ with a random prf key* prfk.

The difference in probability of any adversary $\mathcal{A}$ between winning Game 1 and Game 2 is exactly the PRF-advantage of an adversary $\mathcal{B}$ that works exactly as in the analysis of Game 1 in the proof of Theorem 2. Hence it holds that

$$|w_2 - w_1| = \mathrm{Adv}_{\mathsf{F}}^{\mathsf{PRF}}(\mathcal{B})$$

Game 3 (Redirect to $U_m^{\not\perp}(\mathsf{P},\mathsf{F},H)$). *Game 3 is refactored so that it simulates the* IND-CCA *experiment for* $\mathsf{K}_2 = U_m^{\not\perp}(\mathsf{P},\mathsf{F},H)$ *(which uses implicit rejection and no key confirmation) for the case $b_2 = 0$ (correct key), as follows:*

- *Hash redirection. The oracles H_s resp. H_t used for C resp. $U^\perp$ are redirected to the first ς resp. last τ bits of the hash function H of $U_m^{\not\perp}(\mathsf{P},\mathsf{F},H)$.*
- *The simulator creates a challenge ciphertext c with shared secret k of length $\varsigma + \tau$. It parses this as (k_s, k_t), and gives $\mathcal{A}$ a challenge ciphertext (c, k_t). The challenge shared secret is k_s if $b_1 = 0$, or random if $b_1 = 1$.*
- *The decapsulation oracle D' from Game 2 is changed to use the $U_m^{\not\perp}$ decapsulation oracle internally, as shown in Fig. 9. It is called D''.*

Note that b_2 is fixed, but the adversary is still trying to determine the bit b_1 of the IND-CCA game against K_1.

All the above steps do not change $\mathcal{A}$'s view compared to Game 2, so $w_3 = w_2$.

$\underline{D''((c,t))}:$

1    $r \leftarrow \text{Decaps}_{K_2}(c)$
2   if $r = \bot$: return $\bot$
3   parse r as (k, t')
4   if $t' \neq t$: return $\bot$
5   else: return k

Fig. 9. Decapsulation oracle for Game 3.

Game 4 (Redirect to $U_m^{\not\perp}(\mathsf{P}, \mathsf{F}, H)$ with random keys). *Game 4 is the same as Game 3 except that it now simulates the $b_2 = 1$ (random key) case of the* IND-CCA *experiment against* K_2, *i.e., it always sets* $k \xleftarrow{\$} \{0,1\}^\varsigma$. *This means that for the challenge ciphertext, both* k_s *and* k_t *will be uniformly random.*

Distinguishing Game 3 from Game 4 is exactly the IND-CCA experiment for K_2. Hence,

$$|w_4 - w_3| = \text{Adv}_{K_2}^{\text{IND-CCA}}(\mathcal{A}).$$

In this game the shared secret k is always random, and thereby independent of b_1. Hence, the adversary has no information about b_1 and so $w_4 = \frac{1}{2}$.

Summing up the differences in winning probability from all the games we get

$$\left| w_0 - \frac{1}{2} \right| \leq \text{Adv}_{K_2}^{\text{IND-CCA}}(\mathcal{A}) + \frac{q_{\text{dec}}}{2^\tau} + \text{Adv}_{\mathsf{F}}^{\text{PRF}}(\mathcal{B})$$

and $\text{Adv}_{K_1}^{\text{IND-CCA}}(\mathcal{A})$ is at most twice this value. This completes the proof.   □

Attribute Based Encryption for Deterministic Finite Automata from DLIN

Shweta Agrawal[1(✉)], Monosij Maitra[1], and Shota Yamada[2]

[1] IIT Madras, Chennai, India
{shweta.a,monosij}@cse.iitm.ac.in
[2] AIST, Tokyo, Japan
yamada-shota@aist.go.jp

Abstract. Waters [Crypto, 2012] provided the first attribute based encryption scheme ABE for Deterministic Finite Automata (DFA) from a parametrized or "q-type" assumption over bilinear maps. Obtaining a construction from static assumptions has been elusive, despite much progress in the area of ABE.

In this work, we construct the first attribute based encryption scheme for DFA from static assumptions on pairings, namely, the DLIN assumption. Our scheme supports unbounded length inputs, unbounded length machines and unbounded key requests. In more detail, secret keys in our construction are associated with a DFA M of *unbounded* length, ciphertexts are associated with a tuple $(\mathbf{x}, \mu)$ where $\mathbf{x}$ is a public attribute of *unbounded* length and μ is a secret message bit, and decryption recovers μ if and only if $M(\mathbf{x}) = 1$.

Our techniques are at least as interesting as our final result. We present a simple compiler that combines constructions of unbounded ABE schemes for *monotone span programs* (MSP) in a black box way to construct ABE for DFA. In more detail, we find a way to embed DFA computation into monotone span programs, which lets us compose existing constructions (modified suitably) of unbounded key-policy ABE (kpABE) and unbounded ciphertext-policy ABE (cpABE) for MSP in a simple and modular way to obtain key-policy ABE for DFA. Our construction uses its building blocks in a *symmetric* way – by swapping the use of the underlying kpABE and cpABE, we also obtain a construction of ciphertext-policy ABE for DFA.

Our work extends techniques developed recently by Agrawal, Maitra and Yamada [Crypto 2019], which show how to construct ABE that support unbounded machines and unbounded inputs by combining ABE schemes that are bounded in one co-ordinate. At the heart of our work is the observation that unbounded, multi-use ABE for MSP already achieve most of what we need to build ABE for DFA.

1 Introduction

Attribute based encryption (ABE) [56] is a new paradigm of encryption that enables fine grained access control on encrypted data. In attribute based encryption, a ciphertext of a message m is labelled with a public attribute $\mathbf{x}$ and

© International Association for Cryptologic Research 2019
D. Hofheinz and A. Rosen (Eds.): TCC 2019, LNCS 11892, pp. 91–117, 2019.
https://doi.org/10.1007/978-3-030-36033-7_4

secret keys are labelled with a function f. Decryption succeeds to yield the hidden message m if and only if the attribute satisfies the function, namely $f(\mathbf{x}) = 1$. ABE schemes have a rich and beautiful history [3,8,16,17,19,21,37–39,41,43,50,56,57], with constructions for various classes of functions proven secure under diverse assumptions.

Typically, the function f encoded in the secret key is represented as a Boolean circuit, which necessitates issuing different keys to support different input lengths, even to compute the same functionality. In a breakthrough work, Waters [57] provided the first construction of ABE for regular languages: here, the secret key is associated with a deterministic finite automaton (DFA) and ciphertext is associated with attribute $\mathbf{x}$ of *arbitrary* length. The same secret key can directly decrypt ciphertexts that encode inputs of varying lengths, yielding the first ABE that supports a *uniform* model of computation. Since then, other constructions supporting the uniform model of computation were proposed, supporting even Turing machines [4,9,34], but all these relied on the powerful machinery of multilinear maps [31], indistinguishability obfuscation [15,32] or witness encryption [33], none of which are considered standard assumptions.

While the Waters construction relied on the hardness of assumptions over bilinear maps, which are well understood, the assumption is *parametrized* (also known as "q-type"), which means that the size of the assumption depends on the queries made by the adversary. Achieving a construction of ABE for DFA from standard static assumptions over bilinear maps has remained elusive. Very recently, Agrawal, Maitra and Yamada [5] provided an ABE for *nondeterministic* finite automata from the learning with errors assumption. However, their construction makes use of highly lattice specific machinery (such as reusable garbled circuits [35]) and it is unclear how to use these ideas to improve the state of affairs in the world of pairings.

1.1 Our Results

In this work, we construct the first attribute based encryption scheme for DFA from static assumptions on pairings, namely, the DLIN assumption. Our scheme supports unbounded length inputs as well as unbounded length machines. In more detail, secret keys in our construction are associated with a DFA M of unbounded length, ciphertexts are associated with a tuple $(\mathbf{x}, m)$ where $\mathbf{x}$ is a public attribute of unbounded length and m is a secret message bit, and decryption recovers m if and only if $M(\mathbf{x}) = 1$. Our construction also supports unbounded key requests by the adversary. Additionally, via a simple tweak to our construction, we also obtain the first ciphertext-policy ABE for DFA from the DLIN assumption.

We contrast our results with prior work in Table 1. For brevity, we only compare with constructions of ABE that support uniform models of computation (in particular, handle unbounded input lengths) and rely on standard assumptions. Other relevant work is discussed in Sect. 1.3.

Table 1. Comparison with prior work supporting unbounded input length. KP and CP indicate key-policy and ciphertext-policy respectively.

Construction	Model	KP or CP	Number of keys	Assumption
Waters [57]	DFA	KP	Unbounded	q-type assumption on bilinear maps
Attrapadung [12]	DFA	KP and CP	Unbounded	q-type assumption on bilinear maps
Agrawal-Singh [7]	DFA	KP	Single	LWE
Agrawal-Maitra-Yamada [5]	NFA	KP	Unbounded	LWE
Gong-Waters-Wee [36]	DFA	KP	Unbounded	kLIN
This	DFA	KP and CP	Unbounded	DLIN

1.2 Our Techniques

A natural starting point for constructing (key policy) ABE for DFA is (key policy) ABE for monotone span programs (MSP), which has been studied extensively in the literature. Recall that an MSP is specified by a pair $(\mathbf{L}, \rho)$ of a matrix and a labelling function where $\mathbf{L} \in \mathbb{Z}_p^{\ell \times m}$, $\rho : [\ell] \rightarrow \{0,1\}^*$ for some integer ℓ, m. Intuitively, the map ρ labels row i with attribute $\rho(i)$. Given a set of attributes I as input, the MSP accepts the input iff the sub-matrix of $\mathbf{L}$ restricted to attributes selected by I contains a special target vector in its row span (please see Sect. 2.1 for the precise definition).

Step 1: Leveraging ABE for MSP. Our first observation is that DFA computation is simple enough to be encoded into an MSP. In more detail, given a DFA machine M and an input string $\mathbf{x}$, it is possible to map the DFA M into an MSP $(\mathbf{L}_M, \rho_M)$ and the input $\mathbf{x}$ into a set of attributes $S_{\mathbf{x}}$ such that the MSP $(\mathbf{L}_M, \rho_M)$ accepts attributes $S_{\mathbf{x}}$ iff $M(\mathbf{x}) = 1$. We exhibit such a map in Sect. 4.1 and prove the following theorem:

Theorem 1. *(Informal) Let $(\mathbf{L}_M, \rho_M)$ be the MSP and $S_{\mathbf{x}}$ be the set of attributes obtained by applying the map specified in Sect. 4.1 to M and $\mathbf{x}$ respectively. Then, the MSP $(\mathbf{L}_M, \rho_M)$ accepts attributes $S_{\mathbf{x}}$ iff $M(\mathbf{x}) = 1$.*

This provides a starting point for using ABE for MSP, which can be constructed from static assumptions, as a building block towards constructing ABE for DFA.

Step 2: Handling Unbounded Length. While this seems promising as a first step, the careful reader may have noticed that the above idea fails to address the primary challenge of supporting DFA, namely, that of handling inputs of unbounded length. DFA is a uniform model of computation, which means that the same machine must process inputs of arbitrary length. On the other hand, an MSP can only process inputs of bounded length – in particular, the length of inputs that an MSP can read is clearly bounded above by the number of rows in $\mathbf{L}$.

This appears to make ABE for MSP almost useless for our purposes, since there is no way to guarantee that $|\mathbf{x}|$ is less than the number of rows in $\mathbf{L}$ (denoted by $|\mathbf{x}| \leq |M|$ in the sequel[1]). However, notice that since both the inputs and the machines have unbounded length, it still holds in some cases that $|\mathbf{x}| \leq |M|$, and if we can handle this, it still constitutes progress. More hurdles present themselves – for instance, the syntax of ABE for DFA does not allow the setup algorithm to know the lengths $|\mathbf{x}|$, $|M|$, the key generation algorithm cannot know $|\mathbf{x}|$ and the encrypt algorithm cannot know $|M|$. But this challenge can be overcome by making use of the so called *unbounded* ABE schemes, as described next.

Unbounded ABE schemes (for MSP) [23,54] are those in which the setup algorithm places no restriction on the length of the attributes or the size of the policies that are embedded in the ciphertexts and keys. Moreover, the key generation and encrypt algorithms do not require knowledge of input length or policy size respectively. While significantly more challenging to build than their bounded counterparts, a small number of existing constructions [23,54] achieve this property while relying on standard assumptions.

We show in Sect. 3.2 that unbounded key policy ABE schemes for MSP can indeed be used to construct ABE for DFA so long as $|\mathbf{x}| \leq |M|$. More formally, we define relation $R^{\mathsf{KP}}(S, (\mathbf{L}, \rho)) = 1$ iff the span program $(\mathbf{L}, \rho)$ accepts the attribute set S and $R^{\mathsf{DFA}\leq}(\mathbf{x}, M) = M(\mathbf{x}) \wedge \left(|\mathbf{x}| \overset{?}{\leq} |M|\right)$. Then, we have that:

Theorem 2. *(Informal) Let* kpABE *be a secure unbounded ABE for the relation* R^{KP}. *Then, the construction* dfaABE$^{\leq}$ *provided in Sect. 3.2 is a secure ABE for the relation* $R^{\mathsf{DFA}\leq}$.

Step 3: The Trick of Agrawal, Maitra and Yamada. To construct a full fledged ABE for DFA, our next tool is a recent trick by Agrawal, Maitra and Yamada [5]. In [5], the authors show how to construct an ABE for nondeterministic finite automata (NFA) that supports unbounded inputs and unbounded machines, by running in parallel two restricted ABE for NFA schemes: one that supports unbounded inputs but bounded machines and one that supports bounded inputs but unbounded machines.

Our goal is to construct an ABE scheme dfaABE for the relation $R^{\mathsf{DFA}}(\mathbf{x}, M) = M(\mathbf{x})$. By using the trick of [5], we can construct our dfaABE from two special ABE schemes as follows:

1. An ABE dfaABE$^{\leq}$ for the relation $R^{\mathsf{DFA}\leq}(\mathbf{x}, M) = M(\mathbf{x}) \wedge \left(|\mathbf{x}| \overset{?}{\leq} |M|\right)$.
2. An ABE dfaABE$^{>}$ for the relation $R^{\mathsf{DFA}>}(\mathbf{x}, M) = M(\mathbf{x}) \wedge \left(|\mathbf{x}| \overset{?}{>} |M|\right)$.

It is easy to see that given constructions for the special ABE schemes dfaABE$^{\leq}$ and dfaABE$^{>}$, we may construct dfaABE simply by running them in parallel. In more detail, the setup algorithm of dfaABE simply runs the setup

---

[1] While imprecise, we use this notation here for intuition. Formally, it will turn out to be sufficient to compare $|\mathbf{x}|$ with $|Q|$, where $|Q|$ is the number of states in M.

algorithms of the underlying special ABEs and outputs the public and master secret keys by combining their outputs, the encrypt algorithm encrypts its input $(\mathbf{x}, \mu)$ under both special ABEs, the key generation algorithm produces a key under both special ABEs and the decryption algorithm invokes the decryption of one or the other depending on whether $|\mathbf{x}| \overset{?}{\leq} |M|$. This intuition is formalized in Sect. 3.1, where we prove the following theorem:

Theorem 3. *(Informal) Assume that* $\mathsf{dfaABE}^{\leq}$ *and* $\mathsf{dfaABE}^{>}$ *are secure ABE schemes for relations* $R^{\mathsf{DFA}\leq}$ *and* $R^{\mathsf{DFA}>}$ *respectively. Then, the scheme* dfaABE *constructed in Sect. 3.1 is a secure ABE for relation* R^{DFA}.

Step 4: Plugging the Gap with Ciphertext Policy ABE. We already constructed an ABE for the case of $|\mathbf{x}| \leq |M|$. The case of $|\mathbf{x}| > |M|$ is more challenging, since to use ABE for MSP, it is necessary that the MSP be large enough to read the input as we have discussed above. To handle this, we simply switch the role of key generator and encryptor! In more detail, if the encryptor could instead embed $\mathbf{x}$ into an MSP and the key generator could embed M into a set of attributes, then the dilemma of compatible sizes could be resolved and we would be back in business. We show that this can be done; we provide a maps in Sect. 4.2 that achieves this embedding. More formally, we prove that:

Theorem 4. *Let* $(\mathbf{L}_{\mathbf{x}}, \rho_{\mathbf{x}})$ *be the MSP and* S_M *be the set of attributes obtained by applying the map specified in Sect. 4.2 to* $\mathbf{x}$ *and* M *respectively. Then, the MSP* $(\mathbf{L}_{\mathbf{x}}, \rho_{\mathbf{x}})$ *accepts attributes* S_M *iff* $M(\mathbf{x}) = 1$.

In order to support encryption of an MSP $(\mathbf{L}_{\mathbf{x}}, \rho_{\mathbf{x}})$, we now need an unbounded *ciphertext policy* ABE for MSP. In more detail, we define $R^{\mathsf{CP}}((\mathbf{L}, \rho), S) = 1$ iff the span program $(\mathbf{L}, \rho)$ accepts the attribute set S. Recall that $R^{\mathsf{DFA}>}(\mathbf{x}, M) = M(\mathbf{x}) \wedge (|\mathbf{x}| \overset{?}{>} |M|)$. Then, we show in Sect. 3.3 that:

Theorem 5. *(Informal) Let* cpABE *be a secure unbounded ABE scheme for the relation* R^{CP}. *Then the construction* $\mathsf{dfaABE}^{>}$ *provided in Sect. 3.3 is a secure ABE for the relation* $R^{\mathsf{DFA}>}$.

To summarize, our approach is based on the observation that we must only construct an MSP of length $\max(|\mathbf{x}|, |M|)$, where $|\mathbf{x}|$ is known to the encryptor and $|M|$ is known to the key generator (and neither know the other). When the input vector has size $|\mathbf{x}| \leq |M|$, we embed the DFA into a monotone span program which has number of rows proportional to $|M|$, and the input into a set of attributes – this ensures that the MSP is large enough to support an input of length $|\mathbf{x}|$. We may then leverage an unbounded kpABE scheme to handle this case. On the other hand, when $|\mathbf{x}| > |M|$, we instead embed the input vector into a monotone span program which has number of rows proportional to $|\mathbf{x}|$, and the machine into a set of attributes – this again ensures that the MSP is large enough to support an input of size $|M|$. We may then leverage an unbounded cpABE scheme to handle this case. Of course, neither party knows which case it must support, so it simply provides information for both and leaves it to the decryptor to make the choice!

Step 5: Instantiating the kpABE *and* cpABE. Finally, we must ensure that we can instantiate unbounded ABE schemes kpABE and cpABE for the relations R^{KP} and R^{CP} that we require. While prior work provides constructions of unbounded key policy and ciphertext policy ABE schemes for MSP, these unfortunately cannot be plugged into our compiler out of the box. This is because our construction requires the ABE schemes to support "multi-use" of attributes, i.e. when the map ρ in the MSP is not restricted to be injective. Moreover, the ABE schemes are required to be unbounded, as already discussed above. Finally, we want the schemes to be proven secure from static assumptions such as DLIN, not from q-type assumptions. Schemes achieving all these properties do not exist in the literature to the best of our knowledge.[2] Hence, we must refashion existing schemes to satisfy this. In the full version of our paper [6], we provide constructions for multi-use unbounded key policy and ciphertext policy ABE schemes by modifying the constructions in [23]. Let R^{MUKP} and R^{MUCP} be the same relations as R^{KP} and R^{CP} defined above, but with the requirement that the underlying MSPs in both relations support multi-use of attributes. Then, we obtain the following theorem:

Theorem 6. *(Informal) The constructions* kpABE *provided in [6] (Section 5.2) and* cpABE *provided in [6] (Section 5.4) are unbounded ABE schemes for the relations R^{MUKP} and R^{MUCP} respectively. Security of* kpABE *relies on the* MDDH *assumption and security of* cpABE *relies on the* DLIN *assumption.*

For both KP and CP-ABE schemes, we simply modify the schemes in [23] so that we allow multi-use of the same attribute in an MSP. However, this simple modification ruins the original security proof given by [23] in both cases. The reason is that the core statistical argument in the security proof does not work any more in the multi-use setting. Intuitively, the problem is that the terms used as "one-time pads" in the single-use setting are used multiple times in the multi-use setting. In both KP and CP cases, we switch to weaker security notions than adaptive security and give security proofs by taking advantage of weaker setting.

For KP-ABE scheme, we prove semi-adaptive security. To prove the security, we first use the handy bilinear entropy expansion lemma [23] to create an instance of a multi-use variant of the KP-ABE scheme by [50] (hereafter denoted by LOSTW) in the semi-functional space. To give a proof, we decompose the LOSTW secret key into smaller pieces and gradually add semi-functional randomness to them through a hybrid argument in a way that their distribution depends on the challenge attribute, in a similar manner to [1]. Since this step requires the knowledge of the challenge attribute, we can only prove semi-adaptive security of the scheme. Intuitively, because of this decomposition, we use the "one-time pad" only single time in one hybrid game and can avoid getting into the aforementioned problem of using one-time pads multiple times. Finally, we can use the core statistical step similarly to the case of single-use setting.

---

[2] Only exception is the very recent construction by Kowalczyk and Wee [46]. However, their scheme can only deal with NC_1 circuit instead of general MSP and thus our embedding of DFA into MSP cannot be used.

For CP-ABE scheme, we prove the security notion that we call selective* security, where the adversary is forced to choose its key queries and the challenge attribute after seeing the master public key. The first step of the proof is similar to the KP-ABE case. Namely, we first use the bilinear entropy expansion lemma [23] to create an instance of the LOSTW CP-ABE scheme in the semi-functional space. However, in the next step, we cannot use the above decomposition idea due to technical reasons, which in turn prohibits us from using the statistical argument in the core step. We overcome this by using computational argument instead, which uses the DLIN assumption instead. The idea of using computational argument here was taken from some of prior works [12,13,51].

Putting together these pieces yields our final result – a key-policy ABE for DFA that supports unbounded inputs, unbounded machines and unbounded key requests.

Ciphertext Policy ABE for DFA. In the above description, note that our construction dfaABE uses the underlying kpABE and cpABE in a symmetric way. Thus, by swapping the use of kpABE and cpABE in our construction, we can equivalently construct ciphertext policy ABE for DFA.

In more detail, we exchange the maps used by KeyGen and Enc in the constructions of dfaABE$^{\le}$ and dfaABE$^{>}$ in Sects. 3.2 and 3.3. Please see Sect. 5 for more details. Thus, we obtain

Theorem 7. *There exists a secure key-policy and ciphertext-policy ABE for* R^{DFA} *from the* DLIN *assumption.*

1.3 Related Work

In this section, we discuss the related work in the area, categorized by hardness assumptions. We begin with constructions based on bilinear maps. The first construction of ABE for DFA was given by Waters [57] as discussed above. This scheme achieved selective security, which was improved to adaptive by Attrapadung [12]. For span programs, there have been many constructions [2,12–14,22–25,45,47–50,53–55,58] that achieve various tradeoffs between security (selective versus adaptive), assumptions (static versus parametrized), underlying mathematical structure (prime versus composite order groups), policy embedding (key versus ciphertext policy) and efficiency. In this work, we are particularly concerned with unbounded ABE schemes, in particular those by [23,54].

From the Learning With Errors assumption (LWE), Boyen and Li [20] provided a construction of ABE for DFA, but this was restricted to DFAs with *bounded* length inputs, rendering moot the primary advantage of a DFA over circuits. Recently, Ananth and Fan [8] provided an ABE for random access machines from LWE, but this construction is also restricted to inputs of bounded length. Agrawal and Singh [7] constructed a primitive closely related to ABE for DFA, namely *reusable garbled DFA* from LWE, but their construction is only secure in the single key setting, namely, where the adversary is limited to requesting a single function key. In contrast, we support unbounded key requests in this work.

From strong assumptions such as the existence of multilinear maps [31], witness encryption [34] or indistinguishability obfuscation [15,32], attribute based encryption (or its more powerful generalization – *functional encryption*) has been constructed even for Turing machines [4,10,44], but these are not considered standard assumptions; indeed many candidate constructions have been broken [11,26–30,42,52].

Also relevant to our work are the constructions of [21,40], which provide attribute based encryption for the so called "bundling functionalities". Here, the size of the public parameters does not depend on the length of the input (say ℓ) chosen by the encryptor. However, the key generator must generate a key for a circuit with a fixed input length (say ℓ'), and decryption only succeeds if $\ell = \ell'$. Thus, bundling functionalities do not capture the essential challenge of supporting dynamic data sizes as discussed in [40].

1.4   Concurrent Work

We note that a concurrent work by Gong et al. [36] constructs KP-ABE scheme for DFA relying on the k-LIN assumption. Although there is a qualitative overlap in our final results as shown in Table 1, the approaches and techniques in their work are quite different from ours. They construct KP-ABE from scratch imitating the transition function of a DFA using bilinear maps directly. This, in turn, yields a scheme with better concrete efficiency and security than ours. In particular, in the KP-ABE setting, our ciphertexts and keys scale as $O(|\mathbf{x}|^3)$ and $O(|Q|^2)$ respectively while the ciphertexts and keys in [36] scale linearly as $O(|\mathbf{x}|)$ and $O(|Q|)$ respectively. Also, our construction achieves selective* security based on DLIN assumption, while their construction achieves selective security and relies on the slightly weaker k-LIN assumption. On the other hand, our scheme is a generic compiler, and has conceptual advantages: our construction is modular and simpler and yields CP-ABE essentially for free. Further, it reduces the question of adaptive security for DFA for both KP-ABE and CP-ABE to that of adaptive security for unbounded KP-ABE and CP-ABE for MSP from static assumptions.

Organization of the Paper. In Sect. 2, we provide the definitions and preliminaries we require. In Sect. 3, we provide our ABE for DFA supporting unbounded input and unbounded machines from kpABE and cpABE for monotone span programs. In Sect. 4, we describe how to encode DFA computation into a monotone span program (MSP): Sect. 4.1 shows the encoding procedure for any DFA machine to a MSP (and DFA input to attribute set) while Sect. 4.2 shows the encoding procedure for any input string to a MSP (and DFA machine to attribute set). In the full version of our paper [6], we instantiate our ingredient kpABE and cpABE using techniques from [23]. In Sect. 5 we put together all ingredients to instantiate our ABE for DFA.

2   Preliminaries

In this section, we define some notation and preliminaries that we require.

Notation. We use bold letters to denote vectors and the notation $[a, b]$ to denote the set of integers $\{k \in \mathbb{N} \mid a \leq k \leq b\}$. We use $[n]$ to denote the set $[1, n]$. Concatenation is denoted by the symbol $\|$.

We say a function $f(n)$ is *negligible* if it is $O(n^{-c})$ for all $c > 0$, and we use $\text{negl}(n)$ to denote a negligible function of n. We say $f(n)$ is *polynomial* if it is $O(n^c)$ for some constant $c > 0$, and we use $\text{poly}(n)$ to denote a polynomial function of n. We use the abbreviation PPT for probabilistic polynomial-time. We say an event occurs with *overwhelming probability* if its probability is $1 - \text{negl}(n)$.

2.1 Definitions: Restricted Monotone Span Programs (MSP)

A monotone span program over $\mathbb{Z}_p$ is specified by a pair $(\mathbf{L}, \rho)$ of a matrix and a labelling function where

$$\mathbf{L} \in \mathbb{Z}_p^{\ell \times m} \qquad\qquad \rho : [\ell] \to \mathbb{Z}$$

for some integer ℓ, m. Intuitively, the map ρ labels row i with attribute $\rho(i)$.

A span program takes as input a set of integers and accepts or rejects an input by the following criterion. Let $S = \{u_1, \ldots, u_t\} \subseteq \mathbb{Z}$ be a set of integers. Intuitively, each u_i represents some attribute. For the set S, we define another set $I \subseteq [\ell]$ as $I = \{i \in [\ell] : \rho(i) \in S\}$ and $\mathbf{L}_I$ as the submatrix of $\mathbf{L}$ restricted to set of rows I, i.e. obtained by removing row j of $\mathbf{L}$ for any $j \notin I$. We say that

$$(\mathbf{L}, \rho) \text{ accepts } S \text{ iff } (1, 0, \ldots, 0) \text{ is in the row span of } \mathbf{L}_I.$$

We can write this also as $\mathbf{e}_1 \in \text{span}(\mathbf{L}_I^\top)$.

2.2 Deterministic Finite Automata

A Deterministic Finite Automaton (DFA) M is represented by the tuple $(Q, \Sigma, T, q_{\text{st}}, F)$ where Q is a finite set of states, Σ is a finite alphabet, $T : \Sigma \times Q \to Q$ is the transition function (stored as a table), q_{st} is the start state, $F \subseteq Q$ is the set of accepting states. We say that M accepts $\mathbf{x} = (x_1, \ldots, x_k) \in \Sigma^k$ if there exists a sequence of states $q_1, \ldots, q_{k+1}$ such that $q_1 = q$, $q_{i+1} \in T(x_i, q_i)$ for $i \in [k]$ and $q_{k+1} \in F$. We assume w.l.o.g. that the states are numbered as 1 to $|Q|$, i.e., $Q = \{1, 2, \ldots, |Q|\}$ with $q_{\text{st}} = 1$ along with $\Sigma = \{0, 1\}$ and $F = \{|Q|\}$. Note that any DFA with many accepting states can be converted to a DFA with a single accepting state[3], and states may be renumbered so that the last state is the accepting one.

---

[3] In more detail, we may map any input $\mathbf{x} \in \{0, 1\}^*$ to $\mathbf{x}\|\star$, where $\star$ is a special symbol, and modify M so that we change the accepting state to be $\{|Q| + 1\}$ and add edges from the previous accepting state to $|Q| + 1$, where edges are labelled with $\star$.

2.3 Definition: Attribute-Based Encryption

Syntax. Let $R : A \times B \to \{0,1\}$ be a relation where A and B denote "ciphertext attribute" and "key attribute" spaces. An attribute based encryption scheme for R is defined by the following PPT algorithms:

Setup(1^λ) $\to$ (mpk, msk): The setup algorithm takes as input the unary representation of the security parameter λ and outputs a master public key mpk and a master secret key msk.

Encrypt(mpk, μ, X) $\to$ ct: The encryption algorithm takes as input a master public key mpk, the message bit μ, and a ciphertext attribute $X \in A$. It outputs a ciphertext ct.

KeyGen(msk, mpk, Y) $\to$ sk$_Y$: The key generation algorithm takes as input the master secret key msk, the master public key mpk, and a key attribute $Y \in B$. It outputs a private key sk$_Y$.

Decrypt(mpk, ct, X, sk$_Y$, Y) $\to \mu$ or $\bot$: We assume that the decryption algorithm is deterministic. The decryption algorithm takes as input the master public key mpk, a ciphertext ct, ciphertext attribute $X \in A$, a private key sk$_Y$, and private key attribute Y. It outputs the message μ or $\bot$ which represents that the ciphertext is not in a valid form.

We require the standard correctness of decryption: for all λ, (mpk, msk) $\leftarrow$ Setup(1^λ), $X \in A, Y \in B$ such that $R(X,Y) = 1$, and sk$_Y$ $\leftarrow$ KeyGen(msk, mpk, Y), we have Decrypt(mpk, Encrypt(mpk, μ, X), X, sk$_Y$, Y) $= \mu$.

Security. We now define the security for an ABE scheme Π by the following game between a challenger and an attacker $\mathcal{A}$.

– At first, the challenger runs the setup algorithm and gives mpk to $\mathcal{A}$.
– Then $\mathcal{A}$ may adaptively make key-extraction queries. We denote this phase PHASE1. In this phase, if $\mathcal{A}$ submits $Y \in B$ to the challenger, the challenger returns sk$_Y$ $\leftarrow$ KeyGen(msk, mpk, Y).
– At some point, $\mathcal{A}$ outputs two equal length messages μ_0 and μ_1 and challenge ciphertext attribute $X^\star \in A$. $X^\star$ cannot satisfy $R(X^\star, Y) = 1$ for any attribute Y such that $\mathcal{A}$ already queried private key for Y.
– Then the challenger flips a random coin $\beta \in \{0,1\}$, runs Encrypt(mpk, $\mu_\beta, X^\star$) $\to$ ct* and gives challenge ciphertext ct* to $\mathcal{A}$.
– In PHASE2, $\mathcal{A}$ may adaptively make queries as in PHASE1 with following added restriction: $\mathcal{A}$ cannot make a key-extraction query for Y such that $R(X^\star, Y) = 1$.
– At last, $\mathcal{A}$ outputs a guess β' for β.

We say that $\mathcal{A}$ succeeds if $\beta' = \beta$ and denote the probability of this event by $\Pr^{\mathsf{ABE}}_{\mathcal{A}, \Pi}$. The advantage of an attacker $\mathcal{A}$ is defined as $\mathsf{Adv}^{\mathsf{ABE}}_{\mathcal{A}, \Pi} = |\Pr^{\mathsf{ABE}}_{\mathcal{A}, \Pi} - \frac{1}{2}|$. We say that Π is adaptively secure if $\mathsf{Adv}^{\mathsf{ABE}}_{\mathcal{A}, \Pi}$ is negligible for all probabilistic polynomial time (PPT) adversary $\mathcal{A}$.

Weaker Security Notions. A weaker notion called selective security can be defined as in the above game with the exception that the adversary $\mathcal{A}$ has to choose the challenge ciphertext attribute $X^\star$ before the setup phase but private key queries $Y_1, \ldots, Y_k$ and choice of (μ_0, μ_1) can still be adaptive. The stronger notion of semi-adaptive security lets the adversary output the challenge ciphertext attribute $X^\star$ after seeing the public key but before making any key requests. The still weaker notion of very selective security requires the adversary to output the challenge ciphertext attribute and private key queries at the very start of the game. An intermediate notion to semi-adaptive and very selective, which we term selective*, allows the adversary to receive the public parameters in the first step, but it must specify the challenge ciphertext attribute and private key queries after this step.

ABE for DFA. We then define ABE for DFA by specifying the relation. We define $A^{\mathsf{DFA}} = \{0,1\}^*$ and B^{DFA} as the set of all DFA, also represented as strings over $\{0,1\}^*$. Furthermore, we define the relation $R^{\mathsf{DFA}} = \{A^{\mathsf{DFA}} \times B^{\mathsf{DFA}} \to \{0,1\}\}$ as $R^{\mathsf{DFA}}(\mathbf{x}, M) = M(\mathbf{x})$.

An ABE scheme for the relation R^{DFA} is said to be ABE for DFA. We further define $R^{\mathsf{DFA}\leq} = \{A^{\mathsf{DFA}} \times B^{\mathsf{DFA}} \to \{0,1\}\}$ as

$$R^{\mathsf{DFA}\leq}(\mathbf{x}, M) = M(\mathbf{x}) \wedge \left(|\mathbf{x}| \overset{?}{\leq} |Q| \right),$$

where $|Q|$ is the number of states in M. We also define $R^{\mathsf{DFA}>}$ analogously.

Unbounded ABE for MSP. Here, we define unbounded ABE for MSP. There are distinctions between "single-use" and "multi-use" as well as "key-policy" and "ciphertext-policy". We first define multi-use key-policy unbounded ABE by specifying the relation R^{MUKP}. To do so, we set $A^{\mathsf{MUKP}} := 2^{\mathbb{Z}}$ (i.e., the set of all subsets of $\mathbb{Z}$) and B^{MUKP} as the set of monotone span programs on $\mathbb{Z}_p$ for some prime p, and $R^{\mathsf{MUKP}}(S, (\mathbf{L}, \rho)) = 1$ iff the span program $(\mathbf{L}, \rho)$ accepts the set $S \in A^{\mathsf{MUKP}}$. An ABE for R^{MUKP} is said to be "multi-use key-policy unbounded ABE".

We also define single-use key-policy unbounded ABE by specifying the relation R^{SUKP}. We set $A^{\mathsf{SUKP}} := 2^{\mathbb{Z}}$ and B^{SUKP} as the set of monotone span programs $(\mathbf{L}, \rho)$ such that ρ is injective. We define $R^{\mathsf{SUKP}}(S, (\mathbf{L}, \rho)) = 1$ iff the span program $(\mathbf{L}, \rho)$ accepts the set S. Finally, we can define the ciphertext variant of the above ABE by specifying R^{SUCP} and R^{MUCP}, where we set $A^{\mathsf{xxCP}} = B^{\mathsf{xxKP}}$ and $B^{\mathsf{xxCP}} = A^{\mathsf{xxKP}}$ for $\mathsf{xx} \in \{\mathsf{SU}, \mathsf{MU}\}$ and define the relation analogously.

Unbounded ABE for MSP with Polynomial-Valued Attributes. We can consider a restricted variant of unbounded ABE for MSP where the value of attributes being used is polynomially bounded. Here, we focus on the case of multi-use and key-policy case. Other cases will be defined similarly. Here, we define $A^{\mathsf{MUKP}'}$ and $B^{\mathsf{MUKP}'}$ as

$$A^{\mathsf{MUKP}'} = \left\{ (S, 1^{s_{\max}}) : S \subseteq \mathbb{Z}, s_{\max} = \max_{s \in S} |s| \right\} \qquad \text{and}$$

$$B^{\mathsf{MUKP'}} = \left\{ ((\mathbf{L}, \rho), 1^{\rho_{\max}}) : (\mathbf{L}, \rho) \text{ is a span program over } \mathbb{Z}_p, \ \rho_{\max} = \max_{i \in [\ell]} |\rho(i)| \right\}$$

We define $R^{\mathsf{MUKP'}}(S, (\mathbf{L}, \rho)) := R^{\mathsf{MUKP}}(S, (\mathbf{L}, \rho))$. Here, the reason why we append $1^{s_{\max}}$ to S is somewhat technical. This is to enforce the adversary in the security definition who declares $S \in A^{\mathsf{MUKP'}}$ as its target to choose attributes with polynomially bounded values. Because of the similar reason, we append $1^{\rho_{\max}}$ to $(\mathbf{L}, \rho)$.

For ease of readability in the remainder of the paper, we will overload notation and denote $A^{\mathsf{MUKP'}}$ and $B^{\mathsf{MUKP'}}$ as A^{MUKP} and B^{MUKP} respectively. However, all our constructions will satisfy the constraint of attribute values being polynomially bounded.

2.4 Embedding Lemma for ABE

Here, we introduce a useful lemma that describes a sufficient criterion for implication from an ABE for a given predicate to an ABE for another predicate. The lemma is introduced in [18] and later formally proven in [14]. The presentation here follows that of [14] with some simplifications. The lemma is applicable to any relation family. We consider two relation families:

$$R^{\mathsf{F}} : A \times B \to \{0, 1\}, \qquad\qquad R^{\mathsf{F'}} : A' \times B' \to \{0, 1\}.$$

Suppose that there exists two efficient mappings $f_{\mathsf{e}} : A' \to A$ and $f_{\mathsf{k}} : B' \to B$ which map parameters, ciphertext attributes, and key attributes, respectively, such that for all $X' \in A', Y' \in B'$,

$$R^{\mathsf{F'}}(X', Y') = 1 \Leftrightarrow R^{\mathsf{F}}(f_{\mathsf{e}}(X'), f_{\mathsf{k}}(Y')) = 1. \tag{2.1}$$

We can then construct an ABE scheme $\Pi' = \{\mathsf{Setup'}, \mathsf{Encrypt'}, \mathsf{KeyGen'}, \mathsf{Decrypt'}\}$ for predicate $R^{\mathsf{F'}}$ from an ABE scheme $\Pi = \{\mathsf{Setup}, \mathsf{Encrypt}, \mathsf{KeyGen}, \mathsf{Decrypt}\}$ for predicate R^{F} as follows. Let $\mathsf{Setup'} = \mathsf{Setup}$ and

$$\mathsf{Encrypt'}(\mathsf{mpk}, \mu, X') = \mathsf{Encrypt}(\mathsf{mpk}, \mu, f_{\mathsf{e}}(X')),$$
$$\mathsf{KeyGen'}(\mathsf{msk}, \mathsf{mpk}, Y') = \mathsf{KeyGen}(\mathsf{msk}, \mathsf{mpk}, f_{\mathsf{k}}(Y')),$$

and $\mathsf{Decrypt'}(\mathsf{mpk}, \mathsf{ct}, X', \mathsf{sk}_{Y'}, Y') = \mathsf{Decrypt}(\mathsf{mpk}, \mathsf{ct}, f_{\mathsf{e}}(X'), \mathsf{sk}_{Y'}, f_{\mathsf{k}}(Y'))$.

Lemma 1 (Embedding lemma [14,18]). *If Π is correct and secure, then so is Π'. This holds for very selective, selective, selective* and adaptive security.*

Intuitively, the forward and backward direction of Relation (2.1) ensure that the correctness and the security are preserving, respectively.

3   Attribute-Based Encryption for DFA

We construct an ABE scheme for DFA denoted by $\mathsf{dfaABE} = (\mathsf{dfaABE.Setup}, \mathsf{dfaABE.KeyGen}, \mathsf{dfaABE.Enc}, \mathsf{dfaABE.Dec})$. Following the notation of Sect. 2, we achieve this by constructing an ABE scheme for the relation $R^{\mathsf{DFA}} = \{A^{\mathsf{DFA}} \times B^{\mathsf{DFA}} \to \{0,1\}\}$ which is defined as $R^{\mathsf{DFA}}(\mathbf{x}, M) = M(\mathbf{x})$. Recall that A^{DFA} is the set of all input strings and B^{DFA} is the set of all DFA. Let $|Q|$ be the number of states in M. As described in Sect. 1, our construction relies on two special ABE for DFA as follows:

1. An ABE denoted by $\mathsf{dfaABE}^{\leq}$ for the relation $R^{\mathsf{DFA}\leq} = \{A^{\mathsf{DFA}} \times B^{\mathsf{DFA}} \to \{0,1\}\}$ defined as:

$$R^{\mathsf{DFA}\leq}(\mathbf{x}, M) = M(\mathbf{x}) \wedge \left(|\mathbf{x}| \overset{?}{\leq} |Q| \right)$$

2. An ABE denoted by $\mathsf{dfaABE}^{>}$ for the relation $R^{\mathsf{DFA}>} = \{A^{\mathsf{DFA}} \times B^{\mathsf{DFA}} \to \{0,1\}\}$ defined as:

$$R^{\mathsf{DFA}>}(\mathbf{x}, M) = M(\mathbf{x}) \wedge \left(|\mathbf{x}| \overset{?}{>} |Q| \right)$$

It is easy to see that given constructions for $\mathsf{dfaABE}^{\leq}$ and $\mathsf{dfaABE}^{>}$, we may construct dfaABE simply by running them in parallel. This intuition is formalized in Sect. 3.1.

Then, it suffices to construct the ingredients $\mathsf{dfaABE}^{\leq}$ and $\mathsf{dfaABE}^{>}$ – we do so by leveraging existing constructions of *unbounded* kpABE and cpABE for monotone span programs. Since the intuition was discussed in Sect. 1, we directly provide the constructions in Sects. 3.2 and 3.3 respectively.

3.1   Construction of dfaABE

Below, we describe the construction of our ABE for DFA formally. We denote our construction as dfaABE.

$\mathsf{dfaABE.Setup}(1^{\lambda})$: On input the security parameter 1^{λ}, do the following:
    1. Invoke $\mathsf{dfaABE}^{\leq}.\mathsf{Setup}(1^{\lambda})$ and $\mathsf{dfaABE}^{>}.\mathsf{Setup}(1^{\lambda})$ to obtain $(\mathsf{dfaABE}^{\leq}.\mathsf{mpk}, \mathsf{dfaABE}^{\leq}.\mathsf{msk})$ and $(\mathsf{dfaABE}^{>}.\mathsf{mpk}, \mathsf{dfaABE}^{>}.\mathsf{msk})$ respectively.
    2. Output $\mathsf{dfaABE.mpk} = (\mathsf{dfaABE}^{\leq}.\mathsf{mpk}, \mathsf{dfaABE}^{>}.\mathsf{mpk})$ and $\mathsf{dfaABE.msk} = (\mathsf{dfaABE}^{\leq}.\mathsf{msk}, \mathsf{dfaABE}^{>}.\mathsf{msk})$.

$\mathsf{dfaABE.Enc}(\mathsf{dfaABE.mpk}, \mu, \mathbf{x})$: On input the master public key $\mathsf{dfaABE.mpk}$, a message bit μ, and an attribute $\mathbf{x} \in A^{\mathsf{DFA}}$ of unbounded polynomial length (i.e., bounded by 2^{λ}), do the following:
    1. Compute $\mathsf{ct}_1 = \mathsf{dfaABE}^{\leq}.\mathsf{Enc}(\mathsf{dfaABE}^{\leq}.\mathsf{mpk}, \mu, \mathbf{x})$.
    2. Compute $\mathsf{ct}_2 = \mathsf{dfaABE}^{>}.\mathsf{Enc}(\mathsf{dfaABE}^{>}.\mathsf{mpk}, \mu, \mathbf{x})$.
    3. Output $(\mathsf{ct}_1, \mathsf{ct}_2)$.

dfaABE.KeyGen(dfaABE.msk, dfaABE.mpk, M): On input the master secret key
  dfaABE.msk, the description of a DFA $M \in B^{\mathsf{DFA}}$ do the following:
  1. Compute $\mathsf{sk}_1 = \mathsf{dfaABE}^{\leq}.\mathsf{KeyGen}(\mathsf{dfaABE}^{\leq}.\mathsf{msk}, \mathsf{dfaABE}^{\leq}.\mathsf{mpk}, M)$.
  2. Compute $\mathsf{sk}_2 = \mathsf{dfaABE}^{>}.\mathsf{KeyGen}(\mathsf{dfaABE}^{>}.\mathsf{msk}, \mathsf{dfaABE}^{>}.\mathsf{mpk}, M)$.
  3. Output $(\mathsf{sk}_1, \mathsf{sk}_2)$.

dfaABE.Dec(dfaABE.mpk, dfaABE.ct, $\mathbf{x}$, dfaABE.sk$_M$, M): On input a ciphertext
  encoded under attribute $\mathbf{x}$ and a secret key for DFA M, proceed as follows.
  Let $|Q|$ be the number of states in the machine M.
  1. If $|\mathbf{x}| \leq |Q|$, compute $\mu_1 \leftarrow \mathsf{dfaABE}^{\leq}.\mathsf{Dec}(\mathsf{dfaABE}^{\leq}.\mathsf{mpk}, \mathsf{ct}_1, \mathbf{x}, \mathsf{sk}_1, M)$
     and output it.
  2. If $|\mathbf{x}| > |Q|$, compute $\mu_2 \leftarrow \mathsf{dfaABE}^{>}.\mathsf{Dec}(\mathsf{dfaABE}^{>}.\mathsf{mpk}, \mathsf{ct}_2, \mathbf{x}, \mathsf{sk}_2, M)$
     and output it.

Correctness. Correctness follows directly from the correctness of the ingredient
schemes $\mathsf{dfaABE}^{\leq}$ and $\mathsf{dfaABE}^{>}$, where the former is invoked for the case that
$|\mathbf{x}| \leq |Q|$ and the latter otherwise.

Security. Security of the scheme dfaABE follows directly from the security of
$\mathsf{dfaABE}^{\leq}$ and $\mathsf{dfaABE}^{>}$. In more detail, we have:

Theorem 8. *Assume that* $\mathsf{dfaABE}^{\leq}$ *and* $\mathsf{dfaABE}^{>}$ *are ABE schemes for relations* $R^{\mathsf{DFA}\leq}$ *and* $R^{\mathsf{DFA}>}$ *respectively, that satisfy selective/selective*/adaptive
security. Then,* dfaABE *is an ABE scheme for relation* R^{DFA} *that satisfies selec-
tive/selective*/adaptive security.*

The proof is straightforward: for the case that $|\mathbf{x}| \leq |Q|$, the theorem follows from
security of $\mathsf{dfaABE}^{\leq}$, otherwise from the security of $\mathsf{dfaABE}^{>}$.

3.2   Construction of dfaABE$^{\leq}$

In this section, we construct the ABE scheme dfaABE$^{\leq}$ for the relation $R^{\mathsf{DFA}\leq} =$
$\{A^{\mathsf{DFA}} \times B^{\mathsf{DFA}} \rightarrow \{0,1\}\}$ where $R^{\mathsf{DFA}\leq}(\mathbf{x}, M) = M(\mathbf{x}) \wedge \left(|\mathbf{x}| \overset{?}{\leq} |Q|\right)$. Our construction is built from the following ingredients:

1. An ABE scheme for the relation $R^{\mathsf{MUKP}} : A^{\mathsf{MUKP}} \times B^{\mathsf{MUKP}} \rightarrow \{0,1\}$. Recall
   from Sect. 2, that $A^{\mathsf{MUKP}} := 2^{\mathbb{Z}}$ is the set of attributes, B^{MUKP} is the set
   of monotone span programs and $R^{\mathsf{MUKP}}(S, (\mathbf{L}, \rho)) = 1$ iff the span program
   $(\mathbf{L}, \rho)$ accepts the set $S \in A^{\mathsf{MUKP}}$. We denote such a scheme as kpABE, and
   construct it in the full version of our paper [6] (Section 5.2).
2. A map $f_{\mathsf{e}}^{\mathsf{KP}} : A^{\mathsf{DFA}} \rightarrow A^{\mathsf{MUKP}}$ and a map $f_{\mathsf{k}}^{\mathsf{KP}} : B^{\mathsf{DFA}} \rightarrow B^{\mathsf{MUKP}}$ so that
   $R^{\mathsf{MUKP}}(S_{\mathbf{x}}, (\mathbf{L}_M, \rho_M)) = 1$ iff $R^{\mathsf{DFA}\leq}(\mathbf{x}, M) = 1$, where $S_{\mathbf{x}} = f_{\mathsf{e}}^{\mathsf{KP}}(\mathbf{x})$ and
   $(\mathbf{L}_M, \rho_M) = f_{\mathsf{k}}^{\mathsf{KP}}(M)$. These maps are constructed in Sect. 4.1.

The scheme dfaABE$^{\leq}$ is then defined as follows.

dfaABE$^{\leq}$.Setup(1^{λ}): On input the security parameter 1^{λ}, do the following:
  1. Invoke kpABE.Setup(1^{λ}) to obtain (kpABE.mpk, kpABE.msk).

2. Output $\mathsf{dfaABE}^{\leq}.\mathsf{mpk} = \mathsf{kpABE}.\mathsf{mpk}$ and $\mathsf{dfaABE}^{\leq}.\mathsf{msk} = \mathsf{kpABE}.\mathsf{msk}$.

$\mathsf{dfaABE}^{\leq}.\mathsf{Enc}(\mathsf{dfaABE}^{\leq}.\mathsf{mpk}, \mu, \mathbf{x})$: On input the master public key $\mathsf{dfaABE}^{\leq}.\mathsf{mpk}$, a message bit μ, and an attribute $\mathbf{x} \in A^{\mathsf{DFA}}$ of unbounded polynomial length (i.e. length at most 2^{λ}), do the following:
1. Convert $\mathbf{x}$ to attribute $S_{\mathbf{x}}$ by computing $S_{\mathbf{x}} = f_e^{\mathsf{KP}}(\mathbf{x})$ as described in Sect. 4.1.
2. Compute $\mathsf{ct} = \mathsf{kpABE}.\mathsf{Enc}(\mathsf{kpABE}.\mathsf{mpk}, \mu, S_{\mathbf{x}})$ and output it.

$\mathsf{dfaABE}^{\leq}.\mathsf{KeyGen}(\mathsf{dfaABE}^{\leq}.\mathsf{msk}, \mathsf{dfaABE}^{\leq}.\mathsf{mpk}, M)$: On input the master secret key $\mathsf{dfaABE}^{\leq}.\mathsf{msk}$, the description of a DFA $M \in B^{\mathsf{DFA}}$ do the following:
1. Convert M into an MSP $(\mathbf{L}_M, \rho_M)$ by computing $(\mathbf{L}_M, \rho_M) = f_k^{\mathsf{KP}}(M)$ as described in Sect. 4.1.
2. Compute $\mathsf{sk}_M = \mathsf{kpABE}.\mathsf{KeyGen}(\mathsf{kpABE}.\mathsf{msk}, \mathsf{kpABE}.\mathsf{mpk}, (\mathbf{L}_M, \rho_M))$ and output it.

$\mathsf{dfaABE}^{\leq}.\mathsf{Dec}(\mathsf{dfaABE}^{\leq}.\mathsf{mpk}, \mathsf{dfaABE}^{\leq}.\mathsf{ct}, \mathbf{x}, \mathsf{dfaABE}^{\leq}.\mathsf{sk}_M, M)$: On input a ciphertext encoded under attribute $\mathbf{x}$ and a secret key for DFA M:
1. Compute $S_{\mathbf{x}} = f_e^{\mathsf{KP}}(\mathbf{x})$ and $(\mathbf{L}_M, \rho_M) = f_k^{\mathsf{KP}}(M)$ as described in Sect. 4.1.
2. Compute $\mu \leftarrow \mathsf{kpABE}.\mathsf{Dec}(\mathsf{kpABE}.\mathsf{mpk}, \mathsf{kpABE}.\mathsf{ct}, S_{\mathbf{x}}, \mathsf{sk}_M, (\mathbf{L}_M, \rho_M))$ and output it.

Correctness and Security. Correctness and security follow directly from the "embedding lemma" (Lemma 1) provided in Sect. 2 by setting

$$A' = A^{\mathsf{DFA}}, \quad B' = B^{\mathsf{DFA}}, \quad R^{F'} = R^{\mathsf{DFA}\leq},$$
$$A = A^{\mathsf{MUKP}}, \quad B = B^{\mathsf{MUKP}}, \quad R^F = R^{\mathsf{MUKP}}$$

In more detail, we have the following theorem.

Theorem 9. *Assume that* kpABE *is an ABE scheme for relation* R^{MUKP} *satisfying selective/selective*/adaptive security. Then,* $\mathsf{dfaABE}^{\leq}$ *is an ABE scheme for relation* $R^{\mathsf{DFA}\leq}$ *satisfying selective/selective*/adaptive security.*

3.3   Construction of $\mathsf{dfaABE}^{>}$

In this section, we construct the ABE scheme $\mathsf{dfaABE}^{>}$ for the relation $R^{\mathsf{DFA}>} = \{A^{\mathsf{DFA}} \times B^{\mathsf{DFA}} \to \{0,1\}\}$ where $R^{\mathsf{DFA}>}(\mathbf{x}, M) = M(\mathbf{x}) \wedge (|\mathbf{x}| \overset{?}{>} |Q|)$. Our construction is built from the following ingredients:

1. An ABE scheme for the relation $R^{\mathsf{MUCP}} : A^{\mathsf{MUCP}} \times B^{\mathsf{MUCP}} \to \{0,1\}$. Recall from Sect. 2, that A^{MUCP} is the set of all monotone span programs, B^{MUCP} is the set of attributes and $R^{\mathsf{MUCP}}((\mathbf{L}, \rho), S) = 1$ iff the span program $(\mathbf{L}, \rho) \in A^{\mathsf{MUCP}}$ accepts the set $S \in B^{\mathsf{MUCP}}$. We denote such a scheme as cpABE, and construct it in the full version of our paper [6] (Section 5.4).
2. A map $f_e^{\mathsf{CP}} : A^{\mathsf{DFA}} \to A^{\mathsf{MUCP}}$ and a map $f_k^{\mathsf{CP}} : B^{\mathsf{DFA}} \to B^{\mathsf{MUCP}}$ so that $R^{\mathsf{MUCP}}((\mathbf{L}_{\mathbf{x}}, \rho_{\mathbf{x}}), S_M) = 1$ iff $R^{\mathsf{DFA}>}(\mathbf{x}, M) = 1$, where $(\mathbf{L}_{\mathbf{x}}, \rho_{\mathbf{x}}) = f_e^{\mathsf{CP}}(\mathbf{x})$ and $S_M = f_k^{\mathsf{CP}}(M)$. These maps are constructed in Sect. 4.2.

The scheme $\mathsf{dfaABE}^{>}$ is then defined as follows.

dfaABE$^>$.Setup(1^λ): On input the security parameter 1^λ, do the following:
1. Invoke cpABE.Setup(1^λ) to obtain (cpABE.mpk, cpABE.msk).
2. Output dfaABE$^>$.mpk = cpABE.mpk and dfaABE$^>$.msk = cpABE.msk.

dfaABE$^>$.Enc(dfaABE$^>$.mpk, μ, $\mathbf{x}$):   On   input   the   master   public
key dfaABE$^>$.mpk, a message μ, and an attribute $\mathbf{x} \in A^{\mathsf{DFA}}$ of unbounded
polynomial length (i.e. length at most 2^λ), do the following:
1. Convert $\mathbf{x}$ to MSP ($\mathbf{L_x}, \rho_\mathbf{x}$) by computing ($\mathbf{L_x}, \rho_\mathbf{x}$) = $f_\mathsf{e}^\mathsf{CP}(\mathbf{x})$ as described
in Sect. 4.2.
2. Compute ct = cpABE.Enc(cpABE.mpk, μ, ($\mathbf{L_x}, \rho_\mathbf{x}$)) and output it.

dfaABE$^>$.KeyGen(dfaABE$^>$.msk, dfaABE$^>$.mpk, M): On input the master secret
key dfaABE$^>$.msk, the description of a DFA M do the following:
1. Convert M into an attribute S_M by computing $S_M = f_\mathsf{k}^\mathsf{CP}(M)$ as
described in Sect. 4.2.
2. Compute sk = cpABE.KeyGen(cpABE.msk, cpABE.mpk, S_M) and output
it.

dfaABE$^>$.Dec(dfaABE$^>$.mpk, dfaABE$^>$.ct, $\mathbf{x}$, dfaABE$^>$.sk$_M$, M):   On   input   a
ciphertext encoded under attribute $\mathbf{x}$ and a secret key sk$_M$ for DFA M:
1. Compute ($\mathbf{L_x}, \rho_\mathbf{x}$) = $f_\mathsf{e}^\mathsf{CP}(\mathbf{x})$ and $S_M = f_\mathsf{k}^\mathsf{CP}(M)$ as described in Sect. 4.2.
2. Compute $\mu \leftarrow$ cpABE.Dec(cpABE.mpk, cpABE.ct, ($\mathbf{L_x}, \rho_\mathbf{x}$), sk$_M$, S_M) and
output it.

Correctness and Security. Correctness and security follow exactly as in Sect. 3.2,
by considering the maps defined in Sect. 4.2 instead of Sect. 4.1. In more detail,
we have the following theorem:

Theorem 10. *Assume that* cpABE *is an ABE scheme for relation* R^{MUCP} *satisfying selective/selective*/adaptive security. Then,* dfaABE$^>$ *is an ABE scheme
for relation* $R^{\mathsf{DFA}>}$ *satisfying selective/selective*/adaptive security.*

4   Mapping DFA Computation to Monotone Span Programs

In this section we will describe how to encode DFA computation over a binary
alphabet $\Sigma = \{0, 1\}$ into a monotone span program (MSP). Section 4.1 shows the
encoding procedure for any DFA machine to a MSP and further how to encode
its input to a set of attributes associated with the MSP. In a dual view, Sect. 4.2
shows the encoding procedure for any input string to a MSP while encoding the
DFA machine itself as a set of attributes associated with the MSP. For both
sections, we denote any DFA machine as $M = (Q, \Sigma, T, q_\mathsf{st}, F)$ and $\mathbf{x} \in \Sigma^*$ as
its input of arbitrary (polynomial) length.

4.1 Encoding Deterministic Finite Automata to Monotone Span Programs

In this section, we construct two efficiently computable functions (please see Sect. 2 for the notation):

1. $f_{\mathsf{e}}^{\mathsf{KP}} : A^{\mathsf{DFA}} \to A^{\mathsf{MUKP}}$ to encode $\mathbf{w} \in A^{\mathsf{DFA}}$ as a set of attributes $S_{\mathbf{w}} \in A^{\mathsf{MUKP}}$, and
2. $f_{\mathsf{k}}^{\mathsf{KP}} : B^{\mathsf{DFA}} \to B^{\mathsf{MUKP}}$ to encode $M \in B^{\mathsf{DFA}}$ into a MSP $(\mathbf{L}_M, \rho_M) \in B^{\mathsf{MUKP}}$.

We argue that $R^{\mathsf{MUKP}}(S_{\mathbf{w}}, (\mathbf{L}_M, \rho_M)) = 1$ iff $R^{\mathsf{DFA} \le}(\mathbf{w}, M) = 1$, where $S_{\mathbf{w}} = f_{\mathsf{e}}^{\mathsf{KP}}(\mathbf{w})$ and $(\mathbf{L}_M, \rho_M) = f_{\mathsf{k}}^{\mathsf{KP}}(M)$.

For ease of exposition, we represent the universe of attributes in the following form:

$$A^{\mathsf{MUKP}} := \{\text{``}x_i = b\text{''} \mid i \in [2^\lambda], b \in \{0, 1\}\} \cup \{\text{``String length} = i\text{''} \mid i \in [2^\lambda]\} \cup \{\text{``Dummy''}\}.$$

We assume that these attributes are embedded into $\mathbb{Z}$ via an injective mapping such as

$$\text{``Dummy''} \mapsto 0, \quad \text{``}x_i = b\text{''} \mapsto 3i + b \quad \text{``String length} = i\text{''} \mapsto 3i + 2.$$

However, for maintaining intuitive notation, we make the mapping implicit. An input string $\mathbf{w} = (w_1, \ldots, w_\ell) \in A^{\mathsf{DFA}}$ of length ℓ is encoded to a set of attributes given by $f_{\mathsf{e}}^{\mathsf{KP}}(\mathbf{w}) = S_{\mathbf{w}} \in A^{\mathsf{MUKP}}$ as:

$$S_{\mathbf{w}} := \{\text{``Dummy''}\} \cup \{\text{``}x_i = w_i\text{''} \mid i \in [\ell]\} \cup \{\text{``String length} = \ell\text{''}\}.$$

When we represent $S_{\mathbf{w}}$ as a set of integers, we have $S_{\mathbf{w}} \subseteq [4\ell]$ and thus in particular, all the values in $S_{\mathbf{w}}$ are bounded by $\mathrm{poly}(\ell)$.

A DFA machine $M = (Q, \Sigma, T, q_{\mathsf{st}}, F) \in B^{\mathsf{DFA}}$ is encoded into a MSP given by $f_{\mathsf{k}}^{\mathsf{KP}}(M) = (\mathbf{L}_M, \rho_M) \in B^{\mathsf{MUKP}}$. Here $\mathbf{L}_M \in \{0, \pm 1\}^{\mathcal{R} \times \mathcal{C}}$ with $\mathcal{R} = 1 + (2 \cdot |Q| + 1) \cdot |Q|$ and $\mathcal{C} = 1 + |Q| + |Q|^2$. The label map ρ_M will be implicit in the description of the matrix $\mathbf{L}_M$. Before providing the construction of $\mathbf{L}_M$, we define the following sub-matrices useful in the construction:

- matrix $\mathbf{I}_Q$ denoting the $|Q| \times |Q|$ identity matrix, and
- matrices $\mathbf{Y}^{(b)} \in \{0, -1\}^{|Q| \times |Q|}, \forall b \in \{0, 1\}$ defined as $\mathbf{Y}^{(b)} := \left[y_{i,j}^{(b)}\right]$ such that:

$$y_{i,j}^{(b)} = -1, \text{ if } T(i, b) = j \; (\text{ i.e. there is a transition from state } i \text{ to state } j \text{ upon input } b)$$
$$= 0, \text{ otherwise}$$

We also denote $\mathbf{0}_{Q \times Q}$ to be the all-zero matrix of size $|Q| \times |Q|$ and $\mathbf{0}_Q$ as the column-vector of size $|Q|$ containing all 0s.

We define $\mathbf{L}_M$ and the map ρ_M in Table 2.

Table 2. Encoding a DFA M to matrix $\mathbf{L}_M$

"Dummy" ↦	1	−10...0	0...0	0...0	0...0	...	0...0	0...0
"$x_1 = 0$" ↦	0_Q	I_Q	$Y^{(0)}$	$0_{Q\times Q}$		...	$0_{Q\times Q}$	$0_{Q\times Q}$
"$x_1 = 1$" ↦	0_Q	I_Q	$Y^{(1)}$	$0_{Q\times Q}$		...	$0_{Q\times Q}$	$0_{Q\times Q}$
"$x_2 = 0$" ↦	0_Q	$0_{Q\times Q}$	I_Q	$Y^{(0)}$		...	$0_{Q\times Q}$	$0_{Q\times Q}$
"$x_2 = 1$" ↦	0_Q	$0_{Q\times Q}$	I_Q	$Y^{(1)}$		...	$0_{Q\times Q}$	$0_{Q\times Q}$
⋮	⋮	⋮	⋮	⋮		⋱	⋮	⋮
"$x_{|Q|} = 0$" ↦	0_Q	$0_{Q\times Q}$	$0_{Q\times Q}$	$0_{Q\times Q}$		...	I_Q	$Y^{(0)}$
"$x_{|Q|} = 1$" ↦	0_Q	$0_{Q\times Q}$	$0_{Q\times Q}$	$0_{Q\times Q}$		...	I_Q	$Y^{(1)}$
"String length = 1" ↦	0	0...0	0...01					
"String length = 2" ↦	0		0...00	0...01				
⋮	⋮				⋱			
"String length = $|Q|$" ↦	0						0...00	0...01

We observe that $\max_i \rho_M(i) \le 4|Q|$, where we regard the attributes as integers through the aforementioned injective mapping. In particular, $\mathbf{L}_M$ is associated with attributes bounded by $\mathrm{poly}(|Q|)$.

The last $|Q|$ rows pertaining to attributes "String length $= i$", $i \in [|Q|]$ is a $|Q| \times \mathcal{C}$ submatrix containing all zeros except specific locations filled with 1s in a diagonal form as shown. We prove the following theorem.

Theorem 11. *Let $\mathbf{L}_{M,\mathbf{w}}$ be the submatrix of $\mathbf{L}_M$ restricted to the rows selected by attribute set $S_{\mathbf{w}}$ (please see Definition 2.1). Then, for any DFA $M = (Q, \Sigma, T, q_{\mathsf{st}}, F) \in B^{\mathsf{DFA}}$ and any input $\mathbf{w} \in A^{\mathsf{DFA}}$ we have $\mathbf{e}_1 \in \mathrm{span}(\mathbf{L}_{M,\mathbf{w}}^{\top})$ iff $(M(\mathbf{w}) = 1 \wedge |\mathbf{w}| \le |Q|)$.*

Proof. We first prove "if" direction. For any $\mathbf{w} \in A^{\mathsf{DFA}}$ with $|\mathbf{w}| = \ell \le |Q|$, the submatrix $\mathbf{L}_{M,\mathbf{w}}$ of $\mathbf{L}_M$ restricted by $S_{\mathbf{w}}$ is shown in Table 3.

Since M is a DFA, the matrix $Y^{(b)}$ will always have exactly one "-1" in each of its rows. Let $\mathbf{w} = (w_1, \ldots, w_\ell)$. To prove the theorem, we give an algorithm which constructs a subset of rows $\widehat{\mathbf{L}}_{M,\mathbf{w}}$ of $\mathbf{L}_{M,\mathbf{w}}$ inductively that sums up to $\mathbf{e}_1$ iff $M(\mathbf{w}) = 1$. The algorithm proceeds as follows:

On input $(M, \mathbf{w}, \mathbf{L}_{M,\mathbf{w}})$, it does the following:

1. Initialize $\widehat{\mathbf{L}}_{M,\mathbf{w}}$ with the first row of $\mathbf{L}_{M,\mathbf{w}}$ labelled with attribute "Dummy".
2. For $i \in [\ell]$, do the following:

Table 3. Submatrix $\mathbf{L}_{M,\mathbf{w}}$ defined by $S_\mathbf{w}$ and $\mathbf{L}_M$

	1	$-10\ldots0$	$0\ldots0$	$0\ldots0$	$\ldots$	$0\ldots0$	$0\ldots0$
"Dummy" $\mapsto$	1	$-10\ldots0$	$0\ldots0$	$0\ldots0$	$\ldots$	$0\ldots0$	$0\ldots0$
"$x_1 = w_1$" $\mapsto$	0_Q	I_Q	$\mathbf{Y}^{(w_1)}$				
"$x_2 = w_2$" $\mapsto$	0_Q		I_Q	$\mathbf{Y}^{(w_2)}$			
$\vdots$	$\vdots$				$\ddots$		
"$x_\ell = w_\ell$" $\mapsto$	0_Q					I_Q	$\mathbf{Y}^{(w_\ell)}$
"String length $= \ell$" $\mapsto$	0					$0\ldots0$	$0\ldots01$

(a) If $i = 1$, populate $\widehat{\mathbf{L}}_{M,\mathbf{w}}$ with *second* row of $\mathbf{L}_{M,\mathbf{w}}$ labelled with "$x_1 = w_1$". Discard the remaining $|Q| - 1$ rows in the block labelled with "$x_1 = w_1$". For the chosen row, let $k_1 \in Q$ be such that $T(1, w_1) = k_1$. By construction this implies $y_{1,k_1}^{(w_1)} = -1$ in $\mathbf{Y}^{(w_1)}$.

(b) If $i \in [2, \ell]$, choose the k_{i-1}-th row in the block labelled with "$x_i = w_i$" and add it to $\widehat{\mathbf{L}}_{M,\mathbf{w}}$. Discard the remaining $|Q| - 1$ rows in the block labelled with "$x_i = w_i$". For the chosen row, let $k_i \in Q$ be such that $T(k_{i-1}, w_i) = k_i$. By construction this implies $y_{k_{i-1},k_i}^{(w_i)} = -1$ in $\mathbf{Y}^{(w_i)}$.

3. Add the row labelled "String length $= \ell$" to $\widehat{\mathbf{L}}_{M,\mathbf{w}}$. Output $\widehat{\mathbf{L}}_{M,\mathbf{w}}$ and terminate.

It is easy to see that the above algorithm always terminates. The first two rows of $\mathbf{L}_{M,\mathbf{w}}$ labelled with attributes "Dummy" and "$x_1 = w_1$" are chosen in Step 1 and Step 2(a) of the above algorithm respectively. The last row is chosen in a natural way in Step 3 based on the length of the input string.

Aside from these, note that the way the remaining rows are added to $\widehat{\mathbf{L}}_{M,\mathbf{w}}$ is governed by the transition function T of the DFA M. Essentially, the computation of $\widehat{\mathbf{L}}_{M,\mathbf{w}}$ mirrors the computation of M on input $\mathbf{w}$. In particular, the *order* in which the rows are selected iteratively in Step 2 always follow a loop invariant: at the end of the i-th iteration the chosen rows sum to a vector $\mathbf{v}_i = (1, 0, \ldots, 0, -1, 0, \ldots, 0)$, where -1 appears exactly at the k_i-th position associated with the $|Q| \times |Q|$-sized block matrix $\mathbf{Y}^{(w_i)}$. Hence, when $M(\mathbf{w}) = 1$ with $|\mathbf{w}| = \ell$, the vectors in $\widehat{\mathbf{L}}_{M,\mathbf{w}}$ at the end of the Step 2 sum to $\mathbf{v}_\ell = (1, 0, \ldots, 0, -1)$. Here -1 is at position $|Q|$ associated with $\mathbf{Y}^{(w_\ell)}$ and is also the final state of M. By construction of $\mathbf{L}_{M,\mathbf{w}}$, it follows that the last row selected in Step 3 labelled with "String length $= \ell$" when added to $\mathbf{v}_\ell$ results to $\mathbf{e}_1$, as intended.

We then prove "only if" direction. For any $\mathbf{w} = (w_1, \ldots, w_\ell) \in \Sigma^\ell$ such that $M(\mathbf{w}) \neq 1$ and $\ell \leq |Q|$, note that the description of $\mathbf{L}_{M,\mathbf{w}}$ forces the first two rows corresponding to attributes "Dummy" and "$x_1 = w_1$" to be chosen to build

$\mathbf{e}_1$ progressively. For $i \in [2, \ell - 1]$, let $k_{i-1}, k_i \in Q$ be such that $y_{k_{i-1}, k_i}^{(w_i)} = -1$ in $\mathbf{Y}^{(w_i)}$. Consequently, the only choice left for selecting the next row further to nullify the -1 in $y_{k_{i-1}, k_i}^{(w_i)}$ is restricted to the k_i-th row in the block labelled with "$x_{i+1} = w_{i+1}$" which again forces the emulation of M's computation on input $\mathbf{w}$. Since $M(\mathbf{w}) \neq 1$, the sum of all the rows at the end of the ℓ-th iteration cannot have a "-1" in its $|Q|^{th}$ position. When added to the row labelled "String length $= \ell$", this does not yield $\mathbf{e}_1$ as desired.

We then consider $\mathbf{w} = (w_1, \ldots, w_\ell) \in \Sigma^\ell$ such that $\ell > |Q|$. In this case, the matrix $\mathbf{L}_{M, \mathbf{w}}$ does not have the last row in Table 3. Therefore, we cannot nullify "-1" that appears in the rightmost block as a result of enforced emulation of M's computation. Therefore, we cannot obtain $\mathbf{e}_1$ as desired.

4.2 Encoding DFA Input Strings to Monotone Span Programs

In this case the DFA machine M is encoded into a set of attributes S_M from an appropriately defined attribute universe while the input string $\mathbf{x} \in \Sigma^*$ will be encoded to a MSP $(\mathbf{L}_\mathbf{x}, \rho_\mathbf{x})$.

We construct two efficiently computable functions:

1. $f_\mathsf{e}^\mathsf{CP} : A^\mathsf{DFA} \to A^\mathsf{MUCP}$ to encode $\mathbf{x} \in A^\mathsf{DFA}$ into a MSP $(\mathbf{L}_\mathbf{x}, \rho_\mathbf{x}) \in A^\mathsf{MUCP}$.
2. $f_\mathsf{k}^\mathsf{CP} : B^\mathsf{DFA} \to B^\mathsf{MUCP}$ to encode $M \in B^\mathsf{DFA}$ as a set of attributes $S_M \in B^\mathsf{MUCP}$.

We argue that $R^\mathsf{MUCP}(S_M, (\mathbf{L}_\mathbf{x}, \rho_\mathbf{x})) = 1$ iff $R^{\mathsf{DFA}>}(\mathbf{x}, M) = 1$, where $S_M = f_\mathsf{k}^\mathsf{CP}(M)$ and $(\mathbf{L}_\mathbf{x}, \rho_\mathbf{x}) = f_\mathsf{e}^\mathsf{CP}(\mathbf{x})$.

For ease of exposition, we represent the universe of attributes as follows:

$$B^\mathsf{MUCP} := \{(b, i, j) \mid b \in \{0, 1\}, i, j \in [2^\lambda]\} \cup \{\text{"Size} = \mathsf{s}\text{"} \mid \mathsf{s} \in [2^\lambda]\} \cup \{\text{"Dummy"}\}.$$

We assume that these attributes are embedded into $\mathbb{Z}$ via an injective mapping such as

$$\text{"Dummy"} \mapsto 0, \quad \text{"}(b, i, j)\text{"} \mapsto 4((i+j)^2 + j) + 2b \quad \text{"Size} = \mathsf{s}\text{"} \mapsto 2\mathsf{s} + 1,$$

But for maintaining intuitive notation, we make the mapping implicit.

A DFA $M = (Q, \Sigma, T, q_\mathsf{st}, F) \in B^\mathsf{DFA}$ is encoded as a set of attributes given by $f_\mathsf{k}^\mathsf{CP}(M) = S_M \in B^\mathsf{MUCP}$ as:

$$S_M := \{\text{"Dummy"}\} \cup \{(b, i, j) \in \Sigma \times Q^2 \mid T(i, b) = j\} \cup \{\text{"Size} = |Q|\text{"}\}.$$

When we represent S_M as a set of integers, we have $S_M \subseteq [20|Q|^2]$ and thus in particular, all the values in S_M are bounded by $\mathrm{poly}(|Q|)$.

An input string $\mathbf{x} = (x_1, \ldots, x_\ell) \in A^\mathsf{DFA}$ of length ℓ is encoded into a MSP given by $f_\mathsf{e}^\mathsf{CP}(\mathbf{x}) = (\mathbf{L}_\mathbf{x}, \rho_\mathbf{x}) \in A^\mathsf{MUCP}$. Here $\mathbf{L}_\mathbf{x} \in \{0, \pm 1\}^{\mathcal{R} \times \mathcal{C}}$ with $\mathcal{R} = 1 + \ell^3 + \ell$ and $\mathcal{C} = 1 + \ell + \ell^2$. The label map $\rho_\mathbf{x}$ will be implicit in the description of the matrix $\mathbf{L}_\mathbf{x}$. Before providing the construction of $\mathbf{L}_\mathbf{x}$, we define the following sub-matrices useful in the construction:

– matrix $\mathbf{I}_\ell$ denoting the $\ell \times \ell$ identity matrix and a column-vector $\mathbf{g}_\ell = \underbrace{(1, \ldots, 1)}_{\ell}^\top$

– matrices $\mathbf{S}_\ell$ and $\mathbf{T}_\ell$ such that

$$\mathbf{S}_\ell := \mathbf{I}_\ell \otimes \mathbf{g}_\ell = \begin{bmatrix} \mathbf{g}_\ell & \mathbf{0}_\ell & \ldots & \mathbf{0}_\ell \\ \mathbf{0}_\ell & \mathbf{g}_\ell & \ldots & \mathbf{0}_\ell \\ \vdots & \vdots & \ddots & \vdots \\ \mathbf{0}_\ell & \mathbf{0}_\ell & \ldots & \mathbf{g}_\ell \end{bmatrix}_{\ell^2 \times \ell}, \text{ where } \mathbf{0}_\ell \text{ is the all-zero column-vector of size } \ell$$

and $\mathbf{T}_\ell = -\mathbf{g}_\ell \otimes \mathbf{I}_\ell = [-\mathbf{I}_\ell \| \ldots \| -\mathbf{I}_\ell]^\top$ of size $\ell^2 \times \ell$.

For a fixed $b \in \{0,1\}$, we say "*associate* $[\mathbf{S}_\ell \| \mathbf{T}_\ell]$ *with* b"[4] when we label the rows of $[\mathbf{S}_\ell \| \mathbf{T}_\ell]$ as shown in Table 4.

Table 4. Submatrix $[\mathbf{S}_\ell \| \mathbf{T}_\ell]$ with its row label map

We also denote $\mathbf{0}_{\ell^2}$, $\mathbf{0}_{\ell^2 \times \ell}$ and $\mathbf{0}_{\ell \times \ell}$ to be all-zero column-vector of size ℓ^2 and all-zero matrices of size $\ell^2 \times \ell$ and $\ell \times \ell$ respectively. We now define $\mathbf{L_x}$ with its rows labelled with attributes as specified in Table 5.

We observe that we have $\max_i \rho_{\mathbf{x}}(i) \leq 20\ell^2$, where we regard the attributes as integers through the aforementioned injective mapping. In particular, $\mathbf{L_x}$ is associated with attributes bounded by $\mathrm{poly}(\ell)$.

The last ℓ rows pertaining to attributes "Size $= i$", $i \in [\ell]$ is a $\ell \times C$ submatrix containing all zeros except an identity matrix block $\mathbf{I}_\ell$ located under the rightmost $\mathbf{T}_\ell$ with its i-th row labelled with attribute "Size $= i$", $\forall i \in [\ell]$. We show the following.

---

[4] For brevity, we express this as $b \Leftrightarrow [\mathbf{S}_\ell \| \mathbf{T}_\ell]$ in the final description of $\mathbf{L_x}$.

Table 5. Encoding a string **x** to matrix $\mathbf{L_x}$

"Dummy" $\mapsto$	1	$-10\ldots0$	$0\ldots0$	$0\ldots0$	$\ldots$	$0\ldots0$	$0\ldots0$
$x_1 \Leftrightarrow$	$\mathbf{0}_{\ell^2}$	$\mathbf{S}_\ell$	$\mathbf{T}_\ell$	$\mathbf{0}_{\ell^2\times\ell}$	$\ldots$	$\mathbf{0}_{\ell^2\times\ell}$	$\mathbf{0}_{\ell^2\times\ell}$
$x_2 \Leftrightarrow$	$\mathbf{0}_{\ell^2}$	$\mathbf{0}_{\ell^2\times\ell}$	$\mathbf{S}_\ell$	$\mathbf{T}_\ell$	$\ldots$	$\mathbf{0}_{\ell^2\times\ell}$	$\mathbf{0}_{\ell^2\times\ell}$
$\vdots$	$\vdots$	$\vdots$	$\vdots$	$\vdots$	$\ddots$	$\vdots$	$\vdots$
$x_\ell \Leftrightarrow$	$\mathbf{0}_{\ell^2}$	$\mathbf{0}_{\ell^2\times\ell}$	$\mathbf{0}_{\ell^2\times\ell}$	$\mathbf{0}_{\ell^2\times\ell}$	$\ldots$	$\mathbf{S}_\ell$	$\mathbf{T}_\ell$
"Size $= 1$" $\mapsto$	0						
$\vdots$	$\vdots$	$\mathbf{0}_{\ell\times\ell}$	$\mathbf{0}_{\ell\times\ell}$	$\mathbf{0}_{\ell\times\ell}$	$\ldots$	$\mathbf{0}_{\ell\times\ell}$	$\mathbf{I}_\ell$
"Size $= \ell$" $\mapsto$	0						

Theorem 12. *Let $\mathbf{L}_{M,\mathbf{x}}$ be the submatrix of $\mathbf{L_x}$ restricted to the rows selected by the set S_M (please see Definition 2.1). Then, for any DFA $M = (Q, \Sigma, T, q_{\text{st}}, F) \in B^{\text{DFA}}$ and any input $\mathbf{x} \in A^{\text{DFA}}$ we have $\mathbf{e}_1 \in \text{span}(\mathbf{L}_{M,\mathbf{x}}^\top)$ iff $\big(M(\mathbf{x}) = 1 \wedge |\mathbf{x}| \geq |Q|\big)$.*

Proof. We first remove all the all-zero columns from $\mathbf{L}_{M,\mathbf{x}}$ and call the remaining matrix as $\mathbf{L}_{M,\mathbf{x}}$ w.l.o.g. since these columns do not influence on whether $\mathbf{e}_1 \in \text{span}(\mathbf{L}_{M,\mathbf{x}}^\top)$ or not. This simplification ensures that $\mathbf{L}_{M,\mathbf{x}}$ is given as shown in Table 6. Note that the rows present in $\mathbf{L}_{M,\mathbf{x}}$ is governed by the transition function, T of M (via the row labels in $\mathbf{L_x}$). We also note that the last row in Table 6 will be missing if we have $|\mathbf{x}| < |Q|$. Therefore, the matrix $\mathbf{Y}^{(b)}$ here is the same as that was defined in Sect. 4.1. Hence, the proof follows identically to that of Theorem 11.

Table 6. Submatrix $\mathbf{L}_{M,\mathbf{x}}$ defined by S_M and $\mathbf{L_x}$

"Dummy" $\mapsto$	1	$-10\ldots0$	$0\ldots0$	$0\ldots0$	$\ldots$	$0\ldots0$	$0\ldots0$
$x_1 \Leftrightarrow$	$\mathbf{0}_Q$	$\mathbf{I}_Q$	$\mathbf{Y}^{(x_1)}$				
$x_2 \Leftrightarrow$	$\mathbf{0}_Q$		$\mathbf{I}_Q$	$\mathbf{Y}^{(x_2)}$			
$\vdots$	$\vdots$				$\ddots$		
$x_\ell \Leftrightarrow$	$\mathbf{0}_Q$					$\mathbf{I}_Q$	$\mathbf{Y}^{(x_\ell)}$
"Size $= |Q|$" $\mapsto$	0					$0\ldots0$	$0\ldots01$

5   Putting It All Together: ABE for DFA

In this section, we discuss instantiation of our generic construction of ABE for DFA by putting together all the ingredients developed so far.

As we have seen in Sect. 3.1, ABE for R^{DFA} (i.e., ABE for DFA) can be constructed from ABE for $R^{\mathsf{DFA}\geq}$ and ABE for $R^{\mathsf{DFA}\leq}$. Furthermore, as we have seen in Theorem 10 (resp., Theorem 9), ABE for $R^{\mathsf{DFA}>}$ (resp., ABE for $R^{\mathsf{DFA}\leq}$) is implied by ABE for R^{MUCP} (resp., R^{MUKP}).

To instantiate the ABE for R^{MUKP}, we use the construction in the full version of our paper [6] (Section 5.2). As was shown in [6] (in Theorem 13), this construction is semi-adaptively secure under the MDDH_k assumption. To instantiate the ABE for R^{MUCP}, we use the construction in the full version of our paper [6] (Section 5.4). As was shown in [6] (in Theorem 14), this construction satisfies selective* security under the DLIN assumption. Putting all pieces together, we obtain the following theorem.

Theorem 13. *There exists selective* * *secure key-policy ABE for R^{DFA} from the* DLIN *assumption.*

Ciphertext Policy ABE for DFA. We observe that our construction dfaABE uses the underlying kpABE and cpABE in a symmetric way. Thus, by swapping the use of kpABE and cpABE in our construction, we can equivalently construct ciphertext-policy ABE for DFA. Recall that analogous to ABE for MSP (Sect. 2), the ciphertext-policy variant of ABE for DFA is defined simply by swapping the order of the domains in the relation R^{DFA}. In more detail, we set $A^{\mathsf{CPDFA}} = B^{\mathsf{DFA}}$ and $B^{\mathsf{CPDFA}} = A^{\mathsf{DFA}}$ and define the relation R^{CPDFA} analogously for a ciphertext policy scheme for DFA. Thus, in a ciphertext-policy scheme, the encryptor to encrypt a machine and the key generator to compute a key for an input $\mathbf{x}$.

To modify dfaABE to be ciphertext-policy, we exchange the maps used by KeyGen and Enc in the constructions of dfaABE$^{\leq}$ and dfaABE$^{>}$ in Sects. 3.2 and 3.3 respectively. For instance, to construct a ciphertext-policy variant of dfaABE$^{\leq}$, we modify the encrypt and key generation algorithms so that:

1. The key generation algorithm receives as input an attribute $\mathbf{x}$, converts it to attributes $S_{\mathbf{x}}$ using the map defined in Sect. 4.1 and computes cpABE key for $S_{\mathbf{x}}$.
2. The encryption algorithm receives as input an MSP M, converts it to an MSP $(\mathbf{L}_M, \rho_M)$ using the map defined in Sect. 4.1 and computes cpABE encryption for policy $(\mathbf{L}_M, \rho_M)$.

The modification to dfaABE$^{>}$ is analogous. The compiler dfaABE remains the same.

Thus, we additionally obtain the following theorem:

Theorem 14. *There exists selective* * *secure ciphertext-policy ABE for R^{DFA} from the* DLIN *assumption.*

References

1. Agrawal, S., Chase, M.: A study of pair encodings: predicate encryption in prime order groups. In: Kushilevitz, E., Malkin, T. (eds.) TCC 2016, Part II. LNCS, vol. 9563, pp. 259–288. Springer, Heidelberg (2016). https://doi.org/10.1007/978-3-662-49099-0_10

2. Agrawal, S., Chase, M.: Fame: fast attribute-based message encryption. In: Proceedings of the 2017 ACM SIGSAC Conference on Computer and Communications Security CCS 2017 (2017)

3. Agrawal, S., Freeman, D.M., Vaikuntanathan, V.: Functional encryption for inner product predicates from learning with errors. In: Lee, D.H., Wang, X. (eds.) ASIACRYPT 2011. LNCS, vol. 7073, pp. 21–40. Springer, Heidelberg (2011). https://doi.org/10.1007/978-3-642-25385-0_2

4. Agrawal, S., Maitra, M.: FE and iO for turing machines from minimal assumptions. In: Beimel, A., Dziembowski, S. (eds.) TCC 2018. LNCS, vol. 11240, pp. 473–512. Springer, Cham (2018). https://doi.org/10.1007/978-3-030-03810-6_18

5. Agrawal, S., Maitra, M., Yamada, S.: Attribute based encryption (and more) for nondeterministic finite automata from learning with errors. In: Crypto (2019)

6. Agrawal, S., Maitra, M., Yamada, S.: Attribute based encryption for deterministic finite automata from dlin. Cryptology ePrint Archive, Report 2019/645 (2019). https://eprint.iacr.org/2019/645

7. Agrawal, S., Singh, I.P.: Reusable garbled deterministic finite automata from learning with errors. In: ICALP, vol. 80. Schloss Dagstuhl-Leibniz-Zentrum fuer Informatik (2017)

8. Ananth, P., Fan, X.: Attribute based encryption with sublinear decryption from LWE. Cryptology ePrint Archive, Report 2018/273 (2018). https://eprint.iacr.org/2018/273

9. Ananth, P., Sahai, A.: Functional encryption for turing machines. In: Kushilevitz, E., Malkin, T. (eds.) TCC 2016. LNCS, vol. 9562, pp. 125–153. Springer, Heidelberg (2016). https://doi.org/10.1007/978-3-662-49096-9_6

10. Ananth, P., Sahai, A.: Projective arithmetic functional encryption and indistinguishability obfuscation from degree-5 multilinear maps. In: Coron, J.-S., Nielsen, J.B. (eds.) EUROCRYPT 2017. LNCS, vol. 10210, pp. 152–181. Springer, Cham (2017). https://doi.org/10.1007/978-3-319-56620-7_6

11. Apon, D., Döttling, N., Garg, S., Mukherjee, P.: Cryptanalysis of indistinguishability obfuscations of circuits over ggh13. eprint 2016 (2016)

12. Attrapadung, N.: Dual system encryption via doubly selective security: framework, fully secure functional encryption for regular languages, and more. In: Nguyen, P.Q., Oswald, E. (eds.) EUROCRYPT 2014. LNCS, vol. 8441, pp. 557–577. Springer, Heidelberg (2014). https://doi.org/10.1007/978-3-642-55220-5_31

13. Attrapadung, N.: Dual system encryption framework in prime-order groups via computational pair encodings. In: Cheon, J.H., Takagi, T. (eds.) ASIACRYPT 2016. LNCS, vol. 10032, pp. 591–623. Springer, Heidelberg (2016). https://doi.org/10.1007/978-3-662-53890-6_20

14. Attrapadung, N., Hanaoka, G., Yamada, S.: Conversions among several classes of predicate encryption and applications to ABE with various compactness tradeoffs. In: Iwata, T., Cheon, J.H. (eds.) ASIACRYPT 2015. LNCS, vol. 9452, pp. 575–601. Springer, Heidelberg (2015). https://doi.org/10.1007/978-3-662-48797-6_24

15. Barak, B., et al.: On the (im)possibility of obfuscating programs. In: Kilian, J. (ed.) CRYPTO 2001. LNCS, vol. 2139, pp. 1–18. Springer, Heidelberg (2001). https://doi.org/10.1007/3-540-44647-8_1

16. Bethencourt, J., Sahai, A., Waters, B.: Ciphertext-policy attribute-based encryption. In: IEEE Symposium on Security and Privacy, pp. 321–334 (2007)

17. Boneh, D., et al.: Fully key-homomorphic encryption, arithmetic circuit ABE and compact garbled circuits. In: Nguyen, P.Q., Oswald, E. (eds.) EUROCRYPT 2014. LNCS, vol. 8441, pp. 533–556. Springer, Heidelberg (2014). https://doi.org/10.1007/978-3-642-55220-5_30

18. Boneh, D., Hamburg, M.: Generalized identity based and broadcast encryption schemes. In: Pieprzyk, J. (ed.) ASIACRYPT 2008. LNCS, vol. 5350, pp. 455–470. Springer, Heidelberg (2008). https://doi.org/10.1007/978-3-540-89255-7_28

19. Boneh, D., Waters, B.: Conjunctive, subset, and range queries on encrypted data. In: Vadhan, S.P. (ed.) TCC 2007. LNCS, vol. 4392, pp. 535–554. Springer, Heidelberg (2007). https://doi.org/10.1007/978-3-540-70936-7_29

20. Boyen, X., Li, Q.: Attribute-based encryption for finite automata from LWE. In: Au, M.-H., Miyaji, A. (eds.) ProvSec 2015. LNCS, vol. 9451, pp. 247–267. Springer, Cham (2015). https://doi.org/10.1007/978-3-319-26059-4_14

21. Brakerski, Z., Vaikuntanathan, V.: Circuit-ABE from LWE: unbounded attributes and semi-adaptive security. In: Robshaw, M., Katz, J. (eds.) CRYPTO 2016. LNCS, vol. 9816, pp. 363–384. Springer, Heidelberg (2016). https://doi.org/10.1007/978-3-662-53015-3_13

22. Chen, J., Gay, R., Wee, H.: Improved dual system ABE in prime-order groups via predicate encodings. In: Oswald, E., Fischlin, M. (eds.) EUROCRYPT 2015. LNCS, vol. 9057, pp. 595–624. Springer, Heidelberg (2015). https://doi.org/10.1007/978-3-662-46803-6_20

23. Chen, J., Gong, J., Kowalczyk, L., Wee, H.: Unbounded ABE via bilinear entropy expansion, revisited. In: Nielsen, J.B., Rijmen, V. (eds.) EUROCRYPT 2018. LNCS, vol. 10820, pp. 503–534. Springer, Cham (2018). https://doi.org/10.1007/978-3-319-78381-9_19

24. Chen, J., Wee, H.: Fully, (almost) tightly secure IBE and dual system groups. In: Canetti, R., Garay, J.A. (eds.) CRYPTO 2013. LNCS, vol. 8043, pp. 435–460. Springer, Heidelberg (2013). https://doi.org/10.1007/978-3-642-40084-1_25

25. Chen, J., Wee, H.: Semi-adaptive attribute-based encryption and improved delegation for boolean formula. In: Abdalla, M., De Prisco, R. (eds.) SCN 2014. LNCS, vol. 8642, pp. 277–297. Springer, Cham (2014). https://doi.org/10.1007/978-3-319-10879-7_16

26. Cheon, J.H., Han, K., Lee, C., Ryu, H., Stehlé, D.: Cryptanalysis of the multilinear map over the integers. In: Oswald, E., Fischlin, M. (eds.) EUROCRYPT 2015. LNCS, vol. 9056, pp. 3–12. Springer, Heidelberg (2015). https://doi.org/10.1007/978-3-662-46800-5_1

27. Cheon, J.H., Fouque, P.-A., Lee, C., Minaud, B., Ryu, H.: Cryptanalysis of the new CLT multilinear map over the integers. In: Fischlin, M., Coron, J.-S. (eds.) EUROCRYPT 2016. LNCS, vol. 9665, pp. 509–536. Springer, Heidelberg (2016). https://doi.org/10.1007/978-3-662-49890-3_20

28. Cheon, J.H., Jeong, J., Lee, C.: An algorithm for NTRU problems and cryptanalysis of the GGH multilinear map without a low level encoding of zero. Eprint 2016/139

29. Coron, J.S., et al.: Zeroizing without low-level zeroes: new MMAP attacks and their limitations. In: Gennaro, R., Robshaw, M. (eds.) CRYPTO 2015. LNCS, vol. 9215, pp. 247–266. Springer, Heidelberg (2015). https://doi.org/10.1007/978-3-662-47989-6_12

30. Coron, J.-S., Lee, M.S., Lepoint, T., Tibouchi, M.: Zeroizing attacks on indistinguishability obfuscation over CLT13. In: Fehr, S. (ed.) PKC 2017. LNCS, vol. 10174, pp. 41–58. Springer, Heidelberg (2017). https://doi.org/10.1007/978-3-662-54365-8_3

31. Garg, S., Gentry, C., Halevi, S.: Candidate multilinear maps from ideal lattices. In: Johansson, T., Nguyen, P.Q. (eds.) EUROCRYPT 2013. LNCS, vol. 7881, pp. 1–17. Springer, Heidelberg (2013). https://doi.org/10.1007/978-3-642-38348-9_1

32. Garg, S., Gentry, C., Halevi, S., Raykova, M., Sahai, A., Waters, B.: Candidate indistinguishability obfuscation and functional encryption for all circuits. In: FOCS (2013). http://eprint.iacr.org/

33. Garg, S., Gentry, C., Sahai, A., Waters, B.: Witness encryption and its applications. In: STOC (2013)

34. Goldwasser, S., Kalai, Y.T., Popa, R.A., Vaikuntanathan, V., Zeldovich, N.: How to run turing machines on encrypted data. In: Canetti, R., Garay, J.A. (eds.) CRYPTO 2013. LNCS, vol. 8043, pp. 536–553. Springer, Heidelberg (2013). https://doi.org/10.1007/978-3-642-40084-1_30

35. Goldwasser, S., Kalai, Y.T., Popa, R.A., Vaikuntanathan, V., Zeldovich, N.: Reusable garbled circuits and succinct functional encryption. In: STOC, pp. 555–564 (2013)

36. Gong, J., Waters, B., Wee, H.: ABE for DFA from k-Lin. In: Boldyreva, A., Micciancio, D. (eds.) CRYPTO 2019. LNCS, vol. 11693, pp. 732–764. Springer, Cham (2019). https://doi.org/10.1007/978-3-030-26951-7_25

37. Gorbunov, S., Vaikuntanathan, V., Wee, H.: Attribute based encryption for circuits. In: STOC (2013)

38. Gorbunov, S., Vaikuntanathan, V., Wee, H.: Predicate encryption for circuits from LWE. In: Gennaro, R., Robshaw, M. (eds.) CRYPTO 2015. LNCS, vol. 9216, pp. 503–523. Springer, Heidelberg (2015). https://doi.org/10.1007/978-3-662-48000-7_25

39. Gorbunov, S., Vinayagamurthy, D.: Riding on asymmetry: efficient ABE for branching programs. In: Iwata, T., Cheon, J.H. (eds.) ASIACRYPT 2015. LNCS, vol. 9452, pp. 550–574. Springer, Heidelberg (2015). https://doi.org/10.1007/978-3-662-48797-6_23

40. Goyal, R., Koppula, V., Waters, B.: Semi-adaptive security and bundling functionalities made generic and easy. In: Hirt, M., Smith, A. (eds.) TCC 2016. LNCS, vol. 9986, pp. 361–388. Springer, Heidelberg (2016). https://doi.org/10.1007/978-3-662-53644-5_14

41. Goyal, V., Pandey, O., Sahai, A., Waters, B.: Attribute-based encryption for fine-grained access control of encrypted data. In: ACM Conference on Computer and Communications Security, pp. 89–98 (2006)

42. Hu, Y., Jia, H.: Cryptanalysis of GGH map. Cryptology ePrint Archive: Report 2015/301 (2015)

43. Katz, J., Sahai, A., Waters, B.: Predicate encryption supporting disjunctions, polynomial equations, and inner products. In: Smart, N. (ed.) EUROCRYPT 2008. LNCS, vol. 4965, pp. 146–162. Springer, Heidelberg (2008). https://doi.org/10.1007/978-3-540-78967-3_9

44. Kitagawa, F., Nishimaki, R., Tanaka, K., Yamakawa, T.: Adaptively secure and succinct functional encryption: Improving security and efficiency, simultaneously. Cryptology ePrint Archive, Report 2018/974 (2018). https://eprint.iacr.org/2018/974

45. Kowalczyk, L., Lewko, A.B.: Bilinear entropy expansion from the decisional linear assumption. In: Gennaro, R., Robshaw, M. (eds.) CRYPTO 2015. LNCS, vol. 9216, pp. 524–541. Springer, Heidelberg (2015). https://doi.org/10.1007/978-3-662-48000-7_26

46. Kowalczyk, L., Wee, H.: Compact adaptively secure ABE for NC 1 from k-Lin. In: Ishai, Y., Rijmen, V. (eds.) EUROCRYPT 2019. LNCS, vol. 11476, pp. 3–33. Springer, Cham (2019). https://doi.org/10.1007/978-3-030-17653-2_1

47. Lewko, A.: Tools for simulating features of composite order bilinear groups in the prime order setting. In: Pointcheval, D., Johansson, T. (eds.) EUROCRYPT 2012. LNCS, vol. 7237, pp. 318–335. Springer, Heidelberg (2012). https://doi.org/10.1007/978-3-642-29011-4_20

48. Lewko, A., Waters, B.: New techniques for dual system encryption and fully secure HIBE with short ciphertexts. In: Micciancio, D. (ed.) TCC 2010. LNCS, vol. 5978, pp. 455–479. Springer, Heidelberg (2010). https://doi.org/10.1007/978-3-642-11799-2_27

49. Lewko, A., Waters, B.: Unbounded HIBE and attribute-based encryption. In: Paterson, K.G. (ed.) EUROCRYPT 2011. LNCS, vol. 6632, pp. 547–567. Springer, Heidelberg (2011). https://doi.org/10.1007/978-3-642-20465-4_30

50. Lewko, A., Okamoto, T., Sahai, A., Takashima, K., Waters, B.: Fully secure functional encryption: attribute-based encryption and (hierarchical) inner product encryption. In: Gilbert, H. (ed.) EUROCRYPT 2010. LNCS, vol. 6110, pp. 62–91. Springer, Heidelberg (2010). https://doi.org/10.1007/978-3-642-13190-5_4

51. Lewko, A., Waters, B.: New proof methods for attribute-based encryption: achieving full security through selective techniques. In: Safavi-Naini, R., Canetti, R. (eds.) CRYPTO 2012. LNCS, vol. 7417, pp. 180–198. Springer, Heidelberg (2012). https://doi.org/10.1007/978-3-642-32009-5_12

52. Miles, E., Sahai, A., Zhandry, M.: Annihilation attacks for multilinear maps: cryptanalysis of indistinguishability obfuscation over GGH13. In: Robshaw, M., Katz, J. (eds.) CRYPTO 2016. LNCS, vol. 9815, pp. 629–658. Springer, Heidelberg (2016). https://doi.org/10.1007/978-3-662-53008-5_22

53. Okamoto, T., Takashima, K.: Fully secure functional encryption with general relations from the decisional linear assumption. In: Rabin, T. (ed.) CRYPTO 2010. LNCS, vol. 6223, pp. 191–208. Springer, Heidelberg (2010). https://doi.org/10.1007/978-3-642-14623-7_11

54. Okamoto, T., Takashima, K.: Fully secure unbounded inner-product and attribute-based encryption. In: Wang, X., Sako, K. (eds.) ASIACRYPT 2012. LNCS, vol. 7658, pp. 349–366. Springer, Heidelberg (2012). https://doi.org/10.1007/978-3-642-34961-4_22

55. Rouselakis, Y., Waters, B.: Practical constructions and new proof methods for large universe attribute-based encryption. In: Proceedings of the 2013 ACM SIGSAC Conference on Computer & #38; Communications Security CCS 2013 (2013)

56. Sahai, A., Waters, B.: Fuzzy identity-based encryption. In: Cramer, R. (ed.) EUROCRYPT 2005. LNCS, vol. 3494, pp. 457–473. Springer, Heidelberg (2005). https://doi.org/10.1007/11426639_27

57. Waters, B.: Functional encryption for regular languages. In: Safavi-Naini, R., Canetti, R. (eds.) CRYPTO 2012. LNCS, vol. 7417, pp. 218–235. Springer, Heidelberg (2012). https://doi.org/10.1007/978-3-642-32009-5_14

58. Wee, H.: Dual system encryption via predicate encodings. In: Lindell, Y. (ed.) TCC 2014. LNCS, vol. 8349, pp. 616–637. Springer, Heidelberg (2014). https://doi.org/10.1007/978-3-642-54242-8_26

CPA-to-CCA Transformation for KDM Security

Fuyuki Kitagawa[1]([⊠]) and Takahiro Matsuda[2]

[1] NTT Secure Platform Laboratories, Tokyo, Japan
fuyuki.kitagawa.yh@hco.ntt.co.jp
[2] National Institute of Advanced Industrial Science and Technology (AIST),
Tokyo, Japan
t-matsuda@aist.go.jp

Abstract. We show that chosen plaintext attacks (CPA) security is equivalent to chosen ciphertext attacks (CCA) security for key-dependent message (KDM) security. Concretely, we show how to construct a public-key encryption (PKE) scheme that is KDM-CCA secure with respect to all functions computable by circuits of a-priori bounded size, based only on a PKE scheme that is KDM-CPA secure with respect to projection functions. Our construction works for KDM security in the single user setting.

Our main result is achieved by combining the following two steps. First, we observe that by combining the results and techniques from the recent works by Lombardi et al. (CRYPTO 2019), and by Kitagawa et al. (CRYPTO 2019), we can construct a reusable designated-verifier non-interactive zero-knowledge (DV-NIZK) argument system based on an IND-CPA secure PKE scheme and a secret-key encryption (SKE) scheme satisfying one-time KDM security with respect to projection functions. This observation leads to the first reusable DV-NIZK argument system under the learning-parity-with-noise (LPN) assumption. Then, as the second and main technical step, we show a generic construction of a KDM-CCA secure PKE scheme using an IND-CPA secure PKE scheme, a reusable DV-NIZK argument system, and an SKE scheme satisfying one-time KDM security with respect to projection functions. Since the classical Naor-Yung paradigm (STOC 1990) with a DV-NIZK argument system does not work for proving KDM security, we propose a new construction methodology to achieve this generic construction.

Moreover, we show how to extend our generic construction and achieve KDM-CCA security in the multi-user setting, by additionally requiring the underlying SKE scheme in our generic construction to satisfy a weak form of KDM security against related-key attacks (RKA-KDM security) instead of one-time KDM security. From this extension, we obtain the first KDM-CCA secure PKE schemes in the multi-user setting under the CDH or LPN assumption.

Keywords: Public-key encryption · Key-dependent message security · Chosen ciphertext security · Designated-verifier non-interactive zero-knowledge argument

© International Association for Cryptologic Research 2019
D. Hofheinz and A. Rosen (Eds.): TCC 2019, LNCS 11892, pp. 118–148, 2019.
https://doi.org/10.1007/978-3-030-36033-7_5

1   Introduction

1.1   Background

The most basic security notion for public-key encryption (PKE) is indistinguishability against chosen plaintext attacks (IND-CPA security) [26]. Intuitively, IND-CPA security guarantees that an adversary can obtain no information about a message from its encryption, except for its length. However, in practice, PKE schemes should satisfy the stronger notion of indistinguishability against chosen ciphertext attacks (IND-CCA security) [37,38]. IND-CCA security implies non-malleability [7,20], and provides security guarantees against active adversaries [9].

Since IND-CCA security is stronger than IND-CPA security, the existence of IND-CCA secure PKE implies that of IND-CPA secure one. However, the implication of the opposite direction is not known. While a partial negative result was shown by Gertner, Malkin, and Myers [25], the question whether an IND-CCA secure PKE scheme can be constructed from an IND-CPA secure one has still been standing as a major open question in cryptography from both the theoretical and practical points of view.

In the literature, a number of efforts have been made for (implicitly or explicitly) tackling the problem. Among them, we highlight the two very recent works that make solid progress. Koppula and Waters [33] showed that an IND-CCA secure PKE scheme can be constructed from an IND-CPA secure one by using a pseudorandom generator (PRG) satisfying a special security notion. This additional primitive is called a *hinting PRG*. Subsequently, Kitagawa, Matsuda, and Tanaka [30] showed that a transformation from an IND-CPA secure PKE scheme to an IND-CCA secure one is also possible by using a secret-key encryption (SKE) scheme satisfying one-time key-dependent message security [8] instead of a hinting PRG.

We further study the question of CPA security vs CCA security. Many previous works focusing on this question sought an additional assumption that bridges IND-CPA security and IND-CCA security. In this work, we tackle the question from a somewhat different angle. Concretely, we aim at finding a security notion under which CPA security and CCA security are equivalent. As far as we know, such an equivalence is not known for any security notion for PKE schemes (e.g., leakage resilience, key-dependent message security, and selective opening security). Finding such a security notion is an important question in the theoretical study of public-key cryptography. Moreover, we believe that clarifying for what types of notions CPA security and CCA security are equivalent potentially gives us new insights for the major open question on the equivalence between IND-CPA security and IND-CCA security.

Based on the above motivation, in this work, we study the equivalence of CPA security and CCA security for *key-dependent message (KDM) security* [8]. Informally, KDM security guarantees that an encryption scheme can securely encrypt messages that depend on its own secret key. We can see some connections between IND-CCA security and KDM-CPA security from several previous results [27, 30, 36], and thus KDM security can be considered as one of the best candidates for which CPA security and CCA security could be shown equivalent. Moreover, KDM security is important and interesting enough to be studied in its own right since it has found a number of applications in both theoretical and practical studies in cryptography, e.g., anonymous credentials [15], formal methods [1], hard-disc encryption [10], fully homomorphic encryption [24], non-interactive zero-knowledge proofs [16, 17], and homomorphic secret-sharing [11].

1.2 Our Results

As noted above, we study the equivalence between CPA security and CCA security for KDM security. Then, we obtain the following main theorem.

Theorem 1 (Informal). *Assume that there exists a KDM-CPA secure PKE scheme. Then, there exists a KDM-CCA secure PKE scheme.*

We show this theorem for KDM-CPA security and KDM-CCA security in the single user setting. The underlying scheme needs to be KDM-CPA secure with respect to functions called *projection functions* ($\mathcal{P}$-KDM-CPA secure). The family of projection functions is one of the simplest classes of functions, and KDM security with respect to this function class has been widely studied [5, 10, 12, 13, 22]. The resulting scheme is KDM-CCA secure with respect to all functions computable by circuits of a-priori bounded size. The achieved security notion is the CCA-analogue of the notion called *bounded KDM security* by Barak, Haitner, Hofheinz, and Ishai [6].

We obtain Theorem 1 by combining the following two steps.

Reusable DV-NIZK Based on One-Time KDM Secure SKE. A *designated-verifier non-interactive zero-knowledge* (DV-NIZK) argument system is a relaxation of a standard NIZK argument system in the common reference string model (CRS-NIZK, for short), and allows a verifier to have its own public/secret key pair; The public key is used to generate a proof non-interactively, which can be verified by using the corresponding secret key. A DV-NIZK argument system is said to be *reusable* if its soundness (resp. zero-knowledge property) is maintained even if an adversary can make multiple verification (resp. proving) queries. It was recently shown by Lombardi, Quach, Rothblum, Wichs, and Wu [34] that a reusable DV-NIZK argument system can be constructed from the combination of an IND-CPA secure PKE scheme and a hinting PRG introduced by Koppula and Waters [33].

As the first step for Theorem 1, we observe that we can construct a reusable DV-NIZK argument system based on an IND-CPA secure PKE scheme and an SKE scheme that is one-time KDM secure with respect to projection functions (one-time $\mathcal{P}$-KDM secure), by combining the results and techniques from the recent works by Lombardi et al. [34] and Kitagawa et al. [30].

In fact, this is somewhat obvious from the results [30, 34] and not our main contribution. However, this observation leads to the following interesting implications. A one-time $\mathcal{P}$-KDM secure SKE scheme can be constructed based on the polynomial hardness of the constant-noise learning-parity-with-noise (LPN) assumption [5]. Moreover, we can construct an IND-CPA secure PKE scheme based on the polynomial hardness of the low-noise LPN assumption [2] or the sub-exponential hardness of the constant-noise LPN assumption [41]. Thus, combined together, our observation leads to the first reusable DV-NIZK argument system based on either the polynomial hardness of the low-noise LPN assumption or the sub-exponential hardness of the constant-noise LPN assumption.

We note that the exact same observation (i.e. a reusable DV-NIZK argument system based on IND-CPA secure PKE and one-time $\mathcal{P}$-KDM secure SKE, and the LPN-based instantiation) was very recently made independently and concurrently by Lombardi et al. [35].

Generic Construction of KDM-CCA Secure PKE Using Reusable DV-NIZK. Then, as the second and main technical step for Theorem 1, we show a generic construction of KDM-CCA secure PKE based on the following five building blocks: an IND-CPA secure PKE scheme, an IND-CCA secure PKE scheme, a one-time $\mathcal{P}$-KDM secure SKE scheme, a garbling scheme, and a reusable DV-NIZK argument system.

In the first step above, we show how to construct a reusable DV-NIZK argument system from an IND-CPA secure PKE scheme and a one-time $\mathcal{P}$-KDM secure SKE scheme. Also, IND-CCA secure PKE can be constructed from the same building blocks [30]. Moreover, a garbling scheme can be constructed from one-way functions [40], which is in turn implied by other building blocks. Therefore, through our generic construction, we can construct a KDM-CCA secure PKE scheme based on an IND-CPA secure PKE scheme and a one-time $\mathcal{P}$-KDM secure SKE scheme. Since both of the underlying primitives are implied by $\mathcal{P}$-KDM-CPA secure PKE, we obtain Theorem 1.

We highlight that our construction can "amplify" KDM security in terms of not only the class of functions (from projection functions to circuits of a-priori bounded size) but also the number of KDM-encryption queries allowed for an adversary. Specifically, among the building blocks, the only "KDM-secure" component is the *one-time* $\mathcal{P}$-KDM secure SKE scheme, while our construction achieves the standard *many-time* KDM-CCA security. For more details, see Sect. 2.3.

One might think that if we can use a reusable DV-NIZK argument system, a KDM-CPA secure PKE scheme can easily be transformed into a KDM-CCA secure one by the Naor-Yung paradigm [37]. In fact, if the goal is to achieve an IND-CCA secure PKE scheme, then it is possible to replace a CRS-NIZK argument system in the Naor-Yung paradigm with a reusable DV-NIZK argument system. Furthermore, Camenisch, Chandran, and Shoup [14] showed that (a slight variant of) the Naor-Yung paradigm with a CRS-NIZK argument system can be used to transform a KDM-CPA secure PKE scheme into a KDM-CCA secure one. Unfortunately, however, things are not so easy if we aim at achieving KDM-CCA security using a reusable DV-NIZK argument system via the Naor-Yung paradigm (or its existing variants). The main cause of difficulty is that if we apply the standard Naor-Yung paradigm using a DV-NIZK argument system, the secret verification key of the DV-NIZK argument system is included in the secret key of the resulting scheme, and a circularity involving a DV-NIZK argument system occurs in the KDM-CCA security game. Our main technical contribution is circumventing this difficulty. We will detail the difficulty as well as our techniques in Sect. 2.

KDM-CCA Security in the Multi-user Setting Based on New Assumptions. Although our main focus in this work is on showing that KDM-CPA security and KDM-CCA security are equivalent, through the above results, we obtain the *first* KDM-CCA secure PKE schemes based on the computational Diffie-Hellman (CDH) assumption and the LPN assumption, since KDM-CPA secure PKE schemes can be constructed under these assumptions [13, 21, 22]. These schemes satisfy only KDM-CCA security in the single user setting, since so does our generic construction, as noted earlier.

We then show how to extend our generic construction and achieve a PKE scheme satisfying KDM-CCA security in the multi-user setting under the CDH and LPN assumptions. This is done by requiring the underlying SKE scheme in our generic construction to satisfy a variant of *KDM security against related-key attacks (RKA-KDM security)* [4], instead of one-time KDM security. (We also require a mild property that a secret key is a uniformly distributed random string.) An SKE scheme satisfying our definition of RKA-KDM security can be constructed based on the (polynomial hardness of) constant-noise LPN assumption [4]. Moreover, we show how to construct an SKE scheme satisfying our RKA-KDM security notion based on hash encryption [13, 22], which in turn can be based on the CDH assumption. This construction is an extension of a KDM-CPA secure PKE scheme based on batch encryption proposed by Brakerski, Lombardi, Segev, and Vaikuntanathan [13].

Due to the space constraint, we omit the construction of an RKA-KDM secure SKE scheme using a hash encryption scheme from the proceedings version. For the construction, see the full version.

1.3   Related Work

Generic Constructions for KDM-CCA Secure PKE. To the best of our knowledge, the only existing generic methods for constructing KDM-CCA secure PKE, are the works by Camenisch, Chandran, and Shoup [14], by Galindo, Herrantz, and Villar [23], and by Kitagawa and Tanaka [31]. Camenisch et al. [14] showed how to construct a KDM-CCA secure PKE scheme from a KDM-CPA secure PKE scheme, an IND-CCA secure PKE scheme, and a CRS-NIZK proof (or argument) system. (We will touch it in Sect. 2.) Galindo et al. [23] showed how to construct a KDM-CCA secure PKE scheme from an identity-based encryption scheme which satisfies so-called master-key-dependent message security, via the transformation by Canetti, Halevi, and Katz [18]. However, the only known instantiation of Galindo et al.'s method can achieve security against adversaries that make an a-priori bounded number of master-key-KDM-encryption queries, which is translated to KDM-CCA security against adversaries that make an a-priori bounded number of KDM-encryption queries. Kitagawa and Tanaka [31] showed how to construct a KDM-CCA secure PKE scheme based on a hash proof system [19] satisfying some homomorphic property. It is not obvious how to modify the methods of [23,31] to achieve a generic construction of a KDM-CCA secure PKE scheme starting from a KDM-CPA secure one.

2   Technical Overview

In this section, we provide a technical overview of our main results. As mentioned in the introduction and will be detailed in Sect. 4, we can observe from the previous results [30,34] that a reusable DV-NIZK argument system can be constructed based on the combination of an IND-CPA secure PKE scheme and a one-time KDM secure SKE scheme. Thus, in this overview, we mainly focus on the generic construction of a PKE scheme that is KDM-CCA secure in the single user setting using a reusable DV-NIZK argument system. (From here on, we drop "reusable".) We also briefly explain how to extend it into the multi-user setting by using RKA-KDM secure SKE. We start with why we cannot achieve such a generic construction by using the standard Naor-Yung paradigm [37].

2.1   Naor-Yung Paradigm with DV-NIZK Fails for KDM

Camenisch, Chandran, and Shoup [14] showed that the Naor-Yung paradigm with a CRS-NIZK argument system goes through for KDM security. We first review their construction, and then explain the problems that arise when replacing the underlying CRS-NIZK argument system with a DV-NIZK argument system.

KDM-CCA PKE by Camenisch et al. [14]. The construction uses a KDM-CPA secure PKE scheme PKE, an IND-CCA secure PKE scheme PKE', and a CRS-NIZK argument system NIZK.[1] Using these building blocks, we construct $\mathsf{PKE_{NY}}$ as follows. A public key of $\mathsf{PKE_{NY}}$ consists of $(\mathsf{pk}, \mathsf{pk_{cca}}, \mathsf{crs})$, where pk and $\mathsf{pk_{cca}}$ are public keys of PKE and PKE', respectively, and crs is a CRS of NIZK. The corresponding secret key is sk corresponding to pk. The secret key $\mathsf{sk_{cca}}$ corresponding to $\mathsf{pk_{cca}}$ is discarded and used only in the security proof. When encrypting a message m, $\mathsf{PKE_{NY}}$ generates a ciphertext of the form

$$\left(\mathsf{ct} = \mathsf{Enc_{pk}}(m), \ \mathsf{ct_{cca}} = \mathsf{Enc'_{pk_{cca}}}(m), \ \pi \right),$$

where Enc and Enc' denote the encryption algorithms of PKE and PKE', respectively, and π is a proof of NIZK proving that ct and $\mathsf{ct_{cca}}$ encrypt the same message, generated by using m and random coins used to generate ct and $\mathsf{ct_{cca}}$

---

[1] In their actual construction, a one-time signature scheme is also used. We ignore it in this overview for simplicity, since the problem we explain below is unrelated to it.

as a witness. When decrypting the ciphertext, we first check whether the proof π is accepted or not. If π is accepted, we decrypt ct by using sk, and recover m.

Camenisch et al. showed that PKE_{NY} is KDM-CCA secure for a function class $\mathcal{F}$ with respect to which the underlying PKE scheme PKE satisfies KDM-CPA security.[2]

Circularity Involving DV-NIZK. We now explain why the above construction technique by Camenisch et al. does not work if we use a DV-NIZK argument system instead of a CRS-NIZK argument system.

If we use a DV-NIZK argument system DVNIZK instead of NIZK as a building block of PKE_{NY}, then we need a secret key sk_{dv} of DVNIZK to verify a proof contained in a ciphertext when decrypting the ciphertext. Thus, we have to include sk_{dv} into the secret key of PKE_{NY}.

In this case, an encryption of a message of the form $f(sk\|sk_{dv})$ is given to an adversary in the KDM-CCA security game, where f is a function chosen by the adversary as a KDM-encryption query. Then, there is a circularity problem involving not only encryption schemes but also DVNIZK, since *when encrypting a message $f(sk\|sk_{dv})$, a proof of DVNIZK is generated to guarantee that encryptions of its own secret key sk_{dv} are well-formed.* Even if such a circularity exists, we can use the zero-knowledge property of DVNIZK in the security proof since a reduction algorithm attacking the zero-knowledge property is given a secret verification key sk_{dv} and thus can handle such a circularity. However, we cannot use its soundness property in the security proof unless we solve the circularity, because a secret verification key sk_{dv} is not directly given to an adversary attacking the soundness of DVNIZK.

Due to this circularity problem involving a DV-NIZK argument system, it seems difficult to achieve a KDM-CCA secure PKE scheme using a DV-NIZK variant of the Naor-Yung paradigm.

2.2 How to Solve the Circularity Problem Involving DV-NIZK?

The circularity problem involving a DV-NIZK argument system of PKE_{NY} occurs because in the security game, a message depending on sk_{dv} is encrypted by encryption schemes the validity of whose ciphertexts is proved by the DV-NIZK argument system. In order to solve this circularity problem, we have to design a scheme so that it has an *indirection* that a message is not directly encrypted by encryption schemes related to a DV-NIZK argument system.

The most standard way to add such an indirection to encryption schemes would be to use the hybrid encryption methodology. However, it is difficult to use the hybrid encryption methodology to construct a KDM-CCA secure scheme, since it leads to a dead-lock in the sense that the key encapsulation mechanism and data encapsulation mechanism could encrypt each other's secret key in the presence of key-dependent messages.

---

[2] We note that in this construction, NIZK need not satisfy the simulation soundness property [39], and we can complete the proof based on the ordinary soundness (and zero-knowledge) property of NIZK.

Thus, we use a different technique. We use a *garbling scheme* [40] to realize the indirection that a message is not directly encrypted by encryption schemes related to a DV-NIZK argument system.[3] Concretely, when encrypting a message m, we first garble a circuit into which m is hardwired. Then, we encrypt each of the labels generated together with the garbled circuit by a PKE scheme, and then generate a proof proving that the encryptions of the labels are well-formed by using a DV-NIZK argument system.

In order to realize the above idea using a garbling scheme, we use a one-time KDM secure SKE scheme at the key generation to encrypt (and add to a public key) secret key components of the building block PKE schemes. With the help of a one-time KDM secure SKE scheme, a garbling scheme makes it possible to simulate an encryption of the secret key without directly using the secret key itself, and we can prove the (multi-time) KDM security of the resulting scheme, which has the indirection.

Below, we first show the KDM-CPA variant of our construction without using a DV-NIZK argument system. Then, we show how to extend it into a KDM-CCA secure one.

2.3 KDM-CPA Variant of Our Construction

In the following, we show how to construct a KDM-CPA secure PKE scheme $\mathsf{PKE}^*_{\mathsf{kdm}}$ from a garbling scheme, a one-time KDM secure SKE scheme SKE, and IND-CPA secure PKE schemes PKE and PKE$'$.

Construction Using Garbled Circuits. The key generation algorithm generates a key pair $(\mathsf{PK}, \mathsf{SK})$ of $\mathsf{PKE}^*_{\mathsf{kdm}}$ as follows. It first generates a secret key $s = (s_1, \ldots, s_{\ell_s}) \in \{0,1\}^{\ell_s}$ of SKE. Next, it generates a key pair $(\mathsf{pk}', \mathsf{sk}')$ of PKE$'$ and $2\ell_s$ key pairs $(\mathsf{pk}_{j,\alpha}, \mathsf{sk}_{j,\alpha})_{j \in [\ell_s], \alpha \in \{0,1\}}$ of PKE. Then, it encrypts $\ell_s + 1$ secret keys sk' and $(\mathsf{sk}_{j,s_j})_{j \in [\ell_s]}$ into $\mathsf{ct}_{\mathsf{ske}}$ by SKE under the key s. The public-key PK consists of $2\ell_s + 1$ public keys pk' and $(\mathsf{pk}_{j,\alpha})_{j \in [\ell_s], \alpha \in \{0,1\}}$, and $\mathsf{ct}_{\mathsf{ske}}$. The corresponding secret key SK is just s. Namely, PK and SK are of the form

$$\mathsf{PK} = \Big((\mathsf{pk}_{j,\alpha})_{j \in [\ell_s], \alpha \in \{0,1\}}, \ \mathsf{pk}', \ \mathsf{ct}_{\mathsf{ske}} = \mathsf{E}_s(\mathsf{sk}', (\mathsf{sk}_{j,s_j})_{j \in [\ell_s]}) \Big) \quad \text{and} \quad \mathsf{SK} = s,$$

respectively, where $\mathsf{E}_s(\cdot)$ denotes the encryption algorithm of SKE using the key s.

When encrypting a message m under PK, $\mathsf{PKE}^*_{\mathsf{kdm}}$ first garbles a constant circuit Q that has m hardwired and outputs it for any input of length ℓ_s.[4] This results in a single garbled circuit $\tilde{\mathsf{Q}}$ and $2\ell_s$ labels $(\mathsf{lab}_{j,\alpha})_{j \in [\ell_s], \alpha \in \{0,1\}}$. Then,

---

[3] The following explanations assume that the reader is familiar with a garbling scheme. See Sect. 3.5 for its formal definition.

[4] In the actual construction, we use a garbled circuit and labels that are generated by the simulator of the garbling scheme, instead of those generated by garbling a constant circuit. This makes the security proof simpler. We ignore this treatment here for the simplicity of the explanation.

the encryption algorithm encrypts "0-labels" $\mathsf{lab}_{j,0}$ into $\mathsf{ct}_{j,\alpha}$ by $\mathsf{pk}_{j,\alpha}$ for every $j \in [\ell_\mathsf{s}]$ and $\alpha \in \{0, 1\}$. It finally encrypts $\widetilde{\mathsf{Q}}$ and those encrypted labels $(\mathsf{ct}_{j,\alpha})_{j,\alpha}$ using pk'. The resulting ciphertext CT is of the form

$$\mathsf{CT} = \mathsf{Enc}'_{\mathsf{pk}'} \left(\widetilde{\mathsf{Q}}, \ (\mathsf{ct}_{j,0} = \mathsf{Enc}_{\mathsf{pk}_{j,0}}(\mathsf{lab}_{j,0}), \ \mathsf{ct}_{j,1} = \mathsf{Enc}_{\mathsf{pk}_{j,1}}(\mathsf{lab}_{j,0}))_{j \in [\ell_\mathsf{s}]} \right),$$

where Enc and Enc' are the encryption algorithms of PKE and PKE', respectively. We stress that for every $j \in [n]$, the same label $\mathsf{lab}_{j,0}$ is encrypted under both $\mathsf{pk}_{j,0}$ and $\mathsf{pk}_{j,1}$.

When decrypting the ciphertext CT using the secret key $\mathsf{SK} = s$, we first retrieve the secret keys sk' and $(\mathsf{sk}_{j,s_j})_{j \in [\ell_\mathsf{s}]}$ from $\mathsf{ct}_{\mathsf{ske}}$ contained in PK. Then, using sk', we recover $\widetilde{\mathsf{Q}}$ and $(\mathsf{ct}_{j,\alpha})_{j \in [\ell_\mathsf{s}], \alpha \in \{0,1\}}$. Moreover, we recover the "0-label" $\mathsf{lab}_{j,0}$ from ct_{j,s_j} using sk_{j,s_j} for every $j \in [\ell_\mathsf{s}]$. Finally, we evaluate the recovered garbled circuit $\widetilde{\mathsf{Q}}$ with these ℓ_s "0-labels" by the evaluation algorithm of the garbling scheme. This results in m, since given 0^{ℓ_s}, Q outputs m.

Overview of the Security Proof of $\mathsf{PKE}^*_{\mathsf{kdm}}$. We explain how we prove the KDM-CPA security in the single user setting of $\mathsf{PKE}^*_{\mathsf{kdm}}$. Specifically, we explain that no adversary $\mathcal{A}$ can guess the challenge bit b with probability significantly greater than $1/2$ given an encryption of $f_b(\mathsf{SK}) = f_b(s)$, when $\mathcal{A}$ queries two functions (f_0, f_1) as a KDM-encryption query.[5]

In this construction, the secret keys of PKE corresponding to s, namely $(\mathsf{sk}_{j,s_j})_{j \in [\ell_\mathsf{s}]}$, are encrypted in $\mathsf{ct}_{\mathsf{ske}}$, but the rest of the secret keys $(\mathsf{sk}_{j,1 \oplus s_j})_{j \in [\ell_\mathsf{s}]}$ are hidden from $\mathcal{A}$'s view. Thus, in the security proof, we can always use the IND-CPA security of PKE under the public keys $(\mathsf{pk}_{j,1 \oplus s_j})_{j \in [\ell_\mathsf{s}]}$. By combining the IND-CPA security of PKE under these keys with the security of the garbling scheme, we can change the security game so that the encryption of $f_b(s)$ given to $\mathcal{A}$ can be simulated without using s, without being noticed by $\mathcal{A}$. Concretely, in the modified security game, an encryption of $f_b(s)$ is generated as follows. We first generate $\widetilde{\mathsf{Q}}$ and $(\mathsf{lab}_{j,\alpha})_{j \in [\ell_\mathsf{s}], \alpha \in \{0,1\}}$ by garbling a circuit computing f_b, instead of a constant circuit Q in which $f_b(s)$ is hardwired. Then, we encrypt $\mathsf{lab}_{j,\alpha}$ into $\mathsf{ct}_{j,\alpha}$ by $\mathsf{pk}_{j,\alpha}$ for every $j \in [\ell_\mathsf{s}]$ and $\alpha \in \{0, 1\}$. Finally, we encrypt $\widetilde{\mathsf{Q}}$ and those encrypted labels $(\mathsf{ct}_{j,\alpha})_{j,\alpha}$ using pk', and obtain $\mathsf{CT} = \mathsf{Enc}_{\mathsf{pk}'}(\widetilde{\mathsf{Q}}, (\mathsf{ct}_{j,0}, \mathsf{ct}_{j,1})_{j \in [\ell_\mathsf{s}]})$. We see that we now do not need s to generate CT. The explanation so far in fact works even when $\mathcal{A}$ makes multiple KDM-encryption queries.

After the above change, a ciphertext CT given to $\mathcal{A}$ does not have any information of s, and thus we can use the one-time KDM security of SKE. Although

---

[5] Usually, KDM security requires that an encryption of $f(\mathsf{SK})$ be indistinguishable from that of some constant message such as $0^{|f(\cdot)|}$ instead of requiring encryptions of $f_0(\mathsf{SK})$ and $f_1(\mathsf{SK})$ be indistinguishable, where f, f_0, and f_1 are functions chosen by adversaries. However, these definitions are equivalent if a function class with respect to which we consider KDM security contains constant functions, which is the case in this paper.

the message $(\mathsf{sk}', (\mathsf{sk}_{j,s_j})_{j\in[\ell_s]})$ encrypted in $\mathsf{ct}_{\mathsf{ske}}$ depends on the secret key s, by relying on the one-time KDM security of SKE, we can further change the security game so that $\mathsf{ct}_{\mathsf{ske}}$ is generated as an encryption of some constant message such as the all-zero string. Then, since sk' is now hidden from $\mathcal{A}$'s view, we can argue that $\mathcal{A}$'s advantage in the final game is essentially $1/2$ based on the IND-CPA security of PKE'. This completes the proof for the KDM-CPA security of $\mathsf{PKE}^*_{\mathsf{kdm}}$.

Features of $\mathsf{PKE}^*_{\mathsf{kdm}}$. This KDM-CPA secure construction $\mathsf{PKE}^*_{\mathsf{kdm}}$ has some nice properties. First, all of the building blocks are implied by KDM-CPA secure PKE. (Recall that a garbling scheme can be realized from one-way functions [40].) Moreover, through this construction, we can transform a one-time KDM-CPA secure scheme into a (multi-time) KDM-CPA secure PKE scheme. Also, the resulting scheme satisfies KDM-CPA security with respect to all functions computable by circuits of a-priori bounded size even though the underlying KDM-CPA secure scheme needs to satisfy a much weaker form of KDM-CPA security. Concretely, the underlying scheme needs to be only KDM-CPA secure with respect to projection functions, since the encrypted message $(\mathsf{sk}', (\mathsf{sk}_{j,s_j})_{j\in[\ell_s]})$ can be seen as an output of a function $g(x_1, \ldots, x_{\ell_s}) = (\mathsf{sk}', (\mathsf{sk}_{j,x_j})_{j\in[\ell_s]})$, which can be described as a projection function of an input $x = (x_1, \ldots, x_{\ell_s}) \in \{0,1\}^{\ell_s}$ that has $(\mathsf{sk}', (\mathsf{sk}_{j,\alpha})_{j\in[\ell_s], \alpha\in\{0,1\}})$ hardwired. From these facts, in the single user setting, the construction $\mathsf{PKE}^*_{\mathsf{kdm}}$ in fact improves the previous amplification methods for KDM-CPA secure schemes [3,22,32]. In addition, most importantly, $\mathsf{PKE}^*_{\mathsf{kdm}}$ can be easily extended into a KDM-CCA secure one by using a DV-NIZK argument system.

2.4 KDM-CCA Secure PKE Using DV-NIZK

We extend $\mathsf{PKE}^*_{\mathsf{kdm}}$ into a KDM-CCA secure PKE scheme $\mathsf{PKE}_{\mathsf{kdm}}$ by the following two steps.

First, we use a DV-NIZK argument system DVNIZK for proving that encrypted labels are well-formed. Concretely, we use it in the following manner. When generating a key pair $(\mathsf{PK}, \mathsf{SK})$ of $\mathsf{PKE}_{\mathsf{kdm}}$, we additionally generate a key pair $(\mathsf{pk}_{\mathsf{dv}}, \mathsf{sk}_{\mathsf{dv}})$ of DVNIZK, and add $\mathsf{pk}_{\mathsf{dv}}$ to PK. Moreover, we encrypt $\mathsf{sk}_{\mathsf{dv}}$ into $\mathsf{ct}_{\mathsf{ske}}$ together with $(\mathsf{sk}', (\mathsf{sk}_{j,s_j})_{j\in[\ell_s]})$ by using s. Namely, PK is of the form

$$\mathsf{PK} = \Big((\mathsf{pk}_{j,\alpha})_{j\in[\ell_s], \alpha\in\{0,1\}}, \ \mathsf{pk}', \ \mathsf{pk}_{\mathsf{dv}}, \ \mathsf{ct}_{\mathsf{ske}} = E_s(\mathsf{sk}', \mathsf{sk}_{\mathsf{dv}}, (\mathsf{sk}_{j,s_j})_{j\in[\ell_s]}) \Big).$$

The secret key SK is still only $s = (s_1, \ldots, s_{\ell_s}) \in \{0,1\}^{\ell_s}$. When encrypting a message m, we first generate $\widetilde{\mathsf{Q}}$ and $(\mathsf{ct}_{j,0}, \mathsf{ct}_{j,1})_{j\in[\ell_s]}$ in the same way as $\mathsf{PKE}^*_{\mathsf{kdm}}$. Then, using $\mathsf{pk}_{\mathsf{dv}}$, we generate a proof π of DVNIZK proving that $\mathsf{ct}_{j,0}$ and $\mathsf{ct}_{j,1}$ encrypt the same message for every $j \in [\ell_s]$, by using $\mathsf{lab}_{j,0}$ and random coins used to generate $\mathsf{ct}_{j,0}$ and $\mathsf{ct}_{j,1}$ as a witness.

Next, in order to make the entire part of the ciphertext non-malleable, we require that PKE' satisfy IND-CCA security instead of IND-CPA security, and encrypt $\widetilde{Q}$, the encrypted labels $(\mathsf{ct}_{j,0}, \mathsf{ct}_{j,1})_{j \in [\ell_s]}$, and the proof π, using pk' of PKE'. Therefore, the resulting ciphertext CT is of the form

$$\mathsf{CT} = \mathsf{Enc}'_{\mathsf{pk}'} \left(\widetilde{Q}, \ (\mathsf{ct}_{j,0} = \mathsf{Enc}_{\mathsf{pk}_{j,0}}(\mathsf{lab}_{j,0}), \ \mathsf{ct}_{j,1} = \mathsf{Enc}_{\mathsf{pk}_{j,1}}(\mathsf{lab}_{j,0}))_{j \in [\ell_s]}, \ \pi \right).$$

We perform the decryption of this ciphertext in the same way as before, except that we additionally check whether π is accepted or not by using $\mathsf{sk}_{\mathsf{dv}}$ retrieved from $\mathsf{ct}_{\mathsf{ske}}$, and if it is not accepted, the ciphertext is rejected.

As mentioned earlier (and will be detailed in Sect. 4), by combining the techniques from the two recent results [30, 34], a DV-NIZK argument system can be based on the same building blocks. Moreover, an IND-CCA secure PKE scheme can also be based on the same building blocks [30]. Thus, similarly to $\mathsf{PKE}^*_{\mathsf{kdm}}$, all the building blocks of $\mathsf{PKE}_{\mathsf{kdm}}$ can be based on the combination of an IND-CPA secure PKE scheme and a one-time KDM secure SKE scheme, which are in turn both implied by a KDM-CPA secure PKE scheme.

Overview of the Security Proof of $\mathsf{PKE}_{\mathsf{kdm}}$. At first glance, the circularity involving DVNIZK occurs when encrypting a key-dependent message $f(\mathsf{SK}) = f(s) = \mathsf{sk}_{\mathsf{dv}}$ by $\mathsf{PKE}_{\mathsf{kdm}}$, where f is a function that, given s as input, retrieves $\mathsf{sk}_{\mathsf{dv}}$ from $\mathsf{ct}_{\mathsf{ske}}$ by using s and outputs $\mathsf{sk}_{\mathsf{dv}}$. This is because DVNIZK is used to generate a proof that proves $\mathsf{ct}_{j,0}$ and $\mathsf{ct}_{j,1}$ encrypt the same label, and the labels may contain some information of the key-dependent message $f(s)$ since it is generated by garbling a constant circuit Q into which $f(s)$ is hardwired. However, due to the indirection that $\mathsf{sk}_{\mathsf{dv}}$ is not encrypted by encryption schemes the validity of whose ciphertexts is proved by the DV-NIZK argument system, we can solve the circularity and prove the KDM-CCA security of $\mathsf{PKE}_{\mathsf{kdm}}$ by adding some modifications to the proof for the KDM-CPA security of $\mathsf{PKE}^*_{\mathsf{kdm}}$ explained in the previous section.

First of all, the zero-knowledge property of DVNIZK allows us to change the security game so that we use the simulator for the zero-knowledge property to generate the DV-NIZK key pair $(\mathsf{pk}_{\mathsf{dv}}, \mathsf{sk}_{\mathsf{dv}})$ at the key generation, and we use the simulator also for generating a fake proof π in a ciphertext when responding to KDM-encryption queries. Then, similarly to what we do in the proof for $\mathsf{PKE}^*_{\mathsf{kdm}}$, we can change the security game so that we do not need s for responding to KDM-encryption queries by using the security of the garbling scheme and the IND-CPA security of PKE under public keys $(\mathsf{pk}_{j,1 \oplus s_j})_{j \in [\ell_s]}$. However, differently from the proof for the KDM-CPA security of $\mathsf{PKE}^*_{\mathsf{kdm}}$, we cannot use the one-time KDM security of SKE immediately after this change. This is because we still need s for responding to decryption queries. More specifically, when responding to a decryption query, we have to decrypt the "s_j-side" ciphertext ct_{j,s_j} of PKE using sk_{j,s_j} for every $j \in [\ell_s]$ to recover the labels of a garbled circuit.[6] Thus, before using the one-time KDM security of SKE, we change the security game

---

[6] Strictly speaking, we also use s to retrieve $(\mathsf{sk}', \mathsf{sk}_{\mathsf{dv}}, (\mathsf{sk}_{j,s_j})_{j \in [\ell_s]})$ from $\mathsf{ct}_{\mathsf{ske}}$. However, we can omit this decryption process and use $(\mathsf{sk}', \mathsf{sk}_{\mathsf{dv}}, (\mathsf{sk}_{j,s_j})_{j \in [\ell_s]})$ directly without changing the view of an adversary, and thus we ignore this issue here.

so that we do not need s to respond to decryption queries by relying on the soundness of DVNIZK.

Concretely, we change the security game so that when responding to a decryption query CT, we *always* decrypt the "0-side" ciphertext $\mathsf{ct}_{j,0}$ of PKE using $\mathsf{sk}_{j,0}$ for every $j \in [\ell_s]$. Although we cannot justify this change based solely on the soundness of DVNIZK, we can justify it by combining the soundness and zero-knowledge property of DVNIZK, the one-time KDM security of SKE, and the IND-CCA security of PKE′ using a *deferred analysis* technique. This technique of justifying changes for decryption queries using the deferred analysis originates in the context of expanding the message space of IND-CCA secure PKE schemes [28], and was already shown to be useful in the context of KDM-CCA security [29,31]. In fact, the indirection explained so far makes it possible to use the deferred analysis technique.

Once we change how decryption queries are answered in this way, we can complete the remaining part of the proof based on the one-time KDM security of SKE and the IND-CCA security of PKE′ similarly to the proof for the KDM-CPA security of $\mathsf{PKE}^*_{\mathsf{kdm}}$.

Is It Essential to Encrypt $\mathsf{sk}_{\mathsf{dv}}$ *into* $\mathsf{ct}_{\mathsf{ske}}$? It is *not* essential to maintain $\mathsf{sk}_{\mathsf{dv}}$ (and sk′) in the encrypted form $\mathsf{ct}_{\mathsf{ske}}$ by the key s and make SK consist only of s. In fact, we can consider a variant of $\mathsf{PKE}_{\mathsf{kdm}}$ such that we set $\mathsf{SK} := (s, \mathsf{sk}_{\mathsf{dv}}, \mathsf{sk}')$. In this case, we use $2 \cdot \ell_{\mathsf{SK}} = 2 \cdot (|s| + |\mathsf{sk}_{\mathsf{dv}}| + |\mathsf{sk}'|)$ key pairs of PKE, and we generate $\mathsf{ct}_{\mathsf{ske}}$ as an encryption of $(\mathsf{sk}_{j,\mathsf{SK}_j})_{j \in [\ell_{\mathsf{SK}}]}$ by s, where SK_j is the j-th bit of SK for every $j \in [\ell_{\mathsf{SK}}]$. Even if we adopt such a construction, we can realize an indirection that is sufficient to use the deferred analysis technique, and we can prove its KDM-CCA security similarly to the above.

The security proof for $\mathsf{PKE}_{\mathsf{kdm}}$ is simpler than that for the above variant. Moreover, as we will explain below, we need to encrypt $\mathsf{sk}_{\mathsf{dv}}$ and sk′ and make $\mathsf{SK} = s$ when considering KDM-CCA security in the multi-user setting. For these reasons, we adopt the current construction of $\mathsf{PKE}_{\mathsf{kdm}}$.

2.5   Extension to KDM-CCA Security in the Multi-user Setting

We finally explain how to extend the above construction $\mathsf{PKE}_{\mathsf{kdm}}$ into a scheme that is KDM-CCA secure in the multi-user setting. In fact, we need not change the construction at all. The only difference is that we require a weak variant of *RKA-KDM security* [4] for the underlying SKE scheme SKE, instead of one-time KDM security. We also require a mild property that a secret key is uniformly distributed over the secret key space $\{0,1\}^{\ell_s}$.

Informally, an SKE scheme is said to be RKA-KDM secure if no adversary can guess the challenge bit b with probability significantly greater than $1/2$ given an encryption of $f_b(s)$ under the key $s \oplus \Delta \in \{0,1\}^{\ell_s}$ when it queries two functions (f_0, f_1) and a key shift $\Delta \in \{0,1\}^{\ell_s}$ as an RKA-KDM-encryption query. For our purpose, we need a much weaker form of RKA-KDM security where all key shifts are not chosen by an adversary, but generated uniformly at random in advance by the challenger. We call our RKA-KDM security *passive* RKA-KDM security. For its formal definition, see Definition 3 in Sect. 3.

In the security proof of the KDM-CCA security in the multi-user setting of $\mathsf{PKE}_{\mathsf{kdm}}$, there exist n key pairs of $\mathsf{PKE}_{\mathsf{kdm}}$ for some polynomial n of the security parameter. As the first step of the proof, we change the security game so that n secret keys $s^1, \ldots, s^n$ of $\mathsf{PKE}_{\mathsf{kdm}}$ are generated by first generating a single source key s and n key shifts $(\Delta^i)_{i \in [n]}$ and then setting $s^i := s \oplus \Delta^i$ for every $i \in [n]$. This does not at all change the distribution of the keys due to the requirement on SKE that a secret key is distributed uniformly in the secret key space $\{0, 1\}^{\ell_s}$. We next change the security game so that for every $i^* \in [n]$, an encryption of $f_b(s^1 \| \ldots \| s^n)$ under the i^*-th key can be simulated from f_b and n key shifts $(\Delta^i)_{i \in [n]}$ and *not* the source key s, where (i^*, f_0, f_1) is a KDM-encryption query made by an adversary. This is possible by garbling a circuit into which f_b, i^*, and $(\Delta^i)_{i \in [n]}$ are hardwired,[7] while we just directly garble f_b in the proof for the single user security. Then, we can complete the rest of the security proof in the same way as the proof of the single user security except that we use the (passive) RKA-KDM security instead of one-time KDM security.

Differently from the single user case, it is critical that $\mathsf{sk}_{\mathsf{dv}}$ and sk' are encrypted into $\mathsf{ct}_{\mathsf{ske}}$, and SK consists only of s. If SK is of the form $(s, \mathsf{sk}_{\mathsf{dv}}, \mathsf{sk}')$, it is not clear how we control the multiple secret keys even if SKE is RKA-KDM secure.

KDM-CCA Secure PKE from New Assumptions. An SKE scheme satisfying our definition of RKA-KDM security can be constructed based on the LPN assumption [4]. Moreover, we show how to construct an SKE scheme satisfying our RKA-KDM security definition based on hash encryption [13, 22] which in turn can be based on the CDH assumption. The construction is an extension of that of a KDM-CPA secure PKE scheme based on batch encryption proposed by Brakerski et al. [13]. For the details of the construction and its security proof, see the full version.

In addition to RKA-KDM secure SKE schemes, all other building blocks of our construction can be obtained based on the LPN and CDH assumptions via KDM-CPA secure PKE schemes. Through our generic construction, we obtain the first PKE schemes that are KDM-CCA secure in the multi-user setting based on the LPN and CDH assumptions. Previously to our work, KDM-CCA secure PKE schemes even in the single user setting based on these assumptions were not known.

2.6   On the Connections with the Techniques by Barak et al. [6]

The idea of garbling a constant circuit used in this overview was previously used by Barak et al. [6] in which they constructed a PKE scheme that is KDM-CPA secure with respect to functions computable by circuits of a-priori bounded size (i.e. bounded-KDM-CPA security). They used the technique of garbling a constant circuit together with a primitive that they call *targeted encryption,*

---

[7] To make this change possible, in the formal proof, we need to pad a circuit garbled in the encryption algorithm to some appropriate size depending on n.

which is a special form of PKE and whose syntactical and security requirements have some similarities with hash encryption [22]. In fact, the KDM-CPA variant of our construction $\mathsf{PKE}^*_{\mathsf{kdm}}$ explained in Sect. 2.3 can be described by using the abstraction of targeted encryption in which the targeted encryption scheme is constructed from an IND-CPA secure PKE scheme and a one-time KDM secure SKE scheme.[8]

We note that although we can use the abstraction of targeted encryption for the KDM-CPA variant of our construction, it seems difficult to use it for our main construction of a KDM-CCA secure PKE scheme. The problem is that if we use the abstraction of targeted encryption, we have to prove the well-formedness of ciphertexts of the targeted encryption scheme by using the DV-NIZK argument system. As explained in Sect. 2.5, in the security proof of our KDM-CCA secure PKE scheme, we have to change the security game so that when responding to a decryption query, we recover all labels from "0-side" ciphertexts $(\mathsf{ct}_{j,0})_{j \in [\ell_s]}$ of the underlying IND-CPA secure PKE scheme (instead of "s_i-side" ciphertexts $(\mathsf{ct}_{j,s_i})_{j \in [\ell_s]}$). This key-switching step is not compatible with the syntax of targeted encryption, and it seems difficult to use a targeted encryption scheme in a black-box way.

3 Preliminaries

In this section, we review basic notation and the definitions of cryptographic primitives used in the paper.

3.1 Notations

$\mathbb{N}$ denotes the set of natural numbers, and for $n \in \mathbb{N}$, we define $[n] := \{1, \ldots, n\}$. For a discrete finite set S, $|S|$ denotes its size, and $x \xleftarrow{r} S$ denotes choosing an element x uniformly at random from S. For strings x and y, $x \| y$ denotes their concatenation. For a (probabilistic) algorithm or a function A, $y \leftarrow \mathsf{A}(x)$ denotes assigning to y the output of A on input x, and if we need to specify a randomness r used in A, we denote $y \leftarrow \mathsf{A}(x; r)$ (in which case the computation of A is understood as deterministic on input x and r). λ always denotes a security parameter. PPT stands for *probabilistic polynomial time*. A function $f(\lambda)$ is said to be negligible if $f(\lambda)$ tends to 0 faster than λ^{-c} for every constant $c > 0$. We write $f(\lambda) = \mathsf{negl}(\lambda)$ to mean that $f(\lambda)$ is a negligible function.

3.2 Public-Key Encryption

A public-key encryption (PKE) scheme PKE is a three tuple $(\mathsf{KG}, \mathsf{Enc}, \mathsf{Dec})$ of PPT algorithms. The key generation algorithm KG, given a security parameter 1^λ as input, outputs a public key pk and a secret key sk. The encryption algorithm

---

[8] These connections with the techniques by Barak et al. were pointed out by the anonymous reviewers.

Enc, given a public key pk and a message m as input, outputs a ciphertext ct. The (deterministic) decryption algorithm Dec, given a public key pk, a secret key sk, and a ciphertext ct as input, outputs a message m (which could be the special symbol $\perp$ indicating that ct is invalid). As correctness, we require $\mathsf{Dec}(\mathsf{sk}, \mathsf{Enc}(\mathsf{pk}, m)) = m$ for all $\lambda \in \mathbb{N}$, all $(\mathsf{pk}, \mathsf{sk}) \leftarrow \mathsf{KG}(1^\lambda)$, and all m.

Security Notions for PKE. Next, we review the definitions of key-dependent message security against chosen plaintext attacks/chosen ciphertext attacks (KDM-CPA/CCA security). Note that IND-CPA/CCA security are covered as their special cases.

Definition 1 (KDM-CCA/KDM-CPA Security). *Let* PKE *be a PKE scheme whose secret key and message spaces are* $\mathcal{SK}$ *and* $\mathcal{M}$, *respectively. Let* $n \in \mathbb{N}$, *and let* $\mathcal{F}$ *be a function family with domain* $\mathcal{SK}^n$ *and range* $\mathcal{M}$. *Consider the following* $\mathcal{F}\text{-KDM}^{(n)}$-*CCA game between a challenger and an adversary* $\mathcal{A}$.

1. *First, the challenger chooses a challenge bit* $b \xleftarrow{\mathsf{r}} \{0,1\}$. *Next, the challenger generates* n *key pairs* $(\mathsf{pk}^i, \mathsf{sk}^i) \leftarrow \mathsf{KG}(1^\lambda)$ $(i \in [n])$. *Then, the challenger sets* $\mathsf{sk} := (\mathsf{sk}^1, \ldots, \mathsf{sk}^n)$ *and sends* $(\mathsf{pk}^1, \ldots, \mathsf{pk}^n)$ *to* $\mathcal{A}$. *Finally, the challenger prepares an empty list* L_{kdm}.
2. $\mathcal{A}$ *may adaptively make the following queries.*
   KDM-encryption queries: $\mathcal{A}$ *sends* $(j, f_0, f_1) \in [n] \times \mathcal{F}^2$ *to the challenger. The challenger returns* $\mathsf{ct} \leftarrow \mathsf{Enc}(\mathsf{pk}^j, f_b(\mathsf{sk}))$ *to* $\mathcal{A}$. *Finally, the challenger adds* (j, ct) *to* L_{kdm}.
   Decryption queries: $\mathcal{A}$ *sends* (j, ct) *to the challenger. If* $(j, \mathsf{ct}) \in L_{\mathsf{kdm}}$, *then the challenger returns* $\perp$ *to* $\mathcal{A}$. *Otherwise, the challenger returns* $m \leftarrow \mathsf{Dec}(\mathsf{pk}^j, \mathsf{sk}^j, \mathsf{ct})$ *to* $\mathcal{A}$.
3. $\mathcal{A}$ *outputs* $b' \in \{0,1\}$.

We say that PKE *is* $\mathcal{F}\text{-KDM}^{(n)}$-*CCA secure if for all PPT adversaries* $\mathcal{A}$, *we have* $\mathsf{Adv}^{\mathsf{kdmcpa}}_{\mathsf{PKE}, \mathcal{F}, \mathcal{A}, n}(\lambda) := 2 \cdot |\Pr[b = b'] - 1/2| = \mathsf{negl}(\lambda)$.

$\mathcal{F}\text{-KDM}^{(n)}$-*CPA security is defined similarly, using the* $\mathcal{F}\text{-KDM}^{(n)}$-*CPA game where an adversary* $\mathcal{A}$ *is not allowed to make decryption queries.*

The above definition is slightly different from the standard definition where an adversary is required to distinguish encryptions of $f(\mathsf{sk}^1, \ldots, \mathsf{sk}^n)$ from encryptions of some fixed message. However, the two definitions are equivalent if the function class $\mathcal{F}$ contains a constant function, which is the case for the function families used in this paper (see below). This formalization is easier to work with for security proofs.

Function Families. In this paper, we will deal with the following function families for KDM security of PKE:

$\mathcal{P}$ **(Projection functions):** A function is said to be a projection function if each of its output bits depends on at most a single bit of its input. We denote by $\mathcal{P}$ the family of projection functions.

$\mathcal{B}_{\text{size}}$ (**Circuits of a-priori bounded size** size): We denote by $\mathcal{B}_{\text{size}}$, where size $= \text{size}(\lambda)$ is a polynomial, the function family such that each member in $\mathcal{B}_{\text{size}}$ can be described by a circuit of size size.

$\mathcal{C}$ (**Constant functions**): We denote by $\mathcal{C}$ the set of all constant functions. Note that $\mathcal{C}$-KDM-CCA (resp. $\mathcal{C}$-KDM-CPA) security is equivalent to IND-CCA (resp. IND-CPA) security.

3.3 Secret-Key Encryption

A secret-key encryption (SKE) scheme SKE is a three tuple $(\mathsf{K}, \mathsf{E}, \mathsf{D})$ of PPT algorithms. The key generation algorithm K, given a security parameter 1^λ as input, outputs a key s. The encryption algorithm E, given a key s and a message m as input, outputs a ciphertext ct. The (deterministic) decryption algorithm D, given a key s and a ciphertext ct as input, outputs a message m (which could be the special symbol $\perp$ indicating that ct is invalid). As correctness, we require $\mathsf{D}(s, \mathsf{E}(s, m)) = m$ for all $\lambda \in \mathbb{N}$, all keys s output by $\mathsf{K}(1^\lambda)$, and all m.

Security Notions for SKE. In this paper, we will deal with two types of security notions for SKE: *one-time KDM security* and *passive RKA-KDM security*. We review the definitions below.

One-time KDM security is a weak form of KDM-CPA security in which an adversary is allowed to make only a single KDM-encryption query.

Definition 2 (One-Time KDM Security). *Let* $\mathsf{SKE} = (\mathsf{K}, \mathsf{E}, \mathsf{D})$ *be an SKE scheme whose key and message spaces are* $\mathcal{K}$ *and* $\mathcal{M}$, *respectively. Let* $\mathcal{F}$ *be a function family with domain* $\mathcal{K}$ *and range* $\mathcal{M}$. *Consider the following one-time* $\mathcal{F}$-*KDM game between a challenger and an adversary* $\mathcal{A}$.

1. *First, the challenger chooses a challenge bit* $b \xleftarrow{\text{r}} \{0,1\}$. *Next, the challenger generates a secret key* $s \leftarrow \mathsf{K}(1^\lambda)$ *and sends* 1^λ *to* $\mathcal{A}$.
2. $\mathcal{A}$ *sends a function* $f \in \mathcal{F}$ *as a single KDM-encryption query to the challenger. If* $b = 1$, *the challenger returns* $\mathsf{ct} \leftarrow \mathsf{E}(s, f(s))$ *to* $\mathcal{A}$; *Otherwise, the challenger returns* $\mathsf{ct} \leftarrow \mathsf{E}(s, 0^{|f(\cdot)|})$ *to* $\mathcal{A}$. *(Note that this step is done only once.)*
3. $\mathcal{A}$ *outputs* $b' \in \{0,1\}$.

We say that SKE *is one-time* $\mathcal{F}$-*KDM secure if for all PPT adversaries* $\mathcal{A}$, *we have* $\mathsf{Adv}^{\text{otkdm}}_{\mathsf{SKE},\mathcal{F},\mathcal{A}}(\lambda) := 2 \cdot |\Pr[b = b'] - 1/2| = \mathsf{negl}(\lambda)$.

Remark 1 (On the Message Space of One-Time KDM Secure SKE). Unlike ordinary IND-CPA secure encryption schemes, extending the message space of KDM secure encryption schemes is in general not easy. Fortunately, however, things are easy for $\mathcal{P}$-KDM security. We can extend the message space of a one-time $\mathcal{P}$-KDM secure SKE scheme as much as we want, if the size of the message space of the SKE scheme is already sufficiently large. Specifically, we can show that if there exists a one-time $\mathcal{P}$-KDM secure SKE scheme whose secret key and message spaces are $\{0,1\}^\ell$ and $\{0,1\}^\mu$, respectively, for some polynomials

$\ell = \ell(\lambda)$ and $\mu = \mu(\lambda)$ satisfying $\mu = \Omega(\ell \cdot \lambda)$, then for any polynomial $\mu' = \mu'(\lambda)$, there also exists a one-time $\mathcal{P}$-KDM secure SKE scheme that can encrypt messages of length μ'.

To see this, we observe that the KDM-CPA secure construction $\mathsf{PKE}^*_{\mathsf{kdm}}$ that we described in Sect. 2.3, works also in the secret-key setting. Namely, if we replace the building block IND-CPA secure PKE schemes with IND-CPA secure SKE schemes, then the resulting SKE scheme[9] is (multi-time) $\mathcal{B}_{\mathsf{size}}$-KDM secure where $\mathsf{size} = \mathsf{size}(\lambda)$ is some polynomial that depends on the size of a constant circuit (in which a message is hardwired). In fact, we can make the message space of this construction arbitrarily large since by setting size appropriately, we can hardwire a message of arbitrary length into a circuit to be garbled without compromising the security. Moreover, we only need to assume that the underlying one-time $\mathcal{P}$-KDM secure SKE scheme can encrypt messages of length $\mu = \Omega(\ell \cdot \lambda)$ since it is only required to encrypt $\ell + 1$ secret keys of IND-CPA secure SKE schemes, each of which can be assumed to be λ-bit without loss of generality. This means that, using this construction, we can extend the message space of a one-time $\mathcal{P}$-KDM secure SKE scheme as much as we want if the scheme can already encrypt a message of length $\mu = \Omega(\ell \cdot \lambda)$.

Next, we give a formalization of passive RKA-KDM security, which is a weaker variant of RKA-KDM security formalized by Applebaum [4]. Recall that the original RKA-KDM security of [4] is a slightly stronger form of standard KDM-CPA security (albeit in the presence of a single challenge key) where we consider an adversary that is allowed to ask encryptions of key-dependent messages, encrypted under "related" keys. In this paper, we only consider "XOR by a constant" as related-key deriving functions, and hence give a definition specialized to this setting. On the other hand, however, we only need a weaker "passive" variant of RKA-KDM security where the security game is changed as follows: (1) not the adversary but the challenger randomly chooses the related-key deriving functions (i.e. constants for XORing in our setting), and (2) an adversary has to make its RKA-KDM-encryption queries in one shot.

Definition 3 (Passive RKA-KDM Security). *Let* SKE *be an SKE scheme whose key space is* $\{0,1\}^\ell$ *for some polynomial* $\ell = \ell(\lambda)$ *and whose message space is* $\mathcal{M}$. *Let* $\mathcal{F}$ *be a function family with domain* $\{0,1\}^\ell$ *and range* $\mathcal{M}$. *Let* $n \in \mathbb{N}$ *be an a-priori bounded polynomial. Consider the following passive* $\mathcal{F}$-RKA-KDM$^{(n)}$ *game between a challenger and an adversary* $\mathcal{A}$.

1. *First, the challenger chooses a challenge bit* $b \xleftarrow{\mathsf{r}} \{0,1\}$ *and generates* $s \leftarrow \mathsf{K}(\lambda)$ *and* $\Delta^i \xleftarrow{\mathsf{r}} \{0,1\}^\ell$ *for every* $i \in [n]$. *Then, the challenger sends* $(\Delta^i)_{i\in[n]}$ *to* $\mathcal{A}$.
2. $\mathcal{A}$ *sends* n *functions* $f^1, \dots, f^n \in \mathcal{F}$ *to the challenger. If* $b = 1$, *the challenger computes* $\mathsf{ct}^i \leftarrow \mathsf{E}(s \oplus \Delta^i, f^i(s))$ *for every* $i \in [n]$. *Otherwise, the challenger*

---

[9] If we are only interested in one-time KDM security of the resulting scheme, the SKE-ciphertext $\mathsf{ct}_{\mathsf{ske}}$ that is originally put in a public key of $\mathsf{PKE}^*_{\mathsf{kdm}}$ can be sent as part of a ciphertext.

computes $\mathsf{ct}^i \leftarrow \mathsf{E}(s \oplus \varDelta^i, 0^{|f^i(\cdot)|})$ for every $i \in [n]$. Finally, the challenger sends $\left(\mathsf{ct}^i\right)_{i \in [n]}$ to $\mathcal{A}$.

3. $\mathcal{A}$ outputs $b' \in \{0, 1\}$.

We say that SKE is passively $\mathcal{F}\text{-}RKA\text{-}KDM^{(n)}$ secure, if for all PPT adversaries $\mathcal{A}$, we have $\mathsf{Adv}^{\mathsf{prkakdm}}_{\mathsf{SKE}, \mathcal{F}, \mathcal{A}, n}(\lambda) := 2 \cdot |\mathrm{Pr}[b = b'] - 1/2| = \mathsf{negl}(\lambda)$.

3.4 Designated-Verifier Non-interactive Zero-Knowledge Arguments

Here, we review the definitions for (reusable) designated-verifier non-interactive zero-knowledge (DV-NIZK) argument systems.

Let L be an NP language associated with the corresponding NP relation R. A DV-NIZK argument system DVNIZK for L is a three tuple (DVKG, P, V) of PPT algorithms. DVKG is the key generation algorithm that takes a security parameter 1^λ as input, and outputs a public proving key pk and a secret verification key sk. P is the proving algorithm that takes a public proving key pk, a statement x, and a witness w as input, and outputs a proof π. V is the (deterministic) verification algorithm that takes a secret verification key sk, a statement x, and a proof π as input, outputs either accept or reject.

We require that DVNIZK satisfy the three requirements: Correctness, (adaptive) soundness, and zero-knowledge. In particular, we consider a version of soundness which holds against adversaries that make multiple verification queries, and a version of zero-knowledge which holds against adversaries that make multiple challenge proving queries. A DV-NIZK argument system that satisfies these versions of soundness and zero-knowledge is called *reusable*.

Formally, these requirements are defined as follows.

Correctness. We say that DVNIZK is correct if we have $\mathsf{V}(\mathsf{sk}, x, \mathsf{P}(\mathsf{pk}, x, w)) = \mathsf{accept}$ for all $\lambda \in \mathbb{N}$, all key pairs (pk, sk) output by $\mathsf{DVKG}(1^\lambda)$, and all valid statement/witness pairs $(x, w) \in R$.

Soundness. Consider the following soundness game between a challenger and an adversary $\mathcal{A}$.

1. First, the challenger generates $(\mathsf{pk}, \mathsf{sk}) \leftarrow \mathsf{DVKG}(1^\lambda)$ and sends pk to $\mathcal{A}$.
2. $\mathcal{A}$ may adaptively make verification queries. When $\mathcal{A}$ makes a verification query (x, π), the challenger responds with $\mathsf{V}(\mathsf{sk}, x, \pi)$.
3. $\mathcal{A}$ outputs (x^*, π^*).

We say that DVNIZK is sound if for all PPT adversaries $\mathcal{A}$, we have

$$\mathsf{Adv}^{\mathsf{sound}}_{\mathsf{DVNIZK}, \mathcal{A}}(\lambda) := \mathrm{Pr}[x^* \notin L \wedge \mathsf{V}(\mathsf{sk}, x^*, \pi^*) = \mathsf{accept}] = \mathsf{negl}(\lambda).$$

Zero-Knowledge. Let $\mathsf{S} = (\mathsf{S}_1, \mathsf{S}_2)$ be a pair of PPT "simulator" algorithms whose syntax is as follows.

- S_1 takes a security parameter 1^λ as input, and outputs a fake public key pk, a fake secret key sk, and a trapdoor td.
- S_2 takes a trapdoor td and a statement x as input, and outputs a fake proof π.

Consider the following zero-knowledge game between a challenger and an adversary $\mathcal{A}$.

1. First, the challenger chooses the challenge bit $b \xleftarrow{r} \{0,1\}$. If $b = 1$, then the challenger generates $(\mathsf{pk}, \mathsf{sk}) \leftarrow \mathsf{DVKG}(1^\lambda)$; Otherwise the challenger generates $(\mathsf{pk}, \mathsf{sk}, \mathsf{td}) \leftarrow \mathsf{S}_1(1^\lambda)$. Then, the challenger sends $(\mathsf{pk}, \mathsf{sk})$ to $\mathcal{A}$.

2. $\mathcal{A}$ may adaptively make proving queries. When $\mathcal{A}$ submits a proving query (x, w), if $(x, w) \notin R$, then the challenger returns $\bot$ to $\mathcal{A}$. Then, if $b = 1$, the challenger computes $\pi \leftarrow \mathsf{P}(\mathsf{pk}, x, w)$; Otherwise, the challenger computes $\pi \leftarrow \mathsf{S}_2(\mathsf{td}, x)$. Finally, the challenger returns π to $\mathcal{A}$.

3. $\mathcal{A}$ outputs $b' \in \{0,1\}$.

We say that DVNIZK is zero-knowledge if there exists a PPT simulator $\mathsf{S} = (\mathsf{S}_1, \mathsf{S}_2)$ such that for all PPT adversaries $\mathcal{A}$, we have $\mathsf{Adv}^{\mathsf{zk}}_{\mathsf{DVNIZK}, \mathcal{A}, \mathsf{S}}(\lambda) := 2 \cdot |\Pr[b = b'] - 1/2| = \mathsf{negl}(\lambda)$.

3.5   Garbled Circuits

Here, we recall the definitions of a garbling scheme in the form we use in this paper. We can realize a garbling scheme for all efficiently computable circuits based on one-way functions [40].

Let $\{\mathcal{C}_n\}_{n \in \mathbb{N}}$ be a family of circuits where the input-length of each circuit in $\mathcal{C}_n$ is n. A garbling scheme GC is a three tuple $(\mathsf{Garble}, \mathsf{Eval}, \mathsf{Sim})$ of PPT algorithms. Garble is the garbling algorithm that takes as input a security parameter 1^λ and a circuit $C \in \mathcal{C}_n$, where $n = n(\lambda)$ is a polynomial. Then, it outputs a garbled circuit $\widetilde{C}$ and $2n$ labels $(\mathsf{lab}_{j,\alpha})_{j \in [n], \alpha \in \{0,1\}}$. For simplicity and without loss of generality, we assume that the length of each $\mathsf{lab}_{j,\alpha}$ is λ. Eval is the evaluation algorithm that takes a garbled circuit $\widetilde{C}$ and n labels $(\mathsf{lab}_j)_{j \in [n]}$ as input, and outputs an evaluation result y. Sim is the simulator algorithm that takes a security parameter 1^λ, the size parameter size (where $\mathsf{size} = \mathsf{size}(\lambda)$ is a polynomial), and a string y as input, and outputs a simulated garbled circuit $\widetilde{C}$ and n simulated labels $(\mathsf{lab}_j)_{j \in [n]}$.

For a garbling scheme, we require the following correctness and security properties.

Correctness. For all $\lambda, n \in \mathbb{N}$, all $x = (x_1, \dots, x_n) \in \{0,1\}^n$, and all $C \in \mathcal{C}_n$, we require that the following two equalities hold.[10]

- $\mathsf{Eval}(\widetilde{C}, (\mathsf{lab}_{j,x_j})_{j \in [n]}) = C(x)$ for all $(\widetilde{C}, (\mathsf{lab}_{j,\alpha})_{j \in [n], \alpha \in \{0,1\}})$ output by $\mathsf{Garble}(1^\lambda, C)$.
- $\mathsf{Eval}(\widetilde{C}, (\mathsf{lab}_j)_{j \in [n]}) = C(x)$ for all $(\widetilde{C}, (\mathsf{lab}_j)_{j \in [n]})$ output by $\mathsf{Sim}(1^\lambda, |C|, C(x))$.

Security. Consider the following security game between a challenger and an adversary $\mathcal{A}$.

---

[10] Requiring correctness for the output of the simulator may be somewhat non-standard. However, it is satisfied by Yao's garbling scheme based on an IND-CPA secure SKE scheme.

1. First, the challenger chooses a bit $b \xleftarrow{\text{r}} \{0,1\}$ and sends a security parameter 1^λ to $\mathcal{A}$.
2. $\mathcal{A}$ sends a circuit $C \in \mathcal{C}_n$ and an input $x = (x_1, \ldots, x_n) \in \{0,1\}^n$ to the challenger. Then, if $b = 1$, the challenger executes $(\widetilde{C}, (\mathsf{lab}_{j,\alpha})_{j \in [n], \alpha \in \{0,1\}})$ $\leftarrow \mathsf{Garble}(1^\lambda, C)$ and returns $(\widetilde{C}, (\mathsf{lab}_{j,x_j})_{j \in [n]})$ to $\mathcal{A}$; Otherwise, the challenger returns $(\widetilde{C}, (\mathsf{lab}_j)_{j \in [n]}) \leftarrow \mathsf{Sim}(1^\lambda, |C|, C(x))$ to $\mathcal{A}$.
3. $\mathcal{A}$ outputs $b' \in \{0,1\}$.

We say that GC is secure if for all PPT adversaries $\mathcal{A}$, we have $\mathsf{Adv}^{\mathsf{gc}}_{\mathsf{GC},\mathcal{A},\mathsf{Sim}}(\lambda)$ $:= 2 \cdot |\Pr[b = b'] - 1/2| = \mathsf{negl}(\lambda)$.

4   DV-NIZK via KDM Security

In this section, we explain how to construct a reusable DV-NIZK argument system from the combination of an IND-CPA secure PKE scheme and a one-time $\mathcal{P}$-KDM secure SKE scheme. Specifically, we explain how the following statement can be derived.

Theorem 2. *Assume that there exist an IND-CPA secure PKE scheme and a one-time $\mathcal{P}$-KDM secure SKE scheme that can encrypt messages of length $\Omega(\ell \cdot \lambda)$, where $\ell = \ell(\lambda)$ is the secret key length of the SKE scheme. Then, there exists a reusable DV-NIZK argument system for all NP languages.*

As mentioned in the introduction, this almost immediately follows by combining the results and techniques from the recent works by Lombardi et al. [34] and by Kitagawa et al. [30]. To see this, we first briefly review Lombardi et al.'s work.

Lombardi et al. showed how to construct a reusable DV-NIZK argument system for all NP languages from the combination of an IND-CPA secure PKE scheme and a hinting PRG introduced by Koppula and Waters [33]. The main intermediate technical tool for their construction is what they call *attribute-based secure function evaluation (AB-SFE)*, which can be seen as a generalization (and simplification) of a single-key attribute-based encryption (ABE) scheme (i.e., an ABE scheme secure in the presence of a single secret key). Lombardi et al. formalized two kinds of security notions for AB-SFE: *key-hiding* and *message-hiding*, each notion with strong and weak variants, resulting in total four security notions. Using the notion of AB-SFE, they achieved their result in a modular manner by showing the following steps:

- **(DV-NIZK-from-AB-SFE):** A reusable DV-NIZK argument system can be constructed from an AB-SFE scheme satisfying *strong key-hiding* and weak message-hiding.
- **(Key-Hiding Enhancement):** An AB-SFE scheme satisfying strong key-hiding and weak message-hiding can be constructed from an AB-SFE scheme satisfying *weak key-hiding* and weak message-hiding, by additionally assuming a hinting PRG. This step directly uses the CPA-to-CCA security transformation for ABE using a hinting PRG by Koppula and Waters [33].

– **(AB-SFE-from-PKE):** An AB-SFE scheme satisfying weak key-hiding and weak message-hiding can be constructed from an IND-CPA secure PKE scheme.

On the other hand, Kitagawa et al. [30] showed that an IND-CCA secure PKE scheme can be constructed from the combination of an IND-CPA secure PKE scheme and a one-time $\mathcal{P}$-KDM secure SKE scheme which can encrypt messages of length $\Omega(\ell \cdot \lambda)$, where ℓ denotes the secret key length of the SKE scheme, based on the Koppula-Waters construction [33].

Kitagawa et al.'s result can be understood as showing a technique for replacing a hinting PRG in the Koppula-Waters construction (and its variants) with a one-time $\mathcal{P}$-KDM secure SKE scheme. Hence, we can apply Kitagawa et al.'s technique to the "key-hiding enhancement" step of Lombardi et al. to replace the hinting PRG with a one-time $\mathcal{P}$-KDM secure SKE scheme. This can be formally stated as follows.

Theorem 3 (Key-Hiding Enhancement via KDM Security). *Assume that there exists an AB-SFE scheme that satisfies weak key-hiding and weak message-hiding, and a one-time $\mathcal{P}$-KDM secure SKE scheme that can encrypt messages of length $\Omega(\ell \cdot \lambda)$, where $\ell = \ell(\lambda)$ is the secret key length of the SKE scheme. Then, there exists an AB-SFE scheme that satisfies strong key-hiding and weak message-hiding.*

Then, Theorem 2 follows from the combination of the "DV-NIZK-from-AB-SFE" and "AB-SFE-from-PKE" steps of Lombardi et al. [34] and Theorem 3.

We give the formal proof of Theorem 3 in the full version.

5   Generic Construction of KDM-CCA Secure PKE

In this section, we show our main result: a CPA-to-CCA transformation for KDM security.

More specifically, we show how to construct a PKE scheme that is KDM-CCA secure with respect to circuits whose size is bounded by an a-priori determined polynomial $\mathsf{size} = \mathsf{size}(\lambda)$ and in the single user setting (i.e. $\mathcal{B}_{\mathsf{size}}$-KDM$^{(1)}$-CCA), from the combination of the five building block primitives: (1) an IND-CPA secure PKE scheme, (2) an IND-CCA secure PKE scheme, (3) a reusable DV-NIZK argument system for an NP language, (4) a garbling scheme, and (5) a one-time $\mathcal{P}$-KDM secure SKE scheme.

We have seen in Sect. 4 that a reusable DV-NIZK argument system can be constructed from the combination of an IND-CPA secure PKE scheme and a one-time $\mathcal{P}$-KDM secure SKE scheme. Furthermore, the recent work by Kitagawa et al. [30] showed that an IND-CCA secure PKE scheme can also be constructed from the same building blocks. Moreover, a garbling scheme can be constructed only from a one-way function [40], which is in turn implied by an IND-CPA secure PKE or a one-time $\mathcal{P}$-KDM secure SKE scheme. Hence, our result in this section implies that a $\mathcal{B}_{\mathsf{size}}$-KDM$^{(1)}$-CCA secure PKE scheme can be constructed only from an IND-CPA secure PKE scheme and a one-time $\mathcal{P}$-KDM secure SKE scheme.

Looking ahead, in the next section, we will show that the same construction can be shown to be secure in the n-user setting (i.e. $\mathcal{B}_{\mathsf{size}}$-KDM$^{(n)}$-CCA secure) if we additionally require the SKE scheme to be passively $\mathcal{P}$-RKA-KDM$^{(n)}$ secure.

Construction. Let $\ell_{\mathsf{m}} = \ell_{\mathsf{m}}(\lambda)$ be a polynomial that denotes the length of messages to be encrypted by our constructed PKE scheme. Let $\mathsf{size} = \mathsf{size}(\lambda)$ be a polynomial and let $n \in \mathbb{N}$ be the number of users for which we wish to achieve $\mathcal{B}_{\mathsf{size}}$-KDM$^{(n)}$-CCA security.[11]

We use the following building blocks.

- Let $\mathsf{PKE} = (\mathsf{KG}, \mathsf{Enc}, \mathsf{Dec})$ be a PKE scheme whose message space is $\{0,1\}^{\lambda}$. We denote the randomness space of Enc by $\mathcal{R}$, and the secret key length by $\ell_{\mathsf{sk}} = \ell_{\mathsf{sk}}(\lambda)$.
- Let $\mathsf{PKE}' = (\mathsf{KG}_{\mathsf{cca}}, \mathsf{Enc}_{\mathsf{cca}}, \mathsf{Dec}_{\mathsf{cca}})$ be a PKE scheme whose message space is $\{0,1\}^{*}$. We denote its secret key length by $\ell'_{\mathsf{sk}} = \ell'_{\mathsf{sk}}(\lambda)$.
- Let $\mathsf{SKE} = (\mathsf{K}, \mathsf{E}, \mathsf{D})$ be an SKE scheme whose plaintext space is $\{0,1\}^{\mu}$ for a polynomial $\mu = \mu(\lambda)$ to be determined below and whose secret key space is $\{0,1\}^{\ell_s}$ for some polynomial $\ell_s = \ell_s(\lambda)$.
- Let $\mathsf{GC} = (\mathsf{Garble}, \mathsf{Eval}, \mathsf{Sim})$ be a garbling scheme.
- Let $\mathsf{DVNIZK} = (\mathsf{DVKG}, \mathsf{P}, \mathsf{V})$ be a DV-NIZK argument system for the following NP language

$$L = \left\{ (\mathsf{pk}_{j,\alpha}, \mathsf{ct}_{j,\alpha})_{j \in [\ell_s], \alpha \in \{0,1\}} \;\middle|\; \begin{array}{l} \exists (\mathsf{lab}_j, r_{j,0}, r_{j,1})_{j \in [\ell_s]} \text{ s.t.} \\ \forall (j, \alpha) \in [\ell_s] \times \{0,1\}: \\ \mathsf{ct}_{j,\alpha} = \mathsf{Enc}(\mathsf{pk}_{j,\alpha}, \mathsf{lab}_j; r_{j,\alpha}) \end{array} \right\}.$$

We denote the verification key length of DVNIZK by $\ell_{\mathsf{sk}_{\mathsf{dv}}} = \ell_{\mathsf{sk}_{\mathsf{dv}}}(\lambda)$.

We require the message length μ of the underlying SKE scheme SKE to satisfy $\mu = \ell_s \cdot \ell_{\mathsf{sk}} + \ell'_{\mathsf{sk}} + \ell_{\mathsf{sk}_{\mathsf{dv}}}$. Finally, let $\mathsf{pad} = \mathsf{pad}(\lambda, n) \geq \mathsf{size}$ be a polynomial that is used as the size parameter for the underlying garbling scheme, and is specified differently in Theorem 4 in this section and in Theorem 5 in Sect. 6.

Using these ingredients, we construct our proposed PKE scheme $\mathsf{PKE}_{\mathsf{kdm}} = (\mathsf{KG}_{\mathsf{kdm}}, \mathsf{Enc}_{\mathsf{kdm}}, \mathsf{Dec}_{\mathsf{kdm}})$ whose message space is $\{0,1\}^{\ell_{\mathsf{m}}}$, as described in Fig. 1.

Correctness. The correctness of $\mathsf{PKE}_{\mathsf{kdm}}$ follows from that of the building blocks. Specifically, let $(\mathsf{PK}, \mathsf{SK}) = (((\mathsf{pk}_{j,\alpha})_{j,\alpha}, \mathsf{pk}_{\mathsf{cca}}, \mathsf{pk}_{\mathsf{dv}}, \mathsf{ct}_{\mathsf{ske}}), s)$ be a key pair output by $\mathsf{KG}_{\mathsf{kdm}}$, let $m \in \{0,1\}^{\ell_{\mathsf{m}}}$ be any message, and let $\mathsf{CT} \leftarrow \mathsf{Enc}_{\mathsf{kdm}}(\mathsf{PK}, m)$ be an honestly generated ciphertext. Due to the correctness of PKE, PKE', SKE, and DVNIZK, each decryption/verification done in the execution of $\mathsf{Dec}_{\mathsf{kdm}}(\mathsf{PK}, \mathsf{SK}, \mathsf{CT})$ never fails, and just before the final step of $\mathsf{Dec}_{\mathsf{kdm}}$, the decryptor can recover a garbled circuit $\widetilde{\mathsf{Q}}$ and the labels $(\mathsf{lab}_j)_j$, which must have been generated as

---

[11] As noted earlier, in this section we aim at achieving the security for $n = 1$, and in the next section we will consider more general $n \geq 1$.

$KG_{kdm}(1^\lambda)$:
   $\forall (j,\alpha) \in [\ell_s] \times \{0,1\} : (pk_{j,\alpha}, sk_{j,\alpha}) \leftarrow KG(1^\lambda)$
   $(pk_{cca}, sk_{cca}) \leftarrow KG_{cca}(1^\lambda)$
   $(pk_{dv}, sk_{dv}) \leftarrow DVKG(1^\lambda)$
   $s = (s_1, \ldots, s_{\ell_s}) \leftarrow K(1^\lambda)$
   $ct_{ske} \leftarrow E(s, ((sk_{j,s_j})_j, sk_{cca}, sk_{dv}))$
   $PK \leftarrow ((pk_{j,\alpha})_{j,\alpha}, pk_{cca}, pk_{dv}, ct_{ske}); \quad SK \leftarrow s$
   Return (PK, SK).

$Enc_{kdm}(PK, m)$:	$Dec_{kdm}(PK, SK, CT)$: (*)
$((pk_{j,\alpha})_{j,\alpha}, pk_{cca}, pk_{dv}, ct_{ske}) \leftarrow PK$	$((pk_{j,\alpha})_{j,\alpha}, pk_{cca}, pk_{dv}, ct_{ske}) \leftarrow PK$
$(\widetilde{Q}, (lab_j)_j) \leftarrow Sim(1^\lambda, pad, m)$ (†)	$s = (s_1, \ldots, s_{\ell_s}) \leftarrow SK$
$\forall (j,\alpha) \in [\ell_s] \times \{0,1\}$:	$((sk_{j,s_j})_j, sk_{cca}, sk_{dv}) \leftarrow D(s, ct_{ske})$
$\quad r_{j,\alpha} \xleftarrow{r} \mathcal{R}$	$(\widetilde{Q}, (ct_{j,\alpha})_{j,\alpha}, \pi) \leftarrow Dec_{cca}(pk_{cca}, sk_{cca}, CT)$
$\quad ct_{j,\alpha} \leftarrow Enc(pk_{j,\alpha}, lab_j; r_{j,\alpha})$	$x \leftarrow (pk_{j,\alpha}, ct_{j,\alpha})_{j,\alpha}$
$x \leftarrow (pk_{j,\alpha}, ct_{j,\alpha})_{j,\alpha}$	If $V(sk_{dv}, x, \pi) = $ reject then return $\bot$.
$w \leftarrow (lab_j, r_{j,0}, r_{j,1})_j$	$\forall j \in [\ell_s] : lab_j \leftarrow Dec(pk_{j,s_j}, sk_{j,s_j}, ct_{j,s_j})$
$\pi \leftarrow P(pk_{dv}, x, w)$	Return $m \leftarrow Eval(\widetilde{Q}, (lab_j)_j)$.
$CT \leftarrow Enc_{cca}(pk_{cca}, (\widetilde{Q}, (ct_{j,\alpha})_{j,\alpha}, \pi))$	
Return CT.	

Fig. 1. The proposed PKE scheme PKE_{kdm}. The notations like $(X_{j,\alpha})_{j,\alpha}$ and $(X_j)_j$ are abbreviations for $(X_{j,\alpha})_{j \in [\ell_s], \alpha \in \{0,1\}}$ and $(X_j)_{j \in [\ell_s]}$, respectively. (*) If D, Dec, or Dec_{cca} returns $\bot$, then we make Dec_{kdm} return $\bot$ and terminate. (†) $pad = pad(\lambda, n)$ denotes the size parameter that is specified differently in each of Theorems 4 and 5.

$(\widetilde{Q}, (lab_j)_j) \leftarrow Sim(1^\lambda, pad, m)$. Hence, by the correctness of GC (in particular, correctness of the evaluation of a simulated garbled circuit and labels), we have $Eval(\widetilde{Q}, (lab_j)_j) = m$.

Security. The following theorem guarantees the $\mathcal{B}_{size}$-KDM$^{(1)}$-CCA security of the PKE scheme PKE_{kdm}.

Theorem 4. *Let $\ell_m = \ell_m(\lambda)$ and $size = size(\lambda) \geq \max\{\ell_s, \ell_m\}$ be any polynomials, and let $pad := size$. Assume that PKE is IND-CPA secure, PKE' is IND-CCA secure, SKE is one-time $\mathcal{P}$-KDM secure, GC is a secure garbling scheme, and DVNIZK is a reusable DV-NIZK argument system for the NP language L. Then, PKE_{kdm} is $\mathcal{B}_{size}$-KDM$^{(1)}$-CCA secure.*

One might wonder the necessity of IND-CCA security for the outer PKE scheme PKE'. Suppose the underlying garbling scheme GC has the property that a circuit being garbled is hidden against adversaries that do not see the corresponding labels (which is satisfied by Yao's garbling scheme). Then, among the components $(\widetilde{Q}, (ct_{j,\alpha})_{j,\alpha}, \pi)$, the only component that actually needs to be encrypted is the DV-NIZK proof π, as long as all the components are "tied" together in a non-malleable manner (say, using a one-time signature scheme). Looking ahead, in a sequence of games argument in the security proof, we will consider a modified game in which the key pair (pk_{dv}, sk_{dv}) and proofs π in the challenge ciphertexts are generated by the zero-knowledge simulator of DVNIZK, and we have to bound the probability that an adversary makes a "bad" decryption query CT such that the statement/proof pair (x, π) corresponding to CT is judged valid by V while x is actually invalid (i.e. not in L). This could be done if DVNIZK satisfies (unbounded) simulation soundness, which is not achieved by the DV-NIZK argument system in Sect. 4. By encrypting π with an IND-CCA secure scheme (and relying also on the security properties of the other building blocks), we can argue that the probability of the bad event that we would like to bound, is negligibly close to the probability of the bad event in another modified game in which the key pair $(\mathsf{pk}_{\mathsf{dv}}, \mathsf{sk}_{\mathsf{dv}})$ is generated honestly by DVKG, and proofs π need not be generated for the challenge ciphertexts. The probability of the bad event in such a game can be bounded by the (ordinary) soundness of DVNIZK. For the details, see the proof below.

Proof of Theorem 4. Let $\mathcal{A}$ be an arbitrary PPT adversary that attacks the $\mathcal{B}_{\mathsf{size}}$-KDM$^{(1)}$-CCA security of PKE$_{\mathsf{kdm}}$. We proceed the proof via a sequence of games argument using eight games. For every $t \in [7]$, let SUC$_t$ be the event that $\mathcal{A}$ succeeds in guessing the challenge bit b in Game t. (Game 8 will be used only to bound the probability of a bad event introduced later.)

Game 1: This is the original $\mathcal{B}_{\mathsf{size}}$-KDM$^{(1)}$-CCA game regarding PKE$_{\mathsf{kdm}}$. By definition, we have $\mathsf{Adv}^{\mathsf{kdmcca}}_{\mathsf{PKE}_{\mathsf{kdm}}, \mathcal{B}_{\mathsf{size}}, \mathcal{A}, 1}(\lambda) = 2 \cdot |\Pr[\mathsf{SUC}_1] - 1/2|$.

Game 2: Same as Game 1, except that the challenger uses the simulator $\mathsf{S} = (\mathsf{S}_1, \mathsf{S}_2)$ for the zero-knowledge property of DVNIZK for generating $(\mathsf{pk}_{\mathsf{dv}}, \mathsf{sk}_{\mathsf{dv}})$ and a proof π in generating a ciphertext in response to KDM-encryption queries, instead of using DVKG and P. Namely, when generating PK and SK, the challenger generates $(\mathsf{pk}_{\mathsf{dv}}, \mathsf{sk}_{\mathsf{dv}}, \mathsf{td}) \leftarrow \mathsf{S}_1(1^\lambda)$ instead of $(\mathsf{pk}_{\mathsf{dv}}, \mathsf{sk}_{\mathsf{dv}}) \leftarrow \mathsf{DVKG}(1^\lambda)$. In addition, when $\mathcal{A}$ makes a KDM-encryption query (f_0, f_1), the challenger computes $\pi \leftarrow \mathsf{S}_2(\mathsf{td}, x)$ instead of $\pi \leftarrow \mathsf{P}(\mathsf{pk}_{\mathsf{dv}}, x, w)$, where $x = (\mathsf{pk}_{j,\alpha}, \mathsf{ct}_{j,\alpha})_{j,\alpha}$ and $w = (\mathsf{lab}_j, r_{j,0}, r_{j,1})_j$.
By the zero-knowledge property of DVNIZK, we have $|\Pr[\mathsf{SUC}_1] - \Pr[\mathsf{SUC}_2]| = \mathsf{negl}(\lambda)$.

Game 3: Same as Game 2, except that when responding to a KDM-encryption query, the challenger generates a garbled circuit $\widetilde{\mathsf{Q}}$ and labels $(\mathsf{lab}_j)_j$ by garbling f_b. More precisely, when $\mathcal{A}$ makes a KDM-encryption query (f_0, f_1), the challenger computes $(\widetilde{\mathsf{Q}}, (\mathsf{lab}_{j,\alpha})_{j,\alpha}) \leftarrow \mathsf{Garble}(1^\lambda, f_b)$, instead of $(\widetilde{\mathsf{Q}}, (\mathsf{lab}_j)_j) \leftarrow \mathsf{Sim}(1^\lambda, \mathsf{pad}, f_b(s))$. Moreover, for every $j \in [\ell_s]$ and $\alpha \in \{0, 1\}$, the challenger computes $\mathsf{ct}_{j,\alpha} \leftarrow \mathsf{Enc}(\mathsf{pk}_{j,\alpha}, \mathsf{lab}_{j,s_j})$.[12]
By definition, the circuit size of f_b is $\mathsf{pad} = \mathsf{size}$. Hence, by the security of GC, we have $|\Pr[\mathsf{SUC}_2] - \Pr[\mathsf{SUC}_3]| = \mathsf{negl}(\lambda)$.

Game 4: Same as Game 3, except that when responding to a KDM-encryption query (f_0, f_1), the challenger computes $\mathsf{ct}_{j,1 \oplus s_j} \leftarrow \mathsf{Enc}(\mathsf{pk}_{j,1 \oplus s_j}, \mathsf{lab}_{j,1 \oplus s_j})$ for every $j \in [\ell_s]$. Due to the change made in this game, the challenger now computes $\mathsf{ct}_{j,\alpha} \leftarrow \mathsf{Enc}(\mathsf{pk}_{j,\alpha}, \mathsf{lab}_{j,\alpha})$ for every $j \in [\ell_s]$ and $\alpha \in \{0, 1\}$.

---

[12] Note that in Game 3, the labels of the "opposite" positions, namely $(\mathsf{lab}_{j,1 \oplus s_j})_j$, are not used. They will be used in the subsequent games.

In Games 3 and 4, we do not need the secret keys $(\mathsf{sk}_{j,1 \oplus s_j})_j$ of PKE that do not correspond to $s = (s_1, \ldots, s_{\ell_s})$ (though we need $(\mathsf{sk}_{j,s_j})_j$ for computing $\mathsf{ct}_{\mathsf{ske}}$ and responding to decryption queries). Therefore, by the IND-CPA security of PKE under the keys $(\mathsf{pk}_{j,1 \oplus s_j})_j$, we have $|\mathrm{Pr}[\mathsf{SUC}_3] - \mathrm{Pr}[\mathsf{SUC}_4]| = \mathsf{negl}(\lambda)$.

At this point, the challenger need not use s to respond to KDM-encryption queries. In the next game, we will ensure that the challenger does not use s to respond to decryption queries.

Game 5: Same as Game 4, except that when responding to a decryption query, the challenger computes the labels $(\mathsf{lab}_j)_j$ of a garbled circuit by decrypting $\mathsf{ct}_{j,0}$, instead of ct_{j,s_j}, for every $j \in [\ell_s]$. More precisely, for a decryption query CT from $\mathcal{A}$, the challenger returns $\bot$ to $\mathcal{A}$ if $\mathsf{CT} \in L_{\mathsf{kdm}}$, and otherwise responds as follows. (The change from the previous game is underlined.)

1. Compute $(\widetilde{\mathsf{Q}}, (\mathsf{ct}_{j,\alpha})_{j,\alpha}, \pi) \leftarrow \mathsf{Dec}_{\mathsf{cca}}(\mathsf{pk}_{\mathsf{cca}}, \mathsf{sk}_{\mathsf{cca}}, \mathsf{CT})$, and then set $x := (\mathsf{pk}_{j,\alpha}, \mathsf{ct}_{j,\alpha})_{j,\alpha}$.
2. If $\mathsf{V}(\mathsf{sk}_{\mathsf{dv}}, x, \pi) = \mathsf{reject}$, then return $\bot$ to $\mathcal{A}$.
3. For every $j \in [\ell_s]$, compute $\underline{\mathsf{lab}_j \leftarrow \mathsf{Dec}(\mathsf{pk}_{j,0}, \mathsf{sk}_{j,0}, \mathsf{ct}_{j,0})}$.
4. Return $m \leftarrow \mathsf{Eval}(\widetilde{\mathsf{Q}}, (\mathsf{lab}_j)_j)$ to $\mathcal{A}$.

(By the change made in this game, s is not needed for responding to decryption queries.)

We define the following events in Game $t \in \{4, \ldots, 8\}$.

BDQ$_t$: In Game t, $\mathcal{A}$ makes a decryption query $\mathsf{CT} \notin L_{\mathsf{kdm}}$ that satisfies the following two conditions, where $(\widetilde{\mathsf{Q}}, (\mathsf{ct}_{j,\alpha})_{j,\alpha}, \pi) \leftarrow \mathsf{Dec}_{\mathsf{cca}}(\mathsf{pk}_{\mathsf{cca}}, \mathsf{sk}_{\mathsf{cca}}, \mathsf{CT})$:

1. $\mathsf{V}(\mathsf{sk}_{\mathsf{dv}}, (\mathsf{pk}_{j,\alpha}, \mathsf{ct}_{j,\alpha})_{j,\alpha}, \pi) = \mathsf{accept}$.
2. There exists $j^* \in [\ell_s]$ such that $\mathsf{Dec}(\mathsf{pk}_{j^*,0}, \mathsf{sk}_{j^*,0}, \mathsf{ct}_{j^*,0}) \neq \mathsf{Dec}(\mathsf{pk}_{j^*,1}, \mathsf{sk}_{j^*,1}, \mathsf{ct}_{j^*,1})$.

We call such a decryption query a *bad decryption query*.

Games 4 and 5 are identical unless $\mathcal{A}$ makes a bad decryption query in the corresponding games. Therefore, we have $|\mathrm{Pr}[\mathsf{SUC}_4] - \mathrm{Pr}[\mathsf{SUC}_5]| \leq \mathrm{Pr}[\mathsf{BDQ}_5]$.

Game 6: Same as Game 5, except that when generating PK, the challenger generates $\mathsf{ct}_{\mathsf{ske}} \leftarrow \mathsf{E}(s, 0^\mu)$, instead of $\mathsf{ct}_{\mathsf{ske}} \leftarrow \mathsf{E}(s, ((\mathsf{sk}_{j,s_j})_j, \mathsf{sk}_{\mathsf{cca}}, \mathsf{sk}_{\mathsf{dv}}))$.

In Games 5 and 6, when generating PK, the challenger does not need the secret key s of SKE except for the step of computing $\mathsf{ct}_{\mathsf{ske}}$. Furthermore, the "message" $((\mathsf{sk}_{j,s_j})_j, \mathsf{sk}_{\mathsf{cca}}, \mathsf{sk}_{\mathsf{dv}})$ encrypted in $\mathsf{ct}_{\mathsf{ske}}$ in Game 5 can be described by a projection function of s. Thus, by the one-time $\mathcal{P}$-KDM security of SKE, we have $|\mathrm{Pr}[\mathsf{SUC}_5] - \mathrm{Pr}[\mathsf{SUC}_6]| = \mathsf{negl}(\lambda)$. In addition, whether $\mathcal{A}$ has submitted a bad decryption query can be detected by using $\mathsf{sk}_{\mathsf{cca}}$, $\mathsf{sk}_{\mathsf{dv}}$, and $(\mathsf{sk}_{j,\alpha})_{j,\alpha}$, without using s. Thus, again by the one-time $\mathcal{P}$-KDM security of SKE, we have $|\mathrm{Pr}[\mathsf{BDQ}_5] - \mathrm{Pr}[\mathsf{BDQ}_6]| = \mathsf{negl}(\lambda)$.

Game 7: Same as Game 6, except that when responding to a KDM-encryption query, the challenger computes $\mathsf{CT} \leftarrow \mathsf{Enc}_{\mathsf{cca}}(\mathsf{pk}_{\mathsf{cca}}, 0^{\ell'})$, where $\ell' = |\widetilde{\mathsf{Q}}| + 2\ell_s \cdot |\mathsf{ct}_{j,\alpha}| + |\pi|$.

Recall that in the previous game, we have eliminated the information of $\mathsf{sk_{cca}}$ from $\mathsf{ct_{ske}}$. Thus, we can rely on the IND-CCA security of $\mathsf{PKE'}$ at this point, and straightforwardly derive $|\Pr[\mathsf{SUC_6}] - \Pr[\mathsf{SUC_7}]| = \mathsf{negl}(\lambda)$. Moreover, a reduction algorithm (attacking the IND-CCA security of $\mathsf{PKE'}$) can detect whether $\mathcal{A}$'s decryption query is bad by using $(\mathsf{sk}_{j,\alpha})_{j,\alpha}$, $\mathsf{sk_{dv}}$, and the reduction algorithm's own decryption queries. Thus, again by the IND-CCA security of $\mathsf{PKE'}$, we have $|\Pr[\mathsf{BDQ_6}] - \Pr[\mathsf{BDQ_7}]| = \mathsf{negl}(\lambda)$.

We see that in Game 7, the challenge bit b is information-theoretically hidden from $\mathcal{A}$'s view. Thus, we have $\Pr[\mathsf{SUC_7}] = 1/2$.

We need one more game to bound $\Pr[\mathsf{BDQ_7}]$.

Game 8: Same as Game 7, except that when generating PK, the challenger uses DVKG to generate $(\mathsf{pk_{dv}}, \mathsf{sk_{dv}})$, instead of using $\mathsf{S_1}$. Namely, we undo the change made between Games 1 and 2 for generating $(\mathsf{pk_{dv}}, \mathsf{sk_{dv}})$.[13]

By the zero-knowledge property of DVNIZK, we have $|\Pr[\mathsf{BDQ_7}] - \Pr[\mathsf{BDQ_8}]| = \mathsf{negl}(\lambda)$.

Finally, we argue that the soundness of DVNIZK implies $\Pr[\mathsf{BDQ_8}] = \mathsf{negl}(\lambda)$. To see this, note that in Game 8, $(\mathsf{pk_{dv}}, \mathsf{sk_{dv}})$ is now generated by DVKG. Also, if $\mathcal{A}$ submits a bad decryption query CT such that (1) $\mathsf{V}(\mathsf{sk_{dv}}, (\mathsf{pk}_{j,\alpha}, \mathsf{ct}_{j,\alpha})_{j,\alpha}, \pi) = \mathsf{accept}$ and (2) $\mathsf{Dec}(\mathsf{pk}_{j^*,0}, \mathsf{sk}_{j^*,0}, \mathsf{ct}_{j^*,0}) \neq \mathsf{Dec}(\mathsf{pk}_{j^*,1}, \mathsf{sk}_{j^*,1}, \mathsf{ct}_{j^*,1})$ for some $j^* \in [\ell_s]$, where $(\widetilde{\mathsf{Q}}, (\mathsf{ct}_{j,\alpha})_{j,\alpha}, \pi) \leftarrow \mathsf{Dec_{cca}}(\mathsf{pk_{cca}}, \mathsf{sk_{cca}}, \mathsf{CT})$, then the condition (2) in particular implies $(\mathsf{pk}_{j,\alpha}, \mathsf{ct}_{j,\alpha})_{j,\alpha} \notin L$. Thus $((\mathsf{pk}_{j,\alpha}, \mathsf{ct}_{j,\alpha})_{j,\alpha}, \pi)$ satisfies the condition of violating the soundness of DVNIZK. Note that a reduction algorithm (attacking the soundness of DVNIZK) is not directly given a secret verification key $\mathsf{sk_{dv}}$. However, the reduction algorithm is allowed to make verification queries, which is sufficient to perfectly simulate Game 8 for $\mathcal{A}$. The reduction algorithm can also detect whether $\mathcal{A}$ has made a bad decryption query by using $\mathsf{sk_{cca}}$ and $(\mathsf{sk}_{j,\alpha})_{j,\alpha}$, and verification queries. Hence, by the soundness of DVNIZK, we have $\Pr[\mathsf{BDQ_8}] = \mathsf{negl}(\lambda)$.

From the above arguments, we see that $\mathsf{Adv}^{\mathsf{kdmcca}}_{\mathsf{PKE_{kdm}}, \mathcal{B}_{\mathsf{size}}, \mathcal{A}, 1}(\lambda) = \mathsf{negl}(\lambda)$. Since the choice of $\mathcal{A}$ was arbitrary, we can conclude that $\mathsf{PKE_{kdm}}$ is $\mathcal{B}_{\mathsf{size}}$-$\mathsf{KDM}^{(1)}$-CCA secure. □ (**Theorem** 4)

6   Multi-user KDM-CCA Security from RKA-KDM Security

In this section, we show that for any polynomial $n = n(\lambda)$, our proposed PKE scheme $\mathsf{PKE_{kdm}}$ presented in Sect. 5 can be shown to be $\mathcal{B}_{\mathsf{size}}$-$\mathsf{KDM}^{(n)}$-CCA secure, by choosing a suitable parameter for $\mathsf{pad} = \mathsf{pad}(\lambda, n)$ and additionally requiring the underlying SKE scheme SKE satisfies $\mathcal{P}$-RKA-$\mathsf{KDM}^{(n)}$ security, and its key generation algorithm outputs a uniformly random string in the secret key space. Formally, our result for the multi-user setting is stated as follows.

---

[13] Note that in Games 7 and 8, π is not computed when generating CT, and thus we need not use $\mathsf{S_2}$.

Theorem 5. *Let* $n = n(\lambda)$, $\ell_m = \ell_m(\lambda)$, *and* $\mathsf{size} = \mathsf{size}(\lambda) \geq \max\{\ell_s, \ell_m\}$ *be any polynomials, and let* $\mathsf{pad} := \mathsf{size} + O(\ell_s \cdot n)$. *Assume that* PKE *is IND-CPA secure,* PKE' *is IND-CCA secure,* SKE *is passively* $\mathcal{P}$-*RKA-KDM*$^{(n)}$ *secure and its key generation algorithm outputs a string that is distributed uniformly over* $\{0,1\}^{\ell_s}$, GC *is a secure garbling scheme, and* DVNIZK *is a reusable DV-NIZK argument system for the NP language* L. *Then,* $\mathsf{PKE}_{\mathsf{kdm}}$ *is* $\mathcal{B}_{\mathsf{size}}$-*KDM*$^{(n)}$-*CCA secure.*

The formal proof is given in the full version. A high-level structure of the sequence of the games used in the proof of Theorem 5 is similar to that of Theorem 4. The main differences are as follows.

- Before the game-hop for switching the simulator Sim of the garbling scheme GC to the ordinary algorithm Garble, we introduce a game in which every user's secret key s^i is derived by using a randomly chosen single "main" key $s \in \{0,1\}^{\ell_s}$ and a randomly chosen "shift" $\Delta^i \in \{0,1\}^{\ell_s}$, so that $s^i := s \oplus \Delta^i$. This does not at all change the distribution of the keys due to the requirement on SKE that a secret key is distributed uniformly in the secret key space $\{0,1\}^{\ell_s}$. This enables us to conduct the remaining game-hops as if $s \in \{0,1\}^{\ell_s}$ is the single "main" secret key such that we need to care only its leakage to an adversary via KDM-encryption and decryption queries.
- In the game-hop for switching the simulator Sim of GC to the ordinary garbling algorithm Garble, instead of directly garbling a KDM-function f_b (which is a function of all users' secret keys $S := s^1 \| \ldots \| s_s^\ell$ in the n-user setting) appearing in an adversary's KDM-encryption query (i^*, f_0, f_1), we garble some appropriately designed circuit Q with input length ℓ_s. More specifically, we garble a circuit Q that has the index i^*, the KDM-function f_b, and the shifts $(\Delta^i)_{i \in [n]}$ hard-wired, and satisfies $f_b(S) = \mathsf{Q}(s^{i^*})$.
- In the game-hop for erasing the information of $((\mathsf{sk}^i_{j,s_j})_j, \mathsf{sk}^i_{\mathsf{cca}}, \mathsf{sk}^i_{\mathsf{dv}})$ from $\mathsf{ct}^i_{\mathsf{ske}}$ for every $i \in [n]$, we rely on the passive $\mathcal{P}$-RKA-KDM$^{(n)}$ security of SKE (as opposed to its one-time $\mathcal{P}$-KDM security). Intuitively, passive $\mathcal{P}$-RKA-KDM$^{(n)}$ security suffices here because each user's secret key s^i is computed as $s^i = s \oplus \Delta^i$ where s and each Δ^i are chosen randomly by the challenger, due to the change made in the first item above.

7   Putting It All Together

In this section, we summarize our results.

By combining Theorems 2 and 4, for any polynomial $\mathsf{size} = \mathsf{size}(\lambda)$, a $\mathcal{B}_{\mathsf{size}}$-KDM$^{(1)}$-CCA secure PKE scheme can be constructed from an IND-CPA secure PKE scheme, an IND-CCA secure PKE scheme, a one-time $\mathcal{P}$-KDM secure SKE scheme, and a garbling scheme. From the result by Kitagawa et al. [30], we can realize an IND-CCA secure PKE scheme from an IND-CPA secure PKE scheme and a one-time $\mathcal{P}$-KDM secure PKE scheme. Moreover, a garbling scheme is implied by one-way functions [40], which is in turn implied by an IND-CPA secure PKE scheme. From these, we obtain the following theorem.

Theorem 6. *Assume that there exist an IND-CPA secure PKE scheme and a one-time $\mathcal{P}$-KDM secure SKE scheme that can encrypt messages of length $\Omega(\ell \cdot \lambda)$, where $\ell = \ell(\lambda)$ denotes the secret key length of the SKE scheme. Then, for any polynomial $\mathsf{size} = \mathsf{size}(\lambda)$, there exists a $\mathcal{B}_{\mathsf{size}}$-KDM$^{(1)}$-CCA secure PKE scheme.*

Since both an IND-CPA secure PKE scheme and a one-time $\mathcal{P}$-KDM secure SKE scheme are implied by a $\mathcal{P}$-KDM$^{(1)}$-CPA secure PKE scheme, we obtain the following main theorem.

Theorem 7. (CPA-to-CCA Transformation for KDM Security) *Assume that there exists a $\mathcal{P}$-KDM$^{(1)}$-CPA secure PKE scheme. Then, for any polynomial $\mathsf{size} = \mathsf{size}(\lambda)$, there exists a $\mathcal{B}_{\mathsf{size}}$-KDM$^{(1)}$-CCA secure PKE scheme.*

Similarly to Theorem 6, by combining Theorems 2 and 5, and the previous results [30,40], we also obtain the following theorem.

Theorem 8. *Let $n = n(\lambda)$ be a polynomial. Assume that there exist an IND-CPA secure PKE scheme, and a passively $\mathcal{P}$-RKA-KDM$^{(n)}$ secure SKE scheme that can encrypt messages of length $\Omega(\ell \cdot \lambda)$, where $\ell = \ell(\lambda)$ denotes the secret key length of the SKE scheme, and whose secret key generation algorithm outputs a string that is distributed uniformly over $\{0,1\}^\ell$. Then, for any polynomial $\mathsf{size} = \mathsf{size}(\lambda)$, there exists a $\mathcal{B}_{\mathsf{size}}$-KDM$^{(n)}$-CCA secure PKE scheme.*

Note that a passively $\mathcal{P}$-RKA-KDM$^{(n)}$ secure SKE scheme is also a one-time $\mathcal{P}$-KDM secure SKE scheme.

For any polynomials n and μ, we can construct a passively $\mathcal{P}$-RKA-KDM$^{(n)}$ secure SKE scheme whose message space is $\{0,1\}^\mu$ based on the LPN assumption [4]. In addition, as shown in the full version of this paper, for any polynomials n and μ, we can construct a $\mathcal{P}$-RKA-KDM$^{(n)}$ secure SKE scheme whose message space is $\{0,1\}^\mu$ based on the CDH assumption. The key generation algorithms of the LPN-/CDH-based constructions output a uniformly random string as a secret key. Since an IND-CPA secure PKE scheme can be constructed based on the LPN and CDH assumptions, we obtain the following corollary.

Corollary 1. *Let $n = n(\lambda)$ and $\mathsf{size} = \mathsf{size}(\lambda)$ be any polynomials. There exists a $\mathcal{B}_{\mathsf{size}}$-KDM$^{(n)}$-CCA secure PKE scheme under either the LPN or CDH assumption.*

Acknowledgement. We thank the anonymous reviewers of TCC 2019 for helpful comments, in particular the connections of our techniques with those by Barak et al. [6]. A part of this work was supported by JST CREST Grant Number JPMJCR19F6.

References

1. Adão, P., Bana, G., Herzog, J., Scedrov, A.: Soundness of formal encryption in the presence of key-cycles. In: di Vimercati, S.C., Syverson, P., Gollmann, D. (eds.) ESORICS 2005. LNCS, vol. 3679, pp. 374–396. Springer, Heidelberg (2005). https://doi.org/10.1007/11555827_22

2. Alekhnovich, M.: More on average case vs approximation complexity. In: 44th FOCS 2003, pp. 298–307 (2003)

3. Applebaum, B.: Key-dependent message security: generic amplification and completeness. In: Paterson, K.G. (ed.) EUROCRYPT 2011. LNCS, vol. 6632, pp. 527–546. Springer, Heidelberg (2011). https://doi.org/10.1007/978-3-642-20465-4_29

4. Applebaum, B.: Garbling XOR gates "For Free" in the standard model. In: Sahai, A. (ed.) TCC 2013. LNCS, vol. 7785, pp. 162–181. Springer, Heidelberg (2013). https://doi.org/10.1007/978-3-642-36594-2_10

5. Applebaum, B., Cash, D., Peikert, C., Sahai, A.: Fast cryptographic primitives and circular-secure encryption based on hard learning problems. In: Halevi, S. (ed.) CRYPTO 2009. LNCS, vol. 5677, pp. 595–618. Springer, Heidelberg (2009). https://doi.org/10.1007/978-3-642-03356-8_35

6. Barak, B., Haitner, I., Hofheinz, D., Ishai, Y.: Bounded key-dependent message security. In: Gilbert, H. (ed.) EUROCRYPT 2010. LNCS, vol. 6110, pp. 423–444. Springer, Heidelberg (2010). https://doi.org/10.1007/978-3-642-13190-5_22

7. Bellare, M., Desai, A., Pointcheval, D., Rogaway, P.: Relations among notions of security for public-key encryption schemes. In: Krawczyk, H. (ed.) CRYPTO 1998. LNCS, vol. 1462, pp. 26–45. Springer, Heidelberg (1998). https://doi.org/10.1007/BFb0055718

8. Black, J., Rogaway, P., Shrimpton, T.: Encryption-scheme security in the presence of key-dependent messages. In: Nyberg, K., Heys, H. (eds.) SAC 2002. LNCS, vol. 2595, pp. 62–75. Springer, Heidelberg (2003). https://doi.org/10.1007/3-540-36492-7_6

9. Bleichenbacher, D.: Chosen ciphertext attacks against protocols based on the RSA encryption standard PKCS #1. In: Krawczyk, H. (ed.) CRYPTO 1998. LNCS, vol. 1462, pp. 1–12. Springer, Heidelberg (1998). https://doi.org/10.1007/BFb0055716

10. Boneh, D., Halevi, S., Hamburg, M., Ostrovsky, R.: Circular-secure encryption from decision Diffie-Hellman. In: Wagner, D. (ed.) CRYPTO 2008. LNCS, vol. 5157, pp. 108–125. Springer, Heidelberg (2008). https://doi.org/10.1007/978-3-540-85174-5_7

11. Boyle, E., Kohl, L., Scholl, P.: Homomorphic secret sharing from lattices without FHE. In: Ishai, Y., Rijmen, V. (eds.) EUROCRYPT 2019. LNCS, vol. 11477, pp. 3–33. Springer, Cham (2019). https://doi.org/10.1007/978-3-030-17656-3_1

12. Brakerski, Z., Goldwasser, S.: Circular and leakage resilient public-key encryption under subgroup indistinguishability. In: Rabin, T. (ed.) CRYPTO 2010. LNCS, vol. 6223, pp. 1–20. Springer, Heidelberg (2010). https://doi.org/10.1007/978-3-642-14623-7_1

13. Brakerski, Z., Lombardi, A., Segev, G., Vaikuntanathan, V.: Anonymous IBE, leakage resilience and circular security from new assumptions. In: Nielsen, J.B., Rijmen, V. (eds.) EUROCRYPT 2018. LNCS, vol. 10820, pp. 535–564. Springer, Cham (2018). https://doi.org/10.1007/978-3-319-78381-9_20

14. Camenisch, J., Chandran, N., Shoup, V.: A public key encryption scheme secure against key dependent chosen plaintext and adaptive chosen ciphertext attacks. In: Joux, A. (ed.) EUROCRYPT 2009. LNCS, vol. 5479, pp. 351–368. Springer, Heidelberg (2009). https://doi.org/10.1007/978-3-642-01001-9_20

15. Camenisch, J., Lysyanskaya, A.: Dynamic accumulators and application to efficient revocation of anonymous credentials. In: Yung, M. (ed.) CRYPTO 2002. LNCS, vol. 2442, pp. 61–76. Springer, Heidelberg (2002). https://doi.org/10.1007/3-540-45708-9_5

16. Canetti, R., et al.: Fiat-Shamir: from practice to theory. In: 51st ACM STOC 2019, pp. 1082–1090 (2019)

17. Canetti, R., Chen, Y., Reyzin, L., Rothblum, R.D.: Fiat-Shamir and correlation intractability from strong KDM-secure encryption. In: Nielsen, J.B., Rijmen, V. (eds.) EUROCRYPT 2018, Part I. LNCS, vol. 10820, pp. 91–122. Springer, Cham (2018). https://doi.org/10.1007/978-3-319-78381-9_4

18. Canetti, R., Halevi, S., Katz, J.: Chosen-ciphertext security from identity-based encryption. In: Cachin, C., Camenisch, J.L. (eds.) EUROCRYPT 2004. LNCS, vol. 3027, pp. 207–222. Springer, Heidelberg (2004). https://doi.org/10.1007/978-3-540-24676-3_13

19. Cramer, R., Shoup, V.: Universal hash proofs and a paradigm for adaptive chosen ciphertext secure public-key encryption. In: Knudsen, L.R. (ed.) EUROCRYPT 2002. LNCS, vol. 2332, pp. 45–64. Springer, Heidelberg (2002). https://doi.org/10.1007/3-540-46035-7_4

20. Dolev, D., Dwork, C., Naor, M.: Non-malleable cryptography (extended abstract). In: 23rd ACM STOC 1991, pp. 542–552 (1991)

21. Döttling, N.: Low noise LPN: KDM secure public key encryption and sample amplification. In: Katz, J. (ed.) PKC 2015. LNCS, vol. 9020, pp. 604–626. Springer, Heidelberg (2015). https://doi.org/10.1007/978-3-662-46447-2_27

22. Döttling, N., Garg, S., Hajiabadi, M., Masny, D.: New constructions of identity-based and key-dependent message secure encryption schemes. In: Abdalla, M., Dahab, R. (eds.) PKC 2018, Part I. LNCS, vol. 10769, pp. 3–31. Springer, Cham (2018). https://doi.org/10.1007/978-3-319-76578-5_1

23. Galindo, D., Herranz, J., Villar, J.: Identity-based encryption with master key-dependent message security and leakage-resilience. In: Foresti, S., Yung, M., Martinelli, F. (eds.) ESORICS 2012. LNCS, vol. 7459, pp. 627–642. Springer, Heidelberg (2012). https://doi.org/10.1007/978-3-642-33167-1_36

24. Gentry, C.: Fully homomorphic encryption using ideal lattices. In: 41st ACM STOC 2009, pp. 169–178 (2009)

25. Gertner, Y., Malkin, T., Myers, S.: Towards a separation of semantic and CCA security for public key encryption. In: Vadhan, S.P. (ed.) TCC 2007. LNCS, vol. 4392, pp. 434–455. Springer, Heidelberg (2007). https://doi.org/10.1007/978-3-540-70936-7_24

26. Goldwasser, S., Micali, S.: Probabilistic encryption and how to play mental poker keeping secret all partial information. In: 14th ACM STOC 1982, pp. 365–377 (1982)

27. Hajiabadi, M., Kapron, B.M.: Reproducible circularly-secure bit encryption: applications and realizations. In: Gennaro, R., Robshaw, M. (eds.) CRYPTO 2015, Part I. LNCS, vol. 9215, pp. 224–243. Springer, Heidelberg (2015). https://doi.org/10.1007/978-3-662-47989-6_11

28. Hohenberger, S., Lewko, A., Waters, B.: Detecting dangerous queries: a new approach for chosen ciphertext security. In: Pointcheval, D., Johansson, T. (eds.) EUROCRYPT 2012. LNCS, vol. 7237, pp. 663–681. Springer, Heidelberg (2012). https://doi.org/10.1007/978-3-642-29011-4_39

29. Kitagawa, F., Matsuda, T., Hanaoka, G., Tanaka, K.: Completeness of single-bit projection-KDM security for public key encryption. In: Nyberg, K. (ed.) CT-RSA 2015. LNCS, vol. 9048, pp. 201–219. Springer, Cham (2015). https://doi.org/10.1007/978-3-319-16715-2_11

30. Kitagawa, F., Matsuda, T., Tanaka, K.: CCA security and trapdoor functions via key-dependent-message security. In: Boldyreva, A., Micciancio, D. (eds.) CRYPTO 2019, Part III. LNCS, vol. 11694, pp. 33–64. Springer, Cham (2019). https://doi.org/10.1007/978-3-030-26954-8_2

31. Kitagawa, F., Tanaka, K.: A framework for achieving KDM-CCA secure public-key encryption. In: Peyrin, T., Galbraith, S. (eds.) ASIACRYPT 2018, Part II. LNCS, vol. 11273, pp. 127–157. Springer, Cham (2018). https://doi.org/10.1007/978-3-030-03329-3_5

32. Kitagawa, F., Tanaka, K.: Key dependent message security and receiver selective opening security for identity-based encryption. In: Abdalla, M., Dahab, R. (eds.) PKC 2018, Part I. LNCS, vol. 10769, pp. 32–61. Springer, Cham (2018). https://doi.org/10.1007/978-3-319-76578-5_2

33. Koppula, V., Waters, B.: Realizing chosen ciphertext security generically in attribute-based encryption and predicate encryption. In: Boldyreva, A., Micciancio, D. (eds.) CRYPTO 2019, Part II. LNCS, vol. 11693, pp. 671–700. Springer, Cham (2019). https://doi.org/10.1007/978-3-030-26951-7_23

34. Lombardi, A., Quach, W., Rothblum, R.D., Wichs, D., Wu, D.J.: New constructions of reusable designated-verifier NIZKs. IACR Cryptology ePrint Archive 242 (2019). Accessed 27 Feb 2019. A preliminary version of [35]

35. Lombardi, A., Quach, W., Rothblum, R.D., Wichs, D., Wu, D.J.: New constructions of reusable designated-verifier NIZKs. In: Boldyreva, A., Micciancio, D. (eds.) CRYPTO 2019, Part III. LNCS, vol. 11694, pp. 670–700. Springer, Cham (2019). https://doi.org/10.1007/978-3-030-26954-8_22

36. Matsuda, T., Hanaoka, G.: Constructing and understanding chosen ciphertext security via puncturable key encapsulation mechanisms. In: Dodis, Y., Nielsen, J.B. (eds.) TCC 2015, Part I. LNCS, vol. 9014, pp. 561–590. Springer, Heidelberg (2015). https://doi.org/10.1007/978-3-662-46494-6_23

37. Naor, M., Yung, M.: Public-key cryptosystems provably secure against chosen ciphertext attacks. In: 22nd ACM STOC 1990, pp. 427–437 (1990)

38. Rackoff, C., Simon, D.R.: Non-interactive zero-knowledge proof of knowledge and chosen ciphertext attack. In: Feigenbaum, J. (ed.) CRYPTO 1991. LNCS, vol. 576, pp. 433–444. Springer, Heidelberg (1992). https://doi.org/10.1007/3-540-46766-1_35

39. Sahai, A.: Non-malleable non-interactive zero knowledge and adaptive chosen-ciphertext security. In: 40th FOCS 1999, pp. 543–553 (1999)

40. Yao, A.C.-C.: How to generate and exchange secrets (extended abstract). In: 27th FOCS 1986, pp. 162–167 (1986)

41. Yu, Y., Zhang, J.: Cryptography with auxiliary input and trapdoor from constant-noise LPN. In: Robshaw, M., Katz, J. (eds.) CRYPTO 2016, Part I. LNCS, vol. 9814, pp. 214–243. Springer, Heidelberg (2016). https://doi.org/10.1007/978-3-662-53018-4_9

New Approaches to Traitor Tracing
with Embedded Identities

Rishab Goyal[1][(✉)], Venkata Koppula[2], and Brent Waters[3]

[1] University of Texas at Austin, Austin, USA
rgoyal@cs.utexas.edu
[2] Weizmann Institute of Science, Rehovot, Israel
venkata.koppula@weizmann.ac.il
[3] University of Texas at Austin and NTT Research, Austin, USA
bwaters@cs.utexas.edu

Abstract. In a traitor tracing (TT) system for n users, every user has his/her own secret key. Content providers can encrypt messages using a public key, and each user can decrypt the ciphertext using his/her secret key. Suppose some of the n users collude to construct a pirate decoding box. Then the tracing scheme has a special algorithm, called Trace, which can identify at least one of the secret keys used to construct the pirate decoding box.

Traditionally, the trace algorithm output only the 'index' associated with the traitors. As a result, to use such systems, either a central master authority must map the indices to actual identities, or there should be a public mapping of indices to identities. Both these options are problematic, especially if we need public tracing with anonymity of users. Nishimaki, Wichs, and Zhandry (NWZ) [Eurocrypt 2016] addressed this problem by constructing a traitor tracing scheme where the identities of users are embedded in the secret keys, and the trace algorithm, given a decoding box D, can recover the entire identities of the traitors. We call such schemes 'Embedded Identity Traitor Tracing' schemes. NWZ constructed such schemes based on adaptively secure functional encryption (FE). Currently, the only known constructions of FE schemes are based on nonstandard assumptions such as multilinear maps and iO.

In this work, we study the problem of embedded identities TT based on standard assumptions. We provide a range of constructions based on different assumptions such as public key encryption (PKE), bilinear maps and the Learning with Errors (LWE) assumption. The different constructions have different efficiency trade offs. In our PKE based construction, the ciphertext size grows linearly with the number of users; the bilinear maps based construction has sub-linear ($\sqrt{n}$) sized ciphertexts. Both these schemes have public tracing. The LWE based scheme is a private tracing scheme with optimal ciphertexts (i.e., $\log(n)$). Finally, we also present other notions of traitor tracing, and discuss how they can be build in a generic manner from our base embedded identity TT scheme.

B. Waters—Supported by NSF CNS-1908611, CNS-1414082, DARPA SafeWare and Packard Foundation Fellowship.

ⓒ International Association for Cryptologic Research 2019
D. Hofheinz and A. Rosen (Eds.): TCC 2019, LNCS 11892, pp. 149–179, 2019.
https://doi.org/10.1007/978-3-030-36033-7_6

1   Introduction

Traitor tracing (TT) systems, as introduced by Chor, Fiat, and Naor [14], studied the problem of identifying the users that contributed to building a rogue decoder in a broadcast environment. In a TT system an authority runs a setup algorithm on input a security parameter λ, and the number of users n in the system. This results in generation of a global public key pk, a tracing key key, and n private user keys $(\mathsf{sk}_1, \mathsf{sk}_2, \ldots, \mathsf{sk}_n)$. Each private key is distributed to an authorized user in the system with the guarantee that it can be used to decrypt any ciphertext ct encrypting a message m under the global public key pk. The first security property satisfied by such systems is that the message will be hidden from every unauthorized user, that is one who does not have access to any secret key. The most salient feature of a traitor tracing system is the presence of an additional tracing algorithm which is used to identify corrupt/coerced users. Suppose an attacker corrupts some subset $S \subseteq \{1, \ldots, n\}$ of authorized users and produces a special decryption algorithm/device D that can decrypt the ciphertexts with some non-negligible probability. The tracing property of the system states that the tracing algorithm, on input the tracing key key and oracle access to device D, outputs a set of users T where T contains at least one user from the colluding set S (and no users outside of S).

The initial traitor tracing systems [1,2,6,8,12,14,15,19,27–30,32–34] allowed bounded collusions; we focus on unbounded collusion [9–11,13,20,22,26,31]. While the concept of traitor tracing was originally motivated by catching corrupt users in broadcast systems, the notion of traitor tracing has numerous other applications such as transmitting sensitive information to first responders (or military personnel etc.) on an ad-hoc deployed wireless network, accessing and sharing encrypted files on untrusted cloud storage etc. This propels us to study the problem of traitor traitor more finely with a dedicated focus on understanding the issues that prevent a wider adoptability of such systems.

One major hurdle is that, as per the traditional description of the problem, the tracing portion (that is identifying the corrupt users) is inherently tied to the central authority (key generator) in the system. This is due to the fact that the authority needs to keep track of the users who have been issued private keys, and thus it needs to maintain an explicit mapping (as a look-up table) between the user identification information and the indices of their respective private keys. Otherwise, the output of the tracing algorithm will simply be a subset T of the user indices which can not be linked to actual users in the system, thereby introducing the problem of accountability and circumventing the whole point of tracing traitors. In addition, this not only constrains the authority to be fully stateful (with the state size growing linear with the number of users) by necessitating that the authority *must record* the user information to key index mapping, but also restricts the authority to be the only party which can perform any meaningful notion of tracing if (authorized) user privacy/anonymity is also desired.[1] Therefore, even if the TT system achieves public traceability, that is the tracing key key can be included as part of public parameters, no third party would be able to identify traitors in system due to lack of a public mapping as described above.

Furthermore, in certain situations the user information to key index mapping might be undetermined. For example, suppose all the users in the system obtain their private decryption keys without revealing any sensitive identification information to the key generating authority. (Note that this can be achieved by some sort of two party computation-based transfer between the user and authority.) In such a scenario, it is not clear how tracing would work since the authority would not be able to point to any user in the system as a traitor because the key index to user identity mapping is unknown, even if the tracing algorithm correctly outputs an index of some coerced secret key.

These observations lead to the following question—

Is it possible to embed the user identification information in the private decryption keys such that during tracing the algorithm not only finds the corrupted key indices, but also extracts the corresponding user identities from the pirate decoding device?

Formally, this is captured by giving an additional parameter κ as an input to the setup algorithm, where κ denotes the length of the user identities that can be embedded in the private keys. The setup now outputs a master secret key msk, instead of n private user keys, where msk is used to generate private keys $sk_{i,id}$ for any index-identity pair $(i, id) \in [n] \times \{0,1\}^{\kappa}$. And the tracing algorithm outputs a set of 'user identities' $T \subseteq \{0,1\}^{\kappa}$ where $id \in T$ indicates that id was one of the corrupted users.[2] This interpretation of traitor tracing resolves the above issues of statefulness, third-party traceability, and maintaining a private look-up table for providing user anonymity.

The above-stated question of traitor tracing with embedded information in secret keys was first studied by Nishimaki, Wichs, and Zhandry [31]. Their approach was to directly work with the existing private linear broadcast encryption (PLBE) framework [9], however that resulted in solutions based on non-standard assumptions. Concretely, they assume existence of an adaptively-secure collusion-resistant public-key functional encryption (FE) scheme with compact ciphertexts. Currently all known instantiations are either based on multilinear maps [16,17,21,23], or indistinguishability obfuscation [4,5]. An important open question here is whether the above problem of embedded information traitor

---

[1] Although the problem of statefulness can be avoided by posting the identity of all authorized users along with their respective (decryption key) indices on a public-bulletin board, such a solution is particularly undesirable in practice as the user identities might include highly sensitive information such as passport information, driving license number, etc.

[2] Note that the tracing algorithm could be additionally asked to output the corresponding user index along with the identity, but since the index $i \in [n]$ could itself be encoded in the identity id using only $\log(n)$ bits therefore this seems unnecessary.

tracing can be solved from standard assumptions such as one-way functions, bilinear assumptions, learning with errors etc. In this work, we study this question and provide a general framework for solving this problem with a wide range of parameter choices and assumption families.

Our Results. We give new constructions for traitor tracing systems with embedded identity tracing under the following assumptions.[3]

Public-key encryption. Our first construction is that of an embedded identity TT scheme with public traceability that relies only on regular PKE schemes. The ciphertext size and length of public key grows linearly in both the number of users n as well as the length of embedded identities κ. This is a natural generalization of the basic TT scheme based on PKE, and is provided to serve as a baseline benchmark for comparing efficiency with other instantiations.

Bilinear maps. Second, we show that using a more algebraic approach via bilinear maps we can build an embedded identity TT scheme with a square-root speed-up w.r.t. the PKE-based scheme. Concretely, the size of ciphertexts and length of public key grows linearly in $\sqrt{n}$ and $\sqrt{\kappa}$. And the scheme still achieves public traceability.

Learning with errors. Lastly, we build a *compact* embedded identity TT scheme secure under the learning with errors (LWE) assumption. Here compactness means that the size of ciphertexts and public key scales polynomially with $\log(n)$ and κ. On the flip side, the tracing key needs to be private, that is it only achieves private key traceability.

These are summarized in Table 1. In the next section we elaborate more on our framework and general methodology for breaking down the problem. Below we discuss our results in more detail.

Table 1. Embedded identity traitor tracing. The 'Tr. Mode' column indicates whether tracing is public or private.

Assumption	|ct|	|pk|	|sk|	Tr. Mode	Unbdd
PKE	$n \cdot \kappa \cdot \mathsf{poly}(\lambda)$	$n \cdot \kappa \cdot \mathsf{poly}(\lambda)$	$\kappa \cdot \mathsf{poly}(\lambda)$	Pub	No
Bilinear	$\sqrt{n \cdot \kappa} \cdot \mathsf{poly}(\lambda)$	$\sqrt{n \cdot \kappa} \cdot \mathsf{poly}(\lambda)$	$\log n + \kappa + \mathsf{poly}(\lambda)$	Pub	No
LWE	$(\log n + \kappa) \cdot \mathsf{poly}(\lambda)$	$\mathsf{poly}(\lambda)$	$(\log n + \kappa) \cdot \mathsf{poly}(\lambda)$	Priv	Yes

In this work, we provide three new pathways for realizing embedded identity TT systems, and notably the first constructions relying only on standard assumptions. Our first two constructions from public-key encryption and bilinear maps are novel, where our bilinear map based scheme draws ideas from the

---

[3] Nishimaki, Wichs, and Zhandry [31] used the term "flexible" traitor tracing to refer to schemes where the space of identities that can be traced is exponential. Here we call such TT systems as embedded identity TT schemes (or EITT for short).

trace and revoke scheme of Boneh-Waters [10]. And, for building an LWE-based solution we adapt the recently introduced Mixed Functional Encryption (Mixed FE) schemes [13,26] in our framework to get the desired results.

Furthermore, a very important and useful piece of our approach is that it allows us to avoid subexponential security loss in the transformation (due to complexity leveraging) if we allow an *exponential* number of users in the system and the intermediate primitives used are only *selectively-secure*. Particularly, this is used in our LWE-based solution which relies on mixed FE for which most of the current constructions are only known to achieve selective security. (For example, the first mixed FE construction by Goyal, Koppula, and Waters [26] and two of three follow-up constructions by Chen et al. [13] were proven to be only selectively-secure.) Therefore, our approach also answers the question whether adaptivity is necessary for building embedded identity TT schemes if the system is required to support an unbounded number of users. Note that in the prior work of Nishimaki, Wichs, and Zhandry [31], it was crucial that they start with an 'adaptively-secure' FE scheme for security purposes, but here our approach helps in bypassing the adaptivity requirement. Next, we provide a detailed technical overview of our results.

2   Technical Overview

We start by formally defining the notion of embedded identity traitor tracing (EITT) systems. In order to capture a broader class of traitor tracing systems, we consider three different variants for embedded identity tracing—(1) indexed EITT, (2) bounded EITT, and (3) full (unbounded) EITT. Although the notion of full/unbounded EITT is the most general notion we define and therefore it is also likely the most desirable notion, we believe that both indexed and bounded EITT systems will also find many direct applications as will be evident later during their descriptions. In addition, we also show direct connections between all three notions by providing different transformations among these notions.

Next, we move on to realizing these EITT systems under standard assumptions. To that end, we first introduce a new intermediate primitive which we call *embedded-identity private linear broadcast encryption* (EIPLBE) that we eventually use to build EITT schemes. As the name suggests, the notion of EIPLBE is inspired by and is an extension of *private linear broadcast encryption* (PLBE) schemes introduced in the work of Boneh, Sahai, and Waters (BSW) [9]. BSW introduced the notion of PLBE schemes as a stepping stone towards building general TT systems. In this work, we show that the above-stated extension of PLBE systems can be very useful in that it leads to new solutions for the embedded identity traitor tracing problem.

Finally, we provide multiple instantiations of EIPLBE schemes that are secure under a variety of assumptions (PKE, Bilinear, and LWE). Using these EIPLBE schemes in the aforementioned transformation, we can build various EITT systems with appropriate efficiency metrics.

2.1 Embedded Identity Traitor Tracing Definitions

Let us first formally recall the notion of standard traitor tracing (i.e., without embedding identities in the secret keys). A traitor tracing system consists of four poly-time algorithms—Setup, Enc, Dec, and Trace. The setup algorithm takes as input security parameter λ, and number of users n and generates a public key pk, a tracing key key, and n private keys $\mathsf{sk}_1, \ldots, \mathsf{sk}_n$. The encryption algorithm encrypts a message m using public key pk, and the decryption algorithm decrypts a ciphertext using any one of the private keys sk_i. The tracing algorithm takes tracing key key, two messages m_0, m_1 as input, and is given (black-box) oracle access to a pirate decoding algorithm D.[4] It outputs a set $S \subseteq [n]$ of users signalling that the keys sk_j for $j \in S$ were used to create the pirate decoder D. The security requirements are as described in the previous section.

Let us now look at how to embed identities in the private user keys such that the tracing algorithm outputs a set of identities instead. Below we describe the identity embedding abstractions considered in this work. Throughout this sequel, κ denotes the length of identities embedded (that is, identity space is $\{0,1\}^\kappa$).

Indexed EITT. We begin with indexed EITT as the simplest way to introduce identity embedding functionality in the standard TT framework is as follows. The setup algorithm takes both n and κ as inputs and outputs a master secret key msk. Such systems will have a special key generation algorithm that takes as input msk along with an index-identity pair $(i, \mathsf{id}) \in [n] \times \{0,1\}^\kappa$, and outputs a user key $\mathsf{sk}_{i,\mathsf{id}}$. When the ith user requests a key then it can supply its identity id, and the authority runs key generation on corresponding inputs to sample a secret key for that particular user.

Encryption, decryption, and tracing algorithms remain unaffected with the exception that the tracing algorithm outputs a set of user identities $S \subseteq \{0,1\}^\kappa$ instead.[5] Now the IND-CPA and secure tracing requirements very naturally extend to indexed EITT systems with one caveat that the adversary can only obtain a user key for each index at most once in the traitor tracing game. Comparing this with standard TT schemes in which each corrupted user receives a unique private key depending on its index, this constraint on set of corruptible keys is a natural translation.

Looking carefully at the above abstraction, we observe that using such indexed systems in practice would seem to resolve the 'look-up table' problem thereby allowing third party tracing, but the problem of statefulness is not

---

[4] Traditionally, the tracing algorithm was defined to work only if the decoder box could decrypt encryptions of random messages. However, as discussed in [24], this definition does not capture many practical scenarios. Therefore we work with a broader abstraction where the trace algorithm works even if the decoder can only distinguish between encryptions of two specific messages.

[5] Although one could ask the tracer to output a set of index-identity pairs instead of only identities, this seems unnecessary as the user index can always be embedded in its identity.

yet completely resolved. Concretely, the key generating authority still needs to maintain a counter (that is $\log(n)$ bits) which represents the number of keys issued until that point. Basically each time someone queries for a secret key for identity id, the authority generates a secret key for identity id and index being the current counter value, and it increments the counter in parallel. This constraint stems from the fact that for guaranteeing correct tracing it is essential that the adversary receives at most one key per index $i \in [n]$. Although for a lot of applications indexed EITT might already be sufficient, it is possible that for others this is still restrictive. To that end, we define another EITT notion to completely remove the state as follows.

Bounded EITT. The idea behind bounded EITT is that now the input n given to the setup algorithm represents an upper bound on the number of keys an adversary is allowed to corrupt while the system still guarantees correct traceability. And importantly, the key generation algorithm now only receives an identity id as input instead of an index-identity pair. Thus, the authority does not need to maintain the counter, that is it does not need to keep track of number of users registered. Another point of emphasis is that in a Bounded EITT system if the number of keys an attacker corrupts exceeds the setup threshold n, the attacker may avoid being traced; however, even in this scenario tracing procedure will not falsely indict an non-colluding user. In addition to being a useful property in its own right, the non-false indictment property will be critical in amplifying to Unbounded EITT.

Interestingly, we show a generic transformation from any indexed EITT scheme to a bounded EITT scheme with only a minor efficiency loss. More details on this transformation are provided towards the end of this section. Looking ahead, this transformation only relies on the existence of signatures additionally.

Unbounded EITT. Lastly the most general notion of embedded identity traitor tracing possible is of systems in which the setup algorithm only takes κ the length of identities as input, thus there is no upper bound on the number of admissible corruptions set during setup time. Therefore, the adversary can possibly corrupt an arbitrary (but polynomial) number of users in the system. In this work, we additionally provide an efficient unconditional transformation from bounded EITT schemes to unbounded EITT schemes thereby completely solving the embedded identity tracing problem. More details on this transformation are also provided towards the end of this section.

Next, we move on to building the indexed EITT schemes under standard assumptions. As discussed before, we first introduce the intermediate notion of EIPLBE.

2.2 Embedded-Identity Private Linear Broadcast Encryption

Let us start by recalling the notion of private linear broadcast encryption (PLBE) [9]. Syntactically, a PLBE scheme is same as a traitor tracing scheme as in it consists of setup, key generation, encryption, decryption algorithms with the exception that instead of tracing algorithm it provides an additional encryption algorithm usually referred to as *index-encryption* algorithm. In PLBE systems, the setup algorithm outputs a public, master secret, and index-encryption key tuple (pk, msk, key). As in TT systems, the key generation uses master secret key to sample user private keys sk_j for any given index $j \in [n]$, while the PLBE encryption algorithm uses the public key to encrypt messages. The index-encryption algorithm on the other hand uses the index-encryption key to encrypt messages with respect to an index i. Now such a ciphertext can be decrypted using sk_j only if $j \geq i$, thus one could consider such ciphertexts as encrypting messages under the comparison predicate '$\geq i$'. The security requirements are defined in an 'FE-like' way; that is, if an adversary does not have a key for index i, then index-encryption of any message m to index i should be indistinguishable from index-encryption of m to index $i+1$. Additionally, public key encryptions of any message m should also be indistinguishable from index-encryptions of same message for index 1 (even if adversary is given all keys). And finally, index-encryptions to index $n + 1$ should completely hide any information about the encrypted message.

BSW showed that the PLBE framework could be very useful for building TT systems. At a very high level, their main idea was to use the index-encryption functionality to build the tracing algorithm. The tracing algorithm, given access to a decoding algorithm D, estimates the successful decryption probability of index-encryptions to different indices in 1 to $n + 1$ when decrypted using algorithm D. If it finds an index i such that the probability estimates corresponding to index-encryptions to i and $i+1$ are noticeably far, then the tracing algorithm includes index i to the set of traitors. In prior works [9,26], it was shown that such a transformation preserves IND-CPA security as well as guarantees secure and correct tracing.

An important aspect of the tracing schema described above is that during tracing the algorithm essentially runs a brute force search over set of user indices $\{1, 2, \ldots, n\}$ to look for traitors. This turns out to be problematic if we want to embed polynomial length identities in the secret keys. Because now the search space for traitors is exponential which turns the above brute force search mechanism rather useless. Thus it is not very clear whether the PLBE framework is an accurate abstraction for 'embedded identity' TT.

In this work, our intuition is to extend the PLBE framework such that it becomes more conducive for implementing the embedded identity tracing functionality in TT systems. Hence, we propose a new PLBE framework called embedded-identity PLBE. As in PLBE, an EIPLBE scheme consists of a setup, key generation, encryption, decryption and special-encryption algorithm. (Here special-encryption algorithm is meant to replace/extend the index-encryption algorithm provided in general PLBE schemes.) Semantically, the differences between PLBE and EIPLBE are as follows. In EIPLBE, the user keys are associated with an index-identity pair (j, id). And, special-encryptions are associated with a index-position-bit tuple (i, ℓ, b), where position is a symbol in $[\kappa] \cup \{\bot\}$. The special-encryption ciphertexts can further be categorized into two types:

$(\ell = \bot)$. In this case the special-encryption ciphertext for index-position-bit tuple $(i, \ell = \bot, b)$ behaves identical to a PLBE index-encryption to index i. That is, such ciphertexts can be decrypted using $\mathsf{sk}_{j,\mathsf{id}}$ as long as $j \geq i$.

$(\ell \neq \bot)$. In this case the ciphertext can be decrypted using $\mathsf{sk}_{j,\mathsf{id}}$ as long as either $j \geq i + 1$ or $(j, \mathsf{id}_\ell) = (i, 1 - b)$. In words, these ciphertexts behave same as a PLBE index-encryption to index i, except decryption by the users corresponding to index-identity pair (i, id) is also disallowed if ℓ^{th} bit of their id matches bit value b.

In short, the special-encryption algorithm (when compared with PLBE index-encryption) provides an additional capability of disabling decryption ability of users depending upon a single bit of their identity. The central idea behind introducing this new capability is that it facilitates a simple mechanism for tracing the identity bit-by-bit. The tracing algorithm runs as a two-step process where the first phase is exactly same as in the PLBE to TT transformation which is to trace the indices of corrupt users. This can be executed as before by using the PLBE functionality of disabling each index one-by-one, that is estimate successful decryption probability of encryptions to indices in 1 to $n + 1$ while keeping position variable $\ell = \bot$. This is followed by the core *identity tracing phase* in which the tracing algorithm performs a sub-search on each user index i where it noticed a gap in first phase. Basically the sub-search corresponds to picking a target index obtained during first phase, and then sequentially testing whether the ℓth bit in the corrupted identity is zero or one for all positions $\ell \in [\kappa]$. And, this is where the above additional disabling capability is used.

Next we discuss the expanded set of security properties required from EIPLBE. More details on the above transformation are provided afterwards.

normal-hiding. Standard encryptions are indistinguishable from special-encryptions to $(1, \bot, 0)$.

index-hiding. Special-encryptions to $(i, \bot, 0)$ are indistinguishable from special-encryptions to $(i+1, \bot, 0)$ if an adversary has no secret key for index i.

lower-ID-hiding. Special-encryptions to $(i, \bot, 0)$ are indistinguishable from special-encryptions to (i, ℓ, b) if an adversary has no secret key for index i and identity id such that $\mathsf{id}_\ell = b$.

upper-ID-hiding. Special-encryptions to $(i+1, \bot, 0)$ are indistinguishable from special-encryptions to (i, ℓ, b) if an adversary has no secret key for index i and identity id such that $\mathsf{id}_\ell = 1 - b$.

message-hiding. Special-encryptions to $(n + 1, \bot, 0)$ hide the message encrypted.

Building Indexed EITT from EIPLBE. The setup, key generation, encryption and decryption algorithms for the tracing scheme are same as that for the underlying EIPLBE scheme. Let us now look at how to trace identities from the pirate decoding device. As mentioned before, the tracing proceeds in two phases—(1)

index tracing, followed by (2) identity tracing. The idea is to first trace the set of indices of the corrupted users, say $S_{\text{index}} \subseteq [n]$, and then in the second phase for each index $i \in S_{\text{index}}$, the tracer will (bit-by-bit) extract the corresponding identity corrupted. Formally, the tracing proceeds as follows

Phase 1. For $i \in [n+1]$, do the following:
  A. Compute polynomially many special-encryptions to index-position-bit $(i, \perp, 0)$.
  B. Run decoder D on each ciphertext individually to test whether it decrypts correctly or not. Let $\hat{p}_i$ denote the fraction of successful decryptions.
  Let S_{index} denote the set of indices i of such that $\hat{p}_i$ and $\hat{p}_{i+1}$ are noticeably far.

Phase 2. Next, for each $i \in S_{\text{index}}$ and $\ell \in [\kappa]$, do the following:
  A. Compute polynomially many special-encryptions to index-position-bit $(i, \ell, 0)$.
  B. Run decoder D on each ciphertext individually to test whether it decrypts correctly or not. Let $\hat{q}_{i,\ell}$ denote the fraction of successful decryptions.

Output Phase. Finally, for each $i \in S_{\text{index}}$, it sets the associated traced identity id as follows. For each $\ell \in [\kappa]$, if $\hat{p}_i$ and $\hat{q}_{i,\ell}$ are noticeably far, then set ℓ^{th} bit of id to be 0, else sets it to be 1.

Let us now see why this tracing algorithm works. In the above procedure, the first phase (index tracing) is identical to the PLBE-based tracing algorithm. Thus, by a similar argument it follows that if $i \in S_{\text{index}}$, then it suggests that the decoder D was created using a key corresponding to index-identity pair (i, id) for some identity id. (This part of the argument only relies on normal-hiding, index-hiding and message-hiding security properties.)

The more interesting component of the tracing algorithm is the *identity tracing* phase (i.e., phase 2). The idea here is to selectively disable the decryption ability of users for a fixed index if a particular bit in their identities is 0. Recall that an adversary can not distinguish between special-encryptions to tuple $(i, \perp, 0)$ and $(i, \ell, 0)$ as long as it does not have any secret key for (i, id) such that $\text{id}_\ell = 0$. This follows from 'lower-ID-hiding' property. Similarly, an adversary can not distinguish between special-encryptions to tuple $(i+1, \perp, 0)$ and $(i, \ell, 0)$ as long as it does not have any secret key for (i, id) such that $\text{id}_\ell = 1$. This follows from 'upper-ID-hiding' property. Now whenever $i \in S_{\text{index}}$ we know that $\hat{p}_i$ and $\hat{p}_{i+1}$ are noticeably far. Also, recall that in indexed EITT tracing definition the adversary is allowed to key query for *at most* one identity per index. Therefore, the estimate $\hat{q}_{i,\ell}$ will either be close to $\hat{p}_i$ or to $\hat{p}_{i+1}$, as otherwise one of upper/lower-ID-hiding properties will be violated. Combining all these observations, we can prove correctness/security of the above tracing algorithm.

Next, we move to standard assumption constructions for EIPLBE schemes.

2.3 Building EIPLBE from Standard Assumptions

In this section, we provide three different pathways for securely realizing embedded-identity private linear broadcast encryption systems under standard assumptions. Our first instantiation is based only on general public key encryption, and is provided to serve as a baseline benchmark for comparing efficiency of other schemes. Our second instantiation is based on Bilinear maps, and provides a quadratic improvement over the PKE-based scheme. And finally, our third and last instantiation is based on learning with errors, and it leads to extremely efficient system parameters. See Table 1 for concrete efficiency comparison. Below we discuss these three approaches in greater detail highlighting the main challenges and contributions. Throughout this section, we use n to denote the maximum number of indices and κ to be the length of identities.

EIPLBE via Public Key Encryption. We first present a EIPLBE scheme based on any PKE scheme. In this scheme, the size of the ciphertexts grows linearly with the maximum number of indices n and the length of identities κ. To understand the intuition behind the PKE based EIPLBE construction, let us recall the folklore PLBE construction based on PKE.

PKE-Based PLBE Scheme. The setup algorithm chooses n PKE keys $(\mathsf{pk}_i, \mathsf{sk}_i)_{i \in [n]}$. A secret key for index i is simply sk_i. Standard encryption of message m consists of n ciphertexts, where the ith ciphertext is an encryption of m under public key pk_i. A special-encryption of m for index i^* consists of n ciphertexts; the first i^* ciphertexts are encryptions of a special symbol $\perp$ (under the respective public keys) while the remaining are encryptions of m (under the respective public keys). In summary, the ciphertext consists of n independent and disjoint components, where each component contains one PKE sub-ciphertext. Thus a user can perform decryption by only looking at its dedicated PKE component in the ciphertext. And security follows directly from PKE security since all the PKE sub-ciphertexts are independently created.

Extending This to EIPLBE. Let us now look at how to extend the simple PLBE scheme described above to embed identities as well. Once again, we will have n different strands, and each strand will have 2κ slots. (Here we perform a PKE setup for each slot in each strand.) A secret key for index i and identity id can unlock κ out of the 2κ slots of the ith strand, and using these κ unlocked components, the decryption algorithm tries to reconstruct a message. In particular, the secret key (i, id) can unlock each of the $\{(\ell, \mathsf{id}_\ell)\}_\ell$ slots. This is executed by giving out the PKE secret keys associated with these slots.

To encrypt a message m, one first creates n copies of the message, and secret shares each copy (independently) into κ shares. Let $\{r_{i,\ell}\}_{\ell \in [\kappa]}$ denote the κ shares of the ith copy. In the ith strand, the $(\ell, 0)$ and $(\ell, 1)$ slots encrypt the same message $r_{i,\ell}$. (Here the per-slot per-strand encryption is performed under the corresponding PKE public key.) As a result, a secret key for index i and identity id can recover all the $\{r_{i,\ell}\}_\ell$ components, and therefore the decryption algorithm can reconstruct the message m.

A special-encryption for index-position-bit tuple (i^*, ℓ^*, b^*) is more involved. In the first $i^* - 1$ strands, it has no information about the message m (it secret shares $\perp$ and puts the shares in the 2κ slots). For all $i > i^*$, the ith strand is constructed just as in the standard encryption (secret share message m into κ shares, and put the ℓth share in the slots $(\ell, 0)$ and $(\ell, 1)$). The i^* strand is set up in a more subtle way; here, the encryption algorithm again breaks down m into κ shares $\{r_{i^*,\ell}\}_\ell$. It puts $r_{i^*,\ell}$ in slots $(\ell, 0)$ and $(\ell, 1)$ for all ℓ except ℓ^*. In slot (ℓ^*, b^*) it puts $\perp$, and in slot $(\ell^*, 1 - b^*)$ it puts r_{i^*,ℓ^*}. As a result, a secret key for index i^* and identity id such that $\mathsf{id}_{\ell^*} = b^*$ cannot recover r_{i^*,ℓ^*}, and therefore cannot reconstruct the message.

The security properties follow directly from IND-CPA security of the underlying PKE scheme. Consider, for instance, the index hiding property (special-encryption to $(i, \perp, 0)$ is indistinguishable from special-encryption to $(i+1, \perp, 0)$ if an adversary has no secret keys for index i). The only difference between these two special-encryptions is the ciphertext components in the $\{(\ell, 0), (\ell, 1)\}_\ell$ slots of ith strand. But since the adversary gets no secret keys for index i, it does not have any secret keys to unlock these strand i slots, and hence the index-hiding property holds. The other security properties also follow in a similar manner, except while arguing that the scheme satisfies upper-ID-hiding security we have to additionally use the fact that the message is randomly and independently split in each strand.

The ciphertext size in the above construction grows linearly with both n and κ. Next, we will see how to achieve better parameters using bilinear maps.

EIPLBE via Bilinear Maps. When studying EIPLBE, a natural question to ask is whether it can realized generically from standard PLBE schemes. Since we already have bilinear-map based PLBE constructions [9,10] in which the size of ciphertext grows linearly with $\sqrt{n}$, thus a generic transformation from PLBE to EIPLBE could probably lead to a bilinear-map solution for EIPLBE with similarly efficiency. Here we consider a very natural such transformation from PLBE to EIPLBE and discuss the challenges faced in executing this approach in a black-box way. Starting with this black-box approach we dig deeper into the existing PLBE schemes and extend them directly to a EIPLBE scheme. More details follow.

Why Generic Transformation from PLBE to EIPLBE Does Not Work? Let us first describe a simple candidate EIPLBE scheme based on PLBE. The starting point for this transformation is the PKE-based construction described previously. The intuition is to replace each 'strand' sequence in the PKE-based solution with a single PLBE instantiation while keeping the slot structure intact. That is, during setup the algorithm now runs PLBE setup 2κ times—once for each slot in $\{(\ell, b)\}_{\ell,b}$. The public/master secret key consists of the 2κ public/master secret keys $\{\mathsf{pk}_{\ell,b}, \mathsf{msk}_{\ell,b}\}_{\ell,b}$, one from each slot $(\ell, b) \in [\kappa] \times \{0,1\}$. And, a secret key for index-identity pair (i, id) consists of κ PLBE secret keys, where the ℓth key component is a secret key for index i in the (ℓ, id_ℓ) slot (that is, $\mathsf{sk} = \{\mathsf{sk}_\ell\}_\ell$ where $\mathsf{sk}_\ell \leftarrow \mathsf{KeyGen}(\mathsf{msk}_{\ell, \mathsf{id}_\ell}, i)$). Next, let us look at encryption. A ciphertext consists of 2κ PLBE ciphertexts $\{\mathsf{ct}_{\ell, b}\}_{\ell, b}$. The (standard) encryption algorithm splits message m into κ shares $\{r_\ell\}_\ell$, and then encrypts r_ℓ under the public keys for both $(\ell, 0)$ and $(\ell, 1)$ slots, independently. The special-encryption algorithm on the other hand works as follows—to encrypt m for index-position-bit tuple (i^*, ℓ^*, b^*), the algorithm as before splits m into κ shares $\{r_\ell\}_\ell$, and then computes all but the (ℓ^*, b^*)-slot of the ciphertext as a PLBE index-encryption (of the corresponding share) for index i^*. And, the last remaining ciphertext component (if any[6]) is a PLBE index-encryption (of the corresponding share) for index '$i^* + 1$'. Now decryption can be quite naturally defined. Let us next try to analyze its security.

A careful inspection of the above scheme shows that it satisfies all requisite security properties except one which is upper-ID-hiding security.[7] Recall that upper-ID-hiding security requires that special-encryption to $(i + 1, \bot, 0)$ must be indistinguishable from special-encryption to (i, ℓ, b) if the adversary doed not get any secret key for (i, id) such that $\mathsf{id}_\ell = 1 - b$. Suppose an adversary has two secret keys $\mathsf{sk}_{i, \mathsf{id}}$ and $\mathsf{sk}_{i+1, \mathsf{id}}$, for some identity id such that $\mathsf{id}_\ell = b$. Consider a new secret key $\widetilde{\mathsf{sk}}$ which is equal to $\mathsf{sk}_{i, \mathsf{id}}$, except that the ℓth component is set to be the ℓth component of $\mathsf{sk}_{i+1, \mathsf{id}}$. It turns out that this hybrid key $\widetilde{\mathsf{sk}}$ can decrypt a special-encryption for (i, ℓ, b) but not for $(i + 1, \bot, 0)$, even though both key queries for index-identity pairs (i, id) and $(i + 1, \mathsf{id})$ are permissible as per upper-ID-hiding security game.

As exhibited by the above attack, the main issue with the above (broken) candidate is that there is no mechanism to tie together the different components of a particular secret key. Thus such key mixing attacks, which allow rendering hybrid keys such as $\widetilde{\mathsf{sk}}$ in the aforementioned attack, are unavoidable. In order to prevent such attacks, we dive into the existing PLBE constructions with the goal of exploiting the underlying algebraic structure for linking together the individual PLBE secret keys coming from different subsystems.

Our Intuition and Fixing [10]. Our starting point is the trace and revoke (broadcast) scheme by Boneh and Waters (BW) [10]. We start by presenting a simplified version of the BW PLBE scheme, and then use that as a building block to build our EIPLBE scheme. Along the way we uncover a crucial bug in the security proof provided by BW that renders their theorem as stated incorrect. In this work, we fix the BW security proof while building our EIPLBE scheme, thereby restoring the bilinear map based TT (also trace and revoke) schemes to their original glory.

---

[6] If $\ell^* = \bot$, then all ciphertext slots have already been filled.

[7] Actually there is a pretty simple (related) attack to break the false tracing guarantee if one uses this transformation to build an indexed EITT scheme from standard PLBE. Here we only focus on breaking upper-ID-hiding security.

Revisiting BW Tracing Scheme. Let p, q be primes, $\mathbb{G}, \mathbb{G}_T$ groups of order $N = p \cdot q$ with a bilinear map $e : \mathbb{G} \times \mathbb{G} \to \mathbb{G}_T$, and let $\mathbb{G}_p, \mathbb{G}_q$ denote the subgroups of $\mathbb{G}$ of orders p and q respectively. In the BW tracing scheme for n parties, any index $i \in [n]$ is represented as a pair $(i_1, i_2) \in [\sqrt{n}] \times [\sqrt{n}]$; secret keys and special-encryptions are for pairs $(x, y) \in [\sqrt{n}] \times [\sqrt{n}]$. We say that $(x_1, y_1) \prec (x_2, y_2)$ if either $x_1 < x_2$ or $(x_1 = x_2$ and $y_1 < y_2)$.

The setup algorithm chooses generator $g \leftarrow \mathbb{G}$ and $g_q \leftarrow \mathbb{G}_q$, scalars $\alpha_x, r_x, c_x \leftarrow \mathbb{Z}_N$ for each $x \in [\sqrt{n}]$ and sets $E_x = g^{r_x}$, $G_x = e(g, g)^{\alpha_x}$ and $H_x = g^{c_x}$. It chooses $\beta \leftarrow \mathbb{Z}_N$, sets $E_q = g_q^\beta$, $E_{q,x} = g_q^{\beta r_x}$ and $G_{q,x} = e(g_q, g_q)^{\beta \alpha_x}$. The public key consists of $\{E_x, G_x, E_q, E_{q,x}, G_{q,x}, H_x\}_x$ (together with some additional components); the master secret key consists of $\{\alpha_x, r_x, c_x\}_x$, and the tracing key is the public key itself. A secret key for index (x, y) is set to be $g^{\alpha_x + r_x c_y}$. Special-encryption of message m for index (x^*, y^*) has $4\sqrt{n}$ components $\{R_i, A_i, B_i, C_i\}_{i \in [\sqrt{n}]}$. It chooses $s_x \leftarrow \mathbb{Z}_N$ for each $x \in [\sqrt{n}]$, $t \leftarrow \mathbb{Z}_N$. For $x > x^*$, it sets $R_x = E_{q,x}^{s_x} = g_q^{\beta r_x s_x}$, $A_x = E_q^{s_x t} = g_q^{\beta s_x t}$ and $B_x = m \cdot G_{q,x}^{s_x t} = m \cdot e(g_q, g_q)^{\beta \alpha_x s_x t}$. For $x = x^*$, it sets $R_x = E_x^{s_x} = g^{r_x s_x}$, $A_x = g^{s_x t}$ and $B_x = m \cdot G_x^{s_x t} = m \cdot e(g, g)^{\alpha_x s_x t}$. For $x < x^*$, R_x, A_x, B_x are random group elements. Next, it sets C_y as follows. For $y > y^*$, it sets $C_y = H_y^t = g^{c_y t}$; else it sets $C_y = g^{c_y t} \cdot h_p$, where h_p is a group element in $\mathbb{G}_p$, derived from the public parameters.

For correctness, let $K = g^{\alpha_x + r_x c_y}$ be a key for (x, y), $\mathsf{ct} = \{R_i, A_i, B_i, C_i\}_i$ an encryption of m for (x', y'), where $(x', y') \prec (x, y)$. Consider the terms (R_x, A_x, B_x, C_x). If $x > x'$, then $R_x = g_q^{\beta r_x s_x}$, $A_x = g_q^{\beta s_x t}$, $B_x = e(g_q, g_q)^{\beta \alpha_x r_x s_x t}$ for some β, s_x, t. On pairing R_x with C_y, one obtains $\Gamma_1 = e(g_q, g_q)^{\beta r_x s_x t c_y}$. Here, note that it does not matter whether $y < y'$ or not, because pairing an element in $\mathbb{G}_p$ with an element in $\mathbb{G}_q$ results in identity. Next, pairing A_x with the secret key K results in $\Gamma_2 = e(g_q, g_q)^{\beta r_x s_x c_y t + \alpha_x r_x s_x}$. Finally, note that $B_x \cdot \Gamma_1 / \Gamma_2 = m$. If $x = x'$ but $y > y'$, then pairing A_x and K results in $\Gamma_2 = e(g, g)^{r_x s_x c_y t + \alpha_x r_x s_x}$, and pairing R_x and C_y results in $e(g, g)^{r_x s_x c_y t}$. Therefore $B_x \cdot \Gamma_1 / \Gamma_2$ outputs m.

The main intuition behind the index-hiding security proof is that if an adversary does not have a secret key for index $i = (x, y)$, then the h_p term multiplied to C_y component can be undetectably added or removed. In the actual scheme, the public parameters and the ciphertext includes some additional terms for security purposes. Here we removed them for simplicity of exposition. Next, let us look at how to extend BW for building an EIPLBE scheme.

Our EIPLBE Scheme Based on Bilinear Maps. Our EIPLBE scheme, at a very high level, is inspired by the 2κ-subsystems idea (described in the attempted generic transformation from PLBE to EIPLBE) applied to the BW scheme. However, we will ensure that the adversary cannot mix-and-match different secret keys. Consider 2κ different subsystems of the BW scheme, where all the subsystems share the same $\{\alpha_x, r_x\}_{x \in [\sqrt{n}]}$ values, but each subsystem has its own $\{c_y\}_{y \in [\sqrt{n}]}$ values. So, the public key has $\{E_x, G_x, E_q, E_{q,x}, G_{q,x}\}_x$ (together with some additional components) as in the BW scheme, but instead of $\{H_y\}_{y \in [\sqrt{n}]}$, it now has $\{H_{y,\ell,b}\}_{y \in [\sqrt{n}], \ell \in [\kappa], b \in \{0,1\}}$, where the setup algorithm chooses $\{c_{y,\ell,b}\}_{y\in[\sqrt{n}]}$ values for the (ℓ, b) subsystem and sets $H_{y,\ell,b} = g^{c_{y,\ell,b}}$. The secret key for index $i = (x, y)$ and identity id consists of just one component. The key generation algorithm combines the appropriate $c_{y,\ell,b}$ elements (depending on id) and multiplies with r_x. Let $\gamma_{x,y} = r_x \cdot (\sum_\ell c_{y,\ell,\mathrm{id}_\ell})$. The key generation algorithm outputs $g^{\alpha_x + \gamma_{x,y}}$ as the secret key. Note that unlike the PLBE to EIPLBE transformation, here the components from one key cannot be mixed with the components of another key to produce a hybrid key. An alternate view of the secret key is that it is the BW key, but with c_y value being different for each identity (for identity id, $c_y = \sum_\ell c_{y,\ell,\mathrm{id}_\ell}$).

In the ciphertext/special-ciphertext, we have the $\{R_x, A_x, B_x\}_{x\in[\sqrt{n}]}$ components as in the BW scheme. However, instead of $\{C_y\}_{y\in[\sqrt{n}]}$, we now have 2κ such sets of components. During decryption, one must first combine the $C_{y,\ell,b}$ components depending on the identity id to obtain a term C_y, which is then used to carry out BW-like decryption. We will now present the scheme in more detail.

The setup algorithm chooses $\{c_{y,\ell,b}\}_{y\in[\sqrt{n}],\ell\in[\kappa],b\in\{0,1\}}$. It sets $H_{y,\ell,b} = g^{c_{y,\ell,b}}$ for each $(y, \ell, b) \in [\sqrt{n}] \times [\kappa] \times \{0,1\}$, and the public key consists of the following terms: $\left\{ E_x, G_x, E_q, E_{q,x}, G_{q,x}, \{H_{x,\ell,b}\}_{\ell,b} \right\}_x$, where the $E_x, G_x, E_q, E_{q,x}, G_{q,x}$ terms are computed as in the BW scheme (outlined above). To compute a secret key for index (x, y) and identity id, the key generation algorithm computes $z = \alpha_x + r_x \cdot (\sum_i c_{y,i,\mathrm{id}_i})$ and outputs g^z as the secret key. Finally, the special-encryption of m for index (x^*, y^*), position ℓ^* and bit b^* is computed as follows: for each $x \in [\sqrt{n}]$, the encryption algorithm computes $\{R_x, A_x, B_x\}$ as in the BW scheme. In addition to these components, it computes $\{C_{y,\ell,b}\}$ components for each $y \in [\sqrt{n}], \ell \in [\kappa]$ and $b \in \{0,1\}$ as follows: if $(y > y^*)$ or $(y = y^*$ and $(\ell, b) \neq (\ell^*, b^*))^t$, then $C_{y,\ell,b} = H_{y,l,b}^t$, else $C_{y,\ell,b} = H_{y,l,b}^t \cdot h_p$, where h_p is some element in $\mathbb{G}_p$ computed using the public parameters.

Suppose K is a key for index (x, y) and identity id, and $\left\{ R_x, A_x, B_x, \{C_{x,l,b}\}_{l,b} \right\}_x$ is an encryption of m for $((x^*, y^*), \ell^*, b^*)$. Decryption works as follows: first, compute $C_y = \prod_l C_{y,l,\mathrm{id}_l}$; next, pair C_y and A_x to compute Γ_1, pair K and R_x to compute Γ_2, and output $B_x \cdot \Gamma_1/\Gamma_2$ as the decryption.

The full scheme and security proof is discussed in the full version of our paper. As an alternate approach for constructing an EIPLBE scheme, one could use a functional encryption scheme for quadratic functions. Such a scheme was recently proposed by Baltico et al. [3]. However, one of the contributions of our work is to fix the BW scheme, and hence we chose to provide a direct construction for EIPLBE, based on the BW scheme. Note that in the above outline, the size of ciphertexts grows linearly with $\sqrt{n}$ and κ. In the main body, we optimize the construction such that the size of ciphertexts grows linearly with both $\sqrt{n}$ and $\sqrt{\kappa}$. Finally, we will present a scheme with optimal ciphertext size with only polylogarithmic dependence on n.

EIPLBE via Learning with Errors. In a recent work, Goyal, Koppula, and Waters [26] gave a traitor tracing scheme with compact ciphertexts. Their scheme is based on a new primitive called Mixed Functional Encryption (Mixed FE), which can also be used to build an EIPLBE scheme with optimal parameters. A Mixed FE scheme for a function class $\mathcal{F}$ can be seen as an extension of a secret key FE scheme for $\mathcal{F}$. It has a setup, key generation, encryption and decryption algorithm (as in a secret key FE scheme). In addition, it also has a public encryption algorithm. For the PLBE and EIPLBE schemes, it helps to have keys associated with messages and ciphertexts with functions. The setup algorithm chooses a public key pk and a master secret key msk. The master secret key can be used to generate a secret key for any message m, and can also be used to encrypt any function f. A key for message m can decrypt an encryption of function f if $f(m) = 1$. In addition, the public-encryption algorithm can also generate ciphertexts; it only takes as input the public key pk, and outputs a ciphertext that 'looks like' a secret-key encryption of the 'all-accepting function'. For security, GKW require bounded query FE security, together with the public/secret key mode indistinguishability.

The work of [26] showed a construction of Mixed FE for log-depth circuits. A recent work by Chen et al. [13] showed three different constructions for the same. To construct PLBE, [26] combined a 1-bounded Mixed FE scheme with an ABE scheme. The PLBE encryption of a message m is simply an ABE encryption of m for attribute x being a public-mode Mixed FE encryption. The special-encryption of m for index i^* is again an ABE encryption of m, but with attribute x being a secret-key Mixed FE encryption of the ($>i^*$) function. Finally, to compute a secret key for index i, the key generation algorithm first computes a Mixed FE key k for the message i, and then computes an ABE key for a Mixed FE decryption circuit that has k hardwired, takes a Mixed FE ciphertext ct as input and outputs Mixed FE decryption of ct using k. Note that for this transformation, it suffices to only have a Mixed FE scheme that allows the comparison functionality.

Fortunately (for us), [26] (and later [13]) showed Mixed FE for a much richer class of functions (log-depth circuits), and this will be useful for our construction. Our EIPLBE scheme will also follow the Mixed FE+ABE approach (which is referred to as Mixed FE with messages in [13]). Instead of the comparison function, the Mixed FE ciphertexts in our scheme will be for more expressive functions. In particular, it suffices to have a Mixed FE scheme where the functions are parameterized by (y^*, ℓ^*, b^*), and it checks if input (y, id) either satisfies $y > y^*$, or $y = y^*$ and $\mathsf{id}_\ell \neq b^*$. Since such simple functions can be implemented in log-depth, we can use the ABE+Mixed FE approach for building EIPLBE as well.

2.4 Indexed Embedded-Identity TT to Bounded Embedded-Identity TT

In this part, we discuss our transformation from a tracing scheme with indexed key generation to one where there is no index involved, but the correct trace guarantee holds only if total number of keys is less than an apriori set bound. For technical reasons we require the bounded EITT system to provide a stronger false tracing guarantee, which states there should be no false trace even if the adversary obtains an unbounded (but polynomial) number of keys. Looking ahead, this property will be crucial for the transformation from bounded EITT to its unbounded counterpart.

The high-level idea is to have λ different strands, and in each strand, we have a separate indexed-system with a large enough index bound (that depends on the bound on number of keys n). When generating a key, we choose λ random indices (within the index bound) and generate λ different keys for the same identity in the different strands using the respective randomly chosen indices. Now, we will set the index bound to be n^2, and as a result, at least one strand has all distinct indices (with overwhelming probability). To (special-)encrypt a message, we secret-share the message in the λ different strands, and encrypt them separately. This approach satisfies the correct-trace guarantee, but does not satisfy the false-trace guarantee. In particular, note that the false-trace guarantee should hold even if the number of key queries is more than the query bound. This means the underlying indexed scheme should not report a false trace even if there are multiple identities for a index, which is a strictly stronger false-trace guarantee for the underlying system (and our system does not satisfy it).

There is an elegant fix to this issue. Instead of generating keys for the queried identity id, the key generation algorithm now generates a signature on id, and generates keys for (id, σ). This fixes the false-trace issue. Even if an adversary queries for many secret keys, if it is able to produce a decoding box that can implicate a honest user, then that means this box is able to forge signatures, thereby breaking the signature scheme's security. We describe the scheme a little more formally now.

To build a tracing scheme with bound n, the setup algorithm chooses λ different public/secret/tracing keys for the indexed scheme with index bound set to be n^2. The setup algorithm also chooses a signature key/verification key. It sets the λ different public keys and the verification key to be the new public key, and similarly the master secret key has the λ different master secret keys and the signature key. Encryption of a message m works as follows: the encryption algorithm chooses λ shares of the message, and then encrypts the ith share under the ith public key. To compute a secret key for identity id, the key generation algorithm first chooses λ different indices $j_1, \ldots, j_\lambda$. It then computes a signature σ on id, and generates a key for (id, σ) using each of the λ master secret keys with the corresponding indices. The tracing algorithm uses the underlying indexed scheme's trace algorithm to obtain a set of (id, σ) tuples. It then checks if σ is a valid signature on id; if so, it outputs id as a traitor.

Now, suppose an adversary queries for $t(< n)$ secret keys, and outputs a decoding box D. Let $j_{i,k}$ denote the kth index chosen for the ith secret key. With high probability, there exists an index $k^* \in [\lambda]$ such that the set of indices $\{j_{1,k^*}, j_{2,k^*}, \ldots, j_{t,k^*}\}$ are all distinct. As a result, using the correct-tracing guarantee of the underlying tracing scheme for the k^* strand, we can extract at least one tuple (id, σ).

Next, we need to argue the false trace guarantee. This follows mainly from the security of the signature scheme. Suppose an adversary receives a set of keys corresponding to an identity set $\mathcal{I}$, and outputs a decoding box D. If trace outputs an identity id $\notin \mathcal{I}$, then this means the sub-trace algorithm output a tuple (id, σ) such that σ is a valid signature on id. As a result, σ is a forgery on message id (because the adversary did not query for a key corresponding to id).

2.5   Bounded Embedded-Identity TT to Unbounded Embedded-Identity TT

The final component is to transform a tracing system for bounded keys to one with no bound on the number of keys issued. For this transformation to be efficient, it is essential that the underlying bounded EITT scheme to have ciphertexts with polylogarithmic dependence on the key bound n. The reason is that our core idea is to have λ (bounded) EITT systems running in parallel, where the ith system runs the bounded tracing scheme with bound $n_i = 2^i$, and if the ciphertext size does not scale polylogarithmically with the bound n_i, then this transformation would not work.[8]

More formally, the setup algorithm runs the bounded system's setup λ times, the ith iteration run with bound $n_i = 2^i$. It sets the public key (resp. master secret key and the tracing key) to be the λ public keys (resp. the λ different master secret keys and the tracing keys). The encryption algorithm secret shares the message into λ shares, and encrypts the ith share using the ith public key. The key generation algorithm computes λ different secret keys. Finally, the tracing algorithm runs the bounded system's trace algorithm, one by one, until it finds a traitor. First, note that since the adversary is polynomially bounded, if it queries for t keys, then there exists some i^* such that $t \leq 2^{i^*} < 2t$. As a result, the trace is guaranteed to find a traitor in the i^{*th} system, and hence it runs in time $\mathsf{poly}(2^{i^*}) = \mathsf{poly}(t)$. Second, since every underlying bounded system's false trace guarantee holds even if the adversary queries for more keys than permitted, thus none of the premature sub-traces result in a false trace. At a very high level, the central observation here that allows us in avoiding the need for adaptive security is that: while tracing we simply perform the "tightest" fit search for finding the smallest polynomial bound on keys corrupted and then carry out the tracing procedure rather than tracing on an exponential sized space directly. Similar techniques of combining different *bounded adversary* instances, and invoking the security of the instance with *just high enough* security were used previously in [7,18].

2.6   Comparing Techniques

We conclude by giving some further comparisons between the techniques we introduce and those from the earlier work of NWZ [31]. The closest point for

---

[8] Due to similar reasons, it is essential that the running time of all algorithms (except possibly the tracing algorithm) grows at most polylogarithmically with n.

comparisons are the techniques they use to trace an identity of arbitrary size κ while keeping ciphertexts possibly smaller than κ bits. (We modify their variable names to more closely match ours.) Here they introduce a sub-primitive called private *block* linear broadcast encryption (PBLBE) which can be used as follows. A private key for identity $\mathsf{id} = (\mathsf{id}_1, \mathsf{id}_2 \cdots, \mathsf{id}_\kappa)$ will be associated with a randomly chosen tag s from an exponential sized space. It is then organized into i blocks where each block is associated with the pair (s, id_j) which is embedded by the value $2s + \mathsf{id}_j$. Given a decoding algorithm D the tracing algorithm will perform a search procedure on *each* individual block to recover the set of corrupted tag/identity bit values on each one. The process will essentially perform a search on the j-th block values while leaving all blocks $k \neq j$ alone. At the end, the tracing process will look for a tag s^* that is present in all the individual block searches and use that to reconstruct the traitor identity. An analysis is needed to show that such a tag exists so that one is not just stuck with fragments of many different identities.

At a high level our indexed EITT two part structure (consisting of an index i and identity id) is similar to the two part structure of [31] consisting of a tag s along with the identity. However, there exists some important differences that are closely linked to our goal of realizing embedded traitor tracing from standard assumptions.

- First, our tracing procedure searches in a qualitatively different manner where it first performs a search across the index space (without regard) to identity bits and only when an index is found does it perform a dive into extracting the identity. This is in contrast to the NWZ approach of performing tag/index search per each identity bit, and then combining the identity bits (corresponding to every unique tag) to reconstruct traitor identities. We believe the current way is simpler and has less tracing overhead. In addition, our indexed EITT interface is intended to be a minimalistic which in general helps for realization from more basic assumptions as opposed to full blown functional encryption.
- We consider indices of small range while the tag spaces of NWZ are exponential size. This enables us to access a wider class of traitor tracing realizations from PKE and bilinear maps. There are no known PLBE schemes for exponentially large identity spaces from these assumptions.
- We achieve our scheme for unbounded identities by amplifying from smaller index sized schemes along with an analysis that finds the "tightest fit". The work of [31] requires *adaptive* security of the underlying primitive. The only known scheme from standard assumptions that can handle exponentially large identity space is the [13] which builds the core "Mixed FE" component from lockable obfuscation [25,35]. It is notable that the private constrained PRF-based construction of [13] and the earlier [26] construction of Mixed FE only offer selective security. This suggests that adaptive security may in general be hard to come by and developing techniques to avoid it a worthwhile goal.

Lastly, NWZ also studied the problem in the bounded collusion setting, wherein they provided constructions from regular public-key encryption (instead of full blown FE) where the size of ciphertexts and parameters grew at least linearly in the collusion size. If one sets the collusion size to be the number of users n, then their bounded collusion constructions could be interpreted as collusion-resistant constructions for our indexed EITT notion. However, that approach leads to much less efficient constructions.

3 Traitor Tracing with Embedded Identities

3.1 Indexed Embedded-Identity Traitor Tracing

In this section, we will present the syntax and definitions for traitor tracing with embedded identities where the number of users is bounded, and the key generation is 'indexed'.

Let $\mathcal{T}$ be a (indexed keygen, public/private)-embedded identity tracing scheme for message space $\mathcal{M} = \{\mathcal{M}_\lambda\}_{\lambda \in \mathbb{N}}$ and identity space $\mathcal{ID} = \{\{0,1\}^\kappa\}_{\kappa \in \mathbb{N}}$. It consists of five algorithms Setup, KeyGen, Enc, Dec and Trace with the following syntax:

Setup$(1^\lambda, 1^\kappa, n_{\text{indx}}) \to (\text{msk}, \text{pk}, \text{key})$: The setup algorithm takes as input the security parameter λ, the 'identity space' parameter κ, index space $[n_{\text{indx}}]$, and outputs a master secret key msk, a public key pk, and a tracing key key.

KeyGen$(\text{msk}, \text{id} \in \{0,1\}^\kappa, i \in [n_{\text{indx}}]) \to \text{sk}_{i,\text{id}}$: The key generation algorithm takes as input the master secret key, identity $\text{id} \in \{0,1\}^\kappa$ and index $i \in [n_{\text{indx}}]$. It outputs a secret key $\text{sk}_{i,\text{id}}$.

Enc$(\text{pk}, m \in \mathcal{M}_\lambda) \to \text{ct}$: The encryption algorithm takes as input a public key pk, message $m \in \mathcal{M}_\lambda$ and outputs a ciphertext ct.

Dec$(\text{sk}, \text{ct}) \to z$: The decryption algorithm takes as input a secret key sk, ciphertext ct and outputs $z \in \mathcal{M}_\lambda \cup \{\bot\}$.

Trace$^D(\text{key}, 1^y, m_0, m_1) \to T \subseteq \{0,1\}^\kappa$. The trace algorithm has oracle access to a program D, it takes as input key (which is the master secret key msk in a private-key tracing scheme, and the public key pk in a public tracing algorithm), parameter y and two messages m_0, m_1. It outputs a set T of index-identity pairs, where $T \subseteq \{0,1\}^\kappa$.

Correctness. A traitor tracing scheme is said to be correct if there exists a negligible function $\text{negl}(\cdot)$ such that for all $\lambda, \kappa, n \in \mathbb{N}$, $m \in \mathcal{M}_\lambda$, identity $\text{id} \in \{0,1\}^\kappa$ and $i \in [n]$, the following holds

$$\Pr\left[\text{Dec}(\text{sk}, \text{ct}) = m : \begin{array}{c} (\text{msk}, \text{pk}, \text{key}) \leftarrow \text{Setup}(1^\lambda, 1^\kappa, n); \\ \text{sk} \leftarrow \text{KeyGen}(\text{msk}, \text{id}, i); \\ \text{ct} \leftarrow \text{Enc}(\text{pk}, m) \end{array}\right] \geq 1 - \text{negl}(\lambda).$$

Efficiency. Let T-s, T-e, T-k, T-d, T-t, S-c, S-k be functions. A (indexed keygen, public/private)-embedded identity tracing scheme is said to be (T-s, T-e, T-k, T-d, T-t, S-c, S-k)- efficient if the following efficiency requirements hold:

- The running time of $\mathsf{Setup}(1^\lambda, 1^\kappa, n_{\mathrm{indx}})$ is at most $\mathsf{T\text{-}s}(\lambda, \kappa, n_{\mathrm{indx}})$.
- The running time of $\mathsf{Enc}(\mathsf{pk}, m)$ is at most $\mathsf{T\text{-}e}(\lambda, \kappa, n_{\mathrm{indx}})$.
- The running time of $\mathsf{KeyGen}(\mathsf{msk}, \mathsf{id})$ is at most $\mathsf{T\text{-}k}(\lambda, \kappa, n_{\mathrm{indx}})$.
- The running time of $\mathsf{Dec}(\mathsf{sk}, \mathsf{ct})$ is at most $\mathsf{T\text{-}d}(\lambda, \kappa, n_{\mathrm{indx}})$.
- The number of oracle calls made by $\mathsf{Trace}^D(\mathsf{key}, 1^y, m_0, m_1)$ to decoding box D is at most $\mathsf{T\text{-}t}(\lambda, \kappa, n_{\mathrm{indx}}, y)$.
- The size of the ciphertext output by $\mathsf{Enc}(\mathsf{pk}, m)$ is at most $\mathsf{S\text{-}c}(\lambda, \kappa, n_{\mathrm{indx}})$.
- The size of the key output by $\mathsf{KeyGen}(\mathsf{msk}, \mathsf{id})$ is at most $\mathsf{S\text{-}k}(\lambda, \kappa, n_{\mathrm{indx}})$.

Definition 1. *A traitor tracing scheme $\mathcal{T} = (\mathsf{Setup}, \mathsf{Enc}, \mathsf{Dec}, \mathsf{Trace})$ is said to have* public tracing *if the tracing algorithm* Trace *uses the public key.*

Security. As in the traditional traitor tracing definitions, we have two security definitions. The first security definition (IND-CPA security) states that any PPT adversary should not distinguish between encryptions of different messages. This definition is identical to the INDCPA definition in traditional traitor tracing. The second definition states that if there exists a pirate decoder box, then the tracing algorithm can trace the identity of at least one of the secret keys used to build the decoding box, and there are no 'false-positives'.

Definition 2 (IND-CPA security). *Let $\mathcal{T} = (\mathsf{Setup}, \mathsf{KeyGen}, \mathsf{Enc}, \mathsf{Dec}, \mathsf{Trace})$ be a (indexed keygen, public/private)-embedded identity tracing scheme. This scheme is* IND-CPA *secure if for every stateful PPT adversary $\mathcal{A}$, there exists a negligible function $\mathsf{negl}(\cdot)$ such that for all $\lambda \in \mathbb{N}$, the following probability is at most $1/2 + \mathsf{negl}(\lambda)$:*

$$\Pr\left[\mathcal{A}(\mathsf{ct}) = b \ : \ \begin{array}{l} (1^\kappa, 1^{n_{\mathrm{indx}}}) \leftarrow \mathcal{A}(1^\lambda); (\mathsf{msk}, \mathsf{pk}, \mathsf{key}) \leftarrow \mathsf{Setup}(1^\lambda, 1^\kappa, n_{\mathrm{indx}}); \\ b \leftarrow \{0,1\}; (m_0, m_1) \leftarrow \mathcal{A}(\mathsf{pk}); \mathsf{ct} \leftarrow \mathsf{Enc}(\mathsf{pk}, m_b) \end{array}\right]$$

Definition 3 (Secure tracing). *Let $\mathcal{T} = (\mathsf{Setup}, \mathsf{KeyGen}, \mathsf{Enc}, \mathsf{Dec}, \mathsf{Trace})$ be a (indexed keygen, public/private)-embedded identity tracing scheme. For any non-negligible function $\epsilon(\cdot)$ and PPT adversary $\mathcal{A}$, consider expt. $\mathsf{Expt\text{-}TT\text{-}emb\text{-}index}^{\mathcal{T}}_{\mathcal{A}, \epsilon}(\lambda)$ defined in Fig. 1.*

Based on the above experiment, we now define the following (probabilistic) events and the corresponding probabilities (which are a functions of λ, parameterized by $\mathcal{A}, \epsilon$):

- $\mathsf{Good\text{-}Decoder} : \Pr[D(\mathsf{ct}) = b \ : \ b \leftarrow \{0,1\}, \mathsf{ct} \leftarrow \mathsf{Enc}(\mathsf{pk}, m_b)] \geq 1/2 + \epsilon(\lambda)$
  $\mathsf{Pr\text{-}G\text{-}D}_{\mathcal{A}, \epsilon}(\lambda) = \Pr[\mathsf{Good\text{-}Decoder}]$.
- $\mathsf{Cor\text{-}Tr} : T \neq \emptyset \wedge T \subseteq S_{\mathcal{ID}}$
  $\mathsf{Pr\text{-}Cor\text{-}Tr}_{\mathcal{A}, \epsilon}(\lambda) = \Pr[\mathsf{Cor\text{-}Tr}]$.
- $\mathsf{Fal\text{-}Tr} : T \not\subseteq S_{\mathcal{ID}}$
  $\mathsf{Pr\text{-}Fal\text{-}Tr}_{\mathcal{A}, \epsilon}(\lambda) = \Pr[\mathsf{Fal\text{-}Tr}]$.

Experiment Expt-TT-emb-index$_{\mathcal{A},\epsilon}^{\mathcal{T}}(\lambda)$

- $1^\kappa, 1^{n_{\text{indx}}} \leftarrow \mathcal{A}(1^\lambda)$
- $(\text{msk}, \text{pk}, \text{key}) \leftarrow \text{Setup}(1^\lambda, 1^\kappa, n_{\text{indx}})$
- $(D, m_0, m_1) \leftarrow \mathcal{A}^{O(\cdot)}(\text{pk})$
- $T \leftarrow \text{Trace}^D(\text{key}, 1^{1/\epsilon(\lambda)}, m_0, m_1)$

Each oracle query made by the adversary $\mathcal{A}$ consists of an index-identity pair $(i, \text{id}) \in [n_{\text{indx}}] \times \{0,1\}^\kappa$. Let $S_{\mathcal{ID}}$ the set of identities queried by $\mathcal{A}$. Here, oracle $O(\cdot)$ has msk hardwired and on query (i, id) it outputs $\text{KeyGen}(\text{msk}, \text{id}, i)$ if index i is distinct from all previous queries made by the adversary, otherwise it outputs $\perp$. *In other words, for each index $i \in [n_{\text{indx}}]$, the adversary is allowed to make at most one key query. However, for different indices $i, i' \in [n_{\text{indx}}]$, the identity can be same (that is, (i, id) and (i', id) are valid queries if $i \neq i'$).*

Fig. 1. Experiment Expt-TT-emb-index

A scheme $\mathcal{T}$ *is said to be ind-secure if for every PPT adversary $\mathcal{A}$, polynomial $q(\cdot)$ and non-negligible function $\epsilon(\cdot)$, there exists negligible functions $\text{negl}_1(\cdot)$, $\text{negl}_2(\cdot)$ such that for all $\lambda \in \mathbb{N}$ satisfying $\epsilon(\lambda) > 1/q(\lambda)$, the following holds*

$$\text{Pr-Fal-Tr}_{\mathcal{A},\epsilon}(\lambda) \leq \text{negl}_1(\lambda), \quad \text{Pr-Cor-Tr}_{\mathcal{A},\epsilon}(\lambda) \geq \text{Pr-G-D}_{\mathcal{A},\epsilon}(\lambda) - \text{negl}_2(\lambda).$$

Remark 1. We want to point out that in both IND-CPA and secure tracing games we require the adversary to output the index bound n_{indx} *in unary instead of binary* (i.e., $\mathcal{A}$ outputs $(1^\kappa, 1^{n_{\text{indx}}})$ instead of $(1^\kappa, n_{\text{indx}})$). Now since the running time of the adversary $\mathcal{A}$ is bounded by a polynomial, thus it can only select a polynomially-bounded value for index bound n_{indx}. However, the setup algorithm is given the input n_{indx} *in binary*. This distinction will later be useful in our constructions and security proofs.

4   A New Framework for Embedded-Identity Traitor Tracing

4.1   Embedded-Identity Private Linear Broadcast Encryption

We introduce the notion of embedded-identity private linear broadcast encryption (EIPLBE) as a generalization of private linear broadcast encryption scheme which was introduced by Boneh, Sahai and Waters [9] as a framework for constructing traitor tracing schemes. There are five algorithms in a EIPLBE scheme—Setup, KeyGen, Enc, SplEnc, Dec. The setup algorithm outputs a master secret key and a public key. The key generation algorithm is used to sample private keys for index-identity pairs (j, id). The public key encryption algorithm can be used to encrypt messages, and ciphertexts can be decrypted using any of the private keys via the decryption algorithm. In addition to these algorithms, there is also a special-encryption algorithm SplEnc. This algorithm, which uses the master secret key, can be used to encrypt messages to any index-position-value tuple (i, ℓ, b). A secret key for user (j, id) can decrypt a ciphertext for index-position-value tuple (i, ℓ, b) only if (1) $j \geq i+1$, or (2) $(i, \ell) = (j, \bot)$ or $(i, \text{id}_\ell) = (j, 1 - b)$.

Belowe we first provide the EIPLBE syntax, and then present the security definitions.

Syntax. A EIPLBE scheme EIPLBE = (Setup, KeyGen, Enc, SplEnc, Dec) for message space $\mathcal{M} = \{\mathcal{M}_\lambda\}_{\lambda \in \mathbb{N}}$ and identity space $\mathcal{ID} = \{\{0,1\}^\kappa\}_{\kappa \in \mathbb{N}}$ has the following syntax.

Setup$(1^\lambda, 1^\kappa, n) \to (\text{msk}, \text{pk}, \text{key})$. The setup algorithm takes as input the security parameter λ, the 'identity space' parameter κ, index space n, and outputs a master secret key msk and a public key pk.

KeyGen $(\text{msk}, \text{id} \in \{0,1\}^\kappa, i \in [n]) \to \text{sk}$. The key generation algorithm takes as input the master secret key, an identity id $\in \{0,1\}^\kappa$ and index $i \in [n]$. It outputs a secret key sk.

Enc$(\text{pk}, m) \to \text{ct}$. The encryption algorithm takes as input a public key pk, message $m \in \mathcal{M}_\lambda$, and outputs a ciphertext ct.

SplEnc$(\text{key}, m, (i, \ell, b)) \to \text{ct}$. The special-encryption algorithm takes as input a key key, message $m \in \mathcal{M}_\lambda$, and index-position-value tuple $(i, \ell, b) \in [n+1] \times ([\kappa] \cup \{\bot\}) \times \{0,1\}$, and outputs a ciphertext ct. (Here the scheme is said to be public key EIPLBE scheme if key = pk. Otherwise, it is said to be private key EIPLBE scheme.)

Dec$(\text{sk}, \text{ct}) \to z$. The decryption algorithm takes as input a secret key sk, ciphertext ct and outputs $z \in \mathcal{M}_\lambda \cup \{\bot\}$.

Correctness. A EIPLBE scheme is said to be correct if there exists a negligible function $\text{negl}(\cdot)$ such that for all $\lambda, \kappa, n \in \mathbb{N}$, $m \in \mathcal{M}_\lambda$, and $i \in [n+1]$, $j \in [n]$, id $\in \{0,1\}^\kappa$, $\ell \in ([\kappa] \cup \{\bot\})$ and $b \in \{0,1\}$, the following probabilities are at least $1 - \text{negl}(\lambda)$:

$$\Pr\left[\text{Dec}(\text{sk}, \text{ct}) = m : \begin{array}{c} (\text{msk}, \text{pk}, \text{key}) \leftarrow \text{Setup}(1^\lambda, 1^\kappa, n) \\ \text{sk} \leftarrow \text{KeyGen}(\text{msk}, \text{id}, j) \\ \text{ct} \leftarrow \text{Enc}(\text{pk}, m) \end{array}\right]$$

$$\left(\begin{array}{c} (j \geq i+1) \vee \\ (i, \ell) = (j, \bot) \vee \\ (i, \text{id}_\ell) = (j, 1-b) \end{array}\right) \Rightarrow \Pr\left[\text{Dec}(\text{sk}, \text{ct}) = m : \begin{array}{c} (\text{msk}, \text{pk}, \text{key}) \leftarrow \text{Setup}(1^\lambda, 1^\kappa, n) \\ \text{sk} \leftarrow \text{KeyGen}(\text{msk}, \text{id}, j) \\ \text{ct} \leftarrow \text{SplEnc}(\text{key}, m, (i, \ell, b)) \end{array}\right].$$

Efficiency. Let $\mathsf{T\text{-}s}, \mathsf{T\text{-}e}, \mathsf{T\text{-}\tilde{e}}, \mathsf{T\text{-}k}, \mathsf{T\text{-}d}, \mathsf{S\text{-}c}, \mathsf{S\text{-}k}$ be functions. A EIPLBE scheme is said to be $(\mathsf{T\text{-}s}, \mathsf{T\text{-}e}, \mathsf{T\text{-}\tilde{e}}, \mathsf{T\text{-}k}, \mathsf{T\text{-}d}, \mathsf{S\text{-}c}, \mathsf{S\text{-}k})$- efficient if the following efficiency requirements hold:

- The running time of $\mathsf{Setup}(1^\lambda, 1^\kappa, n)$ is at most $\mathsf{T\text{-}s}(\lambda, \kappa, n)$.
- The running time of $\mathsf{Enc}(\mathsf{pk}, m)$ is at most $\mathsf{T\text{-}e}(\lambda, \kappa, n)$.
- The running time of $\mathsf{SplEnc}(\mathsf{key}, m, (i, \ell, b))$ is at most $\mathsf{T\text{-}\tilde{e}}(\lambda, \kappa, n)$.
- The running time of $\mathsf{KeyGen}(\mathsf{msk}, \mathsf{id}, i)$ is at most $\mathsf{T\text{-}k}(\lambda, \kappa, n)$.
- The running time of $\mathsf{Dec}(\mathsf{sk}, \mathsf{ct})$ is at most $\mathsf{T\text{-}d}(\lambda, \kappa, n)$.
- The size of the ciphertexts is at most $\mathsf{S\text{-}c}(\lambda, \kappa, n)$.
- The size of the key is at most $\mathsf{S\text{-}k}(\kappa, n)$.

q-query EIPLBE Security. Now we provide the security definitions for EIPLBE as a generalization of the PLBE q-query security [26]. Also, see Remark 1.

Definition 4 (q-query Normal Hiding Security). *Let $q(\cdot)$ be any fixed polynomial. A EIPLBE scheme is said to satisfy q-query normal hiding security if for every stateful PPT adversary $\mathcal{A}$, there exists a negligible function $\mathsf{negl}(\cdot)$ such that for every $\lambda \in \mathbb{N}$, the following probability is at most $1/2 + \mathsf{negl}(\lambda)$:*

$$\Pr \left[\mathcal{A}^{\mathsf{SplEnc}(\mathsf{key},\cdot,\cdot),\mathsf{KeyGen}(\mathsf{msk},\cdot,\cdot)}(\mathsf{ct}_b) = b \; : \; \begin{array}{c} (1^\kappa, 1^n) \leftarrow \mathcal{A}(1^\lambda) \\ (\mathsf{pk}, \mathsf{msk}, \mathsf{key}) \leftarrow \mathsf{Setup}(1^\lambda, 1^\kappa, n) \\ m \leftarrow \mathcal{A}^{\mathsf{SplEnc}(\mathsf{key},\cdot,\cdot),\mathsf{KeyGen}(\mathsf{msk},\cdot,\cdot)}(\mathsf{pk}) \\ b \leftarrow \{0,1\}; \; \mathsf{ct}_0 \leftarrow \mathsf{Enc}(\mathsf{pk}, m) \\ \mathsf{ct}_1 \leftarrow \mathsf{SplEnc}(\mathsf{key}, m, (1, \bot, 0)) \end{array} \right]$$

with the following oracle restrictions:

- *SplEnc Oracle: $\mathcal{A}$ can make at most $q(\lambda)$ queries, and for each query $(m, (j, \ell, \gamma))$ the index j must be equal to 1.*
- *KeyGen Oracle: $\mathcal{A}$ can make at most one query for each index position j. That is, let $(j_1, \mathsf{id}_1), \ldots, (j_k, \mathsf{id}_k)$ denote all the key queries made by $\mathcal{A}$, then j_a and j_b must be distinct for all $a \neq b$.*

Definition 5 (q-query Index Hiding Security). *Let $q(\cdot)$ be any fixed polynomial. A EIPLBE scheme is said to satisfy q-query index hiding security if for every stateful PPT adversary $\mathcal{A}$, there exists a negligible function $\mathsf{negl}(\cdot)$ such that for every $\lambda \in \mathbb{N}$, the following probability is at most $1/2 + \mathsf{negl}(\lambda)$:*

$$\Pr \left[\mathcal{A}^{\mathsf{SplEnc}(\mathsf{key},\cdot,\cdot),\mathsf{KeyGen}(\mathsf{msk},\cdot,\cdot)}(\mathsf{ct}) = b \; : \; \begin{array}{c} (1^\kappa, 1^n, i) \leftarrow \mathcal{A}(1^\lambda) \\ (\mathsf{pk}, \mathsf{msk}, \mathsf{key}) \leftarrow \mathsf{Setup}(1^\lambda, 1^\kappa, n) \\ m \leftarrow \mathcal{A}^{\mathsf{SplEnc}(\mathsf{key},\cdot,\cdot),\mathsf{KeyGen}(\mathsf{msk},\cdot,\cdot)}(\mathsf{pk}) \\ b \leftarrow \{0,1\}; \; \mathsf{ct} \leftarrow \mathsf{SplEnc}(\mathsf{key}, m, (i+b, \bot, 0)) \end{array} \right]$$

with the following oracle restrictions:

- *SplEnc Oracle: $\mathcal{A}$ can make at most $q(\lambda)$ queries, and for each query $(m, (j, \ell, \gamma))$ the index j must be equal to either i or $i+1$.*

– KeyGen *Oracle:* $\mathcal{A}$ *can make at most one query for each index position* $j \in [n]$, *and no key query of the form* (i, id). *That is, let* $(j_1, \mathrm{id}_1), \ldots, (j_k, \mathrm{id}_k)$ *denote all the key queries made by* $\mathcal{A}$, *then* j_a *and* j_b *must be distinct for all* $a \neq b$. *And,* $j_a \neq i$ *for any* a.

Definition 6 (*q*-query Upper Identity Hiding Security). *Let* $q(\cdot)$ *be any fixed polynomial. A EIPLBE scheme is said to satisfy q-query upper identity hiding security if for every stateful PPT adversary* $\mathcal{A}$, *there exists a negligible function* $\mathsf{negl}(\cdot)$ *such that for every* $\lambda \in \mathbb{N}$, *the following probability is at most* $1/2 + \mathsf{negl}(\lambda)$:

$$\Pr\left[\mathcal{A}^{\mathsf{SplEnc}(\mathsf{key}, \cdot, \cdot), \mathsf{KeyGen}(\mathsf{msk}, \cdot, \cdot)}(\mathsf{ct}_b) = b \ : \ \begin{array}{c} (1^\kappa, 1^n, i, \ell, \beta) \leftarrow \mathcal{A}(1^\lambda) \\ (\mathsf{pk}, \mathsf{msk}, \mathsf{key}) \leftarrow \mathsf{Setup}(1^\lambda, 1^\kappa, n) \\ m \leftarrow \mathcal{A}^{\mathsf{SplEnc}(\mathsf{key}, \cdot, \cdot), \mathsf{KeyGen}(\mathsf{msk}, \cdot, \cdot)}(\mathsf{pk}) \\ b \leftarrow \{0, 1\}; \ \mathsf{ct}_0 \leftarrow \mathsf{SplEnc}(\mathsf{key}, m, (i+1, \bot, 0)) \\ \mathsf{ct}_1 \leftarrow \mathsf{SplEnc}(\mathsf{key}, m, (i, \ell, \beta)) \end{array} \right]$$

with the following oracle restrictions:

– SplEnc *Oracle:* $\mathcal{A}$ *can make at most* $q(\lambda)$ *queries, and for each query* $(m, (j, \ell, \gamma))$ *the index* j *must be equal to either* i *or* $i+1$.
– KeyGen *Oracle:* $\mathcal{A}$ *can make at most one query for each index position* $j \in [n]$, *and no key query of the form* (i, id) *such that* $\mathrm{id}_\ell = 1 - \beta$. *That is, let* $(j_1, \mathrm{id}_1), \ldots, (j_k, \mathrm{id}_k)$ *denote all the key queries made by* $\mathcal{A}$, *then* j_a *and* j_b *must be distinct for all* $a \neq b$. *And, for every* a, $(\mathrm{id}_a)_\ell \neq 1 - \beta$ *or* $j_a \neq i$.

Definition 7 (*q*-query Lower Identity Hiding Security). *Let* $q(\cdot)$ *be any fixed polynomial. A EIPLBE scheme is said to satisfy q-query lower identity hiding security if for every stateful PPT adversary* $\mathcal{A}$, *there exists a negligible function* $\mathsf{negl}(\cdot)$ *such that for every* $\lambda \in \mathbb{N}$, *the following probability is at most* $1/2 + \mathsf{negl}(\lambda)$:

$$\Pr\left[\mathcal{A}^{\mathsf{SplEnc}(\mathsf{key}, \cdot, \cdot), \mathsf{KeyGen}(\mathsf{msk}, \cdot, \cdot)}(\mathsf{ct}_b) = b \ : \ \begin{array}{c} (1^\kappa, 1^n, i, \ell, \beta) \leftarrow \mathcal{A}(1^\lambda) \\ (\mathsf{pk}, \mathsf{msk}, \mathsf{key}) \leftarrow \mathsf{Setup}(1^\lambda, 1^\kappa, n) \\ m \leftarrow \mathcal{A}^{\mathsf{SplEnc}(\mathsf{key}, \cdot, \cdot), \mathsf{KeyGen}(\mathsf{msk}, \cdot, \cdot)}(\mathsf{pk}) \\ b \leftarrow \{0, 1\}; \ \mathsf{ct}_0 \leftarrow \mathsf{SplEnc}(\mathsf{key}, m, (i, \bot, 0)) \\ \mathsf{ct}_1 \leftarrow \mathsf{SplEnc}(\mathsf{key}, m, (i, \ell, \beta)) \end{array} \right]$$

with the following oracle restrictions:

– SplEnc *Oracle:* $\mathcal{A}$ *can make at most* $q(\lambda)$ *queries, and for each query* $(m, (j, \ell, \gamma))$ *the index* j *must be equal to* i.
– KeyGen *Oracle:* $\mathcal{A}$ *can make at most one query for each index position* $j \in [n]$, *and no key query of the form* (i, id) *such that* $\mathrm{id}_\ell = \beta$. *That is, let* $(j_1, \mathrm{id}_1), \ldots, (j_k, \mathrm{id}_k)$ *denote all the key queries made by* $\mathcal{A}$, *then* j_a *and* j_b *must be distinct for all* $a \neq b$. *And, for every* a, $(\mathrm{id}_a)_\ell \neq \beta$ *or* $j_a \neq i$.

Definition 8 (q-query Message Hiding Security). *Let $q(\cdot)$ be any fixed polynomial. A EIPLBE scheme is said to satisfy q-query message hiding security if for every stateful PPT adversary $\mathcal{A}$, there exists a negligible function $\mathsf{negl}(\cdot)$ such that for every $\lambda \in \mathbb{N}$, the following probability is at most $1/2 + \mathsf{negl}(\lambda)$:*

$$\Pr\left[\mathcal{A}^{\mathsf{SplEnc}(\mathsf{key},\cdot,\cdot),\mathsf{KeyGen}(\mathsf{msk},\cdot,\cdot)}(\mathsf{ct}) = b \ : \ \begin{array}{l} (1^\kappa, 1^n) \leftarrow \mathcal{A}(1^\lambda) \\ (\mathsf{pk}, \mathsf{msk}, \mathsf{key}) \leftarrow \mathsf{Setup}(1^\lambda, 1^\kappa, n) \\ (m_0, m_1) \leftarrow \mathcal{A}^{\mathsf{SplEnc}(\mathsf{key},\cdot,\cdot),\mathsf{KeyGen}(\mathsf{msk},\cdot,\cdot)}(\mathsf{pk}) \\ b \leftarrow \{0,1\}; \ \mathsf{ct} \leftarrow \mathsf{SplEnc}(\mathsf{key}, m_b, (n+1, \bot, 0)) \end{array}\right]$$

with the following oracle restrictions:

- SplEnc *Oracle: $\mathcal{A}$ can make at most $q(\lambda)$ queries, and for each query $(m, (i, \ell, \gamma))$ the index i must be equal to $n+1$.*
- KeyGen *Oracle: $\mathcal{A}$ can make at most one query for each index position i. That is, let $(i_1, \mathsf{id}_1), \ldots, (i_k, \mathsf{id}_k)$ denote all the key queries made by $\mathcal{A}$, then i_a and i_b must be distinct for all $a \neq b$.*

4.2 Building Indexed EITT from EIPLBE

Construction. Consider an EIPLBE scheme $\mathsf{EIPLBE} = (\mathsf{EIPLBE.Setup}, \mathsf{EIPLBE.KeyGen}, \mathsf{EIPLBE.Enc}, \mathsf{EIPLBE.SplEnc}, \mathsf{EIPLBE.Dec})$ for message space $\mathcal{M} = \{\mathcal{M}_\lambda\}_{\lambda \in \mathbb{N}}$ and identity space $\mathcal{ID} = \{\{0,1\}^\kappa\}_{\kappa \in \mathbb{N}}$. Below we provide our embedded identity TT construction with identical message and identity spaces. (Here we provide a transformation for TT schemes with secret key tracing, but the construction can be easily extended to work in the public tracing setting if the special encryption algorithm in the underlying EIPLBE scheme is public key as well.)

$\mathsf{Setup}(1^\lambda, 1^\kappa, n) \to (\mathsf{msk}, \mathsf{pk}, \mathsf{key})$. The setup algorithm runs the EIPLBE setup as $(\mathsf{msk}, \mathsf{pk}, \mathsf{key}) \leftarrow \mathsf{EIPLBE.Setup}(1^\lambda, 1^\kappa, n)$, and outputs master secret-public-tracing key tuple $(\mathsf{msk}, \mathsf{pk}, \mathsf{key})$.

$\mathsf{KeyGen}(\mathsf{msk}, \mathsf{id}, i) \to \mathsf{sk}_{i,\mathsf{id}}$. The key generation algorithm runs the EIPLBE key generation algorithm as $\mathsf{sk}_{i,\mathsf{id}} \leftarrow \mathsf{EIPLBE.KeyGen}(\mathsf{msk}, \mathsf{id}, i)$, and outputs secret key $\mathsf{sk}_{i,\mathsf{id}}$.

$\mathsf{Enc}(\mathsf{pk}, m) \to \mathsf{ct}$. The encryption algorithm runs the EIPLBE encryption algorithm as $\mathsf{ct} \leftarrow \mathsf{EIPLBE.Enc}(\mathsf{pk}, m)$, and outputs ciphertext ct.

$\mathsf{Dec}(\mathsf{sk}, \mathsf{ct}) \to z$. The decryption algorithm runs the EIPLBE decryption algorithm as $z \leftarrow \mathsf{EIPLBE.Dec}(\mathsf{sk}, \mathsf{ct})$, and outputs z.

$\mathsf{Trace}^D(\mathsf{key}, 1^y, m_0, m_1) \to T$. Let $\epsilon = 1/y$. First, consider the Index-Trace algorithm defined in Fig. 2. The sub-tracing algorithm simply tests whether the decoder box uses the user key for index i where i is one of the inputs provided to Index-Trace. Now the tracing algorithm simply runs the Index-Trace algorithm for all indices $i \in [n]$, and for each index i where the Index-Trace algorithm outputs 1, the tracing algorithm adds index i to the *index-set* of traitors T^{index}.[9] Next, consider the ID-Trace algorithm defined in Fig. 3. The identity-tracing algorithm takes as input the index-set T^{index} and uses the decoder box to find the identity of the particular indexed user. Next, the tracing algorithm simply runs the ID-Trace algorithm for all indices $i \in T^{\text{index}}$, and for each index i where the ID-Trace algorithm does not output $\perp$, the tracing algorithm adds the output of the ID-Trace algorithm to the *identity-set* of traitors T.

Concretely, the algorithm runs as follows:

- Set $T^{\text{index}} := \emptyset$. For $i = 1$ to n:
  - Compute $(b, p, q) \leftarrow$ Index-Trace$(\mathsf{key}, 1^y, m_0, m_1, i)$.
  - If $b = 1$, set $T^{\text{index}} := T^{\text{index}} \cup \{(i, p, q)\}$.
- Set $T := \emptyset$. For $(i, p, q) \in T^{\text{index}}$:
  - Compute id $\leftarrow$ ID-Trace$(\mathsf{key}, 1^y, m_0, m_1, (i, p, q))$.
  - Set $T := T \cup \{\mathsf{id}\}$.
- Output T.

Finally, it outputs the set T as the set of traitors.

Algorithm Index-Trace$(\mathsf{key}, 1^y, m_0, m_1, i)$

Inputs: Key key, parameter y, messages m_0, m_1, index i
Output: 0/1
Let $\epsilon = \lfloor 1/y \rfloor$. It sets $N = \lambda \cdot n/\epsilon$, and $\mathsf{count}_1 = \mathsf{count}_2 = 0$. For $j = 1$ to N, it computes the following:

1. It chooses $b_j \leftarrow \{0, 1\}$ and computes $\mathsf{ct}_{j,1} \leftarrow$ EIPLBE.SplEnc$(\mathsf{key}, m_{b_j}, (i, \perp, 0))$ and sends $\mathsf{ct}_{j,1}$ to D. If D outputs b_j, set $\mathsf{count}_1 = \mathsf{count}_1 + 1$, else set $\mathsf{count}_1 = \mathsf{count}_1 - 1$.
2. It chooses $c_j \leftarrow \{0, 1\}$ and computes $\mathsf{ct}_{j,2} \leftarrow$ EIPLBE.SplEnc$(\mathsf{key}, m_{c_j}, (i+1, \perp, 0))$ and sends $\mathsf{ct}_{j,2}$ to D. If D outputs c_j, set $\mathsf{count}_2 = \mathsf{count}_2 + 1$, else set $\mathsf{count}_2 = \mathsf{count}_2 - 1$.

If $\frac{\mathsf{count}_1 - \mathsf{count}_2}{N} > \frac{\epsilon}{4n}$, output $(1, \frac{\mathsf{count}_1}{N}, \frac{\mathsf{count}_2}{N})$, else output $(0, \perp, \perp)$.

Fig. 2. Index-Trace

---

[9] Technically, the set T^{index} contains tuples of the form (i, p, q) where i is an index and p, q are probabilities which are the estimations of successful decryption probability at index i and $i + 1$ (respectively).

Algorithm ID-Trace(key, $1^y, m_0, m_1, (i, p, q)$)

Inputs: Key key, parameter y, messages m_0, m_1, index i, probabilities p, q

Output: id $\in \{0, 1\}^\kappa$

Let $\epsilon = \lfloor 1/y \rfloor$. It sets $N = \lambda \cdot n/\epsilon$, and $\mathsf{count}_\ell = 0$ for $\ell \in [\kappa]$. For $\ell = 1$ to κ, it proceeds as follows:

1. For $j = 1$ to N, it computes the following:
   (a) It chooses $b_j \leftarrow \{0, 1\}$ and computes $\mathsf{ct}_j \leftarrow$ EIPLBE.SplEnc(key, $m_{b_j}, (i, \ell, 0)$) and sends ct_j to D. If D outputs b_j, set $\mathsf{count}_\ell = \mathsf{count}_\ell + 1$, else set $\mathsf{count}_\ell = \mathsf{count}_\ell - 1$.

Next, let id be an empty string. For $\ell = 1$ to κ, do the following:

1. If $\dfrac{p+q}{2} > \dfrac{\mathsf{count}_\ell}{N}$, set $\mathsf{id}_\ell = 0$. Else set $\mathsf{id}_\ell = 1$.

Finally, output id.

Fig. 3. ID-Trace

Correctness. This follows directly from correctness of the underlying EIPLBE scheme.

Efficiency. If the scheme EIPLBE = (EIPLBE.Setup, EIPLBE.KeyGen, EIPLBE.Enc, EIPLBE.SplEnc, EIPLBE.Dec) is a EIPLBE scheme with (T-s, T-e, T-ẽ, T-k, T-d, S-c, S-k)-efficiency, then the scheme TT = (Setup, KeyGen, Enc, Dec, Trace) is a (indexed keygen, public/private)-embedded identity tracing scheme with (T-s', T-e', T-k', T-d', T-t', S-c', S-k')-efficiency, where the efficiency measures are related as follows:

- T-s'(λ, κ, n) = T-s(λ, κ, n),
- T-k'(λ, κ, n) = T-k(λ, κ, n),
- T-e'(λ, κ, n) = T-e(λ, κ, n),
- T-d'(λ, κ, n) = T-d(λ, κ, n),
- T-t'(λ, κ, n, y) = $(2n + \kappa) \cdot \lambda \cdot y \cdot n$,
- S-c'(λ, κ, n) = S-c(λ, κ, n),
- S-k'(λ, κ, n) = S-k(λ, κ, n).

Security. The security proof is included in the full version of our paper.

References

1. Abdalla, M., Dent, A.W., Malone-Lee, J., Neven, G., Phan, D.H., Smart, N.P.: Identity-based traitor tracing. In: Okamoto, T., Wang, X. (eds.) PKC 2007. LNCS, vol. 4450, pp. 361–376. Springer, Heidelberg (2007). https://doi.org/10.1007/978-3-540-71677-8_24

2. Agrawal, S., Bhattacherjee, S., Phan, D.H., Stehlé, D., Yamada, S.: Efficient public trace and revoke from standard assumptions: extended abstract. In: Proceedings of the 2017 ACM SIGSAC Conference on Computer and Communications Security, CCS 2017, Dallas, TX, USA, 30 October–03 November 2017, pp. 2277–2293 (2017). https://doi.org/10.1145/3133956.3134041

3. Baltico, C.E.Z., Catalano, D., Fiore, D., Gay, R.: Practical functional encryption for quadratic functions with applications to predicate encryption. In: Katz, J., Shacham, H. (eds.) CRYPTO 2017. LNCS, vol. 10401, pp. 67–98. Springer, Cham (2017). https://doi.org/10.1007/978-3-319-63688-7_3

4. Barak, B., et al.: On the (im)possibility of obfuscating programs. In: Kilian, J. (ed.) CRYPTO 2001. LNCS, vol. 2139, pp. 1–18. Springer, Heidelberg (2001). https://doi.org/10.1007/3-540-44647-8_1

5. Barak, B., et al.: On the (im)possibility of obfuscating programs. J. ACM **59**(2), 6 (2012)

6. Billet, O., Phan, D.H.: Efficient traitor tracing from collusion secure codes. In: Safavi-Naini, R. (ed.) ICITS 2008. LNCS, vol. 5155, pp. 171–182. Springer, Heidelberg (2008). https://doi.org/10.1007/978-3-540-85093-9_17

7. Böhl, F., Hofheinz, D., Jager, T., Koch, J., Seo, J.H., Striecks, C.: Practical signatures from standard assumptions. In: Johansson, T., Nguyen, P.Q. (eds.) EUROCRYPT 2013. LNCS, vol. 7881, pp. 461–485. Springer, Heidelberg (2013). https://doi.org/10.1007/978-3-642-38348-9_28

8. Boneh, D., Franklin, M.: An efficient public key traitor tracing scheme. In: Wiener, M. (ed.) CRYPTO 1999. LNCS, vol. 1666, pp. 338–353. Springer, Heidelberg (1999). https://doi.org/10.1007/3-540-48405-1_22

9. Boneh, D., Sahai, A., Waters, B.: Fully collusion resistant traitor tracing with short ciphertexts and private keys. In: Vaudenay, S. (ed.) EUROCRYPT 2006. LNCS, vol. 4004, pp. 573–592. Springer, Heidelberg (2006). https://doi.org/10.1007/11761679_34

10. Boneh, D., Waters, B.: A fully collusion resistant broadcast, trace, and revoke system. In: Proceedings of the 13th ACM Conference on Computer and Communications Security, CCS 2006, Alexandria, VA, USA, 30 October–3 November 2006, pp. 211–220 (2006)

11. Boneh, D., Zhandry, M.: Multiparty key exchange, efficient traitor tracing, and more from indistinguishability obfuscation. In: Garay, J.A., Gennaro, R. (eds.) CRYPTO 2014. LNCS, vol. 8616, pp. 480–499. Springer, Heidelberg (2014). https://doi.org/10.1007/978-3-662-44371-2_27

12. Chabanne, H., Phan, D.H., Pointcheval, D.: Public traceability in traitor tracing schemes. In: Cramer, R. (ed.) EUROCRYPT 2005. LNCS, vol. 3494, pp. 542–558. Springer, Heidelberg (2005). https://doi.org/10.1007/11426639_32

13. Chen, Y., Vaikuntanathan, V., Waters, B., Wee, H., Wichs, D.: Traitor-tracing from LWE made simple and attribute-based. In: Beimel, A., Dziembowski, S. (eds.) TCC 2018. LNCS, vol. 11240, pp. 341–369. Springer, Cham (2018). https://doi.org/10.1007/978-3-030-03810-6_13

14. Chor, B., Fiat, A., Naor, M.: Tracing traitors. In: Desmedt, Y.G. (ed.) CRYPTO 1994. LNCS, vol. 839, pp. 257–270. Springer, Heidelberg (1994). https://doi.org/10.1007/3-540-48658-5_25

15. Chor, B., Fiat, A., Naor, M., Pinkas, B.: Tracing traitors. IEEE Trans. Inf. Theory **46**(3), 893–910 (2000). https://doi.org/10.1109/18.841169

16. Coron, J.-S., Lepoint, T., Tibouchi, M.: Practical multilinear maps over the integers. In: Canetti, R., Garay, J.A. (eds.) CRYPTO 2013. LNCS, vol. 8042, pp. 476–493. Springer, Heidelberg (2013). https://doi.org/10.1007/978-3-642-40041-4_26

17. Coron, J.-S., Lepoint, T., Tibouchi, M.: New multilinear maps over the integers. In: Gennaro, R., Robshaw, M. (eds.) CRYPTO 2015. LNCS, vol. 9215, pp. 267–286. Springer, Heidelberg (2015). https://doi.org/10.1007/978-3-662-47989-6_13

18. Döttling, N., Schröder, D.: Efficient pseudorandom functions via on-the-fly adaptation. In: Gennaro, R., Robshaw, M. (eds.) CRYPTO 2015. LNCS, vol. 9215, pp. 329–350. Springer, Heidelberg (2015). https://doi.org/10.1007/978-3-662-47989-6_16

19. Fazio, N., Nicolosi, A., Phan, D.H.: Traitor tracing with optimal transmission rate. In: Garay, J.A., Lenstra, A.K., Mambo, M., Peralta, R. (eds.) ISC 2007. LNCS, vol. 4779, pp. 71–88. Springer, Heidelberg (2007). https://doi.org/10.1007/978-3-540-75496-1_5

20. Freeman, D.M.: Converting pairing-based cryptosystems from composite-order groups to prime-order groups. In: Gilbert, H. (ed.) EUROCRYPT 2010. LNCS, vol. 6110, pp. 44–61. Springer, Heidelberg (2010). https://doi.org/10.1007/978-3-642-13190-5_3

21. Garg, S., Gentry, C., Halevi, S.: Candidate multilinear maps from ideal lattices. In: Johansson, T., Nguyen, P.Q. (eds.) EUROCRYPT 2013. LNCS, vol. 7881, pp. 1–17. Springer, Heidelberg (2013). https://doi.org/10.1007/978-3-642-38348-9_1

22. Garg, S., Kumarasubramanian, A., Sahai, A., Waters, B.: Building efficient fully collusion-resilient traitor tracing and revocation schemes. In: Proceedings of the 17th ACM Conference on Computer and Communications Security, CCS 2010, pp. 121–130. ACM, New York (2010). https://doi.org/10.1145/1866307.1866322

23. Gentry, C., Gorbunov, S., Halevi, S.: Graph-induced multilinear maps from lattices. In: Dodis, Y., Nielsen, J.B. (eds.) TCC 2015. LNCS, vol. 9015, pp. 498–527. Springer, Heidelberg (2015). https://doi.org/10.1007/978-3-662-46497-7_20

24. Goyal, R., Koppula, V., Russell, A., Waters, B.: Risky traitor tracing and new differential privacy negative results. In: Shacham, H., Boldyreva, A. (eds.) CRYPTO 2018. LNCS, vol. 10991, pp. 467–497. Springer, Cham (2018). https://doi.org/10.1007/978-3-319-96884-1_16

25. Goyal, R., Koppula, V., Waters, B.: Lockable obfuscation. In: 58th IEEE Annual Symposium on Foundations of Computer Science, FOCS 2017, pp. 612–621 (2017)

26. Goyal, R., Koppula, V., Waters, B.: Collusion resistant traitor tracing from learning with errors. In: STOC (2018)

27. Kiayias, A., Yung, M.: Traitor tracing with constant transmission rate. In: Knudsen, L.R. (ed.) EUROCRYPT 2002. LNCS, vol. 2332, pp. 450–465. Springer, Heidelberg (2002). https://doi.org/10.1007/3-540-46035-7_30

28. Kurosawa, K., Desmedt, Y.: Optimum traitor tracing and asymmetric schemes. In: Nyberg, K. (ed.) EUROCRYPT 1998. LNCS, vol. 1403, pp. 145–157. Springer, Heidelberg (1998). https://doi.org/10.1007/BFb0054123

29. Kurosawa, K., Yoshida, T.: Linear code implies public-key traitor tracing. In: Naccache, D., Paillier, P. (eds.) PKC 2002. LNCS, vol. 2274, pp. 172–187. Springer, Heidelberg (2002). https://doi.org/10.1007/3-540-45664-3_12

30. Ling, S., Phan, D.H., Stehlé, D., Steinfeld, R.: Hardness of k-LWE and applications in traitor tracing. In: Garay, J.A., Gennaro, R. (eds.) CRYPTO 2014. LNCS, vol. 8616, pp. 315–334. Springer, Heidelberg (2014). https://doi.org/10.1007/978-3-662-44371-2_18

31. Nishimaki, R., Wichs, D., Zhandry, M.: Anonymous traitor tracing: how to embed arbitrary information in a key. In: Fischlin, M., Coron, J.-S. (eds.) EUROCRYPT 2016. LNCS, vol. 9666, pp. 388–419. Springer, Heidelberg (2016). https://doi.org/10.1007/978-3-662-49896-5_14

32. Phan, D.H., Safavi-Naini, R., Tonien, D.: Generic construction of hybrid public key traitor tracing with full-public-traceability. In: Bugliesi, M., Preneel, B., Sassone, V., Wegener, I. (eds.) ICALP 2006. LNCS, vol. 4052, pp. 264–275. Springer, Heidelberg (2006). https://doi.org/10.1007/11787006_23

33. Staddon, J., Stinson, D.R., Wei, R.: Combinatorial properties of frameproof and traceability codes. IEEE Trans. Inf. Theory **47**(3), 1042–1049 (2001). https://doi.org/10.1109/18.915661

34. Stinson, D.R., Wei, R.: Combinatorial properties and constructions of traceability schemes and frameproof codes. SIAM J. Discrete Math. **11**(1), 41–53 (1998). https://doi.org/10.1137/S0895480196304246

35. Wichs, D., Zirdelis, G.: Obfuscating compute-and-compare programs under LWE. In: 58th IEEE Annual Symposium on Foundations of Computer Science, FOCS 2017, pp. 600–611 (2017)

A Unified and Composable Take on Ratcheting

Daniel Jost[✉] [iD], Ueli Maurer, and Marta Mularczyk

Department of Computer Science, ETH Zurich, 8092 Zurich, Switzerland
{dajost,maurer,mumarta}@inf.ethz.ch

Abstract. Ratcheting, an umbrella term for certain techniques for achieving secure messaging with strong guarantees, has spurred much interest in the cryptographic community, with several novel protocols proposed as of lately. Most of them are composed from several sub-protocols, often sharing similar ideas across different protocols. Thus, one could hope to reuse the sub-protocols to build new protocols achieving different security, efficiency, and usability trade-offs. This is especially desirable in view of the community's current aim for group messaging, which has a significantly larger design space. However, the underlying ideas are usually not made explicit, but rather implicitly encoded in a (fairly complex) security game, primarily targeted at the overall security proof. This not only hinders modular protocol design, but also makes the suitability of a protocol for a particular application difficult to assess.

In this work we demonstrate that ratcheting components can be modeled in a composable framework, allowing for their reuse in a modular fashion. To this end, we first propose an extension of the Constructive Cryptography framework by so-called global event histories, to allow for a clean modularization even if the component modules are not fully independent but actually subtly intertwined, as in most ratcheting protocols. Second, we model a unified, flexibly instantiable type of strong security statement for secure messaging within that framework. Third, we show that one can phrase strong guarantees for a number of sub-protocols from the existing literature in this model with only minor modifications, slightly stronger assumptions, and reasonably intuitive formalizations.

When expressing existing protocols' guarantees in a simulation-based framework, one has to address the so-called commitment problem. We do so by reflecting the removal of access to certain oracles under specific conditions, appearing in game-based security definitions, in the real world of our composable statements. We also propose a novel non-committing protocol for settings where the number of messages a party can send before receiving a reply is bounded.

M. Mularczyk—Research supported by the Zurich Information Security and Privacy Center (ZISC).

D. Hofheinz and A. Rosen (Eds.): TCC 2019, LNCS 11892, pp. 180–210, 2019.
https://doi.org/10.1007/978-3-030-36033-7_7

1   Introduction

1.1   Secure Messaging and Ratcheting

Secure-messaging (SM) protocols attempt to provide strong security guarantees to two parties that communicate over an asynchronous network. Apart from protecting confidentiality and integrity of messages, the desired properties include forward secrecy and healing from a state or randomness exposure. The latter properties are addressed by the so-called ratcheting protocols, by having the parties continuously update their secret keys.

The term ratcheting on its own does not carry any formal meaning; rather, it is an umbrella term for a number of different guarantees, somehow related to the concept of updating keys. One notable example of ratcheting is the widely-used Signal protocol [21] with its double-ratchet algorithm, formally analyzed in [1,7]. Furthermore, there exist protocols with much stronger guarantees, but that require the messages to be delivered in order [8–10,24]. Protocols with the stronger guarantee of immediate out-of-order decryption have been proposed in [1]. While the majority of the literature considers secure communication, some works view ratcheting as a property of key exchange instead [2,24].

A number of proposed protocols pursue similar goals, but each achieves a slightly different trade-off between security, efficiency and usability. Moreover, each construction comes with its own—usually fairly complex—security game, intermediate abstractions, and primitives. This renders them hard to compare and hinders achieving new trade-offs that would result from combining ideas from different protocols. This motivates the goal of this work, which is to facilitate a systematic, modular and composable analysis of secure-messaging protocols.

1.2   Composable Security

While a game-based systematization of secure messaging could certainly address some of the aforementioned concerns, composable frameworks, such as [4,14,18,23], provide some distinct advantages.

First, security under (universal) composition is a stronger notion: the guarantees are provided even if a protocol is executed in an arbitrary environment, alongside other protocols. So far, no SM protocol provably achieves this (in fact, even the weaker notion of security under parallel self composition has not been analyzed). Moreover, composable frameworks facilitate modularity. One can define components with clean abstraction boundaries (e.g., a secure channel) and use their idealized versions in a higher-level protocol (and its proof). The overall security of the composed protocol follows from the composition theorem. This stands in contrast with game-based definitions, where security of the components and the overall protocol is expressed by a number of games, and one has to show that winning the security game for the overall protocol implies, via reductions, winning one security game for a component. Finally, guarantees expressed in a composable framework usually have more evident semantics, obtained from directly considering how a protocol is used, rather than a hypothetical interaction of an adversary with a simplified game that encodes excluded attacks.

Unfortunately, secure messaging does not render itself easily to a modular, composable analysis. One reason for this is the difficulty in drawing the right abstraction boundaries. Roughly, the guarantees for a channel heavily depend on other components in the system, for example, we may want to say that the confidentiality of a message is protected only if some memory contents do not leak. This problem also appears in the analysis of some protocols from different contexts (e.g. TLS [12]), which often violate the rules of modularity.

Furthermore, we encounter the so-called "commitment problem" of simulation-based security definitions. Intuitively, the natural composable guarantees are too strong and provide additional security that seems to carry little significance in practice, and that can only be achieved with (stronger) setup assumptions and at an efficiency loss. To address this problem, a number of approaches have been proposed—none of them, however, being able to fully satisfactorily formalize the weaker guarantees achieved by regular schemes. First, the notion of non-information oracles [6] has been proposed that essentially embeds a game-base definition in a composable abstraction module. Second, a line of work considers stronger, i.e., super-polynomial, simulators [3,22,25]. Protocols in those models, however, still have to rely on additional setup and special primitives.

1.3   Contributions

This paper makes both conceptual and technical contributions. Conceptual contributions to composable security frameworks are the notion of global event histories as well as a modeling technique for circumventing the so-called commitment problem. Technical contributions include the modeling of ratcheting (sub-)protocols in a composable framework as well as a novel protocol that achieves adaptive security, i.e., the strongest form of composable security, under certain restrictions.

Global Event Histories. Composable frameworks are based around the idea of independent modules (e.g. channels, keys, or memory resources) that are constructed by one protocol and then used by another protocol in the next construction step. However, in many settings, in particular as they occur in modeling ratcheting protocols, these components are subtly correlated which seems to violate modularity. For example, a channel (one module) can become insecure when a key (another, apparently independent module) is leaked to the adversary.

We address this problem by two conceptual ideas. First, we parameterize resources by several (discrete) parameters—which can be thought of as a switch with two or more positions—which can downgrade the security of a resource, e.g. switch a channel from non-leakable (i.e. confidential) to leakable. Second, we introduce the notion of *global event histories* defined for the entire real (or ideal) world, where a history is a list of events having happened at a module (e.g.

a message being input by Alice or a message having leaked to the adversary). A key idea is now that the switch settings of the modules can be defined by predicates (or, more generally, multi-valued functions) of the global event history. This allows us to draw meaningful abstraction boundaries for secure messaging, but we believe that the concept of event histories is of independent interest and may enable modular analyses for settings where this was previously difficult.

Formally, we use the Constructive Cryptography (CC) framework [15,18], and in particular a slight modification of its standard instantiation to model the event history. Since the composition theorem of CC is proved on an abstract level, we do not need to re-prove it.

Expressing the Guarantees Provided by Ratcheting. Our goal is to capture the guarantees provided by ratcheting (sub-)protocols in a general fashion to make them reusable in different protocols or contexts. This is in contrast to existing game-based definitions, which usually formalize exactly what is required by the next sub-protocol for the overall protocol's security proof to go through.

This goal is achieved by considering parameterized resources as described above and modeling the goal of a (sub-)protocol as improving a certain parameter while leaving the other parameters unchanged, independently of what they are. One can think of a protocol improving certain switch positions (e.g. making a channel confidential), independently of the other switch positions.

In this paper, we consider three ratcheting sub-protocols. We start with a simple authentication protocol in the unidirectional setting which constantly updates keys. As a more involved example, we consider the use of hierarchical identity-based encryption to provide confidentiality. As a third example, we analyze continuous key agreement, a notion introduced by Alwen et al. [1] to abstract the asymmetric ratcheting layer of Signal. On the way, we discover cases where the existing game-based notions are insufficient to prove the stronger, more modular, statements that don't fix the properties (i.e., the switch positions) of the assumed network, but where they can be achieved by simple modifications.

Solutions to the Commitment Problem. When modeling ratcheting protocols, we encounter the so-called commitment problem: the simulator would have to output a simulated value (e.g. a ciphertext) which at a later stage must be compatible with another value (e.g. a leaked key) not initially known to him. Since this is generally impossible, we address this problem in two alternative ways.

On one hand, we propose a technique that allows to transform many standard SM protocols into protocols that achieve full composable security, at the expense of an efficiency lost, as well as being restricted to only sending a bounded number of messages before receiving a reply from the other party. We apply this technique to the HIBE protocol mentioned above and construct its fully composable version.

On the other hand, we can retain composable statements of regular protocols by restricting the adversary's capabilities in the real Roughly, we observe that game-based definitions do not encounter the commitment problem, because they disable certain sequences of oracle calls. For example, if the adversary calls the challenge oracle to obtain a ciphertext, she cannot immediately call the expose oracle that returns the secret key, since this would allow her to trivially win. We give a composable semantic to such conditions by making some real-world components secure by assumption after certain sequences of events. For example, after a message is sent, the memory storing the secret key becomes secure.

1.4   Outline

In Sect. 3 we extend Constructive Cryptography to include the global event history. Based on this, in Sect. 4, we introduce a simple and generic type of security statement for SM protocols. (In the full version [11] we extend it to encompass ratcheting as a key-exchange primitive.) In Sect. 5, we demonstrate how the security guarantees of ratcheting components can be phrased in this model. In Sect. 6, we introduce a novel non-committing ratcheting protocol that achieves full simulation-based security for a bounded number of messages.

2   Preliminaries: Constructive Cryptography

2.1   The Real-World/Ideal-World Paradigm

Many security definitions, and in particular most composable security frameworks [4,14,18,23], are based on the real-world/ideal-world paradigm. The real world models the use of a protocol, whereas the ideal world formalizes the security guarantees that this protocol is supposed to achieve.

The security statement then affirms that the real word is "just-as-good" as the ideal world, meaning that for all parties, no matter whether honest or adversarial, it does not make a difference whether they live in the real or ideal world. Hence, if the honest parties are content with the guarantees they get in the ideal world, they can safely execute the protocol in the real world instead.

2.2   Resources

In each composable framework there is some notion of a module that exports a well-defined interface in a black-box manner to the rest of the world. In the UC framework such a module is called a *functionality*. In the Constructive Cryptography (CC) framework [15,18] such a module is called a *resource*. One of the main differences is that in CC a world consists entirely of resources and the environment (called a distinguisher). So while UC distinguishes between the real world, where the parties can only send messages to each other, and a hybrid world, where they additionally access some ideal functionalities, in CC everything, including communication, is a resource. For example, a security statement about two parties using authenticated encryption to transmit a message is phrased as a real world containing two resources—an insecure channel

Resource InsecCh

Initialization	Interface A
$m_A, m_B \leftarrow \perp$	**Input:** (send, m)
	assume only called once
Interface E	$m_A \leftarrow m$
Input: leak	**output** ok
output m_A	
	Interface B
Input: (inject, m)	**Input:** receive
$m_B \leftarrow m$	**output** m_B
output ok	

Resource Key

Initialization
$k \leftarrow \mathcal{K}$
Interface i, $i \in \{A, B\}$
Input: fetch
output k

Fig. 1. The assumed real-world resources of the authenticated-encryption example: an insecure channel and a shared key. The insecure channel exports three interface A, B, and E, understood to be controlled by the respective parties Alice, Bob, and Eve, whereas the key resource only exports two interfaces.

and a shared key—which are then used by the protocol to construct the ideal world consisting of a secure channel. See Fig. 1 for a description of the real-world resources.

A resource is a reactive system that allows interaction at one or several *interfaces*, i.e. upon providing an input at one of the interfaces, the system provides an output. In this work, we only consider systems where the output is produced at the same interface the input was given. Formally, resources are modeled as random systems [16], where the interface address is encoded as part of the inputs. However, a reader unfamiliar with CC may simply think of a resource with n interfaces as n oracles that share a joint state. Note that there is no formal notion of a party in constructive cryptography; they only give meaning to the construction statements, by thinking of each interface being controlled by some party. Since in this work we make statements about messaging between two honest parties, called Alice and Bob, in the presence of a global adversary, called Eve, we usually label the interfaces accordingly, indicating how the assignment of interfaces to parties should be understood.

A set of resources can be composed into a single one. The interface set of the composed resource corresponds to the union of the ones from the composed resources. Returning to our example of authenticated encryption, in the real world we have both an insecure channel InsecCh and a key Key, where the former has three interfaces and the latter two. The composed resource, denoted [InsecCh, Key], is a resource with five interfaces, each of them addressed by a tuple consisting of the resource's name and the interface's original name.

We describe our resources using pseudo-code (c.f. Fig. 1). The following conventions are followed: each resource has an initialization procedure initializing all the persistent variables (all other variables are understood to be volatile). Formally this initialization is called upon invoking any arbitrary interface for the first time. Each interface exposes one or more capabilities, each of them described by a keyword (e.g. send in case of a channel), and the (potential empty) list of arguments (e.g., m). Furthermore, we use the **assume** command,

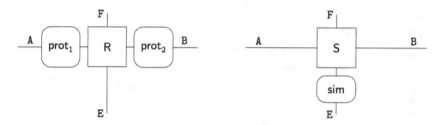

Fig. 2. Execution of the protocol in the real world by Alice and Bob (left) and the ideal world with the simulator attached to Eve's interface (right). The free interface on the top is accessed directly by the environment in both worlds.

which should be understood as a shortcut for explicitly tracking the respective condition and returning an error symbol $\bot$ in case the condition is violated. In Fig. 1, the keyword **assume** is used the specify that the channel is single-use.

2.3   Converters

The protocol execution in CC is modeled by *converters*, each of which expresses the local computation executed by one party. (The name converter derives from the property that a converter attached to a resource converts it into another "ideal" one.) A converter expects to be connected to a given set of interfaces at the "inside", and emulates a certain set of interfaces at the "outside". Upon an input at one of the emulated interfaces, the converter is allowed to make a bounded number of oracle queries to the inside interfaces (recall that a resource always returns at the same interface it was queried), before returning a value at the same emulated interface. For a converter prot and a resource R, we denote by $R' := \text{prot}^{\{I_1,\ldots,I_n\}} R$ the resource obtained from connecting the converter to the subset $\{I_1,\ldots,I_n\}$ of the interfaces. The resource R' no longer exposes those interfaces to the world, but the ones emulated by prot instead. We usually omit specifying the set $\{I_1,\ldots,I_n\}$ and just write for instance $\text{prot}^A R$, denoting that it is connected to all of Alice's interfaces.

2.4   The Construction Notion

Security is then defined following the real-world/ideal-world paradigm, stating that in every environment the real world should behave the same way as the ideal one. The real world, as depicted in Fig. 2, thereby consists of the assumed resource R to which the converters are attached, each to a subset of the respective party's interfaces. The ideal world, on the other hand, consists of the constructed resource S with a simulator (which is a converter) attached to Eve's interfaces.

Behaving the same way is formalized using the notion of a distinguisher, that can make oracle queries to the resource's interfaces and then outputs a bit, indicating whether it believes to interact with the real or ideal world. More formally, in the special case of two honest parties Alice and Bob and a global adversary Eve, the goal of a distinguisher $\mathbf{D}$ is to distinguish the real world $\mathsf{prot}_1^A \, \mathsf{prot}_2^B \, \mathsf{R}$ from the ideal world $\mathsf{sim}^E \, \mathsf{S}$. The advantage of $\mathbf{D}$ is defined as

$$\Delta^{\mathbf{D}}\left(\mathsf{prot}_1^A \, \mathsf{prot}_2^B \, \mathsf{R}, \, \mathsf{sim}^E \, \mathsf{S}\right) := \Pr\left[\mathbf{D}(\mathsf{sim}^E \, \mathsf{S}) = 1\right] - \Pr\left[\mathbf{D}(\mathsf{prot}_1^A \, \mathsf{prot}_2^B \, \mathsf{R}) = 1\right].$$

Let ϵ denote a function mapping distinguishers to values in $[-1, 1]$. Then, the protocol $(\mathsf{prot}_1, \mathsf{prot}_2)$, when attached to A and B, is said to *construct* S from R within ϵ, and with respect to sim attached to E, if

$$\forall \mathbf{D} : \Delta^{\mathbf{D}}\left(\mathsf{prot}_1^A \, \mathsf{prot}_2^B \, \mathsf{R}, \, \mathsf{sim}^E \, \mathsf{S}\right) \leq \epsilon(\mathbf{D}).$$

Note that we require the sets of interfaces controlled by Alice, Bob, and Eve, respectively, to be pairwise disjoint. They however do not have to completely partition the set of interfaces. The remaining interfaces are called *free interfaces* to which the distinguisher has direct access in both worlds.

For simplicity, in this work we consider an asymptotic setting only (although we usually do not make the asymptotics explicit) where all resources and converters are assumed to be efficiently implementable. We then write

$$\mathsf{prot}_1^A \, \mathsf{prot}_2^B \, \mathsf{R} \approx \mathsf{sim}^E \, \mathsf{S},$$

if $\Delta^{\mathbf{D}}\left(\mathsf{prot}_1^A \, \mathsf{prot}_2^B \, \mathsf{R}, \, \mathsf{sim}^E \, \mathsf{S}\right)$ is negligible for every efficient distinguisher $\mathbf{D}$, and simply say that $(\mathsf{prot}_1, \mathsf{prot}_2)$ constructs S from R if there exists an efficient simulator sim achieving this.

Note that the notion of construction is analogous to the notion of secure realization in the UC framework. In contrast to UC, however, the set of all resource instances within a construction statement is fixed. The distinguisher does not instantiate resources or protocols, or assign session identifiers. Dynamic availability properties of resources can obviously still be modeled as part of the resources themselves, though.

2.5 Composition

The notion of construction is composable, which intuitively means that if a protocol $(\mathsf{prot}_1, \mathsf{prot}_2)$ constructs S from R, and another protocol $(\mathsf{prot}_1', \mathsf{prot}_2')$ constructs T from S, then the combined protocol constructs T from R. This is known as *sequential composition*. Additionally, if $(\mathsf{prot}_1, \mathsf{prot}_2)$ constructs $[\mathsf{S}_1, \ldots, \mathsf{S}_i]$ from $[\mathsf{R}_1, \ldots, \mathsf{R}_j]$, for some i and j, then for every set of (efficiently implementable) resources $\{\mathsf{T}_1, \ldots, \mathsf{T}_n\}$ it also holds that $(\mathsf{prot}_1, \mathsf{prot}_2)$ constructs $[\mathsf{S}_1, \ldots, \mathsf{S}_i, \mathsf{T}_1, \ldots, \mathsf{T}_n]$ from $[\mathsf{R}_1, \ldots, \mathsf{R}_j, \mathsf{T}_1, \ldots, \mathsf{T}_n]$, where the interfaces of the additional resources $\mathsf{T}_1, \ldots, \mathsf{T}_n$ are treated as free in the construction. This property is known as *parallel composition*.

Both properties are proven in [18,19] for a more abstract notion of resources being "just-as-good", of which the here introduced indistinguishability notion is a special case. Together, the two properties form the equivalent to the universal composability property of the UC framework.

3   Constructive Cryptography with Events

In this section we generalize the Constructive Cryptography framework to allow for better modularization. More specifically, we introduce another instantiation of resources and the "just-as-good" notion, thereby inheriting the composition theorem of CC that is proven on a more abstract level.

Motivation. Recall that SM protocols are difficult to modularize, because the guarantees for a given message depend on the dynamically changing state of other components in the system, such as whether the state leaked or the adversary tampered with a previous message. In traditional CC, where the abstraction boundary of a resource is just the input-output behavior, properly accounting for those dependencies would essentially force us to model the whole SM application as monolithic resource. In this section, we therefore extend the notions of resources and construction to relax the abstraction boundary in a clean and well-controlled manner, which will allow for such dependencies between different resources. More concretely, we introduce a global event history. Each resource is then allowed to trigger events from a predefined set (e.g. indicating that a party's state leaked), on which the behavior of other resources can then depend. The event history is visible to the environment, the resources, and the simulator.[1]

The Global Event History. We model events as a generalization of monotone binary outputs (MBO) introduced by Maurer et al. [17]. Roughly, an MBO of a resource is an additional output that can change from 0 to 1 but not back. This can be interpreted as a single event, which happens when the MBO changes to 1. We generalize this to many events by the means of a global event history.

Definition 1. *Let $\mathcal{N}$ be a name set. The* global event history $\mathcal{E}$ *is a list of elements of $\mathcal{N}$ without duplicates.*

For $n \in \mathcal{N}$, we use $\mathcal{E}_n$ as a short-hand notation to denote that n is in the list $\mathcal{E}$, and say that the event happened. Analogously, we use $\neg\mathcal{E}_n$ to denote the complementary case. Furthermore, we denote by $\mathcal{E} \xleftarrow{+} \mathcal{E}_n$, the act of appending n to the list $\mathcal{E}$, if $\neg\mathcal{E}_n$, and leaving the list unchanged otherwise.

We also introduce the natural happened-before relation on the events.

Definition 2. *For $n_1, n_2 \in \mathcal{N}$, we say that the event n_1 precedes the event n_2 in the event history $\mathcal{E}$, denoted $\mathcal{E}_{n_1} \prec \mathcal{E}_{n_2}$, if either*

- *both events happened, i.e, $\mathcal{E}_{n_1}$ and $\mathcal{E}_{n_2}$, and n_1 is in the history before n_2,*
- *or only n_1 happened so far.*

---

[1] From a conceptual point of view, this global event history is somewhat reminiscent of the "directory" ITI used in the recent version (as of December 2018) of UC [4] to keep track of which parties are corrupted.

Note that saying that $\mathcal{E}_{n_1} \prec \mathcal{E}_{n_2}$ is true if so far only the former one has happened best matches the type of statement we usually want to make: for instance, if we express the condition that a message is secure if the key has been securely erased before the memory was leaked, then we do not need to insist that the memory actually leaked.

Event-Aware Systems. We consider resources, converters and distinguishers that can (1) read the global event history, and (2) append to the event history from a fixed subset of $\mathcal{N}$. That is, the global event history is an additional component (of both the real and ideal world) that models event-awareness in an abstract manner, rather than formalizing them as outputs that need to be explicitly passed between components.

As a convention, we use as event-name pairs (id, label), where label is a descriptive keyword (e.g., leaked), and id identifies the resource triggering the event, and we use the notation $\mathcal{E}_{id}^{\mathsf{label}}$. Simulators and distinguishers can trigger events with arbitrary id's (looking forward, e.g. a simulator will have to trigger real-world events that do not occur in the ideal world). Still, we require that they do not trigger events that can be triggered by any resources they are connected to (such that, for example, a memory-leaked event really means that it did leak).

Definition 3. *A simulator is* compatible *if it only triggers events that cannot be triggered by the resource it is attached to. For two resources* R *and* S, *a distinguisher* **D** *is* compatible *if it only triggers events that cannot be triggered by neither* R *nor* S.

Converters implementing protocols, on the other hand, do not depend on the event history, since an event is something that *might* be observable, rather than something that is guaranteed to be observable by the honest parties.

Construction Notion. Intuitively, in the context of events, a real-world resource R is "just-as-good" as S if these resources look the same to distinguishers $\mathbf{D}^{\mathcal{E}}$ with read-and-write access to the global event history $\mathcal{E}$. This implies that the sequences of events must be the same in the real and in the ideal world. However, for convenience, we slightly relax this rule and introduce event renaming. For example, if a memory is used to store a key, then the memory-read event in the real world would have in the ideal world a better name key-received. Hence, we use both names to denote the same event (one can think of them as aliases). Moreover, we also allow for multiple aliases for a more fine-grained consideration of events in the ideal world, for instance by separating a message-received event into a successful and unsuccessful one.

We make this renaming explicit in the construction statements by defining a surjection τ that maps events triggered by the ideal-world resource to their real-world counterparts. (Note that in the case of duplicates caused by τ, $\tau(\mathcal{E})$ only contains the first occurrence.) When referring to real-world events for specifying ideal-world guarantees, we will sometimes use $\tilde{\mathcal{E}} := \tau(\mathcal{E})$ as a shorthand notation.

We can now define the construction notion for two resources with events.

Definition 4. *We say that* $(\text{prot}_1, \text{prot}_2)$ *constructs* S *from* R *under the event-renaming* τ, *denoted*

$$\text{prot}_1^A \, \text{prot}_2^B \, R \; \hat{\approx}_\tau \; \text{sim}^E \, S,$$

if there exists an efficient simulator sim, *such that* τ *only renames events triggered by* $\text{sim}^E \, S$, *and for all efficient event-aware distinguishers* $\mathbf{D}^{\mathcal{E}}$, *compatible for* $\text{prot}_1^A \, \text{prot}_2^B$ *and* $\text{sim}^E \, S$ *the following advantage is negligible.*

$$\Delta^{\mathbf{D}^{\mathcal{E}}}\left(\text{prot}_1^A \, \text{prot}_2^B \, R, \; \text{sim}^E \, S\right)$$
$$:= \Pr\left[\mathbf{D}^{\tau(\mathcal{E})}(\text{sim}^E \, S) = 1\right] - \Pr\left[\mathbf{D}^{\mathcal{E}}(\text{prot}_1^A \, \text{prot}_2^B \, R) = 1\right]$$

We stress that this construction notion satisfies the axioms of the more abstract layer on which the composition theorem of CC is proven [18,19], and thus composes as well.

4 Composable Guarantees for Secure Messaging

In this section we introduce the unified type of construction statement—in CC with events—that we make about SM protocols and components thereof.

4.1 The Approach

We opt for the natural choice of an *application-centric approach*, where the security of a cryptographic scheme or primitive is defined as the construction it achieves when used in a particular application. While this approach provides readily understandable and clean security statements, the resulting definitions often turn out to be overly specific. For instance, the statement about an encryption scheme might hard-code a particular assumed authentic communication network, implying that it cannot be directly combined with an authentication scheme achieving slightly different guarantees.

Avoiding such overly specific statements is crucial for a modular treatment of ratcheting protocols, as each sub-protocol of the prior literature achieves slightly different guarantees. We address this problem by making parameterized construction statements, where the assumed real-world resources are parameterized by several "switches" determining their security guarantees. Formally, such a "switch" is represented by a function of the global event history $\mathcal{E}$ (among others), that dynamically defines the behavior of the resource at a given moment in time. For instance, a leakage function $\mathfrak{L}$ may specify to which extent a channel leaks depending on the set of events that happened so far. The goal of a protocol is then expressed as improving certain parameters while leaving the others unchanged, independently of what they were in the beginning. That is, our construction statements will be of the type that a protocol constructs a communication network with certain (stronger) guarantees, assuming a network with certain (weaker) guarantees, where the real-world guarantees are treated as a parameter instead of hard-coding them.

Note that in the context of ratcheting protocols, making such parameterized statement about components—without a-priori assuming any guarantees about the real-world—is mostly not an issue. This is due to the fact that the protocols anyway have to be designed for the setting where the state and randomness could leak at any time, temporarily nullifying all guarantees that the component might try to assume from the underlying sub-protocols.

4.2 Our Channel Model

We now introduce our model of two-party communication networks. It allows us to express flexible security guarantees, but also various usability restrictions or guarantees, such as whether messages can be received out of order or not.

Many Single-Message Channels. We choose to model the communication network between Alice and Bob as the parallel composition of many unidirectional single-message communication channels. Besides being simpler to describe, it allows to have simpler construction steps which only consider a subset of the channels. On the flip side, it results in a world with an arbitrary but bounded number of messages, as the set of resources is static in CC. This is, however, without loss of generality as long as the protocols do not take advantage of this upper bound. Finally, observe that this decision results in a network where messages have implicit (unprotected) sequence numbers, as for instance achieved by TCP.

The Single-Message Channel. We model channels with authenticated data. Since we will use the same type of channel both in the real and ideal world, the channel must hit the right trade-off between giving enough power to the simulator but not too much power to the real-world adversary. On a high level, the channel interfaces and their capabilities are as follows. See Fig. 3 for the formal definition.

- The sender S can issue the command (send, m, ad). Whether she is allowed to do so is determined by the can-send predicate $\mathfrak{S}$. (This predicate will mainly be used to describe situations in which the sender does not have the necessary keys yet.) A successful sending operation triggers the event $\mathcal{E}^{\mathsf{sent}}$. The sender can also query whether the channel is available for transmission.
- The adversary E can then potentially learn m through the **read** command. Whether she is allowed to do so is determined by the can-leak function $\mathfrak{L}$, which outputs either **false** (the adversary is not allowed to read m), **true** (reading is allowed but triggers a leaked event $\mathcal{E}^{\mathsf{leaked}}$), or **silent** (reading is allowed). Moreover, she is always allowed to learn the length of m and the (non-confidential) associated data ad.
- The adversary decides when receiving becomes possible, i.e., the message in principle is delivered. Once this happens, the receiver R can try to fetch the message. This has two possible outcomes: either he receives a message and an according received event is triggered, or he receives $\bot$ and an error event (indexed by an error code from Errors) is triggered. Which case happens is

---

Resource $Ch_{\mathfrak{L},\mathfrak{J},\mathfrak{S},\mathfrak{R},\mathrm{Errors}}^{id,S\to R}$

Parameters:
- Identity id (optionally), and interfaces S (sender) and R (receiver)
- Set of Errors that can occur
- Functions $\mathfrak{L}(\mathcal{E}) \in \{\mathtt{true}, \mathtt{false}, \mathtt{silent}\}$ (can leak), $\mathfrak{S}(\mathcal{E}) \in \{\mathtt{true}, \mathtt{false}\}$ (can send), $\mathfrak{R}(\mathcal{E}) \in \{\mathtt{true}, \mathtt{false}\}$ (can receive) and $\mathfrak{D}(\mathcal{E}, same) \in \mathrm{Errors} \cup \{\mathtt{msg}\}$ (delivery outcome)

Events: $\mathcal{E}^{\mathrm{sent}}$, $\mathcal{E}^{\mathrm{leaked}}$, $\mathcal{E}^{\mathrm{received}(same)}$ and $\mathcal{E}^{\mathrm{error}(err,same)}$ for $same \in \{\mathtt{true}, \mathtt{false}\}$ and $err \in \mathrm{Errors}$

Initialization
$m_S, ad_S, m_R, ad_R, cmd, same \leftarrow \bot$

Interface S

Input: $(\mathtt{send}, m, ad) \in \mathcal{M} \times \mathcal{AD}$
  assume $cmd = \bot$
  if $\neg\mathfrak{S}(\mathcal{E})$ **then output** $\bot$
  $(m_S, ad_S) \leftarrow (m, ad)$
  $\mathcal{E} \overset{+}{\leftarrow} \mathcal{E}^{\mathrm{sent}}$
  output ok

Input: isAvailable
  output $\mathfrak{S}(\mathcal{E})$

Interface R

Input: receive
  assume only called once
  if $\neg\mathfrak{R}(\mathcal{E}) \vee cmd = \bot$ **then**
    output $\bot$

  // same messages (no injection)?
  if $same = \mathtt{check}$ **then**
    $same \leftarrow ((m_R, ad_R) = (m_S, ad_S))$

  // the outcome: an error or the message
  $out \leftarrow \mathfrak{D}(\mathcal{E}, same)$
  if $cmd = \mathtt{dlv} \wedge out = \mathtt{msg}$ **then**
    $\mathcal{E} \overset{+}{\leftarrow} \mathcal{E}^{\mathrm{received}(same)}$
    output (m_R, ad_R)
  else if $cmd = (\mathtt{err}, err, Overw)$
      $\wedge (out = \mathtt{msg} \vee out \in Overw)$ **then**
    $\mathcal{E} \overset{+}{\leftarrow} \mathcal{E}^{\mathrm{error}(err,same)}$
    output $\bot$
  else
    $\mathcal{E} \overset{+}{\leftarrow} \mathcal{E}^{\mathrm{error}(out,same)}$
    output $\bot$

Input: isAvailable
  output $\mathfrak{R}(\mathcal{E}) \wedge cmd \neq \bot$

Interface E

Input: read
  if $\mathfrak{L}(\mathcal{E}) = \mathtt{false}$ **then output** $\bot$
  else if $\mathfrak{L}(\mathcal{E}) = \mathtt{true}$ **then** $\mathcal{E} \overset{+}{\leftarrow} \mathcal{E}^{\mathrm{leaked}}$
  output (m_S, ad_S)

Input: readLength
  output $(|m_S|, ad_S)$

Input: $(\mathtt{deliver}, m, ad, same')$
    $\in (\mathcal{M} \cup \{\mathtt{fwd}\}) \times \mathcal{AD} \times \{\mathtt{check}, \mathtt{false}\}$
  assume $cmd = \bot$

  // handle forwarding request
  if $m = \mathtt{fwd}$ **then**
    if $m_S = \bot$ **then output** $\bot$
    else $m \leftarrow m_S$

  // store for receiving
  $(m_R, ad_R, same) \leftarrow (m, ad, same')$
  $cmd \leftarrow \mathtt{dlv}$
  output ok

Input: $(\mathtt{error}, err, Overw, m, ad, same')$
    $\in \mathrm{Errors} \times 2^{\mathrm{Errors}} \times \mathcal{M} \times \mathcal{AD}$
    $\times \{\mathtt{true}, \mathtt{false}, \mathtt{check}\}$
  assume $cmd = \bot$

  // (m, ad) only to determine same
  if $same' = \mathtt{check}$ **then**
    $(m_R, ad_R) \leftarrow (m, ad)$

  // store for receiving
  $same \leftarrow same'$
  $cmd \leftarrow (\mathtt{err}, err, Overw)$
  output ok

Fig. 3. The single-message channel.

determined by the delivery function $\mathfrak{D}$, which takes into account the event history and on whether the message that R tries to fetch is the same as the one input by S (or an injected value from the adversary). The latter condition is denoted by the flag $same$. The flag $same$ is also exposed as part of the received or error event $\mathcal{E}^{\mathrm{received}(same)}$ or $\mathcal{E}^{\mathrm{error}(err,same)}$, respectively.

– When the adversary decides that receiving is possible, she has two options: schedule the delivery of (m', ad') (command `deliver`), or force an error $err \in$ Errors to be triggered (command `error`). In the first case, she can also request to just forward the sender's message (if one exists), using $m' = \texttt{fwd}$. Moreover, for technical reasons[2], she can also insist that once the receiver fetches the message, $same = \texttt{false}$ is used even if the messages match. In case the adversary forces an error err and the outcome of receiving would anyway be a (different) error, the existing error can either be overwritten or preserved. She can control this by specifying a set $Overw$ of errors that should be overwritten.

A Note on Confidentiality. In our channel, the $\mathcal{E}^{\text{received}(same)}$ and $\mathcal{E}^{\text{error}(err,same)}$ events indicate whether the message that Eve injected was the same as the sender's. Since we assume that those events are in principal observable by everybody, including the adversary, those events can partially breach confidentiality if the communication is not properly authenticated.

However, those events are crucial to phrase the post-impersonation guarantees of certain ratcheting protocols. In fact, in those protocols Eve could usually inject her own message (after exposing the sender's state), observe whether it causes the communication to break down, and thereby deducing whether the sender wanted to send the same message afterwards. Our events simply reflect this.

4.3   Additional Resources: Memory and Randomness

An integral part of secure messaging protocols is the assumption that the parties' state, and sometimes also randomness, can leak to the adversary. In Constructive Cryptography everything that can be accessible by multiple parties, here the honest party and Eve, must be modeled as a resource. As a consequence, all of our converters will be stateless and deterministic. (Stateless means that the converter cannot keep state between two separate invocations at the emulated interfaces.) The statements will contain explicit memory and randomness resources instead.

We consider two types of memory resources: (1) an insecure memory $\mathsf{IMem}^{id,\mathsf{U}}$, and (2) a potentially secure memory $\mathsf{Mem}^{id,\mathsf{U}}$. The main differences are that the latter one can be securely erased at any time, is parameterized in a can-leak predicate $\mathfrak{L}$, and triggers a leaked event $\mathcal{E}^{\text{leaked}}_{\mathsf{Mem}(id,U)}$ once the content actually leaks to the adversary. Since each event can only occur once, we thus model it as a write-once memory. Rewritable secure memory can then be modeled as the parallel composition of many write-once memory cells,[3] where each can be

---

[2] The simulator might need this capability, e.g., if two (abstracted away) ciphertexts decrypt to the same message. Note that providing additional capabilities to the adversary in the real world only strengthens the statement and directly implies the construction where this capability is removed.

[3] The memory requirement of a protocol is not determined by the number of such write-once memories, but rather by the maximal number of them in use at any time.

leaked independently[4]. Analogously, the randomness resource is parameterized by a predicate $\mathfrak{L}$ as well. If allowed, the randomness can leak (triggering $\mathcal{E}_{\mathsf{Rnd}(id)}^{\mathsf{leaked}}$) to the adversary at the moment it is used by the honest party—modeling that it is sampled fresh at this point and is not stored. See the full version [11] for a formal definition of both resources.

5   Unifying Ratcheting: Two Examples

In this section, we get acquainted with how the security guarantees of ratcheting protocols can be phrased within our model. To this end, we model the guarantees of two components of actual ratcheting protocols.

As a first example, we consider a simple authentication scheme that appears in [8–10]. Using this example, we demonstrate how our framework allows for a fine-grained modularization, with the overall security then directly following from composition. As a second example, we consider the use of hierarchical identity-based encryption, as in [9,24]. In this example, we explore a way to work around the so-called commitment issue of composable security.

5.1   A Simple Authentication Scheme

We first consider a simple unidirectional authentication protocol, which is designed with the strong guarantees of secure messaging in mind: the authentication guarantees should not only be forward secure but also heal after a state or randomness exposure of either party. Slight variations of this protocol have been used in [10] (without the hash) and [8] (using signcryption). Essentially the same idea also appeared in [9], where, however, a stronger signature primitive with updatable keys is considered, leading to the protocol being formalized in the bidirectional setting.

The Protocol. In the protocol, whenever the sender wants to send a message, a fresh signing and verification key pair is sampled. The fresh verification key is then signed together with the message—using the prior signing key—and the message, the verification key and the signature are transmitted. Finally, the old signing key is securely erased and the fresh one stored instead. The receiver, on the other hand verifies a received message with the previous verification key and stores the new one. The scheme is depicted in Fig. 4.

Recall that we aim to make a strong construction statement that considers how the scheme enhances any preexisting security guarantees, including confidentiality. Usually preserving confidentiality is not a goal that is considered for an authentication protocol, moreover, it is known that the authenticate-then-encrypt approach used in old versions of TLS is not generally secure [13]. Nevertheless, we show that the scheme actually achieves this at the cost of assuming

---

[4] Technically this leads to more fine-grained statements compared to prior work where it was usually assumed that either the entire state leaks or not. Nevertheless, it does not appear to incur additional significant complications.

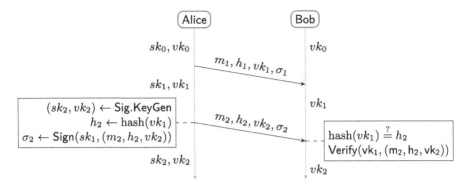

Fig. 4. The simple scheme for unidirectional authentication.

unique signatures instead of unforgeable ones (analogous to [9]), and with a minor modification: with each message, the sender also transmits a hash of the previous verification key. Such a hash is also present in the protocol from [9], and allows the receiver to check whether he is using the correct verification key.

The Guarantees. Clearly, the protocol achieves authenticity if neither party's state is exposed. Moreover, Bob's state only consists of public information. If Alice's state gets exposed, then Eve obtains her current signing key that she can use to impersonate Alice towards Bob at this point in time. However, this key is useless to tamper with previous messages, even if they have not been delivered yet (forward security). More importantly, if, for some reason, Alice's next message containing a fresh verification key still is delivered without modification, then the signing key obtained by the adversary becomes useless thereby achieving the healing property. Hence, the adversary can inject the i-th message if and only if Alice's state between the $(i-1)$-st and i-th message got exposed, or there has already been a successful injection before.

Expressing the scheme's security guarantees in a game-based manner turned out to be surprisingly involved compared to the scheme's simplicity and how easy it seems to intuitively describe its guarantees. Notably, to show its security, in [10] the abstraction of a key-updating signature scheme, as well as its corresponding correctness and security games, have been introduced. This raises a couple of questions: can't we do simpler? What is the right security statement to make about this quite simple protocol, and what happens if the channel already provides certain authenticity or confidentiality guarantees? In the following, we try to answer these questions.

The Construction Statement. First, note that we consider the authentication of messages directly, and do not introduce an intermediate signature notion.

Secondly, we consider authenticating the i-th message only, and to this end consider the $(i-1)$-st message where the fresh verification key is transmitted (we do not authenticate this message here) and the i-th message that is then signed under the corresponding signing key. Authenticating the $(i-1)$-st message, and all others, is then taken care of by iteratively applying the protocol, with the overall security directly implied by the composition theorem. This leads to the following real world resources

$$\mathsf{R}_i^{\mathsf{auth}} := \left[\mathsf{Ch}^{i-1,\mathsf{A}\to\mathsf{B}}, \mathsf{Ch}^{i,\mathsf{A}\to\mathsf{B}}, \mathsf{Rand}^{kg_i,\mathsf{A}}, \mathsf{Mem}^{sk_i,\mathsf{A}}, \mathsf{IMem}^{vk_i,\mathsf{B}} \right], \tag{1}$$

where besides the two channels the sender also has a memory to store the new signing key, and the receiver a (insecure) memory to store the verification key. Furthermore, the sender also has an explicit randomness resource available (note that we only need key-generation randomness, since unique signatures are deterministic). The corresponding protocol converters $(\mathsf{sig}_i, \mathsf{vrf}_i)$ that are connected to Alice's and Bob's interfaces of $\mathsf{R}_i^{\mathsf{auth}}$, respectively, simply implement the previously described protocol. A formal description of those protocol converters can be found in the full version [11].

The goal of the protocol is then phrased as constructing the following ideal-world resource

$$\mathsf{S}_i^{\mathsf{auth}} := \left[\mathsf{Ch}^{i-1,\mathsf{A}\to\mathsf{B}}, \mathsf{Ch}^{i,\mathsf{A}\to\mathsf{B}} \right], \tag{2}$$

in which the channels can also trigger an error sig-err, indicating that the signature verification failed, in addition to the errors from the real-world counterparts.

The authentication guarantees for the i-th channel can then be expressed via the following delivery-function, which guarantees that an injection attempt ($\neg same$) when the key is not known will causes a signature-verification error sig-err, and preserves preexisting authenticity (recall that $\tilde{\mathcal{E}} := \tau(\mathcal{E})$ denotes the real-world's event history):

$$\mathfrak{D}_{\mathsf{Ch}(i,\mathsf{A}\to\mathsf{B})}^{\mathsf{S}_i^{\mathsf{auth}}}(\mathcal{E}, same) := \begin{cases} err & \text{if } \mathfrak{D}_{\mathsf{Ch}(i,\mathsf{A}\to\mathsf{B})}^{\mathsf{R}_i^{\mathsf{auth}}}(\tilde{\mathcal{E}}, same) = err \wedge err \neq \mathbf{msg} \\ \mathbf{msg} & \text{else if } same \vee \mathcal{E}_i^{\mathsf{sk\text{-}known}} \\ \mathsf{sig\text{-}err} & \text{else} \end{cases} \tag{3}$$

where in a slight abuse of notation, we define a composed event $\mathcal{E}_i^{\mathsf{sk\text{-}known}}$, which is triggered as soon as it is not excluded that the signing key corresponding to Bob's verification key is known to Eve:

$$\mathcal{E}_i^{\mathsf{sk\text{-}known}} := \mathcal{E}_{\mathsf{Ch}(i-1,\mathsf{A}\to\mathsf{B})}^{\mathsf{injected}} \vee \mathcal{E}_{\mathsf{Rnd}(kg_i,\mathsf{A})}^{\mathsf{leaked}} \vee \left(\mathcal{E}_{\mathsf{Ch}(i-1,\mathsf{A}\to\mathsf{B})}^{\mathsf{sent}} \prec \mathcal{E}_{\mathsf{Mem}(sk_i,\mathsf{A})}^{\mathsf{leaked}} \prec \mathcal{E}_{\mathsf{Ch}(i,\mathsf{A}\to\mathsf{B})}^{\mathsf{sent}} \right).$$

On the flip side, the scheme limits the availability of the channels to be sequential. While sending messages in order is natural for Alice, the protocol restricts Bob to receive them in order as well. We can express this using the following predicates.

$$\mathfrak{S}^{\mathsf{S}_i^{\mathsf{auth}}}_{\mathsf{Ch}(i,\mathsf{A}\to\mathsf{B})}(\mathcal{E}) := \mathfrak{S}^{\mathsf{R}_i^{\mathsf{auth}}}_{\mathsf{Ch}(i,\mathsf{A}\to\mathsf{B})}(\tilde{\mathcal{E}}) \wedge \mathcal{E}^{\mathsf{sent}}_{\mathsf{Ch}(i-1,\mathsf{A}\to\mathsf{B})}, \tag{4}$$

$$\mathfrak{R}^{\mathsf{S}_i^{\mathsf{auth}}}_{\mathsf{Ch}(i,\mathsf{A}\to\mathsf{B})}(\mathcal{E}) := \mathfrak{R}^{\mathsf{R}_i^{\mathsf{auth}}}_{\mathsf{Ch}(i,\mathsf{A}\to\mathsf{B})}(\tilde{\mathcal{E}}) \wedge \mathcal{E}^{\mathsf{received}}_{\mathsf{Ch}(i-1,\mathsf{A}\to\mathsf{B})}. \tag{5}$$

Note that our model simply forces us to make this restriction explicit, whereas this is often just hard-coded in games.[5]

All other parameters and predicates are preserved, e.g. $\mathfrak{L}^{\mathsf{S}_i^{\mathsf{auth}}}_{\mathsf{Ch}(i,\mathsf{A}\to\mathsf{B})}(\mathcal{E}) := \mathfrak{L}^{\mathsf{R}_i^{\mathsf{auth}}}_{\mathsf{Ch}(i,\mathsf{A}\to\mathsf{B})}(\tilde{\mathcal{E}})$. The security of the protocol can then be phrased as constructing the ideal world $\mathsf{S}_i^{\mathsf{auth}}$ from the real world $\mathsf{R}_i^{\mathsf{auth}}$, as summarized in the following theorem.

Theorem 1. *Let $\mathsf{R}_i^{\mathsf{auth}}$ be as in (1), and let $\mathsf{S}_i^{\mathsf{auth}}$ be as in (2), with the guarantees and restrictions as described in (3), (4), and (5), respectively, and all others guarantees unchanged from $\mathsf{R}_i^{\mathsf{auth}}$. Moreover, let τ map the event $\mathcal{E}^{\mathsf{error}(\mathsf{sig\text{-}err},same)}_{\mathsf{Ch}(i,\mathsf{A}\to\mathsf{B})}$ to $\mathcal{E}^{\mathsf{received}(same)}_{\mathsf{Ch}(i,\mathsf{A}\to\mathsf{B})}$. Then there exists an efficient simulator sim such that*

$$\mathsf{sig}_i^{\mathsf{A}} \, \mathsf{vrf}_i^{\mathsf{B}} \, \mathsf{R}_i^{\mathsf{auth}} \; \hat{\approx}_{\tau} \; \mathsf{sim}^{\mathsf{E}} \, \mathsf{S}_i^{\mathsf{auth}},$$

if the underlying signature scheme is unforgeable with unique signatures, and the hash function is collision resistant.

Proof. The proof is found in the full version [11]. Note that compared to a normal signature-scheme proof it is quite involved, which is the main price we pay for our much stronger statement.

Extending to Many Messages. So far, we only considered a world where Alice sends two messages, of which the second is authenticated. In a realistic setting, Alice can of course send many messages where all of them should be authenticated. In this section, we see how the composition theorem of Constructive Cryptography can be applied to directly get the desired result.

In particular, we start with a sequence of possibly unauthenticated channels $\mathsf{Ch}^{i,\mathsf{A}\to\mathsf{B}}$ for $i \in [n]$, where the authentication of $\mathsf{Ch}^{0,\mathsf{A}\to\mathsf{B}}$ can be seen as a setup assumption (it is standard to assume that Alice and Bob initially share a signing-verification key pair). Then, we iteratively apply the construction for two channels to $\mathsf{Ch}^{0,\mathsf{A}\to\mathsf{B}}$ and $\mathsf{Ch}^{1,\mathsf{A}\to\mathsf{B}}$, then to $\mathsf{Ch}^{1,\mathsf{A}\to\mathsf{B}}$ and $\mathsf{Ch}^{2,\mathsf{A}\to\mathsf{B}}$, etc. (c.f. Fig. 5). The composition theorem of CC guarantees that the composed protocol constructs the ideal world.

Corollary 1. *Let $\mathsf{R}^{\mathsf{auth}}$ and $\mathsf{S}^{\mathsf{auth}}$ denote the following real and ideal worlds*

$$\mathsf{R}^{\mathsf{auth}} := \Big[\big\{ \mathsf{Ch}^{i,\mathsf{A}\to\mathsf{B}} \big\}_{i\in\{0,\dots,n\}}, \big\{ \mathsf{Mem}^{sk_i,\mathsf{A}}, \mathsf{IMem}^{vk_i,\mathsf{B}} \big\}_{i\in[n]} \Big],$$

---

[5] Actually, many recently proposed secure-messaging protocols do have this restriction, which might limit their usability as pointed out by [1].

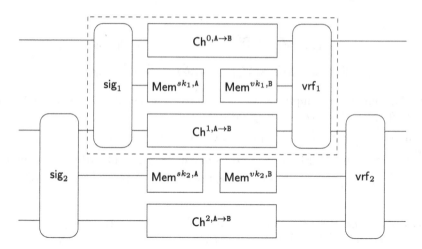

Fig. 5. The first two steps constructing a sequence of authenticated channels: (1) The protocol $(\text{sig}_1, \text{vrf}_1)$ constructs a hybrid world, where the resources in the dashed box are replaced by two channels $\text{Ch}^{0,A \to B}$ and $\text{Ch}^{1,A \to B}$, where $\text{Ch}^{1,A \to B}$ is authenticated as long as $\text{Ch}^{0,A \to B}$ is. (2) $(\text{sig}_2, \text{vrf}_2)$ constructs the ideal world, where $\text{Ch}^{1,A \to B}$ and $\text{Ch}^{2,A \to B}$ are authenticated as long as $\text{Ch}^{0,A \to B}$ is.

and

$$S^{\text{auth}} := \left[\left\{ \text{Ch}^{i,A \to B} \right\}_{i \in \{0,\dots,n\}} \right],$$

respectively. Then, there exists an efficient simulator sim *such that*

$$(\text{sig}_1, \dots, \text{sig}_n)^A \, (\text{vrf}_1, \dots, \text{vrf}_n)^B \, R^{\text{auth}} \approx \text{sim}^E S^{\text{auth}},$$

where for each $i \in [n]$, $\mathfrak{I}^{S^{\text{auth}}}_{\text{Ch}(i,A \to B)}$, $\mathfrak{S}^{S^{\text{auth}}}_{\text{Ch}(i,A \to B)}$, *and* $\mathfrak{R}^{S^{\text{auth}}}_{\text{Ch}(i,A \to B)}$ *are defined as in* (3), (4), *and* (5), *respectively.*

5.2   Confidentiality from HIBE

In the following we discuss a protocol from [9] that uses *hierarchical identity-based encryption (HIBE)* to add confidentiality to a sequence of channels. The protocol was designed for a challenging setting, where we do not assume authentication (as is usually done when talking about encryption). The reason is that in secure messaging authentication cannot be guaranteed when the sender's state is exposed. This situation fits perfectly to our framework.

The protocol is described in the so-called sesqui-directional setting, introduced in [24], meaning that the messages from both directions are considered, but only the guarantees of one of the directions are under concern—here from Alice to Bob. The bidirectional guarantees then follow directly from composition.

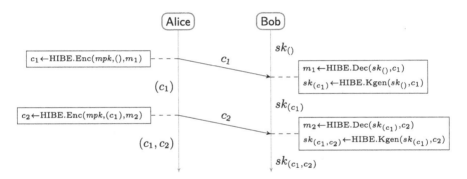

Fig. 6. The first epoch of the sesquidirectional HIBE protocol.

Hierarchical Identity-Based Encryption. A HIBE scheme consists of the following four algorithms:

- A setup generation algorithm $(mpk, msk) \leftarrow$ HIBE.Setup$(1^\kappa; r)$, generating the root master public and secret keys, i.e. $sk_{()} = msk$.
- A key-generation algorithm $sk_{\mathbf{id}\|id_n} \leftarrow$ HIBE.Kgen$(sk_{\mathbf{id}}, id_n)$, where $(\mathbf{id} \| id_n) := (id_1, \ldots, id_{n-1}, id_n)$ for an identity vector $\mathbf{id} = (id_1, \ldots, id_{n-1})$.
- An encryption algorithm $c \leftarrow$ HIBE.Enc$(mpk, \mathbf{id}, m; r)$.
- A decryption algorithm $m \leftarrow$ HIBE.Dec$(sk_{\mathbf{id}}, c)$.

We require the HIBE scheme to be IND-CCA secure with certain additional properties that are not guaranteed by IND-CCA itself, but that most schemes do provide (see the full version [11] for details).

The Protocol Overview. On a high level, the protocol proceeds in epochs, where in each epoch Bob sends one message to Alice, and then Alice sends a sequence of messages to Bob. In particular, Bob's message contains a fresh HIBE public key mpk. For simplicity, consider the first epoch, as depicted in Fig. 6. When Alice sends her i-th message, she encrypts it with mpk, using as the identity (the hashes of) all ciphertexts she sent before. Whenever Bob receives a ciphertext c_i, he decrypts it, derives the secret key for the new identity (with c_i appended) and erases the old key.

In the next epoch, Bob sends a new public key mpk', and we repeat. One subtle issue is how to run the epochs together. Note that, for example, Bob may send a number of public keys without receiving a response, in which case he has to store secret keys from a number of epochs. A fresh secret key is stored for the empty identity, and when Bob receives a ciphertext, he updates all currently stored secret keys. This means that Alice uses for encryption of the i-th message a truncated transcript $(c_r, \ldots, c_{i-1})$. In order for her to compute it, Bob sends with each public key the index r of the last message he received.

Security Intuition. Intuitively, this use of HIBE allows to achieve three goals. The first is healing, achieved by exchanging fresh keys, as in most secure-messaging schemes. The second is forward secrecy: exposing the secret key after the i-th message is received does not affect the confidentiality of messages $m_1, \ldots, m_{i-1}$. This holds, since Bob updated all the secret keys with the identity c_i in the meantime. Healing and forward secrecy could also be achieved by a forward-secure PKE scheme. The last goal is the so-called post-impersonation security: an active injection destroys the decryption keys, so that its leakage exposes no messages. For this we need the hierarchy of identities. Roughly, injecting a message c_i' causes Bob to update his key to $sk_{(c_r, \ldots, c_i')}$. This key gives no information about messages encrypted by Alice, since those will be for another identity $(c_r, \ldots, c_i)$.

The Construction Statement. To formalize these guarantees as a construction statement, we first have to describe the real world in which the protocol is executed. It consists of n channels from Alice to Bob (which the protocol protects) and n channels in the opposite direction on which the master public keys are transmitted. Moreover, Alice has memories to store the public keys and the transcript, and randomness resources for the encryption. Bob, on the other hand, has memories to store the secret keys and randomness resources for the key generation:

$$R^{\mathsf{hibe}} := \Big[\big\{ \mathsf{Ch}^{i,\mathsf{A} \to \mathsf{B}} \big\}_{i \in [n]}, \big\{ \mathsf{Ch}^{j,\mathsf{B} \to \mathsf{A}} \big\}_{j \in [n]}, \mathsf{IMem}^{pk,\mathsf{A}}, \big\{ \mathsf{Rand}^{kg_j,\mathsf{B}} \big\}_{j \in [n]},$$
$$\big\{ \mathsf{Mem}^{tr_i,\mathsf{A}}, \mathsf{Rand}^{enc_i,\mathsf{A}} \big\}_{i \in [n]}, \big\{ \mathsf{Mem}^{sk(j,i),\mathsf{B}} \big\}_{j \in [n], i \in [n+1]} \Big], \quad (6)$$

where the index i indicates that the resource is related to transmitting the i-th message from Alice to Bob, and the index j indicates the j-th epoch. A formal description of the pair of converters implementing the protocol (hibe-enc, hibe-dec) can be found in the full version [11].

The goal of the protocol is to enhance the confidentiality of the channels. Thus, the same set of channels is present in the ideal world, while the memory and randomness resources are used up:

$$S^{\mathsf{hibe}} := \Big[\big\{ \mathsf{Ch}^{i,\mathsf{A} \to \mathsf{B}} \big\}_{i \in [n]}, \big\{ \mathsf{Ch}^{j,\mathsf{B} \to \mathsf{A}} \big\}_{j \in [n]} \Big]. \quad (7)$$

Moreover, the ideal channels can trigger an additional error dec-err, indicating that decryption failed (this error event corresponds to the real-world delivery event when the adversary injects an invalid ciphertext).

We now proceed to formalize the confidentiality guarantees of S^{hibe} by defining in which situations the i-th message might be known to the adversary:

The randomness leaked: If the encryption randomness leaked to the adversary, i.e., $\mathcal{E}^{\mathsf{leaked}}_{\mathsf{Rnd}(enc_i,\mathsf{A})}$, then no PKE scheme can provide (full) confidentiality.

The master public key was set by Eve:] If Alice encrypts using a master public key (potentially) set by Eve, Eve can trivially decrypt. That is, if Alice used the j-th master public key and $\mathcal{E}_{\mathsf{Ch}(j,\mathsf{B}\to\mathsf{A})}^{\mathsf{injected}}$.

The secret key leaked: Assume Alice sent the i-th message during the j-th epoch, and let $sk_{(j,i)}$ denote the secret key that Bob uses to decrypt that message. If Eve learned $sk_{(j,i)}$, the message is obviously not confidential, which either happens if the randomness used to generate the master secret key leaked or a key that allows to compute $sk_{(j,i)}$ leaked from Bob's memory:

$$
\mathcal{E}_{i,j}^{\mathsf{sk\text{-}leaked}} := \mathcal{E}_{\mathsf{Rnd}(kg_j,\mathsf{B})}^{\mathsf{leaked}}
$$

$$
\vee\, \exists k \in [r_j, i] : \left(\mathcal{E}_{\mathsf{Mem}(sk_{(j,k)},\mathsf{B})}^{\mathsf{leaked}} \wedge \forall \ell \in [r_j, k] : \neg\mathcal{E}_{\mathsf{Ch}(\ell,\mathsf{A}\to\mathsf{B})}^{\mathsf{injected}} \right),
$$

where r_j denotes the first message Bob received after sending the j-th public key (r_j is determined by the sent and received events in $\mathcal{E}$). Note that the last condition explicitly encodes the *post-impersonation guarantee*, meaning that $sk_{(j,k)}$ is only useful as long as Eve did not destroy it by injecting her own ciphertext. Forward-secrecy and healing, on the other hand, are encoded implicitly by the order in which those events can happen in the real world. We can make them more explicit by observing

$$
\mathcal{E}_{i,j}^{\mathsf{sk\text{-}leaked}} \iff \mathcal{E}_{\mathsf{Ch}(j,\mathsf{B}\to\mathsf{A})}^{\mathsf{sent}} \prec \mathcal{E}_{i,j}^{\mathsf{sk\text{-}leaked}} \prec \mathcal{E}_{\mathsf{Ch}(i,\mathsf{A}\to\mathsf{B})}^{\mathsf{received}},
$$

where the former condition denotes healing and the latter forward-secrecy.

In summary, we can define the following event denoting that the i-th message is insecure

$$
\mathcal{E}_i^{\mathsf{exposed}} := \mathcal{E}_{\mathsf{Rnd}(enc_i,\mathsf{A})}^{\mathsf{leaked}} \vee \mathcal{E}_{\mathsf{Ch}(j_i,\mathsf{B}\to\mathsf{A})}^{\mathsf{injected}} \vee \mathcal{E}_{i,j_i}^{\mathsf{sk\text{-}leaked}},
$$

where j_i denotes the epoch in which the i-th message has been sent (which is computable from the order of events in $\mathcal{E}$), leading to

$$
\mathcal{L}_{\mathsf{Ch}(i,\mathsf{A}\to\mathsf{B})}^{\mathsf{S}^{\mathsf{hibe}}}(\mathcal{E}) := \begin{cases} \texttt{silent} & \text{if } \mathcal{E}_i^{\mathsf{exposed}} \\ \texttt{false} & \text{otherwise.} \end{cases} \tag{8}
$$

Notice that the above can-leak function fully overwrites any real-world guarantees, and silences the leaked events. This is because in the protocol Alice stores the communication transcript. As a consequence, when her memory leaks, the ciphertext leaks as well, even if the assumed channel was in fact confidential. Moreover, this leakage does not correspond to the channel leaked event.

Analogous to the authentication scheme of the previous section, the HIBE scheme also limits the availability of the channels to be sequential, due to the hash-transcript used as identities. Moreover, Alice can obviously only encrypt using master public keys she received the public key. This could be made formal using the can-send and can-receive predicates $\mathfrak{S}$ and $\mathfrak{R}$, respectively.

Working Around the Commitment Problem. As described so far, the real and ideal world hibe-enc^{A}hibe-dec^{B}R^{hibe} and sim^{E}S^{hibe}, respectively, are easily distinguishable for any simulator sim. The issue is the so-called *commitment problem* of simulation based cryptography: if the distinguisher chooses to first see a ciphertext and then leak the corresponding decryption key, this cannot be simulated, since the simulator first has to output a fake ciphertext, before getting to know the message, and then explain it by outputting a corresponding decryption key. For normal PKE, and especially HIBE, schemes this is impossible.

One solution would be to consider static memory corruptions, where the set of states that can be leaked to the adversary is a parameter of the construction statement. Such a static guarantee is however weaker than the existing game-based definitions and, thus, thwarts our goal of developing a unified model to express the guarantees obtained by existing protocols. We thus opt for the alternative solution to strengthen the real world analogous to how the games disable certain oracles to prevent trivial impossibilities. To this end, we disallow the adversary from obtaining the secret key $sk_{(j,i)}$ if this would allow to trivially identify a fake ciphertext. That is, we assume

$$\mathfrak{L}^{R^{hibe}}_{\mathsf{Mem}(sk_{(j,i)},B)}(\mathcal{E}) := \neg \exists k > i : \left(\mathcal{E}^{committed}_{k,j} \prec \mathcal{E}^{exposed}_k \right), \qquad (9)$$

where $\mathcal{E}^{committed}_{i,j}$ denotes the event that the simulator commits on the i-th ciphertext, and that it was encrypted under mpk_j. More concretely, this happens if the distinguisher

- explicitly asked for the ciphertext;
- requested a hash-transcript that depends on the ciphertext;
- requested a secret key for which the identity depends on the ciphertext;
- actively injected a ciphertext that got decrypted under a secret key whose identity depends on the ciphertext under consideration,

leading to the following definition

$$\mathcal{E}^{committed}_{i,j} := (j_i = j) \wedge \left(\mathcal{E}^{leaked}_{\mathsf{Ch}(i,A \to B)} \vee \mathcal{E}^{leaked}_{\mathsf{Mem}(tr_i,A)} \vee \left(\neg \mathcal{E}^{injected}_{\mathsf{Ch}(i,A \to B)} \right.\right.$$
$$\left.\left. \wedge \exists k \geq i : \left(\mathcal{E}^{leaked}_{\mathsf{Mem}(sk_{(j,k)})} \vee \mathcal{E}^{injected}_{\mathsf{Ch}(k,A \to B)} \right) \right) \right),$$

where again j_i denotes the epoch in which the i-th message has been sent.

While the construction statement loses its evident executional semantics making those restrictions of the real world—it is no longer apparent what guarantees one gets when executing the protocol in the actual world where the memory leakage is obviously not restricted like this—it is analogous to game-based notions where the adversary has to choose beforehand whether a message is a challenge (and then prevents leaking the corresponding randomness or secret keys), or is an insecure message just to advance the state. Phrasing it in a composable framework, however, still has the advantage of modularity and reusability, that is, each subprotocol can be proven secure independently and the overall security directly following from the composition theorem.

Summary and Analysis. The HIBE-based scheme achieves the so far described construction, with one exception: to provide more power to the simulator and make the construction statement provable, we need to silence the real-world channels' leaked events after the message is exposed, i.e, $\mathcal{L}^{\mathsf{R}^{\mathsf{hibe}}}_{\mathsf{Ch}(i,\mathsf{A}\rightarrow\mathsf{B})}$ is arbitrary, except that if $\mathcal{E}^{\mathsf{exposed}}_i$, it no longer evaluates to true.[6]

Observe that while having to silence the leakage event in the real world limits reusability, the statement for instance is still generic enough to be composed with the authentication scheme from the previous section: if the real world is restricted like this (in the end, those events are just a mean to phrase dependencies and carry no real semantics), then the signature scheme, which preserves the can-leak predicate, and afterwards the HIBE scheme can be applied.

Overall, we have the following theorem, proven in the full version [11].

Theorem 2. *Let* $\mathsf{R}^{\mathsf{hibe}}$ *be as in* (6) *with the restrictions to work around the commitment-problem from* (9) *and the restriction described above, and let* $\mathsf{S}^{\mathsf{hibe}}$ *be as in* (7) *with the confidentiality guarantees from* (8)*, and in-order sending and receiving. Let* τ *map the event* $\mathcal{E}^{\mathsf{error}(\mathsf{dec}\text{-}\mathsf{err},\,same)}_{\mathsf{Ch}(i,\mathsf{A}\rightarrow\mathsf{B})}$ *to* $\mathcal{E}^{\mathsf{received}(same)}_{\mathsf{Ch}(i,\mathsf{A}\rightarrow\mathsf{B})}$*. Then there exists an efficient simulator* sim*, such that*

$$\mathsf{hibe\text{-}enc}^{\mathsf{A}}\,\mathsf{hibe\text{-}dec}^{\mathsf{B}}\,\mathsf{R}^{\mathsf{hibe}}\,\,\hat{\approx}_{\tau}\,\,\mathsf{sim}^{\mathsf{E}}\,\mathsf{S}^{\mathsf{hibe}},$$

if the HIBE scheme is IND-CCA secure with our additional assumptions.

6   Adaptive Security

All protocols considered so far, and most of the ones in the literature, only achieve a weakened construction statement, where, due to the commitment problem, we assume that certain sequences of events cannot occur in the real world. Intuitively, this means that the adversary is somewhat static: for example, when she decides to see the contents of a channel (the ciphertext, in the real world), at the same time she decides that she will not look at the contents of certain memory (the secret key). While this is exactly what the standard game-based definitions guarantee, when expressed in a composable framework, it seems rather unsatisfactory.

Hence, in this section, we consider SM schemes that tolerate a fully adaptive adversary, i.e, allow to "explain" ciphertexts whenever needed due to leakage of secret keys. In particular, we present a technique that, given an SM protocol that suffers from the commitment problem, allows to construct an adaptive SM (ASM) protocol with almost the same guarantees, but that achieves fully adaptive security. This comes at the cost of efficiency and being able to send only a fixed number of messages without interaction. Applied to protocols with optimal security [9,24], our technique enables even stronger guarantees.[7] As an example, we apply it to the HIBE protocol from Sect. 5.2.

---

[6] This doesn't affect $\mathcal{E}^{\mathsf{committed}}_{i,j}$, that only considers leakage events before $\mathcal{E}^{\mathsf{exposed}}_i$.

[7] In game-based definitions, one can think of the "corrupt" oracle not being silenced even if the challenge has been issued, but instead outputting the secret state corresponding to the challenge bit 0.

Note that while the technique we use is essentially a general compiler that "removes" the commitment problem, formally phrasing such a theorem would be rather cumbersome for at least two reasons. First, there is not just one game-based definition of an SM scheme that could be lifted and, second, we require the specific simulation technique encoded in most game-based definitions, in contrast to the existential simulator of our constructive SM statements.

6.1   Overview

Receiver Non-committing Encryption. The technical tool we use to construct adaptively-secure secure-messaging (ASM) schemes with optimal security is so-called receiver non-committing encryption (RNCE), introduced by Canetti et al. [5]. Intuitively, in RNCE schemes, key generation outputs an additional trapdoor z, ignored by honest parties and used by the simulator. Then, there are two ways to generate a ciphertext: (1) an "honest" ciphertext is computed in the standard way $c \leftarrow \mathsf{RNCE.E}(pk, m)$ (so, as in any encryption scheme, it is a commitment to the message), (2) a "fake" ciphertext is computed (by the simulator) without the message, but with the secret key sk and the trapdoor z as $\tilde{c} \leftarrow \mathsf{RNCE.F}(pk, sk, z)$. Given a fake ciphertext $\tilde{c}$ and any message m, one can compute a secret key $\tilde{sk} \leftarrow \mathsf{RNCE.R}(pk, sk, z, \tilde{c}, m)$ that explains the message-ciphertext pair (such that $\mathsf{RNCE.D}(\tilde{sk}, \tilde{c}) = m$). Moreover, the distributions (c, sk) (as in the real world) and $(\tilde{c}, \tilde{sk})$ (as in the simulation) are indistinguishable. This allows to explain a single ciphertext per public key.

The Scheme. At a high level, the authors of [5] use RNCE to construct non-committing forward-secure public-key encryption by encrypting with a standard forward-secure public-key scheme RNCE ciphertexts instead of messages. We generalize this idea (and the simulation technique) to SM protocols. In particular, we can construct an ASM scheme by taking a standard SM scheme that suffers from the commitment problem and sending, instead of messages, their RNCE encryptions, where each message is encrypted with a different public key. When a message is received, the secret key is immediately deleted. (For the moment, assume that whenever Alice sends a message, an RNCE key pair is "magically" generated—Alice uses the public key, and the secret key immediately appears stored in Bob's state.) This way, the modified scheme inherits all guarantees of the original SM scheme. Furthermore, it can be simulated in the adaptive setting, as we will see below.

Let us now address the problem of how the RNCE keys are distributed. One trivial solution would be to include ℓ key pairs as part of the setup: the parties send their ℓ public keys at the beginning over an authenticated channel. First, this way we can send only ℓ messages overall. But even worse, the RNCE keys do not heal: when the receiver is corrupted for the first time, the simulator can explain all messages sent so far, but it also has to commit to all RNCE secret keys. Hence, adaptive security is never restored. To deal with this, we use the technique used in all SM schemes: we send with each message an update, consisting of ℓ fresh RNCE public keys. In particular, Alice (Bob will proceed analogously) stores some public keys previously received from Bob. When she sends the i-th message, she RNCE-encrypts it with one of the unused public keys, generates ℓ new key pairs, stores the secret keys, and sends the RNCE ciphertext, the ℓ public keys and i to Bob over the channel constructed by an SM scheme. Bob stores the greatest index i he has seen so far. Whenever he sees a message with a greater i, he ignores all RNCE public keys he has and replaces them by the ℓ newly received ones. Unlike in the first trivial solution, in the above protocol adaptive security is restored as fast as possible: with the first new message delivered from the other party.

Simulation. We give an intuition of how the above protocol can be simulated. Assume that the SM scheme has the standard simulator, as hard-coded in most game-based definitions. In particular, he executes the protocol, and when a memory is exposed, he shows to the distinguisher the real state. For ciphertexts corresponding to confidential messages it shows encryptions of 0's, while for non-confidential ones it shows encryptions of the actual message.

In the adaptive setting, the real and the ideal world are easily distinguishable for that simulator. This is because when a message is sent as confidential, and later the memory is exposed, the distinguisher sees in the ideal world the encryption of 0's. However, we can fix this with our new scheme: the new simulator encrypts, instead of 0's, a fake RNCE ciphertext to generate a ciphertext corresponding to a confidential message. When a memory is corrupted, he receives the message (which, of course, can no longer be confidential) and computes the fake RNCE secret key according to the fake ciphertext. RNCE guarantees that this is indistinguishable from the real world, where we have honest ciphertext and an honest key.

A Note on Efficiency. First, observe that using a symmetric non-committing encryption scheme, such as the one-time pad, instead of RNCE would not work. This is because in many SM schemes corrupting the sender has no effect on confidentiality, implying that upon such a corruption, the simulator needs to output a key of the symmetric non-committing scheme without knowing the messages (which trivially breaks against a distinguisher knowing the message).

Moreover, while our construction of using nested encryption appears to be redundant, it can be observed that using RNCE only would not suffice. This is because SM schemes can provide certain advanced *confidentiality* guarantees not achieved by RNCE alone. For example, the optimal schemes such as [9,24] provide so-called post-impersonation guarantees: once the adversary injects a message to Bob (after corrupting Alice) and then corrupts Bob, all messages sent by Alice afterwards are confidential.

Limitations. Our protocol requires a fixed upper bound on the number of messages a party can send without interaction (in particular, after ℓ messages it needs a new set of public keys from the partner). Unfortunately, overcoming this seems unlikely with our approach. This is due to the impossibility result by Nielsen [20]. It essentially says that a non-committing non-interactive public-key encryption scheme requires that the length of a secret key is at least the overall length of all messages encrypted. This means that we would need non-committing encryption, where the public and secret keys are updated, in other words, a non-committing equivalent of HIBE. To the best of our knowledge, this does not exist yet.[8]

6.2 The Construction: Combining RNCE with HIBE

Recall that the HIBE protocol from Sect. 5.2 is designed for the sesqui-directional setting, where it protects the confidentiality of messages sent by Alice. In the protocol, Bob sends to Alice HIBE master public keys, which results in epochs. In epoch j, Alice uses the j-th master public key to encrypt her messages with the transcript as identity. In this section we consider the analogous setting for the ASM protocol, consisting of RNCE composed with HIBE. That is, Bob sends ℓ RNCE keys alongside the HIBE keys, and Alice uses them to additionally encrypt her messages.

Hence, for the ASM construction we need in the real world the additional randomness $\mathsf{Rand}^{renc_i,\mathsf{A}}$ for RNCE-encrypting the i-th message and $\mathsf{Rand}^{rkg_j,\mathsf{B}}$ for generating the j-th set of ℓ keys, compared to the real world from the HIBE protocol. Moreover, we have memories $\mathsf{Mem}^{rsk_{(j,k)},\mathsf{B}}$ for storing the k-th RNCE secret key, generated in epoch j, and insecure (rewritable) memories $\mathsf{IMem}^{rpk,\mathsf{A}}$ for storing the set of RNCE public keys. Overall, the real-world resources are as follows.

$$\mathsf{R}^{\mathsf{ad\text{-}hibe}} := \Big[\mathsf{R}^{\mathsf{hibe}}, \big\{\mathsf{Rand}^{renc_i,\mathsf{A}}\big\}_{i\in[n]}, \big\{\mathsf{Rand}^{rkg_j,\mathsf{B}}\big\}_{j\in[n]}, \mathsf{IMem}^{rpk,\mathsf{A}},$$
$$\big\{\mathsf{Mem}^{rsk_{(j,k)},\mathsf{B}}\big\}_{j\in[n],k\in[\ell]}\Big], \quad (10)$$

where $\mathsf{R}^{\mathsf{hibe}}$ should be understood as the same set of resources as in Sect. 5.2. The restrictions on those set of resources are dropped, on the other hand, since we no longer need work around the commitment problem. This implies, however, that we have to directly consider security of the overall compiled protocol, instead of using the construction statement for HIBE and composition.[9] A formal description of the converters rnce-enc and rnce-dec implementing the RNCE protocol on top of the HIBE protocol is given in Fig. 7.

In the ideal world, we have the same $2n$ channels: $\mathsf{S}^{\mathsf{ad\text{-}hibe}} := \mathsf{S}^{\mathsf{hibe}}$. Most properties of the constructed channels are the same as in the HIBE construction. In fact, our adaptive protocol only affects (1) availability—only ℓ messages can

---

[8] Note that the impossibility of [20] also rules out a solution where Alice RNCE-encrypts for Bob a new RNCE secret key, used for the next message—this secret key would leave no space for the message.

[9] In general, the simulator for the SM scheme simply does not output the secret state from the commitment-causing memories, and our ASM simulator cannot generate it himself, since this would be inconsistent with the rest of the SM simulation.

Converter rnce-enc

Emulating Interface A of $\mathsf{Ch}^{i,\mathtt{A}\to\mathtt{B}}, i \in [n]$

Input: $(\mathtt{send}, m, ad) \in \mathcal{M} \times \mathcal{AD}$
  assume only called once & isAvailable

  // Read and update the state
  call $(j, k, PK) \leftarrow$ **read** at int. A of $\mathsf{IMem}^{rpk,\mathtt{A}}$
  call $(\mathtt{write}, (j, k+1, PK))$
    at interface A of $\mathsf{IMem}^{rpk,\mathtt{A}}$

  // Encrypt end send
  call $r \leftarrow$ sample at int. A of $\mathsf{Rand}^{renc_i,\mathtt{A}}$
  $c \leftarrow \mathsf{RNCE.E}(PK[k], m; r)$
  call $s \leftarrow (\mathtt{send}, c, (ad, j, k))$
    at interface A of $\mathsf{Ch}^{i,\mathtt{A}\to\mathtt{B}}$
  return s

Input: isAvailable
  call $av \leftarrow$ isAvailable at int. A of $\mathsf{Ch}^{i,\mathtt{A}\to\mathtt{B}}$
  call $(j, k, PK) \leftarrow$ **read** at int. A of $\mathsf{IMem}^{rpk,\mathtt{A}}$
  return $av \wedge (j, k, PK) \neq \perp \wedge k \leq \ell$

Emulating Interface A of $\mathsf{Ch}^{j,\mathtt{B}\to\mathtt{A}}, j \in [n]$

Input: read
  assume only called once
  call $(m, (ad, PK)) \leftarrow (\mathtt{read})$
    at interface A of $\mathsf{Ch}^{j,\mathtt{B}\to\mathtt{A}}$
  call $(j', \_, \_) \leftarrow$ **read** at int. A of $\mathsf{IMem}^{rpk,\mathtt{A}}$

  // Update the state if the keys are newer
  than the stored ones.
  if $j = 1 \vee j' < j$ **then**
    call $(\mathtt{write}, (j, 1, PK))$
      at interface A of $\mathsf{IMem}^{rpk,\mathtt{A}}$
  return (m, ad)

Input: isAvailable
  call $av \leftarrow$ isAvailable at int. A of $\mathsf{Ch}^{j,\mathtt{B}\to\mathtt{A}}$
  return av

Converter rnce-dec

Emulating Interface B of $\mathsf{Ch}^{j,\mathtt{B}\to\mathtt{A}}, j \in [n]$

Input: $(\mathtt{send}, m, ad) \in \mathcal{M} \times \mathcal{AD}$
  assume only called once & isAvailable

  // Generate ℓ new key pairs
  call $r_1, \ldots, r_\ell \leftarrow (\mathtt{sample})$
    at interface A of $\mathsf{Rand}^{rkg_j,\mathtt{B}}$
  for $k \in [\ell]$ **do**
    $(pk_k, sk_k) \leftarrow \mathsf{RNCE.G}(r_k)$
    call $(\mathtt{write}, sk_k)$
      at interface B of $\mathsf{Mem}^{rsk(j,k),\mathtt{B}}$
  call $s \leftarrow (\mathtt{write}, m, (ad, [pk_1, \ldots, pk_\ell]))$
    at interface A of $\mathsf{Ch}^{j,\mathtt{B}\to\mathtt{A}}$
  return s

Input: isAvailable
  call $av \leftarrow$ isAvailable at int. B of $\mathsf{Ch}^{j,\mathtt{B}\to\mathtt{A}}$
  return av

Emulating Interface B of $\mathsf{Ch}^{i,\mathtt{A}\to\mathtt{B}}, i \in [n]$

Input: read
  call $(c, (ad, j, k)) \leftarrow (\mathtt{read})$
    at interface A of $\mathsf{Ch}^{i,\mathtt{A}\to\mathtt{B}}$
  if $(c, (ad, j, k)) = \perp$ **then return** $\perp$

  // Get the secret key and decrypt
  call $sk \leftarrow$ **read** at int. B of $\mathsf{Mem}^{rsk(j,k),\mathtt{B}}$
  if $sk \neq \perp$ **then**
    $m \leftarrow \mathsf{RNCE.D}(sk, c)$
    call erase at int. B of $\mathsf{Mem}^{rsk(j,k),\mathtt{B}}$
  if $m \neq \perp$ **then return** (m, ad)
  else return $\perp$

Input: isAvailable
  call $av \leftarrow$ isAvailable at int. B of $\mathsf{Ch}^{i,\mathtt{B}\to\mathtt{A}}$
  return av

Fig. 7. The RNCE part of the adaptively-secure protocol in the sesqui-directional setting.

be sent without interaction, and (2) confidentiality—we need to account for the additional randomness and memory resources. Recall that the epoch j_i in which message i is sent by Alice is determined by the sent and received events. With this, the restriction (1) can be expressed with the can-send and can-receive predicate in a straightforward way.

Let us now focus on confidentiality. Recall that in the HIBE protocol, the can-leak predicate was defined using the event $\mathcal{E}_i^{\text{exposed}}$, denoting that the i-th message sent by Alice is inherently insecure. We modify this event to account for the additional resources used by RNCE. Specifically, the message is exposed if the RNCE-encryption randomness leaks: $\mathcal{E}^{\text{leaked}}_{\text{Rnd}(renc_i,\text{A})}$, or if the RNCE secret key leaks. The latter happens if Bob's key-generation randomness leaks: $\mathcal{E}^{\text{leaked}}_{\text{Rnd}(rkg_{j_i},\text{B})}$, or if the secret key memory leaks: $\mathcal{E}^{\text{leaked}}_{\text{Mem}(rsk_{(j_i,k_i)},\text{B})}$, where the i-th message was the k_i-th one sent in its epoch. Overall, this leads to the following composed event:

$$\mathcal{E}_i^{\text{exposed-ad}} := \mathcal{E}_i^{\text{exposed}} \vee \mathcal{E}^{\text{leaked}}_{\text{Rnd}(renc_i,\text{A})} \vee \mathcal{E}^{\text{leaked}}_{\text{Rnd}(rkg_{j_i},\text{B})} \vee \mathcal{E}^{\text{leaked}}_{\text{Mem}(rsk_{(j_i,k_i)},\text{B})}.$$

The leakage function $\mathfrak{L}^{\text{S}^{\text{ad-hibe}}}_{\text{Ch}(\text{A}\rightarrow\text{B})}$ is then defined analogously to that of the HIBE construction silent in case of $\mathcal{E}_i^{\text{exposed-ad}}$, and false otherwise. We stress that the need to include these additional cases only arises from our fine-grained modeling of memory and randomness. In reality, it makes sense to consider only one memory storing the whole secret state, only one randomness for RNCE and HIBE encryption, and so on. In such a model, the confidentiality of our adaptively secure scheme and the non-adaptive one would coincide.

The security of our composed protocol is summarized in the following theorem. The proof can be found in the full version [11].

Theorem 3. *Let* $\mathsf{R}^{\text{ad-hibe}}$ *be as in* (10), *and let* $\mathsf{S}^{\text{ad-hibe}}$ *be as in above with the described confidentiality guarantees, in-order sending and receiving, and the restriction to ℓ messages per epoch. If the HIBE scheme is IND-CCA secure with our additional assumptions, then there exists an efficient simulator* sim, *such that*

$$\mathsf{rnce\text{-}enc}^{\text{A}}\mathsf{hibe\text{-}enc}^{\text{A}} \ \mathsf{rnce\text{-}dec}^{\text{B}}\mathsf{hibe\text{-}dec}^{\text{B}} \ \mathsf{R}^{\text{ad-hibe}} \ \hat{\approx}_\tau \ \mathsf{sim}^{\text{E}} \ \mathsf{S}^{\text{ad-hibe}},$$

where τ is the same event mapping as in Theorem 2.

References

1. Alwen, J., Coretti, S., Dodis, Y.: The double ratchet: security notions, proofs, and modularization for the signal protocol. In: Ishai, Y., Rijmen, V. (eds.) EUROCRYPT 2019. LNCS, vol. 11476, pp. 129–158. Springer, Cham (2019). https://doi.org/10.1007/978-3-030-17653-2_5
2. Bellare, M., Singh, A.C., Jaeger, J., Nyayapati, M., Stepanovs, I.: Ratcheted encryption and key exchange: the security of messaging. In: Katz, J., Shacham, H. (eds.) CRYPTO 2017. LNCS, vol. 10403, pp. 619–650. Springer, Cham (2017). https://doi.org/10.1007/978-3-319-63697-9_21
3. Broadnax, B., Döttling, N., Hartung, G., Müller-Quade, J., Nagel, M.: Concurrently composable security with shielded super-polynomial simulators. In: Coron, J.-S., Nielsen, J.B. (eds.) EUROCRYPT 2017. LNCS, vol. 10210, pp. 351–381. Springer, Cham (2017). https://doi.org/10.1007/978-3-319-56620-7_13
4. Canetti, R.: Universally composable security: a new paradigm for cryptographic protocols. In: 42nd IEEE Symposium on Foundations of Computer Science - FOCS 2001, pp. 136–145. IEEE Computer Society (2001)

5. Canetti, R., Halevi, S., Katz, J.: Adaptively-secure, non-interactive public-key encryption. In: Kilian, J. (ed.) TCC 2005. LNCS, vol. 3378, pp. 150–168. Springer, Heidelberg (2005). https://doi.org/10.1007/978-3-540-30576-7_9

6. Canetti, R., Krawczyk, H.: Universally composable notions of key exchange and secure channels. In: Knudsen, L.R. (ed.) EUROCRYPT 2002. LNCS, vol. 2332, pp. 337–351. Springer, Heidelberg (2002). https://doi.org/10.1007/3-540-46035-7_22

7. Cohn-Gordon, K., Cremers, C., Dowling, B., Garratt, L., Stebila, D.: A formal security analysis of the signal messaging protocol. In: 2nd IEEE European Symposium on Security and Privacy, EuroS and P 2017, pp. 451–466 (2017)

8. Durak, F.B., Vaudenay, S.: Bidirectional asynchronous ratcheted key agreement with linear complexity. Cryptology ePrint Archive, Report 2018/889 (2018). https://eprint.iacr.org/2018/889

9. Jaeger, J., Stepanovs, I.: Optimal channel security against fine-grained state compromise: the safety of messaging. In: Shacham, H., Boldyreva, A. (eds.) CRYPTO 2018. LNCS, vol. 10991, pp. 33–62. Springer, Cham (2018). https://doi.org/10.1007/978-3-319-96884-1_2

10. Jost, D., Maurer, U., Mularczyk, M.: Efficient ratcheting: almost-optimal guarantees for secure messaging. In: Ishai, Y., Rijmen, V. (eds.) EUROCRYPT 2019. LNCS, vol. 11476, pp. 159–188. Springer, Cham (2019). https://doi.org/10.1007/978-3-030-17653-2_6

11. Jost, D., Maurer, U., Marta, M.: A unified and composable take on ratcheting. Cryptology ePrint Archive, Report 2019/694 (2019). https://eprint.iacr.org/2019/694

12. Kohlweiss, M., Maurer, U., Onete, C., Tackmann, B., Venturi, D.: (De-)constructing TLS 1.3. In: Biryukov, A., Goyal, V. (eds.) INDOCRYPT 2015. LNCS, vol. 9462, pp. 85–102. Springer, Cham (2015). https://doi.org/10.1007/978-3-319-26617-6_5

13. Krawczyk, H.: The order of encryption and authentication for protecting communications (or: How Secure Is SSL?). In: Kilian, J. (ed.) CRYPTO 2001. LNCS, vol. 2139, pp. 310–331. Springer, Heidelberg (2001). https://doi.org/10.1007/3-540-44647-8_19

14. Kuesters, R., Tuengerthal, M., Rausch, D.: The IITM model: a simple and expressive model for universal composability. Cryptology ePrint Archive, Report 2013/025 (2013). https://eprint.iacr.org/2013/025

15. Maurer, U.: Constructive cryptography – a new paradigm for security definitions and proofs. In: Mödersheim, S., Palamidessi, C. (eds.) TOSCA 2011. LNCS, vol. 6993, pp. 33–56. Springer, Heidelberg (2012). https://doi.org/10.1007/978-3-642-27375-9_3

16. Maurer, U.: Indistinguishability of random systems. In: Knudsen, L.R. (ed.) EUROCRYPT 2002. LNCS, vol. 2332, pp. 110–132. Springer, Heidelberg (2002). https://doi.org/10.1007/3-540-46035-7_8

17. Maurer, U., Pietrzak, K., Renner, R.: Indistinguishability amplification. In: Menezes, A. (ed.) CRYPTO 2007. LNCS, vol. 4622, pp. 130–149. Springer, Heidelberg (2007). https://doi.org/10.1007/978-3-540-74143-5_8

18. Maurer, U., Renner, R.: Abstract cryptography. In: Innovations in Computer Science - ICS 2011, pp. 1–21. Tsinghua University (2011)

19. Maurer, U., Renner, R.: From indifferentiability to constructive cryptography (and back). In: Hirt, M., Smith, A. (eds.) TCC 2016. LNCS, vol. 9985, pp. 3–24. Springer, Heidelberg (2016). https://doi.org/10.1007/978-3-662-53641-4_1

20. Nielsen, J.B.: Separating random oracle proofs from complexity theoretic proofs: the non-committing encryption case. In: Yung, M. (ed.) CRYPTO 2002. LNCS, vol. 2442, pp. 111–126. Springer, Heidelberg (2002). https://doi.org/10.1007/3-540-45708-9_8
21. Open Whisper Systems. Signal protocol library for Java/Android. GitHub repository (2017). https://github.com/WhisperSystems/libsignal-protocol-java. Accessed 01 Oct 2018
22. Pass, R.: Simulation in quasi-polynomial time, and its application to protocol composition. In: Biham, E. (ed.) EUROCRYPT 2003. LNCS, vol. 2656, pp. 160–176. Springer, Heidelberg (2003). https://doi.org/10.1007/3-540-39200-9_10
23. Pfitzmann, B., Waidner, M.: A model for asynchronous reactive systems and its application to secure message transmission. In: Proceedings 2001 IEEE Symposium on Security and Privacy - S&P 2001, pp. 184–200, May 2001. https://doi.org/10.1109/SECPRI.2001.924298
24. Poettering, B., Rösler, P.: Towards bidirectional ratcheted key exchange. In: Shacham, H., Boldyreva, A. (eds.) CRYPTO 2018. LNCS, vol. 10991, pp. 3–32. Springer, Cham (2018). https://doi.org/10.1007/978-3-319-96884-1_1
25. Prabhakaran, M., Sahai, A.: New notions of security: achieving universal composability without trusted setup. In: Proceedings of the Thirty-sixth Annual ACM Symposium on Theory of Computing, STOC 2004, pp. 242–251. ACM, New York (2004). https://doi.org/10.1145/1007352.1007394. http://doi.acm.org/10.1145/1007352.1007394

Continuously Non-malleable Secret Sharing for General Access Structures

Gianluca Brian[1]([✉]), Antonio Faonio[2], and Daniele Venturi[1]

[1] Department of Computer Science, Sapienza University of Rome, Rome, Italy
brian.1615294@studenti.uniroma1.it
[2] IMDEA Software Institute, Madrid, Spain

Abstract. We study leakage-resilient continuously non-malleable secret sharing, as recently introduced by Faonio and Venturi (CRYPTO 2019). In this setting, an attacker can continuously tamper and leak from a target secret sharing of some message, with the goal of producing a modified set of shares that reconstructs to a message related to the originally shared value. Our contributions are two fold.

- In the plain model, assuming one-to-one one-way functions, we show how to obtain noisy-leakage-resilient continuous non-malleability for arbitrary access structures, in case the attacker can continuously leak from and tamper with all of the shares independently.
- In the common reference string model, we show how to obtain a new flavor of security which we dub bounded-leakage-resilient continuous non-malleability under selective k-partitioning. In this model, the attacker is allowed to partition the target n shares into any number of non-overlapping blocks of maximal size k, and then can continuously leak from and tamper with the shares within each block jointly. Our construction works for arbitrary access structures, and assuming (doubly enhanced) trapdoor permutations and collision-resistant hash functions, we achieve a concrete instantiation for $k \in O(\log n)$.

Prior to our work, there was no secret sharing scheme achieving continuous non-malleability against joint tampering, and the only known scheme for independent tampering was tailored to threshold access structures.

Keywords: Secret sharing · Non-malleability · Leakage resilience

---

The first and third authors were supported in part by the research projects "PRIvacy-preserving, Security, and MAchine-learning techniques for healthcare applications (PRISMA)" and "Protect yourself and your data when using social networks", both funded by Sapienza University of Rome, and in part by the MIUR under grant "Dipartimenti di eccellenza 2018–2022" of the Computer Science Department of Sapienza University of Rome.
The second author is supported by the Spanish Government through the projects Datamantium (ref. RTC-2016-4930-7), SCUM (RTI2018-102043-B-I00), and ERC2018-092822, and by the Madrid Regional Government under project BLOQUES (ref. S2018/TCS-4339).

D. Hofheinz and A. Rosen (Eds.): TCC 2019, LNCS 11892, pp. 211–232, 2019.
https://doi.org/10.1007/978-3-030-36033-7_8

1   Introduction

A non-malleable secret sharing for an access structure $\mathcal{A}$ over n parties allows to share a secret message m into n shares $s = (s_1, \ldots, s_n)$, in such a way that the following properties are guaranteed.

Privacy: No attacker given the shares belonging to an arbitrary unauthorized subset $\mathcal{U} \notin \mathcal{A}$ of the players can infer any information on m.

Non-malleability: No attacker tampering with all of the shares via some function $f \in \mathcal{F}$ within some family of allowed[1] modifications can generate a mauled secret sharing $\tilde{s} = f(s)$ that reconstructs to $\tilde{m} \neq m$ related to m.

Sometimes, non-malleability is considered together with leakage resilience. This means that the attacker can additionally leak partial information $g(s)$ from all of the shares (via functions $g \in \mathcal{G}$) before launching a tampering attack. Leakage resilience typically comes in one of two flavors: *bounded leakage* (i.e,. there is a fixed upper bound on the maximum amount of information retrieved from the shares) or *noisy leakage* (i.e., the length of the retrieved information is arbitrary as long as it does not decrease the entropy of the shares by too much).

In this work we focus on leakage-resilient *continuous* non-malleability with *adaptive concurrent reconstruction*, as recently introduced by Faonio and Venturi [19].[2] Here, the attacker can (leak from and) tamper poly-many times with a target secret sharing using functions $f^{(q)} \in \mathcal{F}$ as above, and for each tampering query q it can also choose adaptively the reconstruction set $\mathcal{T}^{(q)} \in \mathcal{A}$ used to determine the reconstructed message. There are only two limitations: First, the attacker is computationally bounded; second, the experiment stops (we say it "self-destructs") after the first tampering query yielding an invalid set of shares. Both limitations are *inherent* for continuous non-malleability [6,19,20].

The only known scheme achieving such a strong flavor of non-malleability is the one by Faonio and Venturi, which tolerates the families $\mathcal{F}$ and $\mathcal{G}$ of *independent tampering/leakage*, i.e. for each query q we have $f^{(q)} = (f_1^{(q)}, \ldots, f_n^{(q)}) \in \mathcal{F}$ where $f_i^{(q)}$ gets as input the i-th share (and similarly $g^{(q)} = (g_1^{(q)}, \ldots, g_n^{(q)}) \in \mathcal{G}$). The access structure $\mathcal{A}$ supported by their construction is the τ-threshold access structure—i.e., any subset of at most τ players has no information about the message—with the caveat that reconstruction works with at least $\tau + 2$ shares, namely a *ramp* secret sharing, thus leaving a minimal gap between the reconstruction and privacy threshold. The following natural question arise:

Problem 1. Can we obtain leakage-resilient continuously non-malleable secret sharing against independent leakage/tampering, for general access structures?

Another open question is whether leakage-resilient continuous non-malleability is achievable for stronger tampering and leakage families $\mathcal{F}, \mathcal{G}$, e.g. in case the attacker can leak from and manipulate subsets of the shares jointly.

---

[1] It is easy to see that non-malleability is impossible for arbitrary (polynomial-time) tampering.

[2] From now on, we omit to explicitly mention the feature of adaptive concurrent reconstruction and simply talk about continuous non-malleability.

Problem 2. Can we obtain leakage-resilient continuously non-malleable secret sharing against joint leakage/tampering?

1.1   Our Contributions

We make significant progress towards solving the above problems. In particular, our first contribution is a positive answer to Problem 1:

Theorem 1 (Informal). *Assuming one-to-one one-way functions, for any access structure $\mathcal{A}$ over n parties there exists a noisy-leakage-resilient continuously non-malleable secret sharing scheme realizing $\mathcal{A}$ against independent leakage and tampering, in the plain model.*

Our second contribution is a positive answer to Problem 2 assuming trusted setup, in the form of a common reference string (CRS). More in details, we put forward a new security notion for secret sharing dubbed continuous non-malleability under *selective k-partitioning*. This roughly means that the attacker, after seeing the CRS, must commit to a partition of the set $[n]$ into β (non-overlapping) blocks $(\mathcal{B}_1, \ldots, \mathcal{B}_\beta)$ of size at most k; hence, the adversary can jointly, and continuously, tamper with and leak from each collection $s_{\mathcal{B}_i}$ of the shares.[3]

Theorem 2 (Informal). *Assuming (doubly-enhanced) trapdoor permutations and collision-resistant hash functions, for any access structure $\mathcal{A}$ over n parties there exists a bounded-leakage-resilient continuously non-malleable secret sharing scheme realizing $\mathcal{A}$ against selective $O(\log n)$-joint leakage and tampering in the CRS model.*

Prior to our work, we had secret sharing schemes unconditionally achieving security either against joint leakage [29] or joint tampering [23,24], but nothing was known for both even in the much simpler case of one-time non-malleability.

1.2   Related Work

Non-malleable secret sharing was introduced by Goyal and Kumar [23]. For any $\tau \le n$, they showed how to realize τ-threshold access structures, against one-time tampering with either all of the shares independently, or jointly after partitioning the players into two non-overlapping blocks of size at most[4] $\tau - 1$. In a subsequent work [24], the same authors show how to extend the result for independent tampering to the case of arbitrary access structures; additionally, for the case of joint tampering, they provide a new scheme realizing the n-threshold access structure (i.e., an n-out-of-n secret sharing) in a stronger model where

---

[3] The only restriction is that no block in the partition can contain an authorized set of players, otherwise trivial attacks are possible.

[4] An additional (artificial) requirement is that the size of the two blocks must be different in order for their technique to work.

the attacker can partition the players into two possibly overlapping blocks of size at most $n - 1$. Srinivasan and Vasudevan [36] built the first non-malleable secret sharing schemes for general access structures against independent tampering, with non-zero rate[5] (in fact, even constant rate in case of threshold access structures). Chattopadhyay et al. [9] construct non-malleable secret sharing for threshold access structures, against affine tampering composed with joint split-state tampering. Lin et al. [31] consider non-malleability against affine tampering in an adaptive setting where the adversary gets to see an unauthorized subset of the shares before launching a single tampering attack.

Badrinarayanan and Srinivasan [6] generalize non-malleability to p-time tampering attacks, where p is an a-priori upper bound on the number of tampering queries the adversary can ask. For each attempt, however, the reconstruction set $\mathcal{T}$ must be chosen in advance at the beginning of the experiment. In this model, they show how to realize arbitrary access structures against independent tampering with all of the shares. Aggarwal et al. [2] were the first to consider p-time non-malleability under *non-adaptive* concurrent reconstruction, i.e. the attacker now can specify a different reconstruction set $\mathcal{T}^{(q)}$ during the q-th tampering query, although the sequence of sets $\mathcal{T}^{(1)}, \ldots, \mathcal{T}^{(p)}$ must be chosen non-adaptively. Kumar, Meka, and Sahai [29] pioneered bounded-leakage-resilient one-time non-malleable secret sharing for general access structures, against independent leakage and tampering with all of the shares.

In the special case of 2-threshold access structures over $n = 2$ parties, the notion of (leakage-resilient) non-malleable secret sharing collapses to that of split-state (leakage-resilient) non-malleable codes [1, 3–5, 10, 11, 15, 17, 18, 20, 30, 32, 34].

Organization. All of our constructions rely on standard cryptographic primitives, which we recall in Sect. 2 (together with some basic notation). The new model of continuous tampering under selective partitioning is presented in Sect. 3.

Our main constructions appear in Sect. 4 (for joint tampering in the CRS model) and Sects. 5–6 (for independent tampering in the plain model), respectively; there, we also explain how to instantiate these constructions with concrete building blocks, thus establishing Theorems 1 and 2. Finally, in Sect. 7, we conclude the paper with a list of open problems and interesting directions for further research.

2   Standard Definitions

Basic Notation. For a string x, we denote its length by $|x|$; if $\mathcal{X}$ is a set, $|\mathcal{X}|$ represents the number of elements in $\mathcal{X}$. When x is chosen randomly in $\mathcal{X}$, we write $x \leftarrow_{\$} \mathcal{X}$. When A is a randomized algorithm, we write $y \leftarrow_{\$} \mathsf{A}(x)$ to denote a run of A on input x (and implicit random coins r) and output y; the value y is a random variable, and $\mathsf{A}(x; r)$ denotes a run of A on input x and randomness r. An algorithm A is *probabilistic polynomial-time* (PPT) if A is randomized and for

---

[5] The rate refers to the asymptotic ratio between the maximal length of a share and that of the message.

any input $x, r \in \{0, 1\}^*$ the computation of $\mathsf{A}(x; r)$ terminates in a polynomial number of steps (in the size of the input).

Negligible Functions. We denote with $\lambda \in \mathbb{N}$ the security parameter. A function p is a polynomial, denoted $p(\lambda) \in \mathsf{poly}(\lambda)$, if $p(\lambda) \in O(\lambda^c)$ for some constant $c > 0$. A function $\nu : \mathbb{N} \to [0, 1]$ is negligible in the security parameter (or simply negligible) if it vanishes faster than the inverse of any polynomial in λ, i.e. $\nu(\lambda) \in O(1/p(\lambda))$ for all positive polynomials $p(\lambda)$. We often write $\nu(\lambda) \in \mathsf{negl}(\lambda)$ to denote that $\nu(\lambda)$ is negligible.

Unless stated otherwise, throughout the paper, we implicitly assume that the security parameter is given as input (in unary) to all algorithms.

Random Variables. For a random variable $\mathbf{X}$, we write $\mathbb{P}[\mathbf{X} = x]$ for the probability that $\mathbf{X}$ takes on a particular value $x \in \mathcal{X}$ (with $\mathcal{X}$ being the set where $\mathbf{X}$ is defined). The statistical distance between two random variables $\mathbf{X}$ and $\mathbf{X}'$ defined over the same set $\mathcal{X}$ is defined as $\mathbb{SD}\,(\mathbf{X}; \mathbf{X}') = \frac{1}{2}\sum_{x \in \mathcal{X}} |\mathbb{P}[\mathbf{X} = x] - \mathbb{P}[\mathbf{X}' = x]|$.

Given two ensembles $\mathbf{X} = \{\mathbf{X}_\lambda\}_{\lambda \in \mathbb{N}}$ and $\mathbf{Y} = \{\mathbf{Y}_\lambda\}_{\lambda \in \mathbb{N}}$, we write $\mathbf{X} \equiv \mathbf{Y}$ to denote that they are identically distributed, $\mathbf{X} \approx_s \mathbf{Y}$ to denote that they are statistically close, i.e. $\mathbb{SD}\,(\mathbf{X}_\lambda; \mathbf{X}'_\lambda) \in \mathsf{negl}(\lambda)$, and $\mathbf{X} \approx_c \mathbf{Y}$ to denote that they are computationally indistinguishable, i.e., for all PPT distinguishers D:

$$|\mathbb{P}[\mathsf{D}(\mathbf{X}_\lambda) = 1] - \mathbb{P}[\mathsf{D}(\mathbf{Y}_\lambda) = 1]| \in \mathsf{negl}(\lambda).$$

We extend the notion of computational indistinguishability to the case of interactive experiments (a.k.a. games) featuring an adversary A. In particular, let $\mathbf{G}_\mathsf{A}(\lambda)$ be the random variable corresponding to the output of A at the end of the experiment, where wlog. we may assume A outputs a decision bit. Given two experiments $\mathbf{G}_\mathsf{A}(\lambda, 0)$ and $\mathbf{G}_\mathsf{A}(\lambda, 1)$, we write $\{\mathbf{G}_\mathsf{A}(\lambda, 0)\}_{\lambda \in \mathbb{N}} \approx_c \{\mathbf{G}_\mathsf{A}(\lambda, 1)\}_{\lambda \in \mathbb{N}}$ as a shorthand for

$$|\mathbb{P}[\mathbf{G}_\mathsf{A}(\lambda, 0) = 1] - \mathbb{P}[\mathbf{G}_\mathsf{A}(\lambda, 1) = 1]| \in \mathsf{negl}(\lambda).$$

The above naturally generalizes to statistical distance (in case of unbounded adversaries). We recall a useful lemma from [12,16].

Lemma 1 ([12], Lemma 4). *Let $\mathcal{O}_{\mathsf{leak}}(x, g)$ be an oracle that upon input a value x and a function g outputs $g(x)$, and let $\mathbf{X}$ and $\mathbf{Y}$ be two independently distributed random variables. For any adversary A, and for any value z, the distributions $(\mathbf{X}|z = \mathsf{A}^{\mathcal{O}_{\mathsf{leak}}(\mathbf{X}, \cdot), \mathcal{O}_{\mathsf{leak}}(\mathbf{Y}, \cdot)})$ and $(\mathbf{Y}|z = \mathsf{A}^{\mathcal{O}_{\mathsf{leak}}(\mathbf{X}, \cdot), \mathcal{O}_{\mathsf{leak}}(\mathbf{Y}, \cdot)})$ are independently distributed.*

Average Min-entropy. The min-entropy of a random variable $\mathbf{X}$ with domain $\mathcal{X}$ is $\mathbb{H}_\infty(\mathbf{X}) := -\log \max_{x \in \mathcal{X}} \mathbb{P}[\mathbf{X} = x]$, and intuitively it measures the best chance to predict $\mathbf{X}$ (by a computationally unbounded algorithm). For conditional distributions, unpredictability is measured by the conditional average min-entropy [14]: $\widetilde{\mathbb{H}}_\infty(\mathbf{X}|\mathbf{Y}) := -\log \mathbb{E}_y[2^{-\mathbb{H}_\infty(\mathbf{X}|\mathbf{Y}=y)}]$. The lemma below is sometimes known as the "chain rule" for conditional average min-entropy.

Lemma 2 ([14], Lemma 2.2). *Let* $\mathbf{X}, \mathbf{Y}, \mathbf{Z}$ *be random variables. If* $\mathbf{Y}$ *has at most* 2^ℓ *possible values, then* $\widetilde{\mathbb{H}}_\infty(\mathbf{X}|\mathbf{Y}, \mathbf{Z}) \geq \widetilde{\mathbb{H}}_\infty(\mathbf{X}, \mathbf{Y}|\mathbf{Z}) - \ell \geq \widetilde{\mathbb{H}}_\infty(\mathbf{X}|\mathbf{Z}) - \ell$. *In particular,* $\widetilde{\mathbb{H}}_\infty(\mathbf{X}|\mathbf{Y}) \geq \widetilde{\mathbb{H}}_\infty(\mathbf{X}, \mathbf{Y}) - \ell \geq \widetilde{\mathbb{H}}_\infty(\mathbf{X}) - \ell$.

2.1 Secret Sharing Schemes

An n-party secret sharing scheme Σ in the common reference string (CRS) model consists of polynomial-time algorithms (Init, Share, Rec) specified as follows: (i) The randomized initialization algorithm Init takes as input the security parameter 1^λ, and outputs a CRS $\omega \in \{0,1\}^*$; (ii) The randomized sharing algorithm Share takes as input a CRS $\omega \in \{0,1\}^*$ and a message $m \in \mathcal{M}$, and outputs n shares $s_1, \ldots, s_n$ where each $s_i \in \mathcal{S}_i$; (iii) The deterministic algorithm Rec takes as input a CRS $\omega \in \{0,1\}^*$ and a certain number of candidate shares, and outputs a value in $\mathcal{M} \cup \{\bot\}$. Given $s = (s_1, \ldots, s_n)$ and a subset $\mathcal{I} \subseteq [n]$, we often write $s_\mathcal{I}$ to denote the shares $(s_i)_{i \in \mathcal{I}}$.

The subset of parties allowed to reconstruct the secrets by pulling their shares together form the so-called access structure.

Definition 1 (Access structure). *We say* $\mathcal{A}$ *is an access structure for* n *parties if* $\mathcal{A}$ *is a monotone class of subsets of* $[n]$, *i.e., if* $\mathcal{I}_1 \in \mathcal{A}$ *and* $\mathcal{I}_1 \subseteq \mathcal{I}_2$, *then* $\mathcal{I}_2 \in \mathcal{A}$. *We call sets* $\mathcal{I} \in \mathcal{A}$ *authorized or qualified, and unauthorized or unqualified otherwise.*

Intuitively, a secure secret sharing scheme must be such that all qualified subsets of players can efficiently reconstruct the secret, whereas all unqualified subset have no information (possibly in a computational sense) about the secret.

Definition 2 (Secret sharing scheme). *Let* $n \in \mathbb{N}$, *and* $\mathcal{A}$ *be an access structure for* n *parties. We say that* $\Sigma = $ (Init, Share, Rec) *is a secret sharing scheme realizing access structure* $\mathcal{A}$ *in the CRS model, with message space* $\mathcal{M}$ *and share space* $\mathcal{S} = \mathcal{S}_1 \times \cdots \times \mathcal{S}_n$, *if it is an* n-*party secret sharing in the CRS model with the following properties.*

(i) **Correctness:** *For all* $\lambda \in \mathbb{N}$, *all* $\omega \in$ Init(1^λ), *all messages* $m \in \mathcal{M}$, *and for all subsets* $\mathcal{I} \in \mathcal{A}$, *we have that* Rec$(\omega, ($Share$(\omega, m))_\mathcal{I}) = m$, *with overwhelming probability over the randomness of the sharing algorithm.*

(ii) **Privacy:** *For all PPT adversaries* $\mathsf{A} = (\mathsf{A}_1, \mathsf{A}_2)$, *we have*

$$\{\mathbf{Privacy}_{\Sigma, \mathsf{A}}(\lambda, 0)\}_{\lambda \in \mathbb{N}} \approx_c \{\mathbf{Privacy}_{\Sigma, \mathsf{A}}(\lambda, 1)\}_{\lambda \in \mathbb{N}},$$

where the experiment $\mathbf{Privacy}_{\Sigma, \mathsf{A}}(\lambda, b)$ *is defined by*

$$\mathbf{Privacy}_{\Sigma, \mathsf{A}}(\lambda, b) := \left\{ \begin{array}{c} \omega \leftarrow_\$ \mathsf{Init}(1^\lambda); (m_0, m_1, \mathcal{U} \notin \mathcal{A}, \alpha_1) \leftarrow_\$ \mathsf{A}_1(\omega) \\ s \leftarrow_\$ \mathsf{Share}(\omega, m_b); b' \leftarrow_\$ \mathsf{A}_2(\alpha_1, s_\mathcal{U}) \end{array} \right\}.$$

If the above ensembles are statistically close (resp. identically distributed), we speak of statistical *(resp.* perfect*) privacy.*

Moreover, we say that Σ is a secret sharing scheme realizing access structure $\mathcal{A}$ in the plain model, if for all $\lambda \in \mathbb{N}$ algorithm Init *simply returns* $\omega = 1^\lambda$.

Remark 1. In the plain model, the above definition of privacy is equivalent to saying that for all pairs of messages $m_0, m_1 \in \mathcal{M}$, and for all unqualified subsets $\mathcal{U} \notin \mathcal{A}$, it holds that $\{(\mathsf{Share}(1^\lambda, m_0))_\mathcal{U}\}_{\lambda \in \mathbb{N}} \approx_c \{(\mathsf{Share}(1^\lambda, m_1))_\mathcal{U}\}_{\lambda \in \mathbb{N}}$.

2.2 Non-interactive Commitments

A non-interactive commitment scheme $\Pi = (\mathsf{Gen}, \mathsf{Com})$ is a pair of polynomial-time algorithms specified as follows: (i) The randomized algorithm Gen takes as input 1^λ and outputs a public key $pk \in \mathcal{K}$; (ii) The randomized algorithm Com takes as input the public key pk and a message $m \in \mathcal{M}$, and outputs a commitment $c = \mathsf{Com}(pk, m; r) \in \mathcal{C}$ using random coins $r \in \mathcal{R}$. The pair (m, r) is called the opening. In the plain model, we omit the algorithm Gen and simply set $pk = 1^\lambda$.

Intuitively, a secure commitment satisfies two properties called binding and hiding. The first property says that it is hard to open a commitment in two different ways. The second property says that a commitment hides the underlying message. The formal definitions follow.

Definition 3 (Binding). *We say that a non-interactive commitment scheme $\Pi = (\mathsf{Gen}, \mathsf{Com})$ is* computationally binding *if the following probability is negligible for all PPT adversaries* A:

$$\mathbb{P}\left[m_0 \neq m_1 \wedge \mathsf{Com}(pk, m_0; r_0) = \mathsf{Com}(pk, m_1; r_1) : \begin{array}{l} pk \leftarrow_\$ \mathsf{Gen}(1^\lambda) \\ (m_0, r_0, m_1, r_1) \leftarrow_\$ \mathsf{A}(pk) \end{array} \right].$$

In case the above definition holds for all unbounded adversaries, we say that Π is statistically binding. *Finally, in case the above probability is exactly 0 (i.e., each commitment can be opened to at most a single message), then we say that Π is* perfectly binding.

Definition 4 (Hiding). *We say that a non-interactive commitment scheme $\Pi = (\mathsf{Gen}, \mathsf{Com})$ is* computationally hiding *if the following holds for all PPT adversaries* A:

$$\left\{ \begin{array}{l} pk \leftarrow_\$ \mathsf{Gen}(1^\lambda); (m_0, m_1, \alpha_1) \leftarrow_\$ \mathsf{A}_1(pk) \\ c \leftarrow_\$ \mathsf{Com}(pk, m_0); b' \leftarrow_\$ \mathsf{A}_2(\alpha_1, c) \end{array} \right\}$$
$$\approx_c \left\{ \begin{array}{l} pk \leftarrow_\$ \mathsf{Gen}(1^\lambda); (m_0, m_1, \alpha_1) \leftarrow_\$ \mathsf{A}_1(pk) \\ c \leftarrow_\$ \mathsf{Com}(pk, m_1); b' \leftarrow_\$ \mathsf{A}_2(\alpha_1, c) \end{array} \right\}.$$

In case the above ensembles are statistically close (resp. identically distributed), we speak of statistical *(resp. perfect) hiding.*

Note that in the plain model the above definition of hiding is equivalent to saying that for all pairs of messages $m_0, m_1 \in \mathcal{M}$ the following holds:

$$\{c : c \leftarrow_\$ \mathsf{Com}(1^\lambda, m_0)\}_{\lambda \in \mathbb{N}} \approx_c \{c : c \leftarrow_\$ \mathsf{Com}(1^\lambda, m_1)\}_{\lambda \in \mathbb{N}}.$$

2.3 Non-interactive Zero Knowledge

Let R be a relation, corresponding to an NP language $\mathcal{L}$. A non-interactive zero-knowledge (NIZK) proof system for R is a tuple of efficient algorithms $\Pi =$ (CRSGen, Prove, Ver) specified as follows. (i) The randomized algorithm CRSGen takes as input the security parameter and outputs a common reference string ω; (ii) The randomized algorithm Prove$(\omega, \phi, (x, w))$, given $(x, w) \in$ R and a label $\phi \in \{0, 1\}^*$, outputs a proof π; (iii) The deterministic algorithm Ver$(\omega, \phi, (x, \pi))$, given an instance x, a proof π, and a label $\phi \in \{0, 1\}^*$, outputs either 0 (for "reject") or 1 (for "accept"). We say that a NIZK for relation R is *correct* if for every $\lambda \in \mathbb{N}$, all ω as output by Init(1^λ), any label $\phi \in \{0, 1\}^*$, and any $(x, w) \in$ R, we have that Ver$(\omega, \phi, (x, \text{Prove}(\omega, \phi, (x, w)))) = 1$.

We define two properties of a NIZK proof system. The first property says that honest proofs do not reveal anything beyond the fact that $x \in \mathcal{L}$.

Definition 5 (Adaptive multi-theorem zero-knowledge). *A NIZK with labels Π for a relation R satisfies adaptive multi-theorem zero-knowledge if there exists a PPT simulator $S := (S_0, S_1)$ such that the following holds:*

(i) S_0 outputs ω, a simulation trapdoor ζ and an extraction trapdoor ξ.
(ii) For all PPT distinguishers D, we have that

$$\left| \mathbb{P}[\mathsf{D}^{\text{Prove}(\omega, \cdot, (\cdot, \cdot))}(\omega) = 1 : \omega \leftarrow_{\$} \text{Init}(1^\lambda)] \right.$$

$$\left. - \mathbb{P}[\mathsf{D}^{\mathcal{O}_{\text{sim}}(\zeta, \cdot, \cdot, \cdot)}(\omega) = 1 : (\omega, \zeta) \leftarrow_{\$} S_0(1^\lambda)] \right|$$

is negligible in λ, where the oracle $\mathcal{O}_{\text{sim}}(\zeta, \cdot, \cdot, \cdot)$ takes as input a tuple (ϕ, x, w) and returns $S_1(\zeta, \phi, x)$ iff R$(x, w) = 1$ (and otherwise it returns $\bot$).

Groth [26] introduced the concept of simulation-extractable NIZK, which informally states that knowledge soundness should hold even if the adversary can see simulated proofs for possibly false statements of its choice. For our purpose, it will suffice to consider the weaker notion of true simulation extractability, as defined by Dodis *et al.* [13].

Definition 6 (True simulation extractability). *Let Π be a NIZK proof systems for a relation R, that satisfies adaptive multi-theorem zero-knowledge w.r.t. a simulator $S := (S_0, S_1)$. We say that Π is true simulation extractable if there exists a PPT algorithm K such that every PPT adversary A has a negligible probability of winning in the following game:*

- *The challenger runs $(\omega, \zeta, \xi) \leftarrow_{\$} S_0(1^\lambda)$, and gives ω to A.*
- *Adversary A can ask polynomially many queries of the form (ϕ, x, w), upon which the challenger returns $S_1(\zeta, \phi, x)$ if $(x, w) \in$ R and $\bot$ otherwise.*
- *Adversary A outputs a tuple (ϕ^*, x^*, π^*).*
- *The challenger runs $w \leftarrow_{\$} K(\xi, \phi^*, (x^*, \pi^*))$.*

We say that A wins iff: (a) (ϕ^*, x^*) was not queried in the second step; (b) Ver$(\omega, \phi^*, (x^*, \pi^*)) = 1$; (c) $(x^*, w) \notin$ R.

3   Continuous Tampering Under Selective Partitioning

In this section we define a new notion of non-malleability against joint memory tampering and leakage for secret sharing. Our definition generalizes the one in [19] which was tailored to threshold access structures and to independent leakage/tampering from the shares.

Very roughly, in our model the attacker is allowed to partition the set of share holders into β (non-overlapping) blocks with size at most k, covering the entire set $[n]$. This is formalized through the notion of a k-partition.

Definition 7 (k-partition). *Let $n, k, \beta \in \mathbb{N}$. We call $\mathcal{B} = (\mathcal{B}_1, \ldots, \mathcal{B}_\beta)$ a k-partition of $[n]$ when: (i) $\bigcup_{i=1}^{\beta} \mathcal{B}_i = [n]$; (ii) $\forall i_1, i_2 \in [\beta]$, with $i_1 \neq i_2$, we have $\mathcal{B}_{i_1} \cap \mathcal{B}_{i_2} = \emptyset$; (iii) $\forall i = 1, \ldots, \beta : |\mathcal{B}_i| \leq k$.*

3.1   The Definition

To define non-malleability, we consider an attacker A playing the following game. At the beginning of the experiment, A chooses two messages m_0, m_1 possibly depending on the CRS ω of the underlying secret sharing scheme, and a k-partition $(\mathcal{B}_1, \ldots, \mathcal{B}_\beta)$ of the set $[n]$. Hence, the adversary interacts with a target secret sharing $s = (s_1, \ldots, s_n)$ of either m_0 or m_1, via the following queries:

- **Leakage queries.** For each $j \in [\beta]$, the attacker can leak jointly from the shares $s_{\mathcal{B}_j}$. This can be done repeatedly and in an adaptive fashion, the only limitation being that the overall amount of leakage on each block is at most $\ell \in \mathbb{N}$ bits.
- **Tampering queries.** For each $j \in [\beta]$, the attacker can tamper jointly the shares $s_{\mathcal{B}_j}$. Each such query yields mauled shares $(\tilde{s}_1, \ldots, \tilde{s}_n)$, for which the adversary is allowed to see the corresponding reconstructed message w.r.t. an arbitrary reconstruction set $\mathcal{T} \in \mathcal{A}$ that is also chosen adversarially. This can be done for at most $p \in \mathbb{N}$ times, and in an adaptive fashion.

The above naturally yields a notion of joint bounded-leakage and tampering admissible adversary, as defined below. Note that, in order to rule out trivial attacks, we must require that the partition $\mathcal{B}$ chosen by the attacker be such that no block of the partition is an authorized set for the underlying access structure.

Definition 8 (Joint bounded-leakage and tampering admissible adversaries).   *Let $n, k, \ell, p \in \mathbb{N}$, and fix an arbitrary message space $\mathcal{M}$, sharing domain $\mathcal{S} = \mathcal{S}_1 \times \cdots \times \mathcal{S}_n$ and access structure $\mathcal{A}$ for n parties. We say that a (possibly unbounded) adversary $\mathsf{A} = (\mathsf{A}_1, \mathsf{A}_2)$ is k-joint ℓ-bounded-leakage and p-tampering admissible ((k, ℓ, p)-BLTA for short) if it satisfies the following conditions:*

(i) *A_1 outputs two messages $m_0, m_1 \in \mathcal{M}$ and a k-partition $\mathcal{B} = (\mathcal{B}_1, \ldots, \mathcal{B}_\beta)$ of $[n]$ such that $\forall j \in [\beta]$ we have $\mathcal{B}_j \notin \mathcal{A}$.*

$\textbf{JSTamper}_{\Sigma,\mathsf{A}}(\lambda,b)$:
$\omega \leftarrow_\$ \mathsf{Init}(1^\lambda)$
$(\mathcal{B} = (\mathcal{B}_1,\dots,\mathcal{B}_\beta), m_0, m_1, \alpha_1) \leftarrow_\$ \mathsf{A}_1(\omega)$
$s := (s_1,\dots,s_n) \leftarrow_\$ \mathsf{Share}(\omega, m_b)$
$\mathsf{stop} \leftarrow \mathsf{false}$
$(\alpha_2, i^* \in [\beta]) \leftarrow_\$ \mathsf{A}_2^{\mathcal{O}_{\mathsf{nmss}}(s,\cdot,\cdot), \mathcal{O}_{\mathsf{leak}}(s,\cdot)}(\alpha_1)$
Return $\mathsf{A}_3(\alpha_2, s_{\mathcal{B}_{i^*}})$
Oracle $\mathcal{O}_{\mathsf{leak}}(s, (g_1,\dots,g_\beta))$:
Return $g_1(s_{\mathcal{B}_1}),\dots,g_\beta(s_{\mathcal{B}_\beta})$

Oracle $\mathcal{O}_{\mathsf{nmss}}(s, \mathcal{T}, (f_1,\dots,f_\beta))$:
If $\mathsf{stop} = \mathsf{true}$
    Return $\perp$
Else
    $\forall i \in [\beta] : \tilde{s}_{\mathcal{B}_i} := f_i(s_{\mathcal{B}_i})$
    $\tilde{s} = (\tilde{s}_1,\dots,\tilde{s}_n)$
    $\tilde{m} = \mathsf{Rec}(\omega, \tilde{s}_{\mathcal{T}})$
    If $\tilde{m} \in \{m_0, m_1\}$
        Return ♥
    If $\tilde{m} = \perp$
        Return $\perp$
        $\mathsf{stop} \leftarrow \mathsf{true}$
    Else return $\tilde{m}$

Fig. 1. Experiment defining leakage-resilient (continuously) non-malleable secret sharing under adaptive concurrent reconstruction. The instructions boxed in red are considered only for continuous non-malleability, in which case the oracle $\mathcal{O}_{\mathsf{nmss}}$ is implicitly parameterized by the flag stop. (Color figure online)

(ii) A_2 outputs a sequence of poly-many leakage queries, chosen adaptively, $(g_1^{(q)},\dots,g_\beta^{(q)})_{q \in \mathsf{poly}(\lambda)}$ such that $\forall j \in [\beta]$ it holds that $\sum_q |g_j^{(q)}(\cdot)| \leq \ell$, where $g_j^{(q)} : \mathsf{X}_{i \in \mathcal{B}_j} \mathcal{S}_i \to \{0,1\}^*$.

(iii) A_2 outputs a sequence of p tampering queries, chosen adaptively, $(\mathcal{T}^{(q)}, (f_1^{(q)},\dots,f_\beta^{(q)}))_{q \in [p]}$ such that $\mathcal{T}^{(q)} \in \mathcal{A}$, and $\forall j \in [\beta]$ it holds that $f_j^{(q)} : \mathsf{X}_{i \in \mathcal{B}_j} \mathcal{S}_i \to \mathsf{X}_{i \in \mathcal{B}_j} \mathcal{S}_i$.

Very roughly, leakage-resilient non-malleability states that no admissible adversary as defined above can distinguish whether it is interacting with a secret sharing of m_0 or of m_1. In the definition below, the attacker is further allowed to obtain in full the shares belonging to one of the partitions, at the end of the experiment. This is reminiscent of augmented (leakage-resilient) non-malleability, as considered in [1,11,20,25].

Definition 9 (Leakage-resilient non-malleability under selective partitioning). *Let $n, k, \ell, p \in \mathbb{N}$ be parameters, and $\mathcal{A}$ be an access structure for n parties. We say that $\Sigma = (\mathsf{Init}, \mathsf{Share}, \mathsf{Rec})$ is an augmented ℓ-bounded leakage-resilient p-time non-malleable secret sharing scheme realizing $\mathcal{A}$ against selective k-joint leakage and tampering in the CRS model (resp., in the plain model)—augmented (k, ℓ, p)-BLR-CNMSS for short—if it is an n-party secret sharing scheme realizing $\mathcal{A}$ in the CRS model (resp., in the plain model) as per Definition 2, and additionally for all (k, ℓ, p)-BLTA adversaries $\mathsf{A} = (\mathsf{A}_1, \mathsf{A}_2)$ we have:*

$$\left\{\textbf{JSTamper}_{\Sigma,\mathsf{A}}(\lambda,0)\right\}_{\lambda \in \mathbb{N}} \approx_s \left\{\textbf{JSTamper}_{\Sigma,\mathsf{A}}(\lambda,1)\right\}_{\lambda \in \mathbb{N}},$$

where, for $b \in \{0,1\}$, experiment $\textbf{JSTamper}_{\Sigma,\mathsf{A}}(\lambda,b)$ is depicted in Fig. 1.

In case the above definition holds for all $p(\lambda) \in \mathtt{poly}(\lambda)$, but w.r.t. all PPT adversaries A (i.e., $\approx_s$ is replaced with $\approx_c$ in the above equation), we call Σ (augmented, bounded leakage-resilient) continuously non-malleable. As shown by [19], already for the simpler case of independent tampering, it is impossible to achieve this notion without assuming self-destruct (i.e., the oracle $\mathcal{O}_{\mathsf{nmss}}$ must stop answering tampering queries after the first such query yielding an invalid reconstructed message).

It is also well-known that computational security is inherent for obtaining continuously non-malleable secret sharing realizing threshold access structures [6]. Unless stated otherwise, when we refer to non-malleable secret sharing in this paper we implicitly assume security holds in the computational setting (both for privacy and non-malleability).

On Augmented Non-malleability. When dropping the adversary A_3 from the above definition, we obtain the standard (non-augmented) notion of (leakage-resilient, continuous) non-malleability. The theorem below, however, says that augmented security is essentially for free whenever non-malleability is considered together with leakage resilience. Intuitively, this is because in the reduction we can simply simulate all leakage queries, and then ask a final leakage query which reveals the output guess of an hypothetical distinguisher attacking augmented non-malleability.[6] A similar proof strategy was used in [29, Lemma 7]. The formal proof appears in the full version [8].

Theorem 3. *Let Σ be a $(k, \ell + 1, p)$-BLR-CNMSS realizing access structure $\mathcal{A}$ for n parties in the CRS model (resp. plain model). Then, Σ is an augmented (k, ℓ, p)-BLR-CNMSS realizing $\mathcal{A}$ in the CRS model (resp. plain model).*

3.2   Related Notions

We finally argue that known definitions from the literature can be cast by either restricting, or slightly tweaking, Definition 9.

Independent Leakage and Tampering. The definition below restricts the adversary to leak/tamper from/with each of the shares individually; this is sometimes known as local or independent leakage/tampering. The condition on leakage admissibility, though, is more general, in that the attacker can leak an arbitrary amount of information as long as the total leakage reduces the uncertainty on each share (conditioned on the other shares) by at most ℓ bits.

Definition 10 (Independent noisy-leakage and tampering admissible adversaries). *Let $n, \ell, p \in \mathbb{N}$, and fix an arbitrary message space $\mathcal{M}$, sharing domain $\mathcal{S} = \mathcal{S}_1 \times \cdots \times \mathcal{S}_n$ and access structure $\mathcal{A}$ for n parties. We say that a (possibly unbounded) adversary $\mathsf{A} = (\mathsf{A}_1, \mathsf{A}_2)$ is independent ℓ-noisy-leakage and tampering admissible $((n, \ell, p)$-NLTA for short) if it satisfies the following conditions:*

---

[6] While we state the theorem for the case of bounded leakage, an identical statement holds in the noisy-leakage setting.

(i) A_1 *outputs two messages* $m_0, m_1 \in \mathcal{M}$ *and the partition* $\mathcal{B} = (\{1\}, \ldots, \{n\})$.

(ii) A_2 *outputs a sequence of poly-many leakage queries (chosen adaptively)* $(g_1^{(q)}, \ldots, g_n^{(q)})_{q \in \mathtt{poly}(\lambda)}$ *such that* $\forall i \in [n]$ *we have* $g_i^{(q)} : \mathcal{S}_i \to \{0,1\}^*$, *and* $\forall m \in \mathcal{M}$ *it holds that:*

$$\widetilde{\mathbb{H}}_\infty \left(\mathbf{S}_i | (\mathbf{S}_j)_{j \neq i}, g_i^{(1)}(\mathbf{S}_i), \cdots, g_i^{(p)}(\mathbf{S}_i) \right) \geq \widetilde{\mathbb{H}}_\infty(\mathbf{S}_i | (\mathbf{S}_j)_{j \neq i}) - \ell,$$

where $(\mathbf{S}_1, \ldots, \mathbf{S}_n)$ *is the random variable corresponding to* $\mathsf{Share}(\mathsf{Init}(1^\lambda), m)$.

(iii) A_2 *outputs a sequence of tampering queries (chosen adaptively)* $(\mathcal{T}^{(q)}, (f_1^{(q)}, \ldots, f_n^{(q)}))_{q \in [p]}$ *such that* $\mathcal{T}^{(q)} \in \mathcal{A}$, *and* $\forall i \in [n]$ *it holds that* $f_i^{(q)} : \mathcal{S}_i \to \mathcal{S}_i$.

When restricting Definition 9 to all PPT $(n, \ell, \mathtt{poly}(\lambda))$-NLTA adversaries, we obtain the notion of (augmented) ℓ-noisy leakage-resilient continuously non-malleable secret sharing against individual leakage and tampering (with adaptive concurrent reconstructions) [19]. Finally, if we consider $n = 2$ and the threshold access structure with reconstruction parameter $\varrho = 2$ (i.e., both shares are required in order to reconstruct the message), we immediately obtain noisy leakage-resilient continuously non-malleable codes in the split-state model [20,34]. In what follows, we write $\mathbf{Tamper}(\lambda, b)$ to denote the random variable in the security experiment of Definition 9 with an (n, ℓ, p)-NLTA adversary.

Leakage-Resilient Secret Sharing. Further, when no tampering is allowed (i.e., $p = 0$), we obtain the notion of leakage-resilient secret sharing [2,12,29,33,36] as a special case. In particular, we write $\mathbf{JSLeak}(\lambda, b)$ to denote the random variable in the security experiment of Definition 9 with a $(k, \ell, 0)$-BLTA adversary, and $\mathbf{Leak}(\lambda, b)$ to denote the random variable in the security experiment of Definition 9 with an $(n, \ell, 0)$-NLTA adversary.

Recall that, by Theorem 3, the augmented variant is without loss of generality as long as leakage resilience holds for $\ell \geq 2$.

4   Construction in the CRS Model

4.1   Description of the Scheme

We show how to obtain leakage-resilient continuously non-malleable secret sharing for arbitrary access structures in the CRS model, with security against selective joint leakage and tampering. Our construction combines a commitment scheme (Gen, Com) (cf. Sect. 2.2), a non-interactive proof system (CRSGen, Prove, Ver) for proving knowledge of a committed value (cf. Sect. 2.3), and an auxiliary n-party secret sharing scheme $\Sigma = (\mathsf{Share}, \mathsf{Rec})$, as depicted in Fig. 2.

The main idea behind the scheme is as follows. The CRS includes the CRS ω for the proof system and the public key pk for the commitment scheme. Given a message $m \in \mathcal{M}$, the sharing procedure first shares m using Share, obtaining shares $(s_1, \ldots, s_n)$. Then, it commits to the i-th share s_i along with the position i using randomness r_i, and finally generates $n-1$ proofs $(\pi_j^i)_{j \neq i}$ for the statement

---

Let $\Sigma = (\mathsf{Share}, \mathsf{Rec})$ be an auxiliary secret sharing scheme realizing access structure $\mathcal{A}$, with message space $\mathcal{M}$ and share space $\mathcal{S} = \mathcal{S}_1 \times \cdots \times \mathcal{S}_n$. Let $(\mathsf{Gen}, \mathsf{Com})$ be a commitment scheme with domain $\{0,1\}^*$, and $(\mathsf{CRSGen}, \mathsf{Prove}, \mathsf{Ver})$ be a non-interactive argument system for the language $\mathcal{L}_{\mathsf{com}}^{pk} = \{c \in \{0,1\}^\gamma : \exists i \in [n], s \in \mathcal{S}_i, r \in \mathcal{R} \text{ s.t. } \mathsf{Com}(pk, i\|s; r) = c\}$ that supports labels in $\{0,1\}^\gamma$. Define the following secret sharing scheme $\Sigma^* = (\mathsf{Init}^*, \mathsf{Share}^*, \mathsf{Rec}^*)$ in the CRS model.

Initialization algorithm Init^*: Sample $\omega \leftarrow_{\$} \mathsf{CRSGen}(1^\lambda)$ and $pk \leftarrow_{\$} \mathsf{Gen}(1^\lambda)$, and return $\omega^* = (\omega, pk)$.

Sharing algorithm Share^*: Upon input $\omega^* = (\omega, pk)$ and a value $m \in \mathcal{M}$, compute $(s_1, \ldots, s_n) \leftarrow_{\$} \mathsf{Share}(m)$. For each $i \in [n]$, generate $r_i \leftarrow_{\$} \mathcal{R}$ and define $c_i = \mathsf{Com}(pk, i\|s_i; r_i)$. For each $i, j \in [n]$ such that $i \neq j$, define $\pi_i^j \leftarrow_{\$} \mathsf{Prove}(\omega, c_j, (c_i, i\|s_i, r_i))$. Return the shares $s^* = (s_1^*, \ldots, s_n^*)$, where for each $i \in [n]$ we set $s_i^* = (s_i, r_i, (c_j)_{j \neq i}, (\pi_i^j)_{j \neq i})$.

Reconstruction algorithm Rec^*: Upon input $\omega^* = (\omega, pk)$ and shares $(s_i^*)_{i \in \mathcal{I}}$ parse $s_i^* = (s_i, r_i, (c_j^i)_{j \neq i}, (\pi_i^j)_{j \neq i})$ for each $i \in \mathcal{I}$. Hence, proceed as follows:
   (a) If $\exists i_1, i_2 \in \mathcal{I}$ and $j \in [n]$ such that $c_j^{i_1} \neq c_j^{i_2}$, output $\bot$; else let the input shares be $s_i^* = (s_i, r_i, (c_j)_{j \neq i}, (\pi_i^j)_{j \neq i})$ for each $i \in \mathcal{I}$.
   (b) If $\exists i \in \mathcal{I}$ such that $\mathsf{Com}(pk, i\|s_i; r_i) \neq c_i$, output $\bot$.
   (c) If $\exists i, j \in \mathcal{I}$ such that $i \neq j$ and $\mathsf{Ver}(\omega, c_j, (c_i, \pi_i^j)) = 0$, output $\bot$.
   (d) Else, output $\mathsf{Rec}((s_i)_{i \in \mathcal{I}})$.

Fig. 2. Leakage-resilient continuously non-malleable secret sharing for arbitrary access structures against selective joint leakage and tampering, in the CRS model.

c_i using each time the value $c_j = \mathsf{Com}(pk, j\|s_j; r_j)$ as label. The final share of player i consists of s_i, along with the randomness r_i used to obtain c_i and all the values $(c_j)_{j \neq i}$ and $(\pi_j^i)_{j \neq i}$. The reconstruction procedure, given a set of shares $s_\mathcal{I}^*$, first checks that for each $i \in \mathcal{I}$ the commits $(c_j)_{j \neq i}$ contained in each share are all equal, and moreover each c_i is indeed obtained by committing $i\|s_i$ with the randomness r_i; further, it checks that all the proofs verify correctly w.r.t. the corresponding statement and label. If any of the above checks fails, the algorithm returns $\bot$ and otherwise it outputs the same as $\mathsf{Rec}(s_\mathcal{I})$.

Intuitively, our scheme can be seen as a generalization of the original construction of continuously non-malleable codes in the split-state model from [20]. In particular, when $n = 2$, the two constructions are identical except for two differences: (i) We commit to each share, whereas [20] uses a collision-resistant hash function; (ii) We include the position of each share in the commitment. Roughly speaking, the first modification is necessary in order to prove privacy (as hash functions do not necessarily hide their inputs). The second modification is needed in order to avoid that an attacker can permute the shares within one of the partitions, which was not possible in the setting of independent tampering. We establish the following result, whose proof appears in the full version [8].

Theorem 4. *Let $n, k \in \mathbb{N}$, and $\mathcal{A}$ be any access structure for n parties. Assume that:*

(i) *Σ is an n-party augmented ℓ-bounded leakage-resilient secret sharing scheme realizing access structure $\mathcal{A}$ against selective k-joint leakage in the plain model;*

(ii) *(Gen, Com) is a statistically hiding and computationally binding commitment scheme with commitment length $\gamma = O(\lambda)$;*

(iii) *(CRSGen, Prove, Ver) is a true-simulation extractable non-interactive zero-knowledge argument system for the language $\mathcal{L}^{pk}_{\mathsf{com}} = \{c \in \{0,1\}^\gamma : \exists i \in [n], s \in \mathcal{S}_i, r \in \mathcal{R} \text{ s.t. } \mathsf{Com}(pk, i||s; r) = c\}$.*

Then, the secret sharing scheme Σ^* described in Fig. 2 is an n-party augmented ℓ^*-bounded leakage-resilient continuously non-malleable secret sharing scheme realizing access structure $\mathcal{A}$ against selective k-joint leakage and tampering in the CRS model, as long as $\ell = 2\ell^* + n\gamma + O(\lambda \log \lambda)$.

4.2   Concrete Instantiation

Finally, we show how to instantiate Theorem 4 from generic assumptions, thus yielding the statement of Theorem 2 as a corollary. It is well known that true-simulation extractable NIZKs can be obtained from (doubly-enhanced) trapdoor permutations [13,21,35], whereas statistically hiding non-interactive commitments—with commitment size $O(\lambda)$ and $2^{-\Omega(\lambda)}$-statistical hiding—can be instantiated from collision-resistant hash functions [27].

As for the underlying leakage-resilient secret sharing, we can use the recent construction from [29] which achieves information-theoretic security in the stronger setting where the attacker can adaptively leak from subsets of shares of size at most $O(\log n)$, in a joint manner. The latter clearly implies leakage resilience against selective $O(\log n)$-joint leakage.

5   Construction in the Plain Model

5.1   Description of the Scheme

We show how to obtain leakage-resilient continuously non-malleable secret sharing for arbitrary access structures in the plain model, with security against independent leakage and tampering attacks. Our construction combines a non-interactive commitment scheme Com with an auxiliary n-party secret sharing scheme $\Sigma = (\mathsf{Share}, \mathsf{Rec})$, as depicted in Fig. 3. The basic idea is to compute a commitment c to the message m being shared, using random coins r; hence, we secret share the string $m||r$ using the underlying sharing function Share, yielding shares $(s_1, \ldots, s_n)$. Hence, the final share of the i-th player is $s_i^* = (c, s_i)$.

We establish the following result. Note that when $n = 2$, we get as a special case the construction of split-state continuously non-malleable codes in the plain model that was originally proposed in [34], and later simplified in [19] by relying on noisy leakage. Our proof can be seen as a generalization of the proof strategy in [19] to the case $n > 2$. We refer the reader to the full version [8] for the details.

Let Com be a non-interactive commitment scheme with message space $\mathcal{M}$, randomness space $\mathcal{R}$, and commitment space $\mathcal{C}$. Let $\Sigma = (\mathsf{Share}, \mathsf{Rec})$ be an auxiliary secret sharing scheme realizing access structure $\mathcal{A}$, with message space $\mathcal{M} \times \mathcal{R}$ and share space $\mathcal{S} = \mathcal{S}_1 \times \cdots \times \mathcal{S}_n$. Define the following secret sharing scheme $\Sigma^* = (\mathsf{Share}^*, \mathsf{Rec}^*)$, with message space $\mathcal{M}$ and share space $\mathcal{S}^* = \mathcal{S}_1^* \times \cdots \times \mathcal{S}_n^*$ where for each $i \in [n]$ we have $\mathcal{S}_i^* = \mathcal{C} \times \mathcal{S}_i$.

Sharing algorithm Share^*: Upon input a value $m \in \mathcal{M}$, sample random coins $r \leftarrow\!\!\$\ \mathcal{R}$ and compute $c = \mathsf{Com}(m; r)$ and $(s_1, \ldots, s_n) \leftarrow\!\!\$\ \mathsf{Share}(m || r)$. Return the shares $s^* = (s_1^*, \ldots, s_n^*)$, where for each $i \in [n]$ we set $s_i^* = (c, s_i)$.

Reconstruction algorithm Rec^*: Upon input shares $(s_i^*)_{i \in \mathcal{I}}$ parse $s_i^* = (s_i, c_i)$ for each $i \in \mathcal{I}$. Hence, proceed as follows:
(a) If $\exists i_1, i_2 \in \mathcal{I}$ for which $c_{i_1} \neq c_{i_2}$, return $\bot$; else, let the input shares be $s_i^* = (s_i, c)$.
(b) Run $m || r = \mathsf{Rec}((s_i)_{i \in \mathcal{I}})$; if the outcome equals $\bot$ return $\bot$.
(c) If $c = \mathsf{Com}(m; r)$ return m, else return $\bot$.

Fig. 3. Leakage-resilient continuously non-malleable secret sharing for arbitrary access structures against independent leakage and tampering in the plain model.

Theorem 5. *Let $n \in \mathbb{N}$, and let $\mathcal{A}$ be an arbitrary access structure for n parties without singletons. Assume that:*

(i) Com *is a perfectly binding and computationally hiding non-interactive commitment;*
(ii) Σ *is an n-party ℓ-noisy leakage-resilient one-time non-malleable secret sharing scheme realizing access structure $\mathcal{A}$ against independent leakage and tampering in the plain model, with information-theoretic security and with message space $\mathcal{M}$ such that $|\mathcal{M}| \in \omega(\log(\lambda))$.*

Then, the secret sharing scheme Σ^* described in Fig. 3 is an n-party ℓ^*-noisy leakage-resilient continuously non-malleable secret sharing scheme realizing access structure $\mathcal{A}$ against independent leakage and tampering with computational security in the plain model, as long as $\ell = \ell^* + 1 + \gamma + O(\log \lambda)$ where $\gamma = \log |\mathcal{C}|$ is the size of a commitment.

6 Statistical One-Time Non-Malleability with Noisy Leakage

Since non-interactive, perfectly binding, commitments can be obtained in the plain model assuming one-to-one one-way functions [22], all that remains in order to derive Theorem 1 as a corollary of Theorem 5 is an unconditional construction of noisy-leakage resilient one-time non-malleable secret sharing for arbitrary access structures against independent leakage and tampering. The only known scheme achieving all these properties unconditionally is the one in [29], but unfortunately that scheme only tolerates bounded leakage, and it is unclear how to generalize the proof to the setting of noisy leakage.[7] Hence, we take a different approach and we instead show how to generalize a recent transformation from [7], which is tailored to the case $n = 2$.

6.1   Asymmetric Noisy-Leakage-Resilient Secret Sharing

Our construction exploits so-called leakage-resilient encryption, as recently introduced by Ball, Guo, and Wichs [7]. To keep the exposition more uniform, we cast their definition in terms of a special 2-out-of-2 leakage-resilient secret sharing satisfying three additional properties: (i) One of the shares is uniformly random, and can be sampled independently from the message; (ii) The shares are almost uncorrelated, namely the distribution of one share in isolation and conditioned on the other share have very similar min-entropy; (iii) The size of the shares are asymmetric, namely one share is substantially larger than the other share. Given a 2-out-of-2 secret sharing scheme $\Sigma = (\mathsf{Share}, \mathsf{Rec})$, abusing notation, for any fixed $s_1 \in \mathcal{S}_1$ and $m \in \mathcal{M}$, we write $s_2 \leftarrow_\$ \mathsf{Share}(m, s_1)$ for the sharing algorithm that computes share s_2 subject to (s_1, s_2) being a valid sharing of m.

Definition 11 (Asymmetric secret sharing). *Let $\Sigma = (\mathsf{Share}, \mathsf{Rec})$ be a 2-out-of-2 secret sharing scheme. We call Σ $(\alpha, \sigma_1, \sigma_2)$-asymmetric, if it satisfies the following properties:*

(i) For any $s_1 \in \mathcal{S}_1$, and any $m \in \mathcal{M}$, it holds that $\mathsf{Rec}(s_1, \mathsf{Share}(m, s_1)) = m$;
(ii) For any message $m \in \mathcal{M}$, and for all $i \in \{1, 2\}$, it holds that $\widetilde{\mathbb{H}}_\infty(\mathbf{S}_i | \mathbf{S}_{3-i}) \geq \log |\mathcal{S}_i| - \alpha$, where $\mathbf{S}_1, \mathbf{S}_2$ are the random variables corresponding to sampling $s_1 \leftarrow_\$ \mathcal{S}_1$ and $s_2 \leftarrow_\$ \mathsf{Share}(m, s_1)$;
(iii) It holds that $\log |\mathcal{S}_1| = \sigma_1$ and $\log |\mathcal{S}_2| = \sigma_2$.

As for security we consider the same security experiment of a leakage-resilient secret sharing, however, we consider a more general class of admissible adversaries:

Definition 12 (Independent noisy-leakage admissibility for asymmetric secret sharing). *Let $\Sigma = (\mathsf{Share}, \mathsf{Rec})$ be a 2-out-of-2 secret sharing scheme. We say that an unbounded adversary $\mathsf{A} = (\mathsf{A}_1, \mathsf{A}_2)$ is independent (ℓ_1, ℓ_2)-asymmetric noisy-leakage admissible $((\ell_1, \ell_2)$-NLA for short) if it satisfies Definition 10 without property (iii), and using the following variant of property (ii):*

(ii) A_2 outputs a sequence of leakage queries (chosen adaptively) $(g^{(q)})_{q \in [p]}$, with $p(\lambda) \in \mathsf{poly}(\lambda)$, such that for all $i \in \{1, 2\}$, and for all $m \in \mathcal{M}$:

$$\widetilde{\mathbb{H}}_\infty\left(\mathbf{S}_i | \mathbf{S}_{3-i}, g_i^{(1)}(\mathbf{S}_i), \cdots, g_i^{(p)}(\mathbf{S}_i)\right) \geq \widetilde{\mathbb{H}}_\infty(\mathbf{S}_i | \mathbf{S}_{3-i}) - \ell_i,$$

where $\mathbf{S}_1$ is uniformly random over $\mathcal{S}_1$ and $\mathbf{S}_2$ is the random variable corresponding to $\mathsf{Share}(m, \mathbf{S}_1)$.

---

[7] This is because [29] relies on lower bounds in communication complexity.

Let $\Sigma' = (\mathsf{Share}', \mathsf{Rec}')$ be a secret sharing scheme realizing access structure $\mathcal{A}$, with message space $\mathcal{M}$ and share space $\mathcal{S}' = \mathcal{S}'_1 \times \cdots \times \mathcal{S}'_n$ where $\mathcal{S}'_i \subseteq \mathcal{M}''$. Let $\Sigma'' = (\mathsf{Share}'', \mathsf{Rec}'')$ be a 2-out-of-2 *asymmetric* secret sharing scheme with message space $\mathcal{M}''$ and share space $\mathcal{S}'' = \mathcal{S}''_1 \times \mathcal{S}''_2$. Define the following secret sharing scheme $\Sigma = (\mathsf{Share}, \mathsf{Rec})$, with message space $\mathcal{M}$ and share space $\mathcal{S} = \mathcal{S}_1 \times \cdots \times \mathcal{S}_n$, where for each $i \in [n]$ we have $\mathcal{S}_i \subseteq (\mathcal{S}''_1)^{n-1} \times (\mathcal{S}''_2)^{n-1}$.

Sharing algorithm Share: Upon input a value $m \in \mathcal{M}$, compute $(s'_1, \ldots, s'_n) \leftarrow_{\$} \mathsf{Share}'(m)$. For each $i \in [n]$ and $j \in [n] \setminus \{i\}$, sample a random share $s''_{i,j,1} \leftarrow_{\$} \mathcal{S}''_1$ and compute $s''_{i,j,2} \leftarrow_{\$} \mathsf{Share}''(s'_i, s''_{i,j,1})$. Return the shares $s = (s_1, \ldots, s_n)$, where for each $i \in [n]$ we set $s_i = ((s''_{j,i,1})_{j \neq i}, (s''_{i,j,2})_{j \neq i})$.

Reconstruction algorithm Rec: Upon input shares $(s_i)_{i \in \mathcal{I}}$ with $\mathcal{I} \in \mathcal{A}$, parse $s_i = ((s''_{j,i,1})_{j \neq i}, (s''_{i,j,2})_{j \neq i})$. Hence, proceed as follows:
(a) Compute $s'_i = \mathsf{Rec}''(s''_{i,\mathsf{nxt}(i),1}, s''_{i,\mathsf{nxt}(i),2})$ for $i \in \mathcal{I}$;
(b) Return $\mathsf{Rec}'((s'_i)_{i \in \mathcal{I}})$.

Fig. 4. Noisy-leakage-resilient one-time statistically non-malleable secret sharing for arbitrary access structures against independent leakage and tampering in the plain model.

Finally, we say that a 2-out-of-2 secret sharing is augmented (ℓ_1, ℓ_2)-noisy-leakage resilient if it is secure as per Definition 9, against the class of all unbounded adversaries that are (ℓ_1, ℓ_2)-NLA. The theorem below says that there is an unconditional construction of such a leakage-resilient secret sharing that is also asymmetric as per Definition 11. The proof appears in the full version [8].

Theorem 6. *For any $\alpha \in \mathbb{N}$, and for any large enough $\ell_1, \ell_2 \in \mathsf{poly}(\lambda, \alpha)$, there exists $\sigma_1, \sigma_2 \in \mathsf{poly}(\lambda, \alpha)$ and an $(\alpha, \sigma_1, \sigma_2)$-asymmetric secret sharing scheme Σ with message space $\{0, 1\}^\alpha$ that is augmented (ℓ_1, ℓ_2)-noisy leakage resilient.*

Construction. Before presenting our scheme, we establish some notation. Given a reconstruction set $\mathcal{I} = \{i_1, \ldots, i_k\}$, we always assume that $i_j \leq i_{j+1}$ for $j \in [k]$. further, we define the function $\mathsf{nxt}_{\mathcal{I}} : \mathcal{I} \to \mathcal{I}$ as:

$$\mathsf{nxt}_{\mathcal{I}}(i_j) := \begin{cases} i_{j+1} & j < k \\ i_1 & \text{otherwise} \end{cases}$$

and the function $\mathsf{prv}_{\mathcal{I}}$ to be the inverse of $\mathsf{nxt}_{\mathcal{I}}$. Whenever it is clear from the context we omit the reconstruction set $\mathcal{I}$ and simply write nxt and prv.

Intuitively, our construction (cf. Fig. 4) relies on a one-time non-malleable (but not leakage resilient) secret sharing Σ', and on an asymmetric leakage-resilient secret sharing Σ'. The sharing of a message m is obtained by first sharing m under Σ', obtaining n shares $(s'_1, \ldots, s'_n)$, and then sharing each s_i independently $n-1$ times under Σ'', obtaining pairs of shares $(s''_{i,j,1}, s''_{i,j,2})_{j \neq i}$; the final share of party i is then set to be the collection of right shares corresponding to i and all the left shares corresponding to the parties $j \neq i$. We can now state the main theorem of this section.

Theorem 7. *Let $n \in \mathbb{N}$, and let $\mathcal{A}$ be an arbitrary access structure for n parties without singletons. Assume that:*

(i) Σ' is an n-party one-time non-malleable secret sharing scheme realizing access structure $\mathcal{A}$ against independent tampering in the plain model, with information-theoretic security;

(ii) Σ'' is an $(\alpha, \sigma_1, \sigma_2)$-asymmetric augmented (ℓ_1, ℓ_2)-noisy leakage-resilient secret sharing scheme.

Then, the secret sharing scheme Σ described in Fig. 4 is an n-party ℓ-noisy leakage-resilient one-time non-malleable secret sharing scheme realizing access structure $\mathcal{A}$ against independent leakage and tampering with statistical security in the plain model, as long as $\ell_1 = \ell + (2n - 3)\alpha$ and $\ell_2 = \ell + (2n - 3)\alpha + \sigma_1$.

The proof to the above theorem appears in the full version [8], here we discuss the main intuition. Privacy of Σ follows in a fairly straightforward manner from privacy of Σ'. In fact, recall that the shares $s''_{i,j,1}$, with $i, j \in [n]$ and $i \neq j$, are sampled uniformly at random and independently of s'. Thus, in the reduction we can sample these values locally and then define the shares $(s_u)_{u \in \mathcal{U}}$ as a function of the shares $(s'_u)_{u \in \mathcal{U}}$. As for the proof of leakage-resilient one-time non-malleability, the idea is to reduce to the one-time non-malleability of Σ' and simulate the leakage by sampling dummy values for the shares $s''_{i,j,1}, s''_{i,j,2}$.

The main challenge is to make sure that the answer to tampering query $f = (f_1, \ldots, f_n)$ is consistent with the simulated leakage. To this end, in the reduction we define the tampering function $f' = (f'_1, \ldots, f'_n)$, acting on the shares $s' = (s'_1, \ldots, s'_n)$, as follows. Each function f'_i, upon input s'_i and given the values $(s''_{i,j,1})_{j \neq i}$, samples $(\hat{s}_{i,j,2})_{j \neq i}$ in such a way that for any j the reconstruction $\mathsf{Rec}''(s_{i,j,1}, \hat{s}_{i,j,2})$ yields a share s'_i that is consistent with the simulated leakage using the dummy values. Noisy-leakage resilience of Σ'' guarantees that the function f'_i samples from a valid distribution (namely, a non-empty one). Note that the function f'_i might not be efficiently computable; however, as we are reducing to statistical non-malleability, this is not a problem.

An additional difficulty is that the functions $(f'_t)_{t \in \mathcal{T}}$ need to communicate in order to produce their outputs. In fact, for any $t \in \mathcal{T}$, the function f'_t returns a tampered share for Σ' that depends on the mauled share $\tilde{s}_{\mathrm{prv}(t),t,1}$ (generated by $f_{\mathrm{prv}(t)}$). To overcome this problem, we let the reduction perform an additional leakage query on the dummy values before tampering. Thanks to this extra leakage, the reduction learns the values $\tilde{s}_{\mathrm{prv}(t),t,1}$ for all $t \in \mathcal{T}$, which can be hard-coded in the description of $(f'_t)_{t \in \mathcal{T}}$. Here is where we rely on the asymmetric property of Σ'', which allows us to leak σ_1 bits from the second share.

At this point, a reader familiar with [7] might notice that the two proofs proceed very similarly. However, our proof requires extra care when bounding the amount of leakage performed by the reduction. The key ideas are that: (i) Each of the shares under Σ' is shared using $n - 1$ independent invocations of Σ''; and (ii) our reconstruction procedure depends only on one of those (chosen as function of the reconstruction set). Property (i) allows to reduce independent leakage on n shares under Σ to independent leakage on 2 shares under Σ'' by sampling locally the missing $n-2$ shares when reducing to noisy-leakage resilience of Σ''. Property (ii) allows to bound the amount of information the reduction needs to simulate the tampering query to a single short leakage from each of the shares (i.e., the value $\tilde{s}_{\mathtt{prv}(t),t,1}$ for $t \in \mathcal{T}$).

7   Conclusions and Open Problems

We have shown new constructions of leakage-resilient continuously non-malleable secret sharing schemes, for general access structures. Our first scheme is in the plain model, and guarantees security against independent noisy leakage and tampering with all of the shares. Our second scheme is in the CRS model, and guarantees security against joint bounded leakage and tampering using a fixed partition of the n shares into non-overlapping blocks of size $O(\log n)$.

The two major questions left over by our work are whether continuous non-malleability against joint tampering is achievable in the plain model, or against adaptive (rather than selective) joint tampering with the shares. Interestingly, our proof strategy breaks down in the case of adaptive tampering, and this holds true even assuming that the inner leakage-resilient secret sharing is secure in the presence of adaptive joint leakage. Intuitively, the reason is that in the reduction we must run different copies of the adversary inside the leakage oracle; in particular, we use each block of the shares in order to simulate the answer to all tampering queries asked by each copy of the attacker, and this is clearly possible only if the adversary does not change the partition within each query.

It would also be interesting to achieve continuous non-malleability under joint selective partitioning for better values of the parameter k (namely, the attacker can tamper jointly with blocks of size super-logarithmic in n). Note that this would follow immediately by our result if we plug in our construction a leakage-resilient secret sharing scheme tolerating joint leakage from subsets of shares with size $\omega(\log n)$. Unfortunately, the only known secret sharing scheme achieving joint-leakage resilience is the one in [29], and as the authors explain improving the parameters in their construction would lead to progress on longstanding open problems in complexity theory. We leave it open to establish whether this holds true even in the case of selective partitioning (recall that the scheme of [29] achieves adaptive leakage resilience), or whether the current state of affairs can be improved in the computational setting (with or without trusted setup).

A further open question is to improve the rate of our constructions. Note that by applying the rate compiler of [19], we do get *rate-one* continuously non-malleable secret sharing for general access structures, against independent tampering in the plain model. However, this is well-known to be sub-optimal in the computational setting, where the optimal share size would be $O(\mu/n)$, with μ being the size of the message [28]. Note that it is unclear whether the same rate compiler works also for our construction against joint tampering under selective partitioning. This is because the analysis in [19] crucially relies on the resilience of the initial rate-zero non-malleable secret sharing against noisy leakage, whereas our construction only achieves security in the bounded-leakage model.

References

1. Aggarwal, D., Agrawal, S., Gupta, D., Maji, H.K., Pandey, O., Prabhakaran, M.: Optimal computational split-state non-malleable codes. In: TCC, pp. 393–417 (2016)
2. Aggarwal, D., Damgård, I., Nielsen, J.B., Obremski, M., Purwanto, E., Ribeiro, J., Simkin, M.: Stronger leakage-resilient and non-malleable secret sharing schemes for general access structures. In: Boldyreva, A., Micciancio, D. (eds.) CRYPTO 2019. LNCS, vol. 11693, pp. 510–539. Springer, Cham (2019). https://doi.org/10.1007/978-3-030-26951-7_18
3. Aggarwal, D., Dodis, Y., Kazana, T., Obremski, M.: Non-malleable reductions and applications. In: STOC, pp. 459–468 (2015)
4. Aggarwal, D., Dodis, Y., Lovett, S.: Non-malleable codes from additive combinatorics. In: STOC, pp. 774–783 (2014)
5. Aggarwal, D., Dziembowski, S., Kazana, T., Obremski, M.: Leakage-resilient non-malleable codes. In: Dodis, Y., Nielsen, J.B. (eds.) TCC 2015. LNCS, vol. 9014, pp. 398–426. Springer, Heidelberg (2015). https://doi.org/10.1007/978-3-662-46494-6_17
6. Badrinarayanan, S., Srinivasan, A.: Revisiting non-malleable secret sharing. In: Ishai, Y., Rijmen, V. (eds.) EUROCRYPT 2019. LNCS, vol. 11476, pp. 593–622. Springer, Cham (2019). https://doi.org/10.1007/978-3-030-17653-2_20
7. Ball, M., Guo, S., Wichs, D.: Non-malleable codes for decision trees. In: Boldyreva, A., Micciancio, D. (eds.) CRYPTO 2019. LNCS, vol. 11692, pp. 413–434. Springer, Cham (2019). https://doi.org/10.1007/978-3-030-26948-7_15
8. Brian, G., Faonio, A., Venturi, D.: Continuously non-malleable secret sharing for general access structures (2019). https://eprint.iacr.org/2019/602
9. Chattopadhyay, E., Li, X.: Non-malleable codes, extractors and secret sharing for interleaved tampering and composition of tampering. Cryptology ePrint Archive, Report 2018/1069 (2018). https://eprint.iacr.org/2018/1069
10. Cheraghchi, M., Guruswami, V.: Non-malleable coding against bit-wise and split-state tampering. In: Lindell, Y. (ed.) TCC 2014. LNCS, vol. 8349, pp. 440–464. Springer, Heidelberg (2014). https://doi.org/10.1007/978-3-642-54242-8_19
11. Coretti, S., Faonio, A., Venturi, D.: Rate-optimizing compilers for continuously non-malleable codes. In: Deng, R.H., Gauthier-Umaña, V., Ochoa, M., Yung, M. (eds.) ACNS 2019. LNCS, vol. 11464, pp. 3–23. Springer, Cham (2019). https://doi.org/10.1007/978-3-030-21568-2_1
12. Davì, F., Dziembowski, S., Venturi, D.: Leakage-resilient storage. In: Garay, J.A., De Prisco, R. (eds.) SCN 2010. LNCS, vol. 6280, pp. 121–137. Springer, Heidelberg (2010). https://doi.org/10.1007/978-3-642-15317-4_9
13. Dodis, Y., Haralambiev, K., López-Alt, A., Wichs, D.: Efficient public-key cryptography in the presence of key leakage. In: Abe, M. (ed.) ASIACRYPT 2010. LNCS, vol. 6477, pp. 613–631. Springer, Heidelberg (2010). https://doi.org/10.1007/978-3-642-17373-8_35
14. Dodis, Y., Ostrovsky, R., Reyzin, L., Smith, A.D.: Fuzzy extractors: how to generate strong keys from biometrics and other noisy data. SIAM J. Comput. **38**(1), 97–139 (2008)
15. Dziembowski, S., Kazana, T., Obremski, M.: Non-malleable codes from two-source extractors. In: Canetti, R., Garay, J.A. (eds.) CRYPTO 2013. LNCS, vol. 8043, pp. 239–257. Springer, Heidelberg (2013). https://doi.org/10.1007/978-3-642-40084-1_14

16. Dziembowski, S., Pietrzak, K.: Intrusion-resilient secret sharing. In: FOCS, pp. 227–237 (2007)
17. Dziembowski, S., Pietrzak, K., Wichs, D.: Non-malleable codes. In: Innovations in Computer Science, pp. 434–452 (2010)
18. Faonio, A., Nielsen, J.B., Simkin, M., Venturi, D.: Continuously non-malleable codes with split-state refresh. In: ACNS, pp. 1–19 (2018)
19. Faonio, A., Venturi, D.: Non-malleable secret sharing in the computational setting: adaptive tampering, noisy-leakage resilience, and improved rate. In: Boldyreva, A., Micciancio, D. (eds.) CRYPTO 2019. LNCS, vol. 11693, pp. 448–479. Springer, Cham (2019). https://doi.org/10.1007/978-3-030-26951-7_16
20. Faust, S., Mukherjee, P., Nielsen, J.B., Venturi, D.: Continuous non-malleable codes. In: Lindell, Y. (ed.) TCC 2014. LNCS, vol. 8349, pp. 465–488. Springer, Heidelberg (2014). https://doi.org/10.1007/978-3-642-54242-8_20
21. Feige, U., Lapidot, D., Shamir, A.: Multiple non-interactive zero knowledge proofs based on a single random string (extended abstract). In: FOCS, pp. 308–317 (1990)
22. Goldreich, O., Micali, S., Wigderson, A.: How to play any mental game or a completeness theorem for protocols with honest majority. In: STOC, pp. 218–229 (1987)
23. Goyal, V., Kumar, A.: Non-malleable secret sharing. In: STOC, pp. 685–698 (2018)
24. Goyal, V., Kumar, A.: Non-malleable secret sharing for general access structures. In: Shacham, H., Boldyreva, A. (eds.) CRYPTO 2018. LNCS, vol. 10991, pp. 501–530. Springer, Cham (2018). https://doi.org/10.1007/978-3-319-96884-1_17
25. Goyal, V., Pandey, O., Richelson, S.: Textbook non-malleable commitments. In: STOC, pp. 1128–1141 (2016)
26. Groth, J.: Simulation-sound NIZK proofs for a practical language and constant size group signatures. In: Lai, X., Chen, K. (eds.) ASIACRYPT 2006. LNCS, vol. 4284, pp. 444–459. Springer, Heidelberg (2006). https://doi.org/10.1007/11935230_29
27. Halevi, S., Micali, S.: Practical and provably-secure commitment schemes from collision-free hashing. In: Koblitz, N. (ed.) CRYPTO 1996. LNCS, vol. 1109, pp. 201–215. Springer, Heidelberg (1996). https://doi.org/10.1007/3-540-68697-5_16
28. Krawczyk, H.: Secret sharing made short. In: Stinson, D.R. (ed.) CRYPTO 1993. LNCS, vol. 773, pp. 136–146. Springer, Heidelberg (1994). https://doi.org/10.1007/3-540-48329-2_12
29. Kumar, A., Meka, R., Sahai, A.: Leakage-resilient secret sharing. Cryptology ePrint Archive, Report 2018/1138 (2018). https://ia.cr/2018/1138
30. Li, X.: Improved non-malleable extractors, non-malleable codes and independent source extractors. In: STOC, pp. 1144–1156 (2017)
31. Lin, F., Cheraghchi, M., Guruswami, V., Safavi-Naini, R., Wang, H.: Non-malleable secret sharing against affine tampering. CoRR abs/1902.06195 (2019). http://arxiv.org/abs/1902.06195
32. Liu, F.-H., Lysyanskaya, A.: Tamper and leakage resilience in the split-state model. In: Safavi-Naini, R., Canetti, R. (eds.) CRYPTO 2012. LNCS, vol. 7417, pp. 517–532. Springer, Heidelberg (2012). https://doi.org/10.1007/978-3-642-32009-5_30
33. Nielsen, J.B., Simkin, M.: Lower bounds for leakage-resilient secret sharing. Cryptology ePrint Archive, Report 2019/181 (2019). https://eprint.iacr.org/2019/181
34. Ostrovsky, R., Persiano, G., Venturi, D., Visconti, I.: Continuously non-malleable codes in the split-state model from minimal assumptions. In: Shacham, H., Boldyreva, A. (eds.) CRYPTO 2018. LNCS, vol. 10993, pp. 608–639. Springer, Cham (2018). https://doi.org/10.1007/978-3-319-96878-0_21

35. De Santis, A., Di Crescenzo, G., Ostrovsky, R., Persiano, G., Sahai, A.: Robust non-interactive zero knowledge. In: Kilian, J. (ed.) CRYPTO 2001. LNCS, vol. 2139, pp. 566–598. Springer, Heidelberg (2001). https://doi.org/10.1007/3-540-44647-8_33
36. Srinivasan, A., Vasudevan, P.N.: Leakage Resilient secret sharing and applications. In: Boldyreva, A., Micciancio, D. (eds.) CRYPTO 2019. LNCS, vol. 11693, pp. 480–509. Springer, Cham (2019). https://doi.org/10.1007/978-3-030-26951-7_17

Interactive Non-malleable Codes

Nils Fleischhacker[1(✉)], Vipul Goyal[2], Abhishek Jain[3],
Anat Paskin-Cherniavsky[4], and Slava Radune[4,5]

[1] Ruhr University Bochum, Bochum, Germany
mail@nilsfleischhacker.de
[2] Carnegie Mellon University, Pittsburgh, USA
[3] Johns Hopkins University, Baltimore, USA
[4] Ariel University, Ariel, Israel
[5] The Open University of Israel, Ra'anana, Israel

Abstract. Non-malleable codes (NMC) introduced by Dziembowski
et al. [ICS'10] allow one to encode "passive" data in such a manner
that when a codeword is tampered, the original data either remains completely intact or is essentially destroyed.

In this work, we initiate the study of *interactive non-malleable codes*
(INMCs) that allow for encoding "active communication" rather than
passive data. An INMC allows two parties to engage in an interactive
protocol such that an adversary who is able to tamper with the protocol
messages either leaves the original transcript intact (i.e., the parties are
able to reconstruct the original transcript) or the transcript is completely
destroyed and replaced with an unrelated one.

We formalize a tampering model for interactive protocols and put
forward the notion of INMCs. Since constructing INMCs for general
adversaries is impossible (as in the case of non-malleable codes), we construct INMCs for several specific classes of tampering functions. These
include bounded state, split state, and fragmented sliding window tampering functions. We also obtain lower bounds for threshold tampering
functions via a connection to interactive coding. All of our results are
unconditional.

1 Introduction

Error correcting codes allow a message m to be encoded into a codeword c, such
that m can always be recovered even from a tampered codeword c' if the tampering is done in a specific way. More formally, the class of tampering functions,
$\mathcal{F}$, tolerated by traditional error correction codes are ones that erase or modify

---

N. Fleischhacker—Funded by the Deutsche Forschungsgemeinschaft (DFG, German
Research Foundation) under Germany's Excellence Strategy - EXC 2092 CASA -
390781972.
Vipul Goyal is supported in part by NSF grant 1916939, a gift from Ripple, a gift from
DoS Networks, a JP Morgan Faculty Fellowship, and a Cylab seed funding award.
Abhishek Jain is supported in part by NSF SaTC grant 1814919 and Darpa Safeware
grant W911NF-15-C-0213.

D. Hofheinz and A. Rosen (Eds.): TCC 2019, LNCS 11892, pp. 233–263, 2019.
https://doi.org/10.1007/978-3-030-36033-7_9

only a constant fraction of the codeword c. However, no guarantees are provided on the output of the decoding algorithm when the tampering function $f \notin \mathcal{F}$. A more relaxed notion, error detecting codes, allows the decoder to also output a special symbol $\bot$ when m is unrecoverable from c'. But here too, the codes can not tolerate many simple tampering functions such as a constant function.

Non-malleable Codes. The seminal work of Dziembowski, Pietrzak, and Wichs [36] introduced the notion of non-malleable codes (NMC). Informally, an encoding scheme code := (Enc, Dec) is an NMC against a class of tampering functions, $\mathcal{F}$, if the following holds: given a tampered codeword $c' = f(\text{Enc}(m))$ for some $f \in \mathcal{F}$, the decoded message $m' = \text{Dec}(c')$ is either equal to the original message m or the original message is essentially "destroyed" and m' is completely unrelated to m. In general, NMCs cannot exist for the set of all tampering functions $\mathcal{F}_{\text{all}}$. To see this, observe that a tampering function that simply runs the decode algorithm to retrieve m and then encodes a message related to m trivially defeats the requirement above. In light of this observation, a rich line of works has dealt with constructing non-malleable codes for different classes of tampering attacks (see Sect. 1.2 for a discussion).

While non-malleable codes have the obvious advantage that one can obtain meaningful guarantees for a larger class of tampering functions (compared to error correcting codes), they have also found a number of interesting applications in cryptography. In particular, NMCs have found a number of applications in tamper-resilient cryptography [36,40,41,60] and they have also been useful in constructing non-malleable encryption [29]. Recently, non-malleable codes were also used to obtain a round optimal protocol for non-malleable commitments [53], as well to build non-malleable secret sharing schemes [51,52].

Interactive Non-malleable Codes. In this work, we seek to generalize the notion of non-malleable codes. Regular non-malleable codes can be seen as dealing with "passive" data in that data is encoded and, upon being tampered, the data either remains completely intact or is essentially destroyed. Now consider the following scenario. Two parties, each holding their own inputs are interested in running a protocol to perform some task involving their inputs, such as computing a joint function on them. Now, say an adversary is able to somehow get access to their communication channel and modify messages being sent in the protocol. We would like to have a similar guarantee: either the original transcript of the underlying protocol remains fully recoverable from the encoded communication, or, very informally, the original transcript is essentially "destroyed" and any transcript possibly recovered is "unrelated" to the interaction that was originally supposed to take place. Hence, we are concerned with encoding "active communication" rather than passive data.

An interesting special case of the above scenario could also occur in terms of computation being performed on a piece of hardware. Suppose several different chips on an integrated circuit board are communicating via interconnecting wires to perform some computation on the secrets stored within them. An adversary could tamper in some way with the communication going through those wires.

We would like to require that either the computation remains intact, or that the original computation is "destroyed" and whatever computation takes place is completely unrelated.

Of course, this basic idea raises a number of questions: What does it actually mean for a computation to be "unrelated" to another computation. How much power can the tampering adversary reasonably be allowed to have? Are we concerned with the secrecy of inputs in this setting?

In the setting of non-interactive non-malleable codes (INMCs), "unrelated" is easily defined as independent of the original message. However, in the interactive setting, things are a bit more complicated since there exists more than one input. Indeed, there are multiple notions of non-malleability that we can envision in the interactive setting. Below, we discuss possible notions of non-malleability.

Suppose, Alice and Bob are holding inputs x and y respectively and they jointly execute a protocol that results in a transcript τ when not tampered with. Now suppose an adversary tampers with the messages sent over the communication channel and Alice and Bob recover transcripts τ_1 and τ_2, respectively. Then, our first notion of non-malleability requires that either $\tau_1 = \tau$ (i.e., the original transcript remains intact) or, the distribution of τ_1 should be completely independent of the distribution of Bob's input y.

We note that this notion still allows an adversary to simply "cut off" Bob from the communication and essentially execute the protocol honestly, but with a different input y'. Clearly, this is not an attack on the notion described above, since y' and thereby the resulting transcript τ_1 is distributed completely independently of y. Nevertheless, one might want to prevent this as well, since the output after tampering still depends on *one* of the inputs.

To this end we consider a strengthening of the above basic definition where a party must receive either the correct transcript τ or $\perp$. This notion is achievable if the tampering function is not strong enough to cut off and impersonate one of the parties. It is easy to see that this notion is stronger than error detection: whether or not a party receives $\perp$ must not depend on the inputs (x, y), i.e. input dependent aborts must be prevented.[1]

We do not explicitly model any secrecy requirements for the inputs (x, y). We view non-malleability of codes in the interactive setting as a separate property and as such it should be studied independently. However, our definitions of encodings work by defining them using simulators relative to an underlying protocol. This formalization ensures that any security properties such as secrecy of inputs of the underlying protocol are preserved under the encoding.

Relationship to Non-malleable Codes. Consider the message transfer functionality where the transcript is simply the transferred message x. An interactive non-malleable coding protocol for this functionality gives the following guarantee: Bob either receives x from Alice or a value x' unrelated to x. It is easy to see that a one round interactive non-malleable coding protocol for this message

---

[1] This is similar in spirit to the definition of non-malleable codes where, whether or not the decoder gets $\perp$, can also not depend upon the original message m.

transfer functionality is the same as a non-malleable code (encoding message x) for the same class of tampering functions. Indeed, the question that we consider in our work can be seen as generalizing non-malleable codes to more complex protocols potentially involving multiple rounds of interaction and both inputs x and y.

Our notion of INMCs is harder to achieve in one sense since more complex functionalities are involved, and yet, is easier to achieve in another sense since one is allowed multiple rounds of interaction and the order of messages introduces a natural limit on the power of an adversary, since she cannot tamper depending on "future" messages.

Similar to non-malleable codes, INMCs are impossible to achieve for arbitrary tampering functions. Very roughly, consider the first message of the protocol transcript which contains non-trivial information about the input x of Alice. The adversary at this point decodes and reconstructs this partial information about the input x, chooses a related input x' consistent with the partial information and simply executes the protocol honestly with Bob from this point onwards (cutting Alice off completely). A similar argument can also be made for the other direction. In fact, we even rule out INMCs for a more restricted class of threshold tampering functions using a very similar argument in Sect. 4. This suggests that, similar to non-malleable codes, we must focus on specific function classes for building INMCs.

One seemingly obvious approach of constructing INMCs even for multi-round protocols would be to directly use non-malleable codes. I.e., encode each message of an underlying protocol independently. The hope would be that this results in an INMC that allows at least independent tampering of each message under the same class of tampering functions as the original NMC. However, this naïve approach fails to produce INMCs for any meaningful class of functions.

As a counter example consider the following protocol: Alice has inputs (x, y) and sends these to Bob in two separate messages. Bob receives the messages and outputs (x, y). With the above approach, x and y would be encoded separately as $\mathsf{Enc}(x), \mathsf{Enc}(y)$. Let f be any tampering function, such that decoding $\mathsf{Dec}(f(\mathsf{Enc}(x))) \neq x$. Such functions exist within the class of tampering functions against which the NMC is supposed to be secure, unless the NMC is in fact error correcting. A valid tampering function against the supposed INMC could then tamper with the first message using f and not tamper with the second message at all. This would result in Bob receiving $z \neq x$ and y and outputting (z, y). Clearly (z, y) and (x, y) are related. Therefore, the protocol is not non-malleable. This counter example works even when more complex constructions such as the NMC against streaming space-bounded tamperings by Ball et al. [11] are used.

An interesting additional hurdle that needs to be overcome when constructing INMCs when compared to non-malleable codes is inherent leakage. Because messages in the protocol are tampered successively, a tampering function can use conditional aborts to communicate some information to future tampering functions. Let $\mathcal{F}$ be some class of tampering functions. Say a tampering function $f \in \mathcal{F}$ looks at message m_i sent in round i of the protocol and aborts unless m_i is "good" in some sense. In future rounds, even if the definition of $\mathcal{F}$ precludes f from having any knowledge of m_i, the tampering function still learns that m_i must have been "good", since the protocol would have otherwise aborted. We deal with this inherent leakage by bounding the leakage and using leakage resilient tools.

Relationship to Interactive Coding. Our notion can be seen as inspired by the notion of interactive coding (IC) [64–66]. Essentially, INMCs are to non-malleable codes what IC is to error correcting codes. In interactive coding, we require that the original transcript must remain preserved in face of an adversary tampering the message over the communication channel. INMCs only require something weaker, namely, that either the transcript must remain preserved or that the original transcript be destroyed and any possibly reconstructed transcript be independent of the inputs to the protocol.

An obvious advantage of such a weaker notion is that one could hope to achieve it for a larger class of tampering functions compared to ICs. Indeed, ICs are achievable only for threshold adversaries, namely, an adversary which only tampers with a fixed threshold number of bits of the communication (typically a constant fraction of the entire communication). All guarantees are lost in the case an adversary tampers with more bits than allowed by this threshold. However, as we discuss later, INMCs are achievable for adversaries which could potentially tamper with *every* bit going over the communication channel. For the specific case of threshold tampering functions, however, we are able to show that lower bounds on the fraction of the communication that can be tampered with transfer from ICss to INMCs.

1.1   Our Results and Techniques

In this work we initiate the study of INMCs. We formalize the tampering model and put forward a notion of securityfor INMC. Since achieving INMC for general adversaries is impossible, we turn our attention to specific classes of tampering functions.

We show both positive and negative results. We first establish a negative result for threshold tampering functions by showing that INMCs for threshold tampering imply ICs for the same class of tampering functions, thereby transferring lower bounds from interactive coding to INMCs. We then provide several positive results for specific classes of tampering functions by constructing general (unconditional) compilers Σ that can encode an arbitrary underlying protocol Π in a non-malleable fashion (for the appropriate class of tampering functions).

Threshold Tampering Functions. A threshold tampering function is not restricted in its knowledge of the protocol transcript or in its computational power, but can only modify a fixed fraction (say $1/4$) of the bits in the transcript. For this class, lower bounds are known for the case of interactive coding. Specifically Braverman and Rao [18] showed that non-adaptive IC can tolerate tampering with at most $1/4$ of the transcript, and Ghaffari, Haeupler, and Sudan

[50] showed that an adaptive IC can tolerate tampering with at most 2/7 of the transcript. When looking for stronger classes of tampering functions, the first natural question to ask is therefore whether the weaker notion of INMCs might allow us to circumvent these lower bounds. However, it turns out that this is not the case.

We show that any INMC for a class of threshold tampering functions that allows only a negligible non-malleability error in fact implies an IC for the same class of functions in the *common reference string* (CRS) model and with parties running in super-polynomial time. While the resulting IC is not efficient and requires a CRS, it turns out that the lower bounds of Braverman and Rao [18] and Ghaffari, Haeupler, and Sudan [50] also apply in this setting, therefore ruling out the existence of such INMCs. This result can be found in Sect. 4. In fact, this impossibility even holds if we apply the notion of INMC to a weaker notion of encodings which does not imply knowledge-preservation. Recall that we are using a strong notion of protocol encoding that ensures that security guarantees of the underlying protocol are preserved. On the flip side, positive results for IC only translate to the positive result for this weaker notion of INMC. Getting meaningful positive result for our stronger INMC definition is an interesting open problem.

Interestingly (and fortunately), the above connection only holds for threshold tampering functions. Indeed, for the remaining families of tampering functions we consider in this paper, IC is naturally impossible and yet we are able to get positive results for INMC.

Bounded State Tampering Functions. For our first positive result we consider the class of tampering functions which can keep a bounded state. In more detail, the adversary is assumed to be arbitrarily computationally powerful, and we do not limit the size of the memory available for computing the tampering function. Instead, a limit is only placed on the size of the state that can be carried over from tampering one message to tampering with the next. That is, an adversary in this model can iteratively tamper with each message depending on some function of *all* previous messages, but the *size* of this information is limited to some fixed number of bits s. It is easy to see that achieving the notion of error correction is impossible for such a tampering function family since an adversary even with no storage can change every protocol message to an all zero string.

Adversaries with limited storage capabilities constitute a very natural model and similar adversaries have been considered before in many settings, starting with the work by Cachin and Maurer [19] on encryption and key exchange secure against computationally unbounded adversaries. In a seemingly related recent work, Faust et al. [39] studied non-malleable codes against space-bounded tampering. However in their setting, a limit is placed on the size of memory available to compute the tampering function (indeed it is meaningless to consider the state carried over from one message to the next in the non-interactive setting).

We give an unconditional positive result for this family of tampering functions: Any underlying protocol Π can be simulated by a protocol Σ which is an INMC against bounded state tampering functions. A naïve way of trying to construct such a compiler would be to try and encode each message of Π using a suitable (non-interactive) non-malleable code. However, this is doomed to fail. For a single message setting, our tampering adversary simply translates to an unbounded general adversary for which designing non-malleable codes is known to be impossible. Hence, getting a positive result inherently relies on making use of additional interaction.

The key technical tool we rely on to construct our compiler is the notion of seedless 2-non-malleable extractors introduced by Cheraghchi and Guruswami [25] as a natural generalization of seeded non-malleable extractors [34]. However, finding an explicit construction of such extractors was left as an open problem by Cheraghchi and Guruswami even for the case when both the sources are uniform. Such a construction was first given by Chattopadhyay, Goyal, and Li [22]. The construction in [22] requires one of the sources to be (almost) uniform, while the other source could have smaller min-entropy. We crucially rely upon a construction of seedless 2-non-malleable extractors where at least one of the sources could have small min-entropy. Our construction can be found in Sect. 5.

Split-State Tampering Functions. The second class we consider are split-state tampering functions where, very roughly, the transcript is divided into two disjoint sets of messages and each set is tampered independently. In more detail, the adversary can decide for each message of the protocol to be either in the first set or the second one. To compute an outgoing message, the tampering function takes all messages (so far) in any one set of its choice as input.

We are able to achieve interactive non-malleability for a strong class of these tampering functions, namely c-unbalanced split-state tampering functions. A c-unbalanced split-state tampering functions can split the transcript into two arbitrary sets, as long as each set contains at least a $1/c$ fraction of the messages (where c can be any polynomial parameter).

This notion is inspired by a corresponding notion in the non-interactive setting. Split-state tampering functions for non-interactive NMC are one of the most interesting and well studied classes of tampering functions in that setting. It was already introduced in the seminal work of Dziembowski, Pietrzak, and Wichs [36] and has since then been studied in a large number of works [2,3,24–26,35,60].

We give an unconditional positive result for this family of tampering functions: Any underlying protocol Π can be simulated by a protocol Σ which is an INMC against split-state tampering functions. The key technical tool we rely on in this case is a new notion of tamper evident n-out-of-n secret sharing we introduce in this work. Such a secret sharing scheme essentially guarantees that any detectable tampering with the shares can be detected when reconstructing the secret. Our construction can be found in Sect. 6.

Sliding Window Tampering Function. In the sliding window model, the tampering function "remembers" only the last w messages. In other words, the tampering function gets as input the last w (untampered) messages of the protocol transcript to compute the tampered message. The sliding window model is very natural and has been considered in a variety of contexts, such as error correcting codes [48] including convolution codes, streaming algorithms, and even in data transmission protocols such as TCP [55].

Our results in fact extend to a stronger model in which we can handle what we call *fragmented sliding window* tampering functions. Functions in this class are allowed to remember *any* w of the previous protocol messages (rather than just the w most recent ones). Thus in some sense, the window of message being stored by the tampering function is not continuous but "fragmented".

Comparing this class of functions with bounded-state tampering functions, we can see, that here the tampering function can no longer retain *some* information about *all* previous messages, but instead *all* of the information about *some* previous messages. Because there is no hard bound on the size of the state, but instead on the number of messages which potentially differ in length, this means that the two models are incomparable.

Comparing this class with c-unbalanced split-state tampering functions, we notice that here the maximum size of the window is fixed and does not scale with the number of messages in the protocol. On the other hand, however, the different sets of messages which the tampering can depend on are not required to be disjoint. E.g., the tampering of each single protocol messages could depend on the first message of the protocol, something that would not be possible in the case of split-state functions.

While this model has important conceptual differences to the our split state model, the techniques used to achieve both of them are almost identical. In particular, essentially the same protocol as in the case of c-unbalanced split-state tampering functions also works in this case, however the proof of security differs slightly. Our construction can be found in Sect. 7.

A Common Approach. A common theme in all of our constructions is the following: We only attempt to transfer a *single* message in a non-malleable way and then use this message to secure the rest of the protocol. In more detail, Alice and Bob essentially exchange a random key k possibly using multiple rounds of interaction such that the following holds. The two parties either agree on the correct key k or receive completely independent keys k_1 and k_2, (or, $\perp$ which leads them to abort the protocol). Subsequently, all future protocol messages will be encrypted with a one-time pad and authenticated with a one-time message authentication code using k (assuming k is long enough). This allows us to achieve non-malleability as long as we can ensure that the tampering function is not capable of predicting the exchanged key in any round. The reason is as follows: as long as the key remains (almost) uniformly distributed from the point of view of the tampering function f, the computation of f cannot depend on the encrypted messages, and any modification of the encrypted messages would be caught by the MAC and cause an abort independently of the inputs. The exact way in which we are able to prevent f from gaining any knowledge of k depends strongly upon the class of tampering functions. This leads to very different constructions of the key-exchange phase using different technical tools.

Given the common approach described above, it may be tempting to abstract a *non-malleable key-exchange* protocol as a new building block. Intuitively, this would allow us to easily extend our construction to new classes of tampering functions simply by designing a new key exchange protocol for said class. However, (maybe counter-intuitively) it turns out that it is very unclear how this abstraction would work. The class of tampering functions $\mathcal{F}_1$ allowed for the full INMC differs a lot from the class $\mathcal{F}_2$ the key-exchange would need to tolerate. Even worse, it is not clear how $\mathcal{F}_2$ can be generically identified from $\mathcal{F}_1$. Or, the other way round, given a key-exchange that is non-malleable relative to a class $\mathcal{F}_2$, it is not clear against which class of functions the full protocol would then be non-malleable. In fact, our constructions for split-state and for sliding-window show that $\mathcal{F}_1$ can be the result of a complex interplay between the properties of $\mathcal{F}_2$ and the round complexities of both the key-exchange and the original protocol itself.

1.2   Related Works

Non-malleable Codes. To the best of our knowledge, there has been no prior work studying non-malleable codes in the interactive setting. In the non-interactive setting, however, there exists a large body of works studying non-malleable codes for various classes of tampering functions as well as various variants of non-malleable codes. We provide a brief, but non-exhaustive, survey here.

The most well-studied class in the non-interactive setting are split-state tampering functions [2–4,24–26,35,57–60]. But other classes of tampering functions have been studied such as tampering circuits of limited size or depth [8,10,11,23,42], tampering functions computable by decision trees [12], memory-bounded tampering functions [39] where the size of the available memory is a priori bounded, bounded polynomial time tampering functions [9] and non-malleable codes against streaming tampering functions [11]. Non-malleable codes were also generalized in several ways, such as continuously non-malleable codes in [4,29–31,38,40,61] and locally decodable and updatable non-malleable codes [21,32,33].

While most work on non-malleable codes deals with the information theoretic setting, there has also been recent work [1,5,6,11] in the computational setting. In the computational setting, the work of Chandran et al. [20] on block-wise non-malleable codes may seem as most closely related to our setting; however, there are important differences. Firstly, Chandran et al. do not consider the setting where both parties may have inputs. Instead their notion is similar to the original notion of non-malleable codes where a single fixed message is encoded. Indeed, the entire communication is from the sender to the receiver (rather than running an interactive bi-directional protocol between two parties). Further, their definitions are weaker, as they inherently allow selective aborts whereas our definitions do not suffer from this problem.

Interactive Coding. Starting with the seminal work of Schulmann [64–66], a large body of works have studied IC schemes for two-party protocols (see, e.g.,

[15,17,18,37,43–45,47,49,50,54]). Most recently, several works have also studied IC for multiparty protocols [7,16,46,56,62] in various models.

Secure Computation without Authentication. We also mention a related work of Barak et al. [13] on secure computation in a setting where the communication channel among the parties may be completely controlled by a polynomial-time adversary. The setting in their work is therefore inherently computational and their techniques rely on using bounded concurrent secure multi-party computation and are unrelated to ours. However, our setting can indeed be seen as being inspired by theirs.

2   Preliminaries

In this section we introduce our notation and recall some definitions needed for our constructions and proofs.

Notation. we denote by λ the security parameter. For a distribution D, we denote by $x \leftarrow_\$ D$ the process of sampling a random variable x according to D. By U_ℓ we denote the uniform distribution over $\{0,1\}^\ell$. For a set S, $x \leftarrow_\$ S$ denotes sampling from S uniformly at random. For a pair D_1, D_2 of distributions over a domain X, we denote their statistical distance by

$$\mathsf{SD}(D_1, D_2) = \frac{1}{2} \sum_{v \in X} \left| \Pr_{x \leftarrow D_1}[x = v] - \Pr_{x \leftarrow D_2}[x = v] \right|.$$

If $\mathsf{SD}(D_1, D_2) \leq \epsilon$, we say that D_1, D_2 are ϵ-close. We denote by replace the function replace : $\{0,1\}^* \times \{0,1\}^* \rightarrow \{0,1\}^*$ that behaves as follows: If the second input is a singular value s then it replaces any occurrence of same in the first input with s. If the second input is a tuple $(s_1, \ldots, s_n)$ then it replaces any occurrence of same$_i$ in the first input with s_i. We will write replace(D, x) for some distribution D to denote the distribution defined by sampling $d \leftarrow_\$ D$ and applying replace(d, x).

Extractors. In our constructions we make use of two types of extractors. We first recall the standard notion of strong two-source extractors. Two source extractors were first implicitly introduced by Chor and Goldreich [27]. An argument due to Barak [63] shows that any extractor with a small enough error ϵ is also a strong extractor. This means we can instantiate strong extractors for example with the two-source extractor due to Bourgain [14].

Definition 1 (Strong 2-source Extractor). *A function* Ext : $\{0,1\}^n \times \{0,1\}^n \rightarrow \{0,1\}^m$ *is a strong 2-source extractor for sources with min-entropy k and with error ϵ if it satisfies the following property: If X and Y are independent sources of length n with min-entropy k then*

$$\Pr_{y \leftarrow_\$ Y}[\mathsf{SD}(\mathsf{Ext}(X, y), U_m) \geq \epsilon] \leq \epsilon \quad and \quad \Pr_{x \leftarrow_\$ X}[\mathsf{SD}(\mathsf{Ext}(x, Y), U_m) \geq \epsilon] \leq \epsilon.$$

Seedless 2-non-malleable extractors were first defined by Cheraghchi and Guruswami [25] but their construction was left as an open problem. The definition was finally instantiated by Chattopadhyay et al. [22]. Such an extractor allows to non-malleably extract an almost uniform random string from two sources with a given min-entropy that are being tampered by a split-state tampering function.

We closely follow the definition from [22].

Definition 2 (2-non-malleable Extractor). *A function* Ext $: \{0,1\}^n \times \{0,1\}^n \to \{0,1\}^m$ *is a 2-non-malleable extractor for sources with min-entropy* k *and with error* ϵ *if it satisfies the following property: If* X *and* Y *are independent sources of length* n *with min-entropy* k *and* $f = (f_0, f_1)$ *is an arbitrary 2-split-state tampering function, then there exists a distribution* D_f *over* $\{0,1\}^m \cup \{$same$\}$ *which is independent of sources* X *and* Y*, such that*

$$\mathsf{SD}\big((\mathsf{Ext}(X,Y), \mathsf{Ext}(f_0(X), f_1(Y))), (U_m, \mathsf{replace}(D_f, U_m))\big) \leq \epsilon$$

where both U_m *refer to the same uniform* m-*bit string.*

Tamper Evident Secret Sharing. We will define a new notion of tamper evident secret sharing in the following. Such tamper evident secret sharing schemes behave the same as regular secret sharing, except that we are guaranteed that the reconstruction algorithm is able to detect any *detectable tampering* of the shares that would lead to a different reconstructed message and will reject them if they have been tampered with.

Intuitively a tampering is detectable if it meets two criteria: First it must leave at least one of the shares unchanged, since otherwise the shares could simply be replaced by a completely independent sharing, which is trivially undetectable. Second, each tampered share must be independent of at least one of the untampered shares, except for some bounded leakage. This is formally defined in the following.

Definition 3 (*n*-**out-of-***n* **Secret Sharing).** *A pair of algorithms* (Share, Reconstruct) *is a perfectly private,* n-*out-of-*n *secret sharing scheme with message space* $\{0,1\}^\ell$ *and share length* ℓ'*, if all of the following hold.*

1. ***Correctness:** Given all shares, the secret can be reconstructed. I.e., for any secret* $m \in \{0,1\}^\ell$*, it holds that* $\Pr[\mathsf{Reconstruct}(\mathsf{Share}(m)) = m] = 1$*.*
2. ***Statistical Privacy:** Given any strict subset of shares, the secret remains perfectly hidden. I.e., for any two secrets* $m_0, m_1 \in \{0,1\}^\ell$ *and any set of indices* $\mathcal{I} \subsetneq \{1, \ldots, n\}$ *it holds that for any (computationally unbounded) distinguisher* $\mathcal{D}$

$$\Pr_{\vec{s} \leftarrow \mathsf{Share}(m_0)}[\mathcal{D}((s_i)_{i \in \mathcal{I}}) = 1] = \Pr_{\vec{s} \leftarrow \mathsf{Share}(m_1)}[\mathcal{D}((s_i)_{i \in \mathcal{I}}) = 1].$$

Definition 4 (Detectable Tampering for Secret Sharing). *Let* (Share, Reconstruct) *be an* n-*out-of-*n *Secret Sharing scheme, let* $m \in \{0,1\}^\ell$ *be a message. A tampering function* f *for a secret sharing* $(s_1, \ldots, s_n)$ *of* m *with* ν *bits* of leakage is described by functions $(f_1, \ldots, f_n)$, sets of indices $\mathcal{I}_1^{in}, \ldots, \mathcal{I}_n^{in}$ and leakage functions $(\mathsf{leak}_1, \ldots, \mathsf{leak}_n)$ such that $\mathsf{leak}_i : \{0,1\}^* \to \{0,1\}^\nu$ and

$$f(s_1, \ldots, s_n) = \Big(f_1\big((s_j)_{j \in \mathcal{I}_1^{in}}, \mathsf{leak}_1((s_j)_{j \notin \mathcal{I}_1^{in}})\big), \ldots, f_n\big((s_j)_{j \in \mathcal{I}_n^{in}}, \mathsf{leak}_n((s_j)_{j \notin \mathcal{I}_n^{in}})\big) \Big).$$

For any fixed secret sharing $\vec{s} \leftarrow \mathsf{Share}(m)$ let $\mathcal{M}$ be the set of indices i, such that $s_i' \neq s_i$ for $(s_1', \ldots, s_n') := f(s_1, \ldots, s_n)$. A tampering function f is called detectable for $\vec{s}$ if it holds that for all $i \in \mathcal{M}$ we have $\mathcal{M} \cup \mathcal{I}_i^{in} \subsetneq \{1, \ldots, n\}$. We define the predicate $\mathsf{Dtct}(\vec{s}, f)$ to be 1 iff f is detectable for $\vec{s}$.

This now allows us to formally define tamper evident n-out-of-n secret sharing.

Definition 5 (Tamper Evident n-out-of-n Secret Sharing). *A perfectly private secret sharing scheme* $(\mathsf{Share}, \mathsf{Reconstruct})$ *is said to be* $\epsilon(\lambda)$-*tamper evident for up to* ν *bits of leakage if the reconstruction algorithm will reject shares with overwhelming probability if they have been tampered detectably with up to* ν *bits of leakage. I.e., for all* $m \in \{0,1\}^\ell$ *and all detectable tampering functions* f *with* ν *bits of leakage it holds that*

$$\Pr_{\vec{s} \leftarrow \mathsf{Share}(m)} \big[\mathsf{Dtct}(\vec{s}, f) = 1 \wedge \mathsf{Reconstruct}(f(\vec{s})) \notin \{m, \bot\} \big] \leq \epsilon(\lambda)$$

Please refer to the full version of this paper for an instantiation of this notion from XOR-based secret sharing and an information theoretic message authentication code. The concept of tamper evident secret sharing may seem superficially similar to non-malleable secret sharing [51] but the two concepts are in fact incomparable. The guarantee of tamper evident secret sharing is very strong, requiring that the secret cannot be changed except to $\bot$, but only holds against a weak class of tamperings that must leave at least one share unchanged. In contrast, NM-secret sharing provides a weaker guarantee, namely that a tampered secret must be unrelated, but against a stronger class of tampering functions.

3   Definitions

In this section we first formally define interactive protocols and encodings of interactive protocols. We then introduce our notions of non-malleability for encodings of interactive protocols.

3.1   Interactive Protocols

We consider protocols Π between a pair of parties P_0, P_1 (also called Alice and Bob, respectively, for convenience) for evaluating functionalities $g = (g_0, g_1)$ of the form $g_b : X \times Y \to Z$, where X, Y, Z are finite domains. Alice holds an input $x \in X$, and Bob holds $y \in Y$, and the goal of the protocol is to interactively evaluate the functionality, such that at the end of the protocol Alice outputs $g_0(x, y)$ and Bob outputs $g_1(x, y)$. The interactive protocol consists of r rounds, in each of which a single message is sent. Without loss of generality we assume that the parties in Π alternate in sending their messages and that Alice always sends the first message. Formally, an interactive protocol Π between two parties is described by a pair of "next message" functions π_0, π_1 (or π_A, π_B) and a pair of output functions out_A and out_B. The next message function π_A (π_B) takes the input x (y), round number i, and message sequence sent and received by Alice (Bob) so far trans_A (trans_B) and outputs the next message to be sent by Alice (Bob). For simplicity of notation, we assume π_A, π_B always output binary strings. Furthermore, we assume that each message output by π_A, π_B is always of the same length ℓ. The output function out_A (out_B) takes as input x (y) and the final message sequence sent and received by Alice (Bob) trans_A (trans_B) and outputs Alice's (Bob's) protocol output. We denote by $\text{Trans}(x, y)$ the function mapping inputs x, y to the transcript of an honest execution of Π between $A(x)$ and $B(y)$. Note that in this setting we do not explicitly consider probabilistic protocols. However, this is not a limitation, since any probabilistic protocol can be written as a deterministic protocol with additional random tapes given as input to the two parties A and B.

This now allows us to define both correctness of a protocol as well as encodings of interactive protocols.

Definition 6 (Correctness). *A protocol Π, is said to ϵ-correctly evaluate a functionality (g_0, g_1) if it holds that without tampering the output of each party $\text{out}_b(x_b, \text{trans}_b) = g_b(x_0, x_1)$ with probability $\geq 1 - \epsilon$.*

Definition 7 (Encoding of an Interactive Protocol). *An encoding Π' of a protocol $\Pi = (A, B)$ is defined by two simulators S_0, S_1 with black-box access to stateful oracles encapsulating the next message functions of A and B respectively. The protocol $\Pi' = (S_0^A, S_1^B)$ is an ϵ-correct encoding of protocol $\Pi = (A, B)$ if for all inputs x, y, $\Pi' = (S_0^{A(x)}, S_1^{B(y)})$ ϵ-correctly evaluates the functionality $(\text{Trans}(x, y), \text{Trans}(x, y))$.*

We note that, given a correct encoding Π' of protocol Π evaluating functionality (g_0, g_1) it is easy to also evaluate (g_0, g_1). To do so, simply run Π' resulting in output $\tau = \text{Trans}(x, y)$ and then evaluate $\text{out}_A(x, \tau)$ and $\text{out}_B(y, \tau)$ respectively. Definition 7 slightly differs from the interactive coding literature [15,65]. In most of the IC literature, encodings are not defined relative to a stateful oracle, but instead relative to a next-message function oracle. This difference is significant, because, as observed by Chung et al. [28] in the context of IC, an encoding as defined in the IC literature can leak the parties' inputs under adversarial errors. I.e., security guarantees of Π are not necessarily preserved under Π'. In contrast, under Definition 7, any security guarantee of Π is preserved under Π'. This follows from the fact that the encoding is defined using a pair of simulators with only black-box access to A and B without the ability to know the inputs or rewind the participants of the underlying protocol. Therefore, access to this oracle is equivalent to communicating with an actual instance of A (or B respectively). Any attacker against Π – whether a man in the middle attacker or an attacker acting as either A or B – always has at least black-box access to the two parties. This means she can easily simulate Π' simply by running S_0, S_1 herself. Thus any attack against some arbitrary security property of Π' directly corresponds to an attack against the same property of Π, implying that security guarantees of Π are preserved under Π'.

Protocols Under Tampering. It may appear tempting to try and define non-malleability in the interactive setting in the same manner as regular non-malleability by, e.g, considering tampering on the full transcript of the protocol. Split-state tampering for an r-round protocol would then for example mean that an adversary could separately tamper on the first $n/2$ and the second $n/2$ of the protocol messages. However, at least in the synchronous tampering setting we're focusing on such a definition would be very problematic. It would allow an adversary to tamper with the first message depending on future messages, which themselves could depend on the first message, therefore potentially causing an infinite causal loop, even if we allow such "time-travelling" adversaries. So instead we make the reasonable restriction that tampering on each message must happen separately and can only depend on past messages.

We formally describe the process of executing a protocol under tampering with a tampering function $f \in \mathcal{F}$, from some family of tampering functions $\mathcal{F}$. First, empty sequences of sent and received messages $\text{trans}_A = \text{trans}_B = \emptyset$ are initialized. Lets assume that it is Alice's turn to send a message in round i. The next message function π_A is evaluated to compute the next message $m_i := \pi_A(x, i, \text{trans}_A)$. Then m_i is added to Alice's transcript $\text{trans}_A := \text{trans}_A \| m_i$. Next the tampering function is applied to compute the tampered message $m_i' := f(m_1, \ldots, m_i)$ and m_i' is added to $\text{trans}_B := \text{trans}_B \| m_i'$. If it is Bob's turn the execution proceeds identically with reversed roles. Finally the output functions of Alice and Bob are evaluated respectively as $\text{out}_A(x, \text{trans}_A), \text{out}_B(y, \text{trans}_B)$. Note that due to tampering it does not necessarily hold for the sequences of messages $\text{trans}_A = m_1^A, \ldots, m_r^A$ and $\text{trans}_B = m_1^B, \ldots, m_r^B$ that $m_i^A = m_i^B$.

We note that this only models "synchronous" tampering, meaning that the adversary cannot drop or delay messages or desynchronize the two parties by first running the protocol with one party and then the other. This choice is partially inspired by the literature on interactive coding and helps keep our definitions simple. However, cryptographic primitives such as non-malleable commitments have been studied in the setting where there is a non-synchronizing man-in-the-middle adversary. We remark that even in these settings, getting a construction for the synchronous case is often the hardest (for example, there exist general compilers for non-malleable commitments to go from synchronous security to non-synchronous security [67]). We leave the study of more general tampering models for INMCs as an interesting topic for future work.

3.2   Interactive Non-malleable Codes

In the non-interactive setting, non-malleability intuitively means that after tampering the result should be either the original input, or the original input should be completely destroyed, i.e., the output should be independent of the original input. In the interactive setting, there are two different outputs and two different outputs and the question is which output (or pair of outputs) should be independent from which input(s). This leads to an entire space of possible notions, however we settle for the strongest possible – and arguably most natural – notion: In this notion we simply call *protocol-non-malleability*, we require that the output of Alice and Bob respectively are either the correct transcript $\mathsf{Trans}(x, y)$ or $\perp$ and that the product distribution over the two is (almost) completely independent of the two parties' respective inputs x and y. It is very important that the decisions whether to output $\perp$ or not must be made independently of x and y, since otherwise an adversary could potentially force selective aborts and thus learn at least one bit of information about the combined input. This means that protocol-non-malleability not only implies error detection, but is even stronger, since in error detection the output distribution over the real output and $\perp$ is not required to be independent of the inputs.

We note, that weaker definitions may still be meaningful and are not necessarily trivial. In Sect. 4 we will show that even for a much weaker notion of protocol-non-malleability strong lower bounds exist in the case of threshold tampering functions. We formally define protocol-non-malleability in the following.

Definition 8 (Protocol Non-malleability). *An encoding $\Pi' = (S_0^A, S_1^B)$, of protocol $\Pi = (A, B)$ is ϵ-protocol-non-malleable for a family $\mathcal{F}$ of tampering functions if the following holds: For each tampering function $f \in \mathcal{F}$ there exists a distribution D_f over $\{\perp, \mathsf{same}\}^2$ such that for all x, y, the product distribution of $S_0^{A(x)}$'s and $S_1^{B(y)}$'s outputs is ϵ-close to the distribution $\mathsf{replace}(D_f, \mathsf{Trans}(x, y))$.*

4   Lower Bounds for Threshold Tampering Functions

Threshold tampering functions are classes of tampering functions where the function is only limited in the fraction of the messages they can tamper with. For these classes of tampering functions, lower bounds are known in the case of interactive codes. Specifically Braverman and Rao [18] showed that non-adaptive interactive codes can tolerate tampering with at most $1/4$ of the transcript, and Ghaffari, Haeupler, and Sudan [50] showed that an adaptive interactive code can tolerate tampering with at most $2/7$ of the transcript. A natural question to ask is whether one can bypass these lower bounds in the case of non-malleable interactive codes. Unfortunately, we show in the following that the known lower bounds for interactive coding translate to identical lower bounds for $\mathsf{negl}(\ell)$-non-malleable interactive coding. In fact, we show that the lower bounds even apply to a much weaker form of protocol-non-malleability, where each party's output by itself (rather than the product distribution of both outputs) only needs to be independent of the *other* party's input.

The basic idea of this lower bound is essentially to show that a non-malleable interactive code is also a regular interactive code. In any encoded protocol, if the output of one party in the underlying protocol depends non-trivially on the other party's input (which should always be the case since otherwise the communication is completely unnecessary) then information theoretically, the transcript must leak this information. If the encoding was not error correcting, then that means that there is a way for a threshold tampering function to cause at least one of the parties to abort. Since the tampering function is unlimited in it's knowledge of the transcript, it can extract the information about one of the parties' input and depending on the function of the input thus revealed either cause the abort or not. This would be an input dependent abort which clearly means that the encoding is not non-malleable.

However, this straightforward approach does not work. The reason is, that the information about the input might only be revealed in say the ith message of protocol, while the threshold tampering function requires tampering with earlier messages to cause the abort. But there is a way around this problem. If we can cleanly define which message in the protocol is the first message that reveals information about the input, then we can construct another INMC in the CRS model, where all previous messages are pushed into the CRS. This is possible since those messages are "almost" independent of the actual input and it is possible for the INMC to (inefficiently) sample a consistent internal state, once it gets the input. This means that now the information about the input is revealed in the very first protocol message and thus the approach described above works.

For the lower bound to translate to INMC, we therefore need that the lower bounds for IC apply also to inefficient interactive encodings in the CRS model. Luckily, this follows easily from the structure of the results in [18] and [50]. We discuss the application of the bounds to the CRS model in a bit more detail in the full version.

As mentioned above, we can in fact show this lower bound for a much weaker form of non-malleability we formally define in the following.

Definition 9 (Weak Protocol Non-malleability). *An encoding $\Pi' = (S_0^A, S_1^B)$, of protocol $\Pi = (A, B)$ is ϵ-weakly-protocol-non-malleable for a family $\mathcal{F}$ of tampering functions if the following holds: For each tampering function $f \in \mathcal{F}$ and for each x (resp. y) there exists a distribution $D_{f,x}^A$ (resp. $D_{f,y}^B$) over $\{\perp, \mathsf{same}\} \cup \{0,1\}^n$ such that for all y (resp. x), the output distribution of $S_0^{A(x)}$ (resp. $S_1^{B(y)}$) is ϵ-close to the distribution $\mathsf{replace}(D_{f,x}^A, \mathsf{Trans}(x,y))$ (resp. $\mathsf{replace}(D_{f,y}^B, \mathsf{Trans}(x,y)))$.*

It is easy to see, that this notion is strictly weaker than protocol-non-malleability as defined in Definition 8. If a distribution D_f as required by Definition 8 exists, then $D_{f,x}^A$ and $D_{f,y}^B$ can easily be sampled by sampling from D_f and throwing away half of the output. On the other hand, since $D_{f,x}^A$ can depend on x, it does not help in sampling a distribution D_f that is required to be (almost) independent of x.

Theorem 1. *Let $\Pi = (A, B)$ be an r-round protocol with inputs $x, y \in \{0,1\}^\ell$ such that there exists at least one triple of inputs (x_1^*, x_2^*, y^*) or (x^*, y_1^*, y_2^*) such that $\mathsf{Trans}(x_1^*, y^*) \neq \mathsf{Trans}(x_2^*, y^*)$ or $\mathsf{Trans}(x^*, y_1^*) \neq \mathsf{Trans}(x^*, y_2^*)$ respectively. Let Π' be an $\delta(\ell)$-correct, $\mathsf{negl}(\ell)$-weakly-protocol-nonmalleable INMC for protocol Π for a family $\mathcal{F}$ of threshold tampering functions. Then there also exists an (computationally unbounded) interactive code $\overline{\Pi}$ in the CRS model for the same protocol Π and the same family of threshold tampering functions $\mathcal{F}$.*

Due to space constraints, the proof of Theorem 1 is deferred to the full version of this paper.

Applying the Lower Bound to Other Tampering Functions. It is natural to ask whether the lower bound stated above also applies to other classes of functions. This would be unfortunate, since it would trivially rule out INMCs for most classes of tampering functions. However, fortunately, this is not the case.

In the proof of Theorem 1, we explicitly use that the tampering function at any point has complete knowledge of the full transcript so far and is completely unbounded in the resources necessary to compute the tampering. It then follows that if the transcript information theoretically reveals *anything* about the inputs, then the tampering function can extract this information and cause a conditional abort, thus allowing for the proof to go through. In each of the classes of tampering functions we consider in the following sections, however, the tampering functions are restricted in one way or another in its view of the full transcript. This means that the proof no longer applies, since even when the full transcript contains information about the inputs, the tampering function is no longer capable of extracting it.

In fact, we explicitly exploit this observation in each of our protocols. Our protocols consist of an initial input-independent phase, where key material is established. This phase is constructed in such a way that in any future round, the established key material will be almost uniform from the point of view of the tampering function. Using information theoretically secure encryption and authentication we can then execute the underlying protocol in such a way that the transcript of that execution is remains independent of the input *from the point of view of the tampering function.*

5   Bounded State Tampering

The first class of tampering functions we consider are tampering functions with bounded state. This is a very natural model in which adversaries are assumed to be arbitrarily powerful, but there exists an a priori upper bound on the size of the state they can hold. Similar adversaries have been considered before in many settings, starting with the work by Cachin and Maurer [19] on encryption and key exchange secure against computationally unbounded adversaries. Recently, in related work, Faust et al. [39] studied non-malleable codes against space-bounded tampering. However, the notion of bounded state tampering we introduce in this section is stronger than one would expect from naïvely extending the notion to interactive non-malleable codes. In particular we do not limit the size of the memory available for computing the tampering function. Instead, a limit is only placed on the size of the state that can be carried over from tampering one message to tampering with the next. I.e., the idea is, that an adversary in this model can iteratively tamper with each message depending on some function of *all* previous messages, *but* the size of this information is limited to some fixed number of bits s. We formally define this in terms of a tampering function in the following.

Definition 10 (Bounded State Tampering Functions). *Functions of the class of s-bounded state tampering functions $\mathcal{F}^s_{bounded}$ for an r-round interactive protocols are defined by an r-tuple of pairs of functions $((g_1, h_1), \ldots, (g_r, h_r))$ where the range of the functions h_i is $\{0,1\}^s$. Let $m_1, \ldots, m_i$ be the messages sent by the participants of the protocol in a partial execution. The tampering function for the ith message is then defined as*

$$f_i(m_1, \ldots, m_i) := g_i\big(m_i, h_{i-1}\big(m_{i-1}, h_{i-2}(m_{i-2}, \ldots)\big)\big).$$

5.1   Interactive Non-malleable Code for Bounded State Tampering

We devise a generic protocol-non-malleable encoding Π for bounded state tampering for any two-party protocol Π_0. The basic idea is to first run a key exchange phase in which Alice and Bob exchange enough key material that they can execute the original protocol encrypted under one-time pad and authenticated with information theoretically secure MACs. The main challenge is to craft the key-exchange phase in such a way, that the adversary's limitations, i.e., having bounded state, preclude her from both, learning any meaningful information about the exchanged key material, as well as influencing the key material in a meaningful way. For bounded state tampering functions, we achieve this using 2-non-malleable extractors. The idea behind this is that each party chooses two random sources that are significantly longer than the size of the bounded state and sends it to the other party. Both parties then apply a 2-non-malleable extractor to each pair of sources and thus extract a key they can use to secure the following communication using information theoretic authenticated encryption. A tampering function with bounded state will not be able to "remember" enough information about the two sources to predict the exchanged key with a any significant probability and thus will not be able to change the authenticated ciphertexts without being caught. Formally this is stated in the following theorem.

Theorem 2. *Let Π_0 denote a correct, r-round protocol, with length-ℓ messages. We assume wlog that Alice sends both the first and last message in Π_0 Let $s \in \mathbb{N}$ be any bound as defined in Definition 10. Let λ' be the target security parameter, then we set $\lambda = \max(\ell, \lambda')$. Let $\mathsf{MAC} : \{0,1\}^{2\lambda} \times \{0,1\}^{\lambda} \to \{0,1\}^{\lambda}$ be a $2^{-\lambda}$-secure information theoretic message authentication code. Let $\mathsf{Ext} : \{0,1\}^n \times$*

Algorithm 1: Protocol Π against bounded state tampering functions

We compile Π_0 into Π below. Let Ext and Π_0 be as in Theorem 2. The communication proceeds in three phases, a key exchange phase, a key confirmation phase and a protocol execution phase. All messages in the following protocol have a fixed length. Whenever a party in the protocol aborts, she outputs $\bot$ instead of a transcript.

Key Exchange Phase: Alice chooses two strings α_1, α_2 and Bob chooses two strings β_1, β_2 all of length n. The two parties then alternatingly send the two strings.

1. First Alice then sends α_1, then Bob sends β_1, Alice sends α_2, and Bob finally sends β_2.
2. Both parties use the extractor to extract $k_1 := \mathsf{Ext}(\alpha_1, \alpha_2)$ and $k_2 := \mathsf{Ext}(\beta_1, \beta_2)$ and set $k := k_1 \oplus k_2$. They then split $k = k_A \| k_B \| k_1^{\mathsf{auth}} \| k_1^{\mathsf{enc}} \| \ldots \| k_r^{\mathsf{auth}} \| k_r^{\mathsf{enc}}$ into substrings, where $|k_A| = |k_B| = |k_i^{\mathsf{auth}}| = 2\lambda$ and $|k_i^{\mathsf{enc}}| = \ell$.

Key Confirmation Phase: Alice and Bob verify that they agree on the exchanged key.

1. Bob chooses a random challenge $c_B \leftarrow_{\$} \{0,1\}^\lambda$ and sends it to Alice.
2. Alice computes $t_B := \mathsf{MAC}(k_B, c_B)$, chooses a challenge $c_A \leftarrow_{\$} \{0,1\}^\lambda$, and sends t_B, c_A to Bob.
3. If $\mathsf{Vf}(k_B, c_B, t_B) = 1$, then Bob sends $t_A := \mathsf{MAC}(k_A, c_A)$ to Alice. Otherwise he aborts.
4. If $\mathsf{Vf}(k_A, c_A, t_A) = 1$ then Alice proceeds to the next phase. Otherwise she aborts.

Protocol Execution Phase: Both parties initialize their view of the underlying protocol as an empty list $\mathsf{trans}_A = \emptyset$ and $\mathsf{trans}_B = \emptyset$. Starting with Alice's first message Alice and Bob proceed as follows for each message:

1. In the ith round, if it is Alice's (resp. Bob's) turn to send a message she invokes the next-message function of the underlying protocol $m_i := \pi_A^0(i, x, \mathsf{trans}_A)$ (resp. $m_i := \pi_B^0(i, y, \mathsf{trans}_B)$) and adds the message to her view $\mathsf{trans}_A := \mathsf{trans}_A \| m_i$ (resp. $\mathsf{trans}_B := \mathsf{trans}_B \| m_i$).
2. Next the party computes the one-time pad encryption $c_i := m_i \oplus k_i^{\mathsf{enc}}$ of m_i as well as an authentication tag $t_i := \mathsf{MAC}(k_i^{\mathsf{auth}}, c_i)$ and sends c_i, t_i to the other party.
3. If the authentication tag verifies, i.e., $\mathsf{Vf}(k_i^{\mathsf{auth}}, c_i, t_i) = 1$ the other party decrypts $m_i := c_i \oplus k_i^{\mathsf{enc}}$ and adds the message to their view, i.e., $\mathsf{trans}_A := \mathsf{trans}_A \| m_i$ or $\mathsf{trans}_B := \mathsf{trans}_B \| m_i$.
4. Finally the underlying protocol terminates and both parties output their respective transcripts trans_A or trans_B or $\bot$ if they aborted at any point during the protocol.

$\{0,1\}^n \to \{0,1\}^{r\ell + (2r+4)\lambda}$ *be a 2-non-malleable extractor for sources with min-entropy* $n - (s + \lambda)$ *and with error* ϵ. *Then there exists a* $r + 7$-*round encoding* Π *of* Π_0 *that is* $5\epsilon + 4 \cdot 2^{-\lambda}$-*protocol-non-malleable against* $\mathcal{F}_{bounded}^s$.

Note that the required extractor can be instantiated using the construction of Chattopadhyay et al. [22], while the MAC can be instantiated with a family of pair-wise independent hash functions.

Proof of Theorem 2. The protocol Π is specified in Algorithm 1. We need to argue that the protocol is correct and protocol-non-malleable.

Correctness: The correctness of Π follows from the fact that the extractor is deterministic and the message authentication code is correct. Since the extractor is deterministic, both parties will extract the same string k. The correctness of the message authentication code then implies neither party will ever abort during the protocol. Further, since the one-time pad is correct it follows that messages of the underlying protocol will always be decrypted correctly and thus both parties are faithfully executing an honest instance of Π_0. Thus at the end of the protocol the collected transcripts correspond to an honest execution of Π_0.

Protocol-Non-malleability: Let f be an s-bounded state tampering function described by $((g_1, h_1), \ldots, (g_r, h_r))$. To prove that the coding scheme is protocol-non-malleable, we need to prove that a distribution D_f as in Definition 8 exist.

Algorithm 2: Sampler of distribution D_f for Algorithm 1

1. Sample four strings $\alpha_1, \alpha_2, \beta_1, \beta_2 \leftarrow_\$ \{0,1\}^n$.
2. Apply the tampering function to the messages as $\alpha'_1 := f_1(\alpha_1)$, $\beta'_1 := f_2(\alpha_1, \beta_1)$, $\alpha'_2 := f_3(\alpha_1, \beta_1, \alpha_2)$, $\alpha'_2 := f_4(\alpha_1, \beta_1, \alpha_2, \beta_2)$ and extract $k_1 := \mathsf{Ext}(\alpha_1, \alpha_2)$ and $k_2 := \mathsf{Ext}(\beta_1, \beta_2)$ as well as $k'_1 := \mathsf{Ext}(\alpha'_1, \alpha'_2)$ and $k'_2 := \mathsf{Ext}(\beta'_1, \beta'_2)$. Set $k := k_1 \oplus k_2$ and $k' := k'_1 \oplus k_2$.
3. If $k' \neq k$ output $(\perp, \perp)$ and stop.
4. If $k' = k$, then simulate a protocol execution tampered with f as follows
   (a) Replace all messages with random strings of appropriate length and apply the tampering function to those messages.
   (b) If for any index $7 < i < r + 7$ it holds that $m_i \neq f_i(m_1, \ldots, m_i)$ output $(\perp, \perp)$ and stop.
   (c) If it holds that $m_{r+7} \neq f_{r+7}(m_1, \ldots, m_{r+7})$ output $(\mathsf{same}, \perp)$ and stop.
5. If the simulated interaction completed successfully, output $(\mathsf{same}, \mathsf{same})$.

The Distribution D_f. When sampling from D_f we need to deal with the problem that in addition to the s bits of state f can keep by design, it can learn additional information by making use of conditional aborts. I.e., in round i the function g_i can force an abort in the protocol unless the message sent in round i is "good". In any future round $j > i$, even if it's s bit state does not retain any information about m_i the function g_j therefore "remembers" that m_i must have been "good", since otherwise the protocol would have aborted.

Technically the tampering function can use conditional aborts to leak an arbitrary amount of information. However, this comes at the expense of having to abort with high probability. Let $1 - \delta(\lambda)$ be the probability of f causing either party to abort *before* the last message in the protocol is sent. Then this allows the tampering function to leak at most $\log \delta^{-1}(\lambda)$ additional bits to future rounds. Note that causing an abort by tampering with the very last message cannot add any additional leakage, since there are no more future rounds to consider. Further note, that either party aborting *before* the last message is sent automatically causes both parties to output $\perp$ in the synchronized setting.

We use the above observation to sample from D_f by sampling differently depending on $\delta(\lambda)$. If $\delta(\lambda) \leq 2^{-\lambda}$, the distribution D_f is sampled by simply outputting $(\perp, \perp)$. Clearly this distribution is $2^{-\lambda}$ close to the real distribution, since f causes both Alice and Bob to abort and output $\perp$ with probability at least $1 - 2^{-\lambda}$. If $\delta > 2^{-\lambda}$, the distribution D_f is sampled as shown in Algorithm 2. The difference between D_f and the real tampered transcript distribution is captured by the event in which the sampler aborts the execution in steps 4b or 4c, but the real execution continues. To see why D_f is close to the tampered transcript distribution, consider the four cases.

1. The tampering function did not change (α_1, α_2) **or** (β_1, β_2)**:** This is the simplest case. Note that the tampering function may store a bounded function of the messages seen so far. That is, the tampering function stores $\gamma = h_4(\beta_2, h_3(\alpha_2, h_2(\beta_1, h_1(\alpha_1))))$ where h_i denotes a memory bounded function as described above. We claim that given γ and up to $\log \delta^{-1}(\lambda) = \lambda$ many bits of additional leakage due to conditional aborts, (k_1, k_2) and hence k is 2ϵ-close to uniform. This follows from the property of strong extractors. Conditioned on γ and the leakage, the sources (α_1, α_2) are still independent and have sufficient min-entropy. This may not be immediately apparent, since future tampering can depend on γ, which technically constitutes joint leakage over (α_1, α_2). However, we can see that this particular joint leakage is not an issue for a 2-nonmalleable extractor by switching to a different but equivalent viewpoint. If we fix $h_1(\alpha_1)$, then α_1 is no longer uniformly distributed but it is still a source with a distribution with at least $n - s$ bits of min-entropy. This is ensured by the fixed upper bound on the size of the leakage. From this viewpoint, since $h_1(\alpha_1)$ is fixed, γ is no longer joint leakage over (α_1, α_2) but merely bounded leakage over α_2. The same applies to additional potential leakage due to conditional aborts, leaving us with a source α_1 with at least $n - (s + \lambda)$ bits of min-entropy. Similarly, the same holds for sources (β_1, β_2).

Now it follows that if the tampering function changes any message in the protocol execution phase, the MAC verification will fail (up to the error $2^{-\lambda}$) causing the receiving party to abort. Unless the tampered message was the one sent in round $r + 7$ this in turn automatically causes the other party to abort as well (corresponding to step 4b). If the tampered message was the one sent in round $r + 7$ then only Bob would abort (corresponding to step 4c). Furthermore, by the property of one-time pads, the probability of the tampering function changing any message is independent of the message itself.

2. The tampering function changed (α_1, α_2) (i.e., changed at least one of them) but not (β_1, β_2): We claim that $k_1 := \mathsf{Ext}(\alpha_1, \alpha_2)$ is ϵ-close to uniform given γ and up to λ many bits of additional leakage due to conditional aborts, $k_1' := \mathsf{Ext}(\alpha_1', \alpha_2')$, and (β_1, β_2). This follows from the fact that k_1 is ϵ-close to uniform given k_1', γ and λ bits of leakage (by the property of 2-non-malleable extractors), and, that (β_1, β_2) are independent of (α_1, α_2). This also implies that k_1 is ϵ-close to uniform given $\gamma, k_1', (\beta_1, \beta_2), k_2$, and λ bits of leakage since k_2 is entirely determined by (β_1, β_2). This in turn implies that k_1 is ϵ-close to uniform given $\gamma, k_1', (\beta_1, \beta_2), k_2, k_2'$, and λ bits of leakage since $k_2' = k_2$. This implies that $k = k_1 \oplus k_2'$ is ϵ-close to uniform conditioned on $\gamma, k_1', (\beta_1, \beta_2), k_2$ and leakage. This finally implies that k is ϵ-close to uniform conditioned on $\gamma, k' = k_1' \oplus k_2$ and leakage. Thus, the MAC verification will fail for Alice in the key confirmation phase (up to the error $2^{-\lambda}$) causing both parties to output $\perp$.

3. The tampering function changed (β_1, β_2) but not (α_1, α_2): This case is symmetric to the previous case.

4. The tampering function changed both (α_1, α_2) and (β_1, β_2): The only difference between this case and case 2 is that now k_2' may not be equal to k_2. As in the previous case, k_1 is almost uniform given $\gamma, k_1', (\beta_1, \beta_2), k_2$ and leakage. But note that k_2' is entirely determined by (β_1, β_2), γ and the (fixed) tampering function. Hence, k_1 is almost uniform given $\gamma, k_1', (\beta_1, \beta_2), k_2, k_2'$ and leakage.

Overall using a union bound over the errors of the extractor and the MAC, we get an upper bound on the statistical distance between D_f and the outputs of a real execution of $5\epsilon + 4 \cdot 2^{-\lambda}$. □

6   Split-State Tampering

Split-state tampering functions are one of the most interesting and well studied families of tampering functions for regular non-malleable codes and were already considered by Dziembowski, Pietrzak, and Wichs [36] in their seminal paper. A 2-split-state tampering function independently tampers on two fixed disjoint parts of a codeword. Transferring this idea to the interactive setting is straightforward. We can divide the transcript of a protocol into two disjoint sets of messages and allow the tampering function to tamper independently on those two sets.

However, we are actually able to achieve protocol non-malleability for a stronger class, namely c-unbalanced split-state tampering functions. In the regular split state setting, the encoding scheme determines the "split". In contrast, a c-unbalanced split-state tampering function can split the transcript into two arbitrary sets, as long as each set contains at least a $1/c$ fraction of the messages.

Definition 11 (c-Unbalanced Split-State Tampering Functions). *Functions of the class of c-unbalanced 2-split-state tampering functions $\mathcal{F}^c_{strong\text{-}split}$ for an r-round interactive protocols are defined by an r-tuple of functions $(g_1, \ldots, g_r)$ and two disjoint sets $\mathcal{I}_0, \mathcal{I}_1$ such that $\min(|\mathcal{I}_0|, |\mathcal{I}_1|) \geq r/c$ and $\mathcal{I}_0 \cup \mathcal{I}_1 = \{1, \ldots, r\}$. Let $m_1, \ldots, m_i$ denote the messages sent by the participants of the protocol in a partial execution. The tampering function for message m_i is then*

$$f_i(m_1, \ldots, m_i) := \begin{cases} g_i((m_j)_{j \in \mathcal{I}_0, j \leq i}) & \text{if } i \in \mathcal{I}_0 \\ g_i((m_j)_{j \in \mathcal{I}_1, j \leq i}) & \text{if } i \in \mathcal{I}_1 \end{cases}$$

As a special case functions in $\mathcal{F}^2_{strong\text{-}split}$ must split the messages into two equal size sets. These functions are also alternatively simply called split-state tampering functions, since the split is not unbalanced.

6.1   INMC for Split-State Tampering

We devise a generic protocol-non-malleable encoding Π for c-unbalanced split-state tampering functions for any two-party protocol Π_0. The basic idea of the encoding will seem similar to the protocol for bounded state tampering functions, however the instantiation is quite different. We again first run a key exchange phase in which enough key material is exchanged to execute the original protocol encrypted under one-time pad and authenticate all messages with information theoretically secure MACs. The main difference is in the implementation of the key exchange phase. Unlike before, where we relied on non-malleable extractors, we use a notion of tamper-evident n-out-of-n secret sharing in this case. The idea behind this is that both parties contribute to the key material $k = \text{Ext}(k_1, k_2)$ and share their part of the key-material into many shares that are sent in separate messages. If we are able to enforce that the tampering function must jointly tamper with almost all of the messages in the key-exchange phase to be able to predict the key with any significant probability, then we can scale the key exchange phase to make sure that such a function would not be c-unbalanced. The tamper-evidence of the secret sharing scheme allows us to ensure that either party's shares must be tampered with jointly to learn anything about the reconstructed secret. However, this is not enough. We must also ensure that the *other party's* messages must also be tampered jointly. We achieve this via a use of

MACs with "successively revealed keys." I.e., each message must be authenticated using a key that is only revealed if one has knowledge of *all* of the other party's previous messages. In this way, each message is "chained" to the other party's previous messages and any successful tampering must necessarily tamper with the full key-exchange phase in a joint manner.

Theorem 3. *Let Π_0 denote a correct, r-round protocol, with length-ℓ messages. Let* (Share, Reconstruct) *be a $\lceil((c-1)(r+5)+1)/2\rceil$-out-of-$\lceil((c-1)(r+5)+1)/2\rceil$ perfectly private, ϵ'-tamper evident secret sharing scheme for up to $\lambda/2$ bits of leakage with message length ℓ'' and share length ℓ' Let λ' be the target security parameter, then we set $\lambda = \max(\ell, \ell', \lambda')$. Let* MAC $: \{0,1\}^{2\lambda} \times \{0,1\}^\lambda$ *be a $2^{-\lambda}$-secure information theoretic message authentication code. Let* Ext $: \{0,1\}^{\ell''} \times \{0,1\}^{\ell''} \to \{0,1\}^{r\ell+(2r+4)\lambda}$ *be a strong two-source extractor for sources with min-entropy $\ell'' - \lambda/2$ with error ϵ''. We assume without loss of generality that Alice sends both the first and last message in Π_0 Then for any c there exists a $c(r+5)$-round encoding Π of Π_0 that is $\epsilon(\lambda) = 2\epsilon' + 3\epsilon'' + (c-1)(r+5)+3) \cdot 2^{-\lambda/2} + 2^{-\lambda+1}$-non-malleable against $\mathcal{F}^c_{strong\text{-}split}$.*

The tamper evident secret sharing scheme can be instantiated using the construction described in the full version of this paper, the MAC can be instantiated with a family of pairwise-independent hash functions and the strong 2-source extractor can be instantiated with the extractor due to Bourgain [14].

Proof of Theorem 3. The protocol Π is specified in Algorithm 3. We need to argue that the protocol is correct and protocol-non-malleable.

Correctness: The correctness of Π follows from the correctness of the secret sharing scheme and the message authentication code. The correctness of the secret sharing scheme implies that when no tampering takes place, Bob and Alice will both reconstruct the correct string k_1 or k_2 respectively. Thus, they will compute the same key k. Combined with the correctness of the message authentication code, this means that neither party will ever abort during the protocol. Further, since the one-time pad is correct it follows that messages of the underlying protocol will always be decrypted correctly and thus both parties are faithfully executing an honest instance of Π_0. Thus at the end of the protocol the collected transcripts correspond to an honest execution of Π_0.

Protocol Non-malleability: Let f be a c-unbalanced split state tampering function described by $(g_1, \ldots, g_{c(r+5)})$ and $\mathcal{I}_0, \mathcal{I}_1$ (refer to Definition 11). To prove that the coding scheme is protocol-non-malleable, we show that a distributions D_f as in Definition 8 exists.

The Distribution D_f: When sampling from D_f we again need to deal with the problem that the tampering function can communicate information through conditional aborts. I.e., in round i with $i \in \mathcal{I}_b$, the function g_i can force an abort in the protocol unless the message sent in round i is "good". In any future round

---

Algorithm 3: Protocol Π against c-unbalanced split-state tampering functions

We compile Π_0 into Π below. Let (Share, Reconstruct), and Π_0 be as in Theorem 3. The communication proceeds in three phases, a key exchange phase, a key confirmation phase, and a protocol execution phase. All messages in the following protocol have a fixed length. Whenever a party in the protocol aborts, she outputs $\perp$ instead of the transcript.

Key Exchange Phase: The number of rounds in the key exchange phase depends on the number of rounds r of the underlying protocol and on the parameter c that determines how unbalanced the states are allowed to be. Let $d = \lceil ((c-1)(r+5)+1)/2 \rceil$.

1. Alice and Bob choose ℓ''-bit strings $k_1, k_2 \leftarrow_{\$} \{0,1\}^{\ell''}$ respectively and secret share them into d shares each as $s_1^A, \ldots, s_d^A \leftarrow \mathsf{Share}(k_1)$ and $s_1^B, \ldots, s_d^B \leftarrow \mathsf{Share}(k_2)$.
2. Alice chooses d random strings $r_{1,1}^A, \ldots, r_{1,d}^A \leftarrow_{\$} \{0,1\}^{2\lambda}$ and sends $m_1^A = (r_{1,1}^A, \ldots, r_{1,d}^A)$ to Bob.
3. For every $1 \leq i \leq d$ Alice and Bob proceed as follows
   (a) Bob chooses $d - i + 1$ random string $r_{i,i}^B, \ldots, r_{i,d}^B \leftarrow_{\$} \{0,1\}^{2\lambda}$, computes the tag $t_i^B := \mathsf{MAC}(r_{1,i}^A \oplus \ldots \oplus r_{i,i}^A, s_i^B)$ and sends $m_i^B = (s_i^B, r_{i,i}^B, \ldots, r_{i,d}^B, t_i^B)$ to Alice.
   (b) Alice verifies that $\mathsf{Vf}(r_{1,i}^A \oplus \cdots \oplus r_{i,i}^A, s_i^B, t_i^B) = 1$ and aborts otherwise.
   (c) Alice chooses $d - i$ random strings $r_{i+1,i+1}^A, \ldots, r_{i+1,d}^A \leftarrow_{\$} \{0,1\}^{2\lambda}$ (note that once $i = d$ this means no random string at all), computes the tag $t_i^A := \mathsf{MAC}(r_{1,i}^B \oplus \ldots \oplus r_{i,i}^B, s_i^A)$ and sends $m_{i+1}^A = (s_i^A, r_{i+1,i+1}^A, \ldots, r_{i+1,d}^A, t_i^A)$ to Bob.
   (d) Bob verifies that $\mathsf{Vf}(r_{1,i}^B \oplus \cdots \oplus r_{i,i}^B, s_i^A, t_i^A) = 1$ and aborts otherwise.
4. Once all the shares have been exchanged, Alice reconstructs $k_2' := \mathsf{Reconstruct}(s_1^B, \ldots, s_d^B)$. If $k_2' = \perp$, she aborts. Otherwise she extracts $k = \mathsf{Ext}(k_1, k_2')$. Bob reconstructs $k_1' := \mathsf{Reconstruct}(s_1^A, \ldots, s_d^A)$. If $k_1' = \perp$, he aborts. Otherwise he extracts $k = \mathsf{Ext}(k_1', k_2)$.
5. Both parties then split $k = k_A \| k_B \| k_1^{\mathsf{auth}} \| k_1^{\mathsf{enc}} \| \ldots \| k_r^{\mathsf{auth}} \| k_r^{\mathsf{enc}}$ into substrings, where $|k_A| = |k_B| = |k_i^{\mathsf{auth}}| = 2\lambda$ and $|k_i^{\mathsf{enc}}| = \ell$.

Key Confirmation Phase: Alice and Bob verify that they agree on the exchanged key.

1. Bob chooses a random challenge $c_B \leftarrow_{\$} \{0,1\}^\ell$ and sends it to Alice.
2. Alice computes $t_B := \mathsf{MAC}(k_B, c_B)$, chooses a challenge $c_A \leftarrow_{\$} \{0,1\}^\ell$, and sends t_B, c_A to Bob.
3. If $\mathsf{Vf}(k_B, c_B, t_B) = 1$, Bob computes $t_A := \mathsf{MAC}(k_A, c_A)$ and sends t_A to Alice. Otherwise he aborts.
4. If $\mathsf{Vf}(k_A, c_A, t_A) = 1$, Alice proceeds to the next phase. Otherwise she aborts.

Protocol Execution Phase: Both parties initialize their view of the underlying protocol as a empty lists $\mathsf{trans}_A = \mathsf{trans}_B = \emptyset$. For each protocol message the parties then proceed as follows:

1. In the ith round, if it is Alice's (resp. Bob's) turn to send a message she invokes the next-message function of the underlying protocol $m_i := \pi_A^0(i, x, \mathsf{trans}_A)$ (resp. $m_i := \pi_B^0(i, y, \mathsf{trans}_B)$) and adds the message to her view $\mathsf{trans}_A := \mathsf{trans}_A \| m_i$ (resp. $\mathsf{trans}_B := \mathsf{trans}_B \| m_i$).
2. Next the party computes the one-time pad encryption $c_i := m_i \oplus k_i^{\mathsf{enc}}$ of m_i as well as an authentication tag $t_i := \mathsf{MAC}(k_i^{\mathsf{auth}}, c_i)$ and sends c_i, t_i to the other party.
3. If $\mathsf{Vf}(k_i^{\mathsf{auth}}, c_i, t_i) = 1$ the other party decrypts $m_i := c_i \oplus k_i^{\mathsf{enc}}$ and adds the message to their view, i.e., $\mathsf{trans}_A := \mathsf{trans}_A \| m_i$ or $\mathsf{trans}_B := \mathsf{trans}_B \| m_i$.

Finally the underlying protocol terminates and both parties output their respective transcripts trans_A or trans_B or $\perp$ if they aborted at some point.

$j > i$, even if $j \in \mathcal{I}_{1-b}$ the function g_j therefore has the information that the message in round i must have been "good". This implies leakage between the two split states. To deal with this problem we sample differently depending on the probability of f causing an abort during a protocol execution. Let $1 - \delta(\lambda)$ be the probability of f causing either party to abort *before* the last message in the protocol is sent. If $\delta(\lambda) \leq 2^{-\lambda/2}$, the distribution D_f is sampled by simply outputting $(\perp, \perp)$. Clearly this distribution is $2^{-\lambda/2} \leq \epsilon(n)$ close to the real distribution, since f causes both parties to abort and output $\perp$ with probability at least $1 - 2^{-\lambda/2}$. If $\delta > 2^{-\lambda/2}$, the distribution D_f is sampled as shown in Algorithm 4.

Analysis. It remains to show that D_f is $2\epsilon' + 3\epsilon'' + (c-1)(r+5) + 3) \cdot 2^{-\lambda/2} + 2^{-\lambda+1}$ close to the tampered transcript distribution. We first note that the protocol Π overall has $((c-1)(r+5)+1)+r+4 = c(r+5)$ rounds, of which $(c-1)(r+5)+2$ form the key exchange phase, 3 the key confirmation phase, and r the protocol execution phase. We therefore have that $|\mathcal{I}_b| \leq (1-1/c) \cdot c(r+5) \leq (c-1)(r+5)$.

Algorithm 4: Sampler of distribution D_f for Algorithm 3

1. Sample $k_1, k_2 \leftarrow_\$ \{0,1\}^{\ell''}$ and share them as $s_1^A, \ldots, s_d^A \leftarrow \mathsf{Share}(k_1)$ and $s_1^B, \ldots, s_d^B \leftarrow \mathsf{Share}(k_2)$.
2. Sample $d^2 + d$ strings
$$r_{1,1}^A, \ldots, r_{1,d}^A, r_{2,2}^A, \ldots, r_{2,d}^A, \ldots, r_{d,d}^A \leftarrow_\$ \{0,1\}^{2\lambda}$$
$$r_{1,1}^B, \ldots, r_{1,d}^B, r_{2,2}^B, \ldots, r_{2,d}^B, \ldots, r_{d,d}^B \leftarrow_\$ \{0,1\}^{2\lambda}.$$
3. Let $m_i^A := (r_{1,1}^A, \ldots, r_{1,d}^A)$ and apply the tampering function as $\bar{m}_i^A = (\bar{r}_{1,1}^A, \ldots, \bar{r}_{1,d}^A) := g_1(m_1^A)$.
4. For $1 \le i \le d$ perform the following steps
   (a) Compute $t_i^B := \mathsf{MAC}(\bar{r}_{1,i}^A \oplus \cdots \oplus \bar{r}_{i,i}^A, s_i^B)$ and let $m_i^B := (s_i^B, r_{i,i}^B, \ldots, r_{i,d}^B, t_i^B)$.
   (b) Apply the tampering function as $\bar{m}_i^B = (\bar{s}_i^B, \bar{r}_{i,i}^B, \ldots, \bar{r}_{i,d}^B, \bar{t}_i^B) := g_{2i}(m_1^A, m_1^B, m_2^A, \ldots, m_i^B)$.
   (c) If $\mathsf{Vf}(r_{1,i}^A \oplus \cdots \oplus r_{i,i}^A, \bar{s}_i^B, \bar{t}_i^B) = 0$, output $(\bot, \bot)$.
   (d) Compute $t_i^A := \mathsf{MAC}(\bar{r}_{1,i}^B \oplus \cdots \oplus \bar{r}_{i,i}^B, s_i^A)$ and let $m_{i+1}^A := (s_i^A, r_{i+1,i+1}^A, \ldots, r_{i+1,d}^A, t_i^A)$.
   (e) Apply the tampering function as $\bar{m}_{i+1}^A = (\bar{s}_i^A, \bar{r}_{i+1,i+1}^A, \ldots, \bar{r}_{i+1,d}^A, \bar{t}_i^A) := g_{2i+1}(m_1^A, m_1^B, \ldots, m_{i+1}^A)$.
   (f) If $\mathsf{Vf}(r_{1,i}^B \oplus \ldots \oplus r_{i,i}^B, \bar{t}_i^A, \bar{s}_i^A) = 0$, output $(\bot, \bot)$.
5. Reconstruct $\bar{k}_1 := \mathsf{Reconstruct}(\bar{s}_1^A, \ldots, \bar{s}_d^A)$ and $\bar{k}_2 := \mathsf{Reconstruct}(\bar{s}_1^B, \ldots, \bar{s}_d^B)$. If $\bar{k}_1 = \bot$ or $\bar{k}_2 = \bot$, output $(\bot, \bot)$.
6. If $\mathsf{Ext}(k_1, k_2) \ne \mathsf{Ext}(\bar{k}_1, k_2)$ or $\mathsf{Ext}(k_1, k_2) \ne \mathsf{Ext}(k_1, \bar{k}_2)$, stop and output $(\bot, \bot)$.
7. Else, if $\mathsf{Ext}(\bar{k}_1, k_2) = \mathsf{Ext}(k_1, \bar{k}_2) = \mathsf{Ext}(k_1, k_2)$, simulate a protocol execution tampered with f
   (a) Replace all messages with random strings of appropriate length and apply the tampering function to those messages.
   (b) If for any index $2d + 4 < i < c(r+5)$ it holds that $m_i \ne f_i(m_1, \ldots, m_i)$ then output $(\bot, \bot)$.
   (c) If $m_{c(r+5)} \ne f_{c(r+5)}(m_1, \ldots, m_{c(r+5)})$ then output $(\mathsf{same}, \bot)$, otherwise output $(\mathsf{same}, \mathsf{same})$.

As noted above, we need to deal with leakage due to conditional aborts for every message being tampered. I.e., the tampered message $\bar{m}_i$ in round i with $i \in \mathcal{I}_b$ can, in addition to all previous messages in $\mathcal{I}_b$, also depend on some joint leakage over all previous messages in $\mathcal{I}_{1-b}$ due to conditional aborts, simply by observing that the protocol has *not* aborted.

Claim 4. *The tampered message $\bar{m}_i$ in round i with $i \in \mathcal{I}_b$ can depend on at most $\lambda/2$ bits of joint leakage over $\{m_j | j \in \mathcal{I}_{1-b} \wedge j \le i\}$.*

Proof. We know that f does *not* cause an abort with probability at least $\delta(\lambda) = 2^{-\lambda/2}$. Therefore, the tampering function g_i learns at most $\log \delta^{-1}(\lambda) = \log 2^{\lambda/2} = \lambda/2$ bits of joint leakage over previous messages in $\mathcal{I}_{1-b}$. $\square$

We will argue that conditioned on the protocol not having aborted and the complete view of any tampering function g_i in the key confirmation and protocol execution phase the key $k = \mathsf{Ext}(k_1, \bar{k}_2)$ computed by Alice in the key exchange phase remains ϵ'' close to uniform. For this we first note that up to step 5 in Algorithm 4 the sampler acts identically to a real execution of the protocol.

Lemma 5. *If Alice, or respectively D_f, does not abort during the key exchange phase, then $\bar{k}_2 = k_2$ except with probability $\epsilon' + (d+1) \cdot 2^{-\lambda/2}$.*

Due to space constraints, the proof of Lemma 5 is deferred to the full version. A completely symmetric argument can be made for $\bar{k}_1 = k_1$, where otherwise Bob aborts with probability $1 - \epsilon' - (d+1) \cdot 2^{-\lambda/2}$, causing Alice to also abort. This means that if Alice does not abort, we have that $k = \mathsf{Ext}(k_1, \bar{k}_2) = \mathsf{Ext}(\bar{k}_1, k_2) = \mathsf{Ext}(k_1, k_2)$ with probability at least $1 - 2(\epsilon' - (d+1) \cdot 2^{-\lambda/2})$.[2]

---

[2] Note that the tampering function cannot influence the values k_1, k_2 at all since they are sampled independently of the protocol transcript.

Now, consider how much information about k_1 and k_2 a tampering function g_i can learn. Let $\mathcal{I}_b$ be the set of indices, such that $i \in \mathcal{I}_b$. Clearly, g_i has complete knowledge of all shares s_j^B with $2j \in \mathcal{I}_b$ and all shares s_j^A with $2j + 1 \in \mathcal{I}_b$. Further, g_i receives joint leakage over shares in $\mathcal{I}_{1-b}$ simply by observing the fact that the protocol has not yet aborted. This leakage is however bounded by Claim 4 by $\lambda/2$ bits. By the perfect privacy of the secret sharing scheme, it follows that $\lambda/2$ bits of joint leakage over all shares can reveal at most $\lambda/2$ bits of the secret.

Since a set of indices with $|\mathcal{I}_b| \geq 2d+1$ would be too large for a c-unbalanced split state tampering function, $\mathcal{I}_b$ cannot possibly contain all the shares. Thus, the maximum amount of information the tampering function g_i can gain about k_1 and k_2 is exactly one of the two strings and $\lambda/2$ bits of the other string. Since Ext is a strong 2-source extractor for sources with min-entropy $\ell'' - \lambda/2$, this implies that in this case with probability at least $1 - \epsilon''$ the extracted key-material remains ϵ'' close to uniform. Overall, this means that with probability at least $1 - 2 \cdot (\epsilon' + (d+1) \cdot 2^{-\lambda/2}) - \epsilon''$, k remains ϵ'' close to uniform from the point of view of any tampering function g_i.

To recap, if any of the key-shares are tampered with in such a way that the original keys are not reconstructed, then the sampling algorithm will always output $(\bot, \bot)$, while the parties in the real protocol will do so with probability at least $1 - 2 \cdot (\epsilon' + (d+1) \cdot 2^{-\lambda/2})$. If the shares were not tampered with and thus $k = \text{Ext}(\bar{k}_1, k_2) = \text{Ext}(k_1, \bar{k}_2) = \text{Ext}(k_1, k_2)$, then since k is distributed ϵ''-close to uniform – the random messages in the simulated protocol execution phase are distributed ϵ'' close to a real protocol execution. Now, if f tampers with any message of the key-confirmation or protocol-execution phase except for the very last one, then the sampling algorithm always outputs $(\bot, \bot)$, whereas if only the very last message is tampered with the sampling algorithm outputs $(\text{same}, \bot)$. In a real protocol execution when tampering with any message, the information theoretic MAC must be computed almost independently of k, since k remains ϵ'' close to uniform. Therefore, if any message is tampered with in a real protocol execution, the receiving party will abort with probability $1 - 2^{-\lambda} - \epsilon''$, causing both parties to output $\bot$, except if it only happens in the very last message, where only Bob will abort with probability $1 - 2^{-\lambda} - \epsilon''$ and output $\bot$ and Alice will retain the correct transcript. On the other hand, if no message is tampered with, the sampling algorithm outputs $(\text{same}, \text{same})$ and both Alice and Bob in a real protocol execution retain the correct transcript. This follows since in this case Alice and Bob agree on a key. Overall a union bound then gives us an upper bound on the statistical distance between D_f and the distribution of both parties' outputs in a real execution of $2\epsilon' + 3\epsilon'' + 2(d+1) \cdot 2^{-\lambda/2} + 2^{-\lambda-1}$. With $d = \lceil((c-1)(r+5) + 1)/2\rceil$, this leads to the claimed bound of $\epsilon(\lambda) = 2\epsilon' + 3\epsilon'' + ((c-1)(r+5) + 3) \cdot 2^{-\lambda/2} + 2^{-\lambda+1}$. □

7   Fragmented Sliding Window Tampering

The sliding window model is a very natural restriction of algorithms and is considered in a variety of contexts, in particular also for error correcting codes [48].

The idea of the sliding window is that an adversary can only watch a stream of data through a window of fixed size. In the context of interactive non-malleable codes this means that the tampering function "remembers" only the last w messages. That is, the tampering function gets as input the last w (untampered) messages of the protocol transcript to compute the tampered message.

We in fact consider a stronger class of functions that we call *fragmented sliding window*. Functions with a fragmented window of size w can depend on *any* w previous messages, not just the *last* w. In a sense the adversary is still watching the transcript through a fixed size window, it can freely choose which fragments of the window remain transparent and which ones become opaque.

Comparing this class with c-unbalanced split-state tampering functions, we note that the size of the window is now fixed and does not scale with the number of messages. On the other hand the different sets of messages tampering can depend on are no longer required to be disjoint. E.g., the tampering of each single message could depend on the first message of the protocol, something that would not be possible in the case of split-state functions.

Definition 12 (Fragmented Sliding Window Tampering Functions).
Functions of the class of w-size fragmented sliding window tampering functions $\mathcal{F}_{frag}^w$ for an r-round interactive protocols are defined by an r-tuple of functions $(g_1, \ldots, g_r)$ and an r-tuple of sets $(S_1, \ldots, S_r)$ such that $S_1 = \emptyset$, $S_i \subseteq S_{i-1} \cup \{i-1\}$ and $|S_i| \leq w$ for $1 < i \leq r$. Let $m_1, \ldots, m_i$ be the messages sent by the participants of the protocol in a partial execution. The tampering function for message m_i is then defined as $f_i(m_1, \ldots, m_i) := g_i(m_i, (m_j)_{j \in S_i})$.

7.1 INMC for Fragmented Sliding Window Tampering

Even though there are important conceptual differences between fragmented sliding window tampering functions and c-unbalanced split-state tampering functions, essentially identical protocol can be used to achieve protocol-non-malleability for fragmented sliding window tampering functions. The difference is how the key exchange phase scales. The window-size is fixed and does not depend on the round complexity of the protocol. This means that d – the number of shares Alice and Bob split their keys into – must scale with w instead of the underlying protocol's round complexity.

Theorem 6. *Let Π_0 denote a correct, r-round protocol, with length-ℓ messages. Let $(\mathsf{Share}, \mathsf{Reconstruct})$ be a $w+2$-out-of-$w+2$ perfectly private, ϵ'-tamper evident secret sharing scheme for up to $\lambda'/2$ bits of leakage with message length ℓ'' and share length ℓ'. Let λ' be the target security parameter, then we set $\lambda = \max(\ell, \ell', \lambda')$. Let $\mathsf{MAC} : \{0,1\}^{2\lambda} \times \{0,1\}^\lambda \to \{0,1\}^\lambda$ be a $2^{-\lambda}$-secure information theoretic message authentication code. Let $\mathsf{Ext} : \{0,1\}^{\ell''} \to r\ell + (2r+4)\lambda$ be a strong two-source extractor for sources with min-entropy $\ell'' - \lambda/2$ with error ϵ''. We assume wlog that Alice sends both the first and last message in Π_0. Then for any w there exists a $r + 2w + 8$-round encoding Π of Π_0 that is $\epsilon(\lambda) = 3 \cdot 2^{-\lambda} + 2\epsilon'(\lambda) + 2\epsilon''$-protocol non-malleable against $\mathcal{F}_{frag}^w$.*

Due to space constraints, the proof of Theorem 6 is deferred to the full version of this paper.

Acknowledgments. We would like to thank the anonymous reviewers for TCC 2019 for suggesting a stronger and more natural notion of non-malleability. We would also like to thank Ran Gelles for helpful comments on an earlier version of our writeup.

References

1. Aggarwal, D., Agrawal, S., Gupta, D., Maji, H.K., Pandey, O., Prabhakaran, M.: Optimal computational split-state non-malleable codes. In: Kushilevitz, E., Malkin, T. (eds.) TCC 2016. LNCS, vol. 9563, pp. 393–417. Springer, Heidelberg (2016). https://doi.org/10.1007/978-3-662-49099-0_15

2. Aggarwal, D., Dodis, Y., Kazana, T., Obremski, M.: Non-malleable reductions and applications. In: 47th ACM STOC, pp. 459–468 (2015)

3. Aggarwal, D., Dodis, Y., Lovett, S.: Non-malleable codes from additive combinatorics. In: 46th ACM STOC, pp. 774–783 (2014)

4. Aggarwal, D., Döttling, N., Nielsen, J.B., Obremski, M., Purwanto, E.: Continuous non-malleable codes in the 8-split-state model. In: Ishai, Y., Rijmen, V. (eds.) EUROCRYPT 2019. LNCS, vol. 11476, pp. 531–561. Springer, Cham (2019). https://doi.org/10.1007/978-3-030-17653-2_18

5. Agrawal, S., Gupta, D., Maji, H.K., Pandey, O., Prabhakaran, M.: Explicit non-malleable codes against bit-wise tampering and permutations. In: Gennaro, R., Robshaw, M. (eds.) CRYPTO 2015. LNCS, vol. 9215, pp. 538–557. Springer, Heidelberg (2015). https://doi.org/10.1007/978-3-662-47989-6_26

6. Agrawal, S., Gupta, D., Maji, H.K., Pandey, O., Prabhakaran, M.: A rate-optimizing compiler for non-malleable codes against bit-wise tampering and permutations. In: Dodis, Y., Nielsen, J.B. (eds.) TCC 2015. LNCS, vol. 9014, pp. 375–397. Springer, Heidelberg (2015). https://doi.org/10.1007/978-3-662-46494-6_16

7. Alon, N., Braverman, M., Efremenko, K., Gelles, R., Haeupler, B.: Reliable communication over highly connected noisy networks. In: 35th ACM PODC, pp. 165–173 (2016)

8. Ball, M., Dachman-Soled, D., Guo, S., Malkin, T., Tan, L.Y.: Non-malleable codes for small-depth circuits. In: 59th FOCS, pp. 826–837 (2018)

9. Ball, M., Dachman-Soled, D., Kulkarni, M., Lin, H., Malkin, T.: Non-malleable codes against bounded polynomial time tampering. In: Ishai, Y., Rijmen, V. (eds.) EUROCRYPT 2019. LNCS, vol. 11476, pp. 501–530. Springer, Cham (2019). https://doi.org/10.1007/978-3-030-17653-2_17

10. Ball, M., Dachman-Soled, D., Kulkarni, M., Malkin, T.: Non-malleable codes for bounded depth, bounded fan-in circuits. In: Fischlin, M., Coron, J.-S. (eds.) EUROCRYPT 2016. LNCS, vol. 9666, pp. 881–908. Springer, Heidelberg (2016). https://doi.org/10.1007/978-3-662-49896-5_31

11. Ball, M., Dachman-Soled, D., Kulkarni, M., Malkin, T.: Non-malleable codes from average-case hardness: AC^0, decision trees, and streaming space-bounded tampering. In: Nielsen, J.B., Rijmen, V. (eds.) EUROCRYPT 2018. LNCS, vol. 10822, pp. 618–650. Springer, Cham (2018). https://doi.org/10.1007/978-3-319-78372-7_20

12. Ball, M., Guo, S., Wichs, D.: Non-malleable codes for decision trees. Cryptology ePrint Archive, Report 2019/379 (2019)

13. Barak, B., Canetti, R., Lindell, Y., Pass, R., Rabin, T.: Secure computation without authentication. In: Shoup, V. (ed.) CRYPTO 2005. LNCS, vol. 3621, pp. 361–377. Springer, Heidelberg (2005). https://doi.org/10.1007/11535218_22

14. Bourgain, J.: More on the sum-product phenomenon in prime fields and its applications. Int. J. Number Theory **1**(01), 1–32 (2005)

15. Brakerski, Z., Kalai, Y.T.: Efficient interactive coding against adversarial noise. In: 53rd FOCS, pp. 160–166 (2012)

16. Braverman, M., Efremenko, K., Gelles, R., Haeupler, B.: Constant-rate coding for multiparty interactive communication is impossible. In: 48th ACM STOC, pp. 999–1010 (2016)

17. Braverman, M., Gelles, R., Mao, J., Ostrovsky, R.: Coding for interactive communication correcting insertions and deletions. In: ICALP 2016, pp. 61:1–61:14 (2016)

18. Braverman, M., Rao, A.: Towards coding for maximum errors in interactive communication. In: 43rd ACM STOC, pp. 159–166 (2011)

19. Cachin, C., Maurer, U.: Unconditional security against memory-bounded adversaries. In: Kaliski, B.S. (ed.) CRYPTO 1997. LNCS, vol. 1294, pp. 292–306. Springer, Heidelberg (1997). https://doi.org/10.1007/BFb0052243

20. Chandran, N., Goyal, V., Mukherjee, P., Pandey, O., Upadhyay, J.: Block-wise non-malleable codes. In: ICALP 2016, pp. 31:1–31:14 (2016)

21. Chandran, N., Kanukurthi, B., Raghuraman, S.: Information-theoretic local non-malleable codes and their applications. In: Kushilevitz, E., Malkin, T. (eds.) TCC 2016-A. LNCS, vol. 9563, pp. 367–392. Springer, Heidelberg (2016). https://doi.org/10.1007/978-3-662-49099-0_14

22. Chattopadhyay, E., Goyal, V., Li, X.: Non-malleable extractors and codes, with their many tampered extensions. In: 48th ACM STOC, pp. 285–298 (2016)

23. Chattopadhyay, E., Li, X.: Non-malleable codes and extractors for small-depth circuits, and affine functions. In: 49th ACM STOC, pp. 1171–1184 (2017)

24. Chattopadhyay, E., Zuckerman, D.: Non-malleable codes against constant split-state tampering. In: 55th FOCS, pp. 306–315 (2014)

25. Cheraghchi, M., Guruswami, V.: Non-malleable coding against bit-wise and split-state tampering. In: Lindell, Y. (ed.) TCC 2014. LNCS, vol. 8349, pp. 440–464. Springer, Heidelberg (2014). https://doi.org/10.1007/978-3-642-54242-8_19

26. Cheraghchi, M., Guruswami, V.: Capacity of non-malleable codes. IEEE Trans. Inf. Theory **62**(3), 1097–1118 (2016)

27. Chor, B., Goldreich, O.: Unbiased bits from sources of weak randomness and probabilistic communication complexity (extended abstract). In: 26th FOCS, pp. 429–442 (1985)

28. Chung, K.M., Pass, R., Telang, S.: Knowledge-preserving interactive coding. In: 54th FOCS, pp. 449–458 (2013)

29. Coretti, S., Dodis, Y., Tackmann, B., Venturi, D.: Non-malleable encryption: simpler, shorter, stronger. In: Kushilevitz, E., Malkin, T. (eds.) TCC 2016-A. LNCS, vol. 9562, pp. 306–335. Springer, Heidelberg (2016). https://doi.org/10.1007/978-3-662-49096-9_13

30. Coretti, S., Faonio, A., Venturi, D.: Rate-optimizing compilers for continuously non-malleable codes. Cryptology ePrint Archive, Report 2019/055 (2019)

31. Coretti, S., Maurer, U., Tackmann, B., Venturi, D.: From single-bit to multi-bit public-key encryption via non-malleable codes. In: Dodis, Y., Nielsen, J.B. (eds.) TCC 2015. LNCS, vol. 9014, pp. 532–560. Springer, Heidelberg (2015). https://doi.org/10.1007/978-3-662-46494-6_22

32. Dachman-Soled, D., Kulkarni, M., Shahverdi, A.: Tight upper and lower bounds for leakage-resilient, locally decodable and updatable non-malleable codes. In: Fehr, S. (ed.) PKC 2017. LNCS, vol. 10174, pp. 310–332. Springer, Heidelberg (2017). https://doi.org/10.1007/978-3-662-54365-8_13

33. Dachman-Soled, D., Liu, F.-H., Shi, E., Zhou, H.-S.: Locally decodable and updatable non-malleable codes and their applications. In: Dodis, Y., Nielsen, J.B. (eds.) TCC 2015. LNCS, vol. 9014, pp. 427–450. Springer, Heidelberg (2015). https://doi.org/10.1007/978-3-662-46494-6_18

34. Dodis, Y., Wichs, D.: Non-malleable extractors and symmetric key cryptography from weak secrets. In: 41st ACM STOC, pp. 601–610 (2009)

35. Dziembowski, S., Kazana, T., Obremski, M.: Non-malleable codes from two-source extractors. In: Canetti, R., Garay, J.A. (eds.) CRYPTO 2013. LNCS, vol. 8043, pp. 239–257. Springer, Heidelberg (2013). https://doi.org/10.1007/978-3-642-40084-1_14

36. Dziembowski, S., Pietrzak, K., Wichs, D.: Non-malleable codes. In: ICS 2010, pp. 434–452 (2010)

37. Efremenko, K., Gelles, R., Haeupler, B.: Maximal noise in interactive communication over erasure channels and channels with feedback. In: ITCS 2015, pp. 11–20 (2015)

38. Faonio, A., Nielsen, J.B., Simkin, M., Venturi, D.: Continuously non-malleable codes with split-state refresh. In: ACNS 2018, pp. 121–139 (2018)

39. Faust, S., Hostáková, K., Mukherjee, P., Venturi, D.: Non-malleable codes for space-bounded tampering. In: Katz, J., Shacham, H. (eds.) CRYPTO 2017. LNCS, vol. 10402, pp. 95–126. Springer, Cham (2017). https://doi.org/10.1007/978-3-319-63715-0_4

40. Faust, S., Mukherjee, P., Nielsen, J.B., Venturi, D.: Continuous non-malleable codes. In: Lindell, Y. (ed.) TCC 2014. LNCS, vol. 8349, pp. 465–488. Springer, Heidelberg (2014). https://doi.org/10.1007/978-3-642-54242-8_20

41. Faust, S., Mukherjee, P., Nielsen, J.B., Venturi, D.: A tamper and leakage resilient von neumann architecture. In: Katz, J. (ed.) PKC 2015. LNCS, vol. 9020, pp. 579–603. Springer, Heidelberg (2015). https://doi.org/10.1007/978-3-662-46447-2_26

42. Faust, S., Mukherjee, P., Venturi, D., Wichs, D.: Efficient non-malleable codes and key-derivation for poly-size tampering circuits. In: Nguyen, P.Q., Oswald, E. (eds.) EUROCRYPT 2014. LNCS, vol. 8441, pp. 111–128. Springer, Heidelberg (2014). https://doi.org/10.1007/978-3-642-55220-5_7

43. Franklin, M., Gelles, R., Ostrovsky, R., Schulman, L.J.: Optimal coding for streaming authentication and interactive communication. In: Canetti, R., Garay, J.A. (eds.) CRYPTO 2013. LNCS, vol. 8043, pp. 258–276. Springer, Heidelberg (2013). https://doi.org/10.1007/978-3-642-40084-1_15

44. Gelles, R., Haeupler, B.: Capacity of interactive communication over erasure channels and channels with feedback. SIAM J. Comput. 46(4), 1449–1472 (2017)

45. Gelles, R., Haeupler, B., Kol, G., Ron-Zewi, N., Wigderson, A.: Towards optimal deterministic coding for interactive communication. In: 27th SODA, pp. 1922–1936 (2016)

46. Gelles, R., Kalai, Y.T.: Constant-rate interactive coding is impossible, even in constant-degree networks. Electronic Colloquium on Computational Complexity (ECCC), TR17-095 (2017)

47. Gelles, R., Moitra, A., Sahai, A.: Efficient and explicit coding for interactive communication. In: 52nd FOCS, pp. 768–777 (2011)

48. Gelles, R., Ostrovsky, R., Roytman, A.: Efficient error-correcting codes for sliding windows. In: Geffert, V., Preneel, B., Rovan, B., Štuller, J., Tjoa, A.M. (eds.) SOFSEM 2014. LNCS, vol. 8327, pp. 258–268. Springer, Cham (2014). https://doi.org/10.1007/978-3-319-04298-5_23
49. Ghaffari, M., Haeupler, B.: Optimal error rates for interactive coding II: Efficiency and list decoding. In: 55th FOCS, pp. 394–403 (2014)
50. Ghaffari, M., Haeupler, B., Sudan, M.: Optimal error rates for interactive coding I: adaptivity and other settings. In: 46th ACM STOC, pp. 794–803 (2014)
51. Goyal, V., Kumar, A.: Non-malleable secret sharing. In: 50th ACM STOC, pp. 685–698 (2018)
52. Goyal, V., Kumar, A.: Non-malleable secret sharing for general access structures. In: Shacham, H., Boldyreva, A. (eds.) CRYPTO 2018. LNCS, vol. 10991, pp. 501–530. Springer, Cham (2018). https://doi.org/10.1007/978-3-319-96884-1_17
53. Goyal, V., Pandey, O., Richelson, S.: Textbook non-malleable commitments. In: 48th ACM STOC, pp. 1128–1141 (2016)
54. Haeupler, B.: Interactive channel capacity revisited. In: 55th FOCS, pp. 226–235 (2014)
55. Jacobson, V., Braden, R., Borman, D.: RFC1323: TCP extensions for high performance. http://www.ietf.org/rfc/rfc1323.txt
56. Jain, A., Kalai, Y.T., Lewko, A.B.: Interactive coding for multiparty protocols. In: ITCS 2015, pp. 1–10 (2015)
57. Kanukurthi, B., Obbattu, S.L.B., Sekar, S.: Four-state non-malleable codes with explicit constant rate. In: Kalai, Y., Reyzin, L. (eds.) TCC 2017. LNCS, vol. 10678, pp. 344–375. Springer, Cham (2017). https://doi.org/10.1007/978-3-319-70503-3_11
58. Kanukurthi, B., Obbattu, S.L.B., Sekar, S.: Non-malleable randomness encoders and their applications. In: Nielsen, J.B., Rijmen, V. (eds.) EUROCRYPT 2018. LNCS, vol. 10822, pp. 589–617. Springer, Cham (2018). https://doi.org/10.1007/978-3-319-78372-7_19
59. Li, X.: Improved non-malleable extractors, non-malleable codes and independent source extractors. In: 49th ACM STOC, pp. 1144–1156 (2017)
60. Liu, F.-H., Lysyanskaya, A.: Tamper and leakage resilience in the split-state model. In: Safavi-Naini, R., Canetti, R. (eds.) CRYPTO 2012. LNCS, vol. 7417, pp. 517–532. Springer, Heidelberg (2012). https://doi.org/10.1007/978-3-642-32009-5_30
61. Ostrovsky, R., Persiano, G., Venturi, D., Visconti, I.: Continuously non-malleable codes in the split-state model from minimal assumptions. In: Shacham, H., Boldyreva, A. (eds.) CRYPTO 2018. LNCS, vol. 10993, pp. 608–639. Springer, Cham (2018). https://doi.org/10.1007/978-3-319-96878-0_21
62. Rajagopalan, S., Schulman, L.J.: A coding theorem for distributed computation. In: 26th ACM STOC, pp. 790–799 (1994)
63. Rao, A.: An exposition of Bourgain's 2-source extractor. Electronic Colloquium on Computational Complexity (ECCC), TR07-034 (2007)
64. Schulman, L.J.: Communication on noisy channels: a coding theorem for computation. In: 33rd FOCS, pp. 724–733 (1992)
65. Schulman, L.J.: Deterministic coding for interactive communication. In: 25th ACM STOC, pp. 747–756 (1993)
66. Schulman, L.J.: Coding for interactive communication. IEEE Trans. Inf. Theory **42**(6), 1745–1756 (1996)
67. Wee, H.: Black-box, round-efficient secure computation via non-malleability amplification. In: 51st FOCS, pp. 531–540 (2010)

Stronger Lower Bounds for Online ORAM

Pavel Hubáček$^{(\boxtimes)}$ [iD], Michal Koucký [iD], Karel Král [iD], and Veronika Slívová [iD]

Computer Science Institute of Charles University,
Malostranské náměstí 25, 118 00 Praha 1, Czech Republic
{hubacek,koucky,kralka,slivova}@iuuk.mff.cuni.cz

Abstract. Oblivious RAM (ORAM), introduced in the context of software protection by Goldreich and Ostrovsky [JACM'96], aims at obfuscating the memory access pattern induced by a RAM computation. Ideally, the memory access pattern of an ORAM should be independent of the data being processed. Since the work of Goldreich and Ostrovsky, it was believed that there is an inherent $\Omega(\log n)$ bandwidth overhead in any ORAM working with memory of size n. Larsen and Nielsen [CRYPTO'18] were the first to give a general $\Omega(\log n)$ lower bound for any *online* ORAM, i.e., an ORAM that must process its inputs in an online manner.

In this work, we revisit the lower bound of Larsen and Nielsen, which was proved under the assumption that the adversarial server knows exactly which server accesses correspond to which input operation. We give an $\Omega(\log n)$ lower bound for the bandwidth overhead of any online ORAM even when the adversary has no access to this information. For many known constructions of ORAM this information is provided implicitly as each input operation induces an access sequence of roughly the same length. Thus, they are subject to the lower bound of Larsen and Nielsen. Our results rule out a broader class of constructions and specifically, they imply that obfuscating the boundaries between the input operations does not help in building a more efficient ORAM.

As our main technical contribution and to handle the lack of structure, we study the properties of *access graphs* induced naturally by the memory access pattern of an ORAM computation. We identify a particular graph property that can be efficiently tested and that all access graphs of ORAM computation must satisfy with high probability. This property is reminiscent of the Larsen-Nielsen property but it is substantially less structured; that is, it is more generic.

Keywords: Oblivious RAM · Bandwidth overhead · Lower bound

This research was supported in part by the Grant Agency of the Czech Republic under the grant agreement no. 19-27871X, by the Charles University projects PRIMUS/17/SCI/9 and UNCE/SCI/004, Charles University grant SVV-2017-260452, and by the Neuron Fund for the support of science.

D. Hofheinz and A. Rosen (Eds.): TCC 2019, LNCS 11892, pp. 264–284, 2019.
https://doi.org/10.1007/978-3-030-36033-7_10

1 Introduction

Oblivious simulation of RAM machines, initially studied in the context of software protection by Goldreich and Ostrovsky [11], aims at protecting the memory access pattern induced by computation of a RAM from an eavesdropper. In the present day, such oblivious simulation might be needed when performing a computation in the memory of an untrusted server.[1] Despite using encryption for protecting the content of each memory cell, the memory access pattern might still leak sensitive information. Thus, the memory access pattern should be *oblivious* of the data being processed and, optimally, depend only on the size of the input.

Constructions. The strong guarantee of obliviousness of the memory access pattern comes at the cost of additional overhead. A trivial solution which scans the whole memory for each memory access induces linear *bandwidth overhead*, i.e., the multiplicative factor by which the length of a memory access pattern increases in the oblivious simulation of a RAM with n memory cells. Given its many practical applications, an important research direction is to construct an ORAM with as low overhead as possible. The foundational work of Goldreich and Ostrovsky [11] already gave a construction with bandwidth overhead $O(\log^3(n))$. Subsequent results introduced various improved approaches for building ORAMs (see [1, 4–6, 9, 11–13, 17, 22, 25, 26, 28, 29] and the references therein) leading to the recent construction of Asharov et al. [2] with bandwidth overhead $O(\log n)$ for the most natural setting of parameters.

Lower-Bounds. It was a folklore belief that an $\Omega(\log n)$ bandwidth overhead is inherent based on a lower bound presented already in the initial work of Goldreich and Ostrovsky [11]. However, the Goldreich-Ostrovsky result was recently revisited in the work of Boyle and Naor [3], who pointed out that the lower bound actually holds only in a rather restricted "balls and bins" model where the ORAM is not allowed to read the content of the data cells it processes. In fact, Boyle and Naor showed that any general lower bound for *offline* ORAM (i.e., where each memory access of the ORAM can depend on the whole sequence of operations it needs to obliviously simulate) implies non-trivial lower bounds on sizes of sorting circuits which seem to be out of reach of the known techniques in computational complexity. The connection between offline ORAM lower bounds and circuit lower bounds was extended to *read-only online* ORAMs (i.e., where only the read operations are processed in online manner) by Weiss and Wichs [30] who showed that lower bounds on bandwidth overhead for read-only online ORAMs would imply non-trivial lower bounds for sorting circuits or locally decodable codes.

The first general $\Omega(\log n)$ lower bound for bandwidth overhead in *online* ORAM (i.e., where the ORAM must process sequentially the operations it has to obliviously simulate) was given by Larsen and Nielsen [18]. The core of their lower

---

[1] Protecting the memory access of a computation is particularly relevant in the light of the recent Spectre [16] and Meltdown [19] attacks.

bound comprised of adapting the *information transfer* technique of Patrascu and Demaine [23], originally used for proving lower bounds for data structures in the cell probe model, to the ORAM setting. In fact, the lower bound of Larsen and Nielsen [18] for ORAM can be cast as a lower bound for the oblivious Array Maintenance problem and it was recently extended to other oblivious data structures by Jacob et al. [15].

1.1   Our Results

In this work, we further develop the information transfer technique of [23] when applied in the context of online ORAMs. We revisit the lower bound of Larsen and Nielsen which was proved under the assumption that the adversarial server knows exactly which server accesses correspond to each input operation. Specifically, we prove a stronger matching lower bound in a relaxed model without any restriction on the format of the access sequence to server memory.

Note that the [18] lower bound does apply to the known constructions of ORAMs where it is possible to implicitly separate the accesses corresponding to individual input operations – since each input operation generates an access sequence of roughly the same length. However, the [18] result does not rule out the possibility of achieving sub-logarithmic overhead in an ORAM which obfuscates the boundaries in the access pattern (e.g. by translating input operations into variable-length memory accesses). We show that obfuscating the boundaries between the input operations does not help in building a more efficient ORAM. In other words, our lower bound justifies the design choice of constructing ORAMs where each input operation is translated to roughly the same number of probes to server memory (common to the known constructions of ORAMs).

Besides online ORAM (i.e., the oblivious Array Maintenance problem), our techniques naturally extend to other oblivious data structures and allow to generalize also the recent lower bounds of Jacob et al. [15] for oblivious stacks, queues, deques, priority queues and search trees.

For online ORAMs with statistical security, our results are stated in the following informal theorem.

Theorem 1 (Informal). *Any statistically secure online ORAM with internal memory of size m has expected bandwidth overhead $\Omega(\log n)$, where $n \geq m^2$ is the length of the sequence of input operations. This result holds even when the adversarial server has no information about boundaries between probes corresponding to different input operations.*

In the computational setting, we consider two definitions of computational security. Our notion of *weak computational security* requires that no polynomial time algorithm can distinguish access sequences corresponding to any two input sequences of the same length – this is closer in spirit to computational security for ORAMs previously considered in the literature. The notion of *strong computational security* requires computational indistinguishability even when the distinguisher is given the two input sequences together with an access sequence corresponding to one of them. The distinguisher should not be able to tell which one of the two input sequences produced the access sequence. Interestingly, our technique (as well as the proof technique of [18] in the model with structured access pattern) yields different lower bounds with respect to the two definitions stated in the following informal theorem.

Theorem 2 (Informal). *Any weakly computationally secure online ORAM with internal memory of size m must have expected bandwidth overhead $\omega(1)$. Any strongly computationally secure online ORAM with internal memory of size m must have expected bandwidth overhead $\Omega(\log n)$, where $n \geq m^2$ is the length of the sequence of input operations. This result holds even when the adversarial server has no information about boundaries between probes corresponding to different input operations.*

Note that even the $\omega(1)$ lower bound for online ORAMs satisfying weak computational security is an interesting result in the light of the work of Boyle and Naor [3]. It follows from [3] that any super-constant lower bound for *offline* ORAM would imply super-linear lower bounds on size of sorting circuits – which would constitute a major breakthrough in computational complexity (for additional discussion, see Sect. 5). Our techniques clearly do not provide lower bounds for offline ORAMs. On the other hand, we believe that proving the $\omega(1)$ lower bound in any meaningful weaker model would amount to proving lower bounds for offline ORAM or read-only online ORAM which would have important implications in computational complexity.

Alternative Definitions of ORAM. Previous works considered various alternative definitions of ORAM. We clarify the ORAM model in which our techniques yield a lower bound in Sect. 2.1 and discuss its relation to other models in Sect. 5. As an additional contribution, we demonstrate an issue with the definition of ORAM appearing in Goldreich and Ostrovsky [11]. Specifically, we show that the definition can be satisfied by a RAM with constant overhead and no meaningful security. The definition of ORAM in Goldreich and Ostrovsky [11] differs from the original definition in Goldreich [10] and Ostrovsky [21], which do not share the issue we observed in the definition from Goldreich and Ostrovsky [11]. Given that the work of Goldreich and Ostrovsky [11] might serve as a primary reference for our community, we explain the issue in Sect. 5 to help preventing the use of the problematic definition in future works.

Persiano and Yeo [24] recently adapted the chronogram technique [8] from the literature on data structure lower bounds to prove a lower bound for *differentially private RAMs* (a relaxation of ORAMs in the spirit of differential privacy [7] which ensures indistinguishability only for input sequences that differ in a single operation). Similarly to the work of Larsen and Nielsen [18], the proof in [24] exploits the fact that the distinguisher knows exactly which server accesses correspond to each input operation. However, as the chronogram technique significantly differs from the information transfer approach, we do not think that our techniques would directly allow to strengthen the [24] lower bound for differentially private RAMs and prove it in the model with an unstructured access pattern.

1.2 Our Techniques

The structure of our proof follows a similar blueprint as the work of Larsen and Nielsen [18]. However, we must handle new issues introduced by the more general adversarial model. Most significantly, our proof cannot rely on any formatting of the access pattern, whereas Larsen and Nielsen leveraged the fact that the access pattern is split into blocks corresponding to each read/write operation. To handle the lack of structure in the access pattern, we study the properties of the *access graph* induced naturally by the access pattern of an ORAM computation. We identify a particular graph property that can be efficiently tested and that all access graphs of ORAM computation must satisfy with high probability. This property is reminiscent of the Larsen-Nielsen property but it is substantially less structured; that is, it is more generic.

The access graph is defined as follows: the vertices are timestamps of server probes and there is an edge connecting two vertices if and only if they correspond to two subsequent accesses to the same memory cell. We define a graph property called ℓ-*dense* k-*partition*. Roughly speaking, graphs with ℓ-dense k-partitions are graphs which may be partitioned into k disjoint subgraphs, each subgraph having at least ℓ edges. We show that this property has to be satisfied (with high probability) by access graphs induced by an ORAM for any k and an appropriate ℓ. To leverage this inherent structure of access graph towards a lower bound on bandwidth overhead, we prove that if a graph has $\frac{\ell}{k}$-dense k-partition for some ℓ and K different values of k then the graph must have at least $\Omega(\ell \log K)$ edges. In Sect. 3, we provide the formal definition of access graph and ℓ-dense k-partitions and prove a lower bound on the expected number of edges for a graph that has many ℓ-dense k-partitions.

In Sect. 4, we prove that access graphs of ORAMs have many dense partitions. Specifically, using a communication-type argument we show that for $\Omega(n)$ values of k, there exist input sequences for which the corresponding graph has $\Omega(\frac{n}{k})$-dense k-partition with high probability. Applying the indistinguishability of sequences of probes made by ORAM, we get one sequence for which its access graph satisfies $\frac{n}{k}$-dense k-partition for $\Omega(n)$ values of k with high probability. Combining the above results from Sect. 4 with the results from Sect. 3, we get that the graph of such a sequence has $\Omega(n \log n)$ edges, and thus by definition, $\Omega(n \log n)$ vertices in expectation. This implies that the expected number of probes made by the ORAM on any input sequence of length n is $\Omega(n \log n)$.

2 Preliminaries

In this section, we introduce some basic notation and recall some standard definitions and results. Throughout the rest of the paper, we let $[n]$ for $n \in \mathbb{N}$ to denote the set $\{1, 2, \ldots, n\}$. A function $\mathsf{negl}(n) \colon \mathbb{N} \to \mathbb{R}$ is *negligible* if it approaches zero faster than any inverse polynomial.

Definition 1 (Statistical Distance). *For two probability distributions X and Y on a discrete universe S, we define* statistical distance *of X and Y as*

$$\mathrm{SD}\,(X, Y) = \frac{1}{2} \sum_{s \in S} |\Pr[X = s] - \Pr[Y = s]| \ .$$

We use the following observation, which characterizes statistical distance as the difference of areas under the curve (see Fact 3.1.9 in Vadhan [27]).

Proposition 1. *Let X and Y be probability distributions on a discrete universe S, let $S_X = \{s \in S \colon \Pr[X = s] > \Pr[Y = s]\}$, and define S_Y analogously. Then*

$$\mathrm{SD}\,(X, Y) = \Pr[X \in S_X] - \Pr[Y \in S_X] = \Pr[Y \in S_Y] - \Pr[X \in S_Y] \ .$$

We also use the following data-processing-type inequality.

Proposition 2. *Let X and Y be probability distributions on a discrete universe S. Then for any function $f \colon S \to \{0, 1\}$, it holds that $|\Pr[f(X) = 1] - \Pr[f(Y) = 1]| \leq \mathrm{SD}\,(X, Y)$.*

Definition 2 (Computational indistinguishability). *Two probability ensembles, $\{X_n\}_{n \in \mathbb{N}}$ and $\{Y_n\}_{n \in \mathbb{N}}$, are* computationally indistinguishable *if for every polynomial-time algorithm D there exists a negligible function $\mathsf{negl}(\cdot)$ such that*

$$|\Pr[D(X_n, 1^n) = 1] - \Pr[D(Y_n, 1^n) = 1]| \leq \mathsf{negl}(n) \ .$$

2.1   Online ORAM

In this section, we present the formal definition for online oblivious RAM (ORAM) we consider in our work – we build on the oblivious cell-probe model of Larsen and Nielsen [18].

Definition 3 (Array Maintenance Problem [18]). *The* Array Maintenance *problem with parameters (ℓ, w) is to maintain an array B of ℓ w-bit entries under the following two operations:*

- *(W, a, d): Set the content of $B[a]$ to d, where $a \in [\ell]$, $d \in \{0, 1\}^w$.   (Write operation)*
- *(R, a, d): Return the content of $B[a]$, where $a \in [\ell]$ (note that d is ignored). (Read operation)*

We say that a machine $\mathcal{M}$ implements the Array Maintenance problem with parameters (ℓ, w) and probability p, if for every input sequence of operations

$$y = (o_1, a_1, d_1), \ldots, (o_n, a_n, d_n), \text{ where each } o_i \in \{R, W\}, a_i \in [\ell], d_i \in \{0, 1\}^w,$$

and for every read operation in the sequence y, $\mathcal{M}$ returns the correct answer with probability at least p.

Definition 4 (Online Oblivious RAM). *For $m, w \in \mathbb{N}$, let $RAM^*(m, w)$ denote a probabilistic random access machine $\mathcal{M}$ with m cells of internal memory, each of size w bits, which has access to a data structure, called* server, *implementing the Array Maintenance problem with parameters $(2^w, w)$ and probability 1. In other words, in each step of computation $\mathcal{M}$ may probe the server on a triple $(o, a, d) \in \{R, W\} \times [2^w] \times \{0, 1\}^w$ and on every input (R, a, d) the server returns to $\mathcal{M}$ the data last written in $B[a]$. We say that RAM^* probes the server whenever it makes an Array Maintenance operation to the server.*

Let m, M, w be any natural numbers such that $M \le 2^w$. An online Oblivious RAM $\mathcal{M}$ with address range M, cell size w bits and m cells of internal memory is a $RAM^*(m, w)$ satisfying online access sequence, correctness, and statistical (resp. computational) security as defined below.

Online Access Sequence: *For any input sequence $y = y_1, \ldots, y_n$ the RAM^* machine $\mathcal{M}$ gets y_i one by one, where each $y_i \in \{R, W\} \times [M] \times \{0, 1\}^w$. Upon the receipt of each operation y_i, the machine $\mathcal{M}$ generates a possibly empty sequence of server probes $(o_1, a_1, d_1), \ldots, (o_{\ell_i}, a_{\ell_i}, d_{\ell_i})$, where each $(o_i, a_i, d_i) \in \{R, W\} \times [2^w] \times \{0, 1\}^w$, and updates its internal memory state in order to correctly implement the request y_i. We define the access sequence corresponding to y_i as $A(\mathcal{M}, y_i) = a_1, a_2, \ldots, a_{\ell_i}$. For the input sequence y, the access sequence $A(\mathcal{M}, y)$ is defined as*

$$A(\mathcal{M}, y) = A(\mathcal{M}, y_1), A(\mathcal{M}, y_2), A(\mathcal{M}, y_3), \ldots, A(\mathcal{M}, y_n).$$

Note that the definition of the machine $\mathcal{M}$ is online, and thus for each input sequence $y = y_1, \ldots, y_n$ and each $i \in [n-1]$, the access sequence $A(\mathcal{M}, y_i)$ does not depend on $y_{i+1}, \ldots, y_n$.

Correctness: *$\mathcal{M}$ implements the Array Maintenance problem with parameters (M, w) with probability at least $1 - p_{\text{fail}}$.*

Statistical Security: *For any two input sequences y, y' of the same length, the statistical distance of the distributions of access sequences $A(\mathcal{M}, y)$ and $A(\mathcal{M}, y')$ is at most $\frac{1}{4}$.*

Computational Security: *For computational security, we consider infinite families of ORAM where we allow m, M, w to be functions of the length n of the input sequence. We distinguish between the following two notions:*

Weak Computational Security: *For any infinite families of input sequences $\{y_n\}_{n \in \mathbb{N}}$ and $\{y'_n\}_{n \in \mathbb{N}}$ such that $|y_n| = |y'_n| \ge n$ for all $n \in \mathbb{N}$, the probability ensembles $\{A(\mathcal{M}, y_n)\}_{n \in \mathbb{N}}$ and $\{A(\mathcal{M}, y'_n)\}_{n \in \mathbb{N}}$ are computationally indistinguishable.*

Strong Computational Security: *For any infinite families of input sequences $\{y_n\}_{n \in \mathbb{N}}$ and $\{y'_n\}_{n \in \mathbb{N}}$ such that $|y_n| = |y'_n| \ge n$ for all $n \in \mathbb{N}$, the probability ensembles $\{(y_n, y'_n, A(\mathcal{M}, y_n))\}_{n \in \mathbb{N}}$ and $\{(y_n, y'_n, A(\mathcal{M}, y'_n))\}_{n \in \mathbb{N}}$ are computationally indistinguishable.*

The parameters of our ORAM model from Definition 4 are depicted in Fig. 1. We use different sizes of arrows on server and RAM side to denote the asymmetry of the communication (the RAM sends type of operation, address, and data and the server returns requested data in case of a read operation and dummy value in case of a write operation). Note that the input sequence y of ORAM consists of a sequence of all operations, whereas the access sequence $A(\mathcal{M}, y)$ consists of a sequence of addresses of all probes.

Arguably, a user of an ORAM might want the stronger notion of computational security whereas the weaker notion is closer to the past considerations. Note that in the case of weak computational security, the adversarial distinguisher does not have access to the input sequences. Thus, it is restricted to contain only constant amount of information about the whole families of input sequences $\{y_n\}_n$ and $\{y'_n\}_n$. In contrast, in the case of strong computational security, the adversarial distinguisher is given also the input sequences. Thus, it is able to compute any polynomial time computable information about the input sequences. This distinction is crucial for our results, as we are able to prove only an $\omega(1)$ lower bound for weak security as opposed to the $\Omega(\log n)$ lower bound for strong security (see Theorems 5 and 4). Nevertheless, we believe that the known constructions of ORAM satisfy the notion of strong computational security.

For ease of exposition, in the rest of the paper we assume perfect correctness of the ORAM (i.e., $p_{\text{fail}} = 0$). However, our lower bounds can be extended also to ORAMs with imperfect correctness (see Remark 1). Finally, our lower bounds hold also for *semi-offline* ORAMs where the ORAM machine $\mathcal{M}$ receives the type and address of each operation in advance and it has to process in online manner only the data to be written during each write operation (see Remark 2).

3   Dense Graphs

In this section, we define an efficiently testable property of graphs that we show to be satisfied by graphs induced by the access pattern of any statistically secure ORAM. This property implies that the overhead of such ORAM must be logarithmic.

We say a directed graph $G = (V, E)$ is *ordered* if V is a subset of integers and for each edge $(u, v) \in E$, $u < v$. For a graph $G = (V, E)$ and $S, T \subseteq V$, we let $E(S, T) \subseteq E$ be the set of edges that start in S and end in T, and for integers $a \leq m \leq b \in V$ we let $E(a, m, b) = E(\{a, a+1, \ldots, m-1\}, \{m, m+1, \ldots, b-1\})$.

Definition 5. *A k-partition of an ordered graph $G = (V = \{0, 1, 2, \ldots, N - 1\}, E)$ is a sequence $0 = b_0 \leq m_0 \leq b_1 \leq m_1 \leq \cdots \leq b_k = N$. We say that the k-partition is ℓ-dense if for each $i \in \{0, \ldots, k - 1\}$, $E(b_i, m_i, b_{i+1})$ is of size at least ℓ.*

There is a simple greedy algorithm running in time $\mathcal{O}(|V|^2 \cdot |E|)$ which tests for given integers k, ℓ whether a given ordered graph $G = (V, E)$ has an ℓ-dense k-partition. (The algorithm looks for the k parts one by one greedily from left to right.)

Lemma 1. *Let $K \subseteq \mathbb{N}$ be a subset of powers of 4. Let $\ell \in \mathbb{N}$ be given. Let $G = (\{0, \ldots, N - 1\}, E)$ be an ordered graph which for each $k \in K$ has an (ℓ/k)-dense k-partition. Then G has at least $\frac{\ell}{2} \cdot |K|$ edges.*

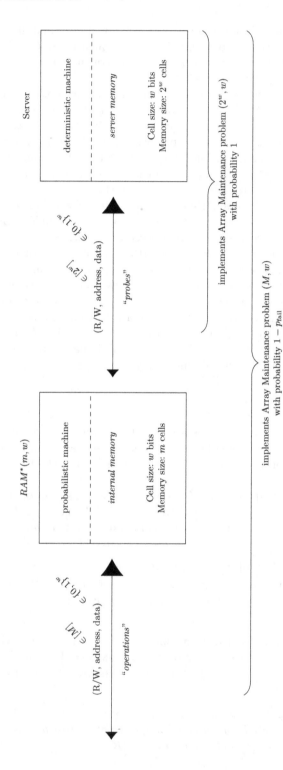

Fig. 1. Schema of online ORAM from Definition 4.

Proof. We use the following claim to bound the number of edges.

Claim. Let $k > k' > 0$ be integers. Let $0 = b_0 \leq m_0 \leq b_1 \leq m_1 \leq \cdots \leq b_k = N$ be a k-partition of G, and $0 = b'_0 \leq m'_0 \leq b'_1 \leq m'_1 \leq \cdots \leq b'_{k'} = N$ be a k'-partition of G. Then for at least $k - k'$ distinct $i \in \{0, \ldots, k-1\}$

$$E(b_i, m_i, b_{i+1}) \cap \bigcup_{j \in \{0, \ldots, k'-1\}} E(b'_j, m'_j, b'_{j+1}) = \emptyset. \tag{1}$$

Proof. For any $j \in \{0, \ldots, k'-1\}$ and $(u, v) \in E(b'_j, m'_j, b'_{j+1})$, if $(u, v) \in E(b_i, m_i, b_{i+1})$ for some i then $b_i < m'_j < b_{i+1}$ (as $b_i \leq u < m'_j \leq v \leq b_{i+1}$.) Thus, i is uniquely determined by j. Hence, $E(b_i, m_i, b_{i+1})$ may intersect $\bigcup_{j \in \{0, \ldots, k'-1\}} E(b'_j, m'_j, b'_{j+1})$ only if $b_i \leq m'_j < b_{i+1}$, for some $j \in \{0, \ldots, k'-1\}$. Thus, such an intersection occurs only for at most k' different i. The claim follows. $\square$

Now we are ready to prove Lemma 1. For each $k \in K$, pick an (ℓ/k)-dense k-partition $0 = b_0 \leq m_0 \leq b_1 \leq m_1 \leq \cdots \leq b_k = N$ of G and define the set of edges E_k:

$$E_k = \bigcup_{i \in \{0, \ldots, k-1\}} E(b_i, m_i, b_{i+1}).$$

For each $k \in K$, we lower-bound $\left| E_k \setminus \bigcup_{k' \in K, k' < k} E_{k'} \right|$ by $\ell/2$. Since K contains powers of 4, $\sum_{k' \in K, k' < k} k' \leq k/2$. By the above claim, for at least $k - \sum_{k' \in K, k' < k} k' \geq k/2$ different $i \in \{0, \ldots, k-1\}$, $E(b_i, m_i, b_{i+1}) \cap \bigcup_{k' \in K, k' < k} E_{k'} = \emptyset$. By density, $|E(b_i, m_i, b_{i+1})| \geq \ell/k$, so $\left| E_k \setminus \bigcup_{k' \in K, k' < k} E_{k'} \right| \geq \frac{\ell}{k} \cdot \frac{k}{2} = \ell/2$. Hence, $\left| \bigcup_{k \in K} E_k \right| = \sum_{k \in K} \left| E_k \setminus \bigcup_{k' \in K, k' < k} E_{k'} \right| \geq |K| \cdot \frac{\ell}{2}$. $\square$

In the following corollary, we show that the property of having many dense partitions with some probability implies proportionally many edges. (Note that the $\lfloor \log_4 t \rfloor - \lceil \log_4 s \rceil$ term corresponds exactly to the number of powers of four between s and t.)

Corollary 1. *Let ℓ, s, t be natural numbers, where $s \leq t$. Let $p \in [0, 1]$ be a real. Let G be an ordered graph picked at random from a distribution such that for each integer k, $s \leq k \leq t$, the randomly chosen ordered graph G has (ℓ/k)-dense k-partition with probability at least p. Then the expected number of edges in G is at least $\frac{p\ell}{2} \cdot (\lfloor \log_4 t \rfloor - \lceil \log_4 s \rceil)$.*

Proof. Let K be the set of integers such that $k \in K$ if and only if k is a power of 4 and G has an (ℓ/k)-dense k-partition. K is a random variable. The expected size of K is at least $p(\lfloor \log_4 t \rfloor - \lceil \log_4 s \rceil)$. By Lemma 1, the expected number of edges in G is at least $\frac{\ell}{2} \cdot p \cdot (\lfloor \log_4 t \rfloor - \lceil \log_4 s \rceil)$. $\square$

4   ORAM Lower Bound

In this section, we fix integers $n, m, M, w \geq 1$ such that $m \leq \sqrt{n}$, $n \leq M \leq 2^w$, and an ORAM $\mathcal{M}$ with address range M, cell size w and m cells of internal memory (see Definition 4). We argue that any statistically secure ORAM $\mathcal{M}$ must make $\Omega(n \log n)$ server probes in expectation in order to implement a sequence of n input operations. We also show that any ORAM $\mathcal{M}$ satisfying Weak Computational Security must make $\omega(n)$ server probes in expectation on any input sequence of length n.

Definition 6. *Let $A(\mathcal{M}, y) = a_0, \ldots, a_{N-1}$ be an access sequence of $\mathcal{M}$ for some input sequence y. We define a directed graph $G(A(\mathcal{M}, y)) = (V, E)$ called* access graph *as follows: $V = \{0, \ldots, N-1\}$ and $(i, j) \in E$ iff $i < j$ and $a_i = a_j$ and for each $k \in \{i+1, \ldots, j-1\}$, $a_k \neq a_i$.*

Notice that every vertex of an access graph has outdegree as well as indegree at most one.

In the following, we consider input sequences of even length $n \in \mathbb{N}$. First, we define a sequence of alternating writes and reads at address $a = 1$ with data $d = 0^w$ as $Y_{n,0} = [(W, 1, 0^w), (R, 1, 0^w)]^{n/2}$. Second, for each $k \in \{1, 2, \ldots, \frac{n}{2}\}$, let $\ell = \lfloor \frac{n}{2k} \rfloor$, we define a distribution $Y_{n,k}$ of input sequences as

$$
\begin{aligned}
Y_{n,k} = &(W, 1, b_{1,1}), (W, 2, b_{1,2}), \ldots, (W, \ell, b_{1,\ell}), (R, 1, 0^w), (R, 2, 0^w), \ldots, (R, \ell, 0^w), \\
&(W, 1, b_{2,1}), (W, 2, b_{2,2}), \ldots, (W, \ell, b_{2,\ell}), (R, 1, 0^w), (R, 2, 0^w), \ldots, (R, \ell, 0^w), \\
&\cdots, \\
&(W, 1, b_{k,1}), (W, 2, b_{k,2}), \ldots, (W, \ell, b_{k,\ell}), (R, 1, 0^w), (R, 2, 0^w), \ldots, (R, \ell, 0^w), \\
&(W, 1, 0^w), (R, 1, 0^w), (W, 1, 0^w), \ldots, (R, 1, 0^w),
\end{aligned}
$$

where each $b_{i,j} \in \{0, 1\}^w$ is an independently uniformly chosen bit string. We define the i-th block of writes $W_i = (W, 1, b_{i,1}), (W, 2, b_{i,2}), \ldots, (W, \ell, b_{i,\ell})$ and the i-th block of reads R_i to be the sequence of operations $(R, 1, 0^w), (R, 2, 0^w), \ldots, (R, \ell, 0^w)$ following right after W_i. Note that after the k-th block of reads the sequence is padded to length n by a sequence of alternating writes and reads. For an ORAM $\mathcal{M}$, we use the notation $G_{n,k} = G(A(\mathcal{M}, Y_{n,k}))$ and $G_{n,0} = G(A(\mathcal{M}, Y_{n,0}))$ when $\mathcal{M}$ is clear from the context.

The following lemma uses only correctness of ORAM and does not depend on its security. The proof of the lemma uses the information transfer technique similarly to Lemma 2 in [18].

Lemma 2. *Let $n, m, M, w, \mathcal{M}$ be as in the beginning of this section, moreover suppose $n \geq 10$ is an even integer. Let $k \geq 1$ be an integer such that $k \leq \frac{n}{10(m+2\log n + 11)}$. Let $A(\mathcal{M}, Y_{n,k})$ be the access sequence of $\mathcal{M}$ and $G_{n,k}$ be the corresponding access graph. ($G_{n,k}$ is a random variable that depends on $Y_{n,k}$ and the internal randomness of $\mathcal{M}$.) With probability at least $1 - \frac{1}{n}$, $G_{n,k}$ has $(n/5k)$-dense k-partition.*

Proof. By our assumption from the beginning of this section, $n \leq M$, and thus for any $k \in \{1, 2, \ldots, \frac{n}{2}\}$ all sequences $Y_{n,k}$ have all addresses in the correct range. Fix any k satisfying the assumptions of this lemma and set $\ell = \lfloor \frac{n}{2k} \rfloor$. As defined before let W_i and R_i be the i-th block of writes and reads in $Y_{n,k}$, respectively. Let U_i be the vertices of $G_{n,k}$ corresponding to W_i, and V_i be the vertices corresponding to R_i. It suffices to prove that for each $i \in \{1, \ldots, k\}$, the probability that there are fewer than $n/5k$ edges between U_i and V_i is less than $1/n^2$. If this holds then by the union bound the lemma follows.

For contradiction, assume there exists $i \in \{1, \ldots, k\}$ such that the probability that there are fewer than $n/5k$ edges between U_i and V_i is at least $1/n^2$. Here, the randomness is taken over the choice of an input sequence $y \leftarrow Y_{n,k}$ and the internal randomness of $\mathcal{M}$. Fix such an i. Fix all the randomness except for the choice of $b_{i,1}, \ldots, b_{i,\ell}$ in $Y_{n,k}$ so that $G_{n,k}$ obtained from this restricted distribution has fewer than $n/5k$ edges between U_i and V_i with probability $\geq 1/n^2$ over the choice of $b_{i,1}, \ldots, b_{i,\ell}$. (This is possible by an averaging argument.) Let $B \subseteq \{0,1\}^{w \times \ell}$ be the set of choices for $b_{i,1}, \ldots, b_{i,\ell}$ which give fewer than $n/5k$ edges between U_i and V_i in $G_{n,k}$. Clearly, $|B| \geq 2^{w\ell}/n^2$.

We use $\mathcal{M}$ to construct a deterministic protocol that transmits any string from B from Alice to Bob, two communicating parties, using at most $\log |B| - 10$ bits. That gives a contradiction as such an efficient transmission violates the pigeon-hole principle.

On input $b \in B$ to Alice, Alice sends a single message to Bob who can determine b from the message. They proceed as follows. Both Alice and Bob simulate $\mathcal{M}$ on $Y_{n,k}$ up until reaching W_i. All the randomness used before the i-th block of writes W_i is fixed and known both to Alice and Bob. Then Alice continues with the simulation of $\mathcal{M}$ on W_i with data $b_{i,1}, b_{i,2}, \ldots, b_{i,\ell}$ set to b. Once she finishes it, she sends the content of the internal memory of $\mathcal{M}$ to Bob using wm bits. Then Alice continues with the simulation of $\mathcal{M}$ on R_i and whenever $\mathcal{M}$ makes a server probe to read from a location that was written last time during the simulation of W_i, Alice sends over the address and the content of that cell to Bob. Overall, Alice sends at most $mw + 2wn/5k$ bits of communication to Bob that can be concatenated into a single message of this size.

On receiving side, Bob uses the internal state of $\mathcal{M}$ communicated by Alice to continue with the computation on R_i, while he uses the state of the server he obtained initially before reaching W_i. He simulates all server probes by himself, except for read operations that match the list sent by Alice, where he initially uses the content provided by Alice. Clearly, Bob can determine b from the simulation.

As $k \leq \frac{n}{10(m + 2\log n + 11)}$, $mw + 2wn/5k \leq (n/2k - 2\log n - 11)w$, so $mw + 2wn/5k \leq (\ell - 2\log n - 10)w$, hence, the number of communicated bits is $mw + 2wn/5k \leq \log |B| - (2w - 2)\log n - 10w$, which is a contradiction. □

Remark 1. Using good error-correcting codes (see for instance [20]), this lemma could be generalized to the case when $\mathcal{M}$ implements Array Maintenance problem with probability $1 - p_{\text{fail}} < 1$, i.e., $\mathcal{M}$ is allowed to return a wrong value for each of its input read operations with a small constant probability p_{fail}. The graph $G_{n,k}$ would still have $(\epsilon n/k)$-dense k-partition with $1 - 1/n$ probability for some $\epsilon > 0$ which depends only on the allowed failure probability p_{fail}.

Remark 2. Note that the randomness of input sequence $Y_{n,k}$ is used only for the data to be written. Moreover, the proof relies only on incompressibility of a random string stored during the write block and it does not rely on the addresses used to store this data. Thus, the same proof goes through even for *semi-offline ORAMs*, i.e., if we allow the ORAM to know the type and address of each input operation in y in advance. On the other hand, as our proof uses interleaved sequences of write blocks and read blocks, it is unlikely that it would be possible to extend it to the *read-only online ORAM* model of Weiss and Wichs [30].

Note that using an averaging argument we can assume that the probability in Lemma 2 is only over the randomness of $\mathcal{M}$. Thus we get the following corollary proving for every k the existence of a single input sequence whose corresponding access graph has $\frac{n}{5k}$-dense k-partition with high probability.

Corollary 2. *For any even integer $n \geq 10$ and an integer $k \geq 1$ such that $k \leq \frac{n}{10(m+2\log n+11)}$ there is an input sequence $y_{n,k}$ of length n such that $G(A(\mathcal{M}, y_{n,k}))$ has a $(n/5k)$-dense k-partition with probability at least $1 - \frac{1}{n}$.*

We show that by statistical security of $\mathcal{M}$, this property holds for a single input sequence and many different values of k.

Lemma 3. *Let $n, m, M, w, \mathcal{M}$ be as in the beginning of this section, and assume n is even and $n \geq 10$. Let y be an input sequence to $\mathcal{M}$ of length n. If $\mathcal{M}$ is a statistically secure online ORAM then for every $k \in \left\{1, 2, \ldots, \left\lfloor \frac{n}{10(m+2\log n+11)} \right\rfloor\right\}$*

$$\Pr\left[G(A(\mathcal{M}, y)) \text{ has an } (n/5k)\text{-dense } k\text{-partition}\right] \geq \frac{3}{5}.$$

Proof. For contradiction, suppose that for some k the probability is less than $3/5$. From the statistical security of $\mathcal{M}$ we know that the statistical distance $\text{SD}\left(A(\mathcal{M}, y), A(\mathcal{M}, y_{n,k})\right) \leq \frac{1}{4}$ where $y_{n,k}$ is given by Corollary 2. By Corollary 2 the sequence $y_{n,k}$ gives us a graph $G(A(\mathcal{M}, y_{n,k}))$ which has an $(n/5k)$-dense k-partition with probability at least $1 - 1/n \geq 9/10$. Define a function $f_{\ell,k}$ on ordered graphs that is an indicator of having an ℓ-dense k-partition. Applying Proposition 2 with $X \leftarrow G(A(\mathcal{M}, y))$, $Y \leftarrow G(A(\mathcal{M}, y_{n,k}))$, and $f = f_{n/5k,k}$, we can conclude that $G(A(\mathcal{M}, y))$ has an $(n/5k)$-dense k-partition with probability at least $3/4 - 1/10 \geq 3/5$. □

We are ready to prove our main theorem for statistically secure ORAM.

Theorem 3. *There are constants $c_0, c_1 > 0$ such that for any integers $m, w \geq 1$ and $M \geq n \geq c_0$ where $m \leq \sqrt{n}$ and $M \leq 2^w$, any statistically secure online ORAM $\mathcal{M}$ with address range M, cell size w bits and m cells of internal memory must perform at least $c_1 n \log n$ server probes in expectation (the expectation is over the randomness of $\mathcal{M}$) on any input sequence of length n.*

Proof. Fix an ORAM machine $\mathcal{M}$. Consider any input sequence y to $\mathcal{M}$ of length n. By Lemma 3 for every k, such that $1 \leq k \leq \left\lfloor \frac{n}{10(m+2\log n+11)} \right\rfloor$, we get that

$$\Pr\left[G(A(\mathcal{M},y)) \text{ has an } (n/5k)\text{-dense } k\text{-partition}\right] \geq \frac{3}{5}.$$

Applying Corollary 1 with $s = 1$, $t = \left\lfloor \frac{n}{10(m+2\log n+11)} \right\rfloor$, $\ell = \lfloor \frac{n}{5} \rfloor$, and $p = 3/5$, we can lower bound the expected number of edges in $G(A(\mathcal{M},y))$ by

$$\frac{3n}{50} \left\lfloor \log_4 \left\lfloor \frac{n}{10(m+2\log n+11)} \right\rfloor \right\rfloor.$$

For $n \geq 1000$, $\left\lfloor \frac{n}{10(m+2\log n+11)} \right\rfloor \geq \frac{\sqrt{n}}{40}$. Hence, the expected number of edges in $G(A(\mathcal{M},y))$ is at least $\frac{3}{100} \cdot n \log \frac{\sqrt{n}}{40} \geq \frac{1}{100} \cdot n \log n$, provided c_0 is large enough. Since the indegree of each vertex of an access graph is at most one, the expected number of vertices in $G(A(\mathcal{M},y))$, which is the same as the expected number of probes in $A(\mathcal{M},y)$, is at least $\frac{1}{100} \cdot n \log n$. □

Next, we prove $\Omega(\log n)$ lower bound for ORAMs satisfying strong computational security from Definition 4.

Lemma 4. *Let $m, M, w \colon \mathbb{N} \to \mathbb{N}$ be non-decreasing functions such that for all n large enough: $m(n) \leq \sqrt{n}$ and $n \leq M(n) \leq 2^{w(n)}$. Let $\{\mathcal{M}_n\}_{n\in\mathbb{N}}$ be a sequence of online ORAMs with address range $M(n)$, cell size $w(n)$ bits and $m(n)$ cells of internal memory which satisfy strong computational security. Let $\{y_n\}_{n\in\mathbb{N}}$ be an infinite family of input sequences where $|y_n| = n$, for each $n \in \mathbb{N}$.*
Then there exists n_0 such that for every $n \geq n_0$ and for every k in the set $\left\{1, 2, \ldots, \left\lfloor \frac{n}{10(m(n)+2\log n+11)} \right\rfloor \right\}$,

$$\Pr\left[G(A(\mathcal{M}_n, y_n)) \text{ has an } (n/5k)\text{-dense } k\text{-partition}\right] \geq \frac{3}{5}.$$

Proof. For contradiction, assume there are infinitely many pairs of integers (n, k), s.t. $k \leq \left\lfloor \frac{n}{10(m(n)+2\log n+11)} \right\rfloor$ and that the probability that y_n has an $(n/5k)$-dense k-partition is less than $3/5$.

Let $\mathcal{D}$ be an algorithm which given two input sequences y and y' of length n and an access sequence $A(\mathcal{M}_n, z)$, where $z \in \{y, y'\}$, does the following:

1. Compute n.
2. Compute k' to be the number of blocks of consecutive reads of length $\lfloor n/k' \rfloor$ in the input sequence y'.
3. If $A(\mathcal{M}_n, z)$ does not have $(n/5k')$-dense k'-partition $\mathcal{D}$ returns "1" (i.e. $\mathcal{D}$ guesses that $z = y$).
4. Otherwise $\mathcal{D}$ returns "1" with probability $1/2$ and "2" with probability $1/2$ (i.e. $\mathcal{D}$ guesses at random).

There is a polynomial time greedy algorithm determining whether the graph $G(A(\mathcal{M}_n, z))$ contains an ℓ-dense k-partition. Thus algorithm $\mathcal{D}$ runs in time polynomial in the length of the access sequence $A(\mathcal{M}_n, z)$.

Let $y_{n,k}$ be a sequence from Corollary 2. So, $G(A(\mathcal{M}_n, y_{n,k}))$ has an $(n/5k)$-dense k-partition with probability at least $1 - 1/n \geq 9/10$. Observe that if $y = y_n$ and $y' = y_{n,k}$ then:

$$|\Pr[\mathcal{D}(y_n, y_{n,k}, A(\mathcal{M}_n, y_n)) = 1] - \Pr[\mathcal{D}(y_n, y_{n,k}, A(\mathcal{M}_n, y_{n,k})) = 1]|$$
$$\geq \left(\frac{2}{5} + \frac{3}{5} \cdot \frac{1}{2} \right) - \left(\frac{1}{10} + \frac{9}{10} \cdot \frac{1}{2} \right) = \frac{3}{20}.$$

By the assumption $\mathcal{D}$ returns "1" in step 3 on $A(\mathcal{M}_n, y_n)$ with probability at least $2/5$. By Corollary 2 $\mathcal{D}$ answers "1" on $A(\mathcal{M}_n, y_{n,k})$ with probability at most $1/10$.

This contradicts the strong computational security of $\mathcal{M}_n$ as $\mathcal{D}$ should not distinguish between y and y' with non-negligible probability. $\qquad \square$

Theorem 4. *Let $m, M, w \colon \mathbb{N} \to \mathbb{N}$ be non-decreasing functions such that for all n large enough: $m(n) \leq \sqrt{n}$ and $n \leq M(n) \leq 2^{w(n)}$. Let $\{\mathcal{M}_n\}_{n \in \mathbb{N}}$ be a sequence of online ORAMs with address range $M(n)$, cell size $w(n)$ bits and $m(n)$ cells of internal memory which satisfy strong computational security. Let $\{y_n\}_{n \in \mathbb{N}}$ be an infinite family of input sequences where $|y_n| = n$, for each $n \in \mathbb{N}$.*

There are constants $c_0, c_1 > 0$, such that for any $n \geq c_0$, $\mathcal{M}_n$ must perform in expectation at least $c_1 n \log n$ server probes on the input sequence y_n.

Proof. The proof is identical to the proof of Theorem 3 but we use Lemma 4 instead of Lemma 3. Note that the different order of quantifiers is caused by different order of quantifiers in Lemma 3 and in Lemma 4. $\qquad \square$

In the rest of this section, we prove an $\omega(1)$ lower bound for ORAMs satisfying weak computational security from Definition 4. Note that in the case of weak computational security it is unclear which k should the adversary use to distinguish y and y'. Thus, we cannot directly conclude that y has $\frac{n}{5k}$-dense k-partition for every n and $k \leq \left\lfloor \frac{n}{10(m(n)+2\log n+11)} \right\rfloor$. On the other hand, for every k there could be only finitely many values n such that there is an input sequence of length n which has no $\frac{n}{5k}$-dense k-partition. This fact allows us to prove the $\omega(1)$ lower bound for weak computational security.

Theorem 5. *Let $m, M, w \colon \mathbb{N} \to \mathbb{N}$ be non-decreasing functions such that for all n large enough: $m(n) \leq \sqrt{n}$ and $n \leq M(n) \leq 2^{w(n)}$. Let $\{\mathcal{M}_n\}_{n \in \mathbb{N}}$ be a sequence of online ORAMs with address range $M(n)$, cell size $w(n)$ bits and $m(n)$ cells of internal memory which satisfy weak computational security. Let $\{y_n\}_{n \in \mathbb{N}}$ be a sequence of input sequences where $|y_n| = n$, for each $n \in \mathbb{N}$.*

For any constant $c_1 > 0$ there is a constant $c_0 > 0$, such that for any $n \geq c_0$, $\mathcal{M}_n$ must perform in expectation at least $c_1 n$ server probes on the input sequence y_n.

In particular there is no computationally secure online ORAM with constant bandwidth overhead $\mathcal{O}(1)$.

Proof. For each $n \in \mathbb{N}$, define $k(n)$ to be the smallest k such that

$$\Pr[G(A(\mathcal{M}_n, y_n)) \text{ has } (n/5k)\text{-dense } k\text{-partition}] < 1/2.$$

Using Corollary 1 we get for each n large enough that the expected number of edges in $G(A(\mathcal{M}_n, y_n))$ is at least $c \cdot n \log k(n)$, for some absolute constant $c > 0$. It suffices to show that $k(n) \to \infty$ as $n \to \infty$. There cannot exist a constant k such that Y_n has $(n/5k)$-dense k-partition with probability less than $\frac{1}{2}$ for infinitely many n. Otherwise $\{y_n\}_n$ would be computationally distinguishable from $\{Y_{n,k}\}_n$ (by the greedy algorithm which has k hard-wired). So, $k(n) \to \infty$ as $n \to \infty$. □

5   Alternative Definitions for Oblivious RAM

In this section, we recall some alternative definitions for ORAM which appeared in the literature and explain the relation of our lower bound to those models.

The Definition of Larsen and Nielsen. Larsen and Nielsen (see Definition 4 in [18]) required that for any two input sequences of equal length, the corresponding distributions of access sequences cannot be distinguished with probability greater than $1/4$ by any algorithm running in polynomial time in the sum of the following terms: the length of the input sequence, logarithm of the number of memory cells (i.e., $\log n$), and the size of a memory cell (i.e., $\log n$ for the most natural parameters). We show that their definition implies statistical closeness as considered in our work (see the statistical security property in Definition 4). Therefore, any lower bound on the bandwidth overhead of ORAM satisfying our definition implies a matching lower bound w.r.t. the definition of Larsen and Nielsen [18].

To this end, let us show that if two distributions of access sequences are not statistically close, then they are distinguishable in the sense of Larsen and Nielsen. Assume there exist two input sequences y and y' of equal lengths, for which the access sequences $A(\mathcal{M}, y)$ and $A(\mathcal{M}, y')$ have statistical distance greater than $1/4$. We define a distinguisher algorithm D that on access sequence x outputs 1 whenever $\Pr[A(\mathcal{M}, y) = x] > \Pr[A(\mathcal{M}, y') = x]$, outputs 0 whenever $\Pr[A(\mathcal{M}, y) = x] < \Pr[A(\mathcal{M}, y') = x]$, and outputs a uniformly random bit whenever $\Pr[A(\mathcal{M}, y) = x] = \Pr[A(\mathcal{M}, y') = x]$. It follows from definition of D, basic properties of statistical distance (see proposition 1), and our assumption about the statistical distance of $A(\mathcal{M}, y)$ and $A(\mathcal{M}, y')$ that

$$|\Pr[D(A(\mathcal{M}, y)) = 1] - \Pr[D(A(\mathcal{M}, y')) = 1]| = \text{SD}\left(A(\mathcal{M}, y), A(\mathcal{M}, y')\right) > \frac{1}{4}.$$

Note that D can be specific for the pair of the two input sequences y and y' and it can have all the significant information about the distributions $A(\mathcal{M}, y)$ and

$A(\mathcal{M}, y')$ hardwired. For example, it is sufficient to store a string describing for each access sequence x whether it is more, less, or equally likely under $A(\mathcal{M}, y)$ or $A(\mathcal{M}, y')$. Even though such string is of exponential size w.r.t. the length of the access pattern, D needs to simply access the position corresponding to the observed access pattern to output its decision as described above. Thus, D can run in linear time in the length of the access sequence (which is polynomial in the length of the input sequence) and distinguishes the two access sequences with probability greater than $1/4$.

The Definition of Goldreich and Ostrovsky. Unlike the original definition of ORAM from Goldreich [10] and Ostrovsky [21], the definition of ORAM presented in Goldreich and Ostrovsky [11] postulates an alternative security requirement. However, the alternative definition suffers from an issue which is not present in the original definition and which, to the best of our knowledge, was not pointed out in the literature. In particular, the definition in [11] can be satisfied by a dummy ORAM construction with only a constant overhead and without achieving any indistinguishability of the access sequences. Given that Goldreich and Ostrovsky [11] might serve as a primary reference for our community, we explain the issue in the following paragraph to help preventing the use of the problematic definition in future works.

Recall the definition of ORAM with perfect security from Goldreich and Ostrovsky (Definition 2.3.1.3 in [11]):

Goldreich-Ostrovsky Security: *For any two input sequences y and y', if the length distributions $|A(\mathcal{M}, y)|$ and $|A(\mathcal{M}, y')|$ are identical, then $A(\mathcal{M}, y)$ and $A(\mathcal{M}, y')$ are identical.*

As we show, this requirement can be satisfied by creating an ORAM that makes sure that on any two distinct sequences y, y', the length distributions $|A(\mathcal{M}, y)|$ and $|A(\mathcal{M}, y')|$ differ. Note that no indistinguishability is required in that case and the ORAM can then reveal the access pattern of the input sequence.

To this end, we describe an ORAM with a constant overhead so that the length $|A(\mathcal{M}, y)|$ is either $2|y|$ or $2|y| + 1$ and the distribution $|A(\mathcal{M}, y)|$ encodes the sequence y. The ORAM proceeds by performing every operation y_i directly on the server followed by a read operation from address 1. After the last instruction in y, the ORAM selects a random sequence of operations r of length $|y|$ and if r is lexicographically smaller than y then the ORAM performs an extra read from address 1 before terminating. Note that this ORAM can be efficiently implemented using constant amount of internal memory by comparing the input sequence to the randomly selected one online. Also, the machine does not need to know the length of the sequence in advance. Finally, the length distribution $|A(\mathcal{M}, y)|$ is clearly different for each input sequence y. Given that the above definition of ORAM of Goldreich and Ostrovsky allows the dummy construction with a constant overhead, we do not hope to extend our lower bound towards this definition.

One could object that the above dummy ORAM exploits the fact that indistinguishability of access sequences must hold only if the length distributions are identical. However, it is possible to construct a similar dummy ORAM with low overhead satisfying even the following relaxation of the definition requiring indistinguishability of access sequences corresponding to any pair of y and y' for which $|A(M, y)|$ and $|A(M, y')|$ are statistically close (i.e., the indistinguishability is required for a potentially larger set of access patterns):

Relaxation of Goldreich-Ostrovsky Security: *For any two input sequences y and y', if the length distributions $|A(\mathcal{M}, y)|$ and $|A(\mathcal{M}, y')|$ are statistically close, then $A(\mathcal{M}, y)$ and $A(\mathcal{M}, y')$ are statistically close.*

We show there is a dummy ORAM $\mathcal{M}$ with a constant overhead such that for any two input sequences y and y' which differ in their accessed memory locations, the statistical distance $\mathrm{SD}\,(|A(\mathcal{M}, y)|, |A(\mathcal{M}, y')|)$ is at least $\frac{1}{nM}$ (where $n = |y| = |y'|$ and M is the size of address range).

The ORAM $\mathcal{M}$ works as follows. At the beginning, the ORAM picks $i \in [n]$ and $r \in [M]$ uniformly at random. Then for $j = 1, \ldots n$, it executes each of the input operations (o_j, a_j, d_j) directly on the server. For each $j < i$, it performs two additional reads from address 1 after executing the j-th input operation. For $j = i$, after the i-th input operation it performs two additional reads from address 1 if $r \leq a_i$, and it performs one additional read from address 1 if $r > a_i$. For $j > i$, it performs each of the input operations without any additional read.

It is straightforward to verify that the distribution of $|A(\mathcal{M}, y)|$ satisfies: for each $i \in [n]$, $\Pr[|A(\mathcal{M}, y)| = n + 2i] = \frac{a_i}{nM}$. Hence, for any pair y and y' of two input sequences of length n, if the sequences of addresses accessed by them differ then the statistical distance between the distributions of $|A(\mathcal{M}, y)|$ and $|A(\mathcal{M}, y')|$ is at least $1/nM$. If M is polynomial in n this means that their distance is at least $\frac{1}{\mathrm{poly}(n)}$. Thus, $\mathcal{M}$ satisfies even the stronger variant of the definition from [11] even though its access sequence leaks the addresses from the input sequence.

It was previously shown by Haider, Khan and van Dijk [14] that there exists an ORAM construction which reveals all memory accesses from the input sequence while satisfying the definition of Goldreich and Ostrovsky from [11]. However, their construction has an *exponential* bandwidth overhead which makes it insufficient to demonstrate any issue with the definition of Goldreich and Ostrovsky. Clearly, any definition of ORAM can disregard constructions with super-linear overhead as a perfectly secure ORAM (with linear overhead) can be constructed by simply passing over the whole server memory for each input operation. Unlike the construction of [14], our constructions of the dummy ORAMs with constant bandwidth overhead exemplify that the definition of Goldreich and Ostrovsky from [11] is problematic in the interesting regime of parameters.

Simulation-Based Definitions. The recent work of Asharov et al. [2] employs a simulation-based definition parameterized by a functionality which implements an oblivious data structure. Our lower bounds directly extend to their stronger definition when the functionality implements Array Maintenance. Moreover, our techniques can be adapted to give lower bounds for functionalities implementing stacks, queues and others considered in [15].

Weak vs. Strong Computational Security. In this work, we distinguish between weak and strong computational security (see Definition 4). Our techniques do not allow to prove matching bounds for ORAMs satisfying the two notions and we show $\Omega(\log n)$ lower bound only w.r.t. strong computational security. Though, as we noted in Sect. 1.1, even the $\omega(1)$ lower bound for online ORAMs satisfying weak computational security is an interesting result in the light of the work of Boyle and Naor [3]. It follows from [3] that any super-constant lower bound for *offline* ORAM would imply super-linear lower bounds on size of sorting circuits – which would constitute a major breakthrough in computational complexity. The main result from Boyle and Naor [3] can be rephrased using our notation as follows.

Theorem 6 (Theorem 3.1 [3]). *Suppose there exists a Boolean circuit ensemble $C = \{C(n, w)\}_{n,w}$ of size $s(n, w)$, such that each $C(n, w)$ takes as input n words each of size w bits, and outputs the words in sorted order. Then for word size $w \in \Omega(\log n) \cap n^{o(1)}$ and constant internal memory $m \in \mathcal{O}(1)$, there exists a secure offline ORAM (as per Definition 2.8 [3]) with total bandwidth and computation $\mathcal{O}(n \log w + s(2n/w, w))$.*

Moreover, the additive factor of $\mathcal{O}(n \log w)$ follows from the transpose part of the algorithm of [3] (see Figs. 1 and 2 in [3]). As Boyle and Naor showed in their appendix (Remark B.3 [3]) this additive factor in total bandwidth may be reduced to $\mathcal{O}(n)$ if the size of internal memory is $m \geq w$. Thus, sorting circuit of size $\mathcal{O}(nw)$ implies offline ORAM with total bandwidth $\mathcal{O}(n + 2\frac{n}{w}w) = \mathcal{O}(n)$. Or the other way around, lower bound $\omega(n)$ for total bandwidth of offline ORAM implies $\omega(nw)$ lower bound for circuits sorting n words of size w bits, each.

We leave it as an intriguing open problem whether it is possible to prove an $\Omega(\log n)$ lower bound for online ORAMs satisfying weak computational security.

Acknowledgements. We wish to thank Oded Goldreich for clarifications regarding the ORAM definitions in [10,11,21] and Jesper Buus Nielsen for clarifying the details of the lower bound for computationally secure ORAMs from [18]. We are also thankful to the anonymous TCC 2019 reviewers for insightful comments that helped us improve the presentation of our results.

References

1. Ajtai, M.: Oblivious RAMs without cryptographic assumptions. In: Proceedings of the 42nd ACM Symposium on Theory of Computing, STOC 2010, Cambridge, Massachusetts, USA, 5–8 June 2010, pp. 181–190 (2010)
2. Asharov, G., Komargodski, I., Lin, W., Nayak, K., Peserico, E., Shi, E.: OptORAMa: optimal oblivious RAM. IACR Cryptology ePrint Archive 2018/892 (2018)
3. Boyle, E., Naor, M.: Is there an oblivious RAM lower bound? In: Proceedings of the 2016 ACM Conference on Innovations in Theoretical Computer Science, Cambridge, MA, USA, 14–16 January 2016, pp. 357–368 (2016)

4. Chung, K.-M., Liu, Z., Pass, R.: Statistically-secure ORAM with $\tilde{O}(\log^2 n)$ overhead. In: Sarkar, P., Iwata, T. (eds.) ASIACRYPT 2014, Part II. LNCS, vol. 8874, pp. 62–81. Springer, Heidelberg (2014). https://doi.org/10.1007/978-3-662-45608-8_4

5. Chung, K., Pass, R.: A simple ORAM. IACR Cryptology ePrint Archive 2013/243 (2013)

6. Damgård, I., Meldgaard, S., Nielsen, J.B.: Perfectly secure oblivious RAM without random oracles. In: Ishai, Y. (ed.) TCC 2011. LNCS, vol. 6597, pp. 144–163. Springer, Heidelberg (2011). https://doi.org/10.1007/978-3-642-19571-6_10

7. Dwork, C., McSherry, F., Nissim, K., Smith, A.: Calibrating noise to sensitivity in private data analysis. In: Halevi, S., Rabin, T. (eds.) TCC 2006. LNCS, vol. 3876, pp. 265–284. Springer, Heidelberg (2006). https://doi.org/10.1007/11681878_14

8. Fredman, M.L., Saks, M.E.: The cell probe complexity of dynamic data structures. In: Proceedings of the 21st Annual ACM Symposium on Theory of Computing, Seattle, Washigton, USA, 14–17 May 1989, pp. 345–354 (1989)

9. Gentry, C., Goldman, K.A., Halevi, S., Julta, C., Raykova, M., Wichs, D.: Optimizing ORAM and using it efficiently for secure computation. In: De Cristofaro, E., Wright, M. (eds.) PETS 2013. LNCS, vol. 7981, pp. 1–18. Springer, Heidelberg (2013). https://doi.org/10.1007/978-3-642-39077-7_1

10. Goldreich, O.: Towards a theory of software protection and simulation by oblivious RAMs. In: Proceedings of the 19th Annual ACM Symposium on Theory of Computing, 1987, New York, USA, pp. 182–194 (1987)

11. Goldreich, O., Ostrovsky, R.: Software protection and simulation on oblivious RAMs. J. ACM **43**(3), 431–473 (1996)

12. Goodrich, M.T., Mitzenmacher, M.: Privacy-preserving access of outsourced data via oblivious RAM simulation. In: Aceto, L., Henzinger, M., Sgall, J. (eds.) ICALP 2011, Part II. LNCS, vol. 6756, pp. 576–587. Springer, Heidelberg (2011). https://doi.org/10.1007/978-3-642-22012-8_46

13. Goodrich, M.T., Mitzenmacher, M., Ohrimenko, O., Tamassia, R.: Oblivious RAM simulation with efficient worst-case access overhead. In: Proceedings of the 3rd ACM Cloud Computing Security Workshop, CCSW 2011, Chicago, IL, USA, 21 October 2011, pp. 95–100 (2011)

14. Haider, S.K., Khan, O., van Dijk, M.: Revisiting definitional foundations of oblivious RAM for secure processor implementations. CoRR abs/1706.03852 (2017). http://arxiv.org/abs/1706.03852

15. Jacob, R., Larsen, K.G., Nielsen, J.B.: Lower bounds for oblivious data structures. In: Proceedings of the Thirtieth Annual ACM-SIAM Symposium on Discrete Algorithms, SODA 2019, San Diego, California, USA, 6–9 January 2019, pp. 2439–2447 (2019)

16. Kocher, P., et al.: Spectre attacks: exploiting speculative execution. CoRR abs/1801.01203 (2018). http://arxiv.org/abs/1801.01203

17. Kushilevitz, E., Lu, S., Ostrovsky, R.: On the (in) security of hash-based oblivious RAM and a new balancing scheme. In: Proceedings of the Twenty-Third Annual ACM-SIAM Symposium on Discrete Algorithms, SODA 2012, Kyoto, Japan, 17–19 January 2012, pp. 143–156 (2012)

18. Larsen, K.G., Nielsen, J.B.: Yes, there is an oblivious RAM lower bound!. In: Shacham, H., Boldyreva, A. (eds.) CRYPTO 2018, Part II. LNCS, vol. 10992, pp. 523–542. Springer, Cham (2018). https://doi.org/10.1007/978-3-319-96881-0_18

19. Lipp, M., et al.: Meltdown: reading kernel memory from user space. In: 27th USENIX Security Symposium, USENIX Security 2018, Baltimore, MD, USA, 15–17 August 2018, pp. 973–990 (2018)

20. MacWilliams, F., Sloane, N.: The Theory of Error-Correcting Codes. North-Holland, Amsterdam (1977)
21. Ostrovsky, R.: Efficient computation on oblivious RAMs. In: Proceedings of the 22nd Annual ACM Symposium on Theory of Computing, Baltimore, Maryland, USA, 13–17 May 1990, pp. 514–523 (1990)
22. Patel, S., Persiano, G., Raykova, M., Yeo, K.: PanORAMa: oblivious RAM with logarithmic overhead. In: 59th IEEE Annual Symposium on Foundations of Computer Science, FOCS 2018, Paris, France, 7–9 October 2018, pp. 871–882 (2018)
23. Patrascu, M., Demaine, E.D.: Logarithmic lower bounds in the cell-probe model. SIAM J. Comput. **35**(4), 932–963 (2006)
24. Persiano, G., Yeo, K.: Lower bounds for differentially private RAMs. In: Ishai, Y., Rijmen, V. (eds.) EUROCRYPT 2019, Part I. LNCS, vol. 11476, pp. 404–434. Springer, Cham (2019). https://doi.org/10.1007/978-3-030-17653-2_14
25. Ren, L., Fletcher, C.W., Kwon, A., Stefanov, E., Shi, E., van Dijk, M., Devadas, S.: Ring ORAM: closing the gap between small and large client storage oblivious RAM. IACR Cryptology ePrint Archive 2014/997 (2014)
26. Stefanov, E., et al.: Path ORAM: an extremely simple oblivious RAM protocol. J. ACM **65**(4), 18:1–18:26 (2018)
27. Vadhan, S.P.: A Study of Statistical-Zero Knowledge Proofs. Ph.D. thesis, Massachusetts Institute of Technology, September 1999
28. Wang, X., Chan, T.H., Shi, E.: Circuit ORAM: on tightness of the Goldreich-Ostrovsky lower bound. In: Proceedings of the 22nd ACM SIGSAC Conference on Computer and Communications Security, Denver, CO, USA, 12–16 October 2015, pp. 850–861 (2015)
29. Wang, X.S., Huang, Y., Chan, T.H., Shelat, A., Shi, E.: SCORAM: oblivious RAM for secure computation. In: Proceedings of the 2014 ACM SIGSAC Conference on Computer and Communications Security, Scottsdale, AZ, USA, 3–7 November 2014, pp. 191–202 (2014)
30. Weiss, M., Wichs, D.: Is there an oblivious RAM lower bound for online reads? In: Beimel, A., Dziembowski, S. (eds.) TCC 2018, Part II. LNCS, vol. 11240, pp. 603–635. Springer, Cham (2018). https://doi.org/10.1007/978-3-030-03810-6_22

Adaptively Secure Garbling Schemes
for Parallel Computations

Kai-Min Chung[1] and Luowen Qian[2(✉)]

[1] Institute of Information Science, Academia Sinica, Taipei, Taiwan
kmchung@iis.sinica.edu.tw
[2] Boston University, Boston, MA, USA
luowenq@bu.edu

Abstract. We construct the first adaptively secure garbling scheme based on standard public-key assumptions for garbling a circuit $C : \{0,1\}^n \mapsto \{0,1\}^m$ that simultaneously achieves a near-optimal online complexity $n + m + \mathsf{poly}(\lambda, \log|C|)$ (where λ is the security parameter) and *preserves the parallel efficiency* for evaluating the garbled circuit; namely, if the depth of C is d, then the garbled circuit can be evaluated in parallel time $d \cdot \mathsf{poly}(\log|C|, \lambda)$. In particular, our construction improves over the recent seminal work of [GS18], which constructs the first adaptively secure garbling scheme with a near-optimal online complexity under the same assumptions, but the garbled circuit can only be evaluated gate by gate in a sequential manner. Our construction combines their novel idea of linearization with several new ideas to achieve parallel efficiency without compromising online complexity.

We take one step further to construct the first adaptively secure garbling scheme for parallel RAM (PRAM) programs under standard assumptions that preserves the parallel efficiency. Previous such constructions we are aware of is from strong assumptions like indistinguishability obfuscation. Our construction is based on the work of [GOS18] for adaptively secure garbled RAM, but again introduces several new ideas to handle parallel RAM computation, which may be of independent interests. As an application, this yields the first constant round secure computation protocol for persistent PRAM programs in the malicious settings from standard assumptions.

1 Introduction

Garbled Circuits. The notion of garbled circuits were introduced by Yao [Yao82] for secure computations. Yao's construction of garbled circuits is secure in the sense that given a circuit C and an input x, the scheme gives out a garbled circuit $\tilde{C}$ and a garbled input $\tilde{x}$ such that it only allows adversaries to recover $C(x)$ and nothing else. The notion of garbled circuits has found an enormous number of

Kai-Min Chung is partially supported by the Ministry of Science and Technology, Taiwan, under Grant no. MOST 106-2628-E-001-002-MY3 and the Academia Sinica Career Development Award under Grant no. 23-17.

D. Hofheinz and A. Rosen (Eds.): TCC 2019, LNCS 11892, pp. 285–310, 2019.
https://doi.org/10.1007/978-3-030-36033-7_11

applications in cryptography. It is well established that garbling techniques is one of the important techniques in cryptography [BHR12b, App17].

Garbled RAM. Lu and Ostrovsky [LO13] extended the garbling schemes to the RAM settings and its applications to delegating database and secure multiparty RAM program computation, and it has been an active area of research in garbling ever since [GHL+14, GLOS15, GLO15, CH16, CCC+16]. Under this settings, it is possible to reduce the size of the garbled program to grow only linearly in the running time of the RAM program (and sometimes logarithmically in the size of the database), instead of the size of the corresponding circuit (which must grow linearly with the size of the database).

Parallel Cryptography. It is a well established fact that parallelism is able to speed up computation, even exponentially for some problems. Yao's construction of garbled circuits is conceptually simple and inherently parallelizable. Being able to evaluate in parallel is more beneficial in the RAM settings where the persistent database can be very large, especially when it is applied to big data processing. The notion of parallel garbled RAM is introduced by Boyle et al. [BCP16]. A black-box construction of parallel garbled RAM is known from one-way function [LO17].

Adaptively Secure Garbling. Bellare, Hoang, and Rogaway [BHR12a] showed that in many applications of garbling, a stronger notion of *adaptive security* is usually required. We note that the notion of adaptive security is tightly related to efficiency.

For the circuit settings, the adversary is allowed to pick the input x to the program C after he has seen the garbled version of the program $\tilde{C}$. In particular, for the circuit settings, we refer to the size of $\tilde{C}$ as *offline complexity* and that of the garbled input $\tilde{x}$ as *online complexity*. The efficiency requirement says that the online complexity should not scale linearly with the size of the circuit[1]. Constructing adaptively secure garbling schemes for circuits with small online complexity has been an active area of investigation [HJO+16, JW16, JKK+17, JSW17, GS18].

For the RAM settings, the adversary is allowed to adaptively pick multiple programs $\Pi_1, ..., \Pi_t$ and their respective inputs $x_1, ..., x_t$ to be executed on the same persistent database D, after he has seen the garbled version of the database $\tilde{D}$, and having executed some garbled programs on the database and obtained their outputs $\Pi_i(x_i)$. Furthermore, he can choose his input after having seen the garbled program. The efficiency requirement is that the time for garbling the database, each program (and therefore the size of the garbled program) and the respective input should depend linearly only on the size of the database,

---

[1] Note that without this efficiency requirement, any selectively secure garbled circuit can be trivially made adaptively secure, simply by sending everything only in the online phase. This also holds similarly for the RAM setting.

the program, and the input respectively (up to poly logarithmic factors). Adaptively secure garbled RAM is also known from indistinguishability obfuscation [CCHR16, ACC+16].

Parallel Complexity of Adaptively Secure Garbling. In two recent seminal works [GS18, GOS18], Garg et al. introduce an adaptively secure garbling scheme for circuits with near-optimal online complexity as well as for RAM programs. However, both constructions explicitly (using a linearization technique for circuits) or implicitly (serial execution of RAM programs) requires the evaluation process to proceed in a strict serial manner. Note that this would cause the parallel evaluation time of garbled circuits to blow up exponentially if the circuit depth is exponentially smaller than the size of the circuit. We also note that the linearization technique is their main technique for achieving near-optimal online complexity. On the other hand, such requirement seems to be at odds with evaluating the garbled version in parallel, which is something previous works [HJO+16] can easily achieve (however, Hemenway et al.'s construction has asymptotically greater online complexity). It's also not clear how to apply the techniques used in [GOS18] for adaptive garbled RAM to garble parallel RAM (PRAM) programs. In this work, we aim to find out whether such trade-off is inherent, namely,

Can we achieve adaptively secure garbling with parallel efficiency from standard assumptions?

1.1 Our Results

In this work, we obtained a construction of adaptively secure garbling schemes that allows for parallel evaluation, incurring only a logarithmic loss in the number of processors in online complexity based on the assumption that laconic oblivious transfer exists. Laconic oblivious transfer can be based on a variety of public-key assumptions [CDG+17, DG17, BLSV18, DGHM18]. More formally, our main results are:

Theorem 1. *Let λ be the security parameter. Assuming laconic oblivious transfer, there exists a construction of adaptively secure garbling schemes,*

- *for circuits C with optimal online communication complexity up to additive $\mathsf{poly}(\lambda, \log |C|)$ factors, and can be evaluated in parallel time $d \cdot \mathsf{poly}(\lambda, \log |C|)$ given w processors, where d and w are the depth and width of circuit C respectively;*
- *for PRAM programs on persistent database D, and can be evaluated in parallel time $T \cdot \mathsf{poly}(\lambda, \log M, \log |D|, \log T)$, where M is the number of processors and T is the parallel running time for the original program.*

This result closes the gap between parallel evaluation and online complexity for circuits, and also is the first adaptively secure garbling scheme for parallel RAM program from standard assumptions. Previous construction for adaptively secure garbled parallel RAM we are aware of is from strong assumptions like indistinguishability obfuscation [ACC+16].

We present our construction for circuit formally in Sect. 4. Please see the full version of our paper for the construction for PRAM.

1.2 Applications

In this section, we briefly mention some applications of our results.

Applications for Parallelly Efficient Adaptive Garbled Circuits. Our construction of parallel adaptively secure garbled circuits can be applied the same way as already mentioned in previous works like [HJO+16, GS18], e.g. to one-time program and compact functional encryption. Our result enables improved parallel efficiency for such applications.

Applications for Adaptive Garbled PRAM. This yields the first constant round secure computation protocol for persistent PRAM programs in the malicious settings from standard assumptions [GGMP16]. Prior works did not support persistence in the malicious setting. As a special case, this also allows for evaluating garbled PRAM programs on delegated persistent database.

2 Techniques

2.1 Parallelizing Garbled Circuits

Our starting point is to take Garg and Srinivasan's construction of adaptively secure garbled circuit with near-optimal online complexity [GS18] and allow it to be evaluated in parallel. Recall that the main idea behind their construction is to "linearize" the circuit before garbling it. Unfortunately, such transformation also ruins the parallel efficiency of their construction. We first explain why linearization is important to achieving near-optimal online complexity.

Pebbling Game. Hemenway et al. [HJO+16] introduced the notion of somewhere equivocal encryption, which enables us to equivocate a part of the garbled "gate" circuits and send them in the online phase. By using such technique, online complexity only needs to grow linearly in the maximum number of equivocated garbled gates at the same time over the entire hybrid argument, which could be much smaller than the length of the entire garbled circuit. Since an equivocated gate can be opened to be any gate, the simulator can simulate the gate according to the input chosen by the adversary, and send the simulated gate in the online phase. The security proof involves a hybrid argument, where in each step we change which gates we equivocate and show that this change is indistinguishable to the adversary. At a high level, this can be abstracted into a pebbling game.

Given a directed acyclic graph with a single sink, we can put or remove a pebble on a node if its every predecessor has a pebble on it or it has no predecessors. The game ends when there is a pebble on the unique sink. The goal of the pebble game is to minimize the maximum number of pebbles simultaneously on the graph throughout the game. In our case, the graph we need to pebble is what is called *simulation dependency graph*, where nodes represent garbled gates in the construction; and an edge from A to B represents that the input label for a piece B is hardcoded in A, thus to turn B into simulation mode, it is necessary to first turn A also into simulation mode. The simulation dependency graph directly corresponds to the circuit topology. The game terminates when the output gate is turned into simulation mode. As putting pebbles corresponds to equivocating the circuit in the online phase, the goal of the pebbling game also directly corresponds to the goal of minimizing online complexity.

Linearizing the Circuit. It is known that there is a strong lower bound $\Omega(\frac{n}{\log n})$ for pebbling an arbitrary graph with n being the size of the graph [PTC76]. Since the circuits to be garbled can also be arbitrary, this means that the constructions of Hemenway et al. still have large online complexity for those "bad" circuits. Thus, Garg and Srinivasan pointed out that some change in the simulation dependency graph was required. In their work, they were able to change the simulation dependency graph to be a line, i.e. the simulation of any given garbled gate depends on only one other garbled gate. There's a good pebbling strategy using only $O(\log n)$ pebbles. On the other hand, using such technique also forces the evaluation to proceed sequentially, which would cause the parallel time complexity of wide circuits to blow up, in the worst case even exponentially.

We now describe how they achieved such linearization. In their work, instead of garbling the circuit directly, they "weakly" garble a special RAM program that evaluates the circuit. Specifically, this is done by having an external memory storing the values of all the intermediate wires and then transforming the circuit into a sequence of CPU step circuit, where each step circuit evaluates a gate and performs reads and writes to the memory to store the results. The step circuits are then garbled using Yao's garbling scheme and the memory is protected with one-time pad and laconic oblivious transfer (ℓOT). This garbling is weak since it does not protect the memory access pattern (which is fixed) and only concerns this specific type of program. Note that with this way, the input and output to the circuit can be revealed by revealing the one-time pad protecting the memory that store the circuit output, which only takes online complexity $n + m$.

Overview of Our Approach. A natural idea is that we can partially keep the linear topology, for which we know a good pebbling strategy; and at the same time, we would use M processors for each time step, each evaluating a gate in parallel. We then store the evaluation results by performing reads and writes on our external memory.

However, there are two challenges with this approach.

- **Parallel writes.** Read procedure in the original ℓOT scheme can be simply evaluated in parallel for parallel reads. On the other hand, since (as we will see later) the write procedure outputs an updated digest of the database, some coordination is obviously required, and simply evaluating writes in serial would result in a blow up in parallel time complexity. Therefore, we need to come up with a new parallel write procedure for this case.

- **Pebbling complexity.** Since now there are M gates being evaluated in parallel and looking ahead, they also need to communicate with each other to perform parallel writes, this will introduce complicated dependencies in the graph, and in the end, we could incur a loss in online complexity. Therefore, we must carefully layout our simulation dependency graph and find a good pebbling strategy for that graph.

Laconic OT. As mentioned earlier, we cannot use the write procedure in laconic oblivious transfer in a black-box way to achieve parallel efficiency. Thus, first we will elaborate on laconic oblivious transfer. Laconic oblivious transfer allows a receiver to commit to a large input via a short message of length λ. Subsequently, the sender responds with a single short message (which is also referred to as ℓOT ciphertext) to the receiver depending on dynamically chosen two messages m_0, m_1 and a location $L \in [|D|]$. The sender's response, enables the receiver to recover $m_{D[L]}$, while $m_{1-D[L]}$ remains computationally hidden. Note that the commitment does not hide the database and one commitment is sufficient to recover multiple bits from the database by repeating this process. ℓOT is frequently composed with Yao's garbled circuits to make a long process non-interactive. There, the messages will be chosen as input labels to the garbled circuit.

First, we briefly recall the original construction of ℓOT. The novel technique of laconic oblivious transfer was introduced in [CDG+17], where the scheme is constructed as a Merkle tree of "laconic oblivious transfer with factor-2 compression", which we denote as ℓOT_{const}, where the database is of length 2λ instead of being arbitrarily large. For the read procedure, we simply start at the root digest, traverse down the Merkle tree by using ℓOT_{const} to read out the digest for the next layer. Such procedure is then made non-interactive using Yao's garbled circuits. For writes, similar techniques apply except that in the end, a final garbled circuit would take another set of labels for the digests to evaluate the updated root digest.

From the view of applying ℓOT to garbling RAM programs, an ℓOT scheme allows to compress a large database into a small digest of length λ that binds the entire database. In particular, given the digest, one can efficiently (in time only logarithmic in the size of the database) and repeatedly (ask the database holder to) read the database (open the commitment) or update the database and obtain the (correctly) updated digest. For both cases, as the evaluation results are returned as labels, the privacy requirement achieves "authentication", meaning the result has to be evaluated honestly as the adversary cannot obtain the other label.

Now, we will describe how we solve these two challenges.

Solving Parallel Writes

First Attempt. Now we address how to parallelize ℓOT writes, in particular the garbled circuit evaluating the updated digest. First, we examine the task of designing a parallel algorithm with M processors that jointly compute the updated digest after writing M bits. At a high level, this can be done using the following procedure: all processors start from the bottom, make their corresponding modifications, and hash their ways up in the tree to compute the new digest; in each round, if two processors move to the same node, one of them is marked inactive and moved to the end using a sorting network. This intuitive parallel algorithm runs in parallel time $\mathsf{poly}(\log M, \log |C|, \lambda)$. By plugging such parallel algorithm back to the single write procedure for ℓOT, we obtain a parallel write procedure for ℓOT.

However, there are some issues for online complexity when we combine this intuitive algorithm with garbling and somewhere equivocal encryption. First, if we garble the entire parallel write circuit using Yao's garbling scheme, we would have to equivocate the entire parallel write circuit in the online phase at some point. Since the size of such circuit must be $\Omega(M)$, this leads to a large block length and we will get high online complexity. Therefore, we will have to split the parallel write circuit into smaller components and garble them separately so that we can equivocate only some parts of the entire write circuit in the online phase. However, this does not solve the problem completely, as in the construction of parallel writes for ℓOT given above, inter-CPU communications like sorting networks take place. In the end, this causes high pebbling complexity of $\Omega(M)$. This is problematic since M can be as large as the width of the circuit.

Block-Writing ℓOT. To fix this issue, we note that for circuits, we can arbitrarily specify the memory locations for each intermediate wires, and this allows us to arrange the locations such that the communication patterns can be simplified to the extent that we can reduce the pebbling complexity to $O(\log M)$. One such good arrangement is moving all M updated locations into a single continuous block.

We give a procedure for handling such special case of updating the garbled database with ℓOT. Recall that in ℓOT, memory contents are hashed together using Merkle trees. Here, to simplify presentation, we assume the continuous block to be an entire subtree of the Merkle tree. In this case, it's easy to compute the digest of the entire subtree efficiently in parallel, after which we can just update the rest of the Merkle tree using a single standard but truncated writing procedure with time $\mathsf{poly}(\log |C|, \lambda)$, as we only need to pass and update the digest of the root of that sub-tree; and the security proof is analogous to that of a single write.

Pebbling Strategy. Before examining the pebbling strategy, we first give the description of the evaluation procedure and our transformed simulation dependency graph using the ideas mentioned in the previous section. In each round, M garbled circuits take the current database digest as input and each outputs a ℓOT ciphertext that allows the evaluator to obtain the input for a certain gate. Another garbled circuit would then take the input and evaluate the gate and output the label for the output for that gate. In order to hash together the output of M values for the gates we just evaluated, we use a Merkle tree of garbled circuits where each circuit would be evaluating a ℓOT hash with factor-2 compression. At the end of the Merkle tree, we would obtain the digest of the sub-tree we wish to update, which would then allow us to update the database and compute the updated digest. We can then use the updated digest to enable the evaluation of the next round.

Roughly, the pebbling graph we are dealing with is a line of "gadgets", and each gadget consists of a tree with children with an edge to their respective parents. One illustration of such gadget can be seen in Fig. 9. One important observation here is that in order to start putting pebbles on any gadget, one only needs to put a pebble at the end of the previous gadget. Therefore, it's not hard to prove that the pebbling cost for the whole graph is the pebbling cost for a single gadget plus the pebbling cost for a line graph, whose length is the parallel time complexity of evaluating the circuit.

Pebbling Line Graph. Garg and Srinivasan used a pebbling strategy for pebbling line graphs with the number of pebbles logarithmic in the length of the line graph. Such strategy is optimal for the line graph [Ben89].

Pebbling the Gadget. For the gadget, the straightforward recursive strategy works very well:[2]

1. To put a pebble at the root, we first recursively put a pebble at its two children respectively;
2. Now we can put pebble at the root;
3. We again recursively remove the pebbles at its two children.

By induction, it's not hard to prove that such strategy uses the number of pebbles linear in the depth of the tree (note that at any given time, there can be at most 2 pebbles in each depth of the tree) and the number of steps is polynomial in the size of the graph.

Putting the two strategy together, we achieve online complexity $n + m + \mathsf{poly}(\lambda, \log|C|, \log M)$, where n, m is the length of the input and the output respectively. Note that M is certainly at most $|C|$, so the online complexity is in fact $n + m + \mathsf{poly}(\lambda, \log|C|)$, which matches the online complexity in [GS18].

2.2   Garbling Parallel RAM

Now we expand our previous construction of garbled circuits (which is a "weak" garbling of a special PRAM program) to garble more general PRAM programs, employing similar techniques from the seminal work of [GOS18]. We start by

---

[2] This strategy is similar to the second strategy in [HJO+16]. However, here the depth of the tree is only logarithmic in the number of processors so we can prevent incurring an exponential loss.

bootstrapping the garbling scheme into an adaptive garbled PRAM with unprotected memory access (UMA).

As with parallelizing adaptive garbled circuits, here we also face the issue of handling parallel writes. Note that here the previous approach of rearranging write locations would not work since due to the nature of RAM programs, the write locations can depend dynamically on the input. Therefore, we have to return to our first attempt of parallel writes and splitting the parallel evaluation into several circuits so that we can garble them separately for equivocation. Again, we run into the issue of communications leading to high pebbling complexity.

Solution: Parallel Checkpoints. Our idea is to instead put the parallel write procedure into the PRAM program and use a technique called "parallel checkpoints" to allow for arbitrary inter-CPU communications. At a high level, at the end of each parallel CPU step, we store all the CPUs' encrypted intermediary states into a second external memory and compute a digest using laconic oblivious transfer. Such digest can then act like a *checkpoint in parallel computation*, which is then used to retrieve the states back from the new database using another garbled circuit and ℓOT.

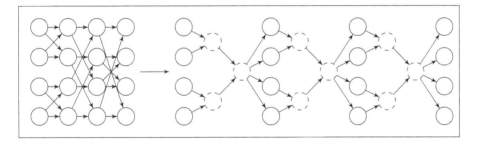

Fig. 1. Transforming a toy sorting network using "parallel checkpoints." The undashed vertices corresponds to the step circuits that do the actual sorting.

To see how this change affects the simulation dependency graph and why it solves the complexity issue, consider the following toy example where we have a small sorting network, as seen in the left side of Fig. 1. Note that applying the two pebbling strategies from [HJO+16] directly on the untransformed network will result in an online complexity linear in either the number of processors M, or the running time T (and in this case also a security loss exponential in T). However, by doing the transformation as shown in Fig. 1, we can pebble this graph with only $O(\log M)$ pebbles, by moving the pebble on the final node of each layer forward (and we can move the pebble forward by one layer using $O(\log M)$ pebbles). We can also see that using this change, the size of the garbled program will only grow by a factor of 2, and the parallel running time will only grow by a factor of $\log M$. In general, this transformation allows us to perform arbitrary inter-CPU communications without incurring large losses in online complexity, which resolves the issue.

For a more extended version of this construction, please refer to the full version.

Pebbling Game for Parallel Checkpoints. As mentioned above, such parallel checkpoints are implemented via creating a database using ℓOT. Thus the same strategy for pebbling the circuit pebble graph can be directly applied here. The key size of somewhere equivocal encryption is therefore only $\mathsf{poly}(\lambda, \log |D|, \log M, \log T)$.

With preprocessing and parallel checkpoints, we can proceed in a similar way to construct adaptively secure garbled PRAM with unprotected memory access. In order to bootstrap it from UMA to full security, the same techniques, i.e. timed encryption and oblivious RAM compiler from [GOS18] can be used in a similar way to handle additional complications in the RAM settings. In particular, we argue that the oblivious parallel RAM compiler from [BCP16] can be modified in the same way to achieve their strengthened notion of strong localized randomness in the parallel setting and handle the additional subtleties there. In the end, this allows us to construct a fully adaptively secure garbled PRAM.

3   Preliminaries

3.1   Garbled Circuits

In this section, we recall the notion of garbled circuits introduced by Yao [Yao82]. We will follow the same notions and terminologies as used in [CDG+17]. A circuit garbling scheme GC is a tuple of PPT algorithms (GCircuit, GCEval).

- $\tilde{\mathsf{C}} \leftarrow \mathsf{GCircuit}\left(1^\lambda, \mathsf{C}, \{\mathsf{key}_{w,b}\}_{w \in \mathsf{inp}(\mathsf{C}), b \in \{0,1\}}\right)$. It takes as input a security parameter λ, a circuit C, a set of labels $\mathsf{key}_{w,b}$ for all the input wires $w \in \mathsf{inp}(\mathsf{C})$ and $b \in \{0,1\}$. This procedure outputs a *garbled circuit* $\tilde{\mathsf{C}}$.
- $y \leftarrow \mathsf{GCEval}\left(\tilde{\mathsf{C}}, \{\mathsf{key}_{w,x_w}\}_{w \in \mathsf{inp}(\mathsf{C})}\right)$. Given a garbled circuit $\tilde{\mathsf{C}}$ and a garbled input represented as a sequence of input labels $\{\mathsf{key}_{w,x_w}\}_{w \in \mathsf{inp}(\mathsf{C})}$, GCEval outputs y.

Correctness. For correctness, we require that for any circuit C and input $x \in \{0,1\}^m$, where m is the input length to C, we have that

$$\Pr\left[\mathsf{C}(x) = \mathsf{GCEval}\left(\tilde{\mathsf{C}}, \{\mathsf{key}_{w,x_w}\}_{w \in \mathsf{inp}(\mathsf{C})}\right)\right] = 1,$$

where $\tilde{\mathsf{C}} \leftarrow \mathsf{GCircuit}\left(1^\lambda, \mathsf{C}, \{\mathsf{key}_{w,b}\}_{w \in \mathsf{inp}(\mathsf{C}), b \in \{0,1\}}\right)$.

Security. We require that there is a PPT simulator GCircSim such that for any C, x, and for $\{\mathsf{key}_{w,b}\}_{w \in \mathsf{inp}(C), b \in \{0,1\}}$ uniformly sampled,

$$\left(\tilde{C}, \{\mathsf{key}_{w,x_w}\}_{w \in \mathsf{inp}(C)}\right) \overset{c}{\approx} \left(\mathsf{GCircSim}\left(1^\lambda, 1^{|C|}, \{\mathsf{key}_{w,x_w}\}_{w \in \mathsf{inp}(C)}, y\right), \{\mathsf{key}_{w,x_w}\}_{w \in \mathsf{inp}(C)}\right),$$

where $\tilde{C} \leftarrow \mathsf{GCircuit}\left(1^\lambda, C, \{\mathsf{key}_{w,b}\}_{w \in \mathsf{inp}(C), b \in \{0,1\}}\right)$ and $y = C(x)$.

Parallel Efficiency. For parallel efficiency, we require that the parallel runtime of GCircuit on a PRAM machine with M processors is $\mathsf{poly}(\lambda) \cdot |C|/M$ if $|C| \geq M$, and the parallel runtime of GCEval on a PRAM machine with w processors is $\mathsf{poly}(\lambda) \cdot d$, where w, d is the width and depth of the circuit respectively.

3.2   Somewhere Equivocal Encryption

In this section, we recall the definition of Somewhere Equivocal Encryption from the work of [HJO+16].

Definition 1. *A somewhere equivocal encryption scheme with block-length s, message length n (in blocks) and equivocation parameter t (all polynomials in the security parameter) is a tuple of PPT algorithms* (KeyGen, Enc, Dec, SimEnc, SimDec) *such that:*

- key $\leftarrow$ KeyGen(1^λ)*: It takes as input the security parameter λ and outputs a key* key*.*
- $\bar{c} \leftarrow$ Enc(key, $\bar{m}$)*: It takes as input a key* key *and a vector of messages $\bar{m} = m_1...m_n$ with each $m_i \in \{0,1\}^s$ and outputs a ciphertext $\bar{c}$.*
- $\bar{m} \leftarrow$ Dec(key, $\bar{c}$)*: It is a deterministic algorithm that takes as input a key* key *and a ciphertext $\bar{c}$ and outputs a vector of messages $\bar{m} = m_1...m_n$.*
- (st, $\bar{c}$) $\leftarrow$ SimEnc((m_i)$_{i \notin I}$, I)*: It takes as input a set of indices $I \subseteq [n]$ and a vector of messages $(m_i)_{i \notin I}$ and outputs a ciphertext $\bar{c}$ and a state* st*.*
- key$'$ $\leftarrow$ SimKey(st, (m_i)$_{i \in I}$)*: It takes as input the state information* st *and a vector of messages $(m_i)_{i \in I}$ and outputs a key* key$'$*.*

It is required to satisfy the following properties:

Correctness. *For every* key $\leftarrow$ KeyGen(1^λ)*, every $\bar{m} \in \{0,1\}^{s \times n}$, we require that*

$$\mathsf{Dec}(\mathsf{key}, \mathsf{Enc}(\mathsf{key}, \bar{m})) = \bar{m}.$$

Simulation with No Holes. *We require that simulation when $I = \emptyset$ is identical to the honest key generation and encryption, i.e. the distribution of $(\bar{c}, \mathsf{key})$ computed via* (st, $\bar{c}$) $\leftarrow$ SimEnc($\bar{m}, \emptyset$) *and* key $\leftarrow$ SimKey(st, $\emptyset$) *to be identical to* key $\leftarrow$ KeyGen(1^λ) *and* $\bar{c} \leftarrow$ Enc(key, $\bar{m}$)*.*

$$\boxed{\begin{array}{l} \mathsf{SimEncExpt}^{b \in \{0,1\}}(1^\lambda, \mathcal{A}) \\ \quad \text{Let } I_0 = I \text{ and } I_1 = I \cup \{j\} \\ \quad (\mathsf{st}, \bar{c}) \leftarrow \mathsf{SimEnc}((m_i)_{i \notin I_b}, I_b) \\ \quad ((m_i)_{i \in I}, \mathsf{st}') \leftarrow \mathcal{A}_1(\bar{c}) \\ \quad \mathsf{key} \leftarrow \mathsf{SimKey}(\mathsf{st}, (m_i)_{i \in I_b}) \\ \quad \text{Output } \mathcal{A}_2(\mathsf{st}', \mathsf{key}) \end{array}}$$

Fig. 2. Simulated encryption experiment

Security. For any non-uniform PPT adversary $\mathcal{A} = (\mathcal{A}_1, \mathcal{A}_2)$, for any $I \subseteq [n]$ s.t. $|I| \leq t$, $j \in [n] - I$ and vector $(m_i)_{i \notin I}$, there exists a negligible function $\mathsf{negl}(\cdot)$ s.t.

$$|\Pr[\mathsf{SimEncExpt}^0(1^\lambda, \mathcal{A}) = 1] - \Pr[\mathsf{SimEncExpt}^1(1^\lambda, \mathcal{A}) = 1]| \leq \mathsf{negl}(\lambda),$$

where $\mathsf{SimEncExpt}^0$ and $\mathsf{SimEncExpt}^1$ are described in Fig. 2.

Theorem 2 ([HJO+16]). *Assuming the existence of one-way functions, there exists a somewhat equivocal encryption scheme for any polynomial message-length n, block-length s and equivocation parameter t, having key size $t \cdot s \cdot \mathsf{poly}(\lambda)$ and ciphertext of size $n \cdot s \cdot \mathsf{poly}(\lambda)$ bits.*

3.3 Parallel RAM Programs

We follow the formalization of parallel RAM (PRAM) programs used in [LO17]. A M parallel random-access machine is a collection of M processors $\mathsf{CPU}_1, ..., \mathsf{CPU}_m$, having concurrent access to a shared external memory D.

A PRAM *program* Π, given input $x_1, ..., x_M$, provides instructions to the CPUs that can access to the shared memory D. The CPUs execute the program until a halt state is reached, upon which all CPUs collectively output $y_1, ..., y_M$.[3]

Here, we formalize each processor as a step circuit, i.e. for each step, CPU_i evaluates the circuit $C_{\mathsf{CPU}_i}^{\Pi}(\mathsf{state}, \mathsf{wData}) = (\mathsf{state}', \mathsf{R/W}, L, \mathsf{rData})$. This circuit takes as input the current CPU state state and the data rData read from the database, and it outputs an updated state state', a read or write bit $\mathsf{R/W}$, the next locations to read/write L, and the data wData to write to that location. We allow each CPU to request up to γ bits at a time, therefore here $\mathsf{rData}, \mathsf{wData}$ are both bit strings of length γ. For our purpose, we assume $\gamma \geq 2\lambda$. The (parallel) time complexity T of a PRAM program Π is the number of time steps taken to evaluate Π before the halt state is reached.

We note that the notion of parallel random-access machine is a commonly used extension of Turing machine when one needs to examine the concrete parallel time complexity of a certain algorithm.

---

[3] Similarly, here we assume the program is deterministic. We can allow for randomized execution by providing it random coins as input.

Memory Access Patterns. The memory access pattern of PRAM program $\Pi(x)$ is a sequence $(\mathsf{R/W}_i, L_i)_{i \in [T]}$, each element represents at time step i, a read/write $\mathsf{R/W}_i$ was performed on memory location L_i.

3.4 Sorting Networks

Our construction of parallel ℓOT uses *sorting networks*, which is a fixed topology of comparisons for sorting values on n wires. In our instantiation, n equals the number of processors M in the PRAM model. As PRAM can simulate circuits efficiently, on a high level, a sorting network of depth d corresponds to a parallel sorting algorithm with parallel time complexity $O(d)$. As mentioned previously, the topology of the sorting network is not relevant to our construction.

Theorem 3 ([AKS83]). *There exists an n-wire sorting network of depth $O(\log n)$.*

3.5 Laconic Oblivious Transfer

Definition 2 ([CDG+17]). *An updatable laconic oblivious transfer (ℓOT) scheme consists of four algorithms* crsGen, Hash, Send, Receive, SendWrite, ReceiveWrite.

- crs $\leftarrow$ crsGen(1^λ). *It takes as input the security parameter 1^λ and outputs a common reference string* crs.
- (digest, $\hat{D}$) $\leftarrow$ Hash(crs, D). *It takes as input a common reference string* crs *and a database $D \in \{0,1\}^*$ and outputs a digest* digest *of the database and a state $\hat{D}$.*
- e $\leftarrow$ Send(crs, digest, L, m_0, m_1). *It takes as input a common reference string* crs, *a digest* digest, *a database location $L \in \mathbf{N}$ and two messages m_0 and m_1 of length λ, and outputs a ciphertext* e.
- $m \leftarrow$ Receive$^{\hat{D}}$(crs, e, L). *This is a RAM algorithm with random read access to $\hat{D}$. It takes as input a common reference string* crs, *a ciphertext* e, *and a database location $L \in \mathbf{N}$. It outputs a message m.*
- $e_w \leftarrow$ SendWrite (crs, digest, $\{L_k\}_{k \in [M]}, \{b_k\}_{k \in [M]}, \{m_{j,c}\}_{j \in [\lambda], c \in \{0,1\}}$). *It takes as input the common reference string* crs, *a digest* digest, *M locations $\{L_k\}_k$ with the corresponding bits $\{b_k\}_k$, and λ pairs of messages $\{m_{j,c}\}_{j \in [\lambda], c \in \{0,1\}}$, where each $m_{j,c}$ is of length λ. It outputs a ciphertext e_w.*
- $\{m_j\}_{j \in [\lambda]} \leftarrow$ ReceiveWrite$^{\tilde{D}}$(crs, $\{L_k\}_{k \in [M]}, \{b_k\}_{k \in [M]}, e_w$). *This is a RAM algorithm with random read/write access to $\tilde{D}$. It takes as input the common reference string* crs, *M locations $\{L_k\}_{k \in [M]}$ and bits to be written $\{b_k\}_{k \in [M]}$ and a ciphertext e_w. It updates the state $\tilde{D}$ (such that $D[L_k] = b_k$ for every $k \in [M]$) and outputs messages $\{m_j\}_{j \in [\lambda]}$.*

It is required to satisfy the following properties:

- **Correctness:** *For any database D of size at most* $\mathsf{poly}(\lambda)$ *for any polynomial function* $\mathsf{poly}(\cdot)$, *any memory location* $L \in [\|D\|]$, *and any pair of messages* $(m_0, m_1) \in \{0, 1\}^\lambda \times \{0, 1\}^\lambda$ *that*

$$\Pr \left[m = m_{D[L]} \middle| \begin{array}{c} \mathsf{crs} \leftarrow \mathsf{crsGen}(1^\lambda) \\ (\mathsf{digest}, \hat{D}) \leftarrow \mathsf{Hash}(\mathsf{crs}, D) \\ \mathsf{e} \leftarrow \mathsf{Send}(\mathsf{crs}, \mathsf{digest}, L, m_0, m_1) \\ m \leftarrow \mathsf{Receive}^{\hat{D}}(\mathsf{crs}, \mathsf{e}, L) \end{array} \right] = 1,$$

where the probability is taken over the random choices made by crsGen *and* Send.

- **Correctness of Writes:** *For any database D of size at most* $\mathsf{poly}(\lambda)$ *for any polynomial function* $\mathsf{poly}(\cdot)$, *any M memory locations* $\{L_j\}_j \in [\|D\|]^M$ *and any bits* $\{b_j\}_j$, *and any pairs of messages* $\{m_{j,c}\}_{j,c} \in \{0,1\}^{2\lambda^2}$, *let D^* be the database to be D after making the modifications $D[L_j] \leftarrow b_j$ for $j = 1, ..., M$, we require that*

$$\Pr \left[\begin{array}{c} m'_j = m_{j, D[L]} \\ \forall j \in [\lambda] \end{array} \middle| \begin{array}{c} \mathsf{crs} \leftarrow \mathsf{crsGen}(1^\lambda) \\ (\mathsf{d}, \hat{D}) \leftarrow \mathsf{Hash}(\mathsf{crs}, D) \\ (\mathsf{d}^*, \hat{D}^*) \leftarrow \mathsf{Hash}(\mathsf{crs}, D^*) \\ \mathsf{e} \leftarrow \mathsf{SendWrite}\left(\mathsf{crs}, \mathsf{d}, \{L_k\}_k, \{b_k\}_k, \{m_{j,c}\}_{j,c}\right) \\ \{m'_j\}_j \leftarrow \mathsf{ReceiveWrite}^{\hat{D}}(\mathsf{crs}, \{L_k\}_k, \{b_k\}_k, \mathsf{e}) \end{array} \right] = 1,$$

where the probability is taken over the random choices made by crsGen *and* Send.

- **Sender Privacy:** *There exists a PPT simulator* $\ell\mathsf{OTSim}$ *such that for any non-uniform PPT adversary* $\mathcal{A} = (\mathcal{A}_1, \mathcal{A}_2)$ *there exists a negligible function* $\mathsf{negl}(\cdot)$ *s.t.*

$$|\Pr[\mathsf{SenPrivExpt}^{\mathsf{real}}(1^\lambda, \mathcal{A}) = 1] - \Pr[\mathsf{SenPrivExpt}^{\mathsf{ideal}}(1^\lambda, \mathcal{A}) = 1]| \le \mathsf{negl}(\lambda),$$

where $\mathsf{SenPrivExpt}^{\mathsf{real}}$ *and* $\mathsf{SenPrivExpt}^{\mathsf{ideal}}$ *are described in Fig. 3.*

$\mathsf{SenPrivExpt}^{\tau \in \{\mathsf{real},\ \mathsf{ideal}\}}(1^\lambda, \mathcal{A})$

  $\mathsf{crs} \leftarrow \mathsf{crsGen}(1^\lambda)$

  $(D, L, m_0, m_1, \mathsf{st}) \leftarrow \mathcal{A}_1(\mathsf{crs})$

  $(\mathsf{d}, \hat{D}) \leftarrow \mathsf{Hash}(\mathsf{crs}, D)$

  If τ is real, $\mathsf{e} \leftarrow \mathsf{Send}(\mathsf{crs}, \mathsf{d}, L, m_0, m_1)$

  If τ is ideal, $\mathsf{e} \leftarrow \ell\mathsf{OTSim}(\mathsf{crs}, D, L, m_{D[L]})$

  Output $\mathcal{A}_2(\mathsf{st}, \mathsf{e})$

Fig. 3. Sender privacy security game

- **Sender Privacy for Writes:** *There exists a PPT simulator* ℓOTSimWrite *such that for any non-uniform PPT adversary* $\mathcal{A} = (\mathcal{A}_1, \mathcal{A}_2)$ *there exists a negligible function* $\mathsf{negl}(\cdot)$ *s.t.*

$$|\Pr[\mathsf{SenPrivWriteExpt}^{\mathsf{real}}(1^\lambda, \mathcal{A}) = 1] - \Pr[\mathsf{SenPrivWriteExpt}^{\mathsf{ideal}}(1^\lambda, \mathcal{A}) = 1]| \leq \mathsf{negl}(\lambda),$$

  where $\mathsf{SenPrivWriteExpt}^{\mathsf{real}}$ *and* $\mathsf{SenPrivWriteExpt}^{\mathsf{ideal}}$ *are described in Fig. 4.*
- **Efficiency:** *The algorithm* Hash *runs in time* $|D|\mathsf{poly}(\log|D|, \lambda)$. *The algorithms* Send, Receive *run in time* $\mathsf{poly}(\log|D|, \lambda)$, *and the algorithms* SendWrite, ReceiveWrite *run in time* $M \cdot \mathsf{poly}(\log|D|, \lambda)$.

$\mathsf{SenPrivWriteExpt}^{\tau \in \{\mathsf{real, ideal}\}}(1^\lambda, \mathcal{A})$
    $\mathsf{crs} \leftarrow \mathsf{crsGen}(1^\lambda)$
    $(D, M, \{L_j\}_{j \in [M]}, \{m_{j,c}\}_{j,c}, \mathsf{st}) \leftarrow \mathcal{A}_1(\mathsf{crs})$
    $(d, \hat{D}) \leftarrow \mathsf{Hash}(\mathsf{crs}, D)$
    $(d^*, \hat{D}^*) \leftarrow \mathsf{Hash}(\mathsf{crs}, D^*)$ where D^* is D after making the modifications $D[L_j] \leftarrow$
    b_j for $j = 1, ..., M$
        If τ is real, $\mathsf{e} \leftarrow \mathsf{SendWrite}\left(\mathsf{crs}, d, \{L_k\}_k, \{b_k\}_k, \{m_{j,c}\}_{j,c}\right)$
        If τ is ideal, $\mathsf{e} \leftarrow \ell\mathsf{OTSimWrite}(\mathsf{crs}, D, \{L_k\}_k, \{m_{j,d_j^*}\}_j)$
    Output $\mathcal{A}_2(\mathsf{st}, \mathsf{e})$

Fig. 4. Sender privacy security game for writes

It is also helpful to introduce the ℓOT scheme with factor-2 compression, which is used in ℓOT's original construction [CDG+17].

Definition 3. *An* ℓOT *scheme with factor-2 compression* ℓOT_{const} *is an* ℓOT *scheme where the database* D *has to be of size* 2λ.

Remark 1. The sender privacy requirement here is from [GS18]. It requires crs to be given to the adversary before the adversary chooses his challenge instead of after, and is therefore stronger than the original security requirement [CDG+17]. But we note that in the security proof of laconic oblivious transfer, such adaptive security requirement can be directly reduced to adaptive security for ℓOT_{const}. And in the construction of [CDG+17], in every hybrid, crs is generated either truthfully, or generated statistically binding to one of 2λ possible positions. Therefore, we will incur at most a $1/2\lambda$ loss in the security reduction, simply by guessing which position we need to bind to in those hybrids. This also applies to the sender privacy for parallel writes we will discuss later.

Theorem 4 ([CDG+17,DG17,BLSV18,DGHM18]). *Assuming either the Computational Diffie-Hellman assumption or the Factoring assumption or the Learning with Errors assumption, there exists a construction of laconic oblivious transfer.*

4 Adaptive Garbled Circuits Preserving Parallel Runtime

In this section, we construct an adaptively secure garbling scheme for circuits that allows for parallel evaluation without compromising near-optimal online complexity. We follow the definition of adaptive garbled circuits from [HJO+16].

Definition 4. *An adaptive garbling scheme for circuits is a tuple of PPT algorithms*
(AdaGCircuit, AdaGInput, AdaEval) *such that:*

- $(\tilde{C}, \mathsf{st}) \leftarrow \mathsf{AdaGCircuit}\left(1^\lambda, C\right)$. *It takes as input a security parameter* λ, *a circuit* $C : \{0,1\}^n \mapsto \{0,1\}^m$ *and outputs a garbled circuit* $\tilde{C}$ *and state information* st.
- $\tilde{x} \leftarrow \mathsf{AdaGInput}(\mathsf{st}, x)$: *It takes as input the state information* st *and an input* $x \in \{0,1\}^n$ *and outputs the garbled input* $\tilde{x}$.
- $y \leftarrow \mathsf{AdaEval}(\tilde{C}, \tilde{x})$. *Given a garbled circuit* $\tilde{C}$ *and a garbled input* $\tilde{x}$, AdaEval *outputs* $y \in \{0,1\}^m$.

Correctness. For any $\lambda \in \mathbf{N}$ *circuit* $C : \{0,1\}^n \mapsto \{0,1\}^m$ *and input* $x \in \{0,1\}^n$, *we have that*

$$\Pr\left[C(x) = \mathsf{AdaEval}(\tilde{C}, \tilde{x})\right] = 1,$$

where $(\tilde{C}, \mathsf{st}) \leftarrow \mathsf{AdaGCircuit}\left(1^\lambda, C\right)$ *and* $\tilde{x} \leftarrow \mathsf{AdaGInput}(\mathsf{st}, x)$.

Adaptive Security. *There is a PPT simulator* AdaGSim = (AdaGSimC, AdaGSimIn) *such that, for any non-uniform PPT adversary* $\mathcal{A} = (\mathcal{A}_1, \mathcal{A}_2, \mathcal{A}_3)$ *there exists a negligible function* negl$(\cdot)$ *such that*

$$|\Pr[\mathsf{AdaGCExpt}^{\mathsf{real}}(1^\lambda, \mathcal{A}) = 1] - \Pr[\mathsf{AdaGCExpt}^{\mathsf{ideal}}(1^\lambda, \mathcal{A}) = 1]| \leq \mathsf{negl}(\lambda),$$

where AdaGCExpt^{real} *and* AdaGCExpt^{ideal} *are described in Fig. 5.*

Online Complexity. The running time of AdaGInput *is called the online computational complexity and* $|\tilde{x}|$ *is called the online communication complexity. We require that the online computational complexity does not scale linearly with the size of the circuit* $|C|$.

Furthermore, we call the garbling scheme is parallelly efficient, if the algorithms are given as probabilistic PRAM programs with M processors, and the parallel runtime of AdaGCircuit is poly$(\lambda) \cdot |C|/M$ if $|C| \geq M$, the parallel runtime of AdaGInput on a PRAM machine to be $n/M \cdot$ poly$(\lambda, \log |C|)$, and the parallel runtime of AdaEval is poly$(\lambda) \cdot d$ if $M \geq w$, where w, d is the width and depth of the circuit respectively.

$\mathsf{AdaGCExpt}^{\tau \in \{\text{real, ideal}\}}[1^\lambda, \mathcal{A}]$

  $(C, s) \leftarrow \mathcal{A}_1(1^\lambda)$

  If τ is real, $(\tilde{C}, \mathsf{st}) \leftarrow \mathsf{AdaGCircuit}\,(1^\lambda, C)$

  If τ is ideal, $(\tilde{C}, \mathsf{st}) \leftarrow \mathsf{AdaGSimC}\,(1^\lambda, 1^{|C|})$

  $(x, s) \leftarrow \mathcal{A}_2(s, \tilde{C})$

  If τ is real, $\tilde{x} \leftarrow \mathsf{AdaGInput}(\mathsf{st}, x)$

  If τ is ideal, $\tilde{x} \leftarrow \mathsf{AdaGSimIn}(\mathsf{st}, C(x))$

  Output $\mathcal{A}_3(s, \tilde{x})$

Fig. 5. Adaptive security game of adaptive garble circuits

4.1 Construction Overview

First, we recall the construction of [GS18], which we will use as a starting point. At a high level, their construction can be viewed as a "weak" garbling of a special RAM program that evaluates the circuit.

In the ungarbled world, a database D is used as RAM to store all the wires (including input, output, and intermediate wires). Initially, D only holds the input and everything else is uninitialized. In each iteration, the processor takes a gate, read two bits according to the gate, evaluate the gate, and write the output bit back into the database. Finally, after all iterations are finished, the output of the circuit is read from the database.

In the garbled world, the database D will be hashed as $\hat{D}$ using ℓOT and protected with an one-time pad r as ℓOT does not protect its memory content. The evaluation process is carried out by a sequence of Yao's garbled circuits and laconic OT "talking" to each other. In each iteration, two read operations correspond to a selectively secure garbled circuit, which on given digest as input, outputs two ℓOT read ciphertexts that the evaluator can decrypt to the input label for the garbled gate, which is a selectively secure garbled circuit that unmasks the input, evaluates the gate, and then unmasks the output. To store the output, the garbled gate generates a ℓOT block-write ciphertext, which also enables the evaluator to obtain the input labels for the updated digest in the next iteration. This garbled RAM program is then encrypted using a somewhere equivocal encryption, after which it is given to the adversary as the garbled circuit. On given input x, we generate the protected database $\hat{D}$ and compute the input labels for the initial digest, and we give out the labels, the masked input, the decryption key, and masks for output in the database.

This garbling is weak as in it only concerns a particular RAM program, and it does not protect the memory access pattern, but it is sufficient for the adaptive security requirement of garbled circuits as the pattern is fixed and public. As we will see in the security proof that online complexity is tightly related to the pebbling complexity of a pebbling game. The pebbling game is played on a simulation dependency graph, where pieces of garbled circuits in the construction correspond to nodes and hardwiring of input labels correspond to edges. As the input labels for every selectively secure circuit is only hardcoded in the previous circuit, the simulation dependency is a line and there is a known good pebbling strategy.

To parallelize this construction, we naturally wish to evaluate M gates in parallel using a PRAM program instead of evaluating sequentially. This way, we preserve its mostly linear structure, for which we know a good pebbling strategy. Reading from the database is inherently parallelizable, but writing is more problematic as the processors need to communicate with each other to compute the updated digest and we need to be more careful.

4.2   Block-Writing Laconic OT

Recall from Sect. 2.1 that we cannot hope to use ℓOT as a black box in parallel, thus we first briefly recall the techniques used in [CDG+17] to bootstrap an ℓOT scheme with factor-2 compression ℓOT_{const} into a general ℓOT scheme with an arbitrary compression factor.

Consider a database D with size $|D| = 2^d \cdot \lambda$. In order to obtain a hash function with arbitrary (polynomial) compression factor, it's natural to use a Merkle tree to compress the database. The Hash function outputs (digest, $\hat{\mathsf{D}}$), where $\hat{\mathsf{D}}$ is the Merkle tree and digest is the root of the tree. Using ℓOT_{const} combined with a Merkle tree, the sender is able to traverse down the Merkle tree, simply by using ℓOT_{const}.Send to obtain the digest for any child he wishes to, until he reaches the block he would like to query. For writes, the sender can read out all the relevant neighbouring digests from the Merkle tree and compute the updated digest using the information. In order to compress the round complexity down to 1 from d, we can use Yao's garble circuit to garble ℓOT_{const}.Send so that the receiver can evaluate it for the sender, until he gets the final output. On a high level, the receiver makes the garbled circuits and ℓOT_{const} talk to each other to evaluate the read/write ciphertexts.

As mentioned in Sect. 2.1, we wish to construct a block-write procedure such that the following holds:

- The parallel running time should be $\mathsf{poly}(\lambda, \log |C|)$;
- For near-optimal online complexity, both the size of each piece of the garbled circuit and the pebbling complexity needs to be $\mathsf{poly}(\lambda, \log |C|)$.

Note that changing the ciphertext to contain all M bits directly do not work in this context, as now the write ciphertext would be of length $\Omega(M)$, therefore the garbled circuit generating it must be of length $\Omega(M)$, which violates what we wish to have. The way to fix this is to instead let the ciphertext only hold the digest of the sub-tree, and the block write ciphertext simply needs to perform a "partial" write to obtain the updated digest, therefore its size is no larger than an ordinary write ciphertext. As it turns out, a tree-like structure in the simulation dependency graph also has good pebbling complexity and we can obtain the sub-tree digest using what we call a garbled Merkle tree, which we will construct in the next section. This way, we resolve all the issues.

Now, we first direct our attention back to constructing block-writes. Formally, we will construct two additional algorithms for updatable laconic oblivious transfer that handles a special case of parallel writes. As we will see later, these algorithms can be used to simplify the construction of adaptive garbled circuit.

- $e_w \leftarrow$ SendWriteBlock $\left(crs, digest, L, d, \{m_{j,c}\}_{j\in[\lambda], c\in\{0,1\}}\right)$. It takes as input the common reference string crs, a digest $digest$, a location prefix $L \in \{0,1\}^P$ with length $P \leq \log|D|$ and the digest of the subtree d to be written to location $L00...0, L00...1, ..., L11...1$, and λ pairs of messages $\{m_{j,c}\}_{j\in[\lambda], c\in\{0,1\}}$, where each $m_{j,c}$ is of length λ. It outputs a ciphertext e_w.

- $\{m_j\}_{j\in[\lambda]} \leftarrow$ ReceiveWriteBlock$^{\tilde{D}}(crs, L, \{b_k\}_{k\in[2^M]}, e_w)$. This is a RAM algorithm with random read/write access to $\tilde{D}$. It takes as input the common reference string crs, M locations $\{L_k\}_{k\in[M]}$ and bits to be written $\{b_k\}_{k\in[M]}$ and a ciphertext e_w. It updates the state $\tilde{D}$ (such that $D[L_k] = b_k$ for every $k \in [M]$) and outputs messages $\{m_j\}_{j\in[\lambda]}$.

The formal construction of block-writing ℓOT is as follows:

- SendWriteBlock $\left(crs, digest, L, d, \{m_{j,c}\}_{j\in[\lambda], c\in\{0,1\}}\right)$
    Reinterpret the ℓOT Merkle tree by truncating at the $|L|$-th layer
    Output ℓOT.SendWrite $\left(crs, digest, L, d, \{m_{j,c}\}_{j\in[\lambda], c\in\{0,1\}}\right)$
- ReceiveWriteBlock$^{\tilde{D}}(crs, L, \{b_k\}_{k\in[2^M]}, e_w)$
    Compute the digest d of database $\{b_k\}_{k\in[2^M]}$
    Reinterpret the ℓOT Merkle tree by truncating at the $|L|$-th layer and $\tilde{D}$ as the corresponding truncated version of the database
    Label $\leftarrow \ell OT$.ReceiveWrite$^{\tilde{D}}(crs, L, \{b_k\}_{k\in[2^M]}, e_w)$
    Update $\tilde{D}$ at block location L using data $\{b_k\}_{k\in[2^M]}$
    Output Label

ℓOTSimWriteBlock$(crs, D, L, \{b_j\}_{j\in[\lambda]}, \{m_{j,digest_j^*}\}_{j\in[\lambda]})$
    Output ℓOTSimWrite$(crs, D, \{L||j\}_{j\in[\lambda]}, \{b_j\}_{j\in[\lambda]}, \{m_{j,digest_j^*}\}_{j\in[\lambda]})$

Fig. 6. Block-writing security simulator

We require similar security and efficiency requirements for block-writing ℓOT. It's not hard to see that the update part of ReceiveWriteBlock can be evaluated efficiently in parallel (and the call to normal ReceiveWrite only needs to run once), and the security proof can be easily reduced to that of SendWrite, and the security simulator is given in Fig. 6.

4.3   Garbled Merkle Tree

We will now describe an algorithm called garbled Merkle tree. Roughly speaking, a garbled Merkle tree is a binary tree of garbled circuits, where each of the circuit takes arbitrary 2λ bits as input and outputs the labels of λ bit digest. Looking ahead, this construction allows for exponentially smaller online complexity compared to simply garbling the entire hash circuit when combined with adaptive garbling schemes we will construct later, since its tree structure allows for small pebbling complexity.

A garbled Merkle tree has very similar syntax as the one for garbled circuit. It consists of 2 following PPT algorithms:

Hashing Sub-Circuit C
  Hardwired Values/Circuit: H, Keys
  Input: $x \in \{0,1\}^{2\lambda}$
  Output $\mathsf{Keys}_{H(x)}$

Fig. 7. Hashing sub-circuit

- GHash$(1^\lambda, H, \{\mathsf{Key}_i\}_{i\in[|D|]}, \{\mathsf{Key}'_i\}_{i\in[\lambda]})$: it takes as input a security parameter λ, a hashing circuit H that takes 2λ bits as input and outputs λ bits, keys $\{\mathsf{Key}_i\}_{i\in[|D|]}$ for all bits in the database D and $\{\mathsf{Key}'_i\}_{i\in[\lambda]}$ for all output bits
    $\mathsf{Keys}_1 \leftarrow \{\mathsf{Key}'_i\}_{i\in[\lambda]}$
    Sample $\{\mathsf{Keys}_i\}_{i=2,...,|D|/\lambda-1}$
    $\{\mathsf{Keys}_i\}_{i=|D|/\lambda,...,2|D|/\lambda-1} \leftarrow \{\mathsf{Key}_i\}_{i\in[|D|]}$
    For $i=1$ to $|D|/\lambda - 1$ do
        $\tilde{C}_i \leftarrow$ GCircuit$(1^\lambda, \mathsf{C}[H, \mathsf{Keys}_i], (\mathsf{Keys}_{2i}, \mathsf{Keys}_{2i+1}))$
    Output $\{\tilde{C}_i\}_{i\in[|D|/\lambda-1]}$

    The circuit C here is given in Fig. 7.
- GHEval$\left(\{\tilde{C}_i\}, \{\mathsf{lab}_i\}_{i\in[|D|]}\right)$: it takes as input the garbled circuits $\{\tilde{C}_i\}_{i\in[|D|/\lambda-1]}$ and input labels for the database $\{\mathsf{lab}_i\}_{i\in[|D|]}$
    $\{\mathsf{Label}_i\}_{i=|D|/\lambda,...,2|D|/\lambda-1} \leftarrow \{\mathsf{lab}_i\}_{i\in[|D|]}$
    For $i=|D|/\lambda - 1$ down to 1 do
        $\mathsf{Label}_i \leftarrow$ GCEval$(\tilde{C}_i, (\mathsf{Label}_{2i}, \mathsf{Label}_{2i+1}))$
    Output Label_1

Later, we will also invoke this algorithm in garbled PRAM for creating parallel checkpoints.

4.4 Construction

We will now give the construction of our adaptive garbled circuits. Let ℓOT be a laconic oblivious transfer scheme, $(\mathsf{GCircuit}, \mathsf{GCEval})$ be a garbling scheme for circuits, $(\mathsf{GHash}, \mathsf{GHEval})$ be a garbling scheme for Merkle trees, and SEE be a somewhere equivocal encryption scheme with block length $\mathsf{poly}(\lambda, \log|C|)$ to be the maximum size of garbled circuits $\left\{ \widetilde{\mathsf{C}}_{i,k}^{\mathsf{eval}}, \widetilde{\mathsf{C}}_{i,j}^{\mathsf{hash}}, \widetilde{\mathsf{C}}_{i}^{\mathsf{write}} \right\}$, message length $2M\ell = O(|C|^2)$ (we will explain ℓ shortly after) and equivocation parameter $\log \ell + 2 \log M + O(1)$ (the choice comes from the security proof).

Furthermore, we assume both M and λ is a power of 2 and λ divides M. We also have a procedure $\{P_i\}_{i \in [\ell]} \leftarrow \mathsf{Partition}(C, M)$ (as an oracle) that partition the circuit's wires $1, 2, ..., |C|$ into ℓ continuous partitions of size M, such that for any partition P_i, its size is at most M (allowing a few extra auxiliary wires and renumbering wires), and every gate in the partition can be evaluated in parallel once every partition P_j with $j < i$ has been evaluated. Clearly $d \leq \ell \leq |C|$, but it's also acceptable to have a sub-optimal partition to best utilize the computational resources on a PRAM machine. We assume the input wires are put in partition 0. This preprocessing is essentially scheduling the evaluation of the circuit to a PRAM machine and it is essential to making our construction's online complexity small.

We now give an overview of our construction. At a high level, instead of garbling the circuit directly, our construction can be viewed as a garbling of a special PRAM program that evaluates the circuit in parallel. The database D will be hashed as $\widehat{D}$ using ℓOT and protected with an one-time pad r as ℓOT does not protect its memory content. In each iteration, two read operations for every processor correspond to two selectively secure garbled circuits, which on given digest as input, outputs a ℓOT read ciphertext that generates the input label for the garbled gate; the garbled gate unmasks the input, evaluates the gate, and then output the masked output of the gate. After all M processors have done evaluating their corresponding gates, a garbled Merkle tree will take their outputs as input to obtain the digest for the M bits of output, and then generate a ℓOT block-write ciphertext to store the outputs into the database. During evaluation, this block-write ciphertext can be used to obtain the input labels for the read circuits in the next iteration. This garbled PRAM program is then encrypted using a somewhere equivocal encryption, after which it is given to the adversary as the garbled circuit. On given input x, we generate the protected database $\widehat{D}$ and compute the input labels for the initial digest, and we give out the labels, the masked inputs, the decryption key, and masks for outputs in the database.

Now we formally present the construction (the description of the evaluation circuit used in the construction is given in Fig. 8). Inside the construction, we omit $k \in [M]$ when the context is clear. It might also be helpful to see Fig. 9 for how the garbled circuits are organized.

- $\mathsf{AdaGCircuit}^{\mathsf{Partition}}\left(1^\lambda, C\right)$:
  $\mathsf{crs} \leftarrow \ell OT.\mathsf{crsGen}(1^\lambda)$

Circuit $C_{\text{eval}}^{\tau \in \{\text{real, ideal}\}}$

Hardwired Values: $\text{crs}, i, j, g, (r_i, r_j, r_g), \text{lab}_0, \text{lab}_1$

Input: d

If τ is real, define for all $\alpha, \beta \in \{0,1\}$, $\gamma(\alpha, \beta) := \text{NAND}(\alpha \oplus r_i, \beta \oplus r_j) \oplus r_g$

If τ is ideal, define for all $\alpha, \beta \in \{0,1\}$, $\gamma(\alpha, \beta) := r_g$

$f_b \leftarrow \text{Send}\left(\text{crs}, d, j, (\gamma(b,0), \text{lab}_{\gamma(b,0)}), (\gamma(b,1), \text{lab}_{\gamma(b,1)})\right)$ for each $b \in \{0,1\}$

Output $\text{Send}(\text{crs}, d, i, f_0, f_1)$

Fig. 8. Description of the evaluation circuit

$\text{key} \leftarrow \text{SEE.KeyGen}(1^\lambda)$

$K \leftarrow \text{PRFKeyGen}(1^\lambda)$

$\{P_i\}_{i \in [\ell]} \leftarrow \text{Partition}(C)$

Sample $r \leftarrow \{0,1\}^{M\ell}$

For $i = 1$ to ℓ do:

   Let $C_{g,1}, C_{g,2}$ denote the two input gates of gate g

$\tilde{C}_{i,k}^{\text{eval}} \leftarrow \text{GCircuit}(1^\lambda, C_{\text{eval}}^{\text{real}}[\text{crs}, C_{P_{i,k},1}, C_{P_{i,k},2}, P_{i,k}, (r_{C_{P_{i,k},1}}, r_{C_{P_{i,k},2}}, r_{P_{i,k}}),$

$\qquad\qquad \text{PRF}_K(1, i, k, 0), \text{PRF}_K(1, i, k, 1)],$

$\qquad\qquad \{\text{PRF}_K(0, i, j, b)\}_{j \in [\lambda], b \in \{0,1\}})$

Let $\text{keyEval} = \{\text{PRF}_K(1, i, k, b)\}_{k \in [M], b \in \{0,1\}}$

Let $\text{keyHash} = \{\text{PRF}_K(2, i, j, b)\}_{j \in [\lambda], b \in \{0,1\}}$

$\{\tilde{C}_{i,j}^{\text{hash}}\}_{j \in [M-1]} \leftarrow \text{GHash}(1^\lambda, \ell OT_{\text{const}}.\text{Hash}, \text{keyEval}, \text{keyHash})$

Let $C_i^{\text{write}} = \ell OT.\text{SendWriteBlock}\left(\text{crs}, \cdot, i, \{\text{PRF}_K(0, i+1, j, b)\}_{j \in [\lambda], b \in \{0,1\}}\right)$

$\tilde{C}_i^{\text{write}} \leftarrow \text{GCircuit}\left(1^\lambda, C_i^{\text{write}}, \text{keyHash}\right)$

$c \leftarrow \text{SEE.Enc}\left(\text{key}, \left\{\tilde{C}_{i,k}^{\text{eval}}, \tilde{C}_{i,j}^{\text{hash}}, \tilde{C}_i^{\text{write}}\right\}\right)$

Output $\tilde{C} := (\text{crs}, c, \{P_i\}_{i \in [\ell]})$ and $\text{st} := (\text{crs}, r, \text{key}, \ell, K)$

– $\text{AdaGInput}(\text{st}, x)$:

   Parse $\text{st} := (\text{crs}, r, \text{key}, \ell, K)$

   $D \leftarrow r_1 \oplus x_1 || ... || r_n \oplus x_n || 0^{M\ell - n}$

   $(\text{d}, \hat{D}) \leftarrow \ell OT.\text{Hash}(\text{crs}, D)$

   Output $(\{\text{PRF}_K(0, 1, j, \text{d}_j)\}_{j \in [\lambda]}, r_1 \oplus x_1 || ... || r_n \oplus x_n, \text{key}, r_{N-m+1} || ... || r_N)$

– $\text{AdaEval}(\tilde{C}, \tilde{x})$:

   Parse $\tilde{C} := (\text{crs}, c, \{P_i\}_{i \in [\ell]})$

   Parse $\tilde{x} := (\{\text{lab}_{0,j}\}_{j \in [\lambda]}, s_1 || ... || s_n, \text{key}, r_{N-m+1} || ... || r_N)$

   $D \leftarrow s_1 || ... || s_n || 0^{M\ell - n}$

   $(\text{d}, \hat{D}) \leftarrow \ell OT.\text{Hash}(\text{crs}, D)$

   $\left\{\tilde{C}_{i,k}^{\text{eval}}, \tilde{C}_{i,j}^{\text{hash}}, \tilde{C}_i^{\text{write}}\right\} \leftarrow \text{SEE.Dec}(\text{key}, c)$

   For $i = 1$ to ℓ do:

      Let $C_{g,1}, C_{g,2}$ denote the two input gates of gate g

      $e \leftarrow \text{GCEval}(\tilde{C}_{i,k}^{\text{eval}}, \{\text{lab}_{0,j}\}_{j \in [\lambda]})$

$$e \leftarrow \ell OT.\mathsf{Receive}^{\hat{D}}(\mathsf{crs}, \mathsf{e}, C_{P_{i,k},1})$$
$$(\gamma_k, \mathsf{lab}_{1,k}) \leftarrow \ell OT.\mathsf{Receive}^{\hat{D}}(\mathsf{crs}, \mathsf{e}, C_{P_{i,k},2})$$
$$\{\mathsf{lab}_{2,j}\}_{j\in[\lambda]} \leftarrow \mathsf{GHEval}(\{\widetilde{\mathsf{C}}_{i,j}^{\mathsf{hash}}\}_{j\in[M-1]}, \{\mathsf{lab}_{1,k}\}_{k\in[M]})$$
$$\mathsf{e} \leftarrow \mathsf{GCEval}(\widetilde{\mathsf{C}}_i^{\mathsf{write}}, \{\mathsf{lab}_{2,j}\}_{j\in[\lambda]})$$
$$\{\mathsf{lab}_{0,j}\}_{j\in[\lambda]} \leftarrow \ell OT.\mathsf{ReceiveWriteBlock}^{\tilde{D}}(\mathsf{crs}, i, \{\gamma_k\}_{k\in[M]}, \mathsf{e})$$
Recover the contents of the memory D from the final state $\hat{D}$
Output $D_{N-m+1} \oplus r_{N-m+1}||...||D_N \oplus r_N$

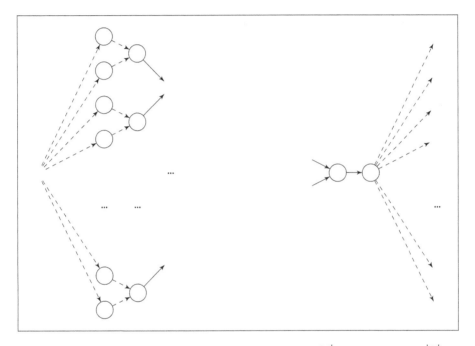

Fig. 9. Illustration of the pebbling graph for one layer: $\widetilde{\mathsf{C}}_{i,k}^{\mathsf{eval}}$ are leaf nodes, $\widetilde{\mathsf{C}}_{i,j}^{\mathsf{hash}}$ are intermediate nodes and the root node, finally $\widetilde{\mathsf{C}}_i^{\mathsf{write}}$ is the extra node at the end. Dotted edges indicate where ℓOT is invoked. Note that WriteBlock is only invoked once and its result is reused M times.

Communcation Complexity of AdaGInput. It follows from the construction that the communication complexity of AdaGInput is $\lambda^2 + n + m + |\mathsf{key}|$. From the parameters used in the somewhere equivocal encryption and the efficiency of block writing for laconic oblivious transfer, we note that $|\mathsf{key}| = \mathsf{poly}(\lambda, \log|C|)$.

Computational Complexity of AdaGInput. The running time of AdaGInput grows linearly with $|C|$. However, it's possible to delegate the hashing of zeros to the offline phase, i.e. AdaGCircuit. In that case, the running time only grows linearly with $n + \log|C|$.

Parallel Efficiency. With a good Partition algorithm and number of processors as many as the width of the circuit, AdaEval is able to run in $d \cdot \mathsf{poly}(\lambda, \log |C|)$ where d is the depth of the circuit.

Correctness. We note that for each wire (up to permutation due to rewiring), our construction manipulates the database and produces the final output the same way as the construction given by [GS18]. Therefore by the correctness of their construction, our construction outputs $C(x)$ with probability 1.

Adaptive Security. We formally prove the adaptive security in the full version.

Acknowledgements. The authors would like to thank Tsung-Hsuan Hung and Yu-Chi Chen for their helpful discussions in the early stage of this research.

References

[ACC+16] Ananth, P., Chen, Y.-C., Chung, K.-M., Lin, H., Lin, W.-K.: Delegating RAM computations with adaptive soundness and privacy. In: Hirt, M., Smith, A. (eds.) TCC 2016. LNCS, vol. 9986, pp. 3–30. Springer, Heidelberg (2016). https://doi.org/10.1007/978-3-662-53644-5_1

[AKS83] Ajtai, M., Komlós, J., Szemerédi, E.: An O(n log n) sorting network. In: Proceedings of the Fifteenth Annual ACM Symposium on Theory of Computing, STOC 1983, pp. 1–9. ACM, New York (1983)

[App17] Applebaum, B.: Garbled circuits as randomized encodings of functions: a primer. In: Lindell, Y. (ed.) Tutorials on the Foundations of Cryptography. ISC, pp. 1–44. Springer, Cham (2017). https://doi.org/10.1007/978-3-319-57048-8_1

[BCP16] Boyle, E., Chung, K.-M., Pass, R.: Oblivious parallel RAM and applications. In: Kushilevitz, E., Malkin, T. (eds.) TCC 2016. LNCS, vol. 9563, pp. 175–204. Springer, Heidelberg (2016). https://doi.org/10.1007/978-3-662-49099-0_7

[Ben89] Bennett, C.H.: Time/space trade-offs for reversible computation. SIAM J. Comput. **18**(4), 766–776 (1989)

[BHR12a] Bellare, M., Hoang, V.T., Rogaway, P.: Adaptively secure garbling with applications to one-time programs and secure outsourcing. In: Wang, X., Sako, K. (eds.) ASIACRYPT 2012. LNCS, vol. 7658, pp. 134–153. Springer, Heidelberg (2012). https://doi.org/10.1007/978-3-642-34961-4_10

[BHR12b] Bellare, M., Hoang, V.T., Rogaway, P.: Foundations of garbled circuits. In: Proceedings of the 2012 ACM Conference on Computer and Communications Security, pp. 784–796. ACM (2012)

[BLSV18] Brakerski, Z., Lombardi, A., Segev, G., Vaikuntanathan, V.: Anonymous IBE, leakage resilience and circular security from new assumptions. In: Nielsen, J.B., Rijmen, V. (eds.) EUROCRYPT 2018. LNCS, vol. 10820, pp. 535–564. Springer, Cham (2018). https://doi.org/10.1007/978-3-319-78381-9_20

[CCC+16] Chen, Y.-C., Chow, S.S.M., Chung, K.-M., Lai, R.W.F., Lin, W.-K., Zhou, H.-S.: Cryptography for parallel RAM from indistinguishability obfuscation. In: Proceedings of the 2016 ACM Conference on Innovations in Theoretical Computer Science, pp. 179–190. ACM (2016)

[CCHR16] Canetti, R., Chen, Y., Holmgren, J., Raykova, M.: Adaptive succinct gar-
          bled RAM or: how to delegate your database. In: Hirt, M., Smith, A.
          (eds.) TCC 2016. LNCS, vol. 9986, pp. 61–90. Springer, Heidelberg (2016).
          https://doi.org/10.1007/978-3-662-53644-5_3
[CDG+17] Cho, C., Döttling, N., Garg, S., Gupta, D., Miao, P., Polychroniadou,
          A.: Laconic oblivious transfer and its applications. In: Katz, J., Shacham,
          H. (eds.) CRYPTO 2017. LNCS, vol. 10402, pp. 33–65. Springer, Cham
          (2017). https://doi.org/10.1007/978-3-319-63715-0_2
[CH16]   Canetti, R., Holmgren, J.: Fully succinct garbled RAM. In: Proceedings
          of the 2016 ACM Conference on Innovations in Theoretical Computer Sci-
          ence, pp. 169–178. ACM (2016)
[DG17]   Döttling, N., Garg, S.: Identity-based encryption from the Diffie-Hellman
          assumption. In: Katz, J., Shacham, H. (eds.) CRYPTO 2017. LNCS, vol.
          10401, pp. 537–569. Springer, Cham (2017). https://doi.org/10.1007/978-
          3-319-63688-7_18
[DGHM18] Döttling, N., Garg, S., Hajiabadi, M., Masny, D.: New constructions of
          identity-based and key-dependent message secure encryption schemes. In:
          Abdalla, M., Dahab, R. (eds.) PKC 2018. LNCS, vol. 10769, pp. 3–31.
          Springer, Cham (2018). https://doi.org/10.1007/978-3-319-76578-5_1
[GGMP16] Garg, S., Gupta, D., Miao, P., Pandey, O.: Secure multiparty RAM com-
          putation in constant rounds. In: Hirt, M., Smith, A. (eds.) TCC 2016.
          LNCS, vol. 9985, pp. 491–520. Springer, Heidelberg (2016). https://doi.
          org/10.1007/978-3-662-53641-4_19
[GHL+14] Gentry, C., Halevi, S., Lu, S., Ostrovsky, R., Raykova, M., Wichs, D.:
          Garbled RAM revisited. In: Nguyen, P.Q., Oswald, E. (eds.) EUROCRYPT
          2014. LNCS, vol. 8441, pp. 405–422. Springer, Heidelberg (2014). https://
          doi.org/10.1007/978-3-642-55220-5_23
[GLO15]   Garg, S., Lu, S., Ostrovsky, R.: Black-box garbled RAM. In: 2015 IEEE
          56th Annual Symposium on Foundations of Computer Science (FOCS),
          pp. 210–229. IEEE (2015)
[GLOS15] Garg, S., Lu, S., Ostrovsky, R., Scafuro, A.: Garbled RAM from one-way
          functions. In: Proceedings of the Forty-Seventh Annual ACM Symposium
          on Theory of Computing, pp. 449–458. ACM (2015)
[GOS18]   Garg, S., Ostrovsky, R., Srinivasan, A.: Adaptive garbled RAM from
          laconic oblivious transfer. In: Shacham, H., Boldyreva, A. (eds.) CRYPTO
          2018. LNCS, vol. 10993, pp. 515–544. Springer, Cham (2018). https://doi.
          org/10.1007/978-3-319-96878-0_18
[GS18]   Garg, S., Srinivasan, A.: Adaptively secure garbling with near optimal
          online complexity. In: Nielsen, J.B., Rijmen, V. (eds.) EUROCRYPT 2018.
          LNCS, vol. 10821, pp. 535–565. Springer, Cham (2018). https://doi.org/
          10.1007/978-3-319-78375-8_18
[HJO+16] Hemenway, B., Jafargholi, Z., Ostrovsky, R., Scafuro, A., Wichs, D.: Adap-
          tively secure garbled circuits from one-way functions. In: Robshaw, M.,
          Katz, J. (eds.) CRYPTO 2016. LNCS, vol. 9816, pp. 149–178. Springer,
          Heidelberg (2016). https://doi.org/10.1007/978-3-662-53015-3_6
[JKK+17] Jafargholi, Z., Kamath, C., Klein, K., Komargodski, I., Pietrzak, K.,
          Wichs, D.: Be adaptive, avoid overcommitting. In: Katz, J., Shacham, H.
          (eds.) CRYPTO 2017. LNCS, vol. 10401, pp. 133–163. Springer, Cham
          (2017). https://doi.org/10.1007/978-3-319-63688-7_5

[JSW17] Jafargholi, Z., Scafuro, A., Wichs, D.: Adaptively indistinguishable garbled circuits. In: Kalai, Y., Reyzin, L. (eds.) TCC 2017. LNCS, vol. 10678, pp. 40–71. Springer, Cham (2017). https://doi.org/10.1007/978-3-319-70503-3_2

[JW16] Jafargholi, Z., Wichs, D.: Adaptive security of Yao's garbled circuits. In: Hirt, M., Smith, A. (eds.) TCC 2016. LNCS, vol. 9985, pp. 433–458. Springer, Heidelberg (2016). https://doi.org/10.1007/978-3-662-53641-4_17

[LO13] Lu, S., Ostrovsky, R.: How to garble RAM programs? In: Johansson, T., Nguyen, P.Q. (eds.) EUROCRYPT 2013. LNCS, vol. 7881, pp. 719–734. Springer, Heidelberg (2013). https://doi.org/10.1007/978-3-642-38348-9_42

[LO17] Lu, S., Ostrovsky, R.: Black-box parallel garbled RAM. In: Katz, J., Shacham, H. (eds.) CRYPTO 2017. LNCS, vol. 10402, pp. 66–92. Springer, Cham (2017). https://doi.org/10.1007/978-3-319-63715-0_3

[PTC76] Paul, W.J., Tarjan, R.E., Celoni, J.R.: Space bounds for a game on graphs. Math. Syst. Theory **10**(1), 239–251 (1976)

[Yao82] Yao, A.C.: Protocols for secure computations. In: 23rd Annual Symposium on Foundations of Computer Science, 1982, SFCS'08, pp. 160–164. IEEE (1982)

Statistical Difference Beyond the Polarizing Regime

Itay Berman[1]($\boxtimes$), Akshay Degwekar[1], Ron D. Rothblum[2], and Prashant Nalini Vasudevan[3]

[1] MIT, Cambridge, USA
{itayberm,akshayd}@mit.edu
[2] Technion, Haifa, Israel
rothblum@cs.technion.ac.il
[3] UC Berkeley, Berkeley, USA
prashvas@berkeley.edu

Abstract. The polarization lemma for statistical distance (SD), due to Sahai and Vadhan (JACM, 2003), is an efficient transformation taking as input a pair of circuits (C_0, C_1) and an integer k and outputting a new pair of circuits (D_0, D_1) such that if $\mathrm{SD}(C_0, C_1) \geq \alpha$ then $\mathrm{SD}(D_0, D_1) \geq 1 - 2^{-k}$ and if $\mathrm{SD}(C_0, C_1) \leq \beta$ then $\mathrm{SD}(D_0, D_1) \leq 2^{-k}$. The polarization lemma is known to hold for any constant values $\beta < \alpha^2$, but extending the lemma to the regime in which $\alpha^2 \leq \beta < \alpha$ has remained elusive. The focus of this work is in studying the latter regime of parameters. Our main results are:

1. Polarization lemmas for different notions of distance, such as *Triangular Discrimination* (TD) and *Jensen-Shannon Divergence* (JS), which enable polarization for some problems where the statistical distance satisfies $\alpha^2 < \beta < \alpha$. We also derive a polarization lemma for statistical distance with any inverse-polynomially small gap between α^2 and β (rather than a constant).

2. The average-case hardness of the statistical difference problem (i.e., determining whether the statistical distance between two given circuits is at least α or at most β), for any values of $\beta < \alpha$, implies

---

This is an extended abstract. The full version of this paper, with formal statements of the theorems and proofs, may be found at: https://eccc.weizmann.ac.il/report/2019/038/.

I. Berman and A. Degwekar—Research supported in part by NSF Grants CNS-1413920 and CNS-1350619, MIT-IBM Award, and by the Defense Advanced Research Projects Agency (DARPA) and the U.S. Army Research Office under Vinod Vaikuntanathan's DARPA Young Faculty Award and contracts W911NF-15-C-0226 and W911NF-15-C-0236.

R. D. Rothblum—This research was supported in part by the Israeli Science Foundation (Grant No. 1262/18).

P. N. Vasudevan—Research supported in part from DARPA/ARL SAFEWARE Award W911NF15C0210, AFOSR Award FA9550-15-1-0274, AFOSR YIP Award, a Hellman Award and research grants by the Okawa Foundation, Visa Inc., and Center for LongTerm Cybersecurity (CLTC, UC Berkeley).

© International Association for Cryptologic Research 2019
D. Hofheinz and A. Rosen (Eds.): TCC 2019, LNCS 11892, pp. 311–332, 2019.
https://doi.org/10.1007/978-3-030-36033-7_12

the existence of one-way functions. Such a result was previously only known for $\beta < \alpha^2$.

3. A (direct) constant-round interactive proof for estimating the statistical distance between any two distributions (up to any inverse polynomial error) given circuits that generate them. Proofs of closely related statements have appeared in the literature but we give a new proof which we find to be cleaner and more direct.

1   Introduction

The STATISTICAL DIFFERENCE PROBLEM, introduced by Sahai and Vadhan [SV03], is a central computational (promise) problem in complexity theory and cryptography, which is also intimately related to the study of statistical zero-knowledge (SZK). The input to this problem is a pair of circuits C_0 and C_1, specifying probability distributions (i.e., that are induced by feeding the circuits with a uniformly random string). YES instances are those in which the statistical distance[1] between the two distributions is at least $2/3$ and NO instances are those in which the distance is at most $1/3$. Input circuits that do not fall in one of these two cases are considered to be outside the promise (and so their value is left unspecified).

The choice of the constants $1/3$ and $2/3$ in the above definition is somewhat arbitrary (although not entirely arbitrary as will soon be discussed in detail). A more general family of problems can be obtained by considering a suitable parameterization. More specifically, let $0 \leq \beta < \alpha \leq 1$. The (α, β) parameterized version of the STATISTICAL DIFFERENCE PROBLEM, denoted $\mathrm{SDP}^{\alpha,\beta}$, has as its YES inputs pairs of circuits that induce distributions that have distance at least α whereas the NO inputs correspond to circuits that induce distributions that have distance at most β.

Definition 1.1 (STATISTICAL DIFFERENCE PROBLEM). *Let $\alpha, \beta \colon \mathbb{N} \to [0,1]$ with $\alpha(n) > \beta(n)$ for every n. The* STATISTICAL DIFFERENCE PROBLEM *with promise (α, β), denoted $\mathrm{SDP}^{\alpha,\beta}$, is given by the sets*

$$\mathrm{SDP}_Y^{\alpha,\beta} = \left\{ (C_0, C_1) \mid \mathrm{SD}(C_0, C_1) \geq \alpha(n) \right\} \ and$$
$$\mathrm{SDP}_N^{\alpha,\beta} = \left\{ (C_0, C_1) \mid \mathrm{SD}(C_0, C_1) \leq \beta(n) \right\},$$

where n is the output length of the circuits C_0 and C_1.[2]

---

[1] Recall that the statistical distance between two distributions P and Q over a set $\mathcal{Y}$ is defined as $\mathrm{SD}(P, Q) = \frac{1}{2} \sum_{y \in \mathcal{Y}} |P_y - Q_y|$, where P_y (resp., Q_y) is the probability mass that P (resp., Q) puts on $y \in \mathcal{Y}$.

[2] In prior works α and β were typically thought of as constants (and so their dependence on the input was not specified). In contrast, since we will want to think of them as parameters, we choose to let them depend on the output length of the circuit since this size seems most relevant to the distributions induced by the circuits. Other natural choices could have been the input length or the description size of the circuits. We remark that these different choices do not affect our results in a fundamental way.

(Here and below we abuse notation and use C_0 and C_1 to denote both the circuits and the respective distributions that they generate.)

The elegant *polarization lemma* of [SV03] shows how to polarize the statistical distance between two distributions. In more detail, for any constants α and β such that $\beta < \alpha^2$, the lemma gives a transformation that makes distributions that are at least α-far be extremely far and distributions that are β-close be extremely close. Beyond being of intrinsic interest, the polarization lemma is used to establish the SZK completeness of $\text{SDP}^{\alpha,\beta}$, when $\alpha^2 > \beta$, and has other important applications in cryptography such as the amplification of weak public key encryption schemes to full fledged ones [DNR04, HR05].

Sahai and Vadhan left the question of polarization for parameters α and β that do not meet the requirements of their polarization lemma as an open question. We refer to this setting of α and β as the *non-polarizing* regime. We emphasize that by *non-polarizing* we merely mean that in this regime polarization is not currently known and not that it is impossible to achieve (although some barriers are known and will be discussed further below). The focus of this work is studying the STATISTICAL DIFFERENCE PROBLEM in the non-polarizing regime.

1.1 Our Results

We proceed to describe our results.

1.1.1 Polarization and SZK Completeness for Other Notions of Distance

The statistical distance metric is one of the central information theoretic tools used in cryptography as it is very useful for capturing similarity between distributions. However, in information theory there are other central notions that measure similarity such as mutual information and KL divergence as well as others.

Loosely speaking, our first main result shows that polarization is possible even in *some* cases in which $\beta \geq \alpha^2$. However, this result actually stems from a more general study showing that polarization is possible for other notions of distance between distributions from information theory, which we find to be of independent interest.

When distributions are extremely similar or extremely dissimilar, these different notions of distance are often (but not always) closely related and hence interchangeable. This equivalence is particularly beneficial when considering applications of SZK—for some applications one distance measure may be easier to use than others. For example, showing that the average-case hardness of SZK implies one-way functions can be analyzed using statistical distance (e.g., [Vad99, Section 4.8]), but showing that every language in SZK has instance-dependent commitments is naturally analyzed using entropy (e.g., [OV08]).

However, as the gaps in the relevant distances get smaller (i.e., the distributions are only somewhat similar or dissimilar), the relation between different statistical properties becomes less clear (for example, the reduction from $\mathrm{SDP}^{\alpha,\beta}$ to the ENTROPY DIFFERENCE PROBLEM of [GV99] only works when roughly $\alpha^2 > \beta$). This motivates studying the computational complexity of problems defined using different notions of distance in this small gap regime. Studying this question can be (and, as we shall soon see, indeed is) beneficial in two aspects. First, providing a wider bag of statistical properties related to SZK, which can make certain applications easier to analyze. Second, the computational complexity of these distance notions might shed light on the computational complexity of problems involving existing distance notions (e.g., $\mathrm{SDP}^{\alpha,\beta}$ when $\alpha^2 < \beta$).

We focus here on two specific distance notions—the *triangular discrimination* and the *Jensen-Shannon divergence*, defined next.

Definition 1.2 (Triangular Discrimination). *The* Triangular Discrimination *(a.k.a. Le Cam divergence) between two distributions P and Q is defined as*

$$\mathrm{TD}(P, Q) = \frac{1}{2} \sum_{y \in \mathcal{Y}} \frac{(P_y - Q_y)^2}{P_y + Q_y},$$

where $\mathcal{Y}$ is the union of the supports of P and Q.

The TRIANGULAR DISCRIMINATION PROBLEM *with promise (α, β), denoted $\mathrm{TDP}^{\alpha,\beta}$, is defined analogously to $\mathrm{SDP}^{\alpha,\beta}$, but with respect to TD rather than* SD.

The triangular discrimination is commonly used, among many other applications, in statistical learning theory for parameter estimation with quadratic loss, see [Cam86, P. 48] (in a similar manner to how statistical distance characterizes the 0–1 loss function in hypothesis testing). Jumping ahead, while the definition of triangular discrimination seems somewhat arbitrary at first glance, in Sect. 2 we will show that this distance notion characterizes some basic phenomena in the study of statistical zero-knowledge. Triangular discrimination has recently found usage in theoretical computer science, and even specifically in problems related to SZK. Yehudayoff [Yeh16] showed that using TD yields a tighter analysis of the pointer chasing problem in communication complexity. The work of Komargodski and Yogev [KY18] uses triangular discrimination to show that the average-case hardness of SZK implies the existence of distributional collision resistant hash functions.

Next, we define the *Jensen-Shannon Divergence*. To start with, recall that the KL-divergence between two distributions P and Q is defined[3] as $\mathrm{KL}(P||Q) = \sum_{y \in \mathcal{Y}} P_y \log(P_y/Q_y)$. Also, given distributions P_0 and P_1 we define the distribution $\frac{1}{2}P_0 + \frac{1}{2}P_1$ as the distribution obtained by sampling a random coin $b \in \{0, 1\}$ and outputting a sample y from P_b (indeed, this notation corresponds to arithmetic operations on the probability mass functions). The Jensen-Shannon divergence measures the mutual information between b and y.

---

[3] To be more precise, in this definition we view $0 \cdot \log \frac{0}{0}$ as 0 and define the KL-divergence to be ∞ if the support of P is not contained in that of Q.

Definition 1.3 (Jensen-Shannon Divergence). *The* Jensen-Shannon divergence *between two distributions P and Q is defined as*

$$\mathrm{JS}(P,Q) = \frac{1}{2}\,\mathrm{KL}\left(P\,\middle\|\,\frac{P+Q}{2}\right) + \frac{1}{2}\,\mathrm{KL}\left(Q\,\middle\|\,\frac{P+Q}{2}\right).$$

The JENSEN-SHANNON DIVERGENCE PROBLEM *with promise (α,β), denoted*
$\mathrm{JSP}^{\alpha,\beta}$, *is defined analogously to* $\mathrm{SDP}^{\alpha,\beta}$, *but with respect to* JS *rather than* SD.

The Jensen-Shannon divergence enjoys a couple of important properties (in our
context) that the KL-divergence lacks: it is symmetric and bounded. Both triangular discrimination and Jensen-Shannon divergence (as well as statistical
distance and KL-divergence) are types of f-divergences, a central concept in
information theory (see [PW17, Section 6] and references therein). They are both
non-negative and bounded by one.[4] Finally, the Jensen-Shannon divergence is a
metric, while the triangular discrimination is a square of a metric.

  With these notions of distance and corresponding computational problems
in hand, we are almost ready to state our first set of results. Before doing so, we
introduce an additional useful technical definition.

Definition 1.4 (Separated functions). *Let $g\colon \mathbb{N} \to [0,1]$. A pair of $\mathrm{poly}(n)$-
time computable functions (α,β), where $\alpha = \alpha(n) \in [0,1]$ and $\beta = \beta(n) \in [0,1]$,
is g-separated if $\alpha(n) \geq \beta(n) + g(n)$ for every $n \in \mathbb{N}$.*

  *We denote by $(1/\mathrm{poly})$-separated the set of all pairs of functions that are
$(1/p)$-separated for some polynomial p. Similarly, we denote by $(1/\log)$-separated
the set of all pairs of functions that are $(1/(c\log))$-separated for some constant
$c > 0$.*

We can now state our first set of results: that both TDP and JSP, with a
noticeable gap, are SZK complete.

Theorem 1.5. *Let (α,β) be $(1/\mathrm{poly})$-separated functions such that there exists
a constant $\varepsilon \in (0,1/2)$ such that $2^{-n^{1/2-\varepsilon}} \leq \beta(n)$ and $\alpha(n) \leq 1 - 2^{-n^{1/2-\varepsilon}}$, for
every $n \in \mathbb{N}$. Then, $\mathrm{TDP}^{\alpha,\beta}$ is SZK complete.*

Theorem 1.6. *For (α,β) as in Theorem 1.5, the problem $\mathrm{JSP}^{\alpha,\beta}$ is SZK complete.*

The restriction on $2^{-n^{1/2-\varepsilon}} \leq \beta(n)$ and $\alpha(n) \leq 1-2^{-n^{1/2-\varepsilon}}$ should be interpreted
as a non-degeneracy requirement (which we did not attempt to optimize), where
we note that some restriction seems inherent. Moreover, we can actually decouple
the assumptions in Theorems 1.5 and 1.6 as follows. To show that $\mathrm{TDP}^{\alpha,\beta}$ and
$\mathrm{JSP}^{\alpha,\beta}$ are SZK-*hard*, only the non-degeneracy assumption (i.e., $2^{-n^{1/2-\varepsilon}} \leq \beta(n)$
and $\alpha(n) \leq 1 - 2^{-n^{1/2-\varepsilon}}$) is needed. On the other hand, to show that these
problems are in SZK we only require that (α,β) are $(1/\mathrm{poly})$-separated.

---

[4] In the literature these distances are sometimes defined to be twice as much as our
   definitions. In our context, it is natural to have the distances bounded by one.

Note that in particular, Theorems 1.5 and 1.6 imply polarization lemmas for both TD and JS. For example, for triangular discrimination, since $\text{TDP}^{\alpha,\beta} \in$ SZK and $\text{TDP}^{1-2^{-k},2^{-k}}$ is SZK-hard, one can reduce the former to the latter.

Beyond showing polarization for triangular discrimination, Theorem 1.5 has implications regarding the question of polarizing statistical distance, which was our original motivation. It is known that the triangular discrimination is sandwiched between the statistical distance and its square; namely, for every two distributions P and Q it holds that (see [Top00, Eq. (11)]):

$$\text{SD}(P,Q)^2 \leq \text{TD}(P,Q) \leq \text{SD}(P,Q) \tag{1.1}$$

Thus, the problem $\text{SDP}^{\alpha,\beta}$ is immediately reducible to $\text{TDP}^{\alpha^2,\beta}$, which Theorem 1.5 shows to be SZK-complete, as long as the gap between α^2 and β is noticeable. Specifically, we have the following corollary.

Corollary 1.7. *Let (α, β) be as in Theorem 1.5, with the exception that (α^2, β) are $(1/\text{poly})$-separated (note that here α is squared). Then, the promise problem $\text{SDP}^{\alpha,\beta}$ is SZK complete.*

We highlight two implications of Theorem 1.5 and Corollary 1.7 (which were also briefly mentioned above).

Polarization with Inverse Polynomial Gap. Observe that Corollary 1.7 implies polarization of statistical distance in a regime in which α and β are functions of n, the output length of the two circuits, and α^2 and β are only separated by an inverse polynomial. This is in contrast to most prior works which focus on α and β that are constants. In particular, Sahai and Vadhan's [SV03] proof of the polarization lemma focuses on constant α and β and can be extended to handle an inverse logarithmic gap, but does not seem to extend to an inverse polynomial gap.[5] Corollary 1.7 does yield such a result, by relying on a somewhat different approach.

Polarization Beyond $\alpha^2 > \beta$. Theorem 1.5 can sometimes go beyond the requirement that $\alpha^2 > \beta$ for polarizing statistical distance. Specifically, it shows that any problem with noticeable gap in the triangular discrimination can be polarized. Indeed, there are distributions (P,Q) and (P',Q') with $\text{SD}(P,Q) > \text{SD}(P',Q') > \text{SD}(P,Q)^2$ but still $\text{TD}(P,Q) > \text{TD}(P',Q')$.[6] Circuits generating such distributions were until now not known to be in the polarizing regime, but can now be polarized by combining Theorem 1.5 and Eq. (1.1).

---

[5] Actually, it was claimed in [GV11] that the [SV03] proof does extend to the setting of an inverse polynomial gap between α^2 and β but this claim was later retracted, see http://www.wisdom.weizmann.ac.il/~/oded/entropy.html.

[6] For example, for a parameter $\gamma \in [0,1]$ consider the distributions R_0^γ and R_1^γ over $\{0,1,2\}$: R_b^γ puts γ mass on b and $1 - \gamma$ mass on 2. It holds that $\text{SD}(R_0^\gamma, R_1^\gamma) = \text{TD}(R_0^\gamma, R_1^\gamma) = \gamma$. If, say, $(P,Q) = (R_0^{1/2}, R_1^{1/2})$ and $(P',Q') = (R_0^{1/3}, R_1^{1/3})$, then $\text{SD}(P,Q) > \text{SD}(P',Q') > \text{SD}(P,Q)^2$ but $\text{TD}(P,Q) > \text{TD}(P',Q')$.

1.1.2   From Statistical Difference to One-Way Functions

We continue our study of the STATISTICAL DIFFERENCE PROBLEM, focusing on the regime where $\beta < \alpha$ (and in particular even when $\beta \geq \alpha^2$). We show that in this regime the $\mathrm{SDP}^{\alpha,\beta}$ problem shares many important properties of SZK (although we fall short of actually showing that it lies in SZK—which is equivalent to polarization for any $\beta < \alpha$).

First, we show that similarly to SZK, the average-case hardness of $\mathrm{SDP}^{\alpha,\beta}$ implies the existence of one-way functions. The fact that average-case hardness of SZK (or equivalently $\mathrm{SDP}^{\alpha,\beta}$ for $\beta < \alpha^2$) implies the existence of one-way functions was shown by Ostrovsky [Ost91]. Indeed, our contribution is in showing that the weaker condition of $\beta < \alpha$ (rather than $\beta < \alpha^2$) suffices for this result.

Theorem 1.8. *Let (α, β) be $(1/\mathsf{poly})$-separated functions. Suppose that $\mathrm{SDP}^{\alpha,\beta}$ is average-case hard. Then, there exists a one-way function.*

The question of constructing one-way functions from the (average-case) hardness of SDP is closely related to a result of Goldreich's [Gol90] showing that the existence of efficiently sampleable distributions that are statistically far but computationally indistinguishable implies the existence of one-way functions. Our proof of Theorem 1.8 allows us to re-derive the following strengthening of [Gol90], due to Naor and Rothblum [NR06, Theorem 4.1]: for any $(1/\mathsf{poly})$-separated (α, β), the existence of efficiently sampleable distributions whose statistical distance is α but no efficient algorithm can distinguish between them with advantage more than β, implies the existence of one-way functions. See further discussion in Theorem 2.1.

1.1.3   Interactive Proof for Statistical Distance Approximation

As our last main result, we construct a new interactive protocol that lets a verifier estimate the statistical distance between two given circuits up to any noticeable precision.

Theorem 1.9. *There exists a constant-round public-coin interactive protocol between a prover and a verifier that, given as input a pair of circuits (C_0, C_1), a claim $\Delta \in [0, 1]$ for their statistical distance, and a tolerance parameter $\delta \in [0, 1]$, satisfies the following properties:*

- **Completeness:** *If $\mathrm{SD}(C_0, C_1) = \Delta$, then the verifier accepts with probability at least $2/3$ when interacting with the honest prover.*
- **Soundness:** *If $|\mathrm{SD}(C_0, C_1) - \Delta| \geq \delta$, then when interacting with any (possibly cheating) prover, the verifier accepts with probability at most $1/3$.*
- **Efficiency:** *The verifier runs in time $\mathsf{poly}(|C_0|, |C_1|, 1/\delta)$.*

(As usual the completeness and soundness errors can be reduced by applying parallel repetition. We can also achieve perfect completeness using a result from [FGM+89].)

Theorem 1.9 is actually equivalent to the following statement.

Theorem 1.10 ([BL13, Theorem 6], [BBF16, Theorem 2]). *For any (α, β) that are $(1/\mathsf{poly})$-separated, it holds that $\mathrm{SDP}^{\alpha,\beta} \in \mathsf{AM} \cap \mathsf{coAM}$.*[7]

It is believed that $\mathsf{AM} \cap \mathsf{coAM}$ lies just above SZK, and if we could show that $\mathrm{SDP}^{\alpha,\beta}$ is in SZK, that would imply SD polarization for such α and β.

Since Theorem 1.9 can be derived from existing results in the literature, we view our main contribution to be the proof which is via a single protocol that we find to be cleaner and more direct than alternate approaches.

Going into a bit more detail, [BL13, BBF16]'s proofs are in fact a combination of two separate constant-round protocols. The first protocol is meant to show that $\mathrm{SDP}^{\alpha,\beta} \in \mathsf{AM}$ and follows directly by taking the interactive proof for SDP presented by Sahai and Vadhan (which has completeness error $(1-\alpha)/2$ and soundness error $(1+\beta)/2$), and applying parallel repetition (and the private-coin to public-coin transformation of [GS89]).

The second protocol is meant to show that $\mathrm{SDP}^{\alpha,\beta} \in \mathsf{coAM}$, and is based on a protocol by Bhatnagar, Bogdanov, and Mossel [BBM11]. Another approach for proving that $\mathrm{SDP}^{\alpha,\beta} \in \mathsf{coAM}$ is by combining results of [GVW02] and [SV03]. Goldreich, Vadhan and Wigderson [GVW02] showed that problems with laconic interactive proofs, that is proofs where the communication from the prover to the verifier is small, have coAM proofs. Sahai and Vadhan [SV03], as described earlier, showed that $\mathrm{SDP}^{\alpha,\beta}$, and SZK in general, has an interactive proof where the prover communicates a single bit. Combining these results immediately gives a coAM protocol for $\mathrm{SDP}^{\alpha,\beta}$ when (α, β) are $\Omega(1)$-*separated*. As for (α, β) that are only $(1/\mathsf{poly})$-separated, while the [GVW02] result as-stated does not suffice, it seems that their protocol can be adapted to handle this case as well.[8]

As mentioned above, we give a different, and direct, proof of Theorem 1.9 that we find to be simpler and more natural than the above approach. In particular, our proof utilizes the techniques developed for our other results, which enable us to give a single and more general protocol—one that approximates the statistical difference (as in Theorem 1.9), rather than just deciding if that distance is large or small.

At a very high level, our protocol may be viewed as an application of the set-lower-bound-based techniques of Akavia et al. [AGGM06] or Bogdanov and Brzuska [BB15] to our construction of a one-way function from the average-case hardness of SDP (i.e., Theorem 1.8), though there are technical differences in our setting. Both these papers show how to construct a coAM protocol for any language that can be reduced, to inverting a *size-verifiable* one-way function.[9]

---

[7] Recall that AM is the class of problems that have constant-round public-coin interactive proofs. coAM is simply the complement of AM.

[8] In more detail, the [GVW02] result is stated for protocols in which the gap between completeness and soundness is constant (specifically $1/3$). In case α and β are only $1/\mathsf{poly}$-separated, the [SV03] protocol only has a $1/\mathsf{poly}$ gap (and we cannot afford repetition since it will increase the communication). Nevertheless, by inspecting the [GVW02] proof, it seems as though it can be adapted to cover any noticeable gap.

[9] Informally, a function f is size-verifiable if given an output $y = f(x)$, there exists an AM protocol to estimate $|f^{-1}(y)|$.

While we do not know how to reduce solving SDP in the worst-case to inverting any specific function, we make use of the fact that associated with each instance of SDP, there is an *instance-dependent* function [OW93], that is size-verifiable on the average.

1.2   Additional Related Works

Barriers to Improved Polarization. Holenstein and Renner [HR05] show that in a limited model dubbed "oblivious polarization", the condition $\alpha^2 > \beta$ on the statistical distance is necessary for polarizing statistical distance.[10] All the past polarization reductions fit in this framework and so do ours. Specifically, Holenstein and Renner show distributions where $\alpha^2 < \beta$ and cannot be polarized in this model. We show a condition that suffices for polarization, even for distributions where $\alpha^2 \leq \beta$. This does not contradict the [HR05] result because their distributions do not satisfy this condition.

In a more general model, [LZ17,CGVZ18] showed lower bounds for SZK-related distribution manipulation tasks. The model they consider allows the reduction arbitrary oracle access to the circuits that sample the distributions, as opposed to the more restricted model of oblivious polarization. In this model, Lovett and Zhang [LZ17] show that efficient entropy reversal is impossible[11], and Chen, Göös, Vadhan and Zhang [CGVZ18] showed that entropy flattening requires $\Omega(n^2)$ invocations to the underlying circuit. Showing lower bounds for polarization in this more general model remains an interesting open question.

Polarization for Other Notions of Distance. In the process of characterizing zero-knowledge in the help model, Ben-Or and Gutfreund [BG03] and Chailloux et al. [CCKV08] gave a polarization procedure that considers two different distances for every $(1/\log)$-separated $\alpha > \beta$: if the statistical distance is at most β, then it decreases to 2^{-k}; and if the *mutual disjointness*[12] is at least α, then it increases to $1 - 2^{-k}$. Fehr and Vaudenay [FV17] raise the question of polarization for the fidelity measure[13] but leave resolving it as an open problem (see Sect. 2.3.3 for details).

---

[10] Roughly speaking, an oblivious polarization is a randomized procedure to polarize without invoking the circuits; it takes as input a bit σ and an integer k, and outputs a sequence of bits $(b_1^\sigma, \ldots, b_\ell^\sigma)$ and a string r^σ. Given a pair of circuits (C_0, C_1), such a procedure defines a pair of circuits (D_0, D_1) as follows: D_σ samples $(b_1^\sigma, \ldots, b_\ell^\sigma)$ and r^σ and outputs $(C_{b_1^\sigma}, \ldots, C_{b_\ell^\sigma}, r^\sigma)$. We are guaranteed that if $\mathrm{SD}(C_0, C_1) \geq \alpha$, then $\mathrm{SD}(D_0, D_1) \geq 1 - 2^{-k}$, and if $\mathrm{SD}(C_0, C_1) \leq \beta$, then $\mathrm{SD}(D_0, D_1) \leq 2^{-k}$.

[11] Entropy reversal refers to the task of given circuit C and parameter t output (C', t') such that when $\mathrm{H}(C) > t$, then $\mathrm{H}(C') < t' - 1$ and if $\mathrm{H}(C) < t - 1$, then $\mathrm{H}(C') > t'$.

[12] For an ordered pair of distributions P and Q, their disjointness is $\mathrm{Disj}(P, Q) = \Pr_{y \sim P}[y \notin \mathrm{Supp}(Q)]$, and their mutual disjointness is $\mathrm{MutDisj}(P, Q) = \min(\mathrm{Disj}(P, Q), \mathrm{Disj}(Q, P))$.

[13] For two distributions P and Q, their fidelity is defined as $\mathrm{Fidelity}(P, Q) = \sum_y \sqrt{P_y \cdot Q_y}$.

SDP *and Cryptography.* We show that average-case hardness of $\text{SDP}^{\alpha,\beta}$ implies one-way functions. In the reverse direction, Bitansky et al. [BDV17] show that one-way functions do not imply even worst-case hardness of $\text{SDP}^{\alpha,\beta}$ in a black-box manner for any (1/poly)-separated α, β.[14]

2   Techniques

We begin in Sect. 2.1 by describing how to construct a one-way function from the average-case hardness of SD with any noticeable gap (Theorem 1.8). The techniques used there are also central in our interactive protocol for SD estimation (Theorem 1.9), which is described in Sect. 2.2, as well as in our proof that triangular discrimination and Jensen-Shannon divergence are SZK complete (Theorems 1.5 and 1.6), which are outlined in Sect. 2.3 below.

2.1   One-Way Function from Statistical Difference with Any Noticeable Gap

We first show the existence of *distributionally* one-way functions. Namely, an efficiently computable function f for which it is hard to sample a uniformly random pre-image for a random output y (rather than an arbitrary pre-image as in a standard one-way function). This suffices since Impagliazzo and Luby [IL89] showed how to convert a distributionally one-way function into a standard one.

Assume that we are given a distribution over a pair of circuits (C_0, C_1) such that it is hard to distinguish between the cases $\text{SD}(C_0, C_1) \geq \alpha$ or $\text{SD}(C_0, C_1) \leq \beta$, for some $\alpha > \beta + 1/\text{poly}$. A natural candidate for a one-way function is the (efficiently computable) function

$$f_{C_0,C_1}(b,x) = C_b(x). \qquad (2.1)$$

Namely, f is parameterized by the circuits (C_0, C_1) (which are to be sampled according to the hard distribution), and the bit b chooses which of the two circuits would be evaluated on the string x. This function appears throughout the SZK literature (e.g., it corresponds to the verifier's message in the SDP protocol of [SV03]).

Assume that f is not distributionally one-way, and let A be an algorithm that given (C_0, C_1) and a random input y—sampled by first drawing a uniformly random bit b and a string x and then computing $y = C_b(x)$—outputs a uniformly random element (b', x') from the set $f_{C_0,C_1}^{-1}(y) = \{(b,x) : C_b(x) = y\}$. For simplicity, we assume that A is a perfect distributional inverter, that is for *every* fixed (C_0, C_1, y) it outputs uniformly random elements of $f_{C_0,C_1}^{-1}(y)$.

Arguably, the most natural approach for distinguishing between the cases of high or low statistical distance given the two circuits and the inverter, is to choose

---

[14] While [BDV17] state the result for constant α, β, the construction and analysis extend to our setting.

x and b at random, invoke the inverter to obtain (b', x'), and check whether $b = b'$. Indeed, if $SD(C_0, C_1) = 1$, then $\Pr[b = b'] = 1$, and if $SD(C_0, C_1) = 0$, then $\Pr[b = b'] = \frac{1}{2}$. Thus, we can distinguish between the cases with constant advantage.

But what happens when the gap in the statistical distance is smaller? To analyze this case we want to better understand the quantity $\Pr[b = b']$. It turns out that this quantity is characterized by the triangular discrimination between the circuits. Let P_b denote the output distribution of C_b. Using elementary manipulations (and the fact that $\frac{1}{2}(P_0 + P_1)$ is a distribution), it holds that[15]

$$
\begin{aligned}
\Pr[b = b'] &= \frac{1}{2} \Pr_{y \sim P_0}[b' = 0] + \frac{1}{2} \Pr_{y \sim P_1}[b' = 1] \qquad\qquad (2.2)\\
&= \frac{1}{2} \sum_y \frac{P_0(y)^2 + P_1(y)^2}{P_0(y) + P_1(y)}\\
&= \frac{1}{4} \sum_y \frac{(P_0(y) + P_1(y))^2}{P_0(y) + P_1(y)} + \frac{1}{4} \sum_y \frac{(P_0(y) - P_1(y))^2}{P_0(y) + P_1(y)}\\
&= \frac{1}{2} + \frac{1}{4} \sum_y \frac{(P_0(y) - P_1(y))^2}{P_0(y) + P_1(y)}\\
&= \frac{1 + TD(C_0, C_1)}{2}.
\end{aligned}
$$

Based on the general bounds between triangular discrimination and statistical distance (Eq. (1.1)), which are known to be tight, all we are guaranteed is

$$SD(C_0, C_1) \geq \alpha \quad \Longrightarrow \quad \Pr[b = b'] \geq \frac{1 + \alpha^2}{2}$$

$$SD(C_0, C_1) \leq \beta \quad \Longrightarrow \quad \Pr[b = b'] \leq \frac{1 + \beta}{2}.$$

So, this approach is limited to settings in which $\alpha^2 > \beta$.

To overcome this limitation we want to find a quantity that is more tightly characterized by the statistical distance of the circuits. This quantity, which we call *imbalance*, will be central in all of the proofs in this work. The imbalance measures how likely it is that an output string y was generated from C_1 versus C_0. Formally,

$$\theta_y \triangleq \Pr[b = 1|y] - \Pr[b = 0|y] = \frac{P_1(y) - P_0(y)}{P_1(y) + P_0(y)}. \qquad\qquad (2.3)$$

---

[15] In Sect. 1 we used P_y to denoted the probability mass a distribution P puts on an element y, while here we use $P(y)$. In the rest of this work we choose which notation to use based on readability and context.

Elementary manipulations yields that

$$\text{SD}(C_0, C_1) = \frac{1}{2} \sum_y |P_1(y) - P_0(y)| \tag{2.4}$$

$$= \sum_y \frac{1}{2}(P_1(y) + P_0(y)) \cdot \frac{|P_1(y) - P_0(y)|}{P_1(y) + P_0(y)}$$

$$= \mathop{\mathbb{E}}_{y \sim (\frac{1}{2}P_0 + \frac{1}{2}P_1)} [|\theta_y|].$$

(Recall that y is sampled by first drawing a uniform random bit b and a string x, and setting $y = C_b(x)$. Hence, using the notation that P_b denotes the output distributions of the circuit C_b, the marginal distribution of y is $\frac{1}{2}P_0 + \frac{1}{2}P_1$.)

Equation (2.4) naturally gives rise to the following algorithm for approximating $\text{SD}(C_0, C_1)$:

Algorithm to estimate $\text{SD}(C_0, C_1)$ using the inverter A:

---

1. Sample polynomially many $y_1, \ldots, y_t$ independently from $\frac{1}{2}P_0 + \frac{1}{2}P_1$.
2. For every y_i:
   (a) Call $\mathsf{A}(y_i)$ polynomially many times to get $b'_1, \ldots, b'_k$.
   (b) Let m be the number of ones in $b'_1, \ldots, b'_k$.
   (c) Set $p_1 = m/k$, $p_0 = (k - m)/k$ and $\widehat{\theta}_i = p_1 - p_0$.
3. Return $\frac{1}{t} \sum_{i=1}^t |\widehat{\theta}_i|$.

The quantities p_1 and p_0 are in fact the empirical distribution of b conditioned on y, computed using k samples. By choosing large enough k, we get that $(p_1, p_0) \approx (\Pr[b = 1|y], \Pr[b = 0|y])$ and so $\widehat{\theta}_i \approx \theta_{y_i}$. By then choosing large enough t, we get that $\frac{1}{t} \sum_{i=1}^t |\widehat{\theta}_i| \approx \text{SD}(C_0, C_1)$. Hence, we can distinguish between the cases $\text{SD}(C_0, C_1) \geq \alpha$ or $\text{SD}(C_0, C_1) \leq \beta$, for any $\alpha > \beta + 1/\mathsf{poly}$.

Essentially the same proof continues to work if A is not a perfect distributional inverter, but is close enough to being so—that is, on input y its output distribution is close to being uniform over $f^{-1}(y)$ for most (but not all) tuples C_0, C_1, y.

The above proof strategy also yields a new proof for the strengthening of [Gol90] by Naor and Rothblum [NR06].[16] See Theorem 2.1 below for a discussion about the differences between our techniques and those of [NR06].

Distributional Collision Resistant Hash Function. As a matter of fact, the above proof also shows that the average-case hardness of $\text{SDP}^{\alpha,\beta}$ also implies that the

---

[16] Namely, that for any $(1/\mathsf{poly})$-separated (α, β), the existence of efficiently sampleable distributions whose statistical distance is α but no efficient algorithm can distinguish between them with advantage more than β, implies the existence of one-way functions.

function $f_{C_0,C_1}(b,x) = C_b(x)$ is a distributional k-multi-collision[17] resistant hash function, for $k = O\left(\frac{\log n}{(\alpha-\beta)^2}\right)$. That is, for a random output y of f, it is difficult to find k random preimages of y. This is because access to such a set of k random pre-images of random y_i's is all we use the inverter A for in the above reduction, and it could handily be replaced with a k-distributional multi-collision finder.

Remark 2.1 (Comparison to [NR06]). *Naor and Rothblum's proof implicitly attempts to approximate the maximal likelihood bit of y; that is, the bit b_{ml} such that $\Pr[b = b_{ml}|y] > \Pr[b = 1 - b_{ml}|y]$ (breaking ties arbitrarily). Indeed, the maximal likelihood bit, as shown by [SV03], is closely related to the statistical distance:*

$$\Pr[b = b_{ml}] = \frac{1 + \mathrm{SD}(C_0,C_1)}{2}. \tag{2.5}$$

To approximate b_{ml}, [NR06] make, like us, many calls to $A(y)$, and take the majority of the answered bits. The idea is that when the statistical distance is large, the majority is likely to be b_{ml}, and when the statistical distance is small, the majority is equally likely to be b_{ml} or $1 - b_{ml}$.

To formally prove this intuition, it must hold that if $\mathrm{SD}(C_0,C_1)$ is large, then $\Pr[b = b_{ml}|y] - \Pr[b = 1 - b_{ml}|y]$ is sufficiently large; putting in our terminology and using Eq. (2.4), if $\mathbb{E}_y\left[\|\theta_y\|\right]$ is sufficiently large, then $|\theta_y|$ should be large for a random y (and the opposite should hold if $\mathrm{SD}(C_0,C_1)$ is small). While these statements are true, in order to prove them, [NR06]'s analysis involves some work which results in a more complicated analysis.

We manage to avoid such complications by using the imbalance θ_y and its characterization of statistical distance (Eq. 2.4). Furthermore, [NR06]'s approach only attempts to distinguish between the cases when $\mathrm{SD}(C_0,C_1)$ is high or low, while our approach generalizes to approximate $\mathrm{SD}(C_0,C_1)$. Lastly, Naor and Rothblum do not construct one-way functions based on the average-case hardness of $\mathrm{SDP}^{\alpha,\beta}$ with any noticeable gap as we do. Using their technique to do so seems to require additional work—work that our analysis significantly simplifies.

2.2 Interactive Proof for Statistical Distance Approximation

We proceed to describe a constant-round public-coin protocol in which a computationally unbounded prover convinces a computationally bounded verifier that the statistical difference of a given pair of circuits is what the prover claims it to be, up to any inverse polynomial (additive) error. Such a protocol simultaneously establishes the inclusion of $\mathrm{SDP}^{\alpha,\beta}$ in both AM and coAM for any $\alpha > \beta+1/\mathrm{poly}$.

Our starting point is the algorithm we described above that used a one-way function inverter to estimate the statistical distance. Specifically, that algorithm

---

[17] Multi-collision hash functions, recently considered in several works [KNY17,KNY18, BKP18,BDRV18], are hash functions for which it is hard to find multiple inputs that all hash to the same output.

used the inverter to estimate θ_y for random y's, and then applied Eq. (2.4). We would like to use the prover, instead of the inverter, to achieve the same task.

In our protocol, the verifier draws polynomially many y's and sends them to the prover. The prover responds with values $\widehat{\theta}_i$'s, which it claims are the genuine θ_{y_i}'s. But how can the verifier trust that the prover sent the correct values? In the reduction in Sect. 2.1, we used k many samples of b conditioned on y to estimate b's true distribution. A standard concentration bound shows that as k grows, the number of ones out of $b_1, \ldots, b_k$, all sampled from $(b|y)$, is very close to $\Pr[b = 1|y] \cdot k$. Similarly, the number of zeros is very close to $\Pr[b = 0|y] \cdot k$. Consider the following *typical set* for any fixed y and arbitrary value θ:

$$T_y^{k,\theta} = \left\{ (b_1, x_1, b_2, x_2, \ldots, b_k, x_k) \,\middle|\, \begin{array}{l} C_{b_i}(x_i) = y \text{ for all } i, \\ \text{and } \frac{\sum_{i=1}^{k} b_i - \sum_{i=1}^{k}(1-b_i)}{k} \approx \theta \end{array} \right\}.$$

Namely, $T_y^{k,\theta}$ contains every k-tuple of (b_i, x_i) such that all map to y, and each tuple can be used to estimate θ well—the difference between the number of ones and the number of zeros, normalized by k, is close to θ. Also consider the *pre-image* set of y: $\mathcal{I}_y = \{(b,x) \mid C_b(x) = y\}$. Since as k grows the estimation of θ_y improves, we expect that T_y^{k,θ_y}—the typical set of y with the value θ_y—to contain almost all tuples. Indeed, standard concentration bounds show that

$$\frac{\left| T_y^{k,\theta_y} \right|}{|\mathcal{I}_y|^k} \geq 1 - e^{-\Omega(k)}. \tag{2.6}$$

On the other hand, the sets $T_y^{k,\theta'}$, corresponding to values θ' that are far from θ_y, should be almost empty. Indeed, if $|\theta' - \theta_y| \geq \Omega(1)$, then,

$$\frac{\left| T_y^{k,\theta'} \right|}{|\mathcal{I}_y|^k} \leq e^{-\Omega(k)}. \tag{2.7}$$

So, for the verifier to be convinced that the value $\widehat{\theta}$ sent by the prover is close to θ_y, the prover can prove that the typical set $T_y^{k,\widehat{\theta}}$ is large. To do so, the parties will use the public-coin constant round protocol for set lower-bound of [GS89], which enables the prover to assert statements of the form "the size of the set S is at least s".

However, there is still one hurdle to overcome. The typical set T_y^{k,θ_y} is only large *relative* to $|\mathcal{I}_y|^k$. Since we do not known how to compute $|\mathcal{I}_y|$ it is unclear what should be the size s that we run the set lower-bound protocol with. Our approach for bypassing this issue is as follows. First observe that the *expected value*, over a random y, of the logarithm of the size of $\mathcal{I}_y$ is the entropy[18] of (b,x) given y. Namely,

---

[18] Recall that the entropy of a random variable X over $\mathcal{X}$ is defined as $(\mathrm{H}(X) = \sum_{x \in \mathcal{X}} \Pr[X = x] \log(1/\Pr[X = x])$. The conditional entropy of X given Y is $\mathrm{H}(X|Y) = \mathbb{E}_{y \sim Y} [\mathrm{H}(X|Y = y)]$.

$$\mathop{\mathbb{E}}_{y} \left[\log |\mathcal{I}_y| \right] = H(B, X|Y), \tag{2.8}$$

where the jointly distributed random variables (B, X, Y) take the values of randomly drawn (x, b, y). Thus, if we draw t independent elements $y_1, \ldots, y_t$, the average of $\log|\mathcal{I}_y|$ gets closer to $t \cdot H(B, X|Y)$, as t grows. Specifically,

$$\Pr \left[\prod_{i=1}^{t} |\mathcal{I}_{y_i}| \approx 2^{t \cdot H(B, X|Y)} \right] \geq 1 - e^{-\Omega(t/n^2)}, \tag{2.9}$$

where n denotes the output length of the given circuits. For large enough t, we can thus assume that the size of this product set is approximately $2^{t \cdot H(B, X|Y)}$, and run the set lower bound protocol for all the y_i's together. That is, we ask the prover to send t estimates $(\widehat{\theta}_1, \ldots, \widehat{\theta}_t)$ for the values $(\theta_{y_1}, \ldots, \theta_{y_t})$, and prove that the size of the product set $\mathcal{T}_{y_1}^{k, \widehat{\theta}_1} \times \cdots \times \mathcal{T}_{y_1}^{k, \widehat{\theta}_1}$ is almost $2^{t \cdot H(B, X|Y)}$.

So far we have reduced knowing the size of $\mathcal{I}_y$ to knowing $H(B, X|Y)$, but again it seems difficult for the verifier to compute this quantity on its own. Actually, standard entropy manipulations show that

$$H(B, X|Y) = (m + 1) - H(Y),$$

where m denotes the input length of the given circuits. It thus suffices to approximate $H(Y)$. Recall that y is the output of the circuit that maps (x, b) to $C_b(x)$, so Y is drawn according to an output distribution of a known circuit. Luckily, Goldreich, Sahai and Vadhan [GSV99] showed that approximating the output entropy of a given circuit is in NISZK, and thus has a constant-round public-coin protocol (since NISZK $\subseteq$ AM $\cap$ coAM).

To conclude, we describe the entirety of our protocol, which proves Theorem 1.9.

Protocol to approximate $SD(C_0, C_1)$, given the circuits (C_0, C_1) as input:

1. First, the prover sends the verifier a claim $\widehat{H}$ of the value of $H(Y)$.
2. The parties execute [GSV99]'s protocol to convince the verifier that this claim—that $\widehat{H} \approx H(Y)$—is correct.
3. The verifier uses $\widehat{H}$ to compute $\widehat{H}(B, X|Y)$ as $((m + 1) - \widehat{H})$.
4. The verifier samples $y_1, \ldots, y_t$ from $\frac{C_0 + C_1}{2}$ and sends them to the prover.
5. The prover responds with $\widehat{\theta}_1, \ldots, \widehat{\theta}_t$ as claims for the values $\theta_{y_1}, \ldots, \theta_{y_t}$.
6. The parties run a set lower-bound protocol to prove that the set $\mathcal{T}_{y_1}^{\widehat{\theta}_1, k} \times \cdots \times \mathcal{T}_{y_t}^{\widehat{\theta}_t, k}$ is almost as large as $(\mathcal{I}_{y_1} \times \cdots \times \mathcal{I}_{y_t})^k$.
   - Here, they use $2^{tk\widehat{H}(B, X|Y)}$ as a proxy for $(|\mathcal{I}_{y_1}| \cdots \cdots |\mathcal{I}_{y_t}|)^k$.
7. If the verifier has not rejected so far, it outputs $\frac{1}{t} \sum_{i=1}^{t} |\widehat{\theta}_i|$.

2.3   TDP and JSP Are SZK-Complete

We show that both $\text{TDP}^{\alpha,\beta}$ and $\text{JSP}^{\alpha,\beta}$ with $\alpha > \beta + 1/\text{poly}$ are SZK-complete. Since the proof of the former uses that of the latter we start by giving an outline that $\text{JSP}^{\alpha,\beta}$ is SZK-complete.

2.3.1   JENSEN-SHANNON DIVERGENCE PROBLEM Is SZK-Complete

We need to show that $\text{JSP}^{\alpha,\beta}$ with $\alpha > \beta + 1/\text{poly}$ is both in SZK and SZK-hard. In both parts we use the following characterization of the Jensen-Shannon divergence, which follows from its definition. Given a pair of circuits C_0 and C_1, consider the jointly distributed random variables (B, X, Y), where B is a uniformly random bit, X is a uniformly random string and $Y = C_B(X)$. Then, it follows from some elementary manipulations that:

$$\text{JS}(C_0, C_1) = 1 - \text{H}(B|Y). \tag{2.10}$$

We use this characterization to tie JENSEN-SHANNON DIVERGENCE PROBLEM to another SZK-complete problem—the ENTROPY DIFFERENCE PROBLEM (EDP) with a gap function g. The input to EDP^g is also a pair of circuits C_0 and C_1. YES instances are those in which the entropy gap $\text{H}(C_0) - \text{H}(C_1)$ is at least $g(n)$ (where n is the output length of the circuits) and NO instances are those in which the gap is at most $-g(n)$. Goldreich and Vadhan [GV99] showed that EDP^g is SZK-complete for any noticeable function g. Our proof that $\text{JSP}^{\alpha,\beta}$ is SZK-complete closely follows the reduction from the reverse problem of SDP (i.e., in which YES instances are distributions that are statistically *close*) to EDP [Vad99, Section 4.4].

$\text{JSP}^{\alpha,\beta}$ **is in SZK:** We reduce $\text{JSP}^{\alpha,\beta}$ to $\text{ED}^{(\alpha-\beta)/2}$. Given C_0 and C_1, the reduction outputs a pair of circuits D_0 and D_1 such that D_1 outputs a sample from (B, Y) and D_0 outputs a sample from (B', Y), where B' is an independent random bit with $\text{H}(B') = 1 - \frac{\alpha+\beta}{2}$. The chain rule for entropy[19] implies that

$$\text{H}(D_0) - \text{H}(D_1) = 1 - \frac{\alpha + \beta}{2} - \text{H}(B|Y) = \text{JS}(C_0, C_1) - \frac{\alpha + \beta}{2},$$

where the second equality follows from Eq. (2.10). Thus, if $\text{JS}(C_0, C_1) \geq \alpha$, then $\text{H}(D_0) - \text{H}(D_1) \geq \frac{\alpha-\beta}{2}$; and if $\text{JS}(C_0, C_1) \leq \beta$, then $\text{H}(D_0) - \text{H}(D_1) \leq -\frac{\alpha-\beta}{2}$. And since $\text{ED}^{(\alpha-\beta)/2} \in \text{SZK}$, we get that $\text{JSP}^{\alpha,\beta} \in \text{SZK}$.

$\text{JSP}^{\alpha,\beta}$ **is SZK-hard:** We reduce $\text{SDP}^{1-2^{-k},2^{-k}}$ to the problem $\text{JSP}^{\alpha,\beta}$, for some large enough k. This is sufficient since $\text{SDP}^{1-2^{-k},2^{-k}}$ is known to be SZK-hard [SV03].[20] In the presentation of related results in his thesis, Vadhan relates the statistical distance of the circuits to the entropy of B given

---

[19] For a jointly distributed random variables X and Y, it holds that $\text{H}(X, Y) = \text{H}(X) + \text{H}(Y|X)$.

[20] For the simplicity of presentation, we are ignoring subtle details about the relation of k to the output length of the circuits. See the full version for the formal proof.

Y [Vad99, Claim 4.4.2]. For example, if $SD(C_0, C_1) = 0$ (i.e., the distributions are identical), then $B|Y$ is a uniformly random bit, and so $H(B|Y) = 1$; and if $SD(C_0, C_1) = 1$ (i.e., the distributions are disjoint), then B is completely determined by Y, and so $H(B|Y) = 0$. More generally, Vadhan showed that if $SD(C_0, C_1) = \delta$, then[21]

$$1 - \delta \leq H(B|Y) \leq h\left(\frac{1+\delta}{2}\right). \tag{2.11}$$

By taking k to be large enough (as a function of α and β), and applying Eqs. (2.10) and (2.11), we have that if $SD(C_0, C_1) \geq 1 - 2^{-k}$, then $JS(C_0, C_1) \geq \alpha$; and if $SD(C_0, C_1) \leq 2^{-k}$, then $JS(C_0, C_1) \leq \beta$. Thus, the desired reduction is simply the identity function that outputs the input circuits.

2.3.2   TRIANGULAR DISCRIMINATION PROBLEM is SZK-Complete

We need to show that $TDP^{\alpha,\beta}$ with $\alpha > \beta + 1/\text{poly}$ is both in SZK and SZK-hard. Showing the latter is very similar to showing that $JSP^{\alpha,\beta}$ is SZK-hard, but using Eq. (1.1) to relate the triangular discrimination to statistical distance (instead of Eq. (2.11) that relates the Jensen-Shannon divergence to statistical distance). We leave the formal details to the body of this paper and focus here on showing that $TDP^{\alpha,\beta}$ is in SZK.

A natural approach to show that $TDP^{\alpha,\beta}$ is in SZK is to follow Sahai and Vadhan's proof that $SDP^{2/3,1/3}$ is in SZK. Specifically, a main ingredient in that proof is to polarize the statistical distance of the circuits (to reduce the simulation error). Indeed, if we can reduce $TDP^{\alpha,\beta}$ to, say, $TDP^{0.9,0.1}$ by polarizing the triangular discrimination, then Eq. (1.1) would imply that we also reduce $TDP^{\alpha,\beta}$ to $SDP^{2/3,1/3}$, which we know is in SZK.

We are indeed able to show such a polarization lemma for triangular discrimination (using similar techniques to [SV03]'s polarization lemma). However, this lemma only works when the gap between α and β is roughly $1/\log$. Actually, the polarization lemma of [SV03] also suffers the same limitation with respect to the gap between α^2 and β.

Still, we would like to handle also the case that the gap between α and β is only $1/\text{poly}$. To do so we take a slightly different approach. Specifically, we reduce $TDP^{\alpha,\beta}$ to $JSP^{\alpha',\beta'}$, where α' and β' are also noticeably separated.

An important step toward showing this reduction is to characterize the triangular discrimination and the Jensen-Shannon divergence via the imbalance θ_y (see Eq. (2.3)), as we already did for statistical distance. Recall that given $Y = y$, the random variable B takes the value 1 with probability $\frac{1+\theta_y}{2}$, and 0 otherwise. Hence, Eq. (2.10) can also be written as

$$JS(C_0, C_1) = 1 - \mathop{\mathbb{E}}_{y \sim Y}\left[h\left(\frac{1+\theta_y}{2}\right)\right]. \tag{2.12}$$

---

[21] The function h is the binary entropy function. That is, $h(p) = -p\log(p) - (1-p)\log(1-p)$ is the entropy of a Bernoulli random variable with parameter p.

As for the triangular discrimination, it follows from the definition that

$$\mathrm{TD}(C_0, C_1) = \underset{y \sim Y}{\mathbb{E}} \left[\theta_y^2 \right]. \tag{2.13}$$

Furthermore, by Taylor approximation, for small values of θ, it holds that

$$h \left(\frac{1 + \theta}{2} \right) \approx 1 - \theta^2. \tag{2.14}$$

As we can see, the above equations imply that if all the θ_y's were small, a gap in the triangular discrimination would also imply a gap in the Jensen-Shannon divergence. Thus, we would like an operation that reduces all the θ_y.

The main technical tool we use to reduce θ_y is to consider the *convex combination* of the two input circuits. Given a pair of circuits C_0 and C_1, consider the pair of circuits D_0 and D_1 such that $D_b = \lambda \cdot C_b + (1 - \lambda) \cdot \frac{C_0 + C_1}{2}$.[22] Let Q_b denote the output distribution of D_b, and recall that P_b denotes the output distribution of C_b. We also let θ_y' be defined similarly to θ_y, but with respect to D_0 and D_1 (rather than C_0 and C_1). Using this notation, we have that $\theta_y = \frac{P_1(y) - P_0(y)}{P_1(y) + P_0(y)}$, and it may be seen that

$$\theta_y' = \frac{Q_1(y) - Q_0(y)}{Q_1(y) + Q_0(y)} = \lambda \cdot \theta_y. \tag{2.15}$$

So, our reduction chooses a sufficiently small λ, and outputs the circuits D_0 and D_1. Some care is needed when choosing λ. Equations (2.13) and (2.15) yield that $\mathrm{TD}(D_0, D_1) = \lambda^2 \cdot \mathrm{TD}(C_0, C_1)$. Hence, the convex combination also shrinks the gap in triangular discrimination. We show that by choosing $\lambda \approx \sqrt{\alpha - \beta}$, the approximation error in Eq. (2.14) is smaller than the aforementioned shrinkage, and the reduction goes through. The resulting gap in the Jensen-Shannon divergence is roughly $(\alpha - \beta)^2$, which is noticeable by the assumption that $\alpha > \beta + 1/\mathrm{poly}$.

This shows that $\mathrm{TDP}^{\alpha,\beta}$ is in SZK if $\alpha > \beta + 1/\mathrm{poly}$. By the relationship between TD and SD (Eq. (1.1)), this implies that $\mathrm{SDP}^{\alpha,\beta}$ is in SZK if $\alpha^2 > \beta + 1/\mathrm{poly}$. This, in turn, by the SZK-hardness of $\mathrm{SDP}^{2/3,1/3}$ and the known polarization lemma that applies for the same, implies polarization for statistical distance for any (α, β) such that $\alpha^2 > \beta + 1/\mathrm{poly}$.

2.3.3   Reflections and an Open Problem

Many f-divergences of interest can be expressed as an expectation, over $y \sim Y$, of a simple function of θ_y. That is, an expression of the form $\mathbb{E}_{y \sim Y} \left[g(\theta_y) \right]$, for some function $g : [-1, 1] \to [0, 1]$. For example:

- $\mathrm{SD}(C_0, C_1) = \mathbb{E}_{y \sim Y} \left[|\theta_y| \right]$ (i.e., $g(z) = |z|$, see Eq. (2.4));

---

[22] This definition of convex combination is more convenient to analyze than perhaps the more natural definition of $D_b = \lambda \cdot C_b + (1 - \lambda) \cdot C_{1-b}$.

- $\text{TD}(C_0, C_1) = \mathbb{E}_{y \sim Y}\left[\theta_y^2\right]$ (i.e., $g(z) = z^2$, see Eq. (2.13)); and
- $\text{JS}(C_0, C_1) = \mathbb{E}_{y \sim Y}\left[1 - h\left(\frac{1+\theta_y}{2}\right)\right]$ (i.e., $g(z) = 1 - h\left(\frac{1+z}{2}\right)$, see Eq. (2.12)).

To reduce TDP to JSP, we took a convex combination of the two circuits and used the fact that $1 - h\left(\frac{1+\theta_y}{2}\right) \approx O(\theta_y^2)$ for small values of θ_y. While this worked for polarization of TD (which corresponds to $g(z) = z^2$), it seems unlikely to yield a polarization lemma for SD for an arbitrarily small (but noticeable) gap. The reason is that the function $g(z) = |z|$—the g-function corresponding to SD—is not differentiable at 0 and in particular does not act like z^2 for small values of z. As we find this similarity between the different notions of distance striking, and indeed our proofs leverage the relations between them, we provide in Fig. 1 a plot comparing the different choices for the function g.

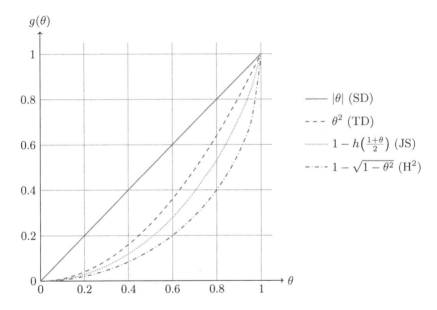

Fig. 1. Comparison between the difference choices of the function g that were discussed. Since all functions are symmetric around 0, we restrict to the domain $[0, 1]$. Recall that $g_1(\theta) = |\theta|$ corresponds to SD, $g_2(\theta) = \theta^2$ to TD, $g_3(\theta) = 1 - h\left(\frac{1+\theta}{2}\right)$ to JS and $g_4(\theta) = 1 - \sqrt{1 - \theta^2}$ to H^2.

Another popular f-divergence that we have not discussed thus far[23] is the *squared Hellinger distance*, defined as $H^2(P, Q) = \frac{1}{2}\sum_y \left(\sqrt{P_y} - \sqrt{Q_y}\right)^2$. It can

---

[23] Actually we will use the squared Hellinger distance to analyze triangular discrimination of direct product distributions (see the full version for details). Also, the squared Hellinger distance is closely related to the Fidelity distance: $\text{Fidelity}(P, Q) = 1 - H^2(P, Q)$.

be shown that $H^2(C_0, C_1) = \mathbb{E}_{y \sim Y} \left[1 - \sqrt{1 - \theta_y^2} \right]$, and so also this distance falls within the above framework (i.e., by considering $g(z) = 1 - \sqrt{1 - z^2}$).

Notably, the squared Hellinger distance also acts like JS (and TD) around 0; namely, $1 - \sqrt{1 - \theta_y^2} \approx O(\theta_y^2)$ for small values of θ_y. However, unlike $\mathrm{TDP}^{\alpha,\beta}$, we do not know how to show that the HELLINGER DIFFERENCE PROBLEM, denoted $\mathrm{HDP}^{\alpha,\beta}$ and defined analogously to $\mathrm{TDP}^{\alpha,\beta}$ (while replacing the distance TD with H^2), is in SZK for all $(1/\mathsf{poly})$-separated (α, β). We do mention that $H^2(P, Q) \leq \mathrm{TD}(P, Q) \leq 2\,H^2(P, Q)$, and thus $\mathrm{HDP}^{\alpha,\beta}$ is in SZK if α and $\beta/2$ are $(1/\mathsf{poly})$-separated. However, the proof described above does not go through if we try to apply it to the Hellinger distance—we cannot guarantee that the gap in the Hellinger distance after taking the convex combination is larger than the error in the Taylor approximation. Indeed, the question whether $\mathrm{HDP}^{\alpha,\beta}$ is in SZK for any $(1/\mathsf{poly})$-separated (α, β), first raised by Fehr and Vaudenay [FV17], remains open.

References

[AARV17] Applebaum, B., Arkis, B., Raykov, P., Vasudevan, P.N.: Conditional disclosure of secrets: amplification, closure, amortization, lower-bounds, and separations. In: Katz, J., Shacham, H. (eds.) CRYPTO 2017, Part I. LNCS, vol. 10401, pp. 727–757. Springer, Cham (2017). https://doi.org/10.1007/978-3-319-63688-7_24

[AGGM06] Akavia, A., Goldreich, O., Goldwasser, S., Moshkovitz, D.: On basing one-way functions on NP-hardness. In: Kleinberg, J.M. (ed.) Symposium on Theory of Computing, pp. 701–710. ACM (2006)

[AH91] Aiello, W., Hastad, J.: Statistical zero-knowledge languages can be recognized in two rounds. J. Comput. Syst. Sci. **42**(3), 327–345 (1991)

[BB15] Bogdanov, A., Brzuska, C.: On basing size-verifiable one-way functions on NP-hardness. In: Dodis, Y., Nielsen, J.B. (eds.) TCC 2015. LNCS, vol. 9014, pp. 1–6. Springer, Heidelberg (2015). https://doi.org/10.1007/978-3-662-46494-6_1

[BBF16] Brakerski, Z., Brzuska, C., Fleischhacker, N.: On statistically secure obfuscation with approximate correctness. In: Robshaw, M., Katz, J. (eds.) CRYPTO 2016, Part II. LNCS, vol. 9815, pp. 551–578. Springer, Heidelberg (2016). https://doi.org/10.1007/978-3-662-53008-5_19

[BBM11] Bhatnagar, N., Bogdanov, A., Mossel, E.: The computational complexity of estimating MCMC convergence time. In: Goldberg, L.A., Jansen, K., Ravi, R., Rolim, J.D.P. (eds.) APPROX/RANDOM -2011. LNCS, vol. 6845, pp. 424–435. Springer, Heidelberg (2011). https://doi.org/10.1007/978-3-642-22935-0_36

[BCH+17] Bouland, A., Chen, L., Holden, D., Thaler, J., Vasudevan, P.N.: On the power of statistical zero knowledge. In: FOCS (2017)

[BDRV18] Berman, I., Degwekar, A., Rothblum, R.D., Vasudevan, P.N.: Multi-collision resistant hash functions and their applications. In: Nielsen, J.B., Rijmen, V. (eds.) EUROCRYPT 2018. LNCS, vol. 10821, pp. 133–161. Springer, Cham (2018). https://doi.org/10.1007/978-3-319-78375-8_5

[BDV17] Bitansky, N., Degwekar, A., Vaikuntanathan, V.: Structure vs. hardness through the obfuscation lens. In: Katz, J., Shacham, H. (eds.) CRYPTO 2017. LNCS, vol. 10401, pp. 696–723. Springer, Cham (2017). https://doi.org/10.1007/978-3-319-63688-7_23

[BG03] Ben-Or, M., Gutfreund, D.: Trading help for interaction in statistical zero-knowledge proofs. J. Cryptol. **16**(2), 95–116 (2003)

[BHZ87] Boppana, R.B., Håstad, J., Zachos, S.: Does co-NP have short interactive proofs? Inf. Process. Lett. **25**(2), 127–132 (1987)

[BKP18] Bitansky, N., Kalai, Y.T., Paneth, O.: Multi-collision resistance: a paradigm for keyless hash functions. In: STOC (2018)

[BL13] Bogdanov, A., Lee, C.H.: Limits of provable security for homomorphic encryption. In: Canetti, R., Garay, J.A. (eds.) CRYPTO 2013. LNCS, vol. 8042, pp. 111–128. Springer, Heidelberg (2013). https://doi.org/10.1007/978-3-642-40041-4_7

[Cam86] Le Cam, L.: Part I. Springer, New York (1986). https://doi.org/10.1007/978-1-4612-4946-7

[CCKV08] Chailloux, A., Ciocan, D.F., Kerenidis, I., Vadhan, S.: Interactive and non-interactive zero knowledge are equivalent in the help model. In: Canetti, R. (ed.) TCC 2008. LNCS, vol. 4948, pp. 501–534. Springer, Heidelberg (2008). https://doi.org/10.1007/978-3-540-78524-8_28

[CGVZ18] Chen, Y.-H., Göös, M., Vadhan, S.P., Zhang, J.: A tight lower bound for entropy flattening. In: CCC (2018)

[DNR04] Dwork, C., Naor, M., Reingold, O.: Immunizing encryption schemes from decryption errors. In: Cachin, C., Camenisch, J.L. (eds.) EUROCRYPT 2004. LNCS, vol. 3027, pp. 342–360. Springer, Heidelberg (2004). https://doi.org/10.1007/978-3-540-24676-3_21

[FGM+89] Fürer, M., Goldreich, O., Mansour, Y., Sipser, M., Zachos, S.: On completeness and soundness in interactive proof systems. Adv. Comput. Res. **5**, 429–442 (1989)

[For89] Fortnow, L.: The complexity of perfect zero-knowledge. Adv. Comput. Res. **5**, 327–343 (1989)

[FV17] Fehr, S., Vaudenay, S.: Personal Communication (2017)

[Gol90] Goldreich, O.: A note on computational indistinguishability. Inf. Process. Lett. **34**(6), 277–281 (1990)

[Gol17] Goldreich, O.: Introduction to Property Testing. Cambridge University Press, Cambridge (2017)

[GS89] Goldwasser, S., Sipser, M.: Private coins versus public coins in interactive proof systems. Adv. Comput. Res. **5**, 73–90 (1989)

[GSV98] Goldreich, O., Sahai, A., Vadhan, S.: Honest-verifier statistical zero-knowledge equals general statistical zero-knowledge. In: STOC (1998)

[GSV99] Goldreich, O., Sahai, A., Vadhan, S.: Can statistical zero knowledge be made non-interactive? Or on the relationship of SZK and NISZK. In: Wiener, M. (ed.) CRYPTO 1999. LNCS, vol. 1666, pp. 467–484. Springer, Heidelberg (1999). https://doi.org/10.1007/3-540-48405-1_30

[GV99] Goldreich, O., Vadhan, S.P.: Comparing entropies in statistical zero knowledge with applications to the structure of SZK. In: CCC (1999)

[GV11] Goldreich, O., Vadhan, S.: On the complexity of computational problems regarding distributions. In: Goldreich, O. (ed.) Studies in Complexity and Cryptography. Miscellanea on the Interplay Between Randomness and Computation. LNCS, vol. 6650, pp. 390–405. Springer, Heidelberg (2011). https://doi.org/10.1007/978-3-642-22670-0_27

[GVW02] Goldreich, O., Vadhan, S., Wigderson, A.: On interactive proofs with a laconic prover. Comput. Complex. **11**(1–2), 1–53 (2002)

[HR05] Holenstein, T., Renner, R.: One-way secret-key agreement and applications to circuit polarization and immunization of public-key encryption. In: Shoup, V. (ed.) CRYPTO 2005. LNCS, vol. 3621, pp. 478–493. Springer, Heidelberg (2005). https://doi.org/10.1007/11535218_29

[IL89] Impagliazzo, R., Luby, M.: One-way functions are essential for complexity based cryptography. In: STOC, pp. 230–235 (1989)

[KNY17] Komargodski, I., Naor, M., Yogev, E.: White-box vs. black-box complexity of search problems: Ramsey and graph property testing. In: FOCS (2017)

[KNY18] Komargodski, I., Naor, M., Yogev, E.: Collision resistant hashing for paranoids: dealing with multiple collisions. In: Nielsen, J.B., Rijmen, V. (eds.) EUROCRYPT 2018. LNCS, vol. 10821, pp. 162–194. Springer, Cham (2018). https://doi.org/10.1007/978-3-319-78375-8_6

[KY18] Komargodski, I., Yogev, E.: On distributional collision resistant hashing. In: Shacham, H., Boldyreva, A. (eds.) CRYPTO 2018. LNCS, vol. 10992, pp. 303–327. Springer, Cham (2018). https://doi.org/10.1007/978-3-319-96881-0_11

[LZ17] Lovett, S., Zhang, J.: On the impossibility of entropy reversal, and its application to zero-knowledge proofs. In: Kalai, Y., Reyzin, L. (eds.) TCC 2017. LNCS, vol. 10677, pp. 31–55. Springer, Cham (2017). https://doi.org/10.1007/978-3-319-70500-2_2

[NR06] Naor, M., Rothblum, G.N.: Learning to impersonate. In: ICML, pp. 649–656 (2006)

[Ost91] Ostrovsky, R.: One-way functions, hard on average problems, and statistical zero-knowledge proofs. In: Structure in Complexity Theory Conference, pp. 133–138 (1991)

[OV08] Ong, S.J., Vadhan, S.: An equivalence between zero knowledge and commitments. In: Canetti, R. (ed.) TCC 2008. LNCS, vol. 4948, pp. 482–500. Springer, Heidelberg (2008). https://doi.org/10.1007/978-3-540-78524-8_27

[OW93] Ostrovsky, R., Wigderson, A.: One-way functions are essential for non-trivial zero-knowledge. In: ISTCS, pp. 3–17 (1993)

[PW17] Polyanskiy, Y., Wu, Y.: Lecture notes on information theory (2017). http://people.lids.mit.edu/yp/homepage/data/itlectures_v5.pdf

[SV03] Sahai, A., Vadhan, S.: A complete problem for statistical zero knowledge. J. ACM (JACM) **50**(2), 196–249 (2003)

[Top00] Topsøe, F.: Some inequalities for information divergence and related measures of discrimination. IEEE Trans. Inf. Theory **46**(4), 1602–1609 (2000)

[Vad99] Vadhan, S.P.: A study of statistical zero-knowledge proofs. Ph.D. thesis, Massachusetts Institute of Technology (1999)

[Yeh16] Yehudayoff, A.: Pointer chasing via triangular discrimination. Electron. Colloq. Comput. Complex. (ECCC) **23**, 151 (2016)

Estimating Gaps in Martingales and Applications to Coin-Tossing: Constructions and Hardness

Hamidreza Amini Khorasgani[(⊠)], Hemanta K. Maji, and Tamalika Mukherjee

Department of Computer Science, Purdue University, West Lafayette, IN, USA
{haminikh,hmaji,tmukherj}@purdue.edu

Abstract. Consider the representative task of designing a distributed coin-tossing protocol for n processors such that the probability of heads is $X_0 \in [0, 1]$. This protocol should be robust to an adversary who can reset one processor to change the distribution of the final outcome. For $X_0 = 1/2$, in the information-theoretic setting, no adversary can deviate the probability of the outcome of the well-known Blum's "majority protocol" by more than $\frac{1}{\sqrt{2\pi n}}$, i.e., it is $\frac{1}{\sqrt{2\pi n}}$ insecure.

In this paper, we study discrete-time martingales $(X_0, X_1, \ldots, X_n)$ such that $X_i \in [0, 1]$, for all $i \in \{0, \ldots, n\}$, and $X_n \in \{0, 1\}$. These martingales are commonplace in modeling stochastic processes like coin-tossing protocols in the information-theoretic setting mentioned above. In particular, for any $X_0 \in [0, 1]$, we construct martingales that yield $\frac{1}{2}\sqrt{\frac{X_0(1-X_0)}{n}}$ insecure coin-tossing protocols. For $X_0 = 1/2$, our protocol requires only 40% of the processors to achieve the same security as the majority protocol.

The technical heart of our paper is a new inductive technique that uses geometric transformations to precisely account for the large gaps in these martingales. For any $X_0 \in [0, 1]$, we show that there exists a stopping time τ such that

$$\mathbb{E}\left[|X_\tau - X_{\tau-1}|\right] \geqslant \frac{2}{\sqrt{2n-1}} \cdot X_0(1 - X_0)$$

The inductive technique simultaneously constructs martingales that demonstrate the optimality of our bound, i.e., a martingale where the gap corresponding to any stopping time is small. In particular, we construct optimal martingales such that *any* stopping time τ has

$$\mathbb{E}\left[|X_\tau - X_{\tau-1}|\right] \leqslant \frac{1}{\sqrt{n}} \cdot \sqrt{X_0(1 - X_0)}$$

Our lower-bound holds for all $X_0 \in [0, 1]$; while the previous bound of Cleve and Impagliazzo (1993) exists only for positive constant X_0.

The research effort is supported in part by an NSF CRII Award CNS–1566499, an NSF SMALL Award CNS–1618822, the IARPA HECTOR project, MITRE Innovation Program Academic Cybersecurity Research Award, a Purdue Research Foundation (PRF) Award, and The Center for Science of Information, an NSF Science and Technology Center, Cooperative Agreement CCF–0939370.

D. Hofheinz and A. Rosen (Eds.): TCC 2019, LNCS 11892, pp. 333–355, 2019.
https://doi.org/10.1007/978-3-030-36033-7_13

Conceptually, our approach only employs elementary techniques to analyze these martingales and entirely circumvents the complex probabilistic tools inherent to the approaches of Cleve and Impagliazzo (1993) and
Beimel, Haitner, Makriyannis, and Omri (2018).

By appropriately restricting the set of possible stopping-times, we
present representative applications to constructing distributed coin-
tossing/dice-rolling protocols, discrete control processes, fail-stop attacking coin-tossing/dice-rolling protocols, and black-box separations.

1   Introduction

A Representative Motivating Application. Consider a distributed protocol
for n processors to toss a coin, where processor i broadcasts her message in round
i. At the end of the protocol, all processors reconstruct the common outcome
from the public transcript. When all processors are honest, the probability of
the final outcome being 1 is X_0 and the probability of the final outcome being 0
is $1 - X_0$, i.e., the final outcome is a *bias-X_0 coin*. Suppose there is an adversary
who can (adaptively) choose to *restart* one of the processors after seeing her
message (i.e., the *strong adaptive* corruptions model introduced by Goldwasser,
Kalai, and Park [20]); otherwise her presence is innocuous. Our objective is to
design bias-X_0 coin-tossing protocols such that the adversary cannot change the
distribution of the final outcome significantly.

The Majority Protocol. Against computationally unbounded adversaries, (essentially) the only known protocol is the well-known majority protocol [5,10,13] for
$X_0 = 1/2$. The majority protocol requests one uniformly random bit from each
processor and the final outcome is the majority of these n bits. An adversary
can alter the probability of the final outcome being 1 by $\frac{1}{\sqrt{2\pi n}}$, i.e., the majority
protocol is $\frac{1}{\sqrt{2\pi n}}$ insecure.

Our New Protocol. We shall prove a general martingale result in this paper
that yields the following result as a corollary. For any $X_0 \in [0,1]$, there exists
an n-bit bias-X_0 coin-tossing protocol in the information-theoretic setting that
is $\frac{1}{2}\sqrt{\frac{X_0(1-X_0)}{n}}$ insecure. In particular, for $X_0 = 1/2$, our protocol uses only
625 processors to reduce the insecurity to, say, 1%; while the majority protocol
requires 1592 processors.

General Formal Framework: Martingales. Martingales are natural models
for several stochastic processes. Intuitively, martingales correspond to a gradual
release of information about an event. A priori, we know that the probability of
the event is X_0. For instance, in a distributed n-party coin-tossing protocol the
outcome being 1 is the event of interest.

A discrete-time martingale $(X_0, X_1, \ldots, X_n)$ represents the gradual release
of information about the event over n time-steps.[1] For intuition, we can assume

---

[1] For the introduction, we do not explicitly mention the underlying filtration for
brevity. The proofs, however, clearly mention the associated filtrations.

that X_i represents the probability that the outcome of the coin-tossing protocol is 1 after the first i parties have broadcast their messages. Martingales have the unique property that if one computes the expected value of X_j, for $j > i$, at the end of time-step i, it is identical to the value of X_i. In this paper we shall consider martingales where, at the end of time-step n, we know for sure whether the event of interest has occurred or not. That is, we have $X_n \in \{0, 1\}$.

A *stopping time* τ represents a time step $\in \{1, 2, \ldots, n\}$ where we stop the evolution of the martingale. The test of whether to stop the martingale at time-step i is a function only of the information revealed so far. Furthermore, this stopping time need *not* be a constant. That is, for example, different transcripts of the coin-tossing protocol potentially have different stopping times.

Our Martingale Problem Statement. The inspiration of our approach is best motivated using a two-player game between, namely, the *martingale designer* and the *adversary*. Fix n and X_0. The martingale designer presents a martingale $\mathcal{X} = (X_0, X_1, \ldots, X_n)$ to the adversary and the adversary finds a stopping time τ that maximizes the following quantity.

$$\mathbb{E}\left[|X_\tau - X_{\tau-1}|\right]$$

Intuitively, the adversary demonstrates the most severe *susceptibility* of the martingale by presenting the corresponding stopping time τ as a witness. The martingale designer's objective is to design martingales that have less susceptibility. Our paper uses a geometric approach to inductively provide tight bounds on the least susceptibility of martingales for all $n \geqslant 1$ and $X_0 \in [0, 1]$, that is, the following quantity.

$$C_n(X_0) := \inf_{\mathcal{X}} \sup_{\tau} \mathbb{E}\left[|X_\tau - X_{\tau-1}|\right]$$

This precise study of $C_n(X_0)$, for general $X_0 \in [0, 1]$, is motivated by natural applications in discrete process control as illustrated by the representative motivating problem. This paper, for representative applications of our results, considers n-processor distributed protocols and 2-party n-round protocols. The stopping time witnessing the highest susceptibility shall translate into appropriate adversarial strategies. These adversarial strategies shall imply hardness of computation results.

1.1 Our Contributions

We prove the following general martingale theorem.

Theorem 1. *Let* $(X_0, X_1, \ldots, X_n)$ *be a discrete-time martingale such that* $X_i \in [0, 1]$, *for all* $i \in \{1, \ldots, n\}$, *and* $X_n \in \{0, 1\}$. *Then, the following bound holds.*

$$\sup_{\substack{\text{stopping time } \tau}} \mathbb{E}\left[|X_\tau - X_{\tau-1}|\right] \geqslant C_n(X_0),$$

where $C_1(X) = 2X(1 - X)$, *and, for* $n > 1$, *we obtain* C_n *from* C_{n-1} *recursively using the geometric transformation defined in Fig. 8.*

Furthermore, for all $n \geq 1$ *and* $X_0 \in [0, 1]$, *there exists a martingale* $(X_0, \ldots, X_n)$ *(w.r.t. to the coordinate exposure filtration for* $\{0, 1\}^n$*) such that for any stopping time* τ, *it has* $\mathbb{E}\left[|X_\tau - X_{\tau-1}|\right] = C_n(X_0)$.

Intuitively, given a martingale, an adversary can identify a stopping time where the expected gap in the martingale is at least $C_n(X_0)$. Moreover, there exists a martingale that realizes the lower-bound in the tightest manner, i.e., all stopping times τ have identical susceptibility.

Next, we estimate the value of the function $C_n(X)$.

Lemma 1. *For* $n \geq 1$ *and* $X \in [0, 1]$, *we have*

$$\frac{2}{\sqrt{2n-1}} X(1-X) =: L_n(X) \leq C_n(X) \leq U_n(X) := \frac{1}{\sqrt{n}} \sqrt{X(1-X)}$$

As a representative example, consider the case of $n = 3$ and $X_0 = 1/2$. Figure 1 presents the martingale corresponding to the 3-round majority protocol and highlights the stopping time witnessing the susceptibility of 0.3750. Figure 2 presents the optimal 3-round coin-tossing protocol's martingale that has susceptibility of 0.2407.

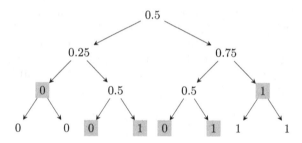

Fig. 1. Majority Protocol Tree of depth three. The optimal score in the majority tree of depth three is 0.3750 and the corresponding stopping time is highlighted in gray.

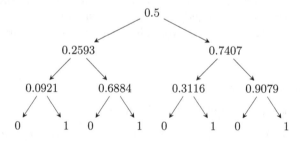

Fig. 2. Optimal depth-3 protocol tree for $X_0 = 1/2$. The optimal score is 0.2407. Observe that any stopping time achieves this score.

In the sequel, we highlight applications of Theorem 1 to protocol constructions and hardness of computation results using these estimates.

Remark 1 (Protocol Constructions). The optimal martingales naturally translate into n-bit distributed coin-tossing and multi-faceted dice rolling protocols.

1. Corollary 1: For all $X_0 \in [0, 1]$, there exists an n-bit distributed bias-X_0 coin-tossing protocol for n processors with the following security guarantee. Any (computationally unbounded) adversary who follows the protocol honestly and resets at most one of the processors during the execution of the protocol can change the probability of an outcome by at most $\frac{1}{2\sqrt{n}}\sqrt{X_0(1 - X_0)}$.

Remark 2 (Hardness of Computation Results). The lower-bound on the maximum susceptibility helps demonstrate hardness of computation results. For $X_0 = 1/2$, Cleve and Impagliazzo [14] proved that one encounters $|X_\tau - X_{\tau-1}| \geqslant \frac{1}{32\sqrt{n}}$ with probability $\frac{1}{5}$. In other words, their bound guarantees that the expected gap in the martingale is at least $\frac{1}{160\sqrt{n}}$, which is significantly smaller than our bound $\frac{1}{2\sqrt{2n}}$. Hardness of computation results relying on [14] (and its extensions) work only for constant $0 < X_0 < 1$.[2] However, our lower-bound holds for all $X_0 \in [0, 1]$; for example, even when $1/\mathrm{poly}(n) \leqslant X_0 \leqslant 1 - 1/\mathrm{poly}(n)$. Consequently, we extend existing hardness of computation results using our more general lower-bound.

1. Theorem 2 extends the fail-stop attack of [14] on 2-party bias-X_0 coin-tossing protocols (in the information-theoretic commitment hybrid). For any $X_0 \in [0, 1]$, a fail-stop adversary can change the probability of the final outcome of any 2-party bias-X_0 coin-tossing protocol by $\geqslant \frac{\sqrt{2}}{12\sqrt{n+1}}X_0(1 - X_0)$. This result is useful to demonstrate black-box separations results.
2. Corollary 2 extends the black-box separation results of [15,16,23] separating (appropriate restrictions of) 2-party bias-X_0 coin tossing protocols from one-way functions. We illustrate a representative new result that follows as a consequence of Corollary 2. For constant $X_0 \in (0, 1)$, [15,16,23] rely on (the extensions of) [14] to show that it is highly unlikely that there exist 2-party bias-X_0 coin tossing protocols using one-way functions in a black-box manner achieving $o(1/\sqrt{n})$ *unfairness* [22]. Note that when $X_0 = 1/n$, there are secure 2-party coin tossing protocols with $1/2n$ unfairness (based on Corollary 1) even in the information-theoretic setting. Previous results cannot determine the limits to the unfairness of 2-party bias-$1/n$ fair coin-tossing protocols that use one-way functions in a black-box manner. Our black-box separation result (refer to Corollary 2) implies that it is highly unlikely to construct bias-$1/n$ coin using one-way functions in a black-box manner with $< \frac{\sqrt{2}}{12 \cdot n^{3/2}}$ unfairness.
3. Corollary 3 and Corollary 4 extend Cleve and Impagliazzo's [14] result on influencing discrete control processes to arbitrary $X_0 \in [0, 1]$.

---

[2] Cleve and Impagliazzo set their problem as an optimization problem that trades off two conflicting objective functions. These objective functions have exponential dependence on $X_0(1 - X_0)$. Consequently, if $X_0 = 1/\mathrm{poly}(n)$ or $X_0 = 1 - 1/\mathrm{poly}(n)$, then their lower bounds are extremely weak.

1.2 Prior Approaches to the General Martingale Problem

Azuma-Hoeffding inequality [6,25] states that if $|X_i - X_{i-1}| = o(1/\sqrt{n})$, for all $i \in \{1, \ldots, n\}$, then, essentially, $|X_n - X_0| = o(1)$ with probability 1. That is, the final information X_n remains close to the a priori information X_0. However, in our problem statement, we have $X_n \in \{0, 1\}$. In particular, this constraint implies that the final information X_n is significantly different from the a priori information X_0. So, the initial constraint "for all $i \in \{1, \ldots, n\}$ we have $|X_i - X_{i-1}| = o(1/\sqrt{n})$" must be violated. What is the probability of this violation?

For $X_0 = 1/2$, Cleve and Impagliazzo [14] proved that there exists a round i such that $|X_i - X_{i-1}| \geqslant \frac{1}{32\sqrt{n}}$ with probability $1/5$. We emphasize that the round i is a random variable and not a constant. However, the definition of the "big jump" and the "probability to encounter big jumps" both are exponentially small function of X_0. So, the approach of Cleve and Impagliazzo is only applicable to constant $X_0 \in (0, 1)$. Recently, in an independent work, Beimel et al. [7] demonstrate an identical bound for *weak martingales* (that have some additional properties), which is used to model multi-party coin-tossing protocols.

For the upper-bound, on the other hand, Doob's martingale corresponding to the majority protocol is the only known martingale for $X_0 = 1/2$ with a small *maximum susceptibility*. In general, to achieve arbitrary $X_0 \in [0, 1]$, one considers coin tossing protocols where the outcome is 1 if the total number of heads in n uniformly random coins surpasses an appropriate threshold.

2 Preliminaries

We denote the *arithmetic mean* of two numbers x and y as A.M.$(x, y) := (x + y)/2$. The *geometric mean* of these two numbers is denoted by G.M.$(x, y) := \sqrt{x \cdot y}$ and their *harmonic mean* is denoted by H.M.$(x, y) := \left((x^{-1} + y^{-1})/2\right)^{-1} = 2xy/(x + y)$.

Martingales and Related Definitions. The *conditional expectation* of a random variable X with respect to an event $\mathcal{E}$ denoted by $\mathbb{E}[X|\mathcal{E}]$, is defined as $\mathbb{E}[X \cdot 1_{\{\mathcal{E}\}}]/\mathbb{P}[\mathcal{E}]$. For a discrete random variable Y, the conditional expectation of X with respect to Y, denoted by $\mathbb{E}[X|Y]$, is a random variable that takes value $\mathbb{E}[X|Y = y]$ with probability $\mathbb{P}[Y = y]$, where $\mathbb{E}[X|Y = y]$ denotes the conditional expectation of X with respect to the event $\{\omega \in \Omega | Y(\omega) = y\}$.

Let $\Omega = \Omega_1 \times \Omega_2 \times \cdots \times \Omega_n$ denote a sample space and $(E_1, E_2, \ldots, E_n)$ be a joint distribution defined over Ω such that for each $i \in \{1, \ldots, n\}$, E_i is a random variable over Ω_i. Let $X = \{X_i\}_{i=0}^n$ be a sequence of random variables defined over Ω. We say that X_j is $E_1, \ldots, E_j$ measurable if there exists a function $g_j \colon \Omega_1 \times \Omega_2 \times \cdots \times \Omega_j \to \mathbb{R}$ such that $X_j = g_j(E_1, \ldots, E_j)$. Let $X = \{X_i\}_{i=0}^n$ be a discrete-time martingale sequence with respect to the sequence $E = \{E_i\}_{i=1}^n$. This statement implies that for each $i \in \{0, 1, \ldots, n\}$, we have

$$\mathbb{E}[X_{i+1}|E_1, E_2, \ldots, E_i] = X_i$$

Note that the definition of martingale implies X_i to be $E_1, \ldots, E_i$ measurable for each $i \in \{1, \ldots, n\}$ and X_0 to be constant. In the sequel, we shall use $\{X = \{X_i\}_{i=0}^n, E = \{E_i\}_{i=1}^n\}$ to denote a martingale sequence where for each $i = 1, \ldots, n$, $X_i \in [0, 1]$, and $X_n \in \{0, 1\}$. However, for brevity, we use $(X_0, X_1, \ldots, X_n)$ to denote a martingale. Given a function $f \colon \Omega_1 \times \Omega_2 \times \cdots \times \Omega_n \to \mathbb{R}$, if we define the random variable $Z_i := \mathbb{E}\left[f(E_1, \ldots, E_n) \mid E_1, \ldots, E_i\right]$, for each $i \in \{0, 1, \ldots, n\}$, then the sequence $Z = \{Z_i\}_{i=0}^n$ is a martingale with respect to $\{E_i\}_{i=1}^n$. This martingale is called the *Doob's martingale*.

The random variable $\tau \colon \Omega \to \{0, 1, \ldots, n\}$ is called a stopping time if for each $k \in \{1, 2, \ldots, n\}$, the occurrence or non-occurrence of the event $\{\tau \leqslant k\} := \{\omega \in \Omega | \tau(\omega) \leqslant k\}$ depends only on the values of random variables $E_1, E_2, \ldots, E_k$. Equivalently, the random variable $\mathbf{1}_{\{\tau \leqslant k\}}$ is $E_1, \ldots, E_k$ measurable. Let $\mathcal{S}(X, E)$ denote the set of all stopping time random variables over the martingale sequence $\{X = \{X_i\}_{i=0}^n, E = \{E_i\}_{i=1}^n\}$. For $\ell \in \{1, 2\}$, we define the *score* of a martingale sequence (X, E) with respect to a stopping time τ in the L_ℓ-norm as the following quantity.

$$\mathrm{score}_\ell(X, E, \tau) := \mathbb{E}\left[\left|X_\tau - X_{\tau-1}\right|^\ell\right]$$

We define the *max stopping time* as the stopping time that maximizes the score

$$\tau_{\max}(X, E, \ell) := \underset{\tau \in \mathcal{S}(X, E)}{\arg\max}\ \mathrm{score}_\ell(X, E, \tau),$$

and the (corresponding) max-score as

$$\mathrm{max\text{-}score}_\ell(X, E) := \mathbb{E}\left[\left|X_{\tau_{\max}} - X_{\tau_{\max}-1}\right|^\ell\right]$$

Let $A_n(x^*)$ denote the set of all discrete time martingales $\{X = \{X_i\}_{i=0}^n, E = \{E_i\}_{i=1}^n\}$ such that $X_0 = x^*$ and $X_n \in \{0, 1\}$. We define *optimal score* as

$$\mathrm{opt}_n(x^*, \ell) := \underset{(X, E) \in A_n(x^*)}{\inf}\ \mathrm{max\text{-}score}_\ell(X, E)$$

Representing a Martingale as a Tree. We interpret a discrete time martingale sequence $X = \{X_i\}_{i=0}^n$ defined over a sample space $\Omega = \Omega_1 \times \cdots \times \Omega_n$ as a tree of depth n (see Fig. 3). For $i = 0, \ldots, n$, any node at depth i has $|\Omega_{i+1}|$ children. In fact, for each i, the edge between a node at depth i and a child at depth $(i+1)$ corresponds to a possible outcome that E_{i+1} can take from the set $\Omega_{i+1} = \{x^{(1)}, \ldots, x^{(t)}\}$.

Each node v at depth i is represented by a unique path from root to v like $(e_1, e_2, \ldots, e_i)$, which corresponds to the event $\{\omega \in \Omega | E_1(\omega) = e_1, \ldots, E_i(\omega) = e_i\}$. Specifically, each path from root to a leaf in this tree, represents a unique outcome in the sample space Ω.

Any subset of nodes in a tree that has the property that none of them is an ancestor of any other, is called an *anti-chain*. If we use our tree-based notation to represent a node v, i.e., the sequence of edges $e_1, \ldots, e_i$ corresponding to the path from root to v, then any prefix-free subset of nodes is an anti-chain. Any anti-chain that is not a proper subset of another anti-chain is called a *maximal anti-chain*. A stopping time in a martingale corresponds to a *unique* maximal anti-chain in the martingale tree.

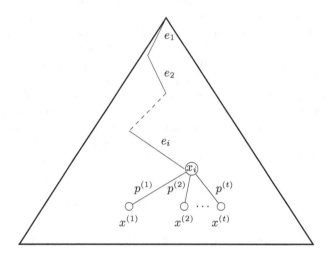

Fig. 3. Interpreting a general martingale as a tree.

Geometric Definitions and Relations. Consider curves C and D defined by the zeroes of $Y = f(X)$ and $Y = g(X)$, respectively, where $X \in [0, 1]$. We restrict to curves C and D such that each one of them have exactly one intersection with $X = x$, for any $x \in [0, 1]$. Refer to Fig. 4 for intuition. Then, we say C is *above* D, represented by $C \succcurlyeq D$, if, for each $x \in [0, 1]$, we have $f(x) \geqslant g(x)$.

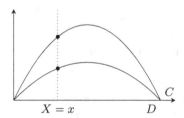

Fig. 4. Intuition for a curve C being above another curve D, represented by $C \succcurlyeq D$.

3   Large Gaps in Martingales: A Geometric Approach

This section presents a high-level overview of our proof strategy. In the sequel, we shall assume that we are working with discrete-time martingales $(X_0, X_1, \ldots, X_n)$ such that $X_n \in \{0, 1\}$.

Given a martingale $(X_0, \ldots, X_n)$, its *susceptibility* is represented by the following quantity

$$\sup_{\text{stopping time } \tau} \mathbb{E}\left[|X_\tau - X_{\tau-1}|\right]$$

Intuitively, if a martingale has high susceptibility, then it has a stopping time such that the gap in the martingale while encountering the stopping time is large. Our objective is to characterize the *least susceptibility* that a martingale $(X_0, \ldots, X_n)$ can achieve. More formally, given n and X_0, characterize

$$C_n(X_0) := \inf_{(X_0, \ldots, X_n)} \sup_{\text{stopping time } \tau} \mathbb{E}\left[|X_\tau - X_{\tau-1}|\right]$$

Our approach is to proceed by induction on n to exactly characterize the curve $C_n(X)$, and our argument naturally constructs the best martingale that achieves $C_n(X_0)$.

1. We know that the base case is $C_1(X) = 2X(1 - X)$ (see Fig. 5 for this argument).
2. Given the curve $C_{n-1}(X)$, we identify a geometric transformation T (see Fig. 8) that defines the curve $C_n(X)$ from the curve $C_{n-1}(X)$. Section 3.1 summarizes the proof of this inductive step that crucially relies on the geometric interpretation of the problem, which is one of our primary technical contributions. Furthermore, for any $n \geqslant 1$, there exist martingales such that its susceptibility is $C_n(X_0)$.
3. Finally, Appendix A proves that the curve $C_n(X)$ lies above the curve $L_n(X) := \frac{2}{\sqrt{2n-1}} X(1 - X)$ and below the curve $U_n(X) := \frac{1}{\sqrt{n}} \sqrt{X(1 - X)}$.

3.1   Proof of Theorem 1

Our objective is the following.

1. Given an arbitrary martingale (X, E), find the maximum stopping time in this martingale, i.e., the stopping time $\tau_{\max}(X, E, 1)$.
2. For any depth n and bias X_0, construct a martingale that achieves the max-score. We refer to this martingale as the *optimal* martingale. A priori, this martingale need not be unique. However, we shall see that for each X_0, it is (essentially) a unique martingale.

We emphasize that even if we are only interested in the exact value of $C_n(X_0)$ for $X_0 = 1/2$, it is unavoidable to characterize $C_{n-1}(X)$, for all values of $X \in [0, 1]$. Because, in a martingale $(X_0 = 1/2, X_1, \ldots, X_n)$, the value of X_1 can be arbitrary. So, without a precise characterization of the value $C_{n-1}(X_1)$, it is not evident how to calculate the value of $C_n(X_0 = 1/2)$. Furthermore, understanding $C_n(X_0)$, for all $X_0 \in [0, 1]$, yields entirely new applications for our result.

Base Case of $n = 1$. For a martingale (X_0, X_1) of depth $n = 1$, we have $X_1 \in \{0, 1\}$. Thus, without loss of generality, we assume that E_1 takes only two values (see Fig. 5). Then, it is easy to verify that the max-score is always equal to $2X_0(1 - X_0)$. This score is witnessed by the stopping time $\tau = 1$. So, we conclude that $\mathrm{opt}_1(X_0, 1) = C_1(X_0) = 2X_0(1 - X_0)$

Inductive Step. $n = 2$ **(For Intuition).** For simplicity, let us consider finite martingales, i.e., the sample space Ω_i of the random variable E_i is finite. Suppose that the root $X_0 = x$ in the corresponding martingale tree has t children with values $x^{(1)}, x^{(2)}, \ldots, x^{(t)}$, and the probability of choosing the j-th child is $p^{(j)}$, where $j \in \{1, \ldots, t\}$ (see Fig. 6).

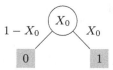

Fig. 5. Base Case for Theorem 1. Note $C_1(X_0) = \inf_{(X_0, X_1)} \sup_\tau \mathbb{E}\left[\|X_\tau - X_{\tau-1}\|\right]$. The optimal stopping time is shaded and its score is $X_0 \cdot |1 - X_0| + (1 - X_0) \cdot |0 - X_0|$.

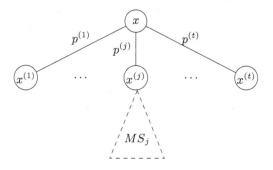

Fig. 6. Inductive step for Theorem 1. MS_j represents the max-score of the sub-tree of depth $n - 1$ whose rooted at $x^{(j)}$. For simplicity, the subtree of $x^{(j)}$ is only shown here.

Given a martingale (X_0, X_1, X_2), the adversary's objective is to find the stopping time τ that maximizes the score $\mathbb{E}\left[\|X_\tau - X_{\tau-1}\|\right]$. If the adversary chooses to stop at $\tau = 0$, then the score $\mathbb{E}\left[\|X_\tau - X_{\tau-1}\|\right] = 0$, which is not a good strategy. So, for each j, the adversary chooses whether to stop at the child $x^{(j)}$, or continue to a stopping time in the sub-tree rooted at $x^{(j)}$. The adversary chooses the stopping time based on which of these two strategies yield a better score. If the adversary stops the martingale at child j, then the contribution of this decision to the score is $p^{(j)}|x^{(j)} - x|$. On the other hand, if she does not stop at child j, then the contribution from the sub-tree is guaranteed to be $p^{(j)}C_1(x^{(j)})$. Overall, from the j-th child, an adversary obtains a score that is at least $p^{(j)} \max\left\{|x^{(j)} - x|, C_1(x^{(j)})\right\}$.

Let $h^{(j)} := \max\{|x^{(j)} - x|, C_1(x^{(j)})\}$. We represent the points $Z^{(j)} = (x^{(j)}, h^{(j)})$ in a two dimensional plane. Then, clearly all these points lie on the solid curve defined by $\max\{|X - x|, C_1(X)\}$, see Fig. 7.

Since (X, E) is a martingale, we have $x = \sum_{j=1}^{t} p^{(j)} x^{(j)}$ and the adversary's strategy for finding $\tau_{\max}$ gives us $\max\text{-score}_1(X, E) = \sum_{j=1}^{t} p^{(j)} h^{(j)}$. This observation implies that the coordinate $(x, \max\text{-score}_1(X, E)) = \sum_{j=1}^{t} p^{(j)} Z^{(j)}$. So, the point in the plane giving the adversary the maximum score for a tree of depth $n = 2$ with bias $X_0 = x$ lies in the *intersection* of the convex hull of the points $Z^{(1)}, \ldots, Z^{(t)}$, and the line $X = x$. Let us consider the martingale defined in Fig. 7 as a concrete example. Here $t = 4$, and the points $Z^{(1)}, Z^{(2)}, Z^{(3)}, Z^{(4)}$ lie on $\max\{|X - x|, C_1(X)\}$. The martingale designer specifies the probabilities $p^{(1)}, p^{(2)}, p^{(3)}$, and $p^{(4)}$, such that $p^{(1)} x^{(1)} + \cdots + p^{(4)} x^{(4)} = x$. These probabilities are not represented in Fig. 7. Note that the point $(p^{(1)} x^{(1)} + \cdots + p^{(4)} x^{(4)}, p^{(1)} h^{(1)} + \cdots + p^{(4)} h^{(4)})$ representing the score of the adversary is the point $p^{(1)} Z^{(1)} + \cdots + p^{(4)} Z^{(4)}$. This point lies inside the convex hull of the points $Z^{(1)}, \ldots, Z^{(4)}$ and on the line $X = p^{(1)} x^{(1)} + \cdots + p^{(4)} x^{(4)} = x$. The exact location depends on $p^{(1)}, \ldots, p^{(4)}$.

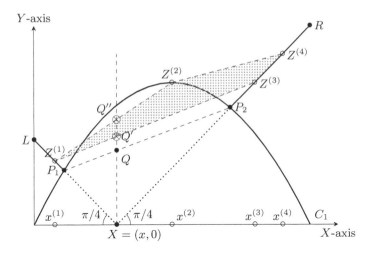

Fig. 7. Intuitive summary of the inductive step for $n = 2$.

The point Q' is the point with minimum height. Observe that the height of the point Q' is at least the height of the point Q. So, in any martingale, the adversary shall find a stopping time that scores more than (the height of) the point Q.

On the other hand, the martingale designer's objective is to reduce the score that an adversary can achieve. So, the martingale designer chooses $t = 2$, and the two points $Z^{(1)} = P_1$ and $Z^{(2)} = P_2$ to construct the optimum martingale. We apply this method for each $x \in [0, 1]$ to find the corresponding point Q. That is, the *locus of the point* Q, for $x \in [0, 1]$, yields the curve $C_2(X)$.

We claim that the height of the point Q is the *harmonic-mean* of the heights of the points P_1 and P_2. This claim follows from elementary geometric facts. Let h_1 represent the height of the point P_1, and h_2 represent the height of the point P_2. Observe that the distance of $x - x_S(x) = h_1$ (because the line ℓ_1 has slope $\pi - \pi/4$). Similarly, the distance of $x_L(x) - x = h_2$ (because the line ℓ_2 has slope $\pi/4$). So, using properties of similar triangles, the height of Q turns out to be

$$h_1 + \frac{h_1}{h_1 + h_2} \cdot (h_2 - h_1) = \frac{2h_1 h_2}{h_1 + h_2}.$$

This property inspires the definition of the geometric transformation T, see Fig. 8. Applying T on the curve $C_1(X)$ yields the curve $C_2(X)$ for which we have $C_2(x) = \mathrm{opt}_2(x, 1)$.

Given. A curve C defined by the zeroes of the equation $Y = f(X)$, where $X \in [0, 1]$.
Definition of the Transform. The transform of C, represented by $T(C)$, is the curve defined by the zeroes of the equation $Y = g(X)$, where, for $x \in [0, 1]$, the value of $g(x)$ is defined below.

1. Let $x_S(x) \in [0, 1]$ be a solution of the equation $X + f(X) = x$.
2. Let $x_L(x) \in [0, 1]$ be a solution of the equation $X - f(X) = x$.
3. Then $g(x) := \mathrm{H.M.}(y^{(1)}, y^{(2)})$, where $y^{(1)} = f(x_S(x))$, $y^{(2)} = f(x_L(x))$, and $\mathrm{H.M.}(y^{(1)}, y^{(2)})$ represents the harmonic mean of $y^{(1)}$ and $y^{(2)}$.

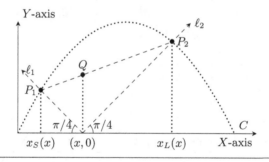

Fig. 8. Definition of transform of a curve C, represented by $T(C)$. The locus of the point Q (in the right figure) defines the curve $T(C)$.

General Inductive Step. Note that a similar approach works for general $n = d \geqslant 2$. Fix X_0 and $n = d \geqslant 2$. We assume that the adversary can compute $C_{d-1}(X_1)$, for any $X_1 \in [0, 1]$.

Suppose the root in the corresponding martingale tree has t children with values $x^{(1)}, x^{(2)}, \ldots, x^{(t)}$, and the probability of choosing the j-th child is $p^{(j)}$ (see Fig. 6). Let $(X^{(j)}, E^{(j)})$ represent the martingale associated with the subtree rooted at $x^{(j)}$.

For any $j \in \{1, \ldots, t\}$, the adversary can choose to stop at the child j. This decision will contribute $|x^{(j)} - x|$ to the score with weight $p^{(j)}$. On the other hand, if she continues to the subtree rooted at $x^{(j)}$, she will get at least a contribution of max-score$_1(X^{(j)}, E^{(j)})$ with weight $p^{(j)}$. Therefore, the adversary can obtain the following contribution to her score

$$p^{(j)} \max \left\{ |x^{(j)} - x|, C_{d-1}(x^{(j)}) \right\}$$

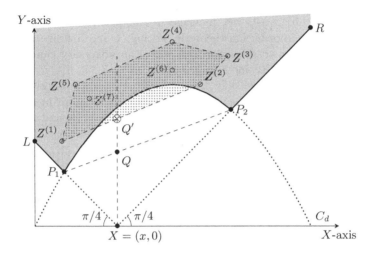

Fig. 9. Intuitive Summary of the inductive argument. Our objective is to pick the set of points $\{Z^{(1)}, Z^{(2)} \ldots \}$ in the gray region to minimize the length of the intercept XQ' of their (lower) convex hull on the line $X = x$. Clearly, the unique optimal solution corresponds to including both P_1 and P_2 in the set.

Similar to the case of $n = 2$, we define the points $Z^{(1)}, \ldots, Z^{(t)}$. For $n > 2$, however, there is one difference from the $n = 2$ case. The point $Z^{(j)}$ need not *lie on the solid curve*, but it can lie on or above it, i.e., they lie in the gray area of Fig. 9. This phenomenon is attributable to a suboptimal martingale designer producing martingales with suboptimal scores, i.e., *strictly above* the solid curve. For $n = 1$, it happens to be the case that, there is (effectively) only one martingale that the martingale designer can design (the optimal tree). The adversary obtains a score that is at least the height of the point Q', which is at least the height of Q. On the other hand, the martingale designer can choose $t = 2$, and $Z^{(1)} = P_1$ and $Z^{(2)} = P_2$ to define the optimum martingale. Again, the locus of the point Q is defined by the curve $T(C_{d-1})$.

Conclusion. So, by induction, we have proved that $C_n(X) = T^{n-1}(C_1(X))$. Additionally, note that, during induction, in the optimum martingale, we always have $|x^{(0)} - x| = C_{n-1}(x^{(0)})$ and $|x^{(1)} - x| = C_{n-1}(x^{(1)})$. Intuitively, the decision to stop at $x^{(j)}$ or continue to the subtree rooted at $x^{(j)}$ has identical consequence. So, by induction, *all stopping times* in the optimum martingale have score $C_n(x)$.

Finally, Appendix A proves Lemma 1, which tightly estimates the curve C_n.

4   Applications

This section discusses various consequences of Theorem 1 and other related results.

4.1   Distributed Coin-Tossing Protocol

We consider constructing distributed n-processor coin-tossing protocols where the i-th processor broadcasts her message in the i-th round. We shall study this problem in the information-theoretic setting. Our objective is to design n-party distributed coin-tossing protocols where an adversary cannot bias the distribution of the final outcome significantly.

For $X_0 = 1/2$, one can consider the incredibly elegant "majority protocol" [5,10,13]. The i-th processor broadcasts a uniformly random bit in round i. The final outcome of the protocol is the majority of the n outcomes, and an adversary can bias the final outcome by $\frac{1}{\sqrt{2\pi n}}$ by restarting a processor once [13].

We construct distributed n-party bias-X_0 coin-tossing protocols, for any $X_0 \in [0,1]$, and our new protocol for $X_0 = 1/2$ is more robust to restarting attacks than this majority protocol. Fix $X_0 \in [0,1]$ and $n \geqslant 1$. Consider the optimal martingale $(X_0, X_1, \ldots, X_n)$ guaranteed by Theorem 1. The susceptibility corresponding to any stopping time is $= C_n(X_0) \leqslant U_n(X_0) = \frac{1}{\sqrt{n}}\sqrt{X_0(1 - X_0)}$. Note that one can construct an n-party coin-tossing protocol where the i-th processor broadcasts the i-th message, and the corresponding Doob's martingale is identical to this optimal martingale. An adversary who can restart a processor once biases the outcome of this protocol by at most $\frac{1}{2}C_n(X_0)$, this is discussed in Sect. 4.3.

Corollary 1 (Distributed Coin-tossing Protocols). *For every $X_0 \in [0,1]$ and $n \geqslant 1$ there exists an n-party bias-X_0 coin-tossing protocol such that any adversary who can restart a processor once causes the final outcome probability to deviate by $\leqslant \frac{1}{2}C_n(X_0) \leqslant \frac{1}{2}U_n(X_0) = \frac{1}{2\sqrt{n}}\sqrt{X_0(1 - X_0)}$.*

For $X_0 = 1/2$, our new protocol's outcome can be changed by $\frac{1}{4\sqrt{n}}$, which is less than the $\frac{1}{\sqrt{2\pi n}}$ deviation of the majority protocol. However, we do not know whether there exists a *computationally efficient* algorithm implementing the coin-tossing protocols corresponding to the optimal martingales.

4.2   Fail-Stop Attacks on Coin-Tossing/Dice-Rolling Protocols

A *two-party n-round bias-X_0 coin-tossing protocol* is an interactive protocol between two parties who send messages in alternate rounds, and X_0 is the probability of the coin-tossing protocol's outcome being heads. *Fair computation* ensures that even if one of the parties aborts during the execution of the protocol, the other party outputs a (randomized) heads/tails outcome. This requirement of guaranteed output delivery is significantly stringent, and Cleve [13] demonstrated a computationally efficient attack strategy that alters the output-distribution by $O(1/n)$, i.e., any protocol is $O(1/n)$ unfair. Defining fairness and constructing fair protocols for general functionalities has been a field of highly influential research [2–4,8,21,22,29]. This interest stems primarily from the fact that fairness is a desirable attribute for secure-computation protocols in real-world applications. However, designing fair protocol even for simple functionalities like (bias-1/2) coin-tossing is challenging both in the two-party and the multi-party setting. In the multi-party setting, several works [1,5,9] explore fair coin-tossing where the number of adversarial parties is a constant fraction of the total number of parties. For a small number of parties, like the two-party and the three-party setting, constructing such protocols have been extremely challenging even against computationally bounded adversaries [12,24,30]. These constructions (roughly) match Cleve's $O(1/n)$ lower-bound in the computational setting.

In the information-theoretic setting, Cleve and Impagliazzo [14] exhibited that any two-party n-round bias-1/2 coin-tossing protocol are $\frac{1}{2560\sqrt{n}}$ unfair. In particular, their adversary is a fail-stop adversary who follows the protocol honestly except aborting prematurely. In the information-theoretic commitment-hybrid, there are two-party n-round bias-1/2 coin-tossing protocols that have $\approx 1/\sqrt{n}$ unfairness [5,10,13]. This bound matches the lower-bound of $\Omega(1/\sqrt{n})$ by Cleve and Impagliazzo [14]. It seems that it is necessary to rely on strong computational hardness assumptions or use these primitives in a non-black box manner to beat the $1/\sqrt{n}$ bound [7,15,16,23].

We generalize the result of Cleve and Impagliazzo [14] to all 2-party n-round bias-X_0 coin-tossing protocols (and improve the constants by two orders of magnitude). For $X_0 = 1/2$, our fail-stop adversary changes the final outcome probability by $\geqslant \frac{1}{24\sqrt{2}} \cdot \frac{1}{\sqrt{n+1}}$.

Theorem 2 (Fail-stop Attacks on Coin-tossing Protocols). *For any two-party n-round bias-X_0 coin-tossing protocol, there exists a fail-stop adversary that changes the final outcome probability of the honest party by at least*
$$\tfrac{1}{12}C_n'(X_0) \geqslant \tfrac{1}{12}L_n'(X_0) := \tfrac{1}{12}\sqrt{\tfrac{2}{n+1}}X_0(1 - X_0), \text{ where } C_1'(X) := X(1 - X) \text{ and}$$
$C_n'(X) := T^{n-1}(C_1'(X)).$

This theorem is *not* a direct consequence of Theorem 1. The proof relies on an entirely new inductive argument; however, the geometric technique for this recursion is similar to the proof strategy for Theorem 1. Interested readers can refer to the full version of the paper [27] for details.

Black-Box Separation Results. Gordon and Katz [22] introduced the notion of $1/p$-*unfair secure computation* for a fine-grained study of fair computation of functionalities. In this terminology, Theorem 2 states that $\frac{c}{\sqrt{n+1}}X_0(1 - X_0)$-unfair computation of a bias-X_0 coin is impossible for any positive constant $c < \frac{\sqrt{2}}{12}$ and $X_0 \in [0, 1]$.

Cleve and Impagliazzo's result [14] states that $\frac{c}{\sqrt{n}}$-unfair secure computation of the bias-1/2 coin is impossible for any positive constant $c < \frac{1}{2560}$. This result on the hardness of computation of fair coin-tossing was translated into black-box separations results. These results [15,16,23], intuitively, indicate that it is unlikely that $\frac{c}{\sqrt{n}}$-unfair secure computation of the bias-1/2 coin exists, for $c < \frac{1}{2560}$, relying solely on the black-box use of one-way functions. We emphasize that there are several restrictions imposed on the protocols that these works [15,16,23] consider; detailing all of which is beyond the scope of this draft. Substituting the result of [14] by Theorem 2, extends the results of [15,16,23] to general bias-X_0 coin-tossing protocols.

Corollary 2 (Informal: Black-box Separation). *For any $X_0 \in [0,1]$ and positive constant $c < \frac{\sqrt{2}}{12}$, the existence of $\frac{c}{\sqrt{n+1}}X_0(1 - X_0)$-unfair computation protocol for a bias-X_0 coin is black-box separated from the existence of one-way functions (restricted to the classes of protocols considered by [15,16,23]).*

4.3   Influencing Discrete Control Processes

Lichtenstein et al. [28] considered the problem of an adversary influencing the outcome of a stochastic process through mild interventions. For example, an adversary attempts to bias the outcome of a distributed n-processor coin-tossing protocol, where, in the i-th round, the processor i broadcasts her message. This model is also used to characterize randomness sources that are adversarially influenced, for example, [11,17–19,26,31–35].

Consider the sample space $\Omega = \Omega_1 \times \Omega_2 \times \cdots \times \Omega_n$ and a joint distribution $(E_1, \ldots, E_n)$ over the sample space. We have a function $f \colon \Omega \to \{0,1\}$ such that $\mathbb{E}\left[f(E_1, \ldots, E_n)\right] = X_0$. This function represents the protocol that determines the final outcome from the public transcript. The filtration, at time-step i, reveals the value of the random variable E_i to the adversary. We consider the corresponding Doob's martingale $(X_0, X_1, \ldots, X_n)$. Intuitively, X_i represents the probability of $f(E_1, \ldots, E_n) = 1$ conditioned on the revealed values $(E_1 = e_1, \ldots, E_i = e_i)$. The adversary is allowed to intervene only once. She can choose to intervene at time-step i, reject the current sample $E_i = e_i$, and substitute it with a fresh sample from E_i. This intervention is identical to *restarting* the i-th processor if the adversary does not like her message. Note that this intervention changes the final outcome by

$$(X_{i-1}|E_1 = e_1, \ldots, E_{i-1} = e_{i-1}) - (X_i|E_1 = e_1, \ldots, E_i = e_i)$$

We shall use a stopping time τ to represent the time-step where an adversary decides to intervene. However, for some $(E_1 = e_1, \ldots, E_n = e_n)$ the adversary may not choose to intervene. Consequently, we consider stopping times $\tau \colon \Omega \to \{1, \ldots, n, \infty\}$, where the stopping time being ∞ corresponds to the event that the adversary did not choose to intervene. In the Doob martingale discussed above, as a direct consequence of Theorem 1, there exists a stopping time τ^* with susceptibility $\geq C_n(X_0)$. Note that susceptibility measures the expected (unsigned) magnitude of the deviation, if an adversary intervenes at τ^*. Some of these contributions to susceptibility shall increase the probability of the final outcome being 1, and the remaining shall decrease the probability of the final outcome being 1. By an averaging argument, there exists a stopping time $\tau \colon \Omega \to \{1, \ldots, n, \infty\}$ that biases the outcome of f by at least $\geqslant \frac{1}{2} C_n(X_0)$, whence the following corollary.

Corollary 3 (Influencing Discrete Control Processes). *Let $\Omega_1, \ldots, \Omega_n$ be arbitrary sets, and $(E_1, \ldots, E_n)$ be a joint distribution over the set $\Omega := \Omega_1 \times \cdots \times \Omega_n$. Let $f \colon \Omega \to \{0, 1\}$ be a function such that $\mathbb{P}\left[f(E_1, \ldots, E_n) = 1\right] = X_0$. Then, there exists an adversarial strategy of intervening once to bias the probability of the outcome away from X_0 by $\geqslant \frac{1}{2} C_n(X_0) \geqslant \frac{1}{2} L_n(X_0) = \frac{1}{\sqrt{2n-1}} X_0(1 - X_0)$.*

The previous result of [14] applies only to $X_0 = 1/2$ and they ensure a deviation of $1/320\sqrt{n}$. For $X_0 = 1/2$, our result ensures a deviation of (roughly) $1/4\sqrt{2n} \approx 1/5.66\sqrt{n}$.

Influencing Multi-faceted Dice-Rolls. Corollary 3 generalizes to the setting where $f \colon \Omega \to \{0, 1, \ldots, \omega - 1\}$, i.e., the function f outputs an arbitrary ω-faceted dice roll. In fact, we quantify the deviation in the probability of any subset $S \subseteq \{0, 1, \ldots, \omega - 1\}$ of outcomes caused by an adversary intervening once.

Corollary 4 (Influencing Multi-faceted Dice-Rolls). *Let $\Omega_1, \ldots, \Omega_n$ be arbitrary sets, and $(E_1, \ldots, E_n)$ be a joint distribution over the set $\Omega := \Omega_1 \times \cdots \times \Omega_n$. Let $f \colon \Omega \to \{0, 1, \ldots, \omega - 1\}$ be a function with $\omega \geqslant 2$ outcomes, $S \subseteq \{0, 1, \ldots, \omega - 1\}$ be any subset of outcomes, and $\mathbb{P}\left[f(E_1, \ldots, E_n) \in S\right] = X_0$. Then, there exists an adversarial strategy of intervening once to bias the probability of the outcome being in S away from X_0 by $\geqslant \frac{1}{2} C_n(X_0) \geqslant \frac{1}{2} L_n(X_0) = \frac{1}{\sqrt{2n-1}} X_0(1 - X_0)$.*

Corollary 3 and Corollary 4 are equivalent to each other. Clearly Corollary 3 is a special case of Corollary 4. Corollary 4, in turn, follows from Corollary 3 by considering "$f(E_1, \ldots, E_n) \in S$" as the interesting event for the martingale. We state these two results separately for conceptual clarity and ease of comparison with the prior work.

4.4 L_2 Gaps and Their Tightness

Finally, to demonstrate the versatility of our geometric approach, we measure large L_2-norm gaps in martingales.

Theorem 3. *Let $(X_0, X_1, \ldots, X_n)$ be a discrete-time martingale such that $X_n \in \{0, 1\}$. Then, the following bound holds.*

$$\sup_{\substack{\text{stopping time } \tau}} \mathbb{E}\left[(X_\tau - X_{\tau-1})^2\right] \geqslant D_n(X_0) := \frac{1}{n} X_0(1 - X_0)$$

Furthermore, for all $n \geq 1$ and $X_0 \in [0,1]$, there exists a martingale $(X_0, \ldots, X_n)$ such that for any stopping time τ, it has $\mathbb{E}\left[(X_\tau - X_{\tau-1})^2\right] = D_n(X_0)$.

We provide a high-level overview of the proof in Appendix B.

Note that, for any martingale $(X_0, \ldots, X_n)$ with $X_n \in \{0,1\}$, we have $\mathbb{E}\left[\sum_{i=1}^n (X_i - X_{i-1})^2\right] = \mathbb{E}\left[X_n^2 - X_0^2\right] = X_0(1 - X_0)$. Therefore, by an averaging argument, there exists a round i such that $\mathbb{E}\left[(X_i - X_{i-1})^2\right] \geq \frac{1}{n}X_0(1-X_0)$. Theorem 3 proves the existence of a martingale that achieves the lower-bound even for non-constant stopping times.

This result provides an alternate technique to obtain the upper-bound to $C_n(X)$ in Lemma 1.

A   Proof of Lemma 1

In this appendix, we summarize a high-level argument proving Lemma 1. For a complete proof, readers are encouraged to read the full version of this paper [27].

Recall that we defined $L_n(X) = \frac{2}{\sqrt{2n-1}}X(1-X)$ and $U_n(X) = \frac{1}{\sqrt{n}}\sqrt{X(1-X)}$. Our objective is to inductively prove that $U_n \succcurlyeq C_n \succcurlyeq L_n$, for $n \geq 1$.

A crucial property of convex upwards curves that we use in our proof is the following. Suppose we have $C \succcurlyeq D$, where C and D are two convex upwards curves above the axis $Y = 0$ defined in the domain $X \in [0,1]$ containing the points $(0,0)$ and $(1,0)$. Then, we have $T(C) \succcurlyeq T(D)$. This result is formalized in Lemma 2 and Fig. 10 summarizes the intuition of its proof.

Lemma 2. *Let C and D be concave downward curves in the domain $X \in [0,1]$, and both curves C and D are above the axis $Y = 0$ and contain the points $(0,0)$ and $(1,0)$. Let C and D be curves such that $C \succcurlyeq D$ in the domain $X \in [0,1]$, then we have $T(C) \succcurlyeq T(D)$.*

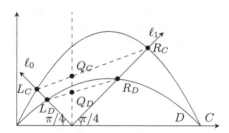

Fig. 10. Summary of the intuition underlying the proof of Lemma 2.

Base Case of $n = 1$. Since, $C_1(X) = L_1(X) = 2X(1 - X)$, it is obvious that $C_1 \succcurlyeq L_1$. Moreover, we know that $U_1(X) = \sqrt{X(1 - X)}$. It is easy to verify that $U_1(X) \geq C_1(X)$ for all $X \in [0,1]$ which is equivalent to $U_1 \succcurlyeq C_1$.

Inductive Argument. Figure 11 pictorially summarizes the intuition underlying our inductive argument.

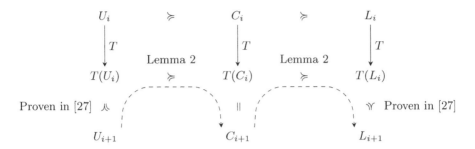

Fig. 11. The outline of the inductive proof demonstrating that if the curves U_i and L_i sandwich the curve C_i, then the curves U_{i+1} and L_{i+1} sandwich the curve C_{i+1}. Recall that the notation "$A \succcurlyeq B$" implies that the curve A lies on-or-above the curve B.

Suppose we inductively have $U_n \succcurlyeq C_n \succcurlyeq L_n$. Then, we have $T(U_n) \succcurlyeq T(C_n) \succcurlyeq T(L_n)$ (by Lemma 2). Note that $C_{n+1} = T(C_n)$. In the full version of the paper [27], we prove that $T(L_n) \succcurlyeq L_{n+1}$, and $U_{n+1} \succcurlyeq T(U_n)$. Consequently, it follows that $U_{n+1} \succcurlyeq C_{n+1} \succcurlyeq L_{n+1}$.

B Large L_2-Gaps in Martingale: Proof of Theorem 3

In Sect. 3 we measured the gaps in martingales using the L_1-norm. In this section, we extend this analysis to gaps in martingales using the L_2-norm. To begin, let us fix X_0 and n. We change the definition of susceptibility to

$$\sup_{\text{stopping time } \tau} \mathbb{E}\left[(X_\tau - X_{\tau-1})^2\right]$$

Our objective is to characterize the martingale that is least susceptible

$$D_n(X_0) := \inf_{(X_0,\ldots,X_n)} \sup_{\text{stopping time } \tau} \mathbb{E}\left[(X_\tau - X_{\tau-1})^2\right]$$

We shall proceed by induction on n and prove that $D_n(X_0) = \frac{1}{n}X_0(1 - X_0)$. Furthermore, there are martingales such that any stopping time τ has $D_n(X_0)$ susceptibility.

Base Case $n = 1$. Note that in this case (see Fig. 5) the optimal stopping time is $\tau = 1$.

$$\mathrm{opt}_1(X_0, 2) = D_1(X_0) = (1 - X_0)X_0^2 + X_0(1 - X_0)^2 = X_0(1 - X_0)$$

General Inductive Step. Let us fix $X_0 = x$ and $n = d \geqslant 2$. We proceed analogous to the argument in Sect. 3.1. The adversary can either decide to stop at the child j (see Fig. 6 for reference) or continue to the subtree rooted at it to find a better stopping time.

Overall, the adversary gets the following contribution from the j-th child

$$\max \left\{ (x^{(j)} - x)^2, D_{d-1}(x^{(j)}) \right\}$$

The adversary obtains a score that is at least the height of Q in Fig. 12. Furthermore, a martingale designer can choose $t = 2$, and $Z^{(1)} = P_1$ and $Z^{(2)} = P_2$ to define the optimal martingale. Similar to Theorem 1, the scores corresponding to all possible stopping times in the optimal martingale are identical.

One can argue that the height of Q is the *geometric-mean* of the heights of P_1 and P_2. This observation defines the geometric transformation T' in Fig. 13. For this transformation, we demonstrate that $D_n(X_0) = \frac{1}{n} X_0(1 - X_0)$ is the solution to the recursion $D_n = T'^{n-1}(D_1)$.

Remark 3. It might seem curious that the upper-bound U_n happens to be the square-root of the curve D_n. This occurrence is not a coincidence. We can prove that the curve $\sqrt{D_n}$ is an upper-bound to the curve C_n (for details, refer to the full version of the paper [27]).

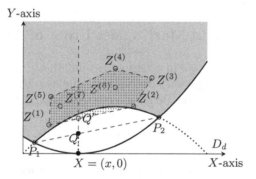

Fig. 12. Intuitive Summary of the inductive argument. Our objective is to pick the set of points $\{Z^{(1)}, Z^{(2)} \dots\}$ in the gray region to minimize the length of the intercept XQ' of their (lower) convex hull on the line $X = x$. Clearly, the unique optimal solution corresponds to including both P_1 and P_2 in this set.

Given. A curve D defined by the zeroes of the equation $Y = f(X)$, where $X \in [0, 1]$.
Definition of the Transform. The transform of D, represented by $T'(D)$, is the curve defined by the zeroes of the equation $Y = g(X)$, where, for $x \in [0, 1]$, the value of $g(x)$ is defined below.

1. Let $x_S(x), x_L(x) \in [0, 1]$ be the two solutions of $f(X) = (X - x)^2$.
2. Then $g(x) := \text{G.M.}(y^{(1)}, y^{(2)})$, where $y^{(1)} = f(x_S(x))$, $y^{(2)} = f(x_L(x))$, and G.M.$(y^{(1)}, y^{(2)})$ represents the geometric mean of $y^{(1)}$ and $y^{(2)}$

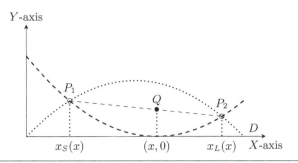

Fig. 13. Definition of transform of a curve D, represented by $T'(D)$. The locus of the point Q (in the right figure) defines the curve $T'(D)$.

References

1. Alon, B., Omri, E.: Almost-optimally fair multiparty coin-tossing with nearly three-quarters malicious. In: Hirt, M., Smith, A. (eds.) TCC 2016. LNCS, vol. 9985, pp. 307–335. Springer, Heidelberg (2016). https://doi.org/10.1007/978-3-662-53641-4_13
2. Asharov, G.: Towards characterizing complete fairness in secure two-party computation. In: Lindell, Y. (ed.) TCC 2014. LNCS, vol. 8349, pp. 291–316. Springer, Heidelberg (2014). https://doi.org/10.1007/978-3-642-54242-8_13
3. Asharov, G., Beimel, A., Makriyannis, N., Omri, E.: Complete characterization of fairness in secure two-party computation of boolean functions. In: Dodis, Y., Nielsen, J.B. (eds.) TCC 2015. LNCS, vol. 9014, pp. 199–228. Springer, Heidelberg (2015). https://doi.org/10.1007/978-3-662-46494-6_10
4. Asharov, G., Lindell, Y., Rabin, T.: A full characterization of functions that imply fair coin tossing and ramifications to fairness. In: Sahai, A. (ed.) TCC 2013. LNCS, vol. 7785, pp. 243–262. Springer, Heidelberg (2013). https://doi.org/10.1007/978-3-642-36594-2_14
5. Awerbuch, B., Blum, M., Chor, B., Goldwasser, S., Micali, S.: How to implement Bracha's O(log n) byzantine agreement algorithm. Unpublished manuscript (1985)
6. Azuma, K.: Weighted sums of certain dependent random variables. Tohoku Math. J. (2) **19**(3), 357–367 (1967). https://doi.org/10.2748/tmj/1178243286
7. Beimel, A., Haitner, I., Makriyannis, N., Omri, E.: Tighter bounds on multi-party coin flipping via augmented weak martingales and differentially private sampling. In: 2018 IEEE 59th Annual Symposium on Foundations of Computer Science (FOCS), pp. 838–849. IEEE (2018)

8. Beimel, A., Lindell, Y., Omri, E., Orlov, I.: $1/p$-secure multiparty computation without honest majority and the best of both worlds. In: Rogaway, P. (ed.) CRYPTO 2011. LNCS, vol. 6841, pp. 277–296. Springer, Heidelberg (2011). https://doi.org/10.1007/978-3-642-22792-9_16

9. Beimel, A., Omri, E., Orlov, I.: Protocols for multiparty coin toss with dishonest majority. In: Rabin, T. (ed.) CRYPTO 2010. LNCS, vol. 6223, pp. 538–557. Springer, Heidelberg (2010). https://doi.org/10.1007/978-3-642-14623-7_29

10. Blum, M.: How to exchange (secret) keys (extended abstract). In: 15th Annual ACM Symposium on Theory of Computing, Boston, MA, USA, 25–27 April 1983, pp. 440–447. ACM Press (1983). https://doi.org/10.1145/800061.808775

11. Bosley, C., Dodis, Y.: Does privacy require true randomness? In: Vadhan, S.P. (ed.) TCC 2007. LNCS, vol. 4392, pp. 1–20. Springer, Heidelberg (2007). https://doi.org/10.1007/978-3-540-70936-7_1

12. Buchbinder, N., Haitner, I., Levi, N., Tsfadia, E.: Fair coin flipping: tighter analysis and the many-party case. In: Klein, P.N. (ed.) 28th Annual ACM-SIAM Symposium on Discrete Algorithms, Barcelona, Spain, 16–19 January 2017, pp. 2580–2600. ACM-SIAM (2017). https://doi.org/10.1137/1.9781611974782.170

13. Cleve, R.: Limits on the security of coin flips when half the processors are faulty (extended abstract). In: 18th Annual ACM Symposium on Theory of Computing, Berkeley, CA, USA, 28–30 May 1986, pp. 364–369. ACM Press (1986). https://doi.org/10.1145/12130.12168

14. Cleve, R., Impagliazzo, R.: Martingales, collective coin flipping and discrete control processes (extended abstract) (1993)

15. Dachman-Soled, D., Lindell, Y., Mahmoody, M., Malkin, T.: On the black-box complexity of optimally-fair coin tossing. In: Ishai, Y. (ed.) TCC 2011. LNCS, vol. 6597, pp. 450–467. Springer, Heidelberg (2011). https://doi.org/10.1007/978-3-642-19571-6_27

16. Dachman-Soled, D., Mahmoody, M., Malkin, T.: Can optimally-fair coin tossing be based on one-way functions? In: Lindell, Y. (ed.) TCC 2014. LNCS, vol. 8349, pp. 217–239. Springer, Heidelberg (2014). https://doi.org/10.1007/978-3-642-54242-8_10

17. Dodis, Y., Ong, S.J., Prabhakaran, M., Sahai, A.: On the (im)possibility of cryptography with imperfect randomness. In: 45th Annual Symposium on Foundations of Computer Science, Rome, Italy, 17–19 October 2004, pp. 196–205. IEEE Computer Society Press (2004). https://doi.org/10.1109/FOCS.2004.44

18. Dodis, Y., Pietrzak, K., Przydatek, B.: Separating sources for encryption and secret sharing. In: Halevi, S., Rabin, T. (eds.) TCC 2006. LNCS, vol. 3876, pp. 601–616. Springer, Heidelberg (2006). https://doi.org/10.1007/11681878_31

19. Dodis, Y., Spencer, J.: On the (non)universality of the one-time pad. In: 43rd Annual Symposium on Foundations of Computer Science, Vancouver, BC, Canada, 16–19 November 2002, pp. 376–387. IEEE Computer Society Press (2002). https://doi.org/10.1109/SFCS.2002.1181962

20. Goldwasser, S., Kalai, Y.T., Park, S.: Adaptively secure coin-flipping, revisited. In: Halldórsson, M.M., Iwama, K., Kobayashi, N., Speckmann, B. (eds.) ICALP 2015. LNCS, vol. 9135, pp. 663–674. Springer, Heidelberg (2015). https://doi.org/10.1007/978-3-662-47666-6_53

21. Gordon, S.D., Hazay, C., Katz, J., Lindell, Y.: Complete fairness in secure two-party computation. In: Ladner, R.E., Dwork, C. (eds.) 40th Annual ACM Symposium on Theory of Computing, Victoria, BC, Canada, 17–20 May 2008, pp. 413–422. ACM Press (2008). https://doi.org/10.1145/1374376.1374436

22. Gordon, S.D., Katz, J.: Partial fairness in secure two-party computation. In: Gilbert, H. (ed.) EUROCRYPT 2010. LNCS, vol. 6110, pp. 157–176. Springer, Heidelberg (2010). https://doi.org/10.1007/978-3-642-13190-5_8

23. Haitner, I., Omri, E., Zarosim, H.: Limits on the usefulness of random oracles. In: Sahai, A. (ed.) TCC 2013. LNCS, vol. 7785, pp. 437–456. Springer, Heidelberg (2013). https://doi.org/10.1007/978-3-642-36594-2_25

24. Haitner, I., Tsfadia, E.: An almost-optimally fair three-party coin-flipping protocol. In: Shmoys, D.B. (ed.) 46th Annual ACM Symposium on Theory of Computing, New York, NY, USA, 31 May–3 June 2014, pp. 408–416. ACM Press (2014). https://doi.org/10.1145/2591796.2591842

25. Hoeffding, W.: Probability inequalities for sums of bounded random variables. J. Am. Stat. Assoc. **58**(301), 13–30 (1963). https://doi.org/10.1080/01621459.1963.10500830

26. Kenyon, C., Rabani, Y., Sinclair, A.: Biased random walks, Lyapunov functions, and stochastic analysis of best fit bin packing (preliminary version). In: Tardos, É. (ed.) 7th Annual ACM-SIAM Symposium on Discrete Algorithms, Atlanta, Georgia, USA, 28–30 January 1996, pp. 351–358. ACM-SIAM (1996)

27. Khorasgani, H.A., Maji, H., Mukherjee, T.: Estimating gaps in martingales and applications to coin-tossing: constructions and hardness. Cryptology ePrint Archive, Report 2019/774 (2019). https://eprint.iacr.org/2019/774

28. Lichtenstein, D., Linial, N., Saks, M.: Some extremal problems arising from discrete control processes. Combinatorica **9**(3), 269–287 (1989)

29. Makriyannis, N.: On the classification of finite boolean functions up to fairness. In: Abdalla, M., De Prisco, R. (eds.) SCN 2014. LNCS, vol. 8642, pp. 135–154. Springer, Cham (2014). https://doi.org/10.1007/978-3-319-10879-7_9

30. Moran, T., Naor, M., Segev, G.: An optimally fair coin toss. In: Reingold, O. (ed.) TCC 2009. LNCS, vol. 5444, pp. 1–18. Springer, Heidelberg (2009). https://doi.org/10.1007/978-3-642-00457-5_1

31. Nisan, N.: Extracting randomness: how and why-a survey. In: CCC, p. 44. IEEE (1996)

32. Nisan, N., Ta-Shma, A.: Extracting randomness: a survey and new constructions. J. Comput. Syst. Sci. **58**(1), 148–173 (1999)

33. Srinivasan, A., Zuckerman, D.: Computing with very weak random sources. In: 35th Annual Symposium on Foundations of Computer Science, Santa Fe, NM, USA, 20–22 November 1994, pp. 264–275. IEEE Computer Society Press (1994). https://doi.org/10.1109/SFCS.1994.365688

34. Trevisan, L., Vadhan, S.P.: Extracting randomness from samplable distributions. In: 41st Annual Symposium on Foundations of Computer Science, Redondo Beach, CA, USA, 12–14 November 2000, pp. 32–42. IEEE Computer Society Press (2000). https://doi.org/10.1109/SFCS.2000.892063

35. Zuckerman, D.: Simulating BPP using a general weak random source. Algorithmica **16**(4–5), 367–391 (1996)

Fully Homomorphic NIZK
and NIWI Proofs

Prabhanjan Ananth[1]([✉]), Apoorvaa Deshpande[2], Yael Tauman Kalai[3],
and Anna Lysyanskaya[2]

[1] UCSB, Santa Barbara, USA
`prabhanjan@cs.ucsb.edu`
[2] Brown University, Providence, USA
`{acdeshpa,anna}@cs.brown.edu`
[3] MIT and Microsoft Research, Cambridge, USA
`yael@microsoft.com`

Abstract. In this work, we define and construct *fully homomorphic* non-interactive zero knowledge (FH-NIZK) and non-interactive witness-indistinguishable (FH-NIWI) proof systems.

We focus on the NP complete language L, where, for a boolean circuit C and a bit b, the pair $(C, b) \in L$ if there exists an input $\mathbf{w}$ such that $C(\mathbf{w}) = b$. For this language, we call a non-interactive proof system *fully homomorphic* if, given instances $(C_i, b_i) \in L$ along with their proofs Π_i, for $i \in \{1, \ldots, k\}$, and given any circuit $D : \{0,1\}^k \to \{0,1\}$, one can efficiently compute a proof Π for $(C^*, b) \in L$, where $C^*(\mathbf{w}^{(1)}, \ldots, \mathbf{w}^{(k)}) = D(C_1(\mathbf{w}^{(1)}), \ldots, C_k(\mathbf{w}^{(k)}))$ and $D(b_1, \ldots, b_k) = b$. The key security property is *unlinkability*: the resulting proof Π is indistinguishable from a fresh proof of the same statement.

Our first result, under the Decision Linear Assumption (DLIN), is an FH-NIZK proof system for L in the common random string model. Our more surprising second result (under a new decisional assumption on groups with bilinear maps) is an FH-NIWI proof system that requires no setup.

Keywords: Homomorphism · Non-interactive zero-knowledge · Non-interactive Witness Indistinguishability

1 Introduction

Homomorphism is a desirable feature that enhances the capabilities of many cryptographic systems. Most notably, the concept of fully homomorphic encryption [13,18,25] has revolutionized the area of cryptography. Other primitives such as homomorphic signatures [10,20] and homomorphic secret sharing [12] have also found useful cryptographic applications [11,22]. In this work, we study homomorphism in the context of non-interactive proof systems. Our goal is to

---

A full version of this paper appears on ePrint [4].

© International Association for Cryptologic Research 2019
D. Hofheinz and A. Rosen (Eds.): TCC 2019, LNCS 11892, pp. 356–385, 2019.
https://doi.org/10.1007/978-3-030-36033-7_14

design homomorphic proof systems with secrecy guarantees; specifically, we focus on the most common secrecy guarantees studied in the literature, namely zero-knowledge [9] and witness indistinguishability [6,17].

Our Work: Fully-Homomorphic NIZK and NIWI Proofs. We introduce the notion of fully-homomorphic non-interactive zero-knowledge (FH-NIZK) and witness-indistinguishable (FH-NIWI) proof systems. In the simplest setting, this proof system allows for combining proofs for the instances A and B into a proof for the instance $A \wedge B$. In the more general setting, this proof system allows for combining proofs for multiple instances $A_1, \ldots, A_n$ using a function f into a single proof for $f(A_1, \ldots, A_n)$.

A naïve attempt to combine proofs for the instances $(A_1, \ldots, A_n)$ using a function f is to simply output the concatenation of the individual proofs on each of the instances $A_1, \ldots, A_n$ together with the function f. However, this combined proof does not resemble an honestly generated proof for the instance $f(A_1, \ldots, A_n)$. Our goal is to combine proofs in a way that is indistinguishable from an honestly generated proof for the instance $f(A_1, \ldots, A_n)$. We call this property *unlinkability*.

There are several reasons why unlinkability is an interesting feature: Firstly, it is often desirable to hide the fact that a proof was obtained by combining multiple proofs. Unlinkability also preserves the privacy of the underlying proof; namely, it ensures that homomorphic evaluation of multiple NIZK (resp., NIWI) proofs still results in a NIZK (resp., NIWI) proof. Moreover, it guarantees that the homomorphic evaluation can be multi-hop, meaning that the proofs can be evaluated upon multiple times. We describe the homomorphic evaluation procedure and unlinkability property below.

We define the notion of a fully-homomorphic proof system for the NP-complete language $L_\mathcal{U}$ which consists of instances (C, b), where C is a boolean circuit with single-bit output and b is a bit, such that there exists a witness $\mathbf{w}$ (a vector of bits) for which $C(\mathbf{w}) = b$. A non-interactive proof system for proving membership in this language consists of the algorithms Prove and Verify. A fully homomorphic proof system additionally has the algorithm Eval defined as follows:

Homomorphic Evaluation (Eval): On input k instances $\{z_i = (C_i, b_i)\}_{i \in [k]}$ accompanied with proofs $\{\Pi_i\}_{i \in [k]}$ for the statements $\{z_i \in L_\mathcal{U}\}_{i \in [k]}$, and a circuit $D : \{0,1\}^k \rightarrow \{0,1\}$, Eval outputs a proof Π^* for the statement $z^* = (C^*, D(b_1, \ldots, b_k)) \in L_\mathcal{U}$, where C^* is defined to be the circuit that on input $(\mathbf{w}_1, \ldots, \mathbf{w}_k)$ outputs $D(C_1(\mathbf{w}_1), \ldots, C_k(\mathbf{w}_k))$.

We define *unlinkability* as follows: A proof Π^* output by Eval on input $\{z_i \in L_\mathcal{U}\}_{i \in [k]}$ accompanied with proofs $\{\Pi_i\}_{i \in [k]}$, where Π_i is output by Prove on input z_i and a valid witness $\mathbf{w}_i$, should be indistinguishable from the output of Prove on input the instance $(C^*, D(b_1, \ldots, b_k))$ and witness $(\mathbf{w}_1, \ldots, \mathbf{w}_k)$. As mentioned above, unlinkability guarantees that the evaluation property preserves zero-knowledge (ZK) or witness-indistinguishability (WI) of an evaluated proof, depending on whether the fresh proof is ZK or WI respectively. We refer the reader to Fig. 1 for an illustrative description of unlinkability, and refer the reader to Sect. 4 for our definition of fully homomorphic proofs.

Our Results. We construct both a NIZK and a NIWI fully homomorphic proof system.

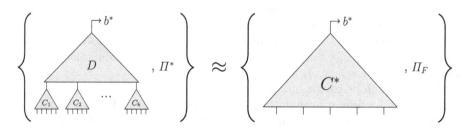

Fig. 1. Unlinkability property of Fully Homomorphic Proofs: Let Π^* be the output of Eval on input $\{(C_i, b_i) \in L_{\mathcal{U}}\}_{i \in [k]}$ accompanied with proofs $\{\Pi_i\}_{i \in [k]}$, where Π_i is output by Prove on input (C_i, b_i) and a valid witness $\mathbf{w}_i$. Let C^* be the circuit that on input $(\mathbf{w}_1, \ldots, \mathbf{w}_k)$, outputs $D(C_1(\mathbf{w}_1), \ldots, C_k(\mathbf{w}_k))$ and let Π_F be an honestly generated proof for the instance $(C^*, b^*) \in L_{\mathcal{U}}$. We require that Π^* is computationally indistinguishable from Π_F.

Theorem 1 (Informal). *Assuming Decisional Linear Assumption (DLIN), there exists a fully-homomorphic non-interactive zero-knowledge proof system in the common random string model.*

We describe the construction of FH-NIZK in the technical sections and defer the proof to the full version [4].

For constructing FH NIWI proofs, we rely on a new decisional assumption on groups with bilinear maps called *DLIN with leakage*, defined in Fig. 2.

A proof of security of the assumption in the bilinear generic model is provided in the full version of the paper [4].

Theorem 2 (Informal). *Assuming DLIN with Leakage, there exists a fully-homomorphic non-interactive witness-indistinguishable proof system in the plain model (i.e. without setup).*

We describe the construction of FH-NIWI in the technical sections and defer the proof to the full version [4].

Related Works. Most relevant to our work is the work on malleable proof systems [14, 16], who studied unary transformations, i.e., when Eval receives a *single* instance-proof pair and outputs a mauled instance along with the corresponding proof. The work of [14] studied malleable proof systems for specific relations, and [16] studied malleability for general relations albeit under knowledge assumptions. Moreover, these works consider NIZK proof systems and thus require trusted setup. We note that [14] satisfies a stronger proof of knowledge property (called controlled-malleable simulation-sound extractability) that we don't achieve in this work.

The notion of malleability, although seemingly limited due to its unary nature, has found many applications, such as verifiable shuffles [14], delegatable anonymous credentials [7,15] and leakage-resilient proof systems [5]. Rerandomizability [7], a special case of malleability, has also been studied in the literature. Following [14,16], Ananth et al. [3] construct *privately* malleable NIZK proof systems, and the works of [1,2] study homomorphic proof systems for specific relations.

Let f, h, g be three random generators in a group $\mathbb{G}$.
The assumption states that $\mathcal{D}_0(1^\lambda) \approx_c \mathcal{D}_1(1^\lambda)$, where:

- $\mathcal{D}_0(1^\lambda)$: Choose $R, S, t \leftarrow \mathbb{Z}_p^*$ and output (f, h, g) along with the following matrix:

$$\begin{bmatrix} f^R & h^S & g^{R+S} \\ f^{R^2} & h^{RS-t} & g^{R(R+S+1)-t} \\ f^{RS+t} & h^{S^2} & g^{S(R+S+1)+t} \end{bmatrix}$$

- $\mathcal{D}_1(1^\lambda)$: Choose $R, S, t \leftarrow \mathbb{Z}_p^*$ and output (f, h, g) along with the following matrix:

$$\begin{bmatrix} f^R & h^S & g^{R+S-1} \\ f^{R^2} & h^{RS-t} & g^{R(R+S-1)-t} \\ f^{RS+t} & h^{S^2} & g^{S(R+S-1)+t} \end{bmatrix}$$

Fig. 2. Description of the DLIN with leakage, with respect to a group $\mathbb{G}$ of prime order p with a bilinear map $e : \mathbb{G} \times \mathbb{G} \rightarrow \mathbb{G}_T$. We refer to this as DLIN with leakage assumption since the first row in both the distributions are indistinguishable assuming DLIN, and the second and third rows can be viewed as leakage.

It is important to stress that all the prior works, even in the case of unary transformations studied in the context of malleable proofs [14,16], assume trusted setup. Thus, in the context of WI proof systems, our results are especially surprising since it allows for combining proofs that were created completely independently, with no shared setup.

We now describe some applications of fully-homomorphic proofs.

Private Incremental Proofs. Incremental proofs, introduced by Valiant [26], allow for merging many computationally sound proofs [23] into one proof which is as short and easily verifiable as the original proofs. Incremental proofs have been applied in several contexts such as proof-carrying data [8] and cryptographic image authentication mechanisms [24]. It is useful in two types of settings: one where the computation dynamically evolves over a period of time, hence a proof of correctness of the entire computation cannot be computed all at once, and the other where different entities wish to compute a proof for the correctness of computation in a distributed setting.

The focus of prior works on incremental proofs was on succinctness whereas the focus of our work is on privacy. While our work does not achieve succinctness, as we will see later achieving privacy alone turns out to be quite challenging (especially, in the context of fully-homomorphic NIWIs). We hope that our tools can be combined with succinct incremental proofs to yield incremental proofs that enjoy both succinctness and privacy guarantees.

Commit-and-Compute Paradigm. Another application of fully-homomorphic proofs is the commit-and-compute paradigm. At a high level, the commit-and-compute paradigm allows a prover to commit to its sensitive data, and later on, prove statements about the committed data. Proofs from different provers can then be combined to infer arbitrary statements about the committed data. We give below an example that illustrates the applicability of this paradigm.

Verifiable Data Analysis. Consulting firms often collect data from different research groups, perform analysis on the joint dataset and then share the analyzed results with different organizations. For instance, there are firms that collect medical data from different research groups and share the analysis on the medical data to pharmaceutical companies. This raises concerns about trusting the research groups and the consulting firms to not lie about their conclusions. We can tackle this concern by using fully homomorphic NIZK or NIWI proofs. The research groups can publish their (committed) data along with a proof that it was collected from valid sources, without revealing the identity of the sources. The consulting firms can then perform analysis on the joint data sets and homomorphically compute a proof that the analysis was performed correctly. Moreover, the homomorphically computed proof will also hide the identities of the research groups involved in sharing the data to the firms.

Commit-and-compute paradigm is formalized by defining the NP language L_{COM}, a modification of $L_{\mathcal{U}}$ so that the instance includes a vector of commitments along with (C, b). The language L_{COM} is defined as follows:

$$L_{\mathsf{COM}} = \left\{ (C, (\mathsf{com}_1, \ldots, \mathsf{com}_n), b) \ \middle| \ \exists\{w_i, r_i\} \text{ s.t.} \ \begin{matrix} C(w_1, \ldots, w_n) = b, \text{ and} \\ \{\mathsf{com}_i = \mathsf{Commit}(w_i, r_i)\} \end{matrix} \right\}$$

The evaluation is defined similarly to that of homomorphic Eval for $L_{\mathcal{U}}$. We define and instantiate the commit-and-compute paradigm using fully-homomorphic proofs in the full version [4].

Roadmap. In Sect. 2, we give an overview of our techniques. In Sect. 3, we describe some notation and definitions. In Sect. 4, we present our definition of fully homomorphic NIZK and NIWI proof systems. In Sect. 5, we define and instantiate the building blocks for our constructions, and describe our DLIN with Leakage assumption (in Sect. 5.3). In Sect. 6, we construct fully homomorphic NIZK proofs for NP from DLIN. In Sect. 7, we describe our main result of fully homomorphic NIWI proofs from the DLIN with Leakage assumption. We refer the reader to the full version of the paper [4] for a detailed description of the constructions.

2   Technical Overview

Let us start with some intuition. Suppose we want to generate a proof for the satisfiability of $C_1 \wedge C_2$ for some circuits C_1, C_2. Given a proof Π_1 for the satisfiability of C_1 and a proof Π_2 for the satisfiability of C_2, clearly $\Pi = (\Pi_1, \Pi_2)$ is a proof for the satisfiability of $C_1 \wedge C_2$. However, such a proof does not satisfy unlinkability. Moreover, the structure of the proof $\Pi = (\Pi_1, \Pi_2)$ may be different from that of a fresh proof computed for the satisfiability of $C_1 \wedge C_2$.

To achieve homomorphism and unlinkability, a natural candidate is a proof system that works gate-by-gate as follows: Commit to all the wire values of the circuit and prove that each gate is consistent with the committed values. Such a proof structure is a good candidate because structurally, a proof of the composed instance $C_1 \wedge C_2$ will be similar to a fresh proof.

Indeed the beautiful work of Groth, Ostrovsky and Sahai [21] (henceforth referred to as GOS) has this proof structure and it is the starting point for our FH NIZK construction as well as our FH NIWI construction. GOS constructed NIZK and NIWI proofs under the decisional linear (DLIN) assumption. First in Sect. 2.1, we describe our FH NIZK construction which builds on the GOS NIZK. Then in Sect. 2.2, we describe our FH NIWI construction which contains the bulk of the technical difficulty in this work.

2.1   Overview: Fully Homomorphic NIZK

Recall that an $L_\mathcal{U}$ instance is of the form (C, out) where $C : \{0,1\}^t \to \{0,1\}$ and $\mathsf{out} \in \{0,1\}$. Let $\mathbf{w} = (w_1, \ldots, w_t)$ be a witness such that $C(\mathbf{w}) = \mathsf{out}$. Let us first recall the GOS NIZK proof for $L_\mathcal{U}$.

GOS NIZK. The GOS NIZK proof system is associated with a commitment scheme with public parameters (as we elaborate on later). The CRS consists of the parameters pp for the commitment scheme. The prover on input (C, out) along with witness $\mathbf{w}$ does the following:

1. Let $w_1, \ldots, w_n$ be the values induced by witness $\mathbf{w} = (w_1, \ldots, w_t)$ on all the wires of the circuit C. Commit to all the wire values with respect to pp, except the output wire. For every $i \in [n-1]$, denote by $\mathbf{c}_i$ the commitment to wire value w_i. Denote by $\mathbf{c}_n = w_n$.
2. For each $i \in [n]$, prove that the commitment $\mathbf{c}_i$ is a commitment to a boolean value. We refer to such proofs by *Bit Proofs*.
3. For each gate in C, prove that the commitments to the input and the output wires of the gate are consistent with the gate functionality. We refer to such proofs by *Gate Proofs*.

In their construction, GOS use a commitment scheme which has two indistinguishable modes of public parameters: perfectly binding and perfectly hiding. Loosely speaking, the perfectly binding mode is used to argue perfect soundness, and the perfectly hiding mode is used to argue zero-knowledge. In addition, they require the commitment scheme to be additively homomorphic and the additive homomorphism is used in the Gate Proofs.

GOS constructed NIWI proof systems for Bit Proofs and Gate Proofs, and proved that this is sufficient for their NIZK construction. Both Bit and Gate Proofs are computed using the openings of the commitments as the witness. Our FH NIZK construction follows a similar template (our NIZK construction is identical to the GOS NIZK) but in order to achieve unlinkability, we need additional properties from the commitment scheme as well as from the Bit Proofs and Gate Proofs, as we explain below.

Homomorphic Evaluation. Homomorphic evaluation works as follows: On input k instances $\{z_i = (C_i, b_i)\}_{i \in [k]}$ along with proofs $\{\Pi_i\}_{i \in [k]}$ where each Π_i is a proof that $z_i \in L_{\mathcal{U}}$, and a circuit D, we want to output a proof that $(C^*, b^*) \in L_{\mathcal{U}}$ where C^* is the composed circuit and $b^* = D(b_1, \ldots, b_k)$. First, compute a fresh proof for the circuit D with witness $(b_1, \ldots, b_k)$. Note that the fresh proof for (D, b^*) together with the proofs $\{\Pi_i\}_{i \in [k]}$, forms a verifying proof with respect to (C^*, b^*). This follows from the fact that in each proof Π_i, the output wire b_i is given in the clear. However this combined proof is distinguishable from a fresh proof (given the individual proofs $\{\Pi_i\}_{i \in [k]}$). Thus, to achieve unlinkability, we randomize this entire proof.

Randomizing the NIZK Proof. A proof system is said to be randomizable [7] if given a proof Π for an instance x, it is possible to randomize the proof Π to obtain a proof Π' for x, such that Π' is indistinguishable from a fresh proof for x. Randomizability of a proof system is sufficient for achieving unlinkability in our construction, as explained above.

At a high level, we randomize the proof Π as follows: Randomize all the commitments in the proof, and then "update" the existing proofs to be with respect to the randomized commitments. Thus, given the original Bit Proofs and Gate Proofs, we need to be able to "maul" them to be with respect to the new randomized commitments in such a way that the updated proofs are distributed as fresh Bit Proofs and Gate Proofs. We refer to such proofs as *malleable proofs*.

Ingredients for Our FH NIZK. In summary, for constructing FH NIZK, we use a commitment scheme (C.Setup, C.Commit, C.Rand) from GOS, which is also randomizable. We also need malleable proof systems for Bit proofs and for Gate proofs. (we define the corresponding proof systems (Bit.Prove, Bit.Verify, Bit.Maul) and (N.Prove, N.Verify, N.Maul) in Sect. 3).

As shown in GOS, both Bit Proofs and Gate Proofs can be reduced to *proofs of linearity* with respect to the NP language L_{Lin}. The language L_{Lin} is parameterized by three random group elements (f, h, g) in some underlying group $\mathbb{G}$ of prime order (which has a bilinear map), and whose instances consists of pairs

(A, B), where $A = (f^{a_1}, h^{a_2}, g^{a_3})$ and $B = (f^{b_1}, h^{b_2}, g^{b_3})$, such that $a_1 + a_2 = a_3$ or $b_1 + b_2 = b_3$[1].

GOS constructed a NIWI proof for L_{Lin}. Recall that for our purposes, we need malleable proof systems for Bit Proofs and Gate Proofs, and as a result we need the underlying NIWI proof for L_{Lin} to be malleable with respect to randomization. Namely given a pair $(\mathbf{A}, \mathbf{B}) \in L_{\mathsf{Lin}}$ with a NIWI proof Π, it should be possible to maul the proof Π for $(\mathbf{A}, \mathbf{B})$ into a proof Π' for a randomization $(\mathbf{A}', \mathbf{B}')$ of $(\mathbf{A}, \mathbf{B})$. We show that the GOS proof for L_{Lin} has the desired malleability property, and we refer the reader to Sect. 3 for the definition of a malleable proof system.

2.2   Overview: Fully Homomorphic NIWI

We now focus on our construction of a FH NIWI proof system for $L_{\mathcal{U}}$. As we will see, this is a significantly harder task compared to the FH NIZK, since NIWI is constructed in the plain model without a CRS.

The GOS NIWI Construction. We will first describe the GOS NIWI proof system. Recall that in the GOS NIZK construction, the CRS consists of the parameters pp of the commitment scheme. In a NIWI construction, there is no CRS. In the GOS NIWI, the prover chooses two parameters $(\mathsf{pp}^0, \mathsf{pp}^1)$ such that it is possible to publicly verify that one of them is binding. The NIWI proof for $(C, \mathsf{out}) \in L_{\mathcal{U}}$ is of the form $(\mathsf{pp}^0, \Pi^0, \mathsf{pp}^1, \Pi^1)$ where Π^b is the NIZK proof with respect to pp^b for each $b \in \{0, 1\}$.

Towards Homomorphic Evaluation and Unlinkability. It is not clear how to use the GOS NIWI construction to construct an FH NIWI. In particular, achieving unlinkability here is significantly harder. Intuitively, the difficulty stems from the fact that even though the GOS NIWI appears to be gate-by-gate, there is an over-arching pair of parameters associated with the entire proof, and this pair is different for different proofs.

In more detail, a fresh GOS NIWI proof as described above has two parameters $(\mathsf{pp}^0, \mathsf{pp}^1)$ associated with it. Thus, if we use an approach similar to the FH NIZK construction for composing proofs, namely if we prove that $(D(C_1, \ldots, C_k), b^*) \in L_{\mathcal{U}}$, given k instances $\{z_i = (C_i, b_i)\}_{i \in [k]}$ along with corresponding proofs $\{\Pi_i\}_{i \in [k]}$, where $b^* = D(b_1, \ldots, b_k)$, then the resulting composed proof will have $2k$ parameters associated with it. It is unclear how to randomize such a composed proof to look like a fresh proof which has only two parameters associated with it.

In order to achieve unlinkability in our construction, we diverge from the GOS construction. Rather than choosing a pair of parameters per proof, we choose a fresh pair of parameters $(\mathsf{pp}_j^0, \mathsf{pp}_j^1)$ for each gate of the circuit. As in the GOS construction, the honest prover chooses one of them to be binding and the other hiding such that one can publicly verify that indeed one of the parameters is binding. Recall that in the GOS NIWI construction, the prover

---

[1] If $a_1 + a_2 = a_3$ then A is said to be a linear tuple.

committed to each wire value with respect to two parameters $(\mathsf{pp}^0, \mathsf{pp}^1)$. Now that we are choosing fresh parameters per gate, the question is which parameters do we use to commit to a wire value?

We associate four parameters $\mathsf{pp}_i^0, \mathsf{pp}_i^1, \mathsf{pp}_j^0, \mathsf{pp}_j^1$ with an internal wire between the ith and the jth gate in the circuit. In our construction, we commit to the wire value with respect to all of these parameters and thus, have four commitments $\mathbf{c}_i^0, \mathbf{c}_i^1, \mathbf{c}_j^0, \mathbf{c}_j^1$ per wire. We compute Bit Proofs with respect to each of the four commitments, and compute Gate Proofs for every gate with respect to both parameters associated with that gate.

Ensuring Soundness. Recall that the GOS NIWI consists of two independent NIZK proofs Π^0, Π^1 with respect to parameters $\mathsf{pp}^0, \mathsf{pp}^1$ respectively. Thus, the commitments, Bit Proofs and Gate Proofs with respect to both the parameters are independent of each other, and Π^0, Π^1 are verified separately. This is not the case in our setting.

Our proof contains a pair of parameters per gate, and has four commitments per wire. Thus, we need to prove that the multiple commitments per wire commit to the same value. In particular for soundness, it is sufficient to prove that among the four commitments per wire, the two commitments corresponding to the two binding parameters commit to the same value.

However the verifier does not know which of the four parameters $\mathsf{pp}_i^0, \mathsf{pp}_i^1, \mathsf{pp}_j^0,$ pp_j^1 are binding. All we are guaranteed is that for every gate j, one of $(\mathsf{pp}_j^0, \mathsf{pp}_j^1)$ is binding. So in our construction, we give four pairwise proofs that *each* commitment with respect to gate i commits to the same value as *each* commitment with respect to gate j. Namely, for all $b_1, b_2 \in \{0, 1\}$, the commitments $(\mathbf{c}_i^{b_1}, \mathbf{c}_j^{b_2})$ with respect to $\mathsf{pp}_i^{b_1}, \mathsf{pp}_j^{b_2}$ commit to the same value. This ensures consistency with respect to the two binding commitments across gates i, j. This, along with the Bit and Gate proofs will ensure that there is a consistent boolean assignment $w_1, \ldots, w_n$ induced by the witness $\mathbf{w}$ across all the wires of the circuit, such that $C(\mathbf{w}) = \mathsf{out}$.

We emphasize that we do not provide consistency proofs between the two commitments $(\mathbf{c}_i^0, \mathbf{c}_i^1)$ for a gate i, and in fact this is crucial for achieving witness indistinguishability, as we explain later. Towards constructing such pairwise proofs, we define the language $L_{\mathsf{TC}}{}^2$ which consists of instances of the form $(\mathbf{c}_i, \mathbf{c}_j, \mathsf{pp}_i, \mathsf{pp}_j)$ where commitment $\mathbf{c}_i$ with respect to parameters pp_i and $\mathbf{c}_j$ with respect to pp_j commit to the same bit.

Arguing Witness Indistinguishability. The main challenge is to prove that the final construction is witness indistinguishable even given the additional L_{TC} proofs for instances of the form $(\mathbf{c}_i, \mathbf{c}_j, \mathsf{pp}_i, \mathsf{pp}_j)$. We note that even if the proof system for L_{TC} satisfies WI, we do not know how to argue that the final construction is WI. Intuitively, the issue is that an L_{TC} statement may have a unique witness, in which case WI offers no secrecy. As we explain below, we need our

---

^{2} TC stands for the language of Two Commitments.

L_{TC} proof system to have a secrecy guarantee of the flavor of strong NIWI (with respect to specific distributions).

To argue WI of our final FH NIWI construction, we prove that a proof Π_0 for $(C, \mathsf{out}) \in L_\mathcal{U}$ with respect to witness wit_0 is indistinguishable from a proof Π_1 with respect to witness wit_1. Let us zoom in on a wire k between gates i, j whose value changes from 0 (for wit_0) to 1 (for wit_1). Both Π_0, Π_1 will contain four commitments to the wire k with respect to parameters $\mathsf{pp}_i^0, \mathsf{pp}_i^1, \mathsf{pp}_j^0, \mathsf{pp}_j^1$, along with the four L_{TC} proofs (see Fig. 3).

Denote by $\mathsf{PP} = (\mathsf{pp}_i^0, \mathsf{pp}_i^1, \mathsf{pp}_j^0, \mathsf{pp}_j^1)$. Denote by $\mathsf{W}(b)$ the four commitments to bit b on wire k, that is $\mathsf{W}(b) = (\mathbf{c}_i^0, \mathbf{c}_i^1, \mathbf{c}_j^0, \mathbf{c}_j^1)$ where all the four commitments are to the bit b. Denote by $\mathbf{\Pi}(b) = (\pi^{00}, \pi^{01}, \pi^{10}, \pi^{11})$ where for all $b_1, b_2 \in \{0,1\}$, $\pi^{b_1 b_2}$ is a proof for $(\mathbf{c}_i^{b_1}, \mathbf{c}_j^{b_2}, \mathsf{pp}_i^{b_1}, \mathsf{pp}_j^{b_2}) \in L_{\mathsf{TC}}$.

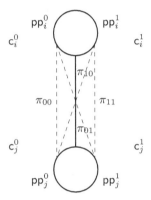

Fig. 3. Zooming in on wire k of circuit C with parameters $\mathsf{PP} = (\mathsf{pp}_i^0, \mathsf{pp}_i^1, \mathsf{pp}_j^0, \mathsf{pp}_j^1)$, commitments $\mathsf{W} = (\mathbf{c}_i^0, \mathbf{c}_i^1, \mathbf{c}_j^0, \mathbf{c}_j^1)$ and L_{TC} proofs $\mathbf{\Pi} = (\pi^{00}, \pi^{01}, \pi^{10}, \pi^{11})$.

To prove WI of the final construction, in particular the following should hold:

$$\big(\mathsf{PP}, \mathsf{W}(0), \mathbf{\Pi}(0)\big) \approx \big(\mathsf{PP}, \mathsf{W}(1), \mathbf{\Pi}(1)\big) \tag{1}$$

This indistinguishability requirement already implies a strong NIWI for L_{TC}, with respect to distributions $\mathcal{D}_0$ and $\mathcal{D}_1$, where $\mathcal{D}_b$ samples L_{TC} instances $(\mathbf{c}_i, \mathbf{c}_j, \mathsf{pp}_i, \mathsf{pp}_j)$ such that $\mathbf{c}_i, \mathbf{c}_j$ commit to the bit b.

For our analysis, Eq. (1) is insufficient since we need Eq. (1) to hold even given the rest of the proof for $(C, \mathsf{out}) \in L_\mathcal{U}$. In other words, we need Eq. (1) to hold given some auxiliary information aux, where given aux it should be possible to efficiently compute the rest of the proof from it. One possible aux is the openings of all the four commitments so that it is then possible to compute Bit and Gate Proofs for the rest of the proof. But if we give the openings with respect to 0 and 1 respectively, then the two distributions in Eq. (1) are clearly distinguishable.

So the question is, what aux can we give? Our key insight is that we can give equivocated openings for the commitments with respect to the two hiding parameters and honest openings with respect to the binding parameters, so that in both the distributions in Eq. (1), two of the openings are to 0 and two of them are to 1. Without loss of generality, we think of $\mathsf{pp}_i^0, \mathsf{pp}_j^0$ as the binding parameters and $\mathsf{pp}_i^1, \mathsf{pp}_j^1$ as the hiding parameters. We strengthen the requirement in Eq. (1) as follows:

$$\big(\mathsf{PP}(0), \mathsf{W}(0), \mathbf{\Pi}(0), \mathsf{O}(0)\big) \approx \big(\mathsf{PP}(1), \mathsf{W}(1), \mathbf{\Pi}(1), \mathsf{O}(1)\big) \tag{2}$$

where $\mathsf{PP}(b) = (\mathsf{pp}_i^b, \mathsf{pp}_i^{1-b}, \mathsf{pp}_j^b, \mathsf{pp}_j^{1-b})$, and $\mathsf{W}(b), \mathbf{\Pi}(b)$ are as before, and where in both the distributions, $\mathsf{O}(b)$ contains openings for the commitments $\mathsf{W}(b)$ to $(0, 1, 0, 1)$ respectively. This is the case since in the left-hand-side parameters $\mathsf{PP}(0)$, the second and fourth parameters are hiding, and we equivocate $\mathbf{c}_i^1, \mathbf{c}_j^1$ to open to 1, whereas in the right-hand-side parameters $\mathsf{PP}(1)$, the first and third parameters are hiding, and we equivocate $\mathbf{c}_i^1, \mathbf{c}_j^1$ to open to 0. Note that the L_{TC} proofs in $\mathbf{\Pi}(b)$ are still computed using the (honest) openings to b.

This is still not sufficient for our WI analysis. In order to argue WI of the final construction, we need to invoke Eq. (2) for every wire k in the circuit for which the value of wit_0 on wire k is different from value of wit_1 on wire k. These invocations are not completely independent since two different wires may be associated with the same gate, and in particular the two wires may be associated with an overlapping set of parameters. Thus, we need to further strengthen Eq. (2) to as follows:

$$\big(\mathsf{PP}(0), \mathsf{W}(0), \mathbf{\Pi}(0), \mathsf{O}(0), \mathsf{W}(1), \mathbf{\Pi}(1), \mathsf{O}(1)\big) \approx$$
$$\big(\mathsf{PP}(1), \mathsf{W}(1), \mathbf{\Pi}(1), \mathsf{O}(1), \mathsf{W}(0), \mathbf{\Pi}(0), \mathsf{O}(0)\big) \tag{3}$$

where $\mathsf{PP}(b), \mathsf{W}(b), \mathbf{\Pi}(b)$ and $\mathsf{O}(b)$ are as described above. We note that in the left-hand-side, $\mathsf{W}(1)$ are four commitments to 1 with respect to $\mathsf{PP}(0)$, $\mathbf{\Pi}(1)$ are the corresponding L_{TC} proofs computed using the honest openings to 1, and $\mathsf{O}(1)$ are the openings to $(1, 0, 1, 0)$ respectively. Similarly, in the right-hand-side, $\mathsf{W}(0)$ are four commitments to 0 with respect to $\mathsf{PP}(1)$, $\mathbf{\Pi}(0)$ are the corresponding L_{TC} proofs, and again $\mathsf{O}(0)$ are the openings to $(1, 0, 1, 0)$ respectively. We refer to the property from Eq. (3) as *Strong Secrecy* of L_{TC}. The Strong Secrecy requirement of L_{TC} as in Eq. (3) is sufficient for our WI analysis. Before explaining our WI analysis, we describe the ingredients for our FH NIWI Construction.

Recall that our NIWI proof for $(C, \mathsf{out}) \in L_{\mathcal{U}}$ is computed as follows: Choose a fresh pair of parameters per gate, commit to all the wire values with respect to all the associated parameters (2 commitments per input wire, 4 commitments per connecting wire), compute Bit Proofs (one per commitment), compute Gate Proofs (two per gate) and compute L_{TC} proofs (four per connecting wire). In order to randomize our NIWI proof, we randomize all the parameters, correspondingly update the commitments and update the proofs to be with respect to the randomized parameters and commitments. Specifically, we need the following ingredients for our final FH NIWI Construction.

Ingredients for our FH NIWI.

- A Commitment Scheme as required in the FH NIZK construction, but with the additional feature that allows for randomizing the parameters and updating the commitments to be with respect to the randomized parameters, so that the randomized parameters and commitments are distributed like fresh commitments.
- Bit Proofs and Gate Proofs as required in the FH NIZK construction, but with the following (modified) malleability property: Given a proof for commitments with respect to some pp, it is possible to efficiently randomize the parameters, correspondingly update the commitments and update the proofs to be with respect to the new parameters and commitments, such that they are all distributed like fresh ones. As in the FH NIZK, we require the Bit and Gate Proofs to satisfy WI.
- A proof system for L_{TC} with the same malleability property as Bit and Gate Proofs, and with the Strong Secrecy property as described in Eq. (3).

We show that the GOS commitment scheme (C.Setup, C.Commit, C.Rand) satisfies the additional feature that we require. The malleability of Bit Proofs and Gate Proofs can be reduced to the malleability of the NP language L_{Lin} described previously (similar to the FH NIZK construction). We then describe the corresponding proof systems (Bit.Prove, Bit.Verify, Bit.GenMaul) and (N.Prove, N.Verify, N.GenMaul).

Jumping ahead, we construct the proof system for L_{TC} also using the proof system for L_{Lin}, and the malleability of L_{TC} follows from the malleability of L_{Lin}. We then argue that the Strong Secrecy follows from our new *DLIN with Leakage* assumption.

WI Analysis. To explain our WI analysis, we describe an algorithm ProofGen that on input a sample from the left-hand-side distribution in Eq. (3), generates an entire proof Π for $(C, \mathsf{out}) \in L_{\mathcal{U}}$ which is indistinguishable from an honest proof generated using wit_0, and on input a sample from the right-hand-side distribution, ProofGen generates a proof Π which is indistinguishable from an honest proof generated using wit_1.

ProofGen *Algorithm.* Without loss of generality, we assume that every circuit is layered; that is, all the gates of the circuit can be arranged in t layers so that for all $i \in [t]$, all the output wires of gates from layer i are input wires to gates in layer $i + 1$. Fix any two witnesses wit_0 and wit_1 for $(C, \mathsf{out}) \in L_{\mathcal{U}}$.

On input $\big(\mathsf{PP}(b), \mathsf{W}(b), \mathbf{\Pi}(b), \mathsf{O}(b), \mathsf{W}(1 - b), \mathbf{\Pi}(1 - b), \mathsf{O}(1 - b)\big)$, ProofGen does the following:

1. Recall that $\mathsf{PP}(b) = (\mathsf{pp}_i^b, \mathsf{pp}_i^{1-b}, \mathsf{pp}_j^b, \mathsf{pp}_j^{1-b})$. Assign parameters $(\mathsf{pp}_i^b, \mathsf{pp}_i^{1-b})$ to all the odd layer gates of the circuit and $(\mathsf{pp}_j^b, \mathsf{pp}_j^{1-b})$ to all the even layer gates of the circuit. We will refer to $\{\mathsf{pp}_i^b, \mathsf{pp}_j^b\}$ as the *Left Parameters* and $\{\mathsf{pp}_i^{1-b}, \mathsf{pp}_j^{1-b}\}$ as the *Right Parameters*.

2. For all the input wires of the circuit C, commit to wit_0 with respect to pp_i^b (Left Parameter) and commit to wit_1 with respect to pp_i^{1-b} (Right Parameter).

3. For every wire k, produce the 4 commitments and 4 L_{TC} proofs for the wire as follows: Denote by $w_{k,0}$ the value induced by wit_0 on wire k, and denote by $w_{k,1}$ the value induced by wit_1 on wire k in the circuit.
   - If $w_{k,0} = w_{k,1}$ then compute the commitments and L_{TC} proofs honestly.
   - If $w_{k,0} = 0$ and $w_{k,1} = 1$ then use $\mathsf{W}(b)$ as the commitments and $\mathbf{\Pi}(b)$ as the L_{TC} proofs.
   - If $w_{k,0} = 1$ and $w_{k,1} = 0$ then use $\mathsf{W}(1-b)$ as the commitments and $\mathbf{\Pi}(1-b)$ as the L_{TC} proofs.

4. Compute the Bit Proofs and Gate Proofs honestly: We have the openings for all the commitments to the input bits (from Step 2). We also have the openings for the commitments to every non-input wire k, namely $\mathsf{O}(b)$ for $\mathsf{W}(b)$ when $w_{k,0} = 0$ and $w_{k,1} = 1$, or $\mathsf{O}(1-b)$ for $\mathsf{W}(1-b)$ when $w_{k,0} = 1$ and $w_{k,1} = 0$, or since we generated the commitments honestly when $w_{k,0} = w_{k,1}$. Note that the openings with respect to the Left Parameters always correspond to wit_0 and the openings with respect to the Right Parameters always correspond to wit_1.
   - Bit Proofs can be computed honestly since all the openings are to 0 or 1.
   - Gate Proofs can be computed honestly since all the openings with respect to the Left Parameters are consistent with wit_0 and all the openings with respect to the Right Parameters are consistent with wit_1.

5. Randomize the entire proof as follows:
   - For every gate, randomize the pair of parameters for that gate.
   - Update all the commitments (2 commitments per input wire, 4 commitments per connecting wire) to be with respect to the randomized parameters.
   - Maul all the Bit Proofs (one per commitment), all the Gate Proofs (two per gate) and all the L_{TC} proofs (four for every connecting wire) to be with respect to the updated parameters and commitments.

Finally output this randomized proof.

So far, we described the ProofGen algorithm that given a sample from the distributions in Eq. (3), generates an entire proof for $(C, \mathsf{out}) \in L_{\mathcal{U}}$. Let Π_{Gen}^0 be a proof output by ProofGen on input a sample from the left-hand-side of Eq. (3) and let Π_{Gen}^1 be a proof output by ProofGen on input a sample from the right-hand-side of Eq. (3).

From Eq. (3), it follows that $\Pi_{\mathsf{Gen}}^0 \approx \Pi_{\mathsf{Gen}}^1$. All that remains is to argue that $\Pi_0 \approx \Pi_{\mathsf{Gen}}^0$ and $\Pi_1 \approx \Pi_{\mathsf{Gen}}^1$, where Π_b is an honestly computed proof for $(C, \mathsf{out}) \in L_{\mathcal{U}}$ using witness wit_b. Note that Π_0 and Π_{Gen}^0 are identical except that Π_{Gen}^0 uses equivocated openings to wit_1 on the Right Parameters to compute the Bit and Gate Proofs. Hence, $\Pi_0 \approx \Pi_{\mathsf{Gen}}^0$ follows from WI of the Bit and Gate Proofs, and in addition follows by the randomizability of the commitment scheme and the malleability of the underlying proofs. By a similar argument, $\Pi_1 \approx \Pi_{\mathsf{Gen}}^1$. Thus, WI of the final construction follows form the Strong Secrecy of L_{TC}.

Constructing the L_{TC} Proof System. We construct a proof system for L_{TC} with the following properties:

1. Strong Secrecy: As defined in Eq. (3).
2. Malleability: Given a proof π for $(\mathbf{c}_1, \mathbf{c}_2, \mathsf{pp}_1, \mathsf{pp}_2) \in L_{TC}$, one can efficiently randomize the parameters to obtain $\mathsf{pp}_1', \mathsf{pp}_2'$, update the commitments to obtain $\mathbf{c}_1', \mathbf{c}_2'$ which are with respect to $\mathsf{pp}_1', \mathsf{pp}_2'$, and then maul π to a proof π' for $(\mathbf{c}_1', \mathbf{c}_2', \mathsf{pp}_1', \mathsf{pp}_2') \in L_{TC}$ such that $(\mathbf{c}_1', \mathbf{c}_2', \mathsf{pp}_1', \mathsf{pp}_2')$ looks like a fresh instance and π' is distributed like a fresh proof.
3. Soundness: We require that soundness holds for all instances $(\mathbf{c}_1, \mathbf{c}_2, \mathsf{pp}_1, \mathsf{pp}_2)$ where both $\mathsf{pp}_1, \mathsf{pp}_2$ are binding. As noted above, this is sufficient for the soundness of the final construction.

We construct such a proof system using the malleable NIWI proof system for L_{Lin} described before. Recall that L_{Lin} is a parameterized language with parameters $\mathsf{pp} = (f, h, g)$ where f, h, g are generators of a group $\mathbb{G}$, and it consists of a pair of tuples $(\mathbf{A}, \mathbf{B})$ such that one of them is of the form $(f^{a_1}, h^{a_2}, g^{a_3})$ where $a_3 = a_1 + a_2$.

We reduce proving that $(\mathbf{c}_1, \mathbf{c}_2, \mathsf{pp}_1, \mathsf{pp}_2) \in L_{TC}$ to proving that $(\mathbf{A}, \mathbf{B}) \in L_{Lin}$ for some $(\mathbf{A}, \mathbf{B})$. However, we only know how to do this reduction for L_{TC} instances $(\mathbf{c}_1, \mathbf{c}_2, \mathsf{pp}_1, \mathsf{pp}_2)$ for which $\mathsf{pp}_1 = \mathsf{pp}_2$. Therefore, we consider an NP-relation for L_{TC} with an additional witness which lets us convert an instance $(\mathbf{c}_1, \mathbf{c}_2, \mathsf{pp}_1, \mathsf{pp}_2)$ into an instance $(\mathbf{c}_*, \mathbf{c}_2, \mathsf{pp}_2, \mathsf{pp}_2)$. The additional witness for $(\mathbf{c}_1, \mathbf{c}_2, \mathsf{pp}_1, \mathsf{pp}_2)$ is a hard-to-compute function of the parameters $\mathsf{pp}_1, \mathsf{pp}_2$, and we refer to it as an "intermediate parameter" pp_* of $\mathsf{pp}_1, \mathsf{pp}_2$. Using the intermediate parameter pp_* we can convert the commitment $\mathbf{c}_1$ with respect to pp_1 into a commitment $\mathbf{c}_*$ with respect to pp_2.

More specifically in our proof, pp_* helps in converting the commitment $\mathbf{c}_1$ with respect to parameters pp_1, into a commitment $\mathbf{c}_*$ (to the same value) with respect to pp_2. Then, we can reduce the instance $(\mathbf{c}_*, \mathbf{c}_2, \mathsf{pp}_2, \mathsf{pp}_2) \in L_{TC}$ to a pair of tuples $(\mathbf{A}, \mathbf{B}) \in L_{Lin}$. The soundness and malleability of the L_{TC} proof system follows from the corresponding properties of L_{Lin} proof system. We refer to the full version [4] for a detailed description of the construction.

Strong Secrecy from DLIN with Leakage. All that remains is to show that the strong secrecy of L_{TC} follows from our new assumption of DLIN with Leakage. We first prove that Strong Secrecy of L_{TC} follows from the fact that the NIWI for L_{Lin} is strong WI with respect to the following distributions $\mathcal{D}_0$ and $\mathcal{D}_1$.

- $\mathcal{D}_0$ generates $(\mathbf{A}, \mathbf{B})$ where $\mathbf{A} = (f^{a_1}, h^{a_2}, g^{a_3})$ for random a_1, a_2, a_3 such that $a_1 + a_2 = a_3$, and $\mathbf{B} = (f^{a_1}, h^{a_2}, g^{a_3+1})$.
- $\mathcal{D}_1$ generates $(\mathbf{A}, \mathbf{B})$ where $\mathbf{A} = (f^{a_1}, h^{a_2}, g^{a_3-1})$ for random a_1, a_2, a_3 such that $a_1 + a_2 = a_3$, and $\mathbf{B} = (f^{a_1}, h^{a_2}, g^{a_3})$.

We then prove that the proof system for L_{Lin} is strong WI with respect to $\mathcal{D}_0$ and $\mathcal{D}_1$ under DLIN with Leakage assumption. We refer to full version [4] for a detailed description of the reduction.

3 Preliminaries

We denote the security parameter by λ. We use PPT to denote that an algorithm is probabilistic polynomial time. We denote by $y \leftarrow A(x)$ if y is the output of a single execution of A on input x. We denote by $y = A(x; r)$ to explicitly mention the randomness used in the execution. We denote $y \in A(x)$ if there exists randomness r such that $y = A(x; r)$.

We use $[n]$ to represent the set $\{1, \ldots, n\}$. Vectors are denoted by $\mathbf{a}$ where $\mathbf{a} = (a_1, \ldots, a_n)$ and a_i is the i th element of $\mathbf{a}$. $|\mathbf{a}|$ denotes the size of $\mathbf{a}$. $\mathbf{a} \circ \mathbf{b}$ denotes concatenation of the vectors $\mathbf{a}, \mathbf{b}$. $\{\mathcal{X}\}_{\lambda \in \mathbb{N}} \approx_c \{\mathcal{Y}\}_{\lambda \in \mathbb{N}}$ will denote that distributions $\{\mathcal{X}\}_{\lambda \in \mathbb{N}}$ and $\{Y\}_{\lambda \in \mathbb{N}}$ are computationally indistinguishable.

3.1 Definition of Proof Systems

Definition 1 (Non-interactive Zero-knowledge Proofs [9]). Let $L \in$ NP and let R_L be the corresponding NP relation. A triplet of PPT algorithms (Setup, Prove, Verify) is called a *non interactive zero knowledge* (NIZK) proof system for L if it satisfies:

- **Perfect Completeness:** For all security parameters $\lambda \in \mathbb{N}$ and for all $(x, w) \in R_L$,

$$\Pr[\mathsf{CRS} \leftarrow \mathsf{Setup}(1^\lambda); \ \pi \leftarrow \mathsf{Prove}(\mathsf{CRS}, x, w) : \mathsf{Verify}(\mathsf{CRS}, x, \pi) = 1] = 1$$

- **Adaptive Soundness:** For any all-powerful prover P^*, there exists a negligible function μ such that for all λ,

$$\Pr[\mathsf{CRS} \leftarrow \mathsf{Setup}(1^\lambda); \ (x, \pi) = P^*(\mathsf{CRS}) : \mathsf{Verify}(\mathsf{CRS}, x, \pi) = 1 \ \wedge \ x \notin L] \leq \mu(\lambda)$$

  When this probability is 0, we say it is *perfectly* sound.
- **Adaptive Zero Knowledge:** There exists a PPT simulator $S = (S_1, S_2)$ where $S_1(1^\lambda)$ outputs (CRS_S, τ) and $S_2(\mathsf{CRS}_S, \tau, x)$ outputs π_s such that for all non-uniform PPT adversaries $\mathcal{A}$,

$$\{\mathsf{CRS} \leftarrow \mathsf{Setup}(1^\lambda) \ : \ \mathcal{A}^{\mathcal{O}_1(\mathsf{CRS}, \cdot, \cdot)}(\mathsf{CRS})\} \approx_c$$

$$\{(\mathsf{CRS}_S, \tau) \leftarrow S_1(1^\lambda) \ : \ \mathcal{A}^{\mathcal{O}_2(\mathsf{CRS}_S, \tau, \cdot, \cdot)}(\mathsf{CRS}_S)\}$$

  where $\mathcal{O}_1, \mathcal{O}_2$ on input (x, w) first check that $(x, w) \in R_L$, else output $\bot$. Otherwise $\mathcal{O}_1$ outputs $\mathsf{Prove}(\mathsf{CRS}, x, w)$ and $\mathcal{O}_2$ outputs $S_2(\mathsf{CRS}_S, \tau, x)$.

Definition 2 (Non interactive Witness Indistinguishable Proofs [6,17]). A pair of PPT algorithms (Prove, Verify) is called a *non interactive witness indistinguishable* (NIWI) proof for an NP language L with NP relation R_L if it satisfies:

- **Completeness:** For all security parameters λ and for all $(x, w) \in R_L$,

$$\Pr[\pi \leftarrow \mathsf{Prove}(1^\lambda, x, w) \ : \ \mathsf{Verify}(1^\lambda, x, \pi) = 1] = 1$$

- **Soundness:** For any all-powerful prover P^*, if $P^*(1^\lambda) = (x, \pi)$ and $x \notin L$, then $\mathsf{Verify}(1^\lambda, x, \pi) = 0$.
- **Witness Indistinguishability:** For all non-uniform PPT adversaries $\mathcal{A}$, there exists a negligible function ν such that for every $\lambda \in \mathbb{N}$, probability that $b' = b$ in the following game is at most $1/2 + \nu(\lambda)$:
   1. $(\mathsf{state}, x, w_0, w_1) \leftarrow \mathcal{A}(1^\lambda)$.
   2. Choose $b \overset{\$}{\leftarrow} \{0, 1\}$. If $R_L(x, w_0) \neq 1$ or $R_L(x, w_1) \neq 1$ then output $\perp$. Else, if $b = 0$ then $\pi \leftarrow \mathsf{Prove}(1^\lambda, x, w_0)$, and if $b = 1$ then $\pi \leftarrow \mathsf{Prove}(1^\lambda, x, w_1)$.
   3. $b' \leftarrow \mathcal{A}(\mathsf{state}, \pi)$.

We say that a pair of PPT algorithms ($\mathsf{Prove}, \mathsf{Verify}$) is called a *non interactive proof system* for an NP language L if it satisfies completeness and adaptive soundness.

For our purposes, we will be using NIWI proofs with respect to parameterized languages of the form $L[\mathsf{pp}]$ where pp denotes some global parameters.

Definition 3 (Non interactive Witness Indistinguishability proofs for Parameterized Languages). Let Setup be a PPT algorithm that takes as input the security parameter and outputs a set of parameters pp. A pair of PPT algorithms ($\mathsf{Prove}, \mathsf{Verify}$) is called a NIWI proof for a parameterized NP language $L[\mathsf{pp}]$, with NP relation $R_L[\mathsf{pp}]$ if it satisfies:

- **Completeness:** For all security parameters λ, for all $\mathsf{pp} \in \mathsf{Setup}(1^\lambda)$ and for all $(x, w) \in R_L[\mathsf{pp}]$, $\Pr[\pi \leftarrow \mathsf{Prove}(\mathsf{pp}, x, w) : \mathsf{Verify}(\mathsf{pp}, x, \pi) = 1] = 1$.
- **Adaptive Soundness:** For any all-powerful prover P^*, there exists a negligible function μ such that for all λ,

$$\Pr[\mathsf{pp} \leftarrow \mathsf{Setup}(1^\lambda) : (x, \pi) \leftarrow P^*(\mathsf{pp}) : \mathsf{Verify}(\mathsf{pp}, x, \pi) = 1 \wedge x \notin L] \leq \mu(\lambda)$$

- **Witness Indistinguishability:** For all non-uniform PPT adversaries $\mathcal{A}$, there exists a negligible function ν such that for every $\lambda \in \mathbb{N}$, probability that $b' = b$ in the following game is at most $1/2 + \nu(\lambda)$:
   1. $\mathsf{pp} \leftarrow \mathsf{Setup}(1^\lambda)$.
   2. $(\mathsf{state}, x, w_0, w_1) \leftarrow \mathcal{A}(\mathsf{pp})$.
   3. Choose $b \overset{\$}{\leftarrow} \{0, 1\}$. If $R_L[\mathsf{pp}](x, w_0) \neq 1$ or $R_L[\mathsf{pp}](x, w_1) \neq 1$ then output $\perp$. Else if $b = 0$ then $\pi \leftarrow \mathsf{Prove}(\mathsf{pp}, x, w_0)$, else if $b = 1$ then $\pi \leftarrow \mathsf{Prove}(\mathsf{pp}, x, w_1)$. Send π to $\mathcal{A}$.
   4. $b' \leftarrow \mathcal{A}(\mathsf{state}, \pi)$.

Definition 4 (Randomizable NIZK and NIWI Proofs [7]). A NIZK proof system for an NP language L with NP relation R_L with algorithms ($\mathsf{Setup}, \mathsf{Prove}, \mathsf{Verify}$) is said to be a randomizable proof system if there exists a PPT algorithm Rand which on input a CRS, an instance x and a proof π, outputs a "randomized" proof π' for x such that for all non-uniform PPT adversaries $\mathcal{A}$, there exists a negligible function ν such that for every $\lambda \in \mathbb{N}$, the probability that $b' = b$ in the following game is at most $1/2 + \nu(\lambda)$:

1. CRS ← Setup(1^λ).
2. (state, x, w, π) ← $\mathcal{A}$(CRS).
3. Choose $b \xleftarrow{\$} \{0,1\}$. If Verify(CRS, x, π) $\neq 1$ or $R_L(x, w) \neq 1$ then output $\perp$.
4. Else if $b = 0$ then $\pi' \leftarrow$ Prove(CRS, x, w), else if $b = 1$ then $\pi' \leftarrow$ Rand(CRS, x, π).
5. $b' \leftarrow \mathcal{A}$(state, π').

More generally, a (WI) proof system (Prove, Verify) is said to be randomizable if there exists a PPT algorithm Rand with the same description and properties as above and where CRS = 1^λ.

Definition 5 (Malleable NIWI Proofs for Parameterized Languages [14]). Let (Prove, Verify) be a NIWI proof system for a parameterized NP language $L[\text{pp}]$ with NP relation $R_L[\text{pp}]$ where pp ← Setup(1^λ) (as per Definition 3). Let $T = (T(C, b), T_{\text{wit}})$ be a pair PPT transformations such that for every $(x, w) \in R_L$ and for every randomness $\sigma \in \{0,1\}^{\text{poly}(\lambda)}$, $(T(C, b)(\text{pp}, x; \sigma), T_{\text{wit}}(\text{pp}, x, w, \sigma)) \in R_L$.

Such a proof system is said to be *malleable* with respect to T, if there exists a randomized PPT algorithm Maul which on input parameters pp, an instance x, randomness σ and proof π, outputs a "mauled" proof π' for $T(\text{pp}, x; \sigma)$ such that the following properties hold:

Malleability. For all non-uniform PPT $\mathcal{A}$, for all pp $\in$ Setup(1^λ), for all $\lambda \in \mathbb{N}$,

$$\Pr\big[(x, \pi) \leftarrow \mathcal{A}(\text{pp}) \; ; \; (\sigma, R) \leftarrow \{0,1\}^{\text{poly}(\lambda)} \; ; \; \pi' = \text{Maul}(\text{pp}, x, \sigma, \pi; R) \; :$$
$$\big(\text{Verify}(\text{pp}, x, \pi) = 0\big) \vee \big(\text{Verify}(\text{pp}, T(\text{pp}, x; \sigma), \pi') = 1\big)\big] = 1$$

Perfect Randomizability. There exists a poly-time function f_T such that for all pp $\in$ Setup(1^λ) and every $(x, w) \in R_L[\text{pp}]$, for every $R, \sigma \in \{0,1\}^{\text{poly}(\lambda)}$,

$$\text{Maul}(\text{pp}, x, \sigma, \text{Prove}(\text{pp}, x, w; R); R') =$$

$$\text{Prove}(\text{pp}, T(C, b)(\text{pp}, x; \sigma), T_{\text{wit}}(\text{pp}, x, w, \sigma); S)$$

where $S = f_T(\text{pp}, w, R, R', \sigma)$. Moreover, if R', σ are uniform, then $f_T(w, R, R', \sigma)$ is uniformly distributed.

Definition 6 (Strong Non-interactive Witness Indistinguishability [19]). Let Setup be a PPT algorithm that takes as input the security parameter and outputs a set of parameters pp. Let $\mathcal{D}_0 = \{\mathcal{D}_{0,\lambda}\}_{\lambda \in \mathbb{N}}, \mathcal{D}_1 = \{\mathcal{D}_{1,\lambda}\}_{\lambda \in \mathbb{N}}$ be distribution ensembles in the support of $R_L[\text{pp}] \cap \{0,1\}^\lambda$ such that for every $b \in \{0,1\}$, $(x_b, w_b) \leftarrow \mathcal{D}_b$ such that $(x_b, w_b) \in R_L[\text{pp}]$.

A NIWI proof system (Prove, Verify) for a parameterized NP language $L[\text{pp}]$ is a *strong* non interactive witness indistinguishable (Strong NIWI) proof with respect to distributions $\mathcal{D}_0, \mathcal{D}_1$, if the following holds:

$$\text{If } \{\text{pp}, x_0\} \approx \{\text{pp}, x_1\} \text{ then } E_0 \approx E_1$$

where $E_b(1^\lambda)$ does the following: Sample $(x_b, w_b) \leftarrow \mathcal{D}_b(\text{pp})$ and compute $\pi_b \leftarrow$ Prove(pp, x_b, w_b). Output (pp, x_b, π_b).

3.2 Bilinear Maps

We will be working with abelian groups $\mathbb{G}, \mathbb{G}_T$ of prime order p equipped with a symmetric bilinear map $e : \mathbb{G} \times \mathbb{G} \mapsto \mathbb{G}_T$. We let $\mathcal{G}$ be a *deterministic* polynomial time algorithm that takes as input the security parameter 1^λ and outputs $(p, \mathbb{G}, \mathbb{G}_T, e, g_p)$ such that p is a prime, $\mathbb{G}, \mathbb{G}_T$ are descriptions of groups of order p, g_p is a fixed generator of $\mathbb{G}$ and $e : \mathbb{G} \times \mathbb{G} \mapsto \mathbb{G}_T$ is a bilinear map with the following properties:

- (Non-degenerate). For any generator g of $\mathbb{G}$, $g_T = e(g, g)$ has order p in $\mathbb{G}_T$
- (Bilinear). For all $a, b \in \mathbb{G}$, for all $x, y \in \mathbb{Z}_p$, $e(a^x, b^y) = e(a, b)^{xy}$

We require that the group operations and the bilinear operations are computable in polynomial time with respect to security parameter.

Assumption 1 (Decisional Linear Assumption). We say that the Decisional Linear (DLIN) Assumption holds for a bilinear group generator $\mathcal{G}$ if the following distributions are computationally indistinguishable:

$$\{(p, \mathbb{G}, \mathbb{G}_T, e, g) \leftarrow \mathcal{G}(1^\lambda) \; ; \; (x, y) \xleftarrow{\$} \mathbb{Z}_p^* \; : \; (r, s) \xleftarrow{\$} \mathbb{Z}_p \; :$$

$$(p, \mathbb{G}, \mathbb{G}_T, e, g, g^x, g^y, g^{xr}, g^{ys}, g^{r+s})\} \text{ and}$$

$$\{(p, \mathbb{G}, \mathbb{G}_T, e, g) \leftarrow \mathcal{G}(1^\lambda) \; ; \; (x, y) \xleftarrow{\$} \mathbb{Z}_p^* \; : \; (r, s, d) \xleftarrow{\$} \mathbb{Z}_p \; :$$

$$(p, \mathbb{G}, \mathbb{G}_T, e, g, g^x, g^y, g^{xr}, g^{ys}, g^d)\}$$

4   Fully Homomorphic Proofs: Definition

In this section we define fully homomorphic NIZK and NIWI proofs for the NP-complete language $L_{\mathcal{U}}$ consisting of instances of the form (C, b) where $C : \{0, 1\}^k \to \{0, 1\}$ is a boolean circuit and $b \in \{0, 1\}$. Formally, $L_{\mathcal{U}}$ is defined as:

$$L_{\mathcal{U}} = \{(C, b) \mid \exists \, \mathbf{w} \text{ such that } C(\mathbf{w}) = b\}$$

Let $R_{\mathcal{U}}$ be the corresponding NP-relation. We first define the notion of composing multiple instances of $L_{\mathcal{U}}$ to get a new instance in $L_{\mathcal{U}}$:

Composing $L_{\mathcal{U}}$ Instances: On input k instances $\{(C_i, b_i)\}_{i=1}^k$ where $C_i : \{0, 1\}^{t_i} \to \{0, 1\}$ and $C' : \{0, 1\}^k \to \{0, 1\}$,

$$\mathsf{Compose}(\{(C_i, b_i)\}_{i=1}^k, C') = (C, b)$$

where $C : \{0, 1\}^T \to \{0, 1\}$ and $T = \sum_{i=1}^k t_i$ and for all $(\mathbf{w_1}, \dots, \mathbf{w_k}) \in \{0, 1\}^{t_1} \times \cdots \times \{0, 1\}^{t_k}$,

$$C(\mathbf{w_1}, \dots, \mathbf{w_k}) = C'\big(C_1(\mathbf{w_1}), \dots, C_k(\mathbf{w_k})\big) \; \wedge \; b = C'(b_1, \dots, b_k).$$

4.1 Definition: Fully Homomorphic NIZK and NIWI Proofs

We now define fully homomorphic NIZK and NIWI proofs for the language $L_{\mathcal{U}}$ defined above.

Definition 7 (Fully Homomorphic NIZK Proofs). A randomizable NIZK proof system (Setup, Prove, Verify, Rand) is a fully homomorphic proof system if there exists a PPT algorithm Eval with the following input-output behavior:

$((C,b), \Pi) \leftarrow$ Eval(CRS, $\{(C_i, b_i), \Pi_i\}_{i=1}^{k}, C')$: The Eval algorithm takes as input the CRS, k instances $\{(C_i, b_i)\}_{i=1}^{k}$ along with their proofs $\{\Pi_i\}_{i=1}^{k}$, and a circuit $C' : \{0,1\}^k \rightarrow \{0,1\}$. It outputs the composed instance $(C,b) =$ Compose($\{(C_i, b_i)\}_{i=1}^{k}, C'$) and a corresponding proof Π such that the following properties hold:

Completeness of Eval: We require that evaluating on valid proofs (proofs that verify), should result in a proof that verifies. More concretely, we require that for all non-uniform PPT $\mathcal{A}$ and for all $\lambda \in \mathbb{N}$,

$$
\Pr\left[
\begin{array}{c}
\mathsf{CRS}\leftarrow\mathsf{Setup}(1^\lambda) \ ; \ (\{(C_i,b_i,\Pi_i)\}_{i=1}^k,C')\leftarrow\mathcal{A}(\mathsf{CRS}) \ ; \\
((C,b),\Pi)\leftarrow\mathsf{Eval}(\mathsf{CRS},\{(C_i,b_i),\Pi_i\}_{i=1}^k,C') : \\
\left(\mathsf{Valid}(C')=0\right) \vee \left(\exists\ i\in[k]\ \mathrm{s.t.}\mathsf{Verify}(\mathsf{CRS},(C_i,b_i),\Pi_i)=0\right) \vee \\
\left((\mathsf{Verify}(\mathsf{CRS},(C,b),\Pi) = 1) \wedge (C,b) = \mathsf{Compose}(\{(C_i,b_i)\}_{i=1}^k,C')\right)
\end{array}
\right] = 1
$$

where $\mathsf{Valid}(C') = 1$ if and only if $C' : \{0,1\}^k \rightarrow \{0,1\}$.

Unlinkability: We require that a proof for $(C, b) \in L_{\mathcal{U}}$ obtained by Eval should be indistinguishable from a fresh proof for the same instance. Namely, for any non-uniform PPT adversary $\mathcal{A}$, there exists a negligible function ν such that for every λ the probability that bit $=$ bit$'$ in the following game is at most $1/2+\nu(\lambda)$:

GAME$_{\mathsf{Eval}}$:

1. CRS $\leftarrow$ Setup(1^λ).
2. (state, $\{((C_i, b_i), \mathbf{w}_i, \Pi_i)\}_{i=1}^{k}, C') \leftarrow \mathcal{A}(\mathsf{CRS})$
3. Choose bit $\xleftarrow{\$} \{0,1\}$. If for any $i \in [k]$, Verify(CRS, $(C_i, b_i), \Pi_i) \neq 1$ or $((C_i, b_i), \mathbf{w}_i) \notin R_{\mathcal{U}}$, output $\bot$.
4. Else if bit $= 0$ then $((C,b), \Pi) \leftarrow$ Eval(CRS, $\{(C_i, b_i), \Pi_i\}_{i=1}^{k}, C')$. Else if bit $= 1$ then compute $(C, b) =$ Compose($\{(C_i, b_i)\}_{i=1}^{k}, C'$) and $\Pi \leftarrow$ Prove(CRS, $(C, b), \mathbf{w}$) where $\mathbf{w} = \mathbf{w}_1 \circ \cdots \circ \mathbf{w}_k$. Send (C, b, Π) to $\mathcal{A}$.
5. bit$' \leftarrow \mathcal{A}(\text{state}, (C, b, \Pi))$.

Definition 8 (Fully Homomorphic NIWI Proofs). A randomizable NIWI proof system (Prove, Verify, Rand) is a fully homomorphic NIWI proof system if there exists a PPT algorithm Eval with the same description and properties as in Definition 7 and where CRS $= 1^\lambda$.

5 Building Blocks for Fully Homomorphic Proofs

In this section we describe the building blocks for our fully homomorphic (FH) NIZK and NIWI constructions. In Sect. 5.1, we define a commitment scheme with additional properties, which we will use in our FH NIZK and NIWI constructions, and we then instantiate it from DLIN.

In Sect. 5.2, we describe a NIWI proof system for the NP language L_{Lin} (defined in Definition 10) based on DLIN. This proof system is the main ingredient in constructing FH NIZK and FH NIWI proofs.

For our FH NIWI construction, we need the NIWI proof for L_{Lin} to have additional properties of malleability and strong WI with respect to specific distributions. We prove that the proof system is malleable and we prove that strong WI holds under a new assumption on bilinear groups: *DLIN with Leakage*. We describe the corresponding bilinear assumption in Sect. 5.3.

5.1 Randomizable Commitment Scheme

Definition 9 (Randomizable Commitment Scheme). A Randomizable commitment scheme for message space $\mathcal{M}$ consists of PPT algorithms COM = (C.Setup, C.Commit, C.Rand) with the following descriptions and properties:

pp $\leftarrow$ C.Setup(1^λ): On input the security parameter, the setup algorithm outputs public parameters pp.

com = C.Commit(pp, $b; o$): Using the public parameters pp, the commit algorithm produces commitment com to message $b \in \{0,1\}$ using randomness $o \leftarrow \{0,1\}^{p(\lambda)}$ for some polynomial p. We will refer to o as "opening" for the commitment com.

com$'$ = C.Rand(pp, com; o'): On input parameters pp, commitment com, randomness o', C.Rand outputs a randomized commitment com$'$ to same value.

We require the following properties from the commitment scheme:

Perfectly Binding: For all $(m_0, m_1) \in \mathcal{M}$ such that $m_0 \neq m_1$ and for all $o_0, o_1 \in \{0,1\}^{\mathsf{poly}(\lambda)}$

$$\Pr[\mathsf{pp} \leftarrow \mathsf{C.Setup}(1^\lambda) \; : \; \mathsf{C.Commit}(\mathsf{pp}, m_0; o_0) = \mathsf{C.Commit}(\mathsf{pp}, m_1; o_1)] = 0$$

Computationally Hiding: Let pp $\leftarrow$ C.Setup(1^λ). For all $(m_0, m_1) \in \mathcal{M}$ and $o_0, o_1 \leftarrow \{0,1\}^{\mathsf{poly}(\lambda)}$, $\big(\mathsf{C.Commit}(\mathsf{pp}, m_0; o_0)\big) \approx_c \big(\mathsf{C.Commit}(\mathsf{pp}, m_1; o_1)\big)$

Perfect Randomizability: Let pp $\leftarrow$ C.Setup(1^λ). There exists an efficient function f_{com} such that for any randomness o, the following holds:
- For every $o' \in \{0,1\}^{\mathsf{poly}(\lambda)}$, C.Rand(pp, C.Commit(pp, $m; o$); o') = C.Commit(pp, $m; s$) where $s = f_{\mathsf{com}}(o, o')$.
- If o' is chosen uniformly at random, then $f_{\mathsf{com}}(o, o')$ is uniformly distributed.

We now describe additional properties that we require from our commitment scheme for our FH NIZK construction:

- **Additive Homomorphism:** We require that if c_1 and c_2 are commitments to m_1 and m_2 respectively, then there exists an efficient function f_{add} such that $c = f_{add}(c_1, c_2)$ is a commitment to $(m_1 + m_2)$.
- **Perfect Equivocation:** There exists a PPT algorithm C.Setup' and a polynomial time algorithm C.Equivocate such that
  - C.Setup' on input the security parameter, outputs pp', such that

$$\{pp \leftarrow \text{C.Setup}(1^\lambda) \; : \; pp\} \approx_c \{pp' \leftarrow \text{C.Setup}'(1^\lambda) \; : \; pp'\}.$$

  - Fix any $r_{pp} \in \{0,1\}^{\text{poly}(\lambda)}$, any $m, m' \in \mathcal{M}$ and any randomness $o \in \{0,1\}^{\text{poly}(\lambda)}$. Let $pp' = \text{C.Setup}'(1^\lambda; r_{pp})$ and $c = \text{C.Commit}(pp', m; o)$. Algorithm C.Equivocate on input (pp', r_{pp}, c, o, m') outputs o' such that $c = \text{C.Commit}(pp', m'; o')$. Also, for truly random o, (c, o') is distributed identically to (c'', o'') where o'' is chosen at random and $c'' = \text{C.Commit}(pp', m'; o'')$.

  Note that the parameters output by $\text{C.Setup}(1^\lambda)$ are *binding* and the parameters output by $\text{C.Setup}'(1^\lambda)$ are *hiding*.

We will denote a randomizable commitment which is also additively homomorphic (aH) and equivocable (E) as described above, by a RaHE-commitment scheme.

Remark 1. We will denote by **1** and **0** the canonical commitments to $1, 0$ respectively, namely the commitments computed with randomness $o = 0$. Given such a commitment it is possible to verify, that the commitment is indeed to 0 or 1.

Additional Functionalities for FH NIWI. In our FH NIWI construction, we use a RaHE-commitment scheme which has additional functionalities (OutParam, ValidParam, RParam, ChangeCom) with properties described below:

- **Outputting hiding parameters**: The deterministic algorithm OutParam takes as input parameters pp^0 and outputs pp^1 such that for all r_{pp}, if $pp^0 = \text{C.Setup}(1^\lambda; r_{pp})$, then $pp^1 = \text{C.Setup}'(1^\lambda; r_{pp})$.
- **Verifying if two parameters are valid**: The algorithm ValidParam is an efficient predicate that outputs 1 if $pp^0 \in \text{C.Setup}(1^\lambda)$ and $pp^1 = \text{OutParam}(pp^0)$. It outputs 0 if both parameters are hiding, namely if $pp^0, pp^1 \in \text{C.Setup}'(1^\lambda)$.
- **Randomization of parameters**: The RParam algorithm takes as input parameters pp, randomness r'_{pp}, and outputs new parameters pp' such that for all r_{pp} and for $pp = \text{C.Setup}(1^\lambda; r_{pp})$, the following properties hold:
  - There exists an efficient function f_{pp}: $f_{pp}(r_{pp}, r'_{pp}) = \sigma$ and $pp' = \text{RParam}(pp; r'_{pp}) = \text{C.Setup}(1^\lambda; \sigma)$.
  - $\text{RParam}(\text{OutParam}(pp); r'_{pp}) = \text{OutParam}(\text{RParam}(pp; r'_{pp}))$.

– **Transformation of commitments with respect to new parameters**: The ChangeCom algorithm takes in parameters pp, randomness r'_{pp}, commitment $\mathbf{c}$, and outputs commitment $\mathbf{c}'$ to the same value, with respect to the parameters $pp' = \mathsf{RParam}(pp; r'_{pp})$.

Proposition 1. *Assuming DLIN, there exists an additively homomorphic randomizable commitment scheme as per Definition 9.*

5.2 Proofs of Linearity

In this section we describe the main ingredient for our fully homomorphic proofs, which is a NIWI proof system with additional properties for the parameterized language $L_{\mathsf{Lin}}[pp]$.

Definition 10 (Linear Tuples). Let $(p, \mathbb{G}, \mathbb{G}_T, e, g_p) = \mathcal{G}(1^\lambda)$ and let f, h, g be any three generators of $\mathbb{G}$. A tuple $\mathbf{A} = (f^{a_1}, h^{a_2}, g^{a_3})$ is said to be *linear* with respect to (f, h, g) if $a_1 + a_2 = a_3$.

Before describing the parameterized language $L_{\mathsf{Lin}}[pp]$, we describe the corresponding setup algorithm for the parameters of the language, given by Lin.Setup.

Lin.Setup(1^λ): Compute $\mathcal{G}(1^\lambda) = (p, \mathbb{G}, \mathbb{G}_T, e, g_p)$. Choose at random $x, y, z \leftarrow \mathbb{Z}_p^*$. Compute $f = g_p^x, h = g_p^y, g = g_p^z$. Output pp $= [p, \mathbb{G}, \mathbb{G}_T, e, g_p, f, h, g]$.

We abuse notation and let pp denote the output of Lin.Setup as well as the output of C.Setup. Note that pp $\leftarrow$ Lin.Setup(1^λ) is a subset of pp $\leftarrow$ C.Setup(1^λ).

We now define the language $L_{\mathsf{Lin}}[pp]$ where pp $\leftarrow$ Lin.Setup(1^λ). $L_{\mathsf{Lin}}[pp]$ is the language consisting of a pair of tuples such that one of them is linear. It is defined as follows:

$$L_{\mathsf{Lin}}[pp] = \big\{ (\mathbf{A}, \mathbf{B}) \mid \exists \, (w_1, w_2, w_3) \, \big((w_1 + w_2 = w_3) \, \wedge$$
$$\big(\mathbf{A} = (f^{w_1}, h^{w_2}, g^{w_3}) \, \vee \, \mathbf{B} = (f^{w_1}, h^{w_2}, g^{w_3})\big)\big\}$$

NIWI Proof from GOS. We first describe the NIWI proof (Lin.Prove, Lin. Verify) for $L_{\mathsf{Lin}}[pp]$ from GOS [21]:

Lin.Prove$(pp, (A_1, A_2, A_3), (B_1, B_2, B_3), (a_1, a_2, a_3))$: Without loss of generality, let (a_1, a_2, a_3) be such that $(A_1, A_2, A_3) = (f^{a_1}, h^{a_2}, g^{a_3})$ and $a_1 + a_2 = a_3$. Choose $t \xleftarrow{\$} \mathbb{Z}_p^*$ and output proof Π which consists of the following matrix:

$$\begin{bmatrix} \pi_{11} = B_1^{a_1} & \pi_{12} = B_2^{a_1} h^{-t} & \pi_{13} = B_3^{a_1} g^{-t} \\ \pi_{21} = B_1^{a_2} f^t & \pi_{22} = B_2^{a_2} & \pi_{23} = B_3^{a_2} g^t \end{bmatrix}$$

Lin.Verify$(pp, (A_1, A_2, A_3), (B_1, B_2, B_3), \Pi)$:
 – Compute $\pi_{31} = \pi_{11}\pi_{21}$ and $\pi_{32} = \pi_{12}\pi_{22}$ and $\pi_{33} = \pi_{13}\pi_{23}$.

- Check $e(A_1, B_1) = e(f, \pi_{11})$, $e(A_2, B_2) = e(h, \pi_{22})$, $e(A_3, B_3) = e(g, \pi_{33})$.
- Finally check $e(A_1, B_2)e(A_2, B_1) = e(f, \pi_{12})e(h, \pi_{21})$, $e(A_2, B_3)e(A_3, B_2) = e(h, \pi_{23})e(g, \pi_{32})$ and $e(A_1, B_3)e(A_3, B_1) = e(f, \pi_{13})e(g, \pi_{31})$.

Proposition 2 ([21]). *Assuming DLIN, the proof system described above is a perfectly sound witness indistinguishable proof system for the language $L_{\mathsf{Lin}}[\mathsf{pp}]$ (as per Definition 3).*

Remark 2. If $\Pi = [\pi_{11}, \ldots, \pi_{33}]$ is a valid proof for $((A_1, A_2, A_3), (B_1, B_2, B_3)) \in L_{\mathsf{Lin}}[\mathsf{pp}]$, then $\Pi^{-1} = [\pi_{11}^{-1}, \ldots, \pi_{33}^{-1}]$ is a valid proof for $((A_1^{-1}, A_2^{-1}, A_3^{-1}), (B_1, B_2, B_3)) \in L_{\mathsf{Lin}}[\mathsf{pp}]$ and for $((A_1, A_2, A_3), (B_1^{-1}, B_2^{-1}, B_3^{-1})) \in L_{\mathsf{Lin}}[\mathsf{pp}]$.

GOS [21] provided a NIWI proof for $L_{\mathsf{Lin}}[\mathsf{pp}]$ as described above. In our work, we need the NIWI proof system to satisfy two additional properties: The first is malleability with respect to randomization, namely given a tuple $(\mathbf{A}, \mathbf{B}) \in L_{\mathsf{Lin}}[\mathsf{pp}]$ with NIWI proof Π, it is possible to randomize $(\mathbf{A}, \mathbf{B})$ to a new tuple $(\mathbf{A}', \mathbf{B}') \in L_{\mathsf{Lin}}[\mathsf{pp}]$ and maul the proof Π to be proof Π' with respect to $(\mathbf{A}', \mathbf{B}')$.

As a second property, we require that the proof system satisfies strong witness indistinguishability with respect to specific distributions (which we describe later in the section).

Malleable Proofs for L_{Lin}. We now show that (Lin.Prove, Lin.Verify) is malleable with respect to the transformation Lin.T = (Lin.Transform, Lin.WitTrans) defined as follows:

$$\mathsf{Lin.Transform}(\mathsf{pp}, \mathbf{A}, \mathbf{B}; (\mathbf{r}, \mathbf{s})) \triangleq ((A_1 f^{r_1}, A_2 h^{r_2}, A_3 g^{r_1+r_2}), (B_1 f^{s_1}, B_2 h^{s_2}, B_3 g^{s_1+s_2}))$$

where $\mathsf{pp} = [p, \mathbb{G}, \mathbb{G}_T, e, g_p, f, h, g]$, $\mathbf{A} = (A_1, A_2, A_3)$ and $\mathbf{B} = (B_1, B_2, B_3)$.

$$\mathsf{Lin.WitTrans}(\mathsf{pp}, (\mathbf{A}, \mathbf{B}), (w_1, w_2, w_3); (r_1, r_2, s_1, s_2)) \triangleq (w_1 + z_1, w_2 + z_2, w_3 + z_1 + z_2)$$
$$(z_1, z_2) = (r_1, r_2) \text{ if } \mathbf{A} = (f^{w_1}, h^{w_2}, g^{w_3}) \text{ else } (z_1, z_2) = (s_1, s_2) \text{ if } \mathbf{B} = (f^{w_1}, h^{w_2}, g^{w_3})$$

Mauled proof for $\mathsf{Lin.Transform}(\mathsf{pp}, \mathbf{A}, \mathbf{B}, (r_1, r_2, s_1, s_2)) = (A_1 f^{r_1}, A_2 h^{r_2}, A_3 g^{r_3}), (B_1 f^{s_1}, B_2 h^{s_2}, B_3 g^{s_3})$ is given by $\mathsf{Lin.Maul}(\mathsf{pp}, (\mathbf{A}, \mathbf{B}), (r_1, r_2, s_1, s_2), \Pi)$: Choose $t \leftarrow \mathbb{Z}_p^*$, and output a proof Π' consisting of the following matrix:

$$\begin{bmatrix} \pi'_{11} = \pi_{11} A_1^{s_1} B_1^{r_1} f^{r_1 s_1} & \pi'_{12} = \pi_{12} A_2^{s_1} B_2^{r_1} h^{r_1 s_2 - t} & \pi'_{13} = \pi_{13} A_3^{s_1} B_3^{r_1} g^{r_1 s_3 - t} \\ \pi'_{21} = \pi_{21} A_1^{s_2} B_1^{r_2} f^{r_2 s_1 + t} & \pi'_{22} = \pi_{22} A_2^{s_2} B_2^{r_2} h^{r_2 s_2} & \pi'_{23} = \pi_{23} A_3^{s_2} B_3^{r_2} g^{r_2 s_3 + t} \end{bmatrix}$$

Proposition 3. *Assuming DLIN, the proof system* (Lin.Prove, Lin.Verify, Lin.Maul) *is a malleable NIWI for $L_{\mathsf{Lin}}[\mathsf{pp}]$ as per Definition 5, with respect to transformation* Lin.T = (Lin.Transform, Lin.WitTrans).

Remark 3. We denote by $\mathsf{Lin.Transform}(\mathsf{pp}, (\mathbf{A}, \mathbf{B}), (r_1, r_2))$ the transformation given by $\mathsf{Lin.Transform}(\mathsf{pp}, (\mathbf{A}, \mathbf{B}), (r_1, r_2, r_1, r_2))$.

Strong NIWI for L_{Lin}. For our FH NIWI construction, we require that the NIWI proofs for $(\mathbf{A}, \mathbf{B}) \in L_{\text{Lin}}[\text{pp}]$ satisfy strong witness indistinguishability with respect to distributions $\mathcal{D}_0(\text{pp}), \mathcal{D}_1(\text{pp})$ for $\text{pp} \leftarrow \text{Lin.Setup}(1^\lambda)$. For every $b \in \{0, 1\}$, distribution $\mathcal{D}_b(\text{pp})$ is defined as follows:

Parse $\text{pp} = [p, \mathbb{G}, \mathbb{G}_T, e, g_p, f, h, g]$. Choose $a_1, a_2 \leftarrow \mathbb{Z}_p^*$, let $a_3 = a_1 + a_2$. Let $\mathbf{A}_b = (f^{a_1}, h^{a_2}, g^{a_3 - b})$ and let $\mathbf{B}_b = (f^{a_1}, h^{a_2}, g^{a_3 - b + 1})$. Output $(\mathbf{A}_b, \mathbf{B}_b)$.

Recall that $(\text{Lin.Prove}, \text{Lin.Verify}, \text{Lin.Maul})$ is said to be strong NIWI with respect to distributions $\mathcal{D}_0(\text{pp}), \mathcal{D}_1(\text{pp})$ (as per Definition 6), if the following holds:

$$\{\text{pp}, (\mathbf{A}_0, \mathbf{B}_0), \pi_0\} \approx \{\text{pp}, (\mathbf{A}_1, \mathbf{B}_1), \pi_1\}$$

where $(\mathbf{A}_b, \mathbf{B}_b) \leftarrow \mathcal{D}_b(\text{pp})$ and where $\pi_b \leftarrow \text{Lin.Prove}(\text{pp}, \mathbf{A}_b, \mathbf{B}_b, (a_1, a_2, a_3))$.

5.3 Assumption: DLIN with Leakage

In this subsection, we state our new assumption on bilinear maps: *DLIN with Leakage*.

Let $\text{pp} \leftarrow \text{Lin.Setup}(1^\lambda)$ and parse $\text{pp} = [p, \mathbb{G}, \mathbb{G}_T, e, f, h, g]$. DLIN with Leakage states that $\mathcal{D}_0'(1^\lambda) \approx_c \mathcal{D}_1'(1^\lambda)$ where $\mathcal{D}_b'(1^\lambda)$ is as follows:

- $\mathcal{D}_0'(1^\lambda)$: Choose $R, S, t \leftarrow \mathbb{Z}_p^*$ and output pp along with the following matrix:

$$\begin{bmatrix} f^R & h^S & g^{R+S} \\ f^{R^2} & h^{RS-t} & g^{R(R+S+1)-t} \\ f^{RS+t} & h^{S^2} & g^{S(R+S+1)+t} \end{bmatrix}$$

- $\mathcal{D}_1'(1^\lambda)$: Choose $R, S, t \leftarrow \mathbb{Z}_p^*$ and output pp along with the following matrix:

$$\begin{bmatrix} f^R & h^S & g^{R+S-1} \\ f^{R^2} & h^{RS-t} & g^{R(R+S-1)-t} \\ f^{RS+t} & h^{S^2} & g^{S(R+S-1)+t} \end{bmatrix}$$

Proposition 4. *The DLIN with Leakage assumption is secure in the generic group model.*

Proposition 5. *Assuming DLIN with Leakage, $(\text{Lin.Prove}, \text{Lin.Verify})$ is strong NIWI for $L_{\text{Lin}}[\text{pp}]$ with respect to $\mathcal{D}_0, \mathcal{D}_1$ (as described in Sect. 5.2).*

6 Fully Homomorphic NIZK Proofs

We use the following ingredients for our FH NIZK construction:

- Randomizable commitment scheme as per Definition 9, which is additively homomorphic and equivocable, denoted by

$$(\text{C.Setup}, \text{C.Commit}, \text{C.Rand})$$

- Malleable NIWI proof system for $L_{\mathsf{com}}[\mathsf{pp}]$ with respect to transformation Bit.Transform, denoted by

$$(\mathsf{Bit.Prove}, \mathsf{Bit.Verify}, \mathsf{Bit.Maul}) \text{ where}$$

$$L_{\mathsf{com}}[\mathsf{pp}] = \{\mathbf{c} \mid \exists\ (b, o) \text{ s.t. } \mathbf{c} = \mathsf{C.Commit}(\mathsf{pp}, b; o)\ \wedge\ b \in \{0, 1\}\}$$

for $\mathsf{pp} \leftarrow \mathsf{C.Setup}(1^\lambda)$, and transformation Bit.T $=$ (Bit.Transform, Bit.WitTrans) is given by $\mathsf{Bit.Transform}(\mathsf{pp}, \mathbf{c}, o') = \mathsf{C.Rand}(\mathsf{pp}, \mathbf{c}; o')$ and $\mathsf{Bit.WitTrans}(\mathsf{pp}, \mathbf{c}, (b, o), o') = f_{\mathsf{com}}(\mathsf{pp}, o, o')$ where o' is fresh randomness.

- Malleable NIWI proof system for $L_{\mathsf{N}}[\mathsf{pp}]$ with respect to transformation N.Transform, denoted by

$$(\mathsf{N.Prove}, \mathsf{N.Verify}, \mathsf{N.Maul}) \text{ where}$$

$$L_{\mathsf{N}}[\mathsf{pp}] = \big\{\{\mathbf{c}_i\}_{i \in [3]} \mid \exists\ \{b_i, o_i\}_{i \in [3]} \text{ s.t. } \mathbf{c}_i = \mathsf{C.Commit}(b_i; o_i)\ \wedge$$
$$(b_3 = b_1 \barwedge b_2)\ \wedge\ \{b_i \in \{0, 1\}\}_{i \in [3]}\big\}$$

for $\mathsf{pp} \leftarrow \mathsf{C.Setup}(1^\lambda)$, and the transformation: N.T $=$ (N.Transform, N.WitTrans) is given by $\mathsf{N.Transform}(\mathsf{pp}, \{\mathbf{c}_i\}_{i \in [3]}, \{o'_i\}_{i \in [3]}) = \{\mathbf{c}'_i\}_{i \in [3]}$ and $\mathsf{N.WitTrans}(\mathsf{pp}, \{\mathbf{c}_i, b_i, o_i, o'_i\}_{i \in [3]}) = f_{\mathsf{com}}(\mathsf{pp}, o, o')$ where $\mathbf{c}'_i = \mathsf{C.Rand}(\mathsf{pp}, \mathbf{c}_i, o'_i)$ for fresh randomness (o'_1, o'_2, o'_3) and where $o = o_1 + o_2 + 2o_3 - 2$ and $o' = o'_1 + o'_2 + 2o'_3 - 2$.

We now describe our construction:

$\mathsf{NIZK.Setup}(1^k)$: Output $\mathsf{pp} \leftarrow \mathsf{C.Setup}(1^\lambda)$.

$\mathsf{NIZK.Prove}(\mathsf{CRS}, (C, \mathsf{out}), \mathbf{w})$: Let $C : \{0, 1\}^t \rightarrow \{0, 1\}$ consist of n wires (including input wires and excluding output wire), one output wire and m NAND gates. Let $w_1, \dots, w_n, w_{\mathsf{out}}$ be the boolean values induced by $\mathbf{w} \in \{0, 1\}^t$ on all (input and internal) the wires of circuit C and where w_{out} is the output wire ($w_{\mathsf{out}} = \mathsf{out}$).

1. For wire i, commit to the value w_i as follows: Choose o_i at random and compute

$$\mathbf{c}_i = \mathsf{C.Commit}(w_i; o_i).$$

For the output wire w_{out}, use canonical commitments so that $\mathbf{c}_{\mathsf{out}} = \mathbf{1}$ if $\mathsf{out} = 1$ and $\mathbf{c}_{\mathsf{out}} = \mathbf{0}$ if $\mathsf{out} = 0$.

2. For each wire i (except output), generate a proof that commitment $\mathbf{c}_i$ commits to a bit. Namely, compute

$$\pi^i_{\mathsf{bit}} = \mathsf{Bit.Prove}(\mathsf{pp}, \mathbf{c}_i, o_i)$$

where o_i is the opening for commitment $\mathbf{c}_i$.

3. For each NAND gate j, let j_1, j_2 be the input wires and j_3 be the output wire with corresponding commitments $\mathbf{c}_{j_i}$ for $i \in [3]$. Compute

$$\pi_{\mathsf{gate}}^j = \mathsf{N.Prove}(\mathsf{pp}, \{\mathbf{c}_{j_i}\}_{i\in[3]}, \{o_{j_i}\}_{i\in[3]}).$$

Finally output

$$\Pi = \left[\{\mathbf{c}_i\}_{i=1}^n, \{\pi_{\mathsf{bit}}^i\}_{i=1}^n, \{\pi_{\mathsf{gate}}^j\}_{j=1}^m, \mathbf{c}_{\mathsf{out}} \right]$$

$\mathsf{NIZK.Verify}(\mathsf{CRS}, (C, \mathsf{out}), \Pi)$:   Parse Π $=$
$\left[\{\mathbf{c}_i\}_{i=1}^n, \{\pi_{\mathsf{bit}}^i\}_{i=1}^n, \{\pi_{\mathsf{gate}}^j\}_{j=1}^m, \mathbf{c}_{\mathsf{out}} \right]$.
1. For each wire $i \in [n]$, check whether $\mathsf{Bit.Verify}(\mathsf{pp}, \mathbf{c}_i, \pi_{\mathsf{bit}}^i) = 1$. Else output 0.
2. For each NAND gate $j \in [m]$, with input wires j_1, j_2 and output wire j_3 and with corresponding commitments $\mathbf{c}_{j_i}$, for $i = 1, 2, 3$. Check that $\mathsf{N.Verify}(\mathsf{CRS}, \{\mathbf{c}_{j_i}\}_{i=1}^3, \pi_{\mathsf{gate}}^j) = 1$. Else output 0.
3. Finally check that $\pi_{\mathsf{out}} = \mathbf{1}$ for $\mathsf{out} = 1$ and $\pi_{\mathsf{out}} = \mathbf{0}$ for $\mathsf{out} = 0$.

$\mathsf{NIZK.Rand}(\mathsf{CRS}, (C, \mathsf{out}), \Pi))$:   Parse Π $=$
$[\{\mathbf{c}_i\}_{i=1}^n, \{\pi_{\mathsf{bit}}^i\}_{i=1}^n, \{\pi_{\mathsf{gate}}^j\}_{j=1}^m, \mathbf{c}_{\mathsf{out}}]$.
1. For each wire i, choose o_i' at random and compute $\mathbf{c}_i' = \mathsf{C.Rand}(\mathsf{pp}, \mathbf{c}_i, o_i')$.
2. Compute $\pi_{\mathsf{bit}}^{i'} \leftarrow \mathsf{Bit.Maul}(\mathsf{pp}, \mathbf{c}_i, o_i', \pi_{\mathsf{bit}}^i)$.
3. For each NAND gate j, with input wires j_1, j_2 and output wire j_3, compute $\pi_{\mathsf{gate}}^{j'} \leftarrow \mathsf{N.Maul}(\mathsf{pp}, \{\{\mathbf{c}_{j_i}, o_{j_i}'\}_{i\in[3]}, \pi_{\mathsf{gate}}^j)$.
4. Finally keep the output proof $\mathbf{c}_{\mathsf{out}}$ same as before. Output

$$\Pi' = \left[\{\mathbf{c}_i'\}_{i=1}^n, \{\pi_{\mathsf{bit}}^{i'}\}_{i=1}^n, \{\pi_{\mathsf{gate}}^{j'}\}_{j=1}^m, \mathbf{c}_{\mathsf{out}} \right]$$

$\mathsf{NIZK.Eval}(\mathsf{CRS}, \{(C_i, b_i, \Pi_i)\}_{i=1}^k, C')$:
1. Compute $(C, \mathsf{out}^*) = \mathsf{Compose}(\{(C_i, b_i, \Pi_i)\}_{i=1}^k, C')$.
2. Let $\pi_{\mathsf{out}}^i \in \Pi_i'$ be the gate consistency proof for the output gate out^i of circuit C_i for $i \in [k]$. Compute $\widehat{\Pi}_i$ as the proof Π_i' without the proof π_{out}^i, namely $\widehat{\Pi}_i = \Pi_i' \setminus \pi_{\mathsf{out}}^i$.
3. Compute a proof for C' with witness $(b_1, \ldots, b_k)$ by computing: $\Pi^* \leftarrow \mathsf{NIZK.Prove}(\mathsf{CRS}, (C', \mathsf{out}^*), (b_1, \ldots, b_k))$ where $\mathsf{out}^* = C'(b_1, \ldots, b_k)$.
4. For each output gate out^i for C_i, $i \in [k]$, let i_1, i_2 be the input wires to the gate and i_3 be the output wire (with value b_i). Let o_{i_3}' be the randomness used in step 2 such that $\mathbf{c}_{i_3}' \in \Pi'$ and $\mathbf{c}_{i_3}' = \mathsf{C.Commit}(\mathsf{pp}, b_i, o_{i_3}')$. Compute $(\pi_{\mathsf{out}}^i)' = \mathsf{N.Maul}(\mathsf{pp}, \{\{\mathbf{c}_{j_i}', o_{j_i}'\}_{i\in[3]}, \pi_{\mathsf{out}}^i)$ where $o_{i_k}' = 0$ for $k \in [2]$.
5. Let $\Pi = [\widehat{\Pi}_1, \ldots, \widehat{\Pi}_k, \Pi^*, (\pi_{\mathsf{out}}^1)', \ldots, (\pi_{\mathsf{out}}^k)']$. Compute $\Pi' \leftarrow \mathsf{NIZK.Rand}(\mathsf{CRS}, (C, \mathsf{out}^*), \Pi)$. Finally output $(C, \mathsf{out}^*, \Pi')$.

Theorem 3. *Assuming DLIN, the construction as described above is a fully homomorphic NIZK proof system for $L_\mathcal{U}$ as per Definition 7.*

We refer the reader to the full version [4] for a proof of Theorem 3.

7   Fully Homomorphic NIWI Proofs

Our **first** *ingredient* for FH NIWI is (C.Setup, C.Commit, C.Rand), a RaHE-commitment scheme with the additional functionalities (OutParam, ValidParam, RParam, ChangeCom, ValidInter, InterParam) as defined in Sect. 5.1.
Our **second** *ingredient* is a malleable proof system (TC.Prove, TC.Verify, TC.Maul) for the language L_{TC} defined as follows:

$$L_{\mathsf{TC}} = \Big\{ (\mathbf{c}_1, \mathbf{c}_2, \mathsf{pp}_1, \mathsf{pp}_2) \mid \exists\ (b, \mathsf{pp}_*, o_1, o_2)\ \text{s.t.}$$
$$\{\mathbf{c}_i = \mathsf{C.Commit}(\mathsf{pp}_i, b; o_i)\}_{i\in[2]} \ \wedge\ \big(\mathsf{ValidInter}(\mathsf{pp}_1, \mathsf{pp}_2, \mathsf{pp}_*) = 1\big) \Big\}$$

Recall that pp_* is the intermediate parameter between $\mathsf{pp}_1, \mathsf{pp}_2$. It is a hard-to-compute function of the parameters which we require as an additional witness for the language.

The malleability is with respect to the transformation $\mathsf{TC.T} = (\mathsf{TC.Transform}, \mathsf{TC.WitTrans})$. $\mathsf{TC.Transform}$ takes as input an instance $(\mathbf{c}_1, \mathbf{c}_2, \mathsf{pp}_1, \mathsf{pp}_2)$, randomness $(r^1_{\mathsf{pp}}, r^2_{\mathsf{pp}}, o_1, o_2)$ and outputs transformed instance $(\mathbf{c}'_1, \mathbf{c}'_2, \mathsf{pp}'_1, \mathsf{pp}'_2)$.

In detail, $\mathsf{TC.Transform}$ on input $(\mathbf{c}_1, \mathbf{c}_2, \mathsf{pp}_1, \mathsf{pp}_2)$, does the following:

- Randomize the parameters as follows: For all $i \in [2]$, compute $\mathsf{pp}'_i = \mathsf{RParam}(\mathsf{pp}_i; r^i_{\mathsf{pp}})$.
- Change the commitment $\mathbf{c}_i$ to be with respect to the new parameters pp'_i, by computing $z_i = \mathsf{ChangeCom}(\mathsf{pp}_i, \mathbf{c}_i; r^i_{\mathsf{pp}})$ for all $i \in [2]$.
- Randomize the commitments as follows: For all $i \in [2]$, compute $\mathbf{c}'_i = \mathsf{C.Rand}(\mathsf{pp}'_i, z_i; o_i)$. Output $(\mathbf{c}'_1, \mathbf{c}'_2, \mathsf{pp}'_1, \mathsf{pp}'_2)$.

Correspondingly,

$$\mathsf{TC.WitTrans}\big((\mathbf{c}_1, \mathbf{c}_2, \mathsf{pp}_1, \mathsf{pp}_2), (b, \mathsf{pp}_*, o_1, o_2), (r^1_{\mathsf{pp}}, r^2_{\mathsf{pp}}, o'_1, o'_2)\big) = (b, \widehat{\mathsf{pp}}, r_1, r_2)$$

where $\widehat{\mathsf{pp}} = \mathsf{InterParam}(\mathsf{pp}_1, \mathsf{pp}_2, r^1_{\mathsf{pp}})$ and where for every $i \in [2]$, $r_i = f_{\mathsf{com}}(o_i, o'_i)$. Recall that $\mathsf{InterParam}$ and f_{com} are as per the definition of the RaHE-commitment scheme described in Sect. 5.1.

Let us look at the soundness and secrecy requirements from this proof system. We weaken the soundness requirement of our NIWI proof system and require a stronger secrecy property from the proof system. We now describe both of these properties:

1. *Weak Soundness:* Rather than requiring soundness to hold for every $(\mathbf{c}_1, \mathbf{c}_2, \mathsf{pp}_1, \mathsf{pp}_2) \in L_{\mathsf{TC}}$, we only require soundness to hold for all instances for which $\mathsf{pp}_1, \mathsf{pp}_2 \in \mathsf{C.Setup}(1^\lambda)$ (when both parameters are binding).
   Note that our construction for NIWI proof of L_{TC} achieves standard soundness, however for the FH NIWI construction it suffices for the proof system to have weak soundness.

2. *Strong Secrecy:* We require that the distributions $\mathcal{D}_{\mathsf{Bind}}$ and $\mathcal{D}_{\mathsf{Hide}}$ (described below) are computationally indistinguishable.

   – $\mathcal{D}_{\mathsf{Bind}}(1^\lambda)$: Choose r_{pp} at random and compute $\mathsf{pp} = \mathsf{C.Setup}(1^\lambda; r_{\mathsf{pp}})$. Compute $\mathsf{pp}' = \mathsf{OutParam}(\mathsf{pp})$. For every $d \in \{0,1\}$, do the following:
      • Choose o_d, o_d'' at random and compute $\mathbf{c}_d = \mathsf{C.Commit}(\mathsf{pp}, d \ ; o_d)$, $\mathbf{c}_d' = \mathsf{C.Commit}(\mathsf{pp}', d; o_d'')$.
      • Compute $\varPi_{\mathsf{TC}}^d \leftarrow \mathsf{TC.Prove}((\mathbf{c}_d, \mathbf{c}_d', \mathsf{pp}, \mathsf{pp}'), (d, \mathsf{pp}, o_d, o_d''))$.[3]
      • Compute $o_d' = \mathsf{C.Equivocate}(\mathsf{pp}', r_{\mathsf{pp}}, \mathbf{c}_d', o_d'', 1 - d)$.
      Output $\left(\mathsf{pp}, \mathsf{pp}', \mathbf{c}_0, \mathbf{c}_0', \mathbf{c}_1, \mathbf{c}_1', o_0, o_0', o_1, o_1', \varPi_{\mathsf{TC}}^0, \varPi_{\mathsf{TC}}^1\right)$.

   – $\mathcal{D}_{\mathsf{Hide}}(1^\lambda)$: Choose r_{pp} at random and compute $\mathsf{pp} = \mathsf{C.Setup}'(1^\lambda; r_{\mathsf{pp}})$. Compute $\mathsf{pp}' = \mathsf{OutParam}(\mathsf{pp})$. For every $d \in \{0,1\}$, do the following:
      • Choose o_d', o_d'' at random. Compute $\mathbf{c}_d = \mathsf{C.Commit}(\mathsf{pp}, 1 - d \ ; o_d'')$ and compute $\mathbf{c}_d' = \mathsf{C.Commit}(\mathsf{pp}', 1 - d; o_d')$.
      • Compute $\varPi_{\mathsf{TC}}^d \leftarrow \mathsf{TC.Prove}((\mathbf{c}_d, \mathbf{c}_d', \mathsf{pp}, \mathsf{pp}'), (1 - d, \mathsf{pp}, o_d'', o_d'))$.
      • Compute $o_d = \mathsf{C.Equivocate}(\mathsf{pp}, r_{\mathsf{pp}}, \mathbf{c}_d, o_d'', d)$.
      Output $\left(\mathsf{pp}, \mathsf{pp}', \mathbf{c}_0, \mathbf{c}_0', \mathbf{c}_1, \mathbf{c}_1', o_0, o_0', o_1, o_1', \varPi_{\mathsf{TC}}^0, \varPi_{\mathsf{TC}}^1\right)$.

Recall that

$$L_{\mathcal{U}} = \{(C, \mathsf{out}) \mid \exists \ \mathbf{w} \text{ such that } C(\mathbf{w}) = \mathsf{out}\}.$$

We will use the following ingredients in our FH NIWI construction:

– A RaHE-commitment scheme (C.Setup, C.Commit, C.Rand) with the additional functionalities (OutParam, ValidParam, RParam, ChangeCom, ValidInter, InterParam) as defined in Sect. 5.1.
– Malleable proof system for L_{TC} with weak soundness and strong secrecy, with respect to the transformation $\mathsf{TC.T} = (\mathsf{TC.Transform}, \mathsf{TC.WitTrans})$ as described before, denoted by (TC.Prove, TC.Verify, TC.Maul).
– Malleable NIWI proof system for $L_{\mathsf{com}}[\mathsf{pp}]$ with respect to the transformation Bit.GenT = (Bit.GenTrans, Bit.GWitTrans).
– Malleable NIWI proof system for $L_{\mathsf{N}}[\mathsf{pp}]$ with respect to the transformation N.GenT = (N.GenTrans, N.GWitTrans).

Theorem 4. *Assuming the existence of the ingredients as described above, the following construction $\varPi_{\mathsf{FHNIWI}}$ is a Fully Homomorphic NIWI proof system as per Definition 8.*

---

[3] Recall that for parameters $\mathsf{pp}, \mathsf{pp}'$ such that $\mathsf{pp}' = \mathsf{OutParam}(\mathsf{pp})$, pp itself is an intermediate parameter between $\mathsf{pp}, \mathsf{pp}'$.

We instantiate the first, third and fourth ingredients from DLIN and instantiate the second ingredient from DLIN with Leakage. This gives the following corollary:

Corollary 1. *Assuming DLIN with Leakage, the following construction Π_{FHNIWI} is a Fully Homomorphic NIWI proof system as per Definition 8.*

We refer the reader to the full version [4] for a proof of Theorem 4 and instantiation of ingredients.

References

1. Acar, T., Nguyen, L.: Homomorphic proofs and applications (2011). https://www.microsoft.com/en-us/research/wp-content/uploads/2011/03/rac.pdf
2. Agrawal, S., Ganesh, C., Mohassel, P.: Non-interactive zero-knowledge proofs for composite statements. In: IACR Cryptology ePrint Archive (2018)
3. Ananth, P., Cohen, A., Jain, A.: Cryptography with updates. In: Coron, J.-S., Nielsen, J.B. (eds.) EUROCRYPT 2017. LNCS, vol. 10211, pp. 445–472. Springer, Cham (2017). https://doi.org/10.1007/978-3-319-56614-6_15
4. Ananth, P., Deshpande, A., Kalai, Y.T., Lysyanskaya, A.: Fully homomorphic NIZK and NIWI proofs. IACR Cryptology ePrint Archive 2019/732 (2019). https://eprint.iacr.org/2019/732
5. Ananth, P., Goyal, V., Pandey, O.: Interactive proofs under continual memory leakage. In: Garay, J.A., Gennaro, R. (eds.) CRYPTO 2014. LNCS, vol. 8617, pp. 164–182. Springer, Heidelberg (2014). https://doi.org/10.1007/978-3-662-44381-1_10
6. Barak, B., Ong, S.J., Vadhan, S.P.: Derandomization in cryptography. IACR Cryptology ePrint Archive 2005/365 (2005). http://eprint.iacr.org/2005/365
7. Belenkiy, M., Camenisch, J., Chase, M., Kohlweiss, M., Lysyanskaya, A., Shacham, H.: Randomizable proofs and delegatable anonymous credentials. In: Halevi, S. (ed.) CRYPTO 2009. LNCS, vol. 5677, pp. 108–125. Springer, Heidelberg (2009). https://doi.org/10.1007/978-3-642-03356-8_7
8. Bitansky, N., Canetti, R., Chiesa, A., Tromer, E.: Recursive composition and bootstrapping for snarks and proof-carrying data. In: Proceedings of the Forty-Fifth Annual ACM Symposium on Theory of Computing, pp. 111–120. ACM (2013)
9. Blum, M., De Santis, A., Micali, S., Persiano, G.: Non-interactive zero-knowledge. SIAM J. Comput. **20**(6), 1084–1118 (1991)
10. Boneh, D., Freeman, D.M.: Homomorphic signatures for polynomial functions. In: Paterson, K.G. (ed.) EUROCRYPT 2011. LNCS, vol. 6632, pp. 149–168. Springer, Heidelberg (2011). https://doi.org/10.1007/978-3-642-20465-4_10
11. Boyle, E., Couteau, G., Gilboa, N., Ishai, Y., Orrù, M.: Homomorphic secret sharing: optimizations and applications. In: Proceedings of the 2017 ACM SIGSAC Conference on Computer and Communications Security, pp. 2105–2122. ACM (2017)
12. Boyle, E., Gilboa, N., Ishai, Y., Lin, H., Tessaro, S.: Foundations of homomorphic secret sharing. In: LIPIcs-Leibniz International Proceedings in Informatics, vol. 94. Schloss Dagstuhl-Leibniz-Zentrum fuer Informatik (2018)
13. Brakerski, Z., Vaikuntanathan, V.: Efficient fully homomorphic encryption from (standard) LWE. SIAM J. Comput. **43**(2), 831–871 (2014)

14. Chase, M., Kohlweiss, M., Lysyanskaya, A., Meiklejohn, S.: Malleable proof systems and applications. In: Pointcheval, D., Johansson, T. (eds.) EUROCRYPT 2012. LNCS, vol. 7237, pp. 281–300. Springer, Heidelberg (2012). https://doi.org/10.1007/978-3-642-29011-4_18

15. Chase, M., Kohlweiss, M., Lysyanskaya, A., Meiklejohn, S.: Malleable signatures: complex unary transformations and delegatable anonymous credentials (2013). http://eprint.iacr.org/2013/179

16. Chase, M., Kohlweiss, M., Lysyanskaya, A., Meiklejohn, S.: Succinct malleable NIZKs and an application to compact shuffles. In: Sahai, A. (ed.) TCC 2013. LNCS, vol. 7785, pp. 100–119. Springer, Heidelberg (2013). https://doi.org/10.1007/978-3-642-36594-2_6

17. Dwork, C., Naor, M.: Zaps and their applications. In: 2000 41st Annual Symposium on Foundations of Computer Science, Proceedings, pp. 283–293. IEEE (2000)

18. Gentry, C.: A fully homomorphic encryption scheme. Ph.D. thesis. International Journal of Distributed Sensor Networks, Stanford University (2009)

19. Goldreich, O.: Foundations of Cryptography: Basic Tools. Cambridge University Press, New York (2000)

20. Gorbunov, S., Vaikuntanathan, V., Wichs, D.: Leveled fully homomorphic signatures from standard lattices. In: Proceedings of the Forty-seventh Annual ACM Symposium on Theory of Computing, pp. 469–477. ACM (2015)

21. Groth, J., Ostrovsky, R., Sahai, A.: Non-interactive Zaps and New Techniques for NIZK. In: Dwork, C. (ed.) CRYPTO 2006. LNCS, vol. 4117, pp. 97–111. Springer, Heidelberg (2006). https://doi.org/10.1007/11818175_6

22. Kim, S., Wu, D.J.: Multi-theorem preprocessing NIZKs from lattices. In: Shacham, H., Boldyreva, A. (eds.) CRYPTO 2018. LNCS, vol. 10992, pp. 733–765. Springer, Cham (2018). https://doi.org/10.1007/978-3-319-96881-0_25

23. Micali, S.: Computationally sound proofs. SIAM J. Comput. **30**(4), 1253–1298 (2000)

24. Naveh, A., Tromer, E.: PhotoProof: cryptographic image authentication for any set of permissible transformations. In: 2016 IEEE Symposium on Security and Privacy (SP), pp. 255–271. IEEE (2016)

25. Rivest, R.L., Adleman, L., Dertouzos, M.L.: On data banks and privacy homomorphisms. Found. Secure Comput. **4**(11), 169–180 (1978)

26. Valiant, P.: Incrementally verifiable computation or proofs of knowledge imply time/space efficiency. In: Canetti, R. (ed.) TCC 2008. LNCS, vol. 4948, pp. 1–18. Springer, Heidelberg (2008). https://doi.org/10.1007/978-3-540-78524-8_1

Lower and Upper Bounds
on the Randomness Complexity
of Private Computations of AND

Eyal Kushilevitz[1], Rafail Ostrovsky[2], Emmanuel Prouff[3,5], Adi Rosén[4(✉)],
Adrian Thillard[5], and Damien Vergnaud[3]

[1] Department of Computer Science, Technion, Haifa, Israel
eyalk@cs.technion.ac.il
[2] Department of Computer Science and Department of Mathematics,
UCLA, Los Angeles, USA
rafail@cs.ucla.edu
[3] Laboratoire d'informatique de Paris 6, LIP6, Sorbonne Université, CNRS,
Paris, France
damien.vergnaud@lip6.fr
[4] CNRS and Université Paris Diderot, Paris, France
adiro@irif.fr
[5] ANSSI, Paris, France
{emmanuel.prouff,adrian.thillard}@ssi.gouv.fr

Abstract. We consider multi-party information-theoretic private protocols, and specifically their randomness complexity. The randomness complexity of private protocols is of interest both because random bits are considered a scarce resource, and because of the relation between that complexity measure and other complexity measures of boolean functions such as the circuit size or the sensitivity of the function being computed [12,17].

More concretely, we consider the randomness complexity of the basic boolean function **and**, that serves as a building block in the design of many private protocols. We show that **and** cannot be privately computed using a single random bit, thus giving the first non-trivial lower bound on the 1-private randomness complexity of an explicit boolean function, $f : \{0,1\}^n \to \{0,1\}$. We further show that the function **and**, on any number of inputs n (one input bit per player), can be privately computed using 8 random bits (and 7 random bits in the special case of $n = 3$

Research of E. Kushilevitz is supported by ISF grant 1709/14, BSF grant 2012378, NSF-BSF grant 2015782, and a grant from the Ministry of Science and Technology, Israel, and the Department of Science and Technology, Government of India. Research of R. Ostrovsky is supported in part by NSF-BSF grant 1619348, DARPA SafeWare subcontract to Galois Inc., DARPA SPAWAR contract N66001-15-1C-4065, US-Israel BSF grant 2012366, OKAWA Foundation Research Award, IBM Faculty Research Award, Xerox Faculty Research Award, B. John Garrick Foundation Award, Teradata Research Award, JP Morgan Chase Faculty Award, and Lockheed-Martin Corporation Research Award. The views expressed are those of the author and do not reflect the position of the Department of Defense or the U.S. Government.

© International Association for Cryptologic Research 2019
D. Hofheinz and A. Rosen (Eds.): TCC 2019, LNCS 11892, pp. 386–406, 2019.
https://doi.org/10.1007/978-3-030-36033-7_15

players), improving the upper bound of 73 random bits implicit in [17]. Together with our lower bound, we thus approach the exact determination of the randomness complexity of **and**. To the best of our knowledge, the exact randomness complexity of private computation is not known for any explicit function (except for **xor**, which is trivially 1-random, and for several degenerate functions).

1 Introduction

A multi-party *private* protocol for computing a function f is a distributed protocol that allows $n \geq 3$ players P_i, for $0 \leq i \leq n-1$, each possessing an individual secret input x_i, to compute the value of $f(x)$ in a way that does not reveal any "unnecessary" information to any player.[1] The protocol proceeds in rounds, where in each round each player sends a message to any other player, over a secure point-to-point channel. The privacy property of such protocol means that no player can learn "anything" (in an information-theoretic sense) from the execution of the protocol, except what is implied by the value of $f(x)$ and its own input. In particular, the players do not learn anything about the inputs of the other players. Private computation in this setting was the subject of considerable research, see e.g., [1,3,6,7,12,16,17]. In addition to its theoretical interest, this setting constitutes the foundation for many cryptographic applications (in information theoretic settings) such as electronic secret ballot.

Randomness is necessary in order to perform private computations involving more than two players (except for the computation of very degenerate functions). That is, the players must have access to (private) random sources. As randomness is regarded as a scarce resource, methods for saving random bits in various contexts have been suggested in the literature, see, e.g., [14,20] for surveys. Thus, an interesting research topic is the design of randomness-efficient private protocols, and the quantification of the amount of randomness needed to perform private computations of various functions and under various constraints. This line of research has received considerable attention, see, e.g., [4,5,11,15–17,19,21].

As in most of the work on the randomness complexity of private computations, we concentrate here on the computation of boolean functions, where the input x_i of each player is a single input bit. Previous work on the randomness complexity of private computations revealed that there is a tradeoff between randomness and time (i.e., number of communication rounds) for the private computation of **xor** [19], or gave lower bounds on the number of rounds necessary to privately compute any function, in terms of the sensitivity of the function and the amount of randomness used [12]. However, if one is allowed an arbitrary number of rounds for the computation then, prior to the present work, there were no known lower bounds on the number of random bits necessary for private protocols computing explicit boolean functions (except that some

---

[1] The two-party case, $n = 2$, is known to be qualitatively different [7].

randomness is indeed necessary, i.e., no deterministic private protocol exists).[2] In fact, Kushilevitz et al. [17] gave a relation between the number of random bits necessary to privately compute a function $f : \{0,1\}^n \rightarrow \{0,1\}$, and the Boolean circuit size necessary to compute f; it is proved, among other things, that the class of boolean functions that have $O(1)$-random, 1-private, protocols is equal to the class of boolean functions that have linear size circuits. This, perhaps surprising, connection to circuit size explains the difficulty of proving $\omega(1)$ lower bounds on the number of random bits necessary for the private computation of any explicit boolean function f, as such a result would imply superlinear lower bounds on the circuit size of f – a notoriously difficult problem.[3] Additional connections between the randomness complexity of the private computation of a function to other complexity measures, such as its sensitivity, have been shown in, e.g., [5, 18, 19].

This leaves the interesting, and perhaps feasible, task to determine the exact randomness complexity of the private computation of boolean functions of linear circuit size, where each player has a single input bit. This class of functions includes quite a few interesting functions f and, in particular, the basic functions xor and and. Indeed, the functions xor and and serve as basic building blocks for private protocols that rely on the boolean-circuit representation of f (more generally, *addition* and *multiplication* are used as building blocks for protocols that use the *arithmetic*-circuit representation of f). In the context of lower bounds for *communication* complexity of private protocols, these building blocks also serve as the center of analysis (as a first step for a more general understanding), see, e.g., [8–10].

It is known that xor can be computed privately using a single random bit, for any number of players, and this is optimal since no deterministic private multiparty protocol can exist (see [19]). To the best of our knowledge, there is no exact determination of the randomness complexity of private computation for any other explicit function. Furthermore, prior to the present paper, there was no lower bound showing for any explicit boolean function that it cannot

---

[2] Recently, a lower bound on the number of random bits necessary for the private computation of the Disjointness function was obtained [21]. However, for the Disjointness function each player has $m \geq 1$ bits of input. Furthermore, the obtained lower bound is of $\Omega(m)$, and the hidden constant is less than 1. Thus, for the special case of and (Disjointness with $m = 1$), the lower bound of [21] only implies, in our context, the trivial claim that and cannot be privately computed by a deterministic protocol.

[3] When the protocol has to be resilient against coalitions of $t > 1$ players (so called t-private protocols) several $\omega(1)$ lower bounds on the number of random bits necessary for private protocols for explicit functions have been proved. Kushilevitz and Mansour [16] proved that any t-private protocol for xor requires at least t random bits. Blundo et al. [5] gave lower bounds for two special cases. Namely, they proved that if $t = n - c$, for some constant c, then $\Omega(n^2)$ random bits are necessary for the private computation of xor, and if $t \geq (2 - \sqrt{2})n$, then $\Omega(n)$ random bits are necessary. Gal and Rosén [13] proved that $\Omega(\log n)$ random bits are necessary for 2-private computation of xor.

be privately computed (in the natural setting that we consider here, i.e., where each player has one input bit) using a single random bit.

In this paper, we give the first such lower bound, showing that the function **and** cannot be privately computed using a single random bit.[4] We further make the first step towards determining the exact randomness complexity of the private computation of **and** by showing an improved upper bound of 8 on the number of random bits necessary for such computation, and we strengthen this upper bound to 7 for the special case of 3 players.

The rest of the paper is organized as follows. In Sect. 2, we define the model and the complexity measures that we consider. In Sect. 3, we prove that the private computation of **and** cannot be performed with a single random bit. In Sect. 4, we give a number of upper bounds on the randomness complexity of private computation of **and**.

2 Preliminaries

Let $f : \{0,1\}^n \to \{0,1\}$ be any Boolean function. A set of n players P_i ($0 \le i \le n-1$), each possessing a single input bit x_i (known *only* to P_i), collaborate in a protocol to compute the value of $f(x)$. The protocol operates in rounds. In each round each player may toss some (fair) random coins, and then sends messages to the other players (messages are sent over private channels so that other than the intended receiver no other player can see them). After sending its messages, each player receives the messages sent to it by the other players in the current round. Without loss of generality (because we are not interested in this paper in the number of rounds), we assume that the messages sent by the players consist of single bits. In addition, each player locally outputs the value of the function at a certain round. We say that the protocol computes the function $f : \{0,1\}^n \to \{0,1\}$ if for every input $x \in \{0,1\}^n$, and for any outcome of all coin tosses, the output produced by each player is always $f(x)$ (i.e., perfect correctness).

To formally define a protocol we first define the notion of a *view* of a player.

Definition 1 (View). *The view of player P_i at round $t \ge 1$, denoted V_i^t, consists of the input bit to player P_i, i.e. x_i, the messages received by P_i in rounds 1 to $t-1$, and the results of the coin tosses performed by player P_i in rounds 1 to t. Let $\mathcal{V}_i^t$ be the set of possible views of player P_i at round t. Let $\hat{V}_i^t$ be the view V_i^t without the coins tossed at round t, and let $\hat{\mathcal{V}}_i^t$ be the set of possible values of $\hat{V}_i^t$.*

Definition 2 (Protocol). *A protocol consists of a sequence of rounds, where each round $t \ge 1$ is formally defined by the following functions:*

---

[4] In a different setting, namely, where there are two input players, Alice and Bob, and a third output player, Charlie, Data et al. [11] also study the randomness (and communication) complexity of secure computation (in particular of the **and** function; see [11, Thm. 11]).

- $S_i^{t,\ell} : (\hat{\mathcal{V}}_i^t \times \{0,1\}^{\ell-1}) \to \{\texttt{stop}, \texttt{toss}\}$, for $\ell \geq 1$, defining if another random coin is to be tossed by player P_i, given $\hat{\mathcal{V}}_i^t$ and the values of the $\ell-1$ random coins tossed so far by player P_i in round t.
- $m_{i,j}^t : \mathcal{V}_i^t \to \{0,1\}$, for $0 \leq i,j \leq n-1$, defining the message P_i sends to P_j at round t.
- $O_i^t : \mathcal{V}_i^t \to \{0,1,\perp\}$, for $0 \leq i \leq n-1$, defining if and what value player P_i outputs at round t. Since the views are increasing, we can require that each player outputs a non-null output only in one round.

Sometimes it is more convenient to model the coin tossing done by each player as a set of binary random tapes R_i, each R_i being provided to player P_i. The number of random coins tossed by player P_i is the number of random bits it reads from its random tape.

We denote by r_i a specific random tape provided to player P_i, by $\boldsymbol{r} = (r_1, \ldots, r_n)$ the vector of random tapes of all the players, and by $\boldsymbol{R} = (R_1, \ldots, R_n)$ the random variable for these tapes. Note that if we fix $\boldsymbol{r}$, we obtain a deterministic protocol.

Definition 3 (Randomness Complexity). *A d-random protocol is a protocol such that, for any input assignment x, the total number of coins tossed by all players in any execution is at most d.*

Our main question in this paper is what is the randomness complexity of the best private protocol (in terms of randomness complexity) for the boolean function **and**.

Informally, *privacy* with respect to player P_i means that player P_i cannot learn anything (in particular, the inputs of other players) from the messages it receives, except what is implied by its input bit, and the output value of the function f being computed.[5] Formally, denote by c_i a specific sequence of messages received by P_i, and by C_i the random variable (depending also on $\boldsymbol{R}$) for the sequence of messages received by P_i. We define:

Definition 4 (Privacy). *A protocol $\mathcal{A}$ for computing a function f is private with respect to player P_i if, for any two input vectors x and y such that $f(x) = f(y)$ and $x_i = y_i$, for any sequence of messages c_i, and for any random tape r_i provided to P_i,*

$$Pr[C_i = c_i | r_i, x] = Pr[C_i = c_i | r_i, y],$$

where the probability is over the random tapes of all other players.

A protocol is said to be private if it is private with respect to all players.

---

[5] In the literature, a more general notion of privacy, called t-privacy, is often considered, where any set of players of size at most t cannot learn anything from the messages received by all of them. In this paper we consider only 1-privacy, and call it "privacy" for simplicity.

3   Lower Bound

In this section we prove that private computation of **and** of n bits, $n \geq 3$, cannot be performed with a single random bit. We note that a lower bound on the number of random bits of private computation for $n > 3$ does not follow from a lower bound for $n = 3$, because, in general, simulating by 3 players a protocol on $n > 3$ players may violate the privacy requirement.

Our result for **and** is in contrast to the situation for the function **xor**, which can be computed privately using a single random bit. Our result constitutes, to the best of our knowledge, the first lower bound that quantifies the amount of randomness needed to privately compute an explicit boolean function (without any limitation on the protocol, such as its round complexity).

In the course of this proof, we denote by **1** the all-1 input of length n, and by e_S, for $S \subseteq \{1, \ldots, n\}$, the input assignment of all 1's except at the coordinates in S. Specifically, we use e_j to denote the vector with 0 at position j and 1's elsewhere[6] and $e_{i,j}$ to denote the vector with 0's at positions i, j and 1's elsewhere.

Assume, towards a contradiction, that π is a 1-random private protocol for **and**. We assume w.l.o.g. that π is in a "canonical form", that we define as follows: A protocol is in canonical form if no message m, sent from player P_i to player P_j at round t, can be inferred from the input x_j, the private randomness of player P_j, and the messages previously received by player P_j (i.e., either received in round $t' < t$, or in round t from a player $P_{i'}$, for $i' < i$). In particular, no message in a protocol in canonical form is a constant message.

Obviously, for π to compute **and** there must be at least one non-constant message defined in π. Consider any such message, m, sent in round $t = 1$ (since π is in canonical form there must be at least one such message in round $t = 1$), say, from player P_i to player P_j. Since the message m is sent in round $t = 1$, it can depend only on x_i and the random bits tossed by P_i by round $t = 1$. To preserve privacy with respect to P_j, the message m has to have the same distribution when $x_i = 0$ and when $x_i = 1$. Since π is 1-random, the number of random bits tossed by any single player, in particular P_i, in any execution of the protocol, is at most 1. It follows that $Pr[m = 0] = 1/2$, and $Pr[m = 1] = 1/2$ regardless of the value of x_i, thus P_i must toss a random bit by round $t = 1$ whether $x_i = 0$ or $x_i = 1$. To conclude, there is some player (the sender of m), w.l.o.g. denote it P_0, that regardless of its input, and in any execution, tosses in π a single random bit, denote it r. Since π is 1-random, no other random bit is tossed in π in any execution (by any player). Thus, since all messages in π can depend only on the input bits, x_i, $0 \leq i \leq n - 1$, and the single random bit r tossed by player P_0, we may consider any message sent in π as a sum of monomials in x_i, $0 \leq i \leq n - 1$, and r. We now analyze some properties of the (assumed) protocol π.

---

[6] Not to be confused with the j-th unit vector.

Lemma 5. *All messages m sent in π are of the form $m = r \oplus \sum_{i \in S \subseteq \{0,\ldots,n-1\}} x_i$ or $m = 1 \oplus r \oplus \sum_{i \in S \subseteq \{0,\ldots,n-1\}} x_i$. No player receives during the execution of π two (distinct) messages.*

Proof. We prove the claim by induction on the round number $t \geq 1$, i.e., we prove that until round $t \geq 1$ all messages are of the form $m = r \oplus \sum_{i \in S \subseteq \{0,\ldots,n-1\}} x_i$ or $m = 1 \oplus r \oplus \sum_{i \in S \subseteq \{0,\ldots,n-1\}} x_i$ and that no player receives by the end of round t two (distinct) messages.

For the basis of the induction consider the first round $t = 1$ and the messages sent and received in this round. Clearly, a (non-constant) message in the first round can be sent only by player P_0 otherwise it consists of only the input bit of the sending player (or its negation) and the privacy property will be violated. Since no message is received before the messages of the first round are sent, the messages sent by player P_0 at round $t = 1$ are a function of only r and x_0. We argue that such message has therefore to be of the form $m = r \oplus x_0$ (or $m = 1 \oplus r \oplus x_0$) or of the form $m = r$ (or $m = 1 \oplus r$): since m depends only on r and x_0, the monomials in m can only be $1, x_0, r$, and rx_0. We claim that if the monomial rx_0 appears in the sum representing m then the privacy property is violated with respect to the player receiving the message, say player P_j. This is because the possible messages that include rx_0 are: rx_0, $rx_0 \oplus x_0 = (r \oplus 1)x_0$, $rx_0 \oplus x_0 \oplus r = (r \oplus 1)(x_0 \oplus 1) \oplus 1$, and $rx_0 \oplus r = r(x_0 \oplus 1)$ (and their negations). Consider the two input assignments $e_{0,j}$ and e_j. Observe that the distribution of each one of these messages on the inputs $e_{0,j}$ and e_j is different, which violates the privacy requirement ("leaking some information" on x_0 to P_j). For example, rx_0 is always 0 in $e_{0,j}$ and uniformly distributed in e_j. The argument for the other cases is similar.

It follows that the messages sent in round $t = 1$ are of the desired form. Since only player P_0 can send messages in round $t = 1$, it also follows that by the end of round $t = 1$ each player receives at most a single message. Thus, the claim holds for round $t = 1$.

We now prove the claim for round $t > 1$, assuming the induction hypothesis holds for round $t - 1$. Consider player P_i and the message $m_{i,j}^t$ that it sends in round t to player P_j. Since this message is computed by player P_i at round t, it can be expressed as a function of x_i, of the single message m that player P_i receives in some round $t' < t$ (if such a message exists) and, if $i = 0$, of the random bit r. We distinguish between two cases: when $i \neq 0$, and when $i = 0$.

When $i \neq 0$, the message $m_{i,j}^t$ sent by P_i is the sum of a subset of the monomials $1, x_i, m, mx_i$. If the monomial mx_i does not appear in the sum, then $m_{i,j}^t$ is of the desired form (otherwise $m_{i,j}^t$ is either a messages that can be inferred by P_j or a message that violates the privacy property with respect to P_j; in any case it cannot be part of the protocol.)[7]

---

[7] By inspection for each of the 8 subsets of $1, x_i$, and m (represented by $\{0,1\}^3$ in the natural way): (000, 100) - 0, 1: constants, not in protocol; (010, 110) - x_i, $1 \oplus x_i$: violates privacy; (001, 101) - m, $1 \oplus m$: of the desired form; (011, 111) - $x_i \oplus m$, $1 \oplus x_i \oplus m$: of the desired form.

On the other hand, we show in the following that any message defined by any of the 8 sums of monomials that include the monomial mx_i violates the privacy property with respect to P_j, and hence such message cannot be part of the protocol. By the induction hypothesis $m = r \oplus \sum_{k \in S \subseteq \{0,\dots,n-1\}} x_k$ (or $1 \oplus r \oplus \sum_{k \in S \subseteq \{0,\dots,n-1\}} x_k$), for some S. Consider the former form, the latter is similar. For the message mx_i (resp., $1 \oplus mx_i$) consider the inputs $e_{i,j}$ and e_j and observe that on the former input the message is always 0 (resp., 1) while on the latter it is m (resp., $1 \oplus m$), and hence does not exhibit the same distribution on the two inputs. Similarly, consider the messages $mx_i \oplus x_i = (m \oplus 1)x_i$, $mx_i \oplus m = m(x_i \oplus 1)$, and $mx_i \oplus x_i \oplus m = (m \oplus 1)(x_i \oplus 1) \oplus 1$ (and their negations), and observe that the message has different distributions on the inputs $e_{i,j}$ and e_j (in each of the cases, for one of these two inputs the value of the message is either m or its negation, i.e., the support of the distribution is of size 2, and for the other input the distribution has support of size 1).

For $i = 0$, player $P_i = P_0$ has also the random bit r, so the message sent by P_0 at round t to player P_j is the sum of a subset of the monomials 1, x_0, m, mx_0, r, rx_0, rm, rmx_i. But, no message m can be received by player P_0 before round t, since any message of the form $r \oplus \sum_{k \in S \subseteq \{0,\dots,n-1\}} x_k$ (or $m = 1 \oplus r \oplus \sum_{k \in S \subseteq \{0,\dots,n-1\}} x_k$) would either violate the privacy (since P_0 knows r), or would be such that P_0 can compute it itself.[8] It follows that the message sent by player P_0 at round t is the sum of a subset of the monomials 1, x_0, r, rx_0. But, we have proved above (when proving the base case of the induction) that in this case $m_{i,j}^t$ must be $r \oplus x_0$ (or $1 \oplus r \oplus x_0$).

We conclude that the messages sent in round t are of the desired form.

Now, assume towards a contradiction that some player P_j receives by the end of round t two (distinct) messages which, as we proved above, must be of the desired form. Denote $q_1 = r \oplus \sum_{i \in S_1 \subseteq \{0,\dots,n-1\}} x_i$, and $q_2 = r \oplus \sum_{i \in S_2 \subseteq \{0,\dots,n-1\}} x_i$. The two messages received by player P_j are therefore $m_1 = q_1$ (or $m_1 = 1 \oplus q_1$) and $m_2 = q_2$ (or $m_2 = 1 \oplus q_2$), for some sets S_1 and S_2. Consider now $Q = m_1 \oplus m_2$. Observe that $Q = \sum_{i \in S' \subseteq \{0,\dots,n-1\}} x_i$ (or $Q = 1 \oplus \sum_{i \in S' \subseteq \{0,\dots,n-1\}} x_i$) for $S' = S_1 \triangle S_2$. If $S' \subseteq \{x_j\}$ then, since π is of canonical form, one of the two messages m_1 and m_2 (the one arriving later) cannot exist in π. It follows that $S' \not\subseteq \{x_j\}$ and the privacy property is violated with respect to player P_j, as Q reveals information on the xor of the inputs in S'.[9] A contradiction to π being private.

Therefore, the claim holds for round t. □

Lemma 6. *Consider the protocol π, an arbitrary player P_j and an arbitrary round $t \geq 1$. Then, player P_j cannot compute the function* and *at the end of round t.*

---

[8] If $S = \{x_0\}$ then P_0 can compute the message itself. If there exists a $k \neq 0$, $k \in S$, consider the two inputs e_0, $e_{0,k}$ to see that the privacy property is violated.

[9] Formally, consider the two inputs $e_{j,k}$ and e_j, for some $k \in S'$, $k \neq j$. These two inputs agree on x_j as well as on the value of the function, but the distributions of the messages that P_j receives on these two inputs are not identical.

Proof. By Lemma 5, player P_j receives by the end of round t at most a single message, and this message is of the form $m = r \oplus \sum_{i \in S \subseteq \{0,...,n-1\}} x_i$ or $m = 1 \oplus r \oplus \sum_{i \in S \subseteq \{0,...,n-1\}} x_i$. We distinguish between two cases.

Case 1: For all $k \neq j$, $k \in S$. Since $n \geq 3$, there exist two distinct $k_1, k_2 \in S$, $k_1 \neq j$, $k_2 \neq j$. Consider the two inputs $\mathbf{1}$ and e_{k_1,k_2}. While $AND(\mathbf{1}) \neq AND(e_{k_1,k_2})$, the view of P_j at the end of round t is the same on $\mathbf{1}$ and e_{k_1,k_2} and hence π must err on at least one of them (note that this in particular holds when $j = 0$; for all other players, who do not know r, the message m is uniformly distributed).

Case 2: There exists an index $k \neq j$, $k \notin S$. Consider the two inputs $\mathbf{1}$ and e_k. As in Case 1, π must err on at least one of these inputs.   □

We conclude that protocol π (a 1-random private protocol for **and**) does not exist.

Theorem 7. *The private computation of the function **and** cannot be performed with a single random bit.*

4   Upper Bounds

In this section, we provide significantly improved upper bounds on the randomness complexity of **and**. Specifically, we show that **and** on any number of players n can be privately computed using 8 random bits, and can be computed with 7 random bits for the special case of $n = 3$ players.

In order to present our protocol, we first present two building blocks which are used in our constructions. They are both implementations of information-theoretic 1-out-of-2 Oblivious Transfer.

4.1   1-out-of-2 Oblivious Transfer

In a 1-out-of-2 Oblivious Transfer (1-2 OT) protocol two parties, Alice and Bob, engage in a protocol that allows Bob to choose which part of the information that Alice holds he wants to learn, in such a way that Alice does not learn which part of her information Bob learned.

More formally, for a 1-out-of-2 Oblivious Transfer protocol Alice has two bits b_0 and b_1, and Bob has a selection bit s. Alice and Bob, together with a set of helper players, $\mathcal{H}$, engage in a protocol at the end of which the following holds:

- Bob knows the value of b_s.
- Bob does not learn any information on $b_{1 \oplus s}$ (i.e., the transcript of Bob, given the values of s and b_s, is identically distributed whether $b_{1 \oplus s}$ is 0 or 1).
- Alice does not learn anything (i.e., the transcript of Alice, given any choice of values for b_0 and b_1, is identically distributed; in particular, it is independent of s).
- The helper players do not learn anything (i.e., the transcript of each of them is distributed independently of the inputs s, b_0, b_1).

We now give two implementations of this building block using a different number of helper players, and a different number of random bits. Both are used in our protocols.

4.1.1   Implementation 1: 3 Random Bits, 1 Helper Player

This implementation is given by Beaver [2].

There is one helper player, denoted by H. The protocol is defined as follows.

1. The helper player H tosses 2 uniformly distributed and independent random bits, r_0 and r_1 (to be used as masking bits), and one additional independent and uniformly distributed random bit p (to define one of the two possible permutations of $\{0,1\}$).
2. H sends both r_0 and r_1 to Alice and it sends p and $r^* = r_p$ to Bob.
3. Bob sends to Alice the message $i = s \oplus p$.
4. Alice sends to Bob the two bits $m_0 = b_0 \oplus r_i$ and $m_1 = b_1 \oplus r_{1 \oplus i}$.
5. Bob "deciphers" the value of the bit he wants to learn (i.e., b_s) by computing $m_s \oplus r^*$.

The fact that Bob learns the value of b_s follows by simple case analysis ($p = 0$ or $p = 1$).

For completeness, we sketch a proof of the privacy of this protocol. A more detailed formal proof is incorporated within the privacy proof for our protocol that uses the OT protocol as a sub-protocol. We observe the following:

- H does not receive any message and hence privacy is preserved with respect to H.
- Alice receives from H the bits r_0 and r_1 and from Bob the bit $i = s \oplus p$. All three are independent and uniformly distributed between 0 and 1 (as r_0, r_1, and p are uniformly distributed and independent random bits).
- Bob receives from H the bits p and $r^* = r_p$ (but not the bit $r_{1 \oplus p}$), and from Alice the bits $m_0 = b_0 \oplus r_i$ and $m_1 = b_1 \oplus r_{1 \oplus i}$. Observe that $b_s = m_s \oplus r^*$, but p and $m_{1 \oplus s}$ are both independent of m_s and r^*, and uniformly distributed.

4.1.2   Implementation 2: 2 Random Bits, 2 Helper Players

Here we assume that there are two helper players, denoted H_0 and H_1. The protocol is defined as follows.

1. Alice tosses two independent random bits p and r.
2. Alice sends the message $m_0 = b_0 \oplus r$ to player H_p, the message $m_1 = b_1 \oplus r$ to player $H_{1 \oplus p}$, and p and r to Bob.
3. Bob sends the bit 1 to player $H_{s \oplus p}$ and the bit 0 to player $H_{1 \oplus s \oplus p}$.
4. If player H_0 (resp., H_1) receives 1 from Bob, it sends to Bob the message m it received from Alice (i.e, either m_0 or m_1).
   Otherwise, if player H_0 (resp., H_1) receives 0 from Bob, it sends to Bob the (constant) message 0.[10]

---

[10] Clearly in this case the relevant helper player does not need to send any message to Alice. However in order to stay coherent with the model we use, we define which bit

5. Bob "deciphers" the value of the bit he wants to learn (i.e., b_s) by computing $b_s = m \oplus r$, where m is the message Bob got from $H_{s \oplus p}$.

The fact that Bob learns the value of b_s follows from the protocol, by inspection.

For completeness, we sketch a proof of the privacy of this protocol. A more detailed formal proof is incorporated within the privacy proof for our protocol that uses the OT protocol as a sub-protocol. We observe the following:

– Alice does not get any message and hence privacy is preserved with respect to Alice.
– Each of H_0 and H_1 gets a single message from Alice, which is one of her input bits xored with r; it also received from Bob a bit which is either 0 or 1, depending on the value $s \oplus p$; since r and p are uniformly random and independent, then privacy is preserved with respect to each one of the helper players H_0 and H_1.
– Bob receives p and r from Alice. Then, given the value of p and the value of s, known to Bob, it receives a constant message from one of H_0 or H_1, and the message $b_s \oplus r$ from the other (if $s \oplus p = 1$ Bob receives the constant message from H_0, and if $s \oplus p = 0$ Bob receives the constant message from H_1.) Hence, given the value of b_s, the transcript of Bob is distributed uniformly.

4.2 The AND Protocol

We first present a protocol, Π_{odd}, applicable to an odd number of players; this protocol uses 8 random bits. This protocol serves to introduce the main ideas of our protocols, and is also the basis for a somewhat improved protocol for $n = 3$, that uses 7 random bits. Extending Π_{odd} to work also for even number of players and keeping the 8 random bits bound requires some more effort, and we give such a protocol in Subsect. 4.2.2, applicable to any $n \geq 4$.

4.2.1 Odd Number of Players

We describe our protocol Π_{odd} for odd number of players, n, denoted $P_0, P_1, \ldots, P_{n-1}$.

Initialization Phase. In the initialization phase player P_0 tosses 3 random bits and plays the role of the helper player of implementation 1 of OT for all pairs of players where Alice is an odd player and Bob is the successive even player. Player P_{n-1} does the same for all pairs of players where Alice is an even player and Bob is the successive odd player. Specifically:

Player P_0 tosses 3 random bits r_0^1, r_1^1, and p^1. It sends the bits r_0^1, r_1^1 to all odd players, and sends the bits p^1 and $r_{p^1}^1$ to all even players.

---

is sent in each round between any two players, unless for all inputs and all random coins values, no message is sent between the two.

Player P_{n-1} tosses 3 random bits r_0^0, r_1^0, and p^0. It sends the bits r_0^0, r_1^0 to all even players, and sends the bits p^0 and $r_{p^0}^0$ to all odd players.

In addition, player P_0 tosses 2 additional random bits q_0 and q_1. It sends q_0 to all odd players, and q_1 to all even players. P_0 also locally computes $y_0 = q_0 \oplus q_1 \oplus x_0$.

Computation Phase. This phase runs in $n-1$ rounds. The inductive invariant that we maintain is that at the end of round $i \geq 1$ player P_i has the value $y_i = q_0 \oplus q_1 \oplus \Pi_{j=0}^{i} x_j$. In each round, the protocol will run an OT protocol. We give a detailed description of the rounds below.

Final Phase. At the end of the computation phase, player P_{n-1} has (by the inductive invariant) the value $y_{n-1} = q_0 \oplus q_1 \oplus \Pi_{j=0}^{n-1} x_j$. It sends this value to P_0 who xors it with $q_0 \oplus q_1$ to obtain $\Pi_{j=0}^{n-1} x_j = AND(x_0, x_1, \ldots, x_{n-1})$. Player P_0 then sends this value to all other players.

We now define how the computation phase is implemented so as to maintain the inductive invariant (and privacy, as we prove later). The invariant clearly holds at the end of round 0 (i.e., before the computation phase starts) since player P_0 has x_0, q_0, and q_1 and hence can compute y_0.

Now, in round $i \geq 1$ players P_{i-1} and P_i engage in a 1-2 OT protocol, using Implementation 1 described above. The values that Alice (i.e., player P_{i-1}) holds for the OT protocol are $b_0 = q_{i \bmod 2}$ and $b_1 = y_{i-1}$. Observe that Alice has b_0 from the initialization phase, and b_1 by the inductive invariant. The selection bit of Bob (i.e., player P_i) is $s = x_i$. The random bits used for the OT protocol are r_0^k, r_1^k, and p^k, where $k = (i+1) \bmod 2$. Observe that P_i and P_{i-1} receive in the initialization phase the random bits needed in order to simulate Alice and Bob of the OT protocol (i.e., r_0^k, r_1^k for Alice and p^k, $r_{p^k}^k$ for Bob). Let v_i denote the output (i.e., the bit learned by Bob) of the OT protocol run in the i-th round.

It follows that at the end of the OT protocol, if the value that player P_i holds is $x_i = 0$, then it gets from player P_{i-1} the value $v_i = q_{i \bmod 2}$, and if $x_i = 1$ then it gets the value $v_i = y_{i-1} = q_0 \oplus q_1 \oplus \Pi_{j=0}^{i-1} x_j$.

Now, if $x_i = 0$ then $\Pi_{j=0}^{i} x_j = 0$, and player P_i has y_i by calculating $q_{i \bmod 2} \oplus q_{(i+1) \bmod 2}$, where the former is just v_i and the latter is received from P_0 in the initialization phase.

If $x_i = 1$ then $\Pi_{j=0}^{i} x_j = \Pi_{j=0}^{i-1} x_j$ and player P_i just sets $y_i = v_i$.

The total number of random bits used in this protocol is 8: the protocol uses 3 bits for each of the two sets of OT protocols, and 2 additional masking bits, q_0 and q_1.

It remains to prove that privacy is preserved with respect to all players. Intuitively, there are $n - 1$ invocations of the OT protocol. Each internal player (i.e., all players except P_0 and P_{n-1}) participates in two OT invocations, once as Alice (with the following player) and once as Bob (with the preceding player), each of these two invocations using different sets of random bits, one set from P_0 and one set from P_{n-1}. Players P_0 and P_{n-1} participate each in a single invocation of the OT protocol, P_0 as Alice with P_1 and P_{n-1} as Bob with P_{n-2}. Hence the number of players must be odd (to guarantee that the random bits used by the OT protocol of P_{n-1} and P_{n-2} come from P_0 and not from P_{n-1}). Formally,

Theorem 8. *The AND protocol Π_{odd} is private for n odd, $n \geq 3$.*

Proof. We first prove the claim for players P_i, $0 < i < n - 1$, and then for P_0 and for P_{n-1}.

For $0 < i < n - 1$, observe that player P_i receives messages pertaining to exactly two OT invocations, one in which it plays the role of Alice, and one where it plays the role of Bob. In addition, P_i receives from player P_0 either the bit q_0 or the bit q_1 and, at the end of the protocol, the computed value of the function.

We prove the claim for i even (the case of i odd is analogous, switching the roles of the random bits, i.e., flipping their superscripts, and switching q_0 and q_1). The messages that such player P_i receives are:

1. During the initialization phase: bits $r_0^0, r_1^0, p^1, r_{p^1}^1, q_0$.
2. During the OT protocol with player P_{i-1} (i.e., when playing the role of Bob):
   - $q_1 \oplus r_j^1$ and $y_{i-1} \oplus r_{1 \oplus j}^1$, where $j = x_i \oplus p^1$.
3. During the OT protocol with player P_{i+1} (i.e., when playing the role of Alice):
   - $x_{i+1} \oplus p^0$.
4. In the final phase, from player P_0, $AND(x_0, x_1, \ldots, x_{n-1})$.

Observing the nine messages received by P_i, one can verify that:

1. The messages received in Stage 1 are just the random bits $r_0^0, r_1^0, p^1, r_{p^1}^1, q_0$.
2. For the messages of Stage 2 we distinguish between two cases depending on the value of x_i.
   If $x_i = 0$ then the first message is $q_1 \oplus r_{p^1}^1$ and the second one is $y_{i-1} \oplus r_{1 \oplus p^1}^1$. We have that the first message includes a xor operation with q_1, and the second one a xor with $r_{1 \oplus p^1}^1$.
   If $x_i = 1$ then the first message is $q_1 \oplus r_{1 \oplus p^1}^1$ and the second one is $y_{i-1} \oplus r_{p^1}^1$. In that case, the first message includes a xor operation with $r_{1 \oplus p^1}^1$ and the second one a xor with q_1 (since by the inductive invariant, $y_{i-1} = q_0 \oplus q_1 \oplus \Pi_{j=0}^{i-1} x_j$.)
3. The message received in Stage 3 includes a xor operation with p^0.
4. The message received in Stage 4 is the value of the function.

Inspecting the distribution of the above messages, the last message (Stage 4) is, by definition, the value of the function; all other 8 messages are independent and uniformly distributed (in correspondence with the 8 random bits that are used): the bits $r_0^0, r_1^0, p^1, r_{p^1}^1, q_0$ in Stage 1, the two messages of Stage 2 one includes a xor operation with $r_{1 \oplus p^1}^1$ and the other with q_1, and the message received in Stage 3 which includes a xor operation with p^0. Hence, the privacy with respect to P_i follows.

Almost the same argument applies to player P_{n-1} as well. It receives a subset of the messages received by players P_i, $0 < i < n - 1$, namely, those of Stages 1, 2, 4 above. In addition it knows the value of the random bit p^0. But, since the message of Stage 3 is not received by P_{n-1}, the privacy with respect to P_{n-1} holds.

As to player P_0, it receives the messages listed under Stages 1 and 3 above, and (from player P_{n-1} at the final phase) the message $y_{n-1} = q_0 \oplus q_1 \oplus \Pi_{j=0}^{n-1} x_j$. In addition, player P_0 knows the values of the random bits r_0^1, r_1^1, q_0 and q_1. We have that the messages received in Stages 1 and 3 each includes a xor operation with an independent (uniformly distributed) random bit not known to P_0. The message received in the final phase is determined by the value of the function, q_0 and q_1. Hence, privacy with respect to player P_0 holds as well.   □

4.2.2   At Least 4 Players

If one attempts to apply the above protocol Π_{odd} to an even number of players then privacy will not be preserved. This is because when players P_{n-2} and P_{n-1} engage in their OT protocol, they will do that with the random bits tossed by player P_{n-1} (while in the case of odd n these bits are tossed by the "helper" P_0).

To remedy this problem, we stop the computation phase one round earlier, that is, we run it for $n-2$ rounds only, at the end of which player P_{n-2} has, as in Π_{odd}, the value $y_{n-2} = q_0 \oplus q_1 \oplus \Pi_{j=0}^{n-2} x_j$. We then perform the last OT protocol of the computation phase using Implementation 2 defined above and fresh random bits. This, however, increases the total number of random bits used, and further requires that the total number of players is at least 4 (as required by Implementation 2 of OT). While requiring at least 4 players is not an issue since we have another variant of the protocol for odd number of players, in order not to increase the total number of random bits used, we generate and distribute the random bits needed for the various OT invocations in a more efficient way. That is, while each internal player still participates in 2 OT invocations, we do not need totally separate 2 sets of random bits. Rather, it is sufficient to ensure that no player will receive two messages (of two different OT invocations) that "use" the same random bit. The resulting protocol uses a total of 8 random bits and is applicable to any $n \geq 4$.

We now formally describe our protocol for $n \geq 4$ players, denoted $P_0, P_1, \ldots, P_{n-1}$. As indicated above, the high level structure of the protocol is the same as that of Π_{odd}, with some modifications, most notably a different way to produce and distribute the random bits.

Initialization Phase. In the initialization phase player P_{n-1} tosses 4 random bits u_0, u_1, u_2, u_4 and defines a sequence of bits $r_0, r_1, \ldots, r_\ell$, for $\ell = 2(n-2)$, recursively as follows:[11]

---

[11] Here and in the following we sometimes abuse notation and consider indices that involve summations over both $\mathcal{N}$ and $\mathcal{F}_2$ (denoted with the operands $+$ and $\oplus$, respectively).

$r_0 = u_0, r_1 = u_1, r_2 = u_2, r_4 = u_4$, and

$$r_j = \begin{cases} r_{j-3} + r_{j-1} & j > 1, j \text{ odd} \\ r_{j-6} + (1 \oplus r_{j-4}) & j > 4, j \text{ even} \end{cases} \tag{1}$$

Player P_{n-1} then sends to each player P_i, $0 \le i \le n-2$ the two bits r_{2i}, r_{2i+1}.

In addition, player P_0 tosses 2 additional random bits q_0 and q_1. It sends q_0 to all odd players, and q_1 to all even players. P_0 also locally computes $y_0 = q_0 \oplus q_1 \oplus x_0$.

Computation Phase. This phase runs in $n-1$ rounds. The inductive invariant that we maintain is that at the end of round $i \ge 1$ player P_i has the value $y_i = q_0 \oplus q_1 \oplus \Pi_{j=0}^{i} x_j$. In each round, the protocol will run an OT protocol. We give a detailed description of the rounds below.

Final Phase. At the end of the computation phase, player P_{n-1} has (by the inductive invariant) the value $y_{n-1} = q_0 \oplus q_1 \oplus \Pi_{j=0}^{n-1} x_j$. It sends this value to P_0 who xors it with $q_0 \oplus q_1$ to obtain $\Pi_{j=0}^{n-1} x_j = AND(x_0, x_1, \ldots, x_{n-1})$. Player P_0 then sends this value to all other players.

The following lemma gives the properties of the sequence of bits r_j, necessary both for the correctness of the protocol and for its privacy. The proof of this lemma is quite technical and the reader may wish to skip this proof.

Lemma 9. *For any $1 \le i \le n-2$, the five bits r_j, $2(i-1) \le j \le 2(i+1)$, are such that*

1. $r_{2i+1} = r_{2(i-1)+r_{2i}}$.
2. *The four bits $r_{2(i-1)}, r_{2(i-1)+1}, r_{2i}, r_{2(i+1)}$ are independent and uniformly distributed.*

Proof. We prove the lemma by induction on i. For the base of the induction ($i = 1$), observe that Point (2) is satisfied since r_0, r_1, r_2, r_4 are set to be u_0, u_1, u_2, u_4, respectively, and these are independent and uniformly distributed random bits tossed by Player P_{n-1}. As to Point (1), r_3 is set to be equal to r_{r_2} according to Eq. (1) (first part, with $j = 3$).

We now prove the lemma for $i+1$ assuming it is correct for i. Note that the 5-tuple that corresponds to $i+1$ partially overlaps the 5-tuple that corresponds to i.

Point (1) holds for $i+1$ because by the first part of Eq. (1) (taking j to be $2(i+1)+1$) $r_{2(i+1)+1} = r_{2i+1+r_{2(i+1)}}$.

As to Point (2), we consider both parts of Eq. (1) and the value of r_{2i}. There are two cases:

1. If $r_{2i} = 0$:
   - $r_{2i+1} = r_{2(i-1)}$ (taking $j = 2i+1$ for the first part of Eq. (1)).
   - $r_{2(i+2)} = r_{2(i-1)+1}$ (taking $j = 2(i+2)$ for the second part of Eq. (1)).
2. If $r_{2i} = 1$:
   - $r_{2i+1} = r_{2(i-1)+1}$ (taking $j = 2i+1$ for the first part of Eq. (1)).
   - $r_{2(i+2)} = r_{2(i-1)}$ (taking $j = 2(i+2)$ for the second part of Eq. (1)).

It follows that the 4-tuple of bits with indices $2i, 2i + 1, 2(i + 1)$ and $2(i + 2)$, i.e., the 4-tuple $(r_{2i}, r_{2i+1}, r_{2(i+1)}, r_{2(i+2)})$ is equal to either the 4-tuple $(r_{2i}, r_{2(i-1)}, r_{2(i+1)}, r_{2(i-1)+1})$ (if $r_{2i} = 0$) or to $(r_{2i}, r_{2(i-1)+1}, r_{2(i+1)}, r_{2(i-1)})$ (if $r_{2i} = 1$), which are two permutations of the same 4 bits. By the induction hypothesis, these 4 bits are independent and uniformly distributed. Hence also Point (2) holds for $i + 1$.   □

We now define how the computation phase is implemented so as to maintain the inductive invariant (and privacy, as we prove later). The invariant clearly holds at the end of round 0 (i.e., before the computation phase starts) since player P_0 has x_0, q_0, and q_1 and hence can compute y_0.

Similarly to protocol Π_{odd}, in round $1 \leq i \leq n - 2$ (but not in round $n - 1$, as is the case for Π_{odd}) players P_{i-1} and P_i engage in a 1-2 OT protocol, using Implementation 1 described above. The values that Alice (i.e., player P_{i-1}) holds for the OT protocol are $b_0 = q_{i \bmod 2}$ and $b_1 = y_{i-1}$. Observe that Alice has b_0 from the initialization phase, and b_1 by the inductive invariant. The selection bit of Bob (i.e., player P_i) is $s = x_i$. The random bits used for the OT protocol are $r_{2(i-1)}$ and $r_{2(i-1)+1}$ held by Alice (player P_{i-1}) and r_{2i} held by Bob (player P_i). Observe that P_i and P_{i-1} receive these bits from P_{n-1} during the initialization phase. Further, by Lemma 9 the bits $r_{2(i-1)}$ and $r_{2(i-1)+1}$, held by player P_{i-1}, and the bit r_{2i}, held by player P_i, all satisfy the properties required for the OT protocol to be correct (and private).

Finally, in round $i = n - 1$, players P_{n-2} and P_{n-1} engage in an OT protocol as in previous rounds, but using Implementation 2 and using additional new random bits.[12] Specifically, P_{n-1} is Bob of the OT protocol and P_{n-2} is Alice; the helper players are P_0 (H_0) and P_1 (H_1), and we denote the two fresh random bits tossed by P_{n-2} by u_5 and u_6 (see Sect. 4.1.2). The use of Implementation 2 of the OT protocol in this round is the reason that the protocol described here works only for $n \geq 4$.

As in protocol Π_{odd}, let v_i denote the output (i.e., the bit learned by Bob) of the OT protocol run in the i-th round, $1 \leq i \leq n - 1$. It follows that at the end of the OT protocol, if the value that player P_i holds as input is $x_i = 0$, then it gets from player P_{i-1} the value $v_i = q_{i \bmod 2}$, and if $x_i = 1$ it gets the value $v_i = y_{i-1} = q_0 \oplus q_1 \oplus \Pi_{j=0}^{i-1} x_j$.

Now, if $x_i = 0$ then $\Pi_{j=0}^{i} x_j = 0$, and player P_i has y_i by calculating $q_{i \bmod 2} \oplus q_{(i+1) \bmod 2}$, where the former is just v_i and the latter is received from P_0 in the initialization phase. If $x_i = 1$ then $\Pi_{j=0}^{i} x_j = \Pi_{j=0}^{i-1} x_j$ and player P_i just sets $y_i = v_i$.

The total number of random bits used in this protocol is 8: u_0, u_1, u_2, u_4 and q_0, q_1 are tossed by player P_0, and u_5, u_6 are tossed by player P_{n-2}.

It remains to prove that privacy is preserved with respect to all players. Intuitively, there are $n - 1$ invocations of the OT protocol. Each internal player

---

[12] It is also possible to perform the OT protocol of this round using Implementation 1 with a separate set of 3 random bits, tossed by another player, say player P_0, but this results in a larger total number of random bits for the protocol.

(i.e., all players except P_0 and P_{n-1}) participates in two OT invocations, once as Alice and once as Bob, and the privacy property with respect to these players will follow from the properties of the sequence of bits r_j (Lemma 9). We now prove that the protocol is private.

Theorem 10. *The AND protocol for $n \geq 4$ is private.*

Proof. We first prove the claim for players P_i, $1 < i < n - 2$, and then for the players having special roles, P_0, P_1, P_{n-2}, P_{n-1}.

For $1 < i < n - 2$, observe that player P_i receives messages pertaining to exactly two OT invocations, one in which it plays the role of Alice, and one where it plays the role of Bob (as implemented in Sect. 4.1.1). In addition, P_i receives from player P_0 either the bit q_0 or the bit q_1 and, at the end of the protocol, the computed value of the function.

We prove the claim for i even (the case of i odd is analogous, switching the roles of q_0 and q_1). The messages player P_i receives are:

1. During the initialization phase: bits r_{2i}, r_{2i+1}, q_0.
2. During the OT protocol with player P_{i-1} (i.e., when playing the role of Bob):
   - $q_1 \oplus r_{2(i-1)+j}$ and $y_{i-1} \oplus r_{2(i-1)+(1\oplus j)}$, where $j = x_i \oplus r_{2i}$.
3. During the OT protocol with player P_{i+1} (i.e., when playing the role of Alice):
   - $x_{i+1} \oplus r_{2(i+1)}$.
4. In the final phase, from player P_0, $AND(x_0, x_1, \ldots, x_{n-1})$.

Observing the seven messages received by P_i, one can verify that:

1. The messages received in Stage 1 are the bits r_{2i}, r_{2i+1}, q_0.
2. For the messages of Stage 2, we distinguish between two cases depending on the value of x_i.
   If $x_i = 0$ then the first message is $q_1 \oplus r_{2(i-1)+r_{2i}}$ and the second one is $y_{i-1} \oplus r_{2(i-1)+(1\oplus r_{2i})}$. In this case, the first message includes a xor operation with q_1, and the second one a xor operation with $r_{2(i-1)+(1\oplus r_{2i})}$.
   If $x_i = 1$ then the first message is $q_1 \oplus r_{2(i-1)+(1\oplus r_{2i})}$ and the second one is $y_{i-1} \oplus r_{2(i-1)+r_{2i}}$. In this case, the first message includes a xor operation with $r_{2(i-1)+(1\oplus r_{2i})}$ and the second one a xor operation with q_1 (since by the inductive invariant, $y_{i-1} = q_0 \oplus q_1 \oplus \Pi_{j=0}^{i-1} x_j$).
3. The message received in Stage 3 includes a xor operation with $r_{2(i+1)}$.
4. The message received in Stage 4 is the value of the function.

The last message (Stage 4) is, by definition, the value of the function. From the observations above, it follows that the distribution of the other 6 messages is the same as the distribution of the tuple $r_{2i}, r_{2i+1}, q_0, q_1, r_{2(i-1)+(1\oplus r_{2i})}, r_{2(i+1)}$ (if $x_i = 0$) or the tuple $r_{2i}, r_{2i+1}, q_0, r_{2(i-1)+(1\oplus r_{2i})}, q_1, r_{2(i+1)}$ (if $x_i = 1$). But, using Lemma 9, we can conclude that both of these 6-tuples are uniformly distributed over the 2^6 possible binary vectors. Thus, privacy is preserved for all players P_i, $1 < i < n - 2$.

Similar arguments apply to the remaining four players. Let $\hat{b}_0 = q_{(n-1) \bmod 2} \oplus u_6$ and let $\hat{b}_1 = y_{n-2} \oplus u_6$ (recall that player P_{n-2} tosses two random bits u_5, u_6, to be used by the OT protocol, Implementation 2, in round $n-1$).

Player P_0: Player P_0 receives the following messages: those listed under Stages 1 and 3 above; in round $n-1$ of the computation phase, when Implementation 2 of OT is invoked, P_0 receives from P_{n-2} either the message $\hat{b}_0 = q_{n-1 \bmod 2} \oplus u_6$ or the message $\hat{b}_1 = y_{n-2} \oplus u_6$ and from P_{n-1} the message $x_{n-1} \oplus u_5 \oplus 1$; and from P_{n-1}, at the final phase, the message $y_{n-1} = q_0 \oplus q_1 \oplus \Pi_{j=0}^{n-1} x_j$. In addition, player P_0 has the values of the random bits q_0 and q_1 tossed by itself. Therefore, the messages received in Stages 1 and 3, as well as the messages received from P_{n-2} and P_{n-1}, each includes a xor operation with an independent (uniformly distributed) random bit not known to P_0. The message received in the final phase is (together with q_0 and q_1) the value of the function. Hence, privacy with respect to P_0 holds.

Player P_1: Player P_1 receives the following messages: the messages listed under Stages 1, 3 and 4 above; in round $n-1$ of the computation phase, when Implementation 2 of OT is invoked, P_1 receives from P_{n-2} either the message $\hat{b}_0 = q_{n-1 \bmod 2} \oplus u_6$ or the message $\hat{b}_1 = y_{n-2} \oplus u_6$ and from P_{n-1} the message $x_{n-1} \oplus u_5$. Therefore, the messages received in Stages 1 and 3, as well as the messages received from P_{n-2} and P_{n-1}, each includes a xor operation with an independent (uniformly distributed) random bit not known to P_1. The message received in Stage 4 is the value of the function. Hence privacy with respect to P_1 holds.

Player P_{n-2}: The set of messages that player P_{n-2} receives is a subset of the messages received by players P_i, $1 < i < n-2$. None of these messages depend on u_5 or u_6 tossed by P_{n-2}. The privacy with respect to player P_{n-2} thus follows from the proof for P_i, $1 < i < n-2$.

Player P_{n-1}: Player P_{n-1} receives a subset of the messages received by the players P_i, $1 < i < n-2$, namely those of Stage 1 and of Stage 4. In addition, it receives, while engaging in Implementation 2 of the OT protocol with player P_{n-2} and helpers P_0, P_1, the following messages:

(1) the messages u_5 and u_6 from player P_{n-2},
(2) the message $M_0 \cdot (x_{n-1} \oplus u_5 \oplus 1)$ from player P_0, where M_0 is the message P_0 receives from P_{n-2} in the OT protocol, Implementation 2,
(3) the message $M_1 \cdot (x_{n-1} \oplus u_5)$ from player P_1, where M_1 is the message P_1 receives from P_{n-2} in the OT protocol, Implementation 2.

We now have four cases depending on the values of x_{n-1} and u_5. In each of the four cases, the two messages received from P_0 and P_1 can be written as follows:

- $x_{n-1} = 0, u_5 = 0$: P_{n-1} receives from P_1 the message 0, and from P_0 the message $M_0 = \hat{b}_0 = q_{(n-1) \bmod 2} \oplus u_6$.
- $x_{n-1} = 0, u_5 = 1$: P_{n-1} receives from P_0 the message 0, and from P_1 the message $M_1 = \hat{b}_0 = q_{(n-1) \bmod 2} \oplus u_6$.
- $x_{n-1} = 1, u_5 = 0$: P_{n-1} receives from P_0 the message 0, and from P_1 the message $M_1 = \hat{b}_1 = y_{n-2} \oplus u_6$.

- $x_{n-1} = 1, u_5 = 1$: P_{n-1} receives from P_1 the message 0, and from P_0 the message $M_0 = \hat{b}_1 = y_{n-2} \oplus u_6$.

It can be verified that, given the values of x_{n-1} and of $AND(x_0, x_1, \ldots, x_{n-1})$, the distribution of the messages received by P_{n-1} is identical in all four cases. Indeed, given the value x_{n-1}, the value of u_5 determines which of the two messages above is a constant, and which includes a xor operation with $q_{(n-1) \bmod 2}$. Now recall that $y_{n-2} = q_0 \oplus q_1 \oplus \Pi_{j=0}^{n-2} x_j$, thus the rest of the messages (except $AND(x_0, x_1, \ldots, x_{n-1})$) include a xor operation with a distinct random bit, other than $q_{(n-1) \bmod 2}$, all are uniformly distributed and independent. Hence, privacy is preserved with respect to P_{n-1}.   □

4.2.3   The Case of $n = 3$

This case can be slightly improved compared to the general case. We can privately compute the and of 3 players using 7 random bits instead of 8.

The protocol is simple to define: run the protocol Π_{odd}, but fix the bit q_1 to be 0 (rather than it being a random bit).

The correctness of the protocol clearly holds since it holds for Π_{odd} with any choice of random bits. To see that privacy is still preserved with respect to all three players, observe that both player P_0 and player P_1 get q_1 in the original protocol (P_0 tosses it, and P_1 gets it in the initialization phase). Therefore, fixing it to 0 leaves the privacy with respect to these two players intact. As to player P_2, note that the OT protocol performed between P_1 and P_2 does not change in the modified protocol. Therefore, if $x_2 = 0$ then P_2 gets q_1 (which is fixed to 0), and no other information. If $x_2 = 1$ then the only information P_2 gets is $q_0 \oplus q_1 \oplus \Pi_{j=0}^1 x_j = q_0 \oplus \Pi_{j=0}^1 x_j$, from which it can compute, using the bit q_0 that it got in the initialization phase, the value of $\Pi_{j=0}^1 x_j$. But this value can be inferred, in the case of $n = 3$ and $x_2 = 1$, from the value of the function and x_2, so privacy is preserved with respect to P_2 too.

5   Conclusions

We consider the randomness complexity of the information-theoretic multi-party private computation of the function and. We show that this computation cannot be done using a single random bit, thus giving the first non-trivial lower bound on the randomness complexity of the private computation of an explicit boolean function. We further give an improved upper bound on the randomness complexity of the private computation of and, thus approaching the exact determination of that measure for and. To the best of our knowledge, for no explicit function f is the exact randomness complexity of the private computation of f known (except for xor, which is trivially 1-random, and degenerate functions). We leave the exact determination of the randomness complexity of private computations of and for further research.

Acknowledgements. We would like to thank an anonymous reviewer of an earlier version of this paper for comments which helped us reduce the upper bound for even number of players from 10 random bits to 8 random bits, and hence also the general upper bound from 10 to 8.

References

1. Asharov, G., Lindell, Y.: A full proof of the BGW protocol for perfectly secure multiparty computation. J. Cryptology **30**(1), 58–151 (2017)
2. Beaver, D.: Precomputing oblivious transfer. In: Coppersmith, D. (ed.) CRYPTO 1995. LNCS, vol. 963, pp. 97–109. Springer, Heidelberg (1995). https://doi.org/10.1007/3-540-44750-4_8
3. Ben-Or, M., Goldwasser, S., Wigderson, A.: Completeness theorems for non-cryptographic fault-tolerant distributed computation (extended abstract). In: Proceedings of the 20th Annual ACM Symposium on Theory of Computing, May 2–4, 1988, Chicago, Illinois, USA, pp. 1–10 (1988)
4. Blundo, C., Galdi, C., Persiano, P.: Randomness recycling in constant-round private computations. In: Jayanti, P. (ed.) DISC 1999. LNCS, vol. 1693, pp. 140–149. Springer, Heidelberg (1999). https://doi.org/10.1007/3-540-48169-9_10
5. Blundo, C., De Santis, A., Persiano, G., Vaccaro, U.: Randomness complexity of private computation. Comput. Complex. **8**(2), 145–168 (1999)
6. Chaum, D., Crépeau, C., Damgård, I.: Multiparty unconditionally secure protocols (extended abstract). In: Proceedings of the 20th Annual ACM Symposium on Theory of Computing, May 2–4, 1988, Chicago, Illinois, USA, pp. 11–19 (1988)
7. Chor, B., Kushilevitz, E.: A zero-one law for Boolean privacy. SIAM J. Discrete Math. **4**(1), 36–47 (1991)
8. Chor, B., Kushilevitz, E.: A communication-privacy tradeoff for modular addition. Inf. Process. Lett. **45**(4), 205–210 (1993)
9. Damgård, I., Nielsen, J.B., Ostrovsky, R., Rosén, A.: Unconditionally secure computation with reduced interaction. In: Fischlin, M., Coron, J.-S. (eds.) EUROCRYPT 2016. LNCS, vol. 9666, pp. 420–447. Springer, Heidelberg (2016). https://doi.org/10.1007/978-3-662-49896-5_15
10. Damgård, I., Nielsen, J.B., Polychroniadou, A., Raskin, M.: On the communication required for unconditionally secure multiplication. In: Robshaw, M., Katz, J. (eds.) CRYPTO 2016. LNCS, vol. 9815, pp. 459–488. Springer, Heidelberg (2016). https://doi.org/10.1007/978-3-662-53008-5_16
11. Data, D., Prabhakaran, V.M., Prabhakaran, M.M.: Communication and randomness lower bounds for secure computation. IEEE Trans. Inf. Theory **62**(7), 3901–3929 (2016)
12. Gál, A., Rosén, A.: A theorem on sensitivity and applications in private computation. SIAM J. Comput. **31**(5), 1424–1437 (2002)
13. Gál, A., Rosén, A.: Omega(log n) lower bounds on the amount of randomness in 2-private computation. SIAM J. Comput. **34**(4), 946–959 (2005)
14. Goldreich, O.: Modern Cryptography, Probabilistic Proofs and Pseudorandomness, vol. 17 of Algorithms and Combinatorics. Springer, Berlin (1998)
15. Jakoby, A., Liśkiewicz, M., Reischuk, R.: Private computations in networks: topology versus randomness. In: Alt, H., Habib, M. (eds.) STACS 2003. LNCS, vol. 2607, pp. 121–132. Springer, Heidelberg (2003). https://doi.org/10.1007/3-540-36494-3_12

16. Kushilevitz, E., Mansour, Y.: Randomness in private computations. SIAM J. Discrete Math. **10**(4), 647–661 (1997)
17. Kushilevitz, E., Ostrovsky, R., Rosén, A.: Characterizing linear size circuits in terms of privacy. J. Comput. Syst. Sci. **58**(1), 129–136 (1999)
18. Kushilevitz, E., Ostrovsky, R., Rosén, A.: Amortizing randomness in private multiparty computations. SIAM J. Discrete Math. **16**(4), 533–544 (2003)
19. Kushilevitz, E., Rosén, A.: A randomness-rounds tradeoff in private computation. SIAM J. Discrete Math. **11**(1), 61–80 (1998)
20. Nisan, N., Ta-Shma, A.: Extracting randomness: a survey and new constructions. J. Comput. Syst. Sci. **58**(1), 148–173 (1999)
21. Rosén, A., Urrutia, F.: A new approach to multi-party peer-to-peer communication complexity. In: Blum, A. (ed.) 10th Innovations in Theoretical Computer Science Conference, ITCS 2019, January 10–12, 2019, San Diego, California, USA, vol. 124 of LIPIcs, pp. 64:1–64:19. Schloss Dagstuhl - Leibniz-Zentrum fuer Informatik (2019)

Leveraging Linear Decryption: Rate-1 Fully-Homomorphic Encryption and Time-Lock Puzzles

Zvika Brakerski[1], Nico Döttling[2], Sanjam Garg[3], and Giulio Malavolta[4(✉)]

[1] Weizmann Institute of Science, Rehovot, Israel
zvika.brakerski@weizmann.ac.il
[2] CISPA Helmholtz Center for Information Security, Saarbrücken, Germany
[3] University of California, Berkeley, Berkeley, USA
[4] Simons Institute for the Theory of Computing, Berkeley, USA

Abstract. We show how to combine a fully-homomorphic encryption scheme with linear decryption and a linearly-homomorphic encryption schemes to obtain constructions with new properties. Specifically, we present the following new results.

(1) Rate-1 Fully-Homomorphic Encryption: We construct the first scheme with message-to-ciphertext length ratio (i.e., rate) $1 - \sigma$ for $\sigma = o(1)$. Our scheme is based on the hardness of the Learning with Errors (LWE) problem and σ is proportional to the noise-to-modulus ratio of the assumption. Our building block is a construction of a new high-rate linearly-homomorphic encryption.

One application of this result is the first general-purpose secure function evaluation protocol in the preprocessing model where the communication complexity is within *additive* factor of the optimal *insecure* protocol.

(2) Fully-Homomorphic Time-Lock Puzzles: We construct the first time-lock puzzle where one can evaluate any function over a set of puzzles without solving them, from standard assumptions. Prior work required the existence of sub-exponentially hard indistinguishability obfuscation.

The full version of this work can be found in https://eprint.iacr.org/2019/720.pdf.

Z. Brakerski—Supported by the Israel Science Foundation (Grant No. 468/14), Binational Science Foundation (Grants No. 2016726, 2014276) and European Union Horizon 2020 Research and Innovation Program via ERC Project REACT (Grant 756482) and via Project PROMETHEUS (Grant 780701).

S. Garg—Supported in part from DARPA/ARL SAFEWARE Award W911NF-15C0210, AFOSR Award FA9550-15-1-0274, AFOSR Award FA9550-19-1-0200, AFOSR YIP Award, NSF CNS Award 1936826, DARPA and SPAWAR under contract N66001-15-C-4065, a Hellman Award and research grants by the Okawa Foundation, Visa Inc., and Center for Long-Term Cybersecurity (CLTC, UC Berkeley). The views expressed are those of the author and do not reflect the official policy or position of the funding agencies.

G. Malavolta—Part of the work done while at Carnegie Mellon University.

D. Hofheinz and A. Rosen (Eds.): TCC 2019, LNCS 11892, pp. 407–437, 2019.
https://doi.org/10.1007/978-3-030-36033-7_16

1   Introduction

Fully-homomorphic encryption (FHE) allows one to evaluate any function over encrypted data. Since the breakthrough result of Gentry [15], the development of FHE schemes has seen a rapid surge [1,6–8,19,32] and by now FHE has become a well-established cryptographic primitive. An FHE scheme gives an elegant solution to the problem of secure function evaluation: One party publishes the encryption of its input under its own public key $\mathsf{Enc}(\mathsf{pk}, x)$ while the other evaluates some function f homomorphically, returning $c = \mathsf{Enc}(\mathsf{pk}, f(x))$. The first party can recover the output by simply decrypting c. The crucial property of this approach is that its communication complexity is proportional to the size of the input and of the output, but does not otherwise depend on the size of f. This distinguishing feature is essential for certain applications, such as private information retrieval [10], and has motivated a large body of work on understanding FHE and related notions [2,29].

Unfortunately, our understanding in secure computation protocol with *optimal* communication complexity is much more limited. Typically, FHE schemes introduce a polynomial blowup factor (in the security parameter) to the ciphertext size, thereby affecting the overall communication rate of the protocol. Given the current state-of-the-art FHE schemes, the only class of functions we can evaluate without communication blowup are linear functions [12]. An FHE scheme with optimal rate, i.e., with a message-to-ciphertext ratio approaching 1, would immediately give us a general-purpose tool to securely evaluate any function (with sufficiently large inputs and outputs) with asymptotically optimal communication complexity. Motivated by this objective, this work seeks to answer the following question:

Can we construct an FHE scheme with rate 1 from standard assumptions?

We also consider the related problem of constructing fully-homomorphic time-lock puzzles (FH-TLP), a primitive recently introduced in [22] to address the computational burden of classical time-lock puzzles [31]. Time-lock puzzles encapsulate secrets for a pre-determined amount of time, and FH-TLP allow one to evaluate functions over independently generated puzzles. The key feature of FH-TLPs is that after a function has been homomorphically evaluated on a (possibly large) number of input TLPs, only a single output TLP has to be solved to recover the function result. Consequently, FH-TLP can be used in the very same way as TLPs, but the solver is spared from solving a large number of TLPs (in parallel) and only needs to solve a single TLP which encapsulates the function result.

FH-TLP have been shown to be a very versatile tool and have several applications, ranging from coin-flipping to fair contract signing [22]. In [22] FH-TLPs were constructed from probabilistic iO [9] and scheme from standard assumptions were limited to restricted classes of functions (e.g., linear functions). Motivated by this gap, the second question that we ask is:

Can we construct an FH-TLP scheme (ideally with rate 1) from standard assumptions?

1.1 Our Results

In this work, we answer both questions in the affirmative. Specifically, we present the following new results:

(1) Our main result is the construction of an FHE which allows compressing many ciphertexts into a *compressed ciphertext* which has rate $1 - 1/\lambda$. In fact, we show that for any a-priori block size $\ell = \mathsf{poly}(\lambda)$, we can construct a scheme where the ciphertext length is at most $\ell + \tau(\lambda)$, where τ is a fixed polynomial (which does not depend on ℓ). Setting $\ell = \lambda \cdot \tau(\lambda)$, the rate claim follows.

   To prove security of this scheme, we only need to assume the hardness of the Learning With Errors (LWE) [30] problem with polynomial modulus-to-noise ratio.[1]

(2) We provide a construction of a fully-homomorphic time-lock puzzle from multi-key FHE and linearly homomorphic time-lock puzzles. The security of the former can be based on the hardness of LWE with superpolynomial modulus-to-noise ratio, whereas the latter can be constructed from the sequential squaring assumption [31] in groups of unknown order.

On a technical level, both of our main results are tied together by the common idea of combining an FHE with a linear decryption algorithm with a linearly-homomorphic encryption (time-lock puzzle, respectively) of optimal rate. The hybrid scheme inherits the best of both worlds and gives us a rate-optimal FHE scheme or an FH-TLP from standard assumptions, depending on the building block that we use. Our techniques are reminiscent of the chimeric scheme of Gentry and Halevi [16], with a new twist to how to encode information without inflating the size of the ciphertexts. Somewhat interestingly, our construction of rate-1 linearly homomorphic encryption from LWE leverages ideas which were originally conceived in the context spooky FHE [13], homomorphic secret sharing [3] and private-information retrieval [14].

Concurrent Work. In a concurrent work, Gentry and Halevi [17] constructed rate-1 FHE schemes using similar ideas as in our work. While the goal of their work is realizing practically efficient high-rate private information retrieval protocols, our constructions are more general and designed to achieve the best possible asymptotic rate.

1.2 Applications

We outline a few interesting implications of our results. We stress that the tools that we develop in this work are of general purpose and we expect them to find more (possibly indirect) applications in the near future.

---

[1] We note that the modulus-to-noise ratio does depend (linearly) on ℓ.

(1) Secure Function Evaluation: FHE yields a very natural protocol for secure function evaluation (SFE) where one party encrypts its input and the other computes the function homomorphically. Given that the input and the output are sufficiently large, rate-1 FHE yields a (semi-honest) SFE scheme where the communication complexity is within *additive* factor from that of the best possible insecure protocol.

(2) Encrypted Databases with Updates: Using rate-1 FHE, it is possible to outsource an encrypted database to an untrusted (semi-honest) cloud provider, without suffering additional storage overhead due to ciphertext expansion. While FHE hybrid encryption (using a non-rate-1 FHE) allows to store a static database without additional storage requirements, as soon as database entries are homomorphically updated they become *FHE-ciphertexts* and consequently their size grows substantially. Keeping the database encrypted under a rate-1 FHE scheme enables the cloud provider to perform updates on the database, while not increasing the size of the encrypted data.

(3) Malicious Circuit Privacy: Instantiating the generic compiler of Ostrovsky et al. [25] with our rate-1 FHE scheme gives the first maliciously circuit-private FHE scheme with rate-1. A maliciously circuit-private scheme does not leak any information to the decrypter about the homomorphically evaluated functions (beyond the function output) for *any choice* of the public parameters. Among others, a rate-1 scheme implies a maliciously statistically sender-private oblivious transfer [4] with the same rate. Previous works [14] were able to achieve rate 1 only for oblivious transfer and only in the semi-honest setting. The prior best known rate in the malicious setting was $\leq 1/2$.

(4) Sealed Bid Auctions: One of the motivating applications of time-lock puzzles is to construct fair sealed bid auctions, where each bid is encrypted in a time-lock puzzle whose opening can be forced by the auctioneer in case the bidder refuses to disclose it. This however involves a computational effort proportional to the number of unopened bids, which can be used as a vector for denial-of-service attacks. Homomorphic time-lock puzzles solve this problem by allowing the auctioneer to homomorphically compute the winner of the auction and only solve a single puzzle. Since this computation cannot be expressed as a linear function, our work provides the first solution from standard assumptions.

1.3 Technical Outline

We present a detailed technical outline of our results in the following. As far as rate-1 FHE is concerned, our focus is on techniques to compress post-evaluation ciphertexts. Compressed ciphertexts can be further expanded (and homomorphically evaluated) via standard bootstrapping techniques.

Schematically, our method for achieving rate-1 FHE is as follows. We consider the "batched-Regev" LWE based encryption scheme (which appears explicitly in the literature, e.g., in [5,28]). This scheme has much better rate than "plain" Regev, but the rate is still asymptotically 0 (i.e., $o(1)$). It can be shown that it is possible to convert plain-Regev ciphertexts into batched-Regev, essentially using the key-switching technique that is frequently used in the FHE literature (see, e.g., [7]). We then show that batched-Regev ciphertexts can be compressed in a way that increases the rate to $1 - o(1)$, but maintains (perfect) decryptability. We do this by combining rounding techniques that appeared previously in the literature [3,13,14] with new techniques that we develop and allow to maintain high rate, perfect correctness, and modest LWE modulus simultaneously. We note that in order to apply key-switching, we need to use batched-Regev in its non-compressed form, and only apply the compression after the switching is complete. This transformation, maintains decryptability but homomorphic capabilities are lost. As mentioned above, these can be restored using bootstrapping in a generic way.

Leveraging Linear Decryption. Our starting point is the observation that, for essentially any FHE construction in literature, decryption (or rather *noisy decryption*) is a linear function in the secret key. More specifically, we can write the decryption operation as a function $L_c(\mathbf{s})$, which is linear in $\mathbf{s}$, the secret key. Typically things are set up in a way such that it holds for correctly formed ciphertexts c that $L_c(\mathbf{s}) = \frac{q}{2} \cdot \mathsf{m} + e$, where m is the plaintext and e is a small noise term. We can then recover m from $L_c(\mathbf{s})$ via rounding.

For many FHE schemes, the choice of the factor $q/2$ is not hardwired into the scheme, but can be provided as an explicit input to the decryption function. More specifically, it holds that

$$L_{\alpha,c}(\mathbf{s}) = \alpha \cdot \mathsf{m} + e,$$

where $L_{\alpha,c}(\cdot)$ is a linear function and e is a small noise term. Assume in the following that $|e| < B$ for some bound B. We refer to this operation as *linear decrypt-and-multiply*. In fact, Micciancio [23] observed that any FHE scheme with linear decryption can be transformed into a scheme which supports linear decrypt-and-multiply.

Equipped with a linear decrypt-and-multiply FHE, our main idea to construct a rate-1 FHE scheme is to run the linear decrypt-and-multiply operation of the FHE scheme inside a high rate linearly homomorphic scheme. Consider an FHE scheme whose secret keys are vectors over $\mathbb{Z}_q$, and a rate-1 linearly homomorphic scheme HE with plaintext space $\mathbb{Z}_q$. Assume we are given as "compression key" the encryption $\mathsf{ck} = \mathsf{Enc}(\mathsf{pk}, \mathbf{s})$ of the FHE secret key $\mathbf{s}$ under the linearly homomorphic scheme HE. Given an FHE ciphertext c encrypting a message $\mathsf{m} \in \{0,1\}$, we can transform c into an encryption of m under the linearly homomorphic scheme by homomorphically evaluating the linear function $L_{\alpha,c}(\cdot)$ on ck, i.e. we compute $\mathsf{HE.Eval}(L_{\alpha,c}(\cdot), \mathsf{ck})$. By homomorphic correctness, this results in an encryption of $\alpha \cdot \mathsf{m} + e$ under the linearly homomorphic scheme HE.

So far, we have not gained anything in terms of rate, as we still have a large ciphertext encrypting only a single bit m. However, we have not yet taken advantage of the fact that we can choose α freely and that the scheme HE has rate 1. Our idea to increase the rate is to *pack* many FHE ciphertexts $(c_1, \ldots, c_\ell)$, each encrypting a single bit m_i, into a single ciphertext of the high-rate linearly homomorphic scheme HE. More specifically, for given FHE ciphertexts $(c_1, \ldots, c_\ell)$ and a parameter t, consider the function $L^*(x)$ defined as

$$L^*(x) = \sum_{i=1}^{\ell} L_{2^{t+i}, c_i}(x).$$

Note that, although we define L^* as a sum of functions, this is not how we compute it. Since L^* is a linear function, we can obtain a matrix-representation of it by, e.g., evaluating it on a basis and then later use the matrix representation to compute the function. By correctness of the FHE scheme it holds that

$$L^*(\mathbf{s}) = \sum_{i=1}^{\ell} L_{2^{t+i}, c_i}(\mathbf{s})$$

$$= \sum_{i=1}^{\ell} 2^{t+i} \cdot \mathsf{m}_i + e,$$

where $e = \sum_{i=1}^{\ell} e_i$ is an ℓB-bounded noise term. Consequently, by homomorphically evaluating L^* on ck, we obtain an encryption $\tilde{c}$ of $\sum_{i=1}^{\ell} 2^{t+i} \cdot \mathsf{m}_i + e$ under the high-rate scheme HE. Given that $2^t > \ell B$, the noise e does not interfer with the encodings of the message bits m_i and they can be recovered during decryption.

The main effect that works in our favor here is that we can *distribute* the message bits m_i into the high order bits by multiplying them with appropriate powers of 2, whereas the decryption noise *piles up in the low order bits*. Consequently, the noise occupies only the lower $\approx \log(\ell) + \log(B)$ bits, whereas the remaining bits of the message space can be packed with message bits. Choosing q as $q \approx (\ell B)^{1/\epsilon}$ for a parameter $\epsilon > 0$ we achieve an encoding rate of $\frac{\log(q) - \log(\ell B)}{\log(q)} = 1 - \epsilon$. Given that the linearly homomorphic encryption scheme has a similarly high rate, we obtain an overall rate of $1 - O(\epsilon)$. Consequently, this construction yields an FHE scheme with rate $1 - O(1/\lambda)$ using, e.g., the Damgård-Jurik cryptosystem or a variant of Regev encryption as linearly homomorphic scheme, where the LWE modulus-to-noise ratio is with (sub-)exponential [28].

Towards a Scheme from Standard LWE. Our next goal is to achieve the same (asymptotic) rate assuming only LWE with polynomial modulus-to-noise ratio. Recall that our packing strategy consisted in encoding the message vector $\mathsf{m} = (\mathsf{m}_1, \ldots, \mathsf{m}_\ell)$ into the high-order bits of a $\mathbb{Z}_q$-element by homomorphically computing $\mathbf{t}^\top \cdot \mathsf{m}$, where $\mathbf{t}^\top = (2^{t+1}, \ldots, 2^{t+\ell})$. However, this is not the only possible strategy. More generally, linear decrypt-and-multiply enables us to homomorphically pack messages $(\mathsf{m}_1, \ldots, \mathsf{m}_\ell)$ into an encoded vector $\mathbf{T} \cdot \mathsf{m}$ for some packing matrix $\mathbf{T} \in \mathbb{Z}_q^{k \times \ell}$. Since linear decryption is inherently noisy, we will require some error correcting properties from such an encoding, i.e., we need to be able to reconstruct m from $\mathbf{T} \cdot \mathsf{m} + \mathbf{e}$, for short noise terms $\mathbf{e}$. With this observation in mind, our next step will be to construct an ad-hoc high-rate linearly homomorphic encryption and pair it with an appropriate packing strategy.

Linearly Homomorphic Encryption with Ciphertext Shrinking. We now discuss new constructions of linearly homomorphic encryption schemes from LWE which allow asymptotically optimal ciphertext sizes. To avoid confusion with our FHE ciphertext compression technique, we will refer to this technique as *ciphertext shrinking*. Our starting point is Regev encryption and its variants. Let q be a modulus. In Regev encryption a ciphertext c consists of two parts, a vector $c_1 \in \mathbb{Z}_q^n$ and a scalar $c_2 \in \mathbb{Z}_q$. The secret key is a vector $s \in \mathbb{Z}_q^n$. Decryption for this scheme is linear, and it holds that

$$c_2 - s^\top \cdot c_1 = \underbrace{\frac{q}{2} \cdot m + e}_{\hat{m}},$$

where e with $|e| < B$ for some bound B is a decryption noise term. We obtain the plaintext m by rounding $\hat{m}$, i.e., by computing

$$\lceil \hat{m} \rfloor_2 = \lceil \hat{m} \cdot 2/q \rfloor$$
$$= \left\lceil \left(\frac{q}{2} \cdot m + e \right) \cdot 2/q \right\rfloor$$
$$= \lceil m + 2e/q \rfloor = m,$$

given that $q > 4B$. We first show how to shrink the component c_2 of the ciphertext into a single bit at the expense of including an additional ring element $r \in \mathbb{Z}_q$ in the ciphertext. Although this procedure does not actually shrink the ciphertext (in fact it increases its size by one $\mathbb{Z}_q$ element), we will later amortize the cost of r across multiple components. The main idea is to *delegate* a part of the rounding operation from the decrypter to a public operation Shrink and it is inspired by recent works on spooky encryption [13], homomorphic secret sharing [3], and private-information retrieval [14].

The algorithm Shrink takes as input the ciphertext $c = (c_1, c_2)$ where $c_2 \in \mathbb{Z}_q$ and proceeds as follows. It first chooses an $r \in \mathbb{Z}_q$ such that $c_2 + r \notin [q/4 - B, q/4 + B] \cup [3/4 \cdot q - B, 3/4 \cdot q + B]$, then it computes $w = \lceil c_2 + r \rfloor_2$ and outputs a compressed ciphertext $\tilde{c} = (c_1, r, w)$. Given a shrunk ciphertext $\tilde{c} = (c_1, r, w)$ and the secret key s, the decrypter computes

$$m' = (w - \lceil s^\top c_1 + r \rfloor_2) \mod 2.$$

We claim that m' is identical to $\mathsf{Dec}(s, c) = \lceil c_2 - s^\top \cdot c_1 \rfloor_2$. To see this, note that since $c_2 - s^\top \cdot c_1 = \frac{q}{2}m + e$, we can write

$$c_2 - e = s^\top \cdot c_1 + \frac{q}{2} \cdot m.$$

Now, since r is chosen such that $c_2 + r \notin [q/4 - B, q/4 + B] \cup [3/4 \cdot q - B, 3/4 \cdot q + B]$ and $e \in [-B, B]$, it holds that

$$\lceil c_2 + r \rfloor_2 = \lceil c_2 + r - e \rfloor_2.$$

Using the above this implies that

$$w = \lceil c_2 + r \rfloor_2 = \lceil c_2 + r - e \rfloor_2 = \left\lceil s^\top \cdot c_1 + r + \frac{q}{2} \cdot m \right\rfloor_2 = (\lceil s^\top \cdot c_1 + r \rfloor_2 + m) \mod 2.$$

It follows that $\mathsf{m} = (w - \lceil \mathbf{s}^\top \mathsf{c}_1 + r \rfloor_2) \mod 2$. Note that after shrinking cipher-texts, we can no longer perform homomorphic operations (unless one is willing to run a bootstrapped ciphertext expansion). As a consequence, in our applications we will only perform the shrinking operation after all homomorphic operations have been computed.

What is left to be shown is how to amortize the cost of including r by shrinking many c_2 components for the same c_1. To achieve this, instead of using basic Regev encryption, we use *batched* Regev encryption. In batched Regev encryption, ciphertexts consist of a vector $\mathsf{c}_1 \in \mathbb{Z}_q^n$ and ring elements $\mathsf{c}_{2,i} \in \mathbb{Z}_q$ for $i \in [\ell]$. To decrypt the i-th message component m_i, we compute

$$\mathsf{m}_i = \lceil \mathsf{c}_{2,i} - \mathbf{s}_i^\top \cdot \mathsf{c}_1 \rfloor_2.$$

where $\mathbf{s}_i$ is the secret key for the i-th component. Consequently, we can use the same shrinking strategy as above for every $\mathsf{c}_{2,i}$. However, now each $\mathsf{c}_{2,i}$ imposes a constraint on r, namely that $\mathsf{c}_{2,i} + r \notin [q/4 - B, q/4 + B] \cup [3/4 \cdot q - B, 3/4 \cdot q + B]$.

Fortunately, given that q is sufficiently large, namely $q > 4\ell B$, there exists an r which fulfills all constraints simultaneously. To find such an r, we compute a union of all *forbidden intervals* modulo q, and pick an r outside of this set. Notice that this procedure can be efficiently implemented even if q is super-polynomially large. The rate of the resulting scheme is

$$\frac{\ell}{(n+1)\log(q) + \ell} = 1 - \frac{(n+1)\log(q)}{(n+1)\log(q) + \ell}.$$

For $q \approx 4\ell B$ and a sufficiently large $\ell = \Omega(\lambda \cdot (n+1)\log(q)) = \mathsf{poly}(\lambda)$, we achieve rate $1 - O(1/\lambda)$.

Notice that while basic Regev encryption is only additively homomorphic, we need a scheme that supports homomorphic evaluation of linear functions. Fortu-nately, this can be achieved by a very simple modification. Instead of encrypting a message m, encrypt the messages $2^i \cdot \mathsf{m}$ for all $i \in [\log(q)]$. Further details are deferred to the main body (Sect. 3.3).

Back to Rate-1 FHE. Returning to our main objective of rate-1 FHE, if we instantiate our generic construction from above with the packed Regev scheme that allows ciphertext shrinking, note that there is a slight mismatch. Recall that our rate 1 FHE construction assumed a linearly homomorphic encryption scheme with plaintext space $\mathbb{Z}_q$ or $\mathbb{Z}_q^k$, whereas our Regev scheme with shrinking has a plaintext space $\{0,1\}^\ell$.

Towards resolving this issue, it is instructive to consider Regev encryption without message encoding and decryption without rounding. That is, we consider only the linear part of decryption where a ciphertext $\mathsf{c} = (\mathsf{c}_1, \mathsf{c}_2)$ decrypts to

$$\mathsf{Dec}(\mathsf{s}, \mathsf{c}) = \mathsf{c}_2 - \mathbf{s}^\top \cdot \mathsf{c}_1 = \mathsf{m}^* + e'$$

where s is the secret key and the message m^* is an element of $\mathbb{Z}_q$. The important observation is that in the construction above the message m^* is the result of a linear decrypt-and-multiply operation. This means that m^* already contains a certain amount of decryption noise and the actual message contained in m^* has already been encoded by the linear decrypt-and-multiply operation.

Assuming for simplicity that $\mathsf{m}^* = L_{\frac{q}{2}, \mathsf{c}^*}(\mathsf{s}^*)$, where c^* is an FHE ciphertext encrypting a message m and s^* the corresponding FHE secret key, we have that

$$\mathsf{Dec}(\mathsf{s}, \mathsf{c}) = \mathsf{c}_2 - \mathsf{s}^\top \cdot \mathsf{c}_1 = L_{\frac{q}{2}, \mathsf{c}^*}(\mathsf{s}^*) + e'$$
$$= \frac{q}{2} \cdot \mathsf{m} + e' + e'',$$

where e'' is a small noise term which is introduced by the inner FHE decryption. Note that above we only had to deal with noise e'' coming from the inner FHE decryption, whereas now we have an additional noise term e' coming from the decryption of the linearly homomorphic scheme. Given that the *compound noise* $e = e' + e''$ is sufficiently small, our shrinking technique for the ciphertext $(\mathsf{c}_1, \mathsf{c}_2)$ still works. The only condition we need for the shrinking technique to work is that $\mathsf{c}_2 - \mathsf{s}^\top \cdot \mathsf{c}_1$ is of the form $\frac{q}{2} \cdot \mathsf{m} + e$ for a B-bounded error e.

To sum things up, all we need to ensure is that the encrypted message is well-formed before ciphertext shrinking via the Shrink procedure. To stay with the notation from above, for this scheme the packing matrix $\mathbf{T}$ which is used to encode plaintexts during the homomorphic decrypt-and-multiply step will be $\frac{q}{2} \cdot \mathbf{I}$, where $\mathbf{I}$ is the identity matrix.

Fully Homomorphic Time-Lock Puzzles. We finally show how ideas from our rate-1 FHE construction can be used to obtain fully homomorphic time-lock puzzles (FH-TLP) from standard assumptions. Very recently, Malavolta and Thyargarajan [22] introduced the notion of homomorphic time-lock puzzles and proposed an efficient construction of linearly homomorphic timelock puzzles (LH-TLP) from the sequential squaring assumption [31]. An LH-TLP allows for evaluations of linear functions on messages encrypted in time-lock puzzles. A key aspect here is that the time-lock puzzles may be independently generated by different players.

The basic idea underlying our construction of FH-TLP is to replace the linearly homomorphic encryption scheme in our rate-1 FHE construction above by an LH-TLP. More concretely, fix an LH-TLP scheme where the message-space is $\mathbb{Z}_q$ and an FHE scheme for which the secret keys are $\mathbb{Z}_q^n$ vectors. We will describe how to generate a puzzle for a message m and time parameter T. First, generate an FHE public key pk together with a secret key $\mathsf{s} \in \mathbb{Z}_q^n$. Next, create a puzzle Z with time parameter T for the LH-TLP scheme encrypting the FHE secret key s. Finally, encrypt the message m under the FHE public key pk obtaining a ciphertext c. The time-lock puzzle consists of $(\mathsf{pk}, \mathsf{c}, \mathsf{Z})$ and can be solved by recovering the secret key s and then decrypting the message m.

While this simple idea allows us to perform homomorphic computations on a single message m, it fails at our actual goal of allowing homomorphic computations on puzzles generated by different puzzle generators. The reason being that every time we generate a new puzzle, we generate a fresh FHE key, and generally homomorphic computations across different keys are not possible. To overcome this issue, we instead use a multi-key FHE scheme, which enables homomorphic computations across different public keys. More specifically, given ℓ puzzles $(\mathsf{pk}_1, \mathsf{c}_1, \mathsf{Z}_1), \ldots, (\mathsf{pk}_\ell, \mathsf{c}_\ell, \mathsf{Z}_\ell)$, encrypting messages $(m_1, \ldots, m_\ell)$, and an ℓ input function f, we can homomorpically compute a ciphertext $\mathsf{c}^* = \mathsf{Eval}(\mathsf{pk}_1, \ldots, \mathsf{pk}_\ell, f, (\mathsf{c}_1, \ldots, \mathsf{c}_\ell))$ which encrypts the message $\mathsf{m}^* = f(m_1, \ldots, m_\ell)$.

We have, however, still not solved the main problem. In order to recover $f(m_1, \ldots, m_\ell)$ from c^*, we first have to recover all secret keys $(\mathsf{s}_1, \ldots, \mathsf{s}_\ell)$ from the LH-TLPs $(\mathsf{Z}_1, \ldots, \mathsf{Z}_\ell)$. Thus, the workload is proportional to that of solving ℓ time-lock puzzles, which is identical to the trivial construction. The final idea is to use a multi-key FHE scheme with linear decryption: If c^* is a (homomorphically evaluated) ciphertext which encrypts a message m^* under public keys $\mathsf{pk}_1, \ldots, \mathsf{pk}_\ell$, we can decrypt c^* using a function $L_{\mathsf{c}^*}(\mathsf{s}_1, \ldots, \mathsf{s}_\ell)$ which is linear in the secret keys $\mathsf{s}_1, \ldots, \mathsf{s}_\ell$. As before, this decryption operation is noisy, i.e.,

$$L_{\mathsf{c}^*}(\mathsf{s}_1, \ldots, \mathsf{s}_\ell) = \frac{q}{2} \cdot \mathsf{m}^* + e,$$

where e with $|e| < B$ is a small noise term. This allows us to homomorphically evaluate the linear function L_{c^*} over the time-lock puzzles $(\mathsf{Z}_1, \ldots, \mathsf{Z}_\ell)$ (recall the Z_i encrypts the secret key s_i) and obtain a time-lock puzzle $\mathsf{Z}^* = \mathsf{Eval}(L_{\mathsf{c}^*}, (\mathsf{Z}_1, \ldots, \mathsf{Z}_\ell))$ encrypting $L_{\mathsf{c}^*}(\mathsf{s}_1, \ldots, \mathsf{s}_\ell) = \frac{q}{2} \cdot \mathsf{m}^* + e$. To recover the computation result m^* we only have to solve Z^*. Note that the final puzzle Z^* is a single compact puzzle for the LH-TLP scheme, thus the overhead to solve this puzzle is that of solving a single LH-TLP and therefore independent of ℓ.

We remark that both multi-key FHE from standard assumptions [11,24] and LH-TLP from standard assumptions [22] need a setup. Consequently, our FH-TLP construction inherits this property. Finally, techniques that we develop to construct rate-1 FHE also apply to our FH-TLP construction.

2   Preliminaries

We denote by $\lambda \in \mathbb{N}$ the security parameter. We say that a function $\mathsf{negl}(\cdot)$ is negligible if it vanishes faster than any polynomial. Given a set S, we denote by $s \leftarrow_\$ S$ the uniform sampling from S. We say that an algorithm is PPT if it can be implemented by a probabilistic machine running in time $\mathsf{poly}(\lambda)$. We abbreviate the set $\{1, \ldots, n\}$ as $[n]$. Matrices are denoted by $\mathbf{M}$ and vectors are denoted by $\mathbf{v}$. We use the infinity norm of a vector $\|\mathbf{v}\|_\infty$, since it behaves conveniently with rounding. For a given modulus q, we define the rounding function $\lceil x \rfloor_2 = \lceil x \cdot 2/q \rfloor$ mod 2.

2.1   Learning with Errors

The (decisional) learning with errors (LWE) problem was introduced by Regev [30]. The LWE problem is parametrized by a modulus q, positive integers n, m and an error distribution χ. An adversary is either given $(\mathbf{A}, \mathbf{s}^\top \cdot \mathbf{A} + \mathbf{e})$ or $(\mathbf{A}, \mathbf{u})$

and has to decide which is the case. Here, $\mathbf{A}$ is chosen uniformly from $\mathbb{Z}_q^{n \times m}$, $\mathbf{s}$ is chosen uniformly from $\mathbb{Z}_q^n$, $\mathbf{u}$ is chosen uniformly from $\mathbb{Z}_q^m$ and $\mathbf{e}$ is chosen from χ^m. The matrix version of this problem asks to distinguish $(\mathbf{A}, \mathbf{S} \cdot \mathbf{A} + \mathbf{E})$ from $(\mathbf{A}, \mathbf{U})$, where the dimensions are accordingly. It follows from a simple hybrid argument that the matrix version is as hard as the standard version.

As shown in [27,30], for *any* sufficiently large modulus q the LWE problem where χ is a discrete Gaussian distribution with parameter $\sigma = \alpha q \geq 2\sqrt{n}$ (i.e. the distribution over $\mathbb{Z}$ where the probability of x is proportional to $e^{-\pi(|x|/\sigma)^2}$), is at least as hard as approximating the shortest independent vector problem (SIVP) to within a factor of $\gamma = \tilde{O}(n/\alpha)$ in *worst case* dimension n lattices. We refer to $\alpha = \sigma/q$ as the *modulus-to-noise* ratio, and by the above this quantity controls the hardness of the LWE instantiation. Hereby, LWE with polynomial α is (presumably) harder than LWE with super-polynomial or sub-exponential α. We can truncate the discrete gaussian distribution χ to $\sigma \cdot \omega(\sqrt{\log(\lambda)})$ while only introducing a negligible error. Consequently, we omit the actual distribution χ but only use the fact that it can be bounded by a (small) value B.

2.2 Homomorphic Encryption

We recall the definition of homomorphic encryption in the following.

Definition 1 (Homomorphic Encryption). *A homomorphic encryption scheme consists of the following efficient algorithms.*

KeyGen(1^λ) : *On input the security parameter 1^λ, the key generation algorithm returns a key pair* (sk, pk).

Enc(pk, m) : *On input a public key* pk *and a message* m, *the encryption algorithm returns a ciphertext* c.

Eval(pk, f, ($c_1, \ldots, c_\ell$)) : *On input the public key* pk, *an ℓ-argument function f, and a vector of ciphertexts* ($c_1, \ldots, c_\ell$), *the evaluation algorithm returns an evaluated ciphertext* c.

Dec(sk, c) : *On input the secret key* sk *and a ciphertext* c, *the decryption algorithm returns a message* m.

We say that a scheme is fully-homomorphic (FHE) if it is homomorphic for all polynomial-size circuits. We also consider a restricted class of homomorphism that supports linear functions and we refer to such a scheme as linearly-homomorphic encryption. We characterize correctness of a single function evaluation. This can be extended to the more general notion of multi-hop correctness [18] if the condition specified below is required to hold for arbitrary compositions of functions.

Definition 2 (Correctness). *A homomorphic encryption scheme* (KeyGen, Enc, Eval, Dec) *is correct if for all $\lambda \in \mathbb{N}$, all ℓ-argument functions f in the supported family, all inputs* ($m_1, \ldots, m_\ell$), *all* (sk, pk) *in the support of* KeyGen(1^λ), and all c_i in the support of $\mathsf{Enc}(\mathsf{pk}, \mathsf{m}_i)$ there exists a negligible function $\mathsf{negl}(\cdot)$ such that

$$\Pr\left[\mathsf{Dec}(\mathsf{sk}, \mathsf{Eval}(\mathsf{pk}, f, (c_1, \ldots, c_\ell))) = f(\mathsf{m}_1, \ldots, \mathsf{m}_\ell)\right] \geq 1 - \mathsf{negl}(\lambda).$$

We require a scheme to be compact in the sense that the size of the ciphertext should not grow with the size of the evaluated function.

Definition 3 (Compactness). *A homomorphic encryption scheme* (KeyGen, Enc, Eval, Dec) *is compact if there exists a polynomial* $\mathsf{poly}(\cdot)$ *such that for all* $\lambda \in \mathbb{N}$, *all ℓ-argument functions f in the supported family, all inputs* $(\mathsf{m}_1, \ldots, \mathsf{m}_\ell)$, *all* $(\mathsf{sk}, \mathsf{pk})$ *in the support of* $\mathsf{KeyGen}(1^\lambda)$, *and all c_i in the support of* $\mathsf{Enc}(\mathsf{pk}, \mathsf{m}_i)$ *it holds that*

$$|\mathsf{Eval}(\mathsf{pk}, f, (c_1, \ldots, c_\ell))| = \mathsf{poly}\left(\lambda, |f(\mathsf{m}_1, \ldots, \mathsf{m}_\ell)|\right).$$

The notion of security is standard for public-key encryption [20].

Definition 4 (Semantic Security). *A homomorphic encryption scheme* (KeyGen, Enc, Eval, Dec) *is semantically secure if for all $\lambda \in \mathbb{N}$ and for all PPT adversaries $\mathcal{A} = (\mathcal{A}_0, \mathcal{A}_1)$ there exists a negligible function* $\mathsf{negl}(\cdot)$ *such that*

$$\Pr\left[b = \mathcal{A}_1(c, \mathsf{st}) \;\middle|\; \begin{array}{l} (\mathsf{sk}, \mathsf{pk}) \leftarrow \mathsf{KeyGen}(1^\lambda) \\ (\mathsf{m}_0, \mathsf{m}_1, \mathsf{st}) \leftarrow \mathcal{A}_0(\mathsf{pk}) \\ b \leftarrow_{\$} \{0,1\} \\ c \leftarrow \mathsf{Enc}(\mathsf{pk}, \mathsf{m}_b) \end{array}\right] = \frac{1}{2} + \mathsf{negl}(\lambda).$$

Finally we define the rate of an encryption scheme as the asymptotic message-to-ciphertext size ratio.

Definition 5 (Rate). *We say that a homomorphic encryption scheme* (KeyGen, Enc, Eval, Dec) *has rate* $\rho = \rho(\lambda)$, *if it holds for all* pk *in the support of* $\mathsf{KeyGen}(1^\lambda)$, *all supported functions f with sufficiently large output size, all messages* $(\mathsf{m}_1, \ldots, \mathsf{m}_\ell)$ *in the message space, and all c_i in the support of* $\mathsf{Enc}(\mathsf{pk}, \mathsf{m}_i)$ *that*

$$\frac{|f(\mathsf{m}_1, \ldots, \mathsf{m}_\ell)|}{|\mathsf{Eval}(\mathsf{pk}, f, (c_1, \ldots, c_\ell))|} \geq \rho.$$

We also say that a scheme has rate 1, if it holds that

$$\liminf_{\lambda \to \infty} \rho(\lambda) = 1.$$

Note that in Definition 5 we need to restrict ourselves to a class of supported functions for which the output size $|f(\mathsf{m}_1, \ldots, \mathsf{m}_\ell)|$ is sufficiently large. E.g., if a function output $f(\mathsf{m}_1, \ldots, \mathsf{m}_\ell)$ is just one bit, we cannot hope to achieve a good rate. Consequently we will only consider functions with a large output domain.

2.3 Multi-key Homomorphic Encryption

A multi-key homomorphic encryption supports the evaluation of functions over ciphertexts computed under different (possibly independently sampled) keys. The result of the computation can then be decrypted using all of the corresponding secret keys. Formally, this introduces a few syntactical modifications. Most notably and in contrast with the single-key variant, multi-key schemes might need a setup which generates public parameters shared across all users.

Definition 6 (Multi-Key Homomorphic Encryption). *A multi-key homomorphic encryption scheme consists of the following efficient algorithms.*

$\mathsf{Setup}(1^\lambda)$: *On input the security parameter 1^λ, the setup algorithm returns the public parameters* pp.

$\mathsf{KeyGen}(\mathsf{pp})$: *On input the public parameters* pp, *the key generation algorithm returns a key pair* $(\mathsf{sk}, \mathsf{pk})$.

$\mathsf{Enc}(\mathsf{pk}, \mathsf{m})$: *On input a public key* pk *and a message* m, *the encryption algorithm returns a ciphertext* c.

$\mathsf{Eval}((\mathsf{pk}_1, \ldots, \mathsf{pk}_\ell), f, (\mathsf{c}_1, \ldots, \mathsf{c}_\ell))$: *On input a vector of public keys* $(\mathsf{pk}_1, \ldots, \mathsf{pk}_\ell)$, *an ℓ-argument function f, and a vector of ciphertexts* $(\mathsf{c}_1, \ldots, \mathsf{c}_\ell)$, *the evaluation algorithm returns an evaluated ciphertext* c.

$\mathsf{Dec}((\mathsf{sk}_1, \ldots, \mathsf{sk}_\ell), \mathsf{c})$: *On input a vector of secret keys* $(\mathsf{sk}_1, \ldots, \mathsf{sk}_\ell)$ *and a ciphertext* c, *the decryption algorithm returns a message* m.

As before, we say that the scheme is fully-homomorphic (MK-FHE) if it is homomorphic for P/poly. The definition of correctness is adapted to the multi-key settings.

Definition 7 (Multi-Key Correctness). *A multi-key homomorphic encryption scheme* $(\mathsf{Setup}, \mathsf{KeyGen}, \mathsf{Enc}, \mathsf{Eval}, \mathsf{Dec})$ *is correct if for all $\lambda \in \mathbb{N}$, all ℓ polynomial in λ, all ℓ-argument functions f in the supported family, all inputs $(\mathsf{m}_1, \ldots, \mathsf{m}_\ell)$, all pp in the support of* Setup, *all $(\mathsf{sk}_i, \mathsf{pk}_i)$ in the support of* $\mathsf{KeyGen}(\mathsf{pp})$, *and all c_i in the support of* $\mathsf{Enc}(\mathsf{pk}_i, \mathsf{m}_i)$ *there exists a negligible function* $\mathsf{negl}(\cdot)$ *such that*

$$\Pr\left[\mathsf{Dec}((\mathsf{sk}_1, \ldots, \mathsf{sk}_\ell), \mathsf{Eval}((\mathsf{pk}_1, \ldots, \mathsf{pk}_\ell), f, (\mathsf{c}_1, \ldots, \mathsf{c}_\ell))) = f(\mathsf{m}_1, \ldots, \mathsf{m}_\ell)\right]$$
$$\geq 1 - \mathsf{negl}(\lambda).$$

Compactness is unchanged except that the ciphertext may grow with the number of keys.

Definition 8 (Multi-Key Compactness). *A multi-key homomorphic encryption scheme* $(\mathsf{Setup}, \mathsf{KeyGen}, \mathsf{Enc}, \mathsf{Eval}, \mathsf{Dec})$ *is compact if there exists a polynomial* $\mathsf{poly}(\cdot)$ *such that for all $\lambda \in \mathbb{N}$, all ℓ polynomial in λ, all ℓ-argument functions f in the supported family, all inputs $(\mathsf{m}_1, \ldots, \mathsf{m}_\ell)$, all $(\mathsf{sk}_i, \mathsf{pk}_i)$ in the support of* $\mathsf{KeyGen}(1^\lambda)$, *and all c_i in the support of* $\mathsf{Enc}(\mathsf{pk}_i, \mathsf{m}_i)$ *it holds that*

$$|\mathsf{Eval}((\mathsf{pk}_1, \ldots, \mathsf{pk}_\ell), f, (\mathsf{c}_1, \ldots, \mathsf{c}_\ell))| = \mathsf{poly}(\lambda, \ell, |f(\mathsf{m}_1, \ldots, \mathsf{m}_\ell)|).$$

The definition of semantic security is identical to that of single-key schemes.

2.4   Linear Decrypt-and-Multiply

To construct our schemes we will need FHE schemes with a more fine-grained correctness property. More specifically, we will require an FHE scheme where for which decryption is a linear function in the secret key. Furthermore, we require that this linear decryption function outputs a the product of the plaintext with a constant ω (which is provided as input to the decryption algorithm). We will refer to such schemes as linear decrypt-and-multiply schemes.

The output of this function may contain some (short) noise, thus we also need an upper bound on amount of noise linear decrypt-and-multiply introduces. This property was explicitly characterized in an oral presentation of Micciancio [23] where he showed that schemes from the literature already satisfy this notion [1, 19] and discussed some applications. A formal definition is given in the following.

Definition 9 (Decrypt-and-Multiply). *We call a homomorphic encryption scheme* (KeyGen, Enc, Eval, Dec) *a decrypt-and-multiply scheme, if there exists bounds* $B = B(\lambda)$ *and* $Q = Q(\lambda)$ *and an algorithm* Dec&Mult *such that the following holds. For every* $q \geq Q$, *all* (sk, pk) *in the support of* KeyGen$(1^\lambda, q)$, *every* ℓ-*argument functions* f *(in the class supported by the scheme), all inputs* $(m_1, \ldots, m_\ell)$, *all* c_i *in the support of* Enc(pk, m_i) *and every* $\omega \in \mathbb{Z}_q$ *that*

$$\text{Dec\&Mult}(\text{sk}, \text{Eval}(\text{pk}, f, (c_1, \ldots, c_\ell)), \omega) = \omega \cdot f(m_1, \ldots, m_\ell) + e \mod q$$

where Dec&Mult *is a linear function in* sk *over* $\mathbb{Z}_q$ *and* $|e| \leq B$ *with all but negligible probability.*

We also consider decrypt-and-multiply for multi-key schemes and we extend the definition below. We note that schemes with such a property were previously considered in the context of Spooky Encryption [13].

Definition 10 (Multi-Key Decrypt-and-Multiply). *We call a multi-key homomorphic encryption scheme* (Setup, KeyGen, Enc, Eval, Dec) *a decrypt-and-multiply scheme, if there exists bounds* $B = B(\lambda)$ *and* $Q = Q(\lambda)$ *and an algorithm* Dec&Mult *such that the following holds. For every* $q \geq Q$, *all* pp *in the support of* Setup$(1^\lambda; q)$, *all* (sk$_i$, pk$_i$) *in the support of* KeyGen(1^λ), *every* ℓ-*argument functions* f *(in the class supported by the scheme), all inputs* $(m_1, \ldots, m_\ell)$, *all* c_i *in the support of* Enc(pk$_i$, m_i) *and every* $\omega \in \mathbb{Z}_q$ *that*

$$\text{Dec\&Mult}((\text{sk}_1, \ldots, \text{sk}_\ell), \text{Eval}((\text{pk}_1, \ldots, \text{pk}_\ell), f, (c_1, \ldots, c_\ell)), \omega)$$
$$= \omega \cdot f(m_1, \ldots, m_\ell) + e \mod q$$

where Dec&Mult *is a linear function in the vector* (sk$_1, \ldots,$ sk$_\ell$) *over* $\mathbb{Z}_q$ *and* $|e| \leq B$ *with all but negligible probability.*

An aspect we have omitted so far is to specify over which domain we require decryption to be linear. For essentially all FHE schemes in the literature, decryption is a linear function over a ring $\mathbb{Z}_q$, which also requires that secret keys are vectors over $\mathbb{Z}_q$. As mentioned before, the main idea behind our constructions will be to perform linear decrypt-and-multiply under a linearly homomorphic encryption scheme. Consequently, we need to match the plaintext space of the linearly homomorphic scheme with the secret key-space of the fully homomorphic scheme. As for some linearly homomorphic schemes we consider, we will need a way to connect the two. Luckily, for essentially all FHE schemes in the literature, the modulus q does not depend on any secret but depends only on the security parameter. Moreover, LWE-based FHE schemes can be instantiated with any (sufficiently large) modulus q without affecting the worst-case hardness of the underlying LWE problem [27].

Consequently, we can consider the modulus q as a system parameter for the underlying FHE scheme. In abuse of notation, we will provide the modulus q as an explicit input to the FHE key generation algorithm.

Schemes with Linear Decrypt-and-Multiply. Micciancio [23] has recently shown that any FHE scheme with linear decryption always admits an efficient linear decrypt-and-multiply algorithm. Notable examples of constructions that support linear decrypt-and-multiply right away are GSW-based schemes [19], e.g., [1,8,11,13,24].

In these schemes, ciphertexts are of the form $\mathbf{C} = \mathbf{A} \cdot \mathbf{R} + \mathsf{m} \cdot \mathbf{G}$, where $\mathbf{A} \in \mathbb{Z}_q^{n \times m}$ is a matrix specified in the public key, $\mathbf{R}$ is a matrix with *small* entries and $\mathbf{G}$ is the so-called gadget matrix. The secret key is a vector $\mathbf{s}$, for which the last component $s_n = 1$, which has the property that $\mathbf{s}^\top \cdot \mathbf{A} = \mathbf{e}^\top$, for a vector $\mathbf{e}^\top$ with small entries. For a vector $\mathbf{v}$ let $\mathbf{G}^{-1}(\mathbf{v})$ be a binary vector with the property that $\mathbf{G} \cdot \mathbf{G}^{-1}(\mathbf{v}) = \mathbf{v}$ ($\mathbf{G}^{-1}(\cdot)$ is a non-linear function). For an $\omega \in \mathbb{Z}_q$ let $\boldsymbol{\omega} \in \mathbb{Z}_q^n$ be a vector which is 0 everywhere but ω in the last component. We can perform the linear decrypt-and-multiply operation by computing

$$\mathbf{s}^\top \cdot \mathbf{C} \cdot \mathbf{G}^{-1}(\boldsymbol{\omega}) = \mathbf{s}^\top \cdot \mathbf{A} \cdot \mathbf{R} \cdot \mathbf{G}^{-1}(\boldsymbol{\omega}) + \mathsf{m} \cdot \mathbf{s}^\top \cdot \mathbf{G} \cdot \mathbf{G}^{-1}(\boldsymbol{\omega})$$
$$= \mathbf{e}^\top \cdot \mathbf{R} \cdot \mathbf{G}^{-1}(\boldsymbol{\omega}) + \mathsf{m} \cdot \mathbf{s}^\top \cdot \boldsymbol{\omega}$$
$$= \omega \cdot \mathsf{m} + e',$$

where $e' = \mathbf{e}^\top \cdot \mathbf{R} \cdot \mathbf{G}^{-1}(\boldsymbol{\omega})$ is a short noise vector. The second equality holds as $\mathbf{s}^\top \cdot \mathbf{A} = \mathbf{e}^\top$, and the third one holds as $\mathbf{s}^\top \cdot \boldsymbol{\omega} = \omega$. We remark that the scheme of Brakerski and Vaikunthanatan [8] satisfies these constraints with a polynomial modulus-to-noise ratio, by exploiting the asymmetric noise growth in the GSW scheme and a specific way to homomorphically evaluate functions.

Since we need a multi-key FHE scheme in our construction of fully homomorphic time-lock puzzles, we briefly discuss a linear decrypt-and-multiply procedure for the MK-FHE construction of Mukherjee and Wichs [24], which in turn is a simplified version of the scheme from Clear and McGoldrick [11]. Recall that the scheme shown in [11,24] is secure against the Learning with Errors problem (with super-polynomial modulo-to-noise ratio) and satisfies the following properties:

(1) The construction is in the common random string model and all parties have access to a uniform matrix $\mathbf{A} \leftarrow_\$ \mathbb{Z}_q^{(n-1) \times m}$.

(2) For any fixed depth parameter d, the scheme supports multi-key evaluation of depth-d circuits using public keys of size $d \cdot \mathsf{poly}(\lambda)$, while secret keys are vectors $\mathbf{s} \leftarrow_\$ \mathbb{Z}_q^n$, regardless of the depth parameter. More concretely, there exists an efficient algorithm MK-FHE.Eval that is given as input:

  (a) Parameters $(\ell, d) \in \mathbb{N}$, where ℓ is the number of public keys that perform depth-d computation.
  (b) A depth-d circuit that computes an ℓ-argument Boolean function $f : \{0,1\}^* \to \{0,1\}$.
  (c) A vector of public keys $(\mathsf{pk}_1, \ldots, \mathsf{pk}_\ell)$ and a fresh (bit-by-bit) encryption of each argument x_i under pk_i, denoted by $c_i \leftarrow \mathsf{MK\text{-}FHE.Enc}(\mathsf{pk}_i, x_i)$.

Then MK-FHE.Eval outputs a matrix $\mathbf{C} \in \mathbb{Z}_q^{n\ell \times m\ell}$ such that

$$\tilde{\mathbf{s}} \cdot \mathbf{C} \cdot \mathbf{G}^{-1}(\boldsymbol{\omega}) = \omega \cdot f(x_1, \ldots, x_\ell) + e \pmod{q}$$

where $\tilde{\mathbf{s}}$ is the row concatenation of $(\mathbf{s}_1, \ldots, \mathbf{s}_\ell)$, $\boldsymbol{\omega}$ is the vector $(0, \ldots, 0, \omega) \in \mathbb{Z}_q^{n\ell}$, and $\mathbf{G}^{-1}$ is the bit-decomposition operator. Furthermore, it holds that

$$|e| \le \beta \cdot (m^4 + m)(m\ell + 1)^d = \beta \cdot 2^{O(d \cdot \log(\lambda))}$$

where β is a bound on the absolute value of the noise of fresh ciphertexts.

(3) By further making a circular-security assumption, MK-FHE.Eval supports the evaluation of circuits of any depth without increasing the size of the public keys. In this case the bound on the noise is $|e| \le \beta \cdot 2^{O(d_{\mathsf{Dec}} \cdot \log(\lambda))}$, where d_{Dec} is the depth of the decryption circuit, which is poly-logarithmic in λ.

Note that that by setting $\ell = 1$ we recover the FHE scheme of [19] except that for the latter we can give a slightly better bound for the noise, namely $|e| \le \beta \cdot m^2 (m+1)^d$. The important observation here is that $\mathbf{C} \cdot \mathbf{G}^{-1}(\boldsymbol{\omega})$ does not depend on the secret key and therefore defining

$$\mathsf{Dec\&Mult}(\tilde{\mathbf{s}}, \mathbf{C}, \omega) = \tilde{\mathbf{s}} \cdot \mathbf{C} \cdot \mathbf{G}^{-1}(\boldsymbol{\omega})$$

gives a syntactically correct linear decrypt-and-multiply algorithm and $B = |e|$ is the corresponding noise bound. Finally we remark that the MK-FHE scheme does not impose any restriction on the choice of q (except for its size) so we can freely adjust it to match the modulus of the companion time-lock puzzle.

2.5 Homomorphic Time-Lock Puzzles

Homomorphic time-lock puzzles generalize the classical notion of time-lock puzzles [31] by allowing one to publicly manipulate puzzles to evaluate functions over the secrets. They were introduced in a recent work [22] and we recall the definition in the following.

Definition 11 (Homomorphic Time-Lock Puzzles). *A homomorphic time-lock puzzle consists of the following efficient algorithms.*

Setup$(1^\lambda, T)$: *On input the security parameter 1^λ and a time parameter T, the setup algorithm returns the public parameters* pp.

PuzGen$($pp, s$)$: *On input the public parameters* pp *and a secret* s, *the puzzle generation algorithm returns a puzzle* Z.

Eval$($pp, f, $(Z_1, \ldots, Z_\ell))$: *On input the public parameters* pp, *an ℓ-argument function f, and a vector of puzzles $(Z_1, \ldots, Z_\ell)$, the evaluation algorithm returns an evaluated puzzle* Z.

Solve$($pp, Z$)$: *On input the public parameters* pp *and a puzzle* Z, *the solving algorithm returns a secret* s.

By convention, we refer to a puzzle as fully-homomorphic (FHTLP) if it is homomorphic for all circuits. We now give the definition of (single-hop) correctness.

Definition 12 (Correctness). *A homomorphic time-lock puzzle* (Setup, PuzGen, Eval, Solve) *is correct if for all $\lambda \in \mathbb{N}$, all $T \in \mathbb{N}$, all ℓ-argument functions f in the supported family, all inputs $(s_1, \ldots, s_\ell)$, all* pp *in the support of* Setup$(1^\lambda, T)$, *and all Z_i in the support of* PuzGen$($pp, $s_i)$ *the following two conditions are satisfied:*

(1) There exists a negligible function $\mathsf{negl}(\cdot)$ *such that*

$$\Pr\left[\mathsf{Solve}(\mathsf{pp}, \mathsf{Eval}(\mathsf{pp}, f, (Z_1, \ldots, Z_\ell))) = f(s_1, \ldots, s_\ell)\right] = 1 - \mathsf{negl}(\lambda).$$

(2) The runtime of Solve$($pp, Z$)$, *where $Z \leftarrow$* Eval$($pp, f, $(Z_1, \ldots, Z_\ell))$, *is bounded by* poly(λ, T), *for some fixed polynomial* poly$(\cdot)$.

In this work we consider the stronger notion of security where time is counted starting from the moment the puzzle is generated (as opposed to the moment where the public parameters of the scheme are generated). This is termed security with reusable setup in [22] and we henceforth refer to it simply as security.

Definition 13 (Security). *A homomorphic time-lock puzzle* (Setup, PuzGen, Eval, Solve) *is secure if for all $\lambda \in \mathbb{N}$, all $T \in \mathbb{N}$, all PPT adversaries $\mathcal{A} = (\mathcal{A}_0, \mathcal{A}_1)$ such that the depth of $\mathcal{A}_1$ is bounded by T, there exists a negligible function* $\mathsf{negl}(\cdot)$ *such that*

$$\Pr\left[b = \mathcal{A}_1(Z, \mathsf{st}) \middle| \begin{array}{l} \mathsf{pp} \leftarrow \mathsf{Setup}(1^\lambda, T) \\ (s_0, s_1, \mathsf{st}) \leftarrow \mathcal{A}_0(\mathsf{pp}) \\ b \leftarrow_\$ \{0, 1\} \\ Z \leftarrow \mathsf{PuzGen}(\mathsf{pp}, s_b) \end{array}\right] = \frac{1}{2} + \mathsf{negl}(\lambda).$$

3   Shrinking Linearly Homomorphic Encryption

In the following section we introduce the useful abstraction of linearly homomorphic encryption with compressing ciphertexts and we discuss several concrete instantiations.

3.1   Definitions

We start by providing relaxed correctness definitions for linearly homomorphic encryption. As discussed before, for Regev-like encryption schemes decryption is a linear operation which, unavoidably, introduces noise. This noise is dealt with by encoding the message accordingly and decoding the result of linear decryption, usually by applying a rounding function. In this section we provide definitions for linearly homomorphic encryption which account for noise, and allow to treat encoding and decoding of the message separately. We assume that a linearly homomorphic encryption scheme is described by four algorithms (KeyGen, Enc, Dec, Eval) with the usual syntax. We further assume that each public key pk specifies a message space of the form $\mathbb{Z}_q^k$.

Definition 14 (Relaxed Correctness). *Let* HE $=$ (KeyGen, Enc, Dec, Eval) *be a linearly homomorphic encryption scheme. Let* $B = B(\lambda)$ *and* $\ell = $ poly(λ). *We say that* HE *is correct with B-noise, if it holds for every* (pk, sk) *in the support of* KeyGen(1^λ), *where* pk *specifies a message space* $\mathbb{Z}_q^k$, *every linear function* $f : (\mathbb{Z}_q^k)^\ell \to \mathbb{Z}_q^k$, *all messages* $(m_1, \ldots, m_\ell) \in \mathbb{Z}_q^k$ *that*

$$\mathsf{Dec}(\mathsf{sk}, \mathsf{Eval}(\mathsf{pk}, f, (\mathsf{Enc}(\mathsf{pk}, m_1), \ldots, \mathsf{Enc}(\mathsf{pk}, m_\ell)))) = f(m_1, \ldots, m_\ell) + e,$$

where $e \in \mathbb{Z}^k$ *is a noise term with* $\|e\|_\infty \leq \ell B$.

Notice that we allow the amount of noise to depend linearly on the parameter ℓ. We also consider linearly homomorphic encryption schemes which allow for shrinking post-evaluation ciphertexts. Such schemes will have two additional algorithms Shrink and ShrinkDec defined below.

Shrink(pk, c) : Takes as input a public key pk and an evaluated ciphertext c and outputs a shrunk ciphertext c̃.

ShrinkDec(sk, c̃) : Takes as input a secret key sk and a shrunk ciphertext c̃ and outputs a message m.

Furthermore, for such schemes we assume that the public key pk contains an *encoding matrix* $\mathbf{T} \in \mathbb{Z}_q^{k \times \ell}$. The encoding matrix $\mathbf{T}$ will specifies how *binary messages are supposed to be encoded in the message space* $\mathbb{Z}_q^k$. We can now define the notion of shrinking correctness for a homomorphic encryption scheme HE.

Definition 15 (Shrinking Correctness). *Let* HE $=$ (KeyGen, Enc, Dec, Eval) *be a linearly homomorphic encryption scheme with additional algorithms* (Shrink, ShrinkDec). *Let* $K = K(\lambda)$. *We say that* HE *is correct up to* K-*noise, if the following holds. For every* (pk, sk) *in the support of* KeyGen(1^λ), *where* pk *specifies a message space* $\mathbb{Z}_q^k$ *and an encoding matrix* $\mathbf{T} \in \mathbb{Z}_q^{k \times \ell}$, *and every* c *with*

$$\mathsf{Dec}(\mathsf{sk}, c) = \mathbf{T} \cdot m + e,$$

where $m \in \{0, 1\}^\ell$ *and* $\|e\| \leq K$, *it holds that*

$$\mathsf{ShrinkDec}(\mathsf{sk}, \mathsf{Shrink}(\mathsf{pk}, c)) = m.$$

In our main construction, we will set the bounds B (in the Definition 14) and K (in Definition 15) in such a way that the amount of noise K *tolerated* by shrinking correctness is substantially higher than the noise B introduced by decryption. Finally, we remark that the notion of shrinking correctness also applies to non-homomorphic encryption, albeit it seems not very useful in this context, as optimal rate can be achieved via hybrid encryption.

3.2 A Ciphertext Shrinking Algorithm

We discuss a ciphertext shrinking technique which applies to a broad class of encryption schemes. Let $(\mathsf{KeyGen}, \mathsf{Enc}, \mathsf{Dec}, \mathsf{Eval})$ be an encryption scheme where the public key specifies a message space $\mathbb{Z}_q^\ell$, the secret key $\mathbf{S}$ is a matrix in $\mathbb{Z}_q^{\ell \times n}$, (evaluated) ciphertexts are of the form (c_1, c_2), and (noisy) decryption computes

$$\mathsf{Dec}(\mathbf{S}, (c_1, c_2)) = F(c_2) - \mathbf{S} \cdot H(c_1),$$

where $F(c_2) \in \mathbb{Z}_q^\ell$, $H(c_1) \in \mathbb{Z}_q^n$. Here the two functions F and H are part of the description of the scheme and publicly known. Assume in the following that q is even. We describe a general method to shrink ciphertexts of schemes that satisfy these conditions. Consider the following algorithms Shrink and $\mathsf{ShrinkDec}$.

$\mathsf{Shrink}(\mathsf{pk}, (c_1, c_2))$: Compute $F(c_2)$ and parse it as $(y_1, \ldots, y_\ell) \in \mathbb{Z}_q^\ell$. Compute the union of intervals

$$U = \bigcup_{i=1}^{\ell} ([q/4 - y_i - B, q/4 - y_i + B] \cup [-q/4 - y_i - B, -q/4 - y_i + B]) \subseteq \mathbb{Z}_q.$$

Pick any $r \in \mathbb{Z}_q \setminus U$. For $i = 1, \ldots, \ell$ compute $w_i = \lceil y_i + r \rceil_2$. Output $\tilde{c} = (r, c_1, w_1, \ldots, w_\ell)$.

$\mathsf{ShrinkDec}(\mathbf{S}, \tilde{c} = (r, c_1, w_1, \ldots, w_\ell))$: Compute $\mathbf{v} = \mathbf{S} \cdot H(c_1)$ and parse $\mathbf{v} = (v_1, \ldots, v_\ell)$. For $i = 1, \ldots, \ell$ set $m_i' = (w_i - \lceil v_i + r \rceil_2) \mod 2$. Output $\mathbf{m}' = (m_1', \ldots, m_\ell')$.

The encoding matrix $\mathbf{T}$ for this scheme is defined to be $\mathbf{T} = \frac{q}{2} \cdot \mathbf{I}$, where $\mathbf{I} \in \mathbb{Z}_q^{\ell \times \ell}$ is the identity matrix. We now state the conditions under which the modified scheme has shrinking correctness.

Lemma 1. *Let* $\mathsf{HE} = (\mathsf{KeyGen}, \mathsf{Enc}, \mathsf{Dec}, \mathsf{Eval})$ *be an encryption scheme as above, let* $(\mathsf{Shrink}, \mathsf{ShrinkDec})$ *be as above and let* $K = K(\lambda)$. *Let* pk *be a public key for* HE *specifying a message space* $\mathbb{Z}_q^\ell$ *with a corresponding secret key* $\mathbf{S} \in \mathbb{Z}_q^{\ell \times n}$. *Then given that* $q > 4\ell \cdot K$ *the scheme has shrinking correctness up to noise* K.

Proof. Let (c_1, c_2) be a ciphertext under pk for which it holds that $F(c_2) - \mathbf{S} \cdot H(c_1) = \frac{q}{2} \cdot \mathbf{m} + \mathbf{z}$ for a $\mathbf{z}$ with $\|\mathbf{z}\| \le K$. Let $\mathbf{y} = F(c_2)$, $\mathbf{v} = \mathbf{S} \cdot H(c_1)$ and parse $\mathbf{y} = (y_1, \ldots, y_\ell)$ and $\mathbf{v} = (v_1, \ldots, v_\ell)$. I.e., it holds that $\mathbf{y} - \mathbf{v} = \frac{q}{2} \cdot \mathbf{m} + \mathbf{z}$. Fix an index $i \in [\ell]$ and write $y_i - v_i = \frac{q}{2} \cdot m_i + z_i$, for a $z_i \in [-K, K]$. This implies that $y_i = v_i + z_i + \frac{q}{2} \cdot m_i$. Note that given that $y_i + r \notin [q/4 - B, q/4 + B]$, $y_i + r \notin [-q/4 - B, -q/4 + B]$ and $z_i \in [-B, B]$, it holds that

$$\lceil y_i + r \rfloor_2 = \lceil y_i + r - z_i \rfloor_2$$
$$= \lceil v_i + r + \frac{q}{2} \cdot m_i \rfloor_2$$
$$= (\lceil v_i + r \rfloor_2 + m_i) \mod 2.$$

Consequently, it holds that $(\lceil y_i + r \rfloor_2 - \lceil v_i + r \rfloor_2) \mod 2 = m_i$.

Thus, given that it holds for all $i \in [\ell]$ that $y_i + r \notin [q/4 - B, q/4 + B]$ and $y_i + r \notin [-q/4 - B, -q/4 + B]$ then decryption of all m_i will succeed. We will now argue that under the given parameter choice such an r always exists. For every index $i \in [\ell]$ it holds that $y_i + r \notin [q/4 - B, q/4 + B]$ and $y_i + r \notin [-q/4 - B, -q/4 + B]$, if and only if $r \notin [q/4 - y_i - B, q/4 - y_i + B]$ and $r \notin [-q/4 - y_i - B, -q/4 - y_i + B]$. I.e., for every index i there are two intervals $[q/4 - y_i - B, q/4 - y_i + B]$ and $[-q/4 - y_i - B, -q/4 - y_i + B]$ of forbidden choices of r. Given that the set of all forbidden choices

$$U = \bigcup_{i=1}^{\ell} ([q/4 - y_i - B, q/4 - y_i + B] \cup [-q/4 - y_i - B, -q/4 - y_i + B])$$

has less than q elements, we can find an $r \in \mathbb{Z}_q$ which satisfies all constraints. By a union bound it holds that $|U| \leq \ell \cdot 4B$. Consequently, since $q > 4\ell B$, it holds that $\mathbb{Z}_q \backslash U \neq \emptyset$, and the compression algorithm will find an r such that decryption will recover every m_i correctly.

3.3 Packed Regev Encryption

We briefly recall the linearly homomorphic packed Regev encryption and augment it with the shrinking procedures provided in the last section. This will give use a linearly homomorphic scheme with rate $1 - O(1/\lambda)$. Let $q = 2q'$ be a k-bit modulus, let (n, m, ℓ) be positive integers and let χ be a B-bounded error distribution defined on $\mathbb{Z}$. Let $\mathbf{G}_i \in \mathbb{Z}_q^{\ell \times k}$ be a matrix which is zero everywhere, but its i-th row is $\mathbf{g}^\top = (1, 2, \ldots, 2^i, \ldots, 2^k)$. For a $y \in \mathbb{Z}_q$ let $\mathbf{g}^{-1}(y) \in \{0, 1\}^k$ be the binary expansion of y, i.e., it holds that $\mathbf{g}^\top \cdot \mathbf{g}^{-1}(y) = y$.

KeyGen(1^λ) : Choose $\mathbf{A} \leftarrow_\$ \mathbb{Z}_q^{n \times m}$ uniformly at random. Choose $\mathbf{S} \leftarrow_\$ \mathbb{Z}_q^{\ell \times n}$ uniformly at random and sample $\mathbf{E} \leftarrow_\$ \chi^{\ell \times m}$. Set $\mathbf{B} = \mathbf{S} \cdot \mathbf{A} + \mathbf{E}$. Set pk $= (\mathbf{A}, \mathbf{B})$ and sk $= \mathbf{S}$.

Enc(pk $= (\mathbf{A}, \mathbf{B}), (m_1, \ldots, m_\ell)$) : Choose a random matrix $\mathbf{R} \leftarrow_\$ \{0, 1\}^{m \times k}$ and set $\mathbf{C}_1 = \mathbf{A} \cdot \mathbf{R}$ and. $\mathbf{C}_2 = \mathbf{B} \cdot \mathbf{R} + \sum_{i=1}^{\ell} m_i \cdot \mathbf{G}_i$. Output $c = (\mathbf{C}_1, \mathbf{C}_2)$.

Eval($(f_1, \ldots, f_t), (c_1, \ldots, c_t)$) : Parse $c_i = (\mathbf{C}_{1,i}, \mathbf{C}_{2,i})$. Compute $\mathbf{c}_1 = \sum_{i=1}^{t} \mathbf{C}_{1,i} \cdot \mathbf{g}^{-1}(f_i)$ and $\mathbf{c}_2 = \sum_{i=1}^{t} \mathbf{C}_{2,i} \cdot \mathbf{g}^{-1}(f_i)$. Output $c = (\mathbf{c}_1, \mathbf{c}_2)$.

Dec(sk $= \mathbf{S}, c = (\mathbf{c}_1, \mathbf{c}_2)$): Compute and output $\mathbf{c_2} - \mathbf{S} \cdot \mathbf{c}_1$.

First notice that under the LWE assumption, the matrix $\mathbf{B}$ in the public key is pseudorandom. Consequently, given that $m > (n + \ell) \cdot \log(q) + \omega(\log(\lambda))$, we can call the leftover-hash lemma [21] to argue that ciphertexts $(\mathbf{C}_1, \mathbf{C}_2)$ are statistically close to uniform [30] and we obtain semantic security.

We now consider the homomorphic correctness of the scheme. Let $\mathbf{f} = (f_1, \ldots, f_t) \in \mathbb{Z}_q^t$ define a linear function and let $(\mathbf{x}_1, \ldots, \mathbf{x}_t) \in \mathbb{Z}_q^t$. For $i \in [t]$ let $\mathsf{c}_i = (\mathbf{C}_{1,i}, \mathbf{C}_{2,i}) = \mathsf{Enc}(\mathsf{pk}, \mathsf{m}_i)$, i.e., it holds that $\mathsf{c}_{1,i} = \mathbf{A} \cdot \mathbf{R}_i$ and $\mathsf{c}_{2,i} = \mathbf{B} \cdot \mathbf{R}_i + \sum_{j=1}^{\ell} x_{i,j} \cdot \mathbf{G}_j$. A routine calculation shows that

$$\mathsf{Dec}(\mathbf{S}, \mathsf{c}^*) = \sum_{j=1}^{t} f_j \mathbf{x}_j + \mathbf{z}$$

where $\mathbf{z} = \mathbf{E} \cdot \sum_{j=1}^{t} \mathbf{R}_j \cdot \mathbf{g}^{-1}(f_j)$. We can bound $\|\mathbf{z}\|_\infty$ by

$$\|\mathbf{z}\|_\infty \le t \cdot k \cdot m \cdot B.$$

Consequently, the scheme HE is correct with $t \cdot k \cdot m \cdot B$-noise. Since HE fulfills the structural criteria of Lemma 1 we can augment the scheme with algorithms Shrink and $\mathsf{ShrinkDec}$ and the resulting scheme has shrinking correctness up to K-noise, given that $q > 4\ell \cdot K$.

Rate. We finally analyze the rate of the scheme for some $K = \mathsf{poly}(\lambda)$ and $q \approx 4\ell K$. Shrunk ciphertexts generated by Shrink have the form $(\mathsf{c}_1, r, w_1, \ldots, w_\ell)$, where $\mathsf{c}_1 \in \mathbb{Z}_q^n$, $r \in \mathbb{Z}_q$ and $w_i \in \{0, 1\}$ for $i \in [\ell]$. Consequently, the ciphertext length is $(n + 1)\log(q) + \ell$. Given that $q = \mathsf{poly}(\lambda)$, we can conservatively bound $\log(q) \le (\log(\lambda))^2$ and observe that indeed the ciphertext is only additively longer than the plaintext. In terms of ratio, we achieve

$$\rho = \frac{\ell}{(n+1)\log(q) + \ell} \ge 1 - \frac{(n+1)\log(q)}{\ell},$$

which translates to $1 - 1/\lambda$ for $\ell \ge n \cdot \lambda \cdot (\log(\lambda))^2$.

4   Rate-1 Fully-Homomorphic Encryption

The following section is devoted to the presentation of our main result, an FHE scheme with optimal rate.

4.1   Definitions

Before presenting the construction of our rate 1 FHE scheme, we will augment the syntax of an FHE scheme by adding a compression algorithm and an additional decryption procedure for compressed ciphertexts. This will facilitate the exposition of our scheme.

428   Z. Brakerski et al.

Definition 16 (Compressible FHE). *Let* $\mathsf{FHE} = (\mathsf{KeyGen}, \mathsf{Enc}, \mathsf{Dec}, \mathsf{Eval})$ *be an FHE scheme and let* $\ell = \ell(\lambda) = \mathsf{poly}(\lambda)$. *We say that* FHE *supports* ℓ-*ciphertext compression if there exist two algorithms* $\mathsf{Compress}$ *and* $\mathsf{CompDec}$ *with the following syntax.*

$\mathsf{Compress}(\mathsf{pk}, \mathsf{c}_1, \ldots, \mathsf{c}_\ell)$: *Takes as input a public key* pk *and* ℓ *ciphertexts* $(\mathsf{c}_1, \ldots, \mathsf{c}_\ell)$ *and outputs a compressed ciphertext* c^*
$\mathsf{CompDec}(\mathsf{sk}, \mathsf{c}^*)$: *Takes as input a secret key* sk *and a compressed ciphertext* c^* *and outputs* ℓ *messages* $(\mathsf{m}_1, \ldots, \mathsf{m}_\ell)$.

In terms of correctness we require the following: Let $(\mathsf{pk}, \mathsf{sk})$ *be a key pair in the support of* $\mathsf{KeyGen}(1^\lambda)$ *and let* $\mathsf{c}_1, \ldots, \mathsf{c}_\ell$ *be valid ciphertexts (i.e., freshly encrypted ciphertext or ciphertexts that are the result of a homomorphic evaluation) such that for all* $i \in [\ell]$ *it holds* $\mathsf{m}_i = \mathsf{Dec}(\mathsf{sk}, \mathsf{c}_i)$. *Then it holds that*

$$\mathsf{CompDec}(\mathsf{sk}, \mathsf{Compress}(\mathsf{pk}, \mathsf{c}_1, \ldots, \mathsf{c}_\ell)) = (\mathsf{m}_1, \ldots, \mathsf{m}_\ell).$$

For compressible FHE schemes, we say a scheme has rate $\rho = \rho(\lambda)$ *if it holds for all* $(\mathsf{pk}, \mathsf{sk})$ *in the support of* $\mathsf{KeyGen}(1^\lambda)$, *all messages* $\mathsf{m}_1, \ldots, \mathsf{m}_\ell$ *and all ciphertexts* $\mathsf{c}_1, \ldots, \mathsf{c}_\ell$ *with* $\mathsf{Dec}(\mathsf{sk}, \mathsf{c}_i) = \mathsf{m}_i$ *(for* $i \in [\ell]$*) that*

$$\frac{|(\mathsf{m}_1, \ldots, \mathsf{m}_\ell)|}{|\mathsf{Compress}(\mathsf{pk}, (\mathsf{c}_1, \ldots, \mathsf{c}_\ell))|} \geq \rho.$$

Note that this rate definition is compatible with Definition 5 when we consider functions f which produce ℓ (bits of) outputs.

4.2 Construction

In the following we describe a compressible FHE scheme which can be instantiated such that compressed ciphertexts achieve rate 1. We assume the existence of an FHE with linear decrypt-and-multiply (and any rate) and a rate-1 linearly-homomorphic encryption scheme. In this scheme, compressed ciphertexts no longer support homomorphic operations, i.e., the scheme is single-hop homomorphic. Later, we briefly discuss how this scheme can be converted into a multi-hop levelled or fully homomorphic scheme.

Notation. Since the linearly homomorphic scheme HE may work with k parallel slots, we need some notation on how to address specific slots. If f is a linear function taking as input a row vector $\mathbf{x}$ we can canonically extend f to take as input matrices $\mathbf{X}$, where the function f is applied to each row individually. In fact, if the function f is represented by a column vector $\mathbf{f}$, we can evaluate f on $\mathbf{X}$ by computing $\mathbf{X} \cdot \mathbf{f}$. Moreover, for a column vector $\mathbf{a}$ and a row vector $\mathbf{b}$ we let $\mathbf{a} \cdot \mathbf{b}$ denote the outer product of $\mathbf{a}$ and $\mathbf{b}$. This allows us to put a row vector $\mathbf{x}$ into a certain slot i by computing $\mathbf{b}_i \cdot \mathbf{x}$, where $\mathbf{b}_i$ is the i-th unit vector. Consequently, this lets us conveniently write $f(\mathbf{b}_i \cdot \mathbf{x}) = \mathbf{b}_i \cdot f(\mathbf{x})$, where f is a linear function taking row vectors as inputs as above. For a linearly homomorphic scheme HE with message space $\mathbb{Z}_q^k$, we denote inputs as column vectors. We can encrypt a message m into the i-th slot by computing $\mathsf{HE.Enc}(\mathsf{pk}_2, \mathsf{m} \cdot \mathbf{b}_i)$, where $\mathbf{b}_i \in \mathbb{Z}_q^k$ is the i-th unit column vector.

Let FHE $=$ (FHE.KeyGen, FHE.Enc, FHE.Eval, FHE.Dec) be a (somewhat or fully) homomorphic encryption scheme with linear decrypt-and-multiply and plaintext space $\{0,1\}$. Let further HE $=$ (HE.KeyGen, HE.Enc, HE.Eval, HE.Dec, HE.Shrink, HE.ShrinkDec) be a packed linearly homomorphic encryption scheme with relaxed correctness in which we can pack ℓ message bits. In abuse of notation we assume that the key-generation algorithm $\mathsf{FHE.KeyGen}(1^\lambda, q)$ takes the modulus q as an explicit input.

$\overline{\mathsf{FHE.KeyGen}}(1^\lambda)$: On input the security parameter 1^λ, the key generation algorithm samples

$$(\mathsf{pk}_2, \mathsf{sk}_2) \leftarrow \mathsf{HE.KeyGen}(1^\lambda).$$

Let q be the modulus of the plaintext space corresponding to pk_2. Compute

$$(\mathsf{sk}_1, \mathsf{pk}_1) \leftarrow \mathsf{FHE.KeyGen}(1^\lambda, q).$$

Let $\mathsf{sk}_1 = (s_1, \ldots, s_n) \in \mathbb{Z}_q^n$. For $i = 1, \ldots, k$ and $j = 1, \ldots, n$ compute

$$\mathsf{ck}_{i,j} \leftarrow \mathsf{HE.Enc}(\mathsf{pk}_2, s_j \cdot \mathbf{b}_i),$$

Set $\mathsf{ck}_i = (\mathsf{ck}_{i,1}, \ldots, \mathsf{ck}_{i,n})$ for $i \in [k]$ and set the compression key to $\mathsf{ck} = (\mathsf{ck}_1, \ldots, \mathsf{ck}_k)$.
Return $\mathsf{pk} = (\mathsf{pk}_1, \mathsf{pk}_2, \mathsf{ck})$ as the public key and $\mathsf{sk} = (\mathsf{sk}_1, \mathsf{sk}_2)$ as the secret key.

$\overline{\mathsf{FHE.Enc}}(\mathsf{pk}, \mathsf{m})$: On input the public key $\mathsf{pk} = (\mathsf{pk}_1, \mathsf{pk}_2, \mathsf{ck})$ and a message $\mathsf{m} \in \{0,1\}$, compute and output $\mathsf{c} \leftarrow \mathsf{FHE.Enc}(\mathsf{pk}_1, \mathsf{m})$.

$\overline{\mathsf{FHE.Eval}}(\mathsf{pk}, f, (\mathsf{c}_1, \ldots, \mathsf{c}_\ell))$: On input the public key $\mathsf{pk} = (\mathsf{pk}_1, \mathsf{pk}_2, \mathsf{ck})$, a function f and ciphertexts $(\mathsf{c}_1, \ldots, \mathsf{c}_\ell)$, compute and output $\mathsf{FHE.Eval}(\mathsf{pk}_1, f, (\mathsf{c}_1, \ldots, \mathsf{c}_\ell))$.

$\overline{\mathsf{FHE.Dec}}(\mathsf{sk}, \mathsf{c})$: On input the secret key $\mathsf{sk} = (\mathsf{sk}_1, \mathsf{sk}_2)$ and a ciphertext c, compute and output $\mathsf{m} \leftarrow \mathsf{FHE.Dec}(\mathsf{sk}_1, \mathsf{c})$.

$\overline{\mathsf{FHE.Compress}}(\mathsf{pk}, (\mathsf{c}_1, \ldots, \mathsf{c}_\ell))$: On input a public key $\mathsf{pk} = (\mathsf{pk}_1, \mathsf{pk}_2, \mathsf{ck})$, where the compression key is of the form $\mathsf{ck} = (\mathsf{ck}_1, \ldots, \mathsf{ck}_k)$, and ciphertexts $(\mathsf{c}_1, \ldots, \mathsf{c}_\ell)$ proceed as follows. Let $\mathbf{T} = (t_{ij})$ be the encoding matrix corresponding to the public key pk. First construct a linear function f which computes

$$f(\boldsymbol{x}_1, \ldots, \boldsymbol{x}_k) = \sum_{i=1}^{k} \sum_{j=1}^{\ell} \mathsf{Dec\&Mult}\left(\boldsymbol{x}_i, \mathsf{c}_j, t_{ij}\right).$$

Note that the function f is specified by the matrix $T = (t_{ij})$ and the ciphertexts $(c_1, \ldots, c_\ell)$.

Compute and output $\tilde{c} = \mathsf{HE.Shrink}(\mathsf{pk}_2, \mathsf{HE.Eval}(\mathsf{pk}_2, f, \mathsf{ck}_1, \ldots, \mathsf{ck}_k))$.

$\overline{\mathsf{FHE}}.\mathsf{CompDec}(\mathsf{sk}, \tilde{c})$: On input the secret key $\mathsf{sk} = (\mathsf{sk}_1, \mathsf{sk}_2)$ and a compressed ciphertext $\tilde{c}$, compute and output $\mathbf{m} = \mathsf{HE.ShrinkDec}(\mathsf{sk}_2, \tilde{c})$.

4.3 Analysis

The security of our scheme is shown in the following. Recall that for LWE-based FHE schemes, e.g., [1,19,24], the LWE modulus is a system parameter which can be provided as an input to the KeyGen algorithm. By [27] that worst-case hardness of the underlying LWE problem is not affected.

Theorem 1 (Semantic Security). *Assume that* FHE *and* HE *are semantically secure encryption schemes, then the scheme* $\overline{\mathsf{FHE}}$ *as described above is also semantically secure.*

Proof (Sketch). Let $\mathcal{A}$ be a PPT adversary against the semantic security of $\overline{\mathsf{FHE}}$. Consider a hybrid experiment where we compute the compression key by

$$\mathsf{ck}_i \leftarrow \mathsf{HE.Enc}(\mathsf{pk}_2, 0)$$

for all $i \in [k]$. By the semantic security of HE the adversary $\mathcal{A}$ will not detect this change. In a second hybrid modification, we replace the challenge ciphertext by an encryption of 0. It follows from the semantic security of FHE that the advantage of $\mathcal{A}$ in this hybrid is at most a negligible amount smaller than in the last hybrid. Since the advantage of $\mathcal{A}$ in this final experiment is 0, it follows that $\mathcal{A}$'s advantage is negligible.

The more interesting aspects of this construction is its correctness.

Theorem 2 (Correctness). *Assume the FHE scheme* FHE *has decryption noise at most* B_{FHE}, *the HE scheme has decryption noise at most* B_{HE} *and that* HE *has shrinking correctness for noise up to* $K \geq \ell \cdot B_{\mathsf{FHE}} + k \cdot n \cdot B_{\mathsf{HE}}$. *Then the scheme* $\overline{\mathsf{FHE}}$ *has compression correctness.*

Proof. Fix a public key $\mathsf{pk} = (\mathsf{pk}_1, \mathsf{pk}_2, \mathsf{ck})$ where pk_2 defines a message space $\mathbb{Z}_q^k$ and a secret key $\mathsf{sk} = (\mathsf{sk}_1, \mathsf{sk}_2)$. Further fix ciphertexts $(c_1, \ldots, c_\ell)$ such that c_i is a valid encryption of m_i. Let $\mathbf{m} = (m_1, \ldots, m_\ell)$. Let the linear function f be defined by

$$f(\mathbf{x}_1, \ldots, \mathbf{x}_k) = \sum_{i=1}^{k} \sum_{j=1}^{\ell} \mathsf{Dec\&Mult}\left(\mathbf{x}_i, c_j, t_{ij}\right).$$

Consider the ciphertext $c' = \mathsf{HE.Eval}(\mathsf{pk}_2, f, (\mathsf{ck}_1, \ldots, \mathsf{ck}_k))$. As $\mathsf{ck}_i = \mathsf{HE.Enc}(\mathsf{pk}_2, \mathbf{b}_i \cdot \mathsf{sk}_1)$, it holds by the relaxed homomorphic correctness of HE that

$$\mathsf{HE.Dec}(\mathsf{sk}_2, c') = f(\mathbf{b}_1 \cdot \mathsf{sk}_1, \ldots, \mathbf{b}_k \cdot \mathsf{sk}_1) + \mathbf{z},$$

where $\|\mathbf{z}\|_\infty \le k \cdot n \cdot B_{\mathsf{HE}}$. Moreover, it holds that

$$f(\mathbf{b}_1 \cdot \mathsf{sk}_1, \ldots, \mathbf{b}_k \cdot \mathsf{sk}_1) = \sum_{i=1}^{k} \sum_{j=1}^{\ell} \mathsf{Dec\&Mult}\,(\mathbf{b}_i \cdot \mathsf{sk}_1, c_j, t_{ij})$$

$$= \sum_{i=1}^{k} \sum_{j=1}^{\ell} \mathbf{b}_i \cdot \mathsf{Dec\&Mult}\,(\mathsf{sk}_1, c_j, t_{ij})$$

$$= \sum_{i=1}^{k} \sum_{j=1}^{\ell} \mathbf{b}_i \cdot (t_{ij} \cdot \mathsf{m}_j + e_{ij})$$

$$= \mathbf{T} \cdot \mathsf{m} + \sum_{i=1}^{k} \mathbf{b}_i \cdot \left(\sum_{j=1}^{\ell} e_{ij} \right)$$

$$= \mathbf{T} \cdot \mathsf{m} + \mathbf{e},$$

where $\mathbf{e} = \sum_{i=1}^{k} \mathbf{b}_i \cdot (\sum_{j=1}^{\ell} e_{ij})$ and $\mathbf{T} = (t_{ij})$ is the encoding matrix. Since it holds that $|e_{ij}| \le B_{\mathsf{FHE}}$, we get that $\|\mathbf{e}\|_\infty \le \ell \cdot B_{\mathsf{FHE}}$. Consequently, it holds that

$$\mathsf{HE.Dec}(\mathsf{sk}, c') = \mathbf{T} \cdot \mathsf{m} + \mathbf{z} + \mathbf{e}.$$

Since $\|\mathbf{z} + \mathbf{e}\|_\infty \le \|\mathbf{z}\|_\infty + \|\mathbf{e}\|_\infty \le k \cdot n \cdot B_{\mathsf{HE}} + \ell \cdot B_{\mathsf{FHE}} \le K$, by the shrinking correctness of HE we have that

$$\mathsf{HE.ShrinkDec}(\mathsf{sk}_2, \mathsf{HE.Shrink}(\mathsf{pk}_2, c')) = \mathsf{m}.$$

This shows that $\overline{\mathsf{FHE}}$ has compression correctness.

4.4 Instantiating with Rate 1

A suitable FHE scheme which readily supports linear decrypt-and-multiply is the GSW scheme [19] and its variants [1,8,24]. For the Brakerski-Vaikuntanathan variant of this scheme [8], we can set things up such that the decryption noise-bound B_{FHE} is polynomial in λ (see Sect. 2.4). Correctness is achieved by choosing a sufficiently large polynomial modulus q.

When instantiating the linearly homomorphic scheme HE with our packed Regev encryption that supports ciphertext shrinking (see Sects. 3.2 and 3.3), we obtain the following. Assume that the decryption noise of the FHE scheme FHE is some polynomial B_{FHE}. Moreover, let $B_{\mathsf{HE}} = \mathsf{poly}(\lambda)$ be the decryption noise of HE for some fixed B-bounded error distribution χ over $\mathbb{Z}$. By Theorem 2 we need to setup HE (via the choice of the modulus q) such that we have shrinking correctness for noise up to $K \ge \ell \cdot B_{\mathsf{FHE}} + k \cdot n \cdot B_{\mathsf{HE}}$. In turn, by Lemma 1 we can achieve this if $q > 4\ell K$. Consequently, since B_{FHE}, B_{HE}, and therefore K are of size $\mathsf{poly}(\lambda)$, we can choose q of size $\mathsf{poly}(\lambda)$ and achieve a polynomial modulus-to-noise ratio $B/q = \mathsf{poly}(\lambda)$ for the underlying LWE problem. For this scheme the encoding matrix $\mathbf{T}$ is given by $\mathbf{T} = \frac{q}{2} \cdot \mathbf{I}$, where $\mathbf{I} \in \mathbb{Z}_q^{\ell \times \ell}$ is the identity matrix (see Sect. 3.3). The overall rate of this scheme is exactly the same as that of HE, which, as we've analyzed in Sect. 3.3. That is, for length ℓ messages we have $\ell + \mathsf{poly}(\lambda)$ length ciphertexts, and thus for a sufficiently large $\ell = \mathsf{poly}(\lambda)$ the rate is $(1 - 1/\lambda)$.

5   Fully-Homomorphic Time-Lock Puzzles

We propose a construction for a fully-homomorphic time-lock puzzle FHTLP. The scheme builds on the similar ideas as our rate-1 FHE construction, except that we have to explicitly use a multi-key fully-homomorphic encryption scheme with linear decrypt-and-multiply, due to the distributed nature of homomorphic time-lock puzzles. Below we describe a simplified construction that encapsulates only binary secrets, however we can easily turn it into a rate-1 scheme by using a high-rate LH-TLP and packing vectors of binary messages into a single puzzle via standard techniques.

Let $\mathsf{FHE} = (\mathsf{MK\text{-}FHE.KeyGen}, \mathsf{MK\text{-}FHE.Enc}, \mathsf{MK\text{-}FHE.Eval}, \mathsf{MK\text{-}FHE.Dec})$ be a (somewhat or fully) multi-key homomorphic encryption scheme with linear decrypt-and-multiply and plaintext space $\{0, 1\}$. Let further $\mathsf{TLP} = (\mathsf{TLP.Setup}, \mathsf{TLP.PuzGen}, \mathsf{TLP.Eval}, \mathsf{TLP.Dec})$ be a linearly homomorphic time-lock puzzle. In abuse of notation we assume that the key-generation algorithm $\mathsf{MK\text{-}FHE.KeyGen}(1^\lambda, q)$ takes the modulus q as an explicit input.

$\mathsf{FHTLP.Setup}(1^\lambda, T)$: On input the security parameter 1^λ and the time parameter T, the setup generates

$$\mathsf{pp}_0 \leftarrow \mathsf{MK\text{-}FHE.Setup}(1^\lambda; q) \qquad \mathsf{pp}_1 \leftarrow \mathsf{TLP.Setup}(1^\lambda, T)$$

where q is the modulus of the plaintext space defined by pp_1, and returns $\mathsf{pp} = (\mathsf{pp}_1, \mathsf{pp}_0)$ as the public parameters.

$\mathsf{FHTLP.PuzGen}(\mathsf{pp}, \mathsf{s})$: On input the public parameters $\mathsf{pp} = (\mathsf{pp}_1, \mathsf{pp}_0)$ and a secret $\mathsf{s} \in \{0, 1\}$ the puzzle generation algorithm samples a fresh key pair

$$(\mathsf{sk}, \mathsf{pk}) \leftarrow \mathsf{MK\text{-}FHE.KeyGen}(\mathsf{pp}_0).$$

Then it encrypts the secret and generates a puzzle where the solution is the secret key

$$\mathsf{c} \leftarrow \mathsf{MK\text{-}FHE.Enc}(\mathsf{pk}, \mathsf{s}) \qquad \tilde{\mathsf{Z}} \leftarrow \mathsf{TLP.PuzGen}(\mathsf{pp}_1, \mathsf{sk})$$

and sets the puzzle to be the following tuple $\mathsf{Z} = (\mathsf{pk}, \mathsf{c}, \tilde{\mathsf{Z}})$.

FHTLP.Eval$(pp, f, (Z_1, \ldots, Z_\ell))$: On input the public parameters $pp = (pp_1, pp_0)$, the circuit representation of a function $f : \{0, 1\}^\ell \to \{0, 1\}$, and a vector of puzzles $(Z_1, \ldots, Z_\ell)$, where each $Z_i = (pk_i, c_i, \tilde{Z}_i)$, the evaluation algorithm computes

$$C \leftarrow \text{MK-FHE.Eval}((pk_1, \ldots, pk_\ell), f, (c_1, \ldots, c_\ell)).$$

Then it evaluates the decrypt-and-multiply function (with C and $q/2$ hardcoded) over the puzzles

$$\tilde{Z} \leftarrow \text{TLP.Eval}(pp_1, \text{Dec\&Mult}(\cdot, C, q/2), (\tilde{Z}_1, \ldots, \tilde{Z}_\ell)).$$

Finally the algorithm returns $\tilde{Z}$ as the evaluated puzzle.

FHTLP.Solve(pp, Z) : We assume without loss of generality that the solving algorithm is given as input an evaluated puzzle Z. The decryption algorithm parses $pp = (pp_1, pp_0)$, solves the input puzzle

$$s \leftarrow \text{TLP.Solve}(pp_1, Z)$$

and returns $\lceil s \rfloor_2$ as the solution.

5.1   Analysis

In the following we analyze the security and the correctness of our scheme.

Theorem 3 (Security). *Let* MK-FHE *be a semantically secure multi-key encryption scheme and let* TLP *be a secure time-lock puzzle, then the scheme* FHTLP *as described above is secure.*

Proof. We analyze only fresh (non-evaluated) puzzles without loss of generality. The distribution ensemble induced by the view of the adversary corresponds to

$$(pp_0, pp_1, pk, \text{MK-FHE.Enc}(pk, s), \text{TLP.PuzGen}(pp_1, sk))$$

over the random choices of the public parameters and the random coins of the algorithms. By the security of TLP it holds that, for all PPT adversaries of depth at most T, the latter distribution is computationally indistinguishable from

$$(pp_0, pp_1, pk, \text{MK-FHE.Enc}(pk, s), \text{TLP.PuzGen}(pp_1, 0)).$$

We are now in the position of invoking the semantic security of the MK-FHE scheme. By a standard reduction, the following distribution

$$(pp_0, pp_1, pk, \text{MK-FHE.Enc}(pk, 0), \text{TLP.PuzGen}(pp_1, 0)).$$

is computationally indistinguishable from the previous one. Although this holds for any PPT adversary, we remark in our case even computational indistinguishability against depth-bounded attackers would suffice. The proof is concluded by observing that the last distribution hides the secret information-theoretically.

What is left to be shown is that the scheme is correct.

Theorem 4 (Correctness). *Assume the MK-FHE scheme* MK-FHE *has decryption noise at most* $B_{\mathsf{MK\text{-}FHE}}$ *and that* $q > 4 \cdot B_{\mathsf{MK\text{-}FHE}}$. *Then the scheme* FHTLP *as described above is (single-hop) correct.*

Proof. We unfold the computation of the solving algorithm of the underlying time-lock puzzle.

$$
\begin{aligned}
\mathsf{s} &= \mathsf{TLP.Solve}(\mathsf{pp}_1, Z) \\
&= \mathsf{TLP.Solve}(\mathsf{pp}_1, \mathsf{TLP.Eval}(\mathsf{pp}_1, \mathsf{Dec\&Mult}(\cdot, \mathsf{C}, q/2), (\tilde{Z}_1, \ldots, \tilde{Z}_\ell))) \\
&= \mathsf{Dec\&Mult}((\mathsf{sk}_1, \ldots, \mathsf{sk}_\ell), \mathsf{C}, q/2) \\
&= \mathsf{Dec\&Mult}((\mathsf{sk}_1, \ldots, \mathsf{sk}_\ell), \mathsf{MK\text{-}FHE.Eval}((\mathsf{pk}_1, \ldots, \mathsf{pk}_\ell), f, (\mathsf{c}_1, \ldots, \mathsf{c}_\ell)), q/2) \\
&= q/2 \cdot f(\mathsf{s}_1, \ldots, \mathsf{s}_\ell) + e \quad \bmod q
\end{aligned}
$$

by the correctness of the TLP scheme and of the MK-FHE decrypt-and-multiply, respectively. By our choice of parameters $|e| \le B_{\mathsf{MK\text{-}FHE}}$ (with all but negligible probability) and therefore the decryption algorithm returns the correct bit with overwhelming probability.

5.2 Instantiation

A linearly-homomorphic time-lock puzzle has been recently proposed in [22]. In this construction, all users in the system share the public parameters

$$
\left(N = p \cdot q, g, h = g^{2^T} \right)
$$

where T is the parameter that dictates the hardness of the puzzle and g is the generator of $\mathbb{Z}_N^*$ (with Jacobi symbol $+1$). For a secret $\mathsf{s} \in \mathbb{Z}_N$, each user can locally generate a puzzle computing

$$
g^r \ (\bmod\ N) \qquad\qquad h^{r \cdot N}(N+1)^{\mathsf{s}} \ (\bmod\ N^2)
$$

where $r \leftarrow_{\$} \mathbb{Z}_{N^2}$. The puzzle can be solved by raising the first element to the power of 2^T and removing the blinding factor from the second term. Once $(N+1)^{\mathsf{s}}$ is known, s can be recovered efficiently using the polynomial-time discrete logarithm algorithm from [26]. The puzzle hides the message up to time T assuming the inherent sequentiality of squaring in groups of unknown order. The scheme is linearly-homomorphic over the ring $(\mathbb{Z}_N, +)$ and can be generalized in the same spirit as the Damgård-Jurik approach to achieve rate 1 (see [22] for more details). As discussed in Sect. 2.4, we can use the LWE-based MK-FHE scheme of [24] (which supports linear decrypt-and-multiply) with an externally provided modulus $q = N$. Hardness of the underlying LWE problem for arbitrary (worst-case) moduli follows by [27].

References

1. Alperin-Sheriff, J., Peikert, C.: Faster bootstrapping with polynomial error. In: Garay, J.A., Gennaro, R. (eds.) CRYPTO 2014. LNCS, vol. 8616, pp. 297–314. Springer, Heidelberg (2014). https://doi.org/10.1007/978-3-662-44371-2_17

2. Boyle, E., Gilboa, N., Ishai, Y.: Breaking the circuit size barrier for secure computation under DDH. In: Robshaw, M., Katz, J. (eds.) CRYPTO 2016. LNCS, vol. 9814, pp. 509–539. Springer, Heidelberg (2016). https://doi.org/10.1007/978-3-662-53018-4_19

3. Boyle, E., Kohl, L., Scholl, P.: Homomorphic secret sharing from lattices without FHE. In: Ishai, Y., Rijmen, V. (eds.) EUROCRYPT 2019. LNCS, vol. 11477, pp. 3–33. Springer, Cham (2019). https://doi.org/10.1007/978-3-030-17656-3_1

4. Brakerski, Z., Döttling, N.: Two-message statistically sender-private OT from LWE. In: Beimel, A., Dziembowski, S. (eds.) TCC 2018. LNCS, vol. 11240, pp. 370–390. Springer, Cham (2018). https://doi.org/10.1007/978-3-030-03810-6_14

5. Brakerski, Z., Gentry, C., Halevi, S.: Packed ciphertexts in LWE-based homomorphic encryption. In: Kurosawa, K., Hanaoka, G. (eds.) PKC 2013. LNCS, vol. 7778, pp. 1–13. Springer, Heidelberg (2013). https://doi.org/10.1007/978-3-642-36362-7_1

6. Brakerski, Z., Gentry, C., Vaikuntanathan, V.: (Leveled) fully homomorphic encryption without bootstrapping. In: Goldwasser, S. (eds.) ITCS 2012, pp. 309–325. ACM, January 2012

7. Brakerski, Z., Vaikuntanathan, V.: Efficient fully homomorphic encryption from (standard) LWE. In: Ostrovsky, R. (eds.) 52nd FOCS, pp. 97–106. IEEE Computer Society Press, October 2011

8. Brakerski, Z., Vaikuntanathan, V.: Lattice-based FHE as secure as PKE. In: Naor, M. (eds.) ITCS 2014, pp. 1–12. ACM, January 2014

9. Canetti, R., Lin, H., Tessaro, S., Vaikuntanathan, V.: Obfuscation of probabilistic circuits and applications. In: Dodis, Y., Nielsen, J.B. (eds.) TCC 2015. LNCS, vol. 9015, pp. 468–497. Springer, Heidelberg (2015). https://doi.org/10.1007/978-3-662-46497-7_19

10. Chor, B., Goldreich, O., Kushilevitz, E., Sudan, M.: Private information retrieval. In: 36th FOCS, pp. 41–50. IEEE Computer Society Press, October 1995

11. Clear, M., McGoldrick, C.: Multi-identity and multi-key leveled FHE from learning with errors. In: Gennaro, R., Robshaw, M. (eds.) CRYPTO 2015. LNCS, vol. 9216, pp. 630–656. Springer, Heidelberg (2015). https://doi.org/10.1007/978-3-662-48000-7_31

12. Damgård, I., Jurik, M.: A generalisation, a simplification and some applications of Paillier's probabilistic public-key system. In: Kim, K. (ed.) PKC 2001. LNCS, vol. 1992, pp. 119–136. Springer, Heidelberg (2001)

13. Dodis, Y., Halevi, S., Rothblum, R.D., Wichs, D.: Spooky encryption and its applications. In: Robshaw, M., Katz, J. (eds.) CRYPTO 2016. LNCS, vol. 9816, pp. 93–122. Springer, Heidelberg (2016). https://doi.org/10.1007/978-3-662-53015-3_4

14. Döttling, N., Garg, S., Ishai, Y., Malavolta, G., Mour, T., Ostrovsky, R.: Trapdoor hash functions and their applications. In: Boldyreva, A., Micciancio, D. (eds.) CRYPTO 2019. LNCS, vol. 11694, pp. 3–32. Springer, Cham (2019). https://doi.org/10.1007/978-3-030-26954-8_1

15. Gentry, C.: Fully homomorphic encryption using ideal lattices. In: Mitzenmacher, M. (eds.) 41st ACM STOC, pp. 169–178. ACM Press, May/June 2009

16. Gentry, C., Halevi, S.: Fully homomorphic encryption without squashing using depth-3 arithmetic circuits. In: Ostrovsky, R. (eds.) 52nd FOCS, pp. 107–109. IEEE Computer Society Press, October 2011
17. Gentry, C., Halevi, S.: Compressible FHE with applications to PIR. Technical report (personal communication) (2019)
18. Gentry, C., Halevi, S., Vaikuntanathan, V.: i-hop homomorphic encryption and rerandomizable Yao circuits. In: Rabin, T. (ed.) CRYPTO 2010. LNCS, vol. 6223, pp. 155–172. Springer, Heidelberg (2010). https://doi.org/10.1007/978-3-642-14623-7_9
19. Gentry, C., Sahai, A., Waters, B.: Homomorphic encryption from learning with errors: conceptually-simpler, asymptotically-faster, attribute-based. In: Canetti, R., Garay, J.A. (eds.) CRYPTO 2013. LNCS, vol. 8042, pp. 75–92. Springer, Heidelberg (2013). https://doi.org/10.1007/978-3-642-40041-4_5
20. Goldwasser, S., Micali, S.: Probabilistic encryption and how to play mental poker keeping secret all partial information. In: 14th ACM STOC, pp. 365–377. ACM Press, May 1982
21. Impagliazzo, R., Levin, L.A., Luby, M.: Pseudo-random generation from one-way functions (extended abstracts). In: 21st ACM STOC, pp. 12–24. ACM Press, May 1989
22. Malavolta, G., Thyagarajan, S.A.K.: Homomorphic time-lock puzzles and applications. In: Boldyreva, A., Micciancio, D. (eds.) CRYPTO 2019. LNCS, vol. 11692, pp. 620–649. Springer, Cham (2019). https://doi.org/10.1007/978-3-030-26948-7_22
23. Micciancio, D.: From linear functions to fully homomorphic encryption. Technical report (2019). https://bacrypto.github.io/presentations/2018.11.30-Micciancio-FHE.pdf
24. Mukherjee, P., Wichs, D.: Two round multiparty computation via multi-key FHE. In: Fischlin, M., Coron, J.-S. (eds.) EUROCRYPT 2016. LNCS, vol. 9666, pp. 735–763. Springer, Heidelberg (2016). https://doi.org/10.1007/978-3-662-49896-5_26
25. Ostrovsky, R., Paskin-Cherniavsky, A., Paskin-Cherniavsky, B.: Maliciously circuit-private FHE. In: Garay, J.A., Gennaro, R. (eds.) CRYPTO 2014. LNCS, vol. 8616, pp. 536–553. Springer, Heidelberg (2014). https://doi.org/10.1007/978-3-662-44371-2_30
26. Paillier, P.: Public-key cryptosystems based on composite degree residuosity classes. In: Stern, J. (ed.) EUROCRYPT 1999. LNCS, vol. 1592, pp. 223–238. Springer, Heidelberg (1999). https://doi.org/10.1007/3-540-48910-X_16
27. Peikert, C., Regev, O., Stephens-Davidowitz, N.: Pseudorandomness of ring-LWE for any ring and modulus. In: Hatami, H., McKenzie, P., King, V. (eds.) 49th ACM STOC, pp. 461–473. ACM Press, June 2017
28. Peikert, C., Vaikuntanathan, V., Waters, B.: A framework for efficient and composable oblivious transfer. In: Wagner, D. (ed.) CRYPTO 2008. LNCS, vol. 5157, pp. 554–571. Springer, Heidelberg (2008). https://doi.org/10.1007/978-3-540-85174-5_31
29. Quach, W., Wee, H., Wichs, D.: Laconic function evaluation and applications. In: Thorup, M. (eds.) 59th FOCS, pp. 859–870. IEEE Computer Society Press, October 2018
30. Regev, O.: On lattices, learning with errors, random linear codes, and cryptography. In: Gabow, H.N., Fagin, R. (eds.) 37th ACM STOC, pp. 84–93. ACM Press, May 2005

31. Rivest, R.L., Shamir, A., Wagner, D.A.: Time-lock puzzles and timed-release crypto. Technical report, Cambridge, MA, USA (1996)
32. van Dijk, M., Gentry, C., Halevi, S., Vaikuntanathan, V.: Fully homomorphic encryption over the integers. In: Gilbert, H. (ed.) EUROCRYPT 2010. LNCS, vol. 6110, pp. 24–43. Springer, Heidelberg (2010). https://doi.org/10.1007/978-3-642-13190-5_2

Compressible FHE with Applications to PIR

Craig Gentry[✉] and Shai Halevi[✉]

Algorand Foundation, New-York City, NY, USA
cbgentry@gmail.com, shaih@alum.mit.edu

Abstract. Homomorphic encryption (HE) is often viewed as impractical, both in communication and computation. Here we provide an additively homomorphic encryption scheme based on (ring) LWE with nearly optimal rate ($1 - \epsilon$ for any $\epsilon > 0$). Moreover, we describe how to compress many Gentry-Sahai-Waters (GSW) ciphertexts (e.g., ciphertexts that may have come from a homomorphic evaluation) into (fewer) high-rate ciphertexts.

Using our high-rate HE scheme, we are able for the first time to describe a single-server private information retrieval (PIR) scheme with sufficiently low computational overhead so as to be practical for large databases. Single-server PIR inherently requires the server to perform at least one bit operation per database bit, and we describe a rate-(4/9) scheme with computation which is not so much worse than this inherent lower bound. In fact it is probably less than whole-database AES encryption – specifically about 2.3 mod-q multiplication per database byte, where q is about 50 to 60 bits. Asymptotically, the computational overhead of our PIR scheme is $\tilde{O}(\log \log \lambda + \log \log \log N)$, where λ is the security parameter and N is the number of database files, which are assumed to be sufficiently large.

1 Introduction

How bandwidth efficient can (fully) homomorphic encryption ((F)HE) be? While it is easy to encrypt messages with almost no loss in bandwidth, the same is generally not true for homomorphic encryption: Evaluated ciphertexts in contemporary HE schemes tend to be significantly larger than the plaintext that they encrypt, at least by a significant constant factor and often much more.

Beyond the fundamental theoretical interest in the bandwidth limits of FHE, a homomorphic scheme with high rate has several applications. Perhaps the most obvious is for private information retrieval (PIR), where bandwidth is of the essence. While HE can clearly be used to implement PIR, even the best PIR implementation so far (such as [1,3]) are still quite far from being able to support large databases, mostly because the large expansion factor of contemporary HE schemes. Another application can be found in the work of Badrinarayanan

---

This work was done while the authors were in IBM Research.

D. Hofheinz and A. Rosen (Eds.): TCC 2019, LNCS 11892, pp. 438–464, 2019.
https://doi.org/10.1007/978-3-030-36033-7_17

et al. [6], who showed that compressible (additive) homomorphic encryption with rate better than $1/2$ can be used for a high-rate oblivious transfer, which in turn can be used for various purposes in the context of secure computation. Alas, prior to our work the only instantiation of high rate homomorphic encryption was the Damgård-Jurik cryptosystem [14], which however is (a) only additively homomorphic, (b) rather expensive, and (c) insecure against quantum computers.

In this work we remedy this situation, devising the first *compressible* fully homomorphic encryption scheme, and showing how to use it to get efficient PIR. Namely, we describe an (F)HE scheme whose evaluated ciphertexts can be publicly compressed until they are roughly the same size as the plaintext that they encrypt. Our compressible scheme can take "bloated" evaluated ciphertexts of the GSW cryptosystem [17], and cram them into high-rate matrix-encrypting matrix-ciphertexts. The ratio of the aggregate plaintext size to the aggregate ciphertext size can be $1 - \epsilon$ for any ϵ (assuming the aggregate plaintext is sufficiently large, proportional to $1/\epsilon^3$). The compressed ciphertexts are no longer GSW ciphertexts. However, they still have sufficient structure to allow additive homomorphism, and multiplication by encryption of small scalars, all while remaining compressed.[1] Just like GSW, the security of our scheme is based on the learning with errors assumption [31] or its ring variant [26]. (Also circular security assumption to get *fully* homomorphic encryption.)

We note that a compressible fully homomorphic encryption easily yields an end-to-end rate-efficient FHE: Freshly encrypted ciphertexts are immediately compressed during encryption,[2] then "decompressed" using bootstrapping before any processing, and finally compressed again before decryption. The resulting scheme has compressed ciphertexts at any time, which are only temporarily expanded while they are being processed.

1.1   Applications to PIR

We describe many optimizations to the basic scheme, yielding a single-server private information retrieval scheme with low communication overhead, while at the same time being computationally efficient. Asymptotically, the computational overhead is $\tilde{O}(\log \log \lambda + \log \log \log N)$, where λ is the security parameter and N is the number of database files, which are assumed to be sufficiently large.

While we did not implement our PIR scheme, we explain in detail why we estimate that it should be not only theoretically efficient but also practically fast. Specifically, we can get a rate $4/9$ single-server PIR scheme,[3] in which the server's amortized work is only 2.3 single-precision modular multiplications for

---

[1] Of course, these operations increase the noisiness of the ciphertexts somewhat.

[2] One could even use hybrid encryption, where fresh ciphertexts are generated using, e.g., AES-CTR, and the AES key is send along encrypted under the FHE.

[3] The rate can be made arbitrarily close to one without affecting the asymptotic efficiency, but the concrete parameters of this solution are not appealing. See discussion at the end of Sect. 5.

every byte in the database. For a comparison point, the trivial PIR solution of sending the entire database will have to at least encrypt the whole database (for communication security), hence incurring a cost of an AES block encryption per 16 database bytes, which is surely more work than what our scheme does. Thus, contra Sion-Carbunar [33], PIR is finally more efficient than the trivial solution not only in terms of communication, but also in terms of computation.

Those accustomed to thinking of (R)LWE-based homomorphic encryption as impractical may find the low computational overhead of our PIR scheme hard to believe. However, RLWE-based HE – in particular, the GSW scheme with our adaptations – really shines in the PIR setting for a few reasons. First, the noise in GSW ciphertexts grows only additively with the degree when the messages multiplied from the left are in $\{0, 1\}$. (The receiver's GSW ciphertexts will encrypt the bits of its target index.) Second, even though we obviously need to do $\Omega(N)$ ciphertext operations for a database with N files, we can ensure that the noise grows only proportionally to $\log N$ (so its bit size only grows with $\log \log N$). The small noise growth allows our PIR scheme to use a small RLWE modulus $q = \tilde{O}(\log N + \lambda)$ that in practice is not much larger than one would use in a basic RLWE-based PKE scheme. Third, we can exploit the recursive/hierarchical nature of the classic approach to single-server PIR [23,35] to hide the more expensive steps of RLWE-based homomorphic evaluation, namely polynomial FFTs (and less importantly, CRT lifting). In the classical hierarchical approach to PIR, the computationally dominant step is the first step, where we project the effective database size from $N = N_1 \times \cdots \times N_d$ down to N/N_1. To maximize the efficiency of this first step, we can preprocess the polynomials of the database so that they are already in evaluation representation, thereby avoiding polynomial FFTs and allowing each $(\log q)$-bit block of the database to be "absorbed" into an encrypted query using a small constant number of mod-q multiplications.[4] Therefore, the computational overhead of the first step boils down to just the overhead of multiplying integers modulo q, where this overhead is $\tilde{O}(\log \log q)$, where (again) q is quite small. After the first step of PIR, GSW-esque homomorphic evaluation requires converting between coefficient and evaluation representation of polynomials, but this will not significantly impact the overhead of our PIR scheme, as the effective database is already much smaller (at most N/N_1), where we will take $N_1 = \tilde{\Theta}(\log N + \lambda)$.

1.2   Related Work

Ciphertext Compression. Ciphertext compression has always had obvious appeal in the public-key setting (and even sometimes in the symmetric key context, e.g., [22]). In the context of (F)HE, one can view "ciphertext packing" [8,9,30,34], where each ciphertext encrypts not one but an array of plaintext elements, as a form of compression. Other prior works included a "post-evaluation" ciphertext compression techniques, such as the work of van Dijk et al. [36] for

---

[4] In the first step, the server generates N_1 ciphertexts from the client's $\log N_1$ ciphertexts, which includes FFTs, but their amortized cost is insignificant when $N_1 \ll N$.

integer-based HE, and the work of Hohenberger et al. for attribute-based encryption [18]. However, the rate achieved there is still low, and in fact no scheme prior to our work was able to break the rate-1/2 barrier. (Hence for example no LWE-based scheme could be used for the high-rate OT application of Badrinarayanan et al. [6].)

The only prior cryptosystem with homomorphic properties that we know of with rate better than 1/2 is due to Damgård and Jurik [14]. They described an extension of the Paillier cryptosystem [29] that allows rate-$(1 - o(1))$ encryption with additive homomorphism: In particular, a mod-N^s plaintext can be encrypted inside a mod-N^{s+1} ciphertext for an RSA modulus N and an arbitrary exponent $s \geq 1$.

Finally, a concurrent work by Döttling et al. [15] and follow-up work by Brakerski et al. [7] also achieves compressible variants of HE/FHE. The former work achieves only weaker homomorphism but under a wide variety of hardness assumptions, while the latter achieves FHE under LWE. The constructions in those works are more general than ours, but they are unlikely to yield practical schemes for applications such as PIR.

Private Information Retrieval. Private information retrieval (PIR) [12] lets a client obtain the N-th bit (or file) from a database while keeping its target index $i \in [N]$ hidden from the server(s). To rule out a trivial protocol where the server transmits the entire database to the client, it is required that the total communication is sublinear in N. Chor et al. provided constructions with multiple servers, and later Kushilevitz and Ostrovsky [23] showed that PIR is possible even with a single server under computational assumptions.

Kiayias et al. [21] (see also [25]) gave the first single-server PIR scheme with rate $(1 - o(1))$, based on Damgård-Jurik [14]. However, Damgård-Jurik is computationally too expensive to be used in practice for large-scale PIR [28,33], at a minimum, PIR using Damgård-Jurik requires the server to compute a mod-N multiplication per bit of the database, where N has 2048 or more bits. The papers [21,25] expressly call for an underlying encryption scheme to replace Damgård-Jurik to make their rate-optimal PIR schemes computationally less expensive.

In terms of computation, the state-of-the-art PIR scheme is XPIR by Aguilar-Melchor et al. [1], with further optimizations in the SealPIR work of Angel et al. [3]. This scheme is based on RLWE and features many clever optimizations, but Angel et al. commented that even with their optimizations "supporting large databases remains out of reach." Concretely, the SealPIR results from [3, Fig. 9] indicate server workload of about twenty cycles per database byte, for a rate of roughly 1/1000. In contrast, our construction yields rate close to 1/2, and the server work-load is roughly 2.3 single-precision modular multiplication per byte (this should be less than 20 cycles).

Organization. Some background information regarding LWE and the GSW scheme is provided in Sect. 2. In Sect. 3 we define compressible HE, in Sect. 4 we describe our compresisble (F)HE scheme, and in Sect. 5, we describe our PIR scheme.

2 Background on Gadget Matrices, LWE, PVW and GSW

Gadget Matrices. Many lattice cryptosystems (including GSW [17]) use a rectangular *gadget matrix* [27], $G \in R_q^{n \times m}$ to add redundancy. For a matrix C of dimension $n \times c$ we denote by $G^{-1}(C)$ a matrix of dimension $m \times c$ with small coefficients such that $G \cdot (G^{-1}(C)) = C \pmod{q}$. Below we also use the convention that $G^{-1}(C)$ is always a *full rank matrix* over the rationals[5]. In particular we denote by $G^{-1}(0)$ a matrix M with small entries and full rank over the rationals, such that $G \cdot M = 0 \pmod{q}$ (so clearly M does not have full rank modulo q). Often G is set to be $I_{n_1} \otimes \boldsymbol{g}$ where $\boldsymbol{g}$ is the vector $(1, 2, \ldots, 2^{\lfloor \log q \rfloor})$ – that is, $m = n_1 \lceil \log q \rceil$ and G's rows consists of shifts of the vector $\boldsymbol{g}$. In this case, one can efficiently find a suitable $G^{-1}(C)$ that has coefficients in $\{0, 1\}$. More generally with $\boldsymbol{g} = (1, B, \ldots, B^{\lfloor \log_B q \rfloor})$, $G^{-1}(C)$ has coefficients in $[\pm B/2]$.

(Ring) Learning With Errors (LWE). Security of many lattice cryptosystems is based on the hardness of the decision (ring) learning with errors (R)LWE problem [26,31]. LWE uses the ring of integers $R = \mathbb{Z}$, while RLWE typically uses the ring of integers R of a cyclotomic field. A "yes" instance of the (R)LWE problem for modulus q, dimension k, and noise distribution χ over R consists of many uniform $\boldsymbol{a}_i \in R_q^k$ together with the values $b_i := \langle \boldsymbol{s}, \boldsymbol{a}_i \rangle + e_i \in R_q$ where $\boldsymbol{s}$ is a fixed secret vector and $e_i \leftarrow \chi$. In a "no" instance, both the $\boldsymbol{a}_i$'s and b_i's are uniform. The decision (R)LWE assumption is that the two distributions are computationally indistinguishable – i.e., that "yes" instances are pseudorandom. Typically, χ is such that $\|e_i\|_\infty < \alpha$ for some size bound α with probability overwhelming in the security parameter λ. The security parameter also lower bounds the ring size and/or the dimension k, and the ratio α/q.

LWE with Matrix Secrets. An LWE instance may (more generally) be associated to a secret *matrix* S', and one can prove via a hybrid argument that breaking the matrix version of LWE is as hard as breaking conventional LWE. In this version, a "yes" instance consists of a uniform matrix A and $B = S'A + E$. Let us give dimensions to these matrices: S' is $n_0 \times k$, A is $k \times m$, B and E are $n_0 \times m$. (See Fig. 1 for an illustration of these matrices.) Set $n_1 = n_0 + k$. Set $S = [S'|I] \in R_q^{n_0 \times n_1}$ and P to be the matrix with $-A$ on top of B. Then $SP = E \bmod q$. The LWE assumption (matrix version) says that this P is pseudorandom.

Regev and PVW Encryption. Recall that in the Regev cryptosystem, a bit $\sigma \in \{0, 1\}$ is encrypted relative to a secret-key vector $\boldsymbol{s} \in \mathbb{Z}_q^{n+1}$ (with 1 in the last coordinate), as a vector $\boldsymbol{c} \in \mathbb{Z}_q^{n+1}$ such that $\langle \boldsymbol{s}, \boldsymbol{c} \rangle = \lceil q/2 \rceil \cdot \sigma + e \pmod{q}$, with $|e| < q/4$. More generally the plaintext space can be extended to R_p for some $p < q$, where a scalar $\sigma \in R_p$ is encrypted as a vector $\boldsymbol{c} \in R_q^{n+1}$ such that $\langle \boldsymbol{s}, \boldsymbol{c} \rangle = \lceil q/p \rceil \cdot \sigma + e \pmod{q}$, with $\|e\|_\infty < q/2p$. (There is also a public key in this cryptosystem and an encryption procedure, but thoese are not relevant to our construction.)

---

[5] More generally, if the matrices are defined over some ring R then we require full rank over the field of fractions for that ring.

Peikert et al. described in [30] a batched variant of this cryptosystem (called PVW), where the plaintext is a vector $\boldsymbol{\sigma} \in R_p^k$, the secret key is a matrix $S = (S'|I) \in R_q^{n \times (n+k)}$ and the encryption of $\boldsymbol{\sigma}$ is a vector $\boldsymbol{c} \in R_q^{n+k}$ such that $S \cdot \boldsymbol{c} = \lceil q/p \rceil \cdot \boldsymbol{\sigma} + \boldsymbol{e}$ with $\|\boldsymbol{e}\|_\infty < q/2p$. For notational purposes, it will be convenient to use a "matrix variant" of PVW, simply encrypting many vectors and putting them in a matrix. Here the plaintext is a matrix $\Sigma \in R_p^{k \times m}$ (for some m), and the encryption of Σ is a matrix $C \in R_q^{(n+k) \times m}$ such that $SC = \lceil q/p \rceil \cdot \Sigma + \boldsymbol{E}$ with $\|\boldsymbol{E}\|_\infty < q/2p$.

The Regev and PVW cryptosystems are additively homomorphic, supporting addition and multiplication by small scalars, as long as the noise remains small enough. The information rate of the PVW cryptosystem is $\frac{|q|}{|p|} \cdot \frac{k}{n+k}$, which can be made very close to one if we use $k \gg n$ and $q \approx p^{1+\epsilon}$. Indeed this forms the basis for one variant of our compressible (F)HE construction.

GSW Encryption with Matrix Secret Keys. We use (a slight variant of) the GSW cryptosystem of Gentry et al. [17], based on LWE with matrix secret as above. Namely the secret key is a matrix S and the public key is a pseudorandom matrix P such that $SP = E \bmod q$ for a low-norm noise matrix E.

The plaintext space of GSW are (small) scalars. To encrypt $\sigma \in R_q$ under GSW, the encrypter chooses a random $m \times m$ matrix X whose entries have small norm, and outputs $C = \sigma \cdot G + P \cdot X \in R_q^{n_1 \times m}$ (operations modulo q). To decrypt, one computes

$$S \cdot C = \sigma \cdot S \cdot G + S \cdot P \cdot X = \sigma \cdot S \cdot G + E' \pmod{q}, \tag{1}$$

where $E' = E \cdot X$ has small norm. Assuming E' has coefficients bounded by an appropriate β, then $E' \cdot G^{-1}(0)$ will have entries too small to wrap modulo q, allowing the decrypter to recover E' (since $G^{-1}(0)$ is invertible) and hence recover $\sigma \cdot S \cdot G$. As $S \cdot G$ has rank n_0 (in fact it contains I_{n_0} as a submatrix), the decrypter can obtain σ.

Matrix GSW? We can attempt to use the same GSW invariant (1) to encrypt matrices, where a ciphertext matrix C GSW-encrypts a plaintext matrix M if $S \cdot C = M \cdot S \cdot G + E \pmod{q}$ for a small noise matrix E. The exact same decryption procedure as above works also in this case, allowing the decrypter to recover E, then $M \cdot S \cdot G$, and then M.

However, the encryption procedure above does not work for matrices in general, it is unclear how to obtain such a GSW-encryption C of M when M is not a scalar matrix (i.e., of the form $\sigma \cdot I$). If we want to set $C = M' \cdot G + P \cdot X$ as before, we need M' to satisfy $S \cdot M' = M \cdot S$, and finding such an M' seems to require knowing S. (For a scalar matrix $M = \sigma \cdot I$, M' is just the scalar matrix with the same scalar, but in a larger dimension.) Hiromasa et al. [20] show how to obtain a version of GSW that encrypts non-scalar matrices, assuming LWE *and a circular security assumption*. In our context, our GSW ciphertexts only encrypt scalars so we rely just on LWE without circular encryptions.

Homomorphic Operations in GSW. Suppose we have C_1 and C_2 that GSW-encrypt M_1 and M_2 respectively (scalar matrices or otherwise). Then clearly

$C_1 + C_2$ GSW-encrypts $M_1 + M_2$, provided that the sum of errors remains β-bounded. For multiplication, set $C^\times = C_1 \cdot G^{-1}(C_2) \bmod q$. We have:

$$S \cdot C^\times = (M_1 \cdot S \cdot G + E_1) \cdot G^{-1}(C_2) = M_1 \cdot M_2 \cdot S \cdot G + M_1 \cdot E_2 + E_1 \cdot G^{-1}(C_2).$$

Thus, $C^\times$ GSW-encrypts $M_1 \cdot M_2$ provided that the new error $E' = M_1 \cdot E_2 + E_1 \cdot G^{-1}(C_2)$ remains β-bounded. In the new error, the term $E_1 \cdot G^{-1}(C_2)$ is only slightly larger than the original error E_1, since $G^{-1}(C_2)$ has small coefficients. To keep the term $M_1 \cdot E_2$ small, there are two strategies. First, if M_1 corresponds to a small scalar – e.g., 0 or 1 – then this term is as small as the original error inside C_2. Second, if $E_2 = 0$, then this term does not even appear. For example, if we want to homomorphically multiply-by-constant $\sigma_2 \in R_q$, we can just set $C_2 = \sigma_2 \cdot G$ (without any $P \cdot X$), and compute $C^\times$ as above. The plaintext inside C_1 will be multiplied by σ_2, and the new error will not depend on either σ_1 or σ_2, which therefore can be arbitrary in R_q.

3   Defining Compressible (F)HE

Compressible (F)HE is defined similarly to standard (F)HE, except that decryption is broken into first compression and then "compressed decryption." Here we present the definition just for the simple case of 1-hop fully homomorphic encryption for bits, but the same type of definition applies equally to multiple hops, different plaintext spaces, and/or partially homomorphic. (See [19] for detailed treatment of all these variations.)

Definition 1. *A compressible fully homomorphic encryption scheme consists of five procedures,* (KeyGen, Encrypt, Evaluate, Compress, Decrypt)*:*

- $(\mathfrak{s}, \mathsf{pk}) \leftarrow \mathsf{KeyGen}(1^\lambda)$. *Takes the security parameter λ and outputs a secret/public key-pair.*
- $\mathfrak{c} \leftarrow \mathsf{Encrypt}(\mathsf{pk}, b)$. *Given the public key and a plaintext bit, outputs a low-rate ciphertext.*
- $\mathfrak{c}' \leftarrow \mathsf{Evaluate}(\mathsf{pk}, \Pi, \mathfrak{c})$. *Takes a public key pk, a circuit Π, a vector of low-rate ciphertexts $\mathfrak{c} = \langle \mathfrak{c}_1, \ldots, \mathfrak{c}_t \rangle$, one for every input bit of Π, and outputs another vector of low-rate ciphertexts $\mathfrak{c}'$, one for every output bit of Π.*
- $\mathfrak{c}^* \leftarrow \mathsf{Compress}(\mathsf{pk}, \mathfrak{c}')$. *Takes a public key pk and a vector of low-rate ciphertexts $\mathfrak{c} = \langle \mathfrak{c}_1, \ldots, \mathfrak{c}_t \rangle$, and outputs one or more compressed ciphertexts $\mathfrak{c}^* = \langle \mathfrak{c}_1^*, \ldots, \mathfrak{c}_s^* \rangle$.*
- $b \leftarrow \mathsf{Decrypt}(\mathfrak{s}, \mathfrak{c}^*)$. *On secret key and a compressed ciphertext, outputs a string of plaintext bits.*

We extend Decrypt *to a vector of compressed ciphertexts by decrypting each one separately. The scheme is correct if for every circuit Π and plaintext bits $\boldsymbol{b} = (b_1, \ldots, b_t) \in \{0,1\}^t$, one for every input bit of Π,*

$$\Pr\left[\begin{array}{c} (\mathfrak{s}, \mathsf{pk}) \leftarrow \mathsf{KeyGen}(1^\lambda), \mathfrak{c} \leftarrow \mathsf{Encrypt}(\mathsf{pk}, \boldsymbol{b}), \mathfrak{c}' \leftarrow \mathsf{Evaluate}(\mathsf{pk}, \Pi, \mathfrak{c}) \\ : \ \Pi(\boldsymbol{b}) \text{ is a prefix of } \mathsf{Decrypt}(\mathfrak{s}, \mathsf{Compress}(\mathsf{pk}, \mathfrak{c}')) \end{array} \right] = 1.$$

$$(2)$$

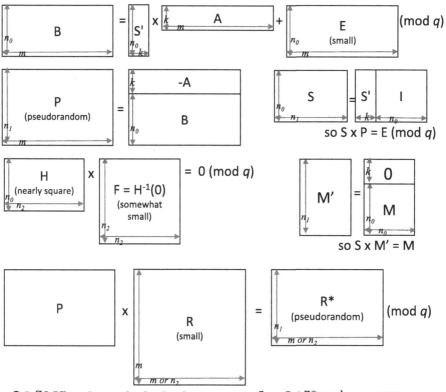

$\sigma \cdot G \in Z_q^{n_1 \times m}$ is a "very redundant" scalar, $C = \sigma G + R^* \bmod q$ is a GSW ctxt

$M^* = M' \times H \in Z_q^{n_1 \times n_2}$ "somewhat redundant" matrix, $C^* = M^* + R^* \bmod q$ compressed ctxt

Fig. 1. An illustration of the matrices in our construction. For some small $\epsilon > 0$ we have $n_1 = n_0 + k \approx n_2 = n_0(1 + \epsilon/2)$ and $m = n_1 \log q$. So, $n_0 \approx 2k/\epsilon$. Also, for correct decryption of ciphertexts with error E using gadget matrix H we require $\|E\|_\infty < q^{\epsilon/2}$.

(We allow prefix since the output of Decrypt *could be longer than the output length of* Π.*)*

The scheme has rate $\alpha = \alpha(\lambda) \in (0,1)$ *if for every circuit* Π *with sufficiently long output, plaintext bits* $\boldsymbol{b} = (b_1, \dots, b_t) \in \{0,1\}^t$, *and low rate ciphertexts* $\boldsymbol{c}' \leftarrow$ Evaluate$(\mathsf{pk}, \Pi, \mathsf{Encrypt}(\mathsf{pk}, \boldsymbol{b}))$ *as in Eq.* (2) *we have*

$$|\mathsf{Compress}(\mathsf{pk}, \boldsymbol{c}')| \cdot \alpha \leq |\Pi(\boldsymbol{b})|.$$

(We note that a similar approach can be used also when talking about compression of fresh ciphertexts.)

4   Constructing Compressible (F)HE

On a high level, our compressible scheme combines two cryptosystems: One is a low-rate (uncompressed) FHE scheme, which is a slight variant of GSW, and the other is a new high-rate (compressed) additively-homomorphic scheme for matrices, somewhat similar to the matrix homomorphic encryption of Hiromasa et al. [20]. What makes our scheme compressible is that these two cryptosystems "play nice," in the sense that they share the same secret key and we can pack many GSW ciphertexts in a single compressed ciphertext.

The low-rate scheme is the GSW variant from Sect. 2 that uses matrix LWE secrets. The secret key is a matrix of the form $S = [S'|I]$, and the public key is a pseudorandom matrix P satisfying $S \times P = E$ (mod q), with q the LWE modulus and E a low norm matrix. This low-rate cryptosystem encrypts small scalars (often just bits $\sigma \in \{0,1\}$), the ciphertext is a matrix C, and the decryption invariant is $SC = \sigma SG + E$ (mod q), with G the gadget matrix and E a low-norm matrix.

For the high-rate scheme we describe two variants, both featuring matrices for keys, plaintexts, and ciphertexts. One variant of the high-rate scheme is the PVW batched encryption scheme [30] (in its matrix notations), and another variant uses a new type of "nearly square" gadget matrix. Both variants have the same asymptotic efficiency, but using the gadget matrix seems to yield better concrete parameters, at least for our PIR application. The PVW-based variant is easier to describe, so we begin with it.

4.1 Compressible HE with PVW-Like Scheme

We now elaborate on the different procedures that comprise our compressible homomorphic encryption scheme.

Key Generation. To generate a secret/public key pair we choose two uniformly random matrices $S' \in R_q^{n_0 \times k}$ and $A \in R_q^{k \times m}$ and a small matrix $E \leftarrow \chi^{n_0 \times m}$, and compute the pseudorandom matrix $B := S' \times A + E \in R_q^{n_0 \times m}$.

The secret key is the matrix $S = [S'|I_{n_0}] \in R_q^{n_0 \times n_1}$ and the public key is $P = \left[\frac{-A}{B}\right] \in R_q^{n_1 \times m}$, and we have $S \times P = S' \times (-A) + I \times B = E$ (mod q).

Encryption and Evaluation. Encryption and decryption of small scalars and evaluation of circuit on them is done exactly as in the GSW scheme. Namely a scalar $\sigma \in R$ is encrypted by choosing a matrix $X \in R^{m \times m}$ with small entries, then outputting the ciphertext $C := \sigma G + PX$ (mod q). These low-rate cipher-texts satisfy the GSW invariant, namely $SC = \sigma SG + E$ (mod q) with $E \ll q$. These being GSW ciphertexts, encryption provides semantic security under the decision LWE hardness assumption [17].

Evaluation is the same as in GSW, with addition implemented by just adding the ciphertext matrices modulo q and multiplication implemented as $C^\times := C_1 \times G^{-1}(C_2)$ mod q. Showing that these operations maintain the decryption invariant (as long as the encrypted scalars are small) is done exactly as in GSW.

Compression. The crux of our construction is a compression technique that lets us pack many GSW bit encryptions into a single high-rate PVW cipher-text. Let $p < q$ be the plaintext and ciphertext moduli of PVW and denote $f = \lceil q/p \rceil$. (The ciphertext modulus q is the same one that was used for the GSW encryption.) Also denote $\ell = \lfloor \log p \rfloor$, and consider $\ell \cdot n_0^2$ GSW ciphertexts,

$C_{u,v,w} \in \mathbb{Z}_q^{n_1 \times m}$, $u, v \in [n_0]$, $w \in [\ell]$, each encrypting a bit $\sigma_{i,j,k} \in \{0,1\}$. Namely we have $S \times C_{u,v,w} = \sigma_{u,v,w} \cdot SG + E_{u,v,w} \pmod{q}$ for low norm matrices $E_{u,v,w}$.

We want to pack all these ciphertexts into a single compressed PVW ciphertext, namely a matrix $C \in \mathbb{Z}_q^{n_1 \times n_0}$ such that $SC = f \cdot Z + E' \pmod{q}$ where $Z \in \mathbb{Z}_p^{n_0 \times n_0}$ is a plaintext matrix whose bit representation contains all the $\sigma_{u,v,w}$'s (and E' is a noise matrix with entries of magnitude less than $f/2$).

Denote by $T_{u,v}$ the square $n_0 \times n_0$ singleton matrix with 1 in entry (u,v) and 0 elsewhere, namely $T_{u,v} = e_u \otimes e_v$ (where e_u, e_v are the dimension-n_0 unit vectors with 1 in positions u, v, respectively). Also denote by $T'_{u,v}$ the padded version of $T_{u,v}$ with k zero rows on top, $T'_{u,v} = \begin{bmatrix} 0 \\ e_u \otimes e_v \end{bmatrix} \in \mathbb{Z}_q^{n_1 \times n_0}$. We compress the $C_{u,v,w}$'s by computing

$$C^* := \sum_{u,v,w} C_{u,v,w} \times G^{-1}(f \cdot 2^w \cdot T'_{u,v}) \pmod{q}. \tag{3}$$

Since $T'_{u,v}$ are $n_1 \times n_0$ matrices, then $G^{-1}(f \cdot 2^w \cdot T'_{u,v})$ are $m \times n_0$ matrices, and since the $C_{u,v,w}$'s are $n_1 \times m$ matrices then $C^* \in \mathbb{Z}_q^{n_1 \times n_0}$, as needed. Next, for every u, v denote $z_{uv} = \sum_{w=0}^{\ell} 2^w \sigma_{u,v,w} \in [p]$, and we observe that

$$
\begin{aligned}
S \times C^* &= \sum_{u,v,w} S \times C_{u,v,w} \times G^{-1}(f \cdot 2^w \cdot T'_{u,v}) \\
&= \sum_{u,v,w} (\sigma_{u,v,w} S\, G + E_{u,v,w}) \times G^{-1}(f \cdot 2^w \cdot T'_{u,v}) \\
&= \sum_{u,v,w} f \cdot 2^w \cdot \sigma_{u,v,w} S\, T'_{u,v} + \overbrace{\sum_{u,v,w} E_{u,v,w} \times G^{-1}(f \cdot 2^w \cdot T_{u,v})}^{E'} \\
&= f \cdot \sum_{u,v} z_{u,v} S\, T'_{u,v} + E' \overset{(*)}{=} f \cdot \overbrace{\sum_{u,v} z_{u,v} T_{u,v}}^{Z} + E', \tag{4}
\end{aligned}
$$

where $Z = [z_{u,v}] \in [p]^{n_0 \times n_0}$. (The equality $(*)$ holds since $S = [S'|I]$ and $T' = \begin{bmatrix} 0 \\ T \end{bmatrix}$ and therefore $ST' = S' \times 0 + I \times T = T$.)

Compressed Decryption. Compressed ciphertexts are just regular PVW ciphertexts, hence we use the PVW decryption procedure. Given the compressed ciphertext $C^* \in \mathbb{Z}_q^{n_1 \times n_0}$, we compute $X := SC = f \cdot Z + E' \pmod{q}$ using the secret key S. As long as $\|E\|_\infty < f/2$, we can complete decryption by rounding to the nearest multiple of f, setting $Z := \lceil Z/f \rfloor$. Once we have the matrix Z, we can read off the $\sigma_{u,v,w}$'s which are the bits in the binary expansion of the $z_{u,v}$'s.

Lemma 1. *The scheme above is a compressible (F)HE cryptosystem with rate* $\alpha = \frac{|p|}{|q|} \cdot \frac{n_0}{n_1}$. $\qquad\qquad\qquad\qquad\qquad\qquad\qquad\qquad\qquad\qquad\qquad\qquad\qquad\qquad\qquad\square$

Setting the Parameters. It remains to show how to set the various parameters – including the matrix dimensions n_0, n_1 and the moduli p, q – as a function of the security parameter k. If we use a somewhat-homomorphic variant of GSW without bootstrapping, then the noise magnitude in evaluated ciphertexts would depend on the functions that we want to compute. One such concrete example (with fully specified constants) is provided in Sect. 5 for our PIR application. Here we provide an asymptotic analysis of the parameters when using GSW as a fully-homomorphic scheme with bootstrapping. Namely we would like to evaluate an arbitrary function with long output on encrypted data (using the GSW FHE scheme), then pack the resulting encrypted bits in compressed ciphertexts that remain decryptable.

We want to ensure that compressed ciphertexts have rate of $1 - \epsilon$ for some small ϵ of our choosing. To this end, it is sufficient to set $n_0 > 2k/\epsilon$ and $q = p^{1+\epsilon/2}$. This gives $n_1 = n_0 + k \leq n_0(1 + \epsilon/2)$ and $|q| = |p|(1 + \epsilon/2)$, and hence

$$\frac{n_0}{n_1} \cdot \frac{|p|}{|q|} \geq \left(\frac{1}{1+\epsilon/2}\right)^2 > (1 - \epsilon/2)^2 > 1 - \epsilon,$$

as needed.

Using $q = p^{1-\epsilon/2}$ means that to be able to decrypt we must keep the noise below $q/2p = p^{\epsilon/2}/2$. Following [11,17], when using GSW with fresh-ciphertext noise of size α and ciphertext matrices of dimension $n_1 \times m$, we can perform arbitrary computation and then bootstrap the result, and the noise after bootstrapping is bounded below αm^2. From Eq. (4) we have a set of $n_0^2 \log p$ error matrices $E_{u,v,w}$, all satisfying $\|E_{u,v,w}\|_\infty < \alpha m^2$. The error term after compression is therefore $\sum_{u,v,w} E_{u,v,w} G^{-1}(\text{something})$, and its size is bounded by $n_0^2 \log p \cdot \alpha m^2 \cdot m = \alpha m^3 n_0^2 \log p$.

It is enough, therefore, that this last expression is smaller than $p^{\epsilon/2}/2$, i.e., we have the correctness constraint $p^{\epsilon/2}/2 > \alpha m^3 n_0^2 \log p$. Setting the fresh-encryption noise as some polynomial in the security parameter, the last constraint becomes $p^{\epsilon/2} > \text{poly}(k) \log p$. This is satisfied by some $p = k^{\Theta(1/\epsilon)}$, and therefore also $q = p^{1+\epsilon/2} = k^{\Theta(1/\epsilon)}$.

We conclude that to get a correct scheme with rate $1 - \epsilon$, we can use LWE with noise $\text{poly}(k)$ and modulus $q = k^{\Theta(1/\epsilon)}$. Hence the security of the scheme relies on the hardness of LWE with gap $k^{\Theta(1/\epsilon)}$, and in particular if ϵ is a constant then we rely on LWE with polynomial gap.

We note that there are many techniques that can be applied to slow the growth of the noise. Many of those techniques (for example modulus switching) are described in Sect. 5 in the context of our PIR application. While they do not change the asymptotic behavior — we will always need $q = k^{\Theta(1/\epsilon)}$ — they can drastically improve the constant in the exponent.

Theorem 1. *For any $\epsilon = \epsilon(\lambda) > 0$, there exists a rate-$(1 - \epsilon)$ compressible FHE scheme as per definition 1 with semantic security under the decision-LWE assumption with gap $\text{poly}(\lambda)^{1/\epsilon}$.* □

More Procedures. In addition to the basic compressible HE interfaces, our scheme also supports several other operations that come in handy in applications such as PIR.

Encryption and additive homomorphism of compressed ciphertexts.
Since this variant uses PVW for compressed ciphertexts, then we can use the
encryption and additive homomorphism of the PVW cryptosystem.

Multiplying compressed ciphertexts by GSW ciphertexts. When p
divides q, we can also multiply a compressed ciphertext $C' \in \mathbb{Z}_q^{n_1 \times n_0}$ encrypting
$M \in \mathbb{Z}_p^{n_0 \times n_0}$ by a GSW ciphertext $C \in \mathbb{Z}_q^{n_1 \times m}$ encrypting a small scalar σ,
to get a compressed ciphertext C'' that encrypting the matrix $\sigma M \bmod p$. This
is done by setting $C'' := C \times G^{-1}(C') \bmod q$ (and note that $C' \in \mathbb{Z}_q^{n_1 \times n_0}$ so
$G^{-1}(C') \in \mathbb{Z}_q^{m \times n_0}$). For correctness, recall that we have $SC = \sigma SG + E$ and
$SC' = q/p \cdot M + E'$ over $\mathbb{Z}_q$, hence

$$S \times C'' = S\, C\, G^{-1}(C') = \sigma SC' + \overbrace{E\, G^{-1}(C')}^{E''} \tag{5}$$

$$= \sigma(q/p \cdot M + E') + E'' = q/p \cdot (\sigma M \bmod p) + \overbrace{\sigma E' + E''}^{E^*} \pmod{q}.$$

This is a valid compressed encryption of $\sigma M \bmod p$ as long as the noise $E^* =
\sigma E' + E\, G^{-1}(C')$ is still smaller than $p/2$.

Multiplying GSW ciphertexts by plaintext matrices. The same technique
that lets us right-multiply GSW ciphertexts by compressed ones, also lets us
right-multiply them by plaintext matrices. Indeed if $M \in \mathbb{Z}_p^{n_0 \times n_0}$ is a plaintext
matrix and M' is its padded version $M' = \left[\frac{0}{M}\right] \in \mathbb{Z}_p^{n_1 \times n_0}$, then the somewhat
redundant matrix $M^* = q/p \cdot M'$ can be considered a noiseless ciphertext (note
that $S \times M^* = q/p \cdot M$) and can therefore be multiplied by a GSW ciphertext as
above. The only difference is that in this case we can even use a GSW ciphertext
encrypting a large scalar: The "noiseless ciphertext" M^* has $E' = 0$, hence the
term $\sigma E'$ from above does not appear in the resulting noise term, no matter how
large σ is.

4.2 High-Rate Additive HE Using Nearly Square Gadget Matrix

We now turn to the other variant of our scheme. Here we encrypt plaintext
matrices modulo q using ciphertext matrix modulo the same q, with dimensions
that are only slightly larger than the plaintext matrix. A new technical ingredient in that scheme is a new gadget matrix (described in Sect. 4.4), that we
call H: Just like the G gadget matrix from [27], our H adds redundancy to
the ciphertext, and it has a "public trapdoor" that enables removing the noise
upon decryption. The difference is that H is a *nearly square matrix*, hence comes
with almost no expansion, enabling high-rate ciphertexts. Of course, an almost
rectangular H cannot have a trapdoor of high quality, so we make do with a
low-quality trapdoor that can only remove a small amount of noise.

The slight increase in dimensions from plaintext to ciphertext in this high-
rate scheme comes in two steps. First, as in the previous variant we must pad
plaintext matrices M with some additional zero rows, setting $M' = \left[\frac{0}{M}\right]$ so as to
get $SM' = M$. Second, we add redundancy to M' by multiplying it on the right

by our gadget matrix H, to enable removing a small amount of noise during decryption. The decryption invariant for compressed ciphertexts is

$$S \times C = M \times H + E \pmod{q},$$

with $S = (S'|I)$ the secret key, C the ciphertext, M the plaintext matrix and E a small-norm noise matrix.

To get a high-rate compressed ciphertexts, we must ensure that the increase in dimensions from plaintext to ciphertext is as small as possible. With $n_0 \times n_0$ plaintext matrices M, we need to add as many zero rows as the dimension of the LWE secret (which we denote by k). Denoting $n_1 = n_0 + k$, the padded matrix M' has dimension $n_1 \times n_0$. We further add redundancy by multiplying on the right with a somewhat rectangular gadget matrix H of dimension $n_0 \times n_2$. The final dimension of the ciphertext is $n_1 \times n_2$, so the information rate of compressed ciphertexts is $n_0^2/(n_1 n_2)$. As we show in Sect. 4.3, we can orchestrate the various parameters so that we can get $n_0^2/(n_1 n_2) = 1 - \epsilon$ for any desired $\epsilon > 0$, using a modulus q of size $k^{\Theta(1/\epsilon)}$. Hence we can get any constant $\epsilon > 0$ assuming the hardness of LWE with polynomial gap, or polynomially small ϵ if we assume hardness of LWE with subexponential gap.

The rest of this section is organized as follows: We now describe on the different procedures that comprise this variant, then discuss parameters and additional procedures, and finally in Sect. 4.4 we describe the construction of the gadget matrix H.

Key Generation, Encryption, and Evaluation. These are identical to the procedures in the variant from Sect. 4.1, using GSW with matrix secret keys. The low-rate ciphertexts satisfy the GSW invariant as GSW, $SC = \sigma SG + E$ $\pmod{q}$ with $E \ll q$, and provides semantic security under the decision LWE hardness assumption [17].

Compression. Compression is similar to the previous variant, but instead of $G^{-1}(f \cdot 2^w \cdot T'_{u,v})$ as in Eq. (3) we use $G^{-1}(2^w \cdot T'_{u,v} \times H)$. Recall that we denote by $T_{u,v}$ the square $n_0 \times n_0$ singleton matrix with 1 in entry (u, v) and 0 elsewhere, and $T'_{u,v}$ is a padded version of $T_{u,v}$ with k zero rows on top

Denote $\ell = \lfloor \log q \rfloor$, and consider $\ell \cdot n_0^2$ GSW ciphertexts, $C_{u,v,w} \in \mathbb{Z}_q^{n_1 \times m}$, $u, v \in [n_0], w \in [\ell]$, each encrypting a bit $\sigma_{i,j,k} \in \{0, 1\}$, we pack these GSW bit encryptions into a single compressed ciphertext by computing

$$C^* = \sum_{u,v,w} C_{u,v,w} \times G^{-1}(2^w \cdot T'_{u,v} \times H) \bmod q,$$

We first note that $T'_{u,v} \times H$ are $n_1 \times n_2$ matrices, hence $G^{-1}(2^w \cdot T'_{u,v} \times H)$ are $m \times n_2$ matrices, and since the $C_{u,v,w}$'s are $n_1 \times m$ matrices then $C^* \in \mathbb{Z}_q^{n_1 \times n_2}$, as needed. Next, for every u, v denote $z_{uv} = \sum_{w=0}^{\ell} 2^w \sigma_{u,v,w} \in [q]$, and we observe that

$$
\begin{aligned}
S \times C^* &= \sum_{u,v,w} S \times C_{u,v,w} \times G^{-1}(2^w \cdot T'_{u,v} \times H) \\
&= \sum_{u,v,w} (\sigma_{u,v,w} S\,G + E_{u,v,w}) \times G^{-1}(2^w \cdot T'_{u,v} \times H) \\
&= \sum_{u,v,w} 2^w \sigma_{u,v,w} S\,T'_{u,v} H + \overbrace{\sum_{u,v,w} E_{u,v,w} \times G^{-1}(2^w \cdot T_{u,v} \times H)}^{E'} \\
&= \sum_{u,v} z_{u,v} S\,T'_{u,v} H + E' \stackrel{(*)}{=} \Bigg(\underbrace{\sum_{u,v} z_{u,v} T_{u,v}}_{Z}\Bigg) \times H + E',
\end{aligned}
\tag{6}
$$

where $Z = [z_{u,v}] \in [q]^{n_0 \times n_0}$. (The equality $(*)$ holds since $S = [S'|I]$ and $T' = \left[\frac{0}{T}\right]$ and therefore $ST' = S' \times 0 + I \times T = T$.)

Compressed Decryption. Compressed ciphertexts in this scheme are matrices $C \in \mathbb{Z}_q^{n_1 \times n_2}$, encrypting plaintext matrices $M \in \mathbb{Z}_q^{n_0 \times n_0}$. To decrypt we compute $X := S\,C = M\,H + E \pmod q$ using the secret key S. This is where we use the redundancy introduced by H, as long as $\|E\|_\infty$ is small enough, we can complete decryption by using the trapdoor $F = H^{-1}(0)$ to recover and then eliminate the small noise E, hence obtaining the matrix M. This recovers the matrix Z, and then we can read off the $\sigma_{u,v,w}$'s which are the bits in the binary expansion of the $z_{u,v}$'s.

Lemma 2. *The scheme above is a compressible FHE scheme with rate* $\alpha = n_0^2/n_1 n_2$. $\qquad\square$

More Procedures. It is easy to see that the current construction supports the same additional procedures as the variant from Sect. 4.1. Namely we have direct encryption and additive homomorphism of compressed ciphertexts, multiplication of compressed ciphertexts by GSW ciphertexts that encrypts small constants, and multiplication of GSW ciphertexts (encrypting arbitrary constants) by plaintext mod-q matrices.

4.3   Setting the Parameters

It remains to show how to set the various parameters — the dimensions n_0, n_1, n_2 and the modulus q — as a function of the security parameter k. As above, we only provide here an asymptotic analysis of the parameters when using GSW as a fully-homomorphic scheme with bootstrapping.

Again from [11,17], if we use fresh-ciphertext noise of size $\mathsf{poly}(k)$ then also after bootstrapping we still have the noise magnitude bounded below $\mathsf{poly}(k)$. After compression as per Eq. (6), the noise term is a sum of $n_0^2 \log q$ matrices $E_{u,v,w}$, all of magnitude bounded by $\mathsf{poly}(k)$, hence it has magnitude below $\mathsf{poly}(k) \cdot \log q$. We therefore need the nearly-square gadget matrix H to add enough redundancy to correct that noise.

On the other hand, to get an information rate of $1 - \epsilon$ (for some small ϵ) we need $n_0^2/(n_1 n_2) \geq 1 - \epsilon$, which we can get by setting $n_1, n_2 \leq n_0/(1 - \frac{\epsilon}{2})$. As we explain in Sect. 4.4 below, a nearly-square matrix H with $n_2 = n_0/(1 - \frac{\epsilon}{2})$ can only correct noise of magnitude below $\beta = \lfloor q^{\epsilon/2}/2 \rfloor$. Hence we get the correctness constraint $\frac{q^{\epsilon/2}}{2} > \mathsf{poly}(k) \log q$ (essentially the same as for the variant from Sect. 4.1 above), which is satisfied by some $q = k^{\Theta(1/\epsilon)}$.

4.4 A Nearly Square Gadget Matrix

We now turn to describing the new technical component that we use in the second variant above, namely the "nearly square" gadget matrix. Consider first why the usual Micciancio-Peikert gadget matrix [27] $G \in \mathbb{Z}_q^{n_1 \times m}$ which is used GSW cannot give us high rate. An encryption of $M \in R_q^{n_0 \times n_0}$ has the form $C = M' \cdot G + P \cdot X$ (for some some M' that includes M), so the rate can be at most n_0/m simply because C has m/n_0 times as many columns as M. This rate is less than $1/\log q$ for the usual G.

The rate can be improved by using a "lower-quality" gadget matrix. For example $G = I \otimes \boldsymbol{g}$ where $\boldsymbol{g} = (1, B, \ldots, B^{\lfloor \log_B q \rfloor})$ for large-ish B, where $G^{-1}(C)$ still have coefficients of magnitude at most $B/2$. But this can at best yield a rate-$1/2$ scheme (for $B = \sqrt{q}$), simply because a non-trivial $\boldsymbol{g}$ must have dimension at least 2. Achieve rate close to 1 requires that we use a gadget matrix with almost the same numbers of rows and columns.

The crucial property of the gadget matrix that enables decryption, is that there exists a known "public trapdoor" matrix $F = G^{-1}(0) \in R^{m \times m}$ such that:

1. F has small entries ($\ll q$)
2. $G \cdot F = 0 \bmod q$
3. F is full-rank over R (but of course not over R_q, as it is the kernel of G).

Given such an F, it is known how to compute $G^{-1}(C)$ for any ciphertext $C \in R_q^{n_1 \times m}$, such that the entries in $G^{-1}(C)$ are not much larger than the coefficients of F, cf. [16].

In our setting, we want our new gadget matrix (that we call H rather than G to avoid confusion) to have almost full rank modulo q (so that it is "nearly square"), hence we want $F = H^{-1}(0)$ to have very low rank modulo q. Once we have a low-norm matrix F with full rank over R but very low rank modulo q, we simply set H as a basis of the mod-q kernel of F.

Suppose for simplicity that $q = p^t - 1$ for some integers p, t. We can generate a matrix F' with "somewhat small" coefficients that has full rank over the reals but rank one modulo q as:

$$
F' := \begin{bmatrix}
1 & p & p^2 & & p^{t-1} \\
p^{t-1} & 1 & p & \cdots & p^{t-2} \\
p^{t-2} & p^{t-1} & 1 & & p^{t-3} \\
& \vdots & & \ddots & \vdots \\
p & p^2 & p^3 & \cdots & 1
\end{bmatrix}
$$

Notice that the entries of F' have size at most $(q+1)/p \approx q^{1-1/t}$ and moreover for every vector $\boldsymbol{v}$ we have

$$\|\boldsymbol{v}F'\|_\infty \leq \|\boldsymbol{v}\|_\infty \cdot (1+p+\ldots+p^{t-1}) = \|\boldsymbol{v}\|_\infty \cdot (p^t-1)/(p-1) = \|\boldsymbol{v}\|_\infty \cdot \tfrac{q}{p-1}. \quad (7)$$

We can use this F' to generate a matrix F with rank $r \cdot t$ over the reals but rank r modulo q (for any r), by tensoring F' with the $r \times r$ identity matrix, $F := F' \otimes I_r$. This yields the exact same bounds as above on the l_∞ norms. Our gadget matrix H is an $r(t-1) \times rt$ matrix whose rows span the null space of F modulo q (any such matrix will do). For our scheme below we will set $n_0 = r(t-1)$ and $n_2 = rt = n_0(1+\frac{1}{t-1})$.

In the decryption of compressed ciphertexts below, we use the "somewhat smallness" of $F = H^{-1}(0)$. Specifically, given a matrix $Z = MH + E \pmod{q}$ with $\|E\|_\infty \leq \frac{p-1}{2}$, we first multiply it by F modulo q to get $ZF = (MH+E)F = EF \pmod{q}$ (since $HF = 0 \pmod{q}$). But

$$\|EF\|_\infty \leq \|E\|_\infty \cdot \frac{q}{p-1} \leq \frac{p-1}{2} \cdot \frac{q}{p-1} = q/2,$$

and therefore $(ZF \bmod q) = EF$ over the integers. Now we use the fact that F has full rank over the reals, and recover $E := (ZF \bmod q) \times F^{-1}$. Then we compute $Z - E = MH \pmod{q}$, and since H has rank n_0 modulo q we can recover M from MH. It follows that to ensure correctness when decrypting compressed ciphertexts, it is sufficient to use a bound $\beta \leq \frac{p-1}{2} = \lfloor q^{1/t} \rfloor / 2$ on the size of the noise in compressed ciphertexts.

The restriction $q = p^t - 1$ is not really necessary; many variants are possible. The following rather crude approach works for any q that we are likely to encounter. Consider the lattice L of multiples of the vector $\boldsymbol{u} = (1, a, \cdots, a^{t-1})$ modulo q, where $a = \lceil q^{1/t} \rceil$. Let the rows of F' be the L-vectors $c_i \cdot \boldsymbol{u} \bmod q$ for $i \in [t]$, where $c_i = \lceil q/a^i \rceil$. Clearly F' has rank 1 modulo q. (We omit a proof that F' is full rank over the integers.) We claim that all entries of F' are small. Consider the j-th coefficient of $c_i \cdot \boldsymbol{u} \bmod q$, which is $\lceil q/a^i \rceil \cdot a^j \bmod q$ for $i \in [t]$, $j \in \{0, \ldots, t-1\}$. If $i > j$, then $\lceil q/a^i \rceil \cdot a^j$ is bounded in magnitude by $q/a^{i-j} + a^j \leq q/a + a^{t-1} \leq 2a^{t-1}$. For the $j \geq i$ case, observe that $\lceil q/a^i \rceil \cdot a^i$ is an integer in $[q, q+a^i]$, and therefore is at most a^i modulo q. Therefore $\lceil q/a^i \rceil \cdot a^j \bmod q$ is at most $a^j \leq a^{t-1}$ modulo q. As long as $q \geq t^t$, we have that $a^{t-1} \leq (q^{1/t} \cdot (1+1/t))^{t-1} < q^{(t-1)/t} \cdot e$ – that is, $\|F'\|_\infty$ is nearly as small as it was when we used $q = p^t - 1$. As we saw above, q anyway needs to exceed β^t where β is a bound on the noise of ciphertexts, so the condition that $q > t^t$ will likely already be met.

5   Application to Fast Private Information Retrieval

Can we construct a single-server PIR scheme that is essentially optimal both in terms of communication and computation? With our compressible FHE scheme, we can achieve communication rate arbitrarily close to 1. Here, we describe a PIR which is not only bandwidth efficient but should also outperform whole-database AES encryption computationally.[6]

5.1   Toward an Optimized PIR Scheme

Our starting point is the basic hierarchical PIR, where the N database entries are arranged in a hypercube of dimensions $N = N_1 \times \cdots \times N_D$ and the scheme uses degree-D homomorphism:

- The client's index $i \in [N]$ is represented in mixed radix of basis $N_1, \ldots, N_D$, namely as $(i_1, \ldots, i_D)$ such that $i = \sum_{j=1}^{D} i_j \cdot \prod_{k=j+1}^{D} N_k$. The client's message is processed to obtain an encrypted *unary representation* of all the i_j's. Namely, for each dimension j we get a dimension-N_j vector of encrypted bits, in which the i_j'th bit is one and all the others are zero.
- Processing the first dimension, we multiply each hyper-row $u \in [N_1]$ by the u'th encrypted bit from the first vector, which zeros out all but the i_1'st hyper-row. We then add all the resulting encrypted hyper-rows, thus getting a smaller hypercube of dimension $N/N_1 = N_2 \times \ldots N_D$, consisting only the i_1'st hyper-row of the database.
- We proceed in a similar manner to fold the other dimensions, one at a time, until we are left with a zero-dimension hypercube consisting only the selected entry i.

We note that the first step, reducing database size from N to N/N_1, is typically the most expensive since it processes the most data. On the other hand, that step only requires ciphertext-by-plaintext multiplications (vs. the ciphertext-by-ciphertext multiplications that are needed in the following steps), so it can sometimes be optimized better than the other steps.

Below we describe the sequence of derivations and optimizations to get our final construction, resulting in a high rate PIR scheme which is also computationally efficient. The construction features a tradeoff between bandwidth and computation (and below we describe a variant with rate 4/9).

The main reason for this tradeoff is that the rate of our scheme is $\frac{n_0}{n_1} \cdot \frac{n_0}{n_2}$, where the secret key matrix S has dimension $n_0 \times n_1$ and the gadget matrix H has dimension $n_0 \times n_2$. Since n_0, n_1, n_2 are integers, we need n_0 to be large if we want n_0/n_1 and n_0/n_2 to be close to one. Recalling that the plaintext matrices M have dimension $n_0 \times n_0$, a large n_0 means that the plaintext is of high dimension. Hence multiplying GSW-ciphertexts C by plaintext matrices M takes more multiplications per entry (e.g., using a cubic matrix multiplication algorithm). A second aggravating factor is that as H becomes closer to square, we can handle smaller noise/modulus ratio. Hence we need the products $C \times M$

---

[6] The "should" is since we did not implement this construction. Implementing it and measuring its performance may be an interesting topic for future work.

to be carried over a larger modulus (so we can later mod-switch it down to reduce the noise), again getting more multiplies per plaintext byte.[7]

Using Our GSW-Compatible Compressible HE Scheme. An advantage of GSW over other FHE schemes is its exceptionally slow noise growth during homomorphic multiplication when the left multiplicand is in $\{0,1\}$. Although GSW normally operates on encrypted bits, GSW's advantage remains when the right multiplicand is a ciphertext of our compressible FHE scheme. So, these schemes are perfect for PIR, where the left multiplicands are bits of the client's query, and the rightmost multiplicands are blocks of the database.

Using Ring-LWE. As usual with LWE schemes, we can improve performance by switching to the ring (or module) variant, where the LWE secret has low dimension over a large extension field. Instead of having to manipulate large matrices, these variants manipulate low-dimension matrices over the same large extension field, which take less bits to describe and can be multiplied faster (using FFTs). To get comparable security, if the basic LWE scheme needs LWE secrets of dimension k, the new scheme will have dimension-k' secrets over an extension field of degree d, such that $k'd \geq k$. (For ring-LWE we have $k' = 1$ and $d = k$.) The various matrices in the scheme consist of extension-field elements, and their dimensions are $n_i' = n_i/d$ and $m' = m/d$ (instead of n_i, m, respectively). Below we use the notation n_i' and m' to emphasize the smaller values in the RLWE context.

Saving on FFTs. One of our most important optimizations is pre-processing the database to minimize the number of FFTs during processing. Our scheme needs to switch between CRT representation of ring elements (which is needed for arithmetic operations) and representation in the decoding basis (as needed for applications of $G^{-1}(\cdot)$). While converting between the two can be done in quasi-linear time using FFTs, it is still by far the most expensive operations used in the implementation. (For our typical sizes, converting an element between these representations is perhaps 10–20 times slower than multiplying two elements represented in the CRT basis.)

As in the XPIR work [1], we can drastically reduce the number of FFTs by pre-processing the database, putting it all in CRT representation. This way, we only need to compute FFTs when we process the client's message to get the encrypted unary representation of the i_j's (which is independent of the size of entries in the database), and then again after we fold the first dimension (so it is only applied to compressed ciphertexts encrypting the N/N_1 database entries).

If we set N_1 large enough relative to the FFT overhead, then the FFTs after folding the first dimension will be amortized and become insignificant. On the other hand we need to set it small enough (relative to N/N_1 and the length-L of the entries) so the initial FFTs (of which we have about $n_1' \cdot m' \cdot N_1$) will also be insignificant.

---

[7] The tradeoffs become harder to describe cleanly when optimizing concrete performance as we do here. For example, a 65-bit modular multiplication is as expensive in software as a 120-bit one.

In the description below we illustrate the various parameters with $N_1 = 2^8$, which seems to offer a good tradeoff. For the other N_i's, there is (almost) no reason to make them large, so we use $N_2 = N_3 = \cdots = N_D = 4$. We note that for the construction below there is (almost) no limit on how many such small N_i's we can use. Below we illustrate the construction for a database with $N = 2^{20}$ entries, but it can handle *much* larger databases. (The same parameters work upto at least $N = 2^{2^{20}}$ entries.)

Client-side Encryption. In the context of a PIR scheme, the encrypter is the client who has the decryption key. Hence it can create ciphertexts using the secret key, by choosing a fresh pseudorandom public key P_i for each ciphertext and setting $C_i := \sigma_i G + P_i \mod q$. This results in ciphertexts of slightly smaller noise, namely just the low-norm E_i's (as opposed to $E \times X_i$ that we get from public-key encrypted ciphertexts).

Since our PIR construction uses small dimensions $N_2 = N_3 = \cdots = 4$, we have the client directly sending the encrypted unary vectors for these dimensions. Namely for each $j = 2, 3, \ldots$ the client sends four ciphertexts $C_{j,0}, \ldots, C_{j,3}$ such that C_{j,i_j} encrypts one and the others encrypt zero.

For the first dimension we have a large $N_1 = 2^8$, however, so the client sends encryptions of the bits of i_1 and we use the GSW homomorphism to compute the encrypted unary vector for this dimension. Overall the client therefore sends $\log N_1 + (N_2 + N_3 + \cdots N_D)$ encrypted bits, in our illustrated sizes this comes up to $8 + 4 \times 6 = 32$ encrypted bits.

Multiple G Matrices. The accumulated noise in our scheme has many terms of the form $E \times G^{-1}(\text{something})$, but not all of them are created equal. In particular, when folding the first (large) dimension N_1, the GSW ciphertexts are evaluated and the noise in them is itself a sum of such. When we multiply these GSW ciphertexts by the plaintext matrix we get $E \times G^{-1}(\text{something}) \times G^{-1}(\text{something}')$, which is larger. For the other (small) dimensions, on the other hand, we multiply by fresh ciphertexts so we get much smaller noise. This imbalance leads to wasted resources.

Moreover, the multiplication by $G^{-1}(\text{something})$ during the initial processing of the client's bits are only applied to a small amounts of data. But the multiplication between the GSW matrices and the plaintext data touches all the data in the database. Hence the latter are much more expensive, and we would like to reduce the dimension of the matrices involved as much as we can.

For all of these reasons, it is better to use different G matrices in different parts of the computation. In particular we use very wide-and-short G matrices (with smaller norm of $G^{-1}(0)$) when we initially process the client's bits, and more-square/higher-norm G matrices later on.

Modulus Switching. Even with a careful balance of the G matrices, we cannot make the noise as small as we want it to be for our compressed scheme. We therefore use the modulus-switching technique from [9,10]. Namely we perform the computation relative to a large modulus Q, then switch to a smaller modulus q before sending the final result to the client, scaling the noise roughly by q/Q.

This lets us be more tolerant to noise, which improves many of the parameters. For example by using $Q \approx q^{2.5}$ we can even replace the G matrix for the actual data *by the identity matrix*. Even if it means using LWE secret of twice the dimension and having to write numbers that are more than twice as large, it would still save a large constant factor. Moreover it lets us use a more square matrix H (e.g. 2×3) thereby getting a higher rate.

We note that using modulus switching requires that we choose the secret key from the error distribution rather than uniformly. (Also, in the way we implement it, for some of the bits σ we encrypt the scalar $q' \cdot \sigma$ rather than σ itself, where $Q = q' \cdot q$.)

5.2 The Detailed PIR Scheme

Our construction is staged in the cyclotomic ring of index 2^{13} and dimension 2^{12}, i.e., $R = \mathbb{Z}[X]/(X^{2^{12}} + 1)$. The ciphertext modulus of the fresh GSW ciphertext is a composite $Q = q \cdot q'$, with $q \approx 2^{46}$ and $q' \approx 2^{60}$ (both with primitive 2^{12}'th roots of unity so it is easy to perform FFTs modulo q, q'). Below we denote the rings modulo these three moduli by $R_Q, R_q, R_{q'}$.

We use ring-LWE over R_Q, in particular our LWE secret is a scalar in R_Q, chosen from the error distribution [4]. (Consulting Table 1 from [2], using this cyclotomic ring with a modulus Q of size up to 111 bits yields security level of 128 bits.)

For the various matrices in our construction we use dimensions $k' = 1$, $n'_0 = 2$, and $n'_1 = n'_2 = 3$, and the plaintext elements are taken from R_q. Hence we get a rate of $(\frac{2}{3})^2 \approx 0.44$. While processing, however, most ciphertexts will be modulo the larger $Q = q \cdot q'$, it is only before we send to the clients that we mod-switch them down to q. We use the construction from Sect. 4.4 with a 2-by-3 matrix H.

We split a size-N database into a hypercube of dimensions $N = 256 \times 4 \times 4 \times \ldots \times 4$. A client wishing to retrieve an entry $i \in [N]$ first represents i as $(i_1, i_2, \ldots, i_D)$, with $i_i \in [256]$ and $i_j \in [4]$ for all $j > 1$. Let $\sigma_{1,0}, \ldots \sigma_{1,7}$ be the bits of i_1, the client then encrypts the scalars $q' \cdot \sigma_{1,0}$ and $\sigma_{1,1}, \ldots, \sigma_{1,7}$ in GSW ciphertexts (modulo Q). For $j = 2, \ldots, D$ the client uses GSW ciphertexts to encrypt the bits of the unit vector e_{i_j} which is 1 in position i_j and zero elsewhere. We use three different gadget matrices for these GSW ciphertexts:

- For the LSB of i_1 (which will be the rightmost bit to be multiplied using GSW) we eliminate that gadget matrix G altogether and just use the identity, but we also multiply the bit $\sigma_{1,0}$ by q'. Namely we have $C_{1,0} \in R_Q^{n'_1 \times n'_1}$ such that
$$SC_{1,0} = \sigma_{1,0} q' S + E \in R_Q^{n'_0 \times n'_1}.$$
- For the other bits of i_1 we use a wide and short $G_1 \in \mathbb{Z}^{n'_1 \times m'_1}$, where $m'_1 = n'_1 \lceil \log_4 Q \rceil = 3 \cdot 53 = 159$. Each bit $\sigma_{1,t}$ is encrypted by $C_{1,t} \in R^{n'_1 \times m'_1}$ such that $SC_{1,t} = \sigma_{1,t} SG_1 + E \pmod{Q}$.
- For the bits encoding the unary representation of the other i_j's $(j > 1)$, we use a somewhat rectangular (3-by-6) matrix $G_2 \in \mathbb{Z}^{n'_1 \times m'_2}$, where $m'_2 = n'_1 \lceil \log_{2^{53}}(Q) \rceil = 3 \cdot 2 = 6$.

The client sends all these ciphertexts to the server. The encryption of the bits of i_1 consists of 9 elements for encrypting the LSB and $7 \cdot 3 \cdot 159 = 3381$ elements for encrypting the other seven bits. For each of the other indexes i_j we use $4 \cdot 3 \cdot 6 = 72$ elements to encrypt the unary representation of i_j. In our numerical example with $N = 2^{20}$ database entries we have 6 more i_j's, so the number of ring elements that the client sends is $9 + 3381 + 6 \cdot 72 = 3822$. Each element takes $106 \cdot 2^{12}$ bits to specify, hence the total number of bits sent by the client is $106 \cdot 2^{12} \cdot 3822 \approx 2^{30.6}$ (a bulky 198 MB).

For applications where the client query size is a concern, we can tweak the parameter, e.g. giving up a factor of 2 in the rate, and getting a 2–4× improvement in the client query size. A future-work direction is to try and port the query-expansion technique in the SealPIR work [3] in our setting, if applicable it would yield a very significant reduction in the client query size.[8]

The server pre-processes its database by breaking each entry into 2-by-2 plaintext matrices over R_q (recall $q \approx 2^{46}$). Hence each matrix holds $2 \cdot 2 \cdot 46 \cdot 2^{12} \approx 2^{19.5}$ bits (92 KB). The server encodes each entry in these matrices in CRT representation modulo Q.[9] Below we let L be the number of matrices that it takes to encode a single database entry. (A single JPEG picture will have $L \approx 4$, while a 4 GB movie will be encoded in about 44 K matrices).

Given the client's ciphertext, the server uses GSW evaluation to compute the GSW encryption of the unit vector e_{i_1} for the first dimension (this can be done using less than $N_1 = 256$ GSW multiplications). For $r = 1, 2, \ldots, 256$ the server multiplies the r'th ciphertext in this vector by all the plaintext matrices of all the entries in the r'th hyperrow of the hypercube, and adds everything across the first hypercube dimension. The result is a single encrypted hyperrow (of dimensions $N_2 \times \cdots \times N_D$), each entry of which consists of L compressed ciphertexts.

The server next continues to fold the small dimensions one after the other. For each size-4 dimension it multiplies the four GSW-encrypted bits by all the compressed ciphertexts in the four hyper-columns, respectively, then adds the results across the current dimension, resulting in a 4-fold reduction in the number of ciphertexts. This continues until the server is left with just a single entry of L compressed ciphertexts modulo Q.

Finally the server performs modulus switching, replacing each ciphertext C by $C' = \lceil C/q' \rfloor \in R_q$, and sends the resulting ciphertexts to the client for decryption. Note that the ciphertext C satisfied $SC = q'MH + E \pmod{q'q}$. Denoting the rounding error by Ξ, the new ciphertext has

$$SC' = S(C/q' + \Xi) = MH + E/q' + S\Xi \pmod{q}.$$

---

[8] Using the SealPIR optimization requires a key-switching mechanism for GSW, which is not straightforward.

[9] While the entries in the plaintext matrices are small (in $[\pm 2^{45}]$), their CRT representation modulo Q is not. Hence this representation entails a $106/46 \approx 2.3$ blowup in storage requirement at the server.

Since the key S was chosen from the error distribution and $\|\Xi\|_\infty \leq 1/2$, then the added noise is small and the result is a valid ciphertext. (See more details below.)

Noise Analysis. For the first dimension, we need to use GSW evaluation to compute the encrypted unary vector, where each ciphertext in that vector is a product of $\log N_1 = 8$ ciphertexts. Hence the noise of each these evaluated ciphertexts has roughly the form $\sum_{u=1}^{7} E_u \times G_1^{-1}(\text{something})$ with E_u one of the error matrices that were sampled during encryption. Once we multiply by the plaintext matrices for the database to get the compressed encryption as in Eq. (5) and add all the ciphertexts across the N_1-size dimension, we get a noise term of the form

$$\sum_{v=1}^{N_1} \left(\sum_{u=1}^{7} E_u \times G_1^{-1}(\text{something}_u) \right) \times \text{plaintext}_v.$$

(Note that on the right we just multiply by the plaintext matrix whose entries are bounded below 2^{45}, but without any G^{-1}.)[10]

The entries of the E_u's can be chosen from a distribution of variance 8 (which is good enough to avoid the Arora-Ge attacks [5]). The entries of $G^{-1}(\cdot)$ are in the range $[\pm 2]$ (because we have $m_1 = n_1 \log_4(Q)$), so multiplication by $G_1^{-1}(\text{something})$ increases the variance by a factor of less than $2^2 \cdot m_1' \cdot 2^{12} < 2^{21.4}$. Similarly multiplying by a plaintext matrix (of entries in $[\pm 2^{45}]$) increases the variance by a factor of $2^{2\cdot45} \cdot n_1 \cdot 2^{12} < 2^{103.6}$. The variance of each noise coordinate is therefore bounded by $2^8 \cdot 7 \cdot 8 \cdot 2^{21.4} \cdot 2^{103.6} < 2^{8+3+3+21.4+103.6} = 2^{139}$. Since each noise coordinate is a weighted sum of the entries of the E_u's with similar weights, it makes sense to treat it as a normal random variable. A good high probability bound on the size of this error is (say) 16 standard deviations, corresponding to probability $\text{erfc}(16/\sqrt{2}) \approx 2^{-189}$. Namely after folding the first dimension, all the compressed ciphertexts have $\|\text{noise}\|_\infty < 16 \cdot \sqrt{2^{139}} = 2^{73.5}$ with high probability.

As we continue to fold more dimensions, we again multiply the encrypted unary vectors for those dimensions (which are GSW ciphertexts) by the results of the previous dimension (which are compressed ciphertexts) using Eq. (5), this time using G_2. We note that the GSW ciphertexts in these dimensions are fresh, hence their noise terms are just the matrices E that were chosen during encryption. Thus each of the N_j noise terms in this dimension is of the form $E \times G_2^{-1}(\text{something})$ for one of these E matrices. Moreover, only one of the four terms in each dimension has an encrypted bit $\sigma = 1$ while the other have $\sigma = 0$.

---

[10] Asymptotically, and disregarding our unconventional way of introducing the plaintexts which optimizes concrete performance, the noise from this step grows linearly with N_1. If we set $N_1 = O(\log N + \lambda)$ for security parameter λ, the noise from this and the remaining steps will be bounded by $O(\log N + \lambda)$, and so q can be bounded by a constant-degree polynomial of these quantities. Given that the complexity of mod-q multiplication is $\log q \cdot \tilde{O}(\log \log q)$, the asymptotic overhead of our PIR scheme will be $\tilde{O}(\log \log \lambda + \log \log \log N)$.

Hence the term $\sigma \cdot$ previousNoise appears *only once* in the resulting noise term after folding the j'th dimension. Therefore folding each small dimension $j \geq 2$ just adds four noise terms of the form $E \times G^{-1}($something$)$ to the noise from the previous dimension.

Since G_2 has $m_2 = n_1 \log_{2^{53}}(Q)$, then each entry in G_2^{-1} is in the interval $[\pm 2^{52}]$, and multiplying by G_2 increases the variance by a factor of less than $(2^{52})^2 \cdot m_2' \cdot 2^{12} = 3 \cdot 2^{117}$ (recall $m_2' = 6$). With $4(D-1) = 24$ of these terms, the variance of each coordinate in the added noise term is bounded by $24 \cdot 8 \cdot 3 \cdot 2^{117} = 9 \cdot 2^{123}$. We can therefore use the high-probability bound $16 \cdot \sqrt{9 \cdot 2^{123}} < 2^{67.1}$ on the size of the added noise due to all the small hypercube dimensions.

The analysis so far implies that prior to the modulus switching operation, the noise is bounded in size below $2^{73.5} + 2^{67.1}$. The added noise term due to the rounding error in modulus switching is $S \times \Xi$, and the variance of each noise coordinate in this expression is $8 \cdot n_1' \cdot 2^{12}/2 = 3 \cdot 2^{15}$. Hence we have a high probability bound $16 \cdot \sqrt{3 \cdot 2^{15}} < 2^{12.3}$ on the magnitude of this last noise term. The total noise in the ciphertext returned to the client is therefore bounded by

$$\|\text{noise}\|_\infty < \frac{2^{73.5} + 2^{67.1}}{q'} + 2^{12.3} \approx 2^{13.5} + 2^{7.1} + 2^{12} \approx 2^{14}.$$

Recalling that we use the nearly square gadget matrix H with $p = \sqrt[3]{q} \approx 2^{46/3}$, the noise is indeed bounded below $(p-1)/2$ as needed, hence the ciphertexts returned to the client will be decrypted correctly with overwhelming probability.

Complexity Analysis. The work of the server while processing the query consists mostly of R_Q multiplications and of FFTs. (The other operations such as additions and applications of $G^{-1}()$ once we did the FFTs take almost no time in comparison.)

With our cyclotomic ring of dimension 2^{12}, each FFT operation is about 10–20 times slower than a ring multiply operation in evaluation representation. But it is easy to see that when N/N_1 times the size L of database entries is large enough, the number of multiplies dwarf the number of FFTs by a lot more than a 20× factor. Indeed, FFTs are only preformed in the initial phase where we process the bits of the index i_i sent by the client (which are independent of L and of N/N_1), and after folding the first dimension (which only applies to $N/N_1 \approx 0.25\%$ of the data). With our settings, the multiplication time should exceed the FFT time once $L \cdot N/N_1$ is more than a few thousands. With $N/N_1 = 4000$ in our example, even holding a single JPEG image in each entry already means that the FFT processing accounts for less than 50% of the overall time. And for movies where $L = 29K$, the FFT time is entirely insignificant.

Let us then evaluate the time spent on multiplications, as a function of the database size. For large $L \cdot N/N_1$, by far the largest number of multiplications is performed when multiplying the GSW ciphertexts by the plaintext matrices encoding the database, while folding the first hypercube dimension. These multiplications have the form $C' := C \times M'H \mod q'q$ with C' a ciphertext of dimension $n_1 \times n_1$ and $M'H$ a redundant plaintext matrix of dimension $n_1 \times n_2$ (where $n_1 = n_2 = 3$). Using the naïve matrix-multiplication algorithm, we need

$3^3 = 27$ ring multiplications for each of these matrix multiplications, modulo the double-sized modulus $q' \cdot q$. Each ring multiplication (for elements in CRT representation) consists of 2^{12} double-size modular integer multiplication, so each such matrix multiplication takes a total of $2 \cdot 27 \cdot 2^{12} \approx 2^{17.75}$ modular multiplications. For this work, we process a single plaintext matrix, containing about $2^{16.5}$ bytes, so the amortized work is about 2.4 modular multiplication per database byte. (Using Laderman's method we can multiply 3-by-3 matrices with only 23 multiplications [24], so the amortized work is only 2 modular multiplications per byte.) Taking into account the rest of the work should not change this number in any significant way when L is large, these multiplications likely account for at least 90% of the execution time.

Two (or even three) modular multiplication per byte should be faster than AES encryption of the same data. For example software implementations of AES without any hardware support are estimated at 25 cycles per byte or more [13,32]. Using the fact that we multiply the same GSW matrix by very many plaintext matrices, we may be able to pre-process the modular multiplications, which should make performance competitive even with AES implementations that are built on hardware support in the CPU.

We conclude that for large databases, the approach that we outlined above should be computationally faster than the naïve approach of sending the whole database, even without considering the huge communication savings. We stress that we achieved this speed while still providing great savings on bandwidth, indeed the rate of this solution is 0.44. In other words, compared to the insecure implementation where the client sends the index in the clear, we pay with only $2.25\times$ in bandwidth for obtaining privacy.

Achieving Higher Rate. It is not hard to see that the rate can be made arbitrarily close to one without affecting the asymptotic efficiency. Just before the server returns the answer, it can bootstrap it into another instance of compressible FHE that has rate close to one. This solution is asymptotically cheap, since this bootstrapping is only applied to a single entry. In terms of concrete performance, bootstrapping is very costly so the asymptotic efficiency is only realized for a very large database. Concretely, bootstrapping takes close to 2^{30} cycles per plaintext byte (vs. the procedure above that takes around 2^4 cycles per byte). Hence the asymptotic efficiency is likely to take hold only for databases with at least $N = 2^{30-4} = 64,000,000$ entries.

Acknowledgment. We thank Yuval Ishai for badgering us over the last four years to figure out the achievable rate in LWE-based constructions, until we could bare it no longer and did this work. We also thank Samir Menon and the anonymous reviewers for their useful comments.

References

1. Aguilar-Melchor, C., Barrier, J., Fousse, L., Killijian, M.-O.: XPIR: private information retrieval for everyone. Proc. Priv. Enhancing Technol. **2016**(2), 155–174 (2016)

2. Albrecht, M., et al.: Homomorphic encryption standard, November 2018. http://homomorphicencryption.org/. Accessed Feb 2019
3. Angel, S., Chen, H., Laine, K., Setty, S.: PIR with compressed queries and amortized query processing. In: 2018 IEEE Symposium on Security and Privacy (SP), pp. 962–979. IEEE (2018)
4. Applebaum, B., Cash, D., Peikert, C., Sahai, A.: Fast cryptographic primitives and circular-secure encryption based on hard learning problems. In: Halevi, S. (ed.) CRYPTO 2009. LNCS, vol. 5677, pp. 595–618. Springer, Heidelberg (2009). https://doi.org/10.1007/978-3-642-03356-8_35
5. Arora, S., Ge, R.: New algorithms for learning in presence of errors. In: Aceto, L., Henzinger, M., Sgall, J. (eds.) ICALP 2011. LNCS, vol. 6755, pp. 403–415. Springer, Heidelberg (2011). https://doi.org/10.1007/978-3-642-22006-7_34
6. Badrinarayanan, S., Garg, S., Ishai, Y., Sahai, A., Wadia, A.: Two-message witness indistinguishability and secure computation in the plain model from new assumptions. In: Takagi, T., Peyrin, T. (eds.) ASIACRYPT 2017. LNCS, vol. 10626, pp. 275–303. Springer, Cham (2017). https://doi.org/10.1007/978-3-319-70700-6_10
7. Brakerski, Z., Döttling, N., Garg, S., Malavolta, G.: Leveraging linear decryption: Rate-1 fully-homomorphic encryption and time-lock puzzles. Private communications (2019)
8. Brakerski, Z., Gentry, C., Halevi, S.: Packed ciphertexts in LWE-based homomorphic encryption. In: Kurosawa, K., Hanaoka, G. (eds.) PKC 2013. LNCS, vol. 7778, pp. 1–13. Springer, Heidelberg (2013). https://doi.org/10.1007/978-3-642-36362-7_1
9. Brakerski, Z., Gentry, C., Vaikuntanathan, V.: Fully homomorphic encryption without bootstrapping. In: Innovations in Theoretical Computer Science (ITCS 2012) (2012). http://eprint.iacr.org/2011/277
10. Brakerski, Z., Vaikuntanathan, V.: Efficient fully homomorphic encryption from (standard) LWE. SIAM J. Comput. **43**(2), 831–871 (2014)
11. Brakerski, Z., Vaikuntanathan, V.: Lattice-based FHE as secure as PKE. In: Naor, M. (ed.) Innovations in Theoretical Computer Science, ITCS 2014, pp. 1–12. ACM (2014)
12. Chor, B., Goldreich, O., Kushilevitz, E., Sudan, M.: Private information retrieval. In: Proceedings, 36th Annual Symposium on Foundations of Computer Science 1995, pp. 41–50. IEEE (1995)
13. Crypto++ 5.6.0, pentium 4 benchmarks (2009). https://www.cryptopp.com/benchmarks-p4.html. Accessed Feb 2019
14. Damgård, I., Jurik, M.: A generalisation, a simpli.cation and some applications of paillier's probabilistic public-key system. In: Kim, K. (ed.) PKC 2001. LNCS, vol. 1992, pp. 119–136. Springer, Heidelberg (2001). https://doi.org/10.1007/3-540-44586-2_9
15. Döttling, N., Garg, S., Ishai, Y., Malavolta, G., Mour, T., Ostrovsky, R.: Trapdoor hash functions and their applications. In: Boldyreva, A., Micciancio, D. (eds.) CRYPTO 2019. LNCS, vol. 11694, pp. 3–32. Springer, Cham (2019). https://doi.org/10.1007/978-3-030-26954-8_1
16. Gentry, C., Peikert, C., Vaikuntanathan, V.: Trapdoors for hard lattices and new cryptographic constructions. In: STOC, pp. 197–206. ACM (2008)
17. Gentry, C., Sahai, A., Waters, B.: Homomorphic encryption from learning with errors: conceptually-simpler, asymptotically-faster, attribute-based. In: Canetti, R., Garay, J.A. (eds.) CRYPTO 2013. LNCS, vol. 8042, pp. 75–92. Springer, Heidelberg (2013). https://doi.org/10.1007/978-3-642-40041-4_5

18. Green, M., Hohenberger, S., Waters, B.: Outsourcing the decryption of ABE cipher-texts. In: Proceedings 20th USENIX Security Symposium, San Francisco, CA, USA, 8–12 August 2011. USENIX Association (2011)

19. Halevi, S.: Homomorphic encryption. Tutorials on the Foundations of Cryptography. ISC, pp. 219–276. Springer, Cham (2017). https://doi.org/10.1007/978-3-319-57048-8_5

20. Hiromasa, R., Abe, M., Okamoto, T.: Packing messages and optimizing bootstrapping in gsw-fhe. IEICE TRANS. Fundam. Electron. Commun. Comput. Sci. **99**(1), 73–82 (2016)

21. Kiayias, A., Leonardos, N., Lipmaa, H., Pavlyk, K., Tang, Q.: Optimal rate private information retrieval from homomorphic encryption. Proc. Priv. Enhancing Technol. **2015**(2), 222–243 (2015)

22. Klinc, D., Hazay, C., Jagmohan, A., Krawczyk, H., Rabin, T.: On compression of data encrypted with block ciphers. IEEE Trans. Inf. Theory **58**(11), 6989–7001 (2012)

23. Kushilevitz, E., Ostrovsky, R.: Replication is not needed: Single database, computationally-private information retrieval. In: Proceedings, 38th Annual Symposium on Foundations of Computer Science 1997, pp. 364–373. IEEE (1997)

24. Laderman, J.D.: A noncommutative algorithm for multiplying 3×3 matrices using 23 multiplications. Bull. Amer. Math. Soc. **82**(1), 126–128 (1976)

25. Lipmaa, H., Pavlyk, K.: A simpler rate-optimal CPIR protocol. In: Kiayias, A. (ed.) FC 2017. LNCS, vol. 10322, pp. 621–638. Springer, Cham (2017). https://doi.org/10.1007/978-3-319-70972-7_35

26. Lyubashevsky, V., Peikert, C., Regev, O.: On ideal lattices and learning with errors over rings. J. ACM **60**(6), 43 (2013). Early version in EUROCRYPT 2010

27. Micciancio, D., Peikert, C.: Trapdoors for lattices: simpler, tighter, faster, smaller. In: Pointcheval, D., Johansson, T. (eds.) EUROCRYPT 2012. LNCS, vol. 7237, pp. 700–718. Springer, Heidelberg (2012). https://doi.org/10.1007/978-3-642-29011-4_41

28. Olumofin, F., Goldberg, I.: Revisiting the computational practicality of private information retrieval. In: Danezis, G. (ed.) FC 2011. LNCS, vol. 7035, pp. 158–172. Springer, Heidelberg (2012). https://doi.org/10.1007/978-3-642-27576-0_13

29. Paillier, P.: Public-key cryptosystems based on composite degree residuosity classes. In: Stern, J. (ed.) EUROCRYPT 1999. LNCS, vol. 1592, pp. 223–238. Springer, Heidelberg (1999). https://doi.org/10.1007/3-540-48910-X_16

30. Peikert, C., Vaikuntanathan, V., Waters, B.: A framework for efficient and composable oblivious transfer. In: Wagner, D. (ed.) CRYPTO 2008. LNCS, vol. 5157, pp. 554–571. Springer, Heidelberg (2008). https://doi.org/10.1007/978-3-540-85174-5_31

31. Regev, O.: On lattices, learning with errors, random linear codes, and cryptography. J. ACM **56**(6), 34:1–34:40 (2009)

32. Schmid, P., Roos, A.: AES-NI performance analyzed; limited to 32nm core i5 CPUs (2010). https://www.tomshardware.com/reviews/clarkdale-aes-ni-encryption,2538.html. Accessed Feb 2019

33. Sion, R., Carbunar, B.: On the practicality of private information retrieval. In: Proceedings of the Network and Distributed System Security Symposium, NDSS 2007, San Diego, California, USA, 28 February–2nd March 2007 (2007)

34. Smart, N.P., Vercauteren, F.: Fully homomorphic SIMD operations. Des. Codes Crypt. **71**(1), 57–81 (2014). Early verion at http://eprint.iacr.org/2011/133

35. Stern, J.P.: A new and efficient all-or-nothing disclosure of secrets protocol. In: Ohta, K., Pei, D. (eds.) ASIACRYPT 1998. LNCS, vol. 1514, pp. 357–371. Springer, Heidelberg (1998). https://doi.org/10.1007/3-540-49649-1_28
36. van Dijk, M., Gentry, C., Halevi, S., Vaikuntanathan, V.: Fully homomorphic encryption over the integers. In: Gilbert, H. (ed.) EUROCRYPT 2010. LNCS, vol. 6110, pp. 24–43. Springer, Heidelberg (2010). https://doi.org/10.1007/978-3-642-13190-5_2

Permuted Puzzles and Cryptographic Hardness

Elette Boyle[1]([✉]), Justin Holmgren[2], and Mor Weiss[1]

[1] Department of Computer Science, IDC Herzliya, Herzliya, Israel
eboyle@alum.mit.edu, mor.weiss01@post.idc.ac.il
[2] Department of Computer Science, Princeton University, Princeton, NJ, USA
justin.holmgren@princeton.edu

Abstract. A *permuted puzzle* problem is defined by a pair of distributions $\mathcal{D}_0, \mathcal{D}_1$ over Σ^n. The problem is to distinguish samples from $\mathcal{D}_0, \mathcal{D}_1$, where the symbols of each sample are *permuted* by a single secret permutation π of $[n]$.

The conjectured hardness of specific instances of permuted puzzle problems was recently used to obtain the first candidate constructions of Doubly Efficient Private Information Retrieval (DE-PIR) (Boyle et al. & Canetti et al., TCC'17). Roughly, in these works the distributions $\mathcal{D}_0, \mathcal{D}_1$ over $\mathbb{F}^n$ are evaluations of either a moderately low-degree polynomial or a random function. This new conjecture seems to be quite powerful, and is the foundation for the first DE-PIR candidates, almost two decades after the question was first posed by Beimel et al. (CRYPTO'00). However, while permuted puzzles are a natural and general class of problems, their hardness is still poorly understood.

We initiate a formal investigation of the cryptographic hardness of permuted puzzle problems. Our contributions lie in three main directions:

- **Rigorous formalization.** We formalize a notion of permuted puzzle distinguishing problems, extending and generalizing the proposed permuted puzzle framework of Boyle et al. (TCC'17).
- **Identifying hard permuted puzzles.** We identify natural examples in which a one-time permutation *provably* creates cryptographic hardness, based on "standard" assumptions. In these examples, the original distributions $\mathcal{D}_0, \mathcal{D}_1$ are easily distinguishable, but the permuted puzzle distinguishing problem is computationally hard. We provide such constructions in the random oracle model, and in the plain model under the Decisional Diffie-Hellman (DDH) assumption. We additionally observe that the Learning Parity with Noise (LPN) assumption itself can be cast as a permuted puzzle.
- **Partial lower bound for the DE-PIR problem.** We make progress towards better understanding the permuted puzzles underlying the DE-PIR constructions, by showing that a toy version of the problem, introduced by Boyle et al. (TCC'17), withstands a rich class of attacks, namely those that distinguish solely via statistical queries.

© International Association for Cryptologic Research 2019
D. Hofheinz and A. Rosen (Eds.): TCC 2019, LNCS 11892, pp. 465–493, 2019.
https://doi.org/10.1007/978-3-030-36033-7_18

1   Introduction

Computational hardness assumptions are the foundation of modern cryptography. The approach of building cryptographic systems whose security follows from well-defined computational assumptions has enabled us to obtain fantastical primitives and functionality, pushing far beyond the limitations of information theoretic security. But, in turn, the resulting systems are only as secure as the computational assumptions lying beneath them. As cryptographic constructions increasingly evolve toward usable systems, gaining a deeper understanding of the true hardness of these problems—and the relationship between assumptions—is an important task.

To date, a relatively select cluster of structured problems have withstood the test of time (and intense scrutiny), to the point that assuming their hardness is now broadly accepted as "standard." These problems include flavors of factoring [RSA78, Rab79] and computing discrete logarithms [DH76], as well as certain computational tasks in high-dimensional lattices and learning theory [GKL88, BFKL93, Ajt96, BKW00, Ale03, Reg05]. A central goal in the foundational study of cryptography is constructing cryptographic schemes whose security provably follows from these (or weaker) assumptions.

In some cases, however, it may be beneficial—even necessary—to introduce and study *new* assumptions (indeed, every assumption that is "standard" today was at some point freshly conceived). There are several important cryptographic primitives (notable examples include indistinguishability obfuscation (IO) [BGI+01, GGH+13] and SNARKs [BCC+17]) that we do not currently know how to construct based on standard assumptions. Past experience has shown that achieving new functionalities from novel assumptions, especially *falsifiable* assumptions [Nao03, GW11, GK16], can be a stepping stone towards attaining the same functionality from standard assumptions. This was the case for fully homomorphic encryption [RAD78, Gen09, BV11], as well as many recent primitives that were first built from IO and later (following a long line of works) based on more conservative assumptions (notably, non-interactive zero-knowledge protocols for NP based on LWE [KRR17, CCRR18, HL18, CCH+19, PS19], and the cryptographic hardness of finding a Nash equilibrium based on the security of the Fiat-Shamir heuristic [BPR15, HY17, CHK+19]). Finally, cryptographic primitives that can be based on diverse assumptions are less likely to "go extinct" in the event of a devastating new algorithmic discovery.

Of course, new assumptions should be introduced with care. We should strive to extract some intuitive reasoning justifying them, and some evidence for their hardness. A natural approach is to analyze the connection between the new assumption and known (standard) assumptions, with the ultimate goal of showing that the new assumption is, in fact, implied by a standard assumption. However, coming up with such a reduction usually requires deep understanding of the new assumption, which can only be obtained through a systematic study of it.

DE-PIR and Permuted Polynomials. A recent example is the new computational assumption underlying the construction of *Doubly Efficient Private Information Retrieval* (DE-PIR) [BIPW17, CHR17], related to pseudorandomness of permuted low-degree curves.

Private Information Retrieval (PIR) [CGKS95, KO97] schemes are protocols that enable a client to access entries of a database stored on a remote server (or multiple servers), while hiding from the server(s) which items are retrieved. If no preprocessing of the database takes place, the security guarantee inherently requires the server-side computation to be linear in the size of the database for each incoming query [BIM00]. Database preprocessing was shown to yield computational savings in the multi-server setting [BIM00], but the goal of single-server PIR protocols with sublinear-time computation was a longstanding open question, with no negative results or (even heuristic) candidate solutions. Such a primitive is sometimes referred to as *Doubly Efficient (DE) PIR.*[1]

Recently, two independent works [BIPW17, CHR17] provided the first candidate constructions of single-server DE-PIR schemes, based on a new conjecture regarding the hardness of distinguishing *permuted* local-decoding queries (for a Reed-Muller code [Ree54, Mul54] with suitable parameters) from a uniformly random set of points. Specifically, although given the queries $\{z_1, \ldots, z_k\} \subseteq [N]$ of the local decoder it is possible to guess (with a non-trivial advantage) the index i which is being locally decoded, the conjectures of [BIPW17, CHR17] very roughly assert that adding a secret permutation can computationally hide i. More precisely, if an adversary instead sees (many) samples of sets of *permuted* queries $\{\pi(z_1), \ldots, \pi(z_k)\}$, where $\pi : [N] \to [N]$ is a secret fixed permutation (the same for all samples), then the adversary cannot distinguish these from independent uniformly random size-k subsets of $[N]$.

This new assumption (which we will refer to as PermRM, see Conjecture 1 in Sect. 6.2) allowed for exciting progress forward in the DE-PIR domain. But what do we really know about its soundness? Although [BIPW17, CHR17] provide some discussion and cryptanalysis of the assumption, our understanding of it is still far from satisfactory.

Permuted Puzzles. The PermRM assumption can be cast as a special case in a broader family of hardness assumptions: as observed in [BIPW17], it can be thought of as an example of an instance where a secret random permutation seems to make an (easy) "distinguishing problem" hard, namely the permutation is the only sources of computational hardness. It should be intuitively clear that such permutations may indeed create hardness. For example, while one can easily distinguish a picture of a cat from that of a dog, this task becomes much more challenging when the pixels are permuted. There are also other instances in which random secret permutations were used to introduce hardness (see Sect. 1.2 below). Therefore, using permutations as a source of cryptographic hardness seems to be a promising direction for research, and raises the following natural question:

---

[1] Namely, computationally efficient for both client and server.

Under which circumstances can a secret random permutation be a source of cryptographic hardness?

1.1   Our Results

We initiate a formal investigation of the cryptographic hardness of permuted puzzle problems. More concretely, our contributions can be summarized within the following three directions.

Rigorous Formalization. We formalize a notion of *permuted puzzle distinguishing problems*, which extends and generalizes the proposed framework of [BIPW17]. Roughly, a permuted puzzle distinguishing problem is associated with a pair of distributions $\mathcal{D}_0, \mathcal{D}_1$ over strings in Σ^n, together with a random permutation π over $[n]$. The permuted puzzle consists of the distributions $\mathcal{D}_{0,\pi}, \mathcal{D}_{1,\pi}$ which are defined by sampling a string s according to $\mathcal{D}_0, \mathcal{D}_1$ (respectively), and permuting the entries of s according to π. A permuted puzzle is *computationally hard* if no efficient adversary can distinguish between a sample from $\mathcal{D}_{0,\pi}$ or $\mathcal{D}_{1,\pi}$, even given arbitrarily many samples of its choice from either of the distributions. We also briefly explore related hardness notions, showing that a weaker and simpler variant (which is similar to the one considered in [BIPW17]) is implied by our notion of hardness, and that in some useful cases the weaker hardness notion implies our hardness notion. Our motivation for studying the stronger (and perhaps less natural) hardness notion is that the weaker variant is insufficient for the DE-PIR application.

Identifying Hard Permuted Puzzles. We identify natural examples in which a one-time permutation *provably* introduces cryptographic hardness, based on standard assumptions. In these examples, the distributions $\mathcal{D}_0, \mathcal{D}_1$ are efficiently distinguishable, but the permuted puzzle distinguishing problem is computationally hard. We provide such constructions in the random oracle model, and in the plain model under the Decisional Diffie-Hellman (DDH) assumption [DH76]. We additionally observe that the Learning Parity with Noise (LPN) assumption [BKW00, Ale03] itself can be cast as a permuted puzzle. This is described in the following theorem (see Propositions 1, 3, and 2 for the formal statements).

Informal Theorem 1 (Hard   Permuted   Puzzles). *There   exists   a computationally-hard permuted puzzle distinguishing problem:*

– *In the random oracle model.*
– *If the DDH assumption holds.*
– *If the LPN assumption holds.*

Statistical Query Lower Bound for DE-PIR Toy Problem. We make progress towards better understanding the PermRM assumption underlying the DE-PIR constructions of [BIPW17, CHR17]. Specifically, we show that a toy version of the problem, which was introduced in [BIPW17], provably withstands a rich class of learning algorithms known as *Statistical Query (SQ) algorithms*.

Roughly, the toy problem is to distinguish randomly permuted graphs of random univariate polynomials of relatively low degree from randomly permuted graphs of random functions. More formally, for a function $f : X \to Y$, we define its 2-dimensional graph $\mathsf{Graph}(f) : X \times Y \to \{0,1\}$ where $\mathsf{Graph}(f)(x,y) = 1 \Leftrightarrow y = f(x)$. For a security parameter λ and a field $\mathbb{F}$, the distributions $\mathcal{D}_0, \mathcal{D}_1$ in the toy problem are over $\{0,1\}^n$ for $n = |\mathbb{F}|^2$, and output a sample $\mathsf{Graph}(\gamma)$ where $\gamma : \mathbb{F} \to \mathbb{F}$ is a uniformly random degree-λ polynomial in $\mathcal{D}_0$, and a uniformly random function in $\mathcal{D}_1$.

We analyze the security of the toy problem against SQ learning algorithms. Our motivation for focusing on learning algorithms in general is that permuted puzzles are a special example of a learning task. Indeed, the adversary's goal is to classify a challenge sample, given many labeled samples. Thus, it is natural to explore approaches from learning theory as potential solvers for (equivalently, attacks on) the permuted puzzle. Roughly speaking, most known learning algorithms can be categorized within two broad categories. The first category leverages linearity, by identifying correlations with subspaces and using algorithms based on Gaussian elimination to identify these. The second category, which is our focus in this work, is SQ algorithms. Informally, an SQ algorithm obtains no labeled samples. Instead, it can make *statistical queries* that are defined by a boolean-valued function f, and the algorithm then obtains the outcome of applying f to a random sample. A statistical query algorithm is an SQ algorithm that makes polynomially many such queries. We show that the toy problem is hard for SQ algorithms (see Theorem 8):

Informal Theorem 2. *The BIPW toy problem is hard for statistical query algorithms.*

We contrast this statistical-query lower bound with the bounded-query statistical indistinguishability lower bound of [CHR17]. That result showed that there is some fixed polynomial B such that no adversary can distinguish B DE-PIR queries from random, even if computationally unbounded. In contrast, our result proves a lower bound for adversaries (also computationally unbounded), that have no a-priori polynomial bound on the number of queries that they can make—in fact, they can make up to $2^{\epsilon\lambda}$ queries where λ is the security parameter and ϵ is a small positive constant. However, they are restricted in that they cannot see the result of any individual query in its entirety; instead, adversaries can only see the result of applying bounded (up to $\epsilon\lambda$-bit) output functions separately to each query.

1.2 Other Instances of Hardness from Random Permutations

There are other instances in which random secret permutations were used to obtain computational hardness. The *Permuted Kernel Problem (PKP)* is an example in the context of a search problem. Roughly, the input in PKP consists of a matrix $A \in \mathbb{Z}_p^{m \times n}$ and a vector $\boldsymbol{v} \in \mathbb{Z}_p^n$, where p is a large prime. A solution is a permutation π on $[n]$ such that the vector $\boldsymbol{v}'$ obtained by applying π to the entries of $\boldsymbol{v}$ is in the kernel of A. PKP is known to be NP-complete in the worst-case [GJ02], and conjectured to be hard on average [Sha89], for sufficiently large $(n - m)$ and p. It is the underlying assumption in Shamir's identification scheme [Sha89], and has lately seen renewed interest due to its applicability to post-quantum cryptography (e.g., [LP12, FKM+18, KMP19]). Despite being studied for 3 decades, the best known algorithms to date run in exponential time; see [KMP19] and the references therein.

1.3   Techniques

We now proceed to discuss our results and techniques in greater detail.

Defining Permuted Puzzles. We generalize and extend the intuitive puzzle framework proposed in [BIPW17], by formally defining the notions of (permuted) puzzle distinguishing problems.

We formalize a *puzzle distinguishing problem* as a pair of distributions $\mathcal{D}_0, \mathcal{D}_1$ over Σ^n, for some alphabet Σ and some input length n. Very roughly, hardness of a puzzle distinguishing problem means one cannot distinguish a single sample from $\mathcal{D}_0$ or $\mathcal{D}_1$, even given oracle access to $\mathcal{D}_0$ *and* $\mathcal{D}_1$. We say that a puzzle problem is (s, ϵ)-*hard* if any size-s adversary distinguishes $\mathcal{D}_0$ from $\mathcal{D}_1$ with advantage at most ϵ. This concrete hardness notion naturally extends to computational hardness of an *ensemble* of puzzles, in which case we allow the distributions to be *keyed* (by both public and secret key information) and require that they be efficiently sampleable given the key.

With this notion of puzzle distinguishing problems, we turn to defining a *permuted puzzle* which, informally, is obtained by sampling a random permutation π once and for all as part of the secret key, and permutating all samples according to π. Hardness of a permuted puzzle is defined identically to hardness of (standard) puzzle distinguishing problems.

We also consider a simpler hardness definition, in which the adversary is given oracle access *only* to a randomly selected $\mathcal{D}_b$ (but not to $\mathcal{D}_{1-b}$), and attempts to guess b. We say that a puzzle distinguishing problem is *weak computationally hard* if every adversary of polynomial size obtains a negligible advantage in this modified distinguishing game. Weak computational hardness captures the security notion considered in [BIPW17], but is too weak for certain applications, as it allows for trivial permuted puzzles, e.g., $\mathcal{D}_0 = \{0^{n/2} 1^{n/2}\}, \mathcal{D}_1 = \{1^{n/2} 0^{n/2}\}$. More generally, and as discussed in Remark 3 (Sect. 3), weak computational hardness is generally weaker than the definition discussed above (which is more in line with the DE-PIR application). Concretely, we show that the definition discussed above implies the weaker definition, and that in certain cases (e.g., when $\mathcal{D}_1$ is the uniform distribution), the weaker definition implies the stronger one. This last observation will be particularly useful in proving security of our permuted puzzle constructions.

Hard Permuted Puzzle in the Random Oracle (RO) Model. Our first permuted puzzle is in the random oracle model. Recall that a permuted puzzle is defined as the permuted version of a puzzle distinguishing problem. For our RO-based permuted puzzle, the underlying puzzle distinguishing problem is defined as follows. There is no key, but both the sampling algorithm and the adversary have access to the random oracle H. The sampling algorithm samples a uniformly random input x_0 for H, and uniformly random seeds $s_1, \ldots, s_n$, where $n = \lambda$, and computes x_n sequentially as follows. For every $1 \leq i \leq n$, $x_i \stackrel{\text{def}}{=} H(s_i, x_{i-1})$. The sample is then $(x_0, x'_n, s_1, \ldots, s_n)$ where $x'_n \stackrel{\text{def}}{=} x_n$ in $\mathcal{D}_0$, and x'_n is uniformly random in $\mathcal{D}_1$. Notice that in this (unpermuted) puzzle distinguishing problem one can easily distinguish samples from $\mathcal{D}_0$ and $\mathcal{D}_1$, by sequentially applying the oracle to x_0 and the seeds, and checking whether the output is x'_n. This will hold with probability 1 for samples from $\mathcal{D}_0$, and only with negligible probability for samples from $\mathcal{D}_1$ (assuming H has sufficiently long outputs). The corresponding permuted puzzle is obtained by applying a fixed random permutation π^* to the seeds $(s_1, \ldots, s_n)$.[2]

Hardness of the Permuted Puzzle. We focus on a simpler case in which the adversary receives only the challenge sample (and does not request any additional samples from its challenger). This will allow us to present the main ideas of the analysis, and (as we show in Sect. 4), the argument easily extends to the general case.

At a very high level, we show that the hardness of the permuted puzzle stems from the fact that to successfully guess b, the adversary has to guess the underlying random permutation π^*, *even though it has oracle access to H.*

We first introduce some terminology. For a random oracle H, input x_0 and seeds $s'_1, \ldots, s'_n$, each permutation π over the seeds uniquely defines a corresponding "output" x_n^π through a length-$(n+1)$ "path" P_π defined as follows. Let $x_0^\pi \stackrel{\text{def}}{=} x_0$, and for every $1 \leq i \leq n$, let $s''_i \stackrel{\text{def}}{=} s'_{\pi^{-1}(i)}$ and $x_i^\pi \stackrel{\text{def}}{=} H(s''_i, x_{i-1}^\pi)$. Then the label of the i'th node on the path P_π is x_i^π. We say that a node v with label x on some path P_π is *reachable* if x was the oracle answer to one of the adversary's queries in the distinguishing game. We note that when $s'_i = s_{\pi^*(i)}$, i.e., the seeds are permuted with the permutation used in the permuted puzzle, then $x_i^{\pi^*} = x_i$ for every $1 \leq i \leq n$. We call P_{π^*} the *special path.*

We will show that with overwhelming probability, unless the adversary queries H on all the x_i's on the special path (i.e., on $x_0^{\pi^*}, x_1^{\pi^*}, \ldots, x_n^{\pi^*} = x_n$), then he obtains only a negligible advantage in guessing b. Hardness of the permuted puzzle then follows because there are $n!$ possible paths, and the adversary has

---

[2] We note that syntactically, this is not a permuted puzzle since the permutation should be applied to the *entire* sample. However, this simplified view of the permuted puzzle captures the fact that in our construction, the permutation essentially operates only over the seeds. In the actual construction, this is achieved by tagging the different parts of the sample (with either "input", "output", or "seed") such that any permutation over the entire sample uniquely determines a permutation over the seeds; see Sect. 4.

a negligible chance of guessing the special path (because π^* is a secret random permutation).

We would first like to prove that all node labels, over all paths P_π, are unique. This, however, is clearly false, because the paths are not disjoint: for example, the label of node 0 in all of them is x_0. More generally, if $\pi \neq \pi'$ have the same length-k prefix for some $0 \leq k < \lambda$, then for every $0 \leq i \leq k$, the i'th nodes on $\mathsf{P}_\pi, \mathsf{P}_{\pi'}$ have the same label. In this case, we say that the i'th nodes *correspond to the same node*. Let Unique denote the event that across all paths there do not exist two nodes that (1) do *not* correspond to the same node, but (2) have the same label. Our first observation is that Unique happens with overwhelming probability. Indeed, this holds when H's output is sufficiently large (e.g., of the order of $3\lambda \cdot \log \lambda$), because there are only $\lambda \cdot \lambda!$ different nodes (so the number of pairs is roughly of the order of $2^{2\lambda \cdot \log \lambda}$).

Let $\mathcal{E}$ denote the event that the adversary queries H on the label of an unreachable node, and let $\mathsf{ReachQ} = \bar{\mathcal{E}}$ denote its complement. Our next observation is that conditioned on Unique, ReachQ happens with overwhelming probability. Indeed, conditioned on Unique, the label of an unreachable node is uniformly random, even given the entire adversarial view (including previous oracle answers). Thus, querying H on an unreachable node corresponds to guessing the random node label. When H's output length is sufficiently large (on the order of $3\lambda \cdot \log \lambda$ as discussed above) this happens only with negligible probability.

Consequently, it suffices to analyze the adversarial advantage in the distinguishing game conditioned on $\mathsf{Unique} \wedge \mathsf{ReachQ}$. Notice that in this case, the only *potential* difference between the adversarial views when $b = 0$ and when $b = 1$ is in the label of the endpoint v_{end} of the special path P_{π^*}, which is x_n when $b = 0$, and independent of x_n when $b = 1$. Indeed, conditioned on Unique, the label of v_{end} appears nowhere else (i.e., is not the label of any other node on any path). Therefore, conditioned on $\mathsf{ReachQ} \wedge \mathsf{Unique}$, the label of v_{end} appears as one of the oracle answers only if v_{end} is reachable, i.e., only if the adversary queried H on all the node labels on the special path.

Hard Permuted Puzzles in the Plain Model. Our second permuted puzzle is based on the Decisional Diffi-Helman (DDH) assumption. The underlying puzzle distinguishing problem is defined over a multiplicative cyclic group G of prime order p with generator g. The public key consists of G, g and a uniformly random vector $\boldsymbol{u} \leftarrow \left(\mathbb{Z}_p^*\right)^n$. A sample from $\mathcal{D}_0, \mathcal{D}_1$ is of the form $(g^{x_1}, \ldots, g^{x_n})$, where in $\mathcal{D}_0$ $(x_1, \ldots, x_n)$ is chosen as a uniformly random vector that is orthogonal to $\boldsymbol{u}$, whereas in $\mathcal{D}_1$ $(x_1, \ldots, x_n)$ is uniformly random. As discussed below, in this (unpermuted) puzzle distinguishing problem one can easily distinguish samples from $\mathcal{D}_0$ and $\mathcal{D}_1$. The corresponding permuted puzzle is obtained by applying a fixed random permutation to the samples $(g^{x_1}, \ldots, g^{x_n})$.

Why are Both DDH and a Permutation Needed? The computational hardness of the permuted puzzles stems from the *combination* of the DDH assumption and the permutation, as we now explain. To see why the DDH assumption is needed, notice that in $\mathcal{D}_0$, all sampled $(x_1, \ldots, x_n)$ belong to an $(n-1)$-dimensional subspace of $\mathbb{Z}_p^n$, whereas in $\mathcal{D}_1$ this happens only with negligible probability, because each sample is uniformly and independently sampled. Consider a simpler version in which $\mathcal{D}_0, \mathcal{D}_1$ simply output the vector $(x_1, \ldots, x_n)$. In this case, one can obtain an overwhelming distinguishing advantage by (efficiently) checking whether all samples $(x_1, \ldots, x_n)$ lie within an $(n-1)$-dimensional subspace, and if so guess that the underlying distribution is $\mathcal{D}_0$. This "attack" can be executed even if the samples are permuted (as is the case in a permuted puzzle), because applying a permutation to the $(x_1, \ldots, x_n)$ is a linear operation, and therefore preserves the dimension of the subspace. Therefore, a permutation on its own is insufficient to get computational hardness, and we need to rely on the DDH assumption.

To see why the permutation is needed, notice that even if the DDH assumption holds in G, given $(g^{x_1}, \ldots, g^{x_n})$ one can efficiently test whether the underlying exponents $(x_1, \ldots, x_n)$ are orthogonal to a known vector $\boldsymbol{u}$, by only computing exponentiations and multiplications in G. Notice that for a sufficiently large p, the exponents of a sample from $\mathcal{D}_1$ will be orthogonal to $\boldsymbol{u}$ only with negligible probability, so this "attack" succeeds with overwhelming probability.

Hardness of the Permuted Puzzle. We now show that the *combination* of the DDH assumption, and permuted samples, gives computational hardness. Notice that it suffices to prove that the permuted puzzle is weak computationally hard, because $\mathcal{D}_1$ is random over G^n (see Sect. 1.3). In this case, the adversarial view $\mathsf{V}_b, b \in \{0, 1\}$ consists of the public key $(G, g, \boldsymbol{u})$, and a polynomial number of permuted samples of the form $(g^{x_1}, \ldots, g^{x_n})$ which were all sampled according to $\mathcal{D}_b$ and permuted using the same random permutation π.

Our first observation is that V_b is computationally indistinguishable from the distribution $\mathcal{H}_b$ in which the public key is $(G, g, \pi'(\boldsymbol{u}))$ for $\pi' \overset{\mathsf{def}}{=} (\pi)^{-1}$, and the samples from $\mathcal{D}_b$ are *unpermuted*.

Our second observation is that the DDH assumption implies that $\mathcal{H}_b$ is computationally indistinguishable from the distribution $\mathcal{H}_b'$ in which the $(x_1, \ldots, x_n)$ additionally lie in a random 1-dimensional subspace $L_{b,v}$. That is, $(x_1, \ldots, x_n)$ are chosen at random from $L_{b,v}$, where in $\mathcal{H}_0'$ $\boldsymbol{v}$ is random subject to $\boldsymbol{v} \cdot \boldsymbol{u} = 0$, and in $\mathcal{H}_1'$ $\boldsymbol{v}$ is uniformly random. Specifically, we show that the problem of distinguishing between $\mathcal{H}_b, \mathcal{H}_b'$ can be efficiently reduced to the task of distinguishing between a polynomial number of length-$(n-1)$ vectors of the form $(g^{y_1}, \ldots, g^{y_{n-1}})$, where the $(y_1, \ldots, y_{n-1})$ are all sampled from a random 1-dimensional subspace of $\mathbb{Z}_p^{n-1}$ or all sampled from the full space $\mathbb{Z}_p^{n-1}$. If the DDH assumption holds in G then a polynomial-sized adversary cannot efficiently distinguish between these distributions [BHHO08]. Consequently, it suffices to show that $\mathcal{H}_0', \mathcal{H}_1'$ are computationally close.

The final step is to show that $\mathcal{H}_0', \mathcal{H}_1'$ are computationally (in fact, statistically) close. The only difference between the two distributions is in the choice of $\boldsymbol{v}$ (which is orthogonal to $\boldsymbol{u}$ in $\mathcal{H}_0'$, and random in $\mathcal{H}_1'$), where all other sampled values are either identical or deterministically determined by the choice of $\boldsymbol{v}$. Notice that in $\mathcal{H}_1'$, $(\pi(\boldsymbol{u}), \boldsymbol{v})$ is uniformly random in $\mathbb{Z}_p^n \times \mathbb{Z}_p^n$. Thus, to show that $\mathcal{H}_0', \mathcal{H}_1'$ are statistically close and conclude the proof, it suffices to prove that $(\pi(\boldsymbol{u}), \boldsymbol{v})$ in $\mathcal{H}_0'$ is statistically close to uniform over $\mathbb{Z}_p^n \times \mathbb{Z}_p^n$. Very roughly, this follows from the leftover hash lemma due to the following observations. First, $\pi(\boldsymbol{u})$ has high min entropy even conditioned on $\boldsymbol{u}$ (because π is random). Second, the family of inner product functions with respect to a fixed vector (i.e., $h_{\boldsymbol{v}}(\boldsymbol{v}') = \boldsymbol{v} \cdot \boldsymbol{v}'$) is a pair-wise independent hash function.

Permuted Puzzles and the Learning Parity with Noise (LPN) Assumption. The argument used in the DDH-based permuted puzzle can be generalized to other situations in which it is hard to distinguish between the uniform distribution and a hidden permuted kernel (but easy to distinguish when the kernel is *not* permuted). This more general view allows us to cast the LPN assumption as a permuted puzzle, see Sect. 5.1.

Statistical-Query Lower Bound. We show that SQ algorithms that make polynomially many queries obtain only a negligible advantage in distinguishing the distributions $\mathcal{D}_0, \mathcal{D}_1$ in the toy problem presented in Sect. 1.1. Recall that a sample in the toy problem is a permuted $\mathsf{Graph}(\gamma)$ where γ is either a uniformly random degree-λ polynomial (in $\mathcal{D}_0$), or a uniformly random function (in $\mathcal{D}_1$), and that the SQ algorithm obtains the outputs of boolean-valued functions f of its choice on random samples. Very roughly, we will show that the outcome of f on (permutation of) a random sample $x \leftarrow \mathcal{D}_b$ is independent of the challenge bit b and the permutation π.

Notice that every permutation π over $\mathsf{Graph}(\gamma)$ defines a partition $\Phi \overset{\text{def}}{=} \{\pi(\{i\} \times \mathbb{F})\}_{i \in \mathbb{F}}$ of $\mathbb{F} \times \mathbb{F}$, where each set in the partition corresponds to a single x value. We say that π *respects* the partition Φ. Notice also that each set contains a single non-0 entry (which is $\pi(i, \gamma(i))$, where i is the value of x that corresponds to the set). Thus, an SQ algorithm can compute this partition, so we cannot hope to hide it. Instead, we show indistinguishability even when the adversary is given the partition.

Our main observation is that for every partition Φ, and any boolean-valued function f, there exists $p_{f,\Phi} \in [0,1]$ such that for every $b \in \{0,1\}$, with overwhelming probability over the choice of random permutation π that respects the partition Φ, the expectation $\mathbb{E}_{x \leftarrow \mathcal{D}_b}[f(\pi(x))]$ is very close to $p_{f,\Phi}$, where $\pi(x)$ denote that the entries of x are permuted according to π. Crucially, $p_{f,\Phi}$ is independent of the challenge bit b, any particular sample x, and the permutation (other than the partition).

We prove this observation in two steps. First, we show that in expectation over the choice of the permutation, $\mathbb{E}_{x \leftarrow \mathcal{D}_0}[f(\pi(x))]$ and $\mathbb{E}_{x \leftarrow \mathcal{D}_1}[f(\pi(x))]$ have the same value. To see this, we write the expectations over $x \leftarrow \mathcal{D}_b$ as a weighted sum $\sum_x P_b(x) f(\pi(x))$, and apply linearity of the expectation over π. To show that this is independent of b, we observe that for any fixed x, the distribution of $\pi(x)$ is the same (i.e. does not depend on x).

Next, we show that for any distribution $\mathcal{D}$, the variance (over the choice of the permutation π) of $\mathbb{E}_{x \leftarrow \mathcal{D}_b}[f(\pi(x))]$ is small. The variance is by definition the difference between

$$\mathbb{E}_{\pi} \left[\mathbb{E}_{x \leftarrow \mathcal{D}_b} [f(\pi(x))]^2 \right] \tag{1}$$

and

$$\mathbb{E}_{\pi} \left[\mathbb{E}_{x \leftarrow \mathcal{D}_b} [f(\pi(x))] \right]^2 . \tag{2}$$

We show that both Eqs. (1) and (2) can be expressed as an expectation (over some distribution of g, g') of $\mathbb{E}_{\pi} \left[\left(f(\pi(\mathsf{Graph}(g))), f(\pi(\mathsf{Graph}(g'))) \right) \right]$. We observe that this depends only on the Hamming distance between g and g'. Finally, we observe that the distribution of (g, g') is uniform in Eq. (2) and two independent samples from $\mathcal{D}_b$ in Eq. (1). To complete the bound on the variance, we show that when g, g' are sampled independently from $\mathcal{D}_b$ (specifically, the interesting case is when they are sampled from $\mathcal{D}_0$), then the distribution of the Hamming distance between g and g' is nearly the same as when g and g' are independent uniformly random functions.

To prove this, we prove a lemma (Lemma 4) stating that when t-wise independent random variables $(X_1, \ldots, X_n)$ satisfy $\Pr[X_i \neq \star_i] = p_i$ for some values of $\star_i$ and p_i such that $\sum_{i \in [n]} p_i \leq \frac{t}{4} \geq \omega(\log \lambda)$, then $(X_1, \ldots, X_n)$ are statistically $\mathsf{negl}(\lambda)$-close to mutually independent. We apply this with X_i being the indicator random variable for the event that $g(i) \neq g'(i)$. This lemma quantitatively strengthens a lemma of [CHR17].

Open Problems and Future Research Directions. The broad goal of basing DE-PIR on standard assumptions was a motivating starting point for this work, in which we put forth the framework of permuted puzzles. In describing hard permuted puzzles, we take a "bottom-up" approach by describing such constructions based on standard cryptographic assumptions. Since these permuted puzzles are still not known to imply DE-PIR, we try to close the gap between the permuted puzzle on which DE-PIR security is based, and provably hard permuted puzzles, by taking a "top-down" approach, and analyzing the security of a toy version of the DE-PIR permuted puzzle, against a wide class of possible attacks.

Our work still leaves open a fascinating array of questions, we discuss some of them below. First, it would be very interesting to construct a hard permuted puzzle based only on the existence of one-way functions, as well as to provide "public-key" hard permuted puzzles, namely ones in which the key generation algorithm needs no secret key, based on standard assumptions. In the context of DE-PIR and its related permuted puzzle, it would be interesting to construct DE-PIR based on other (and more standard) assumptions, as well as to analyze the security of its underlying permuted puzzle (and its toy version) against a wider class of attacks.

2   Preliminaries

For a set X, we write $x \leftarrow X$ to denote that x is sampled uniformly at random from X. For a distribution $\mathcal{D}$, we use $\mathsf{Supp}(\mathcal{D})$ to denote its support. The min entropy of $\mathcal{D}$ is $\mathsf{H}_\infty(\mathcal{D}) \overset{\text{def}}{=} \min_{x \in \mathrm{Supp}(\mathcal{D})} \log \frac{1}{\Pr[x]}$. For a pair X, Y of random variables, we denote their statistical distance by $d_{\mathsf{TV}}(X, Y)$. We use $\cdot$ to denote inner product, i.e., for a pair $\boldsymbol{x} = (x_1, \ldots, x_n), \boldsymbol{y} = (y_1, \ldots, y_n)$ of vectors, $\boldsymbol{x} \cdot \boldsymbol{y} \overset{\text{def}}{=} \sum_{i=1}^n x_i y_i$. We use $[n]$ to denote the set $\{1, \ldots, n\}$, and S_n to denote the group of permutations of $[n]$.

Notation 3 (Permutation of a vector). *For a vector $\boldsymbol{x} = (x_1, \ldots, x_n)$, and a permutation $\pi \in S_n$, we denote:*

$$\pi(\boldsymbol{x}) \overset{\text{def}}{=} \left(x_{\pi^{-1}(1)}, \ldots, x_{\pi^{-1}(n)} \right).$$

3 Distinguishing Problems and Permuted Puzzles

In this section, we formally define (permuted) puzzle problems which are, roughly, a (special case) of ensembles of keyed "string-distinguishing" problems.

We begin in Sect. 3.1 by developing terminology for general string-distinguishing and puzzle problems. In Sect. 3.2 we present the formal distinguishing challenge and define hardness. Then, in Sect. 3.3, we discuss the case of *permuted* puzzles, and present an alternative indistinguishability notion that is equivalent in certain cases.

3.1 String-Distinguishing Problems

At the core, we consider string-distinguishing problems, defined by a pair of distributions over n-element strings. We begin by defining a finite instance.

Definition 1 (String-Distinguishing Problems). *A string-distinguishing problem is a tuple $\Pi = (n, \Sigma, \mathcal{D}_0, \mathcal{D}_1)$, where n is a positive integer, Σ is a non-empty finite set, and each $\mathcal{D}_b$ is a distribution on Σ^n. We call n the* string length, *and Σ the* string alphabet.

More generally, an oracle-dependent *string-distinguishing problem is a function $\Pi^{(\cdot)}$ that maps an oracle $O : \{0, 1\}^* \to \{0, 1\}$ to a string-distinguishing problem Π^O.*

For example, we will consider permuted puzzle string-distinguishing problems relative to a random oracle in Sect. 4. Note that oracle-dependent string-distinguishing problems are strictly more general than string-distinguishing problems, as the distributions can simply ignore the oracle.

Remark 1 (Oracle Outputs). In the above, we modeled the oracle as outputting a single bit for simplicity. However, any (deterministic) oracle with multi-bit output can be emulated given a corresponding single-bit-output oracle, at the cost of making more oracle queries.

We will be interested in distinguishing problems where the distributions $\mathcal{D}_0$ and $\mathcal{D}_1$ may depend on common sampled "key" information. Parts of this key may be publicly available, or hidden from a distinguishing adversary (discussed in Definition 4); these parts are denoted pk, sk, respectively.

Definition 2 (Keyed Families). *A* keyed family *of (oracle-dependent) string-distinguishing problems is a tuple* $(\mathcal{K}, \{\Pi_k\}_{k\in\mathcal{K}})$, *where* $\mathcal{K}$ *is a distribution on a non-empty finite set of pairs* (pk, sk) *and each* Π_k *is an (oracle-dependent) string-distinguishing problem. We refer to the support of* $\mathcal{K}$ *as the* key space, *and also denote it by* $\mathcal{K}$.

Note that any string-distinguishing problem can trivially be viewed as a keyed family by letting $\mathcal{K}$ be a singleton set.

Example 1 (Keyed Family: Dimension-t Subspaces). For a finite field $\mathbb{F}$, and $n \in \mathbb{N}$, consider an example keyed family of string-distinguishing problems $(\mathcal{K}, \{\Pi_k\}_{k\in\mathcal{K}})$ as follows:

- $\mathcal{K}$ samples a random $t \leftarrow \{1, \ldots, n-1\}$, and a random subspace $L \subseteq \mathbb{F}^n$ of dimension t, sets pk $= t$ and sk $= L$, and outputs (pk, sk).
- For a key $k = (t, L)$, the corresponding string-distinguishing problem is $\Pi_k = (n, \mathbb{F}, \mathcal{D}_0, \mathcal{D}_1)$ where $\mathcal{D}_0$ outputs a uniformly random $v \in L$, and $\mathcal{D}_1$ outputs a uniformly random $v \in \mathbb{F}^n$.

Note that in this example, it will be computationally easy to distinguish between the distributions $\mathcal{D}_0, \mathcal{D}_1$ given sufficiently many samples.

We next define a puzzle problem which, informally, is an *efficiently sampleable* ensemble of keyed families of string-distinguishing problems.

Definition 3 (Puzzle problem). *A* puzzle problem *is an ensemble* $\{(\mathcal{K}_\lambda, \{\Pi_k^{(\cdot)}\}_{k\in\mathcal{K}_\lambda})\}_{\lambda\in\mathbb{Z}^+}$ *of keyed families of (oracle-dependent) string-distinguishing problems associated with probabilistic polynomial-time algorithms* KeyGen *and* Samp *such that:*

- *For any* $\lambda \in \mathbb{Z}^+$, KeyGen(1^λ) *outputs a sample from* $\mathcal{K}_\lambda$.
- *For any* $k \in \mathcal{K}_\lambda$, *any* $b \in \{0,1\}$, *and any oracle* $O : \{0,1\}^* \to \{0,1\}$, Samp$^O(k, b)$ *outputs a sample from* $\mathcal{D}_b$, *where* $\Pi_k^O = (n, \Sigma, \mathcal{D}_0, \mathcal{D}_1)$.

*Remark 2 (**Abbreviated terminology**).* Somewhat abusing notation, we will also refer to a *single* keyed family of string-distinguishing problems as a puzzle problem.

3.2   Distinguishing Games and Hardness

We will focus on puzzle problems where it is computationally hard to distinguish between the pair of distributions. This notion of hardness is formalized through the following distinguishing game. Roughly, the distinguishing adversary is given a challenge sample x from a randomly selected $\mathcal{D}_b$, and query access to both distributions (denoted by choices β below), and must identify from which $\mathcal{D}_b$ the x was sampled.

Definition 4 (Distinguishing Game). *Let* $\mathcal{P} = (\mathcal{K}, \{\Pi_k\}_{k\in\mathcal{K}})$ *be a puzzle problem, and let* $\mathcal{O}$ *be a distribution of oracles. The* distinguishing game $\mathcal{G}_{\text{dist}}^{\mathcal{O}}[\mathcal{P}]$ *is run between an "adversary"* $\mathcal{A}$ *and a fixed "challenger"* $\mathcal{C}$, *and is defined as follows:*

1. $\mathcal{C}$ samples a key $k = (\mathsf{pk}, \mathsf{sk})$ from $\mathcal{K}$, and $O \leftarrow \mathcal{O}$, and denote $\Pi_k^O = (n, \Sigma, \mathcal{D}_0, \mathcal{D}_1)$. $\mathcal{C}$ sends pk to $\mathcal{A}$, who is also given oracle access to O throughout the game.
2. $\mathcal{C}$ samples a random bit $b \leftarrow \{0, 1\}$, samples $x \leftarrow \mathcal{D}_b$, and sends x to $\mathcal{A}$.
3. The following is repeated an arbitrary number of times: $\mathcal{A}$ sends a bit β to $\mathcal{C}$, who samples $x' \leftarrow \mathcal{D}_\beta$ and sends x' to $\mathcal{A}$.
4. $\mathcal{A}$ outputs a "guess" bit $b' \in \{0, 1\}$.

$\mathcal{A}$ is said to win the game if $b' = b$. $\mathcal{A}$'s advantage is $Adv_{\mathcal{A}}(\mathcal{G}_{\mathsf{dist}}^{\mathcal{O}}[\mathcal{P}]) \overset{\text{def}}{=} 2 \cdot \left| \Pr[b' = b] - \frac{1}{2} \right|$.

Informally, a permuted puzzle is computationally hard if any polynomial-time adversary wins the distinguishing game of Definition 4 with negligible advantage. We first formalize the notion of *concrete* hardness.

Definition 5 (Concrete Hardness). *A puzzle problem* $\mathcal{P} = (\mathcal{K}, \{\Pi_k\}_{k \in \mathcal{K}})$ *is said to be* (s, ϵ)-hard *(with respect to oracle distribution $\mathcal{O}$) if in the game* $\mathcal{G}_{\mathsf{dist}}^{\mathcal{O}}[\mathcal{P}]$, *all adversaries $\mathcal{A}$ of size at most s have advantage at most ϵ.*

We say a puzzle problem $\left\{ (\mathcal{K}_\lambda, \{\Pi_k^{(\cdot)}\}_{k \in \mathcal{K}_\lambda}) \right\}_{\lambda \in \mathbb{Z}^+}$ *is* $(s(\cdot), \epsilon(\cdot))$-hard *(with respect to an ensemble $\{\mathcal{O}_\lambda\}$ of oracle distributions) if each* $(\mathcal{K}_\lambda, \{\Pi_k^{(\cdot)}\}_{k \in \mathcal{K}_\lambda})$ *is* $(s(\lambda), \epsilon(\lambda))$-hard *with respect to $\mathcal{O}_\lambda$.*

Definition 6 (Asymptotic Hardness). *As usual, we say simply that $\mathcal{P}$ is (computationally)* hard *if for every $s(\lambda) \leq \lambda^{O(1)}$, there exists $\epsilon(\lambda) \leq \lambda^{-\omega(1)}$ such that for every $\lambda \in \mathbb{Z}^+$, $\mathcal{P}$ is* $(s(\cdot), \epsilon(\cdot))$-hard.

$\mathcal{P}$ is statistically *hard if for some $\epsilon(\lambda) \leq \lambda^{-\omega(1)}$, $\mathcal{P}$ is* $(\infty, \epsilon(\cdot))$-hard.

*Remark 3 (**Discussion on Definition**).*
   A slightly simpler and more natural definition would be to give the adversary access to (polynomially-many samples from) *only* a randomly selected $\mathcal{D}_b$, where the adversary must identify b.

   For keyed puzzles, these definitions are in general *not* equivalent. Consider, for example, a modified version of Example 1, where both $\mathcal{D}_0$ and $\mathcal{D}_1$ are defined by random dimension-t subspaces, L_0 and L_1. Then over the choice of the key (including L_0, L_1), the distributions $\mathcal{D}_0$ and $\mathcal{D}_1$ on their own are *identical*: that is, even an unbounded adversary with arbitrarily many queries would have 0 advantage in the simplified challenge. However, given t samples from *both* distributions, as in Definition 4, $\mathcal{D}_0$ and $\mathcal{D}_1$ are trivially separated, and a sample x can be correctly labeled with noticeable advantage. On the other hand, hardness with respect to our definition implies hardness with respect to the simplified notion, by a hybrid argument over the number of queries (see Lemma 1).

   Since our motivation for studying puzzles come from applications where correlated samples from the corresponding distributions can be revealed (e.g., correlated PIR queries on different indices i), we thus maintain the more complex, stronger definition.

The definitional separation in the example above stems from the fact that given access to only one distribution $\mathcal{D}_b$, one cannot necessarily simulate consistent samples from $\mathcal{D}_0$ and $\mathcal{D}_1$. However, in certain instances, this issue does not arise; for example, if one of the two is simply the uniform distribution over strings. We formally address this connection in the following section: presenting the simplified indistinguishability notion in Definition 8, and proving equivalence for certain special cases in Lemma 2.

3.3   Permuted Puzzles and a Related Indistinguishability Notion

In this work we will focus on *permuted* puzzles. This is a special case of puzzle problems, as we now define. Here, the key includes an additional secret random *permutation* on the indices of the n-element strings, and strings output by the distributions $\mathcal{D}_0, \mathcal{D}_1$ will be permuted as dictated by π.

Definition 7 (Permuted Puzzle Problems). *For a puzzle problem* $\mathcal{P} = \{(\mathcal{K}_\lambda, \{\Pi_k^{(\cdot)}\}_{k \in \mathcal{K}_\lambda})\}_{\lambda \in \mathbb{Z}^+}$, *we define the associated* permuted puzzle problem $\mathsf{Perm}(\mathcal{P}) \stackrel{\text{def}}{=} \{(\mathcal{K}'_\lambda, \{\Pi_{k'}^{\prime(\cdot)}\}_{k' \in \mathcal{K}'_\lambda})\}_{\lambda \in \mathbb{Z}^+}$, *where:*

- *A sample from* $\mathcal{K}'_\lambda$ *is* $(\mathsf{pk}, (\mathsf{sk}, \pi))$, *where:*
  - $(\mathsf{pk}, \mathsf{sk})$ *is sampled from* $\mathcal{K}_\lambda$, *and*
  - *If* $\Pi_k = (n, \Sigma, \mathcal{D}_0, \mathcal{D}_1)$, *then* π *is sampled uniformly at random from the symmetric group* S_n.
- *For any key* $k' = (\mathsf{pk}, (\mathsf{sk}, \pi))$, *if* $\Pi_{(\mathsf{pk}, \mathsf{sk})} = (n, \Sigma, \mathcal{D}_0, \mathcal{D}_1)$ *then* $\Pi'_{k'} = (n, \Sigma, \mathcal{D}'_0, \mathcal{D}'_1)$, *where a sample from* $\mathcal{D}'_b$ *is* $\pi(x)$ *for* $x \leftarrow \mathcal{D}_b$.

Recall (Notation 3) for vector $x \in \Sigma^n$ and $\pi \in S_n$, that $\pi(x)$ denotes the index-permuted vector.

As discussed in Remark 3, we now present a simplified notion of indistinguishability, and show that in certain special cases, this definition aligns with Definition 6. In such cases, it will be more convenient to work with the simplified version.

Definition 8 (Weak Hardness of Puzzle Problems). *Let* $\mathcal{P} = (\mathcal{K}, \{\Pi_k\}_{k \in \mathcal{K}})$ *and* $\mathcal{O}$ *be as in Definition 4. The* simplified distinguishing game $\mathcal{G}^{\mathcal{O}}_{\mathsf{dist}, s}[\mathcal{P}]$ *is defined similarly to* $\mathcal{G}^{\mathcal{O}}_{\mathsf{dist}}[\mathcal{P}]$, *except that in Step 3,* $\mathcal{C}$ *samples* $x' \leftarrow \mathcal{D}_b$ *(instead of* $x' \leftarrow \mathcal{D}_\beta$).

A puzzle problem $\mathcal{P} = (\mathcal{K}, \{\Pi_k\}_{k \in \mathcal{K}})$ *is* weak (s, ϵ)-hard *if* $\mathsf{Adv}_\mathcal{A}(\mathcal{G}^{\mathcal{O}}_{\mathsf{dist}, s}[\mathcal{P}]) \leq \epsilon$ *for any size-s adversary* $\mathcal{A}$. *Weak computational hardness is defined similarly to Definition 6.*

Note that *weak* computational (statistical) hardness (with respect to Definition 8) is implied by hardness with respect to Definition 4:

Lemma 1 (Standard $\Rightarrow$ Weak). *Let* $\mathcal{P} = \{(\mathcal{K}_\lambda, \{\Pi_k^{(\cdot)}\}_{k \in \mathcal{K}_\lambda})\}_{\lambda \in \mathbb{Z}^+}$ *be a puzzle problem. If* $\mathcal{P}$ *is computationally (statistically, respectively) hard in the standard sense (Definition 6) then it is weak computationally (statistically, respectively) hard (Definition 8).*

The more interesting direction is that weak hardness implies (standard) hardness in the case that one of the two distributions $\mathcal{D}_0$ or $\mathcal{D}_1$ is efficiently sampleable and *permutation-invariant*, in the following sense.

Definition 9 (Permutation-Invariant Distributions). *Let $n \in \mathbb{N}$, let Σ be a non-empty set, and let $\mathcal{D}$ be a distribution over Σ^n. For a permutation $\pi \in S_n$, let $\mathcal{D}_\pi$ be the distribution induced by sampling $x \leftarrow \mathcal{D}$ and outputting $\pi(x)$. We say that $\mathcal{D}$ is* permutation-invariant *if for a uniformly random $\pi \in S_n$, the joint distribution $\mathcal{D}_\pi \times \mathcal{D}_\pi$ is identical to $\mathcal{D} \times \mathcal{D}_\pi$.*

Remark 4. One example of a permutation-invariant distribution $\mathcal{D}$ particularly useful in this work is the uniform distribution over Σ^n.

Lemma 2 (In certain cases Weak $\Rightarrow$ Standard). *Let $\mathcal{P} = \{(\mathcal{K}_\lambda, \{\Pi_k^{(\cdot)}\}_{k \in \mathcal{K}_\lambda})\}_{\lambda \in \mathbb{Z}^+}$ be a puzzle problem. If:*

- *The corresponding permuted puzzle $\mathsf{Perm}(\mathcal{P})$ is weak computationally hard (Definition 8).*
- *For every λ, every $k = (\mathsf{pk}, \mathsf{sk}) \in \mathrm{Supp}(\mathcal{K}_\lambda)$, and every $\Pi_k = (n, \Sigma, \mathcal{D}_0, \mathcal{D}_1)$:*
  - *$\mathcal{D}_1$ is permutation-invariant.*
  - *One can efficiently sample from $\mathcal{D}_1$ without sk.*

Then $\mathsf{Perm}(\mathcal{P})$ is computationally hard in the standard sense (Definition 6).

Finally, we show that the existence of hard permuted puzzles for which the original distributions $\mathcal{D}_0, \mathcal{D}_1$ are *statistically far* implies the existence of one-way functions. Note that this holds with respect to our standard (strong) definition of computational hardness, but *not* in general for the weaker notion (where, for example, even trivially distinguishable singleton distributions D_0 over $(0,1)$ and D_1 over $(1,0)$ become statistically identical when receiving samples *only* from permuted-D_0 or permuted-D_1).

Lemma 3. *If $\mathcal{P}$ is a puzzle problem that is not statistically hard, but $\mathsf{Perm}(\mathcal{P})$ is computationally hard, then there exists a one-way function.*

The proofs of Lemmas 1, 2 and 3 are deferred to the full version.

4   Hard Permuted Puzzles in the Random Oracle Model

We show that there exist computationally hard permuted puzzles in the random oracle model. We first formally define the notion of a random oracle.

Definition 10 (Random Oracle). *We use the term* random oracle *to refer to the uniform distribution on functions mapping $\{0,1\}^* \to \{0,1\}$.*

Construction 4 (Permuted puzzles in the ROM). *Let H be a random oracle. For a security parameter λ, we interpret H as a function $H_\lambda : \{0,1\}^{m_\lambda + \lambda} \to \{0,1\}^{m_\lambda}$ for $m_\lambda = 2(\lambda+1)\log \lambda$ (also see Remark 1). We define a puzzle problem $\mathcal{P} = \{(\mathcal{K}_\lambda, \{\Pi_k\}_{k \in \mathcal{K}_\lambda})\}$ by the following* KeyGen *and* Samp *algorithms:*

- KeyGen (1^λ) outputs 1^λ as the public key (the secret key is empty).[3]
  We note that for any λ, the corresponding string distinguishing problem $\Pi_\lambda = \left(n, \Sigma, \mathcal{D}_0^{(\cdot)}, \mathcal{D}_1^{(\cdot)}\right)$ has $n = \lambda + 2$ and $\Sigma = \{0,1\}^{m_\lambda} \times \{INPUT, OUTPUT, SEED\}$.
- Samp (k, b) where $k = 1^\lambda$ outputs a sample from $\mathcal{D}_{\lambda,b}^{H_\lambda}$ for $H_\lambda : \{0,1\}^{m_\lambda + \lambda} \to \{0,1\}^{m_\lambda}$ as defined above, where $\mathcal{D}_{\lambda,b}^{H_\lambda}$ is defined as follows.
  - A sample from $\mathcal{D}_{\lambda,0}^{H_\lambda}$ is of the form $(\sigma_1, \ldots, \sigma_{\lambda+2})$, where:
    * For $i \in [\lambda]$, $\sigma_i = (s_i, SEED)$ for uniformly random and independent $s_1, \ldots, s_\lambda$ in $\{0,1\}^{m_\lambda}$.
    * $\sigma_{\lambda+1} = (x_0, INPUT)$, where x_0 is uniformly random in $\{0,1\}^{m_\lambda}$.
    * $\sigma_{\lambda+2} = (x_\lambda, OUTPUT)$, where for each $i \in [\lambda]$, $x_i = H_\lambda(s_i', x_{i-1})$, where s_i' is the length-λ prefix of s_i. (That is, the random oracle uses length-λ seeds, and the rest of the bits in the seed are ignored.)
  - $\mathcal{D}_{\lambda,1}^{H_\lambda}$ is defined identically to $\mathcal{D}_{\lambda,0}^{H_\lambda}$, except that x_λ is uniformly random in $\{0,1\}^{m_\lambda}$, independent of x_0, H_λ, and s_1, ..., s_λ.

Proposition 1. *The puzzle problem $\mathcal{P}$ of Construction 4 is computationally easy, and the corresponding permuted puzzle problem $\mathsf{Perm}(\mathcal{P})$ is statistically hard, with respect to a random oracle.*

We note that $\mathcal{P}$ is computationally easy in an extremely strong sense: a polynomial-sized adversary can obtain advantage $1 - \mathrm{negl}(\lambda)$ in the distinguishing game. The proof of is deferred to the full version.

5   Hard Permuted Puzzles in the Plain Model

In this section we discuss permuted puzzle problems based on hidden permuted kernels. At a high level, these puzzles have the following structure. First, the distributions $\mathcal{D}_0, \mathcal{D}_1$ are associated with a group G with generator g, and a uniformly random public "constraint vector" $\boldsymbol{c}$. Samples from $\mathcal{D}_0$ and $\mathcal{D}_1$ are vectors in G^m, of the form $g^{\boldsymbol{x}}$. Specifically, $\mathcal{D}_1$ samples a uniformly random vector in G^m, whereas $\mathcal{D}_0$ samples a vector $\boldsymbol{x}$ that is uniformly random subject to being orthogonal to $\boldsymbol{c}$. Intuitively, since $\mathcal{D}_1$ is uniformly random, weak computational hardness of the permuted puzzle problem implies computational hardness by Lemma 2.

*Remark 5 (**An alternative formulation of the problem**).* In the high-level blueprint of a permuted puzzle problem described above, the constraint vector $\boldsymbol{c}$ is given "in the clear" (namely, we assume it is public, and indistinguishability does not rely on the secrecy of $\boldsymbol{c}$), and the samples $\boldsymbol{x}$ are permuted according to a random permutation $\pi \in S_n$, namely, the adversary obtains $\pi(\boldsymbol{x})$ (recall that $\pi(\boldsymbol{x}) = \left(x_{\pi^{-1}(1)}, \ldots, x_{\pi^{-1}(n)}\right)$) Let $\mathcal{C}$ denote the set of "good" vectors $\boldsymbol{c}$, i.e., vectors that satisfy the requirement, and let G^n denote the domain over which

---

[3] We note that in this permuted puzzle construction the key generation stage is obsolete.

$\mathcal{D}_0, \mathcal{D}_1$ are defined. Let $\mathcal{D}'_b \overset{\text{def}}{=} \left(c, (\pi(x_i))_{i \in [q]} \right)_{c \leftarrow \mathcal{C}, \pi \leftarrow S_n, x_i \leftarrow \mathcal{D}_b}$ denote the distribution over the adversary's view in the simplified distinguishing game of Definition 8, where b is the challenge bit, and q is the number of samples the adversary receives from the challenger. Denote $\mathcal{D}''_b \overset{\text{def}}{=} \left(\pi(c), (x_i)_{i \in [q]} \right)_{c \leftarrow \mathcal{C}, \pi \leftarrow S_n, x_i \leftarrow \mathcal{D}_b}$. The permuted puzzle problems described in this section will have the property that $\mathcal{D}'_b \approx \mathcal{D}''_b$ for $b \in \{0, 1\}$, which will be used in the security proofs.

5.1 Permuted Puzzles and the Learning Parity with Noise (LPN) Assumption

We now describe how to cast the Learning Parity with Noise (LPN) assumption as a permuted puzzle.

Notation. For $a \in \mathbb{F}_2^n$, we use $|a|$ to denote the Hamming weight of a. For $i \in [n]$, we denote $v_{n,i} = 1^i \cdot 0^{n-i}$ (i.e., a canonical length-n vector of Hamming weight i). For $n \in \mathbb{N}$, let $\mathcal{R}_n$ denote the distribution that outputs a uniformly random $x \leftarrow \mathbb{F}_2^n$. For a fixed $s \in \mathbb{F}_2^n$, and $\gamma \in (0, 1)$, let $\mathcal{D}_{\mathsf{LPN},s,\gamma}$ denote the distribution over $\mathbb{F}_2^n$ that with probability γ outputs a uniformly random $x \leftarrow \mathbb{F}_2^n$, and otherwise (with probability $1 - \gamma$) outputs a uniformly random element of the set $\{x \in \mathbb{F}_2^n : x \cdot s = 0\}$.

Definition 11 (Learning Parity with Noise (LPN)). *Let $\gamma \in (0, 1)$. The γ-Learning Parity with Noise (γ-LPN) assumption conjectures that for every polynomial-sized oracle circuit ensemble $\mathcal{A} = \{\mathcal{A}_\lambda\}_\lambda$ there exists a negligible function $\epsilon(\lambda)$ such that for every λ,*

$$\mathsf{Adv}_{\mathcal{A}}^{LPN}(\lambda) \overset{\text{def}}{=} \left| \Pr_{s \leftarrow \mathbb{F}_2^\lambda} \left[\mathcal{A}^{\mathcal{D}_{\mathsf{LPN},s,\gamma}}(1^\lambda) = 1 \right] - \Pr \left[\mathcal{A}^{\mathcal{R}_\lambda}(1^\lambda) = 1 \right] \right| \leq \epsilon(\lambda).$$

*Remark 6 (**Equivalence to standard LPN formulation**).* Recall that the standard γ-LPN assumption, for $0 < \gamma < \frac{1}{2}$, states that any polynomial-time adversary obtains only a negligible advantage in distinguishing between (polynomially many samples from) the following distributions:

- $(a_i, \langle a_i, s \rangle + e_i)_{i=1}^m$, where for every i, $a_i \leftarrow \mathbb{F}_2^n$ and e_i is sampled from a Bernoulli distribution with $\Pr[e_i = 1] = \gamma$; vs.
- $(a_i, u_i)_{i=1}^m$, where each (a_i, u_i) is sampled uniformly at random from $\mathbb{F}_2^{n+1}$.

We now show that if the standard LPN assumption holds with parameters $(\lambda - 1, \gamma/2)$, then Definition 11 holds with parameters (λ, γ), where the distinguishing advantage increases by at most $2^{-\lambda}$.

- In Definition 11 if $s = 0$ then $\mathcal{D}_{\mathsf{LPN},s,\gamma}$ and $\mathcal{R}_\lambda$ are identically distributed, whereas in the standard LPN formulation they might be distinguishable (with some advantage ≤ 1).

- Conditioned on $s \neq \mathbf{0}$ in Definition 11, there exists at least one nonzero coordinate $i \in [\lambda]$ such that $s_i = 1$, in which case the i'th coordinate of a sample from $\mathcal{D}_{\mathsf{LPN},s,\gamma}$ is a noisy linear function of the other coordinates. That is, with probability $(1 - \gamma) + \frac{\gamma}{2}$, it holds that x is random subject to $x_i = \sum_{j \neq i} x_j s_j$, and with probability $\frac{\gamma}{2}$, the vector x is random subject to $x_i = \sum_{j \neq i} x_j s_j + 1$ with offset noise. Moreover, since s is uniformly random over non-zero vectors, such coordinate is equally likely to occur for any index $i \in [\lambda]$ (in contrast, in the standard LPN formulation the last coordinate always necessary satisfies this "special" structure; i.e., equivalent to $\mathcal{D}_{\mathsf{LPN},s,\gamma}$ with secret $s = (s', 1)$).

Thus, conditioned on the (overwhelming probability) event that $s \neq \mathbf{0}$, we can reduce the problem of distinguishing standard LPN with parameters $(\lambda - 1, \gamma/2)$, to distinguishing our version parameters (λ, γ), by selecting a random $i \leftarrow [\lambda]$ and transposing the i'th coordinate of all received LPN samples with the final coordinate.

We now describe how to cast LPN as a permuted puzzle.

Construction 5 (Permuted puzzle problem from LPN). *For a noise parameter $\gamma \in (0, 1/2)$, we define a puzzle problem $\mathcal{P} = \{(\mathcal{K}_\lambda, \{\Pi_k\}_{k \in \mathcal{K}_\lambda})\}$ by the following* KeyGen *and* Samp *algorithms:*

- KeyGen (1^λ) *samples a weight* w *according to the binomial distribution over* $[n]$. *It outputs* w *as the secret key (there is no public key).*
  For a key k generated by KeyGen (1^λ), *the corresponding string-distinguishing problem* $\Pi_k = (n, \Sigma, \mathcal{D}_0, \mathcal{D}_1)$ *has string length* $n = \lambda$ *and alphabet* $\Sigma = \mathbb{F}_2$.
- Samp (w, b) *outputs a sample from* $\mathcal{D}_{\lambda, b}$, *where* $\mathcal{D}_{\lambda,0} = \mathcal{D}_{\mathsf{LPN}, \mathbf{v}_{\lambda,w}, \gamma}$, *and* $\mathcal{D}_{\lambda,1} = \mathcal{R}_\lambda$.

Proposition 2. *For any constant $\gamma \in (0, 1/2)$, the γ-LPN assumption is equivalent to the computational hardness of the permuted puzzle problem* Perm $(\mathcal{P}_\gamma)$ *of Construction 5.*

Proof. Regarding the equivalence of the γ-LPN assumption and the computational hardness of Perm $(\mathcal{P}_\gamma)$, notice that the permuted distribution $\mathcal{D}'_{\lambda,0}$ of the permuted puzzle is exactly $\mathcal{D}_{\mathsf{LPN},s,\gamma}$, where $s = \pi(\mathbf{v}_{\lambda,w})$ for a uniformly random $\pi \in S_\lambda$, and a weight $w \in [\lambda]$ which was sampled according to the binomial distribution, so s is uniformly random in $\mathbb{F}_2^n$. Therefore, the distinguishing advantage in the distinguishing game of the permuted puzzle corresponds exactly to the γ-LPN assumption (because additionally $\mathcal{D}'_{\lambda,1} = \mathcal{R}_\lambda$). □

*Remark 7 ((**Unpermuted) puzzle problem is computationally easy**).* We note that the (unpermuted) puzzle problem of Construction 5 is computationally easy. Indeed, in the unpermuted puzzle problem there are only λ possible "secret" vectors (i.e., $\mathbf{v}_{\lambda,1}, \ldots, \mathbf{v}_{\lambda,\lambda}$). Given a polynomial number of samples from $\mathcal{D}_{\lambda,0}$ the adversary can determine, with overwhelming probability, which of these is the secret vector used in $\mathcal{D}_{\lambda,0}$, and can then determine (with constant advantage) whether the challenge sample is from $\mathcal{D}_{\lambda,0}$ or $\mathcal{D}_{\lambda,1}$.

5.2   Permuted Puzzles Based on DDH

In this section we describe a permuted puzzle problem based on the DDH assumption. We first recall the standard DDH assumption, and describe an equivalent formulation which we use.

Definition 12 (Group Samplers). *A* group sampler *is a probabilistic polynomial-time algorithm $\mathcal{G}$ that on input 1^λ outputs a pair (G, g), where G is a multiplicative cyclic group of order $p = \Theta(2^\lambda)$, and g is a generator of G. We assume that p is included in the group description G, and that there exists an efficient algorithm that given G and descriptions of group elements g_1, g_2 outputs a description of $g_1 \cdot g_2$.*

Definition 13 (DDH assumption). *For any cyclic group G of order p with generator g, define the following distributions:*

- *$\mathcal{D}_{DDH}(G, g)$ is uniform over the set $\left\{ (g^x, g^y, g^{xy}) : x, y \in \mathbb{Z}_p \right\}$.*
- *$\mathcal{R}_{DDH}(G, g)$ is uniform over G^3.*

For a group sampler $\mathcal{G}$, the DDH assumption over $\mathcal{G}$ *conjectures that for any polynomial-sized circuit family $\mathcal{A} = \{\mathcal{A}_\lambda\}_\lambda$ there exists a negligible function $\epsilon(\lambda)$ such that for every λ:*

$$Adv_{\mathcal{A}}^{DDH(\mathcal{G})}(\lambda) \stackrel{\text{def}}{=} \left| \Pr_{\substack{(G,g) \leftarrow \mathcal{G}(1^\lambda) \\ v \leftarrow \mathcal{D}_{DDH}(G,g)}} [\mathcal{A}_\lambda(v) = 1] - \Pr_{\substack{(G,g) \leftarrow \mathcal{G}(1^\lambda) \\ v \leftarrow \mathcal{R}_{DDH}(G,g)}} [\mathcal{A}_\lambda(v) = 1] \right| \leq \epsilon(\lambda).$$

We will use the matrix version of DDH, defined next. Informally, in matrix DDH the adversary is given many vectors of the form $(g^{x_1}, \ldots, g^{x_n})$, and the conjecture is that no polynomial-time adversary can distinguish between the case that the $(x_1, \ldots x_n)$ are sampled uniformly from $\mathbb{Z}_p^n$, and the case that $(x_1, \ldots, x_n)$ are sampled from a random 1-dimensional subspace of $\mathbb{Z}_p^n$.

Definition 14 (Matrix DDH assumption). *For a cyclic group G of order p, and $n, q \in \mathbb{N}$, define*

$$Rk_i\left(G^{q \times n}\right) = \left\{ g^A = (g^{a_{ij}})_{i \in [q], j \in [n]} \; : \; A \in \mathbb{Z}_p^{q \times n}, rank(A) = i \right\}.$$

Let $\mathcal{G}$ be as in Definition 13, and let $n = n(\lambda), q = q(\lambda)$ be polynomials such that $q(\lambda) \geq n(\lambda)$ for every λ. The matrix DDH assumption over $\mathcal{G}$ *conjectures that for any polynomial-sized circuit family $\mathcal{A} = \{\mathcal{A}_\lambda\}_\lambda$ there exists a negligible function $\epsilon(\lambda)$ such that for every λ:*

$$Adv_{\mathcal{A}}^{M\text{-}DDH(\mathcal{G})}(\lambda) \stackrel{\text{def}}{=} \left| \Pr_{\substack{(G,g) \leftarrow \mathcal{G}(1^\lambda) \\ v \leftarrow Rk_n(G^{q \times n})}} [\mathcal{A}_\lambda(v) = 1] - \Pr_{\substack{(G,g) \leftarrow \mathcal{G}(1^\lambda) \\ v \leftarrow Rk_1(G^{q \times n})}} [\mathcal{A}_\lambda(v) = 1] \right| \leq \epsilon(\lambda).$$

Boneh et al. proved [BHHO08, Lemma 1] that the DDH assumption over $\mathcal{G}$ implies the matrix DDH assumption over $\mathcal{G}$:

Imported Theorem 6 (DDH implies matrix-DDH [BHHO08]). *Let λ be a security parameter, let $\mathcal{G}$ be as in Definition 13, and let $n = n(\lambda), q = q(\lambda)$ be polynomials. Then for any polynomial-sized adversary circuit $\mathcal{A}_{\text{M-DDH}}$ there exists an adversary $\mathcal{A}_{\text{DDH}}$ of size $|\mathcal{A}_{\text{M-DDH}}| + \text{poly}(q, n)$ such that $\text{Adv}_{\mathcal{A}_{\text{M-DDH}}}^{\text{M-DDH}(\mathcal{G})}(\lambda) \leq (n-1) \cdot \text{Adv}_{\mathcal{A}_{\text{DDH}}}^{\text{DDH}(\mathcal{G})}(\lambda)$.*

We are now ready to define the permuted puzzle problem based on DDH.

Construction 7 (Permuted puzzle problem from DDH). *Let $\mathcal{G}$ be as in Definition 13. We define a puzzle problem $\mathcal{P} = \{(\mathcal{K}_\lambda, \{\Pi_k\}_{k \in \mathcal{K}_\lambda})\}$ by the following* KeyGen *and* Samp *algorithms:*

- KeyGen *on input 1^λ samples $(G, g) \leftarrow \mathcal{G}(1^\lambda)$, where $\mathcal{G}$ is the group sampling algorithm of Definition 13. Let p denote the order of G. Then,* KeyGen *samples a uniformly random vector $\boldsymbol{u} \in \mathbb{Z}_p^n$ for $n = \lambda^2$ and outputs $(G, g, \boldsymbol{u})$ as a public key (there is no secret key).*
  We note that for any $k = (G, g, \boldsymbol{u})$, the corresponding string distinguishing problem $\Pi_k = (n, \Sigma, \mathcal{D}_0, \mathcal{D}_1)$ has alphabet $\Sigma = G$.
- Samp (k, b) *for $k = (n, \Sigma, \mathcal{D}_0, \mathcal{D}_1)$ outputs a sample from $\mathcal{D}_b$, where:*
  - *$\mathcal{D}_0$ is uniform over $\{g^{\boldsymbol{x}} \in G^n : \boldsymbol{x} \cdot \boldsymbol{u} = 0\}$.*
  - *$\mathcal{D}_1$ is uniform over G^n.*

Proposition 3. *The puzzle problem $\mathcal{P}$ of Construction 7 is computationally easy. Moreover, if $\mathcal{G}$ is an ensemble of groups in which the matrix DDH assumption of Definition 14 holds, then the corresponding permuted puzzle problem* Perm$(\mathcal{P})$ *is computationally hard.*

We note that $\mathcal{P}$ is computationally easy in an extremely strong sense: a polynomial-sized adversary can obtain advantage $1 - \text{negl}(\lambda)$ in the distinguishing game. The proof of Proposition 3 is deferred to the full version.

6   Statistical Query Lower Bound

In this section we discuss a specific permuted puzzle toy problem introduced by [BIPW17], and study its hardness against a large class of potential adversarial algorithms called *statistical-query algorithms*. We first define this class of algorithms in Sect. 6.1, then present the toy problem in Sect. 6.2 and prove it is secure against such algorithms.

6.1   Statistical Query Algorithms

Definition 15 (Statistical Query Algorithms). *Let $\mathcal{P} = (\mathcal{K}, \{\Pi_k\}_{k \in \mathcal{K}})$ be a puzzle problem. A* statistical q-query algorithm *for $\mathcal{G}_{\text{dist},s}[\mathcal{P}]$ is a stateful adversary $\mathcal{A}$ using an "inner adversary" $\mathcal{A}_{\text{SQ}}$ as follows.*

1. *Upon receiving the public key* pk, $\mathcal{A}$ *forwards it to* $\mathcal{A}_{\mathsf{SQ}}$.
   Recall that pk *is part of the key* k, *and denote* $\Pi_k = (n, \Sigma, \mathcal{D}_0, \mathcal{D}_1)$.
2. *The following is repeated* q *times:*
   (a) $\mathcal{A}_{\mathsf{SQ}}$ *outputs a boolean-valued function* f.[4]
   (b) $\mathcal{A}$ *requests a sample* $x \leftarrow \mathcal{D}_b$ *from the challenger (where* $b \in \{0, 1\}$ *is the challenger's secret bit), computes* $f(x)$ *(this is a single bit), and forwards* $f(x)$ *to* $\mathcal{A}_{\mathsf{SQ}}$.
3. *When* $\mathcal{A}_{\mathsf{SQ}}$ *outputs a "guess" bit* b', $\mathcal{A}$ *forwards* b' *to the challenger.*

Remark 8. We consider only statistical query algorithms for the simplified distinguishing game $\mathcal{G}_{\mathsf{dist},s}$ of Definition 8 because our lower bounds (proven in Sect. 6.2) hold for puzzle problems in which weak computational hardness (i.e., hardness of $\mathcal{G}_{\mathsf{dist},s}$) is equivalent to computational hardness (i.e., hardness of the more standard distinguishing game $\mathcal{G}_{\mathsf{dist}}$ of Definition 4) by Lemma 2.

Statistical Query (SQ) algorithms constitute a broad class of distinguishing algorithms, that is incomparable in power to polynomial-time algorithms. For example, an SQ algorithm can distinguish between a PRG output and a uniformly random string with a single query. On the other hand, SQ algorithms cannot distinguish between a distribution that is uniform on $\{0,1\}^n$ and one that is uniform on a random high-dimensional subspace of $\{0,1\}^n$. These distributions can be distinguished (given many samples) in polynomial time by a simple rank computation.

Still, in the context of distinguishing problems, SQ algorithms seem to be a powerful class of adversarial algorithms. In fact, except for the aforementioned examples of algorithms which exploit algebraic structure, we are not aware of any natural distinguishing algorithms that cannot be simulated by statistical query algorithms. A challenging and important open problem, which we leave for future work, is to formalize a class of algorithms that use algebraic structure (or even only linear algebra), possibly together with statistical queries, and to prove lower bounds against this class.

6.2   The Toy Problem and Lower Bound

The works [CHR17, BIPW17] base the security of their DE-PIR schemes on the PermRM conjecture, for which they also discuss different variants (e.g., noisy versions). Boyle et al. [BIPW17] also put forth a toy version of the problem, for which we will prove a lower bound against SQ algorithms. We first recall the PermRM conjecture and its toy version.

*Conjecture 1 (*PermRM, *Conjecture 4.2 in* [BIPW17]*).* Let $m \in \mathbb{N}$ be a dimension parameter, let $\lambda \in \mathbb{N}$ be a security parameter, let $d = d_m(n)$ be the minimal integer such that $n \geq \binom{m+d}{d}$, and let $\mathbb{F}$ be a finite field satisfying $|\mathbb{F}| > d\lambda + 1$. Define a probabilistic algorithm $\mathsf{Samp}(b, \pi, v)$ that operates as follows:

---

[4] We do not assume any bound on the description size or complexity of f, which will not matter for our lower bounds.

- If $b = 0$:
  1. Select m random degree-λ polynomial $p_1, \ldots, p_m \leftarrow \mathbb{F}[X]$ such that for every $1 \leq i \leq \lambda$, $p_i(0) = v$. Notice that these polynomials determine a curve $\gamma(t)$ in $\mathbb{F}^m$, given by $\{(p_1(t), \ldots, p_m(t)) : t \in \mathbb{F}\}$.
  2. Sample $d\lambda + 1$ distinct points on the curve $\gamma(t)$, determined by non-zero parameters $t_0, \ldots, t_{d\lambda} \leftarrow \mathbb{F}$.
  3. Output the points, in order, where each point is permuted according to $\pi : \mathbb{F}^m \to \mathbb{F}^m$, namely output

$$(\pi(p_1(t_i), \ldots, p_m(t_i)))_{i=0}^{d\lambda} \in (\mathbb{F}^m)^{d\lambda+1} .$$

- If $b = 1$: sample $d\lambda + 1$ random points in $\mathbb{F}^m$ $(w_0, \ldots, w_{d\lambda}) \leftarrow (\mathbb{F}^m)^{d\lambda+1}$, and output $(w_0, \ldots, w_{d\lambda})$.

The PermRM conjecture is that for every efficient non-uniform $\mathcal{A} = (\mathcal{A}_1, \mathcal{A}_2)$ there exists a negligible function $\mu(\lambda) = \mathrm{negl}(\lambda)$ such that:

$$\Pr \left[\begin{array}{l} (1^n, 1^{|\mathbb{F}|}, \mathsf{aux}) \leftarrow \mathcal{A}_1(1^\lambda) \\ \pi \leftarrow S_{(\mathbb{F}^m)}; b \leftarrow \{0, 1\} \\ b' \leftarrow \mathcal{A}_2^{\mathsf{Samp}(b, \pi, \cdot)}(1^n, \mathsf{aux}) \end{array} : b' = b \right] \leq 1/2 + \mu(\lambda)$$

Let $\mathbb{F} = \{\mathbb{F}_\lambda\}_{\lambda \in \mathbb{Z}^+}$ denote an ensemble of finite fields with $|\mathbb{F}_\lambda| = \Theta(\lambda^2)$. Let $q = q_\lambda$ denote $|\mathbb{F}_\lambda|$.

For a function $f : X \to Y$, we define $\mathsf{Graph}(f) : X \times Y \to \{0, 1\}$ such that

$$\mathsf{Graph}(f)(x, y) = \begin{cases} 1 & \text{if } y = f(x) \\ 0 & \text{otherwise.} \end{cases}$$

Define the puzzle problem $\Pi_\lambda = (n, \{0, 1\}, \mathcal{D}_0, \mathcal{D}_1)$, where $n = q^2$, and $\mathcal{D}_0$ and $\mathcal{D}_1$ are defined as follows.

- A sample from $\mathcal{D}_0$ is $\mathsf{Graph}(\gamma)$, where $\gamma : \mathbb{F} \to \mathbb{F}$ is a uniformly random degree-λ polynomial.
- A sample from $\mathcal{D}_1$ is $\mathsf{Graph}(U)$, where $U : \mathbb{F} \to \mathbb{F}$ is a uniformly random function.

Conjecture 2 ([BIPW17]). The permuted puzzle problem $\mathcal{P} \overset{\text{def}}{=} \mathsf{Perm}(\{\Pi_\lambda\}_{\lambda \in \mathbb{Z}^+})$ is computationally hard.

Theorem 8. *The simplified distinguishing game $\mathcal{G}_{\mathsf{dist}, s}[\mathcal{P}]$ is hard for statistical-query algorithms. That is, for all polynomially bounded $q(\cdot)$, the advantage of any statistical $q(\lambda)$-query adversary in $\mathcal{G}_{\mathsf{dist}, s}[\mathcal{P}]$ is at most $e^{-\Omega(\lambda)}$.*

Proof. We will show that even if we give the statistical query adversary additional information about π, it cannot distinguish permuted samples from $\mathcal{D}_0$ from permuted samples from $\mathcal{D}_1$. Specifically, we will give the adversary (for free) the unordered partition $\Phi_1 \cup \cdots \cup \Phi_q$ of $\mathbb{F} \times \mathbb{F}$, where $\Phi_i = \pi(\{i\} \times \mathbb{F})$. (Intuitively, Φ_i is the image under π of all points in which the X coordinate equals i. In particular, $\pi\left(\mathsf{Graph}\left(f\right)\right)$ takes value "1" at exactly one coordinate in Φ_i.) Note that it is indeed possible for a statistical query adversary to learn $\Phi \overset{\text{def}}{=} \{\Phi_1, \ldots, \Phi_q\}$: if (x, y) and (x', y') belong to the same Φ_i, then for a random sample $z \leftarrow \mathcal{D}_b$, it is never the case that $\pi(z)_{(x,y)} = \pi(z)_{(x',y')} = 1$. However, if (x, y) and (x', y') do *not* belong to the same Φ_i, then $\pi(z)_{(x,y)} = \pi(z)_{(x',y')} = 1$ with probability at least $\frac{1}{q^2}$.

We say that a permutation π respects a partition $\Phi = \{\Phi_1, \ldots, \Phi_q\}$ if $\{\pi(\{i\} \times \mathbb{F})\}_i = \Phi$. For any partition Φ, we will write Pr_Φ to denote the probability space in which a permutation π is sampled uniformly at random from the set of permutations that respect Φ. Similarly, we will write $\mathbb{E}_\Phi$ to denote expectations in Pr_Φ, and we write Var_Φ to denote variances in Pr_Φ.

We will show that there is some negligible function $\nu : \mathbb{Z}^+ \to \mathbb{R}$ such that for any function $f : \{0,1\}^n \to \{0,1\}$ and any partition Φ, there exists some $p_{f,\Phi} \in [0,1]$ such that for every $b \in \{0,1\}$, it holds that

$$\Pr_\Phi \left[\left| \underset{x \leftarrow \mathcal{D}_b}{\mathbb{E}} \left[f(\pi(x)) \right] - p_{f,\Phi} \right| \geq \nu(\lambda) \right] \leq \nu(\lambda).$$

Crucially, $p_{f,\Phi}$ is independent of the challenge bit b, the specific sample x, and the secret permutation π (except for its dependence on Φ). Thus, the answer to a query f can be simulated by computing $p_{f,\Phi}$.

The following two observations are at the core of our proof. Recall that Δ denotes the Hamming distance. For a pair of functions $g, g' : X \to Y$, we denote $\Delta(g, g') = |\{x \in X : g(x) \neq g'(x)\}|$.

Claim 1. For any partition Φ, any function $g : \mathbb{F} \to \mathbb{F}$, and any fixed permutation π^* that respects Φ, the distribution of $\pi(\mathsf{Graph}(g))$ under Pr_Φ is identical to the distribution of $\pi^*(\mathsf{Graph}(u))$ when $u : \mathbb{F} \to \mathbb{F}$ is a uniformly random function.

Proof. To sample a random permutation π conditioned on $\{\pi(\{i\} \times \mathbb{F})\}_i = \Phi \overset{\text{def}}{=} \{\Phi_1, \ldots, \Phi_q\}$, one can sample a uniformly random permutation $\sigma : \mathbb{F} \to \mathbb{F}$ and q independent bijections $\pi_i : \mathbb{F} \to \Phi_{\sigma(i)}$, and then define $\pi(j, k) = \pi_j(k)$.

$\pi(\mathsf{Graph}(g))$ is defined by the set of points $\{\pi(j, g(j))\}_{j \in \mathbb{F}} = \{\pi_j(g(j))\}$. It is clear that sampling g uniformly at random corresponds to independently picking each $g(j)$ at random, which produces an identical distribution of $\pi(\mathsf{Graph}(g))$ as picking the bijections $\{\pi_j\}$ independently and uniformly at random. Thus, $\pi^*(\mathsf{Graph}(u))$ for a fixed π^* which respects the partition Φ, and a random u, is distributed identically to $\pi(\mathsf{Graph}(g))$ for a fixed g and a random π that respects Φ. $\quad\square$

Claim 2. For any partition Φ, any functions $g, g' : \mathbb{F} \to \mathbb{F}$, and any fixed permutation π^* that respects Φ, the distribution of $\left(\pi(\mathsf{Graph}(g)), \pi(\mathsf{Graph}(g'))\right)$ under Pr_Φ is identical to the distribution of $\left(\pi^*(\mathsf{Graph}(u)), \pi^*(\mathsf{Graph}(u'))\right)$, where $u, u' : \mathbb{F} \to \mathbb{F}$ are jointly uniformly random conditioned on $\Delta(u, u') = \Delta(g, g')$.

Proof. We first consider the distribution under Pr_Φ of $(x, x') = \left(\pi(\mathsf{Graph}(g)), \pi(\mathsf{Graph}(g'))\right)$, where g and g' are fixed. Because g and g' are functions, both x and x' will consist mostly of zeros, but for each $j \in \mathbb{F}$, they will contain a 1 in exactly one position in Φ_j. Recall from the proof of Claim 1 that π can be sampled by sampling a uniformly random permutation $\sigma : \mathbb{F} \to \mathbb{F}$ and q independent bijections $\pi_i : \mathbb{F} \to \Phi_{\sigma(i)}$, and defining $\pi(j,k) = \pi_j(k)$. Therefore, for any $j \in \mathbb{F}$ if $g(j) = g'(j)$ then x and x' will agree on the position within $\Phi_{\sigma(j)}$ at which they contain a 1 entry. Otherwise, they will disagree. Other than that, the positions are uniformly random within $\Phi_{\sigma(j)}$ because π_j is a random bijection. Moreover, since σ is a random permutation, the set of Φ_i's for which x, x' agree on the 1-entry is a random subset of size $\Delta(g, g')$.

Now consider the distribution of $(y, y') = (\pi^*(\mathsf{Graph}(u)), \pi^*(\mathsf{Graph}(u')))$ where π^* is fixed and defined by σ^* and $\{\pi_i^*\}_{i \in \mathbb{F}}$. The same arguments show that for every $j \in \mathbb{F}$, y, y' agree on the positions within $\Phi_{\sigma^*(j)}$ at which they contain a 1 if and only if $u(j) = u'(j)$. Since u, u' are random and independent, the positions in $\Phi_{\sigma^*(j)}$ in which y, y' have a 1 are otherwise random because these positions are $\pi_j^*(u(j))$ and $\pi_j^*(u'(j))$, respectively. Additionally, the Φ_i's for which y, y' agree on the position of the 1 entry is a uniformly random subset of size $\Delta(g, g') = \Delta(u, u')$, because this set is $\{\sigma^*(j) : u(j) = u'(j)\}$, and u, u' are random and independent. □

Claim 3. If $g_0, g_1 : \mathbb{F} \to \mathbb{F}$ are two independent uniformly random degree-λ polynomials, then $\Delta(g_0, g_1)$ is $e^{-\Omega(\lambda)}$-close to $\Delta(g_0', g_1')$ for uniformly random $g_0', g_1' : \mathbb{F} \to \mathbb{F}$.

Proof. For $i \in \mathbb{F}$, let X_i (respectively, Y_i) be indicator of the event that $g_0(i) = g_1(i)$ (respectively, $g_0'(i) = g_1'(i)$). Then X_i, Y_i are λ-wise independent with $\mathbb{E}[X_i] = \mathbb{E}[Y_i] = |\mathbb{F}|^{-1}$. The claim now follows from Lemma 4 below for $n = |\mathbb{F}|$. □

We now state the lemma used in the proof of Claim 3, the proof is deferred to the full version.

Lemma 4. *Let $X = (X_1, \ldots, X_n)$ and $Y = (Y_1, \ldots, Y_n)$ be t-wise independent $\{0,1\}$-valued random variables with $t \geq 2e^2$, such that for all $i \in [n]$, $\mathbb{E}[Y_i] = \mathbb{E}[X_i] \stackrel{\text{def}}{=} p_i$, let p denote $\frac{1}{n} \cdot \sum_i p_i$, and suppose that $p \leq \frac{t}{4n}$. Then the total variation distance $d_{\mathsf{TV}}(X, Y)$ is at most*

$$(n + 3) \cdot \frac{(4pn/t)^{t/2}}{\prod_{i \in [n]}(1 - p_i)}$$

Now, we will show that $\mathbb{E}_{x \leftarrow \mathcal{D}_0}[f(\pi(x))]$ and $\mathbb{E}_{x \leftarrow \mathcal{D}_1}[f(\pi(x))]$, viewed as random variables that depend on π, have the same expectation and also have very small (negligible) variance.

Claim 4. For any $f : \{0,1\}^n \to \{0,1\}$ and any partition Φ,

$$\mathbb{E}_{\Phi}\left[\mathbb{E}_{x \leftarrow \mathcal{D}_0}[f(\pi(x))]\right] = \mathbb{E}_{\Phi}\left[\mathbb{E}_{x \leftarrow \mathcal{D}_1}[f(\pi(x))]\right].$$

Proof. Consider any $f : \{0,1\}^n \to \{0,1\}$ and any partition Φ. By Claim 1, there is a distribution $\mathcal{U}$ that is equal to the distribution (in $\Pr_\Phi$) of $\pi(\mathsf{Graph}(g))$ for all functions $g : \mathbb{F} \to \mathbb{F}$. Let μ denote $\mathbb{E}_{x' \leftarrow \mathcal{U}}[f(x')]$. Let P_b denote the probability mass function of $\mathcal{D}_b$. Then for any $b \in \{0,1\}$,

$$
\mathbb{E}_\Phi \left[\mathbb{E}_{x \leftarrow \mathcal{D}_b} [f(\pi(x))] \right] = \mathbb{E}_\Phi \left[\sum_x P_b(x) \cdot f(\pi(x)) \right]
$$
$$
= \sum_x P_b(x) \cdot \mathbb{E}_\Phi [f(\pi(x))]
$$
$$
= \sum_x P_b(x) \cdot \mu
$$
$$
= \mu,
$$

which does not depend on b.   □

Now we analyze the variance. Recall that our goal is to show that $\mathrm{Var}_\Phi \left[\mathbb{E}_{x \leftarrow \mathcal{D}_b} [f(\pi(x))] \right]$ is negligible for $b \in \{0,1\}$. Because of Claim 3, this follows from the following more general claim.

Claim 5. Let $\mathcal{D}$ be any distribution on functions mapping $\mathbb{F}$ to $\mathbb{F}$. Suppose that when g and g' are sampled independently from $\mathcal{D}$ and $u, u' : \mathbb{F} \to \mathbb{F}$ are independent uniformly random functions, the distribution of $\Delta(g, g')$ is statistically ϵ-close to that of $\Delta(u, u')$.

Then, for any $f : \{0,1\}^n \to \{0,1\}$, any partition Φ,

$$
\mathrm{Var}_\Phi \left[\mathbb{E}_{g \leftarrow \mathcal{D}} \left[f\big(\pi(\mathsf{Graph}(g))\big) \right] \right] \le \epsilon.
$$

Proof. Let P denote the probability mass function of $\mathcal{D}$, and let π^* be an arbitrary permutation in S_n such that $\{\pi^*(\{i\} \times \mathbb{F})\}_i = \Phi$. By the definition of variance,

$$
\mathrm{Var}_\Phi \left[\mathbb{E}_{g \leftarrow \mathcal{D}} [f(\pi(\mathsf{Graph}(g)))] \right] = \mathbb{E}_\Phi \left[\mathbb{E}_{g \leftarrow \mathcal{D}} [f(\pi(\mathsf{Graph}(g)))]^2 \right] - \mathbb{E}_\Phi \left[\mathbb{E}_{g \leftarrow \mathcal{D}} [f(\pi(\mathsf{Graph}(g)))] \right]^2.
$$

For the first term, we have

$$
\mathbb{E}_\Phi [\, \mathbb{E}_{g \leftarrow \mathcal{D}} [f(\pi(\mathsf{Graph}(g)))]^2] = \mathbb{E}_\Phi \left[\left(\sum_g P(g) \cdot f(\pi(\mathsf{Graph}(g))) \right)^2 \right]
$$
$$
= \sum_{g,h} P(g) \cdot P(h) \cdot \mathbb{E}_\Phi [f(\pi(\mathsf{Graph}(g))) \cdot f(\pi(\mathsf{Graph}(h)))] \qquad \text{(Claim 2)}
$$
$$
= \mathbb{E}_{g,h \leftarrow \mathcal{D}} \left[\mathbb{E}_{\substack{u,v:\mathbb{F}\to\mathbb{F} \\ \Delta(u,v)=\Delta(g,h)}} \left[f(\pi^*(\mathsf{Graph}(u))) \cdot f(\pi^*(\mathsf{Graph}(v))) \right] \right].
$$

For the second term, we have

$$
= \mathop{\mathbb{E}}_{\Phi} \left[\mathop{\mathbb{E}}_{g \leftarrow \mathcal{D}} [f(\pi(\mathsf{Graph}(g)))] \right]^2
$$

$$
= \left(\sum_g P(g) \cdot \mathop{\mathbb{E}}_{\Phi} [f(\pi(\mathsf{Graph}(g)))] \right)^2
$$

$$
= \left(\sum_g P(g) \cdot \mathop{\mathbb{E}}_{u: \mathbb{F} \to \mathbb{F}} [f(\pi^*(\mathsf{Graph}(u)))] \right)^2 \qquad \text{(Claim 1)}
$$

$$
= \mathop{\mathbb{E}}_{u: \mathbb{F} \to \mathbb{F}} [f(\pi^*(\mathsf{Graph}(u)))]^2
$$

$$
= \mathop{\mathbb{E}}_{u,v: \mathbb{F} \to \mathbb{F}} [f(\pi^*(\mathsf{Graph}(u))) \cdot f(\pi^*(\mathsf{Graph}(v)))]
$$

$$
= \mathop{\mathbb{E}}_{g,h: \mathbb{F} \to \mathbb{F}} \left[\mathop{\mathbb{E}}_{\substack{u,v: \mathbb{F} \to \mathbb{F} \\ \Delta(u,v) = \Delta(g,h)}} [f(\pi^*(\mathsf{Graph}(u))) \cdot f(\pi^*(\mathsf{Graph}(v)))] \right] \qquad \text{(law of total expectation)}.
$$

The difference between these two expressions is only in the distribution of g and h over which the (outer) expectation is taken. Furthermore, the value whose expectation is computed lies in $[0, 1]$ and depends only on the Hamming distance between g and h. The claim follows. □

Theorem 8 follows from Claims 3, 4, and 5, and Chebyshev's inequality. □

Acknowledgments. We thank Yuval Ishai for many useful discussions. We thank Fermi Ma for helpful discussions, in particular for pointing out that the blueprint of the DDH-based permuted puzzle extends also to the LPN setting, for simplifying one step of the proof of Proposition 3, and for allowing us to include these observations in the current work. We thank the anonymous TCC reviewers for helpful comments.

References

[Ajt96] Ajtai, M.: Generating hard instances of lattice problems (extended abstract). In: Proceedings of the Twenty-Eighth Annual ACM Symposium on the Theory of Computing, Philadelphia, Pennsylvania, USA, 22–24 May 1996, pp. 99–108 (1996)

[Ale03] Alekhnovich, M.: More on average case vs approximation complexity. In: Proceedings of the 44th Symposium on Foundations of Computer Science (FOCS 2003), Cambridge, MA, USA, 11–14 October 2003. pp. 298–307 (2003)

[BCC+17] Bitansky, N., et al.: The hunting of the snark. J. Cryptol. **30**(4), 989–1066 (2017)

[BFKL93] Blum, A., Furst, M., Kearns, M., Lipton, R.J.: Cryptographic primitives based on hard learning problems. In: Stinson, D.R. (ed.) CRYPTO 1993. LNCS, vol. 773, pp. 278–291. Springer, Heidelberg (1994). https://doi.org/10.1007/3-540-48329-2_24

[BGI+01] Barak, B., et al.: On the (im)possibility of obfuscating programs. In: Kilian, J. (ed.) CRYPTO 2001. LNCS, vol. 2139, pp. 1–18. Springer, Heidelberg (2001). https://doi.org/10.1007/3-540-44647-8_1

[BHHO08] Boneh, D., Halevi, S., Hamburg, M., Ostrovsky, R.: Circular-secure encryption from decision Diffie-Hellman. In: Wagner, D. (ed.) CRYPTO 2008. LNCS, vol. 5157, pp. 108–125. Springer, Heidelberg (2008). https://doi.org/10.1007/978-3-540-85174-5_7

[BIM00] Beimel, A., Ishai, Y., Malkin, T.: Reducing the servers computation in private information retrieval: PIR with preprocessing. In: Bellare, M. (ed.) CRYPTO 2000. LNCS, vol. 1880, pp. 55–73. Springer, Heidelberg (2000). https://doi.org/10.1007/3-540-44598-6_4

[BIPW17] Boyle, E., Ishai, Y., Pass, R., Wootters, M.: Can we access a database both locally and privately? In: Kalai, Y., Reyzin, L. (eds.) TCC 2017. LNCS, vol. 10678, pp. 662–693. Springer, Cham (2017). https://doi.org/10.1007/978-3-319-70503-3_22

[BKW00] Blum, A., Kalai, A., Wasserman, H.: Noise-tolerant learning, the parity problem, and the statistical query model. In: Proceedings of the Thirty-Second Annual ACM Symposium on Theory of Computing, Portland, OR, USA, , 21–23 May 2000, pp. 435–440 (2000)

[BPR15] Bitansky, N., Paneth, O., Rosen, A.: On the cryptographic hardness of finding a Nash equilibrium. In: IEEE 56th Annual Symposium on Foundations of Computer Science, FOCS 2015, Berkeley, CA, USA, 17–20 October 2015, pp. 1480–1498 (2015)

[BV11] Brakerski, Z., Vaikuntanathan, V.: Efficient fully homomorphic encryption from (standard) LWE. ECCC 18(109), 2011 (2011)

[CCH+19] Canetti, R., et al.: Fiat-Shamir: from practice to theory. In: STOC (2019)

[CCRR18] Canetti, R., Chen, Y., Reyzin, L., Rothblum, R.D.: Fiat-Shamir and correlation intractability from strong KDM-secure encryption. In: Nielsen, J.B., Rijmen, V. (eds.) EUROCRYPT 2018, Part I. LNCS, vol. 10820, pp. 91–122. Springer, Cham (2018). https://doi.org/10.1007/978-3-319-78381-9_4

[CGKS95] Chor, B., Goldreich, O., Kushilevitz, E., Sudan, M.: Private information retrieval. In: 36th Annual Symposium on Foundations of Computer Science, Milwaukee, Wisconsin, USA, 23–25 October 1995, pp. 41–50 (1995)

[CHK+19] Choudhuri, A.R., Hubávcek, P., Kamath, C., Pietrzak, K., Rosen, A., Rothblum, G.N.: Finding a Nash equilibrium is no easier than breaking Fiat-Shamir. IACR Cryptology ePrint Archive, 2019/158 (2019)

[CHR17] Canetti, R., Holmgren, J., Richelson, S.: Towards doubly efficient private information retrieval. In: Kalai, Y., Reyzin, L. (eds.) TCC 2017. LNCS, vol. 10678, pp. 694–726. Springer, Cham (2017). https://doi.org/10.1007/978-3-319-70503-3_23

[DH76] Diffie, W., Hellman, M.E.: New directions in cryptography. IEEE Trans. Inf. Theory 22(6), 644–654 (1976)

[FKM+18] Faugère, J.-C., Koussa, E., Macario-Rat, G., Patarin, J., Perret, L.: PKP-based signature scheme. IACR Cryptology ePrint Archive 2018/714 (2018)

[Gen09] Gentry, C.: Fully homomorphic encryption using ideal lattices. In: Proceedings of the STOC 2009, pp. 169–178. ACM (2009)

[GGH+13] Garg, S., Gentry, C., Halevi, S., Raykova, M., Sahai, A., Waters, B.: Candidate indistinguishability obfuscation and functional encryption for all circuits. In: 54th Annual IEEE Symposium on Foundations of Computer Science, FOCS 2013, Berkeley, CA, USA, 26–29 October 2013, pp. 40–49 (2013)

[GJ02] Garey, M.R., Johnson, D.S.: Computers and Intractability, vol. 29. wh freeman, New York (2002)

[GK16] Goldwasser, S., Tauman Kalai, Y.: Cryptographic Assumptions: A Position Paper. In: Kushilevitz, E., Malkin, T. (eds.) TCC 2016. LNCS, vol. 9562, pp. 505–522. Springer, Heidelberg (2016). https://doi.org/10.1007/978-3-662-49096-9_21

[GKL88] Goldreich, O., Krawczyk, H., Luby, M.: On the existence of pseudorandom generators (extended abstract). In: 29th Annual Symposium on Foundations of Computer Science, White Plains, New York, USA, 24–26 October 1988, pp. 12–24 (1988)

[GW11] Gentry, C., Wichs, D.: Separating succinct non-interactive arguments from all falsifiable assumptions. In: STOC, pp. 99–108. ACM (2011)

[HL18] Holmgren, J., Lombardi, A.: Cryptographic hashing from strong one-way functions (or: one-way product functions and their applications). In: 2018 IEEE 59th Annual Symposium on Foundations of Computer Science (FOCS), pp. 850–858. IEEE (2018)

[HY17] Hubávcek, P., Yogev, E.: Hardness of continuous local search: query complexity and cryptographic lower bounds. In: Proceedings of the Twenty-Eighth Annual ACM-SIAM Symposium on Discrete Algorithms, SODA 2017, Barcelona, Spain, Hotel Porta Fira, 16–19 January, pp. 1352–1371 (2017)

[KMP19] Koussa, E., Macario-Rat, G., Patarin, J.: On the complexity of the permuted kernel problem. IACR Cryptology ePrint Archive 2019/412 (2019)

[KO97] Kushilevitz, E., Ostrovsky, R.: Replication is not needed: single database, computationally-private information retrieval. In: 38th Annual Symposium on Foundations of Computer Science, FOCS 1997, Miami Beach, Florida, USA, 19–22 October 1997, pp. 364–373 (1997)

[KRR17] Kalai, Y.T., Rothblum, G.N., Rothblum, R.D.: From obfuscation to the security of Fiat-Shamir for proofs. In: Katz, J., Shacham, H. (eds.) CRYPTO 2017, Part II. LNCS, vol. 10402, pp. 224–251. Springer, Cham (2017). https://doi.org/10.1007/978-3-319-63715-0_8

[LP12] Lampe, R., Patarin, J.: Analysis of some natural variants of the PKP algorithm. In: SECRYPT 2012 - Proceedings of the International Conference on Security and Cryptography, Rome, Italy, 24–27 July 2012, SECRYPT is part of ICETE - The International Joint Conference on e-Business and Telecommunications, pp. 209–214 (2012)

[Mul54] Muller, D.E.: Application of Boolean algebra to switching circuit design and to error detection. Trans. I.R.E. Prof. Group Electron. Comput. **3**(3), 6–12 (1954)

[Nao03] Naor, M.: On cryptographic assumptions and challenges. In: Boneh, D. (ed.) CRYPTO 2003. LNCS, vol. 2729, pp. 96–109. Springer, Heidelberg (2003). https://doi.org/10.1007/978-3-540-45146-4_6

[PS19] Peikert, C., Shiehian, S.: Noninteractive zero knowledge for NP from (plain) learning with errors. IACR Cryptology ePrint Archive 2019/158 (2019)

[Rab79] Michael, O.: Rabin. Digitalized signatures and public-key functions as intractable as factorization. Technical report, MIT Laboratory for Computer Science (1979)

[RAD78] Rivest, R.L., Adleman, L., Dertouzos, M.L.: On data banks and privacy homomorphisms. Foundations of secure computation, Academia Press (1978)

[Ree54] Reed, I.S.: A class of multiple-error-correcting codes and the decoding scheme. Trans. IRE Prof. Group Inf. Theory (TIT) **4**, 38–49 (1954)

[Reg05] Regev, O.: On lattices, learning with errors, random linear codes, and cryptography. In: Proceedings of the 37th Annual ACM Symposium on Theory of Computing, Baltimore, MD, USA, 22–24 May 2005, pp. 84–93 (2005)

[RSA78] Rivest, R.L., Shamir, A., Adleman, L.M.: A method for obtaining digital signatures and public-key cryptosystems. Commun. ACM **21**(2), 120–126 (1978)

[Sha89] Shamir, A.: An efficient identification scheme based on permuted kernels (extended abstract). In: Brassard, G. (ed.) CRYPTO 1989. LNCS, vol. 435, pp. 606–609. Springer, New York (1990). https://doi.org/10.1007/0-387-34805-0_54

Linear-Size Constant-Query IOPs for Delegating Computation

Eli Ben-Sasson[1], Alessandro Chiesa[2(✉)], Lior Goldberg[1], Tom Gur[3], Michael Riabzev[1], and Nicholas Spooner[2]

[1] StarkWare, Tel Aviv, Israel
{eli,lior,michael}@starkware.co
[2] UC Berkeley, Berkeley, USA
{alexch,nick.spooner}@berkeley.edu
[3] University of Warwick, Coventry, UK
tom.gur@warwick.ac.uk

Abstract. We study the problem of delegating computations via interactive proofs that can be probabilistically checked. Known as *interactive oracle proofs* (IOPs), these proofs extend probabilistically checkable proofs (PCPs) to multi-round protocols, and have received much attention due to their application to constructing cryptographic proofs (such as succinct non-interactive arguments). The relevant complexity measures for IOPs in this context are prover and verifier time, and query complexity.

We construct highly efficient IOPs for a rich class of nondeterministic algebraic computations, which includes succinct versions of arithmetic circuit satisfiability and rank-one constraint system (R1CS) satisfiability. For a time-T computation, we obtain prover arithmetic complexity $O(T \log T)$ and verifier complexity polylog(T). These IOPs are the first to simultaneously achieve the state of the art in prover complexity, due to [14], and in verifier complexity, due to [7]. We also improve upon the query complexity of both schemes.

The efficiency of our prover is a result of our highly optimized proof length; in particular, ours is the first construction that simultaneously achieves linear-size proofs and polylogarithmic-time verification, regardless of query complexity.

Keywords: Interactive oracle proofs · Probabilistically checkable proofs · Delegation of computation

1 Introduction

Verifiable delegation of computation is a central goal in cryptography. The complexity-theoretic study of proof systems has enabled significant progress in this area, and the efficiency of numerous delegation schemes crucially relies on the efficiency of the underlying complexity-theoretic objects.

© International Association for Cryptologic Research 2019
D. Hofheinz and A. Rosen (Eds.): TCC 2019, LNCS 11892, pp. 494–521, 2019.
https://doi.org/10.1007/978-3-030-36033-7_19

An influential line of work began with *probabilistically checkable proofs* (PCPs) [5]. These are non-interactive proofs for membership in a language, which admit fast probabilistic verification based on local queries to the proof. While the most prominent application of PCPs is to hardness of approximation [26], seminal works of Kilian [34] and Micali [37] showed that PCPs can also be used to obtain computationally-sound verifiable delegation schemes that are asymptotically efficient.

The application of PCPs to delegation singles out particular design objectives, distinct from those which arise from hardness of approximation. The relevant complexity measures for PCPs in the context of delegation are: *query complexity, verifier time,* and *prover time.* The latter two are self-explanatory, since the proof must be produced and validated; the former arises because in existing delegation schemes based on PCPs, communication complexity depends linearly on the query complexity of a PCP. Note that the running time of the prover is not typically considered in the context of PCPs, because one considers only the existence of a valid PCP and not how it is constructed. For delegation schemes, on the other hand, the time required to generate the proof is often a barrier to practical use.

An ideal PCP for delegation would have *constant* query complexity, *(poly)logarithmic* verifier time and *linear* prover time. State-of-the-art PCPs achieve constant query complexity and polylogarithmic verifier time, but only *quasilinear* ($N \log^c N$) prover time [38]. While the prover time is asymptotically close to optimal, c is a fairly large constant, and more generally the construction uses gap amplification techniques that are not believed to be concretely efficient. The value of c turns out to be very significant in practical settings, but improving it has proven to be a serious challenge in PCP constructions.

In light of these apparent barriers, Ben-Sasson et al. [15] have demonstrated how to obtain computationally-sound delegation schemes from a natural generalization of PCPs known as *interactive oracle proofs* (IOPs) [15,40]. An IOP is an interactive protocol consisting of multiple rounds, where in each round the verifier sends a challenge and the prover responds with a PCP oracle to which the verifier can make a small number of queries (generalizing the "interactive PCP" model studied in [33]). The proof length of an IOP is the total length of all oracles sent by the prover, and the query complexity is the total number of queries made to these oracles. The study of IOPs explores the tradeoff between a new efficiency measure, round complexity, and other efficiency measures. Viewed in this way, a PCP is an IOP with optimal round complexity.

A recent line of works has demonstrated that this additional freedom is valuable, proving a number of results for IOPs that we do not know how to obtain via PCPs alone [6–8,10,11,14]. For example, there are constant-round IOPs with linear proof length and constant query complexity for Boolean circuit satisfiability [10], whereas the best linear-size PCPs known have query complexity N^ϵ [18]. Interaction also enables gains in prover time: the FRI protocol [8] is an $O(\log N)$-round IOP of proximity for the Reed–Solomon code where the prover has *linear* arithmetic complexity. In contrast, state-of-the-art PCPs of proximity for this code have quasilinear arithmetic complexity [13,20]. This theoretical progress has led to IOP-based implementations [7,14], which are significantly more efficient than those based on PCPs [6].

The work of [15] justifies why exploiting the tradeoff between round complexity and other efficiency measures is advantageous for constructing computationally-sound verifiable delegation schemes. In particular, if we could obtain IOPs with constant round complexity that otherwise match the parameters of an ideal PCP (constant queries, polylogarithmic verifier, linear prover), then we would obtain delegation schemes that have the same asymptotic efficiency as those derived from an ideal PCP. Thus, for the purposes of verifiable delegation schemes, it suffices to construct such 'ideal' IOPs.

A recent work [14] constructs IOPs for arithmetic circuits with logarithmic query and round complexity where the prover has $O(N \log N)$ (*strictly quasilinear*) arithmetic complexity, and hence bit complexity $\widetilde{O}(N \log N)$. Because the construction emphasizes concrete efficiency over asymptotics, query and round complexity fall somewhat short of the state of the art, but the prover time, while still not linear, is the best among known schemes with subpolynomial query complexity. However, the IOPs in [14] do *not* achieve polylogarithmic verification time: for the language they target even sublinear verification is impossible (without preprocessing) because the size of the input is the same as the size of the computation.

When the arithmetic circuit can be represented succinctly, however, polylogarithmic time verification *is* possible in principle. Unfortunately the protocol of [14] cannot exploit this property, and the verifier would still run in linear time. Our goal is to achieve an *exponential* improvement in this case.

1.1   Our Results

In this work we construct IOPs for algebraic computations that are "almost" ideal, namely, we achieve constant query and round complexity, polylogarithmic time for the verifier, and $O(N \log N)$ (*strictly quasilinear*) arithmetic complexity for the prover. Our new IOP protocols match the state-of-the-art prover time of [14], while at the same time achieving an *exponential improvement* in verification time for a rich class of computations. We focus on arithmetic complexity as the natural notion of prover efficiency for IOPs for algebraic problems; moving to bit complexity incurs an additional poly(log log) factor to account for the cost of field multiplication.

While the arithmetic complexity of our prover is not linear, the *length* of the proof is linear in the computation size, which is optimal. The single logarithmic factor in our prover's arithmetic complexity comes *solely from fast Fourier transforms*. In particular, if there were a linear-time encoding procedure for the Reed–Solomon code, our prover would run in linear time, and thereby achieve optimal prover efficiency without any other changes in the scheme itself.

Small Fields. All of our results are stated over large fields. Computations over small fields (e.g. $\mathbb{F}_2$) can be handled by moving to an extension field, which introduces an additional logarithmic factor in the proof length and prover time (the same is true of [7,14]). Even with this additional logarithmic factor, our construction matches the state of the art for prover complexity for succinct *boolean* circuit satisfiability, while improving the verifier running time to polylogarithmic.

Delegating Bounded-Space Algebraic Computation. Rank-one constraint satisfiability (R1CS) is a natural generalization of arithmetic circuits that is widely used across theoretical and applied constructions of proof systems (see [24]). An R1CS instance is specified by matrices A, B, C over a finite field $\mathbb{F}$, and is satisfied by a vector w if $Aw \circ Bw = Cw$, where $\circ$ is the element-wise (Hadamard) product. Arithmetic circuits reduce in linear-time to R1CS instances.

Many problems of interest, however, involve R1CS instances where the matrices A, B, C have some structure. For example, many applications consider computations that involve checking many Merkle authentication paths — in this case a hash function is invoked many times, within the same path and across different paths. It would be valuable for the verifier to run in time that is related to a *succinct representation* of such instances, rather than to the (much larger) explicit representation that "ignores" the structure. In light of this motivation, we introduce a notion of *succinctly-represented R1CS instances* that capture a rich class of bounded-space algebraic computations. (Later in the paper we refer to these as *algebraic automata*.)

Definition 1 (informal). *A* **succinct R1CS** *instance is specified by matrices* $A = [A_0|A_1], B = [B_0|B_1], C = [C_0|C_1] \in \mathbb{F}^{k \times 2k}$ *over* $\mathbb{F}$, *and a time bound* T, *and is satisfied by a vector* $z \in \mathbb{F}^{kT}$ *if*

$$
\begin{pmatrix} A_0\ A_1 & & & \\ & A_0\ A_1 & & \\ & & \ddots\ \ddots & \\ & & & A_0\ A_1 \end{pmatrix} w \ \circ\ \begin{pmatrix} B_0\ B_1 & & & \\ & B_0\ B_1 & & \\ & & \ddots\ \ddots & \\ & & & B_0\ B_1 \end{pmatrix} w \ =\ \begin{pmatrix} C_0\ C_1 & & & \\ & C_0\ C_1 & & \\ & & \ddots\ \ddots & \\ & & & C_0\ C_1 \end{pmatrix} w
$$

The relation Succinct-R1CS *is the set of pairs* $(\mathbb{x}, w)$ *such that* $\mathbb{x}$ *is an instance of succinct R1CS which is satisfied by* w.

The size of an *instance* is $O(k^2 + \log T)$, but the size of the computation described is kT. Note that Succinct-R1CS is a PSPACE-complete relation, while the (regular) R1CS relation is merely NP-complete.

To obtain some intuition about the definition, consider the problem of repeated application of an arithmetic circuit $\mathcal{C} \colon \mathbb{F}^n \to \mathbb{F}^n$. Suppose that we want to check that there exists z such that $\mathcal{C}^T(z) = 0^n$, where $\mathcal{C}^T = \mathcal{C}(\mathcal{C}(\cdots \mathcal{C}(\cdot)))$ is the circuit which applies $\mathcal{C}$ iteratively T times. The circuit $\mathcal{C}^T$ has size $\Omega(|\mathcal{C}| \cdot T)$, and if the verifier were to "unroll" the circuit then it would pay this cost in time. However, the R1CS instance corresponding to $\mathcal{C}^T$ is of the above form, with $k = O(|\mathcal{C}|)$, where (roughly) the matrices A_0, B_0, C_0 represent the gates of

$\mathcal{C}$ and A_1, B_1, C_1 represent the wires between adjacent copies of $\mathcal{C}$. (The condition that the output of $\mathcal{C}^T$ is zero is encoded separately as a "boundary constraint".)

Our first result gives a constant-round IOP for satisfiability of succinct R1CS where the verifier runs in time $\mathrm{poly}(k, \log T)$, the prover has arithmetic complexity $O(kT \log kT)$, and the proof length is $O(kT \log |\mathbb{F}|)$ (linear in the computation transcript). In the theorem statement below we take $k = O(1)$ for simplicity.

Theorem 1 (informal). *There is a universal constant $\epsilon_0 \in (0, 1)$ such that, for any computation time bound $T(n)$ and large smooth field family $\mathbb{F}(n)$, there is a 4-round IOP for succinct R1CS over $\mathbb{F}(n)$, with proof length $O(T(n) \log |\mathbb{F}(n)|)$, 4 queries, and soundness error ϵ_0. The prover uses $O(T(n) \log T(n))$ field operations and the verifier uses $\mathrm{poly}(n, \log T(n))$ field operations.*

As in prior work (e.g., [20]), "large smooth field" refers to a field of size $\Omega(N)$, whose additive or multiplicative group has a nice decomposition. For example, ensembles of large enough binary fields have this property, as well as prime fields with smooth multiplicative groups.

Delegating Unbounded-Space Algebraic Computation. While algebraic automata capture a useful class of computations, they are restricted to space-bounded computation (recall Succinct-R1CS $\in$ PSPACE). In particular, using Theorem 1 we can obtain useful delegation protocols for computations whose space usage is much smaller than their running time.

To handle computations which use more space, we introduce the *algebraic machine* relation. This is a natural algebraic analogue of the bounded accepting problem for nondeterminstic random-access machines, where the transition function is an arithmetic (rather than Boolean) circuit. It is NEXP-complete via a linear time reduction from succinct arithmetic circuit satisfiability.

Theorem 2 (informal). *There is a universal constant $\epsilon_0 \in (0, 1)$ such that, for any computation time bound $T(n)$ and large smooth field $\mathbb{F}(n)$, there is a 5-round IOP for the satisfiability problem of $T(n)$-time algebraic machines over $\mathbb{F}(n)$, with proof length $O(T(n) \log |\mathbb{F}(n)|)$, 5 queries, and soundness error ϵ_0. The prover uses $O(T(n) \log T(n))$ field operations and the verifier uses $\mathrm{poly}(n, \log T(n))$ field operations.*

For simplicity, as with Theorem 1 we have stated Theorem 2 for machines whose description is a constant number of field elements, or $\Theta(\log |\mathbb{F}|)$ bits. The proof length is *linear* in the size of the computation trace, which is $N := \Theta(T \log |\mathbb{F}|)$ bits. We stress that the number of queries is 5, *regardless* of the choice of machine.

The above theorem is obtained by bootstrapping Theorem 1. Namely we show that leveraging interaction, we can design an automaton which checks whether a pair of automata have satisfying assignments which are permutations of one another; for more details see Sect. 2.4.

On the Power of Machines. In the linear-length regime, the choice of computational model supported by a proof protocol is important, because reductions between problems typically introduce logarithmic factors. For example, it is not known how to reduce a random-access machine, or even a Turing machine, to a circuit of linear size. Indeed, the sublinear-query PCP of [18] achieves linear proof size for circuits but not machine computations. We thus view Theorem 2 as particularly appealing, because it achieves linear length for a powerful model of computation, algebraic machines, which facilitates linear-size reductions from many other problems; notably, succinct arithmetic circuit satisfiability. We view the identification of a model which is both highly expressive and amenable to efficient probabilistic checking using IOPs as a contribution of this work.

1.2 Relation to Prior Work

There are relatively few works which explicitly deal with prover complexity for PCP and IOP constructions. We present a comparison of the relevant parameters for each construction in Table 1. Since we are concerned with logarithmic factors, it is not sufficient to specify only a complexity class (NP or NEXP) for each one. Instead, for each proof system we give a canonical expressive language for which the given parameters are achieved. In particular, the first three proof systems are for boolean circuit problems, and the latter three are for arithmetic circuit problems. For purposes of comparison, all of the parameters for both boolean and arithmetic constructions are presented in terms of bit complexity.

Table 1. Comparison of PCP/IOP constructions for circuit satisfiability problems for a (fixed) constant soundness. Here N is the size of the circuit *in bits*, which means that for ASAT and Succinct-ASAT, N implicitly includes a factor of $\log |\mathbb{F}|$. For succinct problems, the circuit size N is exponential in the size of its description.

	Rounds	Circuit type	Prover time	Verifier time	Proof length	Queries
[38]	1	Succinct boolean	$N \operatorname{polylog}(N)^*$	$\operatorname{polylog}(N)$	$N \operatorname{polylog}(N)$	$O(1)$
[18]	1	Boolean	$\operatorname{poly}(N)^\dagger$	$\operatorname{poly}(N)^\dagger$	$O_\epsilon(N)$	N^ϵ
[10]	3	Boolean	$\operatorname{poly}(N)$	$\operatorname{poly}(N)$	$O(N)$	$O(1)$
[7]	$O(\log N)$	Succinct arithmetic$^\Diamond$	$\widetilde{O}(N \log^2 N)^\ddagger$	$\operatorname{polylog}(N)$	$O(N \log N)$	$O(\log N)$
[14]	$O(\log N)$	Arithmetic$^\Diamond$	$\widetilde{O}(N \log N)^\ddagger$	$\operatorname{poly}(N)$	$O(N)$	$O(\log N)$
This work	5	Succinct arithmetic$^\Diamond$	$\widetilde{O}(N \log N)^\ddagger$	$\operatorname{polylog}(N)$	$O(N)$	5

$*$: [38] shows a $\operatorname{poly}(N)$ bound; this tighter bound is due to [13].
$\Diamond$: The size of the underlying field must grow as $\Omega(N)$ to achieve the stated efficiency. Problems over smaller fields (e.g. boolean circuits) incur a multiplicative cost of $\log N$ in prover time and proof length.
$\dagger$: The specified time is for *non-uniform* computation (each input size receives $\operatorname{poly}(N)$ advice bits).
$\ddagger$: The notation $\widetilde{O}$ hides $\operatorname{poly}(\log \log N)$ factors, which arise because here we consider the *bit complexity* of the prover (rather than the arithmetic complexity).

From a technical perspective, prover running time is tightly connected to proof length, which is more well-studied. In all constructions, the proof length is a lower bound on the prover running time. Moreover, in the most prover-efficient constructions [7,14], the dominant cost for the prover is in computing Reed–Solomon encodings, which means that for proof length ℓ the arithmetic complexity of the prover is $O(\ell \log \ell)$. Finally, since proof length is an information-theoretic property of the system, it is also usually easier to analyse. We proceed by discussing the state of the art for PCPs and IOPs with *linear* (optimal) proof length, since this is what our construction achieves.

There are two natural approaches that one could follow to simultaneously achieve linear proof length and constant query complexity: (1) start from a construction with constant query complexity and reduce proof length; or (2) start from a construction with linear proof length and reduce query complexity. We summarize prior works that have followed these approaches, and highlight the limitations that arise in each case.

Approach (1). The first approach has been studied extensively [5,17,21,27, 31,39], leading to PCPs for NEXP with proof length N polylog(N) and query complexity $O(1)$ [16,20,25,38]. Later works have reduced the logarithmic factors in the proof length [12,13], but attempts to achieve linear length have failed. Recent work has obtained IOPs with proof length $O(N \log N)$ but at the cost of increasing query complexity from $O(1)$ to $O(\log N)$ [6,7].

Approach (2). The second approach has received much less attention. Insisting on linear proof length significantly restricts the available techniques because many tools introduce logarithmic factors in proof length. For example, one cannot rely on arithmetization via multivariate polynomials and standard low-degree tests, nor rely on algebraic embeddings via de Bruijn graphs for routing; in addition, query-reduction techniques for interactive PCPs [33] do not apply to the linear proof length regime. The state-of-the-art in linear-length PCPs is due to [18], and the construction is based on a non-uniform family of algebraic geometry (AG) codes (every input size needs a polynomial-size advice string). In more detail, [18] proves that for every $\epsilon \in (0, 1)$ there is a (non-uniform) PCP for the NP-complete problem CSAT (Boolean circuit satisfiability) with proof length $2^{O(1/\epsilon)} N$ and query complexity N^ϵ, much more than our goal of $O(1)$.

By leveraging interaction, [10] obtains IOPs for CSAT with proof length $O(N)$ and query complexity $O(1)$. This is a natural starting point for our goal of achieving polylogarithmic-time verification, because we are "only" left to extend this result from CSAT to its succinct analogue, Succinct-CSAT. Unfortunately, the construction in [10] uses AG codes and such an extension would, in particular, require obtaining a succinct representation of a dense asymptotically good family of AG codes over a small field, which is out of reach of current techniques. More generally, we do not know of any suitable code over small fields, which currently seems to prevent us from obtaining linear-size IOPs for Succinct-CSAT. Moreover, obtaining an efficient prover would require efficient encoding and decoding procedures for AG codes.

We now consider arithmetic circuit satisfiability (ASAT) defined over fields $\mathbb{F}$ that are large (of size $\Omega(N)$). In this regime, [14] obtains IOPs for ASAT with proof length $O(N)$ and query complexity $O(\log N)$. The arithmetization, following [20], is based on the Reed–Solomon code and uses the algebraic structure of large smooth fields. Testing is done via FRI [8], a recent IOP of proximity for the Reed–Solomon code with linear proof length and logarithmic query complexity. The construction in [14], which we will build upon, falls short of our goal on two fronts: verification is linear in the size of the circuit rather than polylogarithmic, and query complexity is logarithmic rather than constant.

1.3 Open Questions

We highlight four problems left open by our work.

Optimal Arithmetic Complexity. The prover in our construction has strictly quasilinear arithmetic complexity and produces a proof of linear size. A natural question is whether the arithmetic complexity of the prover can be reduced to linear. To do so with our construction would require a breakthrough in encoding algorithms for the Reed–Solomon code. A promising direction is to build IOPs based on codes with linear-time encoding procedures [23,30,42].

All Fields. The question of whether it is possible to simultaneously achieve linear-length proofs and polylogarithmic-time verifier for Succinct-ASAT over *any* field $\mathbb{F}$ remains open. Progress on this question motivates the search for arithmetization-friendly families of good codes beyond the Reed–Solomon code. For example, the case of $\mathbb{F} = \mathbb{F}_2$, which corresponds to boolean circuits, motivates the search for succinctly-represented families of good algebraic-geometry codes over constant-size fields with fast encoding algorithms.

Zero Knowledge. Zero knowledge, while not a goal of this work, is a desirable property, because zero knowledge PCP/IOPs lead to zero knowledge succinct arguments [15,32]. Straightforward modifications to the protocol, similar to [14], achieve a notion of zero knowledge wherein the simulator runs in time polynomial in the size of the computation being checked, which is meaningful for nondeterministic problems since it does not have access to the witness.

There is a stronger notion of zero knowledge for succinct languages where the simulator runs in *polylogarithmic* time, which is exponentially more efficient. This gap was precisely the subject of a work on designing succinct simulators for certain tests [9]. Whether succinct simulators can be designed for low-degree tests that we could use for our protocol remains an intriguing problem that we leave to future research.

Round Complexity. Our protocol has 5 rounds. Round complexity can be reduced to 4 at the cost of increased (constant) query complexity. Reducing round complexity beyond this while preserving linear proof length and polylogarithmic time verification, or finding evidence against this possibility, remains open.

2   Technical Overview

We discuss the main ideas behind our results. Our goal is to construct an IOP for algebraic machines, over a large field $\mathbb{F}$, with prover arithmetic complexity which is *strictly quasilinear* in the size of the computation (i.e. $O(N \log N)$); and crucially, the running time of the verifier is *polylogarithmic* in the size of the computation (more precisely, polynomial in the machine description). Additionally, we strive to optimize the query and round complexity of this IOP. We stress that no prior work achieves non-trivial strictly quasilinear prover PCPs or IOPs wherein the verifier runs in polylogarithmic time in the size of the computation.

Following [7,14], our construction relies heavily on the Reed–Solomon code, and the dominant cost for the prover is in the encoding procedure. Thus to achieve strictly quasilinear arithmetic complexity in our construction, we *must* achieve a linear proof length. Thus from this point on, discussion will focus primarily on proof length.

The rest of this section is organized as follows. In Sect. 2.1 we discuss our starting point, which is a construction of [14]. In Sect. 2.2 we discuss our approach to overcoming the limitations of prior work by describing a new protocol for checking succinctly-represented linear relations; this achieves an *exponential* improvement over the prior state of the art. In Sect. 2.3 we discuss how to overcome the challenges that arise when attempting to build on this exponential improvement to checking the computation of algebraic automata. In Sect. 2.4, we discuss how to extend these techniques to algebraic machines (which capture succinct arithmetic circuit satisfiability). In Sect. 2.5 we describe a modular framework, which we call *oracle reductions*, in which we prove our results.

2.1   Our Starting Point

The starting point of our work is [14], which obtains IOPs for R1CS with proof length $O(N)$ and query complexity $O(\log N)$, and in which the prover uses $O(N \log N)$ field operations and the verifier uses $O(N)$. Recall that the R1CS problem is as follows: given matrices A, B, C over a finite field $\mathbb{F}$, the problem asks whether there exists a witness vector w, where some entries are fixed to known values, for which the following *R1CS equation* holds: $(Aw) \circ (Bw) = Cw$, where "$\circ$" denotes entry-wise product.

Our initial goal in this paper is to achieve an IOP for satisfiability of algebraic automata. This entails an *exponential* improvement in the running time of the verifier, from linear in the circuit size to polylogarithmic in the circuit size. Moreover, we need to achieve this improvement with proof length $O(N)$ and query complexity $O(1)$ (and a prover that uses $O(N \log N)$ field operations).

The ideas behind our results are better understood if we first briefly recall the IOP of [14]. The prover sends to the verifier four oracles $\pi_w, \pi_A, \pi_B, \pi_C$ that are purported encodings of w, Aw, Bw, Cw. The verifier must now check two subproblems: (a) π_w encodes w then π_A, π_B, π_C respectively encode Aw, Bw, Cw; and (b) if π_A, π_B, π_C encode w_A, w_B, w_C then $w_A \circ w_B = w_C$.

As usual, there is a tension in selecting the encoding used to obtain the oracles $\pi_w, \pi_A, \pi_B, \pi_C$. One needs an encoding that allows for non-trivial checking protocols, e.g., where the verifier makes a small number of queries. On the other hand, the encoding must have constant rate so that proof length can be linear.

The encoding used relies on univariate polynomials: denote by $\mathrm{RS}\,[L, \rho] \subseteq \mathbb{F}^L$ the Reed-Solomon code over a subset L of a field $\mathbb{F}$ with rate parameter $\rho \in (0, 1]$ (that is, the set of all functions $f \colon L \to \mathbb{F}$ of degree less than $\rho|L|$). Also, denote by $\hat{f}$ the unique univariate polynomial of degree less than $\rho|L|$ whose evaluation on L equals f. Given a subset $H \subseteq \mathbb{F}$ (the *domain* of the encoding), a Reed–Solomon codeword f *encodes* $x \in \mathbb{F}^H$ if $\hat{f}(a) = x_a$ for all $a \in H$; for each x, there is a unique encoding f_x of x of minimal rate. We can now restate the aforementioned sub-problems in terms of the Reed–Solomon code.

- **Lincheck:** given a subset $H \subseteq \mathbb{F}$, Reed–Solomon codewords $f, g \in \mathrm{RS}\,[L, \rho]$ that encode $x, y \in \mathbb{F}^H$ respectively, and a matrix $M \in \mathbb{F}^{H \times H}$, check that $x = My$.
- **Rowcheck:** given a subset $H \subseteq \mathbb{F}$ and Reed–Solomon codewords $f, g, h \in \mathrm{RS}\,[L, \rho]$ that encode $x, y, z \in \mathbb{F}^H$ respectively, check that $x \circ y = z$.

The IOP in [14] is obtained by combining sub-protocols for these sub-problems, a *lincheck protocol* and a *rowcheck protocol*. The latter is a simple reduction from the rowcheck problem to testing membership in the Reed–Solomon code, and is implied by standard PCP tools. The former, however, is a novel (and non-trivial) reduction from the lincheck problem to testing membership in the Reed–Solomon code.

While on the one hand the verifier in the rowcheck protocol runs in time that is polylogarithmic in $|H|$ (which is good) the verifier in the lincheck protocol runs in time that is linear in $|H|$ (which is much too slow). In other words, if we simply invoked the IOP in [14] on the circuit described by a succinct R1CS instance, the verifier would run in time that is linear in T, which is exponentially worse than our goal of $\mathrm{polylog}(T)$. This state of affairs in the starting point of our work.

Next, in Sect. 2.2, we discuss how to obtain a succinct lincheck protocol that, for suitable linear relations, is exponentially more efficient. After that, in Sect. 2.3, we discuss the notion of algebraic automata in detail and describe how the succinct lincheck protocol enables efficient probabilistic checking of algebraic automata. Finally in Sect. 2.4 we describe how we can bootstrap our protocol for algebraic automata to check the more powerful algebraic machine model.

Throughout, we present our contributions as *oracle reductions* from some computational task to testing membership in the Reed–Solomon code. Loosely speaking, these are reductions in the setting of the IOP model (and therefore, in particular, allow interaction in which the prover sends PCP oracles). This abstraction allows us to decouple IOP protocol-design from the low-degree test that we invoke at the end of the protocol. See Sect. 2.5 for details.

2.2 Checking Succinctly-Represented Linear Relations

Following the above discussion, we now temporarily restrict our attention to devising a lincheck protocol, which reduces checking linear relations defined by matrices $M \in \mathbb{F}^{H \times H}$ to testing membership in the Reed–Solomon code, in which the verifier runs in time that is *polylogarithmic* in $|H|$. This is not possible in general, however, because the verifier needs to at least *read the description* of the matrix M. We shall have to consider matrices M that have a special structure that can be exploited to obtain an exponential improvement in verifier time. This improvement is a core technical contribution of this paper, and we refer to the resulting reduction as the *succinct lincheck protocol*. We start by describing the ideas behind the (non-succinct) lincheck protocol of [14].

Definition 2 (informal). *In the lincheck problem, we are given a subset $H \subseteq \mathbb{F}$, Reed–Solomon codewords $f, g \in \mathrm{RS}\,[L, \rho]$ encoding vectors $x, y \in \mathbb{F}^H$, and a matrix $M \in \mathbb{F}^{H \times H}$. The goal is to check that $x = My$.*

A simple probabilistic test for the claim "$x = My$" is to check that $\langle r, x - My \rangle = 0$ for a random $r \in \mathbb{F}^H$. Indeed, if $x \neq My$, then $\Pr_{r \in \mathbb{F}^H}[\langle r, x - My \rangle = 0] = 1/|\mathbb{F}|$. However, this approach would require the verifier to sample, and send to the prover, $|H|$ random field elements (too many).

A natural derandomization is to choose r using a small-bias generator over $\mathbb{F}$, rather than uniformly at random. A small-bias generator G over $\mathbb{F}$ is a function with the property that for any nonzero $z \in \mathbb{F}^H$, it holds with high probability over $\rho \in \{0,1\}^\ell$ that $\langle z, G(\rho) \rangle \neq 0$. Now the verifier needs to send only ℓ bits to the prover, which can be much smaller than $|H| \log |\mathbb{F}|$.

A natural choice (used also, e.g., in [5, §5.2]) is the powering construction of [1], which requires sending a *single* random field element ($\ell = \log |\mathbb{F}|$), and incurs only a modest increase in soundness error. In this construction, we define a vector $r(X) \in \mathbb{F}[X]^H$ of linearly independent polynomials in X, given by $(1, X, X^2, \ldots, X^{|H|-1})$. The small-bias generator is then $G(\alpha) := r(\alpha)$ for $\alpha \in \mathbb{F}$. If z is nonzero then $h(X) := \langle r(X), z \rangle$ is a nonzero polynomial and so $\Pr_{\alpha \in \mathbb{F}}[\langle G(\alpha), z \rangle = 0] \leq \deg(h)/|\mathbb{F}|$. The verifier now merely has to sample and send $\alpha \in \mathbb{F}$, and the prover must then prove the claim "$h(\alpha) = 0$" to the verifier. Rearranging, this is the same as testing that $\langle r(\alpha), x \rangle - \langle r(\alpha)M, y \rangle = 0$. The problem is thus reduced to checking inner products of known vectors with oracles.

In the setting of Reed–Solomon codewords, if f_u is an encoding of u and f_v is an encoding of v, then $f_u \cdot f_v$ is an encoding of $u \circ v$, the pointwise product of u and v. Hence, to check that $\langle u, v \rangle = c$, it suffices to check that the low-degree polynomial $f_u \cdot f_v$ sums to c on H, since $\langle u, v \rangle = \sum_{h \in H} f_u(h) f_v(h)$. This can be achieved by running the *univariate sumcheck protocol* ([14]) on the codeword $f_u \cdot f_v$. This protocol requires the verifier to efficiently determine the value of $f_u \cdot f_v$ at a given point in L.

The Inefficiency. The foregoing discussion tells us that, to solve the lincheck problem, the verifier must determine the value of the Reed–Solomon encodings of $r(\alpha) \circ x$ and $r(\alpha)M \circ y$ at a given point in L. The encodings of the vectors x and y are provided (as f and g). Hence it suffices for the verifier to evaluate *low-degree extensions* of $r(\alpha)$ and $r(\alpha)M$ at a given point, and then perform a field multiplication.

This last step is the computational bottleneck of the protocol. In [14], the verifier evaluates the low-degree extensions of $r(\alpha)$ and $M^\top r(\alpha)$ via Lagrange interpolation, which requires time $\Omega(|H|)$. To make our verifier efficient, we must evaluate both low-degree extensions in time $\mathrm{polylog}(|H|)$. In particular, this requires that M be succinctly represented, since computing the low-degree extension of $r(\alpha)M$ in general requires time linear in the number of nonzero entries in M, which is at least $|H|$.

The lincheck protocol in [14] chooses the linearly independent polynomials $r(X)$ to be the *standard* (or *coefficient*) basis $(1, X, \ldots, X^{|H|-1})$. For this basis, however, we do not know how to efficiently evaluate the low-degree extension of $r(\alpha)$. This problem must be addressed *regardless* of the matrix M.

A New Basis and Succinct Matrices. We leverage certain algebraic properties to overcome the above problem. There is another natural choice of basis for polynomials, the *Lagrange basis* $(L_{H,h}(X))_{h \in H}$, where $L_{H,h}$ is the unique polynomial of degree less than $|H|$ with $L_{H,h}(h) = 1$ and $L_{H,\alpha}(\gamma) = 0$ for all $\gamma \in H \backslash \{h\}$. We observe that the low-degree extension of $r(\alpha) = (L_{H,h}(\alpha))_{h \in H} \in \mathbb{F}^H$ has a simple form that allows one to evaluate it in time polylog$(|H|)$ provided that H is an additive or multiplicative subgroup of $\mathbb{F}$. In other words, the Lagrange basis yields a small-bias generator over $\mathbb{F}$ whose low-degree extension can be computed efficiently.

It remains to find a useful class of succinctly-represented matrices M for which one can efficiently evaluate a low-degree extension of $r(\alpha)M \in \mathbb{F}^H$. The foregoing discussion suggests a natural condition: *if* we can efficiently compute a low-degree extension of a vector $v \in \mathbb{F}^H$ *then* we should also be able to efficiently compute a low-degree extension of the vector vM. If this holds for all vectors v, we say that the matrix M is (algebraically) *succinct*. For example, the identity matrix satisfies this definition (trivially), and so does the matrix with 1s on the superdiagonal for appropriate choices of $\mathbb{F}$ and H.

In sum, if we choose the Lagrange basis in the lincheck protocol and the linear relation is specified by a succinct matrix, then, with some work, we obtain a lincheck protocol where the verifier runs in time polylog$(|H|)$. To check satisfiability of succinctly-represented arithmetic circuits, however, we need to handle a more general class of matrices, described next.

Succinct Lincheck for Semisuccinct Matrices. We will relax the condition on a matrix M in a way that captures the matrices that arise when checking succinctly-described arithmetic circuits, while still allowing us to obtain a lincheck protocol in which the verifier runs in time polylog$(|H|)$.

We show that the matrices that we consider are *semisuccinct*, namely, they can be decomposed into a "large" part that is succinct and a "small" part that has no special structure.[1] This structure should appear familiar, because it is analogous to how a succinctly-described circuit consists of a small arbitrary component (the circuit descriptor) that is repeatedly used in a structured way to define the large circuit. Another analogy is how in an automaton or machine computation a small, and arbitrary, transition function is repeatedly applied across a large computation.

---

[1] We actually need to handle matrices that are the *sum* of semisuccinct matrices, but we ignore this in this high-level discussion.

Specifically, by "decompose" we mean that the matrix $M \in \mathbb{F}^{H \times H}$ can be written as the *Kronecker product* of a succinct matrix $A \in \mathbb{F}^{H_1 \times H_1}$ and a small matrix $B \in \mathbb{F}^{H_2 \times H_2}$; we write $M = A \otimes B$. (Succinctly representing a large operator like M via the tensor product of simpler operators should be a natural idea to readers familiar with quantum information.) In order for the product to be well-defined, we must supply a bijection $\Phi \colon H \to H_1 \times H_2$. If this bijection satisfies certain algebraic properties, which preserve the succinctness of the matrix A, we call it a *bivariate embedding*.

We obtain a succinct lincheck protocol for semisuccinct matrices.

Lemma 1 (informal). *There is a linear-length reduction from the lincheck problem for semisuccinct linear relations to testing membership in the Reed–Solomon code, where the verifier runs in polylogarithmic time.*

Next, we discuss how to obtain a reduction from algebraic automata (succinct R1CS) to testing membership in the Reed–Solomon code, where the verifier runs in time that is *polylogarithmic* in the circuit size, by building on our succinct lincheck protocol for semisuccinct matrices.

2.3   Checking Bounded-Space Computations in Polylogarithmic Time

An instance of the *algebraic automaton* relation is specified by three $k \times 2k$ matrices (A, B, C) over $\mathbb{F}$, and a time bound T. A witness $f \colon [T] \to \mathbb{F}^k$ is valid if

$$\forall t \in [T-1] \quad Af(t, t+1) \circ Bf(t, t+1) = Cf(t, t+1), \tag{1}$$

where $f(t, t+1) := f(t) \| f(t+1)$ is the concatenation of the consecutive states $f(t) \in \mathbb{F}^k$ and $f(t+1) \in \mathbb{F}^k$.

We use the term "algebraic automata" since one can think of A, B, C as specifying the transition relation of a computational device with k algebraic registers, and f as an *execution trace* specifying an accepting computation of the device. The relation is PSPACE-complete: it is in NPSPACE because it can be checked by a polynomial-space Turing machine with one-directional access to an exponential-size witness, and recall that NPSPACE = PSPACE; also, it is PSPACE-hard because given an arithmetic circuit specifying the transition relation of a polynomial-space machine, we can find an equisatisfiable R1CS instance in linear time.

If we view the execution trace f as a vector $f = f(1) \| \cdots \| f(T) \in \mathbb{F}^{Tk}$, then we can rewrite the condition in Eq. (1) via the following (possibly exponentially large) R1CS equation:

$$\begin{pmatrix} A_0 \ A_1 & & & \\ & A_0 \ A_1 & & \\ & & \ddots \ \ddots & \\ & & & A_0 \ A_1 \end{pmatrix} f \ \circ \ \begin{pmatrix} B_0 \ B_1 & & & \\ & B_0 \ B_1 & & \\ & & \ddots \ \ddots & \\ & & & B_0 \ B_1 \end{pmatrix} f \ = \ \begin{pmatrix} C_0 \ C_1 & & & \\ & C_0 \ C_1 & & \\ & & \ddots \ \ddots & \\ & & & C_0 \ C_1 \end{pmatrix} f$$

where $A_0, A_1 \in \mathbb{F}^{k \times k}$ are the first half and second half of A respectively; and likewise for B and C. We thus see that algebraic automata are equivalent to Succinct-R1CS.

The matrices in the above R1CS equation have a rigid block structure that we refer to as a *staircase*. Given the discussions in Sects. 2.1 and 2.2, in order to achieve polylogarithmic verification time, *it suffices to show that staircase matrices are semisuccinct* (or, at least, the sum of few semisuccinct matrices).

So let $S(M_0, M_1)$ be the staircase matrix of two given $k \times k$ matrices M_0, M_1 over $\mathbb{F}$. Namely, $S(M_0, M_1)$ is the $Tk \times Tk$ matrix with M_0-blocks on the diagonal and M_1-blocks on the superdiagonal. Observe that:

1. we can write the matrix with M_0-blocks on the diagonal as $I \otimes M_0$, where I is the $T \times T$ identity matrix;
2. we can write the matrix with M_1-blocks on the superdiagonal as $I^{\rightarrow} \otimes M_1$, where $I^{\rightarrow}$ is the $T \times T$ matrix with 1s on the superdiagonal.

Under an appropriate mapping from $[Tk]$ into a subset of $\mathbb{F}$, we prove that both of these matrices are semisuccinct. This tells us that $S(M_0, M_1)$ is the sum of two semisuccinct matrices:

$$S(M_0, M_1) := \begin{pmatrix} M_0 & M_1 & & & \\ & M_0 & M_1 & & \\ & & \ddots & \ddots & \\ & & & M_0 & M_1 \\ & & & & M_0 \end{pmatrix} = I \otimes M_0 + I^{\rightarrow} \otimes M_1 \in \mathbb{F}^{Tk} \times \mathbb{F}^{Tk}.$$

(Note that the above is not exactly the matrix structure we want, because of the extra M_0 block; we handle this technicality separately.) We obtain the following lemma.

Lemma 2 (informal). *There is a linear-length reduction from the algebraic automaton relation to testing membership in the Reed–Solomon code, where the verifier runs in time* poly$(k, \log T)$.

2.4   Checking Machine Computations in Polylogarithmic Time

An instance of the *algebraic (R1CS) machine* relation is specified by two algebraic (R1CS) automata $(\mathcal{A}, \mathcal{A}')$. A witness (f, π), where $f \colon [T] \to \mathbb{F}^k$ is an execution trace and $\pi \colon [T] \to [T]$ is a permutation, is valid if: (1) f is a valid witness for the automaton $\mathcal{A}$, and (2) $f \circ \pi$ is a valid witness for the automaton $\mathcal{A}'$. The algebraic machine relation is NEXP-complete, as the NEXP-complete problem of succinct arithmetic circuit satisfiability reduces to it in linear time.

Execution Traces for Machines. Before we discuss how we reduce from the algebraic machine relation, we briefly explain why the above relation is a natural problem to consider, and in particular why it has anything to do with (random-access) machines. Recall that a random-access machine is specified by a list of instructions, each of which is an arithmetic operation, a control-flow operation, or a read/write to memory. One way to represent the execution trace for the machine is to record the state of the entire memory at each time step; for a time-T space-S computation, such an execution trace has size $\Theta(TS)$ (much more than linear!). Yet, the machine can access only a *single* memory location at each time step. Thus, instead of writing down the state of the entire memory at each time step, we could hope to only write the state of the accessed address — this would reduce the size of the trace to $\Theta(T \log S)$. The problem then is that it is no longer possible to check consistency of memory via local constraints because the same address can be accessed at any time.

Classical techniques of Gurevich and Shelah [29] tell us that one can efficiently represent an execution trace for a machine via *two* execution traces that are *permutations of one another*. Informally, sorting the execution trace by time enables us to check the transition relation of the machine; and sorting the execution trace by the accessed addressed (and then by time) enables us to locally check that memory is consistent. (One must ensure that, for each location, if we write some value to memory and then read the same address, we retrieve that same value.) The transition relation and memory consistency can each be expressed individually as automata. This view of machines immediately gives rise to the algebraic machine relation above.

Checking the Algebraic Machine Relation. We have discussed how to check automata in Sect. 2.3, so it remains to check that the traces are permutations of one another. Historically this has been achieved in the PCP literature using algebraic embeddings of routing networks; e.g., see [12]. The problem is that this increases the size of the representation of the execution trace by at least a logarithmic factor. We instead use an interactive permutation test from the program checking literature [22,36]. The test is based on the observation that $u \in \mathbb{F}^T$ is a permutation of $v \in \mathbb{F}^T$ if and only if the multi-sets given by their elements are equal, which is true if and only if the polynomials $p_u(X) = \prod_{i=1}^T (X - u_i)$ and $p_v(X) = \prod_{i=1}^T (X - v_i)$ are equal. Thus it suffices to evaluate each polynomial at a random point and check equality.

These polynomials require time $\Theta(T)$ to evaluate, which in our setting is exponential. Therefore the prover must assist the verifier with the evaluation. We show that evaluating this polynomial can be expressed as an algebraic automaton, and can therefore be checked again using the protocol from Sect. 2.3.

The reader may believe that by now we have reduced checking an algebraic machine to checking three instances of algebraic automata. Recall, however, that the algebraic automaton relation is PSPACE-complete, whereas the algebraic machine relation is NEXP-complete. What happened? The answer lies in the randomness used in the permutation automaton. In order to check that u is a permutation of v, the prover must first commit to u and v before the verifier chooses his evaluation point α, and then the prover sends the trace of the automaton that evaluates $p_u(\alpha), p_v(\alpha)$. This trace depends on the choice of α, and so we use interaction. This is captured by the *interactive automaton relation*, which is NEXP-complete; it can be checked in essentially the same way as the automaton relation.

We hence obtain the following lemma.

Lemma 3 (informal). *There is a linear-length reduction from the algebraic machine relation to testing membership in the Reed–Solomon code, where the verifier runs in time* $\text{poly}(k, \log T)$.

2.5   Oracle Reductions

Many results in this paper describe IOPs that reduce a computational problem to membership in (a subcode of) the Reed–Solomon code. We find it useful to capture this class of reductions via a precise definition. This lets us prove general lemmas about such reductions, and obtain our protocols in a modular fashion.

We thus formulate a new notion that we call *interactive oracle reductions* (in short, *oracle reductions*). Informally, an oracle reduction is a protocol that reduces from a computational problem to testing membership in a code (in this paper, the code is the interleaved Reed–Solomon code). This is a well-understood idea in constructions of PCPs and IOPs. Our contribution is to provide a formal framework for this technique.

We illustrate the notion of oracle reductions via an example. Consider the problem of testing proximity to the *vanishing Reed–Solomon code*, which plays an important role in a PCP of Ben-Sasson and Sudan [20] and several other PCPs/IOPs. Informally, the goal is to test whether a univariate polynomial f, provided as an oracle, is zero everywhere on a subset H of $\mathbb{F}$.

We describe an oracle reduction that maps the foregoing problem to the problem of testing membership in the Reed–Solomon code of the related polynomial $g := f / \mathbb{Z}_H$. Observe that f is divisible by $\mathbb{Z}_H$ if and only if f is zero everywhere in H, and so g is in the Reed–Solomon code if and only if f satisfies the desired property. But what exactly *is* g? In the oracle reduction framework, we refer to g as a *virtual oracle*: an oracle whose value at any given point in its domain can be determined efficiently by making a small number of queries to concrete oracles. In this case, so long as the domain L we choose for g does not intersect H, a verifier can evaluate g at any point $\alpha \in L$ with only a single query to f. To test that g is low degree, the verifier can invoke any low-degree test on g, and simulate queries to the virtual oracle g via queries to f.

The two main parameters in an oracle reduction are the *proof length*, which is simply the total length of the oracles sent by the prover, and the *locality*, which is the number of queries one would have to make to the concrete oracles to answer a single query to any virtual oracle (in this paper, locality always equals the number of rounds). Using the perspective of oracle reductions, our main theorems (Theorems 1 and 2) follow by combining two main sub-components: (1) a linear-length 3-local oracle reduction from the algebraic automata or machine problem to proximity testing to the Reed–Solomon code (discussed in Sects. 2.3 and 2.4); and (2) a linear-length strictly quasilinear prover 3-query IOP for testing proximity to the Reed–Solomon code from [10].

3   Roadmap

Figure 1 below provides a diagram of the results proved in this paper. The remaining sections in this paper are organized as follows. In Sect. 4 we recall useful notions and definitions. In Sect. 5 we define oracle reductions, and prove how to create IOP protocols from RS oracle reductions and RS proximity tests. In the full version, we define and construct trace embeddings, describe our succinct lincheck protocol, describe an oracle reduction from R1CS automata to testing proximity to the Reed–Solomon code, describe an oracle reduction from R1CS machines to testing proximity to the Reed–Solomon codem, and finally prove Theorems 1 and 2.

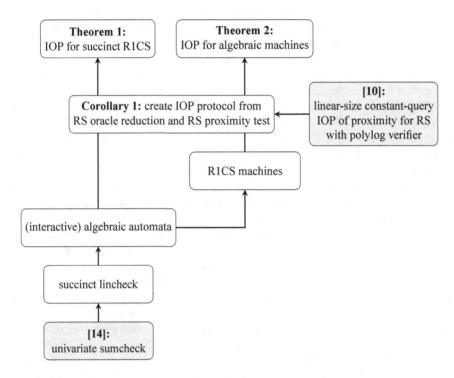

Fig. 1. Diagram of the results in this paper.

4   Preliminaries

Given a relation $\mathcal{R} \subseteq S \times T$, we denote by $\mathcal{L}(\mathcal{R}) \subseteq S$ the set of $s \in S$ such that there exists $t \in T$ with $(s, t) \in \mathcal{R}$; for $s \in S$, we denote by $\mathcal{R}|_s \subseteq T$ the set $\{t \in T : (s, t) \in \mathcal{R}\}$. Given a set S and strings $v, w \in S^n$ for some $n \in \mathbb{N}$, the *fractional Hamming distance* $\Delta(v, w) \in [0, 1]$ is $\Delta(v, w) := \frac{1}{n}|\{i : v_i \neq w_i\}|$. We denote the concatenation of two vectors u_1, u_2 by $u_1 \| u_2$, and the concatenation of two matrices A, B by $[A|B]$. All fields $\mathbb{F}$ in this paper are finite, and we denote the finite field of size q by $\mathbb{F}_q$. We say that H is a *subgroup* in $\mathbb{F}$ if it is either a subgroup of $(\mathbb{F}, +)$ (an additive subgroup) or of $(\mathbb{F} \setminus \{0\}, \times)$ (a multiplicative subgroup); we say that H is a *coset* in $\mathbb{F}$ if it is a coset of a subgroup in $\mathbb{F}$ (possibly the subgroup itself).

4.1 Codes and Polynomials

The Reed–Solomon Code. Given a subset S of a field $\mathbb{F}$ and *rate* $\rho \in (0, 1]$, we denote by $\mathrm{RS}\,[S, \rho] \subseteq \mathbb{F}^S$ all evaluations over S of univariate polynomials of degree less than $\rho|S|$. Namely, a word $c \in \mathbb{F}^S$ is in $\mathrm{RS}\,[S, \rho]$ if there is a polynomial of degree less than $\rho|S|$ that, for every $a \in S$, evaluates to c_a at a. We denote by $\mathrm{RS}\,[S, (\rho_1, \dots, \rho_n)] := \prod_{i=1}^n \mathrm{RS}\,[S, \rho_i]$ the interleaving of Reed–Solomon codes with rates $\rho_1, \dots, \rho_n$.

Representations of Polynomials. We frequently move from univariate polynomials over $\mathbb{F}$ to their evaluations on subsets of $\mathbb{F}$, and back. We use plain letters like f, g, h, π to denote *evaluations* of polynomials, and "hatted letters" $\hat{f}, \hat{g}, \hat{h}, \hat{\pi}$ to denote corresponding polynomials. This bijection is well-defined only if the size of the evaluation domain is larger than the degree. If $f \in \mathrm{RS}\,[S, \rho]$ for $S \subseteq \mathbb{F}$ and $\rho \in (0, 1]$, then $\hat{f}$ is the unique polynomial of degree less than $\rho|S|$ whose evaluation on S equals f. Likewise, if $\hat{f} \in \mathbb{F}[X]$ with $\deg(\hat{f}) < \rho|S|$, then $f_S := \hat{f}|_S \in \mathrm{RS}\,[S, \rho]$ (but we drop the subscript when the subset is clear from context).

Vanishing Polynomials. Let $\mathbb{F}$ be a finite field, and $S \subseteq \mathbb{F}$. We denote by $\mathbb{Z}_S$ the unique non-zero monic polynomial of degree at most $|S|$ that is zero everywhere on S; $\mathbb{Z}_S$ is called the *vanishing polynomial* of S. In this work we use efficiency properties of vanishing polynomials for sets S that have group structure.

If S is a multiplicative subgroup of $\mathbb{F}$, then $\mathbb{Z}_S(X) = X^{|S|} - 1$, and so $\mathbb{Z}_S(X)$ can be evaluated at any $\alpha \in \mathbb{F}$ in $O(\log |S|)$ field operations. More generally, if S is a γ-coset of a multiplicative subgroup S_0 (namely, $S = \gamma S_0$) then $\mathbb{Z}_S(X) = \gamma^{|S|} \mathbb{Z}_{S_0}(X/\gamma) = X^{|S|} - \gamma^{|S|}$.

If S is an (affine) subspace of $\mathbb{F}$, then $\mathbb{Z}_S$ is called an *(affine) subspace polynomial*. In this case, there exist coefficients $c_0, \dots, c_k \in \mathbb{F}$, where $k := \dim(S)$, such that $\mathbb{Z}_S(X) = X^{p^k} + \sum_{i=1}^k c_i X^{p^{i-1}} + c_0$ (if S is linear then $c_0 = 0$). Hence, $\mathbb{Z}_S(X)$ can be evaluated at any $\alpha \in \mathbb{F}$ in $O(k \log p) = O(\log |S|)$ operations. Such polynomials are called *linearized* because they are $\mathbb{F}_p$-affine maps: if $S = S_0 + \gamma$ for a subspace $S_0 \subseteq \mathbb{F}$ and shift $\gamma \in \mathbb{F}$, then $\mathbb{Z}_S(X) = \mathbb{Z}_{S_0}(X - \gamma) = \mathbb{Z}_{S_0}(X) - \mathbb{Z}_{S_0}(\gamma)$, and $\mathbb{Z}_{S_0}$ is an $\mathbb{F}_p$-linear map. The coefficients $c_0, \dots, c_k$ can be derived from a description of S (any basis of S_0 and the shift γ) in $O(k^2 \log p)$ field operations (see [35, Chapter 3.4] and [12, Remark C.8]).

Lagrange Polynomials. For $\mathbb{F}$ a finite field, $S \subseteq \mathbb{F}$, $a \in S$, we denote by $L_{S,a}$ the unique polynomial of degree less than $|S|$ such that $L_{S,a}(a) = 1$ and

$L_{S,a}(b) = 0$ for all $b \in S \setminus \{a\}$. Note that

$$L_{S,a}(X) = \frac{\prod_{b \in S \setminus \{a\}}(X - b)}{\prod_{b \in S \setminus \{a\}}(a - b)} = \frac{L_S'(X)}{L_S'(a)},$$

where $L_S'(X)$ is the polynomial $\mathbb{Z}_S(X)/(X - a)$. For additive and multiplicative subgroups S and $a \in S$, we can evaluate $L_{S,a}(X)$ at any $\alpha \in \mathbb{F}$ in polylog$(|S|)$ field operations. This is because an arithmetic circuit for L_S' can be efficiently derived from an arithmetic circuit for $\mathbb{Z}_S$ [41].

4.2   Interactive Oracle Proofs

The information-theoretic protocols in this paper are *Interactive Oracle Proofs* (IOPs) [15,40], which combine aspects of Interactive Proofs [4,28] and Probabilistically Checkable Proofs [2,3,5], and also generalize the notion of Interactive PCPs [33].

A k-round public-coin IOP has k rounds of interaction. In the i-th round of interaction, the verifier sends a uniformly random message m_i to the prover; then the prover replies with a message π_i to the verifier. After k rounds of interaction, the verifier makes some queries to the oracles it received and either accepts or rejects.

An *IOP system* for a relation $\mathcal{R}$ with round complexity k and soundness error ε is a pair (P, V), where P, V are probabilistic algorithms, that satisfies the following properties. (See [15,40] for details.)

Completeness: For every instance-witness pair (x, w) in the relation $\mathcal{R}$, $(P(x, w),$
$\quad V(x))$ is a k(n)-round interactive oracle protocol with accepting probability 1.
Soundness: For every instance $x \notin \mathcal{L}(\mathcal{R})$ and unbounded malicious prover $\tilde{P}$, $(\tilde{P},$
$\quad V(x))$ is a k(n)-round interactive oracle protocol with accepting probability
$\quad$ at most $\varepsilon(n)$.

Like the IP model, a fundamental measure of efficiency is the round complexity k. Like the PCP model, two additional fundamental measures of efficiency are the *proof length* p, which is the total number of alphabet symbols in all of the prover's messages, and the *query complexity* q, which is the total number of locations queried by the verifier across all of the prover's messages.

We say that an IOP system is *non-adaptive* if the verifier queries are non-adaptive, namely, the queried locations depend only on the verifier's inputs and its randomness. All of our IOP systems will be non-adaptive.

IOPs of Proximity. An IOP *of Proximity* extends an IOP the same way that PCPs of Proximity extend PCPs. An *IOPP system* for a relation $\mathcal{R}$ with round complexity k, soundness error ε, and proximity parameter δ is a pair (P, V) that satisfies the following properties.

Completeness: For every instance-witness pair (x, w) in the relation $\mathcal{R}$, $(P(x, w),$
$V^w(x))$ is a $k(n)$-round interactive oracle protocol with accepting probability 1.
Soundness: For every instance-witness pair (x, w) with $\Delta(w, \mathcal{R}|_x) \geq \delta(n)$ and
unbounded malicious prover $\tilde{P}$, $(\tilde{P}, V^w(x))$ is a $k(n)$-round interactive oracle
protocol with accepting probability at most $\varepsilon(n)$.

Efficiency measures for IOPPs are as for IOPs, except that we also count queries
to the witness: if V makes at most q_w queries to w and at most q_π queries to
prover messages, the query complexity is $q := q_w + q_\pi$.

5 Oracle Reductions

We define *interactive oracle reductions* (henceforth just *oracle reductions*),
which, informally, are reductions from computational problems to the problem
of testing membership of collections of oracles in a code.

The main result in this section is Lemma 4 (and an implication of it, Corollary 1), which enables the construction of IOPs by modularly combining oracle
reductions and proximity tests. The ideas underlying oracle reductions are not
new. Essentially all known constructions of PCPs/IPCPs/IOPs consist of two
parts: (1) an encoding, typically via an algebraic code, that endows the witness
with robust structure (often known as *arithmetization*); and (2) a procedure that
locally tests this encoding (often known as *low-degree testing*).

Oracle reductions provide a formal method of constructing proof systems
according to this framework. We use them to express results in the full version
of the paper, which significantly simplifies exposition. Additionally, expressing
our results as oracle reductions enables us to consider the efficiency of the oracle
reduction itself as a separate goal from the efficiency of the low-degree test. In
particular, future improvements in low-degree testing will lead immediately to
improvements in our protocols.

This section has two parts: in Sect. 5.1 we define oracle reductions; then in
Sect. 5.2, we introduce a special case of oracle reductions where the target code is
the Reed–Solomon (RS) code. For this special case we give additional lemmas: we
show that it suffices to prove a weaker soundness property, because it generically
implies standard soundness; also, we show that all such oracle reductions admit
a useful optimization which reduces the number of low-degree tests needed to a
single one.

5.1 Definitions

Informally, an oracle reduction is an interactive public-coin protocol between
a prover and a verifier that reduces membership in a language to a promise
problem on oracles sent by the prover during the protocol.

In more detail, an oracle reduction from a language $\mathcal{L} \subseteq X$ to a relation
$\mathcal{R}' \subseteq X' \times \Sigma^s$ is an interactive protocol between a prover and a verifier that
both receive an instance $x \in X$, where in each round the verifier sends a message

and the prover replies with an oracle (or several oracles), as in the IOP model. Unlike in an IOP, the verifier *does not make any queries*. Instead, after the interaction the verifier outputs a list of claims of the form "$(\mathbb{x}, \Pi) \in \mathcal{R}'$", which may depend on the verifier's randomness, where $\mathbb{x}' \in X'$ and Π is a deterministic oracle algorithm that specifies a string in Σ^s as follows: the i-th entry in Σ^s is computed as $\Pi^{\pi_1,\ldots,\pi_r}(i)$, where π_j is the oracle sent by the prover in the j-th round. The reduction has the property that if $\mathbb{x} \in \mathcal{L}$ then all claims output by the verifier are true, and if instead $\mathbb{x} \notin \mathcal{L}$ then (with high probability over the verifier's randomness) at least one claim is false.

We refer to each oracle algorithm $\Pi^{(j)}$ as a *virtual oracle* because $\Pi^{(j)}$ represents an oracle that is derived from oracles sent by the prover. We are interested in virtual oracles $\Pi^{(j)}$ where, for each i, the number of queries $\Pi^{\pi_1,\ldots,\pi_r}(i)$ makes to the oracles is small. For simplicity, we also assume that the algorithms are non-adaptive in that the queried locations are independent of the answers to the queries.

A crucial property is that virtual oracles with small locality compose well, which allows us to compose oracle reductions. For this we need an oracle reduction *of proximity* (Definition 5), which we can view as an oracle reduction from a relation $\mathcal{R} \subseteq X \times \Sigma^s$ to another relation $\mathcal{R}' \subseteq X' \times \Sigma^{s'}$. Then we can construct an oracle reduction from $\mathcal{L}$ to $\mathcal{R}'$ by composing an oracle reduction A from $\mathcal{L}$ to $\mathcal{R}'$ with an oracle reduction of proximity B from $\mathcal{R}'$ to $\mathcal{R}''$. Such a reduction may output virtual oracles of the form $\Pi_B^{\Pi_A}$ where Π_B is a virtual oracle output by B and Π_A is a virtual oracle output by A. This can be expressed as a standard virtual oracle with access to the prover messages, and if Π_A and Π_B have small locality then so does $\Pi_B^{\Pi_A}$.

We now formalize the foregoing discussion, starting with the notion of a virtual oracle. Since the virtual oracles in this work are non-adaptive, we specify them via query ("pre-processing") and answer ("post-processing") algorithms. The query algorithm receives an index $i \in [s]$ and computes a list of locations to be queried across oracles. The answer algorithm receives the same index i, and answers to the queries, and computes the value of the virtual oracle at location i. In other words, the answer algorithm computes the value of the virtual oracle at the desired location from the values of the real oracles at the queried locations.

Definition 3. *A* **virtual oracle** Π *of length* s *over an alphabet* Σ *is a pair of deterministic polynomial-time algorithms* (Q, A). *Given any oracles* $\pi_1, \ldots, \pi_r$ *of appropriate sizes, these algorithms define an oracle* $\Pi \in \Sigma^s$ *given by* $\Pi[\pi_1, \ldots, \pi_r](i) := A(i, (\pi_j[k])_{(j,k) \in Q(i)})$ *for* $i \in [s]$. Π *is* ℓ-**local** *if* $\max_{i \in [s]} |Q(i)| \leq \ell$.

Observe that the definition of a virtual oracle given above is equivalent to saying that Π is an algorithm with non-adaptive query access to $\pi_1, \ldots, \pi_r$. Where convenient we will use this perspective.

We now define the notion of an oracle reduction. Since in this work we primarily deal with relations, rather than languages, we define our reductions accordingly.

Definition 4. *An* **oracle reduction** *from a relation $\mathcal{R}$ to a relation $\mathcal{R}'$ with base alphabet Σ is an interactive protocol between a prover P and verifier V that works as follows. The prover P takes as input an instance-witness pair (x, w) and the verifier V takes as input the instance x. In each round, V sends a message $m_i \in \{0,1\}^*$, and P replies with an oracle $\pi_i \in \Sigma_i^*$ over an alphabet $\Sigma_i = \Sigma^{s_i}$; let $\pi_1, \ldots, \pi_r$ be all oracles sent.[2] After the interaction, V outputs a list of instances $(\mathrm{x}^{(1)}, \ldots, \mathrm{x}^{(m)})$ and a list of virtual oracles $(\mathbf{\Pi}^{(1)}, \ldots, \mathbf{\Pi}^{(m)})$ over alphabets $\Sigma_1', \ldots, \Sigma_m'$ respectively, where $\Sigma_i' = \Sigma^{s_i'}$.*

We say that the oracle reduction has **soundness error** *ϵ and* **distance** *δ if the following conditions hold.*

- Completeness: *If $(\mathrm{x}, \mathrm{w}) \in \mathcal{R}$ then, with probability 1 over the verifier's randomness, for every $j \in [m]$ it holds that $(\mathrm{x}^{(j)}, \mathbf{\Pi}^{(j)}[\pi_1, \ldots, \pi_r]) \in \mathcal{R}'$ where $(\mathrm{x}^{(j)}, \mathbf{\Pi}^{(j)})_{j \in [m]} \leftarrow (P(\mathrm{x}, \mathrm{w}), V(\mathrm{x}))$.*
- Soundness:[3] *If $\mathrm{x} \notin \mathcal{L}(\mathcal{R})$ then for any prover $\tilde{P}$, with probability $1 - \epsilon$ over the verifier's randomness, there exists $j \in [m]$ such that $\Delta(\mathbf{\Pi}^{(j)}[\pi_1, \ldots, \pi_r], \mathcal{R}'|_{\mathrm{x}^{(j)}}) > \delta$ where $(\mathrm{x}^{(j)}, \mathbf{\Pi}^{(j)})_{j \in [m]} \leftarrow (P(\mathrm{x}, \mathrm{w}), V(\mathrm{x}))$.*

An oracle reduction is *public coin* if all of the verifier's messages consist of uniform randomness. All of the oracle reductions we present in this paper are public coin. Note that we can always choose the base alphabet Σ to be $\{0,1\}$, but it will be convenient for us to use a larger base alphabet.

This above definition can be viewed as extending the notion of *linear-algebraic CSPs* [11], and indeed Lemma 4 below gives a construction similar to the "canonical" PCP described in that work.

It will be useful to *compose* oracle reductions. As in the PCP setting, for this we will require an object with a stronger *proximity soundness* property.

Definition 5. *An* **oracle reduction of proximity** *is as in Definition 4 except that, for a given proximity parameter $\delta_0 \in (0,1)$, the soundness condition is replaced by the following one.*

- Proximity soundness: *If (x, w) is such that $\Delta(\mathrm{w}, \mathcal{R}|_{\mathrm{x}}) > \delta_0$ then for any prover $\tilde{P}$, with probability $1 - \epsilon$ over the verifier's randomness, there exists $j \in [m]$ such that $\Delta(\mathbf{\Pi}^{(j)}[\pi_1, \ldots, \pi_r], \mathcal{R}'|_{\mathrm{x}^{(j)}}) > \delta(\delta_0)$ where $(\mathrm{x}^{(j)}, \mathbf{\Pi}^{(j)})_{j \in [m]} \leftarrow (P(\mathrm{x}, \mathrm{w}), V(\mathrm{x}))$.*

In the PCPP literature the foregoing soundness property is usually known as *robust soundness*, and the condition is expressed in terms of expected distance. The definition given here is more convenient for us.

Efficiency Measures. There are several efficiency measures that we study for an oracle reduction.

---

[2] Sometimes it is convenient to allow the prover to reply with multiple oracles $\pi_{i,1}, \pi_{i,2}, \ldots$; all discussions extend to this case.

[3] This is analogous to the "interactive soundness error" ε_i in [14].

- An oracle reduction has r *rounds* if the interactive protocol realizing it has r rounds.
- An oracle reduction has m *virtual oracles* and *locality* ℓ if the verifier outputs at most m virtual oracles $\{\mathbf{\Pi}^{(j)} = (Q_j, A_j)\}_{j \in [m]}$, and it holds that $\max_{i \in [s]} | \cup_{j=1}^m Q_j(i)| \leq \ell$. Note that the answer to a single query may consist of multiple symbols over the base alphabet Σ, but we count the query only once.
- An oracle reduction has *length* $s = \sum_{i=1}^r s_i |\pi_i|$ over the base alphabet. Its length in *bits* is $s \log |\Sigma|$.

Other efficiency measures include the running time of the prover and of the verifier.

Oracle reductions combine naturally with proofs of proximity to produce IOPs. The following lemma is straightforward, and we state it without proof.

Lemma 4. *Suppose that there exist:*

(i) an r-round oracle reduction from $\mathcal{R}$ to $\mathcal{R}'$ over base alphabet Σ with soundness error ϵ, distance δ, length s, locality ℓ, and m virtual oracles;

(ii) an r'-round IOPP for $\mathcal{R}'$ over alphabet Σ with soundness error ϵ', proximity parameter $\delta' \leq \delta$, length s', and query complexity $(\mathsf{q}_w, \mathsf{q}_\pi)$.

Then there exists an $(r + mr')$-round IOP for $\mathcal{R}$ with soundness error $\epsilon + \epsilon'$, length $s + s' \cdot m$ over Σ, and query complexity $(\mathsf{q}_w \cdot \ell + \mathsf{q}_\pi) \cdot m$.

5.2   Reed–Solomon Oracle Reductions

In this work we focus on a special class of oracle reductions, in which we reduce to membership in the Reed–Solomon code, and where the virtual oracles have a special form. These reductions coincide with "RS-encoded IOPs" [14, Definition 4.6], which we recast in the language of virtual oracles.

We first define the notion of a *rational constraint*, a special type of virtual oracle that is "compatible" with the (interleaved) Reed–Solomon code.

Definition 6. *A **rational constraint** is a virtual oracle $\mathbf{\Pi} = (Q, A)$ over a finite field $\mathbb{F}$ where $Q(\alpha) = ((1, \alpha), \dots, (r, \alpha))$ and $A(\alpha, \beta_1, \dots, \beta_r) = N(\alpha, \beta_1, \dots, \beta_r)/D(\alpha)$, for two arithmetic circuits (without division gates) $N \colon \mathbb{F}^{\sum_i s_i} \to \mathbb{F}$ and $D \colon \mathbb{F} \to \mathbb{F}$.*

A Reed–Solomon (RS) oracle reduction is a reduction from some relation to membership in the Reed–Solomon code, where additionally every oracle is a rational constraint.

Definition 7. *A **Reed–Solomon (RS) oracle reduction** over a domain $L \subseteq \mathbb{F}$ is an oracle reduction, over the base alphabet $\mathbb{F}$, from a relation $\mathcal{R}$ to the interleaved Reed–Solomon relation*

$$\mathcal{R}_{\mathrm{RS}}^* := \left\{ (\boldsymbol{\rho}, f) \text{ s.t. } \boldsymbol{\rho} \in (0, 1]^*, \, f \colon L \to \mathbb{F} \text{ is a codeword in } \mathrm{RS}\,[L, \boldsymbol{\rho}] \right\}$$

where every virtual oracle output by the verifier is a rational constraint, except for a special instance (ρ_0, Π_0), which the verifier must output. Π_0, over alphabet $\mathbb{F}^{\sum_i s_i}$, is given by $\Pi_0(\alpha) = (\pi_1(\alpha), \ldots, \pi_r(\alpha))$ (i.e., it is a stacking of the oracles sent by the prover).

In this work we will assume throughout that L comes a family of subgroups (of a family of fields) such that there is an encoding algorithm for the Reed–Solomon code on domain L.

Note that Π_0 is not a rational constraint because its alphabet is not $\mathbb{F}$. Later we will also refer to the *non-interleaved* Reed–Solomon relation $\mathcal{R}_{RS} := \{(\rho, f) : \rho \in (0, 1], f \in \mathrm{RS}[L, \rho]\}$.

RS oracle reductions have a useful property: if the soundness condition holds for $\delta = 0$, then the soundness condition also holds for a distance $\delta > 0$ related to the *maximum rate* of the reduction. Informally, the maximum rate is the maximum over the (prescribed) rates of codewords sent by the prover and those induced by the verifier's rational constraints. To define it, we need notation for the *degree* and *rate* of a circuit.

Definition 8. *The **degree** of an arithmetic circuit $C: \mathbb{F}^{1+\ell} \to \mathbb{F}$ on input degrees $d_1, \ldots, d_\ell \in \mathbb{N}$, denoted $\deg(C; d_1, \ldots, d_\ell)$, is the smallest integer e such that for all $p_i \in \mathbb{F}^{\leq d_i}[X]$ there exists a polynomial $q \in \mathbb{F}^{\leq e}[X]$ such that $C(X, p_1(X), \ldots, p_\ell(X)) \equiv q(X)$. Given domain $L \subseteq \mathbb{F}$ and rates $\boldsymbol{\rho} \in (0, 1]^\ell$, the **rate** of C is $\mathrm{rate}(C; \boldsymbol{\rho}) := \deg(C; \rho_1|L|, \ldots, \rho_\ell|L|)/|L|$. (The domain L will be clear from context.) Note that if $\ell = 0$ then this notion of degree coincides with the usual one (namely, $\deg(C)$ is the degree of the polynomial described by C), and $\mathrm{rate}(C) := \deg(C)/|L|$.*

An oracle reduction has **maximum rate** ρ^* if, for every rational constraint (σ, Π) output by the verifier, $\max(\mathrm{rate}(N; \boldsymbol{\rho}_0), \sigma + \mathrm{rate}(D)) \leq \rho^*$. This expression is motivated by the proof of the following lemma; see [14, Proof of Theorem 9.1] for details.

Lemma 5. *Suppose that an RS oracle reduction with maximum rate ρ^* satisfies the following **weak soundness** condition: if $\mathrm{x} \notin \mathcal{L}(\mathcal{R})$ then for any prover $\tilde{P}$, with probability $1 - \epsilon$ over the verifier's randomness, there exists $j \in [m]$ such that $(\rho^{(j)}, \Pi^{(j)}[\pi_1, \ldots, \pi_n]) \notin \mathcal{R}_{RS}$. Then the reduction satisfies the standard soundness condition (see Definition 4) with soundness error ϵ and distance $\delta := \frac{1}{2}(1 - \rho^*)$.*

This means that for the oracle reductions in this paper *we need only establish weak soundness*. Also, one can see that RS oracle reductions have locality r (the number of rounds), since $|Q(\alpha)| = r$ for all $\alpha \in L$.

The following lemma shows that, for RS oracle reductions, it suffices to run the proximity test on a single virtual oracle. This reduces the query complexity and proof length when we apply Lemma 4.

Lemma 6. *Suppose that there exists an r-round RS oracle reduction from $\mathcal{R}$ over domain L, m virtual oracles, soundness error ϵ, maximum rate ρ^*, and distance δ. Then there is an r-round oracle reduction from $\mathcal{R}$ to the* non-interleaved *Reed–Solomon relation $\mathcal{R}_{RS}$ with locality r,* **one** *virtual oracle, soundness error $\epsilon + |L|/|\mathbb{F}|$, maximum rate ρ^*, and distance $\min(\delta, (1 - \rho^*)/3, (1 - 2\rho^*)/2)$.*

Proof. Implicit in [14, Proof of Theorem 9.1], where it follows from [19]. □

Combining Lemmas 4 to 6 yields the following useful corollary. We invoke it, in the full version, on the two main building blocks obtained in this paper in order to prove our main result.

Corollary 1. *Suppose that there exist:*

(i) an r-round RS oracle reduction from $\mathcal{R}$ over domain L, m virtual oracles, length s and rate ρ^* that satisfies the weak soundness condition with soundness error ϵ;
(ii) an r'-round IOP of proximity for $\mathcal{R}_{RS}$ with soundness error ϵ', proximity parameter $\delta' < \min((1 - \rho^*)/3, (1 - 2\rho^*)/2)$, length p and query complexity $(\mathsf{q_w}, \mathsf{q_\pi})$.

Then there exists an $(r + r')$-round IOP for $\mathcal{R}$ with soundness error $\epsilon + \epsilon' + \frac{|L|}{|\mathbb{F}|}$, length $s + \mathsf{p}$ and query complexity $\mathsf{q_w} \cdot r + \mathsf{q_\pi}$.

Acknowledgments. We thank Michael Forbes for helpful discussions. This work was supported in part by: donations from the Ethereum Foundation and the Interchain Foundation.

References

1. Alon, N., Goldreich, O., Håstad, J., Peralta, R.: Simple construction of almost k-wise independent random variables. Random Struct. Algorithms **3**(3), 289–304 (1992)
2. Arora, S., Lund, C., Motwani, R., Sudan, M., Szegedy, M.: Proof verification and the hardness of approximation problems. J. ACM **45**(3), 501–555 (1998). Preliminary version in FOCS 1992
3. Arora, S., Safra, S.: Probabilistic checking of proofs: a new characterization of NP. J. ACM **45**(1), 70–122 (1998). Preliminary version in FOCS 1992
4. Babai, L.: Trading group theory for randomness. In: Proceedings of the 17th Annual ACM Symposium on Theory of Computing, STOC 1985, pp. 421–429 (1985)
5. Babai, L., Fortnow, L., Levin, L.A., Szegedy, M.: Checking computations in polylogarithmic time. In: Proceedings of the 23rd Annual ACM Symposium on Theory of Computing, STOC 1991, pp. 21–32 (1991)
6. Ben-Sasson, E., et al.: Computational integrity with a public random string from quasi-linear PCPs. In: Coron, J.-S., Nielsen, J.B. (eds.) EUROCRYPT 2017. LNCS, vol. 10212, pp. 551–579. Springer, Cham (2017). https://doi.org/10.1007/978-3-319-56617-7_19

7. Ben-Sasson, E., Bentov, I., Horesh, Y., Riabzev, M.: Scalable, transparent, and post-quantum secure computational integrity. Cryptology ePrint Archive, Report 2018/046 (2018)
8. Ben-Sasson, E., Bentov, I., Horesh, Y., Riabzev, M.: Fast Reed-Solomon interactive oracle proofs of proximity. In: Proceedings of the 45th International Colloquium on Automata, Languages and Programming, ICALP 2018, pp. 14:1–14:17 (2018)
9. Ben-Sasson, E., Chiesa, A., Forbes, M.A., Gabizon, A., Riabzev, M., Spooner, N.: Zero knowledge protocols from succinct constraint detection. In: Kalai, Y., Reyzin, L. (eds.) TCC 2017. LNCS, vol. 10678, pp. 172–206. Springer, Cham (2017). https://doi.org/10.1007/978-3-319-70503-3_6
10. Ben-Sasson, E., Chiesa, A., Gabizon, A., Riabzev, M., Spooner, N.: Interactive oracle proofs with constant rate and query complexity. In: Proceedings of the 44th International Colloquium on Automata, Languages and Programming, ICALP 2017, pp. 40:1–40:15 (2017)
11. Ben-Sasson, E., Chiesa, A., Gabizon, A., Virza, M.: Quasi-linear size zero knowledge from linear-algebraic PCPs. In: Kushilevitz, E., Malkin, T. (eds.) TCC 2016. LNCS, vol. 9563, pp. 33–64. Springer, Heidelberg (2016). https://doi.org/10.1007/978-3-662-49099-0_2
12. Ben-Sasson, E., Chiesa, A., Genkin, D., Tromer, E.: Fast reductions from RAMs to delegatable succinct constraint satisfaction problems. In: Proceedings of the 4th Innovations in Theoretical Computer Science Conference, ITCS 2013, pp. 401–414 (2013)
13. Ben-Sasson, E., Chiesa, A., Genkin, D., Tromer, E.: On the concrete efficiency of probabilistically-checkable proofs. In: Proceedings of the 45th ACM Symposium on the Theory of Computing, STOC 2013, pp. 585–594 (2013)
14. Ben-Sasson, E., Chiesa, A., Riabzev, M., Spooner, N., Virza, M., Ward, N.P.: Aurora: transparent succinct arguments for R1CS. In: Ishai, Y., Rijmen, V. (eds.) EUROCRYPT 2019. LNCS, vol. 11476, pp. 103–128. Springer, Cham (2019). https://doi.org/10.1007/978-3-030-17653-2_4. Full version available at https://eprint.iacr.org/2018/828
15. Ben-Sasson, E., Chiesa, A., Spooner, N.: Interactive oracle proofs. In: Hirt, M., Smith, A. (eds.) TCC 2016. LNCS, vol. 9986, pp. 31–60. Springer, Heidelberg (2016). https://doi.org/10.1007/978-3-662-53644-5_2
16. Ben-Sasson, E., Goldreich, O., Harsha, P., Sudan, M., Vadhan, S.: Short PCPs verifiable in polylogarithmic time. In: Proceedings of the 20th Annual IEEE Conference on Computational Complexity, CCC 2005, pp. 120–134 (2005)
17. Ben-Sasson, E., Goldreich, O., Harsha, P., Sudan, M., Vadhan, S.P.: Robust PCPs of proximity, shorter PCPs, and applications to coding. SIAM J. Comput. **36**(4), 889–974 (2006)
18. Ben-Sasson, E., Kaplan, Y., Kopparty, S., Meir, O., Stichtenoth, H.: Constant rate PCPs for circuit-SAT with sublinear query complexity. In: Proceedings of the 54th Annual IEEE Symposium on Foundations of Computer Science, FOCS 2013, pp. 320–329 (2013)
19. Ben-Sasson, E., Kopparty, S., Saraf, S.: Worst-case to average case reductions for the distance to a code. In: Proceedings of the 33rd ACM Conference on Computer and Communications Security, CCS 2018, pp. 24:1–24:23 (2018)
20. Ben-Sasson, E., Sudan, M.: Short PCPs with polylog query complexity. SIAM J. Comput. **38**(2), 551–607 (2008). Preliminary version appeared in STOC 2005

21. Ben-Sasson, E., Sudan, M., Vadhan, S., Wigderson, A.: Randomness-efficient low degree tests and short PCPs via epsilon-biased sets. In: Proceedings of the 35th Annual ACM Symposium on Theory of Computing, STOC 2003, pp. 612–621 (2003)

22. Blum, M., Kannan, S.: Designing programs that check their work. J. ACM **42**(1), 269–291 (1995). Preliminary version in STOC 1989

23. Bootle, J., Cerulli, A., Ghadafi, E., Groth, J., Hajiabadi, M., Jakobsen, S.K.: Linear-time zero-knowledge proofs for arithmetic circuit satisfiability. In: Takagi, T., Peyrin, T. (eds.) ASIACRYPT 2017. LNCS, vol. 10626, pp. 336–365. Springer, Cham (2017). https://doi.org/10.1007/978-3-319-70700-6_12

24. Bowe, S., et al.: Implementation track proceeding. Technical report, ZKProof Standards (2018). https://zkproof.org/documents.html

25. Dinur, I.: The PCP theorem by gap amplification. J. ACM **54**(3), 12 (2007)

26. Feige, U., Goldwasser, S., Lovász, L., Safra, S., Szegedy, M.: Interactive proofs and the hardness of approximating cliques. J. ACM **43**(2), 268–292 (1996). Preliminary version in FOCS 1991

27. Goldreich, O., Sudan, M.: Locally testable codes and PCPs of almost-linear length. J. ACM **53**, 558–655 (2006). Preliminary version in STOC 2002

28. Goldwasser, S., Micali, S., Rackoff, C.: The knowledge complexity of interactive proof systems. SIAM J. Comput. **18**(1), 186–208 (1989). Preliminary version appeared in STOC 1985

29. Gurevich, Y., Shelah, S.: Nearly linear time. In: Meyer, A.R., Taitslin, M.A. (eds.) Logic at Botik 1989. LNCS, vol. 363, pp. 108–118. Springer, Heidelberg (1989). https://doi.org/10.1007/3-540-51237-3_10

30. Guruswami, V., Indyk, P.: Linear-time encodable/decodable codes with near-optimal rate. IEEE Trans. Inf. Theory **51**(10), 3393–3400 (2005). Preliminary version appeared in STOC 2003

31. Harsha, P., Sudan, M.: Small PCPs with low query complexity. Comput. Complex. **9**(3–4), 157–201 (2000). Preliminary version in STACS 2001

32. Ishai, Y., Mahmoody, M., Sahai, A., Xiao, D.: On zero-knowledge PCPs: limitations, simplifications, and applications (2015). http://www.cs.virginia.edu/~mohammad/files/papers/ZKPCPs-Full.pdf

33. Kalai, Y.T., Raz, R.: Interactive PCP. In: Aceto, L., Damgård, I., Goldberg, L.A., Halldórsson, M.M., Ingólfsdóttir, A., Walukiewicz, I. (eds.) ICALP 2008. LNCS, vol. 5126, pp. 536–547. Springer, Heidelberg (2008). https://doi.org/10.1007/978-3-540-70583-3_44

34. Kilian, J.: A note on efficient zero-knowledge proofs and arguments. In: Proceedings of the 24th Annual ACM Symposium on Theory of Computing, STOC 1992, pp. 723–732 (1992)

35. Lidl, R., Niederreiter, H.: Finite Fields, 2nd edn. Cambridge University Press, Cambridge (1997)

36. Lipton, R.J.: New directions in testing. In: Proceedings of a DIMACS Workshop in Distributed Computing and Cryptography, pp. 191–202 (1989)

37. Micali, S.: Computationally sound proofs. SIAM J. Comput. **30**(4), 1253–1298 (2000). Preliminary version appeared in FOCS 1994

38. Mie, T.: Short PCPPs verifiable in polylogarithmic time with O(1) queries. Ann. Math. Artif. Intell. **56**, 313–338 (2009)

39. Polishchuk, A., Spielman, D.A.: Nearly-linear size holographic proofs. In: Proceedings of the 26th Annual ACM Symposium on Theory of Computing, STOC 1994, pp. 194–203 (1994)

40. Reingold, O., Rothblum, R., Rothblum, G.: Constant-round interactive proofs for delegating computation. In: Proceedings of the 48th ACM Symposium on the Theory of Computing, STOC 2016, pp. 49–62 (2016)
41. Shpilka, A., Yehudayoff, A.: Arithmetic circuits: a survey of recent results and open questions. Found. Trends Theor. Comput. Sci. **5**(3–4), 207–388 (2010)
42. Spielman, D.A.: Linear-time encodable and decodable error-correcting codes. IEEE Trans. Inf. Theory **42**(6), 1723–1731 (1996). Preliminary version appeared in STOC 1995

On the (In)security of Kilian-Based SNARGs

James Bartusek[1]($^{(\boxtimes)}$), Liron Bronfman[2], Justin Holmgren[3], Fermi Ma[4],
and Ron D. Rothblum[2]

[1] UC Berkeley, Berkeley, USA
bartusek.james@gmail.com
[2] Technion, Haifa, Israel
{br,rothblum}@cs.technion.ca.il
[3] Simons Institute, Berkeley, USA
holmgren@alum.mit.edu
[4] Princeton University, Princeton, USA
fermima@alum.mit.edu

Abstract. The Fiat-Shamir transform is an incredibly powerful technique that uses a suitable hash function to reduce the interaction of general public-coin protocols. Unfortunately, there are known counterexamples showing that this methodology may not be sound (no matter what concrete hash function is used). Still, these counterexamples are somewhat unsatisfying, as the underlying protocols were specifically tailored to make Fiat-Shamir fail. This raises the question of whether this transform is sound when applied to natural protocols.

One of the most important protocols for which we would like to reduce interaction is Kilian's four-message argument system for all of NP, based on collision resistant hash functions (CRHF) and probabilistically checkable proofs (PCPs). Indeed, an application of the Fiat-Shamir transform to Kilian's protocol is at the heart of both theoretical results (e.g., Micali's CS proofs) as well as leading practical approaches of highly efficient non-interactive proof-systems (e.g., SNARKs and STARKs).

In this work, we show significant obstacles to establishing soundness of (what we refer to as) the "Fiat-Shamir-Kilian-Micali" (FSKM) protocol. More specifically:

  – We construct a (contrived) CRHF for which FSKM is unsound for a very large class of PCPs and for any Fiat-Shamir hash function. The

UC Berkeley—Research conducted while at Princeton University.

Technion—Partially supported by the Israeli Science Foundation (Grant No. 1262/18), a Milgrom family grant, the Technion Hiroshi Fujiwara cyber security research center and the Israel cyber directorate.

Simons Institute—Research conducted while at Princeton University, supported in part by the Simons Collaboration on Algorithms and Geometry and NSF grant No. CCF-1714779.

Princeton University—Supported by the NSF and DARPA. Any opinions, findings and conclusions or recommendations expressed in this material are those of the author(s) and do not necessarily reflect the views of the NSF or DARPA.

The full version of this paper is available at ia.cr/2019/997 [BBH+19].

D. Hofheinz and A. Rosen (Eds.): TCC 2019, LNCS 11892, pp. 522–551, 2019.
https://doi.org/10.1007/978-3-030-36033-7_20

collision-resistance of our CRHF relies on very strong but plausible cryptographic assumptions. The statement is "tight" in the following sense: any PCP outside the scope of our result trivially implies a SNARK, eliminating the need for FSKM in the first place.

- Second, we consider a known extension of Kilian's protocol to an interactive variant of PCPs called *probabilistically checkable interactive proofs* (PCIP) (also known as *interactive oracle proofs* or *IOPs*). We construct a particular (contrived) PCIP for NP for which the FSKM protocol is unsound no matter what CRHF and Fiat-Shamir hash function is used. This result is unconditional (i.e., does not rely on any cryptographic assumptions).

Put together, our results show that the soundness of FSKM must rely on some special structure of *both* the CRHF and PCP that underlie Kilian's protocol. We believe these negative results may cast light on how to securely instantiate the FSKM protocol by a synergistic choice of the PCP, CRHF, and Fiat-Shamir hash function.

1 Introduction

The Fiat-Shamir heuristic [FS86] is an extremely influential approach for eliminating or reducing interaction in a wide variety of cryptographic protocols. First proposed as a practical method for constructing digital signature schemes from identification protocols, it was later generalized to reduce interaction of *arbitrary* (public-coin) protocols. In a nutshell, the idea is to replace the messages from the public-coin verifier (which are uniformly random strings) with a suitable hash of all preceding prover messages.

Identifying whether and when the Fiat-Shamir heuristic is sound has been a focus of cryptographic research for decades. It has been known for over 25 years that security holds in an idealized model where the hash function is modeled as a random oracle [PS96]. While the random oracle is often a useful methodology for designing heuristically secure protocols [BR94], it does not provide any guarantees when the random oracle is replaced with any explicit hash function family. As a matter of fact, results of Barak [Bar01] and Goldwasser and Kalai [GK03] give a strong negative indication. Specifically, these works exhibit sound protocols which become totally insecure after the application of the Fiat-Shamir transform *using any hash function*.

Still, the protocols designed by [Bar01, GK03] were, in a sense, specifically tailored to make the Fiat-Shamir fail. Thus, it is important to understand whether this methodology can be soundly applied to protocols with additional natural structure that we care about. A prominent example for such a protocol is Kilian's [Kil92] beautiful 4-message argument-system for any NP language. Remarkably, this protocol (which relies on a relatively mild cryptographic assumption) can be used to prove the correctness of any NP language with an extremely short proof and with a super efficient verification procedure. A main drawback of Kilian's protocol is that it requires back and forth interaction between the prover and verifier (which is undesirable for some applications) and so this protocol is (arguably) the prime example of a protocol for which we would like to apply Fiat-Shamir.

Indeed, this very idea was advocated by Micali [Mic00] in his construction of CS proofs, which are now more commonly referred to as SNARGs (an abbreviation for Succinct Non-interactive ARGuments). SNARGs are an incredibly powerful and versatile tool that are currently being implemented and adopted in practice (especially in the domain of blockchain technology and cryptocurrencies [BGG17,BGM17,BBB+18]). Some leading SNARG implementation efforts are closely following the basic approach of applying Fiat-Shamir to (suitable extensions of) Kilian's protocol [BCS16,BBC+17,BBHR18a,BBHR18b, BCR+19]. For convenience, throughout this work we refer to the candidate SNARG obtained by applying Fiat-Shamir to Kilian's protocol as the FSKM protocol.

Thus, a basic question that we would like to understand (and was posed explicitly by [GK03]) is the following:

Do there exist hash functions with which the FSKM protocol is sound?

Jumping ahead, we show that the FSKM protocol can potentially be *insecure* when instantiated with *any* Fiat-Shamir hash function family. However, to explain our results more precisely, we first recall some details of Kilian's original protocol and the resulting FSKM protocol.

1.1 Kilian's Protocol and FSKM

First and foremost, Kilian's protocol relies on *probabilistically checkable proofs* (PCPs). Recall that PCPs can be thought of as a way to encode a witness w so that the encoded witness π can be verified by only reading a few of its bits. The celebrated PCP Theorem [ALM+98] shows that such PCPs exist for all NP languages.

Consider some language $\mathcal{L} \in$ NP and let $\Pi_{\mathsf{PCP}} = (\mathcal{P}_{\mathsf{PCP}}, \mathcal{V}_{\mathsf{PCP}})$ be a PCP proof-system for $\mathcal{L}$. To establish that $x \in \mathcal{L}$, and given a witness w, the prover $\mathcal{P}_{\mathsf{Kilian}}$ engages in the following protocol with the verifier $\mathcal{V}_{\mathsf{Kilian}}$:

1. $\mathcal{V}_{\mathsf{Kilian}}$ samples a collision-resistant hash function $h_{\mathsf{CRHF}} \leftarrow \mathcal{H}_{\mathsf{CRHF}}$, and sends h_{CRHF} to $\mathcal{P}_{\mathsf{Kilian}}$.
2. $\mathcal{P}_{\mathsf{Kilian}}$ constructs a PCP π for x's membership in $\mathcal{L}$, and sends a Merkle hash (using h_{CRHF}) of π to $\mathcal{V}_{\mathsf{Kilian}}$.
3. $\mathcal{V}_{\mathsf{Kilian}}$ chooses random coins r for the PCP verifier $\mathcal{V}_{\mathsf{PCP}}$ and sends them to $\mathcal{P}_{\mathsf{Kilian}}$.
4. $\mathcal{P}_{\mathsf{Kilian}}$ computes the locations $i_1, \ldots, i_q$ that $\mathcal{V}_{\mathsf{PCP}}$ would query on randomness r and input x, and "decommits" to the values of $(\pi_{i_1}, \ldots, \pi_{i_q})$.[1]
5. $\mathcal{V}_{\mathsf{Kilian}}$ checks that the decommitments are valid and that the values that were opened make the PCP verifier accept using the random string r.

---

[1] A succinct decommitment to the value π_{i_j} can be accomplished by having $\mathcal{P}_{\mathsf{Kilian}}$ reveal the hash values of all vertices in the tree that are either on, or adjacent to, the path from π_{i_j} to the root in the Merkle tree.

We denote by $\mathsf{FSKM}[\Pi_{\mathsf{PCP}}, \mathcal{H}_{\mathsf{CRHF}}, \mathcal{H}_{\mathsf{FS}}]$ the protocol that results from applying Fiat-Shamir with hash family $\mathcal{H}_{\mathsf{FS}}$ to the above 4 message argument. Observe that $\mathsf{FSKM}[\Pi_{\mathsf{PCP}}, \mathcal{H}_{\mathsf{CRHF}}, \mathcal{H}_{\mathsf{FS}}]$ can be implemented using only 2 messages: in the first message the verifier specifies the collision resistant hash function and the Fiat-Shamir hash function $h_{\mathsf{FS}} \leftarrow \mathcal{H}_{\mathsf{FS}}$, and in the second message the prover reveals the root rt of the Merkle tree together with the relevant decommitments with respect to $r = h_{\mathsf{FS}}(\mathsf{rt})$.

We will also consider a variant of the FSKM protocol that uses a generalization of PCPs called probabilistically checkable *interactive* proofs or PCIPs [BCS16, RRR16a].[2] A PCIP is a type of proof system that combines the locally checkable aspect of PCPs with the multi-round aspect of interactive proofs, thereby generalizing both. More precisely, in a PCIP the prover first sends a PCP proof to the verifier, which can make some queries to this proof string (as in standard PCPs). The difference however is that now the verifier is allowed to respond with a random challenge and the prover sends an *additional* PCP proof string - this process can continue for several rounds.

One of the key benefits of PCIPs (advocated by [BCS16]) is that they can allow for practical efficiency benefits over standard PCPs. As observed by [BCS16], Kilian's protocol can be readily extended to handle PCIPs, by having the prover send a Merkle hash of its entire message in every round, and eventually decommiting to the desired bits as in Kilian's original protocol. It is natural therefore to apply Fiat-Shamir to the resulting protocol and this was shown to be sound by [BCS16] in the *random oracle model*. We extend our notation of FSKM to the more general setting of PCIPs in the natural way (see Line 3 for details).

As mentioned above, the FSKM protocol, when combined with highly efficient PCIPs, is at the heart of current successful implementations of SNARGs [BCS16, BBC+17, BBHR18a, BBHR18b, BCR+19].

1.2   Our Results

Loosely speaking, we show that the FSKM protocol can be insecure when instantiated with *any* Fiat-Shamir hash function unless security relies on specific properties of both (1) the collision resistant hash function, *and* (2) the underlying PCP (or more precisely PCIP). This is established by our two main results which are described next.

Our first main result shows that there exists a collision-resistant hash family $\widetilde{\mathcal{H}}_{\mathsf{CRHF}}$ such that for any "reasonable" PCP Π_{PCP} and *all* candidate Fiat-Shamir hash families $\mathcal{H}_{\mathsf{FS}}$, the protocol $\mathsf{FSKM}[\Pi_{\mathsf{PCP}}, \widetilde{\mathcal{H}}_{\mathsf{CRHF}}, \mathcal{H}_{\mathsf{FS}}]$ is not sound. We refer to such a CRHF as being FSKM-incompatible. The existence of such an FSKM-incompatible CRHF shows that soundness of the FSKM protocol cannot be based on a generic CRHF. Loosely speaking, by "a reasonable PCP," we mean one where it is possible *given the verifier's randomness* to compute a proof string that the verifier would accept.

---

[2] PCIPs are also called *interactive oracle proofs* IOPs.

Unreasonable PCPs *may* exist. For instance, if SNARGs exist, then any PCP for an NP language $\mathcal{L}$ can be modified (in a contrived way) to be an unreasonable PCP for $\mathcal{L}$: Honest proof strings for $x \in \mathcal{L}$ are modified by appending a SNARG π_{SNARG} attesting that $x \in \mathcal{L}$; the verifier is modified so that in addition to performing the original PCP verifier's checks, it also verifies that π_{SNARG} is a valid SNARG. However there is a sense in which such PCPs (already having an embedded SNARG) are the only unreasonable PCPs. We formalize this in Theorem 6.

The collision-resistance of our FSKM-Incompatible CRHF relies on a strong cryptographic assumption: the existence of Succinct Non-Interactive ARguments of Knowledge (SNARKs) with "computationally unique" proofs. By computationally unique we mean that it should be infeasible to find two different proofs corresponding to the same NP witness.

Our result implies that under this assumption, $\mathsf{FSKM}[\Pi_{\mathsf{PCP}}, \mathcal{H}_{\mathsf{CRHF}}, \mathcal{H}_{\mathsf{FS}}]$ cannot be proven to be sound when $\mathcal{H}_{\mathsf{CRHF}}$ is a generic collision-resistant hash family—even if the PCP Π_{PCP} and Fiat-Shamir hash function $\mathcal{H}_{\mathsf{FS}}$ are carefully engineered.

Theorem 1 (Informally Stated, see Theorem 6). *Assume the existence of collision resistant hash functions and (publicly verifiable) SNARKs with computationally unique proofs. Then, there exists a collision-resistant hash family $\widetilde{\mathcal{H}}_{\mathsf{CRHF}}$ such that for every "reasonable" PCP Π_{PCP} and every hash family $\mathcal{H}_{\mathsf{FS}}$, the protocol $\mathsf{FSKM}[\Pi_{\mathsf{PCP}}, \widetilde{\mathcal{H}}_{\mathsf{CRHF}}, \mathcal{H}_{\mathsf{FS}}]$ is not sound.*

We instantiate this theorem with a SNARK constructed in the works of [BCI+13, BCCT13], whose soundness follows from a knowledge of exponent assumption in bilinear groups (along with a more standard "power" discrete log assumption). Such knowledge assumptions are very strong (and are not known to be falsifiable), but are still plausible, and in particular can be proven to hold in the generic group model [Nec94, Sho97, Mau05].[3] In the full version [BBH+19], we show that under the same set of assumptions (we need collision resistant hashing as well, but this follows from either of the assumptions on groups), this SNARK has computationally unique proofs. However, as discussed in [BCCT13], the soundness notion satisfied by this SNARK is slightly weaker than standard soundness. We overcome this difficulty by additionally assuming the existence of injective one-way functions that are exponentially hard.

Moving on, Theorem 1 still leaves open the possibility that a careful choice of $\mathcal{H}_{\mathsf{CRHF}}$ and $\mathcal{H}_{\mathsf{FS}}$ suffices to establish soundness of $\mathsf{FSKM}[\Pi_{\mathsf{PCP}}, \mathcal{H}_{\mathsf{CRHF}}, \mathcal{H}_{\mathsf{FS}}]$. Our

---

[3] The work of [BCPR14] showed that if indistinguishability obfuscation exists, then SNARKs where extraction holds with respect to *arbitrary* unbounded polynomial length auxiliary input do not exist. We therefore rely on a version of the [BCI+13] knowledge of exponent assumption which only requires extraction to hold with respect to auxiliary input from a "benign" distribution (e.g. a uniform distribution); a similar approach was taken in [CFH+15, FFG+16, Gro16, BCC+17]. We are able to rely on this relaxed version since the auxiliary input in our construction essentially just consists of the key for some arbitrary collision resistant hash function. We discuss this issue in further detail in the full version [BBH+19].

second main result shows a significant obstacle to this possibility. Specifically, we show that there exists a PCIP such that for any collision-resistant hash function CRHF *and* any Fiat-Shamir hash function, the resulting FSKM protocol is not sound. We refer to such a PCIP as being an FSKM-incompatible PCIP. The existence of FSKM-incompatible PCIPs implies that the soundness of any FSKM protocol must rely on specific properties of the underlying PCIP. In contrast to Theorem 1, this result is unconditional (i.e., does not rely on any cryptographic assumptions).

Theorem 2 (Informally Stated, see Theorem 7). *There exists a* PCIP $\widetilde{\Pi}_{\mathsf{PCIP}}$ *such that for all hash families* $\mathcal{H}_{\mathsf{CRHF}}$ *and* $\mathcal{H}_{\mathsf{FS}}$, *the protocol* FSKM$[\widetilde{\Pi}_{\mathsf{PCIP}}, \mathcal{H}_{\mathsf{CRHF}}, \mathcal{H}_{\mathsf{FS}}]$ *is not sound.*

In the proof of Theorem 2, we show soundness of FSKM$[\widetilde{\Pi}_{\mathsf{PCIP}}, \mathcal{H}_{\mathsf{CRHF}}, \mathcal{H}_{\mathsf{FS}}]$ is broken in an extremely strong sense. Namely, there exists a polynomial-time adversary that convinces the FSKM verifier to accept *any* input $x \notin L$ with probability 1.

Interpretation of Our Results. We emphasize that our construction of CRHF (in Theorem 1) and PCIP (in Theorem 2) are highly contrived. Thus, it certainly remains a possibility that some special structure of known CRHFs and PCPs/PCIPs might be identified that will allow for the FSKM protocol to be securely instantiated. Indeed, we hope that our results will lead to the identification of special structure that can be leveraged to securely instantiate FSKM.

In fact, we give some initial progress towards this goal. In the full version [BBH+19], we give a sound instantiation (under standard assumptions) of the FSKM protocol when the underlying PCP is a specific PCP for the empty language. In order to bypass our impossibility, we make use of a collision-resistant hash function with special structure: the *somewhere statistically binding* hash function of Hubáček and Wichs [HW15b]. For the Fiat-Shamir hash function, we use a *correlation-intractable* hash function for efficiently searchable relations, recently constructed under the Learning with Errors assumption by Peikert and Shiehian [PS19]. Needless to say, SNARK constructions for the empty language are not particularly interesting. However, we hope that this blueprint will be useful in the future for proving instantiations of FSKM sound when the underlying PCP is defined for more expressive languages.

1.3   Additional Prior Work

Goldwasser and Kalai [GK03] showed that the original application of the Fiat-Shamir heuristic is not sound; there exists a contrived identification protocol such that no matter what hash function is used in the Fiat-Shamir transform, the resulting digital signature scheme is insecure. Since they use a very particular protocol, their result does not yield a negative result for applying Fiat-Shamir to the FSKM protocol (indeed, as mentioned above, finding such a negative result was posed as an open problem in [GK03]).

Another very related work is that of Gentry and Wichs [GW11], who showed a substantial barrier to constructing SNARGs. Our work is incomparable to that of [GW11]. On the one hand [GW11] rule out a very general class of SNARG constructions whereas we focus on a very particular approach (i.e., applying Fiat-Shamir to FSKM with a generic CRHF). On the other hand, when restricting to the foregoing approach, we overcome some significant limitations of [GW11]. First, in contrast to [GW11], our result is not limited to SNARGs whose security holds under a *black-box* reduction from a falsifiable assumption. Second, it applies also to constructions based on *non-falsifiable* assumptions. Third, it rules out protocol achieving standard (i.e., non-adaptive) soundness, whereas [GW11] only rules out adaptively sound protocols. And fourth, our work applies to any NP language whereas [GW11] only rules out SNARGs for particular (extremely) hard NP languages.

A recent line of work [KRR17, CCRR18, HL18, CCH+19, PS19] constructs hash functions that are compatible with Fiat-Shamir, when applied to *statistically sound* interactive proofs. Still, the question of whether the Fiat-Shamir transform can be securely applied to preserve the *computational* soundness of Kilian's argument scheme has remained open.

1.4   Technical Overview

We proceed to an overview of our two main results. First, in Sect. 1.4 we give an overview of our FSKM-incompatible CRHF and then, in Sect. 1.4, we give an overview of our FSKM-incompatible PCIP.

An FSKM-incompatible CRHF. For simplicity, in this overview we describe a weaker result. Specifically, we construct an FSKM-incompatible CRHF for a particular choice of the language $\mathcal{L}$ and for a PCP for $\mathcal{L}$ (rather than handling all languages $\mathcal{L}$ and all "reasonable" PCPs). Nevertheless, this weaker result demonstrates the main ideas that go into the proof of Theorem 1. Specifically, we focus on the empty language $\mathcal{L} = \emptyset$. While this language has a trivial PCP Π_{PCP} (of length 0) in which the verifier always rejects, we will consider a *different* PCP $\widetilde{\Pi}_{PCP}$ for $\mathcal{L}$ (parameterized by a security parameter λ): the PCP proof string is expected to have length 2λ and the verifier uses a random string of length λ, and accepts if the first λ bits of the PCP are equal to its random string. Completeness holds in an empty sense whereas the soundness error is clearly $2^{-\lambda}$. We construct a contrived collision-resistant hash function $\widetilde{\mathcal{H}}_{CRHF}$ such that FSKM$[\widetilde{\Pi}_{PCP}, \widetilde{\mathcal{H}}_{CRHF}, \mathcal{H}_{FS}]$ is not sound for any hash family $\mathcal{H}_{FS}$.

We will construct $\widetilde{\mathcal{H}}_{CRHF} = \{\widetilde{H}_{CRHF}^{(\lambda)} : \{0,1\}^{2\lambda} \to \{0,1\}^{\lambda}\}$ so that it satisfies the following property: Given $\widetilde{h}_{CRHF} \leftarrow \widetilde{H}_{CRHF}^{(\lambda)}$ and any efficiently computable function f, it is possible to efficiently find $(x_0\|x_1) \in \{0,1\}^{2\lambda}$ such that $x_0 = f(\widetilde{h}_{CRHF}(x_0\|x_1))$. This property immediately allows us to break the soundness of FSKM$[\widetilde{\Pi}_{PCP}, \widetilde{\mathcal{H}}_{CRHF}, \mathcal{H}_{FS}]$ as follows. We view $h_{FS} \leftarrow \mathcal{H}_{FS}$ as the function f, and so a cheating prover can produce a valid commitment rt to a string $(x_0\|x_1)$ such that the verifier's randomness is $h_{FS}(\text{rt}) = x_0$. The prover sends rt as the Merkle root but can now decommit to x_0, which makes the PCP verifier accept.

We refer to a CRHF having the foregoing property as a circular tractable (CT-) CRHF.

A CT-CRHF from Ideal Obfuscation. We first illustrate how it is possible to construct a CT-CRHF assuming ideal Turing-machine obfuscation. For readability, we will use collision-resistant hash *functions* (rather than ensembles) in this section.

We will start with any CRHF $h'_{\mathsf{CRHF}} : \{0,1\}^{2\lambda} \to \{0,1\}^{\lambda-1}$, and we construct a CT-CRHF hash function $\tilde{h}_{\mathsf{CRHF}} : \{0,1\}^{2\lambda} \to \{0,1\}^{\lambda}$. The hash function $\tilde{h}_{\mathsf{CRHF}}$ will have two types of outputs: normal outputs, which end in a 1, and special outputs, which end in $0^{\lambda/2}$. On almost all inputs $x_0\|x_1$, we will have

$$\tilde{h}_{\mathsf{CRHF}}(x_0\|x_1) = h'_{\mathsf{CRHF}}(x_0\|x_1)\|1.$$

However, we will guarantee that for every x_0 and special output $y\|0^{\lambda/2}$, x_0 can be extended into a (not efficiently computable) "special" $x_0\|x_1$ such that $\tilde{h}_{\mathsf{CRHF}}(x_0\|x_1) = y\|0^{\lambda/2}$. This is easy to achieve if we augment the description of $\tilde{h}_{\mathsf{CRHF}}$ to include a verification of a (public-key) digital signature scheme, and $\tilde{h}_{\mathsf{CRHF}}$ is defined as

$$\tilde{h}_{\mathsf{CRHF}}(x_0|x_1) = \begin{cases} y\|0^{\lambda/2} & \text{if } x_1 = y\|\sigma, \text{ for } \sigma \text{ a valid signature of } (x_0, y). \\ h'_{\mathsf{CRHF}}(x_0\|x_1)\|1 & \text{otherwise.} \end{cases}$$

In order to actually (efficiently) use the added structure of $\tilde{h}_{\mathsf{CRHF}}$, we will also augment the description of $\tilde{h}_{\mathsf{CRHF}}$ to include an obfuscation $\hat{P}$ of a program P that has the signature signing key hard-wired, and on input the description $\langle f \rangle$ of a function f acts as follows:

1. Computes $y = h''_{\mathsf{CRHF}}(\langle f \rangle)$, where $h''_{\mathsf{CRHF}} : \{0,1\}^* \to \{0,1\}^{\lambda/2}$ is a generic CRHF.
2. Compute $x_0 = f(y\|0^{\lambda/2})$.
3. Compute a signature σ of (x_0, y).
4. Output (x_0, y, σ).

It is clear that the inclusion of $\hat{P}$ in the description of $\tilde{h}_{\mathsf{CRHF}}$ makes $\tilde{h}_{\mathsf{CRHF}}$ circular tractable, but why is $\tilde{h}_{\mathsf{CRHF}}$ collision-resistant?

Suppose that an efficient adversary $\mathcal{A}$ were to output a colliding pair $(x_0\|x_1)$ and $(x'_0\|x'_1)$ of $\tilde{h}_{\mathsf{CRHF}}$. The only new collisions that $\tilde{h}_{\mathsf{CRHF}}$ has compared to h'_{CRHF} (and thus that $\mathcal{A}$ might possibly output) are collisions for special outputs (standard outputs can never collide with special outputs due to their last bit being different). That is, we may assume that $x_1 = y\|\sigma$ and $x'_1 = y\|\sigma'$. The security of the signature scheme and of the ideal obfuscator imply that if $\mathcal{A}$ produced such a collision, it must have queried $\hat{P}$ on two distinct inputs $\langle f \rangle$, $\langle f' \rangle$ such that $P(\langle f \rangle) = (x_0, y, \sigma)$ and $P(\langle f' \rangle) = (x'_0, y, \sigma')$. But this would in particular imply that $h''_{\mathsf{CRHF}}(\langle f \rangle) = h''_{\mathsf{CRHF}}(\langle f' \rangle) = y$, meaning that $\mathcal{A}$ found a collision in h''_{CRHF}, which is a contradiction.

A CT-CRHF *from Unique-Proof* SNARKs. The above construction is tantalizing, but unfortunately we do not know how to prove security (collision-resistance) from any general-purpose notion of obfuscation security (e.g., indistinguishability obfuscation) that is not known to be unachievable. Instead, we show how to use similar ideas to obtain a CT-CRHF using special SNARKs that can be constructed based on a knowledge of exponent assumption.

Taking a closer look at the obfuscation-based construction, we observe that ideal obfuscation was used to ensure that if an adversary $\mathcal{A}$ could come up with an input $x_0\|x_1$ such that $\widetilde{h}_{\mathsf{CRHF}}(x_0\|x_1)$ is the special output $y\|0^{\lambda/2}$, then $\mathcal{A}$ must "know" an f such that $h''_{\mathsf{CRHF}}(\langle f \rangle) = y$ (and $x_0\|x_1$ are a fixed function of f).

With this observation in mind, an alternative way of defining special inputs is as the set of $x_0\|x_1$ that contain a SNARK of this fact. That is, let special inputs be strings x of the form $x_0\|y\|\pi$, where π is a valid proof of knowledge of f satisfying $h''_{\mathsf{CRHF}}(\langle f \rangle) = y \wedge x_0 = f(y)$, and on such inputs let $\widetilde{h}_{\mathsf{CRHF}}(x) = y\|0^{\lambda/2}$.

Is the resulting $\widetilde{h}_{\mathsf{CRHF}}$ collision-resistant? There are two types of collisions that we need to consider. The first type is collisions of the form $x_0\|y\|\pi$, $x_0'\|y\|\pi'$ with $x_0 \neq x_0'$. The second type is collisions in which $x_0 = x_0'$ (but $\pi \neq \pi'$).

The first type of collision is ruled out by the standard SNARK proof-of-knowledge property. If an adversary produces such a collision, then there is an extractor that produces $\langle f \rangle$, $\langle f' \rangle$ such that $h''_{\mathsf{CRHF}}(\langle f \rangle) = h''_{\mathsf{CRHF}}(\langle f' \rangle) = y$ but $f(y) = x_0 \neq x_0' = f'(y)$. The latter inequality implies that $\langle f \rangle \neq \langle f' \rangle$, which means that the extractor is finding a collision in h''_{CRHF}.

To rule out the second type of collision, we require a new "unique proofs" property for the SNARK to ensure that the extracted $\langle f \rangle$, $\langle f' \rangle$ are distinct. Informally, this property says that for any adversary $\mathcal{A}$ that comes up with two distinct valid SNARK-proofs of the same NP claim, there is an extractor $\mathcal{E}$ that comes up with two distinct NP witnesses for the same claim.

An FSKM-incompatible PCIP. For every language $\mathcal{L} \in \mathsf{NP}$ and collision resistant hash function ensemble $\mathcal{H}_{\mathsf{CRHF}}$, we present a contrived PCIP $\widetilde{\Pi}_{\mathsf{PCIP}}$, such that for *any* choice of Fiat-Shamir hash function ensemble $\mathcal{H}_{\mathsf{FS}}$, the resulting protocol $\mathsf{FSKM}[\widetilde{\Pi}_{\mathsf{PCIP}}, \mathcal{H}_{\mathsf{CRHF}}, \mathcal{H}_{\mathsf{FS}}]$ is not sound.

The PCIP construction is inspired by and builds on Barak's [Bar01] beautiful protocol, while taking steps to make the approach compatible with Kilian's protocol. Roughly speaking, our approach is to take an arbitrary PCP for $\mathcal{L}$ (say the one established by the classical PCP theorem) and "tweaking" it so as to maintain its soundness while enabling an attack on the resulting FSKM protocol. Since the tweaking of the PCP will add an additional round, we only obtain a FS-incompatible PCIP rather than a PCP.

In more detail, the first message sent by the honest PCIP prover is $\pi' = b\|\pi$ where b is a single bit and π is a string. The honest PCIP prover *always* sets the bit b to 0 but we add the option of having a malicious prover set b to 1 to facilitate the attack on FSKM.

The PCIP verifier, given this string, first reads the value of b. In case $b = 0$, the verifier simply treats π as a PCP proof string and runs the underlying PCP verifier while redirecting its proof queries to π. This concludes the entire interaction and the PCIP verifier accepts if and only if the PCP verifier accepts. Completeness of the entire protocol as well as soundness for the case that $b = 0$ follow immediately from the construction.

Note however that a malicious prover may indeed send the value $b = 1$. While the verifier could immediately reject in this case, we intentionally make our PCIP verifier do something different. Ignoring π for a moment, the verifier now chooses a random string $r \in \{0,1\}^\lambda$ and sends r to the PCIP prover. The key observation is that when the protocol is compiled via FSKM using a CRHF h_{CRHF} and FS hash function h_{FS}, in the resulting non-interactive argument the value r is fully determined. More specifically, it will always be the case that $r = h_{\mathsf{FS}}(\mathsf{MerkleCom}(h_{\mathsf{CRHF}}, \pi'))$, where $\mathsf{MerkleCom}$ simply computes a Merkle tree of the string π' using the hash function h_{CRHF} and outputs its root. Thus, in order to facilitate the attack, we would like to design our PCIP verifier to accept if it happens to be the case that $r = h_{\mathsf{FS}}(\mathsf{MerkleCom}(h_{\mathsf{CRHF}}, \pi'))$.

What may seem initially problematic is that it is unclear how the PCIP verifier can know which CRHF and FS hash functions will be used in the FSKM protocol. We handle this by simply letting the PCIP prover specify these functions as part of $\pi = (h_{\mathsf{CRHF}}, h_{\mathsf{FS}})$. Thus, after sampling r, we would like for our PCIP verifier to check that $\pi = (h_{\mathsf{CRHF}}, h_{\mathsf{FS}})$ such that $r = h_{\mathsf{FS}}(\mathsf{MerkleCom}(h_{\mathsf{CRHF}}, \pi'))$. Suppose for now that the PCIP verifier does this explicitly (i.e., by reading all of π'). Observe that the PCIP remains sound since r is chosen after the value $h_{\mathsf{FS}}(\mathsf{MerkleCom}(h_{\mathsf{CRHF}}, \pi'))$ is fully determined (and so the probability that r is equal to this value is exponentially vanishing).

On the other hand, we can now demonstrate an attack on the resulting FSKM protocol. Consider a cheating FSKM prover that works as follows. Recall that the FSKM verifier gives the prover descriptions of a CRHF h_{CRHF} and an FS hash function h_{FS}. The prover now sets $\pi = (h_{\mathsf{CRHF}}, h_{\mathsf{FS}})$ and continues as in the FSKM protocol while using $\pi' = (1, \pi)$ as the first PCIP message. In more detail, it computes and sends a Merkle root $\mathsf{MerkleCom}(h_{\mathsf{CRHF}}, \pi')$ to the verifier. By design, the prover and verifier now agree to use the "random" string $r = h_{\mathsf{FS}}(\mathsf{MerkleCom}(h_{\mathsf{CRHF}}, \pi'))$ which makes all of the verifier's tests pass.

A final difficulty that we need to overcome is that the PCIP verifier as described so far has *linear* query complexity since in case $b = 1$ it reads the entire message π. We resolve this by replacing the explicit test done by the verifier with another round of interaction. In more detail, when $b = 1$, after receiving r, the prover is expected to send an *additional* PCP *proving* that $r = h_{FS}(\mathsf{MerkleCom}(h_{\mathsf{CRHF}}, \pi'))$ holds. Actually, a standard PCP will not suffice since a PCP verifier reads its entire input (which in our case is the first PCIP message π). Rather, we will use a PCP *of proximity* (PCPP) [BGH+06, DR06] which is a PCP in which the verifier only reads a few bits of its input and is required to reject inputs that are *far* from the language. To make this approach work, the prover will actually send π encoded under an error-correcting code. We defer further details to the technical sections.

1.5 Organization

In Sect. 2 we give preliminaries. The proof of Theorem 1, via a construction of an FSKM-Incompatible CRHF is presented in Sect. 3. The proof of Theorem 2, via a construction of an FSKM-Incompatible PCIP is presented in Sect. 4. In the full version [BBH+19], we give a sound instantiation of the FSKM protocol for a specific PCP for the empty language, as well as a candidate construction of a SNARK with computationally unique proofs.

2 Preliminaries

We let λ denote the security parameter. Let $[n] = \{1, \ldots, n\}$. Throughout, we will use $\langle P \rangle$ to denote the description of a function/machine/program P. A function $\epsilon(\lambda)$ is said to be negligible, if for every $c \in \mathbb{N}$ it holds that $\epsilon(\lambda) = O(\lambda^{-c})$.

We let $\mathcal{H} = \{\mathcal{H}^{(\lambda)}\}_\lambda$, where $\mathcal{H}^{(\lambda)} = \{h : \{0,1\}^{n(\lambda)} \to \{0,1\}^{m(\lambda)}\}_h$ denote a hash function ensemble, where hash functions $h : \{0,1\}^{n(\lambda)} \to \{0,1\}^{m(\lambda)}$ are sampled as $h \leftarrow \mathcal{H}^{(\lambda)}$.

The *relative distance* between strings $x, y \in \Sigma^\ell$ is $\Delta(x, y) = |\{i \mid x_i \neq y_i\}|/\ell$. The *relative distance* of a string $x \in \Sigma^\ell$ from a (non-empty) set $S \subseteq \Sigma^\ell$ is $\Delta(x, S) = \min_{y \in S}(\Delta(x, y))$.

2.1 Proof Systems

In this work we adhere to the convention in which all proof systems (as well as other cryptographic primitives) are relative to a security parameter λ (given in unary representation to all parties) and with soundness error that is negligible in λ.

Argument Systems (aka Computationally Sound Proofs). The interaction between a prover $\mathcal{P}$, on input x and security parameter 1^λ, and a verifier $\mathcal{V}$, with input y and the same security parameter λ, is denoted by $\langle \mathcal{P}(x, \lambda) \leftrightarrow \mathcal{V}(y, \lambda) \rangle$ and includes a polynomial number of rounds in which each party sends the other a message. The interaction terminates when the verifier $\mathcal{V}$ decides whether to accept or reject its input y. The result of the interaction is the bit $b \in \{0, 1\}$ returned by $\mathcal{V}$ indicating whether it accepted, which is denoted by $\langle \mathcal{P}(x) \leftrightarrow \mathcal{V}(y) \rangle$. If $b = 1$, then we say that $\mathcal{V}$ accepts.

Definition 1 (Argument system). *An* argument system *for a language* $\mathcal{L} \in$ NP, *with soundness error* $s : \mathbb{N} \to [0, 1]$ *is a pair of probabilistic polynomial-time algorithms* $\mathcal{P}$ *and* $\mathcal{V}$ *such that:*

1. **Completeness**: *If* $x \in \mathcal{L}$ *and* w *is a corresponding witness, then for every security parameter* λ *it holds that*

$$\Pr\left[\langle \mathcal{P}(x, w, 1^\lambda) \leftrightarrow \mathcal{V}(x, 1^\lambda) \rangle = 1\right] = 1.$$

2. **Computational soundness**: *If $x \notin \mathcal{L}$, then for all probabilistic polynomial-time malicious prover $\mathcal{P}^*$ and all sufficiently large security parameters λ, it holds that*

$$\Pr\left[\langle \mathcal{P}^*(x, 1^\lambda) \leftrightarrow \mathcal{V}(x, 1^\lambda)\rangle = 1\right] \leq s(\lambda).$$

An argument system $(\mathcal{P}, \mathcal{V})$ is said to be *public-coin* if all messages sent by the verifier $\mathcal{V}$ are random-coin tosses, and $\mathcal{V}$ does not toss any additional random coins.

Probabilistically Checkable Proofs (PCPs). Roughly speaking, a *probabilistically checkable proof* (PCP) is an encoding of an NP witness that can be verified by reading only a few of its bits. More formally:

Definition 2 (Probabilistically checkable proof). *A probabilistically checkable proof (PCP) for a language $\mathcal{L} \in$ NP consists of a polynomial-time algorithm $\mathcal{P}$, which receives a main input x and witness w, and a probabilistic polynomial-time oracle machine $\mathcal{V}$, which receives x and a security parameter 1^λ as explicit inputs, and oracle access to a proof π. The PCP has soundness-error $s : \mathbb{N} \to [0, 1]$ if:*

1. **Completeness**: *If $x \in \mathcal{L}$ and w is a corresponding witness, then for $\pi = \mathcal{P}(x, w)$ and every λ holds that*

$$\Pr\left[\mathcal{V}^\pi(x, 1^\lambda) = 1\right] = 1.$$

2. **Soundness**: *If $x \notin \mathcal{L}$, for every proof π^* and security parameter λ it holds that*

$$\Pr\left[\mathcal{V}^{\pi^*}(x, 1^\lambda) = 1\right] < s(\lambda).$$

In order to query π, the verifier $\mathcal{V}$ tosses $r = r(|x|, \lambda)$ random coins and generates $q = q(|x|, \lambda)$ queries. It will often be convenient to view $\mathcal{V}$ as two separate algorithms $(\mathcal{V}_0, \mathcal{V}_1)$. The first, $\mathcal{V}_0(x; r)$, runs on the instance x and randomness r and outputs the set of queries $\{q_i\}_i$ that $\mathcal{V}$ makes to π. The second algorithm, $\mathcal{V}_1(\{b_i\}_i, x; r)$, takes the corresponding responses $\{b_i\}_i$ as input (as well as the instance x and the same randomness r as $\mathcal{V}_0$), and decides whether to accept or reject.

The following celebrated theorem by [ALM+98] establishes the expressive power of PCPs.

Theorem 1 (PCP theorem). *Every language $\mathcal{L} \in$ NP has a PCP with soundness error $\frac{1}{2}$, constant query complexity, and logarithmic randomness complexity.*

Note that a PCP with negligible soundness error can be easily obtained from Theorem 1 by having the verifier generate $\text{polylog}(\lambda)$ independent query sets.

Probabilistically Checkable Proofs of Proximity (PCPP). In a standard PCP, the verifier is explicitly given the entire input x along with access to an oracle that encodes a "probabilistically checkable" witness. In contrast, in a PCP of proximity (PCPP) [BGH+06, DR06] the goal is for the verifier to decide without even reading the entire input. Thus, the verifier is given oracle access to the input and we count the total number of queries to both the input and the proof.

Since the verifier cannot even read the entire input, the notion of soundness in PCPP is relaxed: the verifier must only reject inputs that "far" from the language (i.e. where distance is measured in Hamming distance).

Following [BGH+06], we define PCPPs with respect to *pair-languages*, which are simply a subset of $\{0,1\}^* \times \{0,1\}^*$. The *projection of a pair-language* $\mathcal{L}$ on x is $\mathcal{L}(x) = \{y \mid (x,y) \in \mathcal{L}\}$.

In our context, we view the first component x of a pair $(x,y) \in \mathcal{L}$ as an *explicit* input for the verifier whereas the second component, y, is an *implicit* input (i.e., the verifier only has oracle access to y). We count the total number of queries to the oracle y, as well as the proof string π. The soundness requirement is that the verifier has to reject words in which the implicit input is far from the projection of $\mathcal{L}$ onto x.

Definition 3 (PCPP). *A probabilistically checkable proof of proximity (PCPP) for a pair-language $\mathcal{L} \in$ NP consists of a polynomial-time prover $\mathcal{P}$ that gets as input a pair (x,y) as well as a witness w, and a probabilistic polynomial-time oracle machine $\mathcal{V}$ that receives x as an explicit input, oracle access to y and oracle access to a proof string π. The verifier also receives (explicitly) a proximity parameter $\delta > 0$ and security parameter 1^λ. The PCPP has soundness error $s : \mathbb{N} \to [0,1]$ if for every proximity parameter $\delta \in [0,1]$, security parameter $\lambda > 0$ and input (x,y):*

1. **Completeness**: *If $(x,y) \in \mathcal{L}$ and w is the corresponding witness, for $\pi = \mathcal{P}((x,y),w)$ it holds that*

$$\Pr[\mathcal{V}^{y,\pi}(x,|y|,|\pi|,1^\lambda,\delta) = 1] = 1.$$

2. **Soundness**: *If $\Delta(y,\mathcal{L}(x)) > \delta$ and oracle π^*, it holds that*

$$\Pr[\mathcal{V}^{y,\pi^*}(x,|y|,|\pi^*|,1^\lambda,\delta) = 1] < s(\lambda).$$

The verifier $\mathcal{V}$ generates $r = r(|x|,\lambda)$ random coins and makes $q = q(|x|,\lambda)$ queries for both oracles. We omit the lengths of the implicit input y and the proof π from the input of the verifier when these are clear from the context.

Ben-Sasson *et al.* [BGH+05] give a construction of PCPP for all of NP (with a suitably efficient verifier).

Theorem 2 ([BGH+05]). *For every language $\mathcal{L} \in$ NTIME(T) and every constant $\delta \in [0,1]$, there exists a PCPP for $\mathcal{L}$ with respect to proximity parameter δ, soundness-error of $\frac{1}{2}$ and proof length poly(T). The verifier runs in time polylog(T) and the prover runs in time poly(T) (i.e., the PCPP proof can be generated in time poly(T) given the NP witness).*

Probabilistically Checkable Interactive Proofs. Probabilistically checkable interactive proofs (PCIPs) [BCS16, RRR16b] (also known as *interactive oracle proofs*) are generalizations of both interactive proofs and PCPs. They allow for multi-round interactions, in which the prover provides the verifier with oracle access to long proof strings, but we only count the number of bits that were actually queried by the verifier. In this work, we will only consider public-coin PCIPs.

Definition 4 (Probabilistically checkable interactive proof). *A probabilistically Checkable Interactive Proof (PCIP) for a language $\mathcal{L} \in$ NP consists of a pair of interactive probabilistic machines $(\mathcal{P}, \mathcal{V})$. The prover $\mathcal{P}$ is a deterministic polynomial-time algorithm, which gets as input x a witness w and a security parameter λ, and the verifier $\mathcal{V}$ is a PPT algorithm, which gets as input x and λ. The interaction consists of the following 3 phases:*

1. **Communication phase**: *The two parties interact for $k = k(|x|, \lambda)$ rounds, in which $\mathcal{V}$ only sends random strings of total length $r = r(|x|, \lambda)$ and $\mathcal{P}$ sends proofs strings $\pi_1, ..., \pi_{k(|x|,\lambda)}$, where π_i is sent in the i-th round.*
2. **Query phase**: *In which $\mathcal{V}$ sends makes a total of $q = q(|x|, \lambda)$ queries to the messages sent by $\mathcal{P}$ in the communication phase.*
3. **Decision phase**: *Based on its random messages in the communication phase, and the answers to its queries in the query phase, the verifier $\mathcal{V}$ decides whether to accept or reject.*

The PCIP $(\mathcal{P}, \mathcal{V})$ has soundness $s : \mathbb{N} \rightarrow [0, 1]$ if:

1. **Completeness**: *If $x \in \mathcal{L}$ and w is the corresponding witness, then for every security parameter λ it holds that*

$$\Pr\left[\langle \mathcal{P}(x, w, \lambda) \leftrightarrow \mathcal{V}(x, \lambda) \rangle = 1\right] = 1.$$

2. **Soundness**: *If $x \notin \mathcal{L}$, then $\forall \mathcal{P}^*$ and security parameters λ, it holds that*

$$\Pr\left[\langle \mathcal{P}^*(x, \lambda) \leftrightarrow \mathcal{V}(x, \lambda) \rangle = 1\right] < s(\lambda).$$

2.2 Kilian's Protocol

Before describing Kilian's protocol, we first recall the definition of collision resistant hash functions and Merkle trees.

CRHF and Merkle Trees. An efficiently computable hash function ensemble $\mathcal{H} = \{\mathcal{H}^{(\lambda)}\}_\lambda$ where $\mathcal{H}^{(\lambda)} = \{h : \{0,1\}^{2\lambda} \rightarrow \{0,1\}^\lambda\}$ is *collision resistant* (CRHF), if there exists a key generation algorithm Gen that on input 1^λ samples h from $\mathcal{H}^{(\lambda)}$ such that for every PPT adversary $\mathcal{A}$ it holds that

$$\Pr_{\substack{h \leftarrow \mathsf{Gen}(1^\lambda) \\ (x,x') \leftarrow \mathcal{A}(h)}} [h(x) = h(x') \wedge x \neq x'] \leq \mathsf{negl}(|\lambda|).$$

Remark 1. The above definition of CRHF is sometimes referred to as a *private-coin* CRHF [HR04] since security is not guaranteed if the adversary sees the coins used by Gen. Nevertheless, for sake of conciseness we will sometimes avoid mentioning Gen explicitly and simply write $h \leftarrow \mathcal{H}^{(\lambda)}$.

We will use the following syntax to describe Merkle tree commitments, which can be built from any CRHF family $\mathcal{H} = \{\mathcal{H}^{(\lambda)}\}_\lambda$. For each of the following algorithms, the input hash function h is drawn uniformly at random from $\mathcal{H}^{(\lambda)}$. For any $d \geq 1$, a Merkle tree commitment allows us to commit to a message $s \in \{0,1\}^m$ where $m := \lambda \cdot 2^d$. That is, we view s as 2^d blocks of λ bits.

- MerkleCom$(h, s \in \{0,1\}^m)$. Write s as $(\ell_1\|\ell_2\| \ldots \|\ell_{2^d})$ where each $\ell_j \in \{0,1\}^\lambda$. Build a binary tree of hash evaluations, starting from the 2^d leaves $(\ell_1\|\ell_2\| \ldots \|\ell_{2^d})$. Output the root com $\in \{0,1\}^\lambda$ of the resulting tree.

A commitment to s can be *locally opened* to the reveal the bits in the ith block by revealing the siblings along the root-to-ith-leaf path:

- MerkleOpen$(h, s \in \{0,1\}^m, i \in [2^d])$. Write s as $(\ell_1\|\ell_2\| \ldots \|\ell_{2^d})$ where each $\ell_j \in \{0,1\}^\lambda$. Determine the path from ℓ_i to the root in the tree of hash evaluations under h, denoted $\{\hat{c}_j\}_{j\in[d]}$ where $\hat{c}_d = \ell_i$. For each $i \in [d]$, determine the sibling sib_i of $\hat{c}_i$. Output open $= \{(\hat{c}_i, \mathsf{sib}_i, p_i)\}_{i\in[d]}$ where $p_i \in \{\mathsf{left}, \mathsf{right}\}$ denotes whether sib_i is a left or right sibling of $\hat{c}_i$.
  For $I \subseteq [2^d]$ we define MerkleOpen$(h, s \in \{0,1\}^m, I)$ as $(\mathsf{MerkleOpen}(h, s \in \{0,1\}^m, i))_{i\in I}$.

These openings can easily be verified by verifying the hash computations with h:

- MerkleVer$(h, \mathsf{com}, \mathsf{open})$ first writes open as $\{(\hat{c}_i, \mathsf{sib}_i, p_i)\}_{i\in[d]}$. Let $\hat{c}_0 = \mathsf{com}$. For each $i \in [d]$, check that $h(\mathsf{sib}_i\|\hat{c}_i) = \hat{c}_{i-1}$ if $p_i = \mathsf{left}$ or that $h(\hat{c}_i\|\mathsf{sib}_i) = \hat{c}_{i-1}$ if $p_i = \mathsf{right}$. Output 1 (accept) if all checks pass, otherwise output 0.

Kilian's Protocol. While Kilian's original protocol relied on PCPs, a natural generalization to PCIPs was suggested by Ben-Sasson *et al.* [BCS16]. This extension proceeds by having the prover repeatedly commit to each of its oracles (rather than sending the entire oracle). At the end of the interaction, the verifier can specify which locations to open and the prover can use the Merkle tree structure to succinctly decommit to these specific locations.

Construction 3. *Let $(\mathcal{P}, \mathcal{V})$ be a public-coin k-round PCIP for $\mathcal{L} \in$ NP. Consider the following argument system for $\mathcal{L}$, denoted by $(\mathcal{P}', \mathcal{V}') = \mathsf{Kilian}[(\mathcal{P}, \mathcal{V}), \mathcal{H}]$, as described in Fig. 1, w.r.t. a CRHF $\mathcal{H}$.*

Theorem 4 (Kilian's protocol). *If (P, V) is a PCIP and $\mathcal{H}$ is a CRHF family, then Construction 3 is a computationally sound argument system with negligible soundness error, communication complexity $\mathsf{poly}(\lambda, \log|x|)$. The verifier runs in time $O(|x| \cdot \mathsf{poly}(\lambda, \log|x|))$ and the prover runs in time $\mathsf{poly}(|x|, |w|, \lambda)$.*

Protocol 1: Kilian's protocol

Common input: $x, 1^\lambda$
Prover's auxiliary input: w

1 $\mathcal{V}'$ generates a hash function $h \leftarrow \mathcal{H}^{(\lambda)}$ and sends h to $\mathcal{P}'$.
2 **for** $j = 1, ..., k$ **do**
3       $\mathcal{P}'$ sends $\mathsf{com}_j = \mathsf{MerkleCom}(h, \pi_j)$, where π_j is the message sent by $\mathcal{P}$ in $(\mathcal{P}(x, w, 1^\lambda), \mathcal{V}(x, 1^\lambda))$ on the j-th round.
4       $\mathcal{V}'$ sends r_j, where r_j is the message sent by $\mathcal{V}$ on the j-th round of $(\mathcal{P}(x, w, 1^\lambda), \mathcal{V}(x, 1^\lambda))$.
5       $\mathcal{P}'$ sends open_j to $\mathcal{V}'$ where $\mathsf{open}_j = \mathsf{MerkleOpen}(h, \pi_j, Q_j)$, where Q_j is the set of queries generated by $\mathcal{V}$ on round j with randomness r_j.
6       $\mathcal{V}'$ computes $v_j \in \{0, 1\}$ where $v_j = \mathsf{MerkleVer}(h, \mathsf{com}_j, \mathsf{open}_j)$.
7 **end**
8 $\mathcal{V}'$ accepts if and only if $\bigwedge_j v_j = 1$ and $\mathcal{V}(x, \{b_1^{i_1}\}_{i_1}, ..., \{b_k^{i_k}\}_{i_k}) = 1$, where $\{b_j^{i_j}\}_{i_j}$ is the set result of the queries revealed in open_j.

Fig. 1. Kilian's protocol

Completeness follows from the correctness of the Merkle tree commitment scheme and the completeness of the PCIP for $\mathcal{L}$.

Soundness follows from the binding property of the commitment scheme and the soundness of the PCP. Note that the soundness of the PCIP was not enough on its own, as without committing to the PCIP proof strings, the prover could have engineered proof strings to make the verifier accept according to its queries.

2.3 Fiat-Shamir

The Fiat-Shamir Heuristic. The Fiat-Shamir heuristic [FS86] is a method for reducing the number of rounds in public-coin interactive proofs. Loosely speaking, the idea is that instead of having the verifier send their random coins, the prover uses a hash function in order to generate the verifier's randomness.

Definition 5 (Fiat-Shamir transform). *Let* $\mathcal{H}_{\mathsf{FS}} = \left\{\mathcal{H}_{\mathsf{FS}}^{(\lambda)} : \{0,1\}^* \to \{0,1\}^*\right\}_{\lambda \in \mathbb{N}}$ *be a hash-function ensemble,* $\Pi = (\mathcal{P}, \mathcal{V})$ *be a public-coin protocol, and*

$$(\alpha_1, \beta_1, ..., \alpha_m, \beta_m)$$

be the set of exchanged messages between $(\mathcal{P}, \mathcal{V})$, *where* $\{\alpha_i\}_{i=1}^m$ *are messages sent by the prover and* $\{\beta_i\}_{i=1}^m$ *the messages sent by the verifier. The Fiat-Shamir transform of* Π, *denoted by* $(\mathcal{P}_{\mathsf{FS}}, \mathcal{V}_{\mathsf{FS}}) = \mathsf{FS}[\Pi, \mathcal{H}_{\mathsf{FS}}]$ *is defined in Fig. 2.*

The FSKM Protocol. The FSKM protocol is obtained by applying the Fiat-Shamir transform to Kilian's protocol (or rather to its extension to PCIPs), to create succinct non-interactive argument systems for NP.

Protocol 2: Fiat-Shamir transform

Common input: $x, 1^\lambda$
Prover's auxiliary input: w
1 $\mathcal{V}_{\mathsf{FS}}$ generates a key $h_{\mathsf{FS}} \leftarrow \mathcal{H}_{\mathsf{FS}}^{(\lambda)}$ and sends it to $\mathcal{P}_{\mathsf{FS}}$.
2 $\mathcal{P}_{\mathsf{FS}}$ sends the following, all in a *single* message

$$\alpha_1, \ \beta_1 = h_{\mathsf{FS}}(\tau_1), \ \alpha_2, \ \beta_2 = h_{\mathsf{FS}}(\tau_2), ..., \alpha_m, \ \beta_m = h_{\mathsf{FS}}(\tau_m)$$

where $\tau_i = (\alpha_1 \| \beta_1 \| ... \| \alpha_i)$ is the transcript thus far.
3 $\mathcal{V}_{\mathsf{FS}}$ checks that $\forall i \in [m] : \beta_i = h_{\mathsf{FS}}(\tau_i)$, and accepts iff $\mathcal{V}(x, \alpha_1, \beta_1, ..., \alpha_m, \beta_m)$
   accepts.

Fig. 2. The Fiat-Shamir transform.

Recall that the FSKM protocol emulates Kilian's protocol, and replaces the verifier's randomness with the application of a FS hash function on the transcript thus far. Regardless of whether it is applied on a PCP or PCIP, the FSKM protocol is a two-round argument system.

Definition 6 (FSKM Protocol). *Given a PCIP Π, a CRHF ensemble $\mathcal{H}_{\mathsf{CRHF}}$, and FS hash function ensemble $\mathcal{H}_{\mathsf{FS}}$, we define*

$$\mathsf{FSKM}[\Pi, \mathcal{H}_{\mathsf{CRHF}}, \mathcal{H}_{\mathsf{FS}}] \triangleq \mathsf{FS}\left[\mathsf{Kilian}[\Pi, \mathcal{H}_{\mathsf{CRHF}}], \mathcal{H}_{\mathsf{FS}}\right].$$

3   An FSKM-Incompatible CRHF

In this section, we obtain our first main result by constructing a specific CRHF family $\widetilde{\mathcal{H}}_{\mathsf{CRHF}}$, for which, loosely speaking, FSKM is not sound. Our CRHF will make use of a *publicly-verifiable succinct non-interactive argument of knowledge* (pv-SNARK) with an additional "unique proofs" property that we formalize in Sect. 3.1. For completeness, we start by providing some background on SNARKs.

3.1   Background on SNARKs

We first define the *universal relation* [BG08] relative to *random-access machines*.

Definition 7 (Universal Relation). *The universal relation is the set $\mathcal{R}_\mathcal{U}$ of instance-witness pairs $(y, w) = \left(\left(\langle M \rangle, x, t\right), w\right)$, where $|y|, |w| \leq t$ and $\langle M \rangle$ is the description of a random-access machine M, such that M accepts (x, w) after at most t steps. We denote by $\mathcal{L}_\mathcal{U}$ the universal language corresponding to $\mathcal{R}_\mathcal{U}$.*

We next define publicly-verifiable succinct non-interactive arguments of knowledge (pv-SNARKs), following [BCCT13]. The following definition is taken verbatim from Bitansky *et al.* [BCCT13], and for more in-depth discussion on SNARKs we refer the reader to [BCCT13].

Definition 8. (pv-SNARKs). *A triple of algorithms* $(\mathcal{G}, \mathcal{P}, \mathcal{V})$, *where* $\mathcal{G}$ *is probabilistic and* $\mathcal{V}$ *is deterministic, is a fully-succinct* pv-SNARK *if the following conditions are satisfied:*

- **Completeness**: *For every large enough security parameter* $\lambda \in \mathbb{N}$, *every time bound* $B \in \mathbb{N}$, *and every instance-witness pair* $(y, w) = ((\langle M \rangle, x, t), w) \in \mathcal{R}_{\mathcal{U}}$ *with* $t \leq B$,

$$\Pr\left[\mathcal{V}(\mathsf{crs}, y, \pi) = 1 : \begin{matrix} \mathsf{crs} \leftarrow \mathcal{G}(1^\lambda, B) \\ \pi \leftarrow \mathcal{P}(\mathsf{crs}, y, w) \end{matrix}\right] = 1.$$

- **Adaptive Proof of Knowledge**: *For every polynomial-sized prover* $\mathcal{P}^*$ *there exists a polynomial-sized extractor* $\mathcal{E}_{\mathcal{P}^*}$ *such that for every auxiliary input* $z \in \{0, 1\}^{\mathsf{poly}(\lambda)}$, *every time bound* $B \in \mathbb{N}$,

$$\Pr\left[\begin{matrix} \mathcal{V}(\mathsf{crs}, y, \pi) = 1 \\ (y, w) \notin \mathcal{R}_{\mathcal{U}} \end{matrix} : \begin{matrix} \mathsf{crs} \leftarrow \mathcal{G}(1^\lambda, B) \\ (y, \pi) \leftarrow \mathcal{P}^*(z, \mathsf{crs}) \\ w \leftarrow \mathcal{E}_{\mathcal{P}^*}(z, \mathsf{crs}) \end{matrix}\right] \leq \mathsf{negl}(\lambda),$$

- **Efficiency**: *There exists a universal polynomial* p *such that for every large enough security parameter* $\lambda \in \mathbb{N}$, *and* $t \leq \lambda^{\log(\lambda)}$,
  - *the generator* $\mathcal{G}(1^\lambda)$ *runs in time* $p(\lambda)$,
  - *the prover* $\mathcal{P}(\mathsf{crs}, y, w)$ *runs in time* $p(\lambda + |M| + |x| + t)$,
  - *the verifier* $\mathcal{V}(\mathsf{crs}, y, \pi)$ *runs in time* $p(\lambda + |M| + |x|)$,
  - *and an honestly generated proof has size* $p(\lambda)$.

Computationally Unique SNARK. In this work we introduce a new security property of SNARKs which we refer to as *computationally unique proofs* (which can be thought of as a particular computational variant of unambiguous proofs [RRR16a]). The requirement here is that if a computationally bounded prover $\mathcal{P}$ can generate two valid proofs $\pi_1 \neq \pi_2$ for the same instance y, it must be possible to extract from $\mathcal{P}$ two distinct witnesses $w_1 \neq w_2$ for y.

Definition 9. (SNARKs with computationally unique proofs). *A SNARK with computationally unique proofs is defined as in Definition 8, but with one additional requirement:*

- **Computationally Unique Proofs**: *For every polynomial-sized adversary* $\mathcal{A}^*$, *there exists a polynomial-sized "extractor"* $\mathcal{E}_{\mathcal{A}^*}$ *such that for every auxiliary input* $z \in \{0, 1\}^{\mathsf{poly}(k)}$, *every time bound* $B \in \mathbb{N}$,

$$\Pr\left[\begin{matrix} \mathcal{V}(\mathsf{crs}, y, \pi_1) = 1 \\ \mathcal{V}(\mathsf{crs}, y, \pi_2) = 1 \\ \pi_1 \neq \pi_2 \\ (y, w_1) \notin \mathcal{R}_{\mathcal{U}} \vee (y, w_2) \notin \mathcal{R}_{\mathcal{U}} \\ \vee w_1 = w_2 \end{matrix} : \begin{matrix} \mathsf{crs} \leftarrow \mathcal{G}(1^\lambda, B) \\ (y, \pi_1, \pi_2) \leftarrow \mathcal{A}^*(z, \mathsf{crs}) \\ (w_1, w_2) \leftarrow \mathcal{E}_{\mathcal{A}^*}(z, \mathsf{crs}) \end{matrix}\right] \leq \mathsf{negl}(\lambda).$$

In the full version [BBH+19], we prove that a preprocessing pv-SNARK constructed in Bitansky *et al.* [BCI+13] from a knowledge of exponent assumption satisfies our notion of computationally unique proofs. We then show that

J. Bartusek et al.

the generic transformation of [BCCT13] from a preprocessing pv-SNARK to fully-succinct pv-SNARK maintains the computationally unique proofs property. Thus, we obtain a fully-succinct pv-SNARK with computationally unique proofs from a knowledge of exponent assumption (and additionally the existence of exponentially-secure one-way functions to address a subtlety in the definition of adaptive proof of knowledge).

3.2 An FSKM-Incompatible CRHF

To formally state our result, we first define a trivial PCP-based 2-message protocol—a protocol that, intuitively, should not be sound. Jumping ahead, at a high level, our main result shows that there exists a collision-resistant hash family $\widetilde{\mathcal{H}}_{\mathsf{CRHF}}$ such that for any $\varPi_{\mathsf{PCP}}$ and any $\mathcal{H}_{\mathsf{FS}}$, the corresponding FSKM protocol is *no more secure* than the corresponding trivial protocol.

The first message of the trivial protocol will be a random string r drawn from some distribution $\mathcal{S}$, which will serve as $\mathcal{V}_{\mathsf{PCP}}$'s randomness. The prover takes r as input and outputs a PCP proof π that will be then verified by $\mathcal{V}_{\mathsf{PCP}}$ using randomness r. Intuitively, since a cheating prover is aware of the verifier's randomness, it can answer queries *adaptively*, so we do not expect the trivial protocol to be sound.

Suppose we have some PCP $\varPi_{\mathsf{PCP}} = (\mathcal{P}_{\mathsf{PCP}}, \mathcal{V}_{\mathsf{PCP}})$. It will be convenient for us to split the verifier $\mathcal{V}_{\mathsf{PCP}}$ into two algorithms: $\mathcal{V}_{\mathsf{PCP}}^{(0)}$ (which outputs the set of query locations) and $\mathcal{V}_{\mathsf{PCP}}^{(1)}$ (which decides whether or not to accept after seeing the prover responses).

Construction 5. (Trivial Protocol). *Let* $\mathsf{Trivial}[\varPi_{\mathsf{PCP}}, \mathcal{S}] = (\mathcal{P}_{\mathsf{Trivial}}, \mathcal{V}_{\mathsf{Trivial}})$ *be the following 2-message protocol, for some PCP* $\varPi_{\mathsf{PCP}} = (\mathcal{P}_{\mathsf{PCP}}, \mathcal{V}_{\mathsf{PCP}}^{(0)}, \mathcal{V}_{\mathsf{PCP}}^{(1)})$ *for a language* $\mathcal{L}$, *and some sampling algorithm* $\mathcal{S}$. *The verifier* $\mathcal{V}_{\mathsf{Trivial}}$ *generates a random string* r *from* $\mathcal{S}$ *and sends* r *to the prover. The prover* $\mathcal{P}_{\mathsf{Trivial}}$, *on input* (x, w, r) *for* $x \in \mathcal{L}$ *runs* $\mathcal{V}_{\mathsf{PCP}}^{(0)}(x; r)$ *to obtain a set of query locations* $\{q_i\}_i$. $\mathcal{P}_{\mathsf{Trivial}}$ *then computes* $b_i \leftarrow \mathcal{P}_{\mathsf{PCP}}(x, w, q_i)$ *for each* i *and sends* $\{b_i\}$ *to the verifier* $\mathcal{V}_{\mathsf{Trivial}}$. *The verifier* $\mathcal{V}_{\mathsf{Trivial}}$ *computes* $\mathcal{V}_{\mathsf{PCP}}^{(0)}(x; r) = \{q_i\}_i$ *and accepts if and only if* $\mathcal{V}_{\mathsf{PCP}}^{(1)}(x, \{(q_i, b_i)\}_i; r)$ *accepts.*

In what follows, we will sometimes view $\mathcal{S}$ as an algorithm that explicitly takes its randomness u as input, and outputs $r = \mathcal{S}(u)$.

For non-contrived choices of a PCP and sampling algorithm we do not expect Construction 5 to be sound. For example, consider Håstad's PCP [Hås01] in which the verifier queries 3 bits of the proof and checks whether their parity is some known fixed value b. Soundness of the trivial protocol can now be violated by having the prover send the answers $(0, 0, b)$.[4]

---

[4] Note that Håstad's PCP only has constant soundness. Nevertheless, the attack can be generalized to the sequential repetition of Håstad's PCP as long as the sampler $\mathcal{S}$ generates random query sets.

Recall (see Line 3) that $\mathsf{FSKM}[\Pi_{\mathsf{PCP}}, \mathcal{H}_{\mathsf{CRHF}}, \mathcal{H}_{\mathsf{FS}}]$ denotes the 2-message argument that results from applying the Fiat-Shamir transform with hash function ensemble $\mathcal{H}_{\mathsf{FS}}$ to $\mathsf{Kilian}[\Pi_{\mathsf{PCP}}, \mathcal{H}_{\mathsf{CRHF}}]$.

The main theorem of this section is the following.

Theorem 6. *Assume the existence of a fully-succinct* $\mathsf{pv}\text{-}\mathsf{SNARK}$ *with computationally unique proofs, where honestly generated proofs have size at most* $p(\lambda)$, *and collision resistant hash functions. Define* $m := 2\lambda \cdot p(\lambda)$. *Then, there exists a collision resistant hash family* $\widetilde{\mathcal{H}}_{\mathsf{CRHF}} = \left\{ \widetilde{\mathcal{H}}_{\mathsf{CRHF}}^{(\lambda)} : \{0,1\}^{2m} \to \{0,1\}^m \right\}_{\lambda \in \mathbb{N}}$ *such that for any* PCP $\Pi_{\mathsf{PCP}} = (\mathcal{P}_{\mathsf{PCP}}, \mathcal{V}_{\mathsf{PCP}})$ *with proof length at most* 2^λ, *and any hash function ensemble* $\mathcal{H}_{\mathsf{FS}}$, *if* $\mathsf{FSKM}[\Pi_{\mathsf{PCP}}, \widetilde{\mathcal{H}}_{\mathsf{CRHF}}, \mathcal{H}_{\mathsf{FS}}]$ *is computationally sound, then* $\mathsf{Trivial}[\Pi_{\mathsf{PCP}}, \mathcal{H}_{\mathsf{FS}}]$ *is computationally sound.*

We believe that for natural choices of PCPs, the trivial protocol will not be sound which, by Theorem 6, means that the corresponding FSKM protocol is not sound. However, actually proving that the trivial protocol is not sound seems to be difficult in case the sampling algorithm generates a peculiar distribution of random strings.[5]

Nevertheless, we can exhibit a *specific* (trivial) PCP for which the trivial protocol is provably not sound. The immediate implication is that for every FS hash function, there exists a PCP and a bounded size CRHF for which soundness of the corresponding FSKM is violated. This is formalized in the following corollary.

Corollary 1. *Assume the existence of a fully-succinct* $\mathsf{pv}\text{-}\mathsf{SNARK}$ *with computationally unique proofs. There exists a language* $\mathcal{L} \in \mathsf{NP}$, *a PCP for* $\mathcal{L}$ *(with* $\mathrm{polylog}(\lambda)$ *query complexity) and a fixed polynomial* $p(\cdot)$ *such that for all efficiently computable hash function ensembles* $\mathcal{H}_{\mathsf{FS}}$, *there exists a CRHF ensemble* $\mathcal{H}_{\mathsf{CRHF}} = \left\{ \mathcal{H}_{\mathsf{CRHF}}^{(\lambda)} : \{0,1\}^{2s(\lambda)} \to \{0,1\}^{s(\lambda)} \right\}_{\lambda \in \mathbb{N}}$ *with* $s(\lambda) \leq p(\lambda)$, *such that* $\mathsf{FSKM}[\Pi_{\mathsf{PCP}}, \mathcal{H}_{\mathsf{CRHF}}, \mathcal{H}_{\mathsf{FS}}]$ *is not sound.*

We first prove Corollary 1 and then go back to the main part—proving Theorem 6.

Proof of Corollary 1. We exhibit a contrived PCP $\Pi_\emptyset$ for the empty language for which the statement holds. Specifically, consider a PCP verifier that samples at random $r \in \{0,1\}^{\log^2(\lambda)}$ and checks whether the $\log^2(\lambda)$-long prefix of the proof is exactly equal to r (by making $\log^2(\lambda)$ queries).

Completeness holds vacuously, and this PCP is sound since the proof must be specified before r was sampled. However, the protocol $\mathsf{Trivial}[\Pi_\emptyset, \mathcal{H}_{\mathsf{FS}}]$ for any sampler $\mathcal{H}_{\mathsf{FS}}$ is clearly not sound, since the cheating prover receives the verifier randomness r as input and simply returns r as its proof. □

---

[5] One would assume that a random choice of FS hash function from the collection would produce a uniformly random string for the verifier. However, since we want to deal with *arbitrary* candidate FS hash functions, we cannot assume that this is the case.

In the full version [BBH+19], we actually give a secure instantiation of FSKM for a variant of the PCP Π_0 that was used to prove Corollary 2. This does not contradict our impossibility, which only rules out security of FSKM with a *generic* CRHF. In particular, our instantiation requires the collision-resistant hash function to also be somewhere statistically binding [HW15a]. Unfortunately, we do not know how to instantiate the FSKM protocol to construct an argument scheme for a non-trivial language.

The remainder of this section will be devoted to a proof of Theorem 6. As described in Sect. 1.4, our strategy centers on a carefully-designed hash function family $\widetilde{\mathcal{H}}_{\mathsf{CRHF}}$, built using two CRHFs and a fully-succinct pv-SNARK with computationally unique proofs (Definition 9). The result then follows immediately from combining Lemma 1, which states that $\widetilde{\mathcal{H}}_{\mathsf{CRHF}}$ is a CRHF family, and Lemma 2, which establishes the soundness implication.

3.3   CRHF Construction

Throughout this construction we will use the notation from the statement of Theorem 6; recall that $p(\lambda)$ is a bound on the proof size of our pv-SNARK, $m := 2\lambda \cdot p(\lambda)$, and $c > 0$ is an arbitrary constant independent of $p(\lambda)$.

We prove Theorem 6 by carefully constructing a CRHF family $\widetilde{\mathcal{H}}_{\mathsf{CRHF}} = \{\widetilde{\mathcal{H}}_{\mathsf{CRHF}}^{(\lambda)} : \{0,1\}^{2m} \to \{0,1\}^m\}_{\lambda \in \mathbb{N}}$. Our construction requires the following:

- A fully-succinct pv-SNARK $\mathcal{S} = (\mathcal{G}, \mathcal{P}, \mathcal{V})$ with computationally unique proofs (Definition 9), where honestly generated proofs have size exactly $p(\lambda)$ (assume that shorter proofs are appropriately padded with zeros).
- A CRHF family $\mathcal{H}_{\mathsf{rt}} = \{\mathcal{H}_{\mathsf{rt}}^{(\lambda)} : \{0,1\}^* \to \{0,1\}^{m/2-\lambda-\log(\lambda)-2}\}_{\lambda \in \mathbb{N}}$.
- A CRHF family $\mathcal{H}_{\mathsf{tree}} = \{\mathcal{H}_{\mathsf{tree}}^{(\lambda)} : \{0,1\}^{2m} \to \{0,1\}^{m-2}\}_{\lambda \in \mathbb{N}}$.

3.4   CRHF Key Generation

We sample a hash function $\widetilde{h}_{\mathsf{CRHF}} \leftarrow \widetilde{\mathcal{H}}_{\mathsf{CRHF}}^{(\lambda)}$ as follows.

1. Sample uniformly random $\$_{\mathsf{rt}} \leftarrow \{0,1\}^m$.
   - Let $\mathsf{pre}_{\mathsf{rt}}$ denote the first two bits of $\$_{\mathsf{rt}}$.
   - Define $\mathsf{pre}_{\mathsf{tree}} := \mathsf{pre}_{\mathsf{rt}} \oplus 10$ and $\mathsf{pre}_{\mathsf{path}} := \mathsf{pre}_{\mathsf{rt}} \oplus 01$.
2. Sample uniformly random $\$_{\mathsf{path}} \leftarrow \{0,1\}^\lambda$.
3. Sample $h_{\mathsf{rt}} \leftarrow \mathcal{H}_{\mathsf{rt}}^{(\lambda)}$ and $h_{\mathsf{tree}} \leftarrow \mathcal{H}_{\mathsf{tree}}^{(\lambda)}$.
4. Define $h'_{\mathsf{tree}} : \{0,1\}^{2m} \to \{0,1\}^m$ such that $h'_{\mathsf{tree}}(x) = (\mathsf{pre}_{\mathsf{tree}} \| h_{\mathsf{tree}}(x))$.
5. Sample $\mathsf{crs} \leftarrow \mathcal{G}(1^\lambda)$.
6. For each $j \in [\lambda]$, compute $\mathsf{com}_j^{(\mathsf{zero})} = \mathsf{MerkleCom}(h'_{\mathsf{tree}}, 0^{m \cdot 2^j})$.
7. Output

$$(\$_{\mathsf{rt}}, \$_{\mathsf{path}}, \mathsf{pre}_{\mathsf{tree}}, \mathsf{pre}_{\mathsf{path}}, h_{\mathsf{rt}}, h'_{\mathsf{tree}}, \mathsf{crs}, \{\mathsf{com}_j^{(\mathsf{zero})}\}_{j \in [\lambda]}),$$

as the description (hash key) of $\widetilde{h}_{\mathsf{CRHF}}$.

CRHF Evaluation. Before we describe how to compute $\widetilde{h}_{\mathsf{CRHF}}(x)$, we need to introduce some specialized notation and definitions.

Notation. We will assume without loss of generality that $m = 2^{m'}$ is a power of 2, and that the PCP Π_{PCP} in fact has proof length bounded by $2^\lambda - m$. Throughout, $\{(q_i, b_i)\}_i$ will denote a set of (index, bit) pairs (representing PCP query/response pairs) where for each i, $q_i \in [2^\lambda - m]$ and $b_i \in \{0,1\}$. We assume without loss of generality that no index appears more than once.

For any set $\{(q_i, b_i)\}_i$ satisfying these conditions, we let $\pi^{\{(q_i,b_i)\}_i}$ denote the length $2^\lambda - m$ bitstring defined bit-wise for each $j \in [2^\lambda - m]$ as:

$$\left(\pi^{\{(q_i,b_i)\}_i}\right)_j := \begin{cases} b & \text{if } (j,b) \in \{(q_i,b_i)\}_i, \\ 0 & \text{else.} \end{cases}$$

In other words, $\pi^{\{(q_i,b_i)\}_i}$ is a PCP proof string that consists of the responses in $\{(q_i, b_i)\}_i$ and 0s everywhere else.

We divide $\pi^{\{(q_i,b_i)\}_i}$ into $2^{\lambda-m'} - 1$ words ℓ_k of $m = 2^{m'}$ bits each, i.e. $\pi^{\{(q_i,b_i)\}_i} = (\ell_1 \| \ell_2 \| \dots \| \ell_{2^{\lambda-m'}-1})$, where each word ℓ_k is in $\{0,1\}^m$. Next, group the words as follows. The first $2^{\lambda-m'-1}$ words will form the first block L_1, the next $2^{\lambda-m'-2}$ words will form the second block L_2, and so on until the last block only consists of only 1 word. We can now write $\pi^{\{(q_i,b_i)\}_i}$ as

$$\left(L_1 \| \dots \| L_{\lambda-m'}\right) := \Big((\ell_1 \| \dots \| \ell_{2^{\lambda-m'-1}})$$
$$\left\| (\ell_{2^{\lambda-m'-1}+1} \| \dots \| \ell_{2^{\lambda-m'-1}+2^{\lambda-m'-2}}) \right\| \dots \left\| (\ell_{2^{\lambda-m'}-1}) \right),$$

where the jth block L_j is exactly twice the length of the $(j+1)$th block L_{j+1}.

We define the helper functions $t(q)$ and $s(q)$ for any $q \in [2^\lambda - m]$ so that the qth bit in $\pi^{\{(q_i,b_i)\}_i}$ is the $t(q)$th bit in block $L_{s(q)}$.

Now define

- $\mathsf{block\text{-}com}(h'_{\mathsf{tree}}, \{(q_i, b_i)\}_i, j) := \mathsf{MerkleCom}(h'_{\mathsf{tree}}, L_j)$, and
- $\mathsf{block\text{-}open}(h'_{\mathsf{tree}}, \{(q_i, b_i)\}_i, i) := \mathsf{MerkleOpen}(h'_{\mathsf{tree}}, L_{s(q_i)}, t(q_i))$.

Note that given $\{\mathsf{com}_j^{(\mathsf{zero})}\}_{j \in [\lambda]}$, if $|\{(q_i, b_i)\}_i| = \mathsf{poly}(\lambda)$, it is easy to compute $\mathsf{block\text{-}com}(h'_{\mathsf{tree}}, \{(q_i, b_i)\}_i, j)$ and $\mathsf{block\text{-}open}(h'_{\mathsf{tree}}, \{(q_i, b_i)\}_i, i)$ in time $\mathsf{poly}(\lambda)$.

Language. We also define a language $\mathcal{L}_{\$_{\mathsf{rt}}, h_{\mathsf{rt}}, h'_{\mathsf{tree}}}$ based on $\$_{\mathsf{rt}}$, h_{rt}, and h'_{tree} (all given in the CRHF description $\tilde{h}_{\mathsf{CRHF}}$). Throughout, we use $\mathsf{bit}_\lambda(j)$ to denote the $\log(\lambda)$-bit binary representation of an integer j.

$\mathcal{L}_{\$_{\mathsf{rt}}, h_{\mathsf{rt}}, h'_{\mathsf{tree}}}$ will be defined by relation $\mathcal{R}_{\$_{\mathsf{rt}}, h_{\mathsf{rt}}, h'_{\mathsf{tree}}}$, which consists of all (instance, witness) pairs of the form

$$\Big((\alpha \| \mathsf{bit}_\lambda(j) \| \mathsf{sib}), (\langle h_{\mathsf{FS}} \rangle \| \langle \mathcal{A}_{\mathsf{Trivial}} \rangle \| \langle \mathcal{V}_{\mathsf{PCP}} \rangle) \Big),$$

which satisfy all of the following conditions:

1. $\langle h_{\mathsf{FS}} \rangle$ and $\langle \mathcal{A}_{\mathsf{Trivial}} \rangle$ can be parsed as descriptions of the (deterministic) circuits h_{FS} and $\mathcal{A}_{\mathsf{Trivial}}$. When used in the proof of Lemma 1, h_{FS} will correspond to the Fiat-Shamir hash function $h_{\mathsf{FS}} \leftarrow \mathcal{H}_{\mathsf{FS}}$, and $\mathcal{A}_{\mathsf{Trivial}}$ will correspond to the adversary breaking the soundness of $\mathsf{Trivial}[\Pi_{\mathsf{PCP}}, \mathcal{H}_{\mathsf{FS}}]$.

2. $\langle \mathcal{V}_{\mathsf{PCP}} \rangle$ can be parsed as the description of a two-part PCP verifier $\mathcal{V}_{\mathsf{PCP}}^{(0)}, \mathcal{V}_{\mathsf{PCP}}^{(1)}$, where $\mathcal{V}_{\mathsf{PCP}}^{(0)}$ outputs a set of query locations, and $\mathcal{V}_{\mathsf{PCP}}^{(1)}$ takes the query responses and outputs a bit indicating accept/reject (see the discussion in Sect. 2.1).
3. $\alpha = h_{\mathsf{rt}} \left(\langle h_{\mathsf{FS}} \rangle \| \langle \mathcal{A}_{\mathsf{Trivial}} \rangle \| \langle \mathcal{V}_{\mathsf{PCP}} \rangle \right)$.
4. $\mathsf{sib} = \mathsf{block\text{-}com}(h'_{\mathsf{tree}}, \{(q_i, b_i)\}_i, j)$ where j is the integer represented by $\mathsf{bit}_\lambda(j)$, and for

$$r := h_{\mathsf{FS}}(\mathsf{rt}) \text{ where } \mathsf{rt} := \$_{\mathsf{rt}} \oplus (0^{\lambda + \log(\lambda) + 2} \| \alpha \| 0^{m/2}),$$

$\{(q_i, b_i)\}_i$ satisfies the requirements
  - $\mathcal{A}_{\mathsf{Trivial}}(r) = x, \{b_i\}_i$,
  - $\mathcal{V}_{\mathsf{PCP}}^{(0)}(x; r) = \{q_i\}_i$,
  - $\mathcal{V}_{\mathsf{PCP}}^{(1)}(x, \{b_i\}_i; r) = 1$.

Since α is the result of applying the CRHF h_{rt} to the witness, which is $\langle h_{FS} \rangle \| \langle \mathcal{A}_{\mathsf{Trivial}} \rangle \| \langle \mathcal{V}_{\mathsf{PCP}} \rangle$, an efficient adversary will only be able to find a single witness corresponding to any given α. The string α fully determines rt and r, which also determines $\{(q_i, b_i)\}_i$ (where $\{q_i\}$ is the set of PCP indices that $\mathcal{V}_{\mathsf{PCP}}$ would check when running on randomness r, and $\{b_i\}_i$ are the PCP responses output by $\mathcal{A}_{\mathsf{Trivial}}$ which cause $\mathcal{V}_{\mathsf{PCP}}$ to accept). This specifies a unique "cheating" PCP proof string consisting of 0's in almost every position, except with b_i's in indices corresponding to the q_i's. sib then corresponds to the label of the off-path node at level j for the rightmost root-to-leaf path in the Merkle tree, and is obtained by applying h'_{tree} to this cheating PCP proof string.

In the proof of Lemma 2, we will rely on the fact that for any j and any witness $\langle h_{FS} \rangle \| \langle \mathcal{A}_{\mathsf{Trivial}} \rangle \| \langle \mathcal{V}_{\mathsf{PCP}} \rangle$, a cheating prover can efficiently compute α, sib such that $((\alpha \| \mathsf{bit}_\lambda(j) \| \mathsf{sib}), (\langle h_{FS} \rangle \| \langle \mathcal{A}_{\mathsf{Trivial}} \rangle \| \langle \mathcal{V}_{\mathsf{PCP}} \rangle))$ is in the relation (by simply applying $h_{FS}, \mathcal{A}_{\mathsf{Trivial}}, \mathcal{V}_{\mathsf{PCP}}^{(0)}, h'_{\mathsf{tree}}$ in the specified way). In the proof of Lemma 1, we use the fact that for each (α, j) pair, an efficient adversary can only find one (sib, w) pair such that $((\alpha \| \mathsf{bit}_\lambda(j) \| \mathsf{sib}), w)$ is in the relation (due to the collision-resistance of h_{rt}).

Hash Computation. Parse input $x \in \{0, 1\}^{2m}$ as

$$\left(\mathsf{sib} \; \middle\| \; (\mathsf{pre} \| \$ \| \mathsf{bit}_\lambda(j) \| \alpha) \; \middle\| \; (\pi_1 \| \dots \| \pi_j \| z) \right),$$

where

  - $\mathsf{sib} \in \{0, 1\}^m$,
  - $(\mathsf{pre} \| \$ \| \mathsf{bit}_\lambda(j) \| \alpha) \in \{0, 1\}^{m/2}$ ($\mathsf{pre} \in \{0, 1\}^2$, $\$ \in \{0, 1\}^\lambda$, $\mathsf{bit}_\lambda(j) \in \{0, 1\}^{\log(\lambda)}$, and $\alpha \in \{0, 1\}^{m/2 - \lambda - \log(\lambda) - 2}$),
  - and $(\pi_1 \| \dots \| \pi_j \| z) \in \{0, 1\}^{m/2}$ ($\pi_i \in \{0, 1\}^{p(\lambda)}$ and $z \in \{0, 1\}^{m/2 - jp(\lambda)}$).

If $\mathsf{pre} = \mathsf{pre}_{\mathsf{path}}$, $\$ = \$_{\mathsf{path}}$, and $z = 0^{m/2 - jp(\lambda)}$, run the SNARK verifier for language $\mathcal{L}_{\$_{\mathsf{rt}}, h_{\mathsf{rt}}, h'_{\mathsf{tree}}}$ on $(\tau, (\alpha \| \mathsf{bit}_\lambda(j) \| \mathsf{sib}), \pi_j)$. If $j \geq 1$ and the verifier accepts, then

– if $j \geq 2$, output

$$\left((\mathsf{pre_{path}} \| \$_{\mathsf{path}} \| \mathsf{bit}_\lambda (j-1) \| \alpha) \;\Big\|\; (\pi_1 \| \ldots \| \pi_{j-1} \| 0^{m/2 - (j-1)p(\lambda)}) \right) \in \{0,1\}^m,$$

– and if $j = 1$, output

$$\left(\$_{\mathsf{rt}} \oplus (0^{\lambda + \log(\lambda) + 2} \| \alpha \| 0^{m/2}) \right) \in \{0,1\}^m.$$

Otherwise, if the input does not parse as above, or the verifier does not accept, output $h'_{\mathsf{tree}}(x)$.

3.5   Proof of Theorem 6

The proof follows easily from these two lemmas, both of which are proven in the full version [BBH+19].

Lemma 1. *Assuming $\mathcal{H}_{\mathsf{rt}}$ and $\mathcal{H}_{\mathsf{tree}}$ are CRHF families and that $\mathcal{S} = (\mathcal{G}, \mathcal{P}, \mathcal{V})$ is a fully-succinct SNARK with computationally unique proofs, then the above construction of $\widetilde{\mathcal{H}}_{\mathsf{CRHF}}$ is a CRHF family.*

Lemma 2. *For any PCP $\Pi_{\mathsf{PCP}} = (\mathcal{P}_{\mathsf{PCP}}, \mathcal{V}_{\mathsf{PCP}})$ and $\mathcal{H}_{\mathsf{FS}}$, if $\mathsf{Trivial}[\Pi_{\mathsf{PCP}}, \mathcal{H}_{\mathsf{FS}}]$ is not sound, then $\mathsf{FSKM}[\Pi_{\mathsf{PCP}}, \widetilde{\mathcal{H}}_{\mathsf{CRHF}}, \mathcal{H}_{\mathsf{FS}}]$ is not sound.*

4   An FSKM-Incompatible PCIP

In this section we show that for every language in NP there exists a probabilistically checkable interactive proof such that for every Fiat-Shamir hash function and every collision-resistant hash function, the resulting FSKM protocol is *not* sound.

Theorem 7. *Let $\mathcal{L} \in$ NP. There exists a PCIP Π for $\mathcal{L}$ with negligible soundness error such that for every collision resistant hash function family $\mathcal{H}_{\mathsf{CRHF}}$ and every Fiat-Shamir hash function family $\mathcal{H}_{\mathsf{FS}}$, the protocol $\mathsf{FSKM}[\Pi, \mathcal{H}_{\mathsf{CRHF}}, \mathcal{H}_{\mathsf{FS}}]$ is not sound.*

As a matter of fact, our attack breaks soundness of $\mathsf{FSKM}[\Pi, \mathcal{H}_{\mathsf{CRHF}}, \mathcal{H}_{\mathsf{FS}}]$ in an extremely strong sense—it is a $\mathsf{poly}(n, \lambda)$-time attack that causes the verifier to accept *any* input $x \notin \mathcal{L}$, with probability 1.

4.1   Proof of Theorem 7

Let $\mathcal{L} \in$ NP and let $\mathcal{H}_{\mathsf{CRHF}} = \left\{ \mathcal{H}_{\mathsf{CRHF}}^{(\lambda)} \right\}_\lambda$, $\mathcal{H}_{\mathsf{CRHF}}^{(\lambda)} = \left\{ h_{\mathsf{CRHF}} : \{0,1\}^{2\lambda} \rightarrow \{0,1\}^\lambda \right\}$ be a collision resistant hash family. The proof will take the following steps.

1. First, we construct a sound PCIP $(\mathcal{P}, \mathcal{V})$ for $\mathcal{L}$. The PCIP will be constructed in a contrived manner (to facilitate the attack in Step 3). This step is done in Sect. 4.1.

2. We briefly describe the argument system $(\mathcal{P}_{\mathsf{Kilian}}, \mathcal{V}_{\mathsf{Kilian}}) = \mathsf{Kilian}[\mathsf{PCIP}, \mathcal{H}_{\mathsf{CRHF}}]$. Its soundness follows from [Kil88, BCS16] (since we are instantiating Kilian's protocol with a sound PCIP and a CRHF). This step is done in Line 7.
3. For every hash family $\mathcal{H}_{\mathsf{FS}}$, we present the protocol $\mathsf{FSKM}[\mathsf{PCIP}, \mathcal{H}_{\mathsf{CRHF}}, \mathcal{H}_{\mathsf{FS}}]$ and show an attack that causes the verifier to accept every possible input $x \notin \mathcal{L}$ with probability 1. This last step is done in Line 7.

A Contrived PCIP for $\mathcal{L}$. We next construct our PCIP $(\mathcal{P}, \mathcal{V})$ for the language $\mathcal{L}$. Before doing so, we first set up some tools that we be used in the construction.

Some Useful Ingredients. Since $\mathcal{L} \in \mathsf{NP}$, by the PCP Theorem (Theorem 1), there exists a PCP $(\mathcal{P}_{\mathcal{L}}, \mathcal{V}_{\mathcal{L}})$ for $\mathcal{L}$ with soundness error $\epsilon_{\mathcal{L}}(\lambda) = \mathsf{neg}(\lambda)$, query complexity $q_{\mathcal{L}} = \mathsf{polylog}(\lambda)$ and randomness complexity $r_{\mathcal{L}} = \mathsf{poly}(\log(n), \log(\lambda))$.

Recall that $\mathsf{MerkleCom}(h, s)$ is the Merkle tree root generated from s using the hash function h (see Sect. 2.2). Let C be an efficiently computable and decodable error correcting code ensemble with constant rate and constant $\delta_0 > 0$ relative distance (for more background on codes and the fact that such codes exist, see the full version [BBH+19]. We define an auxiliary pair language $\mathcal{L}'$ as follows:

$$\mathcal{L}' = \left\{ \left(r, \pi = C\big(\langle h_{\mathsf{CRHF}}\rangle \| \langle h_{\mathsf{FS}}\rangle\big) \right) : \begin{array}{l} r \in \{0,1\}^{\lambda}, \\ \langle h_{\mathsf{CRHF}}\rangle, \langle h_{\mathsf{FS}}\rangle \text{ are Boolean circuits, and} \\ h_{\mathsf{FS}}\big(\mathsf{MerkleCom}(h_{\mathsf{CRHF}}, (1\|\pi))\big) = r \end{array} \right\}$$

In other words, $\mathcal{L}' \subseteq \{0,1\}^* \times \{0,1\}^*$ is a pair language, in which the first part of the input r is a binary string of length λ (which will be the security parameter in the upcoming PCIP), and the second part of the input π is an encoding under C of two Boolean circuits. Jumping ahead, the first circuit h_{CRHF} will play the part of the CRHF used in Kilian's protocol, while the circuit h_{FS} will be the FS hash function. For such (r, π), it holds that $(r, \pi) \in \mathcal{L}'$ if and only if $h_{\mathsf{FS}}\big(\mathsf{MerkleCom}(h_{\mathsf{CRHF}}, (1\|\pi))\big) = r$.

Observe that $\mathcal{L}'$ can be decided by a polynomial time Turing machine (i.e., polynomial in the input length $|r| + |\pi|$). Therefore, by Theorem 2 there exists a PCPP proof-system for $\mathcal{L}'$, denoted by $(\mathcal{P}_{\mathcal{L}'}, \mathcal{V}_{\mathcal{L}'})$ such that for input (r, π) and every proximity parameter $\delta > 0$, the soundness error is $\epsilon_{\mathcal{L}'}(\lambda) = \mathsf{neg}(\lambda)$, query complexity $q_{\mathcal{L}'} = \mathsf{poly}(\log(\lambda), \frac{1}{\delta})$ and randomness complexity $r_{\mathcal{L}'} = \mathsf{poly}(\log(\lambda), \log(t)/\delta)$, where $t = |r| + |\pi|$. Furthermore, the prover $\mathcal{P}_{\mathcal{L}'}$ runs in time $\mathsf{poly}(t, \log(\lambda))$, and $\mathcal{V}_{\mathcal{L}'}$ runs in time $\mathsf{poly}(\log(t), \log(\lambda), \frac{1}{\delta})$.

PCIP *for* $\mathcal{L}$. With these tools in hand, we are ready to present the PCIP. Intuitively (and as hinted on in Sect. 1.4), the verifier $\mathcal{V}$ will accept input x in one of two possible scenarios: The first scenario (denoted by having the prover initially send a bit $b = 0$), is that the prover provides $\mathcal{V}$ with an honest PCP proof for $x \in \mathcal{L}$, thus allowing the honest prover $\mathcal{P}$ to convince the verifier with probability 1. The second scenario (denoted by having the prover send $b = 1$), is that the prover manages to pass the following test (which will act as a backdoor once we compile the PCIP with FSKM):

The prover $\mathcal{P}$ is required to send a description of a Fiat-Shamir hash function h_{FS} which manages to accurately predict r_1, the random coins of $\mathcal{V}$, which *have yet to be sampled*. A cheating PCIP prover has $2^{-|r_1|} = \mathsf{negl}(\lambda)$ probability of passing the challenge.

In contrast, once the FSKM transform is applied, the challenge becomes easy to beat. A malicious prover will simply commit to the FS hash function provided by the verifier, as described in the FSKM transform. Therefore, the malicious prover will be able to predict the randomness of the verifier, thus passing the test.

In order to make the number of queries by $\mathcal{V}$ polylogarithmic in λ, we shall have the prover send its messages via an error-correcting code and run a PCPP checking that the verifier would have accepted had it explicitly read all of π_1.

The PCIP $(\mathcal{P}, \mathcal{V})$ is formally described in Fig. 3. In the protocol we use the convention that messages received by the verifier from the prover, which might be maliciously crafted, are denoted with a tilde.

Protocol 3: PCIP for $\mathcal{L} \in \mathsf{NP}$

Common input: Input $x \in \{0,1\}^n$ and security parameter 1^λ
Prover's auxiliary input: Witness w

1 $\mathcal{P}$ sends $(b\|\pi_1)$, where $b = 0$ and $\pi_1 = \mathcal{P}_{\mathcal{L}}(x,w)$ is the PCP proof.
2 $\mathcal{V}$ receives $(\tilde{b}\|\tilde{\pi}_1)$, where $\tilde{b} \in \{0,1\}$. If $\tilde{b} = 0$, $\mathcal{V}$ generates $r_1 \in_R \{0,1\}^{r_{\mathcal{L}}}$ (i.e., randomness for the PCP verifier $\mathcal{V}_{\mathcal{L}}$). Otherwise, (i.e., $b = 1$) $\mathcal{V}$ chooses uniformly $r_1 \in_R \{0,1\}^\lambda$.
3 $\mathcal{V}$ sends r_1 to $\mathcal{P}$.
4 $\mathcal{P}$ sends an empty string π_2.
5 $\mathcal{V}$ receives the string $\tilde{\pi}_2$.
6 If $b = 0$, then $\mathcal{V}$ runs $\mathcal{V}_{\mathcal{L}}^{\tilde{\pi}_1}(x, 1^\lambda)$, and accepts iff $\mathcal{V}_{\mathcal{L}}$ accepted.
7 Otherwise, (i.e., $b = 1$) the verifier $\mathcal{V}$ runs $\mathcal{V}_{\mathcal{L}'}^{\tilde{\pi}_1, \tilde{\pi}_2}(r_1, 1^\lambda, \delta_0/2)$, where $\tilde{\pi}_1$ is used as the implicit input, $\tilde{\pi}_2$ is used as the proof, and $\delta_0/2$ is the proximity parameter. The verifier $\mathcal{V}$ accepts iff $\mathcal{V}_{\mathcal{L}'}$ accepted.

Fig. 3. $(\mathcal{P}, \mathcal{V})$ a PCIP for $\mathcal{L}$.

We emphasize that while the *honest* prover always sends $b = 0$ and π_2 as the empty string, a cheating prover might not. Indeed, we added the possibility of sending different values here as a kind of backdoor. As we shall show, this backdoor does not violate the soundness of $(\mathcal{P}, \mathcal{V})$ as a PCIP (see Lemma 3) but completely breaks the soundness of the construction after applying Kilian and Fiat-Shamir (see Corollary 2).

Lemma 3. *The protocol $(\mathcal{P}, \mathcal{V})$ is a PCIP for $\mathcal{L}$ with negligible soundness error.*

A proof of this can be found in the full version [BBH+19].

Applying Kilian's Protocol to $(\mathcal{P}, \mathcal{V})$. As our next step (the second step in the outline), we consider the protocol $(\mathcal{P}_{\mathsf{Kilian}}, \mathcal{V}_{\mathsf{Kilian}})$ resulting from applying Kilian's protocol to the PCIP $(\mathcal{P}, \mathcal{V})$.

Ben-Sasson *et al.* [BCS16] showed that applying Kilian's protocol to *any* sound PCIP results in a sound interactive argument. Thus, we obtain the following result as an immediate corollary of Lemma 3:

Corollary 2. *The argument system* $(\mathcal{P}_{\mathsf{Kilian}}, \mathcal{V}_{\mathsf{Kilian}})$ *has negligible soundness error.*

Attack on Fiat-Shamir of $(\mathcal{P}_{\mathsf{Kilian}}, \mathcal{V}_{\mathsf{Kilian}})$. Lastly, consider $(\mathcal{P}_{\mathsf{FS}}, \mathcal{V}_{\mathsf{FS}})$, the result of applying Fiat-Shamir to the previous protocol for hash function ensemble $\mathcal{H}_{\mathsf{FS}} = \left\{ \mathcal{H}_{\mathsf{FS}}^{(\lambda)} \right\}_\lambda$.

Lemma 4. *There exists a malicious prover* $\mathcal{P}^*$ *such that for every input* $x \in \{0, 1\}^n$ *and security parameter* λ, *it holds that* $\mathcal{P}^*$ *runs in time* $\mathsf{poly}(n, \lambda)$ *and*

$$\Pr\left[\langle \mathcal{P}^*(x, 1^\lambda) \leftrightarrow \mathcal{V}_{\mathsf{FS}}(x, 1^\lambda) \rangle = 1 \right] = 1.$$

A proof of this can be found in the full version [BBH+19].

Acknowledgements. We thank the anonymous TCC 2019 reviewers for useful comments.

References

[ALM+98] Arora, S., Lund, C., Motwani, R., Sudan, M., Szegedy, M.: Proof verification and the hardness of approximation problems. J. ACM (JACM) **45**(3), 501–555 (1998)

[Bar01] Barak, B.: How to go beyond the black-box simulation barrier. In: FOCS (2001)

[BBB+18] Bünz, B., Bootle, J., Boneh, D., Poelstra, A., Wuille, P., Maxwell, G.: Bulletproofs: Short proofs for confidential transactions and more. In: 2018 IEEE Symposium on Security and Privacy, pp. 315–334. IEEE Computer Society Press, May 2018

[BBC+17] Ben-Sasson, E., et al.: Computational integrity with a public random string from quasi-linear PCPs. In: Coron, J.-S., Nielsen, J.B. (eds.) EUROCRYPT 2017. LNCS, vol. 10212, pp. 551–579. Springer, Cham (2017). https://doi.org/10.1007/978-3-319-56617-7_19

[BBH+19] Bartusek, J., Bronfman, L., Holmgren, J., Ma, F., Rothblum, R.D.: On the (in)security of kilian-basen snargs. Cryptology ePrint Archive, Report 2019/997 (2019. https://eprint.iacr.org/2018/997

[BBHR18a] Ben-Sasson, E., Bentov, I., Horesh, Y., Riabzev, M.: Fast reed-solomon interactive oracle proofs of proximity. In: 45th International Colloquium on Automata, Languages, and Programming, ICALP 2018, Prague, Czech Republic, 9–13 July 2018, pp. 14:1–14:17 (2018)

[BBHR18b] Ben-Sasson, E., Bentov, I., Horesh, Y., Riabzev, M.: Scalable, transparent, and post-quantum secure computational integrity. IACR Cryptology ePrint Archive **2018**, 46 (2018)

[BCC+17] Bitansky, N., et al.: The hunting of the SNARK. J. Cryptol. **30**(4), 989–1066 (2017)

[BCCT13] Bitansky, N., Canetti, R., Chiesa, A., Tromer, E.: Recursive composition and bootstrapping for SNARKS and proof-carrying data. In: Boneh, D., Roughgarden, T., Feigenbaum, J. (eds.) 45th ACM STOC, pp. 111–120. ACM Press, June 2013

[BCI+13] Bitansky, N., Chiesa, A., Ishai, Y., Paneth, O., Ostrovsky, R.: Succinct non-interactive arguments via linear interactive proofs. In: Sahai, A. (ed.) TCC 2013. LNCS, vol. 7785, pp. 315–333. Springer, Heidelberg (2013). https://doi.org/10.1007/978-3-642-36594-2_18

[BCPR14] Bitansky, N., Canetti, R., Paneth, O., Rosen, A:. On the existence of extractable one-way functions. In: Shmoys, D.B. (eds.) 46th ACM STOC, pp. 505–514. ACM Press, May/June 2014

[BCR+19] Ben-Sasson, E., Chiesa, A., Riabzev, M., Spooner, N., Virza, M., Ward, N.P.: Aurora: transparent succinct arguments for R1CS. In: Ishai, Y., Rijmen, V. (eds.) EUROCRYPT 2019. LNCS, vol. 11476, pp. 103–128. Springer, Cham (2019). https://doi.org/10.1007/978-3-030-17653-2_4

[BCS16] Ben-Sasson, E., Chiesa, A., Spooner, N.: Interactive oracle proofs. In: Hirt, M., Smith, A. (eds.) TCC 2016. LNCS, vol. 9986, pp. 31–60. Springer, Heidelberg (2016). https://doi.org/10.1007/978-3-662-53644-5_2

[BG08] Barak, B., Goldreich, O.: Universal arguments and their applications. SIAM J. Comput. **38**(5), 1661–1694 (2008)

[BGG17] Bowe, S., Gabizon, A., Green, M.D.: A multi-party protocol for constructing the public parameters of the pinocchio zk-SNARK. Cryptology ePrint Archive, Report 2017/602 (2017). http://eprint.iacr.org/2017/602

[BGH+05] Ben-Sasson, E., Goldreich, O., Harsha, P., Sudan, M., Vadhan, S.: Short PCPs verifiable in polylogarithmic time. In: 20th Annual IEEE Conference on Computational Complexity (CCC 2005), San Jose, CA, USA, 11–15 June 2005, pp. 120–134 (2005)

[BGH+06] Ben-Sasson, E., Goldreich, O., Harsha, P., Sudan, M., Vadhan, S.P.: Robust PCPs of proximity, shorter PCPs, and applications to coding. SIAM J. Comput. **36**(4), 889–974 (2006)

[BGM17] Bowe, S., Gabizon, A., Miers, I.: Scalable multi-party computation for zk-SNARK parameters in the random beacon model. Cryptology ePrint Archive, Report 2017/1050 (2017). http://eprint.iacr.org/2017/1050

[BR94] Bellare, M., Rogaway, P.: Entity authentication and key distribution. In: Stinson, D.R. (ed.) CRYPTO 1993. LNCS, vol. 773, pp. 232–249. Springer, Heidelberg (1994). https://doi.org/10.1007/3-540-48329-2_21

[CCH+19] Canetti, R., et al.: Fiat-Shamir: from practice to theory (2019)

[CCRR18] Canetti, R., Chen, Y., Reyzin, L., Rothblum, R.D.: Fiat-Shamir and correlation intractability from strong KDM-secure encryption. In: Nielsen, J.B., Rijmen, V. (eds.) EUROCRYPT 2018. LNCS, vol. 10820, pp. 91–122. Springer, Cham (2018). https://doi.org/10.1007/978-3-319-78381-9_4

[CFH+15] Costello, C., et al.: Geppetto: versatile verifiable computation. In: 2015 IEEE Symposium on Security and Privacy, pp. 253–270. IEEE Computer Society Press, May 2015

[DR06] Dinur, I., Reingold, O.: Assignment testers: towards a combinatorial proof of the PCP theorem. SIAM J. Comput. **36**(4), 975–1024 (2006)

[FFG+16] Fiore, D., Fournet, C., Ghosh, E., Kohlweiss, M., Ohrimenko, O., Parno, B.: Hash first, argue later: adaptive verifiable computations on outsourced data. In: Weippl, E.R., Katzenbeisser, S., Kruegel, C., Myers, A.C., Halevi, S. (eds.) ACM CCS 2016, pp. 1304–1316. ACM Press, October 2016

[FS86] Fiat, A., Shamir, A.: How to prove yourself: practical solutions to identification and signature problems. In: Odlyzko, A.M. (ed.) CRYPTO 1986. LNCS, vol. 263, pp. 186–194. Springer, Heidelberg (1987). https://doi.org/10.1007/3-540-47721-7_12

[GK03] Goldwasser, S., Kalai, Y.T.: On the (in)security of the Fiat-Shamir paradigm. In: 44th FOCS, pp. 102–115. IEEE Computer Society Press, October 2003

[Gro16] Groth, J.: On the size of pairing-based non-interactive arguments. In: Fischlin, M., Coron, J.-S. (eds.) EUROCRYPT 2016. LNCS, vol. 9666, pp. 305–326. Springer, Heidelberg (2016). https://doi.org/10.1007/978-3-662-49896-5_11

[GW11] Gentry, C., Wichs, D.: Separating succinct non-interactive arguments from all falsifiable assumptions. In: Fortnow, L., Vadhan, S.P. (eds.) 43rd ACM STOC, pp. 99–108. ACM Press, June 2011

[Hås01] Håstad, J.: Some optimal inapproximability results. J. ACM 48(4), 798–859 (2001)

[HL18] Holmgren, J., Lombardi, A.: Cryptographic hashing from strong one-way functions (or: one-way product functions and their applications). In: Thorup, M. (eds.) 59th FOCS, pp. 850–858. IEEE Computer Society Press, October 2018

[HR04] Hsiao, C.-Y., Reyzin, L.: Finding collisions on a public road, or do secure hash functions need secret coins? In: Franklin, M. (ed.) CRYPTO 2004. LNCS, vol. 3152, pp. 92–105. Springer, Heidelberg (2004). https://doi.org/10.1007/978-3-540-28628-8_6

[HW15a] Hubacek, P., Wichs, D.: On the communication complexity of secure function evaluation with long output. In: Roughgarden, T. (eds.) ITCS 2015, pp. 163–172. ACM, January 2015

[HW15b] Hub'avcek, P., Wichs, D.: On the communication complexity of secure function evaluation with long output. In: Proceedings of the 2015 Conference on Innovations in Theoretical Computer Science, ITCS 2015, Rehovot, Israel, 11–13 January 2015, pp. 163–172 (2015)

[Kil88] Kilian, J.: Founding cryptography on oblivious transfer. In: Proceedings of the 20th Annual ACM Symposium on Theory of Computing, Chicago, Illinois, USA, 2–4 May 1988, pp. 20–31 (1988)

[Kil92] Kilian, J.: A note on efficient zero-knowledge proofs and arguments (extended abstract). In: 24th ACM STOC, pp. 723–732. ACM Press, May 1992

[KRR17] Kalai, Y.T., Rothblum, G.N., Rothblum, R.D.: From obfuscation to the security of Fiat-Shamir for proofs. In: Katz, J., Shacham, H. (eds.) CRYPTO 2017. LNCS, vol. 10402, pp. 224–251. Springer, Cham (2017). https://doi.org/10.1007/978-3-319-63715-0_8

[Mau05] Maurer, U.: Abstract models of computation in cryptography. In: Smart, N.P. (ed.) Cryptography and Coding 2005. LNCS, vol. 3796, pp. 1–12. Springer, Heidelberg (2005). https://doi.org/10.1007/11586821_1

[Mic00] Micali, S.: Computationally sound proofs. SIAM J. Comput. 30(4), 1253–1298 (2000)

[Nec94] Nechaev, V.I.: Complexity of a determinate algorithm for the discrete logarithm. Math. Notes **55**(2), 165–172 (1994)

[PS96] Pointcheval, D., Stern, J.: Security proofs for signature schemes. In: Maurer, U. (ed.) EUROCRYPT 1996. LNCS, vol. 1070, pp. 387–398. Springer, Heidelberg (1996). https://doi.org/10.1007/3-540-68339-9_33

[PS19] Peikert, C., Shiehian, S.: Noninteractive zero knowledge for NP from (plain) learning with errors. In: Boldyreva, A., Micciancio, D. (eds.) CRYPTO 2019. LNCS, vol. 11692, pp. 89–114. Springer, Cham (2019). https://doi.org/10.1007/978-3-030-26948-7_4

[RRR16a] Reingold, O., Rothblum, G.N., Rothblum, R.D.: Constant-round interactive proofs for delegating computation. In: Wichs, D., Mansour, Y. (eds.) 48th ACM STOC, pp. 49–62. ACM Press, June 2016

[RRR16b] Reingold, O., Rothblum, G.N., Rothblum, R.D.: Constant-round interactive proofs for delegating computation. In: STOC, pp. 49–62. ACM (2016)

[Sho97] Shoup, V.: Lower bounds for discrete logarithms and related problems. In: Fumy, W. (ed.) EUROCRYPT 1997. LNCS, vol. 1233, pp. 256–266. Springer, Heidelberg (1997). https://doi.org/10.1007/3-540-69053-0_18

Incrementally Verifiable Computation via Incremental PCPs

Moni Naor[1]([✉]), Omer Paneth[2], and Guy N. Rothblum[1]

[1] Weizmann Institute of Science, Rehovot, Israel
moni.naor@weizmann.ac.il, rothblum@alum.mit.edu
[2] MIT and Northeastern University, Cambridge, USA
omerpa@mit.edu

Abstract. If I commission a long computation, how can I check that the result is correct without re-doing the computation myself? This is the question that efficient verifiable computation deals with. In this work, we address the issue of verifying the computation as it unfolds. That is, at any intermediate point in the computation, I would like to see a proof that the current state is correct. Ideally, these proofs should be short, non-interactive, and easy to verify. In addition, the proof at each step should be generated efficiently by updating the previous proof, without recomputing the entire proof from scratch. This notion, known as incrementally verifiable computation, was introduced by Valiant [TCC 08] about a decade ago. Existing solutions follow the approach of recursive proof composition and can be based on strong and non-falsifiable cryptographic assumptions (so-called "knowledge assumptions").

In this work, we present a new framework for constructing incrementally verifiable computation schemes in both the publicly verifiable and designated-verifier settings. Our designated-verifier scheme is based on somewhat homomorphic encryption (which can be based on Learning with Errors) and our publicly verifiable scheme is based on the notion of zero-testable homomorphic encryption, which can be constructed from ideal multi-linear maps [Paneth and Rothblum, TCC 17].

Our framework is anchored around the new notion of a probabilistically checkable proof (PCP) with incremental local updates. An incrementally updatable PCP proves the correctness of an ongoing computation, where after each computation step, the value of every symbol can be updated locally without reading any other symbol. This update results in a new PCP for the correctness of the next step in the computation. Our primary technical contribution is constructing such an incrementally

M. Naor—Supported in part by grant from the Israel Science Foundation (no. 950/16). Incumbent of the Judith Kleeman Professorial Chair.

O. Paneth—Supported by NSF Grants CNS-1413964, CNS-1350619 and CNS-1414119, and the Defense Advanced Research Projects Agency (DARPA) and the U.S. Army Research Office under contracts W911NF-15-C-0226 and W911NF-15-C-0236.

G. N. Rothblum—This project has received funding from the European Research Council (ERC) under the European Union's Horizon 2020 research and innovation programme (grant agreement No. 819702).

D. Hofheinz and A. Rosen (Eds.): TCC 2019, LNCS 11892, pp. 552–576, 2019.
https://doi.org/10.1007/978-3-030-36033-7_21

updatable PCP. We show how to combine updatable PCPs with recently suggested (ordinary) verifiable computation to obtain our results.

1   Introduction

Efficient verification of complex computations is a foundational question in the theory of computation. Recent years have seen exciting progress in the study of this problem, from a rich theory of efficient protocols to concrete implementations and new application domains. In the verifiable computation paradigm, the output of a computation is accompanied by a proof of the result's correctness. The proof should be efficient to construct (not much more expensive than simply computing the output), and super-efficient to verify (e.g. verification in nearly-linear time).

Incrementally Verifiable Computation. In this work we revisit the question of *incrementally* verifiable computation, introduced by Valiant [Val08] about a decade ago. To motivate this question, consider the following scenarios:

Intermediate Outputs: Consider a server that executes a long computation for a client. Even before the entire computation terminates, the client may want to obtain intermediate outputs or to audit the server's progress throughout the computation. This is especially significant in the presence of transient faults that are hard to detect: suppose that the computation is so long that faults are likely to occur eventually. Without a methodology for detecting these faults, then the final output is likely to be wrong.

Transferable Computation: We would like to split a long sequential computation between different parties such that every party performs a small part of the computation and passes it on to the next party. Together with the current state of their computation, parties should include a proof that the computation was performed correctly, not only in the last step, but in its entirety. As a compelling example, consider an extremely long computation that would require all of humanity many generations to complete. We would like every generation to perform its part, and pass the state of the computation along to the next generation together with a proof of correctness.

In both examples above we need a correctness proof that can be constructed *incrementally*, so that at any intermediate point in the computation, the current state can be verified. The process of updating the proof must be *fast* and *stateless*, meaning that, first, the time to update the proof is independent of the running time of the computation so far and, second, to update the proof we only need to know the most recent version of the proof and the current state of the computation.

We restrict our attention to non-interactive protocols for deterministic computations, where both the prover and verifier have access to an honestly generated common reference string, and where soundness is only required to hold against computationally bounded adversarial provers. Even without the issue of incremental updates, both of these relaxations are known to be necessary under standard complexity theoretic assumptions (see Goldreich and Håstad [GH98]).

In a verifiable computation protocol an honest prover executes a program M on input y. For every timestep t, let c_t denote the state of the program (including the program's entire memory) after the first t steps. Given the common reference string (CRS) the prover constructs a proof Π_t for the correctness of the state c_t. For security parameter κ, the verifier takes the CRS, the input y, the state c_t and the proof Π_t and decides if to accept the proof in time $(|y| + |c_t|) \cdot \mathrm{poly}(\kappa)$, independently of t. Soundness asserts that, given an honestly generated CRS, no efficient adversarial prover can find an input y, a time t and an accepting proof for any state other then c_t (except with negligible probability).

A verifiable computation protocol is incrementally updatable if there is an update procedure that, given the CRS, the state c_t and the proof Π_t, computes the proof Π_{t+1} for the next state in time $(|y| + |c_t|) \cdot \mathrm{poly}(\kappa)$.

The State of the Art. Valiant presented an approach for constructing incrementally verifiable computation based on the idea of recursive proof composition. Very roughly, given a proof Π_t for state c_t the updated proof Π_{t+1} for the next state c_{t+1} asserts that: (1) there exists a state c_t and a proof Π_t for timestep t that are accepted by the verifier, and (2) the computation starting from state c_t transitions to state c_{t+1}. Constructing the proof Π_{t+1} given c_t and Π_t may potentially be fast since Π_{t+1} only argues about the fast verification algorithm and one step of the computation.

The challenge in implementing this idea is maintaining soundness. Existing solutions are based on the strong notion of succinct non-interactive arguments of knowledge for non-deterministic computations also known as SNARKs [Val08, BCC+17, BCCT13]. Currently such SNARKs are known based on non-standard non-falsifiable assumptions (so-called "knowledge assumptions"). We therefore ask:

Is incrementally verifiable computation possible under standard assumptions?

1.1   This Work

In this work we give a new framework for constructing incrementally verifiable computation. Based on this framework we give new protocols in both the publicly verifiable and designated-verifier settings.

Designated verifier. In the designated-verifier setting the common reference string (CRS) is generated together with a secret key. Only a verifier that holds this secret key can check the proof, and soundness is *not* guaranteed against parties who know the secret key. In this setting we prove the following:

Theorem 1.1 (informal). *Assuming a somewhat-homomorphic encryption scheme for computations of poly-logarithmic degree, there exists a designated-verifier incrementally verifiable computation protocol.*

The protocol is based on the (non-incremental) verifiable computation protocol of Kalai et al. [KRR14] with the improvements of Brakerski et al. [BHK17]. Their construction can use any computational private information retrieval (PIR) scheme. To get incremental updates, we rely on the stronger notion of somewhat-homomorphic encryption. Such encryption schemes are known under the Learning with Errors assumption (see Brakerski and Vaikuntanathan and Gentry et al. [BV11, GSW13]).

Public Verification. In a publicly verifiable protocol, the proof can be verified by anyone who knows the CRS, and there is no secret key. In this setting we prove the following:

Theorem 1.2 (informal). *Assuming a 3-key zero-testable somewhat homomorphic encryption scheme with correctness for adversarially-generated ciphertexts, there exists a publicly verifiable incrementally verifiable computation protocol.*

The protocol is based on the (non-incremental) verifiable computation protocol of Paneth and Rothblum [PR17] and is proven secure under the same assumption as their work. We refer the reader to [PR17] for the definition of the required notion of zero-testable homomorphic encryption. We note, however, that currently, candidates for such homomorphic encryption are only known based on (efficiently falsifiable) assumptions about ideal multilinear maps.

Our framework deviates from the recursive proof composition approach. Instead, our constructions are based on a new type of probabilistically checkable proof (PCP) with *incremental local updates*.

Incrementally Updatable PCP. In contrast to the setting of verifiable computation, known constructions in the PCP model have proofs that are longer than the computation whose correctness is being proved. Verification, on the other hand, is performed by querying only a small number of locations in the proof, and in running time that is nearly-linear in the input length. Moreover, in the PCP model positive results are known even for non-deterministic computations with unconditional soundness. PCPs allow us to prove that for a non-deterministic program M and input y there exists a witness w that will make M reach state c_t after t steps. The proof Π_t is a string of size $\text{poly}(t)$ over some alphabet Σ of size $\text{polylog}(t)$ (our setting requires a non-binary alphabet) and verification queries $\text{polylog}(t)$ symbols of the proof achieving negligible soundness error.

In this setting, the question of incremental updates is as follows: given the proof Π_t for state c_t, and given a state c_{t+1} that follows c_t (for non-deterministic computations, there may be more than one state that follows c_t), we would like to update Π_t and obtain a new proof Π_{t+1} for c_{t+1}. We cannot hope for the update time to be independent of t since, given the error-correcting nature of the proof, every proof symbol must change. Instead we require that every symbol of the proof can "self-update" quickly. That is, given the i-th symbol of Π_t and the states c_t and c_{t+1} we can compute the i-th symbol of the new proof Π_{t+1} in time $(|y| + |c_t|) \cdot \text{polylog}(t)$.

The main technical contribution of this work is a construction of an incrementally updatable PCP. Our construction is based on the classic PCP of Babai, Fortnow, Levin and Szegedy (BFLS) [BFLS91]. We modify their PCP by considering a larger alphabet Σ and augmenting every symbol of the original proof with supplemental values that allow the augmented symbol to self-update.

From PCP to Verifiable Computation, Heuristically. Biehl, Meyer and Wetzel [BMW98] suggested a heuristic transformation from PCPs to verifiable computation protocols. We refer to their technique as the *hidden query heuristic*. Roughly speaking, the idea is to perform the required PCP queries in a manner that does not allow the prover to figure out the query locations. This idea can be implemented by placing random PCP queries in the CRS, encoded using a private information retrieval (PIR) scheme, or, alternatively, encrypted with a homomorphic encryption scheme (where every query is encrypted under a different key). The prover homomorphically evaluates the PCP answers and sends the encrypted results as the proof. The (designated) verifier decrypts the results and checks that the underlying PCP accepts.

We observe that instantiating the hidden query heuristic with a PCP that can be incrementally updated gives a heuristic incrementally verifiable computation protocol. To see this, recall that following the hidden query heuristic, the proof consists of a few PCP symbols encrypted under homomorphic encryption. Since every one of these symbols can self-update, we can homomorphically evaluate the PCP update procedure under the encryption and obtain encryptions of the updated PCP symbols. We note that, while the hidden query heuristic can be implemented with PIR, getting incrementally verifiable computation requires the stronger notion of homomorphic encryption which supports "multi-hop" evaluation. This is because we update the proof by homomorphically evaluating the PCP update procedure over the encrypted PCP answers.

Secure Instantiations. For many years it was not known whether the hidden query technique can be shown to be sound (see Dwork et al. [DLN+00] for the obstacles in proving its soundness, as well as [DNR16] and [DHRW16]). However, recent works give secure instantiations of this heuristic in both the designated-verifier and the publicly verifiable settings. Next, we discuss these instantiations and explain how we turn them into incrementally verifiable computation protocols based on our incrementally updatable PCP.

Starting from the designated-verifiable setting, the works of [KRR13, KRR14, BHK17] prove that the hidden query heuristic is secure, assuming the underlying PCP satisfies a strong form of soundness called *no-signaling* soundness. Our designated-verifier protocol is based on the no-signaling PCP construction of Brakerski, Holmgren and Kalai (BHK) [BHK17], which in turn is based on the PCP of BFLS with several changes that facilitate the proof of no-signaling soundness. Very roughly, their construction has the following structure:

1. Given a program M, define an augmented program $\tilde{M}$ that emulates M while encoding each of its states c_t with a particular error correcting code.

2. The honest prover computes the PCP proof for the augmented program $\tilde{M}$. This proof is essentially the same as in the PCP of BFLS.
3. The verifier locally tests the PCP proof. These tests differ significantly from the tests performed by the original BFLS verifier.

To turn this PCP into a verifiable computation protocol, BHK apply the hidden query technique using any PIR scheme.

To achieve incremental updates, we make the following two changes to the BHK protocol: first, we modify the prover to compute the PCP proof for $\tilde{M}$ using our incrementally updatable PCP instead of the PCP of BFLS. Recall that our PCP augments every symbol of the original BFLS proof with supplemental values. Since these supplemental values are only needed to update the proof, the verifier can simply ignore them. Other than that, our verifier is the same as that of BHK. Second, as discussed above, to turn the PCP into an incrementally verifiable computation protocol we use homomorphic encryption instead of PIR. We note that in our PCP the answers can be computed by a polynomial of poly-logarithmic degree and, therefore, somewhat homomorphic encryption is sufficient [Gen09].

We emphasize that while our honest prover is defined differently, the verification procedure of our incrementally verifiable computation is essentially the same as the one in BHK. Therefore, the soundness of our protocol follows directly from the analysis in BHK. Indeed, the focus of this work is on showing that the *honest proof* can be constructed incrementally. We note that there some minor differences between the BFLS construction that we use and the one used in BHK. However, a careful inspection shows that the analysis in BHK can be easily modified to fit our PCP (see Sect. 2.4 for more detail).

In the publicly verifiable setting, the work of [PR17] gives a verifiable computation protocol based on the hidden query heuristic. While they do not require that the PCP satisfies no-signaling soundness, they need a stronger notion of homomorphic encryption that supports a weak zero-test operation as well as some additional properties. They show that such encryption can be based on ideal multi-linear maps. Similarly to the BHK protocol, in [PR17], the honest prover simply constructs the PCP proof for an augmented program $\tilde{M}$ using the PCP of BFLS. We modify their protocol to use our incrementally updatable PCP instead and use the same verification procedure (ignoring any supplemental values added to the BFLS proof). Therefore, designated-verifiable setting, the soundness of our protocol follows immediately from the proof analysis of [PR17].

On the Locality of Updates. A natural relaxation of incrementally updatable PCP would allow for updating of every proof symbol given the values of a small number of other symbols. PCPs with such local updates may be easier to construct than PCPs with strictly self-updating symbols. Note, however, that in order to go from incrementally updatable PCPs to incrementally verifiable computation following our framework, it is crucial that PCP symbols can self-update. If computing one symbol of the new proof requires the values of even two old symbols, then the number of symbols we need to maintain under every encryption may grow exponentially with the number of updates.

On Strong Soundness. The focus of this work is on constructing PCPs and verifiable computation protocols where the *honest* proof can be computed incrementally. An intriguing question for future research is to design PCPs and verifiable computation protocols where even an adversarially generated proof can be updated. That is, if an adversary produces an accepting proof for timestep t, we can continue updating this proof to get accepting proof for subsequent steps. This strong soundness guarantee is motivated, for example, by the transferable computation scenario described above where multiple mutually distrustful parties incrementally construct the correctness proof.

Our PCP construction does not satisfy this stronger guarantee. Very roughly, the reason is that we augment the standard PCP of BFLS by adding supplemental values encoded into every symbol. These supplemental values are crucial for implementing self-updates, but play no role in the verification of the PCP. In particular, an adversarially generated proof may consist of a good "core PCP" that verifies correctly, together with corrupted supplemental values that would prevent this PCP from updating.

Related Work. In a recent work, Holmgren and Rothblum [HR18] construct designated-verifier argument systems where the prover's space and time complexity are very close to the time and space needed to perform the computation. While their work does not consider or achieve the notion of incrementally updatable PCPs, there are technical similarities in the way the two PCP systems are constructed. Indeed, they consider a related notion where the prover is given streaming access to the computation's tableau. In this related model, they can process additions to the tableau in small *amortized* time. On a technical level, we note that they do not limit the space used by the machine, which leads to significant complications. Further connections between incrementally verifiable computation and argument systems with very efficient provers were explored in [Val08, BCCT13].

In a very recent work (subsequent to ours), Kalai, Paneth and Yang [KPY19] construct a verifiable computation protocol with public verification based on a falsifiable assumption on bilinear groups. While their protocol also relies on the hidden query technique, we do not know how to make it incremental based on our PCP. This is because their protocol also uses a bootstrapping technique (to go from a long CRS to a short CRS) that significantly complicates the prover's strategy.

Future Directions. We leave open the question of constructing incrementally verifiable computation protocols with strong soundness, where even adversarially generated proofs can be updated as discussed above. Another interesting direction is to explore alternative approaches to incrementally verifiable computation based on standard assumptions. One potential path towards this goal is to implement Valiant's idea of recursive proof composition, replacing knowledge assumptions with the recent bootstrapping technique of [KPY19]. We emphasize that the approach proposed in this work is not based on recursive proof composition. In particular, our solution can also be applied in the designated-verifier setting, based on the Learning with Errors assumption.

2   Technical Overview

Next we describe our construction of an incrementally updatable PCP. We start by recalling the PCP of BFLS. In Sect. 2.2 we describe our PCP proof string and in Sect. 2.3 we explain how to update it.

2.1   The BFLS Construction

Our construction builds on the PCP of BFLS [BFLS91]. We recall some of the details of that construction.

Setup. For a non-deterministic polynomial-time Turing machine M and input $y \in \{0,1\}^n$ we construct a proof for the fact that there exists a witness that makes M accepts y. As we know from the Cook-Levin Theorem, it is possible to represent M's computation on an input y by a Boolean 3CNF formula ϕ_y over $N = \mathrm{poly}(n)$ variables such that ϕ_y is satisfiable if and only if there exists a witness that makes M accept y. Let $\mathbb{F}$ be a field of size $\Theta(\log^2 N)$ and let $\mathbb{H} \subset \mathbb{F}$ be a subset of size $\log(N)$. We set $u \in \mathbb{N}$ such that $|\mathbb{H}|^u = N$ and index the variables of ϕ_y by vectors in $\mathbb{H}^u$. Given a witness that makes M accept y we can compute an assignment $X \colon \mathbb{H}^u \to \{0,1\}$ that satisfies ϕ_y.

Arithmetization. The first part of the PCP proof contains the assignment X represented as a multi-variate polynomial $\tilde{X} \colon \mathbb{F}^u \to \mathbb{F}$ of degree at most $(|\mathbb{H}|-1)$ in each variable, that identifies with X on $\mathbb{H}^u$. We also describe the formula ϕ_y algebraically as polynomial $\varphi_y \colon \mathbb{F}^\ell \to \mathbb{F}$ over $\ell = 3(u+1)$ variables, with individual degree $\mathrm{polylog}(N)$. For every 3 variables $\mathbf{h}_1, \mathbf{h}_2, \mathbf{h}_3 \in \mathbb{H}^u$ and 3 bits $b_1, b_2, b_3 \in \{0,1\}$, if the formula ϕ_y contains the clause:

$$(X(\mathbf{h}_1) = b_1) \vee (X(\mathbf{h}_2) = b_2) \vee (X(\mathbf{h}_3) = b_3),$$

then the polynomial φ_y evaluates to 1 on $(\mathbf{h}_1, \mathbf{h}_2, \mathbf{h}_3, b_1, b_2, b_3)$. Otherwise, φ_y evaluates to 0. The polynomial φ_y can be computed by an arithmetic circuit of size $\mathrm{polylog}(N) + O(|y|)$.

The Consistency Check Polynomial. The proof contains a consistency check polynomial $Q^0 \colon \mathbb{F}^\ell \to \mathbb{F}$. For every 3 variables $\mathbf{h}_1, \mathbf{h}_2, \mathbf{h}_3 \in \mathbb{H}^u$ and 3 bits $b_1, b_2, b_3 \in \{0,1\}$ the polynomial Q^0 evaluates to a non-zero value on $(\mathbf{h}_1, \mathbf{h}_2, \mathbf{h}_3, b_1, b_2, b_3)$ if only if the formula ϕ_y contains the clause defined by $(\mathbf{h}_1, \mathbf{h}_2, \mathbf{h}_3, b_1, b_2, b_3)$ and this clause is not satisfied by the assigned values $X(\mathbf{h}_1), X(\mathbf{h}_3), X(\mathbf{h}_3)$. It follows that Q^0 vanishes on $\mathbb{H}^\ell$ if and only if the assignment X satisfies ϕ_y (which implies that there exists a witness that makes M accept y). The polynomial Q^0 is defined as follows:

$$Q^0(\mathbf{h}_1, \mathbf{h}_2, \mathbf{h}_3, b_1, b_2, b_3) = \varphi_y(\mathbf{h}_1, \mathbf{h}_2, \mathbf{h}_3, b_1, b_2, b_3) \cdot \prod_{i \in [3]} \left(\tilde{X}(\mathbf{h}_i) - b_i \right).$$

The Sum-Check Polynomials. To allow the verifier to check that Q^0 vanishes on $\mathbb{H}^\ell$ (and, therefore, M accepts y), the proof contains "sum-check polynomials" $Q^1, \ldots, Q^\ell \colon \mathbb{F}^\ell \to \mathbb{F}$. The j-th polynomial in this sequence is a low-degree extension of Q^0 in its first j variables. In particular, for $0 < j \leq \ell$, the polynomial Q^j is defined as:

$$Q^j (y_1, \ldots, y_\ell) = \sum_{h_1, \ldots, h_j \in \mathbb{H}} \mathsf{ID}_j \left((h_1, \ldots, h_j), (y_1, \ldots, y_j) \right) \cdot Q^0 (h_1, \ldots, h_j, y_{j+1}, \ldots, y_\ell).$$

Where $\mathsf{ID}_j \colon \mathbb{F}^{2j} \to \mathbb{F}$ is the (unique) polynomial with individual degree $(\mathbb{H} - 1)$ such that for every $\mathbf{h}, \mathbf{h}' \in \mathbb{H}^j$, $\mathsf{ID}_j(\mathbf{h}, \mathbf{h}') = 1$ if $\mathbf{h} = \mathbf{h}'$ and $\mathsf{ID}_j(\mathbf{h}, \mathbf{h}') = 0$ otherwise.

The Proof String. The PCP proof string contains, for every $\mathbf{u} \in \mathbb{F}^u$ the value $\tilde{X}(\mathbf{u})$ and for every $\mathbf{v} \in \mathbb{F}^\ell$ the values $Q^0(\mathbf{v}), \ldots, Q^\ell(\mathbf{v})$.

On Verifying the PCP. For the sake of this technical overview, for the most part we ignore the tests run by the verifier (which include various low-degree tests and consistency checks). This is because our focus is on the structure of the proof itself and the procedure that updates it.

2.2   The Incremental PCP Construction

We start by describing the content of the proof at any intermediate timestep and then explain how to update. Our construction relies on the leveled structure of the formula ϕ_y representing the computation. Specifically, if the computation $M(y)$ requires time T and space S, we can view the variables of ϕ_y as organized in a table with $\mathsf{T}' = \mathsf{T} \cdot \beta$ rows and $\mathsf{S}' = \mathsf{S} \cdot \beta$ columns for some constant β. Any assignment $X \colon [\mathsf{T}'] \times [\mathsf{S}'] \to \{0, 1\}$ that satisfies ϕ_y corresponds to an execution of M on input y with some witness as follows: for every timestep $t \in [\mathsf{T}]$ the assignment to the $(t \cdot \beta)$-th row corresponds to the configuration c_t of M after t steps, and rows $(t \cdot \beta) + 1$ through $((t + 1) \cdot \beta) - 1$ contain auxiliary variables used to verify the consistency of the configurations c_t and c_{t+1}.[1] A crucial fact that we will use is that ϕ_y is *leveled*. That is, every clause in ϕ_y only involves variables from two consecutive rows.

Partial Assignments. We set $m, k \in \mathbb{N}$ such that $|\mathbb{H}|^m = \mathsf{T}'$ and $|\mathbb{H}|^k = \mathsf{S}'$ and we index every variable by a pair in $\mathbb{H}^m \times \mathbb{H}^k$. As before, given a witness that makes M accept y we can compute an assignment $X \colon \mathbb{H}^{m+k} \to \{0, 1\}$ that satisfies ϕ_y. For $\tau \in [\mathsf{T}']$ we define the assignment $X_\tau \colon \mathbb{H}^{m+k} \to \{0, 1\}$ that agrees with X on the first τ rows and assigns 0 to all variables in rows larger than τ. As before, we consider a polynomial $\tilde{X}_\tau \colon \mathbb{F}^{m+k} \to \mathbb{F}$ of individual degree at most $(|\mathbb{H}| - 1)$, that identifies with X_τ on $\mathbb{H}^{m+k}$. As discussed above, every step of M's computation determines an assignment for β consecutive rows. After completing

---

[1] These auxiliary rows can be avoided if ϕ_y is a k-CNF formula for some constant $k > 3$. However, for our purpose, it is important that ϕ_y is a 3CNF formula.

only the first t steps of the computation and reaching configuration c_t, we can already compute the assignment X_τ for $\tau = t \cdot \beta$. Moreover, the assignment to the variables in row τ is only a function of the configuration c_t.

The New Formula. Now, to prove that M's computation on input y can indeed reach a configuration c_t after t steps, it is sufficient to prove that both:

1. The assignment X_τ satisfies all of ϕ_y's clauses involving variables of the first $\tau = t \cdot \beta$ rows.
2. The assignment to row τ matches the assignment defined by the configuration c_t.

For a fixed configuration c_t, we therefore define another 3CNF formula ϕ_τ that is satisfied if and only if the assignment of row τ matches c_t.[2] As before, we consider a polynomial $\varphi_\tau \colon \mathbb{F}^\ell \to \mathbb{F}$ describing the clauses of the formula ϕ_τ. We let $\varphi_{y,\tau}$ denote the polynomial $\varphi_y + \varphi_\tau$ describing the clauses of the combined formula $\phi_{y,\tau} = \phi_y \wedge \phi_\tau$.

The Consistency Check Polynomial. Our new consistency check polynomial $Q^0_\tau \colon \mathbb{F}^\ell \to \mathbb{F}$ is defined similarly to Q^0 except that it "ignores" clauses on variables beyond row τ. Recall that every clause in ϕ_y only involves variables from two consecutive rows. We assume WLOG that if $\varphi_{y,\tau}$ contains a clause on the variables $(\mathbf{t}_1, \mathbf{s}_1), (\mathbf{t}_2, \mathbf{s}_2), (\mathbf{t}_3, \mathbf{s}_3) \in \mathbb{H}^{m+k}$ then $\mathbf{t}_2 = \mathbf{t}_3$ is the index of the row immediately before $\mathbf{t}_1$. Therefore, the polynomial Q^0_τ is defined as follows:

$$Q^0_\tau (\mathbf{t}_1, \mathbf{t}_2, \mathbf{t}_3, \mathbf{s}_1, \mathbf{s}_2, \mathbf{s}_3, b_1, b_2, b_3)$$
$$= \mathsf{LE}_m(\mathbf{t}_1, \tau) \cdot \varphi_{y,\tau} (\mathbf{t}_1, \mathbf{t}_2, \mathbf{t}_3, \mathbf{s}_1, \mathbf{s}_2, \mathbf{s}_3, b_1, b_2, b_3) \cdot \prod_{i \in [3]} \left(\tilde{X}_\tau (\mathbf{t}_i, \mathbf{s}_i) - b_i \right).$$

Where $\mathsf{LE}_j \colon \mathbb{F}^{2j} \to \mathbb{F}$ is the (unique) polynomial of individual degree $(|\mathbb{H}| - 1)$ such that for every $\mathbf{h}, \mathbf{h}' \in \mathbb{H}^j$, $\mathsf{LE}_j(\mathbf{h}, \mathbf{h}') = 1$ if the row indexed by $\mathbf{h}$ is smaller than or equal to the one indexed by $\mathbf{h}'$, and $\mathsf{LE}_j(\mathbf{h}, \mathbf{h}') = 0$ otherwise. We purposefully order the input variables to Q^0_τ leading with the row indices. As discussed later in this overview, this simplifies the update procedure of the sum-check polynomials. The sum-check polynomials $Q^1_\tau, \ldots, Q^\ell_\tau$ are defined by Q^0_τ as before.

The Proof String. In our new proof we group together $O(\ell)$ symbols of the original proof into one symbol (over a larger alphabet). This grouping is crucial for allowing this larger symbol to self-update. The PCP proof for the computation up to timestep $t \in [\mathsf{T}]$ is given by Π_τ for $\tau = t \cdot \beta$. The string Π_τ contains one symbol $\sigma^\mathbf{z}_\tau$ for every vector $\mathbf{z} = (\mathbf{t}_1, \mathbf{t}_2, \mathbf{t}_3, \mathbf{s}_1, \mathbf{s}_2, \mathbf{s}_3, b_1, b_2, b_3) \in \mathbb{F}^\ell$. The symbol $\sigma^\mathbf{z}_\tau$ contain the values $\tilde{X}_\tau(\mathbf{t}_1, \mathbf{s}_1), \tilde{X}_\tau(\mathbf{t}_2, \mathbf{s}_2), \tilde{X}_\tau(\mathbf{t}_3, \mathbf{s}_3)$ and the values $Q^0_\tau(\mathbf{z}), \ldots, Q^\ell_\tau(\mathbf{z})$. Further, every symbol contains additional supplemental values that are needed for self-updating. The supplemental values are discussed below, when we detail the update procedure.

---

[2] While ϕ_τ can be described by simple conjunction, in our construction it will convenient to view it as a 3CNF formula.

On Verifying the PCP. The new PCP can be verified via the same tests performed by the original BFLS verifier. The grouping of values into symbols and the supplemental values in every symbol are needed only for updates and are ignored by the verifier. Note that in our new construction every value $\tilde{X}_\tau(\mathbf{u})$ is contained in multiple symbols. When the BFLS verifier queries the value $\tilde{X}_\tau(\mathbf{u})$, it is crucial for soundness that the symbol we read in order to answer this query is chosen as a function of $\mathbf{u}$ alone, independently of the other verifier queries.

2.3   Updating the PCP

We start with the $(t-1)$-th configuration c_{t-1} and one symbol $\sigma^{\mathbf{z}}_{(t-1)\cdot\beta}$ of the proof $\Pi_{(t-1)\cdot\beta}$. Given the next configuration c_t our goal is to compute the symbol $\sigma^{\mathbf{z}}_{t\cdot\beta}$ of the new proof $\Pi_{t\cdot\beta}$. Starting from $\tau = (t-1)\cdot\beta+1$ we show how to update $\sigma^{\mathbf{z}}_{\tau-1}$ to $\sigma^{\mathbf{z}}_\tau$ and we repeat this update β times. Recall that X_τ is our partial assignment to the first τ rows. We first use the new configuration c_t to obtain row τ of X_τ. We denote this assignment by $\gamma_\tau \colon \mathbb{H}^k \to \{0,1\}$. We proceed to update every value in the symbol $\sigma^{\mathbf{z}}_{\tau-1}$. In what follows we denote $\mathbf{z} = (\mathbf{t}, \mathbf{s}, \mathbf{b})$ for $\mathbf{t} = (\mathbf{t}_1, \mathbf{t}_2, \mathbf{t}_3) \in \mathbb{F}^{3m}$, $\mathbf{s} = (\mathbf{s}_1, \mathbf{s}_2, \mathbf{s}_3) \in \mathbb{F}^{3k}$, and $\mathbf{b} = (b_1, b_2, b_3) \in \mathbb{F}^3$.

Updating $\tilde{X}$. The symbol $\sigma^{\mathbf{z}}_{\tau-1}$ contains the evaluations of the assignment polynomial $\tilde{X}_{\tau-1}$ at locations $(\mathbf{t}_i, \mathbf{s}_i)$. We show how to update these evaluations and compute $\tilde{X}_\tau(\mathbf{t}_i, \mathbf{s}_i)$. Recall that $\tilde{X}_\tau$ is a polynomial of individual degree at most $(|\mathbb{H}|-1)$, that identifies with X_τ on $\mathbb{H}^{m+k}$. Equivalently, $\tilde{X}_\tau$ is the unique low-degree extension of X_τ given by the sum:

$$\tilde{X}_\tau(\mathbf{v}) = \sum_{\mathbf{h}\in\mathbb{H}^{m+k}} \mathsf{ID}_{m+k}(\mathbf{h}, \mathbf{v}) \cdot X_\tau(\mathbf{h}). \tag{1}$$

Since the assignment $X_{\tau-1}$ and X_τ only differ on the τ-th row where $X_{\tau-1}(\tau, \cdot)$ is identically zero and $X_\tau(\tau, \cdot) = \gamma_\tau$ we have that:

$$X_{\tau+1}(\mathbf{v}) - X_\tau(\mathbf{v}) = \sum_{\mathbf{h}\in\{0,1\}^k} \mathsf{ID}_{m+k}((\tau, \mathbf{h}), \mathbf{v}) \cdot \gamma_\tau(\mathbf{h}).$$

Therefore, given the old value $X_{\tau-1}(\mathbf{t}_i, \mathbf{s}_i)$ and γ_τ we can efficiently compute the new value $X_\tau(\mathbf{t}_i, \mathbf{s}_i)$ by summing the $O(\mathsf{S}')$ summands above.

Updating Q. The symbol $\sigma^{\mathbf{z}}_{t-1}$ also contains the evaluations of the consistency check and sum-check polynomial $Q^j_{\tau-1}(\mathbf{z})$ for every $0 \le j \le \ell$. We show how to update these evaluations and compute $Q^j_\tau(\mathbf{z})$. The update procedure for Q^j_τ is more involved than the update of $\tilde{X}_\tau$, since the polynomial Q^j_τ is not just linear combination of the values $X_\tau(\cdot)$. For different values of j, we give a different procedures updating Q^j_τ. In this overview we demonstrate the main technical ideas by focusing on some of these cases.

Updating Q^0. For $j = 0$ we can efficiently evaluate the consistency check polynomial $Q^0_\tau(\mathbf{z})$ since the values $X_\tau(\mathbf{t}_i, \mathbf{s}_i)$ have already been computed, the circuit

LE can be efficiently evaluated, and the circuit $\varphi_{y,\tau}$ can be efficiently evaluated given the input y and the assignment γ_τ.

Updating Q^m. For $j = m$ we want to compute:

$$Q_\tau^m(\mathbf{z}) = \sum_{\mathbf{h}_1 \in \mathbb{H}^m} \mathsf{ID}\,(\mathbf{h}_1, \mathbf{t}_1) \cdot Q_\tau^0(\mathbf{h}_1, \mathbf{t}_2, \mathbf{t}_3, \mathbf{s}, \mathbf{b}).$$

In computing this sum, we exploit the fact that the first m inputs to Q_τ^0 are always in $\mathbb{H}$. First, for $\mathbf{h}_1 \in \mathbb{H}^m$ we have $\mathsf{LE}(\mathbf{h}_1, \tau) = 1$ when $\mathbf{h}_1 \leq \tau$ and $\mathsf{LE}(\mathbf{h}_1, \tau) = 0$ when $\mathbf{h}_1 > \tau$. (In contrast for an arbitrary $\mathbf{u} \in \mathbb{F}^m$, $\mathsf{LE}(\mathbf{u}, \tau)$ may not be in $\{0, 1\}$.) Therefore, by the definition of Q_τ^0, we can write the sum above as:

$$\sum_{\mathbf{h}_1 \leq \tau} \mathsf{ID}\,(\mathbf{h}_1, \mathbf{t}_1) \cdot \varphi_{y,\tau}\,(\mathbf{h}_1, \mathbf{t}_2, \mathbf{t}_3, \mathbf{s}, \mathbf{b}) \cdot \left(\tilde{X}_\tau\,(\mathbf{h}_1, \mathbf{s}_1) - b_1 \right) \cdot \prod_{i \in [2,3]} \left(\tilde{X}_\tau\,(\mathbf{t}_i, \mathbf{s}_i) - b_i \right).$$

Since we have already computed the values $\tilde{X}_\tau(\mathbf{t}_2, \mathbf{s}_2)$ and $\tilde{X}_\tau(\mathbf{t}_3, \mathbf{s}_3)$ it is sufficient to compute the following sum denoted by $A_\tau^m(\mathbf{z}, \mathbf{b})$:

$$A_\tau^m(\mathbf{z}) = \sum_{\mathbf{h}_1 \leq \tau} \mathsf{ID}\,(\mathbf{h}_1, \mathbf{t}_1) \cdot \varphi_{y,\tau}\,(\mathbf{h}_1, \mathbf{t}_2, \mathbf{t}_3, \mathbf{s}, \mathbf{b}) \cdot \left(\tilde{X}_\tau\,(\mathbf{h}_1, \mathbf{s}_1) - b_1 \right).$$

Computing the τ summands above from scratch requires time proportional to the running time of the computation so far. Therefore, we instead maintain $A_\tau^m(\mathbf{z})$ as a supplemental value contained in the symbol $\sigma_\tau^\mathbf{z}$. Thus, it is sufficient to compute $A_\tau^m(\mathbf{z})$ from the old value $A_{\tau-1}^m(\mathbf{z})$ given in the symbol $\sigma_{\tau-1}^\mathbf{z}$. Specifically, we show how to efficiently compute the difference $A_\tau^m(\mathbf{z}) - A_{\tau-1}^m(\mathbf{z})$. We observe that most of the summands are equal in $A_\tau^m(\mathbf{z})$ and in $A_{\tau-1}^m(\mathbf{z})$ and, therefore, the difference contains a constant number of summands that we can compute. Specifically we show that for every $\mathbf{h}_1 < \tau - 1$:

$$\varphi_{y,\tau-1}\,(\mathbf{h}_1, \mathbf{t}_2, \mathbf{t}_3, \mathbf{s}, \mathbf{b}) = \varphi_{y,\tau}\,(\mathbf{h}_1, \mathbf{t}_2, \mathbf{t}_3, \mathbf{s}, \mathbf{b})\,. \tag{2}$$

$$\tilde{X}_{\tau-1}\,(\mathbf{h}_1, \mathbf{s}_1) = \tilde{X}_\tau\,(\mathbf{h}_1, \mathbf{s}_1)\,. \tag{3}$$

We first use (2) and (3) to show how to efficiently compute $A_\tau^m(\mathbf{z}) - A_{\tau-1}^m(\mathbf{z})$, and then explain why these equalities hold. Given that (2) and (3) hold for every $\mathbf{h}_1 < \tau - 1$ we can write the difference $A_\tau^m(\mathbf{z}) - A_{\tau-1}^m(\mathbf{z})$ as:

$$A_\tau^m(\mathbf{z}) - A_{\tau-1}^m(\mathbf{z}) = \mathsf{ID}\,(\tau, \mathbf{t}_1) \cdot \varphi_{y,\tau}\,(\tau, \mathbf{t}_2, \mathbf{t}_3, \mathbf{s}, \mathbf{b}) \cdot \left(\tilde{X}_\tau\,(\tau, \mathbf{s}_1) - b_1 \right)$$

$$+ \mathsf{ID}\,(\tau - 1, \mathbf{t}_1) \cdot \varphi_{y,\tau}\,(\tau - 1, \mathbf{t}_2, \mathbf{t}_3, \mathbf{s}, \mathbf{b}) \cdot \left(\tilde{X}_\tau\,(\tau - 1, \mathbf{s}_1) - b_1 \right)$$

$$- \mathsf{ID}\,(\tau - 1, \mathbf{t}_1) \cdot \varphi_{y,\tau-1}\,(\tau - 1, \mathbf{t}_2, \mathbf{t}_3, \mathbf{s}, \mathbf{b}) \cdot \left(\tilde{X}_{\tau-1}\,(\tau - 1, \mathbf{s}_1) - b_1 \right)$$

Recall that the circuits $\varphi_{y,\tau}$ and $\varphi_{y,\tau-1}$ can be efficiently evaluated given the input y and the assignments γ_τ and $\gamma_{\tau-1}$. Therefore, it remains to compute the values:

$$\tilde{X}_\tau\,(\tau, \mathbf{s}_1)\,, \quad \tilde{X}_\tau\,(\tau - 1, \mathbf{s}_1)\,, \quad \tilde{X}_{\tau-1}\,(\tau - 1, \mathbf{s}_1)\,.$$

By (1), for any $\mathbf{h} \le \tau$ the value $\tilde{X}_\tau(\mathbf{h}, \mathbf{s}_1)$ is just a linear combination of the values assigned to the $\mathbf{h}$-th row:

$$\tilde{X}_\tau(\mathbf{h}, \mathbf{s}_1) = \sum_{\mathbf{h}' \in \mathbb{H}^k} \mathsf{ID}_k(\mathbf{h}', \mathbf{s}_1) \cdot X_\tau(\mathbf{h}, \mathbf{h}') = \sum_{\mathbf{h}' \in \mathbb{H}^k} \mathsf{ID}_k(\mathbf{h}', \mathbf{s}_1) \cdot \gamma_{\mathbf{h}}(\mathbf{h}'). \quad (4)$$

Therefore, we can compute the required evaluations of $\tilde{X}_\tau$ and $\tilde{X}_{\tau-1}$ given the assignments γ_τ and $\gamma_{\tau-1}$. To complete the description of the update procedure for Q^m, we argue that (2) and (3) hold. For (2) we first observe that formulas $\phi_{y,\tau-1} = \phi_y \wedge \phi_{\tau-1}$ and $\phi_{y,\tau} = \phi_y \wedge \phi_\tau$ only differ on clauses over variables in rows $\tau-1$ and τ. Therefore, if it was the case that $\mathbf{z} \in \mathbb{H}^\ell$ and $\mathbf{h}_1 < \tau-1$ then (2) would hold. We show how to appropriately modify the definition of the polynomial $\varphi_{y,\tau}$ so that (2) holds for all $\mathbf{z} \in \mathbb{F}^\ell$ as long as $\mathbf{h}_1 \in \mathbb{H}^m$. Recall that the polynomial $\varphi_{y,\tau} = \varphi_y + \varphi_\tau$ describes the formula $\phi_{y,\tau} = \phi_y \wedge \phi_\tau$. We can assume WLOG that every clause in ϕ_τ on variables $(\mathbf{t}_1', \mathbf{s}_1'), (\mathbf{t}_2', \mathbf{s}_2'), (\mathbf{t}_3', \mathbf{s}_3') \in \mathbb{H}^{m+k}$ satisfies $\mathbf{t}_1' = \tau$. Therefore, we can redefine $\varphi_{y,\tau}$ as:

$$\varphi_{y,\tau}(\mathbf{z}) = \varphi_y(\mathbf{z}) + \mathsf{ID}_m(\mathbf{t}_1, \tau) \cdot \varphi_\tau(\mathbf{z}).$$

The new polynomial $\varphi_{y,\tau}(\mathbf{z})$ still represents the same formula $\phi_{y,\tau}$ and (2) holds since for $\mathbf{h}_1 < \tau-1$ we have:

$$\varphi_{y,\tau-1}(\mathbf{h}_1, \mathbf{t}_2, \mathbf{t}_3, \mathbf{s}, \mathbf{b}) = \varphi_y(\mathbf{h}_1, \mathbf{t}_2, \mathbf{t}_3, \mathbf{s}, \mathbf{b}) = \varphi_{y,\tau}(\mathbf{h}_1, \mathbf{t}_2, \mathbf{t}_3, \mathbf{s}, \mathbf{b}).$$

To see why (3) holds, recall that by (4), since $\mathbf{h}_1 \le \tau-1$ the value $\tilde{X}_\tau(\mathbf{h}_1, \mathbf{s}_1)$ is just a linear combination of the values assigned to the $\mathbf{h}_1$-th row and therefore:

$$\tilde{X}_{\tau-1}(\mathbf{h}_1, \mathbf{s}_1) = \sum_{\mathbf{h} \in \mathbb{H}^k} \mathsf{ID}_k(\mathbf{h}, \mathbf{s}_1) \cdot \gamma_{\mathbf{h}_1}(\mathbf{h}) = \tilde{X}_\tau(\mathbf{h}_1, \mathbf{s}_1).$$

Updating Q^j for $j < m$. The final case we consider in this overview is $0 < j < m$. Here we want to compute:

$$Q_\tau^j(\mathbf{z}) = \sum_{\mathbf{h} \in \mathbb{H}^j} \mathsf{ID}(\mathbf{h}, \mathbf{t}_1[:j]) \cdot Q_\tau^0(\mathbf{h}, \mathbf{t}_1[j+1:], \mathbf{t}_2, \mathbf{t}_3, \mathbf{s}, \mathbf{b}),$$

where $\mathbf{t}_1[:j]$ and $\mathbf{t}_1[j+1:]$ denote the j-bit prefix and the $(m-j)$-bit suffix of $\mathbf{t}_1$ respectively. This case is very similar to the case $j = m$ with the added difficulty that now only the first j inputs to Q_τ^0 are in $\mathbb{H}$ (as opposed to the previous case, where the entire first index was in $\mathbb{H}$). In the case where $j = m$ we argued that when $\mathbf{u} \in \mathbb{H}^m$, either $\mathbf{u} \le \tau$ and $\mathsf{LE}(\mathbf{u}, \tau) = 1$, or $\mathbf{u} > \tau$ and $\mathsf{LE}(\mathbf{u}, \tau) = 0$. Now, however, only the first j bits of $\mathbf{u}$ are in $\mathbb{H}$ and the rest may be in $\mathbb{F}$. Thus, it is not immediately clear whether we can say anything about the output of $\mathsf{LE}(\mathbf{u}, \tau)$. We show that in some cases the outcome of $\mathsf{LE}(\mathbf{u}, \tau)$ can be determined given only the prefix of the inputs that is in $\mathbb{H}$. Specifically, using the fact that LE has individual degree $(|\mathbb{H}| - 1)$, we show that for $\mathbf{u} \in \mathbb{H}^j \times \mathbb{F}^{m-j}$ if $\mathbf{u}[:j] > \tau[:j]$ then $\mathsf{LE}(\mathbf{u}, \tau) = 0$. Therefore, we can write $Q_\tau^j(\mathbf{z})$ as:

$$Q_\tau^j(\mathbf{z}) = \sum_{\mathbf{h} \le \tau[:j]} \mathsf{ID}(\mathbf{h}, \mathbf{t}_1[:j]) \cdot Q_\tau^0(\mathbf{h}, \mathbf{t}_1[j+1:], \mathbf{t}_2, \mathbf{t}_3, \mathbf{s}, \mathbf{b}).$$

As before, since we have already computed the values $X_\tau(\mathbf{t}_2, \mathbf{s}_2)$ and $X_\tau(\mathbf{t}_3, \mathbf{s}_3)$, it is sufficient to show how to maintain the sum $A_\tau^j(\mathbf{z}, \mathbf{b})$ as a supplemental value in $\sigma_\tau^\mathbf{z}$:

$$A_\tau^j(\mathbf{z}) = \sum_{\mathbf{h} \leq \tau[:j]} \mathsf{ID}\left(\mathbf{h}, \mathbf{t}_1[:j]\right) \cdot \varphi_{y,\tau}\left(\mathbf{h}, \mathbf{t}_1[j+1:], \mathbf{t}_2, \mathbf{t}_3, \mathbf{s}, \mathbf{b}\right) \cdot \left(\tilde{X}_\tau\left(\mathbf{h}, \mathbf{t}_1[j+1:], \mathbf{s}_1\right) - b_1\right).$$

As before, in order to compute the difference $A_\tau^j(\mathbf{z}) - A_{\tau-1}^j(\mathbf{z})$ we first need to show that, analogously to (2) and (3) above, for every $\mathbf{h} < (\tau - 1)[:j]$:

$$\varphi_{y,\tau-1}\left(\mathbf{h}, \mathbf{t}_1[j+1:], \mathbf{t}_2, \mathbf{t}_3, \mathbf{s}, \mathbf{b}\right) = \varphi_{y,\tau}\left(\mathbf{h}, \mathbf{t}_1[j+1:], \mathbf{t}_2, \mathbf{t}_3, \mathbf{s}, \mathbf{b}\right). \tag{5}$$

$$\tilde{X}_{\tau-1}\left(\mathbf{h}, \mathbf{t}_1[j+1:], \mathbf{s}_1\right) = \tilde{X}_\tau\left(\mathbf{h}, \mathbf{t}_1[j+1:], \mathbf{s}_1\right). \tag{6}$$

The proof of (5) follows the same argument as (2) except that now we also use the fact that for $\mathbf{h} < \tau[:j]$ it holds that $\mathsf{ID}_m((\mathbf{h}, \mathbf{t}_1[j+1:]), \tau) = 0$ even when $\mathbf{t}_1$ is not in $\mathbb{H}^m$. To see why (6) holds recall that by (1) for $\mathbf{h} < \tau[:j]$ and any $\mathbf{u} \in \mathbb{F}^{m-j}$ the value $\tilde{X}_\tau((\mathbf{h}, \mathbf{u}), \mathbf{s}_1)$ is just a linear combination of the values assigned to rows whose indices (in $\mathbb{H}^m$) start with the prefix $\mathbf{h}$ where $\tilde{X}_\tau$ and $\tilde{X}_{\tau-1}$ identify on these rows:

$$\tilde{X}_\tau\left((\mathbf{h}, \mathbf{u}), \mathbf{s}_1\right) = \sum_{(\mathbf{h}', \mathbf{h}'') \in \mathbb{H}^{m-j} \times \mathbb{H}^k} \mathsf{ID}((\mathbf{h}', \mathbf{h}''), (\mathbf{u}, \mathbf{s})) \cdot \gamma_{(\mathbf{h}, \mathbf{h}')}(\mathbf{h}'') = \tilde{X}_{\tau-1}\left((\mathbf{h}, \mathbf{u}), \mathbf{s}_1\right).$$

Let $\mathbf{u}$ denote the vector $(\mathbf{t}_1[j+1:], \mathbf{s}_1) \in \mathbb{F}^{m-j+k}$. Similarly to the previous case, it remains to compute the values:

$$\tilde{X}_\tau\left(\tau[:j], \mathbf{u}\right), \quad \tilde{X}_\tau\left((\tau-1)[:j], \mathbf{u}\right), \quad \tilde{X}_{\tau-1}\left((\tau-1)[:j], \mathbf{u}\right).$$

As explained above, the value $\tilde{X}_\tau\left(\tau[:j], \mathbf{u}\right)$ is a linear combination of the values assigned to rows in whose indices (in $\mathbb{H}^m$) start with the prefix $\tau[:j]$. The number of such rows can be proportional to τ, so this values cannot be efficiently computed from scratch. Instead, we update these values using additional supplemental values, which we place in $\sigma_\tau^\mathbf{z}$ and maintain:

$$\tilde{X}_\tau\left(\tau[:j], \mathbf{u}\right), \quad \tilde{X}_\tau\left((\tau-1)[:j], \mathbf{u}\right).$$

We explain how to compute $\tilde{X}_\tau\left(\tau[:j], \mathbf{u}\right)$ given $\tilde{X}_{\tau-1}\left((\tau-1)[:j], \mathbf{u}\right)$ (updating $\tilde{X}_\tau\left((\tau-1)[:j], \mathbf{u}\right)$ is done similarly). First, recall that the value $\tilde{X}_\tau\left(\tau[:j], \mathbf{u}\right)$ is a linear combinations of the values assigned to rows whose indices (in $\mathbb{H}^m$) start with the prefix $\tau[:j]$:

$$\tilde{X}_\tau\left(\tau[:j], \mathbf{u}\right) = \sum_{\mathbf{h} \in \mathbb{H}^{m-j+k}} \mathsf{ID}(\mathbf{h}, \mathbf{u}) \cdot X_\tau(\tau[:j], \mathbf{h}).$$

When updating $\tilde{X}_\tau\left(\tau[:j], \mathbf{u}\right)$, we distinguish between two cases. First we consider the case where $\tau[:j] = (\tau-1)[:j]$. In this case, both values $\tilde{X}_\tau\left(\tau[:j], \mathbf{u}\right)$ and $\tilde{X}_{\tau-1}\left((\tau-1)[:j], \mathbf{u}\right)$ are computed from the values assigned to the same set of rows whose indices start with the prefix $\tau[:j] = (\tau-1)[:j]$. Since the assignment

$X_{\tau-1}$ and X_τ only differ on the τ-th row where $X_{\tau-1}(\tau, \cdot)$ is identically zero and $X_\tau(\tau, \cdot) = \gamma_\tau$ we have that:

$$\tilde{X}_\tau(\tau[:j], \mathbf{u}) - \tilde{X}_{\tau-1}((\tau-1)[:j], \mathbf{u}) = \sum_{\mathbf{h}' \in \mathbb{H}^k} \mathsf{ID}((\tau[j+1:], \mathbf{h}'), \mathbf{u}) \cdot \gamma_\tau(\mathbf{h}').$$

Therefore, in this case we can compute the value $\tilde{X}_\tau(\tau[:j], \mathbf{u})$ given $\tilde{X}_{\tau-1}((\tau-1)[:j], \mathbf{u})$ by summing the $O(\mathsf{S}')$ summands above. Next, we consider the case where $\tau[:j] \neq (\tau-1)[:j]$. In this case, the τ-th row is the only row that starts with the prefix $\tau[:j]$ and assigned a non-zero value by X_τ. Therefore, in this case we can directly compute the value $\tilde{X}_\tau(\tau[:j], \mathbf{u})$

Updating Q^j for $j > m$. Updating $Q_\tau^j(\mathbf{z})$ for $j > m$ involves many of the ideas described above. The main difference is that in this case we do not only sum over the first row index. To update the sum we rely on the fact that the polynomial $\varphi_{y,\tau}$ evaluates to 0 whenever the indices $\mathbf{t}_2$ and $\mathbf{t}_3$ are different than $\mathbf{t}_1 - 1$. As in the case where $j < m$, here we also need to deal with the cases where only a prefix of the row indices is in $\mathbb{H}$.

2.4   From PCP to Verifiable Computation

As discussed in Sect. 1.1, our designated-verifier incrementally verifiable computation protocol is basically the protocol of BHK [BHK16, Appendix A], where the PCP is replaced by our incrementally updatable PCP. In particular, our verification procedure is essentially identical to that of BHK (ignoring the supplemental values in every symbol that are not part of the original PCP of BFLS). There is, however, a minor differences between our PCP and the PCP in BHK which affects the verification procedure: in our PCP, the sum-check polynomial Q^j is the low-degree extension of Q^0 in its first j variables, while in BHK, Q^j and Q^0 satisfy a different relation. However, the analysis in BHK [BHK16, Appendix B] with only minor changes fits our construction as well.

3   Definitions

In this section we define incrementally updatable PCPs and verifiable computation.

3.1   Incrementally Updatable PCP

We start by recalling the standard notion of a probabilistically checkable proof (PCP) and then define incremental updates. Fix a non-deterministic Turing machine M with running time $\mathsf{T} = \mathsf{T}(n)$. For an input $y \in \{0, 1\}^n$ and a witness string $w \in \{0, 1\}^t$ where $t \in [\mathsf{T}]$, let $M(y; w)$ denote the configuration of M when executing on input y after t steps using w as a witness. The configuration includes the machine's work tapes, state, and the machine's locations on all tapes. Let $\mathcal{L}_M$ be the language that contains a tuple (y, t, c) if there exists $w \in \{0, 1\}^t$

such that $c = M(y; w)$. Let $\mathcal{R}_M$ be the corresponding witness relation. A PCP system for M with alphabet $\Sigma = \{\Sigma_n\}_{n \in \mathbb{N}}$, query complexity $q = q(n)$, and proof length $\ell = \ell(n)$ consists of a deterministic polynomial-time algorithm P and a randomized oracle machine V with the following syntax:

P : given $(x = (y, t, c), w) \in \mathcal{R}_M$ outputs a proof $\Pi \in \Sigma^\ell$.
V : given x and oracle access to the proof Π makes q oracle queries and outputs a bit.

Definition 3.1 *A PCP system* (P, V) *satisfies the following requirements*

Completeness: *For every* $(x, w) \in \mathcal{R}_M$, *let* $\Pi = \mathsf{P}(x, w)$. *It holds that:*

$$\Pr\left[\mathsf{V}^\Pi(x) = 1\right] = 1.$$

Soundness: *For every* $x \notin \mathcal{L}_M$ *and for every* $\Pi \in \Sigma^\ell$:

$$\Pr\left[\mathsf{V}^\Pi(x) = 1\right] \leq \frac{1}{2}.$$

Incremental Updates. In an incrementally updatable PCP, each location in the proof string can be maintained and updated in a step-by-step fashion: given the machine's configuration and the value of the PCP at a certain location z after t steps of the computation, the *updated* value of the PCP at location z after $(t+1)$ steps can be computed *locally*, without looking at any PCP symbols except the symbol in location z. Note that the "updated PCP" proves an "updated claim" about the $(t + 1)$-th configuration. Note also that, while this local update does require knowledge of the entire current configuration (whose size is dominated by the machine's *space* complexity), this can be much smaller than the length of the PCP (which is larger than the machine's *time* complexity). Formally, an incrementally updatable PCP comes with a deterministic polynomial-time algorithm Update with the following syntax: given an instance $(y, t - 1, c_{t-1})$, a witness bit w_t, a position $z \in [\ell]$, and symbol $\sigma_{t-1}^z \in \Sigma$ outputs a new symbol $\sigma_t^z \in \Sigma$. For every $(x = (y, t, c_t), w) \in \mathcal{R}_M$, the PCP proof $\Pi_t = \mathsf{P}(x, w)$ can be constructed by running Update as follows:

1. Let c_0 be the initial configuration of $M(y)$ and let $\sigma_0^z = \bot$.
2. For every $\tau \in [t]$, $z \in [\ell]$, update M's configuration from $c_{\tau-1}$ to c_τ using witness bit w_τ and let:

$$\sigma_\tau^z \leftarrow \mathsf{Update}((y, \tau - 1, c_{\tau-1}), w_\tau, z, \sigma_{\tau-1}^z).$$

3. Output the proof $\Pi_t = (\sigma_t^1, \ldots, \sigma_t^\ell)$.

3.2   Incrementally Verifiable Computation

We start with the definition of verifiable computation and then define incremental updates. Fix a deterministic Turing machine M with running time $\mathsf{T} = \mathsf{T}(n)$. For an input $y \in \{0, 1\}^n$ and $t \in [\mathsf{T}]$, let $M(y; 1^t)$ be the configuration of M when executing on input y after t steps (a configuration includes the machine's work tapes, state, and the machine's locations on all tapes). Let $\mathcal{L}_M$ be the language that contains a tuple (y, t, c) if $c = M(y; 1^t)$. A verifiable computation scheme consists of a randomized polynomial-time algorithm G and deterministic polynomial time algorithms P, V with the following syntax:

G: given the security parameter 1^κ, outputs a pair of keys: a prover key pk and a verifier key vk.

P: given the prover key pk, a time bound 1^t and an instance $x = (y, t, c)$, outputs a proof Π.

V: given the verifier key vk, an instance x and a proof Π, outputs a bit.

We say that the proof is publicly verifiable if the algorithm G always outputs identical prover and verifier keys vk = pk. Otherwise the proof is designated verifier.

Definition 3.2 *A verifiable computation scheme* (G, P, V) *for* $\mathcal{L}_M$ *satisfies the following requirements:*

Completeness: *For every $\kappa \in \mathbb{N}$ and for every $x = (y, t, c) \in \mathcal{L}_M$:*

$$\Pr\left[V(\mathsf{vk}, x, \Pi) = 1 \ \middle| \ \begin{array}{l} (\mathsf{pk}, \mathsf{vk}) \leftarrow G(1^\kappa) \\ \Pi \leftarrow P(\mathsf{pk}, 1^t, x) \end{array}\right] = 1.$$

Efficiency: *In the above honest experiment the length of the proof Π is* $\mathrm{poly}(\kappa, \log(t))$. *The verifier's running time is* $|x| \cdot \mathrm{poly}(\kappa, |\Pi|)$.

Soundness: *For every polynomial* $\mathsf{T} = \mathsf{T}(\kappa)$ *and for every polynomial size cheating prover* P* *there exists a negligible function μ such that for every $\kappa \in \mathbb{N}$:*

$$\Pr\left[\begin{array}{l} x = (y, \mathsf{T}, c) \notin \mathcal{L}_M \\ V(\mathsf{vk}, x, \Pi) = 1 \end{array} \ \middle| \ \begin{array}{l} (\mathsf{pk}, \mathsf{vk}) \leftarrow G(1^\kappa) \\ (x, \Pi) \leftarrow \mathsf{P}^*(\mathsf{pk}) \end{array}\right] \le \mu(\kappa).$$

Incremental Updates. A verifiable computation scheme (with either public or designated verifier) satisfying Definition 3.2 is incrementally verifiable if given the honest proof Π_t for a statement (y, t, c_t) and the configuration c_t we can obtain the next proof Π_{t+1} for the statement $(y, t+1, c_{t+1})$ without repeating the entire computation. Formally, an incrementally verifiable computation scheme also includes a deterministic polynomial-time algorithm Update with the following syntax: given the prover key pk, a statement $(y, t-1, c_{t-1}) \in \mathcal{L}_M$ and a proof Π_{t-1}, Update outputs a new proof Π_t. For every statement $x = (y, t, c) \in \mathcal{L}_M$, the proof $\Pi_t = P(\mathsf{pk}, 1^t, x)$ can be constructed by running Update as follows:

1. Let c_0 be the initial configuration of $M(y)$ and let $\Pi_0 = \bot$.
2. For every $\tau \in [t]$, update M's configuration from $c_{\tau-1}$ to c_τ and let:

$$\Pi_\tau \leftarrow \mathsf{Update}(\mathsf{pk}, (y, \tau - 1, c_{\tau-1}), \Pi_{\tau-1}).$$

3. Output Π_t.

The completeness, efficiency, and soundness requirements of

4   PCP Construction

In this section we introduce notation and describe the PCP system. The update procedure for this PCP is described in the full version of this work. Before reading the full details, we recommend the reader familiarize themselves with the overview in Sect. 2.

4.1   Preliminaries

We start by introducing notations and simple clams that are used throughout the following sections.

Operations on Strings. For an alphabet Σ, a string $\mathbf{v} = v_1, \ldots, v_n \in \Sigma^n$ and $1 \leq i \leq j \leq n$ we denote by $\mathbf{v}[i{:}j]$ the substring $v_i, \ldots, v_j$. We shorthand $\mathbf{v}[1{:}i]$ by $\mathbf{v}[{:}i]$ and $\mathbf{v}[j{:}n]$ by $\mathbf{v}[j{:}]$. We also define $\mathbf{v}[{:}0]$ and $\mathbf{v}[n+1{:}]$ to be the empty string. For a pair of strings $\mathbf{u}, \mathbf{v} \in \Sigma^n$ and $i \in [0, n]$ let $(\mathbf{u}|\mathbf{v})_i$ denote the string $(\mathbf{u}[{:}i], \mathbf{v}[i+1{:}])$.

The Field $\mathbb{F}$. Fix any field $\mathbb{F}$ and a subset $\mathbb{H} \subseteq \mathbb{F}$. (The sizes of $\mathbb{F}$ and $\mathbb{H}$ will be set later in this section.) We also fix a linear order on $\mathbb{H}$ and use the lexicographical order on strings in $\mathbb{H}^m$ for any $m \in \mathbb{N}$. We denote the minimal and maximal element in $\mathbb{H}$ by 0 and $|\mathbb{H}| - 1$ respectively. For $\mathbf{t} \in \mathbb{H}^m$ such that $\mathbf{t} > 0^m$ we denote the predecessor of $\mathbf{t}$ by $\mathbf{t} - 1$.

Arithmetic Circuits. We denote by $C : \mathbb{F}^i \rightarrow \mathbb{F}^j$ an arithmetic circuit over a field $\mathbb{F}$ with i input wires and j output wires. The circuit is constructed from addition, subtraction and multiplication gates of arity 2 as well as constants from $\mathbb{F}$. The size of C is the number of gates in C. We say that C is of degree d if the polynomial computed by C over $\mathbb{F}$ is of degree d or less in every one of its input variables.

Useful Predicates. We make use of arithmetic circuits computing simple predicates.

Claim 4.1. *For every* $i \in \mathbb{N}$ *there exist arithmetic circuits* $\mathsf{ID}_i, \mathsf{LE}_i, \mathsf{PR}_i : \mathbb{F}^{2i} \rightarrow \mathbb{F}$ *of size* $O(i)$ *and degree* $|\mathbb{H}| - 1$ *such that for every input* $\mathbf{u}, \mathbf{v} \in \mathbb{H}^i$, *the circuits' output is in* $\{0, 1\}$ *and:*

$$
\begin{aligned}
\mathsf{ID}_i(\mathbf{u}, \mathbf{v}) = 1 \quad &\Leftrightarrow \quad \mathbf{u} = \mathbf{v} && \textit{(Identity)} \\
\mathsf{LE}_i(\mathbf{u}, \mathbf{v}) = 1 \quad &\Leftrightarrow \quad \mathbf{u} \leq \mathbf{v} && \textit{(Lesser-or-equal)} \\
\mathsf{PR}_i(\mathbf{u}, \mathbf{v}) = 1 \quad &\Leftrightarrow \quad \mathbf{u} - 1 = \mathbf{v} && \textit{(Predecessor)}
\end{aligned}
$$

Proof. For $i = 1$, circuits $\mathsf{ID}_1, \mathsf{LE}_1, \mathsf{PR}_1$ exist by straightforward interpolation. For $i > 1$, $u, v \in \mathbb{F}$ and $\mathbf{u}, \mathbf{v} \in \mathbb{F}^{i-1}$, let $\mathbf{u}' = (u, \mathbf{u})$ and $\mathbf{v}' = (v, \mathbf{v})$. The circuit ID_i is given by:
$$
\mathsf{ID}_i(\mathbf{u}', \mathbf{v}') = \mathsf{ID}_1(u, v) \cdot \mathsf{ID}_{i-1}(\mathbf{u}, \mathbf{v}).
$$

The circuit LE_i is given by:

$$\mathsf{LE}_i(\mathbf{u}', \mathbf{v}') = [\mathsf{ID}_1(u, v) \cdot \mathsf{LE}_{i-1}(\mathbf{u}, \mathbf{v})] + \mathsf{LE}_1(u, v) - \mathsf{ID}_1(u, v).$$

The circuit PR_i is given by:

$$\begin{aligned}
\mathsf{PR}_i(\mathbf{u}', \mathbf{v}') = {} &\mathsf{ID}_1(u, v) \cdot \mathsf{PR}_{i-1}(\mathbf{u}, \mathbf{v}) \\
&+ \mathsf{PR}_1(u, v) \cdot \mathsf{ID}_{i-1}(\mathbf{u}, 0^{i-1}) \cdot \mathsf{ID}_{i-1}(\mathbf{v}, (|\mathbb{H}| - 1)^{i-1})
\end{aligned}$$

We also rely on the following useful property of the circuits $\mathsf{ID}, \mathsf{LE}, \mathsf{PR}$. Intuitively, it says that in some cases, the output of the predicate can be determine from the prefix for the input (even if the rest of the input is not in $\mathbb{H}$).

Claim 4.2. *For every $i \in \mathbb{N}$, $j \in [i]$, $\mathbf{t}_1 = (\mathbf{h}_1, \mathbf{f}_1), \mathbf{t}_2 = (\mathbf{h}_2, \mathbf{f}_2) \in \mathbb{H}^j \times \mathbb{F}^{i-j}$ and $\mathbf{h} \in \mathbb{H}^i$:*

- $\mathbf{h}_1 \neq \mathbf{h}_2 \Rightarrow \mathsf{ID}_i(\mathbf{t}_1, \mathbf{t}_2) = 0.$
- $\mathbf{h}_1 > \mathbf{h}_2 \Rightarrow \mathsf{LE}_i(\mathbf{t}_1, \mathbf{t}_2) = 0.$
- $\mathbf{h}_1 < \mathbf{h}_2 \Rightarrow \mathsf{LE}_i(\mathbf{t}_1, \mathbf{t}_2) = 1.$
- $(\mathbf{h} - 1)[:j] \neq \mathbf{h}_1 \Rightarrow \mathsf{PR}_i(\mathbf{h}, \mathbf{t}_1) = 0.$

The proof of Claim 4.2 follows from the next lemma.

Lemma 4.1. *Let $\varphi \colon \mathbb{F}^i \to \mathbb{F}$ be an arithmetic circuit of degree $(|\mathbb{H}| - 1)$. For every $j \in [i]$, $\mathbf{t} \in \mathbb{H}^j$ and $b \in \{0, 1\}$:*

$$\forall \mathbf{h} \in \mathbb{H}^{i-j} \colon \varphi(\mathbf{t}, \mathbf{h}) = b \quad \Rightarrow \quad \forall \mathbf{f} \in \mathbb{F}^{i-j} \colon \varphi(\mathbf{t}, \mathbf{f}) = b.$$

4.2   The Constraints

In this section we give an algebraic representation of the constraints of a computation through the notion of a constraint circuit.

The Tableau Formula. Let M be a non-deterministic Turing machine with running time $\mathsf{T} = \mathsf{T}(n)$ and space complexity $\mathsf{S} = \mathsf{S}(n)$. By the Cook-Levin theorem the computation of M on some input can be described by $\mathsf{T}' \cdot \mathsf{S}'$ Boolean variables where $\mathsf{T}' = \mathsf{T} \cdot \beta$ and $\mathsf{S}' = \mathsf{S} \cdot \beta$ for some constant $\beta \in \mathbb{N}$. Intuitively, we think the variables as organized in a table with T' rows S' columns. The variables in row $\beta \cdot t$ correspond to the configuration of M after t steps. All other rows, whose indices are not a multiple of β, contain auxiliary variables used to verify the consistency of adjacent configurations. An assignment to the variables describes a valid computation of M (with any witness) if and only if it satisfies a 3CNF "tableau formula" ϕ_y.

Claim 4.3. (Cook-Levin-Karp.) *There exists a constant β such that for every input $y \in \{0, 1\}^n$ there exists a 3CNF formula ϕ_y over the variables $\{x_{t,s}\}_{t \in [\mathsf{T}'], s \in [\mathsf{S}']}$ where $\mathsf{T}' = \beta \cdot \mathsf{T}$ and $\mathsf{S}' = \beta \cdot \mathsf{S}$ such that the following holds:*

Completeness: *For every witness* $w \in \{0,1\}^{\mathsf{T}}$ *there exists an assignment* $X^{y,w} \colon [\mathsf{T}'] \times [\mathsf{S}'] \to \{0,1\}$ *that satisfies* ϕ_y. *Moreover, for any* $t \in [\mathsf{T}]$, *given only the configuration* $c_t = M(y; w[:t])$ *we can compute a row assignment* $\gamma^{c_t} \colon [\mathsf{S}'] \to \{0,1\}$ *such that* $X^{y,w}(t \cdot \beta, \cdot) = \gamma^{c_t}$. *Similarly, for any* $(t-1) \cdot \beta < \tau \leq t \cdot \beta$, *given only the configuration* $c_{t-1} = M(y; w[:t-1])$ *and the witness bit* w_t *we can compute a row assignment* $\gamma_\tau^{c_{t-1}, w_t} \colon [\mathsf{S}'] \to \{0,1\}$ *such that* $X^{y,w}(\tau, \cdot) = \gamma_\tau^{c_{t-1}, w_t}$.

Soundness: *For any assignment* $X \colon [\mathsf{T}'] \times [\mathsf{S}'] \to \{0,1\}$ *that satisfies* ϕ_y *there exists a witness* w *such that* $X = X^{y,w}$. *Moreover, for every* $t \in [\mathsf{T}]$ *and configuration* c, *if* $X(t \cdot \beta, \cdot) = \gamma^c$ *then* $c = M(y; w[:t])$.

Leveled structure: *Every constraint in* ϕ_y *is of the form* $(x_{t_1,s_1} = b_1) \vee (x_{t_2,s_2} = b_2) \vee (x_{t_3,s_3} = b_3)$ *where* $t_1 - 1 = t_2 = t_3$.

The Configuration Formula. For every $\tau \in [\mathsf{T}']$ and a row assignment $\gamma \colon [\mathsf{S}'] \to \{0,1\}$ we define a 3CNF "configuration formula" $\phi_{\tau,\gamma}$ over the same variables as the tableau formula ϕ_y checking that the τ-th row assignment is equal to γ. That is:

- If $\tau = t \cdot \beta$ for some $t \in [\mathsf{T}]$ then $\phi_{\tau,\gamma}$ is satisfied by an assignments $X \colon [\mathsf{T}'] \times [\mathsf{S}'] \to \{0,1\}$ if and only if $X(\tau, \cdot) = \gamma$.
- Otherwise, $\phi_{\tau,\gamma} = 1$ is the empty formula.

For technical reasons, we assume WLOG that all the constraints in $\phi_{\tau,\gamma}$ are of the form $(x_{t_1,s_1} = b_1) \vee (x_{t_2,s_2} = b_2) \vee (x_{t_3,s_3} = b_3)$, where $\tau = t_1$. Additionally we assume that $\phi_{\tau,\gamma}$ has the same leveled structure as the tableau formula. That is, $t_1 - 1 = t_2 = t_3$. For τ that is not a multiple of β, $\phi_{\tau,\gamma}$ is the empty formula so our assumptions on the structure of $\phi_{\tau,\gamma}$ hold vacuously.

Arithmetizing the Constraint Formula. Let $\mathbb{F}$ be a field of size $\Theta(\log^2 \mathsf{T}')$, let $\mathbb{H} \subset \mathbb{F}$ be a subset of size $\lceil \log \mathsf{T}' \rceil$ such that $\{0,1\} \subseteq \mathbb{H}$ and let

$$m = \frac{\log \mathsf{T}'}{\log \log \mathsf{T}'}, k = \frac{\log \mathsf{S}'}{\log \log \mathsf{T}'}.$$

We assume WLOG that m, k and $\log \mathsf{T}'$ are all integers and, therefore, $|\mathbb{H}^m| = \mathsf{T}'$ and $|\mathbb{H}^k| = \mathsf{S}'$. We identify elements of $\mathbb{H}^m$ (with lexicographic order) with indices in $[\mathsf{T}]$, and elements in $\mathbb{H}^k$ with indices in $[\mathsf{S}]$. We view an assignment X for the variables $\{x_{t,s}\}$ as a function $X \colon \mathbb{H}^{m+k} \to \{0,1\}$.

Constraint Circuits. We can implicitly represent a 3CNF formula ϕ over the variables $\{x_{t,s}\}$ using a multivariate polynomial. Intuitively, this polynomial represents the indicator function indicating whether a given 3-disjunction is in the formula. We represent this polynomial via an arithmetic circuit over $\mathbb{F}$.

Definition 4.1. (Constraint circuit). *An arithmetic circuit* $\varphi \colon \mathbb{F}^{3(m+k+1)} \to \mathbb{F}$ *is a constraint circuit representing a 3CNF formula* ϕ *over the variables*

$\{x_{\mathbf{t},\mathbf{s}}\}_{\mathbf{t}\in\mathbb{H}^m,\mathbf{s}\in\mathbb{H}^k}$ if for every $\mathbf{t}_1,\mathbf{t}_2,\mathbf{t}_3 \in \mathbb{H}^m$, $\mathbf{s}_1,\mathbf{s}_2,\mathbf{s}_3 \in \mathbb{H}^k$ and $b_1,b_2,b_3 \in \{0,1\}$ if ϕ contains the constraint:

$$(x_{\mathbf{t}_1,\mathbf{s}_1} = b_1) \vee (x_{\mathbf{t}_2,\mathbf{s}_2} = b_2) \vee (x_{\mathbf{t}_3,\mathbf{s}_3} = b_3),$$

then φ evaluates to 1 on $(\mathbf{t}_1,\mathbf{t}_2,\mathbf{t}_3,\mathbf{s}_1,\mathbf{s}_2,\mathbf{s}_3,b_1,b_2,b_3)$. Otherwise φ evaluates to 0.

Next, we claim that the tableau formula and configuration formula can be efficiently represented as constraint circuits.

Claim 4.4. For every input $y \in \{0,1\}^n$, $\tau \in [\mathsf{T}']$ and assignment $\gamma\colon \mathbb{H}^k \to \{0,1\}$ let ϕ_y and $\phi_{\tau,\gamma}$ be the tableau formula and the configuration formula defined above.

- Given y we can efficiently compute a tableau constraint circuit φ_y of size $O(n) + \mathrm{poly}(m)$ and degree $\mathrm{poly}(m,k)$ describing ϕ_y.
- Given τ and γ we can efficiently compute a configuration constraint circuit $\varphi_{\tau,\gamma}$ of size $\mathsf{S} \cdot \mathrm{poly}(m)$ and degree $O(1)$ describing $\phi_{\tau,\gamma}$.

The Constraint Circuit $\tilde\varphi$. The constraint circuit $\tilde\varphi$ used in our PCP construction is a combination of the constraint circuit and predicates above. Let ϕ_y and $\phi_{\tau,\gamma}$ be the tableau and configuration formulas defined above and let φ_y and $\varphi_{\tau,\gamma}$ be the constraint circuits that describe them, given by Claim 4.4. For $\mathbf{t}_1,\mathbf{t}_2,\mathbf{t}_3 \in \mathbb{F}^m$ and $\mathbf{f} \in \mathbb{F}^{3k+3}$, let $\tilde\varphi_{y,\tau,\gamma}$ be the circuit give by:

$$\tilde\varphi_{y,\tau,\gamma}(\mathbf{t}_1,\mathbf{t}_2,\mathbf{t}_3,\mathbf{f})$$
$$= \mathsf{PR}_m(\mathbf{t}_1,\mathbf{t}_2)\cdot\mathsf{PR}_m(\mathbf{t}_1,\mathbf{t}_3)\cdot(\varphi_y(\mathbf{t}_1,\mathbf{t}_2,\mathbf{t}_3,\mathbf{f}) + \mathsf{ID}_m(\tau,\mathbf{t}_1)\cdot\varphi_{\tau,\gamma}(\mathbf{t}_1,\mathbf{t}_2,\mathbf{t}_3,\mathbf{f})).$$

Claim 4.5. For every $y \in \{0,1\}^n$, $\tau \in \mathbb{H}^m$, $\gamma\colon \mathbb{H}^k \to \{0,1\}$, $\tilde\varphi_{y,\tau,\gamma}$ describes the 3CNF formula $\phi_y \wedge \phi_{\tau,\gamma}$. Moreover, for every $\tau' \in \mathbb{H}^m$, $\gamma'\colon \mathbb{H}^k \to \{0,1\}$, $i < m$, $\mathbf{t}_1,\mathbf{t}_2,\mathbf{t}_3 \in \mathbb{H}^i \times \mathbb{F}^{m-i}$, $\mathbf{h} \in \mathbb{H}^m$ and $\mathbf{f} \in \mathbb{F}^{3k+3}$:

$$\{\mathbf{t}_2[:i],\mathbf{t}_3[:i]\} \neq \{(\mathbf{h}-1)[:i]\} \quad\Rightarrow\quad \tilde\varphi_{y,\tau,\gamma}(\mathbf{h},\mathbf{t}_2,\mathbf{t}_3,\mathbf{f}) = 0,$$
$$\mathbf{t}_1[:i] \notin \{\tau[:i],\tau'[:i]\} \quad\Rightarrow\quad \tilde\varphi_{y,\tau,\gamma}(\mathbf{t}_1,\mathbf{t}_2,\mathbf{t}_3,\mathbf{f}) = \tilde\varphi_{y,\tau',\gamma'}(\mathbf{t}_1,\mathbf{t}_2,\mathbf{t}_3,\mathbf{f}).$$

Proof (Proof sketch). Since the tableau constraints and the configuration constraints are disjoint, the circuit $\varphi_y + \varphi_{\tau,\gamma}$ describes the 3CNF formula $\phi_y \wedge \phi_{\tau,\gamma}$. By the leveled structure of the formulas ϕ_y and $\phi_{\tau,\gamma}$ the circuit $\varphi_y + \varphi_{\tau,\gamma}$ identifies with $\tilde\varphi_{y,\tau,\gamma}$ on $\mathbb{H}^{3(m+k+1)}$. The rest of the claim follows from the leveled structure of the formulas ϕ_y and $\phi_{\tau,\gamma}$ and by Claim 4.2.

4.3   The Proof String

Recall that for every $t \in [\mathsf{T}]$ and $z \in [\ell]$, $\sigma_t^z \in \Sigma$ denotes the z-th symbol of the proof after t updates. We start by specifying the value of σ_t^z and in the next section we describe the procedure Update maintaining it. Next we introduce some notation and describe the different components of the PCP. See Sect. 2 for a high level overview of the construction.

The first part of our construction closely follows the PCP of BFLS. Fix $y \in \{0,1\}^n$ and $w \in \{0,1\}^T$ and let $X^{y,w}$ be the assignment given by Claim 4.3. For $\tau \in \mathbb{H}^m$ we define:

- Let $\gamma_\tau \colon \mathbb{H}^k \to \{0,1\}$ be the row assignment $\gamma_\tau = X^{y,w}(\tau, \cdot)$.
- Let $X_\tau \colon \mathbb{H}^{m+k} \to \{0,1\}$ be the assignment such that $X_\tau(\mathbf{t}, \cdot) = \gamma_\mathbf{t}$ for all $\mathbf{t} \le \tau$ and for all $\mathbf{t} > \tau$, $X_\tau(\mathbf{t}, \cdot)$ is identically zero.
- Let $\tilde{X}_\tau \colon \mathbb{F}^{m+k} \to \mathbb{F}$ be the polynomial of degree $|\mathbb{H}| - 1$ that identifies with X_τ on $\mathbb{H}^{m+k}$:

$$\tilde{X}_\tau(\mathbf{f}) = \sum_{\mathbf{h} \in \mathbb{H}^{m+k}} \mathsf{ID}(\mathbf{h}, \mathbf{f}) \cdot X_\tau(\mathbf{h})$$

- Let $Q_\tau^0 \colon \mathbb{F}^{3(m+k+1)} \to \mathbb{F}$ be the following polynomial. For $\mathbf{z} = (\mathbf{t}_1, \mathbf{t}_2, \mathbf{t}_3, \mathbf{s}_1, \mathbf{s}_2, \mathbf{s}_3) \in \mathbb{F}^{3(m+k)}$, $\mathbf{b} = (b_1, b_2, b_3) \in \mathbb{F}^3$ and $\bar{\mathbf{z}} = (\mathbf{z}, \mathbf{b})$:

$$Q_\tau^0(\bar{\mathbf{z}}) = \mathsf{LE}(\mathbf{t}_1, \tau) \cdot \tilde{\varphi}_{y,\tau,\gamma_\tau}(\bar{\mathbf{z}}) \cdot \prod_{i \in [3]} \left(\tilde{X}_\tau(\mathbf{t}_i, \mathbf{s}_i) - b_i \right).$$

- For $j \in [3(m+k)]$ let $Q_\tau^j \colon \mathbb{F}^{3(m+k+1)} \to \mathbb{F}$ be the polynomial:

$$Q_\tau^j(\mathbf{f}) = \sum_{\mathbf{h} \in \mathbb{H}^j} \mathsf{ID}(\mathbf{h}, \mathbf{f}[:j]) \cdot Q_\tau^0(\mathbf{h}, \mathbf{f}[j+1:]).$$

Next we introduce additional polynomials that are not a part of the BFLS construction). These polynomials define the supplemental values added to the PCP to support updates.

First we define polynomials $A_\tau^0, B_\tau^0, C_\tau^0$ by multiplying together subsets of the factors of Q_τ^0. Let $A_\tau^0, B_\tau^0, C_\tau^0 \colon \mathbb{F}^{3(m+k+1)} \to \mathbb{F}$ be the following polynomials. For $\mathbf{z} = (\mathbf{t}_1, \mathbf{t}_2, \mathbf{t}_3, \mathbf{s}_1, \mathbf{s}_2, \mathbf{s}_3) \in \mathbb{F}^{3(m+k)}$, $\mathbf{b} = (b_1, b_2, b_3) \in \mathbb{F}^3$, and $\bar{\mathbf{z}} = (\mathbf{z}, \mathbf{b})$:

$$A_\tau^0(\bar{\mathbf{z}}) = \tilde{\varphi}_{y,\tau,\gamma_\tau}(\bar{\mathbf{z}}) \cdot \left(\tilde{X}_\tau(\mathbf{t}_1, \mathbf{s}_1) - b_1 \right),$$

$$B_\tau^0(\bar{\mathbf{z}}) = \tilde{\varphi}_{y,\tau,\gamma_\tau}(\bar{\mathbf{z}}) \cdot \left(\tilde{X}_\tau(\mathbf{t}_1, \mathbf{s}_1) - b_1 \right) \cdot \left(\tilde{X}_\tau(\mathbf{t}_2, \mathbf{s}_2) - b_2 \right),$$

$$C_\tau^0(\bar{\mathbf{z}}) = \tilde{\varphi}_{y,\tau,\gamma_\tau}(\bar{\mathbf{z}}) \cdot \left(\tilde{X}_\tau(\mathbf{t}_1, \mathbf{s}_1) - b_1 \right) \cdot \left(\tilde{X}_\tau(\mathbf{t}_2, \mathbf{s}_2) - b_2 \right) \cdot \left(\tilde{X}_\tau(\mathbf{t}_3, \mathbf{s}_3) - b_3 \right).$$

Next we define the polynomials $A_\tau^j, B_\tau^j, C_\tau^j$. Similar to the definition of Q_τ^j via Q_τ^0, the evaluations of A_τ^j, B_τ^j and C_τ^j on input $\bar{\mathbf{z}} \in \mathbb{F}^{3(m+k+1)}$ are given by a weighted sum of evaluations of A_τ^0, B_τ^0 and C_τ^0 respectively, over inputs $\bar{\mathbf{z}}'$ whose prefix is in $\mathbb{H}$ and suffix in equal to that of $\bar{\mathbf{z}}$. However, unlike the definition of Q_τ^j, we do not sum over all possible prefixes in $\mathbb{H}$, but only over prefixes with a certain structure. Specifically:

- A_τ^j sums over prefixes $\mathbf{h} \in \mathbb{H}^j$ such that $\mathbf{h} < \tau[:j]$.
- B_τ^j sums over prefixes $(\mathbf{h}, (\mathbf{h}-1)[:j]) \in \mathbb{H}^{m+j}$ such that $0^m < \mathbf{h} < \tau$.

- C_τ^j sums over prefixes $(\mathbf{h}, \mathbf{h} - 1, (\mathbf{h} - 1)[:j]) \in \mathbb{H}^{2m+j}$ such that $0^m < \mathbf{h} < \tau$.

Formally, for $j \in [m]$ let $A_\tau^j, B_\tau^j, C_\tau^j \colon \mathbb{F}^{3(m+k+1)} \to \mathbb{F}$ be the following polynomials. For $\mathbf{z} = (\mathbf{t}_1, \mathbf{t}_2, \mathbf{t}_3, \mathbf{s}_1, \mathbf{s}_2, \mathbf{s}_3) \in \mathbb{F}^{3(m+k)}$, $\mathbf{b} = (b_1, b_2, b_3) \in \mathbb{F}^3$ and $\bar{\mathbf{z}} = (\mathbf{z}, \mathbf{b})$:

$$A_\tau^j(\bar{\mathbf{z}}) = \sum_{\mathbf{h} < \tau[:j]} \mathsf{ID}\left(\mathbf{h}, \bar{\mathbf{z}}[:j]\right) \cdot A_\tau^0\left(\mathbf{h}, \bar{\mathbf{z}}[j+1:]\right),$$

$$B_\tau^j(\bar{\mathbf{z}}) = \sum_{0^m < \mathbf{h} < \tau} \mathsf{ID}\left((\mathbf{h}, (\mathbf{h} - 1)[:j]), \bar{\mathbf{z}}[:m+j]\right) \cdot B_\tau^0\left(((\mathbf{h}, \mathbf{h} - 1) \,|\bar{\mathbf{z}})_{m+j}\right),$$

$$C_\tau^j(\bar{\mathbf{z}}) = \sum_{0^m < \mathbf{h} < \tau} \mathsf{ID}\left((\mathbf{h}, \mathbf{h} - 1, (\mathbf{h} - 1)[:j]), \bar{\mathbf{z}}[:2m+j]\right) \cdot C_\tau^0\left(((\mathbf{h}, \mathbf{h} - 1, \mathbf{h} - 1) \,|\bar{\mathbf{z}})_{2m+j}\right).$$

Finally, we define polynomials $\bar{A}_\tau^j, \bar{B}_\tau^j, \bar{C}_\tau^j$. These are defined similarly to $A_\tau^j, B_\tau^j, C_\tau^j$ except that we sum over different prefixes:

- $\bar{A}_\tau^j$ sums over prefixes $(\mathbf{h}, (\mathbf{h} - 1)[:j]) \in \mathbb{H}^{m+j}$ such that $0^m < \mathbf{h} < \tau$ and $(\mathbf{h} - 1)[:j] = \tau[:j]$.
- $\bar{B}_\tau^j$ sums over prefixes $(\mathbf{h}, \mathbf{h} - 1, (\mathbf{h} - 1)[:j]) \in \mathbb{H}^{2m+j}$ such that $0^m < \mathbf{h} < \tau$ and $(\mathbf{h} - 1)[:j] = \tau[:j]$.
- $\bar{C}_\tau^j$ sums over prefixes $(\mathbf{h}, \mathbf{h} - 1, \mathbf{h} - 1, \mathbf{h}') \in \mathbb{H}^{3m+j}$ such that $0^m < \mathbf{h} < \tau$ and $\mathbf{h}' \in \mathbb{H}^j$.

Formally, for $j \in [m]$ let $\bar{A}_\tau^j, \bar{B}_\tau^j \colon \mathbb{F}^{3(m+k+1)} \to \mathbb{F}$ be the following polynomials. For $\mathbf{z} = (\mathbf{t}_1, \mathbf{t}_2, \mathbf{t}_3, \mathbf{s}_1, \mathbf{s}_2, \mathbf{s}_3) \in \mathbb{F}^{3(m+k)}$, $\mathbf{b} = (b_1, b_2, b_3) \in \mathbb{F}^3$ and $\bar{\mathbf{z}} = (\mathbf{z}, \mathbf{b})$:

$$\bar{A}_\tau^j(\bar{\mathbf{z}}) = \sum_{\substack{0^m < \mathbf{h} < \tau \\ (\mathbf{h}-1)[:j] = \tau[:j]}} \mathsf{ID}\left((\mathbf{h}, \tau[:j]), \bar{\mathbf{z}}[:m+j]\right) \cdot A_\tau^0\left(((\mathbf{h}, \tau) \,|\bar{\mathbf{z}})_{m+j}\right),$$

$$\bar{B}_\tau^j(\bar{\mathbf{z}}) = \sum_{\substack{0^m < \mathbf{h} < \tau \\ (\mathbf{h}-1)[:j] = \tau[:j]}} \mathsf{ID}\left((\mathbf{h}, \mathbf{h} - 1, \tau[:j]), \bar{\mathbf{z}}[:2m+j]\right)$$
$$\cdot B_\tau^0\left(((\mathbf{h}, \mathbf{h} - 1, \tau) \,|\bar{\mathbf{z}})_{2m+j}\right),$$

For $j \in [3k]$ let $\bar{C}_\tau^j \colon \mathbb{F}^{3(m+k+1)} \to \mathbb{F}$ be the following polynomial:

$$\bar{C}_\tau^j(\bar{\mathbf{z}}) = \sum_{\substack{0^m < \mathbf{h} < \tau \\ \mathbf{h}' \in \mathbb{H}^j}} \mathsf{ID}\left((\mathbf{h}, \mathbf{h} - 1, \mathbf{h} - 1, \mathbf{h}'), \bar{\mathbf{z}}[:3m+j]\right)$$
$$\cdot C_\tau^0\left(\mathbf{h}, \mathbf{h} - 1, \mathbf{h} - 1, \mathbf{h}', \bar{\mathbf{z}}[3m+j+1:]\right).$$

We are now ready to define the PCP proof string. We set $\ell = |\mathbb{F}|^{3(m+k)}$ and identify elements of $\mathbb{F}^{3(m+k)}$ with indices in $[\ell]$.

We first define for every $\tau \in \mathbb{H}^m$ and $\mathbf{z} = (\mathbf{t}_1, \mathbf{t}_2, \mathbf{t}_3, \mathbf{s}_1, \mathbf{s}_2, \mathbf{s}_3) \in \mathbb{F}^{3(m+k)}$ an auxiliary symbol $\bar{\sigma}_\tau^{\mathbf{z}}$. These auxiliary symbols will be useful in defining the update procedure. Then, for every $t \in [T]$, we set the proof symbol $\sigma_t^{\mathbf{z}}$ to be the symbol $\bar{\sigma}_{t \cdot \beta}^{\mathbf{z}}$. The auxiliary symbol $\bar{\sigma}_\tau^{\mathbf{z}}$ contains the values:

1. $\tilde{X}_\tau((\tau|\mathbf{t}_i)_j, \mathbf{s}_i)$ for every $i \in [3]$ and $j \in [0, m]$.
2. $\tilde{X}_\tau((\tau - 1|\mathbf{t}_i)_j, \mathbf{s}_i)$ for every $i \in [3]$ and $j \in [0, m]$. (Only if $\tau > 0^m$.)
3. $Q_\tau^j(\mathbf{z}, \mathbf{b})$ for every $j \in [0, 3(m+k)]$ and $\mathbf{b} \in \{0, 1\}^3$.
4. $A_\tau^j(\mathbf{z}, \mathbf{b}), \bar{A}_\tau^j(\mathbf{z}, \mathbf{b}), B_\tau^j(\mathbf{z}, \mathbf{b}), \bar{B}_\tau^j(\mathbf{z}, \mathbf{b}), C_\tau^j(\mathbf{z}, \mathbf{b})$ for every $j \in [m]$ and $\mathbf{b} \in \{0, 1\}^3$.
5. $\bar{C}_\tau^j(\mathbf{z}, \mathbf{b})$ for every $j \in [3k]$ and $\mathbf{b} \in \{0, 1\}^3$.

The following theorem (that follows from the proof of [BFLS91]) states that the construction above is indeed a PCP proof. In the following sections we prove that this PCP is incrementally updatable.

Theorem 4.6 (Follows from [BFLS91]). *There exists a PCP system* (P, V) *for* M *with alphabet* $\Sigma = \mathbb{F}^{O(m+k)}$, *query complexity* $q = \mathrm{poly}(m + k)$, *and proof length* $\ell = |\mathbb{F}|^{3(m+k)} = \mathrm{poly}(\mathsf{T} \cdot \mathsf{S})$ *such that given* $((y, t, c), w) \in \mathcal{R}_M$, P *outputs the proof* $\Pi = (\sigma_t^1, \ldots, \sigma_t^\ell)$.

References

[BCC+17] Bitansky, N., et al.: The hunting of the SNARK. J. Cryptol. **30**(4), 989–1066 (2017)

[BCCT13] Bitansky, N., Canetti, R., Chiesa, A., Tromer, E.: Recursive composition and bootstrapping for snarks and proof-carrying data. In: STOC, pp. 111–120 (2013)

[BFLS91] Babai, L., Fortnow, L., Levin, L.A., Szegedy, M.: Checking computations in polylogarithmic time. In: Proceedings of the 23rd Annual ACM Symposium on Theory of Computing, New Orleans, Louisiana, USA, 5–8 May 1991, pp. 21–31 (1991)

[BHK16] Brakerski, Z., Holmgren, J., Kalai, Y.T.: Non-interactive RAM and batch NP delegation from any PIR. IACR Cryptology ePrint Archive, 2016:459 (2016)

[BHK17] Brakerski, Z., Holmgren, J., Kalai, Y.T.: Non-interactive delegation and batch NP verification from standard computational assumptions. In: Proceedings of the 49th Annual ACM SIGACT Symposium on Theory of Computing, STOC 2017, Montreal, QC, Canada, 19–23 June 2017, pp. 474–482 (2017)

[BMW98] Biehl, I., Meyer, B., Wetzel, S.: Ensuring the integrity of agent-based computations by short proofs. In: Rothermel, K., Hohl, F. (eds.) MA 1998. LNCS, vol. 1477, pp. 183–194. Springer, Heidelberg (1998). https://doi.org/10.1007/BFb0057658

[BV11] Brakerski, Z., Vaikuntanathan, V.: Efficient fully homomorphic encryption from (standard) LWE. In IEEE 52nd Annual Symposium on Foundations of Computer Science, FOCS 2011, Palm Springs, CA, USA, October 22–25, 2011, pp. 97–106 (2011)

[DHRW16] Dodis, Y., Halevi, S., Rothblum, R.D., Wichs, D.: Spooky encryption and its applications. In: Robshaw, M., Katz, J. (eds.) CRYPTO 2016. LNCS, vol. 9816, pp. 93–122. Springer, Heidelberg (2016). https://doi.org/10.1007/978-3-662-53015-3_4

[DLN+00] Dwork, C., Langberg, M., Naor, M., Nissim, K., Reingold, O.: Succinct proofs for NP ander spooky interactions. Manuscript (2000). http://www.wisdom.weizmann.ac.il/~naor/PAPERS/spooky.pdf

[DNR16] Dwork, C., Naor, M., Rothblum, G.N.: Spooky interaction and its discontents: compilers for succinct two-message argument systems. In: Robshaw, M., Katz, J. (eds.) CRYPTO 2016. LNCS, vol. 9816, pp. 123–145. Springer, Heidelberg (2016). https://doi.org/10.1007/978-3-662-53015-3_5

[Gen09] Gentry, C.: Fully homomorphic encryption using ideal lattices. In: Proceedings of the 41st Annual ACM Symposium on Theory of Computing, STOC 2009, Bethesda, MD, USA, 31 May–2 June, pp. 169–178 (2009)

[GH98] Goldreich, O., Håstad, J.: On the complexity of interactive proofs with bounded communication. Inf. Process. Lett. **67**(4), 205–214 (1998)

[GSW13] Gentry, C., Sahai, A., Waters, B.: Homomorphic encryption from learning with errors: conceptually-simpler, asymptotically-faster, attribute-based. In: Canetti, R., Garay, J.A. (eds.) CRYPTO 2013. LNCS, vol. 8042, pp. 75–92. Springer, Heidelberg (2013). https://doi.org/10.1007/978-3-642-40041-4_5

[HR18] Holmgren, J., Rothblum, R.: Delegating computations with (almost) minimal time and space overhead. In: 59th IEEE Annual Symposium on Foundations of Computer Science, FOCS 2018, Paris, France, 7–9 October 2018, pp. 124–135 (2018)

[KPY19] Kalai, Y., Paneth, O., Yang, L.: How to delegate computations publicly. In: STOC (2019)

[KRR13] Kalai, Y.T., Raz, R., Rothblum, R.D.: Delegation for bounded space. In: STOC, pp. 565–574 (2013)

[KRR14] Kalai, Y.T., Raz, R., Rothblum, R.D.: How to delegate computations: the power of no-signaling proofs. In: Symposium on Theory of Computing, STOC 2014, New York, NY, USA, 31 May–03 June 2014, pp. 485–494 (2014)

[PR17] Paneth, O., Rothblum, G.N.: On zero-testable homomorphic encryption and publicly verifiable non-interactive arguments. In: Kalai, Y., Reyzin, L. (eds.) TCC 2017. LNCS, vol. 10678, pp. 283–315. Springer, Cham (2017). https://doi.org/10.1007/978-3-319-70503-3_9

[Val08] Valiant, P.: Incrementally verifiable computation or proofs of knowledge imply time/space efficiency. In: Canetti, R. (ed.) TCC 2008. LNCS, vol. 4948, pp. 1–18. Springer, Heidelberg (2008). https://doi.org/10.1007/978-3-540-78524-8_1

Author Index

Printed in the United States
By Bookmasters